META-POLITICS

Meta-Politics

City of God, cities of men

CARLOS PERONA CALVETE

Angelico Press

For information, address:
Angelico Press, Ltd.
169 Monitor St.
Brooklyn, NY 11222
www.angelicopress.com

ppr 978-1-62138-933-0
cloth 978-1-62138-934-7

Book and cover design
by Michael Schrauzer

CONTENTS

PRELIMINARIES: General Orientation and Sources 3

PART I: Principles of Spiritual Realization and
  its Political Expression. 7

  I. EPIPHANY AND ECUMENE: Overview and Principles . . . 9
    THE BEING OF BEINGS: THE BEYOND IS BETWEEN 17
    UNITY WITHIN FORMS, OR EVERYTHING HAS
    BORDERS AND BROTHERS 25
      The Hospitable Infinite,
      or the Twin Infinity and Integrity of Forms 32
      How Logocentrism Decentralizes the Cosmos 34
      The Doctrine of Fortunate Absence 41
    UNITY BETWEEN FORMS, OR EVERYTHING
    IN RELATION AND IN RHYTHM 46
      The Absent Center and the Asymptotic Cosmos 52
      The Icon as Logical Necessity,
      or the Irrationality of both Iconoclasm and Idolatry 61
      The Eternal Return of the Different and
      the Eternal Relationship of the Harmonious 65
    THE POLITICS OF APOPHATIC PRESENCE 68
      The King is No-one, Long Live the King,
      or Kenotic Kingship. 78
      The Open Society and its Demons 83
      To Redeem and the Freedom to Deem Again 90
    SAT-CHIT-ANANDA AS THE STRUCTURE OF EPIPHANY:
    THE PLATONIC FIRST INTELLECT, THE DEMIURGE AND
    THE KRATER; THE BIBLICAL ANCIENT OF DAYS,
    THE SON OF MAN AND HIS BRIDE 93
      Chit as Static Masculine, Ananda as Dynamic Feminine . . . 113

PART II: Practices of Spiritual Realization
  and Its Political Expression 119

  II. CORONATIO 121
    THEOPHANY AND MACRANTHROPY 121
      The Four Corners of the Earth 134
      Crucified to the Throne. 137
      Sacrifice of the Cosmic Animal 146
      Oxen of the Sun, or the Horn of Heaven 149

The Greco-Roman Hero and the Cretan Bull,
or How a Hero gets his Horns 161

Saturn as Being and Saturn as Body,
or From the Devouring to the Dialoguing Deity 169

Sacrifice as Kenotic Participation 174

The Cube at the Center, the Creator in the Crater 177

Plato's Crater as the Holy Grail
and Aeneas as Grail Knight. 179

Hell Above is Heaven Beneath,
or Entering the Absent Centre 183

The Centrality of the Sun and the Danger of Idolatry 189

Of Crypts and Chariots. 193

Sacred Rivers in a World without Seas,
or Integrating the Lower and Higher Natures 194

The Throne is the Body. 198

In Stones they Slumber 200

THE MOTHER'S VEGETABLE SUN 202

Milk, the Tree and the Veil 207

The Wandering Mother and the Temple Builder 211

The Morning Star and Heaven's Mandate 215

Sun and Star, Son and Mother 219

THE INITIATE AT MOUNT IDA 222

Theurgy on the Roman Throne 226

Embodiment and Ennead (in the Aeneid) 229

The Psalms and Aeneas. 233

Saint Peter as Sacred King 236

III. COPULATIO. 241

THE LIMPING KING AND THE EPIPHANY OF GENDER . . 241

From the Sexual Wound to Dynastic Fecundity 248

EROTO-THEURGY, OR SPIRITUAL INITIATION
AND SEXUAL INTERCOURSE 249

Eros Completes Epiphany:
The Queen brings the Crown, the Corps becomes King. 255

Eros and the Eschaton:
Chariots of Sex on Judgement Day 258

Black Stones, or the Meteor and the Volcano 270

The Holy Grail and Sexual Initiation. 272

GENDERED METAPHYSICS 273

Unity, Duality, Trinity. 277

The World as Tetrad 280

Quartering and Quintessence 287

The King as Decad 289

THE DIVINE FEMININE AND POLITICAL POWER 291
 The Duality of Femininity 295
 The Duality of Kingship 299
 Lavinia, Rome's Shakti 308
 Roman Sexual Symbolism 309

IV. CORPORATIO 313
 EMBODYING EPIPHANY 313
  The Kingdom and the Corpus Cosmicum 314
  Embodiment and Enculturation,
  or Translating the Transcendent through Tradition 324
  From Heroism as Hubris to Political Heroism 326
  Relations Mystical and Political 328
  Atomized Society and the Holy Fool 333
  Political Representation as Reciprocal Initiation,
  or the Divine and the Demos 337
 CENTER AND PERIPHERY IN ONE BODY 345
  From the Wilderness, a City 345
  The Mystique of the Barbarian 348
  Sacrifice and the Fraternal Foe 352
 SACRED KINGSHIP AND SACRED LAW 353
  Sacred Kingship as Freedom to Legislate,
  or Of God and gods 355
  The True and the Perverse Sacrifice:
  Ex Nihilo Contra Nihilo 372
  The True Sacrifice and the True Body 379
  On Currency and the Cross 382
  Poverty and Property,
  or Heaven Does Not Abolish the Household 384
 THE CORPUS COSMICUM AND THE NARRATIVE BODY . . 388
  The King as Ancestor 388
  Aeneas and the Empire of Heirs 392
  Aeneas's Narrative Body and Biblical Narrative 397
 THE KENOTIC KING'S SOLUBLE STATE,
 OR THE ANARCHY OF MONARCHY AND
 WHERE POWER OVERPOWERS ITSELF 406

V. ECUMENE 413
 TRANSLATION REQUIRES TRANSCENDENCE 413
  Translating the gods:
  Re-Deeming Difference and Rejecting Mimesis 421
  Exiles and Exaltations,
  or Communal Initiation as Theological Translation 424

The Eschaton at Elysium, or the Elysian Ecumene 430

Misremembering Heaven for the Harpy 437

Translating the Ecumene:
From Ethnocentrism to Polycentrism,
or the Absent Center and the Plural Center 438

THE CORPUS COSMICUM AND THE ECUMENE, OR ECUMENIC
INTERNATIONAL RELATIONS 451

Membership as Mediation, not Imitation 461

Maturing in Multiplicity, not Amalgamation 464

Ex Unum et In Unum, Pluribus 469

Theo-Geopolitics:
Misery Loves Uniformity, Joy Loves Unity 473

Ancient Thought and Non-Mimetic Politics,
or Respect over Rivalry 478

BIBLICAL ELECTION AND THE ECUMENE 481

MEDIEVAL EMPIRE AND THE ECUMENE 501

The Holy Roman Empire and the Biblical Concept of Israel:
From "Against the Nations" to Encompassing the Nations . . . 501

The Fractal Empire,
or It's Empires All the Way Down (and Up) 506

Nationalism as Index of a Failed Empire;
Imperialism as Index of a Failed Nation 514

CONCLUSION 527

ADDENDA 549

ADDENDUM I: A Digression on Heliocentrism
and Cosmology as Metaphor 551

ADDENDUM II: The Center at the Periphery:
Crete as the Heart of Europe 555
GREEK PHILOSOPHY AND
BRONZE AGE THEOLOGY 556

ADDENDUM III: On Giants and Incarnation,
or Sacrificial Flesh and Hungry Spirits 561
PROPHETS AGAINST GIANTS 566

ADDENDUM IV: Sacred Authority in European Christendom:
Emperors and Popes 569
THE AMBIVALENCES OF CHRISTIAN EUROPE . . 569
THE ROMAN EMPEROR AS HIGH PRIEST 572
EMPEROR AS THEOLOGICAL
BRIDGE-BUILDER (PONTIFEX) 578

ADDENDUM V: Christian-Roman Emperor 582
 EMPEROR AS GUARDIAN OF THE CHURCH,
 PART I: IMPERIAL ECUMENISM 582
 EMPEROR AS HEAD OF THE CHURCH,
 PART I: FREDERICK II AND THE GHIBELLINES. . 589
 THE EMPEROR AS GUARDIAN OF THE CHURCH,
 PART II: EUROPA REGINA 594
 EMPEROR AS HEAD OF THE CHURCH,
 PART II: HABSBURGS AND HERMETICISTS . . . 597
 THE EMPEROR AND EUROPE 604

ADDENDUM VI: On Europe. 607
 CONTINENT AS CIVILIZATION 607
 EUROPE IS THE FAITH 612
 JAPHETIC HISTORIES 615
 JAPHETH AS SYMBOL. 626

ADDENDUM VII: China and the Ecumene or, the
 Circumference is not the Center. 629

ADDENDUM VIII: The Caliphate and the Ecumene,
 or, the Center is not the Circumference 635
 THE UMMAH: ONE AND MANY 636
 CALIPHAL COLLAPSE AND CALIPHATE
 AS COORDINATION. 640
 THE ARABIC QUR'AN AND
 THE ARCHETYPAL QUR'AN 648

ADDENDUM IX: The Sufis of al-Rum:
 Prophetology and Particularity 652

ADDENDUM X: Europe and the Ecumene 658
 EXPANSIVENESS OVER EXPANSIONISM 665

ADDENDUM XI: Indigenous America and the Ecumene,
 or Imperial Rise and Indigenous Return 676
 THE ASSIMILATION OF CHRISTIANITY AND
 LIBERAL-REPUBLICANISM BY THE MACHA
 AS PRECEDENT TO THE INDIGENIZATION
 OF TECHNOLOGICAL MODERNITY 676
 THE RECONQUISTA OF TEHUANTIN SUYU
 AND THE CONQUEST OF MODERNITY. 679
 IMPERIAL RISE, INDIGENOUS RETURN. 685

ADDENDUM XII: Modern Technological Civilization and
 the Ecumene, or Translating Technology . . . 689
 SIMPLIFYING TECHNOLOGY TO
 REDUCE FUNCTIONAL FIXITY 691

REDUCING FUNCTIONAL FIXITY TO
INCREASE ENCULTURATION 693

INCREASING ENCULTURATION
AS DEVELOPMENT OF SOFT POWER 695

SOFT POWER AS DEVELOPMENT OF
A COMMERCIAL NICHE 697

DEVELOPING A COMMERCIAL NICHE
TO REDUCE MIMETIC RIVALRY 704

INDEX 709

Meta-Politics

City of God, cities of men

PRELIMINARIES:
General Orientation and Sources

I DENTITY AND POLITICAL REPRESENTATION ARE
poised to be epoch-defining questions in the 21st century. How can
distinct cultural identities coexist with each other and with some
wider sense of ecumenicity as opposed to disappearing into a mono-
culture? Will political representation be salvaged from its current crisis
of legitimacy or be replaced by forms of technologically-empowered
direct participation? These questions may seem distinct, but whatever
mechanism allows for a group of people to converge in a representative
is likely to be the same mechanism by way of which different social bodies can be equivalent to each other: If an individual can index a group,
it is because there exists a principle common to individual and group
and, therefore, a principle common to different groups. To justify representative politics is to justify political pluralism. This same principle
justifies exchange or porosity between persons, so that one's particularity
can be translated to another by indexing to a common universal: what
belongs to one or is an extension of one can become of another's or be
an extension of another.

We must attend to how different traditions (civilizations, cultural
trajectories) relate their own cultural particulars to a concept of the
universal. It is in the field of theology—including philosophy and cosmology—where the universal is the subject of inquiry. Here, human
thought will have tended to address that common principle which
serves as the basis for representationalism and ecumenicity. The most
historically and geographically common form that this has taken corresponds to the state-cult of sacred monarchy and its rites of investiture.
Therefore, the present work will (superficially) take the form of a study
into sacred monarchy.

Whatever we write about sacred monarchy and initiation across traditions, however, we write while acknowledging its symbols and operations
often lapsed and gave way to inversion, and even that some may have
originated as mere copies of the genuine article. The initiation whereby
a king embodies a god or receives divine knowledge which he may then
implement (and which we will discuss in terms of Plato's "autozoon,"
αὐτοζῷον) can refer to assimilation into theophany, just as it may describe
possession by another entity, however we interpret this.[1] In such cases,

---

1   It has been proposed that such possession represents the context for the Genesis account of "sons of God" (or angels of God, in the Septuagint) coupling with
"daughters of man." Ancient readers would have understood that spiritual beings

an imminent knowledge of deeper reality is replaced by a horizontal, deviated empowerment, a powerful psychical presence. Another example of such inversion of meaning keeping the external form may be found in the slaughter of an animal as sign of self-sacrifice, not only of the initiate, but of the divine unto humanity, which easily comes to be understood as a procedure for feeding hungry gods and obtaining their favor.

In any case, we attend to the upright meaning, so to speak, of traditional symbols. Whatever their degeneration or accretion, traditions should be taken seriously as expressions of perennial truths, following René Guénon.[2] However, our approach will be to allow for the sprawl of these traditions beyond official canon and into artistic creation and apparently secular speculations when manifesting their insight. There is potential for spurious cultural accretion in religion, just as there is continuity between tradition and institutions or ideas that happened to come into bloom during modernity. What is *officially* heterodox can be *actually* orthodox.

In *Ascent to Heaven in Islamic and Jewish Mysticism*, Algis Uzdavinys described the traditions as "canonized mythologies (be they Jewish, Islamic or secular modernist)." This does not mean we cannot "ritually confirm the orthodox boundaries, the borders of 'property' in the flooded fields of comparative religion" while "at the same time... being unable to follow those rules of courtesy which require one to believe in certain supposedly 'noble' but incredible things simply because they are 'firmly established.'" However, let us add that we emphatically do not include miracles in this category of non-credible things. A certain disregard for the specifics of past events and, especially, of present circumstances, can help open us up to that miracle-accepting faith. The point is not to judge the traditions from a modern, materialistic, limiting perspective. We do not assert them as systems which must be believed wholesale in their official forms, including cultural baggage and superstition—especially insofar as superstition often reverses the spiritually liberating character of religion—but as manifesting in their exoteric form different archetypes and *vast personalities* which humanity is richer for, and which, in their diversity, might catalyze an epiphany of the amplitude of the human-Divine relationship.

The theme of reconciling apparent dichotomies will recur, including, in the case of western civilization, the medieval and the modern, the Christian and the pagan. If we are to position ourselves within a particular current of western history, taking into account our current

---

had recourse to a worthy kingly vessel facilitated through ritual on the eve of sexual union, and that this practice had earned the Bible's condemnation.

2   Frithjof Schuon's essay on his teacher, *René Guénon: Some Observations*, is a good addendum to reading the Frenchman, sorting out Guénon's sometimes comical prejudices from the exegetical main of his work.

lingua anglica, we would think in terms of a retrieval from anglophone modernity of that current represented by King James of England who sought after the Pythagorean-Solomonic temple (through architects like Inigo Jones) against the emerging dichotomies of modernity (as his Archbishop of Canterbury William Laud pointed out). We could make a similar case with regards to Spain's Philip II (see Addendum V). It is in this context that the English translation of the Bible was patronized. Its wake has been modernist and mystical poetry, the greatest light of which is William Blake, who reminds us of the Christian insight that the true temple is the human person. This is both the best of what came to fruit in modernity and its radical correction. "Read Blake or go to hell! That is my message to the modern world," writes Northrop Frye in a letter to his sweetheart.

Among our scholarly coordinates are Eric Voegelin on the study of history and the concept of the Ecumene, Nicholas of Cusa, René Guénon and Frithjof Schuon on the study of religions and metaphysics, Thomas Taylor and Algis Uzdavinys on Platonism, Peter Kingsley on pre-Socratic Greek philosophy,[3] Margaret Barker on Hebrew religion and John Milbank on social and political applications of theological principles. Perhaps our principal referents are William Blake and Henry Corbin,[4] who orient us on the fundamental questions of the human personality's (its agency, imagination) relationship to the Divine, and the point at which religious formulations, however established and traditional they may be, become idolatrous and pose a hindrance to the seeker. Our method is one of "letting the mind play freely around a subject"[5] within the bounds of clear principals, wherefrom a structure emerges, and of course inviting the reader's discernment, just as we exercised ours.

Interviews have been conducted with relevant scholars: Professor of Philosophy and Religion Douglas Hedley, theologian John Milbank. Professor of Indian religions specializing in Tantrism Gavin Flood (the Tantric emphasis on male-female principles being a constant, as well as that on the Divine Feminine), professor of Indian religion specializing in Vaishnavism Edwin Bryant, and historian Eberhard Zangger, specializing in eastern Mediterranean Bronze Age, especially the Luwian context of the historic Troy.[6] Milbank's notion of an alternative, *Proclean*

---

3   Specifically his *Ancient Philosophy, Mystery and Magic: Empedocles and Pythagorean Tradition* (Oxford: Oxford University Press, 1997).
4   Although disagreeing with Corbin's dichotomy between Divine will and necessity (creation vs. emanation) or with the championing of Christian Docetism (while understanding and agreeing with his reasons for it, as it relates to what we call a *fortunate absence*). Blake and Corbin are related through Swedenborg and the correspondences Kathleen Raine details in *Golgonooza: City of Imagination.*
5   Northrop Frye, *Anatomy of Criticism: Four Essays* (Princeton: Princeton University Press, 1990), 3.
6   Hellenism's negotiation of Bronze Age state-cult symbolism provides us with

modernity is our call to action—a modernity based on the philosophy of neo-Platonist Proclus, to whose name we must add Nicholas of Cusa and—perhaps more surprisingly—William Blake, in order to spell out our trajectory.

Finally, my theology is that of St. Dionysius the Areopagite[7] and St. Gregory of Nyssa. Specifically, the understanding of mediation in the former, and the latter's refusal to posit a prime matter. The first allows us to understand spiritual epiphany as able to retain rather than abolish layers of reality, rendering them transparent to what precedes and generous to what follows. The apophatic dimension in Dionysius (and his translator Eriugena) as sustaining diversity of form is, in fact, the core of the present work's argument. The second allows particularity: the essence of a blue circle is not its shape, where color is mere matter; it is not a form imprinted on substance. It is rather an intersection of luminous forms, as Gregory says. Not substance, but the power to substantiate. Matter, when it appears as matter, is always already formed. It does not begin as a preexisting chaotic substrate. This is also why, in using Proclean neo-Platonic theogony as paradigm for initiation, I imagine the *Demiurge* receiving the *autozoon* from the monad, and also discovering it somehow already present in the *Crater*, Juno.

---

a historical framework—further, the spiritual initiatic character of the symbols of monarchical investiture finds its crux, so far as the west is concerned, in the figure of the Trojan hero and imagined ancestor of Caesars, Carolingian and Byzantine emperors, and medieval royals, Aeneas.

7   I refer to author of *Celestial Hierarchy* and *Divine Names*, usually Pseudo-Dionysius. I will simply call him St. Dionysius the Areopagite, but if, for scholarly reasons, some prefix were required, like Samuel Zinner, I would prefer to call him Deutero-Dionysius: "The deutero-canonical are as equally inspired as the primary canonical works. *Our term deutero-dionysius, a term* admittedly used by other scholars in a slightly different sense than employed by us, is intended in the present context in part as a censure of the term Pseudo-Dionysius." Samuel Zinner, *Christianity and Islam: Essays on Ontology and Archetype* (London: The Matheson Trust, 2010), 73, footnote 6.

PART I

Principles of Spiritual Realization and its Political Expression

I. Epiphany and Ecumene:

OVERVIEW AND PRINCIPLES

W E EXPLORE THE *REASON* FOR POLITICAL (OR generally *corporate*) representation and, thereby, the theological understanding that legitimized sacred monarchy in the ancient world. Terms such as *kingly* here refer to the use of monarchical paraphernalia in initiatic ceremonies that need not involve actual dynastic heirs. As far as actual state structures, this is not an apology for any particular monarchical or modern form. Just as the state, or a certain kind of state, manifests the symbolism discussed here, other forms of social organization could do likewise.

Our subject is spiritual overcoming, the *ars regia*, and its communal manifestation. We return to ourselves after ritual death and the experience of transcendent patterns able to provide an example and guide those like us, whoever they may be, according to our vocation. We are shepherds, spiritual kings. Where nations entail strong psychological affinity, this function can conform to political kingship as head of a particular community. Otherwise, we may be called to provide a certain angle on the spiritual quest, ministering to specific personality types, or to people in specific circumstances. [1]

This is implicit in accounts of monarchical investiture, which contain a *doctrine of correspondence* whereby

1. the body of a king is indexed to the body politic, but also,
2. diverse theological systems and the legitimizing principles of states are translatable, because their categories or gods are indexable to common abstract (not culture-specific) principles.

The former explains the idea in the ancient world that the health of a kingdom suffers the fortunes of the health of its king, and the latter constitutes the basis for theological and political conceptions of an *Ecumene*, a harmonious whole.

If a principle can be common to different entities (such as king and kingdom) allowing for political representation, it can also be common to equivalent entities. Several kingdoms can manifest a common principle (order, justice, grandeur, etc.):

---

1   Corbin describes the view that "souls are grouped as it were by spiritual families constituting so many different species in respect to a common genus." Henry Corbin, *Avicenna and the Visionary Recital*, trans. W. Trask (New York: Bollingen Books, 1960), 89.

> If the term is used in the literalist sense, the ecumene can exist
> only in the singular.... If, however, the term is used in its cos-
> mological sense, there may exist an indefinite number of societies
> in which the experience of a fundamental structure in reality will
> be equivalently symbolized.[2]

Identifying a community with an individual representative allows the
personality and discrete bodily existence of the individual human representative to illustrate the community's concreteness as unitary entity, as
well as the idea that the underlying principle it embodies also has personality. "[T]he principle of unity...cannot reside in the multitude...but
in an alterity."[3] Hegel writes, while discussing monarchy, that this is "the
will's ultimate ungrounded self and therefore its similarly ungrounded
existence" that is, the brute fact of the king as actual person, "as the
determination that belongs to nature," and "[i]n this unity lies the actual
unity of the state,"[4] an organic growth, a given constituent of reality.

The doctrine of correspondence, which may also be termed a doctrine
of analogy, translation or indexing, is a metaphysical realism that allows
one corporate structure to link itself to another through their common
underlying principle by way of specific ceremonial operations. As Samuel
Zinner discusses, in the field of semiotics it is the index that best approximates the relation between "Word and words, Idea and articulation."[5]

These operations would entail direct awareness of that underlying
principle on the part of participants and would presumably be constrained by structural affinities between the corporate bodies involved
(the king embodies the *specific* kingdom he rules). This can be described
as a species of what anthropologists term sympathetic magic, which we
may denote *sympathetic theurgy*.

The very idea of political representation and leadership assumes 1) that
an agent may act on behalf of others, implying 2) that this agent may
correspond or represent others, which in turn means 3) that there is a
principle common to both the representing agent and the represented
party by way of which these may correspond so that the former may
represent the latter. This final point constitutes the logic according to
which monarchy was traditionally conceived of as requiring personal
spiritual realization, that is, realization of the underlying principle of
which bodies and communities are expressive, establishing a rule of
three (*a* is to *b* what *b* is to *c*).

---

2   Eric Voegelin. *The Collected Works of Eric Voegelin, vol. 17: Order and History, vol. 4,
The Ecumenic Age* (Columbia, MO: University of Missouri Press, 2000), 340.
3   Jean Hani, *Sacred Royalty: From the Pharaoh to the Most Christian King*, trans. Gustavo
Polit (London: The Matheson Trust, 2011), 43.
4   Georg W. H. Hegel, *Outlines of the Philosophy of Right* (Oxford: Oxford University
Press, 2008), 273.
5   Samuel Zinner, *Christianity and Islam: Essays on Ontology and Archetype*, 12.

In order to apply Unity, or any abstract principle, to a new context, it must be grasped as transcendent by divorcing it from the context in which it is previously encountered, and brought back into the particular. This takes the form of rites of ritual death or ecstatic suspension of the mental oscillations, followed by rebirth, the cross and resurrection, the alchemical *solve et coagula*, and so on. Ritual death is often described as occurring in a sacred mountain, because this latter is the axis mundi, the center wherein the elements of manifestation are not yet differentiated.

This constitutes the basis for religious initiation being linked to social duty: To come to properly perceive that which is transcendent is to come to perceive that which operates in diverse immanent forms (their underlying principle) and, therefore, to become capable of acting towards those forms in ways that concord with their own inherent operations (their reason for being) or, put differently, with the operations of the wider systems of which are parts (as these wider systems would likewise be expressive of the same underlying principle).

This applies to every initiate whose realization of universal selfhood is modulated into conscious occupancy of his social being, whatever that may be, from his own hermit self to family unit to guild or business. The initiate realizes himself as microcosm of the whole cosmos and of all the specific bodies he is a part of, including his specific personality-type, so to speak, a set of concentric and transversal corporate identities constitute a unique view on the whole, a unique perspective which allows him to be a microcosm different from other microcosms, but of the same macrocosm. This assumes social existence can be endowed of, inhabited by, a real being beyond psychological construct or, better, psychologically constructing it in a highest sense, finding the will-towards-it within himself and inhabiting it so that it receives a theatre in his own awareness.

We have the formula of cross and resurrection, or detaching from specific contingent conditions in order to understand the abstract principle (the invisible core, the hollow in the seed mentioned by the *Upanishads*) at work in them and thusly to apply or perceive that principle in different contingent conditions (losing coordinates, gaining the quintessence, and locking it into new coordinates). In Greek Orthodox terms (which I am using inexactly[6]):

- *Katharsis* or ritual death (*annulment* of contingent conditions)
- *Theoria* or perceiving the transcendent (*abstraction* of principle)
- *Theosis* or returning to see the transcendent in the immanent (*application* of abstract principle to new contingent conditions)

Any particular, formal order must be finite, even spatial extension must be discrete, but in so being they are encompassed (in what Proclus calls

---

6 These correspond, respectively, to *Nigredo*, *Albedo* and *Rubedo* in alchemical language. I am omitting the third phase of *Citrinitas* (between Albedo and Rubedo) and assimilating it to Albedo.

a *series*) within the pattern of their commonality (Proclus's *cause*). Being particular, no such discrete extension can present the fullness of a universal (the "unlimited realm of universal possibility" [7]). Thusly is the "quantitative infinite" to be rejected: "Number, space, and time...are determine conditions, and as such can only be finite."[8] This applies even to time, which must be finite, for which reason the traditions speak of infinitely succeeding world periods rather than of a single, ever-unrenewed temporality.

Therefore does Plotinus appear to prefer identifying the term *unbounded* with the Platonic One's power, or describing the One as *source* of infinity, rather than referring to the infinitude of the One itself.[9] Correspondingly, the scholastics distinguish between an *infinitum secundum quid* and an *infinitum absolutum*, as Guénon points out.[10] This is also equivalent to Nicholas of Cusa considering the cosmos *interminatus* where only the divine is properly *infinitus*.[11] Terminological differences notwithstanding, these indicate the same essential distinction.

The infinity of created possibilities is thus fundamentally one of diverse forms, to be distinguished from the Divine simplicity, which is Absolute and not to be conceived of as infinite in spatial terms or in duration. Giordano Bruno, in applying an attribute of God to the world,[12] must confront the paradox that this application becomes a severe contrast: *Divine simplicity* (and Its infinite potential to create) corresponds to infinite *creaturely diversity*. When the Bishop of Paris in 1277, Etienne Tempier, argues that the actual world cannot exhaust God's creativity, but that at the same time the first cause cannot produce an effect equivalent to itself, an effect which is infinite, this is not a contradiction, as Hans Blumenberg suggests,[13] for the infinity of created forms is infinite in its plurality, diverse rather than simple, relative rather than Absolute.

We suggest, with Nicholas of Cusa, that the cosmology of infinite worlds is simply the thorough application of medieval, theistic premises,[14] while pointing out, against Blumenberg, that this does not make the world Divine in the sense of having God's attributes (at least not in the way in which these attributes are held by God in His simplicity). In a sense the world becomes more distinct from God, not less, because a finite

7   René Guénon, *The Symbolism of the Cross*, trans. A. Macnab (Hillsdale, NY: Sophia Perennis, 1996), 10.

8   René Guénon, *The Metaphysical Principle of the Infinitesimal Calculus*, trans. M. Allen and H. Fohr (Hillsdale, NY: Sophia Perennis, 2004), 9.

9   Elizabeth Brient, *The Immanence of the Infinite: Hans Blumenberg and the Threshold to Modernity* (Washington, DC: The Catholic University of America Press, 2002), 114.

10 Guénon, *The Metaphysical Principle of the Infinitesimal Calculus*, 8.

11 Alexandre Koyré, *From the Closed World to the Infinite Universe* (London: John Hopkins Press, 1957), 8.

12 Hans Blumenberg, *The Legitimacy of the Modern Age*, trans. R. Wallace (Cambridge, MA: The MIT Press, 1985), 78–79.

13 Blumenberg, *The Legitimacy of the Modern Age*, 160.

14 Ibid., 518.

world would need to be considered the exclusive icon of His creativity for, despite other worlds being possible, His will was to make only one, *this* one. An infinity of worlds undoes the idolatry inherent in this. This epiphany is one of *harmony, not homogeneity; infinite forms, not formal infinity.* If Unity is transcendent, we are not to find its Divine simplicity in formal manifestation, in infinite entropy, but rather in harmony, which is unity between forms which are themselves unitary (we say a thing is harmonious when it is so with respect to other, distinct things, with its surroundings, etc., so that pluralism or community is implied).

The above implies pluralism and harmony, the unity of things in themselves and the encompassing unity of their relationships. A contrary uniformizing and centralizing occurs when that invisible core which the seeker connects to is reified as a particular being among beings rather than the Being of beings. [15] If a perfect circle were identified with the image of a red circle, or if all circles were red, circularity itself would be defined or become conceptionally confused with the color red. The diversity of circles and a properly transcendent definition of circularity, saves blue and yellow circles from being forced to become red in order to claim to be circles. This is *plurality*, the unity of units in themselves, discontinuous from other units. *Unity as the pluralization of units that shows It is beyond units.*

Rather than imitating a supposedly perfect circle they may express their common shape together by displaying their commonality as that which remains the same across their diversity. This display is *pattern, harmonious relation*: communities throughout the world organize festival processions, presenting themselves to themselves in ordered picturesque. This is *pattern*, that is, *harmonious relations between units* in which they share with each other and preserve in each other what is common and what is contrasting. *Unity as the pattern in which units participate that shows It is between them.*

In the above, color becomes the means through which we know the transcendence of circularity. Extending this, we can conceive of other shapes, and thus understand that shape is a wider transcendent category. We can do the same with color. Ultimately, we arrive at Unity as such, the one Being of the plural beings.

We may read this in the Gospel. Some thinkers (recently Slavoj Zizek) see a Christian atheism in the cross and in Christ's post-resurrection de-emphasizing of the external image of the Father in favor of the Holy Spirit as present within the community of love. But this is precisely metaphysics (as opposed to mega-physics). Here, God (or His unitary Being) is real, for instead of chaos and entropy, the constituents of reality are able to hold together (as individual bodies and as wider encompassing harmonious communities). Further, this occurs not through mechanistic

---

15   Or Beyond Being, superessential for, as Dionysius the Areopagite maintains, "Being," is a name for God as source of all that exists, but in Himself, transcending all things, He can also be described as "not Being."

objective law but in the subjective experience of love. We are here asserting the Unity and Subjectivity of Being of classical metaphysics. Its
consequence is that the community finds Being within itself and is able
to have Being represented to itself. Human cultural imagination and
political participation are justified.

Eric Voegelin's "immanentizing the eschaton" requires idolatry, i.e.,
mistaking the Being of beings for an excellent being among deficient
beings. Older millenarian idolatrous religious sects conceived of the
most-excellent being as out-there, soon to arrive. In contrast, the more
disheartened modern ideological trajectories become, the less they pretend
to even a reified (counter-)metaphysics: If before they had convinced
themselves that there was a perfect circle coming, one which would
teach all other circles how to be likewise perfect, they are now perhaps
more willing to admit that they will have to build that circle, and even,
cynically, *that it will not be perfect* but it *will be the standard.* This is perfectly
consistent, and it is what Nietzsche predicted, as the consequences
of the death of god dawn more fully: if there is no Being, there is no
standard for excellence. We often end up thinking in terms not of a
most-excellent being but a most-powerful or largest being, falling back
upon the gravity of brute force.

We hear it admitted that it is not possible to act without implicitly
assuming metaphysics. The situation is that of a nihilist who, despairing
that human beings are incapable of thinking without transcendent categories, decides to pretend his rationalism is that transcendence. In this
defeat he becomes naked of pretense: There is no Being of beings and
there is not even the possibility of a most-excellent being, because there
is no such thing as excellence. But since human beings need to believe
there is, or disbelieving can nonetheless not act in terms of that disbelief,
they might as well produce the biggest being they can. Frequently, talk
of the technological Singularity seems to mean just this, as do utopian
claims to a future ideal amalgamation of all cultures.

Modern discourse assumes ontology is only in contingent features:
things are only unified if they are made uniform; if things are made to
look the same, then they *are* the same, and if they are the same, they
will not be in conflict, for a thing is not in conflict with itself. Yet this
denial of Being is a reification (an idolatry) of Being: the future sameness
is itself that most-excellent (or rather, biggest) being.

Ideologies that reject Being/Unity as inherent to reality are like
the ego that rejects freedom from its ever-oscillating thoughts. Their
ideological visions of utopia and dystopia are equivalent to the Tibetan
Book of the Dead's wrathful deities, which the ego presents to us during
meditation because it needs us busy pursuing desire and warding off
despair, attraction and aversion, following a model and fighting a scapegoat, for it does not believe that it can survive a perfect, contemplative

freedom from mental strain. It believes we are our mental tension. But refusing to negotiate, argue or react to these wrathful deities, refusing to remain on that tightrope of the mind, we sink into Being.

Here I suggest our rapport with Being (apart from pure absorption) is participative. Instead of the mind's idolatrous deities, transcendent Unity represents Itself formally (the Biblical *Ancient of Days*, the theophany, Indian Vaishnavism's 'bhava' or loving relationship which manifest according to a devotee's desire: Krishna's many forms). The Ancient of Days is, in Orthodox Christianity, still the Second Person of the Trinity, like the Son of Man who meets him in the prophet Daniel's vision. But the Ancient of Days may *represent* the First Person, the Father. It is because Being represents Itself to Itself that It is interactive ("I am in the opinion of my servant" says Allah according to one hadith in the Sahih of al-Bukhari). It is here also where we may locate a philosophy of religious diversity, Schuon's "theophanic individualities." Being is not exhaustible in any one being, and therefore manifests variously.

I suggest that bearing what we could call "apophatic witness" means acknowledging, at least theoretically, the plurality of expressions of Truth, because Truth is inexhaustible in any contingent expression. As with other realizations, generally orthodox religion only approaches it asymptotically. It leaves it outside of itself, like an equation that needs the seeker to add something. When we cross the "thicket of delusion," not even verses from the *Vedas* will do, says the *Gita* (II:52). There is a passage from the Orthodox Christian *Philokalia* that speaks of two kinds of demons, and where those who inspire vices are easy to identify, those who inspire vanity in virtue are harder. Indeed, not only virtue as typically understood, but religious ritualization, pious habit. If we do not bring ourselves to the equation, religious asceticism is mere mechanism, and demonic interference (pushing our buttons) is easy when we rely on mechanical thought patterns. In theology, it is perhaps they who imagine the Divine as an impassible commander who end up considering It an impersonal force, although they would argue the opposite.

This principle of acknowledging the plurality of expressions of Truth as beyond the surface reading of a tradition might have its historic analogue in the detaching of a tradition from its initial outward project (for example, the project of literalizing its universal claim through actual world conversion). We avoid idolatry by acknowledging plurality, because Being is inexhaustible in any being. Our safeguard is a rigorous assertion of Unity as transcendent to any given unit. This might have an analogue in the historical detaching of a tradition from its initial outward project of world-conversion. Such detachment allows it a more pious expression, even in this apparent waning. Understanding plurality as itself a witness to transcendent Unity is a radically different outlook from that of modern discourse, where pluralism is pacification-as-homogenization.

So long as we defend the theophanic individuality of traditions or cultures in these terms, as joyful expressions of Unity, and not as mere restraints against invading forces, we do well. Unfortunately, reactionary religionists frequently present the Good as a mere agonistic resistance against evil, as though the problem of evil came first and the Good were a subsequent solution, so that instead of Good having Being and Evil being only privation, they imply the inverse. In Christian terms, Pentecost is a good in itself, not a mere safeguard against Babel.

Finally, it is worth mentioning that the danger of immanentizing the eschaton is not perforce a mainly political one. Whether we express a true doctrine in a social project or by writing a book is, in principle, the same. Indeed, Biblical eschatology is often expressed as referring to something within history, and therefore affecting the political forces of historical change (see the original language of the Apocalypse 21:24, Luke 21, but also in general Isaiah, Micah, Jeremiah, etc.). The danger is rather mainly one of confusing the planes, of treating unity of principle as uniformity of practice.

Before continuing, we summarize the key points mentioned above, whose import will be iterated throughout the present work:

- *Unity is present* in the coherence of forms.
- *Unity is transcendent* with respect to the plurality of forms. Unity manifests the coherence of forms across varying features. The plurality of forms shows that Unity as such is not exhaustible in any of them.

This leads us to a discussion of what we call the Hospitable Infinite in which coherent and plural forms are sustained.

- *Unity is present* in the harmonious interaction between forms. Harmony encompasses forms in wider unities expressive of Unity. Analogous to the coherence of forms.
- *Unity is transcendent* with respect to the dynamism of patterns between forms. Analogous to the plurality of forms, patterns are dynamic. The patterns of interaction between forms display regularity, often centralizing around a body and repeating a movement, the variation of which shows that this pattern cannot fully express Unity.

This leads us to a discussion of what we call the *Absent Center and Asymptotic Cosmos*, in which there is no definitive centralization and harmonious interactions allow an "apophatic witness" to transcendent centrality, Unity.

Other sections of the Part I explore the above further, until the last section, *Sat-Chit-Ananda*, which locates it more clearly in the context of initiation and comparative religion/mythology. This serves as a transition to Part II, which is focused more on specific symbols and traditions. Here, the main principles under investigation are:

- Political leadership requires the instantiation of the universal in the particular, of the general principle of order or coherence, into a specific context, and therefore of ritual death or dissolution, access of the universal, and its introduction into the particular: political office proper, then, is a spiritual conferment requiring initiatic rebirth.

• In applying the universal (for example in a principle like justice, order, harmony, etc.) to the particular community, the individual must correspond with that particular, accessing the universal that manifests both his individual personhood and the collective, which is why leadership is always representation. Thus, the idea that sacred kings embody their realm and physically share in its health.

• Across traditions, the initiate as perceiver of the universal and introducer of its principle into the particular is presented as male, a sacred king or hero, and the particular which receives the universal as female, the world or kingdom or lady. The universal itself is both, and is bestowed by the Divine Feminine (Rhea, conjoined with Saturn, in neo-Platonism).

• In conducting relations with other polities, a holder of political office must understand them as expressing an underlying principle common to his own, so that, externally, political leadership is the establishment of ecumenical relations. Otherwise, we cannot speak of international *relations*, for there is no basis on which to relate.

  ○ The political always concerns identity and difference, and the respective coherence and peaceability of these depends on a doctrine of correspondence. The transcendence of Unity allows for establishing an analogy between the community and the unitary body of a representative, applying the organic givenness of the individual body to the political community identity. It also legitimizes equivalent expressions of common patterns, so that a community may conceive of others as fellow expressions.

THE BEING OF BEINGS: THE BEYOND IS BETWEEN

According to Plato, the cosmos is a living creature with soul and reason.[16] It is an intelligible animal, and is distinct from what he calls the autozoon (or "essential living being"/intellectual animal[17]). The intelligible animal, that is, the "whole cosmos, both in soul and body," is an image of the autozoon just as time is an image of eternity.[18] The autozoon is the four-cornered center of the cosmos in the sense of being the blueprint for the universe.

Neo-Platonists like Proclus consider the autozoon, the ideal order, the principle of all living creatures, the blueprint for every body and the whole universe, to be contained in the First Paternal Intellect, Saturn, taken by its feminine component, Rhea, to the Second Paternal Intellect, the cosmic architect, the Demiurge, Jove. This place *between* the First and Second Paternal Intellect which is filled by the autozoon is not a place "out

---

16   Plato, *Timaeus*, ed. Richard Archer-Hind (London: Macmillan and Co., 1888), 30b, 93.

17   Proclus, *The Commentaries of Proclus on the Timaeus of Plato in Five Books*, vol. 2, trans. T. Taylor (London: A. J. Valpy, 1820), V; 357.

18   Iamblichus, *Fragments of Iamblichus' Commentary on the Timaeus*, trans. John Dillon (Leiden, Netherlands: E. J. Brill, 1973), III: Fr.66; 177.

there." It is in a sense in the space between manifest forms themselves: the interaction, the ordered relation. It is invisible, a figure of the Divine ineffability. Indeed, transcendence is not one term in a binary between the transcendent and the imminent, but rather is a third, a space *between* the dialoguers, if we speculate an etymology in which *trans-* is taken as indicating the Indo-European root for the number three (bad etymology making for good philosophy, perhaps). The ideal order, the principle of unity, is within each form, for each form manifests it and is a unity in itself, and also *between* manifest forms. Therefore, Luke 17:21 is sometimes translated as *the kingdom of heaven is within you* and also *the kingdom of heaven is in your midst.*

The *autozoon* is the image of that which the awareness of the initiate (in Proclus's schema, Jove) perceives from Being (Kronos-Rhea), that is, the image of ontological Unity, the experience of which is joyful and is realized by recognizing it in the very possibility of formal manifestation/phenomena (Juno). It is an animated image, a sentience, because Unity is ultimately unitary subjectivity, Pure Consciousness, not some pure objectivity devoid of interiority, and so its figure is a *living* creature. Rhea bestows the autozoon on Jove because She is the experience of unitary Being, which is Joy, where Saturn is the Awareness of this Being. (This is very much equivalent in Indian tradition to Shakti and Shiva within Shaivism or Vishnu and Lakshmi in the Vishnu Purana, and we are grounding our exposition in the Indian triad *Sat-Chit-Ananda*, which we are calling Being-Awareness-Joy, or Pure Consciousness, Reflexive Consciousness and Conscious Experience.)

In pure contemplation of Being, Joy and Awareness are in perfect mutual *absorption* (Rhea conjoined with Saturn, as Proclus writes) whereas in a differentiated state of mutual *attraction* they are Juno and Jove. The subjective character or content of this perception of Being is Joy: Unity precludes discord, irreducibility, conflict, and Joy inspires creativity within the indestructible safety of oneness. The initiate's subjectivity is both Awareness and Joy.

We have Being, Awareness and Joy (or Consciousness, its Reflecting and its Experiencing), and *the autozoon is its intellection,*[19] its object of

---

19   Like Sergei Bulgakov's distinction between the three Persons of the Trinity and Sophia. The Divine Sophia suggests Plato's autozoon, which the Demiurge receives but also finally discovers in the Crater: "The Divine Sophia is not only

apprehension, the first psyche, a mind, a composite structure within the subject (a multiplicity expressive of Unity). If we imagine *Sat* as a center, *Chit* as a circumference and *Ananda* as a radius, the autozoon (or representation of *Sat* as multiplicity) would be a point of intersection and, in fact, the whole circumference conceived as points. Awareness reflects Being into an infinitude of points, and Joy allows it to realize these in connection to that center. The radius allows the circumference to conceive of itself as an infinity of beings (points like the center). The radius is simply expansion from the center, which does not lead to individuated, concrete manifestation until it meets with the reflection of the center, which is reflexive awareness. Following the radius, we can also extend or deepen beyond the circumference to draw new wider or narrower versions of that circumference. Treating a point of intersection between radius and circumference as itself a center, it may depart in new directions. And just as the autozoon contains the four elemental ideas which then produce the manifest world as tetrad (four corners, etc.), so it takes four points on the surface of a sphere to define that sphere (to locate its center). *The radius, the very thing that allows Chit to find its center, is also that which allows it to understand itself as a pleroma of potentially infinite points.*

The radius from the center allows the circumference to conceive of itself as an infinity of beings (points alike the center), as a composite body. Therefore *the autozoon the is body of the Demiurge, his presence conceived as discernable parts, anatomized, points each alike the center,* that is, the Eternal Forms which the Demiurge contemplated, wherefrom he made the cosmos in Plato's *Timaeus*. By conceiving of himself as composite, and expanding this body according to its points, the cosmos was made. This may describe the dismemberment of Purusha in India, with the energies of Prakriti, the Lamb slain from the foundation of the earth (Apocalypse 13:8), and the Wife of the Lamb (Apocalypse 21:9). In Biblical terms, *the King is the Demiurge, the Lamb is the autozoon.*

The radius leads both from circumference to center and vice-versa. The autozoon is bestowed on Jove by Rhea but, in a sense, is produced by the contact between these, for it is when the reflexive awareness turns back and reflects on its on Being that the possibility of multiplicity is fathomed, and it is the encounter with Being (specifically the Joy of Being, Rhea) that inspires in Awareness the will to creativity, towards the conception of a multiplicity of expressions of Unity. Awareness does not only encounter/conceive of *multiplicity as expression of Unity* once, in the

---

the Son, just as she is not only the Holy Spirit; rather, she is the bi-unity of the Son and the Holy Spirit as one self-revelation of the Father." She occurs in their "dyadic interpenetration." The autozoon is the essential living creature, whereas the intelligible living creature, or world-soul, would correspond to the creaturely Sophia: "The created world is established in being by God at the 'Beginning,' that is, in the Divine Sophia, as her creaturely image, or the creaturely Sophia." Sergei Bulgakov. *The Comforter*, trans. Boris Jakim (Cambridge, UK: Eerdmans, 2004), 178, 189.

depths of its own Being, but also again, as a second epiphany, at its own
level, out in the phenomenal, where Awareness and Joy are differentiated
(as Jove and Juno) and can experience reunion.

Here it is surprised by the fact that its own will to create is already
at play in the beauty of creation, and it is at play because Joy is already
causing it (she melts forms into revealing themselves as forms of Joy, so
that he may recognize them as that autozoon he saw in contemplation,
and thus participate in formal manifestation in order to bring about that
specific manifestation of the autozoon proper to him—when a man falls
in love with a woman, all his yearnings for spiritual sublimity, retaining
that sublimity, receive a sublime specificity). We can analogize this in
Buddhist meditation terms to *samatha* and *vipassana*. In samatha we bring
single-pointed attention (a thought, a sensation, etc.) to still the mind,
but we can shift to vipassana, observing the whole flux of the mind (in a
sense the mind as receptacle, analogous to Juno) without focusing on any
element of its content. We will find that the one content which is in a
sense inherent, and which is produced when we remove all others, is Joy.

The initiate perceives Unity in contemplative absorption (when mental
or psycho-somatic oscillations cease). His psycho-somatic self has been
slain (this is often presented as the animal self, and across traditions the
initiate is identified with a sacrificial animal, whose four legs can represent the whole world—north, south, east and west, or air, earth, fire
and water—and four basic temperaments of the personality—choleric,
melancholic, phlegmatic and sanguine). That self is subdued and then re-
inhabited (like Greek heroes wearing animal hides), along with the rest of
the formal cosmos, now known as a manifestation of Unity, and therefore
as harmonious, joyful, so that the initiate realizes the cosmos as a manifestation of the same principle manifesting him, and unites with Joy: this is
the king's copulation with the queen as personified kingdom/microcosm.

The king now learns that the cosmos is harmonious, just as the queen
does. But if the king brings this perception, it is because she made it possible. The king has ordered the multiplicity of the queen (the fourfold manifestation of the cosmos—the cardinal directions, the four elements, etc.—is
a function of femininity) around his center (an image of Unity, the fifth
element or literal quintessence) and the queen has previously allowed him
to know that center by pacifying the multiplicity (that of his own sentience,
where contemplation of the object of erotic desire is the same as initiatic
death before rebirth, as we see in Plato or medieval courtly romance).

It is not simply that he is the center and she is the fourfold periphery,
rather, he teaches her that the center is Consciousness and she teaches
him that it is Joy. He absorbs the multiplicity of phenomena into his
Awareness (the Tantric *ahamidam*, where experience is suspended in experiencer), and she clarifies them, makes them transparent, to Joy (idamaham,
where experiencer is absorbed in pure experience): both are a return to

primordial unity. *The autozoon is brought by him, but is already with her.* In their mutual recognition of the autozoon, the four elements whose ideas are in the autozoon, come into manifestation.[20] Juno is already a manifestation of order, coming from the monad, just as Jove is. And being Joy the center encompasses the periphery with exuberance, creativity, dynamism. He finds himself in Pure Being as Awareness/Consciousness and discovers that Pure Being is everywhere as Joy.

The feminine lifts her veils to the spiritual hero, who may renew the world messianically. That this pacification may in turn be a response to him only indicates that Male and Female are mutually superior,[21] just as in Christianity the sacrament of marriage is bestowed by man on wife and by wife on man. Proclus tells us that, for Orpheus, the Demiurge and Crater, Jove and Juno, are equal causes, the one of *being* and the other of *life*. The king initiates the queen by introducing her to the autozoon just as the queen reveals she (the whole cosmos) manifests it. These are the descending and ascending inspirations.

If the autozoon is between the ineffable Oneness of the divine and the multiplicity of the world, it is not itself a thing, but an archetypal reality or pattern manifesting in or as *things*. It is observable, therefore, in the harmonious relatedness of the world's components. Being no-thing it cannot be dwelt on if not in the world. *That which is between human beings and God is between human beings and each other.* To approach God is to approach one another. *Contemplation is compassion, is community.* Thus, Christ's instruction to congregate and promise that He is present where two or more are gathered in His Name (Mathew 18:20). This explains why traditional understandings tended to see spiritual realization as connected to social participation, and that one's duty was itself a spiritual practice, so that perceiving the autozoon is requisite to participating in the political.

Contemplation of the autozoon yields the ability to rule justly, in the case of one set to rule—note the monarchical image of crowns and rods given by Christ to them who overcome in the Apocalypse—or to dwell harmoniously (like Heidegger's *poetic dwelling*). Particulars are instants of a universal, and, sharing Being, may relate on that basis. The universal is manifest in the particular; the beyond-Being and Being of beings is the Being of consciousness (Logos, Son) and its presence there is prior to differentiated creation. This is analogous to

---

20   The primordial Male and Female contain this design and yet manifest it together, where each is one half of the fourfold. Following (Kingsley's reading of) Empedocles, two elements are male (air and fire) and two female (earth and water). If we interpret one of each as stable (air and earth) and one of each dynamic or volatile (fire and water), we may relate this to the active and passive masculinity and the active and passive femininity of Shaivist Tantrism, as a fourfold that together composes the world: *ahamidam* and *idamaham* of the primordial Aham (Male, Reflexive Consciousness) and Idam (Female, Experience).

21   Schuon's term.

St. John's understanding of the Spirit as imparting to the disciples
a knowledge of the Father's dwelling in the Son, and of this knowledge as a beholding of, and sharing in, the glory which the Son
has 'before the foundation of the world' (John 14:10–27; 17:1–26).

Here "the Church perpetuates or renews a Creation prior to all coercion
and conflict—a city, as Origen so repeatedly emphasizes, ruled only by
the persuasive power of the Logos."[22]

The above entails an ethos of patience, what philosopher William
Desmond calls the *passio essendi*.[23] Embracing the dynamism and multiplicity of life requires connecting to the gratuity (the sheer *givenness*)
of things in a joyful spirit (and not in what Nietzsche calls the *spirit of
gravity*[24]). Joy, un-conflicted, cannot but express an "ontology of peace,"
as John Milbank puts it, according to which differences emerge from,
and are expressive of, *Logos*: "differences as analogically related, rather
than equivocally at variance"[25] and do not necessitate discord, as in an
ontology of irreducibly agonistic entities.

To lose sight of this leads to an impatient, simplifying violence. If the
Being of beings is reified into an imagined excellent being among less
excellent beings, if Unity itself is identified with some particular unit, if
the Origin of all is sought in some discrete, single originating event, we
end up violating the matrix of things. Perceiving floridity, the aesthetic of
flowers, an impatient mind eager to schematize reality and be done with
its jarring complexities—eager, that is, to find the unity of an abstract
definition entirely exhausted in one concrete object—may insist on such a
quality being solely or most properly the ambit of flowers. Its presence in
the wings of butterflies, for example, are then considered merely derivative.
In contrast, a patient mind allows the archetypal ingredients of existence to
express themselves as they will, and thus gains a higher-resolution image
of the ordered beauty of creation, one which does not identify this or that
quality exclusively with some given form. Is a deep violet color more properly itself in blueberries or in a viola flower? The question is meaningless.

In practical terms, patient apprehension is preferable to compulsive
criticality because the truth may well appear incongruent to the latter
sensibility. As John Milbank and Adrian Pabst put it, "[a] huge problem
here is that the truth can often look—at least at first sight—*implausible*."[26]

---

22   John Milbank. *The Word Made Strange: Theology, Language, Culture* (Malden, MA:
Blackwell Publishers, 1998), 185.
23   And Proclus's understanding of Plato's *autozoon* is very near Desmond's *metaxy*,
middle.
24   Friedrich Nietzsche. *Thus Spoke Zarathustra: A Book for All and None*, trans. A.
Caro (Cambridge: Cambridge University Press, 2006), I, 29.
25   John Milbank, *Theology and Social Theory: Beyond Secular Reason*, 2nd ed. (Oxford:
Blackwell Publishing, 2006), 279.
26   John Milbank and Adrian Pabst. *The Politics of Virtue: Post-Liberalism and the
Human Future* (London: Rowman and Littlefield, 2016), 262.

Descriptions of any physical structure, dynamic or organism can sound perplexing—openings to a sense of the *uncanny*—to someone who has never encountered the likes of whatever is being described. If one who has never seen an octopus has it described to him, he may, depending on his disposition, take it to be the product of a child's imagination.

There is certainly often an element, a murderous wedge, in culture, that militates against this pacific ontology and ethos of patience. But we do not reject culture in asserting the latter, rather we transform culture as the fires of the burning bush burn but consume not. One autumn, years back, leaving a corner store, crunching laminas of gold leaf underfoot, I walked together with a friend as he explained why he buys candy for Halloween (feeling put upon to justify the thing, as one of his neighbors refused to participate in the celebration for religious reasons):

> "Hay que ser abiertos, por si el diablo..." *We must be open, in case the devil...*

I've written that phrase with a "...," but he meant it as a full stop. Still, I inquired after the folksy wisdom.

> "In case the devil what?"
> "...wants his due." He obliged me, matter-of-factly.

Consider what the Indian perennialist and art historian Ananda Coomaraswamy writes:

> The content of folklore is metaphysical.... We observe, for example, that the primitive craftsman leaves in his work something unfinished, and that the primitive mother dislikes to hear the beauty of her child unduly praised; it is 'tempting Providence,' and may lead to disaster.[27]

The first sentence is true. But where Coomaraswamy distinguishes folklore both from exoteric religion and science, he does not properly parse it from superstition. Folklore might begin with superstition, but it ends with a wink. Andalusians have a saying: "Don't leave to later what you can do now. And so, he shat his pants." The second part is meant to be whispered. The first is directed at the listener, the second is said by the speaker to herself, mocking the listener's potential naiveté. It does not contradict the *practice* of getting on with one's work, but it dispels the idea that it might constitute some universal moral injunction. There are limits. The Sabbath is made for man, not man for the Sabbath (Mark 2:27).

So why are things left slightly unfinished? Why do carpets have fringes? This habit observed by Coomaraswamy lends itself to two readings. The craftsman leaves his work slightly unfinished because if it were entirely complete it would invite death, for all that exists is in a process

27   Ananda Coomaraswamy. *The Essential Ananda K. Coomaraswamy*, ed. R. Coomaraswamy (Bloomington, IN: World Wisdom, 2004), 225.

of becoming perfected, and he himself may be struck down dead if, as an artist, he perfects his craft; or the craftsman leaves his work slightly unfinished—better, slightly *open*—because it is porous, it wants to breath.

Something must suggest to the observer that the work is not only the surface image which he presently sees, that it can pour forth and gives way to the beyond. Houses have windows, and we do not imagine that the ideal house would have none. Even the ideal can be comprehended within an open field. To my friend, I might now say: there are many rooms in Christ's Father's house, and should not each room know itself, in its perfection, to be one of many? Even our images of completeness are inwardly open: they imply dynamism and contain internal variation, like the Buddhist mandala whose center is an embracing divine couple. Which of those two figures is the final stop? Rather, their harmonious interaction, which is not a thing but a pattern, is the final stop. The seed's core is hollow. This we may term *apophatic openness*, openness to our form-transcending intimacy, and to that same intimacy outside us.

The opposite is *apotropaic openness*. The kind of piety that consists of warding-off gestures. This renders openness a danger; a window through which to propitiate hungry superstitions and save ourselves, but by the very same token the window through which those demons may rear their heads. It is why we react to religious imagery with phobic squints. This piety hides from us the aesthetic beauty of openness, relationality, community. Openness becomes a technology and a danger, but not the ecstatic chance at playing with the world and our fellows.

Coomaraswamy discusses a connection between the end of superstitions passed on by prior generations and the degeneration of a culture. However, the radicality of a Christian or similar dispensation is not that it kills a people whose superstitions it banishes and whose polytheistic rites it finishes. Rather, it gives that people new life as an aesthetic good, one that need not justify its existence in terms of, say, the blood-letting it believes makes the sun rise each day. There is life outside the compulsions and necessities it held to. Only if its only reason for being were that blood-letting would it necessarily degenerate. St. Paul, especially in Galatians, emphasizes that there is community outside the law, in fact true community is possible only outside the law, where the law has become an idol (where it is not understood that the Sabbath is made for man, and not vice-versa).

The point of higher spirituality might be that Coomaraswamy's reading phases apocalyptically into the latter interpretation (that a thing is left unfinished in order to indicate its porosity, its transparence to transcendence). The craftsman should not leave a work unfinished to apotropaically ward off death—a death dealt to things too perfect, too beautiful, one intuits, by angry gods who feed on the psychological fear of full relaxation, full relinquishing of fear—let us be clear—*full faith*. These are precisely the gods one faces when the mind begins relaxing in meditation, when it spasms against the cessation of its churning thoughts. Such superstition, folksy as it might be, is precisely the old man, the old law, the Gospel warns against.

The radicality of monotheism, its apocalyptic fire, takes superstitious ritual, an apotropaic compulsion, and extinguishes its reason for being— fear—in the knowledge of the loving God, and of what we will call the *Hospitable Infinite*. It reveals, where such exists to be revealed, a higher and in a sense entirely opposite meaning for that ritual. We assert culture, mythology and folklore but emphatically not the superstitious oxidation on its surface which imitates its contours while hiding its light, like the tyrannical, spiritually ignorant ego upon the true self.

Ultimately, particularity must be defended not as an agonistic necessity but instead asserted in purely positive terms, in an unconflicted spirit of aesthetic beauty. Good, then, the leaving aside of conflict in favor of assertion and celebration of what one positively wants is the path to take. One should avoid the mimetic rivalry that forces one to become like what one is pushing against, more concerned with the competition than the prize, like a man who forgets his love of women in the thrall of obsessive competition with other men (ostensibly for women) and cultivates a sort of counterfeit to sexuality, as philosopher René Girard observed.

Joseph Chilton Pearce writes the following in his *Biology of Transcendence* (a sometimes spurious book, that is precisely not so in its most radical claim):

> Accusation, in any of its forms, is a negative judgment, and a negative judgment in any form ruptures relationship—the classical definition of sin . . . When we accuse or judge another, it has the same effect on us as being judged ourselves. Any judgment we make, no matter of whom, registers in the heart as a disruption of relationship, and the heart dutifully responds on behalf of our defense, shifting neural, hormonal, and electromagnetic systems, from relational to defensive.[28]

UNITY WITHIN FORMS, OR EVERYTHING HAS BORDERS AND BROTHERS

Here we explore the plurality of individualities, heroism,[29] coherence. *Diversity is the epistemology of Unity.* Because the one Being of the plural beings is never fully exhausted in any of them, they each are in themselves legitimate expressions of Being, of Its Unity. Henry Corbin puts this as follows, describing God's Unity:[30]

---

28   Joseph C. Pearce, *The Biology of Transcendence: A Blueprint of the Human Spirit* (Vermont: Park Street Press), 128.

29   I mean the robustness of a thing resting in itself. The word may derive from Hera, the goddess that Proclus understands as the matrix that sustains forms.

30   Discussing the Ismaili (branch of Shia Islam) understanding of *tawhid*, God's Oneness.

He is the 'Unifier' *(muwaḥḥid)*, Who unifies all the Ones, Who 'monadises' all the monads. Thus the *tawḥid* takes on the aspect of a monadology: at the same time that it separates this 'Unifier' from all the Ones He unifies, it also affirms Him through them.[31]

As Frithjof Schuon explains in the context of claims to religious superiority, "[a]s every religion corresponds to a 'divine subjectivity'—a 'theophanic individuality'—it cannot be expected to be 'objective' with regard to another religion...."[32] Nicholas of Cusa discusses diversity in general in *On Learned Ignorance*, arguing that God brings about diversity and each tends to love what is his own so that things tend towards "peace without envy." C. S. Lewis writes prefacing *The Great Divorce*:

> Even on the biological level life is not like a river but a tree. It does not move towards unity but away from it and the creatures grow further apart as they increase in perfection. Good, as it ripens, becomes continually more different not only from evil but from other good.

Let's imagine a series of mirrors, each reflect the sun from different perspectives, being brightest at different parts of the day depending on their angle. Together they teach us about the sun, its position throughout the day, without forcing us to look directly at it.[33] If we take the sun as analogous to an abstract concept like language, just as our eyes are not made to see the sun directly, we can only think about language through a particular language. Unity in itself is not an object of cognition. However, the more languages we know of, the less likely we are to define language as such in terms of some particular grammar. If all mirrors were fused into a single continuum, they would reflect the sun only once and distortedly.

If the spaces between mirrors are fused at a corner, three mirrors can become a triangular continuum, reflecting the sun as a triangle, and four welded in the same way would display a square sun, for example. The shape of the sun would be lost, because such formations would lack a center. The image of discontinuous bodies forming a pattern together allows us to understand each body as a whole in itself and also as a part of a wider whole only *from a wider perspective*—in other words, only *discontinuity and pattern lets us truly convey the idea of a microcosm*.

---

31   Henry Corbin, *Cyclical Time and Ismaili Gnosis* (London: Kegan Paul International, 1980), 174.

32   Frithjof Schuon, *Christianity/Islam: Perspectives on Esoteric Ecumenism*, trans. M. Perry (Bloomington, IN: World Wisdom, 2008), 92.

33   We can also imagine mirrors reflecting mirrors, where some receive more resplendent, less mediated, reflections than others. But ultimacy, the sun, the absent center, is ever beyond the mirrors. This image is relevant to political communities sharing a common paradigm, for example Greco-Roman or Confucian-Buddhist, which is itself a particular reflection on the possibility of a human community ordered towards the Good.

In terms of communities as units expressing Unity (for example through the unitary definition of abstract principles like *justice* or *charity*), the sort of discourse that presents the cultural *melting pot* as somehow superior to, antagonistic towards, or revelatory of deficiencies in, the cultures it draws from, is equivalent to the amalgamation of mirrors described above and is precisely a move against plurality. Instead, the 'melting pot' should constitute itself as a delineated identity with its own 'angle' on the universal, not primarily as a continuum. Peruvian identity, for example, is not a mixture of Spanish and indigenous American identities—that might describe its history, to a point—but its identity is *its own*. And a child's consciousness is as irreducible as that of its parents; a person's consciousness is just as irreducible as the neighbors he lives between.

A discourse that seeks to deconstruct identity is the mirror image of that phenomenon anthropologists have documented according to which elites tend to want to identify as foreign with respect to commoners, claiming the pedigree of conquerors or wealthy magnates. Both use cosmopolitanism as a means of disenfranchisement, both deny ontology to the local, especially village and rural persons, and seek to hide the local as culture-creator or culture-transmitter. In a sense these are the political left and right wings of popular disempowerment, parodying what we will call the twin infinity and integrity of forms.

These discourses of deconstruction can have an existential basis: a cowardly retreat from ritual death and rebirth (Katharsis: suspension of the manifest and ecstatic self-exit; Theoria: perception of the autozoon; Theosis: return with, and recognition of, the autozoon in manifestation). This cowardice is idolatry: we perceive Being as a very powerful being out-there, among weaker beings, rather than as the Being of beings, within them and in their midst. Being just a powerful entity, it might as well be evil or arbitrary in its treatment of us, and so we engage in sacrificial, bartering, appeasement of it. This is what early Christianity criticizes as pagan.

When we begin to contemplate Being, for example by calming the mind in meditation, it throws up at us some fearful impression—the Tibetan Book of the Dead's wrathful deities. The *existential self*, as we saw mentioned in sources from western occultism. This is the very image of our idolatrous view of Being as a powerful, arbitrary *other*. It is produced because the mind does not believe it will survive contemplation: it believes it is identical to our mental tension, and that, without tension, it will die: and insofar as we are identified with the mind, the ego, the false self, we believe that peace, contemplation of unitary Being, will kill us. We would rather forever fight our inner demons than be free and peaceful.

Crucially, the fear of peace and need to be constantly in turmoil leads us to fear stable forms which seem to be at peace in themselves and which, by their beauty and stability, seem to draw us into a pure, calm, contemplation. This disposition has a very specific social and political correlate:

the rejection of stability, beauty. Any stable form that is not in conflict (and specifically in conflict against other stable forms, against stability as such) is viewed as a violent aggressor, for it is trying to steal from us our mental tension, which we believe to be our very life. That this often results in rejecting historically stable institutions and identity is due to the fact that these, by virtue of their continuity, transmit a sense of the ontology of peace, of not requiring tension in order to exist, of annulling mental tension, of ego-death. Whatever antagonisms operated in their history, they have somewhat left behind in course of that long history, and now seem to be mere facts. Joyful admiration of coherent forms that present as discontinuous, as microcosms, as self-so, can therefore be healthy.

This defense of entities as units in themselves, and therefore of their diversity, does not commit us to any particular institutional or definitional framework. Just as the ancient Greeks may choose to express their common Hellenism through an explicit federation, which Plato recommends partly as a function of an external threat, or not, so the diversity to which we refer need not have only one possible political articulation. Neither does the unity of an entity itself constitute a statement concerning how porous or fluid it ought to be with respect to other entities.

The principles here discussed are expressed by a unit being in harmony with its peers and porous to the space of relationship (the in-between as intersubjectivity) where harmonious interaction comes down to gift giving/receiving, to giving something of you and receiving something of the other. We occasionally receive what is not us, but is compatible with us, and can become us, and give what is us, but is compatible with the other, and can become the other. Our definition of us and other allows the flux of gifting. The idea of the absent center also suggests that our unity is not discretely reducible to any one of our features (just as consciousness is not exhausted in any one bodily organ), being instead an invisible presence magnetizing features together, so that a culture or identity should not be simplistically, univocally and hermetically defined.[34]

And yet there may be a consciousness that corresponds to one specific feature, like the color blue,[35] and we may seek to identify completely with the consciousness of blue. We may also find our existential home in a very specific intersection of features, such as "blue circle." But even so, we may occasionally choose to experience that portion of ourselves where blue shifts into *purple* or circle in *oval*. The degree to which we allow our definition of blue to include shades of purple, or of circle to include some ovals, depends on the kind of gifting we want to engage in with others: where their definitions allow us to occasionally share portions of ourselves

---

34   Purism in nationalism is like puritanism in nominalism (religious fundamentalism is often nominalistic, it considers "god" a powerful being among weaker ones). Denying transcendence leads to tyrannical idols.

35   As Henri Bergson suggests in a thought experiment.

(where our blue and their red are the same purple[36]). Foregoing overlap (or acting as though there isn't any) means doing without gifting: solipsism. (We will develop this at the beginning of section I.iii., for it has to do with the harmony between forms rather than their integrity and plurality.)

Continuity is a fact of nature: colors and sounds can be arranged along seamless spectra. But they tend to manifest discontinuously, so that the animal presents bordered patterns of color on its skin and music and language require not a seamless passage from sound to sound but the arrangement of notes or pitches that contrast with each other and are intermittently delineated by silence. This means that intermediate 'angles' are not derivative of others but should be discovered in their own integrity, as having their own reflection of Unity, as being their own mirror for the sun. Approaching an aesthetic form from the vantage of another, and treating it as a liminal space between one's own perspective and some *other* familiar one, will miss what is genuine and unique about it.

The branches of many trees may weave into a continuous texture, but their trunks remain discontinuous. The fact that people share features with each other does not mean they are a single entity and not separate persons. The fact that languages share structural characteristics or loan words does not mean they are not separate systems. To deny the existence of entities due to the continuity of their features—to deny the existence of trees because their branches weave together—is a mistake. Similarly, you can visualize each color on a spectrum, but if you are presented with shapes in continuity with each other, you cannot make them out, because for a specific shape to be *that shape*, it requires a fully enclosed perimeter (a triangle attached to a square is not a triangle, a triangle is only a triangle if it is discontinuous from other shapes). Yet each shape can be drawn in any color, each letter in any font. Separate entities (like shapes) can display features that are on a spectrum (like colors), without thereby ceasing to be separate entitites. There is a tendency today to emphasize that some features are on a spectrum in order to thereby deny the validity of separate identities.

On the other hand, a color along a color spectrum can either be thought of in continuity with or *conceptually* isolated from the rest and just

---

36   If the blue and red circles include all their shades like a spectrum, and they both include purple as one of these shades, then they will seem continuous with each other against a purple background. The commons, resources on which all may draw to build their projects, is like the backdrop against which two circles may stand, side by side, to compare the manner and extent to which their colors are highlighted. Just as a blue circle does not stand out against a blue background, and both a blue and red circle stand out against white, so not every person makes use of every kind of resource a community makes available. But the option should be available, precisely to show where the blue and red contrast together, and are thus comparable and may admire each other, and where the one stands out whereas the other fades, itself a form of comparison.

so, a shape forming the outline of a tube, for example, could be in continuity with other shapes as the tube morphs in shape, likewise *conceptually*
isolatable as a particular cross section of the tube. So, in a sense both form
and feature are conceivable as isolated moments, singular concepts, or as
a wave in the grand flux of reality. Everything, whether shape or color,
form or substance, is ultimately an archetype, a unitary concept. Therefore, matter is not substance in the sense of primary formlessness but is
the ever-adapted, ever-formed, medium in which such interaction occurs,
and which shows us that any unitary concept is in continuity with other
versions of itself and is an intersection of various other concepts, so that
unity belongs not to any concept but to that which is beyond them all.

Henri Bergson writes that we often "...freeze this flux" of life "either
into an immense solid sheet, or into an infinity of crystallized needles,
always into a thing which necessarily partakes of the immobility of a
point of view." But if instead we place ourselves "in the concrete flow of
duration...we shall then find no logical reason for positing multiple and
diverse durations." Essentially, rather than trying to determine how many
points make up a line (the answer is: as many as we want), we take the line,
or the whole duration of a being's movement, as a unit in itself. It is not the
hypothetical stoppages, the infinite possible still-frames of our movement
that define that movement, but the *subjective experience* that animates it and
for which the movement is a unit. *To know is to be,* says the Hermeticist:

> It is not possible for anyone to see anything of the things that
> actually exist unless he becomes like them ... So in this place you
> see everything and do not see yourself, but in that place you do see
> yourself—and what you see you shall become. (*Gospel of Philip*[37])

Bergson proposes a thought experiment:

> ...there might be no other color in the world but orange. But just
> as a consciousness based on color, which sympathized internally
> with orange instead of perceiving it externally, would feel itself
> held between red and yellow, would even perhaps suspect beyond
> this last color a complete spectrum into which the continuity
> from red to yellow might expand naturally, so the intuition of
> our duration, far from leaving us suspended in the void, as pure
> analysis would do, brings us into contact with a whole continuity
> of durations which we must try to follow, whether downwards or
> upwards...In the first we advance towards a more and more atten-
> uated duration, the pulsations of which, being rapider than ours,
> and dividing our simple sensation, dilute its quality into quantity;
> at the limit would be pure homogeneity, that pure repetition by
> which we define materiality. Advancing in the other direction,
> we approach a duration which strains, contracts, and intensifies

---

37 *Nag Hamadi Codex II, 2–7, The Gospel of Philip,* ed. B. Layton and trans. Wesley
W. Isenberg (Leiden: E. J. Brill, 1989), 61:6–62:4, 163.

itself more and more; at the limit would be eternity. No longer conceptual eternity, which is an eternity of death, but an eternity of life. A living, and therefore still moving eternity in which our own particular duration would be included as the vibrations are in light; an eternity which would be the concentration of all duration, as materiality is its dispersion.

Bergson's materiality is analogous to our *color*, which exists as a continuous spectrum, and his eternity is alike what we have called *shape*, the source of unity as discontinuous unity (a triangle is not continuous with a circle, etc.). The Divine is neither, but gives forth both. In Platonic terms: The One gives rise to both the Demiurge and the Crater, the Architect of the cosmos and the cosmic Matrix whence the world is made, Zeus and Hera; both essence and substance, shape and color. The ancients were not reducing what Bergson terms materiality to what he terms eternity, but were perceiving both as derivative of a transcendent One.

Theologically speaking, God is creator, and God is ever the same. God is not in time. For God all moments already are. Therefore, there is always creation. The entirety of His creation is already conceived and created. That which began time must be other than time; that which ends time must be other than time. Therefore, time's beginning and its ending are not events in time. Time is an island within the ocean of eternity. Time did not ever begin nor will time ever end, but time is always already. Time is the sequential experience of a spatial object, so to speak. God is eternally the Creator, therefore "creation...from the divine perspective..." is "itself eternal."[38]

This is how Parmenides understands reality. An extent of time is an artefact, a round or circular artefact, an island among islands floating in the sea of eternity. Henry Corbin's summary of the Ismaili doctrine of cyclical time expresses this:

> We have already stressed the idea that in eternal Time the eternal divine Past *is* eternally actuated and does not fall into the past as a time which 'is no longer.' Thus the procession of archangelical hypostases, which are the events of this past eternally in the present, is manifested to us as the harmony of a perfect hierarchy; there is no retard, no surpassing of one by the other. If such a surpassing does occur, it will bring about a rupture of this eternal Presence in the present; there will be a sort of fraction of pure ether that has become impermeable to the Light.[39]

Each such island is a story when experienced sequentially, when *read*, or a kind of talisman when fathomed as a whole from the vantage of eternity. It is a mandala image, a hieroglyph and narrative, an archetypal

---

38   Catherine Pickstock, *After Writing: On the Liturgical Consummation of Philosophy* (Oxford: Blackwell Publishers, 1998), 247.
39   Corbin, *Cyclical Time and Ismaili Gnosis*, 37.

possibility, among others, for consciousness to experience. The personal
life is also such, if seen as a whole, where tragedy and incidental details are
ornaments in the beauty of the total impression. Consider de Quincey's
recollection of a nine-year-old girl's account from his *Confessions*:

> I was once told by a near relative of mine, that having in her child-
> hood fallen into a river, and being on the very verge of death but
> for the assistance which reached her at the last critical moment,
> she saw in a moment her whole life, clothed in its forgotten
> incidents, arrayed before her as in a mirror, not successively, but
> simultaneously; and she had a faculty developed as suddenly for
> comprehending the whole and every part.

William Blake writes that it is most pernicious to "suppose that before
the Creation all was solitude and chaos," for in truth: "Eternity exists,
and all things in eternity, independent of creation which was an act of
mercy."[40] Where "Error is created, Truth is eternal" and error "is burned
up the moment men cease to behold it."[41] Thus, the unreality of matter and the body consists of being unreal as that which the materialist
perceives them to be. All things endure forever, but not as we perceive
them from behind the doors of our perception, darkly. As the *Bhagavad
Gita* teaches, reality always is, illusion never is.

The Hospitable Infinite, or the Twin Infinity and Integrity of Forms

Eric Voegelin writes:

> The superb irony of the ecumene having the shape of a sphere that
> brings the concupiscential explorer of reality back home to himself,
> and of this sphere being situated in a cosmic Horizon of infinite
> extension and duration, has hardly yet entered the consciousness
> of a mankind that is reluctant to admit concupiscential defeat.[42]

In this vein physicist Arnold Sikkema reflects:

> modern astronomy suggests...that there is no center, much like
> how there is no location on the surface of the earth which could
> rightfully claim such an honor; I consider this to be a superb

---

40   William Blake, *The works of William Blake; poetic, symbolic, and critical.* Edwin
J. Ellis and William Butler Yeats eds. (London: B. Quaritch, 1893), 401. Neville
Goddard was fond of this passage and considered his own mystical experiences
to have confirmed it. What is rejected here is the modern concept of matter, that
is, matter perceived without its inner significance, through the "single vision" of
scientific determinism. This world, born of misperceiving, Blake considered the
realm of a monstrous deity, using language resembling gnostic dualism, similar to
what one finds in the *Gospel of Philip* at one point. Which is not to say that the
world (or the human estate short of spiritual illumination) is not describable as a
creation-to-be-completed.
41   Blake, *The works of William Blake; poetic, symbolic, and critical,* 403.
42   Voegelin, *Order and History Volume IV, The Ecumenic Age,* 272.

poetical analogy of how once Jews claimed they had to worship in Jerusalem, but now God's people worship anywhere in spirit and truth (see John 4:20-24).

Wolfgang Smith would caution against discarding the everyday, spontaneous perception that we have of our place in the cosmos as unmoving observers surrounded by a moving sky[43] and externalizing the esotericism of heliocentrism and a-centralism of the sort de Cusa puts forward. The stability of exotericism is not to be discounted and attacked by esoteric truth. A saint who realizes that the absolute centrality of God is inexpressible by any manifest form should not then go and burn down the village church or town square.

William Desmond's *metaxology* (*metaxylogos*, discourse or logic of *the middle* or *the between*) provides a philosophical expression of what Voegelin sees as the defeat dealt by a spherical earth to the conqueror who went lusting for the edge of the world.[44] Reality will not give us so easy a terminus, so neat a border to conquer and be done with. We need to regain "the horizon of mystery"[45] of the cosmological ecumene precisely in the fact that the horizon shifts as we advance (this mystery is the "internal conclusion" of the Ecumenic age). Here, the trauma of infinity enters human consciousness, with its obvious heralds being Giordano Bruno and Nicholas of Cusa. The trauma is simply that: "...if the whole is infinite, it is not clear how we can have any whole at all. With this new metaphysical homelessness, human finitude appears even more nakedly manifest."

But, "...whereas Pascal felt anguish at an infinite universe, Bruno was intoxicated with infinity and the prospects of endless energy he believed it promised, even in humanity itself."[46] Rather than energy, we may propose this as the very possibility of humanity being safely contained in the infinite. The Infinite as bestower of unity or integrity to beings rather than entropic destroyer of the fluke of our existence, of our temporary reversals of entropy. This requires rejecting the reactionary or calcified image of tradition that is psychologically reliant on finitude as its ground.

---

43 The spontaneous view of being on an unmoving earth and having the cosmos rotate about us is useful. One may draw on its psychological potency. There is something of Nietzsche's perspectivism in this, and William Blake favored viewing the world as a flat disc around us as a way of dispelling mystification. Nothing is hidden from us. In a less empowering vein, we should add, with C. S. Lewis, that the mediaeval view was often that our earthly station was unmoving in the same way as a dead thing is so, and that being at the bottom with the sky on top was analogous to being the anus of the cosmos. In any case, identifying the center of the universe as subterranean fire with the Sun above (an identification implied in Homer or in the Pythagoreans) curbs this paradox.

44 Voegelin's observation is in line with what Gianni Vattimo has called "the weakening of Being."

45 Voegelin, *Order and History Volume IV, The Ecumenic Age*, 342.

46 William Desmond. *Desire, Dialectic, and Otherness: An Essay on Origins.* 2nd ed. (Eugene, OR: Cascade Books, 2014), 162.

Here is the key to the question of why infinity is hospitable to the integrity of finite bodies, rather than being a terrifying expanse suggesting entropy, as it appears to the fearful ego. Infinity is the correlate or physical manifestation of Unity, that is, of the principle of Being, which in its singularity and simplicity must imply an infinite possibility, ever iterating that first simple Unity, ever manifesting unities, as wholes, as coherent bodies. It is the inexhaustibility of God's creativity, and the coherence, integrity, beauty, wholeness of His Logos. It is the nothingness, often perceived as death, in which we find our home, as Heidegger intuited, rather than metaphysical homelessness. This answers the riddle posed by Desmond as to why, if the whole is potentially infinite, there can be a whole at all. It is the reason why whoever loses his life for the sake of the Logos will find it (Matthew 10:39)—because that lost-and-found life is contained in the Logos and is a life (an integral unity, a whole, a moment-to-moment coherence) only because it is an image of the Logos. A never-reified, always-transcendent, ineffable Unity produces unity in creation rather than some flat expanse, some undifferentiated vale.

How Logocentrism Decentralizes the Cosmos

St. Thomas Aquinas reasons as follows in the *Summa Theologica* "... it has to be said that the Divine Person, over and beyond the human nature which He has assumed, can assume another distinct human nature."[47] This refers to the possibility of the Logos uniting hypostatically with a historical personage other than Jesus of Nazareth (with another contingent condition, while the *person*, in a profound sense, is the same):

> ...it may not be said that a Divine Person so assumed one human nature as to be unable to assume another. For it would seem to follow from this that the Personality of the Divine Nature was so comprehended by one human nature as to be unable to assume another to its Personality; and this is impossible, for the Uncreated cannot be comprehended by any creature.[48]

To make one's ultimate center that which is not a thing—the Logos—and to treat the Logos as the 'whole', is to allow for the notions of 'center' or 'whole' and therefore to acknowledge the integrity of this or that manifest body with its own center, acting as its own whole, while also denying any particular body a metaphysical warrant to homogenize others to itself, because no manifest center is the ultimate center, no manifest whole is the totality. The consequence of genuine logocentrism

47   Saint Thomas Aquinas, *Summa Theologica*, vol. 2 Part 2, First Section, trans. Fathers of the English Dominican Province (New York City: Cosimo Classics, 2007), Q.3:Art.7, 64.

48   Saint Thomas Aquinas, *Summa Theologica*, trans. Fathers of the English Dominican Province (London: R. and T. Washbourne, 1913), Q.3:Art.7, 63. Samuel Zinner refers to this in his studies on Christianity and Islam.

is therefore the opposite of what post-structuralists have claimed, which is not entirely their fault, considering how Protestant literalists and Catholic *pura natura* thinking, for example, have tended to reify the Logos.

Biblical tradition consistently provides evidences for the Anthropos, the human archetype, being variously manifested, baptizing diversity by the multitude of his presences, though singular (of course, in a sense every human being is a manifestation of the Anthropos, but what is being referred to is the self-aware missionary presence of the archetype). According to the *Clementine Homilies* (3:20) the Christ, the Anthropos or human archetype, who "alone has" the Holy Spirit (linked to femininity as this often is) "has changed his forms and his names from the beginning of the world, and so reappeared again and again in the world." Various figures, including Simon (Sirach 50), Jacob (Prayer of Joseph) and Enoch (1 Enoch) are presented as such manifestations.[49]

In modern philosophical terms (but contrary to a litany of thinkers) logocentrism precisely cannot deny the equivocal in favor of univocal, the diverse particular in favor of the simple universal, because the latter universal (the Logos, *Word*, even if only as concept and abstraction) is not an eminent *thing* among other *things*. Again, this may be stated in terms of language: language is universal and inherent to the human species but *no particular language* is thusly universal and inherent. A principle is unexhausted in any of its possible manifestations.

Further, *diversity of manifestation is conducive to understanding unity of principle.* Were we unaware of the existence of significantly different grammatical structures (were we to forget that language is a category whose concrete instantiations can vary widely, or that such variation is even possible), we would lose the understanding of the linguistic or communicative function in and of itself as *that which is consistent throughout the diversity of languages but is not exhausted in any of them.* This is the core of any defense of difference. Diverse manifestations of a principle disclose that principle more fully than uniformity would. This idea of a universal linguistic faculty and the particular languages through which we know that universal can be expressed as our titular City of God manifested in and encompassing the plural the cities of men.

The above argument is contained in *The Gospel of Philip.* That which is beyond, language as such in our analogy, or the thing named by names, is not a particular, not a single name itself:

> But truth brought names into existence in the world for our sakes, because it is not possible to learn it (truth) without these names. Truth is one single thing; it is many things and for our sakes to teach about this one thing in love through many things.[50]

---

49 Samuel Zinner, *Christianity and Islam: Essays on Ontology and Archetype,* 138.
50 *The Gospel of Philip,* 54:13–55:5, 149.

It teaches that that which is hidden does not belong to any particular form, whereas that which is revealed is necessarily translatable into different particulars:

> 'Jesus' is a hidden name. 'Christ' is a revealed name. For this reason 'Jesus' is not particular to any language; rather he is always called by the name 'Jesus' While as for 'Christ', in Syriac it is 'Messiah', in Greek it is 'Christ'. Certainly all the others have it according to their own language.

Being hidden and prior to particulars, and being revealed and therefore translatable across particulars, the manifest Logos is the nexus between universal and particular, and contains all things: "'The Nazarene' is he who reveals what is hidden. Christ has everything in himself, whether man, or angel, or mystery, and the Father."[51]

In line with our ubiquitous language-metaphor, Dante writes the following in the *Divine Comedy* (*Paradiso*, 26.130–32):

> That man should speak at all is nature's act,
> but how you speak—in this tongue or in that—
> she leaves to you and to your preference.

Languages may be said to be arbitrary in their differing from each other. It is arbitrary that a certain phonetic configuration (*'chair'*) should denote this or that object (*a four-legged bottom-support*). But this arbitrariness is the only vehicle for expressing a universal (language itself).

To complain of a certain practice or institution's arbitrariness is to have made a false start in one's critique, and to initiate a line of thinking that can just as easily scorn any particular entity for being arbitrary, making of entropy a liberating champion (a sort of parody of the beatific vision's apprehension of reality as sheer gratuity and divine gift). This is Giambattista Vico's *barbarism of reflection* that assails over-critical, rationalized cultures which cannot justify cultural particularity or history and seek instead an immanentized universal. Barbarism of reflection ultimately leads back to the primitive *barbarism of sense*.

Diverse manifestations of a principle exist alongside other actual or possible counterparts and are, in this sense, arbitrary (they differ according to contingencies unrelated to the element that is common between them), but they are the only means by which the principle may manifest, and no less necessary in order to understand that principle.

According to this Pentecostal approach, transcendent things are on a different axis from that along which human culture differentiates. This is not to argue that one culture cannot be more conducive to genuine human flourishing than another. A language can be generally more precise, containing a wider vocabulary, than another. But it is always possible for

---

51   Ibid., 55:37–57:2, 153.

several cultures to be different and equal, in the sense in which two words for *chair* can be just as good as one another at designating that object. Allowing for this difference prevents us from reifying the particulars of one mode of expression and equating it with truth or with the human condition's flourishing as such.

The obvious danger here is in fetishizing diversity to the point of justifying error. The concept 'language' allows for ample manifestations, but a human language not predicated on universal rules, not allowing coherent and complex thoughts to be expresses, is an illegitimate manifestation, it does not edifyingly add to the diversity of language. Equality also allows for *mutual superiorities*. Even if a language is not overall more precise than another, its musicality or vocabulary can be better at transmitting *certain kinds* of meaning.

The whole argument so far may be succinctly restated in theological terms as follows: *Only God is one and the all are His names*, or God is one, and His names infinite. God's Absoluteness requires we abstain from considering any manifest form ultimate or final or exhaustive of His creativity. The notion of an ultimate or unchanging manifest center assumes God's oneness can be fully reified and that God is therefore not Absolute. But if a theme is all encompassing, it bears displaying through infinite permutations. *God is One and every creation plural*, or *if God is one, the worlds are infinite*.

Henri Bergson writes in *An Introduction to Metaphysics*, "... the absolute has often been identified with the infinite." He continues:

> When you raise your arm, you accomplish a movement of which you have, from within, a simple perception; but for me, watching it from the outside, your arm passes through one point, then through another, and between these two there will be still other points; so that, if I began to count, the operation would go on forever. Viewed from the inside, then, an absolute is a simple thing; but looked at from the outside, that is to say, relatively to other things, it becomes, in relation to these signs which express it, the gold coin for which we never seem able to finish giving small change. Now, that which lends itself at the same time both to an indivisible apprehension and to an inexhaustible enumeration is, by the very definition of the word, an infinite. It follows from this that an absolute could only be given in an intuition whilst everything else falls within the province of analysis. By intuition is meant the kind of intellectual sympathy by which one places oneself within an object in order to coincide with what is unique in it and consequently inexpressible. Analysis, on the contrary, is the operation which reduces the object to elements already known, that is, to elements common both to it and other objects. To analyze, therefore, is to express a thing as a function of something other than itself.[52]

---

52   Henri Bergson, *An Introduction to Metaphysics*, trans. T. E. Hulme (London: G. P. Putnam's Sons, The Knickerbocker Press, 1913), 6–7.

Principles, reflecting the unity of the Absolute, are subjective, they occur in consciousness. Anything externalized, anything manifest, anything objective, must be multiple, manifold, composite, diverse. The apprehending subject can draw objects into conceptual unity if they are instances of a type, like multiple glasses all constituting a glass, or grasp the harmony between them if they compose a body. To say humans are in the image of the One, God partly invokes this fact: the human being can unify and grasp as unified what is *objectively* multiple.

As Desmond puts it, "…if there is any return to an origin, it cannot be one origin alone, but rather an origin that is articulated into a plurality of beginnings."[53] And as theologian Catherine Pickstock puts it "…if finite things imitate and participate in transcendent realities," that is, realities beyond the world, in the *between*, "there need be no finite original, and one finds, in this world, a play of repetitions without original, where each variation is equally an original because it is equally a copy."[54] To contradict the 10th century Ismaili theologian Nasir-i Khusraw in his *Knowledge and Liberation*, in God there are many firsts, many beginnings, for an Absolute creative power need not limit itself in the loci of its creation (in the creation of loci). The beginning is not a reified event, the center is absent. Consider that in Genesis the original Hebrew and Greek translation do not speak of the *first day* as they do of the second, third and so on, but of *Day One*, which is set apart by this formula.

God did not create the floral once, and transfer it from flower to butterfly wing. God's Oneness is alone, but generates many beginnings. Eyes evolve in parallel. God creates not in sequence, which implies His singularity is the singularity of His creation, the singularity of a thing, but rather only He is One, and creation is multiple, and the sense in which He is One is not as a thing but precisely because He is beyond time and space.

Few thinkers in the history of Europe expressed this principle as explicitly as Nicholas of Cusa. Chapter twenty-five of *On Learned Ignorance* discusses the pagan deities as different names for God according to His relations to creatures and grants that some pagans understood God as ultimately beyond all these names:

> All the names are unfolding of the enfolding of the one, ineffable name, and as this proper name is infinite, so it enfolds an infinite number of such names of particular perfections. Although there could be many such unfoldings, they are never so many or so great that there could not be more; each of them is to the proper and ineffable name what the finite is to the infinite.[55]

---

53   William Desmond, *Desire, Dialectic, and Otherness: An Essay on Origins*, 175.

54   Pickstock, *After Writing: On the Liturgical Consummation of Philosophy*, 57.

55   Nicholas de Cusa, *Selected Spiritual Writings. On Learned Ignorance*, chapter 25 (New York: Paulist Press, 1997), 124.

To properly assert God's unity requires acknowledging the plurality of everything else. Were creation to consist of only one object or kind of object, the vastness of the creative power of the Divine might be obfuscated; if there were only one language in existence the communicative faculty as such would become excessively identified with the habits of thought facilitated by its grammar.

By understanding the necessarily arbitrary and plural character of manifestation, we understanding that its underlying principle is unitary but non-manifest: that there is such a thing as *language as such*, but that it is not any *specific language*. As the Qur'an (30:22) puts it: "And of His signs is the creation of the heavens and the earth and the diversity of your languages and your colors. Indeed in that are signs for those of knowledge."

In Mark (16:15-20) Jesus teaches that the disciples will speak in new tongues, take up snakes and drink poison without being harmed. Speaking in new tongues can be interpreted both in terms of the phenomena of *glossolalia* and also of the historical emergence of new languages, which illustrates that meaning is not linked to the specificity of any particular means for communicating. It is, then, a call for understating the universal through one's spiritual discipleship. The practice of taking up snakes and drinking poison without suffering harm is potentially related to Tantric practices where the dangers of life are tamed and even utilized. According to the Gospel even the causal link between ingestion of poison and damage to health can be suspended by the disciple, who can detach act from consequence just as word from meaning. Of course, just because we can metabolize a poison does not mean we have a taste for it. A man who can resurrect the dead and heal the trauma of pain does not therefore desire to commit murder. The karmic (cause-and-effect) charge is removed from the act, but the act is still undesirable.

This can be understood not as being a random act of confounding causes and effects, but in terms of calling forth a deeper meaning and appropriating surface casuistry to its ends, like conforming language to the expression of spiritual truth. The deeper meaning is *the good of human flourishing and health* imposing itself even on poison (the telos of the saint, whose freedom is the freedom to be himself, which is the freedom to be incapable of sin, as St. Augustine would say). The realization that a harmful action is not in itself harmful to the disciple whose inner attitude is correct, is like the realization that communication is never exhausted in a language. (This does not justify militant transgression or ignorance of ordinary cause and effect any more than understanding what language is justifies going about speaking an invented idiom which others cannot understand. One may look under the hood, understand how a car works and how to repair it, even invent new types of engines, and still drive normally in conformity to the rules of circulation, although, as one changes others by one's example, these rules might also change.)

In Mark (16:15-20) we see that the inner attitude is beyond the act just as meaning is beyond the word, constituting an esoteric warrant for diversity, as external forms linked to internal truth are multipliable, which may be pursued in terms of great personal feats and cultural creativity (the danger-defying hero who shows others what can be done, the culture-defining artist who gives others new expressions). Following from this, the critique levelled by Christianity, for example in St. Paul's Letter to the Galatians, against *the law*, is, at its root, a critique against reifying particular external forms. It is a critique against identifying specific forms with inner meanings/universal principles to the exclusion of other possible forms.

That there exist unities—coherent bodies or categories—means there is such a thing as Unity (the ubiquity of languages displays the universality of the linguistic ability in humans), and the fact that unities differ between themselves, means that Unity is transcendent, Unity is beyond those unities, they do not define It. The fact that there is such a thing as unity but that it is only observable in diverse unities or bodies displays the truth and transcendence of Unity: There is such a thing as Unity for otherwise there would be no observable unities, therefore it is *true*, but it is nowhere manifested as a terminus, there is no sensible ultimacy to it, instead we fathom an inexhaustible potentiality of unities, therefore it is *transcendent*.

Sometimes Indian Vaishnavism is understood as viewing the Divine in terms of infinite forms, rather than a formless simplicity, as professor Edwin Bryant pointed out to me. But this misses the philosophical necessity of Divine simplicity, which is the depth dimension, inner dimension, of the infinite forms God can produce. The Divine simplicity, that which is beyond form, is precisely that which allows for an infinity of formal manifestation. Because it is not itself a form it represents a principal which can decline into form in infinite configurations. It is like the communicative ability in the abstract which can decline into infinite possible phonetics and grammars without being exhausted by them. The argument for the Divine being beyond form does not proceed, as certain Vaishnavist theologians might have thought, from the idea that form is linked to suffering or sin (an idea resulting from the fact of our encountering form in painful contexts here on earth). In fact, the argument for Divine simplicity is the necessary basis for the argument that the divine can constitute and manifest as infinite forms. That which is beyond form is the vertical or primary (not temporal) cause of that which is formal. That which is beyond form is that which is sustaining form.

Alexander Koyré sums up Nicholas of Cusa's vision: "...neither the earth, nor anything else, can be placed in this center, which does not exist, and...thus nothing in this world can be completely and absolutely at rest."[56] This is expressed by Professor J. Y. Simpson and quoted by

---

56   Alexandre Koyré, *From the Closed World to the Infinite Universe* (London: John Hopkins Press, 1957), 13.

Hugh MacDiarmid at the start of his poem *The Innumerable Christ*: "Other stars may have their Bethlehem, and their Cavalry too."[57] And in Ibn Sina (Avicenna): "a decentralization of the monotheistic universe."[58] We read in Walt Whitman's *Leaves of Grass, Song of Myself*:[59]

> I open my scuttle at night and see the far-sprinkled systems,
> And all I see multiplied as high as I can cipher edge but the rim
>   of the farther systems.

> Wider and wider they spread, expanding, always expanding,
> Outward and outward and forever outward.

> My sun has his sun and round him obediently wheels,
> He joins with his partners a group of superior circuit,
> And greater sets follow, making specks of the greatest inside them.

> There is no stoppage and never can be stoppage,
> If I, you, and the worlds, and all beneath or upon their surfaces,
>   were his moment reduced back to a pallid float, it would not
>   avail the long run,
> We should surely bring up again where we now stand,
> And surely go as much farther, and then farther and farther.

In section III of the *Creed of the Sages*, the 12th century Persian sage Suhrawardi makes a similar argument. Bodies do not originate states (by which he means the contingent features of bodies) and states do not originate bodies. Both are from God.[60] *States*, in Suhrawardi's usage, are like the arbitrary features of a language, and *bodies* are the coherence of each language in itself.

The Doctrine of Fortunate Absence

Beyond their contingent features, manifest centers point to the truly transcendent center. In Christian theology, Christ teaches that none are good but the Father (Mark 10:18; Luke 18:19) instructs His disciples to pray to the Father (Matthew 6:9-13) and serves His disciples by cleaning their feet (John 13:1-17) indeed, by dying for them. More explicitly, He

---

57 Hugh MacDiarmid, *Hugh MacDiarmid: Selected Poetry*, A. Riach and M. Grieve (New York City: New Directions Publishing Corporation, 1993), 15.

58 "...and it was inevitable that in Islam as in Christendom this provoked on the orthodox side a reaction varying in intensity from incomprehension and alarm to the most open hostility" (Corbin, *Avicenna and the Visionary Recital*, 48).

59 Harold Bloom, gnostic pessimism aside, reads the American sublime in this Isaiah-cast poet. If political modernity and Americanism is redeemed beyond its political manifest destiny and imperialism (the way Blake and Cervantes get beyond British and Spanish imperialism), it is in something like this. However, Whitman's political essays fall well short of his poetry, seeming to encourage naïve, potentially dangerous, aspects of liberal modernity.

60 Suhrawardi, *Creed of the Sages*. In: *Illuminationist Texts and Textual Studies: Essays in Memory of Hossein Ziai*, A. Gheissari, A. Alwishah and J. Walbridge (Boston: Brill, 2018), III, 77.

teaches that it is necessary for Him to leave (become absent) so that they receive the Spirit of truth (John 16:7) and asks Mary Magdalene not too cling to Him for He has not yet ascended to His Father (John 20:17) emphasizing that He is ascending to their *common* source ("my God and your God"), which highlights that the injunction is to not clinging to Jesus as empirical person because He and His disciples are in like relation to God. The Spirit allows the fact of the transcendence of the One and absence of Christ to be understood in and through the diversity of creation, and perhaps for this reason receives a name composed of two words, which the *Gospel of Philip* draws attention to:

> 'The Father' and 'the Son' are single names; 'the Holy Spirit' is a double name. For they are everywhere: they are above, they are below; they are in the concealed, they are in the revealed. The Holy Spirit is in the revealed: it is below. It is in the concealed: it is above.[61]

Christ's otherworldly aspect—his absence understood as something positive for the disciples, his celibacy and lack of progeny—precisely *functions to justify the world in its diversity*: He is not a particular among particulars, his lineage is not to enjoy privilege over other lineages, he is absent as a particular and therefore present to all particulars. Here we find the Christian critique of the law in its metaphysical basis: the law being criticized stands for the reification of the link between universal principles and particular practices to the exclusion of others. The meaning of Christ's not leaving a lineage is like the scattered lineages of Aeneas and Muhammad to which many may lay claim, and to the latter's lack of a mature male child (his son Ibrahim died young), so that none retain Muhammad's lineage in the traditional Arab and Islamic sense of patrilineal descent. Another example: In African Yoruba religion, *Ifa*, the divine Orunmila, lord of wisdom, messenger[62] of Olodumare (the Supreme Being in this system), was asked for powers by the many gods. But instead of unilaterally deciding who was to receive what, Orunmila returned to the sky (just as Jesus said that it was good for His disciples that He leave them). The deity then distributed the bounty from above like rain, having sent messengers to announce when this would occur. The gods thus received their distinctions not by simple decree but according to what they gathered as it fell, or picked up from the ground. Here Yoruba metaphysics is interpretable in terms of the Christian understanding of transcendence and participation.

Christ calls His disciples friends, not slaves, reminds them that the slave is not superior to his Lord and then tells them that people who

---

61   *Nag Hamadi Codex II, 2–7, The Gospel of Philip*, 59:6–60:6, 159.

62   Not just a messenger bringing the wisdom of God to earth, Orunmila is said to have been present during creation, and is referred to as *Igbakeji Olodumare*, second in command to Olodumare. It is difficult not to draw a parallel to the Second Person of the Christian Trinity.

would persecute Him will persecute them and the people who would keep His word will keep their word (John 16). He therefore makes them equal to the life He has led (the biography He has inhabited). The contingent should not look to the contingent for salvation, a particular entity is not being told to receive what is transcendent from another particular entity. They are not receiving from that which is ontologically on their level (the life of Jesus, which they are to be equal with) but from the Logos, following its pattern. Thus, Christ as Logos is not a particular idea, but rather Origen of Alexandria's *idea of ideas*, and as St. Irenaeus writes, has "summed up in Himself all nations dispersed from Adam downwards, and all languages and generations of men, together with Adam himself."[63] The Kingdom does not come "by observation," either "here" or "there," but from within and in the midst of the faithful (Luke 17:20–21).

The aloofness of Papal (and proper Imperial) authority that de Lubac emphasizes may be understood in terms of Christ's leaving His disciples as a fortunate absence, as described in John (16:7). The absence leaves the disciples to receive Consoler, a figure the Muslims sometimes identify with Muhammad for bringing worldly, un-monastic consolation through his example, from running a business to righteous martial engagement and polygamy, ending early Christianity's "ascetical panic," as Professor Tim Winter (Abdal Hakim Murad) sees it: "Christianity was providential as *preparatio evangelica*. The Paraclete was indeed the Comforter. We were in a state of ascetical *panic* about ourselves."[64]

Taking this in a direction other than the author intends, we read here that the good news is in part the freedom opened up by Christ, His refusal to take the kingdoms for himself, that is, for his empirical, biographical self, and the sending of the Comforter. This is symbolized by a baptism that is sensed by the mind (water on skin) but does not alter the flesh (St. Peter in Acts 10 baptizes without circumcising), so that bodies are embraced by that which is not a body and has no need of conforming them in their corporeality, or cultures are taken up by a Church that is not a culture and has no need to conform them in their cultural features. Enculturation into modes other than those of Old Testament observance and its cultural context is, in a sense, the natural completion of Christianity, the reception of exotericism in full awareness of the potential plurality of exteriors, the making room for history and culture and peoples' participation in these, in forming the liturgy.

Since Jesus does not create a kingdom in material terms, Jewish or otherwise, and leaves no ruling dynasty to observe and obey, He is, in a sense, letting the disciples get on with the mess of humanity. Muslims

---

63   Saint Irenaeus of Lyon, *Against the Heresies*, III, 22.3, cited in Catherine Pickstock, *Repetition and Identity* (Oxford: Oxford University Press, 2013), 231.

64   Abdal Hakim Murad, *Commentary on the Eleventh Contentions* (Cambridge, UK: Quilliam Press, Contention, 2012), 1:39–40.

understand this as the coming of a religion that justifies family ties, sexual pleasure, political power and the like, mysticism being pursuable in the midst of these. We may in the same vein associate this with the politically involved figure of the emperor. However, this cannot describe that Spirit of truth, the Comforter, only one possible avenue for the reconciliation with politics and the world that can be read in John.

The fact that popes are celibate may be interpreted as responding to this positive absence of Christ, alike the elected character of Holy Emperors. Both avoid the identification of sacred leadership with an empirical lineage, even though, in both cases, lineages have taken up temporary residence in the office, so to speak (from the Medici and Borgias to the Hohenstaufen and Habsburgs). In the case of emperors, the lineage of Aeneas, apart from not having been a formal requirement for election in the west, is a scattered one, made sacred by that scattering, and claimed by whole nations, not an empirical one, and can be interpreted metaphorically.

Even in traditions where the presence of a visible guide is emphasized, such as Shia Islam, the need for such fortunate absence makes itself felt:

> It does indeed seem that the authentic Shiite conception of the Imamate, in addition to its eschatological dimension, also implies the 'invisibility' of the Imam in this world, i.e., his purely spiritual mode of being.[65]

We have already discussed the legitimacy of unified accounts of diverse forms. In fact, these are the basis for translating universals from one particular to another and recognizing the possibility of one body representing another (political representative of political community) and of one body considering itself equivalent to another (one community or culture recognizing others as its legitimate peers). Obviously, René Guénon and related thinkers engage in just such a unified account of diverse forms. One pre-modern example comes from the Ismaili tradition within Shia Islam: Henry Corbin describes how in the *Kitab al-Yanabi'*,

> Abu Ya'qub Sejestani analyses in detail the symbolic concordance between the four branches of the Christian Cross and the four words making up the *shahada*. Then he contemplates the mystery of the Night of Destiny *(laylat al-Qadr)*, whose mystical light transfigures all—things, when suddenly there appears before his mental vision the image—perfectly recognizable to us—of the 'Cross of Light' of Acts of John and Manicheanism.[66]

This goes very far towards a unified account of traditions, in fact, beyond what perennialists typically do. For a Muslim to acknowledge the crucifixion of Christ, interpreting the relevant Qur'anic passage as referring to the fact that Christ died by God's will, not by the action of those who

---

65   Corbin, *Cyclical Time and Ismaili Gnosis*, 176.
66   Ibid., 192.

thought they killed him, for they ultimately lack agency, does not undo Islam, though it renders it in accord with a central claim of Christianity.

Indeed, Ismailism is a particularly integrative strain of Islam. Apart from producing theological exegeses that affirm the cross (the crucifixion of Jesus), this tradition includes texts that consider Lord Krishna, speaking in the *Bhagavad Gita*, as the Eternal Imam, the teacher behind every historical teacher. The Ismaili *Buddh Avatar* (verse 456), by Sayyidna Pir Sadr al-Din, considers Ali, son-and-law and cousin of Muhammad, mystical teacher in Shia as well as Sunni Islam (the latter's Sufi orders frequently trace themselves back to Ali) to be the pre-eternal Vishnu, the Hindu name for God. God is described as taking the form of Krishna by Sayyidna Pir Hasan Kabir al-Din in the *Anant Akhado* (verse 428). The Ahmadiyya also consider Krishna to have been a prophet in the Islamic sense.

There are of course non-Ismaili and non-Shia examples of such broad view. The great fourteenth century Sufi from Iraq, Abd al-Karīm al-Jīlī, who is one of the major expositors of Ibn Arabi's work, linked the Indian brahmin to Abraham, and described Indian religion in his *al-Insan al-Kamil*: "Their worship of the Truth is like that of the prophets before their prophetic mission."[67] He speaks of their four books (presumably the four *Vedas*) written by Abraham's Lord and given them by the patriarch, but also of a fifth book that leads those who read it to become Muslim. The 17th century Moghul Prince Dara Shikoh, heir of the Timurid house, is often cited for his views in this regard, for example apparently regarding the Hindu Upanishads as the "hidden book" mentioned in the Qur'an (56:79–80),[68] although this verse seems to refer to the Qur'an itself, and so locating other theologies within the theology of Islam. The later, renowned 18th century Sufi and poet from Deli, Mirza Mazhar Jan Janan, a member of the Sunni Naqshbandi Sufi order, considered the *Vedas* to be of Divine inspiration,[69] and therefore classified Vedic Hindus as people of the book (*ahl al-kitab*), like Christians and Jews, even distinguishing the Hindu use of images from that of pre-Islamic Arabian Jahiliya due to its being conscious of a supreme, unitary, Divine.[70]

But returning to Ismailism, and Shi'ism in general, depending to the text, it can tend at times to over-emphasize the exclusivity of one lineage as repository of correct spiritual guidance. This largely loses that fundamental Islamic insight of the primordiality of religion and the coming of guidance to all nations. Even Jesus and Muhammad are born to the divergent lineages of Isaac and Ishmael, which should serve to make the point that guidance is not strictly linked to any lineage. Sunni

67   Seyyed Hossein Nasr, *Sufi Essays* (Albany: State University of New York Press, 1972), 139–40.
68   Ibid., 141.
69   Ibid., 139.
70   Asghar A. Engineer, *Islam in Contemporary World* (Berkshire: New Dawn Press, 2007), 59.

decentralization (which in its non-Salafist, traditional form is more akin to Orthodox Christianity than to Protestantism) is in one sense more in line with that insight. In Sunnism, jurists and Sufis of any nation can provide correction and the figure of the generational or periodic restorer of religion, the *mujaddid*, need not be a descendent of Muhammad or belong to any particular lineage at all.

In terms of unified accounts, the cross serves as a symbol for the *multiple states of being*, as René Guénon puts it. The cross as structure of reality, intersection of archetypal elements whose nexuses are every possible entity, its center and peripheral arms branching into other entities, appears in Acts of John (97–102):

> On the evening of Good Friday the Angel Christos, while the multitude below, in Jerusalem, imagines that it is crucifying him, causes the apostle John to go up the Mount of Olives and into the grotto illumined by his presence; and there the angel reveals to John the mystery of the "Cross of Light." This cross is called sometimes Word, sometimes Mind, sometimes Jesus and sometimes Christ, sometimes Door, sometimes Way, sometimes Son, Father, Spirit, sometimes Life, and sometimes Truth. It separates the things on high that *are* from the things below that *become* (the things of birth and of death), and at the same time, being one, streams forth into all things. "This is not the cross of wood which thou wilt see when thou goest down hence: neither am I he that is on the cross, whom now thou seest not, but only hearest his voice. I was reckoned to be that which I am not, not being what I was unto many others...Thou hearest that I suffered, yet I did not suffer; that I suffered not, yet did I suffer...and in a word, what they say of me, that befell me not. But what they say not, that did I suffer."[71]

Along with the doctrine of fortunate absence, this illustrates the refraction of Divine Unity into created multiplicity. Christianity as baptizing existing symbols of Divine authority, institutions, so that their communities see the Christic quality there, rather than setting up a new and singular successor institution.

UNITY BETWEEN FORMS, OR EVERYTHING IN RELATION AND IN RHYTHM

Here we explore the patterns of interaction, harmony, community. Having common ontological ground implies a plane of relationship, a context for interacting. Further, interaction which preserves the diversity of entities involved allows for that common context, that common ontological ground, to be displayed while also shown to be in excess of its particular manifestations. A pattern that displays differently-colored circles illustrates that which is common, *circularity*, and precisely does so

---

71   Corbin, *Cyclical Time and Ismaili Gnosis*, 60.

by displaying it as that which remains the same across different colors. It allows us to grasp that circularity is not identified with any single color, or with color at all. Indeed, it takes us to the realm of transcendence, for we can never draw or physically perceive a colorless circle, and yet we are faced with a concept that is outside color.

Exchange, including that of gifts, implies that what is yours can become mine and vice versa, indeed, what is you can be me and vice versa. It is an instance of our *mutual indexing* to a common principle. If I define myself as *excluding everything that I include in my definition of you, I exclude the gift*, I exclude community. To be a unit is to express Unity, to acknowledge other units is to recognize them as also expressing Unity and, finally, this recognition allows for gift exchange, because *our particularity as units can be indexed to the same principal Unity and thus can translate from one to another:* that which *makes us singular makes us communal.*

When our definition of ourselves includes common features as that of others, we recognize there is an underlying Unity (being a circle is not contingent on being red or blue), and ultimately that our differences are also manifesting that Unity. If we define ourselves as irreducibly different in every feature or in our most essential being, then no exchange with an *other* will be revelatory of Unity. But where our features shade into each other, we recognize reality is not linear or univocal (one can get to purple from the enlargement of the definition of blue and also of red). A red and blue circle that know themselves to both be circles can gift each other the aesthetic experience of contrasting colors in such a way as also reveals circularity is not constrained by color—reveals transcendence—and the perspective of each other's farther reach (purple) being conceivable as a shade of the other. And yet contrast allows one to see oneself as an individual more clearly, and the very move towards seeing the other's perspective on reality allows seeing oneself as a legitimate center of reality. The blue circle can think itself universal by receiving red through purple, so that red is ultimately a shade of blue, and the same is true of the red circle, which can come to conceive of blue as a kind of red.

Let us consider pattern. Whenever we pass our eye across the picturesque pattern of repeating forms and changing features, the *variations on a theme*, we are engaging these in an interaction, the shapes and colors are playing together in our apprehension. We are engaging with what is basically the essence of community. The *simultaneous pleasure at commonality and pride in contrast is the basis of harmonious interaction, of community.* Fusing together and individuating at the same time. The one is *soothing*, the other *sharpening*, the one is like the relaxation of sleep in a familiar setting, the other is like the alertness of wakefulness, excited at sharing or receiving a gift of novelty. Ultimately, this leads us to experiencing the genuine *otherness* of someone combined with their genuine *empathy* (which is a commonality: we share a sense of self such that my getting hurt hurts them too) and this leads us to a religious mystery: the other that is also me, the other that I interact with *as other*, as separate entity, and yet that I do not doubt wants my health.

We tend to consider diversity—the gift of novelty we give and receive—not as a neutral purely objective display but as opening us up to different aesthetic experiences, and different moods as having different harmonious roles to play, like the four humors of medieval medicine. We often integrate the diversity we observe into a schema, just as various ancient peoples assimilated their neighbors into archetypes, like the four corners of the earth corresponding to the four elements, and so on. Observing differently colored circles we will tend to relate the blue one to calm and the red to excitement, for example. The fact that I can perceive a contrast suggests a datum worth distinguishing from other input, and with which I could have some aesthetic involvement eliciting a distinct mood. This allows me to consider myself as prior to mood, as large enough to encompass, and remain constant through the flux of, many moods.

It is not only that contrast emphasizes what is common, it is also that contrast suggests a common archetype to which contrasting features are sub-types: the *differently colored circles show us that shapes are distinct from color*, and that the singular definition of a certain shape must make no mention of color, but *they also suggest what might be the singular definition of color itself*. We are faced with understanding Unity as that which stays the same (circular shape) and also as that which produces difference (but also stays the same as *colorfulness itself*). Not only Unity in form, but in feature; not only of essence but of substance. The One gives forth both the shape-giving Architect, Jove, and the substance-giving Matrix, Juno.

This answers the questions of *why there are many things rather than one thing* (to amend Leibniz's famous *why is there something rather than nothing*). There must be multiple contingencies to bear witness to the fact that unity is beyond them, that God is not His creation. And there must be multiple permutations on a theme to express that there is such a thing as a theme. This serves to conclude the present section.

Before moving on, however, we may highlight the corollary, especially as it concerns politics: *Homogenization* (either as centralization and imperialism or diffusion and entropy) *is sophistry*. It is the equivalent of the following equation: *everything has color; red is a color; everything is (or should be) red*. Or, in political terms: *every human being requires justice; my rule is just; every human being requires my rule*.

An example of this shows up in the political theory of Dante Alighieri. When he argues for global Roman rule, he points out that if Christ took the penalty of all humanity's sins upon himself, the authority that imposed that penalty must have jurisdiction over all humanity. We would add, however, that it had such authority in terms of its principle, and manifestly not in terms of its practice (in terms of its archetype, not its type). The *principle of justice may manifest in Rome, but Rome is not the principle of justice.* In Christian trinitarian terms, it is often explained that God is the Father and God is the Son and God is the Holy Spirit, but that does not mean that the Son is the Father. To the contrary. Rome is the Ecumenic whole, and China is the Ecumenic whole, but Rome is not China nor should it Romanize China.

Recognizing universal principles behind cultural practices requires we recognize that these practices are not an exhaustive manifestation of those principles but also that they are unitary: a certain language like Mongolian or Swahili does not exhaust the possibilities of human oral communication, but in order to manifest that ability at all, they must be coherent in themselves. They must be cogent unities with coherent rules, a grammar, words, etc., but for this very reason *must be translatable, that is, must allow themselves to be indexed to common meanings and to an underlying possibility of grammar that is prior to their specific grammars.* As manifestations of the capacity to communicate they must themselves be able to communicate with each other. *They must be able to extend recognition to each other of a common universal manifesting in each.*

In political terms this is not too different from how Pierre Leroux used the term solidarity to describe a "pre-established harmony between individuals, constituted not through the imposition of any universal rule, but rather through the unique but perfect reflection of the—otherwise transcendent and unrepresentable—whole in each singular person."[72] This is similar to Leibniz's monadology, as Milbank notes. If each monad constituting reality is equipped by the true Reality (which Leibniz arrives at in terms not dissimilar to those of Plato in the Parmenides during his set of apophatic precisions concerning the One), God, with a nature that results in a pre-established harmony among themselves, all are free to follow their inner law, which will make of them convivial partners with all else. They are freest when they become incapable of sinning, per St. Augustine. We may add that this nature becomes occluded and must be rediscovered in course of the spiritual quest (the likeness is marred but the image of God never is). This quest is to make the likeness match the image, to conform the icon to its source, which is the passionate sympathy of seeker to theophany Henry Corbin describes.

Let's refer back to the preceding section, and not that recognizing discontinuity between entities does not require abstaining from unified accounts of these entities: *discontinuity of entities does not entail lack of harmony between them or their being sustained by common underlying structures.* Just as providing a comprehensive, unified archeological, genetic and historical account for the human species and its expansion over the earth does not require that one negate the political and cultural integrity of different

---

72   Milbank, *The Word Made Strange: Theology, Language, Culture,* 273, referring to David Owen Evans's 1948 *Le Socialisme Romantique: Pierre Leroux et ses Compagnons.*

communities, so too providing a comprehensive, unified account of religions and mythologies does not require one to negate differences in rites and symbols. [73] One may describe the substance of the mirrors, how they came about, and the ground on which they rest, thereby emphasizing their common provenance and substrate—indeed, one can describe the fact that they are arranged in relation to each other so as to form a pattern, a harmony—as well as referring to the common object they reflect, without thereby welding them together.

It is in zooming out that discontinuous entities become one, and this zooming out is analogous to seeing wider patterns encompassing multiple entities; from a distance, separate points of light seem to bleed out their shine into a single circumference. The nearer they are the less distance one needs before this occurs. From a granular vantage, points can be discontinuous from each other while, from a grander vantage, they are one. We find a similar image in one of the visions of Black Elk, Lakota medicine man and Catholic convert (currently being investigated for canonization):

> And while I stood there I saw more than I can tell and understood
> more than I saw; for I was seeing in a sacred manner the shapes
> of all things in the spirit, and the shape of all shapes as they must
> live together like one being. And I saw that the sacred hoop of
> my people was one of many hoops that made one circle, wide
> as daylight and as starlight, and in the center grew one mighty
> flowering tree to shelter all the children of one mother and one
> father. And I saw that it was holy. [74]

Our points of light are their own unit and also part of a unit. Perhaps they all face one direction and reflect a common image which itself is a reflection, so that they are properly visible only from the vantage of that reflected image that they, in turn, are mirrors to. One cannot understand a painting without context: art in a given style is understandable by knowing what the artist was doing vis-a-vis how that style attempts to express beauty (what facet of form it emphasizes); Italy is understandable in terms of the Greco-Roman culture, Korea in terms of Confucianism and Buddhism.

The underlying principle of manifestation must always be ever more encompassing than any given form. Even discontinuous universes within a multiverse must exist in relation to each other according to a harmonious pattern expressive of that underlying unitary principle (harmony

---

73   Though not really dealing with the issue of philosophically necessary discontinuity, Voegelin's approach to historiography is admirable as one in which history "must be accorded amplitude wide enough to accommodate all the theophanic events in which the paradox of reality breaks through to consciousness" (*Order and History Volume IV, The Ecumenic Age*, 325).

74   Raymond J. DeMallie, *The Sixth Grandfather: Black Elk's Teachings Given to John G. Neihardt* (Lincoln, NE: University of Nebraska Press. 1984), 97.

expresses unity, but this would be mere accident unless the parts which are harmonious share something in their being). Every microcosm, each a tidy expression of the macrocosm, is so because it is constituted by the same underlying laws. Commonality is emphasized by the fact that there is the possibility of there being something in common at all, a common Being. That principle must be one, unitary, and is therefore prone to producing unities. Rather than realizing commonality by deconstructing the integrity of different entities and trying to amalgamate them, then, unity is realized by granting them their unity, both in themselves as cogent bodies and together in a harmonious relation.

Commonality is best manifested by respecting the integrity of different parts and, indeed, the more they act in relation to each other the more they seem to be distinct, just as a man is most clearly displaying his masculinity when using it functionally, which emphasizes his difference with respect to woman in the context of copulation, and yet is most correspondent with her, most *in relation*, most porous, in that very act.

Key to this is the doctrine that "All things are in everything, though in a way that is appropriate to each thing" (Porphyry's qualification of the Anaxagorean principle).[75] The vision is a fractal one: an expansive and intensive symmetry. Each entity contains all entities: Plato's *intelligible animal*, the universe, is a manifestation of the autozoon or *intellectual animal/essential living animal*—every part of the cosmos and the whole cosmos are manifestations of the autozoon, which we may also call the meta-polis, as it provides the blueprint for every just and harmonious human community—polis, city; it is utopia, the Shiite Iranian *Na Koja Abad/Abode of No-Place*, the Elysium which contains the vision of an *ideal* Rome shown to Aeneas in the *Aeneid*, the non-spatial *One Opening* of Taoism, home of Saints, Buddhas and Immortals according to Liu Yiming,[76] etc. In Platonic terms, the One manifests the All (the All is the icon of the One). Crucially, given that the All can be contained entirely but differently in various entities (its parts), these entities need not be alike or strive for likeness, effacing particularity, in order to be fully expressive of universality.

That *thing* which is singular is *no-thing*. To be a thing (in time, with form, contingent) is to be in some sense composite, divided, multiple. That which is entirely unitary is outside time. Because the All manifests the One it must be unified and yet, because anything manifest must be plural, it need have no single, reified, center. It would not do to accept the existence of a plurality of suns while arbitrarily maintaining that there is only one galaxy, arguing that galactic singularity is expressive of the universal first cause, or

---

75 Gerd van Riel, "The One, The Henads, and The Principles." In: Marije Martijn and Pieter d'Hoine, eds., *All From One: A Guide to Proclus* (Oxford: Oxford University Press, 2017), 86.

76 Fabrizio Pregadio, "The Alchemical Body in Daoism," *Journal of Daoist Studies* 14 (2021): 99–127.

to accept a plurality of galaxies and then to arbitrarily posit the existence of only one galactic super-cluster whose singularity exhausts universal oneness. Rather, the Platonic One can un-problematically be accepted as already articulate in the *fitting in* or harmony, the repeating pattern or *grand vision*, of reality, not requiring that any particular, contingent structure be singular in order to express its own transcendent singularity.

To summarize: the ever-present origin, the center, the expression of oneness, is not ultimate physical centralization but rather harmony throughout. The One is not expressed in centralization but in harmony; harmony is unity, not uniformity. This does not mean physical creation is infinite. Each physical extent must by the nature of physicality, run out, be contained, have its limit. There may therefore be discontinuous temporalities, universes in between which there is nothing physical. However, even these would be organized within a harmony, like adorning gems.

The Absent Center and the Asymptotic Cosmos

A similar shock to that of the spherical world in Voegelin, or the concept of infinity in Pascal, ought today to result from the *hard problem* of consciousness: consciousness as irreducible to any physical thing and therefore constituting an absent center of perception/volition. We should consider the fact that human consciousness experiences the world from the perspective of a complex structure made of many aggregates—the brain. This implies that unification of subordinate unities is real and not just apparent, for consciousness is inexplicable in terms only of those aggregates (why should consciousness not experience only from the level of the quark, the atom, the molecule, the cell? Why should it experience from the vantage of the aggregated, integrated architecture of a brain?). This means unity (the unity of molecules and cells into a brain, for example) is real, but also that the quality which proves that unity, consciousness, is somehow *outside*, as if waiting to inhabit complex structures when these become available.

Consciousness illustrates the absent center, not definable by any one of the body's organic processes, but serving as the body's invisible unity, bearer of volition, expressing the truth that the universal is never exhausted in a particular. Consciousness gives its sanction to the collection of atoms, molecules and brain cells and treats their apparent coherence as a real coherence, a unit, by perceiving out from it: the "unity of consciousness—the 'I think' that under any mental representation of reality as a coherent phenomenon."[77]

As Suhrawardi writes, "... nothing in the world of bodies is a unity," because all is diverse, all allows for and implies by its very existence the possibility of equivalent forms, "so the soul cannot be conceived to exist

---

77   David B. Hart, *The Experience of God: Being, Consciousness, Bliss* (New Haven: Yale University Press, 2013), 182.

in the world of bodies."[78] We are imbued, then, with knowledge of that which cannot be derived from senses, namely the knowledge of unity. To confess that there is Unity is to confess that there is transcendence and correspondingly that imminent manifestation is unified (ordered, coherent, harmonious).

The critique of reductionist (eliminativist or emergentist) accounts of consciousness is implicitly a critique of modern western anthropology. The latter proceeds (maybe, as is often argued, as Christian heresy, by way of Protestantism and Catholic *pura natura* thought) from the rejection of non-relational union with God, for it implies that the human person is conceivable in isolation, whereas non-relationality would mean the human being can know itself at a depth that is, in fact, God's own Being, which also implies a deeper communality—porosity, as Desmond would put it—since persons share each other's beings in that Being. If the fact of our being conscious, and of our consciousness occupying the vantage of the complex composite structure of the brain, is only explicable by its being a priori unitary, then scientific reductionism may prove a stepping stone to a deeper religiosity, may prove to be the danger in which is the saving power, Heidegger's "godless thinking" that is "thus perhaps closer to the divine God."[79]

We find this approach to transcendent Unity through the irreducibility of consciousness to composite, mutable matter in the Persian sage Suhrawardi. Referring to the soul, Suhrawardi quotes the Qur'an (54:55) as follows: "In a seat of truth, a mighty monarch" and from a Sufi hadith commentary, "He who is with God is without place." As Jesus says, the Son of Man has nowhere to rest His head (Matthew 8:20). Suhrawardi argues that the human spirit is not in the world because it can understand unity, which is ever beyond unities, "[y]et, it does have a connection to the body resembling that of a king to his kingdom, and he control it as he wills."[80] This is perfectly in line with our idea that the logic of kingship is one of manifesting Unity as centrality, and of its true character as reflective of the invisible center, that which is not reduced to any part of the system whose unity it serves to express, like consciousness and unitary volition within the body.

Accepting the possibility of non-relational oneness with God at the level where our being is His Being allows for a deeper communal relationality between people, for we share our depths. It is only possible to *overcome atomizing individualism by embracing a certain metaphysical non-relationality* (western Christians do not only need a renewed sense of community and charity, but charity renewed by way of Meister Eckhart

---

78   Suhrawardi, *Creed of the Sages*, VII, 79.
79   Martin Heidegger, *Identity and Difference* (London: Harper and Row Publishers, 1969), 72.
80   Suhrawardi, *Creed of the Sages*, VII, 80.

and other mystics who, following St. Paul, spoke of no longer being themselves, but only God Being).

The *between that is beyond* can also be described as an *absent center*. Complex structures can appear to lack discrete centers: The center of the earth may be its molten core, axis, North Pole, South Pole, equator. The world's center could be double, north and south poles, just as all singularity may be thought of as manifesting outwardly in a gendered dyad (and, adding their union, in a triad). The north celestial pole closely corresponds to the north star, so that a long-exposure photograph displays the stars rotating around it; the same photograph of the south pole shows the stars rotating around a dark center: if we "read" the earth's position metaphorically, the center is both light and darkness, star and space.

Further, given their inhospitability, these places are not closely identified with a particular, historically settled, people in the way other parts of the earth are. They are *topoi*, not nations among nations. Similarly, the center of a body may be its heart, spine, brain, navel, and indeed different organs are central to equally essential functions. Depending on what is valued, different organs will appear central to sustaining the body (the lungs commune with the outside world most directly, the brain performs higher cognition, the genitals store vitality).

As often occurs in complex systems, an entity may not have a single definitional center. Its invisible center—an *apophatic witness* to the absent center at the gap connecting essence and existence, the un-manifest *between*—is at the intersection of many indices, many features. And as a category it will present its own necessary range, like permutations on a theme, the internal diversity of a complex body that allows it to function. Further, for an entity/structure (a person, an architectural style, a civilization) to have its center at the overlap of various more or less measurable factors does not mean its body does not also branch out from that center to include nodes defined by only some of those factors. In any case the invisible, un-measurable, center is, in a sense, the most irreducible of all, for it is a *consciousness* or the awareness of its being a unit.

Even the organic role of a central organ or station—insofar as it manifests centrality—can be thought of as accidental with respect to that centrality. If the centrality of an entity is organic, so to speak, the specific function of a central station can be distinguished from that station: The anatomy of an octopus may award centrality to an organ other than its three hearts, yet these are functionally equivalent to the human heart, which we usually consider central to our anatomy. We may even conceive of creatures in which blood circulation is secondary to the circulation of some bile, and in which blood, while present, does not represent life as it does for us, because the creature in question uses oxygen only secondarily. Referring to the importance of the heart in traditional symbolism, René Guénon can write that such a "localization" is in no wise to be conceived literally once the point of view of corporeal individuality has been transcended, the other modalities being no longer subject to the spatial condition.[81]

This absence of a center is borne out poetically in mandalas whose center is blank or, as appears frequently in the Tantric tradition, occupied by a copulating divine couple, because Unity in and of itself is ineffable and cannot be depicted, but the attaining of unity in the congress of its most fundamental aspects, the eternal masculine and the eternal feminine, is fathomable. Systems that do not discretely centralize (like medieval society), allowing different kinds of centrality (depending on ambit), bear witness to God's ineffability (bear an apophatic witness, where centralized systems bear cataphatic witness, one pluralistic and the other homogenizing, but even accepting these both as legitimate results in a higher pluralism, the way that God's goodness is described as beyond good and evil, and yet also as good in some grander sense).

We may think of the Biblical prophet Daniel's vision of the Son of Man witnessing the heavenly, singular Ancient of Days and then inheriting harmonious, earthly manifold of nations. The latter is a nuptial fulfilment (the kingdoms of the earth as feminine Jerusalem/Church as Bride) and corresponds to what we called an apophatic witness. St. Gregory of Nyssa's proliferation of (mixed) metaphors to convey human relations with God as a safeguard against idolatry is an argument for precisely this *apophatism-as-diverse-cataphatism, negative theology through pluralistic positive theology*, it is an argument for the good of theological diversity and eccentricity of myths.

While having a center permits order by referring peripheral parts to a common core, for Plotinus the "link between the soul and its center is not local."[82] Concerning the "question of the center of all the worlds" Guénon justifies passing "to the supra-sensible order by making an analogical transposition in which space and time no longer bear any but a purely symbolical meaning."[83] Thus, for Guénon "the center is nowhere"[84] just as for Nicholas of Cusa it is everywhere.

The One has no need of an exclusive physical correlate to its oneness in which its productive agency is singularly represented, for it manifests an "eternal and invisible production": Eternal, for that which initiates or terminates time must be other than time, so that, from the vantage of eternity, time cannot be said to be occurring sequentially; invisible,

---

81 René Guénon, *Man and His Becoming According to the Vedanta*, trans. R. Nicholson (Hillsdale, NY: Sophia Perennis, 2004), 33.

82 Bruno Pinchard, "Symbol and Space according to René Guénon." In: Teun Koetsier and Luc Bergmans (eds.), *Mathematics and the Divine: A Historical Study* (London: Elsevier, 2005), 633.

83 René Guénon, *The Symbolism of the Cross*, trans. A. Macnab (Hillsdale, NY: Sophia Perennis, 1996), 16.

84 Ibid., 142.

because that which manifests sensible and physical causation must not be bound by it, and therefore does not proceed along a single, discrete chain of causes and effects, but can issue forth variously.

"Divinity produces all things at once, and eternally," which is not to be taken as justifying a sort of iconoclastic occasionalism that reneges on intelligibility and denies the existence of causal patterns, for "all things being produced at once and eternally... the order of the effects is at the same time preserved... though all things are at once from one cause, yet some have the first, and others a subordinate, dignity."[85] The altar beneath a mantle may equally sustain each of its threads, but these are still woven together in particular relationships, some closer and others farther, presenting a picture together, a causal pattern in which the image of a fount leads the eye into that of springing water. In this context Thomas Whittaker concludes that "[t]o Proclus, the representation of the transcendent idea of the good by a particular physical body in the universe was embarrassing."[86]

For Proclus a monad is known as that which is prior to a multitude. In proposition twenty-one of the *Metaphysical Elements*, Proclus provides the supernal scaffold for this position (roughly what Arthur Lovejoy describes as the "principle of plenitude,"[87] which he traces back to Plato's *Timaeus*[88]). He explains that whatever constitutes commonality between multiple entities (when these are not each other's cause and effect) does not proceed from one of these entities but is prior to, and encompassing of, them. Language is not ideally Mongolian or Swahili—a principle cannot be restricted to one of its expressions over and against the others:

> In each order, therefore, there is one monad prior to the multitude, which imparts one ratio and connection to the natures arranged in it, both to each other and to the whole. For let one thing be the cause of another, among things that are under the same causal chain or series; but that which ranks as the cause of the one series must necessarily be prior to all in that series, and all things must be generated by it as coordinate, not so that each will be a certain particular thing, but that each will belong to this order.[89]

Proclus considers two types of causation: vertical and transversal.[90] Vertical causation produces *different* orders that do not share the essence

---

85   Proclus, *The Commentaries of Proclus on the Timaeus of Plato in Five Books*, vol. 2, III, 1.

86   Thomas Whittaker, *The Neo-Platonists* (Cambridge: Cambridge University Press, 1928), 214.

87   Arthur Lovejoy, *The Great Chain of Being.* (Cambridge, MA: Harvard University Press, 1964), 67.

88   Ibid., 54.

89   Proclus, *Metaphysical Elements*, trans. T. Johnson (Osceola, MO: Press of the Republican, 1909), XXI:20.

90   Marije Martijn and Lloyd Gerson, "Proclus' System." In: Marije Martijn and Pieter d'Hoine, eds., *All From One: A Guide to Proclus* (Oxford: Oxford University Press, 2017), 53–54.

of their cause, being like its reflected image. Transversal causation generates particulars *within* an order of being; a plurality within one principle. In this second mode of generation "things that are 'co-ordinate'...or share (a?) common element"[91] are produced, "intellects proceed from Intellect, souls from Soul."[92]

At each level of reality, a multiplicity of equivalent forms is possible. *Points can exist on a plane equidistant from a center* (which in turn can be on a plane with other centers, all equidistant from some greater center). *Equality is possible*: not every entity occupies a hierarchical position in perfect linear progression from individual entity to individual entity. Ultimate centralization, therefore, commits the same error as homogenization in assuming a finite creation in which everything relates to everything else hierarchically. For Nicholas of Cusa "no individual of any species can possess all the perfection of its nature."[93] Points on a circumference, equidistant to the center are like senses equidistant to the perceiving awareness. There is no meaningful sense in which sight is derivative of hearing or vice versa: *the senses are discontinuous from each other and also all harnessed to a common perceiver.*

Further, microcosm implies the simultaneous presence of all archetypes in a type, the simultaneous presence of anterior principles in a manifestation. So, for example, everything is an interaction of the eternal feminine and eternal masculine. It isn't the case that the male of a species is not also the manifestation of the feminine, and the female also of the male, as all manifestations must be a meeting of the eternal feminine and eternal masculine. And the masculine and feminine are both passive and active, both subject and object, so that no single archetype or principle is devoid of the rest when it manifests in some particular, but rather they are simultaneously present in varying modalities. Archetypes or principles do not manifest into linear, exclusive sequences but simultaneously in each of their derivative manifestations even when one of the latter (a type, a particular) is more explicitly expressive of one of the former (an archetype, a principle), as is the case of the male of a species manifesting the eternal masculine, etc.

Because the One is not exhausted in, or presented exclusively by, any particular entity, there can always be other structures, including other spatial or temporal extents (both as peers, together on one level, and as wider agglutinative wholes): There is no "quantitative infinite," but there is an "indefinite multiplicity,"

---

91 Ibid., 53.
92 Ibid., 53–54.
93 With the exception of Jesus, according to Michael Harrington, although it is difficult to imagine Nicholas of Cusa did not conceive of the historical contingency of Jesus as distinct from the Logos.

> Although Existence is essentially unique because Being in itself
> is one, it nonetheless comprises the indefinite multiplicity of the
> modes of manifestation, for it contains them all equally by the
> very fact that they are all equally possible...Existence comprises
> in its very 'unicity' an indefinitude of degrees corresponding to
> all the modes of universal manifestation...this indefinite multi-
> plicity of degrees of existence implies correlatively a like indefinite
> multiplicity of possible states of manifestation...[94]

Each place or entity manifests that which is neither place nor entity
(each degree of existence manifests that by virtue of which existence can
express *oneness*):

> ...as none of these places can claim an absolutely privileged
> value (for instance, that of being the center of the universe),
> we have to admit the possible existence of different, equivalent
> world-images...[95]

These would nonetheless all have their ground in the One, for there
is no other source. Sharing their ultimate reality, manifesting a single
principle, they would not be disconnected from each other, agonistic and
essentially irreducible, but would be in relation and in harmony. However
many universes there might be, they are always encompassed by a single
harmony, there is always only a *uni*-verse. This is generally the opinion of
the Platonists in rejecting the existence of many worlds and maintaining
that there is only one. Creation is not homogenous so as to blaspheme
God by equating itself with the Divine simplicity, but harmonious to
praise Him in manifold ways, for no one way will do, and a plethora will
testify to the inadequacy of any one of its voices.

Each tradition, for example, may rest upon its peculiar centrality, just
as various cultures self-designate by the generic term for *human being* in
their language, following a kind of "mythological subjectivity" in order "to
remain faithful to the Origin," which "is to place oneself at the Center; it
is to dwell in the primordial Purity."[96] To realize that the *center is everywhere*
is most eminently (and imminently) to realize it is where one happens to
be (it is *what* one happens to be). The latter realization (the center is *here*)
is the only means of mediating the former (the center is *everywhere*). Thus,
the original Ionian map made Delphi the *omphalos* (the center of the world)
whereas the *Book of Jubilees* awarded this position to Jerusalem.[97]

---

94   René Guénon, *The Multiple States of the Being*, trans. H. Fohr and ed. S. Fohr
(Hillsdale, NY: Sophia Perennis, 2004), 28.

95   Alexander Koyré, *From the Closed World to the Infinite Universe* (London: John
Hopkins Press, 1957), 16.

96   Frithjof Schuon, *Light on the Ancient Worlds* (Bloomington, IN: World Wisdom,
2006), 1.

97   Lynn LiDonnici and Andrea Lieber, *Heavenly Tablets: Interpretation, Identity and
Tradition in Ancient Judaism* (Boston, MA: Brill, 2007), 3-4.

It may be concluded from this that created orders must consist of plural forms that are equidistant not only from the One but from their own categorical principle (every monadic term in the tetrad is equally a part of the tetrad: a bull and buffalo, equally bovine; a panther and tiger, equally feline; a wolf and fox, equally canine; Greco-Roman and the Sino-Confucian civilizations, equally human civilizations). Nicholas of Cusa encapsulates in *De Pace Fidei*: "Equality is the unfolding of form in oneness...."[98]

The round table of King Arthur, whose knights are equal and equidistant, and the center of which is occupied by the Holy Grail, which is not of this world, and disappears, provides worthy subject of contemplation along with Cusa's phrase. However, King Arthur also becomes a representative of the center, as the thirteenth knight (consider that twelve is the maximum number of spheres that can be placed around a single central sphere of the same size, which may explain the ubiquity of the number twelve along with an additional king or master in mythology and in the Gospel). The central thirteenth must be a neutral station, yet it has the same size as the twelve around it. It must not have content the way they do, yet must also be alike them in some way. We may manifest it as a neutral institution whose mandate alternates, perhaps.

In terms of reflecting the absent—or remote—center, just as a mirror with no center will reflect a donut-shaped sun and lead us astray in understanding the shape of the sun, we need proximate, contingent centers to understand that there is such a thing as centrality, or unity. Now, someone might argue that a donut shaped mirror precisely reflects the absence of ultimate centrality, however, the mirror's center can be thought to be whichever spot, depending on perspective and time of day, reflects the sun, whose movement is not determined by the mirror. In this sense lacking a center by having an actual hole would precisely be a reification of the transcendent center. The point is that it is perfectly possible to have *both a discrete and a distributed center*, one visible and the other invisible, which forms the *exoteric* and *esoteric* parts of a tradition: like consciousness in the body, which is often spoken of as being in the heart but is really not reducible to any organ, or the liturgy in a medieval society, which can be held in a central cathedral but is also celebrated in every parish church and carried therefrom in the body of every congregant who has taken communion.

Each possible manifested center can be experienced outside time as a still, resting post in eternity. One's being may have its center, but peripheries, that is, farther parts of reality wherein one is more *stretched* and which, experienced in time, are moments of pain or alienation from what one feels is one's center, the integrity of one's being, are also part of the total glory of one's self when felt together with the rest. This

---

98   Nicholas of Cusa, *De Pace Fidei and Cribratio Alkorani*, trans. J. Hopkins (Minneapolis, MN: The Arthur J. Banning Press, 1994), VIII:22, 644-45.

introduces *variety* into the beatific vision, which, in time, is experienced sequentially as *variability*. Each particular, insofar as it is an eternal potential, a thought in the mind of God, endures forever (a person attains *immortality*) and is in this regard itself a universal, but intersecting with other different particulars in different parts of its being, *dilated over eternity*.

Perhaps the center is wherever the specificity of one's being intersects with sublime centrality, for the truest character of contingent things is their un-contingent character, since everything's being is in God's Being. Then the truest expression of blue is where blue appears in the center of a system, etc. Of course, we may share centers, like the couple in the middle of a Tantric mandala, so that our truest character is both centrality and complementarity.

We may consider Hindu descriptions of the eternal Heavens (beyond the temporal heavens whose enjoyment is followed by reincarnation). Divinities occur as regents of different such abodes, including the Shiva-loka of Shiva, the Devi-loka of the Goddess, Vaikuntha of Vishnu and the Go-loka of Lord Krishna. Some traditions provide descriptions of these in which other gods are present in that abode being described, but as secondary figures to make the point that their subject of devotion is supreme. Thus, while one form is supreme where it is central, it is secondary in some other possible configuration, where it is not central.[99] One is thus *dilated over eternity*, as Catherine Pickstock writes quoting St. Gregory, or, we may add, *crucified over eternity*, where the cross is a throne and one reigns in eternity as co-heir with Christ.

The argument for the supremacy of a particular form of the Divine over other forms—like a Vaishnavist claiming Vishnu is supreme or a Shaivist claiming this for Shiva—can be put forward in terms of its being a structure that will always occur in order to sustain other forms. The form considered primary is like the sun which shines energy into the worlds so that life can develop. We can argue that wherever there is a world with life there is a sun shining energy into it. The problem is that a function so abstract or universal seems to resist specific features being attributed to it. The universal function as such is described according to coherent metaphysical schemas, albeit some define it by one theological name and others by another. We also wonder whether Cusa's argument that divine omnipresence renders earth and sun central to the cosmos depending on one's perspective applies here.

Yet if the features being attributed to the primary Divine form are not too specific, its centrality can be defended. For example: the *guna* 'sattva' is that which sustains (where *tattva* destroys and *rajas* creates), it

99   I am referring to the surface aspect of such descriptions, not to the deeper or more ancient meanings of various deities, which may, perhaps, justify considering one as supreme from that perspective, though not ultimately in terms of attributions of formal features which can always bare different meanings and can vary as symbols for those meanings.

therefore symbolizes that which is beyond time, forms unconditioned by the instability of matter, since those archetypal forms need not be created or destroyed. The sustaining guna, as distinct from the destroying and creating ones, better symbolizes the heavenly realms. Vishnu as preserver can, therefore, be understood to be supreme. Another approach, however, might claim that because materiality is ever occurring in the midst of the divine, it is the form which manifests in the earth adorned by the destructive and creative gunas (traditionally Shiva) that is expressing a wider gamut of reality. Which of these two is primary or more fundamental becomes a definitional issue. Perhaps one is more fundamental where is the other is more encompassing. Perhaps one is more central, like the center of a circle, where the other is more radiant, like the radius from center to circumference, or the circumference itself. The Christian Trinity allows for precisely these considerations.

The Icon as Logical Necessity, or the Irrationality of both Iconoclasm and Idolatry

An all-encompassing principle, one constituting the basis for all forms, must also manifest as harmony or pattern between forms. *Harmony is movement and consistency*, that is, movement around, or according to, a fixed or repeating point or pattern. Harmony therefore requires a center. A center can be understood as the equation programming a hyperbola. Harmony can be conceived as revolution/oscillation.

Each center must, in turn, revolve/oscillate, that is, it must vary (the equation itself is subject to higher-order functions), because it is not the ultimate center, because *there is no ultimate center in manifestation*. Each limited system, as microcosm of the whole, can have no ultimate or entirely unchanging center manifested in creation.

When centers shift, when patterns change, they display their capacity to manifest within different contingencies, demonstrating that the principle they manifest is outside contingency, is beyond them. This is the "serpentine reology" of Pickstock (reology deriving from "res," "thing,"): the snake-like quality of all things in general (she could have also called it "rheology" from "rheo," "to flow"). All things must twist and untwist, enter themselves and exist themselves, draw on what is inward while also drawing out into the world, be centripetal and centrifugal, the alchemical *solve et coagula*. In a sense this reproduces the circular, which is the movement of returning to the point of origin, without closing the circle, for nothing in finite existence is entirely closed off, producing instead a spiral or snaking shape. It is here that the snake as Urform[100] is reconciled to, and finds its identity with, the cross. Moses placed a serpent upon a vertical stick to save his people. John's Gospel likens this to Jesus on the cross, the undulations of the snake turned vertical, transcendent.

---

100   Pickstock, *After Writing: On the Liturgical Consummation of Philosophy*, 234.

The color blue may appear both in an orbiting planet covered in water and in an O-type blue star at the center of a planetary nebula, for example. Across different systems of manifest creation (and perhaps across levels of resolution, from higher to lower orders) sets of internally related accidental features repeat themselves. These form narrower and broader layers of complexity approaching the *ultimate center* asymptotically, representing *oneness* in ever wider circles; layers upon layers of hierarchically arranged orders of things.

The cosmos is asymptotically approaching God, or asymptotically approaching the symbol of God's oneness, the final center of everything, which is never finally arrived it, but which is always inspiring new deeper and wider, lower and higher aspirations. Just like the color blue above, a complex entity, understood as a particular objective pattern or subjective disposition, may extend over different systems, sometimes at the center, sometimes at the periphery, for "the perdurance of a thing consists in its non-identical repeatability, and so in a certain style that can persist through different and unpredictable variations."[101]

The more different and abstracted from an entity a center is, the more it will tend to exhibit stability in its accidental features; the less different and abstracted from an entity a center is, the less it will tend to exhibit stability in its accidental features. The sun acts as a center for planets and illustrates centrality to human beings, it also differs a great deal from planets and from human beings and, form their perspective, endures for long eons. The king traditionally acts as a center for the sacred-political order of human beings, he also greatly resembles other human beings, as he is one himself, and lives as long as they do.

A man may manifest a higher principal then other men, either by virtue of symbolic status or actualized vocation, as in the case of a great teacher, but he does not thereby obtain a lifespan so out of proportion to that of other human beings as to justify their confusing his empirical features with the archetype he manifests or, indeed, with the unchanging reality behind all things. In the case of the sun, though we may be tempted to identify it with centrality and therefore with God's oneness, its abstraction with respect to us prevents us from thereby identifying too many accidental features with God. In the case of the king or teacher, though we may be tempted to identify this figure with centrality and therefore with God's oneness, his mortality prevents us from thereby identifying too many accidental features with God.

If the rhythm of the changes in a center's accidental features (in the passing of its representation from one human vessel to another) is too slow to be observed by its peers, facilitating their identification of it with the unchanging function it exerts, it will effectively not be a peer at all, as is the case of the sun with respect to the planets or to human

---

101   Ibid., 160.

beings. Thusly is the cosmos designed to thwart idolatry, beginning with self-idolatry (identification of one's own features with God's oneness). The world is *neither iconoclastic nor idolatrous* and thwarts both tendencies.

This may be behind the apparent seasonal nature of ancient monarchy, recognizing the need to disassociate contingent features of persons from kingship in general, and to allow distance from the political fiction, which is not thereby abolished, but asserted:

> "Within the same population, one could live sometimes in what looks, from a distance, like a band, sometimes a tribe, and sometimes a society with many of the features we now identify with states. With such institutional flexibility comes the capacity to step outside the boundaries of any given social structure and reflect; to both make and unmake the political worlds we live in."[102]

To restate things slightly, we are suggesting that the more accidental a feature is with respect to the entity possessing it, the less often it will tend to manifest in that entity over the ages, across the worlds. As for centrality or harmony itself, an accidental feature with respect to this is everything except sublimity. Each center must in turn revolve around another, and just as it holds certain accidental features, the center to which it attends may hold the features of one of its subordinates, and so forth, so that no specific set of such features is fully identified with centrality and the Divine. Representatives of centrality, experienced sequentially (in time) die, and spatially (in eternity) are peers with others who do not share their accidental features. We may understand this in the shifting of magnetic poles over the ages or the changing of historical protagonists over periods of history. *Thusly is the cosmos designed to maximize both diversity and harmony.*

Henry Corbin sees the twin mistakes of iconoclasm and idolatry in the atheist and literalizing theist (I prefer to describe the erring believer as a *literalist* than as *orthodox*): " ... the twofold error which is at once that of the atheist and the orthodox believer: either he must leave the Divine in pure indetermination *(ta'til),* or else he must make It determinate."[103] The Divine must always be *expressed* by, and never be *equated* with, particular forms. Taking the contingent features of his tradition as identical to the truly transcendent, such a believer will tend to conceive of an immortal god who happens to be immortal, but is not so *by definition*, whose

---

102 This passage continues: "If nothing else, this explains the 'princes' and 'princesses' of the last Ice Age, who appear to show up, in such magnificent isolation, like characters in some kind of fairy-tale or costume drama. Maybe they were almost literally so. If they reigned at all, then perhaps it was, like the kings and queens of Stonehenge, just for a season." David Graeber and David Wengrow, "How to Change the Course of Human History (at least, the part that's already happened)," Eurozine, www.eurozine.com/, retrieved March 15th, 2018.

103 Corbin, *Cyclical Time and Ismaili Gnosis,* 178.

immortality is just an infinite duration of time, but is not outside time. Such a god is a being among beings, albeit writ large, and not the Being of beings, beyond time, is immortal only accidentally.

A thoroughgoing logocentrism would not collapse difference of particular entities into the Logos because the Logos is precisely other than those particulars. In the same way, the more philosophically convinced iconoclasm is that images cannot (not that they *should* not, but that they truly *cannot*) depict the Divine, the more likely it is to embrace images or representation.

Theologically, secondary causation is a direct condescension from primary causation. It is ever subordinate to the Divine but is the means by which human beings are allowed agency, for such agency would be impossible in a cosmos without apparent casuistry and partial occlusion, otherwise everything would occur at once (the possibility of sequential action would be nullified). To consider the direct agency of God as requiring the abolition of other agencies is dangerously iconoclastic. We have here one of the ways in which Muslim thought has tended away from truth, like a mirror image of the west's scientistic denial of primary causation.

We have written that pluralism provides an apophatic witness to the transcendence of the One. The Trinity proves *Tawhid*. Trinitarianism is apophatic and therefore radically monotheistic. If God presents in the *personas/hypostases* of the Trinity it is in part because He is inexpressible in one persona. His Oneness is such that no *persona* can alone describe (although, obviously, the Father's monarchy is privileged in this regard). Nicholas of Cusa's trinitarianism and his certain rapprochement with Islam might signal that he saw these connections. Indeed, Pickstock accounts for pluralism in terms of trinitarianism and precisely in those of Cusa.

Regarding pluralism, then, the above principle applies to the inexhaustibility of theophanic mediations, which Eriugena teaches occur even for the deified soul in its relating to the Divine. The Awareness that knows Being contains its own icon of Being, its own personification of It. The Son of Man sees the Ancient of Days, where the latter is still the Son (Second Person of the Trinity) although representing the Father (First Person). Without theophanic mediation, we conceive of God as a persona, or else (or rather, because of this) end up denying God. Writes Henry Corbin:

> ... by a striking paradox, the orthodox literalistic profession of faith reunites with the absolute negation of the atheist, because the literal monotheistic dogma, by rejecting the theophanic function, destroys the transparency of the Veil; it confuses the Veil with the Divinity that It manifests, in believing that it may predicate of God what is only appropriate to His Veil.[104]

---

104 Ibid., 172.

The Eternal Return of the Different and the Eternal Relationship of the Harmonious

Harmony implies regularity. In every generation of a family there is a father and a mother. The specific sentience filling those roles changes but there is something consistent and archetypal about the consciousness of fatherhood and of motherhood. One consciousness, the archetype, reaches down from above, the other, a specific individual, up from below, so to speak. A doctrine like that of the Mormon pluralization of reality, according to which divine creation consists of an infinite regress of creator gods, ought to render greater deference to the transcendence of unity, so that everything that is not itself God is plural and has its possible counterparts, rather than to deny the transcendent God altogether.[105] When the early Mormon theologian Lorenzo Snow claims that *as man is, god was, as god is, man may become*, this statement could be correct from the Hindu perspective, for example, if it were to refer to the particular god shepherding a particular humanity and not to the true God. Each archetypal post is occupied by a different individual sentience (each age has its *Indra*, as in Indian tradition). In Indian tradition, a mythical hero can be considered the Indra of the age or world to come[106] and, in some texts, can Indra assert he was once the Manu of a past era.[107] And in some Persian, mystical Islamic sources we have a "plurality of Prime Movers. A single divine *ousia* [essence], to be sure—but plurality of *Dii-Angeli*, of divine 'centers' (each occupies the whole of its heaven)."[108]

---

105   Mormonism is, in fact, a kind of theological pan-psychism, considering the *spirit element* or *intelligence* (as consciousness is usually termed in its scriptures) to be a property of matter. Even Orson Pratt, who embraced a pan-psychist pantheism in which the *great god*, as he called it, communicates with every part of its body (the physical cosmos) at the speed of thought, was conceiving of matter as twin and substrate to consciousness, not as occurring *within* the mind of that god. While pan-psychism overcomes the problems of eliminativism (denying such a thing as consciousness altogether) and emergentism (considering consciousness an emergent quality of non-conscious matter/energy, falling afoul of the *ex nihilo nihil fit* principle), it does not account for the fact that consciousness does not rest on the laurels of matter's basest structures, like quarks or atoms, but occupies wider vantages whose physical correlates are complex structures, like the human brain. (With regards to Mormonism, Joseph Smith himself may have actually believed in a truly transcendent Divinity, whom he called the "true light" in the Olive Leaf sermon: see: Samuel M. Brown, "Mormons Probably Aren't Materialists," *Dialogue: A Journal of Mormon Thought* 50(3) (2017): 39–72.)
106   Jai Pal Mittal, *History of Ancient India: From 7300 BC to 4250 BC*, vol. 2 (New Delhi: Atlantic Publishers and Distributors, 2006), 77.
107   Arthur A. Macdonell, *Vedic Mythology* (Delhi: Motilal Banarsidass Publishing, 2002), 57.
108   Henry Corbin on the philosophies (and treatments of Aristotle's *Metaphysics*) of Abu'l-Barakat, ibn-Sina and Suhawardi. He continues: "The result is perhaps a sort of splintering of abstract monotheism; but can the situation be confined within the dilemma monotheism or polytheism? Orthodoxy tended to do so; but,

The particular is always inhabiting archetypes that stretch beyond its narrower ambit.

Some form of this principle occurs in the Buddhist doctrine of dependent origination or mutual arising. There is no single, sensible agent originating the entire sensible cosmos, except it all arises according to the Dharma; there is no single Indra ruling over the universe everywhere and forever, except there is always Indra. "All these worlds with their guardian deities" says the *Bhagavatam Purana*.[109]

The idea that *universal* existential posts are occupied by different *particular* agents does not, however, imply that the former is merely impersonal: both are consciousnesses, one from above and archetypal, the other from below. Therefore, although we have written about the arbitrary element of any particular form (the fact that this or that set of sounds designates a chair in this or that language, for example), it should be added that ultimately even that which is arbitrary is actually archetypal, and whenever things differentiate, they do so according to something beyond the merely apparent (although tradition emphasizes the accidental, perverting and even illusory consequences of sin, such that we may discard aspects of differentiation as extraneous to our true natures). Gender is more than biology and reflects an eternal masculine and feminine; historically stable traditions and civilizations, with their defined aesthetic, should be taken seriously as manifesting prominent archetypal potentials of the human condition; and so on. Thus, the relationship between certain personalities, from the individual to the collective, from the personal to the professional, are recurring.

We find this in multiple traditions, beginning with the ancient Egyptian Book of Gates, when they ascribe archetypal directions or qualities to themselves and their neighboring nations, or when different professions are ascribed to bodily organs and limbs, and so on. Swedenborg writes:

> ...all the parts of the human body have a correspondence with such things as are in heaven...they represent together one person...universal heaven is also called Homo maximus; and hence it is that it has so often been said that one society belongs to one province of the body; another to another, and so forth. The reason is, because the Lord is the only Man, and Heaven represents Him... (*Arcana Coelestia*, 2996[110])

If we think back to the metaphor of differently colored circles, blue and red and yellow are not merely accidental features that display the chaotic flux of color. Rather, we experience color as archetypal: blue is a

---

conversely, the angelology of our philosophers tends to destroy the dilemma" (*Avicenna and the Visionary Recital*, 55).

109   *Bhagavatam Purana*, I:13, 41, 227.

110   Cited by Henry Corbin, *Swedenborg and Esoteric Islam*, trans. L. Fox (West Chester, PA: Swedenborg Foundation, 1999), 60.

calming mood, red an incitement, etc. We speak of language in the same way, as transmitting a feeling. The musicality and mood of a language, its non-discursive character, does the same thing. Something like this is expressed in Vico's *Ancient Italic Wisdom* when he argues for the presence of philosophy in archaic languages, un-codified but implicit in their etymologies and grammars. For an identity to be edifying it should be treated with all the levity and detachment of a beloved color. Detachment occurs, paradoxically perhaps, when we realize its archetypal dimension.

One can study cultural and civilizational continuities (sometimes spanning several related and succeeding iterations) in the way that one waxes poetic about a flower, approximating certain inner states, moods, personalities.[111] Culture as an aesthetic coherence and the experience which that aesthetic elicits. The meaning of a culture will appear in the same terms as the meaning of an orchid or the different meaning of a tulip. It does not *mean* in the way a road sign or a legal treatise has meaning, but in the manner of melody. When towards the end of his *Confessions of an English Opium Eater* de Quincey refers to the inappropriateness of *ideas* in understanding music, and the "language of representative feelings," even speaking of his sensitivity to the music of the Italian language being heightened by his poor understanding of it, he may have been getting at something similar.

The European church organ succeeds its notes and their resonances in the manner of rapid flame movement, but a flame that is ordered, geometric, sublimated, producing a sense of complex but linearly narrated (with super-imposed trains) forward movement: a fire's illuminating path through the night (the organ's uneven pipes even resemble tongues of flame sputtering in the fireplace). The Chinese *qin* played at Taoist temples suspends the listener by the vectors of surface tension in a pool of water, lapsing occasionally into a forward course or trickle, or else whistling with the wind on a wave, but mostly reflecting on a delicate stillness. Both the sounds of organ and qin are elegant, precise and all other appellatives proper to sacred music. It is not in these that they differ. It is in their *mood*, the images they compose.

Another feature of Mormonism that may be removed from that theology's commitment to a kind of *process philosophy* is the doctrine of eternal family relations. A man grows from boyhood and becomes a father in the lineage, or within the family, of his own father. The family he founds has its antecedent in the family he grew from. Particular structures, with their particular center with its particular features remain forever one possible arrangement of reality, one possible expression of the inexpressible centrality or unity of God, and in this sense, remain a node in the being of that creature who is dilated infinitely. Creation is always in kinship: If a saint should discover a cosmos in himself, he

---

111   Like Schuon's theophanic individualities.

remains in that external cosmos he was born to (though insofar as his being is a repeating pattern with possible manifestations in other possible cosmoses, he may discover himself elsewhere as well).

In Christianity, Christ's intercession is not a legal relationship. To pray for something via Christ does not exactly involve Christ imploring on our behalf. Rather, the disciple asks God in the name of Christ and God loves the disciple's loving of Christ (John 16:26–27). The relationship is inherent to the anatomy of things, because Christ is our true vine, rather than a legal fiction somehow extraneous to our being. We really do locate our being in the being of Christ, and must relate to the Divine by way of that grander portion of ourselves which is not our ordinary mind but rather is the mind of Christ. It is not, then, that the Logos is some being like us who arbitrarily has more authority and will advocate for our interests. He is us, in the sense in which the true vine is the same body as the grapes that come from it, so that they cannot get sap from anywhere other than the vine they are organically connected to.

If we ask whether there was a discrete, particular antecedent to the whole of creation, or if, at present, there is a discrete, particular center to the whole of reality, we must conclude that there was not, and is not. God is beyond. His creativity cannot be exhausted in a creation; therefore, it cannot be exhausted in one particular beginning or in one particular physical central location. This does not mean that a particular creation cannot act as microcosm and, in a sense, contain the whole. But other particular conditions, other biographical configurations, other coordinates of contingency, could arise. There could always be parallel centers at a given stratum, or presumably deeper layers with further centers.

THE POLITICS OF APOPHATIC PRESENCE

Each center is a local presencing of the absent center, and the absent center must be searched out in the immediate. Douglas Hedley commented during an interview with me:

> …think of Eliot in *Little Gidding*, with his emphasis on this spot. Which is England but is more than England. I think that sense of encountering the sacred with the particular, through a place that is contingently precious but is thereby the means to recognition of our belonging to a sacred cosmos that transcends the particularity of the tribe or the nation.[112]

T. S. Eliot's point in *Four Quartets* is similar to Voegelin's defeat of the concupiscential conqueror. This defeat is spiritually victory. By returning to our point of origin we know the world is round, so that it has no center and yet we are at our one center, the very place from which we parted, like Paulo Coelho's *Alchemist* who discovers the riches he sought

---

112   Douglas Hedley, "Interview with Carlos Perona," 7th March 2018.

buried in his own home after seeking all around the world. We have traced a circle that can spiral on, snake on, and we have discovered the centrality of home, of place and roots even as we are delivered into the ecumenism of a world without ultimate center.

On the importance of realizing the universal is mediated through the particular, and can only ever be so, and that if God is ever the same, and is a creator and therefore ever a creator, meaning there is always a creation, that is, a realm of particulars mediating the universal, we read the following in G. K. Chesterton's *Manalive*:

> "I think God has given us the love of special places, of a hearth and of a native land, for a good reason."
>
> "I dare say," I said, "what reason!"
>
> "Because otherwise," he said, pointing his pole out at the sky and the abyss, "we might worship that."
>
> "What do you mean?" I demanded.
>
> "Eternity," he said in his harsh voice, "the largest of the idols— the mightiest of the rivals of God."
>
> "You mean pantheism and infinity and all that," I suggested.
>
> "I mean," he said with increasing vehemence, "that if there be a house for me in heaven it will either have a green lamp-post and a hedge, or something quite as positive and personal as a green lamp-post and a hedge. I mean that God bade me love one spot and serve it, and do all things however wild in praise of it, so that this one spot might be a witness against all the infinities and the sophistries, that Paradise is somewhere and not anywhere, is something and not anything. And I would not be so very much surprised if the house in heaven had a real green lamp-post after all."

All religion, as it manifests externally, is partly a cultural construct. We may imagine a meteor whose core is metaphysics but which accrues atmospheric elements and products of chemical reaction as it enters our world, constituting the exoteric tradition. This accrual can be legitimate, the irreducibly arbitrary component of any language that we discussed previously, and which is in fact not arbitrary but archetypal, for we can understand cultural diversity as communicating different moods or personalities, different aesthetic principles. It can also be the result of potentially illegitimate influences. A man whose psyche is not ordered towards the good in terms that are conducive to healthy human sociability, for example, might nonetheless receive genuine metaphysical truth by way of his *nous*, spirit, which he articulates in partially distorted terms by filtering it through his psyche, or in terms that are eccentric and appropriate for only certain individuals and are not compatible with structuring human community.[113] This would not constitute a *religious*

---

113   Perhaps there are subjects whose path to realizing the noetic consists of more violence against their psychic and somatic layers than is ordinary; more a rending

insight, but a *mystical* one, if one of religion's functions is to cultivate persons *in community*.

And it is not only an eccentric mystic, but also a too un-eccentric or un-ecstatic clergy, that endangers a tradition. Exoterism has its social role in communal edification and a communally sustainable way of protecting the esoteric theophany. Writes Voegelin: "dogma is protective symbolization of the original theophanic event." A balance must therefore be struck so that dogma does not close the "openness of the theophanic field" like pharisaic authorities who neither enter nor let others enter the mysteries. In the western case he sees the "originating experiences" as "deeply buried under the millennial accretions of doctrine."[114]

The sage is not necessarily or exhaustively infused with knowledge concerning specialized domains when he gains metaphysical insight. The Buddha presumably did not become an expert at bass fishing upon becoming enlightened. Jesus told his disciples that he did not know the hour of eschatological culmination. Just so, individuals may be ignorant of how human society functions best, and have need of that specialized knowledge, which may come by way of explicitly religious revelation.

However, the fact of a tradition including a fruitful *askesis* and even a correct premise (belief in divine unity, mercy, etc.) does not allow one to conclude its teachings on finer points is valid. Simply judging a religion by the spiritual realization of its adherents, as some readers of Guénon do, appears problematic, since *the spirit blows where it will*, and religion is not exclusively to do with individual gnosis but with principles applicable to human communities. An outwardly irreligious skateboarder could receive the grace of illumination in the throes of practicing his hobby, which then apparently becomes a providential vehicle. Spiritual realization does not necessarily entail correction of every empirical and even ethical error (a saint may remain ignorant of the limits of Newtonian physics even in the midst of his sainthood). Yet we also find examples of *religion beyond mere religion* in the scriptures: spiritual guidance that is not concerned with external trappings. The *Bhagavad Gita* and the Gospel of John are examples of this.

Ultimately all religion necessarily places relationship over ritual, or specificity over generality (the *bhava* or specific type of loving relationship a disciple has to God in Indian Vaishnavism; the specific theophany received by an initiate that Corbin discusses in *Alone with the Alone*). "To the abstract generality of the law, Paul opposes the specificity of divine gift which always takes the form of particular gifts in the senses of specific talents or charismata: these are 'different gifts according to the

---

than a clarification of body and mind to let the Nous shine through. This disposition would presumably be less socially sustainable. We can also use the metaphor of breaking a bone, where some breaks strengthen it while others end up deforming it.
114   Voegelin, *Order and History Volume IV, The Ecumenic Age*, 333.

gift given to us' (Romans 12:6)."[115] In any case, the criticism against religion that it is not necessary, for one can engage in spiritual practices on one's own is spurious for these reasons. We are also seeing that the idea itself of community and of religious practice in culturally specific modes is legitimate.

Sacralizing the particular means seeing it as a node for the universal. A node, that is, a place through which the universal flows, that is, through which the universal is displayed: meaning that the particular must manifest the universal. Consider William Blake's (following Kathleen Raine) using sacred paradigms from the Book of Job and applying them to Albion, preaching to the English nation that it should awake from materialistic sleep and see the world in its spiritual significance. Indeed, in Jerusalem (chapter 1, 16) he one by one identifies the counties of Scotland, Wales and England with the twelve tribes of Israel (Ireland is also included).

Such regard for place is achieved by taking truths from one context, grasping them in their abstraction or universality, and applying them to one's own context. Traditions are in need of periodic historical troughs because, without these, they would continue wedded to particular conditions. In order to come into themselves (repeatedly become themselves, repeating non-identically), they must allow themselves to be crucified, embracing the cross as a technology, the arising and passing away of meditation, the ebb and flow of the tide. They must let their essence be ripped away from the historical conditions it arose in and re-applied (re-deemed). This functions through allegory and analogy, applying a principle or pattern outside the specific scriptural context in which it is recorded.

The Biblical theme of collective division as preamble to exaltation (from the scattering of Israel's tribes to the dividing of Egyptian households in Isaiah (19:2) or Christ speaking of pitting child against parent) is alike that of Rome's foundation through Troy's dispersal (after a war which Homer presents, in John Alvis's reading, as Jove's plan to end hubris and usher in a new sociable heroism of humility and piety, a period of rebirth and sacred politics through collective death, which Dante links to the Biblical narrative in *Il Convivio* by maintaining that Aeneas entered Italy at the same time as king David was born). This applies the logic of crucifixion to collectives, where truths are not limited to specific historical and national contexts but may be reapplied. This will be developed further in later sections (including the historical context of these narratives, which is presumably the end of the Bronze Age).

This communal or *cultural crucifixion* is politically-historically manifested in 1) the loss of a polity or identity, 2) the experience of a universal quality represented by an external entity such as an empire (this quality can be a previously unrealized human capacity in the technological or organizational field) and 3) rebirth of that previous identity in a form

---

115   Milbank, *The Word Made Strange: Theology, Language, Culture,* 227.

that incorporates what was brought by the external entity (brought not necessarily by violent imperial expansion—a local culture might wane due to the peaceful influence of a more prominent culture before undergoing a renaissance). It is like a river going underground and emerging again. We may think of pre-modern identities making modernity their own, from romantic nationalism to assertions of post-colonial Native American identity that do not reject modern technology or organizational capacity, or of the return of Roman provinces as modern European nation-states without contradicting the principle of Empire or trans-national identity.

Yet it is not only the local identity that is 'crucified', but also the foreign novelty. When an empire, for example, brings some technological or organizational innovation, this is closely associated with the imperial polity. As the empire falls or reforms, that which it brought is 'reborn', appropriated, as a feature of former subjects. Consider the Native American brothers Tecumseh and Tenskwatawa who, in the early 1800s, fought the expanding United States. They warned that the suppression of indigenous Americans was analogous to the crucifixion of Jesus and would give way to a return. In articulating this, they were also incorporating modern European concepts of nationhood, statehood and territoriality, which they tried to get other tribal leaders to accept in order to establish a sovereign indigenous territory. Thus, it is not only the Native American people that is predicted to be reborn but also the foreign concept of the state. Way to the south, we find counterparts to Tecumseh and his brother in the 18th century leaders Tupac Amaru and Tupac Katari (born Julian Apaza), who fought against Spain[116] and appealed to the memory of the Incanate. A clearer example is that which we find in Black Elk's visions, including his account of Christ and the future of his people.

The traumatic encounter with the other is one way in which Being discloses to Consciousness (when pursued by a tiger we cannot but be fully present). This trauma marks the consciousness, which is endowed thereafter with a reinvigorated sense of self, gratitude at being alive and the desire to pursue our possibilities to the full. But Being is obviously also encounterable in less potentially deadly forms. Arguably, the incorporation of more or less of the cultural baggage of the dominant *other* during a local reassertion depends on how constructive that *other* was, to refer to Gustavo Bueno's distinction between *generative* and *predatory* empires. This is perhaps too utilitarian, however. We should add that it likely also depends on how compatible the Empire was with the local culture, how much of that native culture was intelligible within its cultural framework, and how much of the local was therefore able to continue thriving and even receiving new life within it. This is consistent with

---

116   Amaru may not have been revolting against Spanish monarchy but against local administrators. He seems to have appealed to the king of Spain and those rights granted him, as descendent of Incan king Tupac Amaru I, under Spanish law.

Plato's *Laws* when they favor participation of Greek city-states inside a Hellenic federation rather than Persian empire.[117]

Anything can be brought into the contemplative search for Being (as St. Dionysius the Areopagite says) for nothing's being is outside God's Being, but that does not mean that some things do not reveal more of our *specific being* as willed by God, than others. We can enter the immediate presence of Being in the jaws of a tiger and in the arms of a beloved. Both may be equally intense. Yet the latter reveals more of our soul, our vocation in creative participation. Choosing a spouse, a craft, a cause for which to fight, affords chances to find Being in aesthetic visions we feel called to, in experiences we help give rise to. A child often perceives the freshness of Being more than adults, and the Gospel teaches to become like children, yet we grow up and receive more responsibilities, more autonomy, more chances to participate in life than when we were children. In this way, we are oriented towards encountering Being through that greater participation.

In terms of the traumatic other and the reinvigorated sense of self (the desire to live fully after surviving a tiger attack): dislocation from a sense of cosmological isolation and centrality allows for a greater sense of identity *as identity*, not simply as what is given or as the universal's preferred vehicle. This new sense of the particular may of course result in a secular nationalism just as damaging as the belief in one's self as metaphysical center of the contingent world, or more so, but, in a third moment, it also allows for a return to the sacred, the sacralization of the particular not over and against other particulars that are assumed to be deficient by virtue of not being proximate to one's self (a position that is not really that of traditional civilization, only of its calcification). This third moment is already arrived at in the mystical core of every tradition, as Eliot's *Little Gidding* illustrates.

Catherine Pickstock describes pious pluralism in the context of European Medieval society, referring to the Christian Roman Rite liturgy (my italics):

> God himself, far from being 'over against' the congregation in the Rite, is represented as ambiguously 'positioned' in relation both to humanity and within the Trinity. This ambiguity of structure seems to mirror the decentred ordering of mediaeval society, for in that period there was no absolute center of sovereignty on an immanent level. *According to a model in which there is only one center of*

---

117   Plato, *Laws*, trans. Robert G. Bury (Cambridge, MA: Cambridge University Press, 1961), III:693; 221–22. In terms of what Plato is describing, the compatibility of native culture (a given Greek city-state) with new wider structure (Hellenic federation), results from a previous centrifugal differentiation of cultures whose common matrix renders them compatible enough to allow for a centripetal reintegration into a self-conscious political project. We could also point to less culturally specific political associations whose shared institutions should therefore be predicated on broader understandings of identity.

sovereignty (a model which could be used to describe the absolutist political structure of the later-medieval, early-modern and baroque periods), there can only be a connection with the transcendent at that central point, so that everything beneath that point is effectively secularized. However, according to the decentred and organic structure of mediaeval society, every social group was... formed by worship.[118]

We may add the fact of multiple emperorships, one western and one eastern, or the mutual dependence of emperor and pope or patriarch to this sense of European medieval poly-centrism. In the Holy Roman Empire, "[p]laces... acquired symbolic importance through events like royal elections, coronations and assemblies, as well as more permanent palaces or tombs. It was a characteristic of the Empire's political order that it used multiple locations rather than a single capital" and "the number of places with imperial associations grew over time,"[119] such that poly-centrism increased organically.

Following from Pickstock's point that, where there is "only one center of sovereignty... everything beneath that point is effectively secularized," exclusive identification of spiritual centrality with one nation secularizes the others. Nietzsche's idea of monotheism leading to nihilism is relevant here. If a universal religion resists its theological translation by the new contexts it spreads to—resists a *sacred enculturation* and a sacralizing of place—it is, in fact, desacralizing the world, with the one exception of that initial culture and place from whence it comes. Writes Blake in his Annotations to Bishop Watson's *An Apology for the Bible*: "The Bible or Peculiar Word of God, Exclusive of Conscience or the Word of God Universal"—that is, the Bible taken in its particular features, "is that Abomination, which, like the Jewish ceremonies, is forever removed...." He writes this after a world-encompassing thrust, "[r]ead the Edda of Iceland, the Songs of Fingal, the accounts of North American Savages (as they are call'd)" (note the distance from dehumanizing prejudices) "Likewise read Homer's Iliad...." And in the *Descriptive Catalogue*: "The antiquities of every Nation under Heaven, is no less sacred than that of the Jews. They are the same thing..."

The society or international system that organizes itself in these terms is centered around a non-center, that is, a liturgy without discrete departure and destination,[120] accepting the non-spatial and non-temporal character of that which it worshipped: "... society has many centers

---

118   Pickstock, *After Writing: On the Liturgical Consummation of Philosophy*, 174.

119   Peter H. Wilson, *Heart of Europe: A History of the Holy Roman Empire* (Cambridge, MA: The Belknap Press of Harvard University Press, 2016), 173.

120   "... our journey towards God cannot begin before its ending, before God Himself has journeyed towards us... to begin is to arrive, the way is the goal. And one can only ever have begun; there is no other way to be than to be on the way" (Pickstock, *After Writing: On the Liturgical Consummation of Philosophy*, 185).

because, as manifest in the theology of the Roman Rite, the true center is unplaceable and lies beyond place itself, in God."[121] Worship, like the burnt offering on an altar, goes nowhere in particular.[122] God, its recipient, is nowhere in particular, so an offering unto Him, like smoke, simply goes *higher* and *all around*. It is precisely observance of divine transcendence that inspires a decentralized (and organically differentiated) social arrangement. Expressing pious pluralism, then, would constitute a new middle age,[123] to use Nicholas Berdyaev's term (or Hedley Bull's,[124] in the context of international relations) and an admittance of what Voegelin describes as "concupiscential defeat," a victory by way of defeat.

Michael Harrington writes that Nicholas of Cusa "had long thought of the division of human beings into distinct regions and nations as an important stimulus to world harmony."[125] Thus, Nicholas of Cusa, "following both Eckhart and the humanists, was able to assess the diversity of human languages non-instrumentally and positively as the different 'points of view' of an 'explicating' and always partial human reason"[126] for which reason there is here "no interest in a mystical ursprache, nor in a 'natural' and universal language."[127] (Without forgetting his Christian faith, so that the "always partial human reason…yet attains a certain 'maximum' exemplarity in the words and actions of Christ.") In the same vein, the tenth century philosopher al-Farabi writes in his *Political Regime*:

> Hence *these things are expressed for each nation in symbols other* than those used for another nation. Therefore, it is possible that excellent nations and excellent cities exist whose religions differ, although they all have as their goal one and the same felicity and the very same aims. *It is possible to imitate these things* for each group and each *nation*, using matters that are different in each case. Consequently, there may be a number of *virtuous nations* and *virtuous* cites whose religions are different, even though they all pursue the very same kind of happiness. For religion is but the impressions of these things or the impression of their images, imprinted in the [individual] soul.[128]

---

121 Ibid., 174.

122 Ibid., 183.

123 Nikolai Berdyaev, *The End of our Time: Together with an Essay on the General Line of Soviet Philosophy* (San Rafael, CA: Semantron Press), 2009.

124 Hedley Bull, *The Anarchical Society: A Study of Order in World Politics* (New York City: Palgrave Macmillan, 2012), 254.

125 Michael Harrington, *Sacred Place in Early Medieval Neoplatonism* (New York: Palgrave Macmillan, 2004), 172.

126 Milbank, *The Word Made Strange: Theology, Language, Culture*, 93.

127 Ibid., 94.

128 al-Farabi, "Political Regime," In: *International Relations in Political Thought: Texts from the Ancient Greeks to the First World War*. Christ Brown, Terry Nardin and Nicholas Rengger, eds. (Cambridge: Cambridge University Press, 2002), 154.

How similar to William Blake's teaching that "[t]he Religions of all Nations are derived from each Nation's different reception of the Poetic Genius, which is everywhere call'd the Spirit of Prophecy" (*All Religions are One*, Principle 5).

This understanding may be the *best* of which relativism is the mirror *worst* (*corruptio optimi pessima*). Whereas relativism disregards the Absolute, it is by assiduous observance of the Absolute *as* Absolute that any contingent form comes to be regarded as only relatively expressive thereof, resulting in what can be described as a pious pluralism, a healthy iconoclasm, an apophatic vocation. Indeed, even quite iconodule civilizations included ritual iconoclasm in their spiritual initiations or investitures, preventing them from too closely identifying their own specific symbols with archetypal realities and the Divine. Consider Bronze Age Hittite ceremonies: "Then they drive out the worshippers of statues, the liturgists, the *psalmodists* and the *kitash*. The king and the queen *sit down on the throne*."[129] Similarly, Plutarch's account of early Roman observance under Numa Pompilius and Tacitus's report of Germanic veneration both describe aniconic religiosity, accounts in which a Muslim might be tempted to see the *fitrah,* the primordial disposition. Again, to abstain from identifying one's own symbols with the things symbolized, even employing ritual iconoclasm, allows one to engage these symbols legitimately. If one thinks a rock is god, it is best to turn from that blasphemy, but if one understands the rock is not god, one can look for god's presence in the rock.

Historically early Christianity sometimes lost sight of the above. It came near, and at times trespassed into, the opposite error of Caesar-worshipers by being iconoclasts in this regard, legitimately rejecting the identification of Caesar with Divine Being but illegitimately rejecting symbolization of being in human affairs. Even a system acknowledging the existence of a host of greater and lesser gods, and dutiful ritual of various sorts, such as that of the *Bhagavad Gita*, entreats worship of the One God alone. There is no need to reject the existence of diverse forms in order to profess radical monotheism. A balanced attitude can respect the symbol, but worship only of the One of whom that symbol is a symbol; veneration of the icon and worship of God alone, as Charlemagne emphasized, ultimately agreeing with Pope Leo III and the Patriarch of Constantinople.

Beholding the Absolute in the contingent is the purpose of the religious life, and is why the faithful try to express the inexpressible in spite of the impossibility of this, that is, why they try to worship God at all. Reaching into the Absolute through the contingent is how culture

---

129   James B. Pritchard, *Ancient Near Eastern Texts relating to the Old Testament*, 3rd ed. (Princeton: Princeton University Press, 1955), iii.25–30, 359; Cited by Marinatos, *Minoan Kingship and the Solar Goddess: A Near Eastern Koine*, 53.

and ritual get imbued with the numinous. And yet this need not mean idolatry, quite the contrary, unless the same divine breath is denied in forms other than those with which one is identified, equating God's presence with one set of contingencies over all others. Pluralism is the proper application of what is good in the iconoclastic instinct.

We cannot discuss Apophatic Presence, or what we will now call Kenotic Kingship, without bringing up its initiatory, spiritual basis, with reference to its striking eruption in the Gospel. *Eli Eli lama sabachtani*, cries Jesus from the cross: *My God, My God, why have you abandoned me?* This implies that to believe in suffering is to disbelieve in the Self, or to feel abandoned by Self (for Christ and God are one, and he may be seen to be calling out to his own Self). It is ultimately the obfuscation of Being. Since the cry on the cross has a crier, a speaker, it also implicitly denies itself: there is a Self, otherwise no one would be speaking. The Self cannot have abandoned Itself. The Self perceived to be gone, is not gone.

That Self is now entirely in the present moment, not projected out, just as, in intense suffering or physically intense stimulus, we notice that we bare it when we come into presence, focusing on the breath, for example. Otherwise, the mind begins to come unhinged and causes us to seek escape (a chattering mind does not see us through an ice-bath, say, but when we quiet down we can relax into it). What has abandoned us in this intensity, and what we may cry out to, is egoic, the support for our actions as a self-projection, the image produced by reflecting on our own Self and in a sense reifying our Self into a personality, a set of mental fixities. We are symbolic creatures, and so legitimately symbolize our own selves. However, in the present moment, on the cross, like meditating under the bodhi tree in Buddhism, that projection is reabsorbed. It is here that the vision of Daniel in the Bible can be read as rendering the Son of Man co-equal to the Ancient of Days, justifying Christianity's focus on depicting the Logos as the young (never over thirty-three) Jesus over the grey-bearded icons of the Ancient One.

Significantly, the sacred king returns from initiation able to bring order, representing the transcendent center, just as Jesus, after his resurrection, told his disciples not to cling to him, and spoke to them of community, of gathering in love and receiving the Spirit, rather than of a definite external God (as though God were merely an excellent being among deficient beings and not the Being of beings). True community, true relationship, true porosity—the harmony of units that represent Unity as inherent to them rather than reifying It into an idol—requires that individuals experience that deep place of self-containment, that cessation of mental chatter in order to bear intense presence, that reabsorption of the external deity and ego into felt immediacy. We are fully one, and therefore can pour out into many. We have ourselves, therefore we gift.

The King is No-one, Long Live the King, or Kenotic Kingship

All this means is that the Absolute does not reify its absoluteness, the One does not reify its oneness by making it identical with one particular thing always and forever. It does not, however, imply that specific structures do not have their apexes and centers (including, perhaps, a particular event being at the center of the history of a world—one history of possible *histories*—as much as the nucleus of the body of a cell is its center) and, of course, it says nothing of how recurring and universal a pattern may be, such as the golden ratio or the cross. The cross, in fact, presents a golden ratio if the vertical length above its horizontal segment is to the bottom length what that bottom length is to the total vertical line. Herein, again, Christ is the *Ratio Rex*, to coin a title: that *King Ratio* ubiquitous—central, in a certain sense—in nature. Christ, the divine *Rex*, is a *ratio*, not a *res*, a ratio governing all things, and not itself a thing. The center not as a particular point but as a ubiquitous pattern. The Biblical, scriptural theme of angels speaking in the first person as the Lord, while also clarifying that they are not the Lord, as occurs in John's Apocalypse, for example, reminds us of the absent center, where local beings can manifest the centrality of the Being of beings, but are, of course, not themselves the Being of beings, and are not even necessarily its clearest representative in a particular order of creation, but locally take on that role in acting as its mouthpiece.

Though present in all, the One, or any abstract principle, also manifests specific centers for specific structures. Krishna declares himself to be the Self, in the hearts of all beings, and to be the beginning, middle, and end of all beings (*Bhagavad Gita*, 10:20), yet also to be specific beings among different groupings, including the lion among beasts (described as their king) (10:30) and Mount Meru among mountains. One way in which these statements are compatible emerges by noting that, in the *Bhagavad Gita*, Krishna switches registers between statements proper to *Nirguna-Brahman*, God in His trans-personality, and *Saguna-Brahman*, God in His personality (in form, interactive).[130]

Further, if Krishna manifests these avatars of centrality, perhaps Radha, His consort, is manifesting in each order as its perimeter, the many points of the circumference to which His icon is a center, like the many gopis, Krishna's shepherd-girl lovers. Indeed, in the *Devi Bhagvatam* (and possibly the *Brahma Vaibtra Purana*) Radha appears as source of the gopis.

Like Krishna, She manifests as foremost exemplar within a group of entities, or is spoken of in these terms: "O Devî Radhike!...Thou art the foremost guide of the Gopîkâs (*Devi Bhagavatam*, IX:50, 5–44, 1003)."[131] But She is also the source of that group (gopikas refer to female cow-herder lovers of Krishna): "...from Her have come out all

---

130   Zinner, *Christianity and Islam: Essays on Ontology and Archetype*, 80.
131   The S'Rimad Devi Bhagavatam, *One of the Upapuranas, devoted to the Devi (Goddess)*, trans. Swami Vijnanananda (Hari Prasanna Chatterji, 1912).

the Gopikas...Her nature is the Highest Bliss, the Highest Contentment, and Excessive Joy" (*Devi Bhagavatam*, IX:1, 48–70, 804). And also, crucially: "Every female in every Universe is sprung from a part of Sri Radha, or part of a part" (*Devi Bhagavatam*, IX:1, 47–70).[132]

The lion may be the point of intersection between archetypal regality and the beastly or animal order (likewise an archetype). If *Isvara*, the personality of God, is a universal regent, it is appropriate that He would manifest in creatures appearing lordly. Elsewhere in the same chapter, however, Krishna's particular manifestations bespeak concern for the most excellent (skilled or efficient) exemplars or means among given orders.

Krishna is the representative monarch in each order, but settles for no single category of entities as His ultimate representative. When referring to a particular entity within a category of entities, He refers to that which most fulfils the category's *telos*. He therefore uses different standards for each category, including standards not necessarily valued in traditional Vedic culture, such as Kubera among the Rakshasas, whose excellence as a Rakshasa is not a result of what would usually be called moral virtue. As well as telos-fulfilment, Krishna refers to archetypes: Mount Meru, one of His manifestations, is best among mountains because it is highest, which is the telos of mountains, but also and distinctly because it is the *axis mundi*.

This may still signify kingship if monarchical pomp and ceremony is understood as the ritual presentation of the panoply of human possibility. In this sense, the center of each order has been made visible as its most outwardly (obviously) revealing microcosm, that is, as that entity most revelatory of the whole order (although to the saint, God's glory is urgent in everything). Among humans He is the King, not a particular king but kingship generally. In any case, He is everything (10:39) and the specific manifestations listed are but indicatory (10:40). Corporate leadership (whether of a city or family or guild or anything else) should therefore be that social function which represents the pattern between functions that is not itself a function.

When the *Rig Veda* lists the castes produced from the different parts of the primordial man's body, no caste corresponds to his heart. The same is true of Jivananda's *Sukranitisana*. No caste is central, being rather four human functions or temperaments, none of which is the fifth element (the *quinta essentia*, quintessence). As the *Mahabharata* puts it, *the castes are equal*. The Jayakhya-samhita's four initiations for four kinds of political actors[133] ought to be considered spiritually equal. This has to do with why Christ emphasizes that it is good for his disciples that He should leave them so that they could receive the Spirit, and with why Krishna

---

132   Ibid., 804.
133   Gavin Flood, *The Tantric Body: The Secret Tradition of Hindu Religion* (London: I. B. Tauris, 2006), 79–80.

emphasizes His presence throughout creation and His responsiveness to devotees irrespective of the names they use to call Him. Insofar as kingship possesses the four castes or corners of the earth (the four horses of the quadriga held by the caesar, the four arrows shot in the four cardinal directions by the Pharaoh, and so on) it is not itself a caste but the center of them all.

Concerning the personality and mere contingency of the subject occupying the throne, John Milbank reads Shakespeare's plays as providing the key to how to approach it non-idolatrously: "the monarch, by virtue of the unchosen destiny of his birth, and his relatively absolute existential freedom, is in fact more everyman than everyman...by dramatically examining the most public of 'thrown' personal destinies, one is also regarding the most acutely private anguish and exuberance."[134] This relates to what was said previously of the need for the accidental features of the person who is king to change over time, avoiding idolatrous identification of monarchy or leadership itself, which symbolizes centrality and therefore a divine attribute, to any set of contingencies. The more arbitrary specific features of a king are understood to be, the less they are identified with kingship itself.

We now return to a previously cited passage from Hegel's Philosophy of Right: "if succession to the throne is rigidly determined," i.e., if it is natural [and hereditary], then faction is obviated when the throne falls vacant."[135] Yet, to contradict the form though not the substance of Milbank and Hegel's argument, it can be added that the non-heritable, elected Holy Roman Emperor or caliph, whose sacred lineage is a scattered and diffuse (respectively Trojan and Banu Quraysh) can serve to emphasize the same point, and is probably truer to how pre-historic monarchy functioned. Indeed, anybody could be elected, in theory, if their character were up to it and, as Joseph de Maistre emphasized, nobility can spring up from humble and obscure places. Indeed, the so-called *good emperors* appointed adoptive sons as successors rather than following a rule of heredity, with the exception of Marcus Aurelius, whose biological son Commodus put an end to a period of good government.

In becoming conformed to and joining with the Demiurge, receiving the autozoon, the initiate obtains that which comes from the First Paternal Intellect who is beyond the Demiurge: "Whoever does not love me does not keep my words; and the word that you hear is not mine but rather that of the Father who has sent me" (John 14:24). That which is received is not a particular but can be manifested as particulars:

> One single name is not uttered in the world, the name which the Father gave to the Son; it is the name above all things: the name

---

134   John Milbank, *Beyond Secular Order: The Representation of Being and the Representation of the People* (Chichester: Wiley Blackwell, 2013), 251.
135   Hegel, *Outlines of the Philosophy of Right*, 273.

of the Father. For the Son would not become Father unless he wore the name of the Father. Those who have this name know it, but they do not speak it. (*Gospel of Philip*)[136]

That gap from First Paternal Intellect to world-soul where the fifth essence or invisible center is found, can be described in terms of Desmond's metaxology. Access to this paradigm of the metaxy is key to monarchical initiation, and so we may characterize traditional understandings of kingship as metaxological monarchy. This also reveals a fundamentally Christian character to Desmond's metaxy, for the Incarnation and the notion of representing humanity is only possibly through the *between*.

The *kenotic king*, the *monarch of the metaxy*, the king who empties out, a sacrificial vessel who accesses higher epiphanies by a willing death and thereby embodies his community, provides ideational basis for the theme of rustic, poor or nude kings in ancient depictions. Apart from the notion that the king is primordial and at one with nature and animality, (mentioned by Nanno Marinatos) cases of royal pomp becoming royal poverty make sense within a Christic framework where the king is a suffering servant whose exaltation comes by way of humility and willing ordeal. In their role of high priests in Minoan rites the king and queen wear animal skins rather than typical monarchical robes and the Egyptian Pharaoh, in a particularly explicit identifications of the king with the sacrificed animal, would wear a ceremonial bull's tail.[137] Self-sacrifice, humility and holy poverty may also relate to an element of simplified, even antimonial, theology in traditions such as the Christian and Tantric, and even with the inner reason behind the fact that the Gospels are written in bad Greek and the Tantras often in bad Sanskrit.

There is a specific political praxis corresponding to the king's kenotic dismemberment: that of Jubilee. The transcendent nature of that which is manifested (the autozoon) requires it not become too closely identified with any given person or institution. It is alike the periodic dissolution of the state through a seasonal oscillation between sedentary and nomadic modes (pointed out by anthropologists like Marcel Mauss) and the state's periodic dissolution of legal/economic bonds like debt (the Biblical Jubilee specified in Deuteronomy 15:1-3). The opposite insoluble state or law, so to speak, would tend to be idolatrous.[138]

The locus of final glorification is not the representation of Being as elder but rather the youth, or *also* the youth, becoming present in that youth—the Son of Man returns as the Ancient One, the resurrected Jesus of the Apocalypse is the Son of Man of Daniel but also resembles

---

136   *Nag Hamadi Codex II, 2–7, The Gospel of Philip* 53:14–54:13, 147.

137   Nanno Marinatos, *Minoan Kingship and the Solar Goddess: A Near Eastern Koine* (Champaign, IL: University of Illinois Press, 2010), 38.

138   This is developed in the final section of *Corporatio*, IV.v: *The Kenotic King's Soluble State*.

the Ancient of Days. The impassible image oscillates with its dynamic counterpart. Subjectivity is not finally sacrificed to impassible, enthroned, ancient Being, but is glorified. Certain reactionary tendencies are dispelled here, which will be a running theme.

Applying this principle to social arrangements, the state that dissolves and whose representation alternates is analogous to the commons, wherein a plurality of forms interact without its ownership falling to any one of them.[139] Just as the state dissolves to show that which it represents is not reducible to its form, so too the state does not extend down into the administration of the commons. If a Jubilee and equivalent phenomena (including alternation in those holding office) correspond to the periodic contemplative subsuming of one's conscious self-representation or ego, then communal property can be analogized to those parts of one that are never determined by that ego—be they the unconscious relations between one's parts in course of carrying out normal physiognomic and psychic functions, or spiritual recesses that remain always in a state of contemplation. And just as the periodic dissolution of the state's explicit structure analogizes contemplation, communal decision-making in relation to the commons allows persons to occupy the vantage of a wider unity—each their own property-owning self and their own commons-owning wider self—and so observe the principle of concentric personhoods.

We may find in the traditional arrangement of farmer-owned cattle and communally-owned grazing land a symbol for the unity of plural forms in themselves and the unity of the harmonious interaction within which they are encompassed. Simon Weil, in *The Need for Roots*, saw how both individual and community property are not only functionally necessary but also psychologically, as representing the entity they belong to:

> Participation in collective possessions—a participation consisting not in any material enjoyment, but in a feeling of ownership—is a no less important need. It is more a question of a state of mind than of any legal formula. Where a real civic life exists, each one feels he has a personal ownership in the public monuments, gardens, ceremonial pomp and circumstance; and a display of sumptuousness, in which nearly all human beings seek fulfilment, is in this

---

139   The commons implicitly posit the local community (village, neighborhood, etc.) as a fundamental unit within greater political associations (given that it owns local resources unitarily). They are often ignored by current political discourse, which compulsively contrasts individual-private and state-public ownership. It is like the *fraternité* of the French Revolution, often deemphasized compared to individual *liberté* and state-guaranteed *égalité*. It represents a middle or third way, whose robustness would potentiate individual entrepreneurship while impeding the harm done by atomized individual interest maximizing, also posing an obstacle to encroachment by the central state while giving state policy-makers more examples of local virtuous innovative solutions worth reproducing.

way placed within the reach of even the poorest. But it isn't just the State which ought to provide this satisfaction; it is every sort of collectivity in turn. A great modern factory is a waste from the point of view of the need of property; for it is unable to provide either the workers, or the manager who is paid his salary by the board of directors, or the members of the board who never visit it, or the shareholders who are unaware of its existence, with the least satisfaction in connection with this need. When methods of exchange and acquisition are such as to involve a waste of material and moral foods, it is time they were transformed...Any form of possession which doesn't satisfy somebody's need of private or collective property can reasonably be regarded as useless. That does not mean that it is necessary to transfer it to the State; but rather to try and turn it into some genuine form of property.[140]

The unitary principle of community finds itself determined in practice by harmonious interactions (shared space whose owners do not overexploit to the detriment of others). This corresponds to medieval or later *municipalist* notions that the state's executive power is determined by local powerholders within their ambit, and that the person occupying the role of head of state cannot violate this without violating their own office.

The Open Society and its Demons

We may formulate our defense of diversity, and specifically *cultural* diversity, in the following terms:

1. *What is inherent and universal is mediated by what is enculturated and particular*: the linguistic ability is universal, but no single language is inherent (we do no spontaneously speak Mongolian, Basque, or Hebrew).
2. *What is necessary for individual expression is received through relationship*: the individual needs complex language to express (and perhaps to have) complex thoughts, but no isolated individual will develop complex language.
3. *The diversity of mediating forms illustrates the universality of what is mediated*: the diversity of languages illustrates the fact that language as such is truly universal (or truly abstract, indeed, transcendent) because it is not reducible to any one instantiation.

We should refrain from incurring the three corollary errors, respectively: 1) seeking to express nature (the inherent) through detachment from inherited culture/identity, 2) seeking to express individuality through isolation (egoism or conflict), 3) seeking to express universality through uniformity.

De facto, the above errors cannot be carried through successfully. Any community will direct its individuals in some way (just as any individual action will affect some context). An acultural society is impossible, just as

---

140 Simon Weil, *The Need for Roots*, trans. A. Wills (London: Routledge Classics, 2002), 34.

a language which is *only language as such* and not some specific language, is impossible. But the search for such a thing *is* possible, and destructive. It is like the myth of Emperor Frederick II isolating newborns, forbidding anyone from speaking to them, in order to determine what language humans speak spontaneously, and so, producing atrophied subjects.

Where the modern left incurs the third error above, the modern right does likewise with the second, and they both commit the first. Each of the errors reifies Being, which we have argued results from identifying with mental tension and fear of contemplation (interpreted as undoing formal structures). Indeed, political modernity, left and right, has tended to treat individual self-interest as its fundamental unit. By defining the individual motive as *contrasting with altruism* (explicitly from Adam Smith on) it has made mental tension *on guard against Being* into the subject of politics (I will argue this in more detail later).

Since we don't want to be undone, openness actually becomes the means for propitiating a hostile outside and thereby saving our inside. It is an uncomfortable reality: we are open but don't want to be. More than this: The self we seek to save, is precisely the self that identifies with this tension, and the dissipation we fear is precisely the rest that would ensue if we were relieved of this tension. We therefore refuse both purely aesthetic openness as ecstatic relationality, and also the rest in our own stabilized selfhood. Thusly do we recoil both from a relaxed aesthetic experience (neither impertinently critical nor excitedly cathartic) and from simple solitude. Apotropaic or appeasement rituals stem from fear of the end of tension, producing obsessive-compulsive mental habits.

Desire is ultimately outward-looking, and so leads to René Girard's *mimetic rivalry*. That which we are bound to desire is outside of us, and being outside, cannot ever be a fulfilment *within*. We therefore lock into this game of pretending to move towards it, finding an excuse that blocks our movement, and perpetuating tension. The tension here is a conflict between us and whatever we have decided blocks us. It is rivalry and scapegoating. The Girardian Subject is just above its own Being, and the tension of Desire and Distress make a tightrope on which he may perch to avoid falling (see the figure below).

Modern discourses around openness (often as "spontaneity," "natural-ity," "being oneself") fall into the first of these understandings of Being. For this reason, they imagine a fulfilment they do not truly desire, for it would mean giving up the tension of opposition. In these discourses, we negatively worship the enemy who we see as occupying the space of Being because we imagine him as capable of blocking our experience of Being (the political opponent is inflated to existential all-reaching neurosis). We prefer agonistic contest. Ours is a heaven made sweet by hell's punish-ments, to which our Girardian Rival will one day be tossed.

If we enter into a state of joyful, wholesome faith, we feel our joy must be compensated by some sorrow, our hubris must be struck down. In politics, this manifests as oikophobia, hatred of the home, as Roger Scruton emphasized. Denying ourselves in this way, we will lash out against those who seem able to walk in confidence. That lashing out allows us to put off dealing with the fact that our own fear is keeping us from joy.

Like a pious believer who fears the god that he loves, and is painfully open to that god in the mode of propitiating sacrifice to avoid being punished, our culture pretends to desire openness while structuring a painful discourse around it: frequently, sexual liberation and sexuality itself are anti-erotically presented as a weapon against old mores or stuffy conservatives; immigration is described as enriching but also as punishment for past colonialism; on the other side, the free market as an open space is sometimes invoked as grueling arena that would bring low the supposedly incompetent leftist political opponent. Openness becomes a punitive discourse.

We identify with tension (between Desire and Distress) and therefore want to maintain it by keeping a Scapegoat to which we can be averse and which justifies our never fully possessing what we desire. We also resent forms that seem stable without being locked in that agonism of Desire and Distress: the very presence of stable forms threatens us with an encounter with Being, that is, a restful, aesthetic contemplation of the unity of things, of reality as a peaceful matrix that sustains differentiated forms in relation, without the need for conflict. The ontology of peace looks like death to one who considers his ontology to be violence; if you think your being is tension, then resting feels like dying (and contemplating wholesome things is always restful in this sense).

We often hear political modernity condemned for believing in a *homo economicus*. Believing that universal good is accessible through the calculative faculty leads both to the left's commitment to automatize the search for the good (and therefore detach from the flux of human interaction, from society, from community) by producing a state (or whatever agent of historical dialectic) that understands the laws of history and material production, as well as to the right's belief that the good will emerge from individual freedom while conceiving of, and cultivating, that freedom in terms of individual economic calculus. Awareness may fall asleep in the wake of beneficent impersonal forces. The result of both is to generate structures or momenta that reify this calculative faculty. This faculty, this narrow calculating ego (and not so much the individual, but a poor understanding of subjectivity), is the protagonist of modern political thought, and is precisely the subject constructed as tension between Desire and Distress.

According to most heirs of classical liberalism, society should produce value (goods and services), on its own, without state interference.

In Marx, the extraneous directing force that should be brushed aside is called *morality*: "morality is not needed in order to transform the pursuit of self-interest into a pursuit that takes the interest of humanity as its guideline."[141] The hidden imperative, however, is that society should never crystallize its vision of the good into a community ethic that is allowed to direct economic dynamics (a crystallization that may occur in the form of the modern state, or in some other form): this is analogous to an individual acting on whatever thoughts it has in his mind without ever stemming their flux and conforming its behavior to a vision for itself. When this crystallization does occur, as it always must, it will be a creature of momentum, of the overall direction which thoughts took, conditioned by external factors or inherent tendencies, without the will having acted upon them: a supposed pure spontaneity. The political analogue is one that takes itself for the neutral expression of the human condition, and so marshals a ferocious universalism.

It is not that the calculative faculty and its use in the pursuit of individual benefits cannot accrue a net benefit for society, as Adam Smith argued (*The Wealth of Nations*, I.2; *The Theory of Moral Sentiments* IV.1). Rather, the question is one of proportion, of the hypertrophy of this rather narrow mode of thinking. Ideologies according to which economic interaction is the primary source of social health, and individual interest the primary source of economic interaction, will tend to encourage such hypertrophy as virtuous. This point is clichéd by now. Argues Ludwig von Mises:

> Social cooperation has nothing to do with personal love or with a general commandment to love one another. People do not cooperate under the division of labour because they love or should love one another. They cooperate because this best serves their own interests. Neither love nor charity nor any other sympathetic sentiments but rightly understood selfishness is what originally impelled man to adjust himself to the requirements of society, to respect the rights and freedoms of his fellow men and to substitute peaceful collaboration for enmity and conflict.[142]

This thesis impoverishes, rather than empowering, the individual. It fails to allow the personality its full range of motives, its full expression in the world, for it excludes that mode of experience and action that does not refer back to the self, that does not stimulate self-reflexive awareness, reifying the ego instead of refreshing it through awe. It can be argued that Mises' definition of subjective value elsewhere is broad enough to include disinterested aesthetic absorption, but then why explicitly exclude terms such as "love," "charity" and "sympathetic sentiment"? This is the

---

141   Harry van der Linden, "Marx and Morality: An Impossible Synthesis?" *Theory and Society* 13.1 (1984): 119–35, 130.

142   Ludwig von Mises, *Human Action: A Treatise on Economics* (Auburn, AL: The Ludwig von Mises Institute, 1998), 168.

core of our argument that the emphasis on individual self-interest is an emphasis on that mode of being that retreats from beauty, fearing the self-so quality of wholes, and ultimately rousing us to resent coherence. It insists on experiencing from the vantage of the ego (habitual thoughts/ mental tension as self-identity) and does not want to experience from the vantage of other, perhaps wider, structures (which are parts of the self anyway). Such structures do not deny the ego, but they are experienced as "charity" or "love," and not as "selfishness." In other words, privileging individual self-interest and understanding it as being in contrast to "sympathetic sentiment" rejects the ecstatic (it tends therefore to view pleasure as mere concession to biology or as an instrumental leisure).

To reiterate, the issue is not that modern political economy tends to use individual self-interest as primary unit of analysis for its thought experiments, but that it contrasts this to altruism, thereby revealing that it is not really describing the individual, but rather a certain faculty of thereof. This is the faculty that does not see Being's Unity as a participatory harmony between beings, does not commune, does not really transcend a survival-mode, does not relax, does not love its neighbor, does not extend and project beyond planning material accrual (understood specifically as monetary accrual, for which reason these paradigms see economic activity as causing social and political arrangements and not vice-versa).

Correspondingly, the commons express Being through harmony between beings. The commons can regulate themselves without an external top-down agent, following Elinor Ostrom's research. They display agency as belonging to the harmony among participants rather than only to the individual participants in isolation or to their commonality as a reified, univocal agency (a state). They assume an ecstatic consciousness that allows for the wider vantage, rather than collapsing into the individual *ego-as-tension* or the reified *Being-out-there* (individual vs. collective, market vs. state). Although we are not rejecting these latter (participants in the commons, of course, also have individual projects and also symbolize their unity through some common identity, with its corresponding institution, some form of statehood). It is understandable, then, that the political doctrines that deny ecstasy, that is, that deny the individual's ability to inhabit wider vantages should also have resulted historically in a simplification of political life and identity, where national identity seemed bound to homogenize the municipal, the regional, and to deny the trans-national (during the early modern period, that is, as things have now progressed further).

If only the ego is the locus of political unfolding, then legal systems that guarantee (negative) freedom, or states that guarantees their needs, are legitimate, but the ways diverse cultural projects direct individual towards their version of the Good will appear problematic. Yet human flourishing includes *political imagination*, *political creativity*, even *political pleasure*, such that part of a person's self-fulfillment occurs in the receiving and bestowing of (aesthetic) good and seeing these manifested in inter-subjective patterns, in interactions, in public spaces. Seeing one's own ideas (or the aesthetics one loves and identifies with) reflected back to one by the community (from the village carnival to the symbols of the state), not only statically but in a participatory way, is an aspect of the individual's self, its agency, its vital project. This is a better, less utilitarian, way to express the issue than the typical formula of needing to balance individual with social needs. But for us to have this freedom, the individuals around us must have cultivated civic virtue, just as one must have learnt to play the piano in order to be free to play the piano.

I would suggest that the way in which the overuse of the narrow calculative egoic mind makes itself evident is not only—not even primarily—in excluding ethical considerations from economic consumption (indeed, it would seem there is a real thirst for this, as highlighted by the environmental movement), or in pursuing self-interested politics (it is often remarked that working classes vote against their interest because the same political factions offering them economic benefits tend to denigrate their religious or national identity—although this point can be overstated). No, the principal manifestation of the above hypertrophy is the ego's fear of beauty—fear of losing itself in aesthetic love for the coherent whole. This is the form in which the pathology is today, and in fact always way, most apparent. Nietzsche's identification of *resentment* as our cardinal sin is closer to the mark than the conservative decrying of liberalism's justifications for individual *self-interest*, but an even better diagnosis is that of fear, *vertigo*, in the face of grandeur, produced from viewing the grand through the eyes of the petty self.

Contemplating beauty induces vertigo, fear, for every recognition of beauty is a relaxation of the critical mind, whose continuous activity we mistake for our very self. Coherent things don't excite us into reflexive problem-solving, mental activity to resolve discord, but pacify, or 'threaten' with pacification. When they do excite mental activity, it is as a creative labor from the starting point of aesthetic pleasure, not problem-solving. The Nietzschean insight sometimes misses the reality that reactions against beauty are often not against its strength, but against its tenderness, delicacy, innocence. Delicacy invites us to appreciate it by being delicate ourselves, that is, by activating subtle sensibilities in ourselves, which requires that we still the mind, and stilling the mind is what we perceive as death.

More superficially, it is a question of fearing that anything healthy might also be a threat. Wholes—aesthetically coherent units, resting in themselves, units manifesting Unity—are perceived as making demands on us or valuing their own vector and therefore potentially piercing us. That which leads to a phobia of religious imagery, for its presenting a large being who may be arbitrary in its treatment of smaller beings—of us—can also lead to a phobia for any whole. But the aura of wholesomeness, of aesthetic coherence, should be perceived not as an invading other but as an inviting partner: invitation to participate in the contemplation of its beauty—a release of one's tightly-clenched egoic tension, perhaps, but also a relationship to which one brings one's own perception, one's own being.

To deny the legitimacy of wholes and assert uniformity instead is to be complicit with the view of Being as big being among little beings. Any willed uniformity, any uniformity perused in definite terms, must have a particular standard to which it will conform other particulars—the color of the perfect circle that justifies changing every other circle's color. Thusly do modern utopian visions of global homogenization feature some mythology of a Singularity. They assert what they are running from.

This hyper-modernism and hostility towards existing structures stems from the fact that historically stable identities often present us with unity more clearly than recent ones because, even where they participated in great conflicts, they have outlived those antagonisms. They seem now to rest in themselves rather than being defined by a rival. They have the aura of the given. More broadly, continuity over time or permanence itself appears as a symbol for Being's Unity (like Daniel's Ancient of Days, the enthroned elder) and therefore induces the phobia discussed above. Prevailing sensibilities favor aesthetic integrity when it is conflictual (the strong female characters as gestures against patriarchy, etc.). Otherwise, it revolts at their coherence.[143]

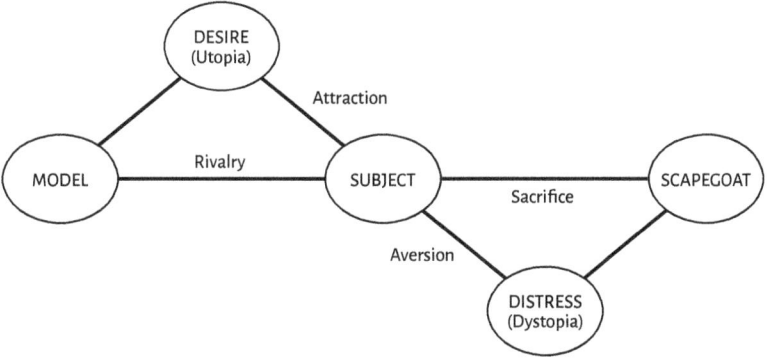

The result is a sacrificial dynamic. Again, it is not straightforward that perceiving forms that subsist independently of one is too much a reminder that one's ego is not supreme. The ego engaged in this violence is not trying to be supreme, for supremacy might mean resting from tension, and therefore death. Such an ego searches for a very specific,

---

143   I recently saw an (otherwise very good) BBC documentary series on Africa which periodically insisted that the Asante are not an ethnic group, or that Swahili culture is part Portuguese, part Arab, part Indian and part Bantu. Without at all denying these influences, such definitions do seem to display an allergy to describing things in their unity rather than in terms of their parts.

precarious point of tension between avoiding aesthetic contemplation of the other and the inward pacification that this entails. Ecstasy is an exit from the self, and also the exit by which the self is entered (Matthew 16:25). It is both too selfless and not selfish enough. It is neither inward- nor outward-going, neither hot nor cold, and its experience is of being constantly cast out, as in John's Apocalypse.

Here we see Girard's triangle of mimetic desire (where I have made "Desire" a vision of Utopia), mirrored by a counter triangle of Distress. I suggest these two converge in a single triangle. Specifically:

- Being as Other is produced through distraction, that is, by barring ourselves from relaxing into the imminent presence of Being.
- Whenever Being is misperceived as "big other," it produces a counterpart: an external god produces an external devil.
- This Being and its contrary, this god and its devil, ultimately coincide:
  - Utopia and Dystopia: The true desire is not for the assumed image of Utopia, but for a future in which the Dystopian vision is fully present to justify punitive action against its agent, the Scapegoat. The Subject does not want to move away from Dystopia but to use it to justify punitive action *as* Utopia. To take sadistic pleasure.
  - Scapegoat and Model: The Subject today pretends that its Scapegoat—typically some demonized portion of society which it is safe to insult—enjoys the privilege of its Model, so that this Subject can claim counter-cultural/rebel status.
  - The primary means for distraction through which we obfuscate Being and generate the image of Being as Other is precisely accusation. In (heterodox) Christian terms, god as big other is the Accuser, Satan.

The above Girardian triangles oppose each other rather than converging like the Star of David. This, I suggest, is the structure of the city of man in its negative sense. *The* city of man, which does not allow multiple *cities* of man, for it does not believe these can be held together on the basis of a single, transcendent city of God. Such transcendence would allow the two to share a center, converging, rather than pushing at each other's vertices. They would not then be Utopia/Desire and Dystopia/Distress, the works of rivalry and sacrifice, but instead something like Blake's Reason and Energy.

To Redeem and the Freedom to Deem Again

But how do we redeem the city built on rivalry and sacrifice? Redemption—to redeem (to *deem* again, to rename)—is to return to what is being named, to the origin, plumb the waters, and find a fresh potential, a new way to designate that essence. A finite being must be dynamic and changing, for this is a necessary part of finitude (of nature, not duration), as St. Gregory of Nyssa seems to indicate when describing the state of salvation as dynamic. It is the creativity given to Adam in Genesis to name creatures in paradise, to deem them, and therefore to re-deem them. It is the freedom humanity has in nature to create language, as Dante notes in *Paradiso* (cited previously).

But pious creativity requires the baptizing of the imagination, as the Inklings put it. Suhrawardi writes:

> Know that when the sciences are vouchsafed to the spiritual adepts and they have pondered with the utmost subtlety... beginning with the Cause of causes... having first weakened their faculties by eating little, that which they think in their hearts will correspond to what they say.... Sometimes they will employ the aid of a soft melody, pleasant scents, and looking at agreeable things. Then they are vouchsafed spiritual lights until that becomes a habit and a Shechinah. Then there appear to them unseen entities with which they soul has a spiritual connection and which act through the imagination in a way appropriate to the state of the imagination. These will be seen in the common sense. Thus it is that they see spiritual figures in the most beautiful forms imaginable and hear sweet speech from which they acquire knowledge. So too they may see hidden things.... Happy is he who apprehends his soul before death and acquires for himself in this world a degree that will give him pleasure in this ephemeral realm and in which he may rejoice in the realm everlasting![144]

This roots *practical* nominalism in *metaphysical* realism. From Catherine Pickstock:

> ... redemption here consists in a continuous and renewed non-identical repetition of history, whose endless allegorical return to the past and ironic removal from the meanings of the past (from Old Testament literal violence, for example) is qualified by the 'witty' and indirect descent of God in human form. This accordingly demands not only our equivalent salvific ascent through deification but also a constant renewal of the meanings of the (Old Testament and pagan) past and our 'dilation' throughout a renewed cosmos.[145]

Indeed, what use is redemption if the past, in all its gore, is not somehow cast in a light to make it beautiful? It is a turn to the origin, the depths, the womb, the word, a building up the spires by digging deeper the foundations—forever. Immortality not only throughout the future and all possible futures, but into the past and all pasts. St. Gregory of Nyssa refers to this as *epektasis*, an extending out (which shares etymological connotations with the word Tantra, the tan- root of which has its equivalent in other Indo-European languages in the phonetically

---

144 Suhrawardi, *Creed of the Sages*, XV, 82–83.
145 Pickstock, *Repetition and Identity*, 227.

similar portions of words like extend, and which designates a tradition that likewise emphasizes the continued finitude, which is to say, individuality, of the being realized in divine infinitude).

A finite being existing in infinity would require movement towards finite stations that nonetheless *are themselves* that finite being. Otherwise, it would become what it is not and cease from being itself. It must therefore become something new but also what it is already in this infinite extension or dilation, an eternal return of the different, a non-identical repetition (Plato's cycle of the different). This is the Pleromatic paradox: Origen's belief that we become what we already are in eternity.

This relates back to what we mentioned previously with regards to time as an island, a mandala, within eternity, to be apprehended either spatially or sequentially, but constituting an archetype, a meaning, a personality, and more specifically, having a circular shape. When we redeem, we go back to the origin and deem again, we find in it a new meaning that we had previously missed (again, bad etymology marshalled to make a point, as the word redeem is not related to the English "deem"):

> Time has the form of a cycle; it is not a rectilinear time indefinitely accumulating a past and leading nowhere, but a time leading back to the origin. There is redemption from the past: the angelic rank is surpassed, it falls into the past, and then again becomes future. To lead back to the origin: this is the exact meaning of the word which designates esoteric spiritual exegesis. *(ta'wil)*, the central operation of Ismaili thought...Thus cyclical time leading back to the origin becomes itself an exegesis, the total exegesis of mankind, the archetype of all exegesis.[146]

More succinctly: "the past is abolished and metamorphosed into the future of Resurrection."[147] This is an "ethic of resurrection...an ethic of struggle against a being-surpassed" against failing to return to the past to redeem it, against leaving the past unredeemed.[148] A work of art is both itself and the self that it receives from the artist. Following Desmond:

> Art can remain true to the difference between us and what is beyond. To praise and preserve this non-identity is the very pathos of art...Thus the artwork may image the aesthetic infinite by embodying the fecund power to suggest a significance that, as inexhaustible, we cannot pin down without residue to one definite prosaic meaning...The artwork may be a whole within itself that is radiant beyond itself, a tense coexistence of centripetal and centrifugal power, an intensive self-sufficiency that is nevertheless the packed suggestion of infinity.[149]

---

146   Corbin, *Cyclical Time and Ismaili Gnosis*, 35–36.
147   Ibid., 54.
148   Ibid., 48.
149   Desmond, *Desire, Dialectic, and Otherness: An Essay on Origins*, 174.

Pickstock discusses this movement as serpentine:

> In order to stay the same, everything must move, since everything else is in constant motion and adaptation. If it is to move…and so preserve itself, a thing must move itself…This means that everything, in some manner, moves after the fashion of a snake…A snake moves by twisting itself up to marshal energy, and by untwisting itself in order to deploy this energy to move forwards.[150]

In this vein, Uzdavinys refers to the great traditions and mythical/theological patterns as "recurring patterns or themes" that "follow the logic of a dynamic arabesque which, nonetheless, is 'static' in its continuity and change."[151]

The idea of being ourselves and also what we receive from beyond ourselves, a serpentine movement that partly regresses, that is, redeems (advancing through the circularity of the sacred dance, like dervishes, like the higher rasa lila) as somehow analogous to a work of art that both presents itself and implies a beyond is not so different from what Henry Corbin, referring to the work of Nasir al-Din al-Tusi, means by redemption or resurrection: the adept is a work of art conforming itself to the beyond that is the artist, that is, the Angel or Archetype whose thought or idea is the adept's spirit, whose word is the adept's psyche and whose action is the adept's body. Spiritual quest is a "combat for the Angel," a going back that is forward going, return, a realizing, of our Archetype.[152] This sort of language is common in Western occultism, appearing the (maybe 15th century) Book of Abramelin the Mage and its instructions to invoke one's angel.

SAT-CHIT-ANANDA AS THE STRUCTURE OF EPIPHANY:
THE PLATONIC FIRST INTELLECT, THE DEMIURGE AND THE KRATER;
THE BIBLICAL ANCIENT OF DAYS, THE SON OF MAN AND HIS BRIDE

In this section we propose the structure of epiphany, whose political character of representationalism is already discernable. We will deal with the traditions around so-called "throne theophany" later, but first we lay out some theoretical background. The recurring equation is of Consciousness (understood as Reflexive Awareness) encountering Being through absorption of a perceived form and of harmonious patterns encompassing forms within a wider unity, or as meditative absorption with no formal support.

This absorption is a self-abnegation for Consciousness, the thinking mind's losing track of itself and its reflection on this or that. It is

---

150 Pickstock, *After Writing: On the Liturgical Consummation of Philosophy*, 53.
151 Algis Uzdavinys, *Ascent to Heaven in Islamic and Jewish Mysticism* (London: The Matheson Trust, 2011), Introduction.
152 Corbin, *Cyclical Time and Ismaili Gnosis*, 51–54.

actually a coming to itself by exiting itself, Katharsis. The resultant vision of virginal forms who reveal being is Theoria and the joyful sense of all encompassed by being and in harmony is Theosis. The interaction is between Being, Consciousness and Joy, the Indian *Sat-Chit-Ananda*. Consciousness encounters Being and this provokes Joy (we could also translate *Sat* as *Pure Consciousness* and *Chit* as *Self-Awareness* or the *Reflecting/Understanding Consciousness*). We may describe the triunity as Pure "I," Awareness and Awe, or, more poetically, "I," Eye and *Aye* (Yes), to use Thomas Traherne's terms, since the eye is the organ that reflects reality and joy is affirmative. Consciousness meets Being, and is therefore Joyous; or, where Consciousness is Joyous it finds its own Being.

The Joy in question is true freedom: the freedom that is not free to sin, in St. Augustine's formula, a subject upon whom is no compulsion, acting with St. Gregory's "pure activity," a creature realizing itself as God's will to be that creature, rather than experiencing only an external will acting upon an internal overpowered will. *Chit* has discovered *Sat*, its own being is Being, and the Joy of this spurs its love, for love is consistent with unity in a way that hatred or sorrow are not, and acts that are unto harmony rather than unto disharmony are expressive of the knowledge of Being's unity. The being is the act of Being, its actions are Being's actions, it therefore participates in the cosmos, and it is paradoxically sustained by Being in this apparently separate existence. *Ananda*, not sorrow or hatred, is in this primordial triune, and the acts of one acting from knowledge of Being are joyful acts.

We contemplate the gift of the present moment and are struck by the beingness of all and ourselves and suddenly are overjoyed at the sheer gratuitous reality of it. The theophanic vision of the human archetype or *(proto-)Anthropos* which occurs across traditions strips naked our doors of perception in precisely this way (this is not only contemplation of an object but of a conscious agent, which is what contemplation of objects opens up to—the subjectivity of reality, all phenomena as having a subjectivity/will and therefore all creation as the names, the acts of will as self-disclosure, of the Creator).

The resultant joy transmits to us the sense that things are in harmony, transmitting also an imperative to engage the world with a care-taking, harmonizing ethos. Such is the autozoon, in Plato's *Timaeus*, the intellectual animal that precedes the manifest cosmos. [153] It is connected to the representation of Being in Consciousness, the heavenly city (Jerusalem) or meta-polis, the archetypal body or Anthropos, and so on. It is that intellection of multiplicity that forms in Consciousness when it encounters the Unity of Being, and therefore wants to express Unity creatively in multiple ways. It is also that which Consciousness encounters when it meets Joy ecstatically (not going inwardly into its own Being but joining

---

153   Proclus, *The Commentary on Plato's Timaeus*, V; 357.

the other), for Joy reveals that one's inner will to creativity is also the very structure of creation around one. It is therefore connected to the erotic theophany. Jove receives the autozoon in the contemplation of Saturn-Rhea but then returns to action by having it reveled in Juno as the possibility of formal manifestation.

The theophany gives to us both a perception of the *Being of beings* and a joyful embrace of beings. In analogous Christian terms, the Son lets us see the un-seeable Father and also bestows through himself the Spirit (from the Father, for without a Being of beings there is no harmony to encompass beings, and no joy as such). In a sense the Anthropos is our own being. But in another sense, constituting a vision, Anthropos is a particular form who, by its porosity to the beyond, which is also a completeness, strikes us dumbfounded with the imminent perception of being as such.[154] We will return to all this later when discussing theophanies.

Ancient sources across traditions indicate that spiritual initiation and specifically monarchical investiture was understood as a sacrificial act in which the empirical ego of the initiate-king died (often being dismembered, although this can also be presented as an ecstatic removal of the illusory ego before its recovery now in harmony with the true self) in order to reveal that which remains, that which is not the empirical self that has died or any of its parts that have been cut away, but rather the un-manifest or transcendent paradigm according to which both that self and the cosmos at large, as well as every other partial body within it, is structured. Having experienced this universal design and understanding the cosmos as one's own body (where consciousness may articulate itself variously in manifested bodies, being itself irreducible to manifestation) the initiate king may then, apart from returning to his own sense of individual bodily self, also inhabit or identify with more or less ample or proximate wholes, given that the capacity to do so has become fluid by attaining access to the underlying ontology of every differentiated body (of wholeness or corporeality itself).

This occurs when he inserts himself and is present within the natural, the worldly. Just as he brings the autozoon, she reveals it. The autozoon does not enter the world as a single origin, but through multiple origins, paying tribute to the ineffable. *The Platonic Demiurge brings the autozoon and finds it already present in the Receptacle.* Matter is always already formal, and has no original pure chaos prior to receiving order. Just as a child is not conceived by a man in a woman, but by both man and woman, both sperm

---

154 Which is a knowledge of our own being. We are reminded of Suhrawardi's *Book of Elucidations*, where the "Helper of souls," the great Imam, "diaphanous light in the likeness of a human being," recommends to "return to yourself," and asks whether your knowledge is a "direct perception of yourself by yourself" or just some external thing. Henry Corbin, *Spiritual Body and Celestial Earth: From Mazdean Iran to Shi'ite Iran*, trans. Nancy Pearson (New Jersey: Bollingen Series, Princeton University Press, 1977), 119.

and egg. Such is consistently attached to the sex act of king with queen, the regularity and fecundity of which are attached to the health of the kingdom. Femininity is linked to nature and to the world or kingdom itself, so that the latter is often the bride and body of the king, just as in Christianity the Church is understood as both of these for Christ. In a sense the revelation received during Theoria is inserted into the world, so that the world is refreshed by its own paradigm of harmony, and the king can truly be present within the world (expressed through insemination of the queen) and inhabit his kingdom as his body/bride, Theosis. "This the nucleus—after the child is born of woman, man is born of woman" (Walt Whitman, *Song of Myself, I Sing the Body Electric*, V).

The insertion of the autozoon or order/harmony, which the king-as-Jove receives from the First Paternal Intellect (specifically from the mother goddess Rhea who, "conjoined with Saturn"[155] is that primordial Intellect) in neo-Platonic thought, into the world through just rule, is a reintroduction of the archetype into the world, and so a leading of the people back into the archetypal world, into the existential home, like Aeneas or Moses. This is analogous to a reconciliation of the straying self-awareness (*Chit*) with Being (*Sat*) through joy (*Ananda*) and often is expressed in terms of a reconciliation to the world, to the feminine (to Juno in the case of Aeneas and his Trojans, or of Hercules). Of course, the universal Demiurge is just subsequent to the unity of First Paternal Intellect, whereas the initiate begins in the Pythagorean Tetrad, the world with its four corners or dimensions. These present us with two modes of autozoon, so to speak: one above is the universal paradigm given to the Demiurge by the First Paternal Intellect (specifically by Rhea, the *Shakti* of that Intellect), and the second is the initial self-sacrifice of the initiate, which self, when sacrificed, reveals that it contained the whole universal paradigm, and so the initiate can read the stars in his own soul.

Plato's autozoon is archetype of order—archetypal body, archetypal city. For this reason, the autozoon contains the four elements of Empedocles, and also the symbolic sacrifice is four-legged and four is the number of scourges undergone in self-sacrifice (the four baboons of the Egyptian *Book of the Dead*). The sacrificial animal is therefore a theophany, while also being the initiate's animal—or psycho-somatic—self, which must be slain (the Lamb of God, the white bull whose form Jove takes and which constitutes a Dionysian vision in ancient Greek rites, the Mesopotamian Bull of Heaven which Gilgamesh slays, etc.).

It is, in a sense, the Divine perceived as separate, which on some level means It is perceived as the same as the world, the rough animal reality out there, rather than as intellectual fountain, supreme subjectivity. We slay our self and we slay the Divine as external, and from that cosmic bull,

---

155   Proclus, *The Theology of Plato*, vol. 1, trans. T. Taylor (London: A. J. Valpy, 1816), V:11, 337.

Mithra makes the cosmos; from that Ymir who drank of the universal cow, Odin makes the world; from the seven parts of the heavenly bull, Gilgamesh distributes meat; after the great flood and end of fourth sun, the Aztec god Quetzalcoatl and Tezcatlipoca destroy the devouring earth monster left over from the receding waters, and the world is made from her parts; from the lamb of Passover Jesus feeds his disciples, and the Lamb is slain from the foundation of the earth, and by it the earth is founded (Apocalypse 13:8). But this theophany and sacrifice from below, which makes the self into a universal body, or (re)makes the universe out of the self, is matched by the Demiurge receiving a pacific paradigm which he installs in the Crater (Plato's *Timaeus*) and makes the cosmos. So, we have a heavenly ascent from below and an earthly descent from above, the rising Jesus and descending Comforter. Both movements described here are demiurgic, are creative, and so creation is from below and above, our agency within Divine agency.

A descending autozoon is the throne with its four legs (as is mentioned in some Islamic traditions as well as in general by the four-cornered structure of the space of spiritual enthronement across traditions), and an ascending autozoon is the four-legged animal (Biblical Lamb, Vedic Cosmic Horse or Heavenly Bull). The latter's epiphany is actually immanentist rather than transcendentalist. Again, prophet Daniel's vision orients us:

> I saw in the night visions, and behold, with the clouds of heaven there came one like a son of man,[156] and he came to the Ancient of Days and was presented before him. And to him was given dominion and glory and a kingdom, that all peoples, nations, and languages should serve him; his dominion is an everlasting dominion, which shall not pass away, and his kingdom one that shall not be destroyed. (Daniel 7:13–14)

The white-haired Ancient of Days is frequently depicted in Christian icons with cruciform aura, indicating He is Christ, the second person of the Trinity, and of course so is the Son of Man. Neither are the first person of the Trinity, the First Parental Intellect of Platonism or *Sat* in Sanskrit, but rather the Second, or *Chit* (Consciousness).[157]

Before continuing in this vein, it may be objected that *Sat-Chit-Ananda* are not persons and so cannot be mapped onto the Trinity. St. Augustine speaks of describes the Trinity as he that loves, and that which is loved, and love, which is very near to the Indian formula. By analogy, consider the person we are when, in meditation, the oscillations of the mind have ceased and we are fully sovereign. Consider the person we are when we are aware of our own self, and cognizant of objects, reflecting upon these. Consider the person we are when, in the midst of a direct, felt experience, we are not aware of ourselves, we are not using our reflexive mind at

---

156   Aramaic *bar enosh* or *bar nasha'* are equivalent to Hebrew *ben Adam*; human being.
157   Some Orthodox do take the Ancient of Days to be the Father.

all, but are present to the flow of experience. Remembering these three states, they register as different modes of being, different personas being inhabited. I suggest that this is analogous to the Trinity.

We resume our discussion of the Ancient of Days and Son of Man in terms of Indian *Sat* and *Chit*. Consciousness being self-reflective, it represents Being to itself within itself. Being itself is never reified in any specific being, or rather, is reified as all beings. The impact of Being must therefore occur within a Consciousness. The Ancient of Days represents Being in Consciousness, ancientness and enthroned impassivity being symbols of Being. That the Son should be dual in this way is consistent with the incarnation's two natures, as though divine regency and human nature itself subsisted in the Son even prior to the incarnation into a particular historical person.

The term "presented" indicates that the Son of Man comes forth as sacrifice to the Ancient of Days, yet He is the locus of glory, he is king and heir to the whole world. In contemplating Being's representation, Consciousness sacrifices its own false self or ego and thereby becomes glorified. We should emphasize that being "presented" means the Son of Man—Consciousness—is fully *present* to the Being within, is not obfuscated. Our consciousness receives rulership in the cessation of mental oscillation (Patanjali).

The *Chit* can be darkened by false ego or it can be glorified. In a sense, there is a duality between Ancient of Days and Son of Man, and there is also a duality between true Son of Man and false, fallen humanity. Daniel (8:17) is himself called "son of man" by the archangel Gabriel, and is fearful in perceiving images of kingship (some of them oppressive). We may therefore consider Daniel, the Son of Man and the Ancient of Days respectively as the ego, the consciousness and the image of Being in consciousness.

It is for consciousness to carry the secret self, the Ancient One, out of the past, out of the buried inner regions, not to leave it asleep there: like Aeneas carrying his father Anchises out of the burning Troy, like Jacob appropriating the concreteness and roughness of Esau and bringing it to the senses of the blind father Isaac. Aeneas's meeting Anchises in Elysium is like the young heir meeting the elder king, Son of Man meeting Ancient of Days. The locus of glorification is the Son of Man, but the glorifier is the Ancient One, our seated unmoving self, and both are *Chit* (in its perceiving *Sat* and in its representing *Sat* respectively[158]). The ego or personhood will finally become royal, its obfuscating parody consumed—the Son of Man comes to rule in John's Apocalypse—albeit with white hair like Daniel's Ancient of Days. But insofar as the Son of Man is sacrificial lamb, it is the Ancient One who is king.

---

158   The ability of Consciousness to represent Bring related to the *bhava* or devotee-specific form taken by the Lord in Vaishnava Indian tradition.

The initiate (Son of Man) enters the throne theophany (Ancient of Days) and understands the latter as revealing the paradigm of all creation, the joy of which epiphany makes it feel itself as at one with that creation and therefore as also itself the paradigm of all creation. It then gives itself kenotically unto ecstatic sacrifice (dismemberment, crucifixion) to be the whole creation.[159] We may also understand absorption into the higher or descending autozoon (the throne[160]) as leading the psyche to experience itself as the whole creation (the nous or spirit being contemplative), and the subsequent realization of the perceiving self as itself also the autozoon (in lower or ascending position) as the realization of itself as a sacrifice (as the Lamb which is actually already sacrificed, for it has already been taken up into the universal self, yet remains). The Ancient of Days or throne theophany is the representative of Being (Indian *Sat*)—again, *representative*, because Being as such is not any *specific* being. It is the representative of *Sat* in *Chit*. *Chit* is the self-awareness, the reflexive consciousness.

In a sense the Ancient of Days is subsequent to the Son of Man, being a representation of Being within the awareness. In this case, theophany is fulfilled when the Son of Man turns from the representation of Being—that image that comes to us to express the stability we discover in contemplation—to the kingdoms of the earth, the new Jerusalem, the Church—the ever-present harmony: the community of love Jesus announces even in his physically leaving it after the resurrection.

Another important element is the duality of kingship as representative of the gods to men and men to the gods. *Chit* is dual, for it is both the Ancient One and the Son of Man or visionary initiate. It is here that we have form. Writes Corbin: "the anthropos is not a simple notion but a dual totality: there are Adam and Phos (or Enos), the celestial and the terrestrial anthropos," referring to Eusebius's distinction between Adam and Enos and Zosimus's distinction between Adam and Phos.[161] He adds: "As Adam is the archetype of all men of flesh, Phos is the archetype not of men in general, but of all men of light." If Adam is the Son of Man and Phos the Ancient One, we should nonetheless remember that Adam is glorified, transformed, not discarded. We have Dante's *Adam subtilis* and *Adam mortalis*, who, in the Divine Comedy, are equivalent to Dante being crowned and mitred by his own self, as Virgil says, *Te sopra te corono e mitrio*. The cross helps illustrate this: There is the higher and

159   Here the Son of Man presented sacrificially in Daniel, the Lamb, is like the sacred Bull of Heaven which Gilgamesh or Mithra in Mesopotamian and Persian traditions distributes communally.

160   Or else contained as the four legs of the throne (per certain Muslim traditions). If the throne represents the Divine Feminine (Rhea), She is the *bestower* of the *autozoon*.

161   Respectively *Praeparatio Evangelica*, xi, 6 and *Scott*, IV, 122, cited in Corbin, *Avicenna and the Visionary Recital*, 232.

lower, the crown and mitre, a fourfold of upper and lower vertical lines, and right and left horizontal arms.

When we are calm as in sleep and collected as in wakefulness, uniting the exhale and inhale, the centrifugal and centripetal, the water that seeks level with the fire that spreads, the female and male (Persephone as water and Hades as fire in Empedocles[162]), the left and right arms of the cross, then we find the central vertical beam: the height and the depth, the heavens and the earth, lofty air and the matrix of matter (Empedocles' aether as Zeus and earth as Hera). The Son of Man encounters the Ancient of Days.

Consciousness/*Chit* has ceased to oscillate between its dual poles, its right and left arm, sacrificing its old animal mind (fight and flight) and thereby encounters Being/*Sat*. There, where consciousness is free of mind, calm and collected, we may delve into a lucid encounter with Being and the new mind is born: St. Paul's *metanoia*, renewal of the mind, the fifth element, between the four arms of the cross. Apollo. The sacred heart in the middle of the cross's four directions. Not Daniel's doubts and fears, but the Son of Man as heir. Not death on the cross, but resurrection. A new mind, born of Consciousness being present to Being and therefore having Joy/*Ananda*.

Since Ernst Kantorowicz uses Dante to draw his study of "The King's Two Bodies"[163] to a close, we may, via our previous parallels, understand these two bodies as Daniel's Ancient of Days and Son of Man. Kantorowicz quotes an English jurist as writing that "[t]o the natural body [of the king] there is conjoined his Body Politic which contains his royal Estate and Dignity,"[164] we would therefore have to add that the "Imbecility of the Body natural" is nonetheless transformed, its duality with respect to the Body Politic retained, in that Son of Man's inheritance from the Ancient One.[165]

In Giorgio Agamben's study of the *homo sacer*, we find the resonance of Ancient of Days in the sovereign and the Son of Man in the homo sacer—a subject who may be murdered with impunity by citizens; a Roman legal category outside the law except in the allowance made by the law with regards to it, that is, exactly the mirror of the sovereign king, who is above the law except in his right to determine its exception.[166] In medieval times this was recovered in the figure of the wolf's

---

162   Following Peter Kingsley's reading.
163   Just before the Epilogue.
164   Ernst Kantorowicz, *The King's Two Bodies: A Study in Medieval Political Theology* (Princeton, NJ: Princeton University Press, 1997), 494–95.
165   According to the Abrahamic/Zoroastrian mystery of Resurrection, albeit with *bodies not of flesh*, as St. Paul says. It is not the paradoxical, joyful play of *becoming* and *Being* that is rejected, but rather becoming's forgetting of Being, and the flesh as manifestation of that forgetfulness.
166   Understandable in Carl Schmitt's terms, which Agamben draws on.

head or *wulfesheud,* as in Edward the Confessor's 11th century writings.

The *homo sacer* is below the law, the king is above it. An animal man who may be killed like an animal. The *homo sacer* cannot be killed in a sacrifice to the gods, however. This reminds us of Christ's death ripping the temple veil. Where the *homo sacer* becomes locus of glorification, heir to the sovereign, we have a reversal of Roman law, a subversion of its absolutes (of the state or household's basis in a master's absolute right over a slave).[167] To be cast out of the law is to become master of the law, not to die in lawlessness (the law now in St. Paul's terms).

The *homo sacer*'s exile from human law and the discovery of his identity with the sovereign who exiled him can be understood as the initiatic experience. During meditation (or contemplation of beauty or some joyful act) we send out our awareness, passed the psychological bounds of seeking after desire and running from aversion. When our inner sovereign, our inner being, sleeps, the faculties seem to rebel wildly and attack our awareness with fears and lusts, trying to crucify it, and it is as if the sovereign had sent them like nightmares in a fevered slumber. But when our awareness does not accept this, does not engage them, observes their threats with detachment, it awakens the Ancient One inside.

Subduing the mind allows its fuller instrumentalization. The animality of the *homo sacer* or wolf-head is what makes it heroic or kingly. Heroes and kings wear the beast: Hercules' lion's skin, Siegfried's dragon blood, the Egyptian Pharaoh's ceremonial bull's tail, etc. These are not animalistic. They are more human for having turned the animal into clothing. They have integrated it in Meister Eckhart's sense: when the lower is integrated by the higher, it transforms into the nature of the higher. When we meditate or contemplate beauty successfully, we feel ourselves coming into the present—our awareness is deliberate and not drawn by this or that tug of instinct—this occurs when the body suddenly calms, the animal is suddenly a garment: "Do not despise the lamb, for without it, it is not possible to see the king. No one will be able to go in to the king if he is naked" (*Gospel of Philip,* 58).

It is not the ferocious play of animals that I am analogizing to an encounter with Being, but that play in which the power of the animal is tamed.

Our awareness is like that *homo sacer* being cast out of the circle of the law, thinking it will die, but realizing its own stability instead. Not only is the exile realized to be kingly, but the king is thereby awakened (the Grail saga's injured Fisher King is restored, Anchises is carried from the burning Troy, etc.). Our awareness does not exist as a function of mental categories (though our ego might).

---

167   This is the medieval shift from the classical and delivers us to the Divine who serves His servants in the Gospel of John.

We have already linked Daniel's Son of Man and Ancient of Days with the Awareness and Being (Indian *Chit* and *Sat*) respectively. In Daniel's vision the Son of Man, who begins as sacrifice, is not condemned but receives the kingdoms of the earth, a harmonious multiplicity (wherein Joy, *Ananda*). The *homo sacer* is realized as paralleling the sovereign (the unity of Being) and thereby redeems political community from legalism and arbitrary power (the psychological oscillation between aversion and attraction; Girard's mimetic desire for the model and sacrifice of the scapegoat;[168] St. Paul's twin mistakes of seeking after signs and thinking up reasons ("For the Jews require a sign, and the Greeks seek after wisdom" [I Corinthians 1:22]); Blake's religious legalist Puritan and rationalist Deist, etc.

This initiatic pattern comes through in archaic Hellenism as well. The Greek *kouros* meets the *kourotrophos*: youth and divine nurturer of the youth. When the sage Parmenides arrives at the Unnamed Goddess, she describes him as a kouros. In Parmenides' hometown of Velia[169] we find the nearly unique inscription of *Pholarchos*—lord of the lair.[170] Lair, *pholeos*, is the den of an animal, a place of hibernation. The initiate is being connected to animality, like the *homo sacer wulfesheud*. The animal inside will be immobilized, the mind's habit to jump from thought to thought will cease. In this way Consciousness will be fully present to Being—*Chit* to *Sat*, the Son of Man fully "presented" to the Ancient of Days. Incubation (*enkoimesis*) in such lairs, in cavernous places, in ancient isolation tanks and volcanic crevasses, was typical in Orphism and Pythagoreanism.

The sun god Apollo is linked to the darkness of the lair of incubation, he is the *Pholeuterios*/God of the Lair, as are the daughters of the Sun with which Parmenides is joined and the *Mansions of Night*, the transcendent place of that Unnamed Goddess whence they come. Plato's Council of Night (not them who apply the law, but them who *understand* the law) meets between early dawn and sunrise.[171] Deep in the darkness we discover a light.[172] The sun is connected to the infernal blaze of volcanos, so important to Sicilian and southern Italian sages like Parmenides or Empedocles. The emphasis on sleeping in holy places and dreams in such

---

168   The false self, that is, the ego which believes our existence to be mental tension (and therefore resists contemplative liberation from tension), is suspended above what it perceives to be death like a tightrope tensed between *putting-off* desire's fulfilment and *warding-off* what it fears. In Girard we don't just have one triangle of desire but two, one of attraction and one of aversion: the Subject-Model-Desire and the Subject-Scapegoat-Fear.

169   Founded in honor of one of Hercules' sons at the indication of the Apollonian oracle. Significant given that Hercules is the quintessential initiate in that context.

170   A priestly position in the cult of Apollo Oulios.

171   Plato, *Laws*, 95 1d7–8, 961b6–8.

172   Peter Kingsley explores all this: *In the Dark Places of Wisdom* (Point Reyes, CA: The Golden Sufi Center Publishing, 2019).

cults may therefore connect us to the trial of lucid sleep: not only lucid dreaming, but remaining lucid into dreamless deep-sleep, the darkness where we encounter the mystery of non-formal awareness, light. The pholeos is a place of *hesychia*, inner silence, the nocturnal sun. Like that "certain night when there was sunlight"[173] on which Hermes ascended in Suhrawardi's *Book of Elucidations*, climbing the "cable" of Divine Irradiation like Parmenides' solar pipes to the heavenly realm. The midnight Apollo, within us. Buddhist tradition tells us the state of deep sleep is the same which we will face upon dying, and if we can remain awake through it, we can transcend.

Plato's autozoon and the cosmos (total ever-encompassing cosmic body/ intelligible animal) that it allows the initiate to perceive (in a sense, to recreate) are somewhat identifiable with the two bodies whose history in Western thought Kantorowicz details. The autozoon manifests as and is perceived through both these bodies, the Ancient of Days is after all the Archetype (Plato's intellectual animal), and the Son of Man is that Lamb that is slain to make the cosmos (Plato's intelligible animal).

The perceiving of the external autozoon (in the enthroned figure as paradigmatic of all order) is joyful (Indian *Ananda*), as is the perception of the perceiver also as autozoon. *Chit*[174] is the masculine (Vishnu in the *Vishnu Purana*, Shiva in Shaivism) and the *Ananda* is the feminine (Lakshmi to Vishnu, Shakti to Shiva). *Ananda* perceived in the enthroned figure is the Feminine as mother (the neo-Platonic Rhea) and in the perceiver himself is the Feminine as lover (Juno in relation to Jove). To the initiate the first is Juno and the second a lover (Lavinia to Aeneas, Hebe to Hercules, Penelope to Odysseus, Sita to Rama, Radha to Krishna, etc.).[175] This is analogous to Bulgakov's divine Sophia and creaturely Sophia,[176] the Heavenly Jerusalem and the new earthly one. Writes Margaret Barker:

> Philo [of Alexandria]... sees the matriarchs as Wisdom, the eternal wife and mother, perhaps an echo of the ancient Wisdom who has been both mother and consort of the ancient kings.... There is a similar picture of Wisdom in the fragments of Jewish Liturgy embedded in the Apostolic Constitutions: God is the Father of Wisdom (7.35.10) and it was to Wisdom God spoke when he said 'Let us make man after our image' (7.34.6).

And the key passage (my italics):

---

173   Corbin, *Spiritual Body and Celestial Earth: From Mazdean Iran to Shi'ite Iran*, 120.
174   Both enthroned Anthropos and archetypal prophet, Ancient of Days and Son of Man.
175   This is fleshed out in a table in the "World as Tetrad" section.
176   Sergei Bulgakov, *The Bride of the Lamb*, trans. B. Jakim (Edinburgh: T&T Clark, 2002), 63.

This implies two Wisdoms, as in the later Kabbalistic tetrad, which comprised Father-Mother and Son-Daughter. The eternal Wisdom in all her aspects as the mother, the consort and the female aspect of the divinity appears in the *Gospel of Philip*: 'There were three who always walked with the Lord: Mary his mother, and her sister, and Magdalene, the one who was called his companion. His sister, his mother and his companion were each a Mary'.[177]

Mother, sister and companion, Magdalene. These three make us think of Orphic poetry in which the initiate discovers the goddess whose milk gives him rebirth, like a "kid in milk," the mother, and two sisters, one Justice and one the understanding of the Law. One is the doing of righteousness and the other the understanding of righteousness, orthopraxy and orthodoxy,[178] and they are with the source of righteousness, the mother. Rhea, Juno and Vesta (goddess of the hearth, stillness, understanding), these latter two being intimately connected in neo-Platonism. When we lose the source, we end up instead with the twin mistakes St. Paul warns of: the mistake of the Hebrews who look for outward omens, and the mistakes of the Hellenes who look for mental reasons (I Corinthians 1:22). The mother of both is despair, existential insecurity, not faith.

These are like the two sandals Moses must take off to enter the presence of the burning bush.[179] The Puritan and Deist of Blake,[180] the horns of that "Two Horn'd Reasoning" "Cloven Fiction" or Satan the false Self,[181] which Blake calls "Doubt" and "Self Contradiction." Gog and Magog/Leviathan and Behemoth. The companion on the right who is wrathful, and on the left who is lethargic, or conflict-seeking and comfort-seeking, the desire to inflict pain and the desire to receive pleasure, and the one ahead of both, who gives us false

---

177   Margaret Barker, *The Great High Priest: The Temple Roots of Christian Liturgy* (London: T &T Clark, 2003), 237. This introduces the Divine Female not only as Mother and Consort, but as Sister too.

178   Like Plato's Nocturnal Guardians as understanding, orthodoxy, and the judges as executing, orthopraxy. Analogous to Roman *auctoritas* and *potestas*.

179   Which in some Sufi commentaries are symbols for the outer and inner, like Paul's outer search for omens of the Hebrew and inner search for reasons of the Hellene. Al-Ghazali in the *Mishkat al-Anwar* says that Moses took off both the material and the spiritual worlds. Everything has an outer and inner, Arabic *zahir* and *batin*, and these can both become impediments. In Suhrawardi's *Book of Elucidations* we read of Hermes that "beneath his feet, was an earth and Heavens" (Corbin, *Spiritual Body and Celestial Earth: From Mazdean Iran to Shi'ite Iran*, 120).

180   Possibly corresponding to the two kinds of men, devourers and producers, in Marriage of Heaven and Hell, but the interaction of these in Blake is positive.

181   Blake's Puritan says *There is no Natural Religion*, denying naturalism/materialism but doing so in favor of sectarian dogma, and his Deist says *All Religions are One*, denying sectarianism but doing so in favor of naturalism/materialism. Blake asserts *both* these phrases at once.

counsel—the mind with its two tendencies of menace and melancholy—in Ibn Sina's *Recital of Hayy ibn-Yaqzan* (VII). Warns Evagrios the Solitary in *On Prayer* (95):

> "You should be aware of this trick: at times the demons split into two groups; and when you call for help against one group, the other will come in the guise of angels and drive away the first, so that you are deceived into believing that they are truly angels."

In this way they might appeal to our two tendencies, which in themselves are legitimate aspects of the human person, one externalizing and one internalizing.

In the poetry of Orphism, *doing* and *understanding* are feminine (like lover and sister), they are *Ananda*, for Joy is Understanding and is an externalizing power, like Shakti in Tantrism. And femininity is also at the level of Being (the mother). Here *Ananda*/Joy is feminine and is the female counterpart of Consciousness. She reconciles consciousness to its own being, for that division was brought about when this reflexive ability to experience joy at one's own being was turned against oneself, becoming ingrown. Consciousness lost that joy and began self-deconstructing/anatomizing. The light tries to shine in on its own source and produces a reified space. Our consciousness is divided from our sentience; our mind turns against us. In Blake's *Four Zoas*, the primordial man, Tharmas, develops an inner life detached from his exterior, a morbid introspection, when the primordial woman, Enion, begins inspecting his motives (actually they mutually divide, accusing each other of what they themselves do). He offers to make a labyrinth for her, just as he has made an inner space in himself.

Our sentience becomes tortuous, labyrinthine. We imagine a problem, try to solve it, and end up creating a problem where, in truth, there was (and in greater truth, still is) none. Now from his various parts, the injured men of the poem, come emanations which enter Tharmas without his wanting them to. We have intrusive thoughts we did not choose. This all happens because Tharmas asked Enion to pity him in his plight, and in that became himself able to pity, but not love. He harbors those thoughts because he somehow pities them. The weakness that keeps us in bondage to the mind, to illusion, to the ego, is linked to what we ordinarily consider a virtue: pity (which we might at times call compassion). Blake is anticipating some of Nietzsche's insights. This shift from love to pity is perceived by the female Enion as far graver: it is a shift from Love to hatred and from Liberty to duty.[182]

We may suggest the following correspondences, where the autozoon is received by the *Chit*, but only in light of *Ananda*:

---

182   Donald Ault, *Narrative Unbound: Re-Visioning William Blake's the Four Zoas* (New York: Barrytown/Station Hill Press, 1995), 30–50.

	Sat (Being or Pure Consciousness)	*Chit* (Self-reflexive Consciousness or Awareness)	*Ananda* (Joy)
Gender[183]	Unity	Male	Female
Correspondence in Kabbalah	Kether	Binah	Hokmah
Indian (Shaivism and Vaishnavism)	Shiva-Shakti, Vishnu-Lakshmi (Krishna-Radha)	Shiva, Vishnu (Krishna)	Shakti, Lakshmi (Radha)
		Being self-reflective, Chit includes both the representation of Being (Being itself is not any particular being) and the perceiver of it:	
Greco-Roman (Pythagorean/ Platonic)	First Paternal Intellect (Saturn-Rhea)	Jove/Demiurge	Juno/Receptacle (Plato's Chora/Krater)
		Hero (Apollo/Hercules/Aeneas/ Dionysus as masculine aspect of world-soul in Proclus)	Heroine (Artemis or Mnemosyne/ Hebe/Lavinia/ Athena as feminine aspect of world-soul in Proclus)
Biblical[184]	El Elyon-Asherah	Ancient of Days/the Lord (Representing El Elyon)	Chariot-Throne (Representing Asherah)
		Son of Man (Archetypal Prophet/Lamb)	*Wife of the Lamb, Church, Jerusalem* in John's Apocalypse (18:23; 19:7–9; 21:2–9; 22:17)

Remembering all three are present in each "layer" of reality as its unity and its masculinity and femininity:

- Monad: *Saturn-Rhea*
- Dyad: *Jove-Juno*
- Triad: *World-Soul* or *Dionysus-Athena*, etc.

Just so, in Christianity, the Trinity is not three different levels of reality, it is throughout reality.

The initial broadened identity through the autozoon or paradigm of all bodies, harmonious, corporeal wholes, is fixed upon a given community, according to the duties of the initiate. This occurs so that the kingdom may be administered according to its deepest nature, the paradigm its king has received, implying a harmony between it, as partial whole, and

---

183   Other systems tend to present *Sat* as masculine and *Chit* as feminine, but here we retain the duality of Father-Son, 'Archetypal Elder'-'Heroic Youth' of Biblical tradition by allowing *Chit* to be divided in its reflexivity. This also keeps *Sat* as transcendent and apophatically avoids considering images of enthroned archetypal kings as Being rather than just representations of Being within Consciousness. They are rather *representations* of Being. The Father is not the Ancient of Days that Daniel sees. In Orthodox Christian terms, the Ancient of Days and Son of Man are both the Son, that is, the Second Person of the Trinity.

184   We could add a further row under "Biblical," with Blake's primary Tharmas-Enion pair, within which is Los-Enitharmon.

other partial wholes, understood as ever encompassed by wider wholes, where wholeness itself is transcendent and nowhere exhaustively externalized (no particular form can definitively represent *the All*) and always manifesting autozoon. This understanding results in an ecumenical ethic. Neither Hegel's "the whole is the true" nor Adorno's "the whole is the untrue,"[185] but the whole is true if it loves its parts and knows them to be their own wholes and itself to be a part in turn, and the part is true in exactly the same way. The eternal feminine is key to this operation. The autozoon is identified in different mythical systems as bestowed on the initiate king by a female entity so that he may properly order the realm or world, which is itself also understood as feminine.

The kingly initiate is matured by a transcendent maternal presence, Rhea in neo-Platonist exegeses, to then consort with the female substrate or matrix of reality, Juno, or, at a lower level, the world-soul, Minerva in Proclus. The correspondent masculine appears as the transcendent source conjoined to that maternal agent (the First Paternal Intellect or Saturn) and as the initiate king's own archetype (the Platonic Demiurge, identified by neo-Platonists like Iamblichus and Proclus with Jove, Jupiter). At the level of the world-soul the masculine deity is Bacchus/Dionysus in Proclus, whose dismemberment is equivalent to the Indian Purusha or Biblical Lamb. At the level of the world-soul the masculine deities can be identified as Mars and Vulcan (as the initiate king at this level can also be identified as Mars and Vulcan [the initiate king is not the universal demiurge but a microcosmic one, engaging in *demiurgy*, per Iamblichus], his station and corresponding queen can also be thought of in mythological terms as those subsequent generations to Juno and Jove).

The ideal, the autozoon, is never fully and finally a created thing. Further, it is dynamic, for it exits the divine simplicity of the First Paternal Intellect and is the basis for creation. What the king receives from Rhea's light is the abstract, universal ideal. The absent center (the Pythagorean central fire and Desmond's *metaxy* middle, between) contains the ideal creation or ideal humanity, because it is the principle of harmony (unity externalized, not the divine simplicity but the divine simplicity unpacking itself into the created cosmos). This is where the theophany occurs: "theophanic event in the Metaxy."[186]

It is also the sight of ordeal, as an encounter with the metaxy elicits from the ego a projection of its fears. Images of crossing a stormy sea (as in the *Aeneid*, which gives an initiatic meaning to the Mediterranean Sea *as metaxy*) and similar crossings of turbulent or murky places relate to this traversing of *the middle*. That metaxy is the center, a place of un-manifest or un-particularized vision of harmony, autozoon, central because it is

---

185   Theodor Adorno, *Minima Moralia: Reflections from Damaged Life* (Verso: London, 2005), 29, 54.
186   Voegelin, *Order and History Volume IV, The Ecumenic Age*, 320.

equidistant to its possible manifestations at any given level of reality. After traversing the metaxy filled with ego-projections and lashes of the disordered soul (the stormy Mediterranean), the metaxy is experienced as a sacred peaceful place (the Platonic *Krater*, feminine counterpart of Jove, represented by actual volcanic craters in the Neapolitan country-side, which Aeneas enters, finally on European soil). There the initiate is given the autozoon, which he will reify into an actual representative center (Aeneas's vision of Elysium and future Rome).

Just as the initiate must cross it *from below*, so to speak, in Proclus the middle between manifest and un-manifest is traversed *from above* by the goddess Rhea, who contains and brings the ideal blueprint for the cosmos, the autozoon, having a feminine character. The initiate, like a new Jove, makes the crossing in being met by the mother, Rhea. The middle, the abyss between transcendence and immanence, is filled by femininity. Jove is like *Chit* (self-awareness) who encounters the monad or Platonic First Parental Intellect, Saturn, *Sat* (Being), and receives *Ananda* (Joy) from that monad (Rhea, the feminine in the monad, in Being). What is gender? Here is one answer: masculinity rests and sends forth; femininity stretches and fills with light.

This exposes that reactionary mentality that views the manifest as a blight on the un-manifest, that scorns becoming for Being, rather than seeing them both as, in a truer sense, Being (this entails rejecting also the mirror-image of this that sees only becoming and mutability and resents any stable form). We reject that metaphysical child-abuse Plotinus accuses world-denying Gnostics of engaging in (hating the child, claiming to love the father, when they should have seen that which they rejected in the child as illusory, healed it, and revealed the imminent presence of Father in child, as the Gospel points to).

Being or Pure Consciousness is always already conscious (capable of reflexive awareness). That which the figure of the Ancient of Days as wise old man represents in Daniel's vision is not really prior to that which the youthful Son of Man represents. The origin is always already generative and therefore co-eternal with the generated (as Meister Eck-hart, St. Thomas Aquinas and St. Dionysius all saw). The Son of Man is not sacrificed to the Ancient One, but self-sacrifices:

> Now my soul is troubled, and what shall I say? 'Father, save me from this hour'? No, it was for this very reason I came to this hour.
> 'Father, glorify your name!' Then a voice came from heaven, 'I have glorified it, and will glorify it again.'
> The crowd that was there and heard it said it had thundered; others said an angel had spoken to him. (John 12:27-29)

The voice of the Father may be interpreted as the Ancient of Days, for it is a representation of the First Person of the Trinity. The Son participates in the will of the Father, and desires to stay upon the cross to complete

His mission. We might understand this as the prototype of Christian martyrdom, like a joyous act of pedagogy rather than a completely alien event which a subject has no understanding of.

Those traditions that identity the eternal masculine with inner experiencer and the eternal feminine with outer experience also often assert *both* as being Divine: masculine Vishnu or Shiva and feminine Lakshmi or Shakti are both beyond the world and make the world. As the *Vishnu Purana* tells us, inner meaning and outer signifier, inner love and outer pleasure, experiencer and experience, masculine Vishnu and feminine Lakshmi, are *both* Absolute, both beyond contingency, both already present in pure interiority (there is no experience except inside the experiencer, so there is no real outside with respect to the inside, no object contrasting the subject). They are both also creators, as in Blake's *Jerusalem*, where the male is time, a present moment which, by its nature, tends to a stillness, an instant in the flow wherein separate forms are discernable, the moment of a concept's manifestation, and the female is space, the substance and matter of manifestation:

> And they conversed together in Visionary forms dramatic, which bright
> Redounded from their Tongues in thunderous majesty, in Visions,
> In new Expanses, creating exemplars of Memory and of Intellect:
> Creating Space, Creating Time according to the wonders Divine
> Of Human Imagination...
> (Blake, *Jerusalem*, IV, 98, 28–32)

Any inner conception is expressible by outer features which will be in continuity with others. If I imagine a triangle, although I can conceive of its geometry as abstract definition (three sides, three angles) I can only really picture it as having some particular color, and that implies the possibility of different shapes with the same color and the same shape with different colors. Where the inner definition, distinction, of a shape from other shapes meets the outer features that inspire the possibility of variation. As soon of Jove the Demiurge wishes to instantiate that cosmic blueprint he received from the great beyond (the Saturn-Rhea monad prior to manifestation in Proclus) he encounters his female counterpart, Juno the Crater, the substrate corresponding to his design.

Like a sculptor whose design already has its ideal marble, wood or clay out there somewhere. A design waiting to join with a series of happy accidents and inspirations out in the world that will see it through to completion. The artist does not deliberately and meticulously make his piece, but collaborates with reality itself as though, in a state of proper inspiration and surrender, all the cosmos conspired in his favor to see that inspiration is expressed. The mystery of matter, the uncanny ecstasy passed the edge of chaos when it turns out not to be. Here we are taken up in a mind bigger than us, which has encompassed us and our creative vision in with a world that contains the material, causal components for that creative vision to become actualized. That mind must know our vision better than our ordinary thoughts, it pours up a deeper portion of our own desire than we can compute. Jove the Demiurge and Juno the Crater are both within that conjoined transcendent unity of Saturn-Rhea which gives them the design for the cosmos (the autozoon) in the first place.

Matter is always already in some particular configuration. There is no neutral matter that is purely formless substrate without any form. Down at that level we have waves that are conspicuously not matter. The mystery of matter is that it has no principal formlessness, as though formlessness could be got at and revealed to be the Ur-form, the original form (Meister Eckhart saw this,[187] likewise ibn-Sina[188]). "Sophia is the thoroughly transparent bottomless abyss of the divine nature...Sophia is God's love for Himself in His self-revelation."[189] It does not pretend that primacy or ultimacy can be reified into a specific form. Rather, it is a mercy unto all forms. Neither can formlessness be reified, for chaos is an appearance, not a real being. It is a space of possibility that takes on form and is, from the start, plural in its possible forms. This plurality from the start, this original pluralism which defines the manifest realm, is its lesson and revelation: any form is already one of many, any materially externalized thing is already within a plurality, and therefore Unity, true Unity, is beyond form. The monotheism of classical metaphysics, the Absolute which cannot be defined in terms of any form, contingent feature or particular, is given us from the start.

The transcendent form-giver beyond matter and matter itself (Demiurge and *prima materia*) are one. Form and Matter disappears into fathomlessness precisely when an impossible *absolutely simple* material particle was to be glimpsed. The form-giver and the externalizer of forms, the eternal masculine and eternal feminine depart the world of manifestation at the same point, so both masculinity and femininity are Divine. What we think of as matter is always formal, Lakshmi is always joined to Vishnu, Shakti to Shiva.

Femininity is esoterism.[190] Masculinity (the initial conscious conception of a form) can tend to identify its unitary concept—the definition

---

187   Following John Milbank's treatment of him in the *Monstrosity of Christ*.

188   "It is extremely difficult to establish, by reasons and arguments, what the quiddity of matter and the quiddity of form are... nevertheless, it must be professed that the origin and cause of all creatural realities are these two things...to which must be added the efficient cause in the final cause." "Know that by itself matter has neither existence nor form, matter becomes existent only because of form" (ibn-Sina, Recital of Hayy ibn-Yaqzan. In: Corbin, *Avicenna and the Visionary Recital*, XI, 320). Form and matter are "the two circumscriptions by which this world is intersected," the great occident and orient in ibn-Sina (Ibid., XII, 324).

189   Bulgakov, *The Bride of the Lamb*, 128.

190   To borrow an expression Henry Corbin uses in his *Swedenborg and Esoteric Islam*, attributing it to the Ismailis.

of a triangle, say—with Unity as such, if it is not perceived, upon externalization, to point to possible variations. Indeed, the only way not to see that any unitary concept must exist in terms of diversity (and that Unity as such is therefore not a concept) would be to never be fully conscious of one's concept, to be in a sort of absorbed trance that idolatrously identifies that one concept with oneness, with the total field of possibilities, and so, what we often call the externalizing element of mythic femininity, is actually the consciousness producer, the means by which there is child and not only parent, Son of Man and not only Ancient of Days, in Indian terms *Chit* (Reflexive Awareness, Conscious Awareness) and not only *Sat* (Being, Pure Consciousness).

Of course, as we will discuss later, if the unitary concept only expresses itself in potentially diverse particulars, by the agency of that merciful material availability of space, of substance—which is itself not some chaotic prime matter but responds to the conceptual design in allowing it to externalize—than it is drawing on concepts too. The triangle can only be drawn in some particular color, but the color is also a concept, a creative work. There is no archetypal concept drawing itself in chaotic substance, but only archetypes crisscrossing the great matrix of reality. The unitary archetype/form is only expressible in a particular type/feature, and particular types are always potentially diverse and always themselves archetypal.

Returning to the ritual of initiation: The autozoon is not a thing, and its no-thingness is sought by ritual death. Here is the drive to expose the hidden hollow at the center of an apple which Yukio Mishima describes in his hybrid critique-confession *Sun and Steel*. His focus stresses an agonistic quality, impressionistically approaching the resurrection, and is a good example of why the desire for transcendence can often look nihilistic.

To be empty, the kenosis that Taoist texts describe so well, elicits as if by nature, like a vacuum abhorred by nature, the presence of our true self. It is out-going, not morbid introspection or splendid isolation, but the finding of ourselves in signs both within and on the horizon (Quran 41:53). Even private sin can be thereby revealed as less real than public work and sacrifice, so that, in the blazes of laboring on behalf of others, we are "changed, changed utterly," as W. B. Yeats eulogizes in *1916*.

The crucifixion of the eternal Word in Christianity corresponds to the dismemberment of the primordial, cosmic man in other systems in which a primordial man is broken apart and the world is made from his limbs (like Ymir in Norse mythology and Purusha in the Indian *Rig Veda*). He is the cosmic man because he is dismembered in his particularity and comes to realize his universality, his identity with the cosmos. Psychologically, this is analogous to the intellectual pain of knowing two apparently contradictory facts forces one, as if by mental dismemberment and re-membermerment, to adopt a broader paradigm able to make sense of both (the term *remembrance* is descriptive of this, and many traditions equate spiritual rebirth with a recovery of memory).

This pattern whereby a particular form (the initiate's individual sense of self) is dismembered like the universal man of various mythologies or crucified like Christ, experiences the universal beyond form, and then is able to fulfil a worldly function by identifying with a particular form other than his narrow initial identity occurs also on the level of cultures, traditions and communities. Again, this is the ecumenic understanding of a translatability of theological categories across theologies. Thusly do communities tend to take particular stories and allegorize them (understanding them as referring to a universal pattern rather than specific event detailed in scripture, for example, applying them to new contexts).

The view *underlying correspondence between one and many also underlies translation*; it is behind both *political representation* and *political reconciliation*, both personal *epiphany* and communal *ecumene*. This is the basis for Egyptologist Jan Assman's contention that theological translatability allowed mutual recognition of political legitimacy among ancient (particularly Bronze Age Near Eastern) rulers. Writes Goethe:

> We are so pious, we lovers…
> We are like you, ye victorious Romans, in this: for we offer
> Gods of all peoples and tribes, over the whole world, a home—
> May the Egyptian, black and austere out of primeval basalt,
> Or from the marble a Greek, form them charming and white—
> Yet the eternal ones do not object to particularism
> (*Erotical Romana*, sixth elegy)

Here, Roman victory—ecumenic truth—embraces diversity: both the Egyptian and Greek form of archetypal realities. In the context of Abrahamic religion, and specifically Christianity, this translatability of theological/metaphysical categories can occur in the notion of national election being translatable from one context to another, as in the Roman Pontificate and Christian Roman Empire, or Ethiopian emperorship as presented in the *Kebra Nagast* representing Solomonic, Biblical monarchy.

Further, apart from peers on one level, the same principle can also manifest as different rungs or modes, occurring as the layers of a structure, as in Kantorowicz's detailing of the idea of the *mystical body* corresponding variously to different kinds of corporate entities (ecclesial, republican, etc.),[191] which we can also relate to how medieval monarchs would sometimes refer to themselves as emperors even while recognizing a wider Empire, so that the community is fractal, constituted by microcosms which are macrocosms with respect to their constituents.

---

191   Kantorowicz, *The King's Two Bodies*.

Chit as Static Masculine, Ananda as Dynamic Feminine

This movement, this dynamism, revealed by the radii, is in God: "This cannot be emphasized enough: The Christian God, who is infinite, is also infinitely *formosus*, the supereminent fullness of all forms."[192] Jove (*Chit*, circumference) does not truly receive the autozoon from Rhea, but only when he recognizes it in Juno, at his own level, the radii in superposition with himself, no longer with the center. This is made possible by first contemplating the center (like Eve coming from Adam after a sleep comes over him, where sleep is understood as contemplation).

In the Proclean triad (*On-Zoe-Nous*: Being-Life-Intellect), Life follows Being and precedes Intellect. Life is Being's ability to move back on Itself and so "produce" Intellect. This seems analogous to *Sat* reflecting on Itself (*Chit*) to "produce" *Ananda*. In fact, all three are simultaneous. Here, product is always present with producer, for a light source or a flame is always consubstantial with its light rays, per St. Athanasius. Proclus presents these three as layers of reality and also as facets present within each level.

As *layers*, they are the three Shaivist Pure Creations, the Pythagorean monad-dyad-triad, and so on. Here, Pure Consciousness or Being produces the beingness of the many beings (including inanimate ones), Experiential Consciousness or Life produces the living beings (the vitality of organic lifeforms) and Reflexive Consciousness or Intellect produces the intellective beings (the self-awareness of humans).

As *facets* (which, again, are all present within each layer of reality) they are equivalent to *Sat-Chit-Ananda*. Joy is synonymous here with Understanding (the satisfaction, so to speak, of grasping the object of apprehension and, ultimately, one's very Being). It is, as Proclus would say of Life, like a returning movement.

Chit then appears as the result of this movement, a reflexive moment, a reflection of Being. It is by Rhea that Jove knows Saturn, by the Shakti of the Divine that knowledge is arrived at. We preserve the idea of Life or *Ananda* as feminine, given that Life is connected by Proclus to Rhea, the vivific source. *Chit*, or Jove, proceed therefrom, along with Juno. Similarly, in Christianity the Spirit mediates between Father and Son, but the Spirit is said to also flow through the Son.

In addressing the question of whether Joy leads to Consciousness by enjoying Being, or Consciousness leads to Joy by being conscious of Being—apart from recalling these three are one and so we speak here only of how they *appear* as discernable elements—we treat the issue as analogous to the fact that some schools call the Supreme Shakti, and others Shiva, or that alchemy speaks of a wet path and a dry path.

In any case, Joy is not a static product but Joy precisely *at Being*, which is therefore a movement about Being. *Ananda* as Understanding or

192 David Bentley Hart, *The Beauty of the Infinite: The Aesthetics of Christian Truth* (Cambridge, UK: William E. Eerdmans Publishing Company, 2003), 177.

Experience (the very possibility of understanding/experiencing), equivalent to Proclus's Life, is the returning movement, the dynamic power, the Shakti of Being, and *Chit* is the static, whether arrived at as "product" of Joy or known as the always already existent reflection of Being, always already *at a distance* from Being, (the Logos as mirror to the Father) wherein the gap is filled by *Ananda* (the light that shines from Father and reflects from Son, Spirit as the bond of love between Logos and Father). Consider:

> …in its fullness, being must also be consciousness, because the highest power to act—and hence the most unconditioned and unconstrained reality of being—is rational mind. Absolute being, therefore, must be absolute mind.

And,

> If indeed to exist is to be manifest—to be intelligible and perceptible—and if to exist fully is to be consciously known, then God, as infinite being, is also an act of infinite knowledge.[193]

And the following,

> God's being—esse, on, sat, wujud—is also consciousness—ratio, logos, chit, wijdan. As Ramanuja would have it, Brahman, as the fullness of all being, must possess immediate knowledge of all reality within himself, and so be the fullness of all consciousness as well, the "personal" source in whom being achieves total manifestation, total actuality. Or, in the language of Plotinus, the One ceaselessly generates the eternal reflective consciousness of the divine mind, nous, from which emanates all the rationally coherent diversity of the cosmos. Or, in the terms of Philo of Alexandria or the Gospel of John, God is never without his Logos, the divine Wisdom, in and through whom the world is created, ordered, and sustained.[194]

Chit's path to *Sat* being through the dynamism of experience/understanding (the purest experience being joy): "the only way to know the truth of things is, necessarily, the way of bliss"[195] and

> It only makes sense…that consciousness should be made open to being by an implausible desire for the absolute, and that being should disclose itself to consciousness through the power of the absolute to inspire and (ideally) satiate that desire.[196] (Here truth is *Sat*, consciousness is *Chit* and bliss is *Ananda*.)

---

193   David B. Hart, *The Experience of God: Being, Consciousness, Bliss* (New Haven: Yale University Press, 2013), 236.

194   Ibid., 235.

195   Ibid., 249.

196   Ibid., 248–49.

Thus, in his discussion of *Ananda*, Bentley Hart expresses its movement in drawing *Chit* to *Sat* in terms analogous to Proclus's understanding of Life drawing Intellect to Being:

> It is bliss that draws us toward and joins us to the being of all things because that bliss is already one with being and consciousness, in the infinite simplicity of God…
>
> The Father knows his own essence perfectly in the mirror of the Logos and rejoices in the Spirit who is the 'bond of love' or "bond of glory" in which divine being and divine consciousness are perfectly joined…
>
> The restless heart that seeks its repose in God (to use the language of Augustine) expresses itself not only in the exultations and raptures of spiritual experience but also in the plain persistence of awareness. [197]

So that *Ananda*/Awe is the movement, dynamic, and *Chit*/Awareness the persistence, static. In this sense, *Chit* displays a masculine character as stillness, and *Ananda* a feminine character as dynamism.

Insofar as *Chit* relates to *Sat* through *Ananda*, *Ananda* is a duality, consistent with her character as dynamic power and with her appearing as a second term, subsequent to the unity of Being in Proclus. She is known to *Chit in Sat*, and also in himself as the reflection of *Sat*. She flows to him and back from him. These correspond to Rhea and Juno, respectively. We have here the Egyptian (and, according to Raphael Patai, also Hebrew) quaternary of father-mother-daughter-son (*Sat*, *Ananda*-in-*Sat*, *Ananda*-with-*Chit*, *Chit*).

Ananda-with-*Chit* produces the impression of a mirroring surface, space, a matrix, Plato's Crater. It positions *Chit* towards *Sat* so that he knows he is the reflexive mind of *Sat*, so to speak. This mirror or matrix is the body and feminine counterpart of *Chit*, the manifestation of *Ananda* in *Ananda*-with-*Chit*. Writes Bulgakov,

> The first action of the Holy Spirit in creation is that in the void of nothing reality arises (in *ouk on* there appears *me on*) as a certain preliminary actuality: i.e., precisely the earth as the ontological place of future creation, and then different species of being. [198]

I have argued that the Demiurge does not simply receive the autozoon from Rhea but discovers it in Juno. It is in this latter, fuller consolidation of the autozoon that we see a parallel between the autozoon and Bulgakov's Divine Sophia, who is present in the "dyadic interpenetration" of Son and Holy Spirit. That the autozoon would be feminine makes sense, given the feminine character of the Shekinah in the Bible, for example. This is what the initiate receives during his death and rebirth,

---

197   Ibid., 248.
198   Bulgakov, *The Comforter*, 192–93.

and whose presence he must then recognize in the world. As for the
creaturely Sophia, she would then correspond to Plato's intelligible
(rather than *essential*) living creature, or to Athena as Proclus's world-soul.

Bulgakov himself identifies the first spatio-temporal matrix as being
"full of all the seeds of being, an organism of forms is formed," which
sounds like the autozoon, and as being made beautiful with a beauty that
"is an effect of the Holy Spirit... and Beauty is Joy, the joy of being,"[199]
precisely what is meant by *Ananda*. We should distinguish here between
Juno as a name for *Ananda-with-Chit* and Juno already manifesting as the
matrix of space-time, the "the ontological place of future creation."[200]
Whereas we will use Juno to refer to Plato's Crater as this latter, her
name is also applied to the preceding feminine principle.

We may further consider Rhea and Juno the archetypes of centripetal
and centrifugal motion, where *Chit* is the stationary *sattva* as distinct from
rajas and *tamas* in terms of the Indian *gunas*. This lower triad would be
the Platonic hyparxis-dynamis-nous in Proclus (dynamis is apparently
called *zoe* in Porphyry) and the alchemical salt-mercury-sulphur. The
presence of these three (centrifugal, stable and centripetal) tendencies in
higher orders are also relatable to the fact that in Proclus, Jove/Demiurge
(the dyadic masculine) nonetheless contains three deities, Poseidon, a
lesser Jove, and Pluto.

We may now provide greater detail concerning the several goddesses
that have been mentioned, invoking the image used by Schuon to describe
the Trinity as center, radius and circumference (Father, Son, Spirit; *Sat,
Chit, Ananda*) (see table opposite):

The two modes of *Ananda-with-Chit* correspond to the duality of *Chit*
(Ancient of Days and Son of Man) and are symbolized by the Orphic Justice and Understanding, and the *Gospel of Philip*'s "sister" and "companion."
Whereas *Ananda-in-Sat* corresponds to pure contemplative absorption
in Being, these latter two are modes of consciousness in which we know
ourselves in relation to Being, Vesta, and perceive Being in ourselves,
Juno (we may also think of these as the "vestal" and "venusian" modes
of a singular Juno). The latter represents a fuller "discovery" of Being
in Consciousness. Whereas Vesta seems to represent monadic quietude,
Juno provides a more complete epiphany, a participatory experience of
Being (this is analogous to that principle according to which Adam's
prelapsarian state was not higher than that of the post-lapsarian resurrection). A simple way to distinguish between these is that Rhea is
known at the center, Vesta between the circumference and the center
(or in the circumference's stillness which mimics the singularity of the
center), and Juno at the circumference itself (or in its movement, whose

199   Ibid., 201.
200   The latter could be considered equivalent to the Divine Sophia, but Bulgakov
does not make this equivalence.

Ananda **At one with *Sat***			
Likened to radii identical to central point; the latent potential of the center to radiate out			
Joy of unity/ Divine simplicity	Leads *Sat* to eternally beget *Chit*; Beckons *Chit* to contemplate *Sat*	Apophatic (represented by throne/mother)	Rhea
Together with *Chit*			
Likened to radii at circumference; allowing for a spectrum of movement along which circumference may contract/expand;[1] movement illustrates circle's relation to center and to its own points/states of dilation:			
Relation to its center (Circle as shape whose points are equidistant from its center)			
Joy of union/ harmony with one's being	Leads *Chit* to know itself as distinct, but harmonious with *Sat*	Chariot-throne	Hestia/ Juno
Relation between its parts/states (Circle as shape with constant curvature; rate of rotation is proportional to distance travelled)			
Joy of harmony with one's parts/states	Leads *Chit* to know itself as image of *Sat*	Bride/Wife of the Lamb	Juno/ Celestial Venus
Divine Sophia[2]			
Likened to points on a circumference, realized as the intersection of radius with circumference; circumference conceived as individual points which may be extended out beyond it			
First intellection of *Chit* and *Ananda*[3]	"material" of creation, points as harmonious multiplicity, "body"[4]	City/Book	Autozoon[5]
Creaturely Sophia			
Likened to extension of radii past circumference to produce peripheral centers for new circles			
Creation	Ordered creation (six circles around a seventh, etc.)	Earthly Paradise/ New Earth	World-Soul[6]

1   Thus the three gunas of stability, expansion and contraction, which may map onto the triad of Jove in Proclus (Poseidon, Jove and Pluto).

2   Bulgakov's Divine and creaturely Sophia imitate *Ananda* at one with *Sat* and *Ananda* with *Chit*, but on a lower level.

3   Dyadic interpenetration of Son and Spirit in Bulgakov.

4   Creation as dismemberment of a divine body or as the fall of Sophia in Gnostic myths.

5   The Joy of harmony with one's self (Juno/Venus) is prior to conceiving of oneself as composite, because that Joy is the principle behind later manifestation. First the circumference is understood as harmonious with the center, then as harmonious in itself, then as conceivable as individual points.

6   Plato's intelligible living creature, as distinct from the autozoon (the essential living creature).

consistency of form across states of dilation mimics the singularity of the center). Alternatively, the vestal is ascent or return, the venusian descent or procession.

Vesta being eldest among the gods, and yet a sister of Zeus, represents the prior generation (*Sat*) without being identical to it. Being a virgin, she appears as a type for the woman dressed in the sun in the Apocalypse, as distinct from the wife of the lamb. The "sister" reminds one of parentage, not to return to the origin, for she is of one's own generation, but to retain harmony with that origin. Here, the definition of the circle refers to the inward-looking orientation of each part of the circumference towards its center. Hestia as goddess of the hearth relates to this sense of origin and stability.

The "companion," or wife, causes one to become harmonious in oneself by being an image of one's origin (the circumference as a "dilated" image of the single point at its center). That is, a wife turns a man into a father, and so makes him an image of his father. Here, by describing a circle as a shape whose curvature is constant, we seem to exclude its center from its definition, focusing on the circumference's features. But the *constancy* of curvature reflects the *singularity* of the central point, so that the circle appears as "dilated" center. Without referring to the center, it nonetheless arranges itself around it, just as a man need not conform to his father for his wife to make him an image of the father. It is the orientation of each part of the circumference with respect to each other part. This orientation is the radius at the circumference, because in order to retain a constant curve, every "point" of the circle must align itself with its own vector, a degree intermediate to that of adjacent points.

PART II

Practices of Spiritual Realization and Its Political Expression

So turn whereto it dies,
Pulse of a draining sun:
The face of daylight's guise
The yield that night has won.
See on the far-west front,
Goes trotting godly fame:
The bull called occident.
His white hide bears a name—
By what light is yet sparred
(Again, he is Jove paired!)
It reads: *she, wide of brow*;
Or maybe: *she, of dusk.*
Set on, she will avow
The birth of this *cultus.*
It spells out *Europa,*
(Decorous, ridding brusque)
God's virgin mineral
(With frankincense for musk)
Fair consort of the bull.
Kingly initiate,
Oh regal neophyte—
The gods part you from blame,
Buried to be raised up.
Birthed thus into your name:
Son of Zeus and Europe. [1, 2]

---

1   Euripides, *Cretans,* cited by Porphyry in *On Abstinence from Animal Food,* IV:xix.
2   Poem first published under the title *Son of Europe* on the Society of Classical Poets website.

We now proceed according to four moments of royal ordination and the political consequence of the ethos they imply.

II. Coronatio, or enthronement—a divinizing operation taking place on the seat of a regent or archetypal human form, in a flame-ridden, quadrangular (sometimes cuboidal) space, often described as a mountain and identified as the Divine Feminine as Mother (described as luminous, divine hypostasis or personality). Subterranean, infernal features may be associated with the space, being the usurping selfhood resisting epiphany.

III. Copulatio—Epiphany becomes corporealized, the transcendent is translated into a tradition. Here that which was received as epiphany (harmony as such), is introduced into the world, which is revealed as a manifestation (as harmonious). This is presented in terms of a female initiatrix, the Divine Feminine as Lover representing the world into which a male initiate introduces epiphany (through the symbolism of penetrative coitus and insemination as creative act).

IV. Corporatio—As a consequence of the preceding, the incumbent initiate perceives cosmic corporeality (the universe as coherent, organic unit) and epiphanically identifies the universal ensemble with his own body (the two being anatomically analogous).

V. Ecumene—A political ethic of respect for boundaries derives from this ordeal, given that each social entity is experienced as an organ in a common body whose health would be adversely affected by tumorous aggression. In Western terms this ethic is describable as the principle of subsidiarity or sphere sovereignty inwardly, and as ecumenism outwardly.

II. Coronatio

W E WILL DISCUSS THE RITUAL DEATH ASSO-
ciated with spiritual initiation and monarchical investiture
across traditions (*Theophany and Macranthropy*), focusing on
the Divine Feminine as Mother and the hero's rebirth from Her (*The
Mother's Vegetable Sun*), before exploring the presence of this paradigm
in the story of Aeneas and more broadly in Greco-Roman myth (*The
Initiate at Mount Ida*).

THEOPHANY AND MACRANTHROPY

The sun is the transcendent, ever-shining *deus absconditus* whose empyrean abode is unreachable by mortal flesh on pain of immolation, but
who condescends, reaching out his light and heat, who fills the gap
between eternity and time by emanation, and leaves a ray of light, caught
in lower planes, in the dense obscurity of the world, of storm clouds,
becoming focused, active, wrathful, a lightning rod to gift primitive man
with direct understanding of the remote Sun by way of storm-ignited
flames, symbol of the *deus revelatus*, flames alike those of the burning
solar orb. The sun is almost always a symbol of God's equanimity and
constancy, whereas storm deities are almost always kings, present to the
affairs of mortals. In Platonic terms, especially those of Iamblichus and
Proclus, the sun stands for the First Paternal Intellect or the Monad,
and the storm-god for the Second Paternal Intellect, also referred to
as the Demiurge, Jupiter and the Logos. The mortal king is assimilated
into the heavenly king, the Second, in order to gain access to the First.

A king must have his throne. None is king unless he occupies a seat
of power, an unmoving center to represent the cosmic authority around
which all else revolves. This is his trial, this is the privilege to which he
aspires, from Egypt, where the Pharaoh is seen "shining on his throne
like Ra," imitating Osiris, ruler of the underworld, whose descent is
prerequisite to attaining union with the empyreal deity,[1] to India, where
the *Jayakhya-Samhita* teaches that the Divine Lord, the *Sadasiva*, must
be visualized upon His throne[2] by the spiritual aspirant, during an
enthronement that occurs within the visualizer.

The Greek roots of western culture hearken back to the throne of
sacred kingship. The Mysteries of the *Curetes*, cited by Plato and elucidated by Proclus, iterate the same mystical operation as other archaic

---

1   Algis Uzdavinys, *Philosophy as a Rite of Rebirth: From Ancient Egypt to Neoplatonism*
(Wiltshire: Promethean Trust, 2008), 193.
2   Flood, *The Tantric Body: The Secret Tradition of Hindu Religion*, 143.

traditions: "In the Euthydemus [Plato] makes mention of the collocation on a throne which is performed in the Corybantic mysteries..." which imitates the position of the "Demiurge of wholes"[3] who is king of the gods, Jove.[4, 5]

But before his coronation, the king-to-be must scale his people's sacred mountain, alone and humbly robed, donning nothing but an animal skin and the dread of his animal self—that primal fear of death pulsing like the heat from subterranean ore underfoot, leaving a film of sweat on his skin. He carries a rope around his hand to harness the sacrificial beast anointed for the occasion. Reaching the top, he lifts the critter to pass over the rim of a crater. Now begins the descent. He enters the place of initiation through that cavernous opening and finds himself in the entrails of the mountain, dark like a womb but for the flames of the underworld, like the red pulse of embryonic life, poised to stage a second birth. Scaling the mountain corresponds to a descent into darkness, as St. Gregory comments on Moses's climbing of Sinai. The holy of holies at the temple of Jerusalem will eventually correspond to the peak of the mountain, which is also the depth of its womb-like caverns.

The Platonic *Crater* (spatiotemporal matrix, or principle of space and time, which is therefore outside both, identified by neo-Platonists with the goddess Juno) is symbolized and experienced in both a craterous, cavernous depth and the dome of the sky. Therefore, the practice of incubation in deep underground caves (Greek *enkoimesis*) leads to the experience of heavenly ascent. Incubation can also refer to sleeping in sacred places generally, as in the case of King Solomon (I Kings 3), but the cave or underground chamber is a particularly suggestive environment. We begin in the womb-like environment of the cave and are transported to the womb-like cosmic opening all about the earth. This is the *katabasis-anabasis* process, descent and ascent.

As mentioned, the association of the sun with the underworld, the underworld with practices of incubation, and incubation with dreams and Apollo, leads us to relate Pythagorean-Orphism/Apollonian tradition with dream yoga, as found in Buddhism: retaining lucidity through the sleep cycle and into deep-sleep, where the conscious encounter with formless, dreamless deep-sleep—like the formless realm encountered after death—is experienced as a radiance analogous to the solar orb. This justifies the idea of a nocturnal sun or sun in the underworld—Helios in Hades. The midnight Apollo.

From the underground we rise as in a chariot, the solar chariot of Parmenides with its solar maidens, the Jewish *Merkabah*, the *Buraq*

---

3   Proclus, *The Six Books of Proclus The Platonic Successor, On The Theology of Plato*, vol. 1, trans. T. Taylor (London: A. J. Valpy, 1816), VI:13, 49.

4   Iamblichus, *Fragments of Iamblichus' Commentary on the Timaeus*, Fragment 3a, 65–66.

5   Proclus, *On the Theology of Plato*, V:25; 383.

creature on which Muhammad and other prophets rode according to Islam. Uzdavinys refers to this as the "hermeneutical descent into the womb-like chariot."[6] The fact that in New Kingdom Egyptian theology, specifically the *Book of the Heavenly Cow*, the god Ra retires from the earth after the end of the Golden Age upon a sacred cow, and so the initiate must likewise ride the holy cow into theurgic exaltation,[7] reinforces this idea of heavenly descent and ascent through a womb, a maternal presence, which means it is a return to conception and a rebirth. This relates to the artistic motif of king-as-child seated upon the mother's lap (from ancient Egypt and Crete to later Christian depictions of the child Jesus on mother Mary's lap).

On another level, the chariot also represents a female consort of the male, like the fiery chariot-throne of the Ancient of Days, which, if this latter is a paternal image, is like the mother of the Son of Man, so that when the Son sits on the Ancient One's throne, it is like sitting on his mother, on her lap, his own consort being Jerusalem. In ancient Israel, the queen mother ascended to her position when her son took on the role of king, whose principal wife will be the future queen mother. We may think of Solomon's having a throne brought out for his mother Bathsheba in 1 Kings 2:19. The initiate is both a demiurge, a Jove, within Rhea's Cretan Mount Ida, and also a Jove with princess Europe who has been taken to Crete.

According to *On Nature*, Parmenides, who practices Greek incubation, reaches the dwelling of a goddess in a place beyond opposites like day and night (translated alternatively as Nature, Wisdom, etc.). According to some hadiths, Muhammad "was sleeping in ... the sacred enclosure" near the Kaaba "used as a place for the practice of oracular incubation"[8] before his heavenly ascent. Enoch also incubated prior to ascent (I Enoch 13 [incubation "by the waters of Dan"] and 14 [ascent]). The scholar Ioan Culianu[9] distinguished between Biblical prophets who are called from above, those who are victims of accident, and those who themselves seek out revelation, these last ones being celebrated in "Quest Apocalypses":

> Enoch combines the Call and the Quest ...[10] Unlike some other visionaries (such as Isaiah), Enoch is not formally invested or

---

6   Uzdavinys, *Ascent to Heaven in Islamic and Jewish Mysticism*, 46.

7   *Pyramid Texts*, 273–74. Cited by Algis Uzdavinys, *Philosophy as a Rite of Rebirth: From Ancient Egypt to Neoplatonism* (Wiltshire: Promethean Trust, 2008), 85.

8   Uzdavinys, *Ascent to Heaven in Islamic and Jewish Mysticism*, 30.

9   Ioan Culianu, *Psychanodia I* (Leiden, 1983), 6; cited by J. Collins (see below).

10   "The Quest aspect appears in his incubation by the waters of Dan, where he reads out the petition until he falls asleep. Dan, of course, was an old sacred site in Israelite tradition, and was also close to the Hellenistic shrine of Pan" (George Nickelsburg, "Enoch, Levi, and Peter. Recipients of Revelation in Upper Galilee," JBL 100 (1981): 575–600; cited by J. Collins). "It is possible that some form of incubation ritual was associated with the site. Other apocalyptic visionaries of the Hellenistic

commissioned in heaven,[11] but the authorization of his message
and role must be reckoned nonetheless among the functions of
his ascent.[12]

Here, we are emphasizing the Call and Quest of the above scholarly
distinction as a katabasis and anabasis—descent and ascent. This is not
only a descent and ascent of the initiate (descending down to a cave
and up to heaven) but of the Divine descending down, *calling*, and the
initiate ascending up, *questing*. Alternatively, the initiate descends to a
cave and is then *picked up*, ascended, by the Divine. The two meet. We
find the theme of "immortalization, and ascent to heaven, as a result of
throwing oneself into a krater"[13] that occurs in figures such as Empedocles at Etna or Aeneas at Pozzuoli. The Name and its speaker, to put
it in Henry Corbin's terms, finally coincide.

After experiencing the emptiness (or rather, utter plenitude) of the
Crater, we experience the stars, points of light, definite form within that
potential. We return having recreated the whole cosmic architecture for
ourselves, *as* ourselves, represented by our particular star, that is, the
rising sun which, with its light, illumines the sensible, formal plane of
existence, the earth, daytime (thus the solar-hero and sun-king motif).

This solar king, the legislator who can rule a people justly, is universally
identified with a sacred (solar) mountain, wherein he incubated. Like
Moses descending Mount Sinai with divine commandments or king
Gilgamesh encountering the lord of the living mountain. As Gregory
of Nyssa writes, the Mosaic ascent up the mountain is a descent into
divine darkness. It is a going into the trans-formal, returning with the
paradigm of order, autozoon, the law. The Egyptian *Duat* or underworld
is identified with the primordial mound out from which the world was
first formed[14] and, in turn, with the royal seat: the hieroglyph meaning *enthronement* consists of the sun rising behind a mound.[15] Likewise,
the heavenly *sanctum sanctorum* into which the Biblical Enoch enters is
described as a high mountain whose summit is like the throne of the

---

and Roman periods also take measures to initiate their experiences. (Daniel fasts
in Daniel 10, and Ezra eats the flower that is in the field, in 2 Esdras 9:26). These
measures distinguish the apocalyptic visionaries from the classical biblical prophets."
11   This last point introduces a dichotomy which is not essential. Not only does
Enoch subvert it somewhat, but in the case of Muhammad and Islamic theology,
for example, practicing active incubation, including perhaps his praying in a cave
as a *Hanif* prior to receiving the Qur'an, and actively seeking revelation, does not
contradict his also being a prophet "formally invested or commissioned in heaven."
Presumably this is also the case for the *mantias theo-phonas* (messengers of the Divine
sound) of Pythagorean-Platonic tradition.
12   John J. Collins, *Apocalypse, Prophecy, and Pseudepigraphy: On Jewish Apocalyptic
Literature* (Cambridge: William B. Eerdmans Publishing Company, 2015), 185.
13   Kingsley, *Ancient Philosophy, Mystery and Magic*, 244.
14   Uzdavinys, *Philosophy as a Rite of Rebirth: From Ancient Egypt to Neoplatonism*, 238.
15   Toby Wilkinson, *The Egyptian World* (New York City: Routledge, 2007), 308-9.

Lord (1 Enoch 25:3). Hermes/Mercury, identified with the prototypical initiate (like Odin/Woden[16]) is born from the mountain nymph Maia, whose name she shares with the Sanskrit term for sensible reality, and, in the Homeric hymn to Hermes, receives a whip to herd cattle from Apollo, symbolic of spiritual mastery.

This volcanic crater, simmering with death, is a symbol for the *Crater* in Plato's *Timaeus*, the divine mixing-bowl and receptacle at the beginning of time in which the Jove combined the elements to create the world, the hot furnace in which the alloys and compounds of mortal life are forged, the womb of the female consort of Jove, Juno, who births the cosmos. Proclus quite clearly identifies Juno with Mount Ida and refers to her as the mother of souls.[17] That which proceeds from the higher conjoined masculine and feminine principles, Saturn and Rhea, is the pair of Jove and Juno who produce souls, but also Hestia/Vesta, who is identified with the cuboid fire at the center of the cosmos according to Pythagoreans, so that "a subsistence in self is the peculiarity of Vesta, but in another of Juno."[18] We may think of the divine feminine below the level of Rhea as both Vesta and Juno: Vesta in the stillness as the cube-throne of the Lord (as in Egyptian art) and Juno in her dynamic producing of souls as a mother. The king himself will be newly minted in this way, birthed afresh, if he submits.

That which Jove, the Demiurge, receives from Rhea and matures into Juno (having himself become mature by his mother Rhea and thereby made ready for the marital encounter) we identify with Plato's autozoon, the form of the universe as living organism. Being carrier of divine designs, the feminine power proceeds from the head, the intellective center, of the eternal masculine. This is so not only in the image of Minerva's birth from Jove's head but also appears in the Bible when Lady Wisdom (Hokmah, המכה; Sophia, Σοφία) is described as coming from the divine mouth (that is, the mouth of the Most High, El Elyon, וְיִלְעָ לֹא not the Lord, YHWH, הוָֹהיְ) (Sirach 24:3)[19] and, more comprehensively, as being breath and power (*Shakti*) (Wisdom 7:25-27), which entails the image of a mouth and head, and again in the New Testament when the Holy Spirit (likely a feminine word in Jesus's original utterance) is imparted by Christ through his breath (John 20:22). Rhea proceeds from

---

16   Who gives his name to Wednesday, named after Mercury in Romance languages.

17   Proclus, *The Commentaries of Proclus on the Timaeus of Plato in Five Books*, vol. 1, trans. T. Taylor (London: A. J. Valpy, II, 1820), 344.

18   Proclus, "Scholia of Proclus on the Cratylus of Plato," In: Thomas Taylor, *Theology of Plato: Proclus* (Somerset, UK: Prometheus Trust, 2017), 682.

19   Sirach's privileging of YHWH, the god of Israel, despite distinguishing between him and the Most High (in Barker's reading) can be understood in terms of Frithjof Schuon's *divine subjectivity* or *theophanic individuality* where scriptures express their teachings in exclusivist terms, but also in terms of Christian theology, where the gods of the nations did not succeed in keeping their wards from idolatry, except that Israel was preserved to a greater degree than others.

Saturn to Jove, and Jove in turn produces the world-soul or Minerva from his head as a blueprint/design/architecture (autozoon) with which he makes pregnant the Receptacle, Juno.

The theme of Wisdom, of a *Gnosis* which the architect Demiurge receives and imparts, is linked to royalty, to Jove as king, to the imparting of knowledge as rulership. In some traditions the original sacred kingship finds declinations in the figure of the teacher, the sage and legislator, emphasizing this sense of passing on knowledge, such as the Biblical Moses and prophets after King David, or Chinese sages Sima Qian and Mencius who continue the work of the Duke of Chou outside the political-aristocratic sphere.

Jove's ceremonial throne at Mount Ida may be identified with the Crater of Plato's *Timaeus* (this association is developed further below). This is consistent with a tradition according to which the Platonic Crater or mixing bowl is represented by actual volcanic craters, constituting a flaming province, with the god Vulcan (bearing a mixing cup) being a Demiurgic type. Further, Plato seems to identify volcanoes (and thereby Jove's throne) with Tartarus, mentioning Sicily in the *Phaedo* when referring to Tartarus and possibly evoking the region under Mount Etna, a Sicilian volcano.[20] Etna was related to the mysteries of Persephone—the Divine Feminine—and in some accounts was the entry through which Hades took her to the underworld. The association of the divine seat with Tartarus mirrors Osirian regency over the subterranean realms. Here Osiris and Jove represent the same archetype and, insofar as Dionysius is a Greek version of many of the myths surrounding Osiris, he is partially assimilated to Jove as well, although usually operating at a lower level.

The king has entered what the Egyptians call the *Duat*. It is not clear now whether the underworld has risen or else the king has descended, or whether its rising and his falling have met in this place where ceremony forgets itself and exits time. Indeed, the Egyptians believed the mountain to be the highest point of the underworld—high, yet still a province of hellish jurisdiction.

Before the as-yet-uninitiated ruler is the image of everything he aspires to be. All about him an august scene unfolds in a fiery rage. Infernal proceedings bow their heads to the god who judges souls,[21] the one king whose authority no mortal can avoid. Him who the Egyptians know as Osiris, the Greeks as Jove and Demiurge of wholes, the Biblical Ancient of Days beheld by the patriarch Enoch upon his heavenly throne (I Enoch 47:3; 60:2). It is for the king to become the thing beheld that the Lord of judgement has manifested. He must do as Enoch who sat on the celestial throne (2 Enoch 25:5), as the Tantric sage who visualizes enthronement as locus of divinization.

20   Kingsley, *Ancient Philosophy, Mystery and Magic*, 74.
21   G. Pinch, *Magic in Ancient Egypt* (London: British Museum Press, 1994), 27.

The Ancient of Days is equivalent to the prophet's "heavenly double" [22] in such apocrypha as "Joseph and Aseneth," and to Metatron in Enochic texts. The "Visions of Ezekiel" (*Re'uyot Yehezkel*), one of the earlies Merkabah texts, equates Metatron to the Ancient of Days. The interpretation of Metatron's title of "youth" in the 3 Enoch according to which the angel is constantly rejuvenated after reaching old age [23] is similar to the Bride of Christ becoming youthful after appearing an old woman in the *Shepherd of Hermas*, and the Son of Man appearing as a youthful version of the Ancient of Days (sharing the latter's attributes) in John's Apocalypse. The Ancient of Days and Son of Man in Daniel's vision are an archetypal representation of that which, at a lower level, occurs between the theophany of the Lord (or "Lesser Lord") and human initiate, respectively:

> Enoch's celestial alter ego, the supreme angel Metatron, was often depicted in the Hekhalot and Shi'ur Qomah [Midrashic] materials as a very distinguished operator or even as the embodiment of the divine Name, the office that is briefly and accurately summed up in his striking title...the Lesser YHWH. [24]

Because this theophany represents the monad to the initiate, like Saturn-Rhea to Jove, it is from it that the autozoon is received.

The elements of a mountain, light, bestowal of rulership and the assertion of divine origins occur in the Gospel as well. Jesus was subsumed in light, perhaps the feminine Shekinah, on Mount Tabor, wherein appeared initiated Saints, Elijah and Moses, and a cloud (like that which Daniel refers to in which the Son of Man was to come, perhaps, linked to typical monarchical storm-imagery) wherefrom a voice declared Christ's Divine sonship and dominion, instructing the disciples to obey Him (Matthew 17:1–8; Mark 9:2–8; Luke 9:28–36). In the Apocryphal *Gospel According to the Hebrews*, there is a link between the divine feminine and Mount Tabor when Jesus says to Satan: "It is written again, Thou shalt not tempt the Lord thy God. Just now my mother the Holy Spirit took me by one of my hairs and here me up on to the great mountain Tabor." [25] Further, in the Apocalypse (21:9–10) John is shown the wife of "the suckling lamb" when the disciple is taken to a holy mountain. This seems to display the relationship between sacred femininity and mountains we have been discussing.

The celestial throne has been witnessed, its occupancy held by the human archetype, the *Anthropos*, the hypostasis by which the human

---

22 Andrei Orlov, *The Greatest Mirror: Heavenly Counterparts in the Jewish Pseudepigrapha* (Albany, NY: SUNY Press, 2017).

23 Andrei Orlov, *The Greatest Mirror*, 29.

24 Andrei Orlov, *The Greatest Mirror*, 32.

25 W. E. Byron Nicholson, *The Gospel according to the Hebrews: its fragments translated and annotated with a critical analysis of the external and internal evidence relating to it* (London: C. Kegan Paul and Co., 1879), 76.

condition becomes plural, that true vine of which individual personhood is a sprout. This is the content of the theophanic vision consistent across traditions. A vision for the dead, for the newly living.

That figure our king has laid eyes on appears in Christian art, often reminding admirers of the Greek Zeus or Roman Jove. This is no coincidence and should not be understood as mere iconographic translation from the Classical pagan to the Christianity, having no theological importance, or worse, as a theological embarrassment. Storm-god symbolism already appears in the Book of Daniel, where the prophet sees the Ancient of Days with a face like lightning (Daniel 10:6). Some Christians identified accounts of an archetypal human figure (including those of Ezekiel 1:26, Exodus 24:10 and Isaiah 6:1) with the pre-incarnate Christ.[26] It is the "more primary, paradisal incarnation" from "the eternal time when the incarnate Logos walks (as the Fathers taught) with Adam and Even in the dressed and kept garden (Genesis 2:15)."[27]

Whenever Christian art features an aged, bearded divinity, it is the Ancient of Days, the Logos as the prophet Daniel saw Him, the pre-incarnate form of Christ which continues to manifest, as in the AD 410 mosaic at Santa Pudenziana or the fourth-century Basilica San Giovanni in Fonte (Napoli) where it appears as elderly black-bearded Jesus accompanying a youthful blonde Christ. In Orthodox icons these images often appear with a cruciform aura, as we have mentioned previously, making it clear that they are God the Son, even if in the guise of an old man. In the Catholic West, instances such as the centerpiece of the Sistine Chapel should be interpreted as the Ancient of Days reaching out to man, not as depictions of God the Father, which would be blasphemous. Not all theologians agree that the Ancient of Days is the Second rather than First Person of the Trinity, and indeed, we agree He is a *representation* of the Father.

The Lord—the vision of Anthropos or Ancient of Days, Christ, the Divine human form, the throne theophany—are all the Son in Christian Trinitarian terms, or YHWH in the Old Testament, rather than the Father, or High One/El Elyon.[28] Indeed, in John's Apocalypse, the Son, Jesus upon

---

26   Paul A. Patterson, *Visions of Christ: The Anthropomorphite Controversy of 399 CE* (Tubingen: Mohr Siebeck, 2012), 79–80.

27   Pickstock, *After Writing: On the Liturgical Consummation of Philosophy*, 249.

28   "If we read the Hebrew Scriptures in the way that the first Christians read them, we should understand that Yahweh was the son of God Most High (El Elyon), the Second Person (to use an anachronism), and that Yahweh was incarnate in Jesus. Thus Gabriel announced to Mary, 'He shall be called Son of God Most High' (Luke 1.32). We should know why Paul could proclaim one God, the Father, and one LORD, Jesus the Messiah (1 Corinthians 8:6). We should know why two early texts of the New Testament came to describe Jesus as the one who brought Israel out of Egypt (Jude 5). We should know why the Fourth evangelist believed that Isaiah's vision of the LORD had been a vision of Jesus (John 12:41). We should know why Justin regarded the Old Testament theophanies as pre-incarnation appearances of Jesus,

his return, is described with features of Daniel's Ancient of Days, such as white hair. This may be understood if we understand the Second Person of the Trinity as corresponding with reflexive consciousness, whose reflecting on Being or pure consciousness it represents to itself through, or receives as, the stability of the elder, the archetype of the wise king.

The Son, or *Chit*, reflexive consciousness, is dual in that it is eternally proceeding from *Sat* and is also reflecting back upon *Sat*. We may view this duality of Son of Man and Ancient of Days as indicating the dual nature of Jesus, human and Divine. A similar duality occurs between the woman dressed in the sun in the Apocalypse (the heavenly archetype of Mary), on the one hand, and the Wife of the Lamb (21:9) or Church as Bride in The Shepherd of Hermas, on the other (this latter also becomes a young woman in the second vision of Hermas, yet retains white hair, like the white-haired Christ). This resembles the Father-Mother-son-daughter quaternary Raphael Patai identifies in Egyptian mythology and the Hebrew Tetragrammaton.

In the Old Testament, we find the angel of the Lord as theophany rather than messenger, and later Judaism features such a vision, identified with Metratron, in chariot-throne or Merkabah mysticism. Even in Islam, apart from anthropomorphic terminology and that of kingship reminiscent of the Ancient of Days to describe Allah, the emphasis on the radical transcendence of God has not entirely precluded the vision of a, somehow divine, human form which we may associate with the Son of Man.[29] An account with admittedly weak *isnad*,[30] presumably originating with A'isha, one of Muhammad's wives[31] reads, "The Prophet saw his Lord under the form of a young man seated on a footstool, his foot in verdure made of twinkling light."[32]

In Daniel, the Son of Man is "presented" to the Ancient of Days. The implied relation is one of prince to king, young man to old regent. The idea that the young heir completes the system—that the newer, which lacks precedence in time (even if only symbolically) is nonetheless the center of the whole game—seems to provide a profound justification for

why Irenaeus, Hippolytus and Novatian read the Old Testament in the same way, and why Constantine's mother erected a Christian church at Mamre, the place where the Lord appeared to Abraham. We should also understand why ikons of Christ have in the halo *ho on*, the Greek form of Yahweh" (Barker, *The Great High Priest: The Temple Roots of Christian Liturgy*, 309–10).

29 Wesley W. Williams, *Tajalli Wa-Ru'ya: A Study of Anthropomorphic Theophany and Visio Dei in the Hebrew Bible, the Qur'an and Early Sunni Islam* (PhD Thesis: The University of Michigan, 2008), 275–77.

30 Line of succession for the passing down of a teaching or instructive event from prophet Muhammad.

31 By way of Safwan b. Sulaym to 'Abd al-Malik b. 'Abd al-'Aziz b. Jurayj, provided in al-Suyuti's *al-La'ali al masnu'a fi al-ahadith al-mawdu'a* quoting from al-Tabarani's *Kitab al-Sunnah*.

32 Williams, *Tajalli Wa-Ru'ya*, 193.

creation, nature, humanity. Crucially, and unlike myths of violent generational overthrow and foundational patricide in which a god replaces
his predecessor, Daniel's double theophany of Ancient One and Son
does not pit these against one another.

Perhaps the Ancient of Days is the human archetype at a prior level
of reality, and the Son of Man is the same at a subsequent but therefore crowning, more inclusive, one. As Plotinus writes, criticizing those
dualists who wanted to break with the world and all bodily things: one
cannot love the parent without loving the child. This also reminds us
of the idea that the fourth heaven, the sun, is also the pole (*qutb*) of
the seven heavens for Ibn Arabi. It is not the highest, not the *eldest*, so
to speak, and for this reason it is the center. Religion often subverts
our more reactionary instincts. It is not a question of hierarchy in the
ordinary sense: "Those who say, 'There is a heavenly man and there is
one above him' are wrong... For it would be better for them to say, 'The
inner and outer...'" (*Gospel of Philip*[33]).

We should note here the appearance of feminine forms in the mystical vision. The demiurgic plane (which is derivative of the monad but
represents monadic unity to us since our being is in turn derivative of
it—like consciousness experiencing joy when reflecting on being) includes
both Jove and Juno. Proclus writes the following in his *Commentaries of
Proclus on the Timaeus of Plato in Five Books*:

> For souls indeed, according to the being which is in them, were
> produced by the Demiurgus; but according to the life which is
> in them, from the Crater...Orpheus celebrates this vivific deity
> as equal to the Demiurgus, and connecting and conjoining with
> him, makes it to be the one mother of all things of which Jupiter
> is the father. But Plato calls it the Crater, as being the fountain
> of the psychical life.[34]

Adding, "But the theologist of the Greeks"—Socrates—"denominates
this vivific cause Juno...."[35]

There is the theophany of the Anthropos, and the encounter with the
Divine Feminine, ideal humanity and its principle in person.

> There in his bosom Sapience doth sit,
> The sovereign darling of the Deity,
> Clad like a queen in royal robes, most fit
> For so great power and peerless majesty,
> And all with gems and jewels gorgeously
> Adorn'd, that brighter than the stars appear,
> And make her native brightness seem more clear. (From Edmund
> Spenser *An Hymn of Heavenly Beauty*)

---

33   *Nag Hamadi Codex II, 2–7, The Gospel of Philip*, 67:23–68:17, 177.
34   Proclus. *The Commentaries of Proclus on the Timaeus of Plato in Five Books*, vol. 2, V, 376.
35   Ibid., vol. 2, V, 377.

The Divine is approached via femininity in traditions like Shaktism. In the case of the Ancient of Days, we may identify Her with his fiery chariot-throne. Later we will see how the final realization of that ideal occurs through femininity-as-lover: its experience and activation in the world through penetration of the world-in-person, that is, the queen consort, revealing its true character. This corresponds to the kingdoms of the earth, the ideal Jerusalem, which are the consort of the Son of Man. Again, the king as Son of Man sits upon his mother's lap, throne of his father, and his reign is presided by the queen-mother following Israelite tradition, but as Ancient of Days, his chariot-throne is his feminine counterpart, so that, Jerusalem/the Church becomes the throne of the Son of Man when this one returns with features of the Ancient One to consummate his mission (compare Daniel 7:9 to John's Apocalypse 1:14).

For now, however, the initiate knows death and absorption into the beyond, and on the way, a blinding vision of being, Anthropos, and the paradigm of all creation therefrom. The vision itself can be thought of as the autozoon in a perfect microcosm which manifests its impossible plenum, so that we can speak of a vision of the autozoon and the demiurge who possesses and shines with it. Pure possibility is experienced but is mediated by a figure of divinity. The apophatic darkness of contemplation wherein shines the light of all possible manifestation, the *light of order*, the autozoon, and the cataphatic theophany accompany each other. Theophany facilitates apophatic contemplation just as a reflexive consciousness is lit up with joy by an experience of pure being. The experience of pure being is not the form of the theophany but the sheer gratuity of being it opens us up to, just as two lovers contemplating each other's irreducibility receive insight into the nature of that being which is both their beings and, in truth, all beings.

True apophatic absorption is not of the autozoon, but of the monad and the One, beyond what we can experience, beyond experience. Yet it is on the way and way back, as a sacrifice like the Son of Man presented to the Ancient of Days, that the initiate visions that figure and receives the autozoon. The absolute irreducibility of theophany can expose us to the sovereignty of that which is beyond us or our capacity to control and even understand, and give us the means for understanding the world—analogizing in Christian terms, to see the Son is to have seen the Father who cannot be seen, and through the Son one may receive the Spirit.

Union with the transcendent, the First Paternal Intellect, which Uzdavinys calls the "paternal harbor," the "Nous Patrikos" and "paternal intellect," using the language of Platonism, attains to His "luminous epiphany" which "is tantamount to the irradiation (*ellampsis*) and creation of the psycho-somatic cosmos."[36] Union with the transcendent allows embodiment of the cosmic body (the cosmic human body, the *macranthropos*).

---

36   Uzdavinys, *Ascent to Heaven in Islamic and Jewish Mysticism*, 34.

The archetypal human figure bestows identity with the cosmic body (as explored in the following section). Although not appearing cosmically large, it is at one with the entire creation, being the personification of divine creative agency. It is not a historically contained person but the pre-manifest body whereby the manifest universe is constructed (the pre-incarnate Logos and the post-incarnate one, for revelation is neither in some vast *before* or *after*, but is an Eschaton outside and within).

Before moving on, we will briefly outline the historical tension between theophany and iconoclasm in Abrahamic tradition:

> The seventh-century BCE reformers in the time of Josiah were the first to obscure the world of the temple. This situation was reinforced by the triumph of the group who returned from Babylon in the sixth century and set up the second temple, 'Ezra'—condemned by the Enoch tradition and by all who regarded the second temple period as the age of wrath. It was reinforced yet again with the formation of the Hebrew canon and the text which became modern theology—'Ezra', and eventually the Western Old Testament.

In such a theological context, theophany is treated with suspicion. Contrastingly,

> The world of the first temple and its high priestly tradition survived into the early Church, in many of the allusions in both early Rabbinic and early Christian texts, and in so much of what has been identified as deviation from Christianity or Judaism. The world of the first temple and its high priesthood survived in the Hekhalot texts, which, as Schäfer observed, seem to be independent of the canonical Hebrew Scriptures. It underlies the Gnostic systems, the Kabbalah and Sufism. It also shaped the Liturgy of the Church.

It is not merely first temple Judaism that Christianity restores, but the first temple *prior* to a degradation in which Israelites began practicing human sacrifices, and which the Bible tells us was a contagion from neighboring cults. This had affected first temple ritual and was in part the cause for its reform by king Josiah. Those sources that Barker identifies as critical of that reform, simultaneously appeal to a non-sacrificial form of the religion. Texts identified as continuing pre-Josianic tradition also present the Adamic and Enochic ritual offerings as bloodless, as in the *Book of Jubilees* (2:20; 2:28), or at least as limited to animal offerings, as in 2 Enoch (more on this in Addendum III).

This would be the true core of Christian dispensation, a possible initial context for Islamic polemic against the *Ahl al-Kitab*, People of the Book (Christians and Jews) having corrupted their scriptures,[37] and the

---

37 Jewish opponents of king Josiah's reform who were loyal to the first temple "...settled not only in Egypt but also in Arabia, among the sons of Ishmael. This tradition was known when the Jerusalem Talmud was compiled in the fourth century

ongoing source of the Enochic, Hekhalot, Kabbalist stream within Judaism. In the cases of mainstream Islam and Judaism, as well as Christian Protestantism, more of Josiah's iconoclasm is retained, and less of the prior temple symbolism is recovered. Even non-Protestant Christianity has, on the surface, conformed its scripture to this paradigm:

> An unacknowledged problem at the heart of Western Christian biblical study is that the Church, and especially the Western Church, has as its Scriptures the Jewish canon and text of the Old Testament, when the evidence shows clearly that the earliest Church used very different Scriptures.[38]

"Christian origins" are not in the canon attributed to Ezra,[39] which seems to bypass "the temple and the priesthood as described in the books of Moses," yet Christians ended up partly adopting scriptures,[40]

CE, i.e., when Christians and Jews were still arguing over the text and canon of the Scriptures. Since 'Ezra' and his heirs were associated with the new ('apostate') ways in Jerusalem and with the rejection of Wisdom, it would not be surprising if hostility to his tradition and Scriptures survived among 'the sons of Ishmael'. The faithful ones described in Isaiah warned the returned exiles in Jerusalem that their name would become a curse, and that the faithful servants would have a new name (Isa. 65:15). Even though the accusations have been made relevant to the new situation after the advent of Muhammed, the pattern of accusation is recognizable in Muslim texts. The enigmatic and allusive nature of the text of the Qur'an makes certainty impossible, but there are striking passages, not least the frequent references to the falsification of the text (*tahrif*), and to 'the Book and Wisdom' (3:81; 4:113; 5:110) which had been given, together with a great kingdom, to the people of Abraham (4:54). They were also given to Jesus (3:48; 3:79). This could be an allusion to the roots of Christianity being in the older faith of Abraham and 'Wisdom', and in the cult of the first temple. It is quite clear that the earliest Christians had Scriptures other than those in the present Old Testament, and the story of Ezra in 2 Esdras 14 shows that Wisdom had been lost along with the other secret books.... Parts of Moses' Book had been concealed (6:91) and parts had been changed (7:162), so that the covenant of the Book has been taken from them (7:169). This had been a Christian accusation as early as the Letter of Barnabas" (Barker, *The Great High Priest: The Temple Roots of Christian Liturgy*, 311-12).

38 Barker, *The Great High Priest: The Temple Roots of Christian Liturgy*, 298.

39 Which "described itself thus: 'Moses received the Law from Sinai and committed it to Joshua, and Joshua to the elders, and the elders to the prophets, and the prophets committed it to the men of the Great Synagogue' (m. Aboth 1.1). This tradition bypasses the temple and the priesthood as described in the books of Moses..." (Ibid., 307).

40 Partly in order to limit their arguments to texts used by the mainstream of Jewish religion at the time in order to proselytize on that basis: "Origen made his 'improved' text of the Greek Old Testament on the basis of the MT and the Greek translations made by Jews after the Christians had adopted the [Septuagint] — Theodotion, Aquila and Symmachus. Theodotion and his successor Aquila aimed to produce a Greek text closer to the Hebrew of their time, i.e., closer to that Hebrew text which became the modern theology. In other words, Origen was using various versions of the post-100 CE Hebrew to 'improve' the older Greek" (Ibid., 305). William Blake's intuition about a degradation of tradition, according to which the

which we may interpret as an exoteric safeguard against the kind of degradation that once polluted first temple religion. We can, in this sense, treat Josiah as overseeing a reformation that overcorrected, in light of Barker's research, while also following the tradition that considers him a genuine reformer. In order to maintain social, moral and, indeed, spiritual health, some things are kept from the foreground, that they may not be wrongly applied due to a confusion of planes.

The Four Corners of the Earth

In a sense, to truly be in the central mountain, the axis mundi, is already to be quartered, because it is beyond the four corners of the earth, it is that hollow of the seed, the mountain whence the four primordial rivers spring. If you enter the central mountain, you are in the place where the four elements have not yet emerged. It is the crater of the volcano wherein infernal fire ascends and the crater of the meteor wherein celestial fire descends: it is the symbol of Jove and Juno before the world-soul's creation, of the horizontal and vertical lines, to use the symbol of the cross, which is Christianity's equivalent of the holy mountain. To be there is to be beyond the four temperaments of the soul.

Porphyry relates that Pythagoras was initiated at Mount Ida, witnessing there the yearly establishment of Jove's throne.[41] It is therefore worth probing Pythagorean doctrine. According to Simplicius the term *Jupiter's throne* designates the fire Pythagoreans believed to occupy the center of the world or cosmos.[42] Anatolius relates that the Pythagoreans attributed the shape of a cube to this central fire[43] (apparently identified with the goddess Vesta). This corresponds to the Biblical Holy of Holies entered into by Enoch; a likewise cuboidal pyric estate wherein deity sits enthroned, with its corners flanked by four angels akin to the four figures of the Duat (1 Enoch 40:9). The central flame-cube presents the eternal feminine as radiant and fiery, the Shekinah, or the pre-Josianic figure of Asherah (or Ashratah, as Barker renders) in Hebrew religion, possibly Vesta (Greek Hestia) in Pythagorean terms. The cuboidal shape reminds of the forge where a metal is broken down and given new shape, and therefore of what would become alchemical symbolism.

Inside the sacred mountain, where we last left him, if the would-be monarch looks around, he will see that this underworldly court is a rectilinear, four-cornered hall. Each corner of the earth—north, south, east and west—is one of the elements, fire, earth, air and water. These are

---

theophanic story of Moses and the Burning Bush is at odds with Mosaic law *as passed down*, would be in line with this.

41   Porphyry, *Life of Pythagoras*. In: trans K. S. Guthrie and ed. D. Fideler, *The Pythagorean Sourcebook and Library* (Grand Rapids, MI: Phanes Press, XVII, 1988), 126.
42   Simplicius, *On Aristotle, On the Heavens*, cited in Kingsley, *Ancient Philosophy, Mystery and Magic*, 187.
43   Anatolius, *De Decade*, cited in Kingsley, *Ancient Philosophy, Mystery and Magic*, 183.

the subtle components that make physical reality. The aspiring king can see the god of kingship calling forth the forces of the four corners and creating new forms, new bodies, just as Plato writes that Jove unites the four primordial elements in the Crater.[44] The king watches and wonders whether he too will soon have a new body made new according to the divine regent's plan, one worthy of being his steward above, capable of bringing a portion of that power back to his people.

Prosperity and righteous rule are identified with the feminine mother here, for she is manifest in this four-cornered court room. Old Testament prophets would have warned of the disasters befalling Israel as related to the cessation of veneration of Lady Wisdom after King Josiah's reforms and use of the book of Deuteronomy, and Christianity would have brought it back[45] (in her work, Margaret Barker investigates the layers of suppression of this veneration[46]). Barker points out instances of identification of Lady Wisdom with the Virgin Mary in her work.

Christ tells His disciples that Mary is their mother (19:27) would have a profound meaning. The Spanish city of Seville's Patroness, the Virgin of Kings, is depicted with the inscription "Per me Reges Regnant" in the city's Cathedral, a phrase that occurs in Proverbs 8:15, voiced by Wisdom, that is, Sophia. Here the Virgin Mary is being identified with Old Testament Wisdom and with monarchical rulership, both in its capacities, which is to say, investiture, and in its diversity, for the word king appears in the plural form. It is a remarkable example of the themes we are discussing, one in which Barker would find confirmation for some of her theses.

Returning to the fourfold, the *Papyrus of Ani* (a version of the *Book of the Dead* dating from about 1250 BC) preserves a record of this realm: It is a rectangular lake of fire with four baboons markings its vertices. The same principle inspires the motif of cube-shaped thrones in Egyptian sculpture.[47] In India these protectors of the cosmic mountain are

---

44   Plato, *Timaeus*, 33c, 100–1.

45   As sources for the Hebrew understanding of Lady Wisdom, Barker cites *Ben Sira* and the *Wisdom of Solomon*.

46   My italics: "There are far more problems recovering the Lady than with other aspects of Old Testament study. The first problem is that *the primary sources in the Hebrew Scriptures were transmitted for the most part by the heirs of the Deuteronomists*, and so the Lady has disappeared or survived only as an abomination.... The second of the problems is that *when the canon of the Hebrew Scriptures was formed* after the destruction of the second temple, the *key texts for the Lady, such as Ben Sira, were not included.* They only survived through transmission in the Greek Scriptures that were adopted by the Church. The third problem is that *when Protestant scholars in Europe began to translate the Scriptures into the vernacular, they adopted the Hebrew canon,* and thus excluded the Lady yet again. Since it was largely Protestant scholars who developed modern critical study of the Bible, they worked with a canon that did not include the Lady, a Hebrew text that had obscured her, and an innate suspicion of anything that smacked of Rome and Mary." Barker, *The Great High Priest: The Temple Roots of Christian Liturgy*, 232–33.

47   Kazimierz Michalowski, *Great Sculpture of Ancient Egypt* (New York City: Reynal, 1978), 97.

known as the four divine kings who look out from Mount Meru in the cardinal directions,[48] Mount Qaf in Persian and Arabic traditions,[49] and in China they are springs at the Kunlun Mountain, fountain of the four rivers which souse the earth's quarters,[50] the four rivers mentioned by Socrates in Plato's *Phaedo* (Oceanus, Acheron, Pyriphlegethon and Cocytus)[51] or the four streams of milk Ymir observes from the primordial cow *Auðumbla in Norse mythology*. The macrocosmic character of the central mountain and its four rivers is pointed out by Plato who writes in the Phaedo that Pyriphlegethon is associated with anger, we can therefore deduce the four moods (melancholic, sanguine, choleric and phlegmatic or the four medieval virtues of prudence, fortitude, temperance and justice) in these rivers and the mountain as human being. The tradition would predate Plato:

> In his commentary on the Phaedo myth Damascius explains Plato's selection of four underworld rivers—unusual from the point of view of Homeric tradition—as a sign of his indebtedness to Orphism. He states that a similar arrangement of underworld rivers was described 'at some length' by Orpheus; and he adds on Proclus's testimony, that according to 'Orphic tradition' it was interpreted symbolically by correlating each river with an element.[52]

The four rivers of Eden appear above one as one enters the Cathedral at Aachen built by the re-founder of Rome in the west, Charlemagne. If this modern mosaic is a reconstruction of a medieval-era piece, it may suggest a parallel to the four sacred buildings at four rivers of Charlemagne's Empire: Cologne (the Rhine), Maastricht (the Maas, a Basilica), Aachen (the Meuse) and Paris (the Seine). All except the cathedral of Cologne belong to Mary (indeed, Aachen was the first Cathedral dedicated to Mary north of the Alps), and Cologne includes a St. Mary's Chapel. The feminine character of sacred rivers and mountains is consistent across traditions.

The king looks at each of the corners, each of the subtle elemental powers, and performs a rite of banishing towards them, entreating these

---

48   John C. Huntington, J. and Dina Bangdel, *The Circle of Bliss: Buddhist Meditational Art* (Chicago: Serindia Publications, 2003), 82.

49   Since Qaf is presented as surrounding the earth in some accounts, it includes the four cardinal points: "*traditions specifically describe the mountain Qaf* as the mountain surrounding our universe and as formed entirely of emerald." And the dimension of the cities beyond Qaf—Jabarsa and Jabalqa—in al-Tabari's histories, "express quaternity," like the Heavenly Jerusalem (Corbin, *Spiritual Body and Celestial Earth: From Mazdean Iran to Shi'ite Iran*, 73-74).

50   Tony Allan and Charles Phillips, *Ancient Chinese Myths and Beliefs* (New York City: Rosen Publishing Group, 2012), 36.

51   Plato, *Phaedo*, trans. E. M. Cope (Cambridge: Cambridge University Press, 1875), 112e-113d, 100-1.

52   Kingsley, *Ancient Philosophy, Mystery and Magic*, 120.

cardinal beings to join his cause and help him send away untoward influences, dismissing all that might deviate him and usurp the place of the Lord in his desire. The Jayakhya-Samhita teaches that when the Sadasiva is visualized on His throne,[53] a protective wall must be erected around Him and repeated purges performed in "the directions,"[54] presumably the four corners.

Crucified to the Throne

The king may now proceed to the throne. If he is to be born again, he first has to die, just as a seed has to be buried like the dead before it can grow (John 12:24). The Duat is a place of torment in which souls are subjected to beings with "alarming or grotesque names."[55] The grotesques guarding cathedrals, the gargoyles protecting water in fountains, these are alive here, revealed as the same Titanic villains that ripped Dionysus to shreds, the god that murdered Osiris and the maddened women who attacked Orpheus. Just as Set is Osiris's brother, and just as Orpheus was driven to homosexuality by grief for his lost wife, fleeing from women only to be killed by them, so too do these mystical torturers take the form of the king's own double, his own mental specters, the things he fears and loathes, the things he wants to suppress for the sorrow they bring.

It may be at this point that the king hears a voice offering him a path forward. The chance to make a deal. To be empowered. He should offer up the sacrificial beast he has brought, but not as a symbol of self-sacrifice, or of the beneficent Lord who gives forth his bounty. Rather, it is to be food for powerful spirits who will favor him in return. And yes, he should embrace new life, the dawning of wisdom. But this new life within him is to be a god, a principality, an angel whose desire is to inhabit the flesh of the monarch, and who, in return, will give him knowledge and influence, the kingdoms of the earth. Is it the specter of his own ego, the vacuum of worldly attachments sucking him into non-being? Is it the guardian angel, the tutelary deity, of his realm, who has become desirous of human tabernacle and human pleasure? Is it some hungry demon cunningly interspaced between the king and higher realms at this so crucial a juncture?

Writes the 3rd century Zosimos of Panopolis, emphasizing agreement between his Egyptian teachings (the *Treaty of Isis to her Son Horus*) and the Jewish Book of Enoch on fallen angels or Nephilim (which he calls "overseers"):

> In former days, powerful men kept the overseers at bay. In order to receive prayers, the overseers "hid" (ekrupsan) the art of natural tinctures [natural or edifying alchemy] and replaced them with a

53   Flood, *The Tantric Body: The Secret Tradition of Hindu Religion*, 143.
54   Ibid., 188.
55   Pinch, *Magic in Ancient Egypt*, 34.

"non-natural" one (aphusikon), asking for sacrifices in exchange for success in these tinctures. After a "revolution of the astrological zones (klimatōn)" and a war, the human race disappeared from "this zone" (ek tou klimatos ekeinou). The temples were deserted and the sacrifices offered to the overseers were consequently neglected. Contacting those left as if in dreams and sending them omens, the overseers continued to exchange success in tincture for the offering of sacrifices.[56]

How many nations have fallen into idolatry—how many kings have thought themselves gods, how many bloody rites installed, how many cults of state tyranny have blighted the earth—all because initiates took this terrible deal? "Have you come to die and be reborn? Do you search for Wisdom's Womb? Then offer mother Nature death, that she may reward you with life."

If we think the world a primal chaos, if we ignore that matter is always already formed, that there is no primordial formless substrate (a notion both quantum physics and St. Gregory of Nyssa dissuade us from), we will tend to fear nature and anticipate her entropic hunger through sacrifice. "What is your purpose here," the demonic voice persists, "to be reborn as a great one? To be a proper bridegroom to your kingdom, and sire powerful heirs? We can give you powerful heirs, and knowledge with which to rule."

Now the young initiate remembers his mother's words. As a child, she told him stories of foreign suitors. Men of renown, princes whose people praised them as gods, magnates possessed by ancient spirits. All these the queen mother rejected, for her son and future lord of the realm was not to be under their influence.

> In the Enochian myth, which is based on Genesis 6:1–4, the angels mate with human women and beget a race of giants called the Nephilim. Isis's claims [in the myth Zosimos relates] that such breeding is "against the order of nature" and "engenders monsters" are in full agreement with the sentiments of the Jewish scriptures.[57]

William Blake intuited such a degradation. For Blake the theophanic story of Moses and the Burning Bush is at odds with Mosaic law as passed down. Yet Blake precisely points to tree-worship and human sacrifice as a degeneration (one from the Age of Moloch, as he calls it, and not new to the Age of Jehovah in which Moses lived), so he is neither celebrating a pre-Josianic Hebrew rite or a reformed Deuteronomic legalism, but directing us to the Gospel proper (which he views as perennial, the Ur-religion).

---

56 Olivier Dufault, *Early Greek Alchemy, Patronage and Innovation in Late Antiquity* (Berkley: University of California, 2019), 129.
57 Shannon L. Grimes, *Zosimos of Panopolis: Alchemy, Nature and Religion in Late Antiquity* (Syracuse University Dissertation. 2003), 1056.

This agrees with Barker, who at one point refers to the original Adamic covenant as not including blood sacrifice. Neither Enoch nor Adam offer blood, but incense in *Jubilees* (2:20; 2:28). And whereas she finds a reference to blood sacrifice in Exodus (22:29), Hosea (6.6–7) presents the Lord as saying "I desire steadfast love, not sacrifice, and knowledge of the angels, rather than burnt offerings. But like Adam they transgressed the covenant". When our awareness is divorced from the phenomenal (when *Chit* and *Ananda* are not united, in Indian terms), we perceive the cosmos or nature as a vast other, and we desire to appease nature through sacrifices in order to anticipate and placate its chaotic power. This is what Blake calls "female will" and "the Druidic age." The reaction against it in Roman and Mosaic legalism would be a male equivalent to the prior female nature cult, and the Gospel would heal both. Addendum III explores this further.

If our king gives in to these profane sacrifices, he engages with idolatry, the path of Blake's Druidic bloodshed, the post-Adamic covenant of sacrifice in Barker. If he runs away and does without initiation, ruling from his ego, he falls into iconoclasm, a statist legalism. But if he attains the true initiation, then he may act as an icon. And indeed, he recalls his teachers, recites the exorcistic psalms of his people, and refuses the demonic attack.

Now he looks upon the throne. All about Osiris, the Demiurge, the Ancient of Days, is a fire scolding the would-be monarch and ghouls clawing at his flesh. They are the monsters Heaven employs to test its saints. Fear is too heavy a thing to take into the second birth, and must be exited, exorcised, brought out, scrutinized and discarded if one is to approach the throne of resurrection. It is a necessary rending apart of the initiate, taking each limb of his body away until he realizes that the essence which remains is not reducible to this or that part, but is beyond parts: it is non-spatial, consciousness itself.

Ritual death is entry into the metaxy, which in western occultism is named the Abyss, and which is well known to the hesychasts and saints. It is the place of him who prays, with Job,

> I am counted with them that go down into the pit…whom thou rememberest no more: and they are cut off from thy hand. Thou hast laid me in the lowest pit, in darkness, in the deeps. Thy wrath lieth hard upon me, and thou hast afflicted me with all thy waves. (Psalm 88, 4–7)

"All thy waves" are the chaotic waters, reality's substratum interpreted as pure chaos. Job feels he has been made an abomination. Again, it is a wrath like water, arbitrary movements of formless substance, except for their malevolence.

> I am afflicted and ready to die from my youth up: while I suffer thy terrors I am distracted. Thy fierce wrath goeth over me; thy terrors have cut me off. They came round about me daily like water; they compassed me about together. (Psalm 88, 15–17)

As the veil of distractions is allowed to fall, the mind apotropaically throws up its worst fears, as if to anticipate the emptiness, for who knows what monsters populate emptiness? Indeed, tradition teaches that engaging in spiritual struggle excites our enemies, "[i]f you cultivate prayer, be ready for the attacks of demons and endure them resolutely; for they will come at you like wild beasts and maltreat your whole body" writes Evagrios the Solitary in his treatise *On Prayer* (91), adding (92–99):

> ...do not be alarmed. Should you see even some loathsome and bloody figure, do not panic; but stand fast, boldly affirming your faith, and you will be more resolute in confronting your enemies. He who bears distress patiently will attain joy, and he who endures the repulsive will know delight. Take care that the crafty demons do not deceive you with some vision. He who practices pure prayer will hear the demons crashing and banging, shouting and cursing; yet he will not be overwhelmed or go out of his mind. But he will say to God: "I will fear no evil, for Thou art with me" (Ps. 23:4), and other words of this kind. At the time of such trials, use a brief but intense prayer. If the demons suddenly threaten to appear out of the air, to make you panic and *to take possession of your intellect*, do not be frightened and pay no attention to their threats. For they are trying to terrify you, to see if you take notice of them or scorn them utterly.

"To take possession of your mind," is the intent of the enemy during this great trial. The guardian of the abyss comes forth, the vapors of the void, the fog of war. We are also fighting a specter of ourself, as Blake would say. The "Existential Self at the last gasp," for "the 'personality' on the brink of the Abyss will do anything, say anything and find any excuse to avoid taking this disintegrating step into 'non-being.'"[58] Aleister Crowley described this as

> more or less...the gap in thought between the Real, which is ideal, and the Unreal, which is actual. In the Abyss all things exist, indeed, at least *in posse*, but are without any possible meaning; for they lack the substratum of spiritual Reality. They are appearances without Law. They are thus Insane Delusions.[59]

But although this "is not really an individual," since "[t]he Abyss is empty of being," it is,

> filled with all possible forms, each equally inane, each therefore evil in the only true sense of the word—that is, meaningless but malignant, in so far as it craves to become real. These forms swirl

---

58   Grant Morrison, "Pop Magic!" In: Richard Metzger, *Book of Lies: The Disinformation Guide to Magick and the Occult* (New York, NY: Disinformation Books, 2003).
59   Aleister Crowley, *Little Essays Towards Truth*, "Man: Neschamah" (Phoenix AZ: Falcon Press, 1996), 13.

senselessly into haphazard heaps like dust devils, and each such chance aggregation asserts itself to be an individual and shrieks, "I am I!" though aware all the time that its elements have no true bond; so that the slightest disturbance dissipates the delusion just as a horseman, meeting a dust devil, brings it in showers of sand to the earth.

Evagrios says not to visualize anything at all, but to keep the prayerful attention fixed on the intellect. We must practice *nepsis*, wakefulness. The trial involved in this womb-like cave of rebirth relates to what the Bible calls "without form and void" (Gen.1:2), but which is so "not in the sense of the absence of form and forms but only in the sense of their unrevealedness."[60] Hippolytus writes in *The Refutation of All Heresies*:

> ... the perfect Word of the light on high, having been made like the beast, the serpent, entered into the unpurified womb, beguiling it by its likeness to the beast, so that it might loose the bands which encircle the Perfect Mind which was begotten in the impurity of the womb by the first-born of the water, (to wit) the serpent, the beast. This ... is the form of the slave and this the need for the descent of the Word of God into the womb of a Virgin. But it is not enough, he says, that the Perfect Man, the Word, has entered into the womb of a virgin and has loosed the pangs which were in that darkness. But in truth after entering into the foul mysteries of the womb, He was washed and drank of the cup of living bubbling water, which he must needs drink who was about to do off the slave-like form and do on a heavenly garment.[61]

In Sufism, we find the terms *nafs* (ego) and *fana'* (annihilation), where the spiritual life is a moving from former to latter, a descent from a mountain into a valley, as Ibn al-Arif says. The Spanish *muladi*[62] Ibn al-Husayn Ibn Qasi gives us the image of two mountains separated by a valley, which we can understand as Ibn al-Arif's valley of fana', the two mountains being the high place of the nafs and the true elevation of the Divine, between which is a gap that the Sufi must leap over. The Sufi's path is therefore different from the narrow shadow-covered passage between the mountains, a merely dogmatic (exoterically religious) trek whose route may never lead up the mountains (neither to the false elevation of ego nor, however, to the true elevation of the Divine):

> In order to cross this chasm (and thereby reach God) one must first destroy the self by leaping into the abyss—essentially, a mystical suicide of all desires. In this way, the mystic becomes nothing

---

60   Bulgakov, *The Comforter*, 202.
61   Hippolytus, *Philosophumena, or The Refutation of all Heresies*, trans. F. Legge (London: Society for Promoting Christian Knowledge, 1921), "Book V: The Ophite Heresies, III: The Sethiani," 216, 164–65.
62   Local convert to Islam.

and consequently crosses the gap between himself and God, thus becoming everything.[63]

And,

...the ultimate goal of the mystic...is to achieve this condition of self-destruction (fana) as the prelude to its restoration to its original condition of eternity (baqa), from which creation in time has robbed it.[64]

We will see the importance of the bull as symbol of the sun and of the initiate later on, but for now we should recall the symbol of a cave, a crater wherein the initiate incubates and from which he rises in a womb-like chariot. This place of death and rebirth is alike the Holy Grail, which collected Christ's blood but is also identified as the bowl from which Jesus ate lamb during the last supper—it is the place where we consume ourself.

In the underground cave the initiate faces an externalization of his fears (the ancient Taoist practice of spending days in total darkness is a perfect systematized example of this ordeal). During this phase, the incubation chamber is a labyrinth and initiation or the cosmic bull (of Mithraism)/sun-bull (initiation is alike birth from the goddess Hathor as bull-god Apis, etc.) is a scourge, the minotaur of the labyrinth:[65] "The true purpose of the myth is revealed: the goddess through her agent strikes the great solar bull in its cave. The labyrinth is the cave of the sun..."[66] We are the sun that will be reborn from the goddess, but after enduring the non-entity, the minotaur, who usurps the image of initiation, the solar bull. The principle according to which the goddess Juno first opposes and later embraces heroes such as Hercules and Aeneas are the same: the solar or cosmic bull, already found in the *Rig Veda* as composing the entire cosmos, is first perceived as a separate and oppositional reality by the individual ego, but then is united with upon spiritual awakening. Juno is the underlying principle of reality and the cosmic bull is the male counterpart (Jove, the Demiurge) or, at a lower level, the sensible universe and true body of the initiate. The labyrinthine image is particularly apt, in that it reminds us that the constant meandering and complexifying tendency of the mind is not the path to spiritual victory.

---

63   Describing Ibn Qasi's doctrine: William Elliott, *The Career of Ibn Qasi as Religious Teacher and Political Revolutionary in 12th Century Islamic Spain*, PhD Thesis (Edinburgh: University of Edinburgh, 1979), 81.

64   Majid Fakhry, *A History of Islamic Philosophy* (New York: Columbia University Press, 1970), 267. Cited by Elliott, *The Career of Ibn Qasi*, 82.

65   Although, as we will see later, the minotaur can represent the excessive growth of the egoic false self which can be avoided by sacrificing the solar bull at an earlier phase.

66   Adrian Bailey, *The Caves of the Sun: The Origin of Mythology (Myth and Mankind)* (London: Jonathan Cape, 1998).

And the mad rushing non-entity wishes of one in confrontation with it "to obsess him, to live in his life."[67] Indeed, as one begins to perceive the infinite field of sheer gratuity, one is met also by the ego's vertigo and desire for retreat. This retreat takes the form of mental restriction, it seeks to save us from giving our life away, to save us from receiving life (Matthew 16:25). It is a compulsive if often oscillating fixity upon this or that idea which prevents contemplation, but in its course, should one allow oneself to be absorbed by some form of this fixity, it seems to end in chaotic despair; a tight control meant to placate the vision of gratuity which actually disintegrates order, for order and control and not the same. Obsession and chaos, though obsession seems single-pointed and definite while chaos seems ample and diffuse, are intimate, like a road to perdition and the cliff it leads to.

This experience of vertigo, or desire for retreat, of restriction, this Dark Night of the Soul, follows ascent up the mountain, and precedes a heavenly ascent and triumphant descent or return/resurrection. Often, we receive a taste of liberation before its stark and painful absence. In this case we must move closer, endure, but it is an endurance that resists not evil (for to obsess us as object of antagonism or otherwise is what it seeks), but overcomes evil with good. And in this overcoming with good even when good is occluded from us there is a tremendous creative work, a work of faith that imitates creation from nothing. We discover truth not neutrally, but by choosing what is true in us, in spite of us. We do not cross through solving problems, the complexes presented us, but through will and faith:

> The Atman (true self) cannot be attained by one devoid of strength or by excitement or by *tapas* (austerities, disciplines) devoid of *linga*.[68] But of the knower who strives with these aids, the *Atman* enters into the *Brahman* (the universal, divine self). (*Mundaka Upanishad*, 3.2.4, this is also the *Bhagavad Gita*'s teaching)

The gap, the *metaxy*, in order to be the place of the ideal, the autozoon, must be traversed in its negative image. Instead of sustaining creativity,

---

67   In part IV, chapter 66 of Aleister Crowley's *Confessions*. We are not commenting on the specifics of this passage or the operation they describe, only the principle illustrated. Of such overcoming and the inability of the habitual or calculating mind to see one through, the same author writes in the poem *Aha!*: "The path of the abyss runs through/Things darker, dismaller than death!/Courage and will! What boots their force?/The mind rears like a frightened horse..../Then I dropped my reasoning./Vacant and accursed thing!/By my Will I swept away/The web of metaphysic, smiled/At the blind labyrinth, where the grey/Old snake of madness wove his wild..."
68   Here Sri Sankara identifies *linga* with *Sanyusa* (the fourth stage of life, renunciation). Penance and discipline thus requiring genuine letting go, renunciation, of mental compulsion and activity. We may read into *linga* the meaning of the phallus (often a symbol of Shiva), creativity, virility and will-power, where austerity avoids morbid life-denying renunciation.

co-participation as a demiurge in the work of theurgy/demiurgy, here possibility is encountered as chaos. The minotaur of the labyrinth, of the *Bhagavad Gita*'s "thicket of delusion," St. John of the Cross's prison guards in the Dark Night of the Soul, a persecutor in a half-understood Kafkaesque complex of oppression, the monster-god and Specter in Blake's poetry. Just when we are ready to trust in the goodness of the Divine, our inner fear that reality is an oppressive or chaotic monstrosity will assail. The *metaxy* is filled with its parody, the insecurity of our own existential self, which will try to sustain itself on the law, what St. Paul calls the Elementals, on ritual religious prescription or mental habits. But as the *Bhagavad Gita* warns, we cannot use these for support. We must rest in faith, on the true content of the metaxy the autozoon, the harmonious blueprint of reality seen aright as ordered and beautiful, for when *Chit* encounters *Sat* (reflexive awareness encounters Being), it knows Joy (*Ananda*).

To the initiate there comes a vision of an enthroned monarch: "No farther, young prince. Go no farther now. Rest here with your god. I will no vainglories for you, no worldly duties. Return not and hope not and pray not for bounty, neither you nor your kingdom will have it. Stay here, secluded in contemplation, for holy is the renouncer of toil and joy." So speaks the vapor of the void, formed perilously into the silhouette of a lordly host, the very "lifeless dejection" Lord Krishna warns against in the Gita, and against which one's weapon is a joyful certainty. The ancient fiend lodged in the back of our mind, clawing at every beauty we perceive with moralistic gossip, for beauty is too much a surrender into un-conflicted selfhood, wherein that fiend exists not: "You see the abyss of joy? After me is deluge, so go no farther than me. Solid land is a well-kept law. Solid land is a mental fixity, for what is the soul and immortality if not a densely weaved obsession? Lay out your hope, all trust in goodness, lay out all things in the hopeless, faithless surrender that is my altar. Trust not in prayer nor in Divine mercy, but give all up and stay safe in the laws of holiness. Lay out especially that emanation, that work of creative glory, which men fulfil in love of woman, in pleasure unrestrained, slay all soft and easy things. Pleasure is sin."

So it speaks, for its way is "delighting in cries and tears and clothed in holiness and solitude" (Blake, *Jerusalem*, I, 10, 48). The initiate shrinks at the prospect of a life spent in hermitage, away from all bright and happy things, "Withering the Human Form by laws of sacrifice for sin" (Jerusalem, II, 49, 25). But the future king believes not in that vision of fear, and will give himself over to the abysmal ego-death in faith of its being a womb of mercy. He takes the fear into himself as into a furnace, and feels himself burn there, like Christ on the cross he endures through the moment of perceived abandonment, he consumes in himself that anti-god (*Eli, Eli, lama sabachthani*). Death is tolerated here because it is utterly denied in resurrection.

As we have said before, if this follows Daniel's vision, then it is the end of the idolatry of God the Father as that enthroned Ancient of Days, and the imminent communality of the kingdoms of the earth which, in Daniel, the Son inherits. Apart from a prophecy, quoting Psalm 22, the cry on the cross is a lesson that we will experience the lack (suffering) of that which we have chosen (Life), and must endure and ignore such appearances to prove we are already beyond appearances. Further, it implies the reabsorption of the image of the external deity, the psychological support of the large *other*, into the immediacy of our own felt presence (an immediacy that can be facilitated by intense physical pain). Relationship to the other is real, but must come after realizing full selfhood. Then can the Divine be related to without fear of idolatry, knowing It is us (like Vyasa, after ages of perfect self-absorbed meditation, deciding to return to phenomena, and to write the *Vedas*), and then can true, non-ego-driven community be experienced: for it is after the cross that Jesus tells his disciples not to cling to him, and to find God by gathering together in love, receiving the Spirit.

"When your intellect crosses beyond the thicket of delusion, then you shall become disgusted with that which is yet to be heard and with that which has been heard (in the *Veda*)." The *Bhagavad Gita* (II:52[69]) here relates the crossing not to a theistically prescribed behavior but to the efforts of the initiate, adding "When your intellect stands fixed in deep meditation, unmoving, disregarding Vedic doctrine, then you shall attain self-realization" (II:53) emphasizes that the locus of action is internal, not external. The initiate is not using Vedic religion as support. We are not looking for external confirmation because all signs are averse anyway, the mind's fears and insecurities are projected out, and so we must have true faith, the kind that has internalized the promise and no longer needs it repeated. The seeker must be as the soul in Limbo (Bardo) in the Tibetan Book of the Dead, unafraid of those wrathful deities, knowing they are merely a projection.

Like the Gospel teaching that we are forgiven when we forgive, we cannot rely on receiving a *metanoia* (*change of consciousness*) while the mind remains busy (albeit with lofty religious content): we will receive if we believe it and internalize so fully as to paradoxically have it already, "...whatever you ask in prayer, believe that you have received it, and it will be yours" (Mark 11:24). And as reality is not an ontology of violence, we can only step into our own redemption as co-demiurges, co-heirs, if we renounce all resentment, all debts, for prayer requires that we follow the command "If you keep my commands, you will remain in my

---

69   Winthrop Sargeant's translation, which helpfully draws attention to certain terms and their context. Namely "yada te mohakalilam" as "when of thee the delusion-thicket; "srutivipratipanna te" as "disregarding ritual-centered revelation (i.e., of the *Veda*), of thee."

love...whatever you ask in my name the Father will give you. This is my command: Love each other" (John 15: 5–17). Mercy to them who show mercy, the tree of life to them who plant it, the true temple to them that build it: here is the whole meaning of demiurgy/theurgy, that is, receiving heavenly ascent by participating in the heavenly patterns (the Egyptian-rooted Proclean Platonism we have been emphasizing).

Sacrifice of the Cosmic Animal

The king has brought with him an offering. Animal death often precedes the initiate's ritual death. A pet to represent his ritual slaughter, to die vicariously. Dismemberment is carried out at the feet of the throne. But the true sacrifice is a self-sacrifice. The sacrificial animal analogizes the body of the initiate and its death and dismemberment (sometimes given out as a meal) represents the initiate's ritual death and realization of a wider identity. It is also a manifestation of the Divine, which gives forth to sustain the people. Just as the sacrificial animal is sometimes eaten, the ritually dead and reborn person identifies his body as the whole cosmos and, more especially, as a political community, that is, as those who participate in the eating of the sacrifice, including it in their body, are included in the sacrificed king's body.

Identification between slain animal and king is explicit in Vedic rites, "[i]n the Ashvamedha ritual of the Sanskrit tradition, after the sacrifice of the horse the ranking queen was symbolically married to the sacrificed horse."[70] Just as the dismembered parts of Heaven's bull are used to make or sustain the city by Gilgamesh in Mesopotamian myth and Mithraism, the Vedic horse sacrifice of *Ashvamedha* involves having a horse wander around a territory, during which time any pretender may challenge the armed company accompanying this horse, following which, if the king to whom that sacrifice belongs is undefeated, he may slay it and be considered legitimate. The horse is therefore identified with the kingdom it has wandered through and its presence there with the king's rulership, so that the link between king and sacrificial animal and specifically between the latter and the king's authority is quite clear. Equivalents to this horse sacrifice exist in other cultures. However, the bull is also a cosmic animal in the *Vedas*.[71]

Zagreus, son of Jove, is slain at Mount Ida in the form of a bull and attains immortality thanks to Minerva. Dionysus, of the same parentage, born a horned child, is likewise ripped apart by titans and resurrected by Rhea. This reminds us of the bull god and son of Hathor, the Egyptian Apis. Pythagoras is said by Porphyry to have performed a sacrifice at

---

70   Thomas Gamkrelidze and Vjaceslav Ivanov, *Indo-European and the Indo-Europeans: A Reconstruction and Historical Analysis of a Proto-Language and Proto-Culture* (New York: Walter de Gruyter, 1995), 402.

71   Leroy A. Campbell, *Mithraic Iconography and Ideology* (Leiden: Brill, 1968), 129.

Mount Ida,[72] as did King Solomon at the temple (2 Chronicles 7), remembering that the temple corresponds to mount Sinai. In a heartwarming passage from the Gospel according to Luke (22:8-15), Jesus orders his disciples to prepare the meal of Passover, lamb, wherein an animal is slain for religious purposes, saying to them "I have eagerly desired to eat this Passover with you before I suffer." Here, Jesus is the model, the prototype, for the initiate. The animal is eaten, connecting the religious symbol according to which its slaughter is analogous to the initiate's facing death, with the immediate utility of feeding the community. Here the Passover sacrifice is not salvific like the self-sacrifice taught by Christ, but is maintained as communal feast. This connection emphasizes the initiate's social function, for his initiation benefits the community and is not an isolated individual pursuit. Ritual death renders one able to do good for others, like a good king. Further, the Passover lamb becomes part of the disciples' bodies when they eat it, just as the initiate will realize identity with others, and with the whole cosmos, all a part of him, himself a part of all.

The imagery according to which the sacrificial lamb and divine monarch are identified is clarified by Christian imagery. The four corners, like the four arms of the cross, are the crucible within which the aspirant dies, is crucified or quartered, before resurrection, like Christ, the fifth point that is the axis mundi in between the four corners of the earth, the fifth essence, quintessence (the caesar leading his quadriga of four horses, the pharaoh shooting four flaming arrows during his investiture, the Turkish patriarch Oghuz Khagan sending letters in the four directions announcing himself ruler, etc.).

The four arms of the Christian cross indicate a quartering of the personality, where that which can pass from death to resurrection is the Self which was not contained in any part, a hidden center. Indeed, Christ's garments are divided upon his crucifixion into four parts, so He is in a sense quartered (John 19:23). Its center, the *Sacred Heart* in Catholic terms, in the middle of the cross, the essential self, preserved through dismemberment—that blood collected in the Holy Grail—is invisible, as the Upanishads state repeatedly, for it is not a manifest part to be removed from other parts, but what is left when those parts are absent, on the basis of which the primordial man can be reconstituted as cosmos, the Christ can resurrect. This relates to the absence of a caste corresponding to the heart in the *Rig Veda* (other parts of the cosmic man make the castes, but not the heart) so that the *Mahabharata* can state that all castes are equal (for none is the heart, none is the center) and the teaching from the Gospel of John that it is good for Christ to be absent, leaving his disciples, so that the Spirit of truth may come to them.

That monarchy is understood across traditions to require the ritual death of its possessor, who can thus exit the particular, including his body,

---

72   Porphyry, *Life of Pythagoras*, XVII, 126.

and receive the universals that his office requires he act in accordance with, reveals some of the meaning of the Christian imagery in which royalty and sacrifice are joined together, such as the crown of thorns or the cross which is sometimes referred to in Christian texts as a throne. To link symbols of holy poverty and endurance to political leadership is key. The king must become absent just as Christ became so.

Mesopotamian religion contains this paradigm in its Tammuz or Dumuzid liturgies, which describe the "death of the king-god," "his triumphal return"[73] and includes a "list of deified kings of the third dynasty of Ur" (22nd and 21st centuries BC) who are said to participate in the god king's return and whose historicity is archeologically attested to.[74] As John Milbank writes: "[i]f Christ is to return, then so too is Arthur, so also Charlemagne, Frederick II and King Sebastian of Portugal."[75] The empirical king unites with the archetype. The triumphal return of Tammuz, or Christ, is that of the king who united with him, or the resurrection of the faithful.

There is evidence for a "... connection between the establishment of the office of kingship and the well-documented elaboration of elite death rituals"[76] in Mesopotamia between 2,600 and 2,230 BC (Early Dynastic periods IIIa and IIIb). These death rituals refer to actual funerals, but may constitute a response to the expectation of the king's return (storing up, as they do, provisions for the corpse) stemming from the above paradigm.

In light of this necessary dismemberment and consequent return with new insight, it may be stated that political leadership and generally spiritual initiation is always Christological. The Bronze Age Aegean and Near East provide clear examples. Drawing on Ugaritic and Hittite equivalents, for example, Nanno Marinatos agrees with Martin Nilsson that the mummy-like image on the Minoan Hagia Triada sarcophagus is a dead king.[77] Marinatos adds that the imagery associated with this figure is not consistent with a single personage and mere recollection, but with a religious, mythical observance.[78] The dead king to whom reverence is paid, and who is alive despite having died, and through devotion to whom the present king may likewise attain a sort of death and new life is, in all these respects, remarkably Christ-like.

According to Gregory Shaw's reading of Iamblichus,[79] this sacrificial

---

73   Samuel H. Hooke, "Myth, Ritual and History." *Folklore* 50(2), (1939): 137-47, 138 (Taylor & Francis, Ltd. on behalf of Folklore Enterprises).

74   Ibid., 141.

75   John Milbank, *Beyond Secular Order: The Representation of Being and the Representation of the People* (Chichester: Wiley Blackwell, 2013), 250.

76   Andrew Cohen, *Death Rituals, Ideology, and the Development of Early Mesopotamian Kingship* (Boston: Brill, 2005), 3.

77   Marinatos, *Minoan Kingship and the Solar Goddess: A Near Eastern Koine*, 46.

78   Ibid., 48.

79   Gregory Shaw, "The Sphere and the Altar of Sacrifice." In: M. Berchman and

dynamic opens linearity (the sides of a square or rectangle, the shape of the Duat), which represents finitude, into infinity (symbolized by the circle, points on whose circumference cannot be said to be closer to or farther from its ending or its beginning, there being no vertices, which is why it illustrates infinity). Thusly is the underworld rectilinear and sacrificial whereas the celestial dome and sun are round. Descent into the former is a closing and ascent into the latter is an opening.[80]

The fact that the infernal throne-room is a fiery abode which is both ennobling and also a place of imprisonment and torture, or rather purgation, points to the Orthodox Christian understanding of hell as the presence of the same divine light as Heaven, only experienced by the sinner, the soul in need of humility. Hell is the black lightning that haunts a selfish soul in William Golding's novel *Pincher Martin*, subtitled "A Study of Self and Its Terror of Negation," taking its limbs and senses away, leaving a stump like a dismembered Osiris, storing gifts it would bestow where the egoist but ready to open up and resist not. In a sense this is the *Eli, Eli, lama sabachtani* moment, Jesus crying out on the cross for pain of feeling abandoned by God, but as one who does not surrender, does not accept his quartering or crucifixion upon the four corners and therefore does not discover the quintessence.[81]

The same cry that is the body and mind asking us to reengage with them, suggesting to us that the detachment of meditation is a forsaking of the works of the mind, an abandoning of the pities and beauties of the empirical self. This we must ignore, just as we must ignore our own temptation to cry the same cry when we notice that the path of spiritual heroism has begun to take from us that external psychological support which we previously had in our image of God, and in the pious scriptures and rituals that sustained us.

Oxen of the Sun, or the Horn of Heaven

The pre-incarnate king, the lamb slain from the foundations of the earth according to John's Apocalypse (13:8), is represented by both the spiritual aspirant willing to die and the animal he brings to slay. In the

---

J. Finamore (eds.), *History of Platonism: Plato Redivivus* (New Orleans, LA: University Press of the South, 2003).

80 It follows, then, that the base of temples or cathedrals be square, representing the four-edged Duat, whereas the copula is circular, like the solar disk or horizon line. The one fire is subterranean, the other celestial. The rectilinear base, further, is stable, for it may rest still on any side, whereas the sphere will tend to roll, as does the sun ever around the earth. These two shapes therefore provide a recurring symbolic polarity (René Guénon, *Reign of Quantity* [Hillsdale: Sophia Perennis, 2001], 137–39).

81 The cry on the cross is actually a quote from Psalm 22, which goes on to assert faith in God: "But thou art he that took me out of the womb... Deliver my soul from the sword; my darling from the power of the dog.... Save me.... They shall come, and shall declare his righteousness unto a people that shall be born, that he hath done this."

Mediterranean world the sacrifice of choice was often a bovine. The ox is a telluric animal in that it ploughs the field, it works the earth, and so it's being revealed as Heavenly communicates the mystery of identity of samsara with nirvana, of creation as the Creator's names. In Christian tradition, St. Zeno of Verona reinterprets the constellation of Taurus as the meek sacrificial calf and so identifies the bull with Christ. This is the form taken by Greek, and specifically Minoan, tradition's equivalent to the Ancient of Days, in the myth of Jove becoming a white bull. This was also true of northern Europe, where the *aurochs* bull was a symbol of coming of age, so that the *Ur* rune may derive from this archaic bovine (one of its meanings being "wild ox"),[82] and south into ancient Iraq, where the bull of heaven is slayed by Gilgamesh.

The root Ur- (appearing from the Norse rune to Gilgamesh's city Uruk) is also related to the word *origin*, which is fitting, given that it is with a bull that the initiate's life begins again. Indeed, in Sumerian myth, the god Enki is said to have his origin or birth from a bull.[83] Assyrian monarchical sacrifice was also linked to the bovine.[84] Correspondingly, in the case of Vedic horse sacrifice, which confirms the king's authority, the horse is identified with the sun.[85] In the Zoroastrian *Bundahishn* (7:4) Tishtar becomes man, horse and bull, and is distinguished in brilliance, reminding us of the link between horse/bull sacrifice and the sun. In this same text (*Bundahishn,* 30:25) the resurrection of the dead occurs by a drink of *Haoma* (like the Vedic *Soma,* fruit of the tree of life) mixed with fat from the slain ox Hadhayosh.[86] Margaret Barker explores the evidence of sacred animals in the early Hebrew faith, highlighting humanoid figures with bovine heads found in archaeological digs, matching Ezekiel's descriptions, "the head of a calf on [Solomon's] throne in Jerusalem" (1 Kings 10:19), "elsewhere described as the throne of the Lord" (1 Chronicles 29:23), so that "the calf must have been an important symbol in the royal cult in Jerusalem."[87] And referencing 1 Enoch (89:12 and 90:37-38):

> Bovines were important in the Enoch tradition. All the patriarchs from Adam to Isaac were described as bulls, but from Jacob onward they were sheep. In the future, when the true temple was

82   Raymond I. Page, *Reading the Past: Runes* (Berkley, CA: University of California Press/British Museum, 1987), 15.

83   Alan W. Bernthal-Hooker, '*You Shall Know Yahweh': Divine Sexuality in the Hebrew Bible and Beyond,* PhD thesis (Exeter: University of Exeter, 2017), 66.

84   Mehmet-Ali Atac, *The Mythology of Kingship in Neo-Assyrian Art* (Cambridge: Cambridge University Press, 2010), 68.

85   Roshen Dalal, *Hinduism: An Alphabetical Guide* (New Delhi: Penguin Books India, 2010), 399.

86   Bundahishn, trans. Edward William West, from *Sacred Books of the East,* vol. 5 (Oxford: Oxford University Press, 1897).

87   Barker, *The Great High Priest: The Temple Roots of Christian Liturgy,* 231.

restored, first the Messiah and then all the generations would be transformed again into white bulls.[88]

As in Iranian tradition, the bull is a cosmic animal in the *Vedas*. Leroy Campbell lays this out with reference to the *Rig Veda*, noting that "...it is probable that the idea of a cosmic bull is considerably earlier" than the second millennium BC: "The Pardsanja ox of the thunderstorm creates the young brood and shoots of plants" and "nothing else is greater than the Ox which carries Heaven and Earth...."[89]

We may think of the above as rendering the cosmic body bull-shaped, *tauromorphic* (it can of course be described as a lamb, or cosmic Vedic horse, as well, but ultimately anthropomorphic). The Vedas include reference to the world-tree as well, and are connected to Iranian versions of an "Ox-horn tree with its surrounding wall and vegetation...located in the midst of the world-wide sea." Porphyry mentions Venus in connection with a cosmic bull in his commentary on the cave of the nymphs in Homer (this is one of the few sources for Roman Mithraism, as distinct from the ancient Iranian *Mithra* deity, though related): "...Mithras...is conveyed on Taurus of Aphrodite, as the bull also is a demiurgos and Mithras a *despotes* of genesis,"[90] Mithras is "riding the bull of Aphrodite because he is just like the bull the demiurgos and the Lord of generation,"[91] and "the Bull or Pneuma is the most divine element...the demiurgic stuff of the world."[92] Its relation to the sacrificing king or Mithra: "The bull a moisture was essentially generative and Mithra as fire was essentially ordering" (here Mithra is the demiurge, "creativity and ordering," and the bull is despot, "life-force," which is more consistent than the previous passage).[93] The bull as cosmic substance which

---

88   Margaret Barker, *The Mother of the Lord Volume I: The Lady in the Temple* (London: Bloomsbury, 2012), 157.

89   My italics: "The ancient Vedic poets sang of the Ox (Varsan) of fire and light (*Rig Veda* 4.I.II-12) which bellowed loud on the wide ways when Heaven and Earth built the two great worlds (*Rig Veda* 4.56.I), or of the Ox that shot out the thousand rays and mounted upward from the sea (*Rig Veda* 7.55.7). *The Pardsanja ox of the thunderstorm creates the young brood and shoots of plants.* His seed is the rain that impregnates mother earth and brings forth mankind and all other things (*Rig Veda* 6.101). In a rather obscure cosmological poem (*Rig Veda* 10.31) it is said that the Cow arose from the abundance that resides in the place of Asura, and asks whether Earth and Sky were constructed out of a forest or a great tree. 'Nothing is as great, *nothing else is greater than the Ox which carries Heaven and Earth....* Like a shaft he pierces through the Earth's habitation and strews living beings as the Wind strews the cloud; decked out like Varuna and Mitra, he causes the light to stream forth like fire in a forest.'" Leroy Campbell, *Mithraic Iconography and Ideology* (Leiden: Brill, 1968), 129.

90   Campbell, *Mithraic Iconography and Ideology*, 249.

91   Maarten J. Vermaseren, *Mithriaca III: The Mithraeum at Marino* (Leiden: Brill, 1982), 75.

92   Campbell, *Mithraic Iconography and Ideology*, 249.

93   Ibid., 248.

the hero or initiate uses to create the universe or attain cosmic identity, or as method of communion and realizing corporate unity like the last supper, echoes in the Gilgamesh myth, when the Mesopotamian hero distributes the parts of the slain bull of heaven.

On the bull's relation to Venus, comments Campbell: "The Aphrodite whose bull was also a Demiurgos of Genesis...can have little to do with the classical Greek Aphrodite."[94] But this is perhaps the celestial Venus, the Venus Caelestis. The connection may have to do with the position of the planet Venus in relation to the Taurus constellation,[95] but it also relates to our observations concerning the king (in this case, in the mold of Mithras) in relation to the morning star, Venus (as in the Psalms or *Aeneid*), because Venus announces the rising sun during part of its cycle. The hero is connected to the bull and to Venus, the morning star. This connection appears in the Gilgamesh myth too, as Gilgamesh receives the bull of heaven because of goddess Inanna. In Hebrew tradition, the bull was also the sacrificial animal whose blood was sprinkled by the priest emerging from the Holy of Holies, and in King Solomon's Temple the font rested on twelve oxen (1 Kings 7:23–26).

Ra rides on the Heavenly Cow, the initiate is a "falcon-bull,"[96] the "Memphite bull" or Apis being the image of the soul of Osiris.[97] Read the *Pyramid Texts* (334 and 405, rendered by Algis Uzdavinys):

> I have grasped your tail (or Ra in bull shape) for myself, for I am a god and the son of god...
>   O Ra...I am you and you are I...if you shine in me I will shine in you...for I am the eye of Yours which is on the horns of Hathor...[98]

In Mithraism slaying the cosmic animal and making the universe, like Odin from the body of Ymir (who fed on the milk of the cosmic cow), are connected, and so we have a body that is cosmic but not yet realized as such, and whose slaying allows its becoming realized as the substance of the whole universe. Here the initiate is both Mithras and the cosmic bull whose unpacked body is the cosmic body of the realized hero and is demiurgic, creative. "The sacrificial horse is a symbol of Prajapati and consubstantial with Prajapati [the Lord of Creation]...so that what is said to the horse is said to Prajapati 'face to face'...."[99] The initiate and the Lord of whom the initiate is an image, is both sacrificer and holy animal sacrificed. It is a kenotic creativity, but in these myths, the part

94   Ibid., 71.
95   Vermaseren, *Mithriaca III: The Mithraeum at Marino*, 75.
96   Uzdavinys, *Philosophy as a Rite of Rebirth: From Ancient Egypt to Neoplatonism*, 29.
97   Ibid., 105.
98   Ibid., 199.
99   Ananda Coomaraswamy, *The Essential Ananda K. Coomaraswamy*, ed. R. Coomaraswamy (Bloomington, IN: World Wisdom, 2004), footnote 22; Cf. 243.

of the initiate that does the ordering and the part that is dismembered are distinguished. These are the imagination, Los, and its Specter, in Blake's poetry. The animal, having four legs, contains the four elements we discussed, and its ordering occurs in the feminine shakti. We may also think of Virgil's Georgics and re-enlivening nature through ox sacrifice.

Apart from its initial context of ritual death, sacrifice can be understood as turning the injunction to give life away (Matthew 10:39) into an attitude of ongoing generosity. The cultivation of a sense of openness, porosity, detachment from what one holds and willingness to give things up, a breaking of the fearful psychology of hoarding and cultivating a sense of faith in receiving, a sense of abundance. This might have operated as a kind of sympathetic magic. The bottle of wine is smashed against the side of our ship in a spirit of levity and release, of ecstatic communing with the source to which we consign the thing, rather than in an anxious spirit of need, begging that it be accepted in return for a desired end.

Such acts may have the effect of reminding us of the porosity of our being with respect to other beings and the world around us. Such a realizing of lack of self-sufficiency, or, seen from another perspective, the will to experience a wider whole rather than the isolated whole of ourselves alone, can involve the enactment of loss, of opening up the self, which is to say, producing an apparent lack (the smashed bottle). Here, knowledge willingly participates in illusion. Ignorant states of being (perception of lack) are instrumentalized. *Maya* as magic rather than illusion. Every sacrifice is a self-sacrificing, an opening to kenotically experience manifestation.

This realization is active, a making of the cosmos. The sacred, cosmic or solar animal is like the human mind, which contains the whole pattern of creation, just as the Intellect, or pure consciousness, or inner will, is alike the agency that makes that universe. The mind can of course be as a wild animal, and needs to be tamed just like an animal, at which point we have slain its wildness and are free of its wondering attachments and repulsions, free to use it for good, creative, work. The Reflective Awareness (*Chit*) is free to reflect on Being (*Sat*) and therefore receive Joy (*Ananda*), because its substance (mental stuff, thought) is transparent, no longer turbulent, no longer oscillating and obfuscating its perception. Therefore, it can create from joy—the knowledge of Being which does not depend on thought—rather than legalistic, moralistic and sacrificial compulsion. This is borne out in the myth of the minotaur.

There is a positive reading of the animal-human chimera which is linked to the *homo sacer* of Roman law or werewolf of medieval codes: a human rendered animal in being cast out of the protection of the law, and thereby—in being outside the law—being like the sovereign king. We have these creatures of carnival who mark the lengthening days of the year and Hebrew inscriptions:

The inscriptions at Kuntillet 'Ajrud... seem to read: 'I bless you by
yhwh of Samaria and by 'srth'... accompanied by a rough drawing
of three figures.... Two of the figures are humanoid figures with
bovine heads, a male and a female, and these have been variously
explained. The most obvious explanation is that they were the
golden calves who represented the deities of Israel. We tend to
imagine the golden calves as life-like representations of the young
animal, but these strange humanoids may have been how they were
actually made. Ezekiel described similar creatures in his vision of
the throne (Ezek. 1.5-10).... When Jereboam set up shrines to
rival Jerusalem as centres of worship, he made golden calves and
set them at Bethel and Dan (1 Kgs 12.28-29), and there he offered
sacrifices to the calves (1 Kgs 12.32). Why attempt to rival Jerusalem in this way? When Jehu wiped out the cult of Baal he did not
destroy the calves (2 Kgs 10.28-29), and Solomon had the head of a
calf on his throne in Jerusalem (1 Kgs 10.19). Since this is elsewhere
described as the throne of the LORD (1 Chron. 29.23), the calf must
have been an important symbol in the royal cult in Jerusalem. The
two humanoids with bovine heads were probably yhwh and 'srth,
animals representing deities as does the Lamb in Christian art.[100]

The sacred king, as both sovereign and animal, is Agamben's *homo
sacer*, the *wulfesheud* we described earlier, like Christ denied by the sovereign authority and its law and given over to the mob for execution.
Agamben's linking of sovereign to *homo sacer* is consistent with the
use of animal symbols for sacred kings throughout traditions, and the
casting of the king in the role of sacrificed animal. Agamben deals with
the homo sacer as a creature of *zoe*, outside *bios*. But here, in the king's
taking up of the sacrificial animal who is outside the laws that protect
life in the human real, is finally denying the possibility of pure *zoe*—or
mere animal life—outside *bios*—or political, cultural, human life. This
is like Christ going outside the law—outside the law of Pontius Pilate
and indeed, outside the law as St. Paul speaks of it—revealing that the
utter dehumanization or death that dwells there is an illusion. Animals
exist not outside the human, and were part of Man's body until cruel
sacrifices separated them, as Blake declared. Animality is integrated and
transformed by humanity inside the initiate himself, *zoe* in *bios*. Writes
Porphyry in line with Blake:

But the Egyptian priests, through the proficiency which they made
by this exercise, and similitude to divinity, knew that divinity does
not pervade through man alone, and that soul is not enshrined
in man alone on the earth, but that it nearly passes through all
animals. On this account, in fashioning the images of the Gods,
they assumed every animal, and for this purpose mixed together
the human form and the forms of wild beasts, and again the

---

100   Barker, *The Great High Priest: The Temple Roots of Christian Liturgy*, 231.

bodies of birds with the body of a man...For they venerated the power of God which extends to all things through animals which are nurtured together, and which each of the Gods imparts. (*De Abstinentia* IV:9[101])

That the head is an animal's allows us to intuit the antitype of the minotaur: the human organism has defeated the chattering mind (the head) and made it into a domesticated pet, on one level, and a noble expression of nature/animality, for it no longer seeks to lead us astray as the thinking ego did. In this way, Egyptian depictions of animal-headed human figures may be equivalent to the headless Dionysus, or the god Ganesh, whose father, Shiva, rids him of his head and replaces it with that of a peaceful and wise animal, the elephant.

It is important to sacrifice this cosmic animal, to enter into a state of detachment and give forth creatively the whole cosmos from ourselves. Otherwise we are like king Minos, who does not slay the white bull which was given as a sign of his kingship, whereupon it breeds with his wife and gives forth a monster, the minotaur, that demands sacrifice and receives young boys and girls (failing the inner or *mental sacrifice*, as Blake calls it, we enter into *cruel sacrifices*): the legalistic, bartering economy of blood which represents the egoic consciousness seeking to assuage its existential insecurity with apotropaic acts. This legalistic mentality is well represented by the labyrinth, a thicket of thought in which we become lost when we rely on signs or reasons (the twin error of the Jews and Greeks in St. Paul) and are stalked by the minotaur of the mind, the compulsive ego and its ever-pressing need for appeasement. The beauty of the white bull we give forth to make the cosmos like Mithra, to be made royal like Minos.

The depths—the subconscious, the waters, Poseidon's domain—gift us a beautiful but wild creature analogous to the heavens (the white bull, a solar beast). We may show our spiritual royalty thereby, as Minos was to prove his legitimacy to rule. If we do not slay this beautiful idea, give it forth, create from it (the most beautiful idea of all being the idea of our own selves: the ego) and instead become fixated on it, obsessed, then our passions, our nature, soul—the wife of the king—breeds with it. Now we give rise to something monstrous, the Minotaur. The white bull is now our head, our whole mind is that beast, and the human part of us, the body, is usurped by it.

That path which avoids making ideas sacred (*sacrificing* them), and instead hordes them, wishes to keep them as they are, and ultimately falls into lust with them, is the path which leads to making the mind complicated, labyrinthine: the instinct that avoids being done with a beautiful

---

101   Thomas Taylor's translation. This has its correspondence in the body politic: "...also, a lion is worshipped as a God, and a certain part of Egypt, which is called Nomos, has the surname of Leontopolis [or the city of the lion], and another is denominated Busiris [from an ox], and another Lycopolis [or the city of the wolf]."

idea, wishing to keep rather than slay it, will forever vacillate, create extra steps, put off the true work, and thus builds up a maze of psychological motivations. It is the path of the Tibetan Book of the Dead's wrathful deities: the labyrinth prevents simple spiritual epiphany. Here we end up having to provide a different sort of sacrifice, that of infant joys, nascent energies: the young men and women the minotaur demands. Fixation on the ego keeps us from developing our faculties. The way out reverses the mistake of Minos and the queen—a weak man and abandoned woman: it is the way of Theseus and Ariadne working together. Theseus kills the monstrous ego by stabbing its throat, for we must cease listening to the ego's chatter in order to stop it. Theseus then finds his way out of the maze not by thinking but by feeling. He does not escape through the ego, through his own devices or by thinking, but by the sense of touch, following the thread given him by the feminine, the sensual.

But just as King Minos went astray, Theseus does likewise. He rejects Ariadne, who had helped him so. The reflexive faculty must take a new form after it defeats the ego. It receives a new identity, one worthy of the feminine. The reflexive mind is that which undergoes death and rebirth. By defeating itself in the form of ego, it recreates itself. It makes itself divine. Thus, to Ariadne comes a husband, a god. Specifically, the god of nature's renewal and ecstasy, Dionysus. She becomes his mate. This transformation is also indicated by the myth of Theseus's descent to Hades, from which realm he is rescued by Hercules.

We should not hold on to ourselves too tightly, we should not fall too passionately in love with our ideas. We should defeat the ego, and any strong or beautiful idea, at the outset, subduing its tendency to becoming autonomous from our will, keeping its automatic, instinctual, animal reflexes from hijacking us, slaying the beast, and thereby displaying the sovereignty of our will: "Do not despise the lamb, for without it, it is not possible to see the king. No one will be able to go in to the king if he is naked."[102] We could imagine that the historic church has at times lost sight of the king, however, and like King Minos's bride, has bred a monstrous ego by emphasizing the sacrificial animal over the spiritual royalty it is meant for.

In some sources (as in Robert Graves) the Cretan bull Hercules slays during his seventh trial is identified with the one Minos failed to sacrifice, and so a hero puts things right ultimately. The king is Hercules, Mithra (a successful Minos) and the lamb is the cosmic (white/solar) bull. We are not naked but clothed in the cosmic body, unpacked into the wider self, that is, made into a clothing. Failing this we breed our inner minotaur.

Our self must slay its minotaur-like need for sacrifices, for the young (like the children sacrificed to cruel Druidic rites in Blake's poetry, as a metaphor for works of art and joy being torn by a heavy moralism). We

---

102   *Nag Hamadi Codex II, 2–7, The Gospel of Philip*, 58:8–59:6, 157.

must slay and make the cosmos as our own body, we must be creative with it: "If you bring forth what is within you, what you bring forth will save you. If you do not bring forth what is within you, what you do not bring forth will destroy you" (*Gospel of Thomas*).

This bovine is often solar in character. The Cretans on whose island Europa and Jove united apparently referred to the sun as a bull,[103] the white color of which would represent luminescence. Jove is a solar god, and the initiate is a son of Europa and Jove's counterpart Juno includes the cow among her symbols. Zagreus, son of Jove, who also took the form of a bull at Ida and overcomes by the agency of the female wisdom deity, is associated with Cretan monarchical rites as well.

This does not discount the storm-king image Jove is typically taken to represent. For Minoans the divine king was a thunder god,[104] as well as solar.[105] The monarch is lightning. He is the active manifestation of the equanimous and ecumenical ray of the sun. The latter shines steadily on all from far above, whereas lightning comes from nearer storm clouds and touches down at particular spots, starts fires, gets involved in mortal life directly.

In any case, Jove is solar and, correspondingly, according to J. G. Frazer "[t]he moon rising from the sea was the fair maiden Europa coming across the heaving billows from the far eastern land of Phoenicia...."[106] Europa's evasiveness would have to do with the moon's distance from the sun, and their final union, culminating the chase, with the conjunction of the two during the interlunar period (between old and new moons), apparently considered an auspicious time for marriage ceremonies.[107] Lucian of Samosata also apparently considered Europa to be represented by the moon, understanding her as equivalent to the goddess Astarte (equivalent to Inanna, whose brother Utu is the sun-god, so she is a feminine counterpart to the solar, and is associated with planet Venus).

The etymology according to which Europa means wide-of-countenance would therefore relate specifically to the full moon (which gives her a solar character, for the full moon fully reflects and resembles the sun). The theme of a heavenly ox depicted carrying the solar disc and sometimes the moon, is not exclusively Cretan Minoan, appearing in Near Eastern and Egyptian mythology as well.[108] The solar Jove is contemplative radiance, and is perhaps a superior principle to the ordinary lightning-wielding form of this deity, justifying Plutarch's apparent raising up of Apollo over Jove in *De E Apud Delphos* (if he is doing this). Elsewhere,

---

103   Bekker, *Anecdota Graeca*, I:344; cited by James G. Frazer, *The Golden Bough*, vol. 3: *The Dying God* (Cambridge: Cambridge University Press, 2012), 72.
104   Marinatos, *Minoan Kingship and the Solar Goddess: A Near Eastern Koine*, 185.
105   Ibid., 14–16.
106   Frazer, *The Golden Bough*, vol. 3: *The Dying God*, 72.
107   Ibid., 73.
108   Marinatos, *Minoan Kingship and the Solar Goddess: A Near Eastern Koine*, 120.

discussing the Egyptian system as corresponding with Pythagoreanism, Plutarch tells us that Apollo is the monad and Artemis the dyad, so that Apollo is the first principle. Virgil considers the return of the Golden Age (fulfilment of the Cumaean prophecy) to be a return to the rule of Apollo (as well as of the Virgin and Saturn, as if Apollo were the manifestation of that transcendent monad) (*Eclogue*, IV, 1–10).

In Cretan Mount Ida the form of the Ancient of Days an initiate would encounter is that of Jove, whose animal form is the bull. The bull, specifically the slaughtered bull whose power is appropriated by the initiate (who has slain it, that is, has defeated the ego, overcoming those ravenous, animalistic parts of the psyche and integrating their energies, like Zagreus who is ripped apart by the Titans covered in gypsum and then enters an immortal body precisely made of gypsum by Minerva, indicating those destroyers are not integrated by him), is represented by its horns—the obvious sign of his power. In Biblical scripture, horns are often associated with the successful spiritual initiate and kingship (in the person of King David): "You have exalted my horn like that of a wild ox; fine oils have been poured on me" (Psalm 92:10). And, "Here I will make a horn grow for David and set up a lamp for my anointed one" (Psalm 132:17).

Just like the *morning star*, the symbol of the horn sometimes represents Heavenly anointing and others the satanic parody thereof (the little horn of John's Apocalypse). Perhaps for this reason Greek tradition associates the material of horn, such as from a bull, with true dreams, that is, genuine inspiration, as opposed to ivory, the gate of false dreams (Penelope discusses this in Homer's Odyssey, and Virgil includes it in the *Aeneid*).

In a well-known series of events, the impressionist painter van Gogh cut his own ear off and offered it by way of macabre gesture of devotion to a prostitute whose attentions he desired, just as the matador cuts off the defeated bull's ear after a bullfight and gives it to whatever woman in the audience he finds comeliest. This practice, surviving in southern France, where the celebrated artist found himself, echoes the distant past, but van Gogh would make that echo resound clearer. When he subsequently painted himself as a Christ figure, the severed ear of his sacrifice visibly patched-up, complete with a background Fuji to stand for Cavalry and three Geishas to represent the Virgin Mary, Mary Magdalene and Martha, he was understanding the link between the salvific king—the Christ—as sacrificial animal, and those practices of bull slaughter by way of which Egyptians, Minoans and other bronze and iron age cultures would consecrate their divinized monarchs.

As Cyril of Alexandria writes (*Letter* 41) "We must perceive the Immanuel" the presence of the Lord, usually in the sacred king, "in the slaughtered goat...." In line with this, Margaret Barker quotes Cyril in this context. She considers the slaughtered goat in Leviticus to represent the Lord rather than being a sacrifice to the Lord as usually understood:

"the sacrificed goat must have represented the Lord. The *le* meant '*as* the Lord' not '*for* the Lord.'"[109] Christ is this very slaughtered Lord and, as Barker notes, the argument of the *Letter to the Hebrews* is that the older animal sacrifice is no longer needed. She continues:

> Hence when the 'Last Supper' was repeated in early worship, they prayed for the return of the high priest to complete the great atonement: '*Maranatha*'. As time passed and the Parousia hope faded, the significance of the original *epiklesis* changed, and what had begun as a temple ritual fulfilled in history, returned to being a ritual. The roots of the Christian Eucharistic Liturgy lie mainly in the Day of Atonement, understood as the renewal of the creation, and this ... passed into the words of the Liturgies.[110]

Yet the Parousia does occur in the sacrament of holy communion, and Day One of Genesis, and the Day of Atonement are present in the congregation even as they are present at the end of the Age. The sacrifice of bread and wine in the Liturgy continues as the presence of the Lord. It is like Joseph Danquah's formulation of the African Akan doctrine as a "discovered," not "expected," Messiah.

The *Gospel of Philip* provides some further elucidation of all this. The self-sacrificial is not abolished. Spiritual realization is not presented as outside that fleshy self, for "[i]t is necessary to rise in this flesh, since everything exists in it." The spiritual realization being taught is one in which the creaturely self, so to speak, is present but submitted to the inner self:

> He [Christ] said on that day in the thanksgiving, "You who have joined the perfect light with the Holy Spirit, unite the angels with us also, as being the images." Do not despise the lamb, for without it, it is not possible to see the king. No one will be able to go in to the king if he is naked.[111]

We recall Corbin's highlighting of Eusebius's distinction between Adam and Enos and Zosimus's distinction between Adam and Phos. The creaturely, the thing which is sacrificed, is the lamb, and the revealed theophanic divine presence is the king. To be naked in the above likely refers to having no body, being in a postmortem state without a body. The lamb or bodily self is the image which is united to the angel, where this latter is the kingly or inner self. Again, the sacrifice or submission of image to angel, lamb to king, is not any longer an agonistic suffering, but what we previously called the technology of the cross, cross now as throne, a

---

109   Barker, *The Great High Priest: The Temple Roots of Christian Liturgy*, 83. This also means that no goat is being sacrificed to Azazel, the evil one, but rather a second goat is being used to represent the driving out of evil from the assembly: one is killed and its blood used in the temple and another is driven into the desert.

110   Ibid., 84.

111   *Nag Hamadi Codex II, 2–7, The Gospel of Philip*, 58:8–59:6, 157.

joyful perpetual surrender of the outgoing breath and perpetual faith in the possibility of a returning inhale. The initiate remains his own sacrifice, in a sense, where that animal self is the horns adorning his helm.

Nietzsche saw this in his way, when in *Beyond Good and Evil* (225) he warned against those whose pity is for the creature in man ("...in man there is matter, fragment, excess, clay, mud, madness, chaos... your pity is for the 'creature in man', for that which has to be formed, broken, forged, torn, burned, annealed, refined—that which has to suffer and should suffer..."), rather than the creator in man ("but in man there is also creator, sculptor, the hardness of the hammer, the divine spectator and the seventh day"). To pity the creature and ignore the divine spectator within is to prevent that creature from suffering and therefore from becoming what it must in relation to the inner or higher in human beings. Nietzsche was warning against the kind of compassion that is in reality a shield ("the worst of all pampering and weakening") against initiatic ordeal and spiritual realization.

While the depth is in abject contemplation of the mystery beyond form, a surface portion may express that contemplation in form,

> In the Kingdom of Heaven, the free will minister to the slaves: the children of the bridal chamber will minister to the children of the marriage. The children of the bridal chamber have just one name: rest. Altogether, they need take no other form, because they have contemplation...[112]

The depth is beyond form, at rest, contemplative, slaves in surrender, and that which serves them, that which is derivative, remains in form (is contrasted to their rest and contemplation). That outer self, the image, must be at ease too, in that it must be surrendered to the inner contemplative self, or angel:

> ...children...originate in a moment of ease. ...You will find that this applies directly to the image. Here is the man made after the image accomplishing things with his physical strength, but producing his children with ease.[113]

That which is strong, beastly, the outer animal self, is in truth given up, a lamb to be slaughtered by the king. Creation is contrasted with begetting in the *Gospel of Philip*, where begetting—as in producing children not "with his physical strength" but "with ease" in submission to the Lord—is superior. This is the mysticism of Meister Eckhart: God always begets the Son, and in us, if we surrender, if we are restful, the Son is always being born.

We may address the meaning of the horns themselves, those two daggers, a symbol of double danger. The bull or horned beast as holy sacrifice

---

112   Ibid., 71:28–72:24, 187.
113   Ibid.

identified with the sun appears in Ibn Sina's *Recital of Hayy ibn-Yaqzan*. As one approaches the Orient's Rising Sun (spiritual rebirth), one sees it is flanked by two demon's horns, and these have to do with the demons that inspire anger in us and that lead us to seek pleasure: the conflict-seeker and the comfort-seeker, the desire to *inflict* pain and the desire to *receive* pleasure. Elsewhere we have identified these with the extroverted and the introverted, the outgoing search for signs and omens in the world, and the cerebral search for reasons in the mind. Compulsion and Obsession. Paul's double critique of Jews and Greeks in I Corinthians. The two sandals we must remove in Sufi commentaries, like Moses. Blake's religious hypocrite Puritan, and rationalist Deist. Behemoth and Leviathan. And these are drawn together by the nihilistic, faithless disposition. "Two Horn'd Reasoning, Cloven Fiction, In Doubt, which is Self-contradiction." The grasping, attached, mind. Such is the double-beast we must slay, and wear those horns transformed, by harnessing them to the true center, the spiritual Sun. Like Hercules, once we slay the three-souled Geryon Titan, we have access to the solar bulls.

The Greco-Roman Hero and the Cretan Bull, or How a Hero gets his Horns

Hercules, as paradigmatic hero of Classical antiquity, and fundamental referent of the Italic, Orphic and Pythagorean milieu in which pre-Socratics like Empedocles moved, leads us organically to a digression on Greco-Roman heroes in relation to the solar bull. In Euripides' *Cretans* (fragments of which are provided by Porphyry in *On Abstinence from Animal Food*[114]) the narrator recounts his being initiated to the Jove of Mount Ida, thereby becoming a *bacchant*, that is, a follower of Dionysius. The Dionysian initiate embraces death and receives life, becoming a solar king (Dionysus-Jove, Osiris-Ra). Like Orpheus, he follows Dionysus, is ripped apart and thereby enters into Apollonian devotion. Euripides refers to Mount Ida as mother or as maternal, reiterating the femininity of the sacred space. Further, the initiate is described as a child of Jove and Europa. Like Zagreus who becomes immortal after dismemberment at Ida. In light of Proclus's identification of Juno with holy mountains and that goddess's correspondence with Jove, as well as her association with the cow (wide of countenance) which also symbolizes Juno, this serves to assimilate Europa to Juno.

We can integrate the oppositional force of life as a technology rather than experiencing it as tragic, celebrating instead of decrying the fact that we perceive from a limited vantage. Python and his serpentine mate, Delphyne, are integrated and celebrated by Apollo's cult after he slays them (or at least Python). We may also think of Hercules defeating Ladon to attain Juno's apples of Hesperides from the daughters of Atlas, or the presence of one end of the Titanic serpent Typhon at Mount Etna in Sicily and the other at Cumae in Naples according to Pindar, so that

---

114   Porphyry, *On Abstinence from Animal Food*, trans. T. Taylor (Whitefish, MT: Kessinger Publishing, 2006).

heroes who descend into these volcanoes (Empedocles in Etna, Aeneas in Cumae) are engaging the serpent. But they do so through descent, death.

Indeed, Jove deems Apollo's slaying of Python to have been impious (occurring in a sacred place, Delphi, the oracle of Mother Earth, Gaia) and so orders the sun god to go to Tempe for purification, as well as instituting the Pythian games in honor of the snake hero. Later, Jove further binds Apollo to a year's service in the court of King Admetus of Therae and his sheep-herders for various transgressions, after which Apollo and his cult acquire their fundamental character of moderation.[115] It is through purgation that we finally gain dominion over what is below us.

In this way, the solar may take up the chthonic and earthly, to the point that so distinguished a member of the solar priesthood as Pythagoras bears the name of Python. Gaia's center is embraced. The result of Apollo's travail is a truer synthesis:[116] the feathered snake of the Toltec, the eagle and snake forms of Odin, the purity of doves and cunning of serpents Jesus advises. Since it was Juno who opposed Apollo, and in some versions, created and sent Python, we may see here a reconciliation to Juno, to the Divine Feminine, alike those of Aeneas and Hercules. Python is sometimes identified with the Egyptian Set, and so Apollo as "Greek Horus" reflects a paradigm similar to that of the Egyptians.

Chapter XII of Homer's *Odyssey* sees its hero thwarted by his crew. After swearing not to harm the cattle of Apollo on the island of *Thrinacia*, and making his men do likewise, he falls asleep. They then betray him and, consequently, are smitten by Jove, who Apollo entreats to avenge the offence. Odysseus is alone and returns home late and beleaguered. An esoteric reading: the clamoring voices of our divided psyche break the oaths we made in lucid moments, and we sleepwalk through life, slaughtering sacred things, until that contemplative inner truth (represented by the sun) becomes active judgement (represented by the lightning god), our conscience perhaps, and manifest nature itself (the feminine, an angry Minerva, in the above episode) seems to have turned against us. In the end, however, the experience is purifying, we learn from it. It is a gestation of our better self, as James Joyce's chapter "oxen of the sun" in *Ulysses*, a metaphor for conception and pregnancy, grasped.

The sacrifice of those bulls of Helios is a sacred affair, not to be eaten ravenously the way the desecrating crew does. Contrast this with the pious crew of those Cretans whom Apollo, in his Homeric hymn, leads passed the island with the cattle of Helios and who do not have

---

115   Graves, *The Greek Myths*, 21, p. 79.
116   Robert Graves speculates that the historical context is one of religious conflict between Hyperborean religionists and a central Greek Gaia-focused cult. Pindar describes Libyans as Hyperboreans in the *Pythian Odes* (X, 50–55) and other sources refer to parts of Palestine and northern Europe as following this cult. Hecataeus (Diodorus Siculus, ii.47) refers to the British as Hyperborean and generally describes different countries who follow this religion as enjoying close relations.

the opportunity to rampage, led as they are by a wind sent by Jove, to Delphi where they will serve as Apollonian disciples. In fact, in the hymn, we read that these Minoan sons are sailing to the dawn, they are thus rightly guided and successful initiates, already passed ritual death, whose destiny is rising with the sun.

But despite his crew's sin, in a sense sacrifice yields its proper end: Odysseus experiences a death of sorts and matures from it. He is alone, his will awake, and on returning to himself (his home and wife) he must now undertake the cutting away of distraction directly, rather than relying on an external agent. Jove freed him from his crew the first time. Now he realizes the voices of a fragmented psyche, the desires and repulsions that act on us, are not his crew but usurpers, represented by those pretenders abusing his household's hospitality and trying to woo his wife. Realizing this, Odysseus kills them himself. It is when our desires (the crew's hunger) lead us to destroy something beautiful or sacred in our life (the solar cattle) that we begin to realize that those desires are not our crew but usurpers (the suitors clamoring for Penelope's attention, wanting to consume her like the crew did those holy cows). Penelope, then, is the sacred, identified as she is with Apollo's oxen by her pronouncement that true dreams come by gates of horn.

Another transgressor who stole the cattle of the sun, specifically of Apollo, is Hermes in the Homeric hymn to Hermes. Here, as in the Odyssey, the initiatic theme is clear. Hermes is born in the Cyllene Mountain from its nymph, Maia, equivalent to other mountain goddesses, and steals the sacred animals, which he sacrifices in a manner wholly in keeping with proper order. The hymn tells us that he did not eat their flesh despite feeling tempted to do so, and that, like Gilgamesh with the parts of the bull of Heaven, he distributed their remains. Specifically, he divides these into twelve parts, placing him, Christ-like, between twelve, just as the saved enter a Heavenly city of twelve gates in John's Apocalypse. Thus, Hermes, unlike Odysseus's crew, succeeds. After ritual death the initiate is reborn. Hermes thus returns to the mountain of his birth's innards with his mother and wraps himself in a cradle, like those ancient Greek incubation tanks spiritual seekers would enter.

But the element of transgression is not absent. Just as the king must face his demons, those scourges of the Duat that constitute his true dismemberment, the sense of abandonment perceived by Jesus on the cross, so too Hermes is found out by the wronged Apollo. The two go to their common father, Jove, and are instructed to work together to find the cattle. Eventually all is discovered and Hermes learns to tell Apollo the truth. The two become united. Hermes gives Apollo his lyre, the creative voice is given over to the higher spiritual principle, and Apollo gives Hermes dominion, the sort of mastery that is received by the king who submits to Heaven, in the form of a whip to keep the grazing animals ordered. Other examples of heroes slaying animals like lions, whose solar association is consistent, as is the case of Hercules, may bare a similar meaning.

A descendent of Hermes, Jason, also engaged in the quest for a sacrificial solar beast, namely the golden fleece. The link to kingship is explicit, as Jason is the son of the rightful ruler of Iolcos, Aeson. After gathering a crew, the Argonauts, which includes Hercules, Jason sailed to Lemnos, where the sort of sexual dysfunction occurring in Orpheus's tale plays out. The women of that island neglected their veneration of Venus, who turns them foul of smell, so that their husbands seek women in Thrace, the land of Orpheus. These scorned wives kill their husbands in retaliation. The proper relation of the sexes has collapsed. Hercules, like Odysseus, is offended by the crew, who revel with the women of Lemnos. The men later land among the Doliones, but after fighting monsters there they sail off at night, inadvertently landing again in the same place and fighting with the locals, both sides mistaking the other for an enemy in the darkness. We have here the theme of sleepwalking into an act of murder, like the crew of Odysseus blinded by hunger, or Hercules himself, while maddened.

Later, like a knight of the Holy Grail, Jason encounters a sort of king Anfortas called king Phineas. He kills the harpies that have been appointed to eat the king's meals. Given the female character of harpies, Phineas is like king Anfortas in being sexually wounded. In return for his help king Phineas instructs Jason on how to arrive safely at Colchis, where the golden fleece waits for him. There, a woman, Medea, anoints him like a king so that the heat from fire-breathing oxen—who we may identify as solar animals in their trying, infernal mode—does not burn him. Medea goes on to instruct Jason on how to defeat the beasts. Like Apollo, Jason slays his final trial, a dragon, using a potion given him by Medea. As with Odin, a luminous maid is key to learning the arts needed to gain the prize. She also helps him to escape her father and household, but as she kills her own brother to do so, Jove sends a storm to scourge their ship, and purification has to be sought from a nymph called Circe. They overcome the same sirens Odysseus encountered with the help of Orpheus's lyre playing (the two stories of Odysseus and Orpheus are clearly in the background). Together, by Medea's magic, they also defeat the bronze man Talos in Crete, finally returning to Jason's homeland. However, because he tries to marry Creusa, heiress to Corinth, for political reasons, and does not so much as apologize to Medea for breaking his vow of loyalty to her, she poisons his wife to be, leaves on a chariot of dragons sent by Helios, her grandfather, and he loses the favor of Hera. His whole enterprise literally rots and crushes him, when a piece of the Argo ship collapses and kills him in his sleep.

This tragic end for Jason, a hero who had, but then lost, Hera's support, is the inverse of Aeneas. Jason slayed the oxen of the sun, or dragon-bulls, but perhaps the true solar boon, the solar beast to be tamed, even through love, the luminous Tantric initiation he rejects for the sake of politics, was the descendent of Helios himself, the means to all his victories, his very own shining Shakti, Medea. The story has hinted that reconciling with femininity is the end of his journey, and indeed, after the ritual death of self-sacrifice represented by the killing of the solar animal, the initiate is meant to return to the world, to be drawn in by a woman. This Jason fails to do, because he puts the world as *mere world*, that is, political alliance, first. He has not learnt the lesson and therefore scorns a solar consort.

The ritual slaughter of bulls occurs several times in the *Aeneid*. Early on, in Book II, the Trojan Laocoon who speared the wood horse delivered by the Greeks and told the others not to trust it, officiates such a slaughter. While acting as priest of Neptune (a rotating post), the sacred duty is cut short as sea serpents rise from the water and attack, killing him and his sons. These are a species of dragon. They are described as having flaming crests, seeming to burn the seas, and sputtering flame. Virgil presents their slaying of Laocoon as the very beast he was slaying, for he dies like a sacrificial bull. The killing of the bull, often a solar animal, is interrupted and reversed by fiery monsters, a kind of lower form of the solar epiphany, denizens of the subterranean rather than celestial fire, the sort that assail the king and hero as he lets himself be taken apart before second birth. Here are the monsters Jason slew by means of Medea's know-how. The connection with the solar rites is made strong by the fact that some, like Sophocles, relate the story with Laocoon as priest of Apollo rather than Neptune. It is Laocoon, the presiding priest and, in a sense, representative, of the Trojans, who becomes the sacrificial animal, indeed, it is the Trojans as a people, all of Troy, that is soon to be slain and dismembered like the bull.

Another Trojan falling short of the Apollonian height is Cassandra, the prophetess who, in resisting Apollo, is cursed to foretell a future none will heed. She, like Laocoon, warns of the wooden horse, but is ignored. In fact, the disaster of the sea serpents convinces the Trojans to take that Greek subterfuge into the city, thinking that it was Laocoon's spearing and scorning of it that caused the attack. Just as the disaster of Odysseus's crew savaging the oxen of the sun leads ultimately to a proper end for the hero, so too this disaster leads ultimately to the Trojans becoming Romans. It is a fortunate failure, a *felix culpa*.

In Book III of the *Aeneid* a bull sacrifice to Jove sees the earth turn its water and sap into blood as the Trojans head for Thrace, and more like sacrifices to Neptune and Apollo while they direct themselves to Crete see them end up in Carthage instead. Sacrifice does not deliver what they want but each time the wondering nation comes to resemble the

dismembered animal by being flung further into perdition. In keeping
with this, truth comes in an ugly guise, for it is the queen of the harpies
that informs the shipwrecked lot that Italy is to be their promised land. In
Book V, Aeneas's people hold sporting games to inaugurate or renew their
voyage. Bulls are again sacrificed, especially by winners. Indeed, Cloanthus,
who wins a naval race, does so after promising to slay a white bull which,
given its associated with the Cretan Jove, is probably a solar symbol.

In Book VI the priestess Deiphobe, the Cumaean Sibyl, guides Aeneas
into the underworld. This is the Trojan king's initiation. His walking of
that perennial path, entering into darkness, facing and conquering death,
like Jesus after the cross. As is typical during ritual death, the priestess
recommends animal sacrifice. Seven bulls are slain to Phoebus Apollo, the
god over whose oracle at Cumae, near Naples, the Sibyl presides. There
are others besides, including dark bulls without a streak of white, that is,
bulls symbolizing not the solar but the earthly or lunar. These the Sibyl
kills for Hecate. She is, after all, opening the door to Hades for the initiate.

There will be more examples before the *Aeneid* is through. The bull
hide itself appears constantly, like a symbol of the fact that the sacrificed
animal, the defeated beast, is incorporated into the one who overcomes,
like armor. In addition, in Book VIII bulls are released from monstrous
captivity, in Book X Aeneas's rival, Turnus, sees a speeding bull and likewise speeds into battle, there is sacrifice in Book XI and in XII warriors
are described as bulls fighting for a female. Indeed, Aeneas is not the
solar bull. He has died and therefore lives, and will contend for and win
Lavinia and the Latin country. The solar character of this overcoming
is borne out by the fact that Aeneas is Apollo's favored hero and that
Lavinia's hair catches fire during a ritual.

Virgil provides a useful commentary on the possible meaning of the
bull and its slaughter as a means for renewing peoples. It is common
for commentaries on Virgil's work to note an association between bees
and humanity.[117] This may be approached in terms of duality, subordination and pollination (standing in between two realities and, therefore,
being a subordinate principle to the higher, but also acting as bridge
between the higher and the lower). In terms of duality, as has already
been discussed, in Homer (via Porphyry's reading) bees represent the
generative function of Minerva's nymphs who weave mortal vessels
and whose work is both the pain of the stinger and the sweetness of
honey, containing as it does the tension of temporal existence, which
corresponds to the often-cited ambiguity with which Virgil seems to
treat the birth of bees in the Georgics[118] (where bees are engendered
by the ritual slaughter of a bull—perhaps the ancients suffered from

117   Llewelyn Morgan, *Patterns of Redemption in Virgil's Georgics* (Cambridge: Cambridge University Press, 1999), 130.
118   Jasper Griffin, *Latin Poets and Roman Life* (London: Duckworth, 1985), 176.

bee colony collapse syndrome).

Regarding the subordinate character of humanity-as-hive: the un-differentiation proper to a swarm of insects whose movements are mechanical and interchangeable, contrasts with the clearly discernable personhood of each soul Aeneas encounters in the Elysian Fields. In the Roman paradise individuality is preserved,[119] or rather, perfected, transcending the dualism of stinger and honey. The ox may be partly identified with Elysium, representing a sacred principle, one higher than the bees, given that Virgil is observant of bovine sanctity. In Book II of his *Georgics* the poet teaches that these animals were not eaten during the golden age.[120] Therefore, Book IV of the *Georgics* is detailing the ritual savaging of what is understood to be a holy beast (although, granted, acknowledgement of such holiness is ascribed to the aegis of Saturn, whereas the rite in question takes place during that of Jove: the one is undivided contemplation whereas the other actively engages in cosmic construction).

Virgil is perhaps presenting a paradigm according to which higher forms decline into lower ones (the ox into bees), where the latter is more numerous than the former, and consists of individuals whose anonymity or similitude may represent their manifesting a common principle, just as ontologically superior types encompass several subordinates (there are fewer archetypes than types, gods than mortals, ox than bees), an essentially traditional doctrine. Entering into, or focusing on, a lower rung of being can obfuscate the higher, thus the death of the ox and an apparently sacrificial dynamic at play in the natural world and in the human psyche.

Another angle on the humble bee is that, as a pollinator, it bridges plant life with human life, using pollen to make honey, which serves as human food, nourishing higher types. It is this pontifical function that humanity, located between and bridging earth and Heaven, exercises (pontifical, *pons-facere*, bridge-making). Thus, Virgil may be referencing the renewal of this role after epochs of ignorance during which it has been forgotten. The symbol of the ox is the same to which was paid deference during the golden age, but it has now become only an echo, poorly understood, thereof. That the ox has been presented as sacred may be no contradiction, then, but, less severely, a metaphor: sacred oxen (calcified dogma) need goring to renew men's minds.

Drawing the topic of the solar bull to a close, we return to the center, Mount Ida. Etymologically, the name Europa may derive from the Greek for broad-faced or from the Assyrian for sunset.[121] Both of these would relate to Hathor, who is called broad-faced, being represented by a cow,

---

119   Rajesh Mittal, *Time and History in Virgil's Aeneid*, PhD thesis (Michigan: University of Michigan, 2011), 237.
120   Virgil, *Georgics*, II:536; 174.
121   Daniel Gilman, Harry Peck and Colby Frank (eds.), *New International Encyclopedia*, vol. 7 (New York City: Dodd, Mead and Company, 1903), 42.

and is associated with the setting sun (the king orients himself towards her and dies with the daylight before his rebirth at morning) and the west.[122] Additionally, given the myth in which Jove takes Europa while in the form of a white bull, she is perhaps acting as feminine counterpart to the bovine which, again, links her to the Egyptian Hathor. There has been some suggestion that horns are identified with the holy mountain in Minoan art (which would be consistent with Hathor and Europa as bovine goddesses, or Jove as solar bull going to Mount Ida). Nearby, the name of *Italy* is speculated to derive from the bullock by several authors.[123] This view is attributed, via a footnote in *The Library*, to Marcus Terentius Varro in his *De Re Rustica* (II.1:9) and to Dionysius of Halicarnassus in his Greek work, *Roman Antiquities* (I.35:6). Following Margaret Barker, we may also note that the Lady of Jerusalem has horns and hooves, being symbolically bovine, and these are made of metal and used to defend her nation (Micah 4:13).

The Yellow Emperor of China is also said to have encountered solar or fiery beasts, including a phoenix and, interestingly, a *qilin*, a sort of dragon with hooved feet like an ox. Here he died to the mortal world but is presently, following certain Chinese observances, a Taoist immortal. The peripherally sexual character of the solar bull, given its link to Penelope and Medea, but more clearly in the case of Europa's conjoining with Jove as sun-bull, might occur here as well, given that the Yellow Emperor had mastered Taoist sexual techniques as part of his spiritual discipline.

In closing this section, we note that its theme also echoes in Spain's wintery masquerades or *mascaradas invernales*, during which locals of small towns throughout the peninsula dress up in gothic attire (the term *invernal*—wintery—reminds of *infernal*), often as some folkloric were-bull (half man half bull), from the *Devils of Luzon* in central Castile to the Basque-Navarrean *Momotxorros*. The Sardinian *Arestes e s'Urtzu* and German figure of the horned *Krampus* may have to do with this as well. They are like reversed minotaurs, not the animal usurping the human but the human wearing the animal. Like a modern version of "Indus Valley figures of therianthropic males with horns and tales (which go back in turn to Mesopotamian representations of bull-men)" possibly involving vows to act as a bull in the context of spiritual ascesis, they are Mithras, having slain and made the world anew from the cosmic bull.[124]

These seem to honor the solar bull in its subterranean scourging of the initiate, as well as displaying the initiate's victory, donning the

---

122   Wallis E. A. Budge, *The Gods of the Egyptians: Or, Studies in Egyptian Mythology*, vol. 1 (New York City: Dover Publications, 1969), 514.

123   *Apollodorus: The Library* (London: William Heinemann, 1921), II.v:10, 217.

124   Thomas McEvilley, *The Shape of Ancient Thought, Comparative Studies in Greek and Indian Philosophies* (New York: Allworth Press, Open Source, 2002).

animal's hide and horns to signal its sacrifice and integration by the human, like Siegfried drinking dragon blood. This reminds us of the Spanish 11th century church of Saint Pelayo in Puentedey,[125] which features above its entrance a human figure fighting a snake, where the figure's arm and sword are themselves extended and snake-like, teaching, perhaps, that the hero can integrate into himself the enemy's character as an instrument or limb. It is fitting that these occur around the time when nights are longest, at the threshold of the resurrection of the sun after winter solstice and the lengthening of daylight, like heat salvaged in the hearth, like Halloween leading to Christmas.

Saturn as Being and Saturn as Body, or From the Devouring to the Dialoguing Deity

The sacrificial animal *as divine*, like the goat which represented the Lord giving himself for his people's sustenance in Biblical temple worship, can coincide with its symbolizing the *initiate's own animal self* and so self-sacrifice. We may address this ambiguity through the symbol of Saturn in alchemical tradition, which is both pure or original Being (leading some to speculate an etymological relationship between Saturn and the Sanskrit for Being, *Sat*) and also the body, matter or minerality. These are connected in that the body's solidity can serve to symbolize Being's stability. Further, contemplation of Being can be attained through attention to the body and bringing awareness into the senses until these are absorbed (the noise of sensory input gradually reduced).

When habitual psychic oscillations, deeply embedded in physiognomic processes, are arrested by meditation, these are released from their ordinary course with a momentum that may manifest in hallucinations or otherwise powerful impressions. These impressions, animated by the primordial strata of physical existence, will threaten to flood our consciousness, shattering the contemplative state. Such a trial should be met with impassibility by the meditator.

At the level of the greater rather than lesser mysteries, so to speak, this threat of "flooding" occurs again in the possibility that the initiate will prefer form-transcending contemplation to re-entering the world and pursuing his vocation. In Hermetic tradition, one rejects dissolution in form-transcending Being just as, analogously and on a lower level, one rejects absorption into the formless energies that animate the life of the body.

The medieval and renaissance alchemical symbol of Saturn is therefore

---

125   In *Las Merindades* (Burgos), cradle (along with La Rioja) of Castile. For a (in some ways flawed but fascinating and endowed of spiritual force) study on rural, Romanesque, Spanish art and the social relations, and the general philosophy communicated therein, see: Felix Rodrigo Mora, *Tiempo, Historia y Sublimidad en el Románico Rural* (Madrid: Potlatch, 2012).

consistent with the Greek myth of Zeus who rejects staying in the belly (primordial womb) of his father. The devouring of Zeus, like entering the tomb after crucifixion, is Katharsis, and absorption into pure Being or into the body is rejected during Theosis, following Theoria. The castration of Saturn represents a fixation of the deeper layers of the self so that they cease to generate a rebellious ego, that is, so that Saturn will not sire for Zeus a usurping sibling to contest his position as king of the gods.

We find something similar in the Egyptian tale of Isis making a serpent from the drool of Ra as he sleeps. This serpent is able to poison Ra with its bite, for it is made from him, and as he agonizes, Isis grants him the cure to his affliction only after he tells her his secret name, which she only passes on to her son, Horus. The base of our being sleeps, and for this reason drools, but we may learn its true essence and release its power by allowing it to suffer until this is revealed—during meditation and certain spiritual ordeals, it may feel like our whole being is shouting out in agony.

That from which we seem to emanate (the body as support for our consciousness) is not to be deferred to, but overcome, such that the dependent relationship of consciousness to the body is inverted. The completion of the work is in the young man, not the old man, in the Son of Man, not the Ancient of Days.

The philosophical transition from experiencing Being as a *powerful being among beings*, as in literalist readings of scripture, to a universal essence, the *Being of beings*, corresponds to the initiatic breaking of the awareness's (Sanskrit *Chit*'s) identification with the ego/body. This also stops the body (or simpler layers of one's self) from continuing to deviate its energy, instead fixing them on us: the generative power of earlier strata of our own self are fixed on the generated, summit, of the self. The body becomes the temple in which *Chit* sacrifices itself (its false self, its restricted identity) to *Sat*.

Breaking its identification with the body allows reflexive consciousness or *Chit* to contemplate universal Being and inhabit the perspective of other bodily structures as manifesting the same unitary Being. Saturn, the Ancient of Days, and related symbols, can represent the body, prior to the Son of Man's sacrifice, prior to Jove's surviving the scourging of his father. Here the body is a prison, and so Being is experienced as a tyrant. Thereafter they correspond to the particular vision of Being and the ability of an awareness to identify with a wider corporeal structure according to its vocation, its dharma. Here we have the bhava, or a vision of Being chosen by the initiate. The symbol of Saturn/Ancient of Days thereby passes from external tyrant to being at one with the initiate. To be at one with the image of external deity is, in the Gospel, a question of faith, such that the disciple experiences complete confidence in that external deity and so renders it no longer truly external.

This is analogous to what Varro, quoted by St. Augustine in *City of*

God, and Livy, have to say about the god Janus. Indeed, both Janus and Saturn are elsewhere identified as ancient kings of Italy during the golden age, and so are somewhat equivalent. For Varro, Janus is the god of beginnings, but Jove is the god of summits, and so the latter is properly called the king:

> Because the beginnings (*prima*) are in the power of Janus, and the summits (*summa*) in that of Jupiter. So Jupiter is rightly regarded as king of all. For beginnings are inferior to summits, since, though the precede in time, they are surpassed in dignity by the summits. (Varro quoted in St. Augustine's *City of God* 7.9 [126])

Janus, with his two faces, the beginning and end, can also be understood as manifested in the king, in the summit, in the vision of the young man, which justifies the use of his image to symbolize Christ in the Middle Ages as Alpha and Omega, divine and human. In this case, his image is understood as containing the third term, beyond his two faces, and drawing these together, like the thrice-greatness of Hermes or the third term at the root of *transcendence*, and so on. A three-faced Janus is equivalent to Jove in his relation to Saturn. [127]

As an aside, Prometheus sometimes fits the mold assigned to his fellow Titan Saturn. He can be interpreted as a failed initiate who the fire of the gods condemns because, we may infer, he was not ready for it. When the liquification of the alchemical process has been undergone, the fire must be intensified and brought to the earth, as the *Turba Philosophorum* puts it, but woe to him who has not properly undergone that first stage of purgation and reaches for the fire all the same. [128]

However, Prometheus may also be understood not as a failed initiate ultimately rescued, but also—or for this very reason—as representing a certain phase of initiation. He is the immobilized body, either during the trial of death and rebirth, the incubation ritual, or generally understood as the human condition tied to the body/mind and its suffering. If Prometheus's plight is the human condition as such, we share the understanding of Zosimus of Panopolis concerning this myth, where Prometheus is the original spirit that becomes locked in the body and Epimetheus is the spirit liberating itself and ascending again. In the former, initiatic understanding, Prometheus, with his liver eaten out,

---

126 Georges Dumezil, *Archaic Roman Religion* (Chicago: University of Chicago Press, 1996), 100.

127 The Christ parallel is suggested by the case of the Knights Templar, who were accused of venerating a three-faced idol. At the church that served as their Spanish center in Toledo, we find a three-faced statue of Christ holding a downward facing triangle (this is not displayed, given its non-canonical imagery, but is in the basement of the church and a viewing can be requested).

128 *The Turba Philosophorum*, trans. Arthur Edward Waite (London: George Redway, 1806), Twenty-Sixth Dictum, 91-92.

becomes equivalent to the fisher king Anfortas, wounded on his side and immobilized, restored by the grail knight, or to Christ on the cross, immobile and speared on the side. Hercules, who rescues Prometheus, is the grail knight, or the witness that suffers not, like the Christ that acts on himself, the cross of light that presents itself in the apocryphal *Acts of John* and is apart from the crucifixion.[129]

The practical correlate of complete, formless absorption is complete renunciation of formal duties, and the conception of a divinity that gives no warrant to forms, to manifestation. Such a divinity often appears wrathful. Theological narrative at times subverts this conception of deity. We may consider how the skillful averting of one's gaze before the overwhelming presence of the Divine, thereby avoiding complete absorption, is identified with the *Salat* prostration by some Sufi discourses: it is both a gesture of self-annulment and of self-preservation. Likewise, when the Canaanite woman comes to Jesus and He is harsh with her at first but, seeing her faith, heals her daughter (Matthew 15:21–28), human agency and petition are taken up as the locus for revealing Divine mercy. This same ethos comes through in St. Dionysius's *The Celestial Hierarchy* (VIII):

> The name given to the holy Dominions signifies, I think, a certain unbounded elevation to that which is above, freedom from all that is of the earth, and from all inward inclination to the bondage of discord, a liberal superiority to harsh tyranny, an exemptness from degrading servility and from all that is low: for they are untouched by any inconsistency.... The name of the holy Powers, co-equal with the Divine Dominions and Virtues, signifies an orderly and unconfined order in the divine receptions, and the regulation of intellectual and supermundane power which never debases its authority by tyrannical force, but is irresistibly urged onward in due order to the Divine. It beneficently leads those below it, as far as possible, to the Supreme Power which is the Source of Power, which it manifests after the manner of Angels in the well-ordered ranks of its own authoritative power.

There are also stories in which there is some ambiguity as to whether the divine being petitioned is not the calcified bedrock of our being, nature in its forgetful, fallen state. We think of Numa Pompilius using humor to avoid a prescription of human sacrifice from Jove in order to attain power over storms (in Plutarch's account), so that his agency and the linguistic faculty are being utilized to disarm the image of wrathful divinity and attain a warrant for formal manifestation and the good of humans (obtaining favorable weather, doing without human sacrifice, etc.).

A final note on Christianity and the myths, for we risk appearing too conciliatory, papering over real contradictions: Where Saturn is the fallen image of Being as lethargic bodily existence, he is not

---

129 Corbin, *Cyclical Time and Ismaili Gnosis*, 60.

symbolizing true Being. In such cases, we do not have a correspondence with the Indian *Sat*, or with the Christian First Person of the Trinity. The Ancient of Days and Son of Man are parodied by the devouring father and beastly son; the entropic cosmos (actually chaos) and the animalistic (reactive) ego (not self-slaying, unalike the Biblical lamb). Indeed, we should not ignore that in a myth such as this—and there are many—the malevolence or neutrality of a primordial deity and its violent overthrow leaves no room for the concept of a primordial ontological unity, or else makes of malevolence and violence the ground of being. But in Christianity, *the Son of Man does not do violence against the Ancient of Days*, and the grail knight restores the fisher king. The Father is not at odds with the Son.

There is truth, then, in the polemic according to which Christianity confronted nations whose religious imagination would have found its ontology of peace quite alien—I mean the popular myths, not the philosophical schools, although even here, to the degree that the Divine was conceived of as impersonal and creation as automatic, transcendence is not ascribed to qualia such as love. This maps well onto the Biblical narrative that fallen angels began receiving idolatrous worship from the nations they were to guide after the destruction of the Tower of Babel. This idolatry would need to justify itself against the prior order, or rather, against primordial reality. Myths of foundational violence against the first generation of gods were, from the Christian perspective, quite straightforwardly taken to be Satanic propaganda, and they can hardly be treated as less grave a misunderstanding of reality from a philosophical perspective that does not consider chaos irreducible.

When we draw parallels between traditions, such as between the Biblical YHWH and Ugaritic Baal, we should nonetheless remember that accounts of a foundational patricide—those succession myths involving forceful overthrow of old divinity by new, so common across traditions—represent an existentially alienated perception, or outright parody, of the glorifying of generated by generator, of the divine hierarchy St. Dionysius describes so beautifully, and ultimately an exclusion of love and devotion, *bhakti*, from our relationship to the Divine.[130]

We have written that sacrifice, beyond the context of ritual death, can become an ongoing willingness to give things up, like the pouring over of an ever-full cup. Here, we do not fear falling into death if we become too perfect, thinking that things that reach completion must die (following that superstition Ananda Coomaraswamy notes). Instead, we exit the contemplative state and enter into the world, leaving that belly of Saturn with neither fear nor agonistic violence.

---

130   See the work of the Orthodox priests, Fathers Stephen De Young and Andrew Stephen Damick.

Sacrifice as Kenotic Participation

In Indian tradition, we have the example of Vyasa, who reached perfect contemplation, but chose to return to manifestation where he penned the *Vedas*. Edwin Bryant writes that "…the very notion of liberation itself…is rejected in the higher stages of bhakti"—devotion to God—"also because the bliss bhakti bestows far surpasses the bliss of the atman's immersion in its own nature of pure consciousness, the culmination of the generic path of yoga."[131] This highlights existential porosity: of a particular body or unity continuing to interact with other unities and therefore be part of wider unities as a means for expressing transcendent Unity. It presents the spiritual legitimacy of participation and sacrifice, conjugal relations and the life of the polis.

In the specific case of the Eucharist, what is given up is bread and wine, which becomes flesh and blood, and is received back. This elevates, in a sense destroying by fulfilling, human sacrifice, where the human order admits its porosity by asserting human—not merely animal—mortality. In addition, as an act of eating it is a surrender of the sense of self-containment, a choice to participate in the cycle of life that includes receiving from outside our bodies what sustains those bodies, and from outside our spirits what sustains those spirits, a choice that expresses what already is, the truth that Being always lends itself to beings.

We can therefore assert, as the *Bhagavad-Gita* does, that devotion is superior to full absorption into the unconditioned. It is not the case, as some scholars have claimed, that devotion to the personal God is a temporary phase preceding the initiate's experience of the unconditioned Divine, like passing through a gate. Rather, the initiate's being relates to the personal God structurally; it is not a separate being who happens to be bigger, more important, and bearer of the keys to the beatific vision. Being (*Sat*) (and what is beyond being) always produces a consciousness (*Chit*) of itself, a reflexive self-awareness, and in that consciousness is understanding, a satisfaction, the joy of knowing (*Ananda*), for there is always joy in reflecting on a thing and understanding it.

This also explains why warrior spirituality, as articulated in the *Gita*, is devotional. The rejection of devotion and desire for total formless contemplation would precisely undo the conditions for play, creativity, involvement in the world and the whole of the warrior disposition. Western *perennialists* who considered devotion an inferior mode of realization (*Jnana* as superior to *Bhakti*, knowledge above devotion) have been mistaken.[132] What is reproachable in vulgar religiosity is not devotion as distinct from

---

131   Edwin Bryant, *Bhakti Yoga: Tales and Teachings from the Bhagavata Purana* (New York: North Pole Press, 2017), 27.
132   Unless what is meant is devotion as relationship to an external entity which is never perceived as one with our being. That would be inferior to contemplative knowledge of the nature of reality, but that is not what Bhakti properly refers to.

contemplation, but moral morbidity as distinct from levity. Nietzsche was correct to identify the spirit of heaviness or gravity as the primary foe. Here the first chapters of the Gita communicate the correct attitude and it is a joyful heart that Christ recommends in the Gospel as well.

When we approach the topic of ritual death and rebirth, we do not speak of a sterile operation without love, but of an operation in which a subjective ecstatic encounter with the great Other as true Self occurs. We suffer with the Dionysiac, we receive the autozoon from the Divine as Parent, and are returned. Proclus writes:

> What is the cause of this initiation except that faith? For on the whole the initiation does not happen through intellection and judgement, but through silence which is unifying and is superior to every cognitive activity. Faith imparts this... (*Platonic Theology*, iv.31).[133]

The initiate, a new demiurge, receives and instantiates the autozoon in the world, engaging in a creative manifestation. As Christ teaches, "If you remain in me and my words remain in you, ask whatever you wish, and it shall happen for you. By this my Father has been glorified: that you bear plentiful fruit and will become my disciple." The keeping His words is followed by the injunction to "keep my commandments" and "This is my commandment: that you love one another as I have loved you" (John 15:7–12).

The ability to ask and have it granted, that is, to engage in the creative works of the Divine in the world, requires the sacrificial ordeal of the king who experiences his ritual death or dismemberment, the keeping of Jesus's commandment, which is to love as he loves, that is, unto death: to embrace death as sacrifice, death as love, "No one has greater love than this: that he should lay down his soul for his friends" (John 15:13). That one does so for the sake of one's friends, that a universal love is expressed locally in the context of one's particular, personal friendships, is the king's circumscribing his cosmic realization of identity with the whole universe to one particular realm that he is tasked with ruling.

We manifest, we do works, we bring the autozoon—order, wholesomeness—into our world, but we chose a noble death if it comes to that, if it serves to display glory through one who values love more than survival and appearances, brave unto the grave. Do glorious things, and chose a glorious death if it saves loved ones and shows the world.

As for that world, that twisted creation, it is a figure of the autozoon into which the autozoon must be brought back in by kingly initiates, because it has fallen away from itself. It is still made in the image, but has lost the likeness, in Christian terms: the world acts badly (John 16:20)

---

133   Martin Laird, *Gregory of Nyssa and the Grasp of Faith: Union, Knowledge, and Divine Presence* (Oxford: Oxford University Press, 2007), 12.

yet bringing life into the world as a disciple, like a woman giving birth, is a good thing (John 16:21). It is imperfect, but it is not to be abolished, rather it is to be perfected. The game is to conquer the world (John 16:33), that the world may have faith (John 17:21).

This, then, is the dialectic of death and deliverance, that one can only have life by embracing death delivers us into an exquisite reciprocity: we should be willing to die for our friends (John 15:13) and we are died for, that is, we are counted as Christ's friends and covered by His blood, by doing as He commands, that is, by being willing to die (John 15:14).

Acting as the Jovial king, the co-demiurge, the co-heir with Christ, is not a self-directed, hubristic or tight-chested sort of acting. It remains fully submitted, in a sense still crucified, ruling from the *cross as throne*, from *self-surrender as self-mastery*, still apprehending the autozoon, the archetypal order beyond the world, but also in the world, ready to instantiate the archetypes by works that are beyond us. Desmond expressed this idea to me as follows:

> Often our endeavoring is ungrateful to the receiving and then things get out of alignment...but there can be an endeavoring that in its own way keeps open that porosity to the more original source out of which it receives its own energy of self-surpassing. [134]

Our endeavoring must be an outpour from our receiving and the experience of alignment between endeavor and reception—type and archetype—is gratitude: to be grateful is to be aligned with the original source; to be grateful is to receive the energy of self-surpassing from that source.

To sum up and conclude this section, the legalistic and sacrificial (usually apotropaic but at least compulsively seeking security and perceiving insecurity) mentalities are intimately connected. They have to do with acting upon forms—the world as it is encountered—so as to manufacture a sense of order by foisting mental categories, rather than allowing the vertigo-inducing moment of recognition that order, the very possibility of sustained coherent and beautiful existence, does not rely on our ego but on the structure of reality; that we must surrender to—that is, accept—the gift.

Crucially: no sacrifice or payment was ever required. Such is an artefact of the ego wishing to invent stability rather than experience the death of its control by accepting that stability is already given, a gift; that reality is already stable and does not need to be *thought about into being set right*. Jesus teaches the embrace of death and the acceptance of this, which is the relinquishing of sacrifice, including the sacrifice of the firstborn which the payment that in His case was never made represented.

Letting go of external sacrifices (even of mental habits) as a psychological strategy for feeling secure in the world is only possibly by fully accepting death, which is what the initiatic ordeal entails, so Jesus is does

---

134   William Desmond, "Interview with Carlos Perona," 7th July 2018.

not attenuate or satisfy the need for sacrifice, He teaches how to end it.

The kind of sacrifice that leads to this epiphany and genuine king-ship is not vicarious or legalistic, it is only self-sacrifice and embrace of death, receiving the true life. In the prophet Daniel's vision, the Son of Man Jesus identifies with and the Ancient of Days, who in Ortho-dox Christianity is the Logos in human form prior to the Incarnation, are separate beings. The Son of Man is said by Daniel to be presented to the Ancient of Days, which is a term sometimes denoting sacrifice, and which is used by Luke (2:22–24) to describe the infant Jesus being presented in the temple, but, crucially, not paying the usual monetary compensation for firstborn sons.

It is a sacrifice in the correct sense of making sacred, not a sacrifice in the sense of incurring a loss apotropaically, of debt, and of blood (since firstborn animals were slaughtered, firstborn human sons paying this price was the substitute for human sacrifice). Thusly is the Son of Man initiated in Daniel as monarch—receiving the kingly symbol of the throne. The Son of Man—we may identify this with Jesus of Nazareth, the man—united with the archetypal king, the Ancient of Days—the Christ—not in a barter, a legal fiction, a paying of a debt, but in an initiatic making sacred, the self-sacrifice and embrace of death whence comes new life, for which there is no substitute. This is expressed by Micah (6:7–8), with reference to the ancient sacrifice of the firstborn son:

> Would the Lord be pleased with thousands of rams, with ten thousand rivers of oil? Shall I present my firstborn for my trans-gression, the fruit of my body for the sin of my soul? He has shown you, O Mankind, what is good. And what does the Lord require of you, but to act justly, to love devotion, and to walk humbly with your God?

The Cube at the Center, the Creator in the Crater

Returning to the central fire, later we will explore its association with the sun, but this does not account for its being cuboid or quadrangular. Pythagoras, being an initiate of the Cretan Jove, would have known of the (probably) solar character of Jove in what survived of Minoan mythology. Yet his school presents the central fire as square or cube. Thomas Taylor writes in a footnote to Proclus's *Commentary on Plato's Timaeus*:

> ... five figures are the five regular bodies, viz. the dodecahedron, the pyramid, the octahedron, the icosahedron, and the cube. But the five centers are the northern, southern, eastern and western centers, and the center of the universe.

Here, the cube seems to be the central center.[135] The cube's importance is further elucidated as follows.

---

135 Proclus, *The Commentaries of Proclus on the Timaeus of Plato in Five Books*, vol. 2, III, 86.

...the beginning from the monad gives to the soul a progression from intellect; but the termination in these cubes, evinces the harmony of all the celestial orbs, for they produce by their composition the celestial harmony. Each of them likewise is a harmony. For the Pythagoreans are accustomed to call a cube harmony, because it is the only figure that has equal angles, analogous to the sides of the superficies.[136]

Again, following Proclus in his Scholia on the Cratylus, this central cube is feminine and is Vesta, were its demiurgic production of souls with Jove is Juno. The terminus of harmonious creation, then, is the cube. The cube can be conceived as the filled-in space of a cross extended on several planes, or something similar to Salvador Dali's *Corpus Hypercubus* (Hyper-Cuboidal Body) in one of his paintings of the Crucifixion. We have the motif in Egyptian art of sitting upon a cube, the throne or created completion of the transcendent Lord, the cube of the Kaaba as central in Islam, the central cube of the Bible and Pythagoreans, and so on. Christian descriptions of the cross as Christ's throne are likewise consistent with this, for an out-folded cube revealing its six faces on a plane can take the form of a cross, as can a fourth-dimensional cube, the tesseract, which may be represented by the three-dimensional so-called *Dali cube*, on which the surrealist artist depicted Christ.

As for the association of the central cuboidal fire with the sun, this probably relates to the widespread identification of cross with sun: The Celtic cross or sun-wheel where the solar body is pointing in four directions attests to the connection. The luminosity of the sun and its round infinity is attained by way of crucifixion, of the four corners, and the transcendent or solar intellect contains in itself the design for the world—that is, the four corners.

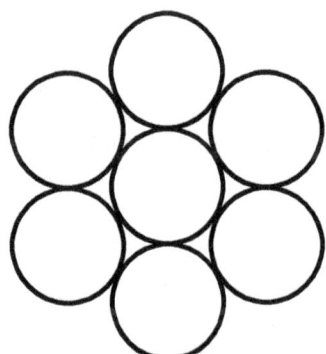

We may gain insight into the cube and circle by looking at numbers associated with the heavenly city or estate in sacred traditions. Its twelve gates and the seventy-two nations of Genesis or Islamic heavenly wives,

---

136   Ibid., 100.

and the one-hundred forty-four thousand sealed souls, are all divisible by six and three. This applies to the three-hundred sixty degrees of a circle as well. (All but the number twelve are divisible by nine, the number of worlds in Norse myth and curates around the throne in some Greek traditions, the gates of the body.)

Six is a circular number, a number that expresses the perfection of the circle, because it takes six circles to surround a circle of the same size. As the Shepherd of Hermas says: "the six men, and the glorious and mighty man in the midst of them, him that walked about the tower.... The glorious man...is the Son of God, and those six are the glorious angels who guard Him on the right hand and on the left..." (Parable 9, 12:7–8).

Five is too few, seven too many (see illustration, left). This implies the number seven, where the seventh circle is the center of the rest, like white light and the six colors of the rainbow. Let us repeat the same exercise in three dimensions. Consider a sphere: how many equally sized spheres can be in contact with a central one? The answer was provided by Johannes Kepler and argued for by Isaac Newton: twelve (sometimes called the *Newton number*).

These twelve can be collocated in a *cubic packing* arrangement, though other configurations are possible. If we start thinking of the central shape for the Bible and Pythagoras, we note that six is also the number of faces on a cube, and twelve is its number of edges. The cube has twelve edges and eight vertices, so the twelve gates of the new Jerusalem and the eight signs around the central circle of the Taoist *I Ching*, the octagonal Holy Roman Imperial crown and Frederick Barbarossa's chandelier at Aachen representing the new Jerusalem find themselves in that shape too. They complete creation, representing the eighth day of resurrection after the six days of creation and seventh day of rest in Genesis. So, the cube seems to be the gate (be it twelve edges or eight vertices) and surrounding (six faces like six circles around a seventh), around an inner circularity, a heavenly sphericity, a secret spiritual sun which nonetheless is also a secret quadrangle, in that it contains the four ideas (like Platonism's Crater, like the sun-wheel).

Plato's Crater as the Holy Grail and Aeneas as Grail Knight

The Platonic Crater as divine feminine can be linked to the holy grail symbol. Some accounts of that mythos include seeing the world, with all its crevices and smoothness, in the holy grail, just as the Crater, Juno, gives forth the world, created with the Demiurge, Jove. This reminds us of Bulgakov's essay on the grail, where he maintains that the blood that fell upon the ground during Christ's crucifixion renders the whole earth the holy grail. The Crater in Plato's *Timaeus* is the matrix of manifestation (Juno) upon which the Demiurge Jove acts. Since the Crater constellation is traditionally said to be Apollo's, we are dealing with an identification of the higher solar intellect rather than its particular, initiatic monarchical function (the First rather than Second Paternal Intellect, in neo-Platonic terms, or else the Second Paternal Intellect or Demiurge as distinct from the individual initiate, if we translocate the schema onto a lower ontological plane). Proclus describes the Crater as a grail, *fontal*:

> This Crater, therefore, is a fontal Crater; since it is the cause of souls so far as they are souls, and not of all life.... Plato likewise elsewhere calls soul itself the fountain of prudence.... Much more therefore, should we call according to him, the first soul fontal, and the Crater fontal, if there is a Crater established with the Demiurgus of wholes.[137]

Other craters include that from which Hebe pours wine and from which Vulcan drinks, distributing nectar to all the gods.[138] We are dealing with a metaphysical component of reality symbolized as dish or cup, that is, a chalice, a grail, which manifests at different levels: At one level it is prior to the world-soul, which Jove the Demiurge brings about in Juno the Receptacle by receiving its paradigm (the autozoon) from his mother Rhea; and at another level it is the empowering drink that makes a king powerful over his realm (common in Irish folklore), that is, his specific part in (re-)creating the world, his *demiurgia* (demiurgic-work, as Iamblichus calls it).

The Platonic Crater of the *Timaeus*, identified by neo-Platonists as goddess Juno, "mother of souls," and also with goddess Vesta in its connection with the cosmic center of the Pythagoreans[139] is the place to which spiritual initiates go to be judged, undone in ritual death and reborn. It is a tomb to die in and a womb to be born from. The fact that Plato's Greek word *Krater* can refer both to a dish or cup and, as its meaning in English indicates, to a volcanic crater or opening in the earth made by a celestial object, provides the relevant associations. The spiritual significance of the holy grail myths and of mountains like the Cretan and Anatolian Ida or Sicilian Etna are the same (thus Empedocles' relationship to Etna and Hecate-related symbolism, such as the leaving behind of a single bronze sandal, which we know through the Paris

137   Ibid., V, 377.
138   Ibid., V, 378.
139   Which is described as a cube and indicates four corners, corresponding to the underworld's purgative crucifixion—the four-cornered Egyptian *Duat*—as well to exaltation and the Divine throne—the Duat being the throne-room of Osiris, who is at one with Ra. Which is described as a cube and indicates four corners, corresponding to the underworld's purgative crucifixion—the four-cornered Egyptian *Duat*—as well to exaltation and the Divine throne—the Duat being the throne-room of Osiris, who is at one with Ra. Plato describes the *autozoon* as containing the ideas of the four Empedoclean elements, and as Jove receives this from Rhea we can think of these four as contained in a transcendent non-space or Womb (since She is the First Paternal Intellect along with Saturn).

Magical Papyrus was a sign of Hecate and perhaps a way to indicate one had not simply wondered off, but rather ascended, leaving clothing items behind[140]). The meaning is death and rebirth—resurrection.

That goddess Juno should be presented as initially at enmity with the hero, as in the stories of Hercules and Aeneas, apart from other meanings, indicates the fact that ego-death is difficult: one must endure against the seeming opposition of external reality (nature with its typically feminine association), until resistance is overcome. Insofar as the holy grail is the Platonic Crater, the European Christian medieval search for the grail is identical to the Greco-Roman tradition of heroes reborn from or reconciled to Juno (Aeneas and Hercules). This is consistent with the Hebraic religiosity inherited by the classical world,[141] specifically in the demiurgic association of the king with the Lord and the role of a Divine Mother. The Jewish philosopher Philo of Alexandria "knew of a divine couple who had been parents of the King"[142] (where the king represents the Lord, YHWH, and the parents represent the High One, El Elyon, and His feminine counterpart, Wisdom or Asherah[143]).

While we may struggle to reconcile demigods with the Biblical opposition to angelic unions with human females, the provenance of Greco-Roman heroes is given different interpretations. Obviously, Aeneas is Christianized by Constantine and the conversion of the empire. In *Against Symmachus* (1.539-44), Prudentius repeats the words spoken by Jupiter to Venus concerning Rome's destiny, claiming that they are fulfilled thanks to the empire's conversion. In the case of Hercules, Jewish sources somewhat integrated him. Philo of Alexandria praises his virtues in *Embassy to Gaius* and is elsewhere favorable to him, celebrating his stories as allegories for virtue. The 2nd century BC Cleodemus Malchus writes that Heracles's lineage married that of Abraham. Other sources seem to claim Heracles was the father of Melchizedek. Epiphanius reports this in his *Panarion* (55.2.1) while discussing heresies that attribute a high

---

140 He left behind a single bronze sandal, which, via the magical Papyri, we know is a symbol of Hecate (Kingsley, *Ancient Philosophy, Mystery and Magic*, 250-51).

141 Although not always in the scriptures as handed down.

142 Barker, *The Great High Priest: The Temple Roots of Christian Liturgy*, 237.

143 They *represent* these, because El Elyon and Asherah would be equivalent to the "First Parental Intellect" in neo-Platonism, consisting of Saturn conjoined with Rhea, but the hero in Greco-Roman tradition relates to Jove and Juno, the Second Paternal Intellect. The parental images are therefore a representation of a transcendent principle just as the king manifests but does not exhaust the Lord, YHWH, in early Hebrew theology (following Margaret Barker's reconstruction). In Christian Trinitarian terms, the Ancient of Days (who the prophet Daniel sees as a bearded elder) is not the Father, but the Son, for the Father is beyond being depicted, and yet this Ancient One might *represent* the Father through his aged demeanor. The Son of Man in Daniel's vision is also the Son in Christian terms, but here representing the initiate who rises to the Ancient One's throne (so we have an ascending and a descending current, equivalent to the Islamic Sufi idea of the Qur'an's *descent* to prophet Muhammad as equivalent to Muhammad's Mi'raj or heavenly *ascent*).

spiritual station to Melchizedek, even above Jesus, writing of "a man called Heracles" considered the priest's father.

The pagans also present a more Jewish-compatible Heracles (not intentionally, but as a function of their own philosophical intuitions). The 1st century Stoic philosopher Lucius Annaeus Cornutus writes in section 31 of *On Greek Theology* that the name Hercules refers to universal reason, and that later stories should not scandalize us: the reason why the son of Alkmene and Amphitryon was identified with this name is that he was known for his virtue. Thus, the hero's human lineage is emphasized, and his union to the name Hercules is a matter of brave and godly conduct, not of lascivious divinities interacting with humans. Epictetus, in his second Discourse, writes that Hercules counted God as his greatest friend, and so came to be known as a son of God. Dio Chrysostom, who does identify Hercules as son of Zeus, writes in his first Discourse that Hermes showed the hero two visions upon a mountain. One was of Lady Royalty, and with her Justice, the other of Lady Tyranny. Hercules chose the first. The idea of mountains linked with femininity comes up again and again.

In some late German Romances, the son of Parzival, Lohengrin, is sent by King Arthur (for King Arthur features frequently in this genre) *from the Grail*. Here, the Grail is the mountain in which Arthur awaits the end days or some future time of reckoning, according to that widespread theme of great kings sleeping in mountains. This adds credence to the idea that the Holy Grail is Plato's Crater, the substrate of creation as well as the world-soul, represented by actual craters. Records of German prayers referring to the *Mary of the Grail* reiterate this idea of the Grail as the feminine womb of the world or of holiness.

A likely candidate for the historical Christian relic of the holy grail is a cup which was held in the province of Huesca of northern Aragon in Spain, at the monastery in a cave of St. John de la Peña (St. Lawrence would have died a martyr refusing to reveal where it had been taken). Consistent with this, in the Parsifal opera, Richard Wagner places the castle of the grail south of the Pyrenees. The cave of St. John de la Peña, birthplace of the kingdom of Aragon, is also where King Alfonso I the Battler retired after being injured on his side, so that he may be the historical origin of the Anfortas character.[144] The cup in question, which is now in Valencia, has been dated to between the first centuries AD and BC, and would be the product of workshops in Palestine or nearby (interestingly, the custodian of the Ark of the Covenant according to Ethiopian tradition, Emperor Haile Selassie, visited the cup in Valencia and was gifted with a reproduction of it by the Spanish royal family). Inscription on its bottom in Arabic characters have been identified as

---

144   King Alfonso contributed to the *Reconquista* and attempted to unify the Iberian kingdoms.

spelling the words *luminous, Mary* and *merciful*. Thus, the link between Mary and the Grail, and between the Grail and femininity (and the constantly recurring theme of femininity as luminous) occurs here.

The volcanic area around Pozzuoli, the ancient Greek colony at Cumae northwest of Naples where Aeneas entered the underworld according to Virgil, is identified as "Venusberg" and as the Holy Grail by certain German texts from the 15th and 16th centuries (including a translation of Rabelais from 1575).[145] The connection with the epic of Aeneas, son of Venus, is further suggested by holy grail stories where one is taken up to the third heaven, that of Venus (following what St. Paul has to say in II Corinthians about a man who was taken up into the third heaven).

The pleasures and revelries in Venusberg described by German texts may constitute a recurrence of the language associated with Elysium, which Aeneas discovers through the volcanic openings, taken by Virgil from Orphic literature (specifically, the Gold Leaf found at Thurii presents us with strong parallels). This includes gymnastics and dance in meadows and fields. The German texts sometimes suggest a perverse inversion of the terrestrial or transcendent paradise, however, one constructed by mischievous or malicious faeries as a counterfeit: the seeker must be discerning. Indeed, this provides a useful orientation when relating to paganism: while Nicholas of Cusa intuitively understands the names of gods as names of the one God designating His different relations to creation, vulgar paganism might well have allowed entities of another sort, including psychological complexes and projections, to substitute for the genuine name and the spiritual epiphanies represented by it.

Hell Above is Heaven Beneath, or Entering the Absent Centre

Margaret Barker notes the occurrence in Hebrew literature of equivalents to the three titles of the central cosmic fire according to Pythagoreanism, as mentioned by Simplicius:[146] Jove's throne, Jove's watchtower, and Jove's prison. She thereby draws a parallel between the Pythagorean central fire and the holy of holies (also indicating their common shape and substance: a quadrangular flame). The holy of holies, however, is celestial and not at the earth's center, which is not necessarily consistent with Pythagoreanism, as Peter Kingsley writes: "the overall probability must remain that in origin the Pythagorean central fire did occupy the middle of the earth."[147]

The link between a central fire and the earth's midpoint readily evokes the Egyptian Duat. The primordial mound previously mentioned is, in

---

145   Richard Barber, *The Holy Grail: Imagination and Belief* (Cambridge: Harvard University Press, 2004), 191–92.
146   Barker, *The Great Angel: A Study of Israel's Second God*, 269–70.
147   Kingsley, *Ancient Philosophy, Mystery and Magic.* 182.

fact, the upper Duat, or highest reach of the underworld,[148] such that
the base of the mountain (or stepped pyramid: a temple as stylized
mountain) corresponds to the throne at the world-center. The holy
mountain and throne is a portal to the underworld, as indicated by
its being an open volcanic crater. In Minoan culture, the mountain is
a gate to the underworld,[149] the portal by which the sun descends at
dusk and rises at dawn.[150] The Egyptians, in fact, considered Crete
the land of the setting sun,[151] which would link it to ritual death (the
initiate following the sun into the underworld at dusk). Because the
underworld contains the central fire its gate or upper limit—the holy
mountain—represents that same center as axis mundi. It is not only
the womb whence the dead are reborn but the kingly staff, like a pole
around which the world may symbolically turn, according to whose
archetype those reborn initiates become kings in their own rights. The
correspondence of mother goddess and father god, of birth canal and
staff, Juno and Jove, presents sexual symbolism.

This view appears voiced by Empedocles in the medieval Arabic *Mushaf
al-Jama'a*, translated into Latin as *Turba Philosophorum*, or Assembly of
Philosophers, with Pythagoras presiding, attributed to Archelaos, student
of Anaxagoras and teacher of Socrates. Here, Empedocles describes our
world as the surface shell of an egg. Below are the waters, the oceans of
the earth, like the egg-white. The point of the sun in the middle of the
world is the yoke, and the yoke is a chick: "Solis autem punctus I medio
rubei, qui est pullus."[152] Thus, the center of the cosmos is the sun, and
is linked to rebirth, to being as a babe, a chick ("pullus").

The underworld is also identified with sunlight in Plato's *Republic*:
our world is actually the underworld, and the apparent descent of the
initiate is an ascent into true light. Plato's work (the *Gorgias*, the *Phaedo*)
"consists of different strata." These would present us with the same
double-reading as Empedocles' philosophy, namely "the level at which
the earth's surface is still the earth's surface and Hades has not yet been
projected allegorically into the world in which we live"[153] and the level
at which it has.

The same occurs in Blake's *Marriage of Heaven and Hell* (including the
association with the inverted tree, as in Indian tradition, or the tree as
symbol for entry and exit from the world, as in Porphyry's commentary
on Homer's description of the island Ithaca):

---

148   Diethelm Eigner, *Die monumentalen Grabbauten der Spätzeit in der thebanischen
Nekropole* (Vienna: OAW, 1984), 169.
149   Marinatos, *Minoan Kingship and the Solar Goddess: A Near Eastern Koine*, 112.
150   Ibid., 115.
151   Ibid., 2.
152   Quoted in Kingsley, *Ancient Philosophy, Mystery and Magic*, 57.
153   Ibid., 113.

> ...down the winding cavern we groped our tedious way, till a void
> boundless as a nether sky appeared beneath us, and we held by the
> roots of trees.... By degrees we beheld the infinite abyss, fiery as
> the smoke of a burning city; beneath us at an immense distance
> was the sun, black but shining;

Cosmological models in which the center above is the center within (the sun is the central fire) serve as occasion for metaphysical contemplation. Writes Nicholas of Cusa: "It is no less true that the center of the world is within the Earth than that it is outside the Earth...the Blessed God is also the center of the Earth, of all spheres, of all things in the world."[154]

The central fire is sometimes located in a certain direction, although this can vary. A direction can be meant as pointing to a pole or axis mundi, which is often the case of north, or else can be *merely* directional. The central fire is sometimes identified as northern: A north staked out in fire, both purgatorial and Heavenly, like the Duat and Mount Ida: "...the northern point of the ecliptic is the region of fire (purgatory and the entrance to the Anu-heaven)," writes Carl Jung concerning Babylonian tradition, just as Mithras, the bull-slaying savior (a slaughter marking rebirth through death), is described in some texts by "endless fire-attributes" for he "obviously hails from the north," and, in Egypt, the scourge of Set, the crucible but also benediction of the four sons of Horus, Heaven's prince, are all found in the north.[155] Jung also locates the image of archetypal fish in the north, which he partly identifies with the dying and resurrecting god, such as Osiris whose phallus is swallowed by a fish, or Christ whose symbols include the fish.

According to Frithjof Schuon, however, the southern extremity sometimes receives the same Edenic symbolism among the Amerindian Lakota peoples as does the north in those traditions cited above. The Sioux also apparently invert the attributes of east and west as articulated by other cultures.[156] This indicates the relativity of these attributions, so that the central fire, which apparently also appears in Lakota cosmology,[157] is not definitively associated with one direction or another (though interestingly, it is identified with one or another of the earth's poles).

Were the Pythagorean central fire to be located outside the earth, as it is in the system of Philolaus, even this, Kingsley argues, would not extirpate its chthonic character. It would remain, in some significant wise, subterranean. The line from Homer's Iliad cited by Anatolius as the support invoked by Pythagoreans for their doctrine of the central fire

---

154 Nicholas of Cusa, *On Learned Ignorance*, trans. J. Hopkins (Minneapolis: Banning, 1985), 115.

155 Carl Jung, *Aion: Researches into the Phenomenology of the Self*, trans. R. Hull (London: Routledge, 1981), 124.

156 Frithjof Schuon, *Language of the Self* (Bloomington, IN: World Wisdom Books, 1999), 191–92.

157 Ibid., 186.

takes for granted that this fire is Tartarus,[158] locating it "as far beneath Hades as heaven is high above the earth."[159] Tartarus is outside Hades to the same degree that Heaven is outside the earth. A non-geocentric cosmos of this kind is therefore not alien to the Hellenic canon.

Therefore, the same Homeric stroke that renders the central fire extra-terrestrial also identifies it with Tartarus. Situating the center outside the earth does not cease its status as nether-realm: it remains beneath the earth but is so much beneath as to have fallen out (so to speak). This is manifested by its continuing to be described in terms of under-worldly attributes.[160] In fact, according to Kingsley, the association of the sun with an infernal blaze is notable in ancient Greek thought.[161] Minoan religion, at the root of Hellenism, likewise identifies the sun with the underworld.[162] This provides an answer to the question posed by Marinatos as to why the symbol of the Minoan goddess is used by that Bronze Age culture's iconography in relation both to the underworld and to the sky,[163] also being identified with the sun: it is because the place of torture and death is also the site of rebirth:[164] Jove's prison is also Jove's throne.

The Egyptian Duat is consistent with the above Homeric-Pythagorean imagery, which is unremarkable, given that the traditional biographies[165] of Homer, Pythagoras and Plato refer to them as students of Egyptian theology. The Duat is beneath the earth yet is in the sky. Commenting on an inscription dated to about 1280 BC, James Allen writes that it "locates the Duat within the body of Nut—that is, somehow 'inside' the sky."[166] This reminds of the association between the fiery entry into Hades at the Sicilian volcano Etna and the goddesses Hecate, Persephone or Demeter. According to the *Pyramid Texts*, the Duat at times encircles stellar constellations.[167] The notion expressed in Empedocles' fragments that the stars

---

158   Kingsley, *Ancient Philosophy, Mystery and Magic*, 183.
159   Homer, *The Iliad*, trans. I. Johnston (Nanaimo, British Colombia, Canada: Richer Resources Publications, 2006), VIII, 159.
160   Kingsley, *Ancient Philosophy, Mystery and Magic*, 181.
161   Ibid., 54–56.
162   Ibid., 46.
163   Ibid., 124.
164   "This 'central fire', as [the Alchemists] sometimes called it, was considered by them the key to the alchemical transformation process. According to them it was the real source of light—so much so that they referred to it as the 'sun in the earth', the 'subterranean' sun. on the one hand this 'earthly' or 'invisible sun' was the 'fire of hell', the 'black sun', the 'darkness of purgatory'. On the other, as the sun that 'rises out of the darkness of the earth', it was the origin not only of the visible sun but also of the light of the stars. And, significantly, they indicated that the nature of this hidden, generative fire was volcanic" (Ibid., 55–56).
165   Diodorus Siculus, *The Library of History*, vol. 1 (Cambridge, MA: Loeb Classical Library, 1933), I:96, ii; 327.
166   James Allen, *Genesis in Egypt: The Philosophy of Ancient Egyptian Creation Accounts* (New Haven: Yale University, 1988), 5–6.
167   Samuel Mercer (trans.), *The Pyramid Texts* (Online: Public Domain, 2010), 151a–c.

are trapped fire bubbles originating from an inferno beneath the earth[168] echoes the Egyptian doctrine that perfected souls unite with the stars[169] after a purgative sojourn through the subterranean realm. Further, the Duat is ever merging with (sunset) and birthing (sunrise) the Heavenly fire, Ra's disk, so that its flames are in Heaven even as it remains a necropolis. Osiris is both at one with the revolving motions of the sun and with the immobile, earthly court of the deity Ptah-Tanen (more on this later).

This is consistent with the two translations of Aristotle's *On the Heavens* that Kingsley singles out as, in his view, coming close to Philolaus's system and to the original Pythagorean doctrine of the central fire. These are the translations penned by Gerard of Cremona and by the so-called Syriac commentator. Kingsley's favor is owed to their paying due respect to the expression *Jupiter's prison*.[170] The central fire is treated as the place in which fallen angels are bound and souls judged. Kingsley argues Philolaus would have characterized the central fire in these terms (with Titans replacing fallen angels) inspired by Hesiod's *Theogony*, whereas Gerard and the Syriac commentator, being Christians, did so via the New Testament. We should recall the Orthodox Christian notion of hell and heaven as one place, experienced respectively by the yet-selfish ego and by the unselfish saint. Kingsley traces both Hesiodic Greek mythology and the New Testament to the older, common, source of Babylonian religion. Resemblances with the Egyptian Duat suggest a parallel origin.

The central fire is the absent center, a metaphysical reality often symbolized by the sun. Finding it means accepting its absence in form, dying to form. After being ripped apart until nothing is left, something *is* left. The initiate is outside all sense, no form remains, yet there is a light, the light of consciousness. Zagreus's heart—symbol of the essential self—is saved by Minerva after his dismemberment by the Titans at Mount Ida, and placed in an immortal body. From dismemberment comes awareness of the light of the inner sun. This idea occurs throughout traditions, including Christianity. The hypothesis that the Thracians considered their kings to be "Dionysus incarnate"[171] would (treating Dionysus as the Greek Osiris, a dismembered god) present a direct correspondence to Egyptian kingship's Osirian character.

The Thracian Orpheus's passage into the exclusive worship of the sun god Apollo after having been under the patronage of Dionysus, as the myth relates, may symbolize union with Ra through the tribulation of Osiris. *The Birth of the Sun and the Triumph of Bacchus*, a painting by the 18th century artist Corrado Giaquinto which decorates one of the ceilings

---

168 Kingsley, *Ancient Philosophy, Mystery and Magic*, 51.
169 Uzdavinys, *Philosophy as a Rite of Rebirth: From Ancient Egypt to Neoplatonism*, 130.
170 Kingsley, *Ancient Philosophy, Mystery and Magic*.
171 Arthur B. Cook, *Zeus: A Study in Ancient Religion*, vol. 2, Part 1 (Cambridge: Cambridge University Press, 1925), 270.

at Madrid's Royal Palace, provides an encapsulation of the intimate relationship between the dismembered and ecstatic Dionysus and the luminous Apollo. The unity of the vegetable with the solar can also be encountered a few miles south from Giaquinto's piece, in Toledo, at the far side of the city's Cathedral, which houses a golden sun with what looks like a golden rose as its center, a bloom and a blaze, the unity of rose and fire with which T. S. Eliot concludes his *Four Quartets*.

Incidentally, one can read this tradition as containing an accurate cosmology. If the center of the world by night is the sun in the sky by day, the myths correspond to reality insofar as the sun really is the center of the world, understanding *the world* as referring to the orbital plane of the earth. In this line, in their book *Hamlet's Mill*, the controversial researchers Giorgio de Santillana and Hertha von Dechend suggest that ancient models of a flat earth echoed or were superseded by knowledge of the heliocentric terrestrial orbit [172] (they argue axial precession was known to humans in the megalithic, which is beyond the present speculation). [173] As for the symbolism of the earth as flat, it may be this: that the entirety of its dynamics are perceived at one glance, like a mandala or, indeed, a map. In this way nothing is left unseen on the other side of the orb. This may be why William Blake affirmed the perception of the world as bordered by the horizon, that is, entirely gathered into man's perception and not left up to mystery or obfuscation. It fits with the stories of epiphany presenting the initiate with a flat world (St. Peter seeing the corners of the earth gathered up, for example, in *Acts*).

But an accurate cosmology confirms the metaphysics of initiation. Our searching, like a "concupiscent conqueror" finally comes to rest in the fact that going far is a return, a rounding off of the spherical earth, and so the epiphany of discovering that the world is round has a spiritual impact, as Eric Voegelin argues in his *Ecumenic Age*. [174] That deep-down fiery center to which one descends, revealed as the transcendent celestial light (represented by the sun), turns out to be unmoving (relative to the earth). It is the profound stillness, the unmoving mover whose gravity keeps the surface self—the earthly realm—orbiting around it.

But the initiate who goes around the world to find home also goes inwardly to find the heights. The initiate is itself the sacrificial animal of archaic rites. In that animal's lair and place of deathly hibernation, the Greek *pholeos*, like ancient Orphic and Pythagorean rituals of incubation (*enkoimesis*), beneath the earth, in cavernous isolation, in volcanic openings, mastering sleep itself, the initiate enters the underworld in

---

172   Giorgio de Santillana and Hertha von Dechend, *Hamlet's Mill: An Essay Investigating the Origins of Human Knowledge and Its Transmission Through Myth* (Boston: Nonpareil Books, 2014).

173   For a digression on heliocentrism see Addendum I.

174   Voegelin, *Order and History Volume IV, The Ecumenic Age*, 272.

the manner of Buddhist dream yoga: *retaining lucidity*. If the practitioner remains lucid even into dreamless deep-sleep, alike formless death itself, there shines a radiance only a clear mind may perceive. A radiance in the dead of night, in the place of incubation, in the depth of sleep. Thusly is the sun-god also the god of the animal lair (Apollo the *Pholeuterios*).[175] The sun in the underworld.

The Centrality of the Sun and the Danger of Idolatry

The sun is also *conceptually* central to various traditions. In the case of Egyptian myth, the focus is on the drama of Osiris becoming gerent of the underworld—the *Duat*—and thereby also uniting with the solar deity, Ra. In the Greek case, it is the lineage of Pythagoras and Plato (including their exegetes) that is addressed: both Pythagoras[176] and Plato[177] being identified by their successor lineage as Apollonian (solar) incarnations. Indeed, Pythagoras was born on a Greek island whose colonization was ordered by Apollo's oracle, and upon his birth word was sent to his parents from that oracle pertaining to his destiny. He was further recognized as an incarnated Apollo by one journeying from the sun god's far-north: Abaris the Hyperborean. Melchizedek to his Abraham. This mysterious teacher and witness to the status of Pythagoras, "Abaris, alleged to be a Hyperborean, who carried the arrow over the whole world, fasting all the while" (Herodotus, *Histories*, 4:36, 2) bestowed that arrow, or spear or lance, on the Hellene, and, with it, healed the Greeks from a plague which was then afflicting them. In the Hebrew case, it is to the partisans of Enoch that attention is given. This seventh antediluvian Biblical patriarch may be linked to the heliacal figure of the seventh pre-deluge Mesopotamian monarch Enmeduranki, "king of Sippar, the city of the sun god Shamash" by way of common epithets,[178] as Andrei Orlov establishes (Algis Uzdavinys agrees with the Mesopotamian link,[179] as does Peter Kingsley,[180] and there is evidence that the ancient Mesopotamian throne room at Mari near the Euphrates was imitated by various Bronze Age cultures, indicating that Mesopotamia exerted great influence).

---

175   Peter Kingsley explores all this: *In the Dark Places of Wisdom* (Point Reyes, CA: The Golden Sufi Center Publishing, 2019).

176   Iamblichus, *Life of Pythagoras or Pythagoric Life*, trans. T. Taylor (London: John M. Watkins, 1818), II, 2–3.

177   Olympiodorus, *The Life of Plato and On Plato First Alcibiades*, 1–9, trans. Michael Griffin (London: Bloomsbury, 2016), 25–30, 72.

178   Andrei Orlov, *The Enoch-Metatron Tradition*, Texts and Studies in Ancient Judaism (Book 107). (Tubingen: Mohr-Siebeck, 2005), 26.

179   Algis Uzdavinys, *Chaldean Divination and the Ascent to Heaven*. In: Patrick Curry, *Seeing with Different Eyes: Essays in Astrology and Divination* (Newcastle: Cambridge Scholars Publishing, 2007), 30.

180   Kingsley, *Ancient Philosophy, Mystery and Magic*, 211.

Enoch's lifespan reflects the solar year, consisting as it does, according to the Bible, of 365 (year-long) days (Genesis 5:23), and the Islamic tradition places him in the fourth Heaven, the solar circle which, for the Ibn Arabi, is the pole of the other six heavenly spheres, being the middle heaven. This is consistent with the suggestion that the Qumran texts are critical of the second Jerusalem temple for following a lunar rather than a solar calendar.[181]

Andrei Orlov identifies a substantial literature of anti-Moses polemic in pro-Enoch texts,[182] such that Enochic Judaism (heir to Mesopotamian heathenry) can be contrasted with the historic mainstream of Mosaic Judaism (and, via Barker, contrasted specifically with Moses considered as author of Deuteronomy and therefore as the basis for the seventh century BC proto-Protestant iconoclastic reformation, identified with the canon of scripture defined by the figure of Ezra). The link between Enoch and Mesopotamian religion also allows us to guess at the motives of those Jewish loyalists of the pre-Josianic temple who joined the Babylonian army against their own countrymen.[183] The roots of this antagonism could be further situated within Margaret Barker's account of the reform to which King Josiah subjected Jerusalem temple observance in the seventh century BC.[184]

Under the guidance of a certain priest Hilkiah, Josiah used a supposedly newly discovered book of Deuteronomy to reform practices, including removing and destroying the tree in the temple courtyard that represented the goddess Asherah and collapsing the figure of the High God El Elyon into YHWH. Barker has argued that prior to this subversion the prevailing *cultus* was consistent with Enochic lore (as found in the Book of Enoch).[185] (Emphasizing the Enochic literature is perhaps also justified by the fact of the Book of Enoch being set in a pre-Abrahamic period, prior to the Biblical distinction between Israel and gentiles and for this reason readable in a universalist light, emphasizing the commonality between this Hebrew religion and other traditions.[186])

This traumatic episode of iconoclasm would have been undergone in compliance with the book of Deuteronomy, bearing Moses's patronage. It echoes Akhenaten's savaging of the Egyptian cult centuries before, and may be invoked as the descendent of Amarna theology, following

181   Hanan Eshel, "4Q390, the 490-Year Prophecy and the Calendric History." In: Gabriele Boccaccini (ed.), *Enoch and Qumran Origins: New Light on a Forgotten Connection* (Grand Rapids, MI: Eerdmans, 2005), 110.
182   Orlov, *The Enoch-Metatron Tradition*, 254.
183   Barker, *The Great Angel: A Study of Israel's Second God*, 319.
184   Margaret Barker, *Temple Theology: An Introduction* (London: The Society for Promoting Christian Knowledge, 2004), 76–78.
185   Margaret Barker, *The Older Testament: The Survival of Themes from the Ancient Royal Cult in Sectarian Judaism and Early Christianity* (Sheffield: Sheffield Phoenix Press, 2005).
186   Although these texts often emphasize Israel, as Metatron is presented as intervening on behalf of that nation.

Jan Assman[187] (although the contour of a possible line of descent is not the present discussion's object).

Accounts concerning the fleeing by loyalists to the previous Solomonic rite into Arabia and southern Egypt, whose temple was considered ritually correct, and siding with Babylonians against their heretical co-religionists, as well as the general conformity of a reconstructed pre-Josianic Jerusalem temple cosmology with other religious systems, supports a perennialist view. This corresponds to the somewhat widespread late antique view, expressed by Julian the Apostate, for example, that Abraham was a Chaldean star-gazer and that his religiosity was not at odds with other ancient religions.[188] However, this would ignore the explicit theology of the Abraham account, according to which Babylon had fallen into idolatry, so that the patriarch's migration to the levant is required to establish a separate nation. In the Biblical narrative, if the nations were originally righteous following the destruction of the tower of Babel, a general apostasy had now occurred. Far later, after the Josianic reform, the Babylonians would, despite their continued idolatry, be an instrument for correction.

The Amarna reform, possibly constituting an antecedent to that reform, may be conceptually related to an error that recurs throughout history, and which Jean Hani warns against,[189] when kingship is not understood as the paradoxical representation of the absent center and, instead, the person who is king identifies *as kingship*. As Henry Corbin writes:

> If worship can be directed toward a theophanic person, it is because that person, by refusing divinity for himself, thereby renders himself transparent to the Divinity, Who nevertheless can only be worshipped through that theophany.[190]

(Although the word *veneration* is more appropriate than *worship*, where veneration of an icon is expressive of worship given only to God.)

Akhenaten focused his devotion on the sun, as did Egyptian state religion prior to him, as well as the Ramesside theology that followed him, and as do traditions throughout the world. However, he apparently did so to a fault, excluding the rest of the faith and seemingly addressing the divinity of the sun as a sensible, imminent object, falling into idolatry, as well as correspondingly concentrating the mediation of divine realities to his people in his own person.

The correct view is to relativize the link between king and kingship. The individual occupying the post of king is not always in a state of ritual action upon the world. As Marinatos notes, ritual vestments, washing and

---

187   Jan Assman, *Moses the Egyptian: The Memory of Egypt in Western Monotheism* (London: Harvard University Press, 1998).
188   James Kugel, *The Bible as It Was* (London: The Belknap Press of the Harvard University Press, 2001), 139.
189   Jean Hani, *Sacred Royalty: From the Pharaoh to the Most Christian King.*
190   Corbin, *Cyclical Time and Ismaili Gnosis*, 172.

actions indicate that kingship was a state of being into which the king
and queen could enter and from which they could exit, so that they were
not necessarily always in a theurgic state of empowerment.[191] This state
is therefore distinct from the individuals involved. Indeed, in Minoan
culture, it was the dead king, not the living, who received offerings, so
that the possible identification of a particular encounterable individual
with the principle of kingship that is paid tribute to is avoided.[192] The
theme of the *devi* (deity) as corpse, just like the Christian saint who has
died to himself and to worldly things, is also found in Tantric Indian.

This is the principle that allows the universal archetype of king to
be divided or translated, as in the translatability Jan Assman observes
in ancient Egypt's dealings with foreign rulers, or in the case of Diocletian's dividing the personal title of *Augustus* between east and west.
The Augustus is not exhausted in any one person, so there can be more
than one individual holder of that office, while the office itself remains
singular. When Jesus tells His disciples that it is good that He leave
them, His words can be interpreted in these terms, where the absence
of an empirical person they have identified with the Logos allows for
the universality of the Logos to be properly received.

The above does not, therefore, contradict the doctrine of the Incarnation in Christianity or Divine Avatars in India, as realization includes a
movement upward from the perspective of what is lower and downward
from what is higher, and it is one thing to reach a fountain at the top of
a mountain and another to receive its water in a river that courses down.
There is he who forgets and is reminded, and there is He who remembers
and comes to remind. The Incarnation or the Avataric descents remind
us that agency is of God, with eruptions of the miraculous interrupting
the religious life, which risks seeming like a completely managed and
ritualized relationship with the Divine, just as one does not always
encounter absorption into contemplation of God when one wants or at
places laid apart for it but can find oneself flung into it or pulled in by
it at an unsuspected moment's notice. The Gospel of John teaches us to
be active, to ask and seek and perform works, while in full submission
to the agency of God, as does the *Bhagavad Gita*.

John Milbank describes this confusion occurring in Byzantium's
iconoclasm "... there has always been a danger here of an over-realized
eschatology, with the king claiming a plenitude of iconic presence: in
Byzantium this was one factor in the iconoclastic attempt to ban sacred
images, thereby focusing all mediation on the person of the emperor."[193]
These words could almost be read as describing Akhenaton's Amarna

---

191   Marinatos, *Minoan Kingship and the Solar Goddess: A Near Eastern Koine*, 35.
192   Ibid., 48.
193   Milbank, *Beyond Secular Order: The Representation of Being and the Representation
of the People*, 198.

reform. Indeed, modern theological trajectories have also sometimes erred in failing to distinguish between levels, as, for example, the over-stated claim that Haile Selassie of Ethiopia is the unique second coming of Christ by Rastafarians, rather than an example of Christological kingship (which traditional Ethiopian monarchy can claim to be, without commenting on this particular monarch's reign).

If Christian liturgy is a continuation of pre-seventh century BC Jerusalem patterns of worship,[194] (or more accurately, of the Adamic covenant as presented in *Jubilees* or Hosea) and if this latter is one expression of broader tradition (consistent in salient features with Egyptian, Greek and Indian practices), then discussion of the split between Christianity and paganism (glossing over the inexactitude of this second term) is less descriptive than is that of the contrast between iconodule forms of religiosity and both idolatrous and iconoclastic ones. Where such iconodulism is present, a Christian may search for instances of *praeparatio evangelica*.

Of Crypts and Chariots

The revelation of infernal as celestial occurs in the coincidence of images associated with initiation such as tomb and womb or crypt and chariot. The image of the chariot is widespread. According to Plato via Socrates, the chariot is a metaphor for the human person, driven by the divine center who must be given the reigns to appetitive portions of the soul, where our conscious awareness is a passenger, like Prince Arjuna in the *Bhagavad Gita*, who must awaken by learning from his driver, Lord Krishna. In the Greek, Apollonian tradition we have the account of Parmenides, priest of Apollo, who describe his journey into Heavenly realms on a chariot driven by the daughters of the sun, which connects it to the solar chariot of Egyptian religion. The image features prominently in Jewish Merkabah mysticism as well, with its roots in the throne epiphanies of Old Testament prophets who see the divine human form upon a throne-chariot. The "cosmic crypt"[195] ceases to be a crypt once we are passed its stellar firmament and realize the starry courses as symbolic of principles in ourselves, so that the crypt was both our birth into cosmic consciousness and is the body born of that dazzling darkness beyond the stars in which the stars and earth now appear as our own body, and the astral courses are like fiery wheels in a chariot which is like a human vehicular body.

Ritual death leaves the initiate poised for second birth, and in this sense is a planting rather than a burial. As Christ says, the seed must die in order to sprout (John 12:24). The imagery of the infernal fire to which one descends before realizing its identity with celestial light emphasizes that the former phase is one of apparent burial, of venturing bravely

194 Barker, *The Great High Priest: The Temple Roots of Christian Liturgy*.
195 Corbin, *Avicenna and the Visionary Recital*, 16–28.

into the underworld and facing fear, especially the fear of death. It is fitting, then, that this appears in the form of actual burial chambers, in which the initiate is suspended in isolation, as was apparently the case of the Eleusinian Mysteries. Isolation, the deprivation of sensory stimuli, forces the mind to project one's psychic matter out, even producing hallucinations. This matter can then be confronted. The Tibetan Book of the Dead tells us that upon dying, losing its support in the material/ gross body, the subtle/psychic body will find its contents animated all about it in the Bardo realm, equivalent to the Western Limbo. Over-coming these mental fixations, these hopes and fears, the third, noetic or properly speaking spiritual component of the personality is liberated.

The practice of reciting specific formula recommended by the Tibetan and Egyptian Books of the Dead, as well as Kabbalist texts, seems to indicate that disciplining the mind, which is an auxiliary result of spiritual asceticism, is necessary to *keep it together*, so to speak, and overcome ritual or actual death without being swept away by sleep and unconscious forces, to walk rather than drown in the waters. This sometimes involves *sleep yoga*, where one retains consciousness through falling asleep, dreaming and into deep sleep, which is considered a nightly experience of the unconditioned light encountered at death. However, discipline should not be considered a matter of mere mental rigor. Christ teaches that his yoke is easy. By relinquishing flights of affect for and against this or that, one is disciplined by default. Simple surrender makes one master. Self-surrender is self-mastery. Letting go of the monsters of desire and aversion ensures they are not there to haunt one, at night or at death.

The burial, the isolation of the crypt which is actually initiatic incu-bation, a tomb that is a womb, especially given the maternal character of the mountains that symbolize it, is a head-on dive into deep sleep and the clearing of whatever nightmares dwell in our un-distracted mind, a facing up to and exorcising of these specters, Nietzsche's spirit of heaviness, so that it cannot weigh us down and, like Parmenides, we may be light enough to travel on that solar chariot with the daughters of Apollo to meet and be reborn from what he calls the Unnamed Goddess.

Sacred Rivers in a World without Seas, or Integrating the Lower and Higher Natures

In order to attain rebirth, the hero must reconcile with the Divine feminine as mother. This is conveyed in the above idea of surrender to *amor fati*, the death of Odin, and so on. Enjoyment of creation as feminine form comes from recognizing it as deriving from the Eternal Feminine. Receiving the consort and becoming king will first require accepting and being reborn from the prior strata of reality. In the *Deva Bhagavatam* (IX:13, 114–125),[196] Ganga (the being represented by the

---

196   The S'Rimad Devi Bhagavatam, *One of the Upapuranas, devoted to the Devi (God-dess)*, 861.

Ganga river, whose forms include the watery sustenance of life, and who is apparently a *gopi*, a female lover of Krishna) flees from Radha when she is caught with Krishna, and hides under Krishna's feet, knowing it is Radha's intention to drink her whole.

In hiding, the worlds are denied water, and so the creator god, Brahma, along with Vishnu and a form of Shiva, go looking for her. The problem is solved by having Ganga learn how to worship Radha, revealing that Ganga is a declination of Radha, deriving from her and Krishna as their liquid form. Thus, instead of being reintegrated into the Divine femininity, retreating from the created order back into the prior reality or plenary form (being drunk in by Radha), Ganga can become involved in the creation of new worlds thereafter. Brahma speaks:

> 'O Radha! Ganga, appeared from Thee and the Lord Sri Krishna. Both of you were transformed before into the liquid forms in the Rasa Mandalam, on hearing the music of Shankara. And That Liquid Form is Ganga. So She is born of Thee and Sri Krishna. Hence She is like Thy daughter and to be loved as such. She will be initiated in Thy Mantra and She will worship Thee. The four-armed Lord of Vaikuntha will be Her husband. And when She will appear in parts on earth, the Salt Ocean will be Her husband. O Mother! The Ganga that dwells in Goloka, is dwelling everywhere. O Governess of the Devas! Thou art Her mother; and She is always Thy Self born daughter.' Hearing thus, the words of Brahma, Radha gave Her assent towards the protection of Ganga.

In order to 'forgive' the pairing of creation (or the *water*, the substrate of creation, Ganga) with the Divine Bridegroom (Krishna) creation must be understood (or must understand itself) as a form or extension (a limb, adornment) of the Divine Bride which is beyond creation and its waters (Radha). In Christian terms: creation and humanity are the bride of Christ if it submits and is revealed as Sophia, the earthly form of the Heavenly feminine. Creation begins anew. Lord Krishna speaks to Brahman Vishnu and Shiva:

> Now the Kalpa is going to expire. So in the other regions than Goloka and Vaikuntha, the Brahmas, etc., that were existing in all other Universes, have all now dissolved in My Body. O Lotus-born! Save Goloka and Vaikuntha, all are now under water, the pre-state of earth. Better go and create your own Brahmandas and Ganga will go to that newly created Brahmanda. I will also create other worlds and the Brahmas thereof. Now you all better go with the Devas and do your own works respectively. You have waited here for a long interval. As many Brahmas that have fallen all appear again. (*Deva Bhagavatam*, IX:13, 126–36)[197]

---

197   Ibid., 861–62.

Therefore, chapter 3 of book 9 of the *Deva Bhagavatam* seems to explain what Greco-Roman tradition tells us of its heroes (although in the tradition of the Deva Bhagavatam, the Goddess Radha expresses the Divine feminine in general, probably exceeding the role of Juno in Greco-Roman myth). The created order and specifically their life's mission within the world are perceived egotistically, which is to say, with reference to the ordinary self rather than to the Divine. Juno opposes their undertakings because they do not understand these as a form of her own self, albeit at a lower level of reality. However, by recognizing their life and nature as a form of the Divine, Juno accepts them and they overcome. One cannot proceed with one's engagement with the world if one treats the Divine as separate, absent from it all.

The Ganga here connects to a general symbolism for water. Water is feminine and sometimes symbolizes the oscillations (which the *Yoga Sutras* tell us must cease) of the unenlightened self (an obscure perception; not perceiving the Divine). Water is made holy when it is internalized by the subject and is no longer a force *out there*. Thus, the Biblical idea that rivers are holy and oceans are to be abolished: the river circulates in land, the ocean is outside human dwelling:

> In apocalyptic symbolism we have the "water of life," the fourfold river of Eden which reappears in the City of God, and is represented in ritual by baptism. According to Ezekiel the return of this river turns the sea fresh, which is apparently why the author of Revelation says that in the apocalypse there is no more sea. Apocalyptically, therefore, water circulates in the universal body like the blood in the individual body. Perhaps we should say "is held within" ... [198]

The crater, grail, or cup likewise contains liquid and its association with femininity and the fourfold relates to the holiness of the four rivers from the Chinese mountain of immortals to Eden. Waters contained in this way are living waters, as in the Gospel. That is, they are not outside life, not mere chaotic force imagined to be outside Logos. Water is remembered not to be chaos but a projection of consciousness. As discussed elsewhere, the mystery of matter is that there is no chaotic pre-formal *prima materia*, but matter is always already formed, it always has some particular form, the Matter, the Mother, is always already paired to the Paternal Intellect of Platonism. This is a macranthropic epiphany because once the body is made global, all water is within it. It thus ceases to be salty, it becomes fresh, as in Ezekiel, it is no longer unconsumable by the human subject (corresponding with the Gospel's doctrine of apostles drinking poison without damage).

---

198   Frye, *Anatomy of Criticism: Four Essays*, 146.

Water must be remembered (the water in us must remember itself) to be at one with the Divine, to be extensions of Radha/Juno. This involves death and rebirth. Aeneas and his people take a new form favored by Juno, as Latins rather than Trojans. As son of Venus, Aeneas sees the reconciliation of Venus to Juno, equivalent to the reconciliation of Ganga to Radha above. Heroes often overcome the waters by sailing across a stormy sea, as in the case of Aeneas who finally makes it north of the Mediterranean, like the *metaxy* filled with our wrathful projections, the abyss of occultism, between the conditioned self of Carthaginian luxury and the awakened, active consciousness of Rome. Poseidon and Aeolus attack, they are the holders of deviated or un-integrated powers (the fire-crested sea snakes, representing initiation through the image of fire, but in a wild, watery form) and the four parts of the whole, like the four rivers of Eden or corners of the earth, but not yet Edenic, not yet parceled in St. Peter's vision (the four winds Aeolus releases on Aeneas).

After overcoming these Aeneas is glorified by the deity of the Tiber River, so like Ezekiel's imagery and Biblical symbolism, his spiritual progress passes from sea to river. Further, what was once a gap to cross (the stormy Mediterranean) will be encompassed by the fruit of its crossing, imperial Rome, ecumenic peace, *pax Romana*, rendering the Mediterranean, which is the ordeal or abyss in Aeneas's quest, as the *mare nostrum*. Here we grasp Virgil's metaphor of Roman rule as initiatic epiphany (the stormy sea with its many waves framed in the political intrigue of Greek, Carthaginian and Italic tribes is like the desert of Jahiliya idolatry with its many deities in the narrative of early Islam, framed by the rival interests of Abyssinian, Persian and Byzantine empires).

It occurs after a war that ends the heroic age, the age of heroism as personal glory and hubris, introducing, per John Alvis's reading of Homer, an age of heroic humility and piety, following Jove's plan, a theme which Virgil's later account of Aeneas as the pious one conforms to. The Trojans' new Latin identity allows for new creativity, new interface with the feminine matrix of the world, producing, in the case of the Trojans, an Empire. It involves dissolution, returning to the fundamentals of reality, an initiatic death like the trials of Hercules or the journey to the underworld of Aeneas (which, at a grand scale, occurs during the end of a great cycle and re-creation of the worlds mentioned above). Hercules likewise is re-birthed in Olympus as son of Juno. In the Heavenly realms of the Vaikuntha, the Goddess of Fortune, Lakshmi, "stays (permanently) in Hari's residence giving up her noxious quality (of fickleness)" (*Bhagavatam Purana*, 3.15:21),[199] she is entirely devoted to the Lord (Hari) Krishna, and in that place, the devotees of Krishna are embraced in salvation.

---

199   (Delhi: Motilal Banarsidass, 1950), 306.

The Throne is the Body

And now, after losing track of life itself, the king is in his body again. Freshly born from the cosmic mother Rhea, innocent and sensitive to the world, worthy of ruling, for "a little child shall lead them" (Isaiah 11:6). Whether he only thought himself dead or did actually die, he does not know, only that he is alive presently, but not as before, not so as to forget what he is.

The king is very much alive in the conventional sense—embodied. The "supreme Lord" is established within the practitioner, as described in the Jayakhya-Samhita and Lakshmi Tantra.[200] The Pythagorean appellations of Jove's throne, tower and prison, as well as their being associated with mountains, can be forthrightly understood as indicating the body itself. It is a prison in that one is bound to the limitations and privations of mortality and finitude (there are many traditional accounts in which the body is referred to as a prison); it is a throne in that one may attain to spiritual realization within it, and; it is a watchtower in that the ascetic practice requires mindful and impassible observation of sense perception from within the body. Finally, it is a mountain, dual like the Pythagorean central fire, both high and low, reaching to the Heavens and also a cavernous or volcanic opening into nether-regions, granting the duality of the human experience, and of realization itself, which is an out-going and an in-going, a supreme ecstasy and an *instasy*, a discovery of one's deepest recess, which is precisely gifted by the transcendent.

The body of the initiate as mountain occurs in Taoist tradition, such as in the Chinese painter Liang Kai's 13th century depiction of a *Drunken Celestial*, which appears to use motifs proper to representations of mountains,[201] or the *Inner Meaning of the Wondrous Scripture of the Upper Chapters on Salvation* (*Duren shangpin miaojing neiyi*), which presents human anatomy upon the depiction of a mountain.[202]

As the *Bhagavad Gita* (5:13) teaches: the soul of the yogi is seated as a god (divinely enthroned) inside a town of nine gates (the body). The nine corybantic dancers at the Cretan Mount Ida correspond to the nine orifices of the human body (ears, eyes, nostrils, mouth, urethra and anus) and to the nine months of pregnancy through which the human person enters the world: Mount Ida, the upper Duat and all holy mountains in which the divine feminine incubates initiates are in this sense a womb leading to spiritual rebirth. The Sumerian goddess Ninkur's name means something like Lady Mountain, and one of her alternative names, Nin-imma, Lady Vulva. The Holy Mountain is the Holy Mother's organ, and death in its volcanic catacombs is the second birth of initiation.

---

200   Flood, *The Tantric Body: The Secret Tradition of Hindu Religion*, 116.
201   Fabrizio Pregadio, *The Encyclopedia of Taoism: A–Z* (New York City: Routledge, 2008), 76.
202   Ibid., 767.

The number of the body also recurs in Odin's story, precisely high-lighting the fact that the spiritual quest requires facing mortality. The god of war and poetry hangs for nine nights and learns "nine mighty songs."[203] Mortality, constituted by the "nine worlds… home where dead men dwell"[204] is below the three abodes of immortality, three heavens (the highest of which includes *Gimlé* and is inhabited by the angelic species of light-elves).[205] Yet this mortality in which dwell the dead (for many who seem alive are sleep-walkers, like the dead whom Christ would let bury the dead) is elevated, revealed as sacred by the nine songs Odin attains from below, that is, from the roots of the tree of life: magic or sanctity, the eternal arcana or archetypes, are at the roots of temporality. The dwelling of the goddess Freya is in "the ninth" world, "Folkvang" where she "decrees who shall have seats in the hall."[206] The eternal feminine is at the threshold of the nine mortal worlds and the three heavens, she mediates mortality and immortality. This female mediation is already contemplated by Odin when he learns women's sorcery and receives the Mead of Poetry from a woman. In the Norse context, and being related to femininity, we may also refer to the eschaton-foreseeing god Heimdallr, "son of nine mothers."[207]

Odin hangs on the world-tree Yggdrasil, "I was offered to Odin, myself to myself,"[208] an initiation prefaced by his learning of female sorcery, receiving the Mead of Poetry from the giantess Gunnloth,[209] possibly in the context of a sacred marriage[210] (there is also some indication of a temporary marriage between Odin and Freya[211]) by a golden stool.[212] In the Odinic journey, the overcoming of the tree of Mimir's guard is said to require the use of the *Laevatein* wand, a weapon that "nine locks fasten,"[213] possibly signifying its being held as secret treasure in the castle of nine gates, the body. This weapon is forged by Loki, which adds credence to the notion that the latter Titan is related to the underworld's fire, assuming the Hall of Lyr and its resident goddess represent the sort

203 Anonymous, *The Poetic Edda*, trans. Henry Adams Bellows (New York City: Princeton University Press, 1936), "The Ballad of the High One," 141, 61.

204 Ibid., *The Poetic* Edda, "The Ballad of Vafthruthnir," 43, 80.

205 Rudolf Simek, *A Dictionary of Northern Mythology*, trans. A. Hall (Rochester, NY: D. S. Brewer, 2000), 109.

206 Anonymous, *The Poetic Edda*, "The Ballad of Grimnir," 14, 90–91.

207 Snorri Sturluson, *The Prose Edda: Tales from Norse Mythology*, trans. A. Brodeur (Mineola, NY: Dover Publications, 2006), "The Poesy of Skalds": VIII, 113.

208 Anonymous, *The Poetic Edda*, "The Ballad of the High One," 139, 60.

209 Ibid., 106, 51.

210 Lee Hollander, *The Poetic Edda* (Austin, TX: University of Texas Press, 1990), notes, 28, 30.

211 Rudolf Simek, *A Dictionary of Northern Mythology*, trans. A. Hall (Rochester, NY: D. S. Brewer, 2000), 250.

212 Anonymous, *The Poetic Edda*, "The Ballad of the High One," 106, 51.

213 Ibid., *The Ballad of Svipdagsmol*, 42, 245.

of beatific infernality touched on previously, and assuming their connection to Mimir's tree. This can be compared to Odin's hanging on the world-tree and the already mentioned association with Mimir.

Another lesson can be drawn from the fact that the structure we have been discussing (at once mountain, throne, tower and prison) is, for Proclus, the *axis mundi*: "The Pythagoreans call the middle 'the tower of Zeus'..."[214] (—by *middle* he means the center of the earth). It is a prison, therefore, also in the sense of being the inescapable, necessary center without which no coherent action is possible, but for this very reason it is a throne: *amor fati*, the embrace of life as it truly is, represents a crowning achievement resulting in inward freedom, as Nietzsche observed. The initiate finds such a center inside, within and beyond the very contingent features he happens to inhabit, even in the midst of the bodily.

In Stones they Slumber

Before moving on, we should avoid giving the impression through the preceding that ritual death and rebirth are a one-off experience to be overcome forever. This may be true in terms of the dramatic character of ego-death. But as a technology, they are also ever-utilizable. A king may 'die' for a few centuries until he is needed again. The idea of ritual death in a mother mountain of the kingly initiate sheds light on the recurring theme of a king who is not truly dead but dormant, usually in a mountain, as if fused with the cavernous depths, awaiting an hour of need in which to rise and save his people. Examples abound: Frederick Barbarossa at Kyffhäuser; the fourteenth century Serbian prince Marco Mrnjavčević who was also mothered by a Slavic mountain nymph or *vila* according to legend, like Hermes in the Homeric hymns and Aeneas for the first five years of his life (mothered by the goddess Venus but also tended to by nymphs in Mount Ida); Ogier the Dane, sleeping king of the mountain at Kronborg; the fifteenth century Balkan Slavic king Matjaž buried under a mountain; Frederick II in Sicily's Mount Etna; Constantine XI turning to marble under Constantinople's golden gate; etc. Some stories also involve king Arthur and Charlemagne in this motif, or St. John, author of the Apocalypse, at Ephesus. The theme appears outside the west as well. The Kukai, founder of Shingon Buddhism, is said to be meditating in Mount Koya in Japan, for example. In Peru we have the legend of Inkarri, based in part around the historical figure of Atahualpa, according to which Inkarri, founder of the city of Cuzco, was decapitated and his head buried. That head germinates underground, growing a new body, and once complete, the returning Inkarri will put the world in order.

---

214   Proclus, *Commentary on Plato's Timaeus*, II 106.15-23, trans. Dirk Baltzly, quoted by John F. Finamore and Emilie Kutash, "Proclus on the Psyche." In: M. Martijn and P. d'Hoine, *All From One: A Guide to Proclus* (Oxford: Oxford University Press, 2017), 127.

It is not only the initiate who dies and is reborn but the realized initiate as well, then. The resurrected Christ has already spent three days gone, defeating death, but still He absents Himself and is set to return differently. Their fortunate fall is an *exitus dubius*. They are not quite gone.

The theme is palpably Christian, as well as pagan, for these sacred mountains are also holy temples, and Christ's very body is the temple. Old Testament prophecies of rivers running through the temple occur in His very body, as His side is pierced, and water and blood gushes. When Christ dies, the temple veil rips analogously. Byzantine Emperor Constantine XI, for example, follows Christ in turning his body into a temple, for he turns to marble, like the Greek and Roman temples of his people, and follows Christ in leaving his disciples to return one day.

Here is the technology of the cross, the temporary entry into death before history is forced to submit again, to be transparent again. Rhythmically by the seasons of history, those realized individuals whose fusion with their own archetypal recess has made the stains and accidents of biography into filigreed décor, die to return, like a centrifugal end to their earthly enterprise bidding its time before centripetally recollecting itself in some other form, perhaps more fully.

The meaning of these myths is the same as that of the Chinese Huangdi, the Yellow Emperor, drying up during his time at Mount Bowang as described by the Taoist *Huangdi Sijing* (the *Four Scriptures* or *Classics of the Yellow Emperor*, discovered recently and reflecting a Huangdi-focused Taoism, also articulated in the figure of Huang Lao which combines Huangdi with Lao Tse). Becoming dry, fusing with the stones and unmoving mountain, the *axis mundi*, is the abandoning of the waters of ever-ebbing and flowing motion, ceasing the oscillations of the mind as Patanjali puts it in the *Yoga Sutras*. There, in deep meditation, the kings can wait for their season, even beyond seasons, they can turn the wheel, even at its center.

They are gone from the factionalism of history until the wheat and chaff have grown up sufficiently to be separated. An excellent expression of this principle concludes a certain essay concerning the prophecies associated with the Druid Merlin and a returning King Arthur that circulated in 13th century Italy in the context of the Emperor Frederick II: "Merlin, neither Guelph nor Ghibelline…joins his patrons Arthur and Frederick, the ranks of those of whom the Sibyl sounds the rumor, 'Vivet et non vivet.'"[215]

The king returns to a state of embryonic dormancy, but he is also the father Jove in the mountain Ida who is Juno, his wife. He is in deep meditation, incubation, in the presence of what we have called the infernal sun and midnight Apollo where the consciousness is absorbed

---

215   Donald Hoffman, "Was Merlin a Ghibelline? Arthurian Propaganda at the Court of Frederick II." In: Martin Shichtman and James Carley (eds.) *Culture and the King: The Social Implications of the Arthurian Legend* (Albany, NY: SUNY Press, 1994), 123.

in its own being. From this comes Joy. Thus, the male consciousness and the female joy, the king Jove and the mountain Juno, are united—contemplating Being.

He is the *Aham* of Tantrism, with *Idam*: Subjectivity with Objectivity, I and Thou, Consciousness and Bliss, the Awareness and the Awe, all within contemplation of Being. In a sense he has entered the bedrock of history, the archetypal substratum underneath its tumult, waiting to emerge, reborn to re-engender his kingdom, re-people the earth. Consider the phenomena of mummification, which Algis Uzdavinys describes in terms of preserving a sort of psycho-somatic anchor for the noetic aspect of the deceased initiate to use as a vehicle, should contact be sought by the living.

THE MOTHER'S VEGETABLE SUN

After his ritual death the king is not reabsorbed forever into nameless potentiality. The generative principle has brought him back into the world, like Rhea protecting her son, the infant king Jove, in Mount Ida where he would be enthroned, so that Saturn would not find and devour the child, and putting the horned Dionysus child together again after the Titans had dismembered him, or Venus preserving the heart of Dionysus after the latter was cut to pieces, or Minerva saving the heart of Zagreus at Ida. Here is the Minoan goddess mentioned above who is both underworld and solar rebirth.

This motherly protection, the maternal facet of God, is associated with the theatre of investiture. In the Egyptian case, the shinning king emerges "out of the fiery furnace of the goddess Nut."[216] The furnace of Nut, also described as her womb, is identified with the Duat by Uzdavinys,[217] which is substantiated by the previously referenced Egyptian inscription from the 13th century BC that situates the Duat inside Nut's body.[218] It is worth reflecting on the symbol of Nut's womb. An internal organ, it provides a rationale for understanding the tendency discussed above to project sub-terrestrial features out onto the super-terrestrial firmament: the celestial dome and all space-time is, like a womb, the site of gestation for a seed which is external to it—a transcendent design. The regal neophyte descends into this most primordial of states in order to be likewise gestated in proper conformity to such a design. Proclus likewise describes "the Demiurge of wholes when he was unfolded into light from Rhea" in the Curetic mysteries[219] (Rhea being his mother).

This role of shining forth from the First Paternal Intellect, where the goddess radiates the light of wisdom (the *autozoon*, the archetypal

---

216   Uzdavinys, *Philosophy as a Rite of Rebirth: From Ancient Egypt to Neoplatonism*, 193.
217   Ibid., 233.
218   Allen, 1988, 5–6.
219   Proclus, *On the Theology of Plato*, VI:13, 49.

world) upon the intellect of the initiate, like the warmth and light of the sun bridging the vast gap between it and us, explains why the mother goddess of initiation is associated with the sun. The mother goddess of many Aegean and Near Eastern pantheons is often solar, as Nanno Marinatos has pointed out,[220] but the theme is more widespread even than this. She is the Leto of the Greeks, mother of Apollo, Amaterasu of the Japanese, ancestor of the Emperor, Sól of the Norse, Arinna or Hepat of the Hittites, Shapshu (or Shapash) and Athirat of the Ugarit people, Hathor with her possible solar associations in the Egyptian case, possibly the Chinese sun goddess Xihe, Inanna whose brother in Mesopotamian religion, Utu, is the solar god, and the Lady of ancient Hebrew religion according to Margaret Barker, represented by the sun.[221] She is the progenitor of kings, including the king-god himself, which closely parallels traditional Japanese religion, in which the solar goddess Amaterasu is the ancestor of Japan's emperors. We may also think of Sól in Norse myth, a solar goddess important in Odin's initiatic career. The ancient Israelite queens seem to have been identified with Asherah, who was associated with the palm tree, a typically solar symbol.[222] Asherah's maternal function is that of the Mother (Jerusalem) who comforts the inhabitants of the city in Isaiah 66 (10-11):

> Rejoice with Jerusalem and be glad for her, all you who love her; rejoice greatly with her, all you who mourn over her. For you will nurse and be satisfied at her comforting breasts; you will drink deeply and delight in her overflowing abundance.

Later in Isaiah 66 (12-13) the role of comforter is taken on by the Lord, which Samuel Zinner reads as an indication that Mother Zion is the feminine aspect of the Lord: "For this is what the Lord says... As a mother comforts her child, so will I comfort you, and you will be comforted over Jerusalem."

The goddess Cybele was apparently also represented in the conjunction of sun and moon. Her prominence is noteworthy: Cybele is described as *Magna Mater*, *Mater Deum*, *Magna Mater deorum Idaea* and, in an ancient Phrygian language, the *Matar Kubeleya*, which means mother of the mountain. Her worship is linked to a black, possibly meteoric stone, which was taken to Rome in the context of war with Carthage, and she was prominent in Caesar Augustus's formulation of Roman religion. The link between Mount Ida and the Mother Goddess also reminds us of the link between Mount Etna and the mysteries of Persephone, Demeter and Hecate:[223] "the craters and volcanic phenomena of Sicily—includ-

---

220 Marinatos, *Minoan Kingship and the Solar Goddess: A Near Eastern Koine*, 191.
221 Barker, *The Mother of the Lord* vol. 1, 152-53.
222 Marinatos, *Minoan Kingship and the Solar Goddess: A Near Eastern Koine*, 47.
223 The bronze sandal said to have been left behind by Empedocles in his entering Etna "points directly to Hecate and...to the mysteries of Persephone." There is

ing Etna itself—were not just viewed as entrances to the underworld but were associated specifically with the mythology and the mysteries of Persephone," the underworld fire reached via these entryways being associated with the sun too.[224]

Hathor in Egypt, critical to Horus's exaltation, may have had a solar character as well.[225] Apollo is described by Robert Graves as "a Greek Horus," which would draw parallels between Hathor or Isis and Leto as solar goddess.[226] We may also think of the Heavenly Lady dressed in the sun in John's Apocalypse. Although the sun is also often associated with the masculine principle, traditional associations would lead us to identify solar goddesses with the luminosity and nurturing quality of the sun, and masculinity with other features thereof, such as its stillness and remoteness.

These symbols and the operation they facilitate are also observable in native Bolivian culture. Images of a holy tree are identified with the goddess Pachamama, who is also represented by the local Sumaj Urqu mountain. With the coming of Christianity this mountain became associated with the Virgin Mary, and the related figure of the child Huayna Potosi, to the Christ Child.[227] Here is the perennial symbol of feminine tree and mountain associated with the sun and the child king. This is all liturgically expressed:

> The functions and meaning of solar symbolism within Andean Christianity can be clearly detected in the ethnographic record. Today, as in the eighteenth century, the feast of Corpus Christi— celebrated by Macha Indians at the climax of the maize-harvest in the North Potosi valleys—can be understood as a covert mass for the sun. Addressed as 'Our Father' (tatanchej) and equated with the Holy Sacrament, the sun is here explicitly identified with the Body of Christ, the 'sun' of God Himself who (as we have seen) reactivates organic growth after the harvest by fertilizing the Pachamama, symbolized by the town square and helping to nourish the sacred tree which grows there.[228]

Of course, when in the above passage we read 'God' we are dealing with a demiurgic operation, Jove and Juno, not with the Platonic One (the Second rather than First Paternal Intellect, in neo-Platonic terms).

---

some indication of "a Sicilian origin for Hecate and Persephone material embodied in the magical papyri…the divine name Pasikrateia…only occurs in this form in the Paris papyrus and in the great Gaggera sanctuary of Demeter, Hecate, and Persephone at Selinus up the south coast of Sicily from Acragas" (Kingsley, *Ancient Philosophy, Mystery and Magic*, 240, 243).

224   Kingsley, *Ancient Philosophy, Mystery and Magic*, 240.

225   Marinatos, *Minoan Kingship and the Solar Goddess: A Near Eastern Koine*, 47.

226   Robert Graves, *The Greek Myths* (London: Penguin, 1992), 21.2, 80.

227   Tristan Platt, *Simon Bolivar, the Sun of Justice and the Amerindian Virgin. Andean conceptions of the Patria in 19th century Potosí* (Cambridge: Cambridge University Press, 1993), 173.

228   Ibid., 176.

It is interesting to note Vidya Dehejia's observation that the presence of the *ashoka* tree in or near temples in India may relate to the inclusion of the Surasundari (female celestial beauty, heavenly maiden) in temple sculptures, perhaps as a protective presence.[229] The eleventh century Shilpa Prakasha, a (probably Tantric) architectural treaty, states that without the Surasundari a temple fails to bear fruit, like a frolic without a woman or a house without a wife. The Buddhist equivalent of the Surasundari, the Yakshi, is traditionally associated with the ashoka tree. This would mean the ashoka tree is feminine. It is not an equivalent to the tree representing Asherah in ancient Hebrew religion, given that a Surasundari is not generally presented as so high a goddess, but it may be related. If the ashoka tree is connected to Sita, wife of Rama, given that it appears in the *Mahabharata* in relation to her, and given that Sita is an incarnation of the divine feminine where Rama is the masculine godhead incarnate, there may be evidence for the ashoka tree being connected to divine femininity in the manner of the tree at the pre-Josianic Jerusalem temple.

The goddess, the throne, kingship, radiance, the mountain, the tree, and sacrifice all occur in Minoan culture as well. The king is made king by a goddess, to which the royal throne belongs,[230] identified with a sacred mountain, which is itself a throne.[231] She is luminous in that she is a solar goddess, represented by a solar tree.[232] The tree in question is usually a palm tree, as is also the case in Egyptian and Mesopotamian mythology,[233] whose connection to the sun is likely to do with the radiating configuration of palm leaves. This survives Minoan culture and Mycenaean Greece in the Bronze Age, appearing in Iron Age Greek religion in the figure of palm-tree goddess Leto, mother of the sun-god Apollo.[234] The Minoan king leads animals to sacrifice[235] and the queen is depicted as officiating these as well (an example is the Hagia Triada Sarcophagus, dated to 1400 BC),[236] similar to how, in Vedic India, the chief queen and consorts would clean the sacrificial horse.

Marinatos considers Rhea the closest equivalent to this solar goddess in Greek mythology, who we have precisely highlighted as representing the radiant mother of the divine king Jove and, therefore, of every anointed king, according to neo-Platonic exegetes. The goddess's scarce presence in ancient Greece's popular religious manifestations should not be allowed to detract from the likelihood of her being a local expression of the same

---

229   Dehejia, Vidya. *The Body Adorned: Sacred and Profane in Indian Art* (New York: Columbia University Press, 2009), 101–2.
230   Marinatos, *Minoan Kingship and the Solar Goddess: A Near Eastern Koine*, 53.
231   Ibid., 153.
232   Ibid., 109.
233   Ibid., 62.
234   Ibid., 191.
235   Ibid., 25.
236   Ibid., 16.

goddess as is prominent in other systems. Rhea's importance may simply have remained more or less hidden as a matter of initiatic doctrine, as her prominence in the commentaries of Iamblichus and Proclus, who understand the Greek religion as anchored in Minoan rite, seems to indicate. This does not mean that Marinatos is wrong to consider many of these parallels "echoes across time, rather than translations," and to therefore view Greek religion as a "mutated" version of the Minoan and Mycenean system.[237] But it is interesting to note that neo-Platonic exegesis on that mutated system seem to preserve an awareness of the original, concurring with modern archeological and textual scholarship in describing that Bronze Age system's underlying view of reality, the metaphysical categories signified by its various stories, gods and so on.

In Hebrew tradition, Enoch was raised up by way of the Shekinah, the femininely connoted divine presence that the Holy One retired from among the generation to be drowned in the Biblical flood (3 Enoch 6:3). Enoch therefore ascends on the wings of the Shekinah (3 Enoch 7:1) before being enthroned in Heaven (3 Enoch 10:1–3; 16:1). The Shekinah is described as radiant (3 Enoch 5:1-6), and seems to assimilate Enoch into her light, as his face shone like that of the Lord (2 Enoch 37), his flesh turned into flame and his body into a blaze (3 Enoch 15). The Shekinah also came to King Solomon with fire and light at the holy of holies (2 Chronicles 7). The space itself, the holy of holies, may also be identified as "mother of the sons of God."[238] The similarities between King Solomon and his ritual work in the Bible and that of Minoan and Mycenaean kings (the rites which Platonism explicates, according to Proclus) are noted by Marinatos.[239] The link between feminine radiance and solar language, as well as an understanding of creation as proceeding from interplay of male and female (Vishnu-Lakshmi, Shiva-Shakti) appears in esoteric Shia Islam as well.[240]

The fundamentally feminine character of thrones and monarchical investiture may serve to reconcile Arthur Evans's view of the throne room

---

237   Ibid., 191.
238   Barker, *The Great Angel: A Study of Israel's Second God,* 156–57.
239   Marinatos, *Minoan Kingship and the Solar Goddess: A Near Eastern Koine,* 34.
240   "The couple 'Ali-Fatima is the exemplification, the epiphany on earth, of the eternal couple Logos-Sophia. Hence, we can foresee the implications of their respective persons. The Logos ('aql)…is the hidden…suprasensory calling for visible Form in order to be manifested…like the archetypal body, the inner astral mass of the sun, invisible to human perception, in relation to the visible Form, which is its aura, brilliance and splendor. The *maqam* (this word signifying state, rank, degree, plane, also the pitch of a note in music)—the maqam of Fatima corresponds exactly to this visible form of the sun, without which there would be neither radiance nor heat. And this is why Fatima has been called by a solar name: Fatima al-Zahra', the brilliant, resplendent Fatima. The totality of the universes consists of this light of Fatima, the splendor of each sun illuminating every conceivable universe" (Corbin, *Spiritual Body and Celestial Earth: From Mazdean Iran to Shi'ite Iran,* 64).

at Knossos belonging to a king with that of Helga Reusch, who identifies elements that implicate it with a goddess.[241] The throne room and the throne itself are indeed associated with the goddess, but that does not mean a priestess sits upon it, but precisely that the king's kingship comes by way of the feminine, as Marinatos concludes: "...the king sat on the throne of the goddess to establish his relationship with her as her earthly representative and son, just as the pharaoh sat on the lap of Isis."[242] The enactment of rites by a priestess may be similar to feminine initiations in other traditions such as the congress of a priestess of Inanna with the Mesopotamian king, although the priestess par excellence is the queen herself.

Milk, the Tree and the Veil

Apart from this broad outline, there are other symbols attributed to the eternal feminine as deputy of royal ordination that recur across traditions. These are milk, tree and the veil or act of weaving. Milk may represent the mother goddess's light, that resplendence into which the initiate is immersed. Goddesses associated with the cow, like Hathor and Hera/Juno (described as *boopis*, cow-eyed, in Greek) or Europa, are mothers to the initiate and, in the case of the latter, also identified with the moon as feminine principle. Theia/Euryphaessa, the mother of the Sun Helios, is also described as cow-eyed. The Bacchic/Orphic gold plates found at Thurii contain passages in which a mortal becomes a god and is as a kid in milk and goes to drink the milk of the goddess of the underworld (Persephone or Demeter). This reminds us of the primordial cow *Auðumbla* in Norse mythology, from whose milk fed the giant Ymir whose body made up the whole cosmos, so that the cosmic identity or universal body which the initiate realizes is sustained by this essential divine cow. The milky light of the moon may have rendered a poetic symbol for the cow, divine milk-bearer and mate of the solar bull (like the Minoan Jove, a sun god and heavenly white ox).

Rome's remembrance of its founder's precarious infancy centered on the place of his being breastfed, whereon stood a *Ficus Ruminalis*, the fig tree sacred to Rumina, goddess of lactation. This follows the Egyptian paradigm in which the eventual Pharaoh faced the sycamore tree of Hathor, a cow-goddess and therefore likewise a milk-bearing deity. Drinking milk in Persephone's realm (sometimes assimilated to Venus) during ritual descent into the underworld (via caves and caverns) was also part of the Dionysian mysteries[243] to which Pythagoreanism is intimately bonded.[244] This image of milk bearing tree may relate to the "fruit...like a bunch of grapes when it is white" of the Tree of

---

241 Marinatos, *Minoan Kingship and the Solar Goddess: A Near Eastern Koine*, 53.

242 Ibid., 65.

243 Ibid., 270–71.

244 Ibid., 262.

Eternal Life mentioned in the Biblical Apocryphon *On the Origin of the World*.[245] The symbol of milk may easily occur in the context of the fig tree given the milky white secretion its tips produce when one of its fruits is picked early. (In addition, a general maternal connotation may have resulted from the fig's cross-section resembling a womb.)

Remembering that the fig tree is identified with the divine feminine in Greco-Roman myth, it is interesting to note a verse from the Sibylline Oracles that "Fitting things now will I sing: That there shall be on the fig-tree a many-colored flower" (354–55). This passage seems to then reference the post-deluge world and three sons of Noah. Though the Sibylline Oracles mention four human races (in addition to others of partly inhuman provenance), these are representatives of successive degeneration during historical eons: From the early denizens of Eden, who were "darkened not with passion" (45), to a second, "very subtle race That cared for lovely works" (110), to a "third strong-minded race...of overbearing men And terrible, who wrought among themselves Many an evil" (130) and finally, "from these afterward another race Proceeded, late-completed, youngest born, Blood-stained, perverse in counsel; of men these Were in the fourth race" (135 onwards). The verse about the fig tree, however, contrastingly presents a legitimate diversity, and identifies it with the feminine.

The tree as cosmic body or world-tree appears in the writings of the Sufi Ibn Arabi. The trunk is the *axis mundi* and a kingly symbol, potentially to be identified as perfect man or archetypal prophet.[246] Ibn Arabi's exegesis of Qur'anic passages concerning a tree presents it as containing the possibilities for human and cosmic manifestation, including duality and, through the symbol of four perching birds, the four principal qualities of the four cardinal directions, four elements and four temperamental dispositions.[247] Ibn Arabi further conforms to other traditions in associating the tree-as-cosmic-body with the feminine. One of the four birds on this tree is identified as ringdove and the receptive feminine,[248] and another, the '*anqa' (gryphon)*, is the feminine matrix of reality or prime matter.[249] Ibn-Arabi's 'Anqa' al-Mughrib reads: "The Anqa is the Dust in which God reveals/opens the bodies of the world." This is very similar to the Platonic Chora or Receptacle in the *Timaeus*.

It also corresponds to the Lyr hall in Norse myth, belonging to the goddess Mengloth, a "sun-bright maid."[250] It is a place "encom-

245   Anonymous, "On the Origin of the World: The Untitled Text," trans. Hans-Gebhard Bethge and Bentley Layton. In: ed. James M. Robinson, *The Nag Hammadi Library* (San Francisco: Harper Collins, 1990), 288.
246   Ibn Arabi, *The Universal Tree and the Four Birds*, trans. Angela Jaffray (Oxford: Anqa Publishing, 2006), 82.
247   Ibid., 82.
248   Ibid., 97.
249   Ibid., 91–92.
250   Anonymous, *The Poetic Edda*, "The Ballad of Svipdagsmol," 58, 249.

passed...with flickering magic flames"[251] whose name means *heat-holding* and which is connected to *Lyjaberg*, a mountain on which the lady rests (like the Egyptian Nut and Greco-Latin Juno, with their fiery abodes and mountainous dwellings). The hall is also associated with the tree of Mimir, as the two appear together.[252] This tree is possibly an alternative appellation for the world-tree *Yggdrasil*. The world-tree corresponds to Wisdom in the Biblical Proverbs and to Minerva's olive tree. Mimir is connected to Odin, for it is from his well that the god drinks to acquire wisdom. Further, the severed head of another mythic personage by the name of Mimir is kept by Odin for the counsel it gives. As previously noted, the wanderer and father god also commends himself to the eternal feminine in gaining wisdom (learning womanly sorcery,[253] drinking the mead of poetry given him by a giantess,[254] and possibly participating in sacred marriages[255, 256]). Thus, Norse poems describe similar journeys to those of Osiris, Jove, Enoch-Metatron and others. In terms of Hebrew sources, Margaret Barker presents elements of a pre-Josianic (pre-seventh century BC) female deity recognized in the Jerusalem temple as mother of Yahweh and consort of El Elyon, the High God.[257] Named Asherah, she was apparently identified with a tree (apart from other potential areas of overlap between her and the Egyptian Hathor).[258]

In his commentary *On the Cave of the Nymphs in the Thirteenth Book of the Odyssey*,[259] Porphyry highlights the symbolic triad of goddess, tree and coronation in an essentially Hellenic, Homeric context: "The olive...sacred to Minerva; supplies the victors in athletic labors with crowns..." (a reference to the Olympic wreath). Minerva is goddess of proverbial (3:19) wisdom, born of the divine king's head, by which the earth's foundations were laid, femininely connoted (Proverbs 1:20-21; 8:1-3; 9:1-4). She saves the heart of the initiate who dies and becomes immortal, Zagreus. That "tree of life" (Proverbs 3:18) may be the stuff of which not only bodies but the mortal abode is made, since it the Minervic olive tree's roots that weave above the cave at Ithaca, where flesh is spun, according to Porphyry's reading of the *Odyssey*.

This relates to the cosmic Banyan tree of Indian tradition, whose branches grow downward and constitute mundane, gross nature, having its roots in the heavens (*Bhagavat-Gita*, 15:1). Given the significance of

---

251 Ibid., 47, 246.
252 Ibid., 23-30, 240-42.
253 Ibid., "The Ballad of the High One," 106, 51.
254 Ibid.
255 Hollander, *The Poetic Edda*, notes, 28; 30.
256 Rudolf Simek, *A Dictionary of Northern Mythology*, trans. A. Hall (Rochester, NY: D. S. Brewer, 2000), 250.
257 Barker, *The Mother of the Lord Volume I: The Lady in the Temple*, 123.
258 Ibid., 114.
259 Porphyry, *On the Cave of the Nymphs in the Thirteenth Book of the Odyssey*, XV; 36-38.

the fig tree in the west, associated with the divine feminine which bodies forth as the sensible cosmos, it is worth noting that Greeks identified the Indian banyan tree with the fig during Alexander's campaigns.[260] The tree as solar symbol of the feminine whereby kings are initiated was prominent in the Bronze Age Aegean, as in a seal from Naxos whereon the Minoan king, wearing a feathered headdress and holding court, makes offerings to a palm tree, the solar tree of the goddess.[261]

Porphyry's commentary transitions into another persistent symbol of the womanly actor who bestows royal honors: the veil and the act of weaving. Minerva's nymphs, at the Ithacan cave, beneath her olive tree, weave the purple garments of mortal bodies. Purple, too, is the color of the *peplos*, Minerva's garment woven on occasion of a yearly festival in Athens by the goddess's female virginal devotees in the course of nine months. This last fact makes clear that the garment represents the corporeal vessel, consistent with Porphyry's interpretation of Homer's nymph-woven webs of "purple hue."[262]

That a virgin-goddess, Minerva, should be responsible for weaving a body over nine months reminds of the virgin mother, Mary, weaving the temple veil covering the entrance to the Holy of Holies in the apocryphal *Infancy Gospel of James*, a parallel strengthened by the garment's being described as partially purple[263] and also enjoying the attention of a host of temple virgins.[264] Margaret Barker identifies a tradition of young women weaving linen for Asherah before Josiah's reforms,[265] and also considers there having been some significance in the color of the veil.[266] This significance would seem to be that it is the color of flesh or blood, a royal color.

In this context, Tristan Platt's description of the commonplace planting of a tree in front of churches in Bolivia, where it grows from a square and stands for the indigenous Pachamama or Virgin Mary[267] is remarkable. We have here the central square, the four cornered shape associated with the tree and radiant (solar) goddess highlighted across mythic systems. Its presence before churches is like the tree of Asherah which was removed from the temple of Solomon's courtyard by King Josiah and priest Hilkiah. Further, as Platt notes, the Pachamama, in her receiving the Sun and becoming newly and cyclically fertile, gives

---

260   Zénaïde A. Ragozin, *History of Vedic India* (New Delhi: Mittal, 1984), 29.

261   Marinatos, *Minoan Kingship and the Solar Goddess: A Near Eastern Koine*, 63–64.

262   Porphyry, *On the Cave of the Nymphs in the Thirteenth Book of the Odyssey*, I; 5.

263   Pseudo-James (brother of Jesus), *Infancy Gospels of James and Thomas*, ed. R. Hock. (Santa Rosa, CA: Polebridge Press, 1996), X:7-8, 51.

264   *Infancy Gospel of James*, X:2;6, 51.

265   Barker, *The Mother of the Lord Volume I: The Lady in the Temple*, 43.

266   Ibid., 319.

267   Platt, *Simon Bolívar, the Sun of Justice and the Amerindian Virgin. Andean conceptions of the Patria in 19th century Potosí*, 174.

the tribes harvest, that is, self-sufficiency and the ability to hold fast to their land. It is a tribal identification with land similar to that which the Bible describes in the case of Israel, the loss of which, in Margaret Barker's reading, seems to follow, according to some prophets, from the cessation of veneration for the female, Asherah. The king who restores fertility and represents a people's territoriality is able to do so by way of this solar goddess.

The use of a veil to cover the temple's innermost, and its association with a female deity finds its Egyptian version at Sais in the Goddess Neith (assimilated to Minerva by the Greeks) said to have been covered by a shroud (which may be identified with the *peplos* at Athens, perhaps as predecessor to its Greek counterpart[268]). Since the sun is presented as the offspring of Neith behind the covering,[269] her temple at Sais establishes the link between the image of the shroud and the previously discussed kingship ceremonies in which the Osirian initiate is re-birthed from the body of the goddess, Nut, now at one with the sun disk of Ra.

The Wandering Mother and the Temple Builder

Wandering and exile is equivalent to crucifixion, dismemberment and scattering as a symbol of ritual death before rebirth, and is represented by the pregnant woman ready to give birth but denied asylum until she finds her own promised land wherein the new child, patron of the initiate, may finally be born. The theme of the wandering people whose exile prepares them for holy promise occurs in Israel's being scattered by Assyria, carried off into Babylon, enslaved in Egypt and wandering the desert with Moses before entering the fertile crescent, or the Trojans losing their city, ship-wrecking on Carthaginian shores and eventually making their way to Italy.

Returning to the theme of Consciousness encountering Being, *Chit* returning to *Sat*, we may analogize the theme of exile as the alienated self-awareness (the exile) re-encountering his own true Being (coming home). The Trojan returns to Italy, which is the land of his ancestors (where Dardanus was born, Virgil's *Aeneid*, VII, 238–43) and becomes a Latin, adopting local culture by Jove's decree and Juno's wish (Juno, the feminine, is thus appeased in this return to the land, to the origin). The Israelites who stayed on the land were the yeomen stock, whereas those carried off into Babylonian captivity were elites and scholars who seem to criticize those left behind[270] for clinging to what, in light of

---

268   Assman, *Moses the Egyptian*, 87.
269   Ibid.
270   "The exiles for whom Ezekiel and his disciples wrote constituted both a social and an intellectual elite, and it is not difficult to detect...their contempt for the peasantry of the homeland. It is of those still in Judah that Yahweh says 'surely those who are in the waste places shall fall by the sword...' Extermination, no less, is to be the fate of all who refuse to adhere to Yahweh alone and remain obstinately polytheistic": Norman Cohn, *Cosmos, Chaos and the World to Come: The Ancient Roots of*

Barker's research, may be pro-Lady Wisdom, pre-iconoclastic forms of the religion (for although militant priests left after Josiah's reforms, the countryside may have remained unreformed).

Yet other prophets celebrate that older form of the faith, so that some prophets can be analogized as the mind raging against Being (legalism and iconoclasm are appropriate to such an attitude, wanting to simplify the world), whereas others are the pacific embrace thereof. The latter hearken back to Lady Wisdom (again, according to Margaret Barker): Those Biblical authors who want to return and do not consider exile a source of superiority in itself (those who do not fetishize suffering, which is often religion's vice) would be devoted to the Lady, just as those who return in the *Aeneid* reconcile with Juno: the divine feminine is again the agent of initiation. The king who receives the autozoon or joy/harmony from the mother after a confrontation with the First Paternal Intellect, in Platonism, and is able to rule justly according to that autozoon, is thereby in a sense leading his people back to the archetypal home, because he is putting that archetype into the world, where it has become occluded. It is the feminine, Rhea, who carries to Jove the autozoon from Saturn: The feminine transmits to consciousness (*Chit*), the joy/harmony (*Ananda*)

Apocalyptic Faith, 2nd ed. (London: Yale University Press, 2001), 150–51). Thus, "... the law became of central importance.... After the exile this new kind of religion was established.... Ezra 'the scribe' was empowered by the Persian monarch...a thorough-going religious reform was introduced" (Ibid., 145). We may also read Ezekiel more positively and with an eye to spiritual analogy, but *the context pointed out by Cohn is interesting in its relation to Barker's work and to the Aeneid, where the return home is an embrace rather than a rejection of local ways and specifically of the Divine Feminine.* "Given that 2 Esdras was written about 100 CE, what the legend of Ezra is actually describing is the process by which the Hebrew canon was formed after the destruction of the temple in 70 CE. The excluded texts that survived only did so because they were preserved by Christian scribes..." (Barker, *The Great High Priest*, 106); "The Christians in Palestine must have known what was being done to the Scriptures hence the 'Ezra' story—and Justin was the first to raise this issue of altering texts. The Christian telling of this story showed that they did not accept the Ezra canon as exclusive.... There is good reason to believe that this 'Ezra' not only determined the canon but also gave the Hebrew text the form which superseded all earlier texts and became modern theology....This dispute was also remembered, as we shall see, and appeared in later accusations that the Scriptures had been rewritten by Ezra. Thus Porphyry, the Neoplatonist from Syria, wrote at the end of the third century CE that nothing of the original Mosaic Torah remained; it had been burned with the temple. The Mosaic writings had actually been composed by Ezra and his disciples. He must have known the story in 2 Esdras" (Ibid., 299); "Since the original Ezra had led the 'men of the great synagogue', and represented the traditions which came back from Babylon, the story of Ezra dictating the Scriptures may be describing how the Babylonian tradition eventually determined the Hebrew canon" (Ibid., 306); "The early Church read 1 Enoch as Scripture; Clement and Origen both knew and quoted from it. 1 Enoch, however, has a very different estimate of the people who returned from Babylon, the Ezra tradition. Far from restoring the true temple and the true Scriptures, they were a generation of impure apostates who had forsaken wisdom and lost their vision (1 En. 89:73; 93:8–9)" (Ibid., 308).

from Being (*Sat*). It is profound, therefore, that the paradigmatic exile who finds safe harbor and gives birth to the initiate, the sacred king or prophet, is a wondering mother (Virgin Mary, Abraham's concubine Hagar, Apollo's mother Leto, the mother of the ancestor of the Asante nation in modern Ghana, who had to take the child into exile, etc.).

The same occurs in the Biblical story, where the Virgin Mary is rejected, finally giving birth in a barn. In the Qur'anic account, she finds an apparently inauspicious resting place under a palm tree (Surah Maryam 19:23). The rejection and desert exile of Hagar, Abraham's concubine, is an equivalent story in Islamic tradition, telling of the birth of Ishmael (Isma'il), co-builder of the Kaaba and ancestor of Muhammad. In Greek tradition, we find the story of Leto, represented by palm trees (which reminds us of the Qur'anic account of Jesus's birth) mother of Apollo, in the Homeric hymn to Apollo. Like Hagar, rejected by Sarah, wife of Abraham, Leto becomes pregnant by Jove but is forced to wander by Hera, his wife, who warns all not to accept the pregnant mother on pain of enduring the goddess's wrath. Like other heroes, including Hercules and Aeneas, the pains of nature, of the world, represented by Juno, must be endured. Indeed, Apollo begins life enduring these with his mother. Leto finally finds a suitable place and, like Jesus and Ishmael, the resulting child accomplishes great things. This reminds us that the *axis mundi*, the mother mountain where initiates are reborn, is not really a particular place, just as that mother is not fixed in any spot, but is a gate to what we have called the absent center, the kingly center that is everywhere and nowhere.

Where Jesus presents his disciples with the true temple in his own body, prophesizing the destruction of the one in Jerusalem, and where Ishmael builds the Kaaba in Mecca along with his father Abraham, to which Muslims continue to go on pilgrimage, so too, Apollo builds a temple at Delphi, constituting an *omphalos* or world-navel, a spiritual center which is universal, for the hymn refers to every nation of humans paying tribute there, and also specifically for the Greek islands and the mainland (the language used by the Homeric hymn is, in fact, the first historical instance of the term Europe as geographic category, so that this Apollonian refuge is the European Mecca). Further, it is represented by a stone with fishing net ropes carved into it, because Apollo took the form of a dolphin to lead Cretan sailors to it. The fishermen officiate there and become fishers of men, like St. Peter in the Gospel, and as in early Christianity, fishing and fish becomes a pertinent symbol of Apollo's *cultus*.

The idea of the body as true temple is significant, as is the link of great spiritual patriarchs and religious founders to the building of a temple (often a place of incubation), from Abraham to Apollo. Relevant here is R. A. Schwaller de Lubicz's insight into the Egyptian temple as analogous to the human body.[271] The rationale for building the temple

---

271   S. de Lubicz, *The Temple of Man* (Rochester: Inner Traditions, 1998).

to correspond with the human body is in fact the same as that which produces the perennial analogy, throughout traditions, between the kingdom and the body of its king. As Margaret Barker has noted, the instruction on building the temple in Exodus 40 corresponds to the six days of creation in Genesis, so that the temple is a micro-cosmos. The initiate's body is the sight of liturgy, is the temple, but initiation does not abolish the institution of the temple any more than relationship with Christ abolishes the liturgy in Christianity. This theme is brought up by Henry Corbin with respect to his very specific comparison between Swedenborg's *Homo Maximus* and the Ismaili Shiite *Temple of Light*.[272]

In this light we may understand the search by certain European kings for a restored Solomonic temple as reconnecting the royal and ecclesial in Davidic-Biblical (which they associated with the Hermetic and Pythagorean) terms without denying the more antinomian character of Christian theology which seeks personal relationship with the true *temple as person* (*Jesus*). "If the antitype of the temple is the body of Christ, the antitype of the ark of the covenant could be the infant Christ. The manger, with its fertility overtones, contains a vestige of Noah's ark in the animals inhabiting." [273] Everything structural becomes about the human person. Christ reveals the purpose of the Sabbath by teaching that it was made for man, and not man for it (Mark 2:27). The Sabbath is not a day like any other, not one among the other six, just as white light from the sun is not one of the six colors of the rainbow: the Sabbath is set apart from work and so is the seventh beyond the six, the center of the six points of the star of David. And since Jesus teaches not to be slavish to the point of not doing one's works on that day, we may understand that the thing beyond manifestation, in its reified symbol (the Sabbath as represented of the thing which is at rest beyond the six days of creation) does not violate the particular, does not force creation. We do not take the sacred as a procrustean amputation on the particulars of men's work. To recognize the transcendent absent center is not to deny the manifest particular center, so long as the latter is not absolutized. The erection of temples by Britain's King James I and Spain's Philip II, for example (James's architectural projects and Madrid's Escorial), can be read as an expansion of the church to again encompass the secular precisely when modernity was desacralizing politics (more on this in Addendum V.iv).

The representative and mediating function of the sacred king can also be carried out by a symbol, indeed, by a temple, where the temple is a body and presents worshipers with their correspondence to the *corpus cosmicum*, the cosmos as body: what the cosmos is to the temple the temple is to the individual believer and community of believers, where

---

272   Corbin, *Swedenborg and Esoteric Islam*, 59.
273   Northrop Frye, *The Great Code: The Bile and Literature* (Toronto: University of Toronto Press, 2006), 198.

the underlying ratio and paradigm they all manifest is the autozoon, bodily order beyond particular bodies. The temple at a people or religion's capital, their center, can fill the role of the king.

Pythagoras, whose very birth was arranged by Apollo's oracle (his parents being colonists of an island whose peopling she ordered) is related to fishermen by an episode recounted by Iamblichus which somewhat parallels that involving Jesus in Luke (5:1–11) during which the philosopher was able to accurately number the fish caught in a net, and preserve their life despite long exposure to dry air, having them returned and paying the men their full price. [274] Pythagoras, Socrates and Plato would all be priests of this rite, so that the importance of their philosophy to Christianity is perfectly of a piece with the essence of that religion.

In fact, apart from recruiting fishermen, paralleling the Gospel, in the Homeric hymn to Apollo the god tell his Cretan disciples at Delphi not to worry over provisions, for these will be brought to them so long as they do not speak or act spuriously, to leave their old homes behind and to sacrifice white barley (like bread). The text also shows a Biblical concern for geography and sequence of events. It is thus quite in keeping with Christian scripture.

Finally, the wonderer, apart from an exiled people pregnant with promise and a scorned woman ready to give birth to a prophet or savior, also appears as an individual wise man, a hermit and teacher, like the god Odin, or Jesus spending forty nights fasting in the desert, equivalent to the forty years of exile for Israel. This manifests the Son of Man with nowhere to lay His head, even before being born. Indeed, the biography of spiritual teachers generally includes a period of isolation and wondering.

That a wondering mother with nowhere to rest, scorned by those she meets, should birth a temple builder who gives humanity a stable center, a place in which to have refuge despite its lack of hospitality, returning love for hate, constitutes a lesson in compassion, a Christian, alchemical paradigm.

The Morning Star and Heaven's Mandate

The duality or ambiguity of the goddess comes through in the symbol of the morning star. The morning star refers to the planet Venus (or Phosphorus, Venus seen at dawn) and is identified with the Roman goddess Venus (Greek Aphrodite) and Inanna in Babylonian myth. Aeneas is made king by his mother Venus, just as Gilgamesh (Sumerian Bilgamesh) engages the self-sacrifice, slaughtering a heavenly bull while being identified with the bull, through the action of goddess Inanna. John's Apocalypse concords with these myths, presenting the morning star as bestowal of kingship:

---

274 Iamblichus, *Life of Pythagoras or Pythagoric Life*, VIII, 23.

But that which ye have already hold fast till I come. And he that overcometh, and keepeth my works unto the end, to him will I give power over the nations: And he shall rule them with a rod of iron; as the vessels of a potter shall they be broken to shivers: even as I received of my Father. And I will give him the morning star. He that hath an ear, let him hear what the Spirit saith unto the churches. (Apocalypse 2: 25–29)

The morning star is given by the Lord to one who overcomes, an initiate, and entails kingship, being expressed in terms of political power (reigning over the nations), which is rulership over one's own self as microcosm containing all the world.

The link between the morning star and Heaven-mandated, legitimate, monarchical investiture (here represented by King David), on the one hand, and divine femininity (the "bride" or "Spirit and the bride" given that the Hebrew word for Spirit, *ruach*, as well as Shekinah, is feminine), on the other, is confirmed later in Apocalypse 22 (16–17):

'I, Jesus, have sent my angel to give you this testimony for the churches. I am the Root and the Offspring of David, and the bright Morning Star.' The Spirit and the bride say, 'Come!' And let the one who hears say, 'Come!' Let the one who is thirsty come; and let the one who wishes take the free gift of the water of life.

Again, this is consistent with the stories of Gilgamesh and Aeneas.

In Ugaritic religion the king is suckled by the wives of El, who together are the solar goddess, and he becomes an earthly counterpart of the morning star, Venus, who is a son to the goddess and is called Athtar. That the initiate should become as the divine son identified with Venus presents a close parallel to Christianity. Indeed, Margaret Barker sees this Ugaritic paradigm occurring in the pre-Josianic Hebrew religion that Christianity would be a recovery of.[275] In Hebrew religion, we may consider how the heavenly image of the patriarch Joseph who comes to his future bride, the Egyptian Asaneth, does so through the morning star, which seems to be the entry point for heavenly influx:

And as Aseneth finished her confession to the Lord, lo, the morning star rose in the eastern sky. And Aseneth saw it and rejoiced and said, 'The Lord God has indeed heard me, for this star is a messenger and herald of the light of the great day.' And lo, the heaven was torn open near the morning star and an indescribable light appeared. And Aseneth fell on her face upon the ashes; and there came to her a man from heaven and stood at her head; and he called to her, 'Aseneth.' (*Joseph and Aseneth*, 14:1–4)

The fact that the term morning star also appears as a descriptor of the devil in scripture reminds us that spiritual ordeal can be a path to

275   Barker, *The Mother of the Lord Volume I: The Lady in the Temple*, 80–81.

perversity as well as purity. One can succeed like Hercules or fail (at least temporarily) like Prometheus. The Holy Grail myth, according to which the grail is both a gem from Lucifer's crown detached as the angel fell and the cup into which Christ's blood was collected when He was on the cross, communicates this same duality. A thing in a fallen, diabolical state, can be pursued by faithful knights and put right again, just as Prometheus was liberated by Hercules and is no longer chained and tormented.

The clearest light in the sky at morning, a light left over from the night's sky—Venus—is identified with initiation because the spiritual quest is often presented as a dying at dusk and being reborn at dawn, having descended to that midnight underworld whereto the sun goes when it is not visible. Poetically, in another case of true cosmogony confirming ancient mythological tropes, the representative of sunset and death, the Greek Hesperos, turned out to be the same planet as the morning star Phosphoros (both are Venus, just seen at different times and during different seasons), although this was perhaps known by the Babylonians, and as the Ugaritic Shahar and Shalem.

A good description of the meaning of this planet, to which we must add its passing from the west to the east, from the place of dusk to that of dawn, depending on the time of year, follows:

> Venus taught... the process of human alchemy through Her planetary cycles. Venus's 'alchemical' cycle of eight years begins with its sunset position when it is just above the horizon, an event that symbolizes a person's spiritual darkness preceding his or her alchemical transformation. Venus's subsequent transit below the horizon and 'under the Earth' represents a person's passage through the hellish underworld regions of their own subconscious and his or her corresponding 'death'. And finally the planet's reappearance as the Morning star that precedes the light of the rising Sun symbolizes the rebirth and 'dawn' of the transfigured immortal.[276]

Aeneas, as son of Venus, is relevant here. Apart from the fact that, like Jacob, Odin and Christ, they are both wounded on their side or groin, there are other parallels between Anfortas and Aeneas, and the *Aeneid* is relevant to the Holy Grail myth. The Holy Grail is equivalent to previously addressed symbols of initiation: the volcanic (*Vulcanic*) cavern, Plato's Receptacle, Juno before the birth of the world and so forth. The story of the Holy Grail allows for this association, identifying the sacred relic as having fallen from Lucifer's forehead,[277] Lucifer being an appellative of Venus (which Virgil uses[278]). A dislocated Heavenly thing,

276   Mark. A. Pinkham, *Guardians of the Holy Grail: The Knights Templar, John the Baptist and the Water of Life* (Kempton, IL: Adventures Unlimited Press, 2004), 48–49.
277   Wolfram von Eschenbach, *Parzival: A Knightly Epic*, trans. J. Weston (New York City: G. E. Stechert and Co., 1912), IX:665–68, 271.
278   Virgil, *Aeneid*, II:712, 91.

fallen as when Venus is injured while rescuing Aeneas, to be justified or restored in course of the spiritual quest (so that setting humanity right implies a Heavenly restoration as well). Awareness of this link comes through in German sources (including the *Tannhäuser Saga*, from 14th century versions to Wagner's opera), which refer to the Holy Grail being at an Italian "mountain of Venus"[279] or Venusberg (though here there is a confusion between the Earthly Paradise and that which lies beyond, accessed by Aeneas through the volcanic openings of that Neapolitan countryside German accounts call Venusberg and the Grail, and realms of another order elaborated in fairy tales, intercourse with which can be spiritually distracting or damaging).

The Luciferian fall is like the fallen star Wormwood in the Apocalypse that turns waters bitter like the plant of the same name, the Swedenborgian understanding of which is as a parody of divine intelligence which sours spiritual teaching or, as water often represents, the mental faculty or creation's sustenance, and which we could read as a parody of the holy stones that come from heaven in various traditions.

Lucifer, light-bringer, sometimes called morning star or daystar, in the un-fallen state is mentioned in Psalm 110:3, which may be rendered as "from the womb before the daystar I begot thee." This precisely refers to the kind of enthronement explored previously, including the luminous and feminine agency. The next verse, which St. Paul quotes in reference to Christ, and which in this context refers to King David, specifies the monarchical and sacral-monarchical character of being begotten: "The Lord hath sworn and will not repent: Thou art a priest forever, after the order of Melchisedek," Melchisedek being a king. Commenting on Psalm 110 and Paul's reference to it, Margaret Barker discusses evidence that, for the patriarchs, "Melchizedek was a heavenly being who could 'appear' in or as the king."[280]

It has been interpreted in terms of the glorification of Jesus as well as of the Virgin: "[t]he daystar is the light-bearer, in Latin 'Lucifer'. Therefore, this begetting, this birth is immaculate, for it occurs before Lucifer's 'fall'."[281] The verse can be read as meaning that the begetting—which in Psalmist terms often means enthroning, and in the vase of this verse, is connected to the king of Israel, applied to Jesus later—occurs in the presence of, connected to, or prior in time to the daystar or morning star. If we connect it to the bestowing of the morning star by Christ on the saints who overcome and keep His works, where it is clearly a bestowal of kingship or power over the nations, we have the enthronement and

279   Arthur E. Waite, *The Holy Grail: History, Legend and Symbolism* (Mineola, NY: Dover Publications, 2006), 290.

280   Margaret Barker, *Who Was Melchizedek and Who was His God?* (Temple Studies Group, 2008), 12.

281   Zinner, *Christianity and Islam: Essays on Ontology and Archetype*, 116.

rebirth not merely prior to but connected with (indeed, receiving) the morning star, a Lucifer that is not fallen. That which is unfallen here is received by one who embraces his fall with surrender, keeping the works of Christ, which is the transcending of the cross, rather than refusing to be humble and therefore falling through hubris, as the adversary.

Manifesting historically, this is the Immaculate Conception that in turn leads to the conception of Jesus. Given those traditional commentaries that identify the Virgin Mary as daystar through the above Psalm verse, and Venus being called Lucifer or daystar, Aeneas, son of Venus, receives a Christic character.

Sun and Star, Son and Mother

We encounter a coincidence between stars and suns, planets and plants. Mythological associations of Venus to a goddess implicitly identify the king with the sun, as the sun's rising is heralded by the morning star, Venus. But mythology often associates the mother goddess with the sun, as we have seen. Indeed, Margaret Barker understands ancient Hebrew religion as conceiving of morning star as the male son of the female solar and (apparently lunar) male deities. This Venusian male son would be Jehovah and the king in Jerusalem. This is consistent with the Lady dressed in the sun in the Apocalypse and references to Christ as, and bestower of, the morning star. It is difficult to ignore the solar associations of Christ, however, whose face shines like the sun (Apocalypse 1:16), for they seem to be articulated precisely through the imagery that so clearly associates the Mother with the sun. In fact, the Old Testament often associates the king with the sun.

The Greek word *anatole* (ἀνατολή), which appears in Luke 1:78–79 in the context of Old Testament references to the coming of the messiah, can apparently describe dawn as well as sprouting: the rising of the sun or a star or planet on the horizon, as well as of a plant's shoot. Holy kingship involves *germination*. We have here the *feminine image of a solar tree*, perhaps. But this sprout is precisely the Messiah who is described in relation to Wisdom and is therefore another entity (the male son and king, not the female mother): "a righteous branch" who is a descendant of David and a just king ruling with wisdom (Jeremiah 23:5–6); "a man whose name is Branch" (Zechariah 6:12). Old Testament references to the coming king are taken up in the New Testament as prophecies of Christ. Apart from the references to a shoot from David and to light shining, the King has seven stars in his right hand according to the Apocalypse (1:16) just as the Branch, high priest of Joshua, in Zechariah (3:9) is associated with a stone set before Joshua with seven eyes upon it.

Even if Biblical sun-imagery has been made to refer to figures other than Lady Wisdom due to the iconoclastic turn under king Josiah, as Margaret Barker believes, this would not mean that the same imagery was not being used to prophesize the Messiah, associating him with the sun and not just with the morning star. She is the sun and tree of life but the Son is the branch, the sprout thereof, and also our "true vine." Of course, if She is symbolized by the sun, the king's being a branch follows neatly, for the sun causes plants to grow. Just as goddesses who birth kings are often solar as well as arboreal, the resultant king may be a representative of that solar arboreality on earth, its fruition.

In Christian tradition, the male-female pair of Bridegroom-Bride, Christ-Church is often rendered such that Christ is solar. See Gregory of Nyssa's commentary on the erotic-mystical Song of Songs:

> Perhaps (if I may venture a rather bold conjecture) in seeing the beauty of the Bridegroom in the Bride they are really admiring the invisible and incomprehensible as it is in all creatures.... [I]n her [the Bride] they see more clearly that which is invisible. It is like men who are unable to look upon the sun, yet can see by its reflection in the water. So the friends of the Bridegroom see the Sun of Justice by looking upon the face of the Church as though it were a pure mirror, and thus He can be seen by His reflection.[282]

Barker notes the presence of white bulls in 1 Enoch, and the lordly station of the king Messiah who is a lamb and becomes a horned creature along with the other lambs who become oxen (1 Enoch 90:37–38). This reminds of the widespread theme of oxen of the sun, and given its relationship to the messianic kingly figure in Enoch, we may suggest that the passage is invoking themes of solar kingship. Malachi 4:2 is relevant here as well: "But for you who fear my name, the Sun of Righteousness will rise with healing in his wings. And you will go free, leaping with joy like calves let out to pasture." There is no reason to deny that the king is solar simply on the basis that Lady Wisdom is associated with the sun as well. Both seem to be the case.

We may think of the herald of the sun, Venus, as its predecessor and mother, with its remoteness and slower cycles, or we may interpret the smaller size and dimmer illumination of Venus as justifying its being thought of as offspring to the sun (indeed, the sun is, in a sense, parent to every planet, and the morning star is not really a star, but since it seems to announce sunrise it can be thought of as closely associated thereto). Venus's disappearance behind the sun can be seen as its gestation within the sun's light, or its being prior in the order of generations.

As Geraldine Pinch writes, reflecting this ambiguity, concerning the Egyptian deity Hathor, house of Horus: "As the Eye of Ra, she could be identified with the solar disk or the morning or evening star (Venus)."[283]

---

282   Gregory of Nyssa, "Commentary on Song of Songs," in *From Glory to Glory* (London: John Murray, 1962), 219, cited by John Milbank, *The Word Made Strange*, 208.
283   Geraldine Pinch, *Handbook of Egyptian Mythology* (Santa Barbara, CA: ABC-Clio, 2002), 137.

Although the Egyptian king is identified with Ra's solar character, it also seems that "[i]n Pyramid Text spell 245, the sky goddess Nut assigns the dead king a place in heaven as the Lone Star [Venus?]"[284] (it may be that, in receding from earthly life, the king moves from sun to morning star).

The point, in any case, is that in whatever way the king is the morning star among his people (representing cycles and heralding the light of day) or the sun (shining upon the land and making it fertile, illuminating people's vision) he is so precisely *among* his people: the principle of Venus or the sun are taken to represent is represented by the king at the level of the earth (or the New Earth of the Apocalypse). We should therefore not hold on too tightly to the images presented here but grasp what they convey and what they say about initiation and just rule.

Morning star, sun and tree/branch apply to mother as well as son, therefore, but at different levels of reality, so to speak. Some of the examples of solar goddesses provided by Marinatos in her study on Minoan solar kingship, specifically the Mesopotamian goddess Inanna, are considered equivalent to the Greco-Roman Venus/Aphrodite by some authors, and so would refer to the morning star. Meanwhile, the ancient patriarchs who were bulls according to 1 Enoch and the coming generations made into white bulls with the Messiah would therefore be solar in the same sense in which the Messiah is solar: as children of the solar goddess. They are akin to the Cretan Jove or Zagreus, or Dionysus who, apart from being horned at birth was apparently also represented as a white bull in Thrace, all of whom overcome death thanks to a goddess.

Given the above, then, we are now in a position to suggest the following order and associations:

- archetypal motherhood or womb, represented by the formless darkness of space, which is "before the morning star" and from which kings or spiritual initiates are begotten by the Lord in Psalm 110 (this is the formless matrix or Crater, that is, goddess Juno, according the Platonists);
- the stars, possibly including the Milky Way, and the morning star or Venus, whose day is longer than that of the sun because it rises in the east during part of the year, like the sun, and is seen in the west during another part, and which is the first light of morning, leading or heralding the nearer, more visible solar orb, and which in the Bible is given to those who overcome and receive dominion, and in pagan traditions seems to be linked to a goddess who births rulers (this is the world-soul of the Platonists, identified with Venus by Bernard Sylverstris who calls that goddess the "music of the world" in his commentary on the *Aeneid*, and Nicholas of Cusa, who writes of the Roman view that "Venus is the daughter of an omnipotent Jupiter, from whom Nature and all her company

---

284   Ibid., 207.

descend"[285]—in Proclus the world soul is more readily identified with Athena);

- and the sun itself, linked to the monarch himself, as a life-giving light, nearer than the stars, a masculine form corresponding to the feminine earth and moon (this is the male solar king, from pharaoh to caesar; the Tetrad or ideality of our imminent realm, of which the earth is an imperfect play—thus the widespread association of utopian "solar" cities and Apollo in European literature).

In Greco-Roman terms we can hazard that the first of these is Juno, the second Venus (or Leto and other solar goddesses) and the third Apollo, whose specifically Roman representative is Aeneas, champion of Apollo, rescued by the solar god in the *Aeneid*. The heavenly Joseph who comes from a rip in the sky near the morning star ("heaven was torn open near the morning star") and shines intensely would then be using the morning star as channel or "birth canal" between the heavenly and earthly realms, himself being a solar personage. Of course this is only one set of associations (we can put the whole schema forward or backward, so to speak, so that Juno can represent in the world soul in some texts, or the feminine principle in general elsewhere).

THE INITIATE AT MOUNT IDA

We have already mentioned the yearly rite of Jove's enthronement whose significance is cited by Plato and his successors. This rite was performed, among other places but pre-eminently, at Mount Ida in Crete, the island from which a continent gets its name, for it is here that Jove absconded with princess Europa and where the son of Jove, Zagreus, died and became immortal. Proclus highlights the centrality of this observance for Hellenism:

> For who that is in the smallest degree acquainted with the divine wisdom of the Greeks, does not know that in their arcane mysteries and other concerns respecting the Gods, the order of the Curetes is in a remarkable manner celebrated by them.... [286]

Indeed, it is in Crete, not Athens or anywhere in mainland Greece, that Plato's final dialogue, *The Laws*, is set. Medieval Europeans in the sixth and seventh century also understood this, associating the origin of the religious cult of Jupiter with Crete, as St. Isidore of Seville writes in his Etymologies, discussing various pre-Christian devotions, "Isis in Egypt, Jupiter in Crete...."[287] (See Addendum II for more on Minoan culture's foundational importance.)

---

285   Nicholas de Cusa, *Selected Spiritual Writings. On Learned Ignorance* (New York: Paulist Press, 1997), 124.
286   Proclus, *On the Theology of Plato*, V:35, 408.
287   St. Isidore of Seville, *Etymologies*, VIII.xi.1, 183.

The great Greek philosophers were priests of Apollo's rite and, in the case of Pythagoras and Plato, as discussed below, were considered partial incarnations of the solar god by their followers (including by Proclus's teacher Iamblichus). Porphyry writes that "[i]t is well known that he showed his golden thigh to Abaris the Hyperborean, to confirm him in the opinion that he was the Hyperborean Apollo, whose priest Abaris was."[288] They are messengers of the sound of God, mantias theophonas and priests of Apollo, *Apollonos hetairon*. Pythagorean-Platonism is religious and initiatic. Philosophy, including that component which requires mental exertion, is meant to lead to encountering metaphysical truths, as Pierre Grimes demonstrates.

Apollo's eminence is also linked to Crete. To begin with, the Homeric hymn to Apollo informs us that its hero led a group of sailors from Knossos in Crete to his temple at Delphi so that they would officiate there as his priests. We have here a possible transference of the Idaean mysteries to mainland Greece. Further, as will also be explored in detail later, the Minoan observance at Crete originating the myth of Europa riding upon Jove in the form of a white bull, seems to have consisted of a solar Jove, with the motif of a solar or heavenly bull being quite widespread during the Bronze Age. It is interesting that the connection between the solar deity and Crete should occur in a hymn which apparently presents the first example of the word *Europe* being used to designate a contiguous landmass, as well as in the story of princess Europa. The usage of Europe in the hymn to Apollo, then, may be a conscious reference to the myth of that island from which it tells us Apollo recruited his first disciples, and whose cult of Jove was likely solar in character.

Aeneas is perhaps the quintessential initiate of the Greco-Roman tradition,[289] the prototypical hero of the west. After Troy's defeat he is guided by Jove to encounter his mother Venus at the Anatolian Mount Ida.[290] Here he is sheltered by Venus just as his grandfather was by Rhea at the Cretan Ida. Aeneas is retracing the pattern that led to his birth, for the Olympian monarch inspired lust for Venus in the hero's father at the feet of this very mountain[291] (a *monte di venere*, or Venusian mount—as Italians refer to subcutaneous fat protecting the

---

288   Porphyry, *Life of Pythagoras*, trans. K. S. Guthrie, 28.
289   Of course, as Algis Uzdavinys notes, this role properly falls to Hercules, and Peter Kingsley gives us reason to award it to Empedocles, and we have Orpheus and the hagiographies of Pythagoras by Iamblichus and Olympiodorus (although Pythagoreanism is often imitation of Hercules, and Empedocles' stories follow Hercules' labors for example in diverting a river at Silenus, which purified plague-infested waters). Yet we focus on Aeneas because, being the founder of Rome, the initiatic themes of his story and implicit political critiques by Virgil *suggest to us the redemption of Empire from imperialism*, into ecumenism.
290   Virgil, *The Aeneid*, II:712–14, 91.
291   Anonymous, *Hesiod, the Homeric Hymns and Homerica*, trans. H. Evelyn-White (Cambridge, MA: Loeb, 1914), II:1008–1010, 35 (Hymn to Aphrodite).

female pubic bone—perfectly fitting, given that Aeneas begins life at this site). Meeting his mother at the place of his own providentially arranged conception is therefore an encounter with his divine origin: an appropriate description of spiritual epiphany.

Christ's divine sonship is declared by a voice during the Transfiguration, also on a mountain, Tabor, amidst a light we may interpret as the feminine, Shekinah. Jove himself was enthroned at a similarly named Mount Ida (Cretan counterpart to the Anatolian), the place where his mother, Rhea, left him as a child. It seems, then, that the archetypal pattern of kingship involves recovering one's childhood (Matthew 18:3).

The enthronement of Jove and the refuge of future king Aeneas suggest Ida is a monarchically significant name. The Icelandic bard Snorri Sturluson's testimony of Norse religion links the latter to Aeneas and Rome, for Odin assembles the rulers of the earth at a site called Ida,[292] albeit a field rather than a mountain. Ida, then, is the name for the stage of kings. Further, according to Sturluson, the historic Odin was a descendent of Aeneas's Trojan company, part of which arrived in Scandinavia.

The Idaean Venus shares her mount's name with another Ida who, like the Greco-Roman deity, was also born of the sea, frothing out from its waters in the Indian *Satapatha Brahmana*.[293, 294] She came to populate the world with Manu, the Indian Noah, after a catastrophic flood. Using this parallel for creative fodder, it may be suggested that, as Venus's son, conceived at Mount Ida, Aeneas re-presents that first post-diluvian generation, the generation in which humanity had its new beginning. As a Roman, Classical Japheth (parentage over Europe is ascribed to both), Aeneas is born fresh from the flood, coming through Asia Minor to populate Europe. The image of renewer-king anchoring his realm in human primordially after catastrophe (flood) is a perennial one.

Aeneas can lead his people into a post-diluvian age (a state beyond confrontation with the waters of the unconscious, in Jungian, psychological terms which are analogous to the spiritual), because the waters do not overwhelm him, he does not drown. When Juno searches out Aeolus in order to commission his aid in thwarting Aeneas, the wind god appears dwelling in a cave, among the four winds. He is a quintessence drawing the quaternary in and keeping it under control. (Indeed, in the course of almost ninety-nine full moons, that is, every eight years, the planet Venus, symbol of Aeneas's mother, traces a fivefold curved star pattern in the sky.[295])

292   Sturluson, *The Prose Edda*, "The Beguiling of Gylfi": XIV; 25.
293   Anonymous, *Satapatha Brahmana, according to the text of the Madhyandina School*, trans. J. Eggeling (Oxford: Clarendon Press, 1882), First Kanda: Eighth Adhyaya, 7, 218.
294   Dated to anywhere between 700 and 300 BC, depending on the part and on whether dating refers to the age of an oral tradition or to its being written down.
295   Miranda Lundy, *Sacred Number: The Secret Qualities of Quantities* (Glastonbury, England: Wooden Books, 2009), 32.

Aeneas's surviving of the winds marshaled by Aeolus at Juno's behest represents his confrontation with the divine feminine in her terrible aspect. The winds, usually identified as proceeding from the four cardinal directions, are the four streams of Eden (Genesis 2:10) that Wisdom has poured out (Sirach 24:40), the four founts of the Kunlun Mountain, like Mount Ida, where divine femininity enthrones the worthy, the corners of her glorifying quadrangle. They are the tetrad of mundane manifestation, personified and linked to their divine source by Sophia, but appearing as scourge to one who has not yet undergone ordeal, not yet been purged and readied for enthronement, not yet followed into crucifixion: death by the four directions. As for the one who does follow: "[a]t first she will walk in twists and turns with them. She will bring fear and dread upon them, and she will torture them with her discipline" (Sirach 4:17), "[s]he seems very harsh to the undisciplined ... she is not readily perceived by many" (Sirach 6:20; 6:22), and eventually he will "put her on like a splendid crown" (Sirach 6:31).

Like Egyptian grotesques in the Duat or Greek titans in Tartarus, the winds are held in a vast cave,[296] ever the entrance to nether-realms, chained and imprisoned[297] by a presiding king,[298] like Osiris in the depths or Jove at the central, cosmic fire which is also somehow infernal. It is by agency of the divine feminine that the four are released, that one ceases from coherence, with the phlegmatic, choleric, sanguine and melancholic elements of the self, in medieval terms, becoming discordant, risking one's sinking into the waters, into instability, like a shipwrecked Aeneas. They are made chaotic that they might become cosmic, disordered into a truer order; *solve et coagula* in the Hermetic formula, the cross and resurrection. Overcoming the four winds renders Aeneas a representative of the *axis mundi*, the center between four corners (that the north wind is not mentioned as being a part of the simultaneous convolution in which the other three at one point assail the Trojan fleet indicates Aeneas's affinity with Apollo of the far north, and that his destined course is that way bound). Just as Wisdom crowns one in the midst of the four elements, it also purges one by means of them. Insofar as mountain represents the unmoving axis and the rivers about it are the rotating, moving creation, Aeneas's overcoming of four winds and water marks his being anchored in that existential center.

Attaining *demiurgy*, as Iamblichus calls it, the work of Jove,[299] a deserving subject identifies with the anatomy of the cosmos.[300] Initiate

---

296 Virgil, *The Aeneid*, I:61, 34.

297 Ibid., I:63–64, 35.

298 Ibid., I:61, 34.

299 Gregory Shaw, "Theurgy as Demiurgy: Iamblichus' Solution to the Problem of Embodiment." In: *Dionysius*, vol. 12 (Halifax City, Canada: Dalhousie University Press, 1998), 37.

300 Iamblichus, *De Mysteriis Aegyptiorum*, trans. E. Clarke, J. Dillon and J. Hershbell (Atlanta: Society of Biblical Literature, 2003), X:6.

becomes Jove, the macro-anthropos[301] of Orphism. Emergent, born of mountainous womb, he is that child of Jove and Europa in Euripides' song,[302] the latter princess revealed by this association as an avatar of Juno, wife of the king, source of souls at Ida.[303] The white bull courts his counterpart, a northern Hathor.[304] Jove fathers the martyr who falls with the sun at dusk, the deathly west of which his consort is goddess, that he might be born again, solar, at dawn. Where Jove's thunderstone meets Juno's volcanic crater, the sky meets infernal depth, Europe's *omphalos* and umbilical connection to divine parents.

Different traditions present common appellations for the site of enthronement, including fearsome facet of a prison, as well as a watch-tower. Apart from the symbolic value of understanding exaltation as overcoming the ordeal or ritual death, a place of imprisonment, descent into the underworld, and the like, there is imagery here which points to Mount Ida. Simplicius[305] relates that, according to Aristotle, the Pythagoreans referred to the throne of Jove as his defense tower and prison (all three designations—throne, tower and prison—belonging to the Pythagorean central fire). Given that Pythagoras himself is said to have encountered the (ceremonial) throne of Jove at Mount Ida, it is worth considering whether the other two epithets (prison and tower) are attributable to this mountain. The title of *defense tower* may refer to the peak being an elevated place from which to anticipate threats or encroaching disorder. The symbol of the tower may therefore be linked to the equally recurrent image of a mountain, as in Egyptian and Hebrew tradition, according to what has already been cited.

As for the term *Jupiter's prison*, this may also fit Mount Ida, given that it is the mythical haven wherein Jove is forced to spend his childhood to avoid the scourge of his father, thereby acting as a prison of sorts. More generally, caverns (and the inside of mountains) often appear in fable as openings into Hades. The connection between Heavenly monarchy and the underworld is worth examining.

Theurgy on the Roman Throne

Sources in the background of Virgil's composition may shed light on the *Aeneid*'s view of spiritual realization. Aeneas gains initiation and kingship by means of descent (*katabasis*), which Virgil appears to narrate in terms of traditions in which descent into Heaven and kingship rites

---

301   Uzdavinys, *Philosophy as a Rite of Rebirth: From Ancient Egypt to Neoplatonism*, 88.

302   Porphyry, *On Abstinence from Animal Food*, trans. T. Taylor (Whitefish, MT: Kessinger Publishing, 2006). We recall that Euripides considered that "the nous in each one is god for man" (fragment 839.19) and so has spiritual initiation in mind.

303   Proclus, *The Commentary on Plato's Timaeus*, III, 14.

304   Page, *Reading the Past: Runes*, 15.

305   Simplicius, *On Aristotle, On the Heavens*, cited in Kingsley, *Ancient Philosophy, Mystery and Magic*, 187.

are accompanied by macranthropic realization (a vision of, or identification with, the macro-anthropos, cosmic body). These traditions are the Orphic and, possibly, the Enochic. As Jan Brenner concludes in his exploration of the topic, it is not implausible that Virgil incorporated literature of "Orphic katabaseis with Enochic influence."[306]

Possible instances of the former influence (via the Orphic Gold Leaf from Thurii, Pindar and other sources) include the encounter with nameless dead,[307, 308] jubilation at Elysium,[309] the experience of perpetual light, Heaven's gymnastics and dance,[310] and the presence of meadows and fields.[311, 312] These depict a Paradise of *Lila*, divine play, that reminds of Lord Krishna's Goloka, like a deathless Arcadia. As for the connection with Enoch, Aeneas's journey places him in the same position as the eponymous patriarch of *1 Enoch*. The records of their beatitude exhibit common rhetorical and stylistic features, namely the presence of a guide (the Sybil in Aeneas's case), which is "a recurring feature of…tours of hell…going back to 1 Enoch," and the travailing initiate's posing of questions regarding souls encountered on the way (in the form of "who are these?"),[313] being answered by the guide (Dante will make bountiful use of this format in his *Divine Comedy*). This, again is "a phenomenon that can equally be traced back to Enoch's cosmic tour in 1 Enoch," establishing a link, for "…these demonstrative pronouns also seem to occur in the *Aeneid*."[314]

Thusly is Aeneas prepared for a divinized afterlife and, like the prophet Enoch, for the heavenly spiriting away of his body upon death, which presents a further suggestive indication of Aeneas's Enochic heroism or prophethood. The Greek historian Dionysus of Halicarnassus notes that the body of Aeneas was never found after a battle against the Rutuli indicating it had been taken to Paradise:

> A severe battle took place not far from Lavinium and many were slain on both sides, but when night came on, the armies separated; and when the body of Aeneas was nowhere to be seen, some concluded that it had been translated to the gods and others that it had perished in the river beside which the battle was fought. And the Latins build a hero-shrine to him with this inscription:

---

306   Jan Brenner, "The Golden Bough: Orphic, Eleusinian, and Hellenistic-Jewish Sources of Virgil's Underworld in *Aeneid* VI," *Kernos* 22 (2009): 183–208, Section 40.
307   Ibid., Section 14.
308   Virgil, *Aeneid*, VI.551–57, 196.
309   Brenner, *The Golden Bough: Orphic, Eleusinian, and Hellenistic-Jewish Sources of Virgil's Underworld in Aeneid VI*, Section 25.
310   Virgil, *Aeneid*, VI.570–572, 198.
311   Brenner, Section 26.
312   Virgil, *Aeneid*, VI.569–71, 198; VI.580–85, 198.
313   Ibid., VI.275–78, 185–86; VI.496–97, 194.
314   Brenner, Section 6.

To the father and god of this place, who presides over the waters
of the river Numicius.[315]

But even the account of the faithless contains a truth, for what per-
ished of Aeneas in that river was what was perishable in him. The river
deity Numicius carried Aeneas into his divinization, or carried from
Aeneas all that was superfluous, and this at the request of Venus according
to Livy. Ovid relates the episode in his *Metamorphoses* (XIV, 598–608):

> The horned river-god performed the commands of Venus and
> purified all that was mortal of Aeneas and cleansed it with his
> waters. The best part of Aeneas remained. His mother anointed
> the purified body with divine perfume; she touched his face with
> ambrosia and sweet nectar and made him a god. Him the people
> of Quirinus [i.e., the Romans] hailed as 'Indiges,' and received him
> with a temple and altars.[316]

This is similar to the revelation of Christ's Divinity to the crowd
during his baptism at the river Jordan, with Orthodox Christian icons of
the event often including an anthropomorphic figure personifying that
river, as though local river-deities were somehow related to apotheosis
or *apocalypsis* (revelation) of divinity, maybe marking the overcoming of
the waters, of changeability, as well as a cleansing.

Aeneas renamed *Jupiter Indiges*, an *Indigenous Jupiter* (Jove-Pater, Jove-
Father). Like Jesus, he is at one with the Father. Aeneas is a local manifestation of that principle. We may remind ourselves that Jupiter, Aeneas's
grandfather via Venus, was probably a solar god in the ancient Minoan
rite (and that Aeneas is connected to that rite, for his initial refuge was
to be sought in Crete, whose Mount Ida is twin to the Anatolian Mount
Ida in which he was conceived). The name Jupiter Indiges is therefore
connected to the solar deity *Sol Indiges*, into whose family Aeneas married, for princess Lavinia, as has been noted, was the descendent of Sol
Indiges. This then is the founding of a solar dynasty very much akin to
Egyptian or Japanese links to the sun.

In the traditions that Virgil seems to draw upon, the end of such
visionary ventures is an experience of universal corporeality. It is therefore justified to hazard Aeneas's status as a realizer of this cosmic body.
Again, these epiphanies are serviceably circumscribed to a king's particular realm, so that he may embody and attend to it especially, and since
Aeneas is Rome's founder, his monarchy most properly embodies this
sphere and its heirs (Europe, for again, per T. S. Eliot, Aeneas is to Rome
as Rome is to Europe). Aeneas's operation in the European imagination
(via poetry and pseudo-history) as generous progenitor of many peoples

---

315   Dionysus of Halicarnassus, *Roman Antiquities*, I:64, 5, 213.
316   Mark Morford and Robert Lenardon, *Classical Mythology*, 6th ed. (New York:
Oxford University Press, 1999), 508.

and dynasties, serves to manifests the above. The stories of his lineage and descendants are the temporal, historical, horizontal reflection of his personification of a particular cultural space.

Embodiment and Ennead (in the Aeneid)

We have seen the identification of mountains not only with the mother but with the body. Given that the mother is the means by which physicality is generated this is no arbitrary symbolic coincidence. The mother-mountain is the initiate's body in its latency, in its initial retirement from the world and revivification, whereas later, his queen or consort, will be his body in its triumphal return to the world. Likewise, it makes sense that the prototype of classical initiation, Aeneas, associated with Mount Ida as with his divine mother, and to the initiatrix-consort, Latin princess Lavinia, descendent of the sun-deity Sol Indiges, is associated with bodily divinization. This occurs by way of Virgil's ample use of the number nine, the significance of which seems to be the body with its nine openings. (I would also recall Blake's conception of the, technically unfinished, *Four Zoas* or *Vala*—fittingly feminine—in nine nights of dreams.)

The rise of Aeneas to kingship over Latium was preceded by an initiatic descent into the underworld and the Elysian fields, Virgil's telling of which invokes Orphic and Enochic tropes[317] that imply realization of the macranthropic Jove or cosmic body of Metatron and prelapsarian Adam which these traditions attain (to be addressed later). The appearance of the number nine during initiatic descent (the nine windings of the river Styx,[318] for example) corresponds with the nine dancers around Jove's throne, nine openings of the body and nine months of pregnancy. It is a statement of corporeal hallowedness. Indeed, Dante, the great student of Virgil, writes the name of Beatrice, his Heavenly guide, sixty-three times in the *Divine Comedy*, a number which, by mystical addition (adding its digits), a technique we know Dante was familiar with and used elsewhere, gives us the product of nine. The divine feminine is being linked to the number of exalted corporeality in the course of the Italian poet's initiatic travel.

The natal and therefore corporeal character of this number is borne out by its near ubiquitous appearances in the *Aeneid*. As noted, the obvious attribution of this number is to the gestation period of nine months and to the nine openings of the body, being that its purpose is birth (incarnation, a corporeal fruition, touching eternity inside mortality). This is consistent with Bernard Sylvestris's medieval interpretation of the name Aeneas, according to which it means *embodied* (*ennos-demas*; dweller-body).[319] The poet Prudentius, writing during the second half

---

317   Brenner, *The Golden Bough: Orphic, Eleusinian, and Hellenistic-Jewish Sources of Virgil's Underworld in Aeneid VI*, Section 40, 22.

318   Vigil, *The Aeneid*, VI:385; 190.

319   David Thompson, "Dante and Bernard Sylvestris." In: Lynn White Jr. (ed.),

of the fourth century, likewise read Christian themes in the *Aeneid*, as did Petrarch and Tasso, and as comes through in Raphael's fresco in the Vatican Stanza dell'Incendio, and Dante himself referred to the *Aeneid* as his teacher.

The Ennead as featured in the *Aeneid* relates to mountains, Mount Ida specifically, the underworld, rebirth and femininity, that is, to many of the staples of initiatic ordeal discussed in the preceding. Antenor escapes disaster by sailing the waters of the Timavus that split into "nine mouths, a bursting flood, with a gigantic roar of the mountain."[320] In this context, the number nine appears not only as related to a mountain but to water, often a symbol for generation and the stream of life or contingency. In terms of Mount Ida, apart from its Cretan instance featuring nine dancing Corybantes (which is not mentioned by Virgil), this number is linked to Mount Eryx in Sicily, which is treated as an analogue of Ida. When Aeneas and his company are present at the site, it features a statue of Venus of Idalia upon its peak[321] (which epithet derives from Ida[322]).

In this way it is not only associated with Ida but with Venus, which for Aeneas signifies maternity. The festival at this mountain (*qua* mother) is said to last nine days.[323] The latter number is thus linked not only to mountains and Ida in particular, but now also to motherhood and generally to femininity. (The availing of a male initiate by a woman also occurs when the Sybil oracle guides Aeneas through a cave into the underworld.) This theme is related to the tradition of the nine (female) muses who inspire artists (which Virgil partly alludes to when he calls on Calliope to inspire his narration[324]). Consistent with this, Aristaeus's Bougonia ritual in Book IV of Virgil's *Georgics*, which was previously linked to birth and renewal, also lasts nine days.[325] Again, in such instances the number nine appears to relate most relevantly to the months of pregnancy.

In terms of that association of mountains and the underworld, an explicit association of depth with height may be drawn from Virgil's description of a sun and stars at the recess of the underworld where the Elysian Fields are found.[326] In addition, by mentioning the "nine windings of the Styx"[327] (the river that leads the dead into nether-realms) the *Aeneid* associates the number nine with infernal interiors as well as

---

Viator: Medieval and Renaissance Studies, vol. 1 (Berkley, CA: University of California Press, 1970), 203.

320   Virgil, *The Aeneid*, I:271–72; 42.

321   Ibid., V:645–46; 165.

322   The reasons for which attribution the translator Barry Powell describes as "unclear" in a footnote thereto. It is, however, perfectly intelligible in light of the following.

323   Vigil, *The Aeneid*, V:649; 165.

324   Ibid., IX:457; 286.

325   Virgil, *Georgics*, IV:552; 235.

326   Vigil, *The Aeneid*, VI:570; 198.

327   Ibid., VI:385; 190.

high peaks (as above), so that these two are further connected. It may be suggested that the inward journey whereby one meets the injunction "know thyself" is a venture into Tartarus (implying as it does a potentially frightening confrontation with the often-tenebrous psychic-scape) and that discovering a kinship between the self and the celestial, the subterranean and supernal lights, is its yield. The means to this worthy end is the paradigmatic death before dying through which the initiate is reborn. The descent whereby ascent is attained corresponds to the previously explored symbol of saving wound.

By way of negative contrast, just as Promethean defeat has served to illustrate Herculean success, so too Aeneas's encountering of Tityus in the land of the dead (again in Book VI of the *Aeneid*) presents an example of abortive initiation. This erstwhile child of Jove is guilty of attempted rape (illegitimate appropriation of the spiritual prize, perhaps) and is punished for it by having his liver and guts repeatedly fed on by a vulture, where the tissue ever renews itself[328] (as in the case of Prometheus). The wound upon the side bespeaks initiation, whereas its being constantly regenerated and reopened implies a lack of acceptance or acquiescence thereof. This makes for an arrested development whereby the initiate never submits to his wounding and consequently never matures passed it. Rather than rebirth in the body, Tityus's body lies "across nine acres"[329] in a state of living death whose association with the number nine parodies the period of gestation and highlights what potential is being denied actuality, what process is being thwarted (the process of rebirth). Perhaps for this reason he is the "foster-child of the mother of all"[330] rather than being described as her biological spawn.

Although more tenuous than the foregoing, it may be telling that, towards the *Aeneid*'s completion, fighting erupts as a consequence of a young man, one of "nine handsome brothers,"[331] suffering injury when a "spear pierced his ribs."[332] The ensuing clash sees Aeneas in turn injured on his side (an arrow to the leg) and healed by Venus. Both instances, then, make reference to wounding and birth. This can be interpreted as being the case not only because these traumas occur in the wake of a reference to the number nine with its link to gestation, but also because the mother of the nine brothers is explicitly mentioned in the cited passage, and obviously given that Venus is Aeneas's mother. Although the young man struck by a spear may have died, it causes his brothers to fight and, ultimately, his people are triumphant. The bearer of the number nine is the tenth, the initiate: the eye of the heart, in Orthodox Christian terms,

---

328   Ibid., VI:531–33; 195.
329   Ibid., VI:529–30; 195.
330   Ibid., VI:529; 195.
331   Ibid., XII:245; 362.
332   Ibid., XII:249; 362.

as tenth (non-)bodily opening which completes the other nine corporeal ones. In higher terms, this is Horus among the ennead of Egyptian gods.

Briefly, before moving on, we may note that the number seven also endears itself to the *Aeneid*'s verse. Aeolus's collaboration with Juno, liberating the four winds to scourge Aeneas, involves receiving the loveliest of "twice seven" nymphs, *Deiopeia*,[333] so that the holy couple would constitute the center of four winds and the center of the two sets of seven (fourteen) nymphs. The fact that the latter is doubled but expressed in terms of seven might refer to its operating at the level of duality, yet pegged to unity by the marriage of its loveliest exemplar to the *quintessential* wind god. Aeneas is worthy of all that is ascribed to Aeolus from the moment that he survives the god's bane. Specifically, Aeneas's alliance to the seven principles represented by the nymphs comes through in the recurrence of that number in the triumphant Trojan's vicinity.

Of his storm-wrecked fleet there survive seven ships,[334] and his people are fed thereafter on seven stags.[335] Later, his wandering is noted for entering its seventh year.[336] There are other instances besides,[337] some referring to mortality, as in the case of the layers of Turnus's shield,[338] which is pierced to deadly effect by Aeneas, or in that of human sacrifice,[339] and others to its overcoming, as in the cases already cited, to which may be added Rome's seven hills, Aeneas's supreme earthly prize. Having a similar function, but more forcefully represented, is the number nine, connoted as it is with both death and immortality.

These are precisely the numbers that recur in the context of Wisdom. As has been discussed, she is often associated with a mountain and a monarch in between four cardinal directions, sometimes presented as rivers (again, mountains are stability and rivers a pouring forth). The central mountain where the king is enthroned can also be identified as the central pillar of Wisdom's house, which she has built with seven pillars (Proverbs 9:1), sending out her maidens to call on those worthy of its feast (Proverbs 9:3), maidens identifiable with Juno's seven or twice seven nymphs. Given that it is by Wisdom that God laid the foundations of the earth (Proverbs 3:19), her house can be considered as the manifest abode, creation, the Cosmos, in its un-fallen or ideal state (it is in these terms that Sophia is usually described by theologians). Seven are the most obviously discernable colors of the rainbow—that is, the atmospheric diversity of creation, six in number—combined with the seventh, their originating white resplendence—that is, the stratospheric unity of the

---

333   Ibid., I:84, 35.
334   Ibid., I:193–94, 40.
335   Ibid., I:216, 40.
336   Ibid., I:789–90, 62.
337   Lee M. Fratantuono and R. Alden Smith, *Aeneid 5* (Leiden: Brill, 2015), 191.
338   Vigil, *The Aeneid*, XII:775, 381.
339   Ibid., VI:20, 173.

sun as representative of the divine beyond. As for the number nine, it is the worlds of death the border of which is presided by Freya; the Egyptian ennead is completed by the tenth term, Horus, who is birthed by Hathor (whose name means "house of Horus").

The Psalms and Aeneas

In this section we will continue discussing the figure of Aeneas, relating him to David and both to the schema developed in "Sun and Star, Son and Mother." The connection between a goddess and kingship which is explicit in (not only Tantric) Indian sources is in fact the basis of European civilization, which connects emperorship with Venus/Aphrodite, being that emperors descend from her via Aeneas. Further, the Bible in many places connects imagery of kingship and the dominion given to the faithful to the morning star, which is Venus, and is also used to describe Christ himself. In a sense the pagan Roman connection of emperorship with Venus and the Christian Biblical connection of kingship with the morning star presents us with a startling continuity from two different traditions which come together in Europe.

Indeed, the Psalms (110:3) speak of the womb before the morning star whence the king is begotten by the Lord (originally referring to king David and therefore to the Davidic model which the Bible treats as paradigmatic of rightful monarchy), which connects Venus (the morning star) to motherhood of kings, just as in Roman tradition Venus is the mother of emperors. From this perspective, Dante's claim in *Il Convivio* that Aeneas entered Italy at the same time as king David was born points to the connection between the two as expressing the same principle.

The morning star bestowed by Christ in the Apocalypse would be the autozoon of Plato's *Timaeus*, making one capable of just rule, just relation with creation (because it is the paradigm of ordered bodies). Just as the autozoon or "essential living animal" is prior to the manifest world or "intelligible living animal," the morning star rises prior to the sun, the lighting up of forms by daylight. The womb before the morning star is Rhea for the cosmic Demiurge, who bestows the autozoon to him from the First Paternal Intellect, and it is Juno to the co-demiurge, the kingly initiate, like Aeneas.

In any case, prior to Juno (and to Vesta, who is the divine feminine at rest rather than in its giving-forth mode, but is at the same ontological grade as Juno, according to Proclean understanding) is Rhea, conjoined to her masculine counterpart Saturn. We could see these as symbols for the various realms that precede our world in Pythagoreanism: the Monad is beyond all these; the Dyad or Juno is the Crater represented by the celestial dome, like a womb; the Triad or Venus (and Minerva) is the world-soul represented by the morning star which announces the coming day of manifestation, rising just before the sun in the east; the

Tetrad, with its four corners, is the earth, our realm, whose ideal-type is represented by the sun, Apollo, which reminds us of the 16th century literary theme of describing utopias through a meeting with Apollo (Boccalini's *De' Raggugagli di Parnaso*, Tommaso Campanella's *City of the Sun*, etc.).

Egyptian mythology seems to approximately confirm this schema, with its symbolism apparently tending to show the morning star as feminine and prior to the sun in order of generation (although also sometimes presenting these two as creative and destructive aspects of the Eye of Atum/Ra or as two Eyes). The primordial god Atum sent light into darkness to find Shu and Tefnut, who had become lost, causing what was possibly "the first sunrise":

> The moment when Atum was united with Ra to become the creator sun god. In the earliest versions of the myth, the Eye that was sent forth may have been thought of as the morning star that precedes the sunrise. The Eye returned with Shu and Tefnut, but wept with rage when she saw that Ra-Atum had grown a new solar eye: the Glorious One. Human beings were created from the tears of the angry Eye or from the tears of joy shed by Ra-Atum's new eye...Ra-Atum placated the angry Eye by placing her on his forehead as the *uraeus*. Shown as a cobra coiled around the sun disk, she was more powerful than all other deities.[340]

To go searching for Shu and Tefnut is to return by birth through the vision of Atum, the uraeus, and like a pharaoh, to have an uraeus oneself. One born of the morning star, like Aeneas, can only really be at peace with his inheritance by dying (entering the underworld) and being born of the "womb before the morning star," that is, being born from the formlessness which is prior to form (prior to the morning star which heralds daylight, in which all forms become crisp and clear). And the *Pyramid Texts* (412): "You belong to the Stars who surround Ra, who are before the morning star, you are born in your months as the moon. Ra leans upon you on the Horizon...the Imperishable Stars follow you. Make yourself ready until Ra comes that you may be ready when you ascend to Ra."[341]

We receive the morning star, the power to rule, to be in the world, to enjoy form, after going into formlessness and returning from it. This plays out in Toltec mythology where Quetzalcoatl, who also loved his people (refusing human sacrifice), dies willingly, becoming identified with the planet Venus as Lord of Dawn[342] (he is also associated with the feathered snake, so that the Egyptian association of serpent and Venus

---

340   Pinch, *Handbook of Egyptian Mythology*, 129.
341   Cited by Uzdavinys, *Philosophy as a Rite of Rebirth: From Ancient Egypt to Neo-platonism*, 198.
342   Lee Irwin, *Coming Down from Above: Prophecy, Resistance, and Renewal in Native American Religions* (Norman, OK: University of Oklahoma Press: 2008), 80.

recurs).[343] Therefore was Aeneas not at peace with Juno. Aeneas, to receive his proximate cause and lordship over forms, Venus, had to die and be reborn, at peace with the prior cause and formless matrix, Juno. It seems the correct order of things needed to be put in place, and this king with a great destiny had to die ritually, go to the formless womb and only then receive the morning star, his inheritance as a son of Venus, founding Rome and ruling the nations as Rome did (or does, metaphorically, in terms of what Rome represents: the Elysian ideal of Rome shown to Aeneas during his death-journey) alike one who receives the morning star and can rule over the nations in the Bible (Apocalypse 2:26–27).

This finds its devotional correlate in the emergence of a certain cult. Approaching the above epiphany through the story of Aeneas can be understood as rendering Venus, his mother, in continuity with the great female deities prior to Venus, including Juno. This would be expressed by the form of *Venus Caelestis*, Heavenly Venus, whose shrine was precisely at Pozzuoli, where Aeneas descended into the underworld and would have realized the divine matrix (the Crater, womb), a ritual death and rebirth, realizing the morning star, his mother, as proceeding from that prior layer of reality, Juno, and returning with a new form (the communal correlate of which is the Trojan transformation into Latins). The rites of Venus Caelestis included the taurobolium, or sacrifice of the bull, performed at Pozzuoli, which is relevant for the following section, in which we explore the significance of bull slaying.

The morning star can be understood as representing the umbilical cord connecting the king to the darkness of the womb beyond the stars, the Crater that the dark night's sky evokes (and the Milky Way a sort of supernal source of nourishment as he goes into or returns from formlessness), and also as representing the third eye (wherein Ra places her according to the previous passage), like inner vision connecting the king to transcendent knowledge, for it is from the head of the Crater's male counterpart, Jove, that feminine wisdom at the next generation proceeds (Minerva springing from Jove's head). This image of the celestial dome as not only a Crater above us and dark womb but also the skull of a male counterpart, so that all is occurring inside the mind of that Demiurge, occurs in Norse mythology, where the sky consists of Ymir's head: "The sky from the frost cold giant's skull,"[344] which is consistent with the theme of the macro-anthropic Jove as Greco-Roman equivalent. Another account of one related to a macro-anthropic form and giving forth from his forehead occurs in the Indian Devi Bhagavatam (I am

---

343   Also, according to historian Enrique Florescano, the feathered serpent/Venus was part of a triad which included the mother goddess: Enrique Florescano, *El mito de Quetzalcóatl* (Baltimore: Johns Hopkins University Press, 1999).

344   Anonymous, *The Poetic Edda*, trans. A. Bellows (New York City: Princeton University Press, 1936), Vafthruthnismol, 21, 74.

condensing the passage quite a bit, but the full version should be read to understand the theological vision contained):

> That youth Janârdan of the form of the Great Cosmos...Brahmâ took his birth in His navel...began to travel...came back to his former place and began to meditate on the lotus feet of Sri Krisna. Then, in meditation, with his introspective eye...he saw the God Sri Krisna in Goloka with Gopas and Gopis. He then began to praise the Lord of Goloka when He granted boons...and he began to do the work of creation...from his forehead eleven Rudras sprang. (IX:3, 45–58, 818)

Saint Peter as Sacred King[345]

Peter's vision in Acts is highly instructive, as it presents many of the symbols of sacred kingship:

> And he beholds the sky opened, and an object descending, like a great sheet being let down to the ground by four corners, On which were all the quadrupeds and reptiles of the earth and birds of the sky. And a voice came to him: 'Arise, Peter, sacrifice and eat.' But Peter said, 'Certainly not, Lord, for I have never eaten anything profane and impure.' And again, for a second time, there came a voice to him: 'Do not deem profane what God has made pure.' And this happened three times, and at once the object was taken up into the sky. (Acts of the Apostles 10:11–16)

St. Peter seems to have a vision of the autozoon consistent with sacred kingship imagery across traditions:

1. It is in between the four corners of the earth, constituting a fifth element (quintessence), and comprehends all things, in the form of animals both kosher and non-kosher, which is therefore consistent with the theme of the monarchical axis mundi between the four corners, such as Caesar with his four horses or Pharaoh shooting four flaming arrows, or Ezekiel's vision with its four faces, and specifically with the understanding that the fifth term manifests all worldly things, all the animals St. Peter sees;
2. It is, in a way, dismembering him, for he is losing a prior exclusivist conception of religion, equivalent to kingly ordeals of death before rebirth. This brings an antinomian, we might say Tantric, element that presumably must de-emphasize specific cultural strictures in part so as to emphasize the universality of the principle being glimpsed itself;
3. It renders him universal representative by receiving that which is

---

345 Although dealing with a different topic, this discussion appears as sub-section to the Initiate at Mount Ida because sacred authority in Europe derives both from the Roman account of its Empire and the Christian account of St. Peter—the emperor/pope dichotomy. We therefore want to associate the two rather than having it be a stand-alone.

a paradigm of all things and, indeed, he includes these in himself, like the cosmic man in various traditions that comprehends all manifest forms, for he sees all animals related to that supernal object, and is told to eat them, that is, include them in his person corporeally;

4. It contains a sacrifice—a direct injunction to perform sacrifice—whose inner significance we have interpreted as the removal of the empirical self to allow for perception of the formless before returning to that self with new insight. This sacrifice occurs by presenting him with various forms for it transcends form and therefore leads Peter to adopt a pluralistic, ecumenical vision.

In terms of this last point especially, Acts tells us that Peter does not accept a Roman centurion's subordination to himself, of gentile to Jew or of profane student to holy teacher, saying "Stand up; I too am a man" (Acts 10:26), "God also showed me that I must not call any man profane or impure" (10:28), "...in every people, whoever revers Him and performs works of righteousness is accepted by Him" (10:35, referring to God), "The word that he sent to the sons of Israel...Jesus the Anointed—this one is the Lord of everyone" (10:36), "And the faithful among the circumcised...were astonished, because the gift of the Holy Spirit has been poured out even upon the gentiles" (10:45).

We may treat this vision as foundational to the Papacy because it occurs as a sign and lesson to Peter that his work is universal in character and specifically, in terms of the historical unfolding of the Christian Church, that it is Roman, given that it is predicted by an angelic vision given to a Roman centurion called Cornelius, precisely belonging to a cohort by the name of *Italic*, who is told to meet Peter by an angel. Roman popes[346] are arguably spiritual descendants of Peter (and Paul) as well as of the *Italic*'s Centurion Cornelius, or else the Centurion is a type for the emperor, with whom Peter asserts his own equality, as has been asserted about Emperor Constantine through the title *Equal to the Apostles.* Conversely, a Christian emperor could quite coherently claim the type of St. Peter, as well as Cornelius, as model for his own office.

Peter, and all legitimate rulers, receives the vision, the intellectual illumination, that the Logos is not a thing among things whose qualities must be imposed on things but is beyond things and can encompass these in their own qualities. They become representatives of unity by analogy.

---

346   It is not only the bishop of Rome who succeeds St. Peter according to St. Cyprian of Carthage (33rd Epistle), and given Peter's role in founding Antioch directly and Alexandria through St. Mark, these others are also Petrine, "in three places is the See of one," as Pope St. Gregory the Dialogist says. Neither am I here asserting Vatican I's view on papal authority, which is not the same as that "primacy of honor" that the Roman bishop did definitely hold in the early church. We also have the 34th Apostolic Canon, according to which the bishops must not act without the consent of the first among them, nor him without their consent.

In this sense, the above does not necessarily constitute an argument for papal supremacy or infallibility, albeit a special honor is implied for the Roman pontiff. The design in the mind of the Logos is harmony, it is not a quality to be compared to other qualities. Acts 10 tells us St. Peter perceived that the Holy Spirit had descended on gentiles and that he baptized them but did not have them circumcised. The Jewish members of his company remained so and the gentiles remained so, yet both were encompassed in a unity that is at another level, an ecumenic unity. Thusly was it fortunate for Jesus to leave us, as He says, so that His disciples may receive the Spirit, the Advocate, for now Jesus's empirical biography, with its many particulars, is not confused for Him. This vision of Ecumene is the whole of legitimate authority.

St. Peter's vision, so consistent with that of the sacred king *as* high priest across traditions, renders him a royal figure, which is confirmed by his general warrior zeal and the fact that his epiphany corresponds and leads him into mutual exchange with a man likewise prompted by a Heavenly vision who is also a warrior. Indeed, the epiphany of Acts 10 does not inaugurate a pure contemplative praxis but actually instructs St. Peter to sacrifice. In Christ is the ultimate sacrifice, comprehending all others, and yet "Arise, Peter, sacrifice and eat." It is an active practice and participation in holy things.

St. Peter was a married man and wielded one of the swords Jesus explicitly instructed the apostles to carry with them (Luke 22:36), although sometimes doing so impetuously, earning his master's reprimand. He is not a priestly figure in a world-denying sense (and neither were many popes).

There is weirdly not much warrant for the division of Roman high pontiff and Roman emperor in all this. It is sensible to divide the day-to-day operations of politics from sacred representation, but in that case the imagery of traditional monarchy and emperorship belong in the latter, not the former category. It would also make sense to separate a universal representative of humanity from a local one, where the latter ceases to conflate universal archetype with actual aspirations to global hegemony, but this is not what was meant by the Pope-Emperor distinction in medieval Europe. The result was perhaps somewhat idiosyncratic as respects other traditions.

The current system of Papal election by cardinals alone is one thousand years old. In the prior means of election, which had lasted for a couple of centuries, the Papacy was not as divorced from the Empire and the local Roman aristocracy. Apart from granting power to Roman aristocrats in choosing a pope, a dual dependence used to exist whereby the pope would swear loyalty to the Emperor and the Emperor would be crowned by the pope in Rome.

A parallel case would play out in East Asia.[347] The relationship between state and church, or two nations as depositories of each, under the Mongolian Kublai Khan and Tibetan Lama Pagspa established a *two powers* or *dual law* doctrine. This was recovered by the Altan Khan. Khutukhtu Setsen Khung Taiji popularized a text called *Arban Buyantu Nom-un Chayaan Teukey (The Tenfold Virtuous White Chronicle of the Faithful,* or *White History of the Tenfold Dharma*), dating it to the late thirteenth century, attributing it to the Kublai Khan and celebrating the relation between the head of the Yellow Faith in Mongolia and the Khan.[348] The Altan Khan conferred the title of the Dalai Lama to the head of the Yellow Faith, originating this term, which is partly Mongolian and partly Tibetan. The Dalai Lama in turn claimed to be a reincarnation of the Pagspa Lama, and the Altan Khan to be the reincarnated Kublai Khan, hearkening back to Mongolian prosperity and, in fact, unity with China, given that the Kublai Khan had ruled China. This more or less displaced the actual, nominal Emperor of the Mongols, the Jasagtu Khan, and it would be Altan's dynasty that took hold. In 1577 the Abdai Khan followed Altan's example and received the title of Khan from the Dalai Lama and presided over continued reciprocity between khan and lama, emperor and pope.

China was never wholly left out, however. Despite a tradition that tried to build him up and present him as exalted both in Mongolian and Tibetan—secular and sacred—terms, the Ligdan Khan seems to not have lived up to this mission, behaving abusively towards his vassals and failing to build up Mongol supremacy. China therefore remained the overriding center of effective statecraft in the region, and even of religious authority. This was manifest by the 17th century, when the son of Tushetu Khan was raised up by the Mongols but took refuge with the Manchu emperor of China from his Oirat enemies in 1688. The Manchu Emperor then restored him and made him the Grand Lama over the Yellow Faith in Mongolia. Here, the relation of Tibetan Buddhist clergy to Mongolian aristocracy and kingship is superseded by the Chinese Emperor, who manifested both temporal and religious authority, and rendered the Mongolian Buddhist church independent of Tibet while unifying it to Mongolian kingship.

Back in the west, it was a certain Archbishop Hildebrand, by way of his Norman allies, who changed the method of Papal election after deposing the antipope Benedict X. It is interesting that such a complete severing of Papal election from the political community came as part of a general reform attempting to impose celibacy on priests (the south of

---

347   Charles Bawden, *Modern History of Mongolia* (New York: Routledge: 2009).
348   Vesna A. Wallace, "Legalized Violence: Punitive Measures of Buddhist Khans in Mongolia." In *Buddhist Warfare*, Michael Jerryson and Mark Juergensmeyer, eds. (Oxford: Oxford University Press, 2010), 92.

Italy, largely Byzantine, was to have this rule imposed upon its clergy by Norman strength, and in the north, Milan, with its own liturgical tradition, resented the reform) as well as *clerical autocracy*, as Norwich calls it.

Hildebrand became Pope, taking the name Gregory VII, and proposed that all popes from that time forward be considered saints. Fittingly, imperial authority, in the form of Henry IV, king of the Germans (becoming emperor later) entered into conflict with Pope Gregory VII, who twice excommunicated Henry and fought against the latter's own selection for pope, antipope Clement III. Gregory brought allies from the south and with them, the Saracen and Norman rape of Rome, leaving his flock so embittered with its pontiff that he had to leave with the Norman king Robert after winning a Pyrrhic victory, such was the damage done to the city. Gregory VII died in exile. There is perhaps a lesson in the fact that a vision of pristine priestly purity and supremacy ended up allied with heresy and holocaust and filled the souls it was meant to save with such hatred. Of course, the opposite vision of a purely secular authority has led to disaster as well.

III. Copulatio

WE DISCUSS THE STATE OF THE INITIATE
after ritual death and experience of transcendence (*The Limping King*), his restoration through erotic union (*Eroto-Theurgy*), more theoretically, the meaning of gender in terms of metaphysical categories (*Gendered Metaphysics*) and the political corollaries of the kingly initiate's union to his consort as instantiation and paradoxical discovery of his epiphany in the world (*The Divine Feminine and Political Power*).

THE LIMPING KING AND THE EPIPHANY OF GENDER

The king returns at sunrise, coming home with the dawn, crawling, a reeling silhouette heavy with volcanic fumes mixed with sweat and bloody gore, now dry and caked. He is him who was "transformed into a golden embryo,"[1] a Hiranyagarbha, described in the *Atharva Veda*. This return involves emergence from a makeshift vaginal passage in various tribal cultures according to Mircea Eliade, which also appears in Hellenic mythical accounts of apotheoses:

> [Zeus] persuaded Hera to adopt Heracles by a ceremony of rebirth: namely, going to bed, pretending to be in labor, and then producing him from beneath her skirts—which is the adoption ritual in use among many barbarian tribes.[2]

The initiate's emergence from a holy mountain, such as Mount Ida which Proclus identifies with Juno, would be precisely a rebirth/adoption by this goddess.

The king will be ritually bathed, tattered skin replaced with purple robe. Yet he is not worthy yet. After knowing infinity and understanding that no particular, finite form can exhaust its potentials, the king is left wounded. The intelligible archetype he perceived arising in that ineffable consciousness after his outward self had been shredded are uncontainable in any particular manifestation, in this or that place or practice. This is the secret of ecumenism. He has been given the invisible vision that reveals everything to be an expression of the same pattern, every worldly thing an echo of a name of God, a designation for He who remains forever unnamable. The king should therefore sit upon his throne, for he is now capable of just rule, of not confusing his power with God's power, his laws for cosmic order itself, or his realm for the *Ecumene*, the entire human creation.

---

1   Mircea Eliade, *Rites and Symbols of Initiation: The Mysteries of Birth and Rebirth* (London: Harper Colophon Books, 1975), 56.
2   Graves, *The Greek Myths*, 145.i, 565.

Enoch is assimilated into Metatron, Pythagoras into the Demiurge, Aeneas into Jove, the Pharaoh into Osiris and Ra. And yet, to feel the love of God is not always to love his creation as we ought, especially if we are tempted by release, by the sweetness of escape, of never again becoming mired in lesser things. To one who knows the divine, who has even once been alone with the Alone, death can be so sweet a thing as to sour life.

The king now understands that his realm is not the world, and is only one possible expression of cosmic order. He lacks the motivation of simple fanaticism, the concupiscent conquering hunger that Voegelin decries in a figure like Alexander the Great.[3] It is easy to motivate one who believes all paths but his own are devoid of value. It is another thing entirely to endure on one's path while knowing there are other, valid routes available. But this endurance is no mean labor, no heavy yoke, it is the play of outpouring creativity. The king has lost the first motivation and has not quite found the second. He is not swept up in love for finite things in the light of infinite principles, willing to give himself to the heroic pursuit of glory in the full understanding that glory fades—at least in its contingent forms. He has not yet discovered why he should rule, why he should do his duty, as Lord Krishna entreats Arjuna to do in the *Bhagavad Gita*. Why the aesthetic joy of his *particular* realm and *particular* life's work are supremely justified and sustained rather than absorbed and dissolved against the backdrop of that universal principle he has encountered. He does not understand why God lets human beings live and act, rather than abolishing the whole of creation. He does not know why there is something rather than nothing or, indeed, many things rather than a single thing, all this confusing plurality rather than a simple uniformity.

He has seen that forms are meaningless from the vantage of eternal principles. All things end, yet there is that which is beyond all things and which remains forever the same, so why endeavor to do anything at all in this twittering world, as Eliot called it? If he took power now, it would be to end it all. To close history and particularity forever and force the world to imitate the divine simplicity by becoming less vexing, by being violently levelled—he would do what Voegelin's lustful conquerors but for different reasons which are, in the end, the same reason. Like certain modern revolutionaries, the king resents the world and would have all the fruits of human culture and politics, that rotten bounty for which he has no taste, undone. Afterwards—or right now, for why should he bother abolishing the world when he can simply abdicate his role in it?—he would spend his time conversing with the pure, innocent

---

3 Although in western tradition this figure is presented as somehow holy. In the medieval Alexander Romances we see him build a chariot and attach it to four griffins—the four elements/corners—ascending until he sees the world disc surrounded by the outer ocean like an ouroboros snake. He is told to go no higher. Perhaps this means he sees the limitations of trying to conquer the world politically, preferring instead a world-encompassing perspective.

creatures of the forest, like the wild man Enkidu of Mesopotamian epic. But, like Enkidu, he will be won back to the side of humanity by a woman.

At this stage, the king is like a painter who looks at the white resplendence of sunlight refracted by water droplets in the air after it rains to suspend a rainbow across the sky and decides to mix the colors of his paint pallet in the hope of igniting the same solar resplendence on his canvas. He has confused the stratospheric for the mesospheric; one layer of reality for another. Instead of honoring sunlight by painting beautiful images of the forms it illumines, images for it in turn to illumine, he makes a mess. He has become confounded and precisely missed the point that because transcendent, eternal things are beyond imminent, temporal ones, they are not expressed by the latter in isolation only, the way a letter expresses a sound, but are always wider, more encompassing, and therefore are expressed in the relations, the patterns, between forms. God's unity manifests in the harmony of created things, not in their uniformity. The Logos is not this or that thing, but the Golden Ratio, the ordered pattern encompassing all things. He is not ready for the work of rulership, of making the kingdom beautiful, just as that painter would not know how to make a beautiful image.

A common example of this confusion is to pass from unity of principle to desiring uniformity of the practices expressing that principal, or from the sense of reality as joyful creative exuberance, to denying not just that some expressions of human creativity are invalid, but even that they cause pain or cause one's health to suffer. If all is ultimately arbitrary, for the contingent form rests on a trans-formal absolute, then all is valid, and if at root reality is the joyful outpouring of a creative agent (as traditional theologies would agree), then bending one's arm the wrong way should not result in pain or trauma—it is just another way of experiencing reality.

This can all be concluded from studying the book of nature. Theologically, secondary causation is a direct condescension on the part of God ("every Natural Effect has a Spiritual Cause ... for a Natural Cause only seems," Blake, *Milton*, 26, 45). It is ever subordinate to Him but is the means by which God allows human beings agency, for such agency would be impossible in a cosmos without apparent casuistry and partial occlusion, otherwise everything would occur at once and the possibility of sequential action would be nullified. To consider the direct agency of the Lord as requiring the abolition of other agencies is dangerously iconoclastic. The correct view is one that treats Occasionalism and Aristotelianism as compatible.

To reject culture and proclaim oneself animal (albeit a rational, if not a human, one), as some Franciscans have done, ends in submission to the momentum of unexamined cultural residues (in practice, much more than mere residue, for human beings can never be acultural) or psychological and instinctual pursuits. It is still mediated by culture, for culture never goes away, but embarrassedly and therefore in an attenuated manner, leaving more room for whatever is considered a fait accompli of human nature, conceding more of its vicious expressions, the result being just as socially-constructed, but less self-confident and therefore less willing to orient itself towards the Good. To reject culture and proclaim oneself animal (albeit a rational one), as some Franciscans did, ends up in the same dialectic between reaction and revolution, power and liberation, restraining Dystopia and gesturing towards Utopia. It engages in that which forces its reaction, the way a libertine may give himself over to the iron-clad law of abstinence in order to restrain the chaotic power whose consequences he has come to fear. Writes Adorno in *Minima Moralia*:

> The refined are drawn to the unrefined, whose coarseness decep-
> tively promises what their own culture denies. They do not know
> that the indelicacy that appears to them as anarchic nature, is
> nothing but a reflex-action produced by the compulsion they
> struggle to resist.[4]

There is always culture and political association, just as an a-linguistic commune would point and grunt its way into language. The cases of John Duns Scotus and Peter John Olivi, "outspoken defenders of Franciscan poverty" and at the same time "articulators of proto-liberal economic and political reasoning"[5] would be an example. We may also refer to certain abuses of native Americans by Europeans as proceeding from literalized Franciscan beliefs about the apocalypse, and seeing the natives as neutral vessels near the Adamic state[6] (Eric Voegelin's immanentizing of the eschaton).

Since culture (or the particular) is always multiform and always organic, the king should legitimately direct himself to one particular culture on

---

4   Adorno, *Minima Moralia*, 117, 195.

5   John Milbank, "The Franciscan Conundrum." *Communio: International Catholic Review* 42 (2015): 477.

6   "A 1521 papal bull issued by Leo X authorized the Franciscans...to preach, baptize and give sacraments.... Led by apocalyptic visions, the twelve Franciscan friars" who met with Hernan Cortes in America "proceeded to evangelize the Nahuatl-speaking peoples" of Mexico "as a new 'primitive and reborn church' whose poverty and simplicity recalled the original founding of Christianity and the promised spiritual renewal of Joachim of Fiore.... The final renewal of the world required a deliverance of Native peoples...wiping the slate clean of all pagan beliefs and instilling salvation.... This aggressive *tabula rasa* approach is built on a foundation that denies the authenticity, rights and complexity of alternative spiritual epistemologies and the legitimacy of Native religious traditions. According to Franciscan historian Geronimo de Mendieta (c. 1590s), Native peoples were 'like soft wax' that could be molded into any form" (Irwin, *Coming Down from Above*, 87–88). While illustrating a certain mentality worthy of criticism, we should supplement this passage by recalling that Franciscans and Jesuits historically made a point of learning Nahua and preaching in the native tongue.

the basis of its apparent coherence, form, history, just as each person can legitimately pursue their life's story, shop, make friends, work, on the simple basis of its being there.

But it is not only the king's intellect that is marred, and the solution to his stagnation does not rest with clever arguments. He has been robbed of his pride, of believing himself unique, of believing his kingdom and work a pinnacle of human achievement. Or at least of believing in the possibility of becoming unique, or of finding something which is, some cause representing the end of human understanding. Instead, now he knows the transcendent always has new potentials in store, and is never exhausted, so that there is no end to its emanations, and no end that seems worthy of pursuing. He is like Alexander in the medieval romances, who rises on a carriage upon four griffins (again, the Grail/Crater is fourfold). His initial will is to conquer the horizon, but at a certain point a voice tells him to go no further. It is as though he had discovered the earth is round and one will be delivered up to the starting point if one goes far enough. The immanent (the world) cannot be occupied completely and thus made absolute; one must relate to the particular without wishing to turn it into an absolute and paradoxically receive the absolute thereby (Blake's *infinity in a grain of sand*). He has reached a point, integrated an epiphany, that the self-assured modern man—perhaps thousands of years ahead of him in time—has not fully come into.

Excessive concern for abstract or universal things and a desire to flee from worldly affairs is represented in the image of a king who is asymmetrically wounded on the thigh, side, or groin. His priorities have become lopsided, he is unbalanced, and as a consequence he cannot rule. Yet it is through this ordeal that greater wisdom and capacity for just rule is achieved.

Popular wisdom recommends sex as the cure for excessive abstraction, that cerebral affliction and flight from life, a sort of *dispositional gnosticism*. It is the eternal feminine that urges forward. Correspondingly, those asymmetric lesions that present in heroes and kings across traditions usually have a clear psycho-sexual character. During the events of the Trojan War, a man of Troy by the name of Anchises, father of Aeneas who would be founder of Rome according to Virgil, had been left lame, having been struck on a foot or thigh by Jove for revealing his secret courting of Venus,[7] Aeneas's divine mother. That he was wounded in a context related to his union with the goddess of beauty emphasizes the erotic character of the wound. Aeneas himself was revived at Apollo's temple after this god rescued the injured hero,[8] who is the solar deity's champion, just as Aeneas carried his injured father from the burning Troy.[9]

---

7   Virgil, *The Aeneid*, II:585 (B. Powell's footnote), 86.
8   Homer, *The Iliad*, V:529–32; 107.
9   Virgil, *The Aeneid*, II:635–36, 88.

One who, when injured, is saved by the gods, as Aeneas was on his hip, knows to in turn carry tradition, the broken-footed inheritance, upon his back, even as his home burns. Thus, after having his side sliced, and being rescued by Venus and Apollo, the hero then carried his injured father out of the burning Troy, despite the risk entailed. This episode is significant. Venus descends to the level of mortals for the sake of her son. Her rescue of Aeneas leads to her injury,[10] so that it is a mutual wounding of divinity's manifestation and humanity that allows for their contact (a very Christian idea). After descent to the mother goddess of the holy mountain and ritual death (marked here by injury), the initiate enters into the secret center, the spiritual sun: it is Apollo who is able to revive Aeneas.

His later exaltation occurs by sexual union: having ritually died and been reborn from the divine mother he is mature enough to earn the solar princess for his wife. Aeneas marries Lavinia, whose burning hair[11] reveals her luminous role as initiatrix. Lavinia is the Shakti, *power*, of the divine initiate Aeneas, the erotic spiritualization of the body (her name reminds of the *Laevatein*, magic wand-weapon of Norse myth, and of lava, externalized inner—infernal—heat).

That the hero receives trauma to his side may be understood as referring to the sexual function, with the hip, thigh and rib approximating the groin. Awareness of the sexual organ and its function is awareness of one's incompleteness, one's self as half of a pair. Such is the transcendent openness of Eros, a vulnerability that leads to venture. In addition, losing balance as a result of asymmetrical injury implies falling out from the rhythm of a given station and potentially finding a new equilibrium, so that the hero is ruined for a prior mode of life but may attain to a new, more complete one. Finally, the laceration could, in this context, signify rebirth, that is, a caesarian section whereby one becomes spiritual Caesar, (re)birthed out from one's previous self.

The Mesopotamian god Tammuz or Dumuzid was said to be wounded yearly, so that his death and rebirth may have been recapitulated in the person of a mortal king. A rite of annual wounding, a seasonal metaphor, also corresponds to the evidence from "Hittite rock carvings…which celebrate the king's yearly ritual death and resurrection in the gorge of Yasilikaya near Hattusas" which greatly resemble images found at the royal Minoan site of Knossos in Crete.[12] That the king's wound is a sexual one is reinforced by the fact that in some bovine sacrifices the bull was castrated in Mesopotamian or Assyrian rites, for example.[13]

---

10   Homer, *The Iliad*, V:403; 104.

11   Virgil, *The Aeneid*, VII.56-63, 212.

12   Vincent Scully, *The Earth, the Temple, and the Gods: Greek Sacred Architecture* (San Antonio, TX: Trinity University Press, 2013).

13   Mehmet-Ali Ataç, *The Mythology of Kingship in Neo-Assyrian Art* (Cambridge: Cambridge University Press, 2010), 68.

Examples of this include the yearly wounding of the Mesopotamian king-god Tammuz, commemorated by the king having ritual intercourse with the high priestess of the goddess Inanna; Osiris missing his phallus after being recomposed and receiving a new one from his wife Isis (in Plutarch's version she makes a new one, otherwise she finds his severed member and reattaches it); Jacob whose hip is dislocated after wrestling the angel of the Lord; Aeneas injured on his hip by Diomede (*Iliad* II:5); the legend of Pythagoras having a golden thigh; Empedocles breaking his right thigh upon descent to Mount Etna following an account provided by Diogenes Laertius;[14] king Anfortas in the Holy Grail myth; Odin who gave up one eye and, along with Jesus, was speared on one side.

This image also appears in Catholic eschatology, and specifically, again in the records of Anne Catherine Emmerich, who describes a vision according to which the future restorer-emperor will be injured at his hip by an angel, limping slightly thereafter.[15] There is a similar story in the Arabian (1,001) Nights. It concerns a prince whose kingdom is made up of four mountains: one populated by Muslims, one by Christians, one by Jews and one by Zoroastrians. Here we have a metaphor for the whole of humanity. The prince is immobilized from the waist down by his evil wife, who is an adulteress and black magician, and also turns his mountains into watery islands and their denizens into fish. This is like the motif of the fisher-king motif of king Anfortas and of the fish that swallows Osiris's manhood. When the prince is finally restored, his subjects turn back into humans, an appropriate wife is given him and the former one is beheaded.

As in all heroic tales, discovery follows disaster in the *Aeneid*. This is manifest in the motif of a saving wound, a *felix culpa*. At one point in the Iliad Aeneas is wounded on his side, specifically the hip,[16] eliciting divine condescension from Venus[17] and Apollo.[18] It is in the context of what may be described as a Christic tradition of spiritual kingship being restored in the person of a wounded king that Aeneas functions in the manner of the Biblical Jacob, and can be further linked to Odin, who was wounded with a spear presumably upon his side.[19] The same image occurs in the Holy Grail mythos, in which the fisher king, Anfortas, is injured at his side (leg or groin),[20] and is in need of healing in order to resume his duty as guardian of the grail.

Using the story of Aeneas as guide, the key is that the mother cannot help beyond maturation, because the hero's side-injury is a discovery

14   Kingsley, *Ancient Philosophy, Mystery and Magic*, 254.
15   Carl E. Schmöger, *The Life and Revelations of Anne Catherine Emmerich*, vol. 2 (Charlotte, NC: TAN Books & Publishers, 2004).
16   Homer, *The Iliad*, V:361; 102.
17   Ibid., V:371–76, 103.
18   Ibid., V:406, 104.
19   Anonymous, *The Poetic Edda*, "The Ballad of the High One," 139, 60.
20   Von Eschenbach, *Parzival: A Knightly Epic*, IX:799, 275.

of sexual asymmetry, it is the freshly reborn subject growing up, so to speak, and coming to know himself as a gendered being. Coming to know gender and entering into sexual union is, in a sense, the end of pristine, childhood innocence, but also the opportunity for a new, adult, experience of the divine: erotic ecstasy. Ultimately Apollo can only give him the vision of the transcendent. It will be marriage to a solar, fire woman, the Latin princess Lavinia (whose name and hair catching fire testify to the association) that will complete Aeneas's journey.

From the Sexual Wound to Dynastic Fecundity

The Egyptian myth according to which Horus was pursued and sexually predated upon by his uncle Set presents the latter as something like a counterforce to the father Osiris, belonging to the same family and generation but seeking an opposite end for the son Horus, namely sexual submission to himself rather than maturation into reproductive heterosexuality. The objective is to take from Horus his birthright of kingship, so that rule over Egypt falls to Set instead. That Set is identified as a god of foreigners in some Egyptian texts, as well as chaos, suggests that politically this stands for the disintegration of Egypt. Similar to the Thracian Orpheus who is altered by his wife's death and later passes into the worship of Apollo, also reuniting with his deceased wife in some versions, Horus overcomes his rape and is recognized as rightful king by the sun god Ra.

The way this occurs is significant. The hands of Horus touched Set's semen, and so the future king's mother replaces these with new hands of her own making. Consistent with initiatic symbolism across traditions, the mother goddess re-births the initiate, that is, re-engenders him. Here, she specifically re-makes that part of him that had become corrupted, polluted and submissive, so that he may be spared from becoming passive in life and instead return kingly and fertile. In ancient Egypt hands were often associated with the phallus.[21] The above event is therefore both distinct and alike Isis's making a new penis for her husband. Man is initiated by his mother into good behavior (possibly represented by hands), including what will constitute sexual propriety (the association of hands with the sexual organ), and then he is initiated into sexuality proper by his wife (the phallus of Osiris).

The initiate turns back, starts over, as it were, to be reborn and then re-matured into adult relations. It may also represent introverted, unfertile sexual practice in general (the hands as masturbatory instrument, the debilitating side wound of the king, from Jacob to Anfortas, as energy wasted in onanism) which is then replaced by externalized, fertile engagement with the word (the new hands of a twice-born initiate king). This represents Horus's initiatic dismemberment. Broken by life

21   Alan William Bernthal-Hooker, *"You Shall Know Yahweh": Divine Sexuality in the Hebrew Bible and Beyond*, PhD thesis (University of Exeter, 2017), 114-15.

we must willingly break fully, be dismembered and allow the mother to birth us anew. Horus is dismembered like the cosmic man or Christ, having his hands chopped off and remade.

In this context, Set appears as that necessary oppositional force that attempts to deviate the initiate from his path as intended by his mother and father (rulership, fertility) but which, if overcome, earns him recognition by Ra, spiritual triumph symbolized by the sun and rule over Egypt. Such opposition, the counterforce to our vocation, can be treated as part of the game of life, the adventure of overcoming, so long as one is not defeated by it.

Cultures that actually institutionalized predation of this sort are guilty of the same obscenity as rites of passage actually leading to death or damaged health, and to child sacrifice. This may be at the root of cultures that have celebrated the sort of pederasty Plato condemns in the Republic, Symposium and Laws. They have inverted the meaning of the myth above. It is the equivalent of celebrating murder rather than ritual death for the sake of new life.

EROTO-THEURGY, OR SPIRITUAL INITIATION AND SEXUAL INTERCOURSE

Rites of death and rebirth are ubiquitous across traditions, as is their link to maternal divinity. The present discussion concerns what comes after. The initiate has been born again; now he must mature again. The light of mother Rhea, the Hebrew Shekinah,[22] the furnace of Nut, the solar goddess (mother to the king, from the Minoan Bronze Age state-cult to the Japanese Amaterasu) has receded. In neo-Platonic terms,[23] he has seen the autozoon, the Essential Living Creature: the paradigm of organism/organization which *precedes specific organisms*. This is carried to the cosmic architect Jove/Demiurge by Rhea, the mother-goddess conjoined with the transcendent "First Paternal Intellect" (Saturn).[24]

---

22   The term Shekinah does not appear in the Bible, although there are allusions to her in Isaiah 60:2, Matthew 17:5, Luke 2:9 and Romans 9:4. The term first appears in the Targums, with the possible exception of the word "σκηνὴ" in John's Apocalypse (21:3), usually translated as "tabernacle" but which could be a Greek transliteration of the Hebrew Shekinah. See: Moshe Weinfeld, "Feminine Features in the Imagery of God in Israel: The Sacred Marriage and the Sacred Tree," *Vetus Testamentum*, 46, no. 4 (1996): 515-29.

23   The language of Proclean neo-Platonism is used throughout, as well as that of sacred monarchy, where the sacred king and queen stand for the spiritual initiate and their kingdom for one's vocation. Reference to this tradition is consistent with our subject matter: the relationship between masculine and feminine—king and queen as high priests—was prominent in Minoan Crete and Mycenaean southern Greece (according to Nanno Marinatos, *Minoan Kingship and the Solar Goddess: A Near Eastern Koine*, 33-49). Hellenic culture, which according to Proclus centers on Cretan (presumably Bronze Age Minoan) ritual survivals into the iron and classical ages, would likewise derive from a pre-Hellenic Mediterranean monarchism.

24   Proclus, *The Six Books of Proclus The Platonic Successor, On The Theology of Plato*, vol. 2, trans. T. Taylor (London: A. J. Valpy, 1816), V:11; 337.

The initiate is therefore reborn as a little Jove.[25] He must now engage in the labor of creation, the work of the Demiurge. In order to sustain his kingdom, he must create it, for all things are created anew every instant, and apparent creation is also discovery of what already is. This is one of the epiphanies he had during his initiation. Nothing exists, even for a split instant, but by Divine consent and the work of the Divine powers, powers with which he has now merged, work which he must now participate in, as "co-heir" with the Logos: "unless one is born again he cannot see the Kingdom of God" (John 3:3). It is the kingdom, the order, the Divine intends and continuously brings about. Being reborn one is a child again, and "if we are children, then we are heirs" (Romans 8:17).

We have already referred to final realization occurring through femininity-as-lover. As Barker writes of Philo of Alexandria, "He presented the story of the patriarchs and their wives as a complex allegory, in which the wife of each patriarch in turn was Wisdom. Sarah was the motherless Wisdom (*On Gen.* 4.145), Rebecca was also Wisdom (*On Gen.* 4.146)."[26] Mystics often envision a beautiful woman, just as the Anthropos is manifested not only as Ancient of Days but as Son of Man. In the vision of beauty and coherence we gain the autozoon. "Nature awaits its humanization, which can arrive through the spirit bearing man."[27]

The Demiurge must instantiate the autozoon in his female counterpart Juno. She goes to "Mount Ida, from which all the series of souls is derived,"[28] joining Jove. Juno herself is "the fountain of the soul"[29] and therefore is in some regard associated with the mountain. She is brought there by him, yet is already its true essence. Indeed, Jove the Demiurge brings Juno the autozoon he received from mother Rhea, but Juno pre-exists that, she is not Jove's creation. Juno is *already* the manifestation of Rhea at the level of Jove.

Mount Ida is the site wherein the initiatic enthronement is held, is the stage for Jove and Juno's consorting (during Homer's *Iliad*, 14:292–351). Proclus understands Juno as the *Krater* (Greek crater, cup) or Receptacle of Plato's *Timaeus*,[30] to which Plato assigns the feminine appellations "nurse...of all becoming"[31] and "mother...of creation."[32] She is the substrate of materiality, whereas Jove, as referenced previously, is the Demiurge. What is occurring at this enthronement recapitulates the ordering of the cosmos Plato describes in the *Timaeus*. It is the work of Saturn and Rhea at a lower ontic octave, a lower level.

---

25   Per Iamblichus and theurgic neo-Platonism.
26   Barker, *The Great High Priest: The Temple Roots of Christian Liturgy*, 237.
27   Bulgakov, *The Comforter*, 202.
28   Proclus, *Commentaries on Plato's Timaeus*, II, 344.
29   Ibid., III, 14.
30   Ibid., II, 262.
31   Plato, *Timaeus*, 49a, 171.
32   Ibid., 51b, 179.

Our king, as a little demiurge, must in his turn become as that "blameless king, who like a god, maintains justice; to whom the black earth brings forth wheat and barley, whose trees are bowed with fruit, and his sheep never fail to bear, and the Sea gives him fish" (Homer's *Odyssey*, XIX). These fertile elements, black earth and sea, are often symbolically feminine. In most traditions the health of the land and kingdom depend on the king, his conjugal coitus with the queen ignites a country's fertility. In Sumer, the god Enki's phallus is described as an instrument used to irrigate the fields, which act constitutes his lovemaking with the goddess, "mother of the country," Ninhursag.[33] Words for water, which brings life to the fields, and semen, related in various languages including ancient Egyptian (respectively *mw* and *mtwyt*).[34]

Juno is the spatiotemporal matrix out from which physicality emerges. The resultant universe resembles its paradigm:[35] "[T]he nature that the Demiurge shows the soul, Juno, is that source-like nature that pre-exists in the life-giving Goddess, Rhea."[36] Juno receives an "intellectual essence" from Jove which elevates her "to the fountain of her nature."[37] She is ordered according to the form of the autozoon, which the Demiurge learns from Rhea. Rhea is the bosom of the Saturnian power[38] and is at one, or conjoined, with Saturn.[39] She is the "Goddess, being conjoined with Saturn...called Rhea,"[40] in whom nature pre-exists even the Demiurge[41] and who brings that nature to the Demiurge to aid in his ordering of the world. She proceeds, bringing inspiration, from Saturn through his son, the Demiurge (a formula corresponding to the Orthodox Christian understanding of the Trinity). This, then, supports the notion that the place of ritual death prior to rebirth is also the world-soul,[42] a proto-cosmos: Juno with Jove prior to cosmic conception.

But our king is not aware of this, he has only perceived the proto-cosmos, not the cosmos, and has yet to sacralize the universe. He is weary. He leans over on one side to nurse his wound and sits uncomfortably on the seat he earned so dearly. The kingdom he has inherited is not yet truly his, for he does not perceive it as his body. Here is the widespread theme of the injured king. Jacob, Odin, Aeneas, Jesus: all injured on their

---

33 Bernthal-Hooker, *"You Shall Know Yahweh": Divine Sexuality in the Hebrew Bible and Beyond*, 57.

34 Ibid., 111.

35 Iamblichus, *Fragments of Iamblichus' Commentary on the Timaeus*, II: Fr.43; 145–47.

36 Proclus. *The Commentaries of Proclus on the Timaeus of Plato in Five Books*, vol. 1, II, 395.

37 Ibid., II, 344.

38 Proclus, *The Theology of Plato*, V:XI; 335.

39 Ibid., V:XI: 337.

40 Proclus, 1816. *The Theology of Plato*, vol. 1, trans. T. Taylor (London: A. J. Valpi), V:11; 337.

41 Marije Martijn, *Proclus on Nature: Philosophy of Nature and Its Methods in Proclus' Commentary on Plato's Timaeus* (Leiden: Brill Academic Publishers, 2010), 51.

42 Uzdavinys, *Philosophy as a Rite of Rebirth: From Ancient Egypt to Neoplatonism*, 48.

side. Like Anfortas, fisher-king, he is without his Holy Grail, the Crater, a Juno to his Jove, personal herald of nature and worldly splendor. He knows the feminine as a child, not as a man. He knows the mother, not the consort. He knows the principle that originates, not the principle by which he may participate in originating life. He cannot know the autozoon as anything other than a transcendent archetype until he can serve as its conduit, until he can give it forth and know it as ever-fecund source of manifestation. Reality is rendered or, more properly, *revealed*, as a harmonious whole in terms of that paradigm, autozoon.

Plato's *Timaeus*, especially in Proclus's Commentaries, suggests that this occurs through a female consort, as do other traditions. Indeed, the theme that a kingdom is the female counterpart and at once the body of the monarch is a recurring one. It is therefore through sexual congress with the queen that the king becomes active and brings what he has received into the world, ceasing to be wounded on his side, that is, imbalanced and biased in favor of the otherworldly or masculine and against the dynamism and particularism of the world, the feminine. Just as Dante, after enduring his tour of Hell, had need of his beloved Beatrice to enter Heaven, so the traditions follow ritual death and its hellish ordeal with union, "...the high priestess can be no other person than the queen or queen mother in a palatial society."[43] Static epiphany takes its final leap, from the white resplendence of some vista over infinity, a perch from which no blood flows back to the loins, to the royal color, the burning reds and purples of courtly life. From the savior, martyred and entombed, to the resurrected and king, with mitre and enthroned.

In Biblical texts, the Anthropos, the archetypal human form understood as pre-incarnate Logos,[44] the Ancient of Days in Daniel's vision, appears consistently in the (literal) light of feminine power, which illustrates the coincidence of Logos and Sophia. Jacob Boehme specifically connects God's Wisdom, Sophia, to the throne (on which the Ancient One is seen during theophanies, and which is also often a chariot, bespeaking dynamism) and, indeed, to the "infinite multiplicity" and "many millions without number" unfolding from there (justifying the title of *true vine*, for a multitude stem from the one Archetype).[45] In fact, Robert Fludd links Sophia not only to Jesus but also to the angelic Metatron of Enoch-centered apocrypha.[46]

The theophany of a beautiful woman can be understood as the Son of Man's turning from Ancient of Days to inherited kingdoms, the world being a feminine manifestation. This is the wife of the Lamb

43   Marinatos, *Minoan Kingship and the Solar Goddess: A Near Eastern Koine*, 65.
44   Paul A. Patterson, *Visions of Christ: The Anthropomorphite Controversy of 399 CE* (Tubingen: Mohr Siebeck, 2012), 79–80.
45   Michael Martin, *The Submerged Reality: Sophiology and the Turn to a Poetic Metaphysics* (Kettering, OH: Angelico Press, 2015), 44.
46   Ibid., 87.

from John's Apocalypse. She is the female counterpart of Christ, for just as Even came from Adam's rib, it is through the spear-wound to the side of Christ that the Church proceeds (St. Augustine, *City of God*, 22:17), spilling on the earth as blood and water, rendering the world a holy grail, per Bulgakov. She is the Bride or Church in the Shepherd of Hermas's Ninth Parable (1, 78:1), where she is identified as the Holy Spirit and the Son of God, being a manifestation of the Divine and so a feminine theophany: "the angel of repentance, he came to me and said, 'I wish to explain to you what the Holy Spirit that spake with you in the form of the Church showed you, for that Spirit is the Son of God.'" In the Second Vision (4, 8:1) we read that her form as "Church" is created but preeminent: "she was created before all things; therefore is she aged; and for her sake the world was framed." Her agedness is here equivalent to that of the Ancient of Days (a form representing the eternity of the Divine through the appearance of venerable antiquity), and her appearing as a young woman with white hair later on seems to relate to Christ having hair "white like wool" in John's Apocalypse, the same as the Ancient One in Daniel 7 (the Son of Man as being properly assimilated to the Ancient of Days, having the latter's wisdom).

Just as the Son and Spirit come forth from the font of the Father, and the Son does only what he hears (John 5:19), his wisdom (white hair) is that of the Ancient of Days (symbol of the Father). This is in turn given to the world as revelation by the Son. Rhea's bestowing of the autozoon to Jove or the Islamic *Umm al-Kitab* (Mother of the Book) of which the Qur'an is a particular enliteration, are equivalent to the book which the Son/Spirit in the form of the Lady Church give the seer: "Whom thinkest thou the aged woman, from whom thou receivest the book, to be?" (Second Vision 4, 8:1). This book is equivalent to the construction of a holy tower (the temple) in Hermas.

In the Bride/Church, singularity of the principle is finally located in the harmony of practices. The autozoon was received in the theophany of Ancient of Days/Metatron, with its feminine equivalents (Saturn and Rhea), but now the autozoon is truly *discovered*, rather than *received*, in its immediate presence. Vladimir Solovyov recounts experiences in *Three Encounters* that may relate to either level. Ibn Arabi's experience, by way of the daughter of a Persian acquaintance who seemed to him like a princess of the Greeks when, through her, he perceived Wisdom speaking, seems clearly related to the Bride rather than the Mother. We detect the same in Goethe's sixth elegy of *Roman Erotica*:

> Therefore we gladly confess to singling a special immortal
>
> . . .
>
> Sweet Opportunity, that is her name. You should meet her.
>   Often will she turn up, ever in a new form.
>
> . . .

Once she appeared to me, too: a dark-skinned girl, tumbling
Over her forehead the hair down in waves heavy and dark.
Round about a delicate neck curled short little ringlets;
Up from the crown of her head crinkled the unbraided hair.
When she dashed by me I seized her, mistaking her not. Lovingly
Kiss and embrace she returned, knowing and teaching me how.
O how enraptured I was! Ah, say now no more. It's a bygone.
But, O pigtails of Rome, still I'm entrammled in you.

The romantics in general had this intuition (as Michael Martin has
emphasized in his work):

Both heaven and earth obey unto her will,

. . .

They all partake, and do in state remain
As their great Maker did at first ordain,
Through observation of her high behest,
By which they first were made, and still increast.
The fairness of her face no tongue can tell;
For she the daughters of all women's race,
And angels eke, in beauty doth excel,
Sparkled on her from God's own glorious face,
And more increas'd by her own goodly grace,
That it doth far exceed all human thought,
Ne can on earth compared be to aught
            (from Edmund Spenser, *An Hymn of Heavenly Beauty*)

Here is Corbin's "Eternal Womanly as an Image of the Godhead"[47]
which he gets from Ibn Arabi's *Fusus*. Corbin writes of the "Madonna
Intelligenza in the meditation of the *Fedeli d'amore*. Among the Ishraqi-
yun it is the Angel of humanity, the celestial archetype of the human
creature (*rabb al-naw'-e insani*)."[48]

Recall what we have already written about the ideal which is grasped
by the initiate king. It is the paradigm of creation which is heroically
reintroduced to refresh creation, to remind it of itself, by the returning
king after his ordeal of initiation. The autozoon is carried from the
monad to the demiurgic realm by femininity-as-mother, goddess Rhea.

In Shia Islam, world-soul (and the Divine Feminine in genera) are
identified with the daughter of Muhammad, Fatima. "Fatima is the
Sophia of Shi'ite theosophy":

    ...the ontological rank of the Soul and the reality of the Soul
    are the very rank and reality of Fatima-Sophia. The Imams are
    masculine as agents of cosmogony, since creation is their soul; as
    authors of spiritual creation they are feminine, since they are the

47   Henry Corbin, *Alone with the Alone: Creative Imagination in the Sufism of Ibn 'Arabi*,
      trans. R. Manheim (Princeton, NJ: Princeton University Press, 1997), 159.
48   Corbin, *Cyclical Time and Ismaili Gnosis*, 76.

Soul and since the Soul is Fatima. This, therefore, is why we read that Fatima is the theophany of the supreme pleroma, and that is why the theophanic and initiatic function of the holy Imams is precisely their "Fatimic" degree of being (their *fatimiya*, which we faithfully translate as "Sophianity"), and this is how Fatima comes to be called Fatima *Fatir*, Fatima the Creator.[49]

This latter term appearing, for example, in Ismailism. The world-soul also appears in connection to the feminine angel of the earth in Mazdeism, which Corbin sees as informing later Persian Shia theology.

The work of creation, the union that renders the country fertile, the *sacrament of the bedchamber*, as the *Gospel of Philip* terms it, will seduce the king with love for the particular, a sense of the preciousness of finite things as receptacles for the infinite rather than somehow opposed to it. This is the mystery of eroticism, where a thing so powerfully universal blatantly becomes love for a particular person and where the particular person is so completely endowed of an ideal aura. The mystery of the beyond, where the king had no body for it was dismembered in the underworld (ritual death frequently enacts dismemberment), the mystery of Rhea's light, which is the autozoon, is brought down to earth. By knowing order *as such*, organism *in and of itself*, the king understands that his body is that, and so is the body politic, and so is the whole of humanity and the cosmos.

For the king, this phase represents his true maturation. In Virgil's *Aeneid*, after losing his wife Creusa and leaving queen Dido, the eponymous hero courts Lavinia, holds court in Rome and sires a lineage of Emperors. King Anfortas receives the Holy Grail, Orpheus reunites with his wife by entering Hades, Jacob begets the line of David into which Jesus is born after the angel of the Lord dislocates his hip. Healed hips sire kings. The initiate will no longer pursue ascetical perfection against, rather than with, the feminine principle.

Eros Completes Epiphany: The Queen brings the Crown, the Corps becomes King

After his ritual dismemberment, the king bears within himself the principle of universal order. He has become endowed with a felt perceptual awareness of the archetype of organic life, the idea of harmony which naturally draws diversity into collaborative life, the pattern that reminds different bodies of their pertinence in grander bodies, including the whole of the universe. He has seen and continues to see the autozoon.

This dismemberment or quartering is a subduing of mental oscillations, traditionally regarded as a fourfold (anger, melancholy, sanguine and phlegmatic). It need not be violent, and is sometimes suggested as ecstatic. Indeed, the fourfold is sometimes a manifestation of the initiate's feminine consort, where a romantic devotion leads him to transcendence.

---

49   Corbin, *Spiritual Body and Celestial Earth: From Mazdean Iran to Shi'ite Iran*, 68.

This is still prior to union with the feminine, for after purgative devotion the transcendent is perceived and then brought into the world (the world understood as female counterpart of the king). The world must still receive the king and the king the world: like the four terms of the Tantric formula *ahamidam-idamaham*: the active and passive Male (Awareness) and the active and passive Female (Sentience): Absorption of awareness in sentience, where we forget ourselves in pure joyful experience, and absorption of sentience in awareness, where there is no experience but contemplation. Sentience is here properly understood as Joy.

If the king does not enter the world he cannot unfold this principle of order there, giving the world a new impetus, in a sense reminding it of what it already is, of the truth it pours forth from, just as a plant will die and its form will cease to manifest in the world unless it is given water. He has become—or rather has awakened to being—a son of the Divine and, having order within himself, the Logos that according to Proclus is the divine king Jove, son of the First Paternal Intellect or Heavenly Father, is now given over to the world that it may not perish, as the Gospel says (John 3:16).

The king must introduce this principle into the world and activate it, which is why his regular copulation with the queen or high priestess is so essential to the health of the world and of the kingdom (the particular part of the world that represents the whole as microcosm, be it in a household or in an ancient state-cult). The queen is manifestation, physicality, dynamism, becoming, nature. She is Juno, who for the neo-Platonists is the spatiotemporal receptacle in which the world is made, a microcosm of goddess Inanna who for Mesopotamians was the universe, Isis who is Egypt and Osiris's bride and body, Shakti who is the externalized physical reality and power for the Tantrists, Lady Philosophia, whose dress for Boethius is all of nature.

To close the circuit whose electricity was received during initiation, the king must introduce it into the world by entering his queen. The unity of transcendence and imminence is enacted, as when Dante is one with his Beatrice at the end of *La Vita Nuova*, where the woman is Heaven or the ideal earth, and the man is the earth or the striving towards heaven (femininity is a vector towards manifestation but for that very reason is already Heavenly—women are native to Paradise as the Muslim poets say—and man is a vector towards Heaven and therefore strives from earth) or Lord Krishna with Radha at the end of the *Govinda Gita* by the almost contemporary 12th century Indian poet Jayadeva.

The king must penetrate the world—the feminine principle of manifestation—and leave himself there so that the universal order he represents may be active within nature. "Great is the mystery of marriage! For without it, the world would not exist ..." (*Gospel of Philip*[50]). The

---

50   *Nag Hamadi Codex II, 2-7, The Gospel of Philip*, 64:31–65:32, 183.

king's penetration of the world is understood as coitus, for during this act the king is present inside another being, one who represents the world, feminine nature, and the generative presence of the king outside himself in nature is understood as the reproductive consequences of coitus where the king's semen is present in the queen and may produce royal heirs there.

The real subject of initiation is this unity, for in it the world is entered and renewed with its own principle: "Through the Holy Spirit we are indeed begotten again, but we are begotten through Christ in the two."[51] The transcendent vision received by the king saves him and the queen together:

> If the woman had not separated from the man, she should not die with the man. His separation became the beginning of death. Because of this, Christ came to repair the separation, which was from the beginning, and again unite the two, and to give life to those who died as a result of the separation, and unite them. But the woman is united to her husband in the bridal chamber. Indeed, those who have united in the bridal chamber will no longer be separated. We are anointed through the Spirit. When we were begotten, we were united.[52]

This last sentence is crucial. He is born again, but in truth, his being born again, his being begotten from above, is a uniting with the queen. They are one flesh; they are image and angel. His bringing to her is a revelation in her.

Here is the alchemy by which the species is renewed, the turning of mercury into gold—like the god Mercury, Hermes, entering into proper relation with the golden sun god Apollo—fulfilled when the initiate's quicksilver merges with the forge that is the womb of his consort and becomes a new person (entertaining an analogy between mercury and semen, considering that sexual energy is considered the basis for spiritual transformation in many traditional systems).

Sexual union serves as a reminder of formless transcendence, a recurrence of the epiphany of ritual death, indeed, a *petite mort,* the death by which a kernel ceases to be single and gives forth many (John 12:24) for, like Aeneas, the king has left that mountain that birthed him near Troy, for the mountain of Rome, the hill of his Lavinia. In that Rome husband and wife may know each other and be reborn nightly from the Divine in a formlessness of erotic ecstasy, the joy of knowing the Logos, the encompassing of forms that is not itself a form and by whose mystery their two forms fit.

Perhaps the king has glimpsed a peasant girl, one day by chance as he let himself roam outside to alleviate ennui, and his heart has been arrested ever since, so he has asked his men to bring her to him and

---

51 Ibid., 64:31–65:32, 183.
52 Ibid., 69:7–70:4, 181.

compensate the family abundantly. Or else he has been informed it is incumbent upon him, for the good of his subjects, that he should marry the princess of a neighboring state to avoid hostilities and cement ecumenic familiarity. Or maybe he must be joined to the young female scion of a wealthy and politically important family in order to consolidate order in his realm, and decides to go along with the charade out of compassion for his subjects, who might suffer otherwise.

Indeed, it is not a matter of politics alone, or of politics as it has come to be understood. The officiators of rites, the priestly caste, have asked him to marry soon, for he is the highest representative of their own order (there is no high priest higher than the king), and the union of king and queen is essential to the prosperity of kingdom and nature, which are in continuity. Just as Dante, after enduring his tour of Hell, had need of his beloved Beatrice to enter into Heaven, parting with the noble Virgil, so the traditions follow ritual death and hellish ordeal with ritual copulation of king and queen. A queen must be taken for religious reasons, that she might carry out ceremonies, for "...the high priestess can be no other person than the queen or queen mother in a palatial society."[53] The king needs a queen, and as high priest, a high priestess.

However, it comes about, one day a company appears, escorting minstrels and armed entourage in formal configuration around a young woman. His posture changes as their eyes meet and for the first time since taking occupancy, he fits that seat of power properly. There are announcements and celebrations, and before long, she lays a hand on his and leads him away, from throne-room to bedchamber, where his stagnant epiphany takes its final leap, from the white resplendence of some vista over infinity, a perch from which no blood flows back to the loins, to the royal color, the burning reds and purples of courtly life and statecraft, of worldly duty. From the savior, martyred and entombed, to the resurrected and triumphant Christ the King. Later, keen to show his new bride the sight of his life-changing death, the king takes her to their kingdom's sacred mountain, and they consecrate it together.

Eros and the Eschaton: Chariots of Sex on Judgement Day

We return to the principle, introduced during the introduction, of eternal relationship, as well as to the issue of *eros* as completing initiation and allowing political representation. Any categorization of diverse forms assumes an underlying unitary principle *in terms of which* they can be categorized. *But the unitary principle needs diversity of presentation too.* By way of their diversity and harmony the presence and at the same time transcendence of that unity is known.

> Spoke Hermes to Asclepius: And if you (Asclepius) wish to see the reality of this mystery, then you should see the wonderful

---

53   Marinatos, *Minoan Kingship and the Solar Goddess: A Near Eastern Koine,* 65.

representation of the intercourse that takes place between the male and the female. For when the semen reaches the climax, it leaps forth. In that moment, the female receives the strength of the male; the male, for his part, receives the strength of the female, while the semen does this. (Asclepius 21–29/Nag Hammadi Codex VI.8)[54]

The idea of Divine creation, passed the horizon of soteriology, as always requiring harmony, which is to say, relationship, and therefore the legitimacy of conceiving of Divine things in terms of engagement with the world and sacrifice, can be explored by way of Indian tradition, specifically Vaishnavism. The *Vishnu Purana* and *Bhagavatam Purana* describe the Heavenly realm *Vaikuntha*, which is beyond the changeability of the three *gunas* so that its forms are not temporary, its pleasures not a respite before further reincarnation, as is the case of lower heavens. Vaikuntha is home to those who are spiritually liberated. They dwell there with beautiful spouses, un-distracted from God. In Vaikuntha are "devotees of Vishnu along with their beautiful wives in the aerial cars..."[55] (*Bhagavatam Purana*, 3.15:17).

However, only an obtuse exegesis would take this to mean that their beauty and married status is incidental, not engaging one another and focusing instead on God's formal manifestation before them in a *physical, spatial* sense. After all, the dwellers of heaven "disregard the fragrant wind even though their minds are distracted by the fragrance of the blossoming..." (*Bhagavatam Purana*, 3.15:17). A portion of the self participates in that fragrant pleasure while one remains anchored in contemplation, and as this is occurring in heaven, it is without the inner conflict we would associate with a divided, earthly experience. This explains how we can have descriptions of "...damsels of big hips and beautifully smiling faces..." which emphasize sensual beauty, but also learn that these "cannot with their beguiling smiles and other allurements, excite passion in those devotees whose minds are fixed on Krishna" (3.15:20). And just as these male devotees are fixed on Krishna, so we immediately read that "[t]he goddess of Wealth (Lakshmi) of beautiful form...stays (permanently) in Hari's"—the Lord's—"residence" and "in her own garden, the goddess Lakshmi attended upon by her maid-servants, was worshipping the Lord" (3.15:21). We see then that the beauty and coupling of male with female is included in the salvific state while these are simultaneously entirely absorbed in Divine contemplation.

Again, exclusive centralization around one form, along with the notion that engagement with God somehow contradicts engagement with persons, are a misunderstanding of metaphysics and a fall into iconoclasm.[56]

---

54 Translated by James Brashler, Peter A. Dirkse, and Douglas M. Parrott.
55 Motilal Banarsidass (Delhi: West Bengal Public Library, 1950), 305-6.
56 The Hare Krishna movement, although it may also have done excellent work, has in this sense championed somewhat crass understandings.

Some such commentaries have it that the only sex in heavenly realms is between Isvara and female devotees, which in a sense is correct, if this is understood as the saint realizing itself as Isvara *and* as devotee to Isvara. The consciousness of such a being may inhabit both its own form and that of its spouse, both the mystery of centrality and that of harmony, both Christ and Church. Indeed, for heaven to include, per the Vishnu Purana, units consisting of spouses, husband with wife, on aerial vehicles in contemplation of the Divine couple, is revelatory of the metaphysical meaning of eros: Heaven consists of couples contemplating a divine couple. And to contemplate the Divine couple is to become one: "Bridegrooms and brides belong to the bridal chamber. No one shall be able to see the bridegroom with the bride unless he become such a one."[57]

In Vaishnavism the types of spiritual liberation different from contemplative absorption into the formlessness of the Self (and not lower, but more ecstatic than such absorption) include sharing the same form as, and opulence of, God's manifestation,

> ...residing in the same abode as Vishnu (salokya), having the same opulence as Him (sarsti), being close to Him (samipya), having the same form as Him (sarupya), and merging into Him (ekatvam). (*Bhagavatam Purana* III:29:12–14)[58]

This appears as something similar to the Abrahamic paradigm of resurrection, with bodies that are superior to flesh and blood, as St. Paul highlights. In Vaishnavism:

> ...when bhakti yoga to Isvara is practiced rather than jnana or yoga, the Bhagavata tradition (and Vaishnavism in general) posits that there are four other types of liberation that become available in addition to ekatvam and that these bestow divine (Brahman) personal transcendent forms and qualities on the individual atman when liberated.[59]

Although this body and its abode are outside the world of prakriti, changeable materiality, it is also maintained that forms in prakriti are like a rendering in smoke of that which is in the permanent realms. Our world, "the realm of nonconscious prakriti can be seen as something of a dull and imperfect reflection of those Brahman realms."[60] Since *prakriti* is feminine counterpart to *purusha*, and the scriptural descriptions of the realms of Vaikuntha and Goloka prominently include male-female interplay, we may consider the material world (the lower expression of the feminine) as somehow taken up as a surface décor by those archetypal forms, which is compatible with the Abrahamic and Zoroastrian doctrine of resurrection.

---

57   *The Gospel of Philip*, 82:7–83:2, 207.
58   Bryant, *Bhakti Yoga: Tales and Teachings from the Bhagavata Purana*, 117–18.
59   Ibid., 119.
60   Ibid.

This is relatively consistent across traditions, where some are more prone to emphasize that spiritual liberation is a liberation that includes the liberty to manifest on the lower planes, albeit in a *vertical* rather than horizontally-conditioned manner—in Christianity the resurrected body is genuinely a body, genuinely physical, but it is, apparently, to judge from St. Paul, not really *flesh*. Chinese Taoist texts use expressions such as the body being permeated in Tao, melted spirit, and no longer dying.

The idea of the resurrection is often rejected as being less refined than the standard account one finds in certain Indian traditions of how a liberated person progresses spiritually. Yet something subtle is missed. If higher states are in continuity with the lower, one experiencing those higher states can simultaneously, in other parts of his being, be experiencing lower ones. Since materiality is unfolding in the midst of the Divine, a saint who has reached what Indian tradition refers to as the Brahman realms, where forms are beyond matter, may nonetheless continue to perceive matter as a superficial part of reality and of his own extended self. Resurrection then is a revealing of the true identity of matter and material bodies as the surface mist of a vast and profound pool. Receiving a body like that of God (His infinite capacity for producing forms), as Vaishnavism puts it, would, like His creation, include a material portion.

Continuing on the topic of gender, St. Thomas Aquinas points out that it is not a deficiency and therefore bodies in the resurrection will have gender (Question 81, Article 3 of the *Summa Theologica*). We understand D. H. Lawrence when, according to Milbank, he "worried about Christianity because it appeared to him illogically (and differently from Islam in this respect) to exclude sexual relationship from the life of the resurrected body" adding that "the pre-Cartesian Catholic metaphysical vision permits a much more literally sexy account of the universal possibility of love."[61] Milbank references Jean-Louis Chretien's *Symbolique du Corps* to the effect that the sexual imagery of the Song of Songs is not to be taken metaphorically. The Zoroastrian *Bundahishn* (30:26) states that in the resurrection "...all men become immortal forever and everlasting...and they give to everyone his wife, and show him his children with the wife; so they act as now in the world, but there is no begetting of children," which seems to mean that married spouses are in familial proximity to their descendants without creating new children although they "act as now in the world" (presumably having sexual relations). Their possibilities (children) are fully present and do not need to be experienced gradually in time but can be related to in the present moment.

What Indian Vaishnavism's heavenly bodies mean should be clarified: "God too has a divine bodily form, or more precisely, being unlimited, has

---

61   John Milbank and Slavoj Zizek, *The Monstrosity of Christ* (Cambridge, MA: MIT, 2009), 225.

unlimited divine forms, and these inhabit divine abodes, also unlimited"
that is, the Vaikuntha. This form and those akin to it that the saved
receive in such realms are "inconceivable: they cannot be fathomed or
conceived of by the rational mind…limited to the spatial, temporal
and physical conditions of prakriti."[62] Receiving a body alike that of
God's forms is referred to as *sarupya*. We may think of God's body as a
conscious inhabiting the complex crisscrossing of every archetype that
makes reality, and the atman, those individual manifestations of God, in
their exaltation, would likewise be aware of themselves as coordinates
of manifest reality, feeling the sprawling of out reality from their coordinate as their own body.

That which is below is as that which is above, a reflection thereof, and
given the emphasis on relationality in Vaishnavism, relationship must
exist among such forms. If there is form, relationality and mediation in
our world, it is because it is so also in the archetypal realm, so the saved
"receive Brahman minds, forms and relationships, and situations in the
Vaikuntha realm that reflect the nature of their bhakti."[63] This can be
thought of in terms of "merging into Krishna's actual body and relishing
the bliss of this (*Bhagavat-sayunja*)" being a little Demiurge (though on
a higher level) as Iamblichus describes, or a co-heir with Christ, per St.
Paul. Even as concerns the lower worlds, the devotee "need not reject
the world of prakriti" but can "enjoy it as Shiva enjoying an expression
of Himself" (understanding Shiva as "non-different" from Krishna, as
Srila Sanatana writes in the *Brhad Bhagavatamrta*[64]). To share the opulence
and form of Vishnu or Krishna, including heavenly relationship, then,
would include engagement or communality with others, including that of
the erotic mode Krishna shares with Radha and the *gopis*, understood as
absorption into and experience as Krishna or becoming a little Krishna
in the *sarupya* mode of dual moksha (dual liberation, a spiritual liberation
that maintains duality of subject-object).

The Islamic notion of Heaven as one in which the believer is sexually
engaged with the heavenly maidens, the *houris*, while fully conscious of
the existence of, in submission to, Allah, is actually the subtler doctrine
compared to radically ascetical and literalizing approaches to the above
Indian tradition. Eros is a particularly stark evidence for relatedness and
relatedness's spiritual import. As Abdal Hakim Murad (Tim Winter)
writes of Islam in his *Commentary on the Eleventh Contentions*: "Our Paradise
shows that the Dionysian mysteries were proleptic" (1:63); "Unless there
is Paradise, eros is a trick" (9:11) and; "Celibacy is an anticipation of hell,
for there is no eros there" (9:98). The spiritual meaning of this act and
a reason for its inclusion in descriptions of Heavenly realms in Indian

---

62   Bryant, *Bhakti Yoga: Tales and Teachings from the Bhagavata Purana*, 120.
63   Ibid., 119.
64   Ibid., 122.

and Islamic traditions can be illumined with recourse to what Ibn'Arabi writes in his *al-Futuhat al-Makkiyya* (remembering when we read the word "pleasure" that the Sufi is referring to an exalted "spiritual station"):

> The consummation of sexual intercourse is itself commended in the Law ... and the sexual act of the one in this spiritual station is like the sexual union of the people of Paradise, only for the sake of pleasure, for it is the greatest manifestation which has been hidden from men and jinn, except for those servants whom God has specially chosen for it.... If it did not have complete nobility indicating the weakness appropriate to servanthood, it would not have such an overwhelming pleasure which causes a person to pass away from his own strength and pretensions. It is a pleasurable subjugation, although subjugation precludes pleasure in the one who is subjugated ... except in this act in particular. This nobility has escaped people, who have made it an animalistic passion from which they refrain.... So what they have deemed ugly with regard to themselves is the very thing that is praiseworthy for the perfect.... [65]

Here, the Sufi transcends the Indian contrast between Tantric sex as means to spiritual liberation and non-Tantric sex where pleasure is a goal in itself but distinct from spiritual liberation. [66] In the passage above erotic enjoyment is a goal in itself and for this reason is spiritual and spiritually liberated (rather than liberat*ing*, that is, spiritual liberation occurs *in* it, not *through* it). Indeed, given that traditional non-Tantric Indian erotic arts (*kama shastra*) are not taboo-breaking, which the Tantric approach to spiritual liberation often is, they are closer to ibn-Arabi's approach to erotic relations, so that the Indian categories are confounded further: It is normal and non-instrumental eroticism (eroticism that is not as a technology to which pleasure is incidental, and which is not directed at deconditioning the participants from social — or even personal — taboos) that is presented as spiritually significant. Making social taboo or expectation a determinant of the personal and private can severe us from the exalted intimacy of the present moment, and even trying to decondition one's mind from excessive hang-ups by transgressing them can cause more resistance and neurosis than anything else (our personal taboos may be perfectly healthy, only they should be borne with a light touch and not turned into phobias, but this attitude of levity does not require that they be transgressed, only that we not make them the object of excessive thinking). Instead, we become aloof and detached from these hang-ups by simply going where they are not: beyond the mind, whereto the erotic naturally invites us.

---

65   Muhyi'l-Din Ibn-al-Arabi, *al-Futuhat al-makkiyya* (Beirut: Dar Sadir, 1966), II, 573-74.
66   Flood, *The Tantric Body: The Secret Tradition of Hindu Religion*, 86-87.

It is not what D. D. Shulman calls the "barren eroticism"[67] of (early) Tantric practices as magical-spiritual operations for which enjoyment is not the point, but liberation. It is a latter-day Tantrism for which *bhukti* is *mukti*, pleasure is liberation. The eleventh century architectural treaty the *Shilpa Prakasha* presents this Tantric perspective, more compatible with non-Tantric kama shastra. It helps explain the erotic sculptures in temples such as Khajuraho and Konarak, which, as Gavin Flood notes, do not seem to be like Christian cathedral grotesques, meant to ward off obscenity by depicting it, because they are actually beautiful. The *Shilpa Prakasha* recommends depictions of celestial maidens, the Surasundari, like the Buddhist Yakshi, possibly equivalent to the Muslim Houris, Greek Kóres Sōteíras, and Norse Valkyries. Without these, it says, a temple will yield no fruit. It further recommends the presence of love images (*kama kala*) between *maithuna* couples and considers their absence as rendering a place worthy of being shunned.[68] However, it does not consider actual depictions of penetrative coitus appropriate in this context, which reminds us of its non-transgressive emphasis and the idea that we are discussing spiritually edifying eroticism, not pornography (although the depictions of the temples mentioned above do include examples that go beyond this particular limit as stated by the *Shilpa Prakasha*).

The *Shilpa Prakasha* reminds us of de Lubicz's *Temple of Man* study of Egyptian temples in that it refers to temples as being like bodies and therefore seems to bring out the spiritual meaning of the body. The fact that it recommends erotic coupling connects the divinization of the body through temple to a spirituality of sexual union. As for Ibn Arabi, sexual union is paradisal and spiritual, not a means to an end, but occurring in the midst and awareness of the spiritual. In an excellent concluding paragraph, Gavin Flood puts it like this:

> ...what is significant is that maithuna couples are here directly linked to the kamasastra, an important shift in relocating eroticism to a context of aesthetics. With the erotic carvings on temple walls, eroticism is stripped of its violence and link with death that we find in early tantric appeasement and taboo breaking. The depiction of the body on temple walls is a representation of the body in an idealised eroticism that is grounded in text; an eroticism which rejoices in the body yet which points beyond itself to a divine transcendence. The body's representation here is divinised and textualized in a way that goes beyond transgression or protection. Indeed, such representation points to the sexualised body as a manifestation of the deity, as other deities on temple

67   David D. Shulman, *Tamil Temple Myths: Sacrifice and Divine Marriage in the South Indian Saiva Tradition* (Princeton, NJ: Princeton University Press, 1980), 261–62. Cited by Flood, *The Tantric Body: The Secret Tradition of Hindu Religion*, 85.
68   Vidya Dehejia, *The Body Adorned: Sacred and Profane in Indian Art* (New York: Columbia University Press, 2009), 103.

facades are manifestations: the temple is the body of the deity
and is not devoid of sexuality.[69]

(This is not to imply that early Tantrism was limited to liberation via
taboo-breaking and to rituals of protection, or that its practitioners
necessarily or as a rule fell into the errors of unedifying transgression
which was highlighted before.)

The play between male-female is archetypal and not reducible to
apparent effects, be they procreative (as in standard *religion cum morality* and
morality cum social utility) or liberational (as in transgressive "underground"
spiritual practices), any more than the love elicited by a child or the awe
at a sunset are reducible to biological imperatives, despite there being a
certain kind of religionist who is happy to grant the transcendence of
these sooner than that of erotic attraction. Ibn Arabi's statement that
heavenly sex is not for procreation or for utilitarian ends but "only for
the sake of pleasure" corresponds to the *Bundahishn*'s "they act as now
in the world, but there is no begetting of children," for the children
already are. We are not in the stream earthly, temporal disclosure but
in a temporality that is more malleable, so to speak.

This also relates to the Gospel's teaching that "those who are consid-
ered worthy to attain to that age and to the resurrection from the dead
neither marry nor are given in marriage, for they cannot die anymore"
(Luke 20:34–36). (In Islam the saved soul receives marriage not only
before death but also upon entry into Paradise, and we need not read the
Gospel in literal terms or as referring to pre- and post-mortem estates.)
They need not enter marriage once having entered salvation if, as the
Gospel of Philip says, the unit which enters salvation (the presence of the
"bridegroom with the bride") is itself already a unit of bridegroom and
bride. This unit is an icon for Son and Spirit, Word and Wisdom, for
the crucified one revealed to be king and the world revealed as holy grail,
or for the blood and water that flowed from Christ's wound.

In *Sophia in Exile*,[70] Michael Martin cites Pope Benedict XIV's *Deus
Caritas Est* encyclical to the effect that the purpose of human eros is iconic:

> Marriage based on exclusive and definitive love becomes the icon of
> the relationship between God and his people and vice versa...This
> close connection between eros and marriage in the Bible has
> practically no equivalent in extra-biblical literature.

And from the Eastern Orthodox Jonathan Tobias:

> The exclusiveness of marriage is not a limit, a temporary dispensa-
> tion, or even a prophetic symbol whose identity will be subsumed
> by the eschaton. Rather, the "exclusiveness" that chastity establishes,

---

69   Flood, *The Tantric Body: The Secret Tradition of Hindu Religion*, 87.
70   Michael Martin, *Sophia in Exile* (Brooklyn, NY: Angelico Press, 2021), 44.

in cooperation with Grace, is a new body with an identity that will remain and grow ever in deification.[71]

As we have quoted from Thomistic, Zoroastrian and Islamic eschatologies, we should add the poet-prophet William Blake and his account of triumphal, apocalyptic sex. First, the narrow ego and its corresponding orientation (of utilitarian ends and rigorously linear experience of time) is defeated, revealed to be a non-entity in the light of noetic vision: "The Druid Spectre was Annihilate, loud thund'ring, rejoicing terrific... and at the clangor of the Arrows of Intellect..." mark the coming of the host of beatific Eros:

> The innumerable Chariots of the Almighty appear'd in Heaven...
> ...A Sun of blood red wrath surrounding heaven on all sides around,
> Glorious, incomprehensible by Mortal Man, and each Chariot was Sexual Twofold.
> And every Man stood Fourfold, each Four Faces had, One to the west...
> east...south...north, the Horses Fourfold. (Blake, *Jerusalem*, Chapter IV, 98, lines 6–13)

Recall the Ancient of Days as male counter to the female chariot-throne, and the returning Son of Man *as* Ancient One during the apocalyptic consummation (Apocalypse 1:14). Blake is of course proceeding from Ezekiel's vision, and we are also reminded of the Indian motif of four-faced deity (with Egyptian and Chinese equivalents), and particularly of the story of the patriarch Svayambhuva Manu who develops four faces that he may gaze on the beauty of his wife Shatarupa no matter what direction she is in: transforming into an encompassing, universal being through romantic love. The chariots remind us of the Indian tradition's *Vimana* flying vehicles, whereon those couples in the heavenly Vaikuntha worlds may contemplate the Divine. As in the Persian *Bundahishn*, the *Gospel of Philip*, Islam and currents of Indian tradition, for Blakean Christianity the unit of salvation is sexual.

The idea that the bodily, the formal, is sacralized, taken up into the spiritual, through eroticism, relates to the salvation imagery in Biblical and Qur'anic scripture. The total seventy-two nations listed in Genesis are divisible by the twelve gates of the Heavenly city in the New Earth of the Apocalypse, wherein the kings of the nations enter, which might imply their integral inclusion. The same number appears as comprising human (vocational rather than national) diversity in some accounts of Indian tradition which refer to seventy-two castes[72] (indeed, in the 1,001

---

71   Jonathan Tobias, "The Persistence of Nuptial Union: Desire, Joy, and Spiritualization in Eternity," in *Jesus the Imagination, Volume II: The Being of Marriage* (Kettering, OH: Angelico Press, 2018): 7–12, at 8.
72   Concerning the region of Kerala: Nair R. Raman and L. Sulochana Devi,

Nights, Indian travelers tell Sinbad the Sailor that there are seventy-two castes in their home country). There are seventy-two colors in the *Gospel of Philip* which are dyed and come out white.[73]

Salvation is understood as a wedding between humanity and savior, Church and Christ as bride and bridegroom. The divine feminine is linked with human plurality elsewhere, as we have seen, and ideal humanity is personified in a feminine person, a certain manifestation of the divine feminine. Just as the Bible lists seventy-two nations descending from Noah through his three sons, Islam speaks of seventy-two houris, or heavenly maidens, married by a Muslim man in paradise (according to strong hadiths). (These can include his earthly spouse, as Muhammad's wives in paradise are said by one hadith to include A'isha.) We are reminded of the hadith according to which there are to be seventy-three sects of Islam, whereof seventy-two are hell-bound. That there are more women than men sent to hell, per another hadith, is connected to the tradition that those condemned women may enter heaven through soteriological polygamy in the afterlife: seventy of the believer's seventy-two wives are said to proceed from those women sent to hell. Interpreting this in terms of metaphysical principles: Plurality, or the feminine, is redeemed along with singularity, the masculine, in its being *indexed* to the singular, so to speak, diversity as witness to unity.

The Isvara, or eternal masculine, manifests in relation to the *Isvari*, or eternal feminine, that is, Vishnu with the Goddess of Fortune, Krishna with Radha (where the latter relates to multiplicity and dynamism, the many gopis, the cow-herding women who are the highest of yogis devoted to Krishna, engaging in *parakiya-rasa*, or erotic play with Him) and the former to singularity and stillness. This highlights my running argument that physicality or location, which is to say, relatedness, can never exhaust the singularity of the Divine, but must give forth a plurality of forms which express singularity by being taken up in an ever *encompassing* and ever *excessive* harmony. They also express the transcendence of singularity by showing that no single set of contingent features can fully express the Divine potential. The Islamic understanding of Heavenly relatedness as producing a multiplicity of households, each with its singularity (the masculine) and plurality (the feminine) follows coherently as an exegesis on the Indian descriptions concerning Vaikuntha and Goloka (the Heaven of Vishnu and Krishna, respectively).

Importantly, Divine simplicity or oneness is not itself the principle of centrality any more than it is that of harmonious relationality; it is not masculinity any more than femininity; it is not the center (which is everywhere) any more than the circumference (which is nowhere). The

---

Chattampi Swami: An Intellectual Biography (Kudappanakunnu Trivandrum: Center for South Indian Studies, 2010), 22.

73 *The Gospel of Philip*, 62:34–63:34, 167.

Divine couple around which the saved assemble—the essential form of that formal Heaven—is *both* Isvara and Isvari.

Further, centrality and harmony are not only expressed in the conjugal mode. Love is the *movement of relatedness* of peripheries to centers with the potential for ever-finer and ever more encompassing circles: The child moves or "rotates" around the parent in the mode of filial piety, neither *eros* nor *thumos*; the soldier "rotates" around his chief in the mode of *thumos* and battle-ready fealty, not erotic attraction; the wife around her husband in that of eros, not martial obedience (I am using the sorts of images one finds in scripture and traditional exegeses). In Vaishnavist terms, these reflect different forms of worship of the personal God according to different *bhava* (meaning loving relationships to God, as parent to child, friend, lover, etc.).[74]

Focusing on the romantic-erotic, however, it is a stark highlighting of universal love within the particular loved one, who is utterly unique to us, the conjoining of opposite and complementary types of equal dignity, providing each other reciprocal, conscious spiritual epiphanies, and, in earthly, temporal terms, serving as the locus of new life, the nexus to other (future and past) persons. We are not, then, a single point of centrality, but rather manifest the apophatic inscrutability of the Divine in our relationship, the correspondence between forms, the very possibility of which implies an invisible, encompassing harmony (again, like the empty space at the center of the Rose-Cross or the coitus-scene at the center of some Buddhist mandalas) Since love is universal but so very particular, the *Parousia* (the Arrival) at the source of love, the original love, is also an arrival at a particular. Recall Desmond's "…any return to an origin…cannot be one origin alone, but rather an origin that is articulated into a plurality of beginnings."[75] The universal is always already the particular, the one is always already the many (insofar as it is at all manifest, it can only manifest as particulars, which are irreducibly diverse).

Henry Corbin writes that for Ibn Arabi

> The union of the masculine and the feminine is only the aspect, in the sensible world, of a structure repeated on every plane of being. (Modelled on this same type: the union of the *fedele d'amore* and his Lord. The "appeased" soul does not return to God in general, but to its Lord of love. To this context we should also relate Ibn-Arabi's extraordinary dream, in which a nuptial union is concluded with each of the cosmic powers, the stars of the Sky…

The return to a specific form of God, the Lord of love, that is, not formlessness but the superior forms of liberation according to Vaishnavism in which the saint remains an individual able to relate to the Divine and play games (*Lila*), imply different ways to relate to the Divine,

---

74   Bryant, *Bhakti Yoga*, 115.
75   Desmond, *Desire, Dialectic, and Otherness: An Essay on Origins*, 175.

for the Divine's Oneness is not a form among others. The Heavenlies are therefore "heterogenous and, in principle, unlimited array of liberated possibilities reflecting the free will and partialities of the living entities. This might be expected if the Absolute is to be deemed unlimited and all-inclusive."[76] Apart from the hierarchies of spiritual states, "the Absolute, being infinite and unlimited, must be unlimitedly diverse and multifaceted for the Bhagatava."[77] As Christ says, in His Father's house there are many mansions. In the *Acts of Peter*, the disciples see Christ in different forms, and the *Gospel of Philip* teaches the following:

> Jesus took them all by stealth, for he did not appear as he was, but in the manner in which they would be able to see him. He appeared to them all. He appeared to the great as great. He appeared to the small as small. He appeared to the angels as an angel, and to men as a man. Because of this, his word hid itself from everyone. Some indeed saw him, thinking that they were seeing themselves, but when he appeared to his disciples in glory on the mount, he was not small. He became great, but he made the disciples great, that they might be able to see him in his greatness.[78]

The final sentence is significant as emphasizing the correspondence and likeness of devotee to Divinity (indeed, there is a whole theme in Biblical apocrypha of becoming alike the figure through which the Divine manifests, wherein prophets see Abraham in the likeness of Adam, or themselves in that of Abraham, etc.). To see the Great, we must be great. We do not only relate to the Divine in some of its manifestations, but crucially, we re-propose the Divine manifestation. In this sense the relationship to the Divine as a relationship between one form and another is ultimately a beautiful absurdity, paradisal paradox. Rather, the complete transcendence of the Divine makes itself imminently present in our self, when that self is inclusive of other selves, other forms, so that no single form can be confused with an ultimate center, and so that the harmony of forms bares apophatic witness to the transcendent (indeed, every form is made of other forms, bodies of cells and cells of molecules, until there is no form at all but a wave of potential). Theophany (vision of Divinity) is theomorphy (taking the form of Divinity). Writes Henry Corbin:

> *Talem eum vidi qualem capere potui.* The community of vision will be established not by reference to an external object, an evidence uniformly and fully given to all, but by reason of a dimension of being that is common to this or that group or family of souls... the conception of the metamorphoses of the Logos, no doubt derived from Philo and frequent in the works of Origen, according to

76   Bryant, *Bhakti Yoga,* 122.
77   Ibid., 123.
78   *The Gospel of Philip,* 57:2–58:8, 155–57.

which the Saviour appears to men as a man and to the angels as
an angel[79]

We end, then, having linked our discussion of the erotic with a vision
of spiritual realization as *diverse*, each seeker receiving a vision of the
Divine which is ever-beyond-vision, appealing to the person as microcosm,
containing a mandalic cosmos of revelatory forms to be borne witness
to, not at all as an atomizing pursuit, but with crisscrossing affinities
(Corbin's "families of souls") that structure our spiritual vocation into a
grander harmony ultimately encompassing every other seeker. As Blake
writes in *The Everlasting Gospel*: "The Vision of Christ that thou dost see
Is my Vision's Greatest Enemy. Thine has a great hook nose like thine;
Mine has a snub nose like to mine"[80] and in *Jerusalem*, "Let the Human
Organs be kept in their perfect Integrity… Everyone knows, we are One
Family! One Man blessed forever."[81]

Black Stones, or the Meteor and the Volcano

To further render the copulative character of the initiatic site, it may
be noted that during Pythagoras's initiation at Mount Ida, he was purified with a "meteoric thunderstone,"[82] according to Porphyry. Thunder
(even if only symbolically alluded to by this stone, which need have no
literally meteoric origin) is the touching down of the paternal, demiurgic, lightning-wielding deity (Ju-piter; Theos-Pater, God-father), upon
the feminine site or holy of holies (meteoric to volcanic stone; solar
to infra-terrestrial flame). Their meeting produces offspring (saintly
initiates) and is marked by an *omphalos*, a navel: an umbilical link to
the origin of a culture, in observance of which this culture remembers
the divine coupling that brought it about. Enthronement of the initiate
(Jove meeting Juno) is also rebirth (Jove born from Rhea). The omphalos
at Delphi, for example, marks Apollo's enthronement, a temple devoted
to the heights of the (male) solar deity as well as to the earthly depth,
wherefrom fumes rise to inspire female oracular utterings.

The theme of the black stone also relates to the Semitic *Baetyl*,[83]
etymologically sharing its root with *Bethel* meaning *dwelling of the Lord*.
Such a site is feminine and births archetypal humanity by contact with
the divine masculine, thus the Egyptian goddess Hathor's name means

---

79   Corbin, *Cyclical Time and Ismaili Gnosis*, 61.
80   Although this passage seems to compare an esoteric to exoteric understanding
of Christ, it can also be taken in terms of the Indian doctrine of bhavas, so that
Christ appears differently to different devotees.
81   William Blake, "Jerusalem, Emanation of Giant Albion," *Blake: The Complete
Poems* (London: Pearson Longman, 2007), 36, 781.
82   Porphyry, *The Life of Pythagoras*, 17, 126.
83   Wendy Doniger, *Merriam-Webster's Encyclopedia of World Religions* (Springfield,
MA: Merriam-Webster, 2000), 106.

House of Horus (Horus as divine heir, archetype of the realized initiate) and thusly is Jesus born at Bethlehem.

Thus, stones representing divine contact are often described as black (representing meteoric and volcanic rock, one masculine, the other feminine, respectively) as in the case of the *"Idaean* Mother," the goddess at Mount Ida itself, who took the form of a black stone,[84] which would be identified with or related to the *Lapis Niger* or Black Stone at the Roman Forum which was precisely paired with the *Vulcanal* shrine to Vulcan, the volcanic god, in the ancient public hall or *Comitium* of Rome. In Rome we also have Numa Pompilius's shield, given him by Jove god of thunder, whose runic inscriptions he deciphered with the help of a nymph, and which we may identify with a meteoric or thunder-stone (the procession of this shield originates the Ides of March, according to Plutarch in *Parallel Lives*).

In his *Roman Antiquities*, Dionysus of Halicarnassus discusses the likelihood that the vestals do indeed guard a real holy item between the Capitoline and Palatine hills of Rome where king Numa Pompilius set up their sacral office. Dionysus notes that some consider this central relic of Roman veneration to be

> ...the Palladium that fell from Heaven, the same that was in possession of the people of Ilium; for they hold that Aeneas, being well acquainted with it, brought it into Italy, whereas the Achaeans stole away the copy.[85]

Since it fell from Heaven, the Palladium may be yet another instance of a meteoric stone at the cultic center of civilization. Indeed, there having been a copy, it follows the same pattern as Numa's forgeries of the shield he received from Jove, meant to confound would-be thieves. This Palladium brought by Aeneas remained at the core of the Roman state even into its Christian rebirth, when Emperor Constantine included it, along with Biblical relics, at his forum in the new Rome, Constantinople.

Much later in Roman history, during the 3rd century AD, the cult of Sol Invictus was also represented by a black, possibly meteoric, stone. It was identified with the deity Elagabalus, of Syrian provenance, which figure was merged with Sol Invictus. The name Elagabalus Latinizes *Ilah* and *gabal* from Semitic (Syrian) words for god and mountain. The connection to a mountain is interesting given all we have noted concerning the initiation rites occurring in volcanic craters and this latter's metaphysical symbolism. Further, the assimilation of mountain and sun related deities reminds us that the mountain as entry or extension of the underworld coinciding with

---

84   Kirk Summers, "Lucretius' Roman Cybele." In: Eugene N. Lane, ed., *Cybele, Attis and related cults: essays in memory of M. J. Vermaseren* (Leiden: Brill, 1996), 363.
85   Dionysus of Halicarnassus, *Roman Antiquities*, trans. Earnest Cary (on basis of E. Spelman) (Cambridge, MA: Harvard University Press, 1937), II:66, 5-6, 505.

the sun above us is paramount to ancient Egyptian ritual: Ra is accessed by Osiris; the infernal and celestial flames are revealed to be one. The word *Ilah* here is the same as occurs in the Arabic Allah (*al-llah*, *the* God, equivalent to the Greek *ho*-theos, to emphasize the true and transcendent Divine). It is fascinating, then, that this worship was associated with a black stone, so clearly equivalent to the black stone of Kaaba at Mecca.

The importance of Sol Invictus as native to Rome should be highlighted as well. It is a return to the early *Sol Indiges* deity, whose cult had been occluded over time. The wife of Aeneas, Lavinia, daughter of king Latinus, was granddaughter to Circe, mother of Latinus and daughter of the sun god. Therefore, Aeneas was marrying into the solar royalty of the Latins. By way of Syrian religion, Rome was in a sense rehabilitating its early observances and doing justice to its origins. Indeed, there is now good evidence for strong continuity between the old Sol Indiges and later Sol Invictus.[86, 87, 88] Perhaps Emperor Constantine's long-lived relationship to the Sol Invictus movement was spurred by similar considerations.

How the sun relates to the thunder-stone (meteor) is that the sun is a contemplative and equanimous shinning down, whereas the storm or lightning is the sun ray made active and even wrathful, bestowing the scourge and inestimable gift of fire when it strikes. The sun is a symbol for the distance of God and lightning for God's agency in human affairs. It should be remembered that the Cretan Jove whose form as a white bull is associated with princess Europa and certain Minoan rites was likely a solar deity (corresponding to Europa as lunar), so that this deity is not only a lightning wielder but also equivalent to the solar gods of other pantheons. Aeneas was deified by the name *Jupiter Indiges*, which may connect him to that anciently Roman *Sol Indiges* given the solar mode of Jupiter (Jove, Zeus). The black stone represents the storm and lightning, meteor, the bearing down of Heaven, its involvement and presence on earth, which is a presence of that contemplative distant radiance of the Divine represented by the sun. Such is the meaning of a black stone being associated with Sol Invictus (or with a potentially solar Jove in the case of the meteoric shield given to king Numa Pompilius).

The Holy Grail and Sexual Initiation

The Holy Grail heals the side-wound of king Anfortas. The theme of the Holy Grail as restoring one who has realized his own partiality and need for completion—that is, his need of combining with a correspondent

86   Steven Hijmans, "The Sun which did not rise in the East. The Cult of Sol Invictus in the Light of Non-Literary Evidence." *Babesch. Bulletin Antieke Beschaving* 71 (1996): 115–50.

87   Stefan Berrens, *Sonnenkult und Kaisertum von den Severern bis zu Constantin I (193–337 n. Chr.)* (Stuttgart: Historia Einzelschriften 2004), 185.

88   Petra Matern, *Helios und Sol: Kulte und Ikonographie des griechischen und römischen Sonnengottes* (Istanbul: Ege, 2001).

opposite—can be approached in terms of the Platonic image of a crater, which can be formed by both a volcanic eruption *from below* or meteor *from above*. It also appears in the Grail's association with the Crater constellation (given Wolfram von Eschenbach writes that the sage Flagetanis derived the human narrative of the Grail by reading it in the stars, this constellation is a worthy candidate). Crater is traditionally pictured as occurring between Hydra and Corvus constellations, the snake and the crow, opposite images (which suggests an Odinic connection, since Odin became both a snake and an eagle to steal the precious mead, which appears to be a version of the Holy Grail).

The lance or sword which often appear in grail stories, along with the dish or grail, symbolize sexual correspondence, as Dhira Mahoney notes, seeing in the Celtic version of the Holy Grail narrative, *Peredur*, something like the Indian *Lingam-Yoni*, Phallus-Vulva, symbol[89] (which is also similar to what Anne Catherine Emmerich describes inside the Ark of the Covenant in her visions). Mahoney sees a parallel between the *Lingam-Yoni* or head/orb upon a dish/grail and the symbol of a solar orb resting on a crescent moon to show the conjunction of male and female deities.

The severed head upon the grail-dish in the Welsh Peredur, also reminds of the story of a headless St. Dionysius the Areopagite, and Valentine Tomberg's interpretation of the headless man in the Tarot cards as one who has stopped allowing his intellections, the oscillations of the mind, to rule his direction. It is the advanced meditator, so to speak. Perhaps Orpheus sang best after his head was severed.

John Waddell discusses Irish stories, including the *Niall of the Nine Hostages*, in which a goddess personifies the land itself, and a potential ruler makes love to her. In that story she appears grotesque, but in being properly copulated with, she becomes beautiful, as the land or community are beautified by good governance.

The initiate discovers the divine feminine, the protean creativity or matrix, the Crater, and is reborn from it, but also, becoming a demiurge, finds his own Juno, his own Crater, at the level of reality he operates within (the world, his kingdom): in Irish tales, the king receives a cup from a woman as sign of his becoming ruler and drinks from it. He brings her the autozoon, his particular vision thereof, with which she is already mysteriously acquainted, for she has the autozoon already, and they fall in love.

GENDERED METAPHYSICS

Much of the above presents a gendering of metaphysical categories. Each such category is defined by the relationship of subjectivity to objectivity, so that each is gendered according to its masculine principle and mode or degree of feminine externalization. Before these is ineffability.

---

89   Glenys W. Goetinck, "The Quest for Origins." In: *The Grail: A Casebook*, ed. Dhira B. Mahoney (Routledge: London, 2000), 134.

Iamblichus describes this as the "prior cause even of the first god and king" to which "no object of intellection is linked...nor anything else"[90] wherein, in Shaivist terms, Shiva and Shakti are undifferentiated.[91] It is the Egyptian primordial waters or flood from which Atum comes.[92]

Non-Shaivist, Vaishnavist, Hinduism, centered on Vishnu-Krishna, presents the same idea. Vishnu is with Lakshmi, Krishna with Radha, (indeed, these incarnate variously, so that the Rama avatar of the *Ramayana*, prior to the events of the *Mahabharata*, also had his consort, Sita, incarnation of the feminine principle):

> In the seventh heaven, the shepherds' heaven (go-loka), the one absolute supreme Self, Krishna, unable to enjoy the pleasure of love because he was alone, manifested himself in dual form, a black light and a white light. From Radhika, the white light, impregnated by Krishna, the black light, were born Universal Intellect (Mahat-tattva), Basic-Nature (Pradhana), and the Embryo-of-Splendor (Hiranya-garbha), which is the principle and totality of all subtle bodies. The love [of Krsna for Radha] is an allegory of the union of Supreme-Man (purusa) and Nature (prakrti), from which the universe gradually arose.[93]

Here the eternal male and female produce three realities (Universal Intellect, Basic-Nature and the Embryo-of-Splendor), which are different from the world as we know it. This is consistent with Shaivism, in which Shiva and Shakti produce three pure-creations prior to the mortal world, impure creation, and with Proclus, according to which the masculine and feminine produce three layers prior to the world. We will explore these in the following section.

All begins with One, which contains the triad insofar as it is creative. As the Orthodox Christian theologian Nikitas Stithatos writes, "God is both Monad and Triad."[94] Nicholas of Cusa describes the triadic structure of creation (implicitly emphasizing the tetrad or number four as the manifest world): "When a man is summoned by Omnipotence from out of not-being, there first of all arises a oneness, then an equality and then the union of both."[95]

---

90   Iamblichus, *De Mysteriis Aegyptiorum*, VIII.2; 307.

91   Mark Dcyzkowski, *The Doctrine of Vibration: An Analysis of the Doctrines and Practices of Kashmir Shaivism* (New York City: State University of New York Press, 1987), 166.

92   Uzdavinys, *Philosophy as a Rite of Rebirth: From Ancient Egypt to Neoplatonism*, 43.

93   Karapatri, Sri Bhagavati tattva, Siddhanta, V, 1944-5, cited by Alain Danielou, *The Myths and Gods of India: The Classic Work on Hindu Polytheism* (Rochester, VT: Inner Traditions, 1991), 177.

94   Nikitas Stithatos, "On Spiritual Knowledge, Love and the Perfection of Living: One Hundred Texts." In: St. Nikodemos of the Holy Mountain and St. Makarios of Corinth (compilers), G. E. H. Palmer, Philip Sherrard, and Metropolitan Kallistos Ware (eds.), *Philokalia: The Complete Text*, vol. 4 (London: Faber and Faber, 1995), 173:100, 252.

95   Nicholas of Cusa, *De Pace Fidei and Cribratio Alkorani*, J. Hopkins trans. (Minneapolis, MN: The Arthur J. Banning Press, 1994), VIII:22, 644.

There is 1) a principle, 2) a plurality of particular expressions (equidistant from their principle, for being a *principle* it is not exhausted in any single *particular*) and 3) the union of both.

The distinction between triad and tetrad is borne out by several traditions. The Pythagorean Tetractys is complete after arriving at this tetrad, its fourth term (1;2;3;4). According to Iamblichus the threshold of manifestation is triadic, for it is in the term following the triad (the number four, following three) that gross reality begins.[96] The triad is "wisdom"[97] to the Platonist, just as Wisdom laid the foundations of the earth according to Proverbs, for which reason (in the Chinese *Tao te Ching*) the number three "begets the myriad creatures."[98] In Egyptian religion, Atum declares:[99] "After I developed as One God, that was three gods with respect to me." In the words of the Sophiologist Pavel Florensky "with the fourth hypostasis there begins a completely new essence."[100] The fourth or tetradic level is the cosmos proper, that is, Plato's intelligible animal, which is preceded by the intellectual animal or autozoon.

The three terms preceding the world (monad, dyad and triad) constitute pre-manifest or pre-formal reality. In the *Metaphysical Elements*, Proclus distinguishes, after the Ineffable One (which is not the monad, indeed, in a sense the Ineffable is not One either, being beyond number, except the neo-Platonists intend this meaning by distinguishing Ineffable One from monad) between the intelligible (Proposition CLXII), intellectual (Proposition CLXIII) and supermundane (Proposition CLXIV).[101] Following these, there comes the mundane. He writes in his commentary on Plato's *Timaeus*: "...You have therefore, in the intelligible, in the intellectual, and in the supermundane gods, the harmonious conjunction of the male with the female."[102] *And elsewhere,*

> *Hence Juno proceeds* together with Jupiter, generating all things in conjunction with the father. Hence, too, she is said to be equal in rank with Jupiter, *as is* likewise Rhea with Saturn (Κρόνος). For this Goddess is the bosom of all the Saturnian (Kronian) power. Earth also is equal in dignity with Heaven (Οὐρανός). For Earth is the mother of all things of which Heaven is the father.[103]

---

96 Attributed to Iamblichus, *Theologumena arithmeticae*, R. Waterfield trans. (Grand Rapids, MI: Phanes Press, 1988), II; 42; III; 50.

97 Attributed to Iamblichus, *Theologumena arithmeticae*, III; 51.

98 Lao Tse, *Tao-Teh-Ching* (Boston, MA: Gnomad Publishing, 1996), chapter 42.

99 The Bremmer-Rhind Papyrus, cited by Uzdavinys, *Philosophy as a Rite of Rebirth: From Ancient Egypt to Neoplatonism*, 169.

100 Pavel Florensky, *The Pillar and Ground of Truth: An Essay in Orthodox Theodicy in Twelve Letters*, B. Jakim trans. (Princeton, NJ: Princeton University Press, 1997), 38. Cited by Martin, *The Submerged Reality*, 152–53.

101 Proclus, *Metaphysical Elements*, T. Johnson trans. (Osceola, MO: Press of the Republican, 1909), CLXII-CLXIV, 119–21.

102 Proclus, *The Commentary on Plato's Timaeus*, I, 39.

103 Ibid., vol. 1, I, 39.

In Proclus's theology this male and female is the *Bound* and *Infinite*, or *Limit* and *Unlimit*—the Platonic *Peras* and *Apeiron* and Empedocles' Strife and Love[104]—corresponding to Shiva and Shakti. They are masculinity and femininity as components of reality, coordinates within which all becomes, and not specifically either Saturn and Rhea, Jove and Juno or any other particular dyad of deities. The following passage presents this gendering:

> Bound indeed is a guard proceeding to the intelligible summit, the imparticipable and first God, measuring and defining all things, giving subsistence to every paternal, connective and undefiled genus of God. But Infinite is the never-failing power of this God, unfolding into light all the generative orders, and all infinity, which is prior to essence, and that which is essential, and also that which proceeds as far as to the last matter.[105]

Proclus associates the "paternal" to the agency of Peras, whereas Apeiron receives symbolic descriptors related to the feminine, including "power of this God," just as Shakti is Shiva's power, "light," "generative" and "matter" or materiality. The *Henads*, that is, the unities that mediate the One's unity to creation, are in some sense subordinate to these two poles, while being indistinct from the One, though also distinct from each other and continuous with creation (similar to the names of God in Islamic theology, which are also gendered, in God and continuous with creation).

In Shaiva Tantra, as in Proclus, there are three modes of conjoining between the eternal masculine and feminine prior to the emergence of the world, corresponding to the three levels cited from Proclus above. In Tantrism these three are the states of *Sadasiva, Isvara* and *Suddhavidya* and together constitute pure-creation, called *Suddhasrsti* (which is often listed as also including the principles of Shiva and Shakti, male and female, in themselves, totaling five constituents of pure-creation) after which begins the world: impure, mundane, creation (*asuddhasrsti*).[106]

If Saturn corresponds to Rhea as top and bottom of reality, Jove to Juno are the immediately preceding levels from that top and bottom, and so forth, then it is not a pyramidal shape of monad, dyad, triad and tetrad that is being described. Rather, each level is both above and below (both masculine and feminine): "the whole of reality may therefore be thought of as a diamond, rather than a pyramid, with the simplest entities at the top

---

104   The fifth century neo-Platonist Syrianus considered Empedocles' terms equivalent to the monad and dyad, Love and Strife, but we can take this, as does Uzdavinys (*Philosophy as a Rite of Rebirth: From Ancient Egypt to Neoplatonism*, 171), as that which is whole in itself and unchanging, and that which is dynamic and changing (able to multiply, divisive, thus, dyadic): the resting consciousness and the externalizing joy, Shiva and Shakti.

105   Proclus, *On The Theology of Plato*, III:12, 177–78.

106   Dyczkowski, *The Doctrine of Vibration*, 166.

and bottom, and the greatest complexity in the middle."[107] Each level has a "double mediation, descending and ascending."[108] This is expressed by the duality of kingship, that sacerdotal and monarchical role of representing both the divine to the congregants and the congregants to the divine.

Indeed, the Christian duality of king and bride, Christ and Church, is one between the masculine and feminine. In terms of Proclus and the pagan past, Nicholas of Cusa takes up the centrality of male-female interaction to metaphysics in strands of pre-Christian philosophy and views it as compatible with the Christian faith.

> Hermes maintained that two sexes are to be found in all things, animals and nonanimals alike; therefore, he declared that the cause of all things, God, enfolds in Godself both the masculine and feminine sex, of which Hermes believed Cupid and Venus were the unfolding. Valerius the Roman concurred and sang of Jupiter omnipotent, God the Father and Mother.[109]

Unity, Duality, Trinity

In Tantrism, the Sadasiva state is typified by the formula "I am this (universe)" ("*aham-idam*"): consciousness encompasses sentience or objectified being. The Sadasiva may be identified as the Monad. In Iamblichus, it is the "self-sufficient god" which "has autonomously shone forth" from the previous ineffability as "first principle... a monad springing from the One."[110] *Ex uno non proven it nisi unum.* On this level consciousness "views the All in a state of withdrawal," and is "at one with its own nature."[111] Given that, at each existential estate, Shakti is the means by which the proceeding is made manifest, a Shaktic dimension must be present even in the Monad, albeit indiscernible except in its acting to bring about the dyad. This is described by Proclus as the "Goddess, being conjoined with Saturn... called Rhea,"[112] in whom nature pre-exists even the Demiurge.[113]

In terms of this transcendent estate, the Monad, or indeed, in terms of the personality of the Divine irrespective of the specific state it is manifesting (for Shiva and Shakti are discussed in Shaivism even as independent of the various existential modalities such as the Sadasiva), the (non-Shaivist) *Devi Bhagavatam* exalts the Divine Feminine, Radha, as follows:

---

107   Marije Martijn and Lloyd Gerson, *Proclus' System*, 54.
108   St. Nikodemos of the Holy Mountain and St. Makarios of Corinth (compilers), *Philokalia: The Complete Text*, 253.
109   Nicholas de Cusa, *Selected Spiritual Writings. On Learned Ignorance* (New York: Paulist Press, 1997), 124.
110   Iamblichus, *De Mysteriis*, VIII:2; 307.
111   Dcyzkowski, *The Doctrine of Vibration*, 166.
112   Proclus, *The Theology of Plato*, vol. 1, trans. T. Taylor (London: A. J. Valpy, 1816), V:11; 337.
113   Martijn, *Proclus on Nature: Philosophy of Nature and Its Methods in Proclus' Commentary on Plato's Timaeus*, 51.

> She is the Lady of the Râsa Lîlâ, the Foremost of the Jovial, humor-
> ous (witty) persons and dwells always in Râsa. Her abode is in
> Goloka and from Her have come out all the Gopîkâs. Râsa—the
> circular dance of Krisna and the cow-herdesses of Vrindâvana.
> Her nature is the Highest Bliss, the Highest Contentment, and
> Excessive Joy; She transcends the three Sattva, Rajo and Tamo
> Gunas and is Nirâkâra (without any particular form); but She
> dwells everywhere but unconnected with any. She is the soul of
> all. She is without any effort to do anything and void of Ahamkâra.
> She assumes forms only to show Her favor to Her Bhaktas. The
> intelligent learned men (Pundits) read Her Mahimâ (glories) in
> meditating on Her according to the *Vedas*. (*Devi Bhagavatam*, IX:1,
> 48–70, 804)

And,

> It was Bhagavân Srî Krisna, The Highest Spirit, that worshipped,
> first of all, the Devî Râdhâ within the Râsa Mandalam, the enclo-
> sure, within which the Râsa Lîlâ was performed (the circular dance)
> in the region Goloka. Then under the command of Srî Krisna, all
> the Gopas (cow-herds), Gopîs, all the boys, girls, Surabhî, the queen
> of the race of the cows, and the other cows worshipped Her. (*Devi
> Bhagavatam*, IX:1, 144–59, 810)

An important point here is that the eternal feminine is not only externalizing. Even when the Divine is praised without reference to creation
or Its agency in creation the feminine aspect is present. Likewise, we read
in the *Vishnu Purana* that both Vishnu and his consort Goddess Lakshmi
are God according to classical definitions, that is, both eternal masculine
and feminine are described as Absolute and beyond contingency: "Sri,
the bride of Vishnu, the mother of the world, is eternal, imperishable.
In like manner as he is all-pervading, so also is she...omnipresent."[114]

Even so, throughout traditions the feminine is often described as the
reflexive, externalizing awareness of the Divine, which is rendered by
the term wisdom, intelligence or sentience. In the Vishnu Purana, which
describes reality in terms of male-female Divinity, "Hari [The Lord] is all
that is called male; Lakshmi is all that is termed female" (*Vishnu Purana*,
I.8[115]), we encounter a long list of correspondences, including Him as
meaning and Her as speech, and Vishnu as Love and Goddess Lakshmi
as Pleasure (She is the sentience to a consciousness: an externality which
nonetheless cannot exist unless it is internal, that is, unless it is being
experienced by an *experiencer* with an inner life).

Being the externalizing aspect or agency of the Divine, created things
are Hers (Wisdom was with God at the foundation of the earth; Sophia

---

114   vol. 1, trans. Horace Hayman Wilson and ed. Fitzedward Hall (London:
Trubner and Co., 1864), 118.
115   Ibid., 120.

personifies creation and humanity). We encounter all this in the *Devi Bhagavatam*:

> So when this Intelligence of the nature of Brahmâ, beyond the three attributes, gets tinged with the above three Gunas and becomes omnipotent, then She is superior (Pradhânâ) in the work of creation. Hence She is styled as Prakriti. (*Devi Bhagavatam*, IX:1, 4–18, 797)

Onward then: The Monad has condescended unto the dyad. Isvara, is expressed by the formula "this (universe) is me" ("*idam-aham*"): "The All now becomes more clearly manifest as an independent reality," consistent with the separateness of the Demiurge from Receptacle, Jove from Juno, so that the masculine and feminine are distinguishable. Born of the unitive Saturn-Rhea, Jove (again, the Platonic Demiurge[116, 117]), that is, the divine agency as separate from, and capable of acting upon, creation. This corresponds with the Shaivist *Isvara*[118] wherein Divine personality becomes discernable. At this declination Shakti is that potentiality into which consciousness "unfolds externally full of the creative power of action,"[119] equivalent to Juno, who, Proclus teaches, "becomes the receptacle of an intellectual essence, and receives the mundane intellect, which proceeds into her from the thigh of Jupiter."[120]

In the third place, "both subjective and objective aspects share an equal status..." so that "I am this (universe) and this (universe) is me (*ahamidamidamaham*)."[121] After this begins impure-creation (*asuddhasrsti*),[122] or the worldly realm. The "mundane intellect" received by Juno from Jove, "becoming participable by her... elevates her to the intelligible, and to the fountain of her nature,"[123] such that Juno births the world-soul (she is referred to as receptacle and world-soul, for both are expressions of the same eternal feminine), initiating the triad. It is her own nature that she receives, for she is a form of Rhea (*Shakti*), and it is Rhea who constitutes the intellect she is acquiring, which is prior to, though moving through, Jove, that he may instantiate it.

This third degree of being is Juno after her being elevated to the fountain of her nature, in Proclean terms, that is, no longer Plato's Receptacle but here the world-soul, with a declination of Jove appropriate

---

116 Iamblichus, in *Studies on the 5th and 6th Essays of Proclus' Commentary on the Republic* (*Hypomnemata*), trans. A. Sheppard (Göttingen, Germany: Vandenhoeck & Ruprecht, 1980), 65–66.
117 Proclus, *Theologia Platonica*, V:25; 383.
118 Dyczkowski, *The Doctrine of Vibration*, 166.
119 Ibid.
120 Proclus. *The Commentaries of Proclus on the Timaeus of Plato in Five Books*, vol. 1, II; 344.
121 Dcyzkowski, *The Doctrine of Vibration*, 166.
122 Ibid.
123 Proclus, *In Timaeum*, II; 344.

to this lower station. In Proclus these seem to be Minerva and Bacchus. It is, however, also implicitly fourfold. Following the Shaivist expression cited above, according to which the subject is the universe and vice-versa (*ahamidam-idamaham*), there is subjectivity that is active over the object, the object passive to subjectivity, the subject passive to the objective and the objective active over the subject. Put in terms of artistic production, the first phase is conception, then follows concretization and, in the third place, the artist must at times affect his piece by ornamenting as he will, but at other times must be passive to his work, allowing himself to trace its already existing lines and add finishing touches per its promptings (the piece must be allowed to *speak* to its artist). The function of the final generation of deities can be understood as neither contemplation (Saturn and Rhea) nor concretization (Jove and Juno), but rather conservation.

In Plato this third mode is the intellectual animal or autozoon, which contains the four primary ideas: "...so far as [the universe] is an animal, it is the image of animal itself, and so far also as it consists of four parts [i.e., of the four elements]."[124] Although, in some subtler sense, the autozoon was present in the dyad, with the Demiurge receiving it from Rhea. The autozoon, with its four ideas[125] (the concepts underlying the four elements) may be related to the four-faced creature of Ezekiel's vision in Hebrew tradition[126] and to Egyptian religion's four sons of Horus, four horns of the Bull of Ra,[127] or four-faced god.[128] These latter are all related to the four cardinal directions. Plotinus, describing the "ideal paradigm of physical reality" as Uzdavinys puts it, writes of the "well-rounded whole," "a globe of faces radiant with faces all living."[129] Analogues abound, including the four-faced form of Janus, *Mercurius Quadratus* and Astrampsychos's invocation of Mercury by way of the four cardinal directions. Four is therefore the number of manifestation, again, wherein four elements or corners structure themselves into the world.

The World as Tetrad

The four corners composing the final, pre-mundane, generation could be tentatively identified with the Greco-Roman gods Mars, Minerva, Vulcan and Venus (respectively the masculine and feminine expressions of separation and conjoining, the two basic dynamics of the physical

124   Ibid., II, 338; V, 357.
125   Ibid., III, 105.
126   Margaret Barker, *The Great High Priest: The Temple Roots of Christian Liturgy* (London: T &T Clark, 2003), 289.
127   *Pyramid Texts*, 470a.
128   Ibid., 1207b.
129   Ennead, VI:7.15. Cited by Uždavinys, *Ascent to Heaven in Islamic and Jewish Mysticism* (London: The Matheson Trust, 2011), 2.

universe they maintain). While the names of these deities are sometimes used by traditional exegetes to describe functions quite apart
from those presently being considered, they also present close affinity
to the four ideas of the Shaivist Suddhavidya, as understood above.
Mars, as warmonger, separates, whereas Vulcan, as forger, joins and
constructs: "…both Vulcan and Mars…operate about the universal
world… Mars indeed separates…[b]ut Vulcan adorns"; "…each of
these deities requires the assistance of Venus; Mars that he may insert
order…Vulcan that he may induce beauty."[130] Vulcan also has need of
Minerva. In "Vulcan and Minerva" (the latter is sometimes identified
with the world-soul), "the cause of all arts is primarily comprehended…."[131] Vulcan "…being in love with Minerva, emitted his seed on
the earth, and from thence the race of the Athenians blossomed forth,"
indeed, "Vulcan is always in love with Minerva,"[132] such that worldly
creation is spawned continuously thereby. (The duality of Mars and
Vulcan as masculine separator and joiner is also perhaps equivalent to
the way Empedocles uses the names Hades to refer to fire's destructive function, and Hephaestus to refer to its constructive function,[133]
which matches the juxtaposition of Persephone and Aphrodite, mates
of Hades and Hephaestus, in the Bacchic/Orphic lead plates found
at Selinus.[134])

Minerva, in this context, is also identified with war and therefore
separation: "Minerva…is a friend to war indeed, because she is allotted
the summit of separation; but she is a lover of contrarieties…."[135] In
contrast, Venus, goddess of romantic love, joins things together, which
is the effect of erotic attraction. Since Shiva is consciousness and Shakti
is sentience in Tantrism (respectively subjectivity and objectivity, though
the latter is never understood in materialist terms as entirely insentient,
but rather as apprehended phenomena) the male deities Mars and Vulcan may be identified as the two subjective modes of the third tier, one
active over objectivity and the other passive to it.

Correspondingly, Minerva and Venus would be the active and passive modes of objectivity in this scheme. The autozoon precedes the
intelligible animal, or living cosmos (the *idea* of the four elements that
make up the universe precedes those elements). These four deities,

---

130 "The Latter Platonists, The History of the Restoration of the Platonic Theology," trans. T. Taylor. In: Proclus, *The Philosophical And Mathematical Commentaries
Of Proclus On The First Book Of Euclid's Elements*, vol. 2, ed. Thomas Taylor (London:
Printed for the Author, 1966), Section II, 305.
131 Proclus, *Theologia Platonica*, V:24, 377.
132 Ibid., I;121.
133 Following Peter Kingsley's interpretation. I'm using the Greek names here.
134 Kingsley, *Ancient Philosophy, Mystery and Magic*, 270–71.
135 Proclus, *The Six Books of Proclus The Platonic Successor, On The Theology of Plato*,
vol. 2, XXI, 167.

therefore, are followed by the earthly abode. They also would constitute the tetrad as its four corners in their exterior aspect, while
pre-existing as triad in subtler form. The masculine in its active and
passive modes with respect to the active and passive forms of the
feminine (the combinations of Shaivist ahamidam-idamaham, the *I*
and *that* of *I am that*, and the *I* and *that* of *that is I*; Vulcan as forger,
Mars as divider, Venus as joiner, Minerva as discerner) also correspond
that that quaternity of Sufi mystics which appears in the work of Ibn
Arabi of Adam-Eve-Mary-Jesus, where Eve is born from Adam (his
rib) and Jesus is born from Mary: a producing and a born masculine,
a birthing and a produced feminine. [136]

We may also think of them as conjoining the extremes of the seven
Heavenly spheres, where Saturn and the Moon (seventh and first) represent the male-female pair of the first pure-creation (the Sadasiva of
Shaivism or super-mundane of Proclus), followed by the sixth and second
Heavens, Jupiter and Mercury (Shaivist *Isvara* or Proclus's Intellectual),
then the fifth and third, Mars and Venus (*Suddhavidya* or the Intelligible),
with the solar Heaven being at the very heart, the pole of the Heavens,
as Ibn Arabi conceives of it, and meant for unity with the earth, to be
ruled by solar monarchy (an image ibn-Arabi uses, associating it with
Muhammad). This idea is expressed by Franz Cumont in *Astrology and
Religion Among the Greeks and Romans*,[137] while discussing Chaldean cosmology and politics, whence the traditional order of the seven spheres,
which Gregory Lipton considers the origin of ibn-Arabi's conception
of solar centrality.[138]

Following the above, a punctual correspondence between the Platonic
and Shaivist-Tantric schemas emerges, one facilitated by the pious regard
in which certain neo-Platonists held the old myths. The same can be
said for other traditions mentioned, but these two seem to be preserved
in a particularly complete, and therefore correspondent, form.

Uzdavinys presents these layers of reality in a similarly gender-
symmetrical scheme by following the Egyptian Ennead of gods, after
the One, wherein also the male and female principles of *Hu* and *Sia*
(Hu is related to the Egyptian verb "to announce," and Sia, the feminine, is Perception or Wisdom,[139] so they match the Christian Word
and Wisdom, Logos and Sophia): the monad as Atum; the dyad as Shu
and Tefnut; the triad as Geb and Nut and their embrace ("Geb and
Nut were united in tight marital embrace, until Father Shu separated

---

136   Henry Corbin, *Alone with the Alone: Creative Imagination in the Sufism of ibn-Arabi*,
trans. R. Manheim (Princeton, NJ: Princeton University Press, 1997), 163.
137   Franz Cumont, *Astrology and Religion Among the Greeks and Romans* (New York:
Putnam, 1912), 128.
138   Gregory Lipton, *Rethinking Ibn 'Arabi* (Oxford: Oxford University Press, 2018).
139   Uzdavinys, *Philosophy as a Rite of Rebirth: From Ancient Egypt to Neoplatonism*, 169.

them"[140]); the tetrad as Osiris, Isis, Set and Nephthys.[141] This is suggestive of the Kabbalah's *Sephirot*. The Zohar presents the four syllables of the name YHWH, the Kabbalistic tetrad (which Barker discusses in connection to the Pythagorean Tetractys[142]) as consisting of a father, mother, son and daughter.[143] Barker refers to the two instants of Lady Wisdom (one as mother and one as consort corresponding to the male father and son). Raphael Patai refers specifically to this understanding of the Tetragrammaton as paralleling the Egyptian gods Shu and Tefnut (father and mother) with their children Geb and Nut (son and daughter),[144] that is, the first four gods following the source, Atum, who are similarly gendered and generationally structured.

These deities are in turn followed by a lower, subsequent tetrad also composed of two male and two female persons (Isis, Osiris, Set and Nephthys). The same appears in Empedocles, fragment 6 of whose verses gives us the four elements of air, earth, fire and water respectively as the parental gods Zeus and Hera, and the subsequent Hades[145] and Nestis (the latter probably being an indigenous Sicilian equivalent to Persephone). A lower younger tetrad in Empedocles (supplementing with Bacchic Sicilian texts, namely the lead plates at Selinus) might consist of Aphrodite, Hephaestus, Hades and Persephone/Nestis. Even the first of these tetrads, given the relation of Osiris and Set, on the one hand, and Zeus and Hades on the other, both sets of brothers, is equivalent to Isis, Osiris, Set and Nephthys.[146]

According to the above, Geb is Jove at the level of world-soul and Nut is Juno as world-soul rather than Receptacle, or rather, more in keeping with Proclus, these are Dionysus and Athena. Mars-Vulcan and Minerva-Venus would correspond to Osiris, Isis, Set and Nephthys as tetrad.

We may suggest a table of correspondences at this point:

---

140 Raphael Patai, *Hebrew Goddess* (Detroit: Wayne State University Press, 1990), 118.
141 Algis Uzdavinys, *The Heart of Plotinus: The Essential Enneads* (Bloomington, IN: World Wisdom, 2009), 12: "the structure of the noetic cosmos constituted by four ontological levels: 1. Ayum, 2. Shu and Tefnut, 3. Geb and Nut, 4. Osiris, Isis, Seth and Nephtys."
142 Barker, *The Great High Priest: The Temple Roots of Christian Liturgy*, 262.
143 Raphael Patai, *Hebrew Goddess*, 117.
144 Ibid., 118.
145 Though Hades is the brother of Zeus, Zeus is described as "dazzling" and Hera as "life-bearing," so that there seems to be a preeminence for these two—air and earth. On the other hand, the order of the elements seems to be air, fire, earth and water, so the equivalent of Zeus and Hades may be not with the Egyptian Shu and Geb but with Osiris and Set.
146 We even get a certain similarity in the names of the Sicilian *Nestis* and Egyptian *Nephthys*. Note also I am using Greek names consistent with Empedocles rather than my usual Roman Jove, Juno and so on.

ONTIC NUMBERS	EGYPTIAN TRADITION	INDIAN TRADITION (ABHINAVAGUPTA'S SHAIVISM)	GREEK TRADITION	PLATONISM (PROCLEAN)	KABBALAH	ASSOCIATED IMAGERY	HEAVENLY ASCENT (DANTE)
One					Ain Sof		
Male-Female principles and Trinity (Sat-Chit-Ananda[1]) manifesting throughout	Hu and Sia (Heka, the magical power, is somewhere described as prior to Atum[2])	Shiva and Shakti (Vishnu and Lakshmi in Vaishnavism, Krishna and Radha in Krishna-centered Vaishnavism, Aham and Idam in Shaivism)[3]		Peras and Apeiron (Limit and Un-limit)			God surrounded by nine Angelic Circles[4]
Monad	Atum	Sadasiva (aham-idam) / Pure Creation	Saturn and Rhea conjoined	Super-Mundane (First Paternal Intellect) / Autozoon[6] as transcendent paradigm sacrificed into lower reality by Demiurge (Rhea dispensation to Jove)	Kether	Sky Dome (as Female Womb & Male Skull/Mind)	Empyrean and Immaculate Rose[5]
Dyad	Shu and Tefnut	Isvara (idam-aham)	Demiurge (Jove) and Crater (Juno)	Intellectual (Second Paternal Intellect)	Hokmah	Stars (especially Morning Star, as Umbilical Opening and Eye[7])	Prime Mover
Triad	Geb and Nut	Suddhavidya (ahamidam-idamaham)	World-Soul	Intelligible	Binah	Sun (as ever-reborn King and Vision of Apollonian utopia)	Fixed Stars

Autozoon (Intellectual Animal/Essential Living Animal) as paradigm in body of initiate sacrificed into higher reality. The correspondence between the autozoon here and above is that between the heavenly ascent of the initiate and the earthly descent of revelation. The Islamic Muhammadan mi'raj (ascent) and Quranic descent. It is analogous to ibn-Sina's double explanation for knowledge: one bottom up speculative abstraction from sense-data to general principle, and one top-down illumination of the soul by the Agent Intellect. Here, the autozoon is the Book (Heavenly/Archetypal Qur'an, the Mother Book, Umm al-Kitab), Temple, City (Meta-Polis, Heavenly Jerusalem, Elysian Rome, Na-Koja Abad, Taoist One Opening, Henry Corbin's mundus imaginalis). Gap between Pure to Impure Creation (Shaivism). (the Abyss of some occultist system). Sacrifice of one's selfhood as holy animal or giant (white bull given to king Minos, cosmic bull slain by Mithra, Ymir slain by Odin and his brothers, the heavenly bull whose parts are distributed by Gilgamesh, the holy Lamb). The autozoon contains the fourfold of the tetrad and Tetragrammaton which is symbolized by the four-legged animal. If this sacrifice is not undergone the ego becomes tyrannical (Voegelin's egophany—as opposed to theophany—of Hegelianism and modern philosophy; the Minotaur after Minos fails to sacrifice the white bull; Blake's Specter in his poetry) and must be defeated. The ideal relation is sacrificial (sacred-making) but ecstatic, not agonistic, for Chit is ever going joyfully into the Sat (flowing in and out, until the flow is perceived as a single movement within Sat); the Lamb is slain from the world's foundation (Apocalypse); the Lamb makes a covering or dress for the King (Gospel of Philip). Insofar as the sacrificial animal appears as a theophany (the white bull/oxen of the sun as sacrifice in the Hellenic Mediterranean, a form taken by Jove; the Lamb which is Christ) it reveals a stage prior to full theophany (the human form, King) wherein the Divine is perceived as separate from the initiate, and its death may present as a condescension to the initiate (Christ as servant of His disciples, His body as their sustenance, and similar statements in the Bhagavatam Purana and elsewhere) wherein the devotee realizes itself as being at one with its Lord.

Tetrad[8]	Osiris, Isis, Set and Nephthys	Asuddhasrsti	Impure Creation	Mars, Venus, Minerva, Vulcan	Mundane (Intelligible Living Being/Animal, Corpus Cosmicum)	Seven lower sephirot	Earth (ideally "made solar," as Kingdom)	Seven Ptolemaic Planetary Spheres

The Solar King: Jesus Christ, Horus, tenth sephirah of the Kabbalah, Ibn Arabi's understanding of Muhammad, possibly Blake's Orc, completes the system as a reification of transcendence (which nonetheless occludes itself).

1   Interaction of Male and Female (*Sat* as Masculine, *Chit* as Feminine and *Ananada* as Joyful interplay, or *Chit* as "child" of *Sat* and *Ananda* as feminine counterpart of *Chit*, whereas the masculine and feminine in *Sat* are conjoined and not differentiated). In considering *Chit* masculine and *Ananda* feminine, we are consistent with Porphyry's triad of *hyparxis, nous* and *zoe*: the first is energy at rest, the second centripetal and the third centrifugal (like the Indian gunas sattva-rajas-tamas, and the alchemical salt-mercury-sulphur). They express, respectively, being, consciousness and bliss. The Platonic version of *Sat-Chit-Ananda* is thus Being-Intellect-Life.

2   Uzdavinys, *Philosophy as a Rite of Rebirth: From Ancient Egypt to Neoplatonism*, 170.

3   Meaning and Speech, Love and Pleasure (Vishnu Purana), Peras and Apeiron (Proclus), Nous and Zoe, the Egyptian paired-concepts of order-life (maat-ankh), sameness-recurrence (djet-neheh), stasis-development (unun-kheper) (Uzdavinys, *Philosophy as a Rite of Rebirth: From Ancient Egypt to Neoplatonism*, 171–72).

4   Perhaps as the ideas of the Ennead manifested subsequently.

5   The rose and fire being a male-female pair as in T. S. Eliot's *Four Quartets*.

6   Autozoon given to the Demiurge (Jove) by Rhea for him to make the world in the Crater (Juno). The shift from Monad to Dyad therefore is recapitulated by initiate in gap between Triad and Tetrad, Pure and Impure Creation. This can also be understood as the gap between The One and the Monad.

7   Morning star (Venus) as announcer of day, rising before the sun, so that spiritual realization symbolized by the sun is birth associated with morning star (Psalm 110:3); founder-hero Aeneas born of Venus. The morning star appears as the uraeus or third-eye/snake upon the brow of Atum in Egyptian mythology. Here Atum sent a light to find Shu and Tefnut in the darkness. Thus, at the dyadic level, him who goes to find that primal pair may return through the uraeus, born from the spiritual vision of Atum.

8   Ideally the Apocalyptic New Earth, Blake's Golgonooza-Allamanda-Bowlahoola, etc. The various images Northrop Frye presents as Apocalyptic in his *Anatomy of Criticism* (stone, temple, city, tree, lamb) are both the archetypal vision of the autozoon and their manifestation.

The Tetrad "reifies" the four modes present in the Triad: the *aham-idam* and *idam-aham* of Shaivism, which is triadic insofar as a mutual recognition occurs and produces a third as joy (the realization of *Ananda* between *Sat* and *Chit* which here manifests as the I-Thou relation); the subject (or consciousness) and object (or sentience) in their active and passive forms. Here we interpret the dyadic deities in Egyptian mythology as also present in the triad as active modes of masculine and feminine (the passive Geb in relation to active Tefnut and the passive Nut in relation to active Shu). This is consistent with Raphael Patai's considering the two parental and two filial Egyptian deities (respectively our dyadic and triadic levels), as the Hebrew Tetragrammaton, the four letters of which would then manifest at a lower level as the four corners of mundane reality. The "I" that identifies the "thou" as itself has a certain protagonism, corresponding to Los in Blake's Four Zoas, or Jove, so that the initiate is a "little Jove." In this sense the Tetrad is the epiphany of Isvara by representing a connection with the "trans-personal" Sadasiva. All levels are simultaneous, but this is the monad (*Sadasiva, aham-idam*) in awareness of the personal god *Isvara* (idam-aham). The "I" having realized unity with the Divine and relating to the Divine not only as a separate entity (*Isvara*).

The dual function of monarchy consisting of representing the divine to the human and the human to the divine may also be conceptualized in terms of the above, that is, the subject conditioning objectivity and the object conditioning subjectivity. The former is compactly diffuse whereas the latter is diffusely compact. These different syntheses correspond to the four-fold of active and passive subject and active and passive object. There is also clear evidence that these pre-historic social arrangements were already distinctly monarchical. As discussed, the monarch is a fifth term between the four corners.

We have here a metaphysics of complementarity. This also corresponds to Desmond's metaxology, which concords with traditional metaphysics in ways most idealist and dialectical theories do not. For Desmond, both terms of the dyad *equivocity-univocity* are allowed to differentiate internally, both self-determining and determining the other (as opposed to their reconciliation in Hegelian dialectic, where only univocity assimilates equivocity or, in the above terms, only *Shiva* includes *Shakti*, but *Shakti* does not condition *Shiva*).[147] This allows us to avoid what some authors approaching tradition have done, which is to assert Being by rejecting becoming, leading to a sort of metaphysics of misogyny in which the masculine principle is considered spiritually true and femininity is devalued (an error not unknown to medieval thinkers).

To distil this section: it was noted that femininity is both the substance and prior conception of manifest reality, Juno and Rhea, whereas masculinity is the constructor and prior conceiver, Jove and Saturn. Being

147   Desmond, *Desire, Dialectic, and Otherness: An Essay on Origins*, 141.

born aright, one matures properly and becomes a demiurge: being born from Rhea, one may grow up to court Juno, being a son of Saturn, one may become Jove. Femininity is engaged differently at different levels, in the manner appropriate to that level, as is masculinity.

To pervert the above is to rebel against life and the conditions necessary for life. To reject the multiform cosmos and to desire its homogenization is to rend the betrothed (Juno) and assail the mother goddess (Rhea), incorrectly expressing the unity of the monad (Rhea conjoined with Saturn) by rejecting the plurality born of the dyad (interplay of Juno with Jove). This misunderstands the monad because it construes it as a physical reality (immanentizing the eschaton, in Voegelin's terms), precisely rejecting its transcendent truth, consciousness (Saturn, the masculine), and only perceiving the objective (Rhea, who, without Saturn, cannot but be misperceived). This oedipal abomination is the psychodrama of cultural decline: refusal of maturity and monarchy, responsibility and rightful rule (Jove); rejection of difference and of heterosexuality (the male-female, Jove-Juno interaction), and; materialistic rejection of consciousness, accounting for subjectivity as, at most, an epiphenomenon (as if Rhea could exist without Saturn).

Quartering and Quintessence

One is quartered by having the four constituents of manifestation (four elements, four directions, four humors, etc.) removed, one perceives the transcendent, which contains these (the autozoon contains the idea of the four elements), and in bringing it back into manifestation, rediscovering/remaking manifestation according to one's vocation, one paradoxically discovers the autozoon already out there (in one's feminine counterpart, in the case of the male initiate: Jove brings the autozoon and discovers it is there already in Juno, as according to Proclus, Orpheus teaches these two are equal causes of the world, and both are caused by the First Parental Intellect—he brings it, she reveals it; he initiates her and she initiates him). Jesus resurrects and points the disciples to His Bride, the loving community, the Church.

According to an Indian myth, Brahma split into the first male and female, respectively Svayambhuva Manu and his consort Shatarupa, and the latter, in turn, split into four goddesses (Sarasvati, Gayatri, Savitri and Brahmani), associated with the four cardinal points.[148] Her husband developed four faces that he might gaze upon her beauty no matter what direction he turns towards. The first king or primordial Adam is thus at the center of the four cardinal directions, and the world is a woman. The story's romantic motif illustrates eroticism's capacity to awaken one.

Parallels with Egypt may be sought in the fact that both Ptah and Osiris are in some wise identified with the Djed. The Djed was a pillar

---

148   Kathiresan Ramachanderam, *The Sacred Texts: Mandukya Upanishad and Isha Upanishad.* (Bloomington, IN: Partridge Publishing, 2016).

of four horizontal planes intersected vertically and erected on occasion
of royal investitures and renewal ceremonies, from which the king fired
flaming arrows in the four cardinal directions.[149] Thusly does the Pharaoh's body or domain extend to the four corners, just as the gods of these
four directions sustain the risen Osiris according to the *Pyramid Texts*.[150]
He is therefore a fifth term centering the four corners. Guénon refers
to this in the context of the five-lettered name *Jesus*, which, according
to him, consists of the Tetragrammaton with the Hebrew letter "*shin*"
added to the middle.[151] This name would therefore express the four
arms of the cross and the sacred heart at its center.

Something similar is recounted in the *Devi Bhagavatam*. Goddess
Radha, consort to Lord Krishna, is described as the "fifth Shakti" (IX:1,
41–47).[152] We read, "This is the fifth Prakriti and She is denominated as
Râdhâ" (IX:1, 48–70).[153] The fourfold character of creation, the Tetrad,
the "Creator Brahma" or his creation, receives nourishment (primordial
water, the Ganga) by praising the Divine Feminine (IX:13, 108–13): "The
Creator Brahma, the Compiler of the Four *Vedas*, the Four-faced One
praised Radha with His Four heads…" [154]

This occurs in the context of a creation story involving dismemberment. In the *Devi Bhagavatam* (IX:13, 52–107), the gopis—shepherdess
lovers of Krishna—are divided, their parts being spread throughout
creation. After joining with Krishna they flee from Krishna's female
counterpart, Radha. Their flight takes them to different locations. Subsequently, out of the pain of separation, Krishna then divides them, their
parts going to various places, including sometimes Radha herself.[155] This
also occurs to Ganga (whose gives her name to the famous holy river in
India and who seems to be the watery substance that nourishes creation).
Ganga hides under Krishna's feet, causing water to retreat from creation,
but is forgiven by Radha when Brahma recalls that Ganga is the liquid
form of Radha and Krishna themselves, and teaches Ganga to worship
Radha, whereupon the waters are then used to create new worlds. Lord
Krishna speaks to the creator Brahma and Vishnu and Shiva (the creator,
preserver and destroyer):

> Ganga has taken refuge under My feet out of fear for Radha. Seeing
> Ganga by My side, Radha wanted to drink Her up, However I will

---

149   Hani, *Sacred Royalty*, 12–13.
150   *Pyramid Texts*, 464, cited in J. G. Griffiths, *The Origins of Osiris and His Cult*
(Leiden: Brill, 1980), 148.
151   René Guénon, *Miscellanea*, trans. F. Bethell and M. Schiff (Hillsdale, NY:
Sophia Perennis, 1976), 47.
152   The S'rimad Devi Bhagavatam, *One of the Upapuranas, devoted to the Devi (Goddess)*.
153   Ibid., 804.
154   Ibid., 861.
155   Ibid., 858–59.

give over Ganga to the hands of you all; but you will have to pray
to Radha, so that Ganga becomes fearless of Her. (IX:13, 108–13)[156]

Dismemberment is both the falling into created forms, scattering the
self's awareness into multiplicity, but also the means of creation, realizing
the true self and therefore seeing the macrocosm as one's body: Creation
as fall into ignorance and as initiatic return to knowledge. An initial
dismemberment results from perceiving the self as separate from the
Divine (Ganga as separate from Radha; the oscillating waters of creation
as separate from the quintessence, the essential self), and is resolved by
recalling unity, whereupon one experiences the self as universal and can
participate in the creation of worlds (Ganga goes on to produce new
worlds; the initiate participates in the neo-Platonic demiurgy).

Since "[e]very female in every Universe is sprung from a part of Sri
Radha, or part of a part" (*Devi Bhagavatam*, IX:1, 47–70),[157] the dismembered gopis who Krishna, out of the pain of separation, scatters
throughout the worlds, and Ganga, who participates in creation of worlds,
would seem to realize their true selves in Radha, no longer subject to Her
reproach, by way of dismemberment.

There is a Christ-like element here. Again, Krishna experiences the
pain of separation which leads Him to scatter the *gopis*. Their dismemberment is like a spiritual awakening, reminding them of the truth
of their selves in Radha and ending that pain of separation. Krishna's
experience of separation's pain is like Christ's passion, and just as Christ
says he has come to bring a sword and to divide, Krishna divides the *gopis*,
but it is a spiritual realization that is being bestowed. In the end, just
as the Christian is a member of the Church, Bride of Christ, Krishna
reconciles these individuated forms to His consort, Radha.

The King as Decad

We have mentioned the fifth element or quintessence (*quinta essentia*,
fifth essence), but the king is also presented as the tenth term after the
divine Ennead. The king not only recapitulates the immediately preceding
cause of the world (the tetrad or four elemental ideas) but also the subtler,
prior causes (the entire Ennead, including not only the tetrad but also the
monadic, dyadic and triadic principles), joining all of them and thereby
re-presenting their singular originating source. The morning sun (with
which the king is united post-Osirian descent) is "king of the Ennead":[158]

...the Ennead, a group of nine...Horus did not belong to the group.
He was the god who stood over against the other deities and thus

---

156   Ibid., 860–61.
157   Ibid., 804.
158   Jan Assman, *The Search for God in Ancient Egypt* (Ithaca: Cornell University
Press, 2001), 105.

the point from which the entirety was conceived. The starting
point was the king. He was the incarnation of the god Horus…[159]

The Ennead does not, then, include Horus, but begins with Atum, so
that in Horus (the king, fruit of Osiris's dismemberment, reconstitution
and seeding of Isis) the origin reifies itself in the midst of its creation.
The Egyptian Ennead is completed by a tenth term, like the Pythagorean
Tetractys or the *Sephirot* of the Kabbalistic tree of life. For this reason,
Uzdavinys considers the Tetractys as having Egyptian provenance.[160] The
notion that Pythagoreanism begins with Egyptian theology[161] enjoys
a long pedigree, appearing in Herodotus's *Histories*.[162] This contrasts
with Barker's tendency to see the origin of Pythagoreanism—including
the Tetractys—in the Hebrew prophets, a position which concords with
that Christian polemic that seems to assume eternal truths should be
limited to the strictures of a particular tradition (so that everything of
value must have been learnt from the prophets mentioned in the Bible)
and which conflates the transcendent (truth, mathematical disclosure)
and the immanent (a particular prophetic lineage).[163]

The Orthodox Christian expression of the principle of completion on
a tenth term appears in a previously quoted passage from Nikitas Stithatos: "God begins with the Monad and, as Decad, He completes Himself
through a cyclic movement."[164] This schema, with Christian precedent
in St. Dionysius the Areopagite,[165] views the human being (locus of
Incarnation) as the tenth term in which the preceding is completed.[166]

159   Ibid., 122.
160   Uzdavinys, *Philosophy as a Rite of Rebirth: From Ancient Egypt to Neoplatonism*, 59.
161   For an exploration of the origin of the Kabbalah as possibly rooted in Egypt,
developed in Greece and incorporated by Hebrew tradition, see: Kieren Barry,
Greek Qabalah: Alphabetical Mysticism and Numerology in the Ancient World (York, ME:
Weiser, 1999).
162   Herodotus, *Histories*, II.81. cited in Uzdavinys, *Philosophy as a Rite of Rebirth:
From Ancient Egypt to Neoplatonism*, 30. This is part of a general attribution of origins
to Egypt: Plutarch also considers Pythagoreanism as equivalent to the Egyptian
system, and even the Homeric verses so often cited by Pythagoreans in esoteric
exegeses are linked to Egypt, as in the legend, found in Heliodorus of Emesa's
Aethiopica, writing in the third or fourth century AD, that Homer was the son of
Hermes Trismegistus (born of a priest's wife as she slept in Thebes). Uzdavinys,
Philosophy as a Rite of Rebirth: From Ancient Egypt to Neoplatonism, 89.
163   Pharoah put Joseph in charge of Egypt (Genesis 41:40-41), and "Moses was
learned in all the wisdom of the Egyptians" (Acts 7:22). Not that the relationship
need be one-way. There may well have been Israelite influence on Egyptian learning, and enduring ties. The Bible does not at all present Egypt as consistently
antagonistic, and the opponents of Josian reform would eventually choose Egypt
as a place of refuge.
164   Nikitas Stithatos, *On Spiritual Knowledge, Love and the Perfection of Living: One
Hundred Texts*, 173:100, 252.
165   St. Nikodemos of the Holy Mountain and St. Makarios of Corinth (compilers),
Philokalia: The Complete Text, 253.
166   Ibid.

In terms of the purpose of there being multiple worlds and levels, if it is Minerva's veil from whose poetry the dress worn by Lady *Philosophia* in Boethius's *Consolation* is spun, then Minervic contrariety represents the opportunity to engage in a revelatory gradualism: subsequent disclosures[167] at each rung of nature's embroidery, as described by Boethius.[168] Duality, therefore, exists as a function of concealment, and concealment at one tier is revelation at the next. In these concentric epiphanies the divine plan reveals itself elegantly and by degrees, relative obfuscations constituting the parameters of play and an opportunity to venture. As the *Gospel of Philip* says: "Truth did not come into the world naked, but it came in types and images." Creation is adventure, the necessary fall into ignorance in order to attain the joy of discovery: "The eternal God eternally repeats the order of time: unfallen, fallen, and redeemed"[169] and yet, also, seeing the drama from the eternal vantage, all of that is redeemed.

It should be noted that the resulting schema is not pantheistic, but rather *panentheistic*. The cosmos is referred to as being subject to ordering, and is therefore changeable, meaning it cannot be the supreme identity. It is not a simple spatial extension of consciousness that is described. Conscious awareness does not merely annex new physical loci (such would represent a quantitative rather than qualitative change; awareness of more phenomena and not of what is more *than* phenomena). Rather, what is being indicated is awareness of the idea underlying spatial reality: the subjective modes that constitute types of outward manifestation (whose presence in specific physical locations is of necessity ever in flux). Realization is not merely of Shiva's body, but of that state in which "...Shiva does not confront any reality outside Himself, He has no body at all."[170] Supreme realization is not, then, the final rung on a ladder, although each rung may disclose it to a greater degree than the last.

THE DIVINE FEMININE AND POLITICAL POWER

The queen sees her husband's sacrifice through to good effect, like Isis recomposing and returning virility to Osiris, or the Vedic queen spending the night with the sacrificed horse that confirms her husband's rule.[171] In Tantrism, Shakti is Shiva's power, and is the light that anoints kings who become living icons of Shiva. The correlate is that these kings draw their power to rule, including the power to conquer, from the feminine (not from the mother, but from the consort, that is, not from femininity at the level of the higher pure-creation, in Shaivist terms, but as it

---

167 Boethius, *The Consolation of Philosophy*, trans. W. Cooper (Public Domain: Ex-Classics Project, 2009), V.4; 66.
168 Ibid., I.1: 8.
169 Pickstock, *After Writing: On the Liturgical Consummation of Philosophy*, 249.
170 Dcyzkowski, *The Doctrine of Vibration*, 141.
171 Thomas Gamkrelidze and Vjaceslav Ivanov, *Indo-European and the Indo-Europeans: A Reconstruction and Historical Analysis of a Proto-Language and Proto-Culture*, 402-3.

manifests lower down the scale of things, not from Rhea but from Juno).
As Gavin Flood writes, "[t]he erotic violence of the Goddess is contained
within the king and controlled through a political structure that is
scripturally and ritually legitimate,"[172] and "[t]he king is the analogue
of Kulesvara and his queen, from whom he derives power through sex,
the analogue of Kulesvari"—(Tantric deities)—"Power flows from her to
the king to the deities of the clan and so to the wider community."[173]
This reminds of the role of the Chinese Goddess Jiutian Xuannu, deity
of sex, war and longevity, who teaches the great Yellow Emperor in the
Xuannu Jing text. In the European context, John Waddell, exploring Celtic
and specifically Irish paganism, refers to "the goddess of sovereignty."[174]

In native African religion, the Asanti (Akan) people conceive of the
"divinely creative king and elder (Nyame, or Sky-God)" whose anointing
union to a king and elder (Nana) Joseph B. Danquah proposes in his
The Akan Doctrine of God: "...the speculative effort to connect the Asanti
'Jehovah' with the Golden Stool as the sacramental covenant between
deified nana and the Deity Himself...."[175] The Golden Stool being an
altar to the Sky-God.[176] There "is the idea of a Nana"—king—"standing
between the heaven god and mortal men and pleasing for them or serving
as an exemplar...and...the conception of the Nana as originally feminine,
or at least female under the name *Nana*...." In addition, among Akan
peoples the right to rule was apparently traditionally matrilineal. We
are also reminded of the 13th century Chinese traveler to Angor Wat
in Cambodia, Zhou Daguan, who writes that the king of that splendid
Khmer palatial complex would every night sleep with a magical nine-
headed naga (snake person) at the top of his tower, and that should he
fail to do so, it bodes badly for the kingdom.[177]

Incan tradition also considered the female regent as necessary to
political power. There is the male Inca and the female Kolla. We have
also the Iniakas, the female representatives of the various regions of
the Incan state, like the 72 virgins in Islam who match the 72 nations

---

172   Flood, *The Tantric Body: The Secret Tradition of Hindu Religion*, 78.
173   Ibid., 79.
174   John Waddell, *Archeology and Celtic Myth: An Exploration* (Portland, OR: Four
Courts Press, 2014), 110.
175   J. B. Danquah, *The Akan Doctrine of God: A Fragment of Gold* (London: Routledge, 2006), 8.
176   A holy stool that came down to the first Asanti emperor Osei Tutu, after
his establishment of the empire, by means of the magic of his companion Okomfo
Anokye.
177   I cite this as yet another example of linking sovereignty to femininity, which
does not refute the idea that the consorting of human with non-human was a
practice in need of ending by religious reform or a new dispensation. Certainly, it
is entirely incompatible with Christianity and Islam. The naga princess in this case
might represent the deific feminine as such, or an alliance of human with spiritual
entity. The latter seems likely.

of Genesis in number, or the daughters of Jerusalem who provide the chorus to king Solomon's congress with Queen Sheba. Historian Maritza Villavicencio and others distinguish between the Incan figures of Mama Ocllo and Mama Waco. She suggests Mama Ocllo was the wife of Tupac Yupanki and mother of Uaina Kapac, the second to last Inca monarch. The earlier, foundational queen would be Mama Waco, a semi-mythical matriarch and wife of Manco Kapac.[178] These would be the most significant women in Incan political history: the founder of the state and the expander of the empire.

Divine femininity as politically empowerment relates to the recurrence of solar goddesses. Maidens related to the sun are often the origin of royalty, and failing to court them results in botched political career, as for Jason and his mistreatment of Medea, daughter of Helios. Just as Japanese emperorship descends from the sun goddess Amaterasu, the Roman Emperor descends from the Trojan hero Aeneas, who married the Latin princess Lavinia, great-granddaughter of Sol Indiges, the archaic Italic sun cult deity to which the later Sol Invictus cult harkens back. Waddell sees "[m]ythological associations" linking "sacral kingship, a sovereignty goddess, solar cosmology and a perception of the Otherworld" in Irish literature as explicating the symbolism of certain archaeological finds.[179] The Amazonian Tukano tribe relate their ancient arrival to the Amazon as being led by the *daughter of the sun* and the *helmsman* who steered a boat with the tribe's ancestors, whereupon they received civilizing instruction and Ayahuasca. The daughter of the sun and the helmsman remind of Lavinia and Aeneas. Again, political agency and civilizational enterprising are connected to a solar or radiant woman across traditions.

The relationship between kingship, the divine feminine, and political power, holds true in near eastern mythology and monarchy as well:

> Just as Anat sustained the ordered world by helping Ba'al to overthrow the gods of the unruly waters and of drought, so she sustained it by defeating and slaughtering the enemies of whatever state was worshiping her. It was not for nothing that in Egypt her cult was observed by the warrior pharaohs of the nineteenth dynasty, or that Ramses II named his sword "Anat is victorious." Anat was in fact a western counterpart of the Mesopotamian goddess of victory Inanna/Ishtar.[180]

---

178   The Aimara historian and political militant Felipe Quispe Huanca suggests husband and wife as a political unit lasting into the modern era, pointing to the importance of the wives of latter day indigenous leaders, such as Tupac Amaru's wife Micaela Bastida and Tupac Katari's wife Bartolina Sisa. Pedro Portugal and Carlos Macusaya, *El Indianismo Katarista: Un Analisis Critico* (Buenos Aires: Fundación Friedrich Ebert, 2016), 557–58.

179   Waddell, *Archeology and Celtic Myth*, xii–xiii.

180   Cohn, *Cosmos, Chaos and the World to Come: The Ancient Roots of Apocalyptic Faith*, 127–28.

In perfect conformity to the Tantric rite described by Gavin Flood, the king of Mesopotamia is linked to the goddess Inanna, whose body was thought to be the entire cosmos, and has ritual intercourse with her high priestess.[181]

This sometimes is expressed in terms of the conjunction of sun and moon, a ubiquitous alchemical symbolism, representing the joining of the masculine and feminine, which constitutes the initiatic meaning and sacred foundation of Cretan rite of the solar bull Jove joining the lunar Europa. As Parmenides puts it in *On Nature* (XII), during a passage that reminds us of Rhea giving Jove the cosmic plan for him to penetrate Juno with it:

> ...the divinity that directs the course of all things; for she rules over all painful birth and all begetting, driving the female to the embrace of the male, and the male to that of the female.[182]

In *The Body of God: An Emperor's Palace for Krishna in Eighth Century Kanchipuram* D. Dennis Hudson writes about the panels on the end of the southern sequence of a graven depiction:

> The analogy of the king to Emusha the Boar and his realm to Earth, and Varuna's address to Earth as his mother, reveal four ideas about kingship in the rajasuya:
>   1) The king's realm is his wife, and his subjects their progeny;
>   2) a brutish king may tear apart his realm;
>   3) a realm may "shake off" a brutish king;
>   4) the king's realm is his mother.[183]

The ambiguity between the first and fourth points here can be cleared up with recourse to our previous discussion: the realm is body and bride of the king, his kingship derives from his rebirth from a prior hypostasis, which can be understood as the soul of manifest creation, of the world itself, and even prior to that. But to make the epiphany of that prior relevant to the world he must bring it in, making his being one with the realm of worldly things, represented by the queen consort.

The sexual formula of kingship becomes explicit in the Tamil poem *Netunalvatai*, which presents a royal bedchamber sacrament: "Inside the house of the Pandya king there stood another *house*," an apt description for the holy of holies, "in which... the territory of his kingdom as a person was present," this refers to the king's consort, the queen, who, in being *his kingdom as a person*, reminds again of the Christian Church, in

181   Samuel Noah Kramer, *The Sacred Marriage Rite* (Bloomington, IN: Indiana University Press, 1970).
182   Parmenides, "On Nature." In: *Parmenides and the Way of Truth*, trans. and commentator R. Geldard (Rhinebeck, NY: Monkfish Book Publishing Company, 2007), 50.
183   Dennis Hudson, *The Body of God: An Emperor's Palace for Krishna in Eighth Century Kanchipuram* (Oxford: Oxford University Press, 2008), 245.

which the body of believers, Christ's kingdom, is also His bride. The poem continues: "This house...like the inner sanctum, the womb-house of the Hindu temple...was a bedroom...the bed is the round Vedic fire altar that symbolizes the earth and the queen the Vedic fire..."[184] That this space should represent flame and womb is consistent with the Egyptian lake of fire, the Duat, as Nut's womb, the volcanic Crater as Juno mother of souls, and the flaming holy of holies as mother of the sons of God. Further, the Tantric king of the tradition to which this poem belongs conquers the four cardinal directions by performing this fire sacrifice before walking the perimeter of his domain.[185] The only discrepancy with respect to prior accounts is that here the central fire is round and not rectilinear. There are examples from India of the temple, site of religious devotion, being presented as a sexual union as well: "A stone inscription of thirty Sanskrit verses composed in the late twelfth century speaks of the earth, the sky, and a temple in terms of human erotic love."[186]

Political power relates to sex because both exhibit porosity, human relatedness. This is an end, not just means, as Vaishnavism makes clear with its doctrine of fully liberated spiritual states in which one remains in relation to God—having realized the true Self is God, one chooses to *encounter* it. Consciousness continues to exist in individuated states representing the whole in themselves and relating to the whole or that which is beyond the whole (God) as an *other*, which must be done symbolically, for that *beyond* is not itself a form.

The Duality of Femininity

The feminine seems to be the personality of formal manifestation. Such is explicit in the Tantric Shaivist understanding of Shakti as counterpart and means of manifestation for Shiva.[187] She is the "vibration or pulse of consciousness"[188] of which all forms are moments. The symbol of the veil stands for the weaving of mortal life, yet also for the state of relative ignorance inherent in such an existence (a figurative veiling, for cloaks necessarily occlude). Shakti can receive either the prefix Vidya or Avidya, with the first referring to the capacity to lead towards knowledge and the second to the ability to cause ignorance.[189] Equivalent names for Shakti are "Nibodhika and Nirodhika" where "[t]he first means the Giver of Knowledge, and the second That which obstructs," as Sir John

184   David G. White, *Tantra in Practice* (Delhi: Motilal Banarsidass Publishing, 2001), 27-28.
185   Ibid., 25.
186   Vidya Dehejia, *The Body Adorned: Sacred and Profane in Indian Art* (New York: Columbia University Press, 2009), 6.
187   Dcyzkowski, *The Doctrine of Vibration*, 99.
188   Ibid., 21.
189   Swami Narayanananda, *The Primal Power in Man, or The Kundalini Shakti* (Rishikesh, India: Messrs N. K. Prasad and Company, 1990), 41.

Woodroffe (pseudonym Arthur Avalon) notes.[190] Consistent with this, Proclus describes the veil of Minerva as "the last image of the whole contrariety of things."[191] Minervic duality is highlighted in Plato's *Cratylus*[192] when Socrates reminds his interlocutor that the goddess has two names after being questioned as regards her nature. She is identified as "cause of both" war and wisdom[193] by Iamblichus, an association which Proclus bolsters in observing that "[t]he theologians praise two powers...of our lady [Minerva]...[t]his is why in the Timaeus Plato analogously praises [Minerva] as both a 'lover of war' and a 'love of wisdom.'"[194] In Blake's poetry, Vala, the shadow of Jerusalem, the Divine Feminine, can likewise be of both "vegetated" and "animated" or "sweet reposing" disposition.

From Bernardus Sylvestris to Ficino and C. S. Lewis, the goddess Venus is often presented as likewise including both an earthly and carnal avatar and as being Heavenly and archetypal. Ficino describes these as *Venus naturalis* and *Venus coelistis*. In the Bible, the title "morning star," which refers to the planet Venus, is both the fallenness of spiritual ignorance, more specifically, pride, in Isaiah (14:12) and a title for Christ Himself (Apocalypse 22:16) as well as that which Christ bestows on the saints (Apocalypse 2:25–29) and the spiritual truth that dawns in the hearts of the faithful (2 Peter 1:19).

Why this dually inclined character should constitute itself into a quadrangular space (Nut's body containing the rectangular Duat; Juno as the Crater combining the four elements; the Shekinah as the cuboidal holy of holies) is perhaps clarified with further recourse to the Indian tradition: "The shape of the *vatsu* for Gods and Brahmanas is prescribed as square"[195] and the fire-altar in a Hindu temple "is spoken of as the womb, and its cube holds the entire manifested universe"[196] because "[t]he square, form of finality, is at the same time that of the pairs of opposites; manifestation is only through the pairs of contraries and in their balance lies the perfection of the square," thusly can it be described as the square throne of divinity.[197] Rectitude represents finality for Iamblichus as well, and is likewise the basis of form and creation. This, again, provides a rationale for this symbol's recurrence.

---

190   Arthur Avalon (John George Woodroffe), *The Serpent Power* (Glastonbury, UK: The Lost Library, 1919), 183.

191   Proclus, *The Commentary on Plato's Timaeus*, I; 113.

192   Plato, *Cratylus*, C. D. C. Reeve, trans. In: *Complete Works*, ed. J. Cooper (Indianapolis, IN: Hackett Publishing Company, 1997), 124–25.

193   Iamblichus, *Commentary on Plato's Timaeus*, I:21, 125.

194   Proclus, *Commentary on Plato's Cratylus*, trans. Brian Duvick (London: Bloomsbury Publishing, 2007), 107.

195   *Mayamata*, III:1, cited by Stella Kramrisch and Raymond Burnier, *The Hindu Temple*, vol. 1 (Delhi, India: Motilal Banarsidass Publishers, 1976), 22.

196   Stella Kramrisch and Raymond Burnier, *The Hindu Temple*, vol. 1, 26–27.

197   Ibid., 43.

Its duality may be understood in terms of the world-soul itself tending towards order while the grosser portion of its own being (the body as opposed to the soul) is entropic, or as being orderly due to its being under Demiurgic tutelage while also preserving the chaotic bent described by Plato[198] as belonging to the Receptacle upon which it is founded (Juno before being elevated to the fountain of her own nature,[199] in Proclean terms). The link between Plato's Receptacle and Sophia comes through in the Sophiologists' description of the latter as a looking glass or "mirror of the divinity,"[200] a mirror being eminently receptive.

It is thus capable both of rebelling against, and of submitting to, higher designs, becoming obscure or diaphanous. Vladimir Solovyov,[201] discussing the world-soul, a lower octave, as it were, of Sophia, provides a similar account of her dual temperament.[202] The "earthly and the heavenly aspects of Sophia" appear also in the work of other theologians, including that of Sergei Bulgakov,[203] where one proceeds from the other: "...the radiation of the energies of the creaturely Sophia from the darkness of the transcendental unfathomability of the divine Ousia-Sophia."[204] The creaturely and transcendental divine feminine Wisdom are, respectively, Juno and Rhea in the neo-Platonic theology of Iamblichus and Proclus.

Bulgakov emphasizes the multiplicity of the feminine, her agency as one of externalizing a diverse creation. In the above citation, he uses the word "energies" in terms of St. Gregory Palamas's theology, according to which the divinized Christian is united to and transformed by God's uncreated energies, a Divine plurality which is at one with God yet is the basis for creation's diversity (similar to the ninety-nine names of Allah in the Islamic tradition). During my interview with Gavin Flood[205] he summarized the Tantric view of oneness with God and the role of the feminine Shakti in terms strikingly similar to those of Palamas and

198   Plato, *Timaeus*, 30a, 93.

199   Proclus, *The Commentary on Plato's Timaeus*, II; 344.

200   J. Martin Newsome, "True and Truer Gnosis: The Revelation of the Sophianic in Hans Urs von Balthasar." In: Michael Martin, *The Heavenly Country: An Anthology of Primary Sources, Poetry, and Critical Essays on Sophiology* (Kettering, OH: Angelico Press/ Sophia Perennis, 2016), 347–48.

201   Solovyov may be treated as in some wise heir to Iamblichus and Proclus, given his significant ideational continuity with St. Dionysius the Areopagite: John Milbank, "Sophiology and Theurgy: The New Theological Horizon." In: Adrian Pabst and Christoph Schneider (eds.), *Encounter Between Eastern Orthodoxy and Radical Orthodoxy: Transfiguring the World through the Word* (Farnham: Ashgate Publishing Company, 2009), 78. For the similarities between St. Dionysius and these neo-Platonists: Gregory Shaw, "Neoplatonic Theurgy and Dionysius the Areopagite." *Journal of Early Christian Studies* 7(4) (1999): 573–99.

202   Vladimir Solovyov and Judith Deutsch-Kornblatt, *Divine Sophia: The Wisdom Writings of Vladimir Solovyov* (Ithaca, NY: Cornell University Press, 2009), 114.

203   Martin, *The Heavenly Country*, 112.

204   Bulgakov, *The Bride of the Lamb*, 63.

205   Oxford University Professor of Comparative Religion and Hindu Studies.

Bulgakov, as a "participation in the energies of the Divine, in the Saktis of God."[206] One realizes spiritual autonomy from the body and matter, yet thereby accesses the energies which are God's agency and from which the body and matter congealed, so that paradoxically one is in greater communion with the body. Distance from a thing often permits the sort of perspective needed to understand it holistically. This provides a rationale for the doctrine of resurrection, the proper alignment of world and bodily existence, which in the Bible often appears linked to God's Wisdom.[207]

---

206   Gavin Flood, "Interview with Carlos Perona," 16th April 2018.

207   Some might object to discussing Palamas in line with Pythagorean-Platonism. In Metochites we begin to see the misreading of Plato that makes philosophy a rationalistic alternative to religion rather than experiential theurgy. There is also an early naturalistic, pantheistic reading of Platonism in which god and the universe are the same, falling afoul of the kind of essence-energy distinction found in Palamas (true, in Proclus there is no real such distinction, but this might be an issue of emphasis). Thus, in *Radical Platonism in Byzantium*, Nikitas Siniossoglou contrasts Metochites to St. Dionysius the Areopagite and Gregory Palamas (*Radical Platonism in Byzantium: Illumination and Utopia in Gemistos Plethon* [Cambridge Classical Studies: Cambridge University Press, 2016], 91–92). The Hesychastic attempt to recreate the transfiguration at mount Tabor may be considered the Christian equivalent to the initiatory configuration we have been discussing, given the feminine and motherly presence (explicit in the Gospel according to Hebrews), radiance and mountain-theme. Hesychasm would then be an initiation in line with multiple traditions. Indeed, its navel-gazing meditation, described disapprovingly by Barlaam of Calabria, is similar to Taoist breathwork—sometimes called embryonic breathing—and much of Hesychasm seems in line with the Eleusinian mysteries (Siniossoglou, *Radical Platonism in Byzantium*, 94). It is interesting, therefore, that Barlaam attacks Hesychasm precisely from a position favorable to Greek philosophy. The actual contention, in any case, was probably one of language, with some serious pantheistic error on the pagan side and the occasional dualist on the Christian side. Indeed, Gemistos Plethon, arch-representative of the pagan revival in Byzantium, actually omits reference to grace in his *Nomoi* (Siniossoglou, 157). Overall, the fact that revivals of paganism tended towards naturalism, pantheism and rationalism, in opposition to actual theurgic, initiatic practice and experience, serves to illustrate the point that rediscovering the Pythagorean-Platonic tradition is best done through Christianity, not against it. To shore up the contention that the real conflict is one of language, and that there is nothing anti-Platonic in Palamas (misunderstandings of Platonism notwithstanding) we may attend to David Bentley Hart:

> "I am not at all convinced that Palamas ever intended to suggest a *real* distinction between God's essence and energies; nor am I even confident that the energies should be seen as anything other than sanctifying grace by which the Holy Spirit makes the Trinity really present to creatures. I take the distinction to mean only that God's transcendence is such that he is free to be the God he is even in the realm of creaturely finitude, without estrangement from himself and without the creature being admitted thus to an unmediated vision of the divine essence." David B. Hart, *The Beauty of the Infinite: The Aesthetics of Christian Truth* (New York, NY: Eerdmans, 2004), 204, footnote 74.

Like traditional Sunni Muslims, therefore, we simply draw a veil over conflicts between honored members of the *Sahabah*, and treat Platonists and Palamas as getting at the same thing.

Sophia vouchsafes the material, the concreteness of the mineral, the carnality of the animal and human kingdoms, as trophies for Heaven. This comes through in the way theologian-poets observant of her have represented a current against *pure nature* theology, that is, against the idea that a nature entirely outside the super-nature of the Divine can exist, the idea that something can be incapable of salvation but capable of subsistence without God.[208] Thusly is femininity associated with the material cosmos: both with its substance (its veiled form) and with its design or the origin of its design (behind the veil). In the Platonism of Iamblichus and Proclus the former is Juno and the latter Rhea.

A slight digression on the issue of the initiate realizing himself as Jove: this can be lost sight of in those occultist systems that present the feminine lover as whore rather than maiden, putting forward an esotericism of prostitution and considering the orgy rather than the marital bedchamber to be the locus of erotic epiphany. We can think of the consort embracing all forms of her lover. But the doctrine of virginity and marital privacy conveys that the feminine only ever joins herself to the same consort, for the initiate is only an initiate in his having de-personalized and accomplished himself as the Demiurge, and insofar as his realization is new (ever-new, ever-renewing) so is her becoming conjoined to him, so that she is ever his virgin (the virginity of the mother is distinct from this, and has to do with her never being tarnished by a fall from immediate apprehension of Divine reality, giving birth by virtue of that ever-pure contemplation). Insofar as he is at all able to interact with Shakti, he is Shiva. Again: "Bridegrooms and brides belong to the bridal chamber. No one shall be able to see the bridegroom with the bride unless he becomes such a one" (*Gospel of Philip*[209]).

Whatever in him remains the unregenerate past, peculiar, petty self, cannot touch Shakti. Thusly does radical antinomianism risk falling below rather than rising above the strictures it transgresses. In this regard, traditional, conservative morality presents a true image of metaphysical reality.

The Duality of Kingship

Henceforth, during a yearly rite of sacrifice, the king and queen will dispense with their purple robe, a product of cotton or silk and rare pigments, of arduous and specialized agriculture and trade, to don instead the simple raiment of an animal's hide, the basic cloth won by hunt, for they rule the sedentary city and also the hunting party, the two modes between which humanity oscillated by seasons in remote antiquity. Donning their animal skins, the robes of the hunter, of the barbarian, of the mysteries outside the circle of human civility, they sacrifice one or several animals,

---

208 Martin, *The Submerged Reality.*
209 *The Gospel of Philip*, 82:7–83:2, 207.

to have their hides, hoofs, organs and meat distributed widely, and each year the king will die with that animal, like the yearly wounding of the Mesopotamian god Tammuz, refreshing his vision of the great beyond on the other side of ritual death, reconfirming his mission as king with his consort, like the annual enthronement of Jove at Mount Ida.

A duality of role is inherent in the king's identification with universal patterns in both their universality and locality (the specific realm he presides over), for these entail a mediation, like a golden ratio's middle term (John 20:21), between cosmos and kingdom, Heavenly choir and human congregation. This is represented, for example, in the two heads of Janus whose honorific month of January was, according to Plutarch, installed in the Roman Calendar by Rome's Pythagorean initiate-king Numa Pompilius.[210] Janus was appropriately adopted, according to Jean Hani, to depict Jesus and the two natures of the Christ in certain early iconography.[211] It is the basis for the medieval doctrine of the king's two bodies, as Ernst Kantorowicz presents it, noting its pre-medieval, Biblical and Pythagorean, parallels.[212] Without a proper understanding of organic differentiation, this doctrine could flatten into emphasizing mere grandeur in some depthless sense, justifying monarchical absolutism[213] (*corruptio optimi pessima*).

According to John Alvis, through tragic loss and thwarting of ambition, in the Iliad Achilles discovers the human condition as neither animal nor divine, but a middle way.[214] The subject is neither a pure archetype of this or that sort but a microcosm containing all archetypes, all the gods, and not subject to them. His very body is a place in which to practice, a blessing, for by way of it, spiritual awakening can be achieved, as Indian systems teach.

This yearly return to the primeval womb of smoldering sacred mountain, death and rebirth, is seasonally enacted by the winter solstice. The progression from shortening to elongating days: The chthonic sun and celestial Tartarus of Greek tradition the infernality of a central fire revealed to be anything but; Apollo's midnight sun of the north (counterpoint to midday's southerly arc as seen from north of the equator) preceding dawn's kingly rebirth; the worshipful hearth of winter in which fire is scarce, familiar, guarded, gathered and un-promiscuous, turned into a furnace for experimenting and affecting change, consuming and rekindling, the oven of alchemy. The hearth coincides with the symbol of the forge to represent fabrication (with its Faustian danger, should creativity become a merely willful enterprise) and the process of change

---

210   Plutarch, *Lives*, Bernadotte Perrin trans. (Cambridge, MA: Harvard University Press, 1914), Numa:18; 367–68.
211   Hani, *Sacred Royalty*, 129.
212   Kantorowicz, *The King's Two Bodies*, 499–500.
213   Ibid., 499.
214   Alvis, 61.

(a sort of yearly re-incubation in the heated shelter) before winter's end and nature's rebirth.

Just as Jove can be assimilated into Apollo, being the white sun-bull of Cretan myth, so too Odin—whom it is difficult not to associated with Christmas—becomes a fire deity as master of *wut* (root of the name Wotan, presumably), the sacral heat and religious furor (and fire). *Wotan, id est furor*, in the words of Adam von Bremen (quoted by Mircea Eliade).[215] The link between storm god (Jove, Odin) and metallurgy occurs in Ezekiel's vision of a cloud from the north whose center is as molted or heated metal (Ezekiel 1:4). We could also cite Juno, the Demiurge's Receptacle, as cosmic forge, indicating a metallurgic dimension to Jove, like Thor as storm god who carries a hammer. This would be why "the conception of stone and metal skies was common to the Indo-Europeans."[216]

The cuboidal central fire of Biblical scripture evoking a forge and paralleling the four-cornered fiery underworld whence ordeal leads to rebirth in mythologies like the Egyptian, European folk-stories of Christ as forge-master rejuvenating mortals in his furnace,[217] and the Hermetic interpretation of the crucifixion's titular INRI as "Ignis Natura Renovatur Integram" (*nature is integrally renewed by fire*) all identify the rended-and-renewed, burnt-and-born initiate with the solar-fire. The Christmas hearth is the Hermetic forge. It is there that the initiate travels, for he goes to the center of his being, and of Being generally. The initiatic journey ultimately enters into that fire which is the Empyrean beyond the seven heavens, and which Dante observes in the Divine Comedy presents him with a sense of going deeper rather than higher up as had been his perception when scaling the spheres. The Pythagorean central fire, which is Hestia, the most ancient goddess according to Proclus's commentary on Plato's Cratylus.

Today the king wears a hide. He is the sacrificial animal. Today he enters in by sacred water, the place of purity, and offers up sacrifice, for only the sacrificed should sacrifice. Once a year, on a day like today, he remembers the epiphany of the beyond, losing his body to holy fire and altar, to return again renewed by that transcendent vista.

It is like the medieval knight who slays the dragon but keeps with him its tooth around his neck or skin about his back. He takes on the animalistic and the terrible, defeating it, becoming it, rendering it an accessory to the human. The king is Siegfried slaying the dragon and drinking its blood. He is the champion of Apollo, first dragon slayer according to the Homeric hymn to Apollo, getting his solar character

---

215   Mircea Eliade, *The Forge and the Crucible: The Origins and Structure of Alchemy*, trans. S. Corrin (Chicago: The University of Chicago Press, 1978), 106.
216   Ibid., 201.
217   C. M. Edsman, *Ignis Divinus: Le Feu comme moyen de rajeunissement et d'immortalité: Contes, légendes, mythes et rites* (Lund: C. W. K. Gleerup, 1949), 40, 82. Cited by Eliade, *The Forge and the Crucible*, 107.

from the ordeal, for it is the down-bearing heat of Helios, the sun, that consumes the remains of the monster. We have here a solar king defeating chthonic snake-like powers, but keeping their vapors of the deep to inspire his serpentine oracle Pythia, named after the Python. Here Apollo faces a dragon, and was led there by a duplicitous nymph who wanted to steer him away from her shrine at Parnassus, being jealous of the god. Yet Apollo ultimately speaks his truths through a female oracle and therefore is reconciled to the feminine, just as Juno tried to thwart his birth by causing people to reject the pregnant mother of the god, Leto, a wandering and scorned woman in search of a place to birth her divine son, like a Marian figure anticipating the Gospel. The undulations of life, of the snake, are conquered and taken up, placed vertical on a wooden stake as Moses did, made into the nature of the higher agent who integrates them, as Meister Eckhart would say.

The recurring duality of monarchical symbolism in Bronze and Iron Age states may be related to these two modes of social organization. In the case of the Bronze Age, kings and queens alternated royal robes with animal skins, wearing the latter during priestly ceremonies, themselves being the high priests (as mentioned already in the context of Nano Marinatos's exploration of Cretan ceremonial). The king is both civilized and possesses that "liminality"[218] represented by animal skins manifest in Enkidu's wilderness existence when described in the Epic of Gilgamesh as wearing a lion's skin, as does Gilgamesh when he journeys to the underworld, also developing his own body hair like an animal, for the skin is associated with the bestial creature it came from and with its death. It is animality and death, placing one between these and human civility and life.

Thus, the monarch has a dual function corresponding to different raiment in which one function is associated with the animal and requires less refinement (perhaps the shepherd or hunter) and the other to the farmer and to more refinement (the difficulty of producing purple pigments for royal robes belongs to the sphere of cultivators). Mehmet Ali-Atac refers to the Babylonian Khorsabad palace depictions of Sargon II as being somewhat ambiguous in terms of whether they are portraying a sacrifice or a hunt.[219] The two are one to the monarch, where sacrifice brings wilderness into civilization, hunt into the temple.

Consider that the mind interprets magenta color as corresponding with green: if green light is shone upon an object, its shadow seems purple to us, and when we shine two lights on the same surface, perhaps using light pointers, one red and one yellow, we perceive magenta, not green, although green is in between those two on the light spectrum.

---

218   Mehmet-Ali Ataç, *The Mythology of Kingship in Neo-Assyrian Art* (Cambridge/ New York: Cambridge University Press, 2010), 43.
219   Ibid., 51.

The mind interprets the space green occupies as magenta, so to speak. This is unlike what occurs when we shine a green and red light together, which results in our perceiving yellow. The human brain, then, associates magenta with green. Goethe made this point in his theory of colors. It illustrates that royalty, associated with purple, is a corresponding reality to nature, associated with green. It is the human completion or complementation of nature.

We have here the lyre and the whip of the Homeric hymn to Hermes. In the Homeric hymn to Hermes, Hermes appears as a Promethean figure, for he is both thief and the first to make fire. His becoming reconciled to his brother Apollo and made of one mind with him by their father Jove is like Prometheus's liberation by Hercules. The fire-maker and the sun god become united. The celestial, contemplative and the dynamic earthly, potentially dangerous, fires, which are of one substance, become aligned. The ecstatic character of Hermes, playing a song on his lyre that captivates Apollo and that brings wisdom to those who hear it if they experience it joyfully rather than seeking hard-work and drudgery (a Tantric polemic), makes Hermes a Dionysian figure as well, so that this reconciliation is also between the Apollonian and Dionysian cultural forms, as Nietzsche saw it.

Finally, that the fire-maker is redeemed and forgiven for his initial transgression (theft) against Apollo also corresponds to Biblical language concerning the similarly named light-maker, Lucifer. Images associated with Lucifer, including the morning star (Venus) are also used to describe Christ and Heaven's mandate, as is also the case in the Holy Grail story, where the Grail is found and used to good effect, as the cup that collected the blood of Jesus upon the cross, like a Sacred Heart, even though it is, in some versions, made with a jewel that fell from Lucifer's crown as that angel fell.

In the end, Hermes delights Apollo with his song and the lyre he gifts, and Apollo in turn gives Hermes his whip to hold power over cattle, legitimizing his sacrifice of the solar beasts. Just as the barbarian gives the civilized state his vital creativity and the latter gives the barbarian refined technology, so too the initiate evokes religious epiphany through poetic mania and gives the spiritual depths a medium to manifest through himself, and those depths in turn allow him self-mastery and right action in the world.

The duality of monarchy is also the transcendent and the imminent, like Jove receiving protection from his mother Rhea and Jove uniting to his wife Juno. The beyond and the world are also represented in the king, who has his transcendent vision of the autozoon, and the queen, who is the cosmos into which that vision enters. The king and queen were both priestly officiators in Bronze Age cultures like that of Crete, and Holy Roman Emperors were generally anointed by popes along with their wives, who were Empresses.

Desmond's "packed suggestion of infinity" and the artwork's tension of centripetal and centrifugal power, occurs culturally in the contrast between the free outburst of tribal nomadism and the contained refinement of cities. As David Graeber and David Wengrow write, there is evidence that humanity knew these two organizational behaviors as seasonal modalities:

> Anthropologists describe societies of this sort as possessing a "double morphology." Marcel Mauss, writing in the early twentieth century, observed that the circumpolar Inuit, "and likewise many other societies ... have two social structures, one in summer and one in winter, and that in parallel they have two systems of law and religion."

Thus Inuits "dispersed into small patriarchal bands in pursuit of freshwater fish, caribou, and reindeer, each under the authority of a single male elder" during the summer, when "[p]roperty was possessively marked and patriarchs exercised coercive, sometimes even tyrannical power over their kin" but then,

> ...in the long winter months, when seals and walrus flocked to the Arctic shore, another social structure entirely took over as Inuit gathered together to build great meeting houses of wood, whale-rib, and stone. Within them, the virtues of equality, altruism, and collective life prevailed...

The same is described in the context of other native Americans, though sometimes swapping mode and seasons.

> Within the same population, one could live sometimes in what looks, from a distance, like a band, sometimes a tribe, and sometimes a society with many of the features we now identify with states. With such institutional flexibility comes the capacity to step outside the boundaries of any given social structure and reflect; to both make and unmake the political worlds we live in. If nothing else, this explains the "princes" and "princesses" of the last Ice Age, who appear to show up, in such magnificent isolation, like characters in some kind of fairy-tale or costume drama. Maybe they were almost literally so. If they reigned at all, then perhaps it was, like the kings and queens of Stonehenge, just for a season.[220]

This allows for greater sensitivity to the contingent nature of the features cloaking the central office as reflective of the absent center and, indeed, of every office, as well as establishing a balance and mutual receptivity between masculine and feminine.

---

220   David Graeber and David Wengrow, *How to Change the Course of Human History (at least, the part that's already happened)*. https://www.eurozine.com/change-course -human-history/.

Anthropological research, therefore, furnishes us with a holistic basis for synthesizing barbarity and civility, hunter and farmer. It is the ideal of the seasonal shift between nomadism and sedentarism and the later Bronze Age king who wears his robe when ruling and his animal skin when sacrificing, literally inhabiting both modes of human community. Neither is anti-state or anti-king (it would be absurd to think so, since we have evidence for kingship even in the remote past among nomadic bands). Yet the barbaric or hunter ideal is not concerned with day-to-day administration or the dispensing of justice. It is a general religious sacrifice, a jubilee involving all the community, just as all must eat of the meat the hunter brings back. It is a priestly role, which is paradoxical to the modern mentality since the warrior or hunter is often thought of as opposite to the priest.

Knowing that in the remote past peoples shifted between nomadism and the polis, and that more recently kings wore both robe and animal skin, however, we can view the imperial or statist structure as drawing from or emanating out of that simpler office of hunter-priest, dropping conceptual opposition.

This suggests an interpretation of the Genesis story of Cain and Abel, where Abel is a priest figure, favored by the Lord, as well as being a shepherd involved in the slaughter of animals, compared to his agricultural and jealous brother Cain. It should be remembered, however, that in Biblical narrative, the chosen people do not descend from Abel rather than Cain, but from neither of these, their father being a third brother, Seth, perhaps indicating a synthesis or an office beyond opposition. The barbaric hunter-priest is apolitical in the sense that the priest or hunter hearkens to the band of nomads rather than to the settled city, the *polis*, which explains why the less refined (though not quite nomadic) ancient and medieval Germans are identified, from Dante to Nietzsche, with anti-imperial politics.

The duality of robe and hide, of court proceedings and priestly sacrifice, corresponds to the double crown of the Pharaoh, representing upper and lower Egypt, the double monarchy of Israel and Judea in the Bible and, in Europe, to the ever-sought-after concord between Pope and Emperor, or between western Latin-German and eastern Greco-Slav empires, or between the barbarous German and the civilized Roman. In some countries the Holy Roman Empire is referred to as *Holy Roman-Germanic Empire*. This might have conjured the idea of a synthesis between the vitality of the northern tribes and refinement of the meridional classical world (like a recurrence of the synthesis between meso/paleolithic hunter gatherers and more sedentary/civilized Neolithic Anatolian farmers, or between the latter and the Indo-Europeans). In the east, Byzantine thinkers present a running theme of their civilization as synthesis of the Roman and the Greek trajectories.[221] Of course, not all barbarian incursions into the south during late antiquity were Germanic. Some, like the Alans, were Iranian/Scythian. But Germans are generally identified with barbarism in the European imagination just as the term Goth gives its name to the "barbarous" style of architecture.

The triple coronation of Holy Roman Emperors, and the dual monarchy of Egypt, for example, implying a third encompassing element, also finds equivalence in the Papal tiara or triple crown, which has not been used since Pope Paul VI in the 1960s. Its second component, possibly originating with Innocent III, would have explicitly referred to temporal, in addition to sacred, authority.

In Spain, a second century BC silver dish belonging to the Oretanian culture of central-southern Iberia depicts what must have been a widespread paradigm: its wild mandala in relief centers on the face of a wolf eating a man. Warriors would drink from such cups. Here, the fierce mouth that eats man becomes his helmet. The force that can swallow us up becomes our armor and advantage. This simple image elegantly sums up the point. It may occur in the medieval poem *El Mio Cid*, when after aiding a leper, the latter reveals itself as St. Lazarus to the story's hero, giving him the ability to receive a mysterious heat that enters his body after drinking warm wine, thereby becoming invincible in battle, as if possessing a berserker rage. The Christic warrior, king and priest, allows himself, like Jonah in the belly of the whale, to be consumed by terrors and ordeals, surrenders to fate, for what one resist persists, as Carl Jung writes, and we are taught to resist not evil (Matthew 5:39). Once it has done its worse, it is exhausted, and that victorious warrior rises, cutting a path through the beast's entrails, integrating all those psychic forces that had grown unruly and autonomous from his will, and rendering demons and mockers impotent by his faith.

Gilgamesh (*Bilgames or Pabilga-mes* in the earlier Sumerian texts) is described as a bull by the goddess Inanna before the bull of Heaven is released by her father on her request and slaughtered by the hero. Later, in the presence of the lord of the living mountain, Utu—the mountain

---

221   Emperor Constantine XI describes his people as "descendants of the Greeks and the Romans"; the mid-13th c. Georgios Akropolites, in *Against the Latins*, 2.27 writes "No other nations were ever as harmonious as the Greeks—Graikoi—and the Italians... for science and learning came to the Italians from the Greeks. And after that point, so that they need not use their ethnic names, a New Rome was built to complement the Elder one, so that all were called Romans.... And just as they received the most noble name from Christ, so too did they take upon themselves the national (ethnikon) name"; the 4th c. Constantius II, in his *Address to the Senate concerning Themistios*, 21a writes "in receiving from us a Roman rank, he offers us Hellenic wisdom in exchange"; the 2nd c. Aristeides, in the *Panathenaic Oration* maintains that Rome is supreme in rule, in law, and Greece in culture. Much of this proceeds from the 1st c. BC Dionysus of Halikarnassos.

featuring as a symbol of monarchy and the *axis mundi*—he is again likened to the sacrificial animal, being described as beleaguered and resembling an ox. The phrasing implies he is occupying the whole earth and its four cardinal points, for he was on all fours on the "Great Earth," and therefore is the self-sacrificed initiate, dismembered, scattered to the four corners but thereby discovering the fifth element, the secret corner, the corner stone holding the earth together, which is the axial center between those four.[222] Gilgamesh, king of Uruk, is both himself the bull and the slayer of the bull. This is an early example of the dynamic according to which kings officiate the sacrifice even as they are identified with the sacrificial animal. It is also the means by which the man is reconciled to the divine feminine, for Gilgamesh has scorned Inanna but offers libations to her with the horns of the beast she released on him. Some interpretations of this myth see an anti-imperialistic theme at play (Uruk resisting the hegemony of Kish), so that the sacrificial ritual precipitating a vision of transcendence and reconciliation with femininity inspires an ecumenical worldview, consistent with our understanding.

A modern survival of this theme occurs in the use by Spanish monarchy of the symbol of the golden fleece from the myth of Jason and the Argonauts. The Catholic order of the Golden Fleece is association with Spanish and Austrian monarchies whose heirs represent its grand masters. A pendant symbolizing this legendary hide is one of the Spanish royal family's primary treasures, along with its crown. Before realizing its Hellenic provenance, this author grew up thinking the animal skin depicted hanging from Spain's royal coat of arms represented the lamb of God. In light of the traditional identification of the monarch with the sacrificial animal and of exaltation with ritual death, that childhood misapprehension does not, however, seem so unreasonable.

It is manifest in Henry VII's early 14th-century triple coronation as king of the Germans, king of the Romans, and finally Holy Roman Emperor which encompasses both the Germanic and Latin halves of the Empire (though after crossing the Alps to subdue rebellious Florence in 1310, like a reverse Hannibal restoring Roman rule, Henry's career was botched by an early death due to malaria or possibly poisoning near Siena). In his letter defending Henry VII, Dante scorns the Lombards for rejecting that Emperor, drawing attention to their Scandinavian, northern barbarian blood as the cause of this error, and asking them to recall what Roman-Trojan ancestry they have in order to rekindle loyalty for the Imperial ideal.[223] In the *Birth of Tragedy*, Nietzsche likewise identifies Germans with the un-civilized:

---

222   *The Epic of Gilgamesh: The Babylonian Epic Poem and other Texts in Akkadian and Sumerian*, trans. Andrew George (London: Penguin Books, Penguin Classics, 2003), 153.
223   Barbara Reynolds, *Dante: the Poet, the Political Thinker, the Man* (London: IB Taurus, 2013), 237.

Beneath this restlessly palpitating civilized life and educational
convulsion there is concealed a glorious, intrinsically healthy
primeval power.... It is from this abyss that the German reformation came forth.[224]

He links this character with Dionysus, adding that from this "...abyss
the Dionysian song"[225] lets us know what manner of dreams are dreamt by
the sleeping German knight. Roman culture would, counter-wise, be Apollonian. Here Nietzsche celebrates a rebirth of the un-civilized, German-
Dionysian disposition. In later works, after the Birth of Tragedy he would
prefer to integrate what he viewed as a Latin love for clarity rather than
(what he perceived as) the German affection for murky or stormy vistas.

The idea that the Holy Roman Emperor is dual, which is to say, that
he occupies the *metaxy*, the middle between two poles, will be discussed
later in a section devoted specifically to the history of this institution.
He leads the state but also takes on the mantle of barbarism, the hunter,
the un-refined animal hides of the king in his priestly office, which
is in a sense outside the state. For now, it suffices to note that Holy
Romans Emperorship can be conceived of as functioning in between the
sub-political or apolitical localism of kingdoms and principalities and
the hyper or trans-political universalism of the Papacy, the decentralizing or centrifugal element identified with German vitalism and the
centralizing centripetal element identified with Roman civilization (in
its Christian, medieval form).

Lavinia, Rome's Shakti

Aeneas again illustrates the principles being explored. Here, we are
dealing with the divine feminine and political power, which occurs at
the very basis as Roman civilization, according to Virgil. After all his
travails, Aeneas lives to see victory, which comes when Juno relents and
ceases from enmity towards him, so long as the Trojans adopt Latin,
which they do, by Jove's happy consent, in a sense being birthed anew
as a people, now Roman. Juno, the often-oppositional feminine presence in nature, has been won over, and Aeneas has become king, like
Jove, receiving his queen, his Juno, princess Lavinia. Unlike Jason and
his ill-treatment of Medea, daughter of Helios, but alike Odin and his
knowledge of the solar maiden, Aeneas marries Lavinia and produces
issue with that descendent of the sun god Sol Indiges. Becoming worthy
of regency, becoming a king, requires observance of the disciplining travails, the counter-forces which nature, the feminine, Wisdom (6:17-21)
unleashes: "So thee, you that rule the nations, if you value your thrones
and symbols of authority, honor Wisdom so that you may rule forever."

---

224   Frederic Nietzsche, *The Birth of Tragedy, or Hellenism and Pessimism* (London: G.
Allen and Unwin: 1923), Section 23, 176.
225   Nietzsche, *The Birth of Tragedy*, Section 24, 185.

Aeneas's amorous career summarizes the holy tread. The Trojan knows three women intimately: Creusa he loses, Dido he leaves, Lavinia he wins. The first teaches him powerlessness in the wake of fate, the second his power to choose a path, and the third is his end, a synthesis of submission to fate and choice of destiny. Aeneas attains her through surrender to the divine plan, pressing on into Italy as Jove ordained, and by conquest over human impediments: "Thou art conqueror...Lavinia is thine in marriage."[226] He has self-mastered through self-surrender, and she is initiation's culmination. This is highlighted by the hero's Tantric prayer to Sun and Earth, Jove and Juno, when approaching the Latins and calling on his future wife.[227] Further, Lavinia's initiatic character is on display when her hair catches fire during a sacrificial rite,[228] taken as auspicious omen, and revealed by an oracle as signaling her impending union to a foreigner (the Trojan Aeneas).[229] During this episode she is seen to embody the source of light and heat, as well as flame's destructive agency, burning dross, tempering metal: the fiery furnace, the volcanic receptacle Juno, the Lord's Shekinah who comes with fire and light; and Aeneas is Jove, the Lord to which this Shakti corresponds. Having received knowledge of providential designs from Rhea (the mother; Venus in Aeneas's case), Aeneas as Demiurge (creator, co-heir) is ready to instantiate it into his Juno, Lavinia. Depending on the account, their offspring was named Silvius, and possibly Ascanius, and through these came many lines of kingship.

Lavinia catches the ritual's sacred fire like the lunar Europa reflecting celestial flame. She is the descendent of the sun and its mirror. Aeneas receives that light after hardship. He is the redemption of Troy in Rome, *as* Rome. He has undergone ritual death, both during his battlefield injury and subsequent descent to the underworld. He is a new self, reborn. Juno is no longer opposed to his people, for just like their leader they are reborn with a new identity, *Romans*. Just as Prometheus stole fire and Hermes the solar cattle, just as Faustus fell into lust for knowledge beyond his mortal remit, so Paris of Troy stole Helen, and the guilt from this falls on the whole city. But Aeneas sets it right, he does not stay with she who was not intended for him, Dido. He suffers the consequence of his people's sin and receives what is rightfully assigned to him, the fire princess, Lavinia, and Italy.

Roman Sexual Symbolism

The *Ancile* and the *Fascinus*, sacred objects of Rome, display sexual symmetry. Tradition holds that Vesta's worship was introduced to Italy by Aeneas and the Trojans, at their first settlement in Lavinium. Thus,

---

226 Virgil, *The Aeneid*, XII.784–86, 383.
227 Ibid., XII.161–64, 359.
228 Ibid., VII.56–63, 212.
229 Ibid., VII.76–79, 213.

her name of *Vesta Iliaca*, or Trojan Vesta, and her Trojan fire, or *Ilaci foci* (from Ilus, son of Dardanus and founder of Troy). The Trojan connection is emphasized by the fact that the Penates—those Trojan gods Jove allowed Rome to retain—were honored by Roman magistrates at Lavinium along with Vesta during the same rites.

It would be Numa Pompilius who made her cult official in the early Roman state, taking up the Trojan legacy and, we may add, uniting her phallic symbol to the feminine symbolism of the Ancile, the heavenly shield given to him. The eleven forgeries made by Numa to confound would-be thieves relates to the story of Odysseus's ancient theft of the Palladium, which was but a copy, so that the Ancile is presented as Rome's Palladium, and therefore might be related to Minerva as well. The arcs on either side of it, making an hour-glass or eight-shape, may imitate the female figure, providing further speculative support for its feminine character.

In *Parallel Lives*, Plutarch refers to the link between the shield and the female Egeria, the muses and the Vestal priestesses:

> ...a bronze buckler fell from heaven, which came into the hands of Numa, and a wonderful account of it was given by the king, which he learned from Egeria and the Muses. The buckler came, he said, for the salvation of the city...He said further that the spot where it fell, and the adjacent meadows, where the Muses usually had converse with him, must be consecrated to them; and that the spring which watered the spot should be declared holy water for the use of the Vestal virgins, who should daily sprinkle and purify their temple with it. Moreover, they say that the truth of all this was attested by the immediate cessation of the pestilence.

Of course, the Ancile is related to Mars as well, who sends it down in some accounts (in others it is Jove), and whose priests, in any case, are charged with its protection (the Salii are priests of Mars, or at least half of them are). This martial association also belongs to the sacred phallus of Vesta's cult—the Fascinus (*Fascinus populi Romani*). This object was guarded by vestal priestesses. They would place an image of it under the chariots of victorious generals, and St. Augustine writes that it was taken out in procession to guard the fields from malignant spells. Vesta herself was identified with a fire stick inserted into hollow wood to light sacred flames—which reminds us of the united Lingam and Yoni of Indian tradition.

Before king Numa, we find that Rhea Silvia, mother of Romulus and Remus and Vestal priestess, became pregnant with the twins by this supernatural phallus when it appeared in the Vestal flame. It is sometimes identified as belonging to Mars. Both the Ancile and the Fascinus, then, are related to Minerva and Mars, and both are housed in the houses of the prior generation of deities, Vesta (who for Proclus is one with Juno) and Jove (if we interpret the place where the Ancile was kept, the *Regia*, house of the Pontifex Maximus, as related to the king of the gods, given its name and function are monarchical). Indeed, the *Regia* domicile is near the Temple of Vesta, within the *precinct of Vesta*, and the *Domus Publica* and Hall of Vestals were connected at one point:

> This precinct contained the temple of Vesta, the dwelling of the Vestals, the sacred grove, and the Regia or house of the king. This group was called both Regia and *Atrium Vestae* (Ovid, *Fasti*, VI.263–64).... Like the Temple of Vesta with its Palladium, the Regia housed a sacred object bound up with the well-being of Rome, in this case the Ancile, a sacred shield with an archaic figure-8 design.... The Regia was thus an important site...the Temple of Vesta and...the Regia...along with the Hall of the Vestals and the *Domus Publica* ("Public Residence"), are also connected to each other by more than just physical proximity, and may even be another sort of bridge, this one historical, between the public and the private spheres.... The clearest connection between these sites is the figure of the Pontifex Maximus, who was not only the head of the priestly order in Rome, which had its central offices and important religious observances in the Regia, but oversaw the Vestals as well (indeed, Horace, reaching for an image to express how long his poetry will last, says, in what turns out to be a conservative estimate, "as long as the Pontifex Maximus and the silent Vestal climb the Capitolium together"). His residence, moreover, called the Domus Publica, was adjacent to the Hall of the Vestals (and eventually attached to it, probably at the upper end), at least until Augustus...moved the residence to his own quarters on the Palatine, uniting the post of chief priest with the position of princeps. It has been suggested, however, that these sites were even more closely connected originally, as functions of the palace of Rome's kings, an original Regia, or "Royal Palace," more extensive than the portion now known as the Regia.[230]

The male kingly high-priest kept the Ancile in his Regia, whereas the Fascinus was at Vesta's temple, which indicates symbolic symmetry.

We note a Herculean, as well as Martial, character to the Fascinus. Concerning Hercules' consorting with the Thespiads, daughters of Thespius—during that episode which led to the establishment of a

---

230 Samuel Ball Platner, *A Topographical Dictionary of Ancient Rome*, rev. Thomas Ashby (London: Humphrey Milford. Oxford University Press, 1929), 58–60. He continues: "After the fall of the monarchy, the complex was split and rendered public, but still retained its religious functions, transformed, however, into public rituals and posts. Some of the king's original religious duties split off, perhaps originally to a 'rex sacrorum' but eventually to the post of Pontifex Maximus. The Vestals occupied part of the old palace, now called the *Atrium Vestae*, and the chief pontiff another part that, no longer the residence of the ousted king, was appropriately called the Domus Publica."

temple in Hercules' honor, after he had slain a lion in the manner of
sacred monarchical investitures—Robert Graves speculates that they
were priestesses of Hestia/Vesta. Thespius would be a masculinization
of *thea Hestia*, goddess Hestia. He would then be the name of their order,
not their literal father. Further, "Hyginus (*Fabula*, 162) mentions only
twelve Thespiads," rather than fifty-one, "perhaps because this was the
number of Latin Vestals who guarded the phallic Palladium and who
seem to have celebrated a similar annual orgy on the Alban Hill, under
the early Roman monarchy."[231] If this is the case, the number of female
Vestals correspond to that of male Salii: priestesses guarding the male
symbol, and priests the female.

Hercules' relation to the Thespiads connects with the idea that "[t]he
Pontifex Maximus had what Dumezil calls 'an obscure, now unknown
duty' toward the Vestal Virgins," so "[o]ne might suppose that his 'way'
was something like the Way of eastern sex-sacraments; that is, he built
the 'bridge' between Father Heaven and Mother Earth (Vesta),"[232] so
the vestal priestess "symbolically married, through the Pontifex, the
phallic deity of the Palladium."[233]

We turn to the Palladium, which was also kept at the Temple of Vesta,
and has sometimes been characterized as phallic (by Robert Graves, for
example). If this is the case, being carved with an image of Pallas (or
Minerva, taking the name of Pallas), it is nonetheless also feminine, and
would represent the monadic unity of male and female, rather than the
dyadic separateness and interactivity of male and female symbolized by
Ancile and Fascinus. Correspondingly, the Palladium represents the origin, and these latter two the heir: the Palladium is a symbol of Rome's
origin in Troy rather than Rome proper, whose symbols—those that
appeared in Rome herself—are the Ancile and Fascinus. If the Palladium
represents this unity, like "a protean, androgynous deity," that "occupied
the Holy of Holies in the Roman temple of Vesta,"[234] we find a parallel
to the Indian yoni-lingam.

---

231   *Greek Myths II* (London: Penguin Books, 1955), 120.2, 96.
232   Barbara G. Walker, *The Woman's Encyclopedia of Myths and Secrets* (San Francisco:
Harper, 1983), 1046.
233   Manuela Dunn-Mascetti, *The Song of Eve: Mythology and Symbols of the Goddess*
(New York: Simon & Schuster, 1990), 194.
234   Barbara G. Walker, *The Woman's Encyclopedia of Myths and Secrets*, 764. Walker
continues: "Athene's androgynous idol represented by a lingam-yoni, showing her
union with Pallas, Pales, or Pan. The Vestal Virgins were married to the spirit
of Rome by means of an artificial phallus in the Palladian shrine; thus it seems
probable that Pallas was a sacred lingam signifying AMOR, the secret name of
ROMA in reverse."

IV. Corporatio

W E DEAL WITH HOW THE BODY POLITIC IS structured. We begin with the meaning that the initiatic experience, including the sense of cosmic corporeality, gives to the body politic (*Embodying Epiphany*), the relationship of the body politic to the proverbial *barbarian* outside its order (*Center and Periphery in One Body*), the relationship of the initiate to the concept of sacred law and the meaning of his role as legislator (*Sacred Kingship and Sacred Law*) and to the idea of semi-mythical patriarchal lines of descent (*The Corpus Cosmicum and the Narrative Body*), before ending with a brief statement concerning the political modes that may express kingship's absent center (*The Kenotic King's Soluble State*).

EMBODYING EPIPHANY

The king consummates the marriage to his queen on their wedding night. It shows him he exists in relation to another, and paradoxically this heals his imbalance. Although it confirms he is, indeed, lopsided, for any gendered being must be so, it is not really him who is lopsided. It is his body, but if that body is understood as part of a grander body, one with two poles, king and consort, there is no insufficiency.

The king uses his body functionally for the first time since returning from his metaphysical flight. He understands the instincts of the body and those of his queen, but as one who knows the ordering principle in all things. The union of king and queen results in the enthroned subject recognizing the cosmos as a body, and as *his* body, whereas before he had only understood what it is that defines a body, namely coherence or unity, the underlying order of things.

The perceptual shift corresponding to this act of congress is a *recognition*, that is, becoming cognizant of a thing for a second time but in a context different from the initial one and, moreover, a context which one is present within, whereas the initial awareness was purely theoretical. It is the difference between learning a mathematical formula and holding its beauty and coherence in the mind, initially, and subsequently realizing what that formula looks like when it structures the patterns on fruit or the spirals of a galaxy. The Demiurge instantiates the autozoon into the Crater and thereby crafts the intelligible universe.[1] Before this act of theurgy, or enactment, the autozoon is only intelligible. After touching the Crater, the receptacle, Juno, it is sensible.

---

1 "Each Soul is at once turned toward the Angel and occupied with drawing its heaven into the motion of its desire" (Corbin, *Avicenna and the Visionary Recital*, 85).

To hold a seed is not the same as tasting fruit from the tree it becomes.

He knew that transcendent order (the autozoon) is not contained in a particular form or even every particular form. But now the king's vision reveals itself as not contained in some metaphysical no-man's land between the transcendent Divine and the imminent world either. It is, in fact, right here, in the gap between forms. Its manifestation is the harmonious relation, the pattern that arranges bodies in relation to each other, the complex system irreducible to the qualities of its components.

This harmonious relationship is starkly obvious in the way man and woman fit together and in their fitting being the rite by which new life is generated. The transcendent principle he approached during initiation, when body and mind were dismembered and taken away, is the singularity and rectitude of his form, whereas the dynamic, imminent principle of manifestation is the curvature and generosity of his wife's form. Reality is metaphorical. The two are not distinct but in a state of mutual pursuit and desire. The interaction of being and becoming is not agonistic, reducing one to the other, but ecstatic, joyful. Here is the key to why God, as he thought to understand God, does not abolish the world and end its terrible, jarring multiplicity. God is not a pole in some monstrous contest between two poles. Indeed, each principle becomes more itself in relation to the other, and the Divine encompasses and exceeds both.

The king's being has been externalized and extended into another. Being is porous. He can, therefore, legitimately extend himself and the epiphany received during initiation out into the kingdom, that is, into multiplicity and manifestation, which his wife represents and has activated for him. The human community is the feminine principle, not the mother who births the initiate but the consort who allows him to extend his being, most obviously by producing progeny with her, and also in the context of political participation. Thusly does Pericles recommend a political actor, a citizen of the *polis*, engage that city with *erotic* love. The community is the reassembled body of Osiris yet also his consort, Isis, receiving Osiris,[2] the cosmic body of Inanna, the Church receiving Christ as bridegroom.

The Kingdom and the Corpus Cosmicum

In sitting at the initiatic throne and being enveloped by Rhea's light, the kingly aspirant receives the same *autozoon* as the Demiurge on the eve of cosmic genesis, and in uniting to Juno he recognizes that cosmos as deriving from the same design as his own form, perceiving the prototype for both his human body and the universe as a whole. Such is the mechanism at play. An apt description is provided in Tantric sources: "As the universe is populated with multiple worlds, levels and beings, so the practitioner's body is populated with worlds, levels and

---

2   Uzdavinys, *Philosophy as a Rite of Rebirth: From Ancient Egypt to Neoplatonism*, 105.

beings,"[3] such that what is aspired to is "universalisation of the body through locating the universe of beings within it."[4] Turning again to the *Jayakhya-Samhita* and *Lakshmi Tantra*, they guide the practitioner through visualizations to map the cosmos (its various parts with their corresponding deities) onto his own body.[5]

As early as 2000 BC, Mesopotamian sources present the cosmos as an anthropomorphic body and emphasize the correspondence between microcosm and macrocosm where the state imitates the heavens:

> In terms of Mesopotamian cultural history, macranthropy is an aspect of the idea of a correspondence between macrocosm and microcosm. As early as the third millennium BC the state seems to have been conceived in correspondence to the astronomical heavens.... [6]

Turning to Platonism, a hierarchy of contemplation and participation in the divine work that is the cosmos is found in, among others, the work of Iamblichus when he addresses the plurality of world-orders.[7] Likewise, Solovyov posits a complex nesting whereby

> ... organisms find their center in another entity with a still more general, or broader, idea, and thus become parts or organs, of a new organism of a higher order...Thus, gradually ascending, we reach the most general and broadest idea...of absolute goodness, or more precisely, absolute love.[8]

In the same way, the Shaivist Vidyacakravartin, in his commentary of the contemplative work the *Virupaksapancasika*, describes how a yogi may come to identify with, and exist as, "forms of entities, such as the sun" which serves as one stage in a work whose goal is to exist "as identical with the universe."[9] The Papyrus *Graecae Magicae* (IV.155–284) provides an example of theurgy as union with the sun in the Greco-Egyptian world.[10] David Lawrence expounds on this, holding that although identification of "one's I-hood or I-concept with a specific cosmic agency" may be reached, yogic success requires that the consciousness and powers associated with this station become "consolidated and subsumed...within

---

3   Flood, *The Tantric Body: The Secret Tradition of Hindu Religion*, 130.
4   Ibid., 131.
5   Ibid., 116.
6   McEvilley, *The Shape Of Ancient Thought, Comparative Studies In Greek And Indian Philosophies.*
7   Iamblichus, *De Mysteriis*, I:8; 33.
8   Vladimir Solovyov, *Lectures on Divine Humanity* (Hudson, NY: Lindisfarne Press, 1995), 53.
9   David Peter Lawrence, *The Teachings of the Odd-eyed One: A Study and Translation of the Virupaksapancasika, With the Commentary of Vidyacakravartin* (Albany: SUNY Press, 2008), 37.
10   Cited by Uzdavinys, *Philosophy as a Rite of Rebirth: From Ancient Egypt to Neoplatonism*, 201.

the absolute power gained through corporifying the universe."[11] As Vidyacakravartin teaches, "[u]nlimited awareness" corresponds to the universal body,[12] where the yogi's "body is the universe, the sum total of all spiritual extensions and world-orders."[13] Identification with various cosmic entities poses, therefore, a hierarchical progression.

Writes Henry Corbin describing the visionary recitals of the Persians Ibn Sina (Avicenna) and Suhrawardi: "...the Event carries us to the utmost limit of the world; at this limit, the cosmos yields before the soul, it can no longer escape being interiorized into the soul, being integrated with it."[14] Crucially for Corbin this is linked to the vision of the Anthropos, which reminds us of the link between theophany and macranthropy. Just as knowing the autozoon allows us to see that which it manifests in the macro as corresponding to the micro (our own body), "the mystical pilgrimage progresses by virtue of a transmutation of these data into symbols, a transmutation that realizes progressive interiorization of the cosmos, emergence from the cosmic crypt"[15] so that the heavenly ascent where "the visionary rises from sphere to sphere of the 'cosmic crypt'"[16] is its interiorization, not a physical displacement. The crypt is no longer a dead world but a living emblem, the initiate's body. And in Whitman (*Leaves of Grass*, "Song of Myself"):

> This day before dawn I ascended a hill and look'd at the crowded heaven,
> And I said to my spirit *When we become the enfolders of those orbs, and the pleasure and knowledge of every thing in them, shall we be fill'd and satisfied then?*
> And my spirit said *No, we but level that lift to pass and continue beyond.*

The Tantric understanding maintains that just "[a]s the universe is populated with multiple worlds, levels and beings, so the practitioner's body is populated with worlds, levels and beings,"[17] such that what is aspired to is "universalisation of the body through locating the universe of beings within it."[18] And in the Indian tradition of devotion to Krishna:

> ...the ceremony for engendering a king (rajasuya) does construct him from "all beings." A realm is like a wheel (chakra): a wheel moves because of its picot, a realm flourishes because of its king.

This can turn despotic, but "...the Bhagavata understanding of kingship subordinates the king's pleasure to God's pleasure."[19]

---

11 Lawrence, *The Teachings of the Odd-eyed One*, 37.
12 Ibid., 34.
13 Dyczkowski, *The Doctrine of Vibration*, 141.
14 Corbin, *Avicenna and the Visionary Recital*, 32.
15 Ibid., 125.
16 Ibid., 176.
17 Flood, *The Tantric Body: The Secret Tradition of Hindu Religion*, 130.
18 Ibid., 131.
19 Dennis Hudson, *The Body of God: An Emperor's Palace for Krishna in Eighth Century Kanchipuram* (Oxford: Oxford University Press, 2008), 143.

Identification of human microcosm with cosmic macrocosm is not, however, merely contemplative, but is an active work, given that the cosmic rungs are phenomenal realms and therefore subject to being affected, and specifically, of being ordered so as to more perfectly express their own character. In Shaivism a view is taken of "...[t]he body as symbolic system for ordering the cosmos...."[20] Likewise, the Platonist "theurgist's highest good was not realized by escaping from materiality but by embracing matter and multiplicity in a demiurgic way,"[21] that is, in an ordering activity through which "the theurgist would participate in the ordering of matter, which was the specific function of the Demiurge as described in Plato's *Timaeus*."[22] Both agree upon an active co-ordering of the cosmos by individuals who realize their identity with it.

The shift from experiencing ever-broadening phenomenal estates and their subjective depths to the principle which exceeds them would be incongruence unless the created order were itself extended out from that principle. This is necessitated by the understanding of cosmos as divine agency, power or Shakti of God, and therefore as a divine guise.[23] Paradoxical formulations display this in both traditions. In the Shaivist context, Abhinavagupta teaches that God "moves not" yet "manifests as motion,"[24] whereas the Platonist Iamblichus expresses this in terms of "the first god and king, remaining unmoved in the singularity of his own unity" yet shinning forth creative agency.[25]

The capacity of the human being to venture out, and inwardly know, the cosmos is possible because the two (human being and cosmos) share an underlying identity and, outwardly, are analogously structured. Plato presents the human being as microcosm, both in soul[26] and body,[27] to the cosmos as living being.[28] Tantric Shaivism shares this doctrine,[29] teaching "identification of the body with the cosmos."[30] Such analogy is owed to embodiment, for "(w)ithout a body...liberation cannot be attained."[31] The tally of human and cosmic anatomies enables a relationship between microcosm and macrocosm wherein the former recognizes itself in the latter. It is encompassed by myths in which a primordial man

---

20   Flood, *The Tantric Body: The Secret Tradition of Hindu Religion*, 26.
21   Gregory Shaw, *Theurgy and the Soul: The Neoplatonism of Iamblichus* (University Park, PA: Pennsylvania State University Press, 1995), 24.
22   Ibid., 23.
23   Sir John Woodroffe, *Principles of Tantra II* (Madras, India: Ganesh and Company, 2003), 139.
24   Dyczkowski, *The Doctrine of Vibration*, 81.
25   Iamblichus, *De Mysteriis*, VIII:2; 307.
26   Plato, *Timaeus*, 43d; 33.
27   Ibid., 88c–d; 93.
28   Ibid., 37c–d; 25.
29   Dyczkowski, *The Doctrine of Vibration*, 100; 135.
30   Flood, *The Tantric Body: The Secret Tradition of Hindu Religion*, 107.
31   Ibid., 125.

is dismembered, his re-assembled portions inaugurating the universe.

For the initiate king to realize identity with the cosmos and micro-cosmos of his kingdom, is only possible because he realizes identity with the pattern behind these, the autozoon or Word (if Proclus identifies Jove as the Logos, Jove also in a sense receives a Logos from Rhea). Gavin Flood's description of *entextualization* of the Tantric practitioner's body whereby mantras/scripture is mapped onto the anatomy is in keeping with Christian mystery (Word becoming flesh).

This prototypal operation—for the lamb is slain from the foundation of the world (Apocalypse 13:8)—belongs to the Firstborn and human archetype whose body is said to encompass humanity. Spiritual or, more properly, religious realization is reaped when the individual emulates (Mathew 16:24) the foundational drama of re-membrance (Luke 22:19) or re-linkage (*re-ligion*) unto a higher ontic level,[32] identifying his body with the cosmos *in toto*. This explains why the model emulated in real-izing identity with the cosmic body is male, yet the feminine character of the corporate whole is also retained in various traditions.

The Vedic horse sacrifice discussed previously in which the horse is identified with king and kingdom also, in some related Indo-European equivalents, identifies horse with queen and therefore perhaps kingdom with queen, just as the community is a bride in Christianity. There is evidence for the king, rather than queen, symbolically marrying the sacrificial horse in Celtic tradition, for example.[33]

An example of female rather than male dismemberment also presents the kingdom as the queen and highlights a correspondence between Christian and Tantric images: The sacred topography of Tantric India consists of spots whereon part of the dismembered goddess Sati fell, uniting with the multiplied phalluses of her husband Shiva. Thus, the world results from divine dismemberment, and the complex of temples and holy sites (the church, the world as sacred complex) is a vast femi-nine body mated to the divine Lord.[34] Similarly, the forty-two pieces of the dismembered Osiris were identified with the forty-two provinces of ancient Egypt,[35] and given their unity in one state this can be understood as forty-two pieces held together by Isis, where the goddess is essential to political power (consistent with the previous discussion on that topic).

Egypt also provides several examples of the cosmic body with which the prospective king becomes identified may be provided. The *Instruction for King Merikare* (dated from between 2025 BC and 1700 BC) describes

3 2   Uzdavinys, *Philosophy as a Rite of Rebirth: From Ancient Egypt to Neoplatonism*, 244.

3 3   Thomas Gamkrelidze and Vjaceslav Ivanov, *Indo-European and the Indo-Europeans: A Reconstruction and Historical Analysis of a Proto-Language and Proto-Culture*, 403.

3 4   Anway Mukhopadhyay, *The Goddess in Hindu-Tantric Traditions: Devi as Corpse* (New York: Routledge, 2018).

3 5   Geraldine Pinch, *Egyptian Mythology: A Guide to the Gods, Goddesses, and Traditions of Ancient Egypt* (Oxford: Oxford University Press, 2004).

human beings as "the herd of God...his images, they have come forth from his body."[36] In the ba-theology of Amun, a hidden God animates the universe from within, so that the visible world is His body, as recounted in a hymn from the 13th century BC: "Ra himself is united with His body."[37] The imagery of a hymn to Ptah-Tanen from about 1100 BC is more explicitly corporeal:

> Thy feet are upon the earth and thy head is in the heights above in thy form of the dweller in the [D]uat...The upper part of thee is heaven and the lower part of thee is the [D]uat...The winds come forth from thy nostrils, and the celestial water from thy mouth, and the staff of life (i.e., wheat, barley, etc.) proceeds from thy back...[38]

Ptah is the crafter of the seat or primordial mound mentioned previously, for which reason he is a craftsman god.[39] Ptah is partly identified with the demiurgic intellect of Platonism by Iamblichus.[40] Tanen, or Ta-Tenen, refers to risen land, that is, the primordial mound, or perhaps to the inert, immobile earth,[41] which would refer to the cube or rectangle as a stable block upon which to construct (in contrast to the sphere's tendency to roll). Ptah-Tanen, then, is both craftsman and the thing crafted, both demiurge and cosmos as demiurgic body. Osiris, after his dismemberment and re-assemblage, is joined both with Ra in the solar orbit and with the "Court of Ptah-Tanen," ruling where Ptah rules, inside the earth,[42] according to the *Memphite Theology*.[43] He may therefore be considered to have identified with Ptah-Tanen's universal body.

In the Greek tradition, occupancy of the seat of Jove may be characterized as theurgy or demiurgy[44] (god-work or specifically the work of the Demiurge, Jove). In *De Mysteriis* Iamblichus writes of this work that "when it has conjoined the soul individually to the parts of the cosmos and to all the divine powers pervading them, this leads and entrusts the soul to the keeping of the universal demiurge."[45] This conveys the vision of the Orphic hymn fragment 168, in which Jove is described

---

36   Jan Assman, *Religio Duplex: How the Enlightenment Reinvented Egyptian Religion* (Cambridge: Polity, 2014), 166.

37   Assman, *Moses the Egyptian*, 196.

38   Sir Ernest Alfred Wallis Budge, *The Gods of the Egyptians, or Studies in Egyptian Mythology*, vol. 1 (London: Methuen and Co., 1904), 509-11.

39   Ibid., 500.

40   Iamblichus, *De Mysteriis*, VIII:3.

41   Wallis Budge, *The Gods of the Egyptians*, 509.

42   Henri Frankfort, *Kingship and the Gods: A Study of Ancient Near Eastern Religion as the Integration of Society and Nature* (Chicago: University of Chicago Press, 1978), 31.

43   Miriam Lichtheim (trans.), *Ancient Egyptian Literature: A Book of Readings*, vol. 1. (Berkley, CA: University of California Press, 2006).

44   Gregory Shaw, "Theurgy as Demiurgy: Iamblichus' Solution to the Problem of Embodiment." In: *Dionysius* 12 (1988): 37.

45   Iamblichus, *De Mysteriis*, X:6.

as constituting the various regions of the sensible world, albeit as their root and foundation. Therefore, imitating Jove's enthronement in rites such as the Cretan observance at Mount Ida would imply identity also with this "macranthropic" Jove[46] of the Orphic hymns.

In the case of Enoch, sitting on the throne results in his being "made big" (2 Enoch 39), matching the world in size: "I was raised and enlarged to the size of the length and width of the world" (3 Enoch 9:1-2). This is presented as the body of Metatron or of the prelapsarian Adam, so that Enoch's embodiment as the cosmic totality reverses the expulsion from Eden,[47] at which time, presumably, man's perception of his being a microcosm (a micro-cosmos analogous to the total cosmos) dimed.

This Hebraic version of the macranthrope is invoked by Blake in *Jerusalem* when he addresses the teaching that "...Man contained in his limbs all animals...and they were separated from him by cruel sacrifices..." (*To the Jews*, closing paragraph). His subsequent pronouncement on the coming of Christ reminds us of the idea that the world, animals and the rest, is made of a dismembered primordial man and can be recognized as unitary in the body of Christ. Animals and plants are themselves manifest portions of the human person, such that human salvation implies their presence in a likewise Heavenly estate. The non-human, the world, is transfigured in its human corporeality.

The cosmic body often appears oriented along, or extended unto, the four cardinal points. In some texts Adam, the first man, was initially a mass extending from the east to the west and from the north to the south (*Genesis Rabbah*, 8:1), which four directions are mentioned following the same order in 2 Enoch (30:13).[48] This order (east, west, north and south) is significant in that the name *Adam* serves as an acronym for these four words, according to Zosimus of Panopolis. The acronym functions in Greek and not in Hebrew, which Andrei Orlov suggests indicates a Hellenic origin.[49]

There is also the medieval European theme of the Giant Christ, St. Ambrose's expression *gigas germinae substantiae*,[50] which Kantorowicz calls the *Christus Gigas*.[51] This appears for example in an eleventh century inscription on an illustration in a Gospel from Bamberg which reads, "Lo, the greatest giant strides over the stars in his triumph." St. Augustine writes in his commentary on Psalm 91 that Christ sits in Heaven on the right hand of the Father, but his feet and limbs are "struggling on earth."[52] The late 10th-century Aachen Gospel features an Emperor-as-Christ (Otto

---

46   Uzdavinys, *Philosophy as a Rite of Rebirth: From Ancient Egypt to Neoplatonism*, 88.
47   Orlov, *The Enoch-Metatron Tradition*, 248.
48   Ibid., 242.
49   Ibid.
50   Kantorowicz, *The King's Two Bodies*, 70.
51   Ibid., 73.
52   St. Augustine, *Enarrationes in Psalmos* XCI, 11, quoted by Kantorowicz, *The King's Two Bodies*, 71.

II) sat in this manner, and dividing heaven from earth is a sky-curtain perched, following Biblical imagery, on the four corners of the earth. This is the separation veil between the Holy of Holies and outer temple in the Bible, and the emperor is therefore the high priest who enters into that inner sanctum during sacrifice, like Christ, the high priest, sacrifice and king. Thus, this theme unites sacrifices and the priestly function of monarchy, cosmic corporeality or the macro-anthropos, and deification. In later Christian esoterism, we have Swedenborg's Homo Maximus:

> ...all the parts of the human body have a correspondence with such things as are in heaven, insomuch that there is not even the smallest particle in the body...which has not heavenly communities corresponding to it...they represent together one person...universal heaven is also called Homo maximus.
>
> (*Arcana Coelestia*, 2996[53])

And also, Blake's Eternal Man (note his scattering or extending to the four corners, like so many traditions, like the cross):

> So Man looks out in tree and herb and fish and bird and beast
> Collecting up the scatter'd portions of his immortal body
> Into the Elemental forms of every thing that grows,
> He tries the sullen north wind...
> The sultry south...the angry east
> ...in the gentle West
> ...in the center weeps
> ...till he reassumes his ancient bliss.
>
> (Blake, *Four Zoas*, Night 8, II)

And in Whitman's *Leaves of Grass*, "Song of Myself" is also a description of the *macranthrope*:

> I make appointments with all...
>
> Do you guess I have some intricate purpose?
> Well I have, for the Fourth-month showers have, and the mica
>   on the side of a rock has.
>
> Do you take it I would astonish?
> Does the daylight astonish? does the early redstart twittering
>   through the woods?
> Do I astonish more than they?
>
> This hour I tell things in confidence,
> I might not tell everybody, but I will tell you.

Wandering north, we intuit a macranthropic Odin by reading the Norse creation myth allegorically. The giant Ymir grew evil, like a personality becoming obscure, no longer diaphanous to the divine. As a

---

53   Cited by Corbin, *Swedenborg and Esoteric Islam*, 60.

consequence, Odin and his two brothers, by working together as a triadic, balanced composite (like the three *gunas* of Indian tradition in proper relation to each other) slew Ymir and made the world from his parts, the narrow sense of selfhood was subdued and a cosmic identification emerged in the wake of this saintly self-sacrificing violence.

If a link between Ymir and Mimir (which some commentators have suggested due to the two being referred to by a common appellative, apart from their sounding alike[54]) is entertained, then Odin's close association with the latter adds to the reading of Ymir's as the old, defeated, Titanic self of the Odinic initiate (the Mimir to whom Odin gives up an eye to drink from the well of wisdom is not the Mimir whose severed head he keeps, but the name recurs in the context of sacrifice and knowledge).

The epiphany of cosmic corporeality can be read in the overcoming of the giant Ymir as narrow self, Odin being the conscious agency by which the grander, cosmic identity is inhabited, and by the association of Ymir with Mimir, Odin reveals the initiate's ritual death to himself, to the mental and its constructs, carrying the head of the old self as instrument, but not enslaved to its thoughts, to the oscillations of its substance, and able, therefore, to fully assimilate the bodily (indicated by the appearance of the number nine, the nine night hanging on the world-tree, the nine songs or spells of Odin, and the fact that mortality and immortality are separated by Freya in the ninth world).

By preserving Mimir's severed head and receiving knowledge from it[55] the divine wayfarer Odin may be reabsorbing the intellectual function without allowing it to usurp his will, avoiding an excessively cerebral disposition that saps vitality. In this, Mimir's decapitation and Odin's bearing of the head is alike the balancing of a defenestrated tightrope walker in some tarot card representations of *the magician*. This tarot figure keeps equilibrium precisely by abstaining from the head, the mental monologue, that is, "oscillations of the mental substance" as Patanjali puts it in his *Yoga Sutras*, and as Valentin Tomberg quotes while discussing this tarot pictograph.[56] Tomberg also references the beheading of, and miraculous taking up of his own detached head by, St. Dionysius the Areopagite, which according to the relevant hagiography occurred before a statue of Mercury,[57] a god traditionally identified with Odin (for which reason Wednesday derives

54   The Norroena Society, *The Asatru Edda: Sacred Lore of the North* (New York City: iUniverse Inc., 2009), note 38 on L. III Baldr, 312.

55   Snorri Sturluson, *Heimskringla*, vol. 1, trans. A. Finlay and A. Faulkes. London: Viking Society for Northern Research (London: University College London, 2011), 13 (Chapter 4); 8.

56   Patanjali, Yoga Sutras, I.2, cited in Anonymous (known to be Valentin Tomberg), *Meditations on the Tarot: A Journey into Christian Hermeticism*, trans. Robert Powell (New York City: Jeremy Tarcher/Putnam, 2002), 8–9.

57   Jacobus de Voragine, *Legenda Aurea: Vulgo Historia Lombardica dicta ad Optimorum Librorum Fidem* (Leipzig: Impensis Librariae Arnoldianae, 1850). Cited in *Meditations on the Tarot: A Journey into Christian Hermeticism*, 10.

its name from the name of Odin—Woden—in Germanic languages and from Mercury in Romance tongues—*Mercredi* in French, *Miercoles* in Spanish and so on).

From north to Far East, we see the same theme in Taoism. The following is from the sixth century *Essays to Ridicule the Dao (Xiaodao lun)* (Fabrizio Pregadio's translation):

> Laozi transformed his body. His left eye became the sun; his right eye, the moon; his head, Mount Kunlun; his beard, the planets and constellations; his bones, the dragons; his flesh, the quadrupeds; his intestine, the snakes; his stomach, the sea; his fingers, the five peaks (wuyue); his hair, the trees and the herbs; his heart, the Flowery Canopy (huagai, i.e., Cassiopea in heaven and the lungs in the body); and his kidneys, the Real Father and the Real Mother of humanity.[58]

As the 3rd/4th-century *Baopu Zi Neipian* by Ge Hong teaches: "Methods leading to immortality call for us to extend our love the very frontiers of the universe and to view others as we do ourselves."[59]

The Chinese Huangdi or Yellow Emperor also receives initiation at a mountain, the Kongtong, where he is said to have learnt of the Tao from the mythical Guangchengzi, according to the 4th-century BC scholar Zhuangzi. His titles include that of Huangdi Simian which, with appropriate accents, translates to Yellow Deity with Four Faces as well as Zhongyuedadi, or Grand Deity of the Central Peak, the axis mundi.

Academic accounts of the Huangdi' origin conform quite well with the paradigms we are exploring. Mark Edward Lewis's apparently idiosyncratic etymology links the title *Huangdi* to the word *wang*, presumably for phonetic similarity.[60] A *wang* is a burnt shaman in the Shang religion's rainmaking ritual, from ancient Chinese tradition. Here, the emperor's death and fusion with the solar principal brings fertility. Sarah Allen's theory of the figure of the Huangdi having been an underworld deity[61] also fits our discussion, for the shinning king is, like Osiris, a knower of death and regent of the infernal.

Macranthropic epiphany is solar, the Huangdi who is cosmic-bodied is linked to fiery and solar initiation, because the sun, as lofty remote center, is expressive of the body to which it is center, the peripheral spheres illumined by its light. The union with Ra is union with the court of Ptah-Tanen. The poet Wallace Stevens seems to connect with these images in his *Like Decorations*:

58   Pregadio, *The Encyclopedia of Taoism*, 76.
59   James Ware's translation. Fabrizio Pregadio, *Seeking Immortality in Ge Hong's Baopuzi neipian*. In: ed. David Chai, *Dao Companion to Xuanxue* (New York: Springer, 2019), 27.
60   Mark E. Lewis, *Sanctioned Violence in Early China* (Albany, NY: SUNY Press, 1990).
61   Sarah Allan, "The Myth of the Xia Dynasty," *The Journal of the Royal Asiatic Society of Great Britain and Ireland* 2 (1984): 242–56.

In the far South the sun of autumn is passing
Like Walt Whitman walking along a ruddy shore.
He is singing and chanting the things that are part of him,
The worlds that were and will be, death and day.
Nothing is final, he chants. No man shall see the end.
His beard is of fire and his staff is a leaping flame.

Embodiment and Enculturation, or Translating the Transcendent through Tradition

The king is about to bring his insights from the land beyond death to the land of his birth (and rebirth). He is to refresh the cultic observance, the tradition and the kingdom. In fact, the way in which he was set up for initiatic death, the site and rite by which it came, were all also culturally specific. The body is itself is enculturated. As Gavin Flood writes:

> Throughout the history of Indian society (and arguably of all human societies) the body is a sign of social location. The subject of first-person predicates not only has but is a body for the traditional Brahmanical community within the sphere of vedic teaching; a body that marks a person as belonging to a particular endogamous social grouping or caste, the property of the body one is born with. While some tantric traditions believed that initiation could eliminate caste, the body nevertheless remains an index of social identity through the marks of one's cult, one's gender and one's practices.[62]

The value of this is partly that

> There is arguably a wisdom here that has implications across cultures: that subjective transformations occur not through the assertion of individuality but through subjecting self and body to a master and to tradition.[63]

The body is not fully reified. As Flood observed in my interview, the body includes a subtle anatomy that is accessed through imagination and can therefore actually be accessed in different ways, varying in its visual—visualized—manifestations. This elevates the exercise of subjective, inner, imaginative work and yet also the communal, tradition-specific inheritance that teaches a certain map for doing this work. Again, the universal is accessed within the particular, as the depth-dimension of a surface. In Tantrism one follows the visualization exercises and cosmic map of a specific initiatic lineage or tradition, which differs from other such traditions but leads to the same prize.

Modernity, post-modernity and certain pre-modern imperialisms are partly an effort to de-enculturate the body and allow its features to be

---

62   Flood, *The Tantric Body: The Secret Tradition of Hindu Religion*, 36.
63   Ibid., 187.

conceived not in terms of new cultural connotations but of culture-less spontaneity. Post-modernity purports to allow for the individual to do this as he or she wills, whereas other universalizing efforts, including the Enlightenment project, explicitly prescribed a set of what it considered universal principles. This is no less an aesthetic vision, an ideal-type, than the canon of faces and dwellings—the protagonists—we find in ancient Greek or Edo period Japanese artistic canons (canons even of physiognomic aesthetic). It entails particular cultural features, it has an inherited aesthetic: modernity does privilege a certain form of Western cultural assumptions, it just pretended or pretends not to.

If we use the language metaphor, Flood's point does not seem so strange. The corpus cosmicum appears in microcosms in a manner appropriate to them (again, Porphyry's Anaxagorean principle). A universal principle or reality cannot be decoded into grosser, communicable terms without some degree of choice, of imaginative play in how this is done, just as a concept cannot be communicated without using language and, therefore, using a certain language which differs from others.

The idea here is consistent with Jesus dispensing teaching on the basis of how people interact with him and the questions posed, Qur'anic revelation coming as a response to situations Muhammad and his community were in, Krishna adopting interactive modes appropriate to the devotee, and so on. As Henry Corbin writes concerning theophany:

> This vision presupposes and actualizes the eternal co-dependence...
> of this Lord with the being who is also His being, for whom and
> by whom He is the Lord...since the totality of a divine Name
> comprises the Name and the Namer, the one supplying being, the
> other revealing it.[64]

If humanity is called to a theurgic, culturally creative enterprise of taking universal, subtle realities and revealing them down through the great chain of being, giving them form, color, building monuments to them with mud and stones, paint and filigree, then this can necessarily be done in many possible different ways (for Flood, this includes experiencing and activating the subtle anatomy of chakras within, which can be perceived in different ways).

So long as we understand and allow for that diversity, we can engage in it joyfully and non-antagonistically. And a lot of what we do will be inherited: a lonely feral child does not develop linguistically complex behavior, he or she needs family and community to be reared by and to interact with. If we embrace that inheritance and chose it consciously, we prevent thinking about it as though it were a universal, default human setting and unconsciously imposing it on others or viewing them as deficient for not sharing it.

---

64   Corbin, *Alone with the Alone: Creative Imagination in the Sufism of Ibn 'Arabi*, 158.

Given that individuals are part of communities, also sharing professional vocations and personality types across communities, it is appropriate that there be multiple, collective ways to mediate the universal to the individual. There will therefore be those who find beauty in engaging with, and adding to, what is passed down, participating in inherited projects, working within a tradition for aesthetic (as well as practical) reasons. On the other hand, there may be personalities whose vocation implies being relatively aloof from inherited identities. This emphasizes both the fact of collective mediation of universals—of tradition and heritage—and also the fact that this mediation is subject to human creativity and that one can engage it as a two-way structure. One might even be a syncretist or pioneer of new forms.

From Heroism as Hubris to Political Heroism

The ceremonial of sacrifice in sacred kingship integrates barbarism with civilization, it takes the vigor or refinement of life and places it within the pacific context of religious humility. The youthful drive at self-aggrandizement contains an earnest virtue and willingness to self-sacrifice. It can carry the initiate to the threshold of ritual death and the giving up of all things that it represents. But this life crisis must be the end of that age of blunt heroics and the maturation of a truer heroism, a sociable, political responsibility. In the Iliad, the personification of the heroic age and its defect, a defect that reveals its purpose and rightful ending, is Achilles. Being partly divine makes Achilles a moral cripple, "...the result of his mixed origin is his inclination to crave distinction and to feel anger when honors appear to fall short...."[65] Being aware of humanity's high dignity can lead us to lose the attitude with which that dignity is expressed.

Thus, as in the Zen koans, we must pass from not knowing the transcendent, to knowing it, to again not knowing, or rather, knowing in a manner that sees it in imminent and humble things rather than requiring any grand ascetic feat. This hero can have the great renown he craves, but in the act of self-surrender and an opening to human porosity, interdependence and humility to the Divine: "Zeus will keep his honors unimpaired only if in arranging Thetis's marriage"—the union of goddess to mortal man that engenders Achilles—"he also arranges to have her offspring's achievements testify to Zeus's sovereignty... to human insufficiency...."[66] The felix culpa here is that "Achilles' blindness and his ruin proceed from his preoccupation with proving his self-sufficiency."[67] Such an attitude can only give way, but it is a beautiful and, indeed, heroic path, to endure in folly until one is wise, as Blake writes. In a sense this is all human beings can do, for their first steps towards wisdom will always be

---

65   John Alvis, *Divine Purpose and Heroic Response in Homer and Virgil: The Political Plan of Zeus* (London: Rowman and Littlefield Publishing, 1995), 25.
66   Ibid., 27.
67   Ibid., 34.

missteps from the perspective of a more knowledgeable subject, for their starting point is one of ignorance and therefore of reliance on the Divine.

Achilles learns that the promises made to him are subject to an "irksome contingency,"[68] and so he becomes "beset by dilemmas."[69] But the solution, as in the *Bhagavad Gita*, is not simply to cease from the activity that heroism beckons towards. Achilles, like Prince Arjuna (also a demigod), tries this. He wants to avoid Troy, offended by Agamemnon, and save himself from dying in that conflict. This is partly a matter of pique at not receiving the esteem he feels owed,

> Because he fails to conceive how he might repudiate the heroic code for a moral principle, he attempts instead merely to remove the contractual element. His exploit...will exact recognition without returning Achilles to any obligation to the Achaeans. He will have forced them to an acknowledgement of his preeminence...[70]

Granted that Arjuna was moved more by what we would consider morality, although actually mere sentiment no more deserving of admiration than Achilles' desire for fame beyond any moral responsibility. In both cases, however, a surface instinct, a psychological fixation, supersedes duty and genuine inner vocation. For Achilles, the focus on self-will, which is the desire to be seen and admitted, often erupting in anger, contributes to the death of his friend Patroclus. Anger in battle causes forgetfulness of a prophecy given him by his mother that the best of the Myrmidons would leave the light of the sun by Trojan hands (*Iliad*, 13:10-11). Thus, for Homer, "passion exalts the self I relation to others while inducing forgetfulness of human interdependence."[71] So "Homer places Achilles in situations that display the dependency of even the strongest fighter.... Achilles finds he succeeds, when he succeeds, by divine aid and, alternately, he is baffled by divine opposition."[72]

This is made explicit when Trojans begin, apparently utterly gratuitously, to outperform Achaeans (*Iliad*, 12:629-32); "with the reversal in favor of Trojan fighters, Zeus has arranged a more public exhibition of the inferiority of heroic prowess to divine purpose." In the *Iliad*, this leads to humility, to recognition of human openness to other humans and to Heaven, by way of painful loss. This also affects others: "Achilles, envisioning self-sufficiency, loses Patroclus; Hector perceives too late that his similar preoccupation has ruined his people..."[73]

Achilles' attempts to savage the body of Hector and sacrifice enemy captives gives Homer occasion to show how the barbarity of certain rites,

---

68 Ibid., 28.
69 Ibid., 32.
70 Ibid., 38.
71 Ibid., 42.
72 Ibid., 49.
73 Ibid., 56.

and the vulgar spectacle of power, is not a noble honoring of the dead, an appropriate means for mourning, but always selfish. The departed Patroclus appears to Achilles, whose actions are being justified as a vengeance on behalf of the apparition's former life, and reproaches him in just such terms. Jove does not simply take Hector away, but attempts to reconcile Achilles' mother, Thetis, to Juno, and to get Achilles to agree to give the body up. [74] Reconciliation and humility, it seems, are the purpose of ending the age of heroes by means of this war. Apollo's protecting of Hector's body, and convincing Jove that Achilles should allow the body to be ransomed (24:107), indicates Hector's redemption. His funeral pyre is prepared for nine days, and he is cremated on the tenth, nine days being an indication of nine months of pregnancy and therefore of spiritual rebirth.

The correct way to mourn is not vengeance. Deviated attempts at transcendence, the merely epic bombast, a grasp at self-sufficiency, give way to a political, corporate enterprise in the funeral, a new-found solidarity, where martial prowess during the games that honor the dead subordinate competitiveness to deference and religion. [75] Achilles seems to embrace common effort from thenceforth. [76]

Relations Mystical and Political

The above suggests a thought experiment. Because the sacred king represents spiritual centrality, the ways in which the many (the community, kingdom, subjects) relate to his office can be taken as analogizing ways in which mystical epiphany of spiritual centrality are attained. This also allows us to critique the kind of city—since we have just arrived at the polis from the wilderness, humility from hubris—that political modernity thrusts upon us.

As we have seen, theophany takes different forms for different seekers. This may be taken as support for political participation (relationship to the king) via differentiated social groupings and partial associations. The crucial question implied here is that of the legitimacy of modern theoretical conceptions of citizen-state relationship as isonomic and corresponding modern sociological processes in which atomization effaces non-institutionalized social differentiation as well (an idea expressed from Hannah Arendt's *Origins of Totalitarianism* to Putnam's *Bowling Alone*).

Henri Bergson makes the point that identical repetition is not good, because it is not open to the needs of the present moment enough to do actual good as it is actually called for. Rather, it imposes its prior abstract categories on the present and is therefore selfish. But absorption into being does not occur in the isolated moment but often in the moment as *type*. One experiences the particularity of the present moment while

---

74   Ibid., 60.
75   Ibid., 63.
76   Ibid., 62.

also experiencing that which relates it to the experience itself: If one is making love to one's spouse, it is not only the present moment but the fact of sexual congress that grabs consciousness and confronts it with radiant being, and we will relate that experience to other instances, however disconnected in time, in the same way as we relate our presence in a room to other times we have entered that same room, however much these entries may have occurred at different times.

Thus, the absorption into being one experiences from sculpting, hunting, sex, or lifting weights constitute archetypal experiences of being, archetypes that mediate, not just disconnected moments. Such is analogous to the role of *the few* in a mixed (in Aristotelean terms, *democratic-monarchic*) system. If we consider a parade in which military and civil bodies are displayed, or a village procession in which local fraternities and associations go on the march, these provide their community with a show of its parts. The community displays itself to itself.

Because the community is differentiated, its municipal, regional and sectional/professional subunits as well as units that cut across the community and other communities, should have representatives who mediate how community and representative interact, ensuring each part of the former is represented by the latter. These can be organically arising leaders, not necessarily normative arrangements[77] but this requires that established institutions be open to such organic shepherding of particular necessities towards political articulation. This amounts to a defense of a mixed constitution and civic engagement.

Experiencing being without its presence in some archetypal act proper to our particularity (the specific gifts we are given in Saint Gregory's terms, or the particular vision of the divine we are inflamed by, the Indian bhava or Henry Corbin's Lord of love) would correspond to the renunciatory path and the formlessness which some Indian schools consider derivative of Divine form just as sunlight and heat are derivative of the spherical body of the sun.

If we experience the actual trans-formal, the unconditioned that allows for there to be an infinite potential of forms[78], this will tend to return to form, as in the story of the scribe of the *Vedas*, Vyasa, spending eons in unconditioned contemplation before desiring to interact with God in form again (although Vaishnavist accounts may consider the scribe to have been experiencing a derivative formlessness and not an ultimate state beyond form), or it will tend to perceive form from within that which is trans-formal. God in His isolation is also Creator.

The formal possibility of play and devotion is considered higher than a contemplative absorption that cancels (swallowing actual into potential)

---

77   Milbank and Pabst, *The Politics of Virtue*, 83.

78   Whereas becoming absorbed by an experience in the midst of it is corresponds to *Ananda*, this state would correspond to *Sat*.

the formal, exterior self. The self, in a sense, is not really itself when it is all within itself: the self is itself when it is interacting with other selves, with *its own* other selves, for all shares in one Being, God's. The same is true of the Christian tradition:

> Going inward to attain contemplative unity is not, for Eckhart, the final goal, as it never is, for all authentic Christian mystics. To the contrary, the attainment of perfect detachment, or a kind of refusal to let contingent circumstances alter one's fundamental abiding mood of openness to God, is a way of allowing the divine love to come to constant new birth in one's soul, and so of proceeding ecstatically outward toward others. The "emptied" soul is also the fertile soul, the soul open to performing God's will as its own and so of acting creatively, which means precisely to act without egotism, although still with personal distinctness—in fact for the first time with personal distinctness... [79]

The theophany—the vision of the Anthropos, the archetypal human, the Christ, Logos-in-person—is, to use Corbin's terms, an encounter with that which is the actor of our action, reciter to of word. It is analogous to a word becoming aware of its pronouncer, an action becoming aware of its agent. This would be analogous to the ultimate word, the Logos, being in relation to the Father, and to reflexive consciousness being aware of its ever-present, undivided consciousness. The theophanic vision of the Anthropos is understood as a vision of the Son, Christ, yet presents us with the principle of the Father, which is consistent with the Gospel: whomsoever has seen Christ has seen the Father (John 14:9) and as the Father sends the Son, the Son sends the disciples (John 20:21).

If the initiate-king is representative of the theophany, a sort of provisional theophanic stand-in (also representative of the demos to the divine in a high-priestly mediation) then the community's contemplation of the sacred king is analogous to the consciousness reflecting on its own being, seeing in the sacred king their own unity (as a people, as an ecumene, as a cosmos), and "where there is no vision, the people perish" (Proverbs 29:18).[80] It is appropriate to recall here that the principles discussed in terms of sacred kingship are not only applicable to actual institutional monarchy or to the state executive in general, indeed, sometimes they may not be applicable to that context, manifesting instead in myriad other ways: the *pater familias*, the matriarch, the abbot of a monastery, the guru, the teacher, the natural leader of any group, etc.

When overwhelmed by the virgin form of unity—a perfect tree, a radiant morning, an impossible smile, ultimately the theophanic vision—reflexive consciousness is suddenly made one. Its usual diversity of thought

---

79   Milbank and Zizek, *The Monstrosity of Christ*, 207.
80   Using Margaret Barker's translation in *Creation: A Biblical Vision for the Environment* (London: T&T Clark International, 2010), 3.

and even the diversity of object-subject dries up. What is really going on here is that naked being and the thinker are known to be one. The cosmos and the psyche share a Logos, and so the vision of being out there is a vision of the inner being too. In this is joy. Discovery of the truth of things is joyful. We have *Sat, Chit* and *Ananda*. In a sense the encounter with the unitary body of sacred kingship, the pomp meant to recapitulate the whole cosmic order, is to the diversity of a community that which encountering itself in the being of outer gratuity is to the diversity of the thinking mind. Joy is the bond and the secret unity of things is the site of it all (my being is the being of that perfect other whose vision pierces my doors of perception, the Logos of cosmos and psyche where through I can know that cosmic being is my being).

On the problem of political modernity: For Voegelin the denial of God does not efface the God-man dichotomy or, analogously, what we are describing as *Chit* reflecting on *Sat*, but pretends to internalize both into man (his ego and instinct) who becomes a "divided self." He finds Nietzsche and Hegel guilty of this. The result is egophany replacing theophany. Like a consciousness (*Chit*) that refuses to reflect on Being (its own and that of others, which are revealed to be one) because it does not consider Being (*Sat*) to be real or harmonious, and so does not derive an experience of essential joy (*Ananda*) but tries to *invent* joy, harmony, order (a rationalistic counterfeit of the autozoon).

In itself, the divided self can be a simple case of our having both *speculative* and *practical* intelligences, which Corbin discusses as reflecting spiritual realities,[81] and which we would approach as analogous to the division of *Chit* (consciousness) between its primary awareness and the representation of Being in itself that identified with the Son and Ancient One in Daniel's vision. However, in Voegelin's egophany, *Chit*'s practical intelligence usurps the rest—the initiate never stops thinking, and he thinks himself up an idol.

Heidegger's critique of certain modern technologies is relevant here because the pleasure of understanding a mechanism is an instance of consciousness experiencing joy from turning to being, so that technologies that unnecessarily hide their mechanics will cultivate the egophany—indeed, digital technology is particularly expert at prompting the mind to create its own worlds without having to encounter Being.

Unity or form (the consciousness that is able to mentally encompass the diversity of things into unified categories and tends to grasp the coherence of reality) and diversity or substance—or the discontinuity of shapes and the continuity of the color spectrum—cease to have a common ground of Being: they are irreducible, and one colonizes the other. Conceiving of Being as inert chaos separates it from consciousness and the experience of joy (as joy always perceives order rather than chaos). They may define each

---

81   Corbin, *Avicenna and the Visionary Recital*, 71.

other as dialectical opposites but are not upheld by an underlying One. For this reason, Milbank rejects Hegelian dialectics in favor of Eckhart's paradoxical knowledge in *The Monstrosity of Christ*. In Christian terms, both the Son of Man and the Ancient of Days are the second person of the trinity whereas the first person is beyond them both, or all the persons of the trinity have a common Divinity which is not itself a fourth persona.[82]

All this helps us grasp the political consequences of modern philosophies in which consciousness does not care for Being. For the egophanist, since harmony is not inherent but can only be thought up and imposed, and since reality is chaotic and likely composed of predatory natures in need of appeasing, tyranny and bloody sacrifice come to make sense, as does revolutionary violence. Writes Voegelin:

> The mystery of cosmic-divine reality that must be lived through, and died through, can be speculatively solved and actively abolished by men whose existence has been disordered by their *libido dominandi*. The enterprise is, of course, grotesque; and this strand of the grotesque in Western deculturation cannot be stressed strongly enough.

And,

> The revolution in "history" is made to substitute for the theophanic event in reality. The turbulence of the encounter between God and man is transformed into the violence of an encounter between man and man. In the imaginary reality of the ideologists, this killing of men in revolutionary action is supposed to produce the much desired transfigurative, or metastatic, change of the nature of Man as an event in "history."[83]

There is no whole, except we may invent wholes, where part and whole are antagonistic, having no common ontic basis. Contrariwise, if the unity of Being is the basis on which joyful work of diversification proceeds, many bodies are represented by or indexed to a single body, and their doing so is according to the differentiation of that single body into organs, such that society is not only an aggregate of individuals but also of families, municipalities, professional associations and the like, which order the many into a body analogous to the representative singular body. We have here the many, the one and the few, following Milbank and Pabst in *The Politics of Virtue*. Augustine's *True Religion* (VIII:13) refers to the triadic structure of

---

82   When Theodore Adorno, in section 44 of *Minima Moralia*, describes dialectical thought as producing propositions which are all equidistant to their object, so that there is no gradual disclosure, first principles or procession from archetypes, he is risking entropy against the gradual disclosures we have described. Post-modernism often takes that route. The point is that there is no paradoxical (non-reified) common principle if we cannot move from anterior principle to derivative proposition. Such a dialectic would reject paradoxical compatibility of propositions.

83   Voegelin, *Order and History Volume IV, The Ecumenic Age*, 319.

things as what a thing is in its particularity, what it is as distinct from other things and what it is within a wider order. It is a one in itself, it is part of a relational many, and an instance of order.

Atomized Society and the Holy Fool

The individual citizen interacting with the state in the same way as every other citizen (formlessly) in modern, liberal theory is perhaps more analogous to a formlessness that is derivative of the trans-formal than it is to the experience of the trans-formal itself. The entire communality of the heavenly city would be occurring within the latter awareness of that which is beyond form. (In the harmonizing joy that says something of the unity of Being that the individual representative of the many represents to the many.) A particular form of interaction would not stand for that experience of the trans-formal any more than other forms of interaction.

It is already represented by interaction as such, harmony in itself. Structures in which the many (citizens) interact with the individual (the state, executive) isonomically symbolize the kind of formless state some have called *naïve enlightenment*, or else an experience of the undifferentiated energies. These latter may nonetheless be analogous to that which is beyond form (in some systems, access to that beyond, wherein is the potential for infinite forms, is denied as a possibility).

We have already seen that the individuated consciousness's relation to and experience of Being is structurally mediated by the archetype of consciousness, the Logos, Anthropos. But this would also be mediated by the individual's specific vision of the Anthropos, a specific orientation to it, a *bhava*, a theophany. Therefore, any isonomic relation to the state (the symbol of theophany) not proceeding through partial association (*dharma*, civic bodies, etc.) would *not* be analogizing the mystical experience of an unconditioned, trans-formal Divine. But it can be analogizing the mystical experience of formless energies subsequent to the formal persona or Logos, of the trans-formal Divine. Isonomic citizenship would be analogous to the equal reception of the formless energies.

Again, these formless energies might in turn be analogizing the trans-formal, so there is really no particular reason to draw too hard a distinction except to say that modern political theory and individualism are not analogous to a higher spiritual principle than traditional political formation in which individuals relate to the sacred king by way of a differentiated plurality of social groupings. The relationship of many to one, citizens or subjects to individual representative, may include a vocation that does without any intervening partial associations, namely that of the renunciate or priestly advisor. In doing without partial associations, the modern atomized society-state relation is describable as monastic or priestly to the detriment of other vocations.

In any case, sacred kingship is not only manifest in the initiate-king, and spiritual epiphany may be encountered elsewhere. Even if the state is meant to reflect cosmic order under sacred monarchy, the paradox that the center represented by the initiate-king is ultimately apophatically approached and beyond the cosmos should make us reject totalitarian conclusions in which the spiritual life of every subject is fully central-ized in the figure of the king: the true king is never fully reified. And the forms and loving relationships manifesting with exalted devotees are various (bhavas). Yet, metaphysically speaking, all spiritual epiphany comes by that archetypal king, that idea of ideas which is the Logos, so all spiritual life is centralized around the invisible center, which none-theless makes itself absent for the sake of fixing worship upon Being and Beyond-Being ("Why do you call me good?" Jesus answered. "No one is good—except God alone . . ." [Mark 10:17]). But within a corpo-rate system, a particular microcosm, every part may be in relation to a particular form expressive of the transcendent center.

Yet even recognizing different estates, duties, partial associations of all sort, etc., there can be functions of the state that are equally accessible to all citizens, and these can be taken to represent the sustaining of all things by their first cause (the table holding up a tablecloth whose patterns imply causation and order but whose threads are, in truth, all touched and sustained by the same altar beneath). It is in these terms that Milbank sees a radically democratic dimension in Meister Eckhart's recognition of the presence of the first cause in all things (like Proclus and St. Dionysius), while also recognizing inequality (the differentiated pattern on the table cloth: the first cause produces apparent secondary causation) and therefore rejecting Franciscan radical egalitarianism. To assert the presence of the table equally to all threads on the cloth by burning the cloth would be to confuse different levels of reality, to love the parent by hating the child (which is impossible, as Plotinus warns).

It is a question of expressing that which is common to all by pro-viding equal sustenance to all (Milbank wants to express this as a "rad-ical extension of social welfare"[84]) and yet also the mediation of the beyond in the formal. This is what Milbank means by paradox rather than dialectic (his disagreement with Zizek). Since the sustaining of all things equally is carried out by a radically transcendent cause, yet we paradoxically see that radical transcendence manifest in actual causes and centers, including, traditionally, the sacred king, we can understand this modern idea of the state providing equal services to all citizens as contained in ancient thought (and probably it was realized in some ancient polities). It is only a symbolic equanimity, just as his stripping down for sacrifice and dressing-up in pomp are symbolic for the plenitude of theophanic vision. He is symbolizing just as Jesus refers to the sun and

---

84   Milbank and Zizek, *The Monstrosity of Christ,* 207.

rain as symbolizing the Father's action "...love your enemies, and pray for those who persecute you, that you may be sons of your Father in heaven. He causes His sun to rise on the evil and the good, and sends rain on the righteous and the unrighteous" (Matthew 5:45).

But we should remember this is an impossible equanimity, for it cannot be infinitely expanded and its imitation of the first cause is limited by that first cause itself, by the specific nature and limit it has bestowed upon the creature. The heart pumps blood around the whole body but no farther. But where is the praxis of equal and non-formal relation, and what is its purpose? In him we may find something of what egalitarianism, taken far enough, yields. Who is the renunciate who plays the equanimity game most fully, most absurdly? Who personally relates to the Divine without reference to family, society, profession and form? He is a hermit, a solitary monk or a holy fool. Or perhaps the carnival in whose season ordinary ritual is turned on its head and the jester by whom the king is critiqued in his own court. His game is an important game, because by reminding us everything is a game, he can engender in us the desire to play properly. During carnival in Europe a donkey was typically inserted into church just as Christ rode a donkey to the land of pagan oppression, Egypt, which had become a safe haven from the promised land, Israel, which had become a land of pagan oppression. Carnival is the reversal that renews order. Just so, egalitarianism allows us to be other than ourselves and try on the vocation of others, it is a sort of carnival.

Modernity, beginning with the Reformation and certain Catholic strands, abolished the carnival only to unleash the hypertrophic carnival of revolution and the hypertrophic seriousness of modern bureaucracy. The modern city is built against the clown and becomes all clown, all inversion of tradition, but in a hyper-serious, puritanical way, with its political correctness, proliferation of laws and technologically-enabled surveillance. Play became puritan, and is open to an opposite reversal.

Mikhail Bulgakov, in *The Master and Margarita*, turns jesters into Apocalyptic horsemen (his Behemoth was a clown, for example) and this occurs during a storm, indeed, the term Harlequin may derive from the Germanic *Herla Cyning*, king of the raiders, analogue to Odin, storm god. The wanderer, the hidden one who is not what he seems, the dispossessed of haughtiness, the revealer of inner truth who returns chaos to order through apparent chaos. We may think of this as the *solve* prior to *coagula*, dissolving errant calcifications prior to coagulating the true form.

We may also think of the 13th-century *Romance of Silence*, wherein a wild-man Merlin who returns to human society, laughs at various pretensions which he thereby, by his mirth, reveals in their true character (a grieving father and priest at a boy's funeral, where the priest is in truth the biological father of the deceased; a nun at court who is in truth a man disguised who the queen is taking as her lover, etc.).[85] Here revelation, *apocalypsis*, is comedic—the arcadian revelry that puts an end to misunderstanding and stuffy, stifling in classical and Shakespearean comedy. Apocalypse is heralded by the clown. And in the holy city of the Apocalypse there is no sanctuary, for God and the hypostatic lamb are its light. The holy city is open to the beyond, not enclosed. It is illumined by the beyond. It does not claim to be the full presence of the Divine, just as it differentiates between God and the sacrificial lamb, and speaks of the throne of God and God's light.

The Absolute, which is not exhausted in any particular, inspires a vertiginous fear in the enclosed ego, which is always trying to idolatrously, exclusively identify Absolute with particular (a particular religious tradition, for example). Such vertigo, such fear, is too heavy to take into contemplation of the Absolute, and so must be left with the grotesques our mind mushrooms forth around the holy place, a confrontation with which is typical of spiritual initiation. This gargoyle-flank around the ordeal of death and subsequent rebirth is the carnivalesque.[86] Europe in "semi-barbarity,"[87] in the chaos that allows it to not feel at home in any historic mode, any *costume*, and therefore allows it to judge all as if from a distance, these "parodists of world history," "god's clowns"[88] may by that very carnival of detachment from costumes and consorting with their many forms actually end up returning to the stable costume.

Again, the clown reminds us that we play also, and makes us want to play properly. The clown plays so absurdly, he shows us what a game with no rules would be like, and again sparks in us the desire for rules—for roles and stable costumes/personae. Modernity, then, may be returning to the medieval, just as the clown returns us to order after carnival. From persisting in folly, comes wisdom. This takes the form of rediscovering corporate, differentiated, mediated modes of individual-state interaction, which can appear like a becoming less rationalized and rediscovering the supposed barbarism of the past in which apparently-gratuitous social differentiation and association is recognized institutionally.

---

85   See Jonathan Pageau's excellent YouTube channel, "The Symbolic World".
86   Like the presently quite pervasive fear of clowns, for example, or of grey aliens, the accounts of which may be somehow carnivalesque, although complex theorizing and lore focused around technology can fix the mind on quasi-materialist explication rather than reaching into what is beyond thought and effecting a return to religion, which is carnival's role. Here, then, this role can, like anything else, be mirrored by a parodic opposite which obfuscates its true purpose—*being* in the mode of *hiding being*, as Heidegger would put it—and which, like all illusion/ignorance, is ultimately a chance for the initiate to see through it with adventurous piety and humble courage.
87   Friedrich Nietzsche, *Beyond Good and Evil* (Oxford: Oxford University Press, 1998), Section 224; 114.
88   Ibid., Section 223; 114.

Political Representation as Reciprocal Initiation, or the Divine and the Demos
During an interview with John Milbank, he noted the following in relation to corporate representation in the Christian context:

> I think the idea of representation (I've learnt this from Anglican theologian Oliver O'Donovan) is very much to do with Christian theology and the idea that the Son represents the Father, Jesus Christ represents humanity to God and God to humanity. And then the Bishop is representing God to the people and the people to God. Or the sacrament is representative. So this has the idea of a kind of sort of shared symbolic horizon, if you like. So I think within that outlook, which implies a sort of basic mystical consensus in unity...[89]

As Milbank highlights, Christian theology very clearly articulates this principle. Yet it is not unique to historic Christianity. Norman Cohn writes the following, employing terms extremely similar to those used by Milbank and Oliver O'Donovan: "Like a Mesopotamian king, a king of Ugarit both represented the people before the gods and represented the gods to the community."[90] This is also consistent with ancient Indo-European languages' *middle voice*, where a verb is modulated to express Divine agency by human action.[91] Spiritual realization can be indexed to political representation, so that political representationalism is not a modern invention but constitutes the basis of politics itself with its necessary metaphysical basis.

Here is the duality of the political representative: it represents earth to Heaven and Heaven to earth, being both feminine (the bride, ideal humanity and the dynamism of nature) and masculine (the bridegroom, humanity's savior and the unmoving beyond), king and queen, patriarchal band of hunters and matriarchal settlement of agriculturalists, centripetal congealment of human designs and centrifugal escape into the wilderness wherein humans gain inspiration. For this reason, upon returning from his renewed sacrifice and vision of what is beyond, the king must re-enter the role of regent by entering his queen during the conjugal act.

Although on a lower plane, this corresponds to the principle expressed by Meister Eckhart in his *Sermon IV*, when he writes that the eye with which he sees God and the eye with which God sees him are the same, there being one sight, one knowledge, one love, but we may add, two perspectival currents passing through that same node. Politically these two currents pass through the representative, the congregation leader. As Corbin writes when discussing layers of reality

---

89   John Milbank, "Interview with Carlos Perona," 16th March 2018.
90   Cohn, *Cosmos, Chaos and the World to Come: The Ancient Roots of Apocalyptic Faith*, 120.
91   The Spanish political theorist and art historian Antonio Garcia Trevijano explores this in his *Pure Theory of the Republic*.

(in Ismaili Angelology, paralleling Proclus's Metaphysical Elements):

> At once act and passion, at once the Veil that conceals and the Name that names and reveals, at once adoring (in respect to the Principle that actuates it) and adored (by those to whom it reveals the Principle).[92]

Representationalism is the perennial principle of politics, not only the representation of a people but of that which is beyond the people. The kingdom is the king's extended body, where particular body and body politic correspond. Politics, understood as the human community creating together, having common projects and projecting itself into individuals, is a necessarily perennial feature. Representationalism is simply a fact of the human mind. This principle shows up in the 34th Apostolic Canon,

> The bishops of every nation must acknowledge him who is first among them and account him as their head, and do nothing of consequence without his consent but neither let him (who is the first) do anything without the consent of all; for so there will be unanimity...

As representative of Heaven and earth, of gods and humans, the sacred king or initiate is a nexus between the downward and upward streams. Sacred kingship is a stand-in for the theophany. Again, for Margaret Barker, "Melchizedek was a heavenly being who could 'appear' in or as the king."[93] She identifies this with the Lord and Christ, and writes that *The Apocalypse of Abraham*:

> ...describes Yahweh-El as the high priest, appearing to Abraham immediately after the meeting with Melchizedek. I suspect that the writer of the Apocalypse knew that Yahweh-El was Melchizedek...The Apocalypse also knew that Yahweh-El had the form of a man...

And was sent unto Abraham and his descendants. She adds:

> Ambrose, writing in Milan at the end of the fourth century CE, also knew that Melchizedek was the Lord. "Can a man be king of righteousness when he himself can hardly be righteous? Or a king of peace when he can hardly be peaceable?... The sacrament your received is the gift not of man but of God, brought forth by him who blessed Abraham..." (Ambrose, *On the Mysteries*, 8:46). Melchizedek here is the Lord, the Son of God, and Ambrose regarded the appearance of Melchizedek to Abraham as a theophany...[94]

---

92   Corbin, *Cyclical Time and Ismaili Gnosis*, 38.
93   Barker, M., 2008. *Who Was Melchizedek and Who was His God?*, 12. Available from: http://www.templestudiesgroucom/Papers/Melchizedek_Barker.pdf.
94   Ibid., 13.

The idea of king as stand-in for mystical theophany corresponds to how, across traditions, God acts *in terms of* his creatures, allowing Himself to be (apparently) affected. Thus, the initiate (the sacred king) is a nexus between the divinizing and democratic currents. Indeed, this principle manifests in the history of the imperial office, which is consistent with republic and popular will, not contradictory of these. Caesar Augustus and the form of emperorship he articulates—to which medieval Holy Roman and Byzantine counterparts would always hearken—was not rejecting the Republic. "Caesar's heir Octavian (i.e., Augustus) clearly assumes the ancient republican role of *Tribunus Plebis* 'protector of the people'...." This gave him power to veto the senate and thus impose imperial authority,[95] but it was not a formal break with the civic structure of republicanism. It was, in some sense, sacred monarchy, especially given Augustus's explicit mission to restore religion, but in its specific actions it assumed a state of emergency based on an already established normative framework. It can therefore not in itself be characterized as the end of that prior framework.

Here the manifesto to the Romans issued by Manfred, son of Frederick II, is relevant. Its references to the Gospel, to the Divine Kingdom as partly disclosed by Empire and Rome in a process of election emanating from the people, is remarkable.

> Rise up, oh Rome, and with frequent meditation consider within the recesses of your heart how hitherto Caesar was publicly elected to the throne of the Empire by the decree of your generals, by the authority of the Senate, and by the affirmation of your people, without any intervening act by the prelates of the Roman Church...O most happy root of the founding of the Empire, the first to conceive a Caesar, oh great Rome...the monarchy of our power...proclaims to your attentive obedience that which was written: "For to you it has been given to know the mystery of the Kingdom of God"—both of the restoration of the Empire and of the heling of your Republic—"but to the others only in parables".... Accompanied by our greatest power, and having invoked the name of Christ, we hasten to come to you...[96]

Something like this view was apparently held by Dante, a nominal Guelph whose politics are *de facto* popular Ghibelline. Indeed, even the Anjou who defeated Manfred and his relative Conrad, heir to Frederick II, appealed to the Roman Senate and people as a form of legitimacy in the coins they minted, possibly during the 1260s.

This ancient unity of Republic and Empire recurred at the dawn of political modernity with Cola di Rienzo. In this context we should view

---

95   Amanda Collins, *Greater Than Emperor: Cola Di Rienzo (ca. 1313–54) and the World of Fourteenth Century Rome* (Ann Arbor: University of Michigan Press, 2002), 40.
96   Peter Armour, "Dante and Popular Sovereignty." In: ed. John Woodhouse, *Dante and Governance* (Oxford: Clarendon Press, 1997), 27–28.

medieval imperial authority and the emergence of early modern republicanism, inspired by old Roman republicanism, not as discontinuous
realities but as having been potentially compatible and as presenting an
avenue for a more self-consciously medieval modernity and, now, post-
modernity. Modern processes have at times returned to classic principles
and are not to be rejected merely for being modern. Republicanism
and emperorship are, in their origin, a unity—not, perhaps, one in
which sovereignty emanates from popular desire, but one in which the
sovereign is legitimate as *tribunus plebis*, the people's protector. Modern
republicanism in its nationalist form rejecting transnational unities is
a historical falsity.

But what can representing earth to Heaven entail? Consider how
Jesus dispenses lessons and miracles as a result of being prompted, or
Muhammad's negotiation with Allah for a number of daily prayers that
will be manageable for his *ummah*. As John Alvis writes of Homer's Iliad,

> If we think of the plan of Zeus as an unfolding of providence
> adjusting at need to human choices, we perceive how divine purpose
> does not cancel human freedom in Homer's view and, hence, why
> the grammar of the poem does not subordinate human causation
> to divine, but, rather, sets forth the two orders of causes, as it
> were, paratactically.[97]

The human level is involved in Divine instruction and command, the
latter does not reveal itself unilaterally. Of course, the correct way to
phrase this is that the Divine plan includes in Itself both human choice
and the direct, explicit demiurgic agency of Heaven, and even beyond
this that the human perception of its inner will and total surrender to
the Divine are in fact the same (total freedom from any compulsion on
our will is total absorption into the Divine will *for us*, or, as St. Augustine
says, freedom to be incapable of sin).

The community, and not just its king, must see the autozoon, for
they must perceive their corporate collectivity as indexed to the body of
their representative. All Israel is present at Mount Sinai. The principle
of correspondence requires an abstract paradigm that the corresponding
entities both manifest, an abstract principle *in terms of which they correspond*.
Thus, the will of a group who are defining themselves, even if implicitly
and in terms of practice, as a group, is key. The community must perceive
the clear, delineated corporeal existence of the king's body, receiving
this principle of bodily, unitary cohesion, and attribute it to their own
communal existence, rendering the latter likewise clearly delineated. In
this very act, the community is implicitly recognizing the autozoon—the
possibility of some particular entities corresponding to others in terms of
common, underlying universals principles—that is, they are recognizing

---

97   Alvis, *Divine Purpose and Heroic Response in Homer and Virgil*, 14.

metaphysics and *becoming virtual, if not actualized, initiates*. The profundity of the act of political participation is expressed by Greek philosophers who considered it key to the good life. It comes through as well in the myriad of stories of a community's scattering and exile followed by new found land and glory, where the initiatic ritual of death and rebirth, the crucifixion, occurs collectively.

The founder of a tradition indexes a community to a sacred paradigm, just as Jesus contains the spiritual principle of Israel, fasting for forty days where Israel wandered the desert for forty days, for example, and allows access to that principle outside its specific historical coordinates. An example of this principle is the case of the Native American Tenskwatawa, or *open door*, whose surviving falling into a fire and overcoming of alcoholism is likened to the trials of Native Americans in dealing with European culture and its negative impact. Just as the initiate does not imagine or decide what to give up during ritual death, but dies fully (though not literally/physically), so too the political community should not be understood in terms of pure social constructivism and changing concerns. There is a deeper, historically rooted, substance to how we articulate political communities, like initiates returning to sensible awareness of the empirical body inhabited prior to ritual death.

We close by returning to the underlying issue here, that of God acting in terms of His creatures, the paradoxical granting of autonomy and response to their creative endeavor. A metaphysics of *bhavas*. There is always a moment of response or activity in the subject to the reality around it. Wilfrid Sellers shows that there is no independent semantic base on which inference is a superstructure. Inference is always present. If a phenomenalist describes how things appear to be and claims to withhold the commitment required to make a statement about what is ("the leaf *appears* green, but I do not say it *is* green"), he is, in truth, parasitic on meaning, not really detached from it.[98] Tweets Milbank: "...thought is ultimately feeling, as Hume and Whitehead and arguably also Plato thought (or felt). But feeling reflected on and refined is integral reason." And Northrop Frye writes, "[a]nyone who, like Descartes, begins by doubting everything except his own doubts, will never end in certainties...."[99] Such a one ends up in Blake's "Two Horn'd Reasoning, Cloven Fiction, In Doubt, which is Self-contradiction."

To seek the truth in absolutely neutral terms is annihilation. We always bring something to the truth and must choose what is true in our

---

98   Further, Sellers argues that scientific casual models should not be imported into accounts of the manifest image of reality: The mechanics of causation involved in a glass falling to the floor are not appropriate to the kind of causation a conscious decision involves. You cannot describe the subject's actions as though there were no such thing as subjectivity.

99   Frye Northrop, *Fearful Symmetry: A Study of William Blake*, vol. 14, ed. N. Halmi (Toronto: University of Toronto Press, 1991), 25.

bringing. The vision of totality must include the self and the self's activity insofar as agency is given to that self within existential architecture,
so that the self must be active in that vision. Insofar as our capacity to
choose is a part of the whole—is in fact the choosing of consciousness
at the particular rung of the cosmos occupied by us—we must be exercising it. We cannot refuse ourselves as theatre of choosing that which
the Divine chooses: beauty, mercy, love, the good. If we treat these latter
as neutral realities to be disclosed neutrally, we precisely cease to seek
them, for they are subjective and must be sought subjectively. Strikingly,
even choice can feel like a choice, for when we begin to truly chose the
good over the demands of a compulsive mind and a disordered soul, we
quickly *experience* the degree to which our past state of despondency or
anger was, in fact, a choice, but from within that state it felt like an
iron-clad imposition and not at all a choice.

The Divine Names manifest forms and are manifested by forms,
give being to beings and are revealed by those beings, which suggests "a
twofold, active and passive dimension...pathetic and poietic...receptive
and creative"[100] and which "synchronize" in theophany,[101] both sensible and subtle. In Islam, a Hadith Qudsi (a hadith from the perspective
of Allah, rather than Muhammad) teaches that Allah has prohibited
oppression, even making it haram to Himself. Islam also teaches that a
believer may hold Allah to His promises. Further, Allah says according
to a hadith[102] that He is in the opinion of His servant, "I am as My
servant expects Me to be":

> Allah the Almighty said: I am as My servant thinks I am. I am
> with him when he makes mention of Me. If he makes mention
> of Me to himself, I make mention of him to Myself; and if he
> makes mention of Me in an assembly, I make mention of him in
> an assembly better than it. And if he draws near to Me an arm's
> length, I draw near to him a cubit, and if he draws near to Me
> a cubit, I draw near to him a fathom. And if he comes to Me
> walking, I go to him at speed.

This relates to the teaching[103] that prayer (du'a) should not be fearful
but confident: "None of you should say 'Oh Allah forgive me if you
wish', 'Oh Allah be merciful to me if you wish'; but he must appeal to
Allah with determination, for nobody can force Allah to do something
against his will" and "Invoke Allah while you are certain to be answered
and know that Allah does not answer a du'a from a heart which is inat-
tentive and unmindful," and also "Oh worshipper, ask and you will be

100   Corbin, *Alone with the Alone: Creative Imagination in the Sufism of Ibn 'Arabi*, 159.
101   Ibid., 150–51.
102   via Abu Hurayrah, appearing in *Sahih al-Bukhari* and elsewhere.
103   Also narrated in a hadith via Abu Hurayrah, appearing in *Sahih al-Bukhari*,
6339, and *Sahih -Muslim*, 2679.

answered."[104] The mentality of scarcity, even scarcity of mercy, which holds faith back in a veneer of monstrously false piety, must be cast off:

> Oh my servants, were the first of you and last of you, the human of you and jinn of you to rise up in one place and make a request from me, and were I to give everyone what they requested, that would not decrease what I have any more than a needle decreases the sea if put into it.[105]

We have also the interpretation of the Islamic teaching that humanity or the Muslim ummah are made a "middle nation," according to which this middle is between full (apparent) human egoic autonomy and full extinction in the Divine Sovereignty.

This is similar to the attitude of friendship with, and abundance in, God that Christ teaches his disciples, at times altering what he says on the basis of being challenged. It is the teaching that

> ...if you have faith and do not doubt... even if you say to this mountain, "Be lifted up and thrown into the sea," it will happen. If you believe, you will receive whatever you ask in prayer. (Matthew 21:21–22)
>
> ...whatever you ask in prayer, believe that you have received it, and it will be yours. (Mark 11:24)
>
> But let him ask in faith, with no doubting, for the one who doubts is like a wave of the sea that is driven and tossed by the wind. For that person must not suppose that he will receive anything from the Lord. (James 1:6–7)
>
> Very truly I tell you, my Father will give you whatever you ask in my name. Until now you have not asked for anything in my name. Ask and you will receive, and your joy will be complete. (John 16:23–24)
>
> If you remain in me and I in you, you will bear much fruit; apart from me you can do nothing.... If you remain in me and my words remain in you, ask whatever you wish, and it will be done for you. This is to my Father's glory, that you bear much fruit, showing yourselves to be my disciples.
>
> As the Father has loved me, so have I loved you. Now remain in my love. If you keep my commands, you will remain in my love, just as I have kept my Father's commands and remain in his love. I have told you this so that my joy may be in you and that your joy may be complete. My command is this: Love each other as I have loved you. Greater love has no one than this: to lay down one's life for one's friends. You are my friends if you do what I command. I no longer call you servants, because a servant does not know his master's business. Instead, I have called you friends, for everything that I learned from my Father I have made known

---

104   in al-Albani.
105   Hadith Qudsi, narrated via Abu Dharr, in *Sahih-Muslim*.

to you. You did not choose me, but I chose you and appointed you
so that you might go and bear fruit—fruit that will last—and so
that whatever you ask in my name the Father will give you. This
is my command: Love each other. (John 15: 51–7)

In the *Bhagavatam Purana*, we learn that

The quality of submission to His devotees was demonstrated by
Hari [God], despite the fact that He is only constrained by His
free will. (X:919)

In the *Gita* (7:20–21), Lord Krishna tells us that

Those whose knowledge has been carried away by various desires
take refuge in other deities...disciplined by faith who seek the
favor of that deity or form, receive from it their desires because
those desires are decreed by Me But temporary is the fruit for
those with small understanding.

But again, it need not be done by one with small understanding, and
it need not be onto a deity considered separate from the seeker and
separate from the Lord. It can be the demiurgic, co-creative work of a
"man of pure mind":

Whatever worlds he covets by his mind, and whatever objects he
wishes for the man of pure mind, he gains those worlds and those
objects; therefore, let him who longs for *Bhuti* (manifested power)
worship him who knows the *atman*. (*Mundaka Upanishad* 3.1.10)

One who meditates on God with "a calm mind" can also "form his will"
(here the context is like that of the bhavas, taking post-mortem shapes
depending on our desire):

All this is Brahman. From It the universe comes forth, in It the
universe merges and in It the universe breathes. Therefore, a man
should meditate on Brahman with a calm mind. Now, verily, a
man consists of will. As he wills in this world, so does he become
when he has departed hence. Let him with this knowledge in mind
form his will. (*Śāṇḍilya Vidya*, in the *Chandogya Upanishad* 3.14.1)

Also, in the *Chandogya Upanishad* (3.14.4), as in the *Mandaka Upanishad*,
in the Gospel and in Islam, creative desire is the playful participation
of the pacified soul, for God "embraces all this":

He whose creation is this universe, who cherishes all desires, who
contains all odors, who is endowed with all tastes, who embraces
all this, who never speaks and who is without longing—He is
my Self within the heart, He is that Brahman. When I shall have
departed hence, I shall certainly reach Him: one who has this faith
and has no doubt will certainly attain to that Godhead. Thus said
Sandilya, yea, thus he said.

Proclus writes of *The Chaldean Oracles*:

> The Oracles often give victory to our own choice, and not to the Order alone of the Mundane periods. As, for instance, when they say, "On beholding thyself, fear!" And again, "Believe thyself to be above the Body, and thou art so." And, still further, when they assert, "That our voluntary sorrows germinate in us the growth of the particular life we lead."[106]

The initiate, the saint, the believer, the sacred monarch, is therefore not a one-way instrument, not a passer of law to subjects, but a responsive communal lover, an interceder, where the Divine is also in the agency of the human towards it, in the upward as well as downward motions, in harmony.

CENTER AND PERIPHERY IN ONE BODY

The Anthropos, receiver and dispenser of the autozoon, from eternal feminine, who in turn proceeds from the First Paternal Intellect, to the particular beings of the intelligible living organism (that is, denizens of the universe), is not any one particular being among them, but is ontologically prior, nor is He the total cosmic organism, for such organism is never totally defined (again, as Guénon puts it, there is no quantitative infinite). The final *unio mystica* cannot be a union with a definite cosmic body. This truth appears in the Eucharist.

Experience of the cosmic body is 1) a *reception* 2) of the (autozoon) body that precedes the (whole and parts of the) intelligible cosmos 3) and, by analogy (since both parts and whole are made according to the autozoon) awareness that one's own ordinary sentient self is a part of the universal whole, re-introducing one's self into the circuit, so to speak (penetrating and being present in the realm of becoming as expressed by sexual union of king and queen, Jove and Juno). The gift of their common paradigm produces a perception of all intelligible things as correspondent. Such is the autozoon, the design whereby the large and the small, the above and the below, the without and the within, are made and sustained. One not only knows the body of the All, but the body that precedes the all, the body that is more fundamental than the physical, intelligible creation. Such entails understanding one's ordinary sentience as one of the cosmic body's components.

From the Wilderness, a City

This is the *Eucharist*. The three elements highlighted above testify to it: 1) it is the receiving of a gift (via Rhea outflowing from the First Paternal Intellect, in Platonic-Proclean terms, which reminds of the

---

106 William Wynn Westcott, *The Chaldean Oracles of Zoroaster* (Philadelphia, PA: Dalcassian Publishing Co., 2018), 44.

Holy Spirit's feminine character in some Christian understanding); 2) the gift is of Christ's body, Christ preceding the creation (as Logos); 3) the receiver of this body is a part of the Church, the manifest body of Christ (and, indeed, is continuous with the un-manifest body as well, for only by means of this is the former realization possible).

The sending forth of the autozoon in the Paternal Intellect's Rhea to the new Jove can only occur in a gap between pre-manifestation and manifestation, between "...the *essence*...'accidents'...and their *existence* as signifying manifestations of the substance of Christ's Body."[107] Catherine Pickstock writes (expounding on St. Thomas Aquinas, using his categories):

> From essence, no existence follows, and existence is received from elsewhere, from God who exists of his very nature and not in this or that manner. Hence every creature is "pulled" by its participation in *esse* beyond its own peculiar essence—it exceeds itself by receiving existence—and no created substance is truly substantial, truly self-sufficient, absolutely stable or self-sustaining.

Each thing is expressive of the One's creative paradigm, the autozoon, just as the total *thing* (the universe) is. The All is in all things, and the All proceeds only from the One, so that all things constantly receive the All (in that manner appropriate to them) from the One.

> It follows that the violation of the substance/accident contrast and the gap between *esse* and essence in the case of transubstantiation is only an extreme case of what, for Aquinas, always applies. All substances are "accidents" in contrast to divinity, and become signs which, in their essence, realize a repetition and revelation of the divine "substance."

This serves as St. Thomas's justification for the doctrine of transubstantiation, but also presents the Eucharistic rite as a rite that summarizes, as it were, the operations of creation as such (the autozoon's activity in producing the intelligible animal that is the cosmos). It is therefore a rite for making participants aware of how creation works, indeed, how it occurs at all:

> One should note also that since the subject of the Body and Blood of Christ is the second hypostasis of the Trinity, identical with *esse*, this body and blood is *not* simply the body and blood of an "individual."[108]

The monarch endowed of this awareness is consummate high priest, mediating the mystery of incarnation, that is, of the correspondence between every manifest form and the absent center or autozoon—the

---

107   Pickstock, *After Writing*, 260.
108   Ibid., 261.

un-manifest whole in the gap between essence and existence, in St. Thomas or Pickstock's language, which is Desmond's *between*—to the local, the region, which realizing its correspondence to the monarch's body must also realize a universal pattern behind both kingdom and king, manifesting both. Thusly can John Milbank write that "...in the end it is Christ's kingly role which is eternal, and not his mediating priestly role,"[109] for, in a sense, the kingly role is the fulfilment of mediation:

> ...if the ruler has responsibility for positive natural functions...that would exist irrespective of sin, and if he must have an eye to the further coordination of these things with the supernatural life of charity, then in a real sense it is the ruler who is most concerned with the whole human person, body, soul and spirit, and the ruler who most anticipates our resurrection in glory...[t]he emperor or king as it were "diagonalises out" of his proper subordination to the Curia or the Pope...the king and the concerns of kingship are symbolically more ultimate, since they are a remote foreshadowing of the eschaton.[110]

Frithjof Schuon makes a similar point in the specific context of Christian Roman emperorship, noting that "[t]he emperor, as opposed to the Pope, incarnates temporal power; but more than that he also presents, by virtue of his pre-Christian but nevertheless celestial origin, an aspect of universality, whereas the Pope is identified by his function with the Christian religion alone..." He concludes: "one might well think that the Pope had recognized this ambiguity—or this aspect of superiority paradoxically accompanying an inferiority—by prostrating himself before Charlemagne after his coronation."[111]

Priests and especially celibate monks are like the oxygen between people, or like stem cells as distinct from differentiated cells. They do not necessarily represent any particular function outside of universal human charity the way a parent does insofar as it is organically linked to a particular child, or a person with a given profession. In this sense they are somehow more universal but also congealing fewer human energies than the political agent, and are a sustaining element available to the body, rather than expressing the realized body of humanity.

As St. Paul writes (Hebrews 5:5-6), quoting Psalms (110:4), Christ is "a priest forever according to the order of Melchizedek," that is, sacred monarchy (Melchizedek is king of Salem). This is confirmed in ancient tradition, as Nanno Marinatos points out with respect to the Aegean

---

109 John Milbank, "Power is Necessary for Peace: In Defence of Constantine." ABC Religion and Ethics, 29 October 2010. Available from: http://www.abc.net.au/religion/articles/2010/10/29/3051980.htm. Accessed on: 17/03/2018.

110 Milbank, *Beyond Secular Order*, 249.

111 Frithjof Schuon, *The Essential Frithjof Schuon* (Bloomington, IN: World Wisdom, 2005), note 8, 180.

and Near East, where there was no high priest higher than the king[112] and in a Christian context it is why the fall occurs, so as to bring about not only the garden of paradise but the city, the exalted polity which is not a sort of *givenness* in nature but also a creature of human ingenuity and artifice, "…the Son's redemptive act reveals, and incomprehensibly ensures, that the garden is relocated within eternally civic Jerusalem."[113] Here is the Rome of Aeneas, the sacred civility his story conveys.

The true city is built just as the Eucharist requires human addition, labor and creativity (wine is not just grapes, bread is not just wheat). The sacrifice where the king wears skins and identifies with animal nature, accessing that which is beyond human culture, precisely allows him to bring wisdom from that beyond back with him and to make human culture better, to build the holy city. He accesses a vision of the *metapolis* to inform his ordering of the polis. That this follows union with the queen relates to the womanly role of domesticating man and motivating him (like Enkidu), the eternal feminine urges us forward, as Goethe put it.

The Mystique of the Barbarian

Let us now turn to the exogenous force that cracks the city open to complete it, renewing it with the sorts of apparent disorder that forces baroque, medieval structures on excessively atomizing, rationalizing civilization. The previous duality of wilderness and city is precisely what we discussed before as the duality of kingship. It manifests in the attraction of the nomadic or tribal people for the settled and civilized, and vice-versa. Medieval historians determining which European nations descended from which of the seven sons of Japheth, son of Noah, were earnest enough in their classificatory endeavors to count political enemies as brethren, as in the case of "the Goths who were recently raging in our land"[114] and who had once "presented Rome with major threats,"[115] as St. Jerome writes in his fourth century *Hebrew Questions on Genesis*, and as St. Isidore of Seville would confirm in his influential 7th century *Etymologies*.

It is alike the great 2nd-century BC Chinese scholar Sima Qian listing those nations descended from the Yellow Emperor, a progeny that includes northern proto-Turkic or Mongolian Xiongnu barbarians despite this latter's enmity with China. This is perhaps a similar concession to St. Jerome's in the case of the Goths as fellow descendants of Japheth. A feeling of kinship for certain savage tribes—the sentiment that these may be barbarians, but that they are *"our barbarians"* —warrants a short divagation.

This conception is consistent with a phenomenology of civilization analogous to traditional anthropology, according to which a human

---

112   Marinatos, *Minoan Kingship and the Solar Goddess: A Near Eastern Koine*, 53.

113   Pickstock, *After Writing: On the Liturgical Consummation of Philosophy*, 249.

114   Saint Jerome, *Hebrew Questions on Genesis*. Gen. 10:2; 39.

115   Ibid., Chapter 9 verse 2, 139.

person consists of body, soul and spirit (*soma, psuche*, and *nous*). Civilization would have its savage, empire-builder and sage; the vitality of youth, the discipline of maturity and the wisdom of old age. These seem to enter the stream of history inversely, like principle preceding practice, beginning with Greek philosophical bloom, Roman discipline and Gothic incursion. An East Asian equivalent under the Manchurian Qing might be proposed as consisting of Mongol barbarism, Han civilization and Tibetan spiritual technology: "...the fighting prowess of Mongol allies and the spiritual ministration of Tibetan lamas...the traditional bureaucratic system...the Confucian classics...."[116]

In the case of Europe, and of the barbarians mentioned by St. Jerome and St. Isidore (the Goths) one line of historical narrative views incursion by the boreal barbarian as the means through which a second civilizational cycle, the medieval out from the Classical, was catalyzed. This highlights a certain meaning of *Germanic* as germ, germination, sprouting (which in itself may simply refer to their lack of civilizational refinement).[117] St. Isidore provides this etymology for the land "called Germania (cf. *germinare*, 'germinate')"[118] and it relates to the English expression "german brother" to mean biological brother.

At this point it is also interesting to highlight the continuity of Odin's presence in the intellectual life of Europe. Like St. Jerome, Snorri Sturluson (the scholar to whom the *Prose Edda* is owed), links Goth to Roman, presenting an account according to which Odin is an offshoot of Rome's founder, Aeneas's Trojan company.[119] The barbarian people who, according to Edmund Burke, introduce that "Germanic or Gothic customary"[120] essential to European culture, bear his name (Goths, after *Gothan*, a rendering of *Wotan* or *Odin*).

Centuries after Sturluson, thinkers continued to refer to this figure. Donoso-Cortés, for example, praises Odin in similar terms to those invoked by Thomas Carlyle's study on heroism. Odin, he imagines, was a Moses-like leader, but one who ruled as poet-bard rather than legislator. Donoso-Cortés proclaims the Scandinavian deity an incarnation of *intelligence* itself, by which he means the civilization-building instinct, a reciprocal action by which tribe molds individual and individual molds tribe.[121] The notion of his being a god of intelligence is consistent

---

116   Peter Zarrow, *China in War and Revolution: 1895–1949* (New York City: Routledge, 2005), 55.
117   Francis E. J. Valpy, *Etymological Dictionary of the Latin Language* (London: G. B. Whittaker, 1828), 174–75.
118   St. Isidore, *The Etymologies of St. Isidore of Seville*, XIV.iv.4, 289.
119   Sturluson, 1842, Foreword, 8, 106.
120   Edmund Burke, "The First Letter on a Regicide Peace," cited by Milbank and Pabst, *The Politics of Virtue*, 361.
121   Juan Donoso-Cortés, *Obras de Don Juan Donoso Cortés, Marqués de Valdegamas*, vol. 1 (Madrid: Imprenta de Tejado, 1854), 212–13.

with Odin's steadfast search for wisdom. It is a sort of intelligence the Castilian Catholic seems to suggest was kept fresh and unperturbed, if also unfulfilled, among the people of Odin prior to their confronting Rome and entering into her mercenary service.

In this context architectural Gothicism may be said to present a complete symbolic fulcrum of Europe. This is the case firstly because the organic understanding of human community so essential to Platonic thought finds itself manifested in the Gothic cathedral:

> An art which, like that of the gothic, is at once seemingly natural and organic in its endlessly varied adaptation of form and functionality, and yet also highly artificial in its subordination of structure to ornament and instruction.... [122]

The structure is arboreal, tree-like, yet man-made. It is cultivated as much as it is constructed. It can always be altered: arches added between towers, towers added at the seams of arches, even taking on asymmetries for practicality's sake, just as a tree can grow in all sorts of wanton ways without losing overall coherence and symmetrical semblance.

Naming this style after the Gothic tribes was meant to convey the barbarity and monstrous aspect of the new aesthetic. In this sense it combines the refinement or maturity of civilization (technical competence) with the vitality or youth of savagery, while also housing the wisdom, the religious reflectivity, of old age, since the cathedral is for religious contemplation. In addition, related to this sacred dimension, the name Gothic itself derives from the principal deity after whom those tribesmen and their native Swedish fief were named. The quintessential symbol of European Christianity, therefore, is indirectly named after the immortal wisdom-seeker, Odin. It is a temple of reconciliation between plant and construct, between pagan and Christian.

In the spirit of a sort of poetic *essayism*, it can be suggested that the Latin conceptualization of German barbarity and its historical trajectory illustrate the sense among civilized peoples that they have need of savage vitality, and that the often-subliminal figure of Odin highlights this psychological category in individual terms, where it is wilderness outside civilization that yields wisdom for the seeker. We have here a drive for synthesis between the civilized and the barbaric which comes through in many historical processes and echoes that ancient state of fluidity between the nomadic and the sedentary modes. When the Mongol desires to retain his nomadism even as rulership over complex civilizational structures is attained, or the Arab looks askance at the urbanism of the nations he conquers, they are pointing to the same thing. Thus, the analogy drawn by some historians between the "German federate princes of the early medieval period" as "western counterpart of the

---

122   Milbank, *Beyond Secular Order*, 210.

Arabs,"[123] where apparently less culturally refined incursions infused empires with a new civilizational impetus and, at the same time, ended their own cultural stagnation or regression.

To muse indulgently on history's slaughter bench, it may be said that the barbarian comes endowed of childlike regard for the fruits of civilization, having been ignorant of them. The enthusiasm that spurs his raids is partially consequent of the harshness of his home. His is a marriage of vitalism with refinement. The European synthesis is specifically one of medieval Germanism and Greco-Latinity.[124] Refinement's myriad offerings contrast with the savage desert, a reflective habitat symbolizing the undifferentiated source, a mirror for the sun:

> In the sensorial domain, the blinding light of the sun is the most fitting symbol for the unmanifest being of the archetypes, at least from the earthly perspective; and upon the earth, the fullest revelation of the archetypal energies behind forms is revealed by the unrelenting light of the desert sun.[125]

A kind of echo of primordiality is carried out, be it from the sun-reflecting Arabian desert of sand, the Germanic snow cape, or the Mongolian steppe.

Ibn 'Abd al-Barr writes in his *al-Inbah* that Umar, the second rightly guided caliph in Sunni Islam, said the following (note that Umar is often identified with early Arab imperialism, being rejected by Shi'ism altogether, and even in Sunnism, having his example tempered by the examples of the other three rightly guided caliphs, as well as by fundamental religious principles. In terms of the following quotation, however, his opinion would seem to be consistent with Qur'anic statements):

> Learn your genealogies...so that you may make your ties of blood-kinship close; and do not be like the Nabataeans of the plains of

---

123   Irfan Shahid, *Byzantium and the Arabs in the Sixth Century*, Vol. 1, Part I (Washington, DC: Dumbarton Oaks, 1995), 488.

124   Writes Kantorowicz of the 12th and 13 centuries: "...everything Sicilian had worn a halo of romance in German eyes, and his German contemporaries cherished a vision of a fairy prince living in distant Sicily. Since the wanderings of the old Germanic peoples, Sicily had exercised on the imaginations of men a peculiar fascination. The further the Northern invaders penetrated south into regions of ever-increasing wealth and luxuriance the nearer they seemed to approach the Garden of Eden: a dream-fulfilment of an Earthly Paradise. The very beginning of the Germanic epoch had seen the figure of the lion-like young king, Alaric of the Western Goths, who with scanty knowledge but the sure instinct of an animal had fought his way towards the southern Paradise where he was to find his grave. The end of the same Germanic age provided a fitting parallel in that young Conrad of Hohenstaufen who lost his life in Sicily, the fate of the Germans seemed bound up with the south of Italy. In one way or another almost all the medieval emperors had sought to win it, until the luck turned and Barbarossa's scheming obtained it for his son Henry as his bride's dower." *Frederick the Second 1194-1250*, E. O. Lorimer trans. (New York: Frederick Ungar Publishing, 1957), 20.

125   Zinner, *Christianity and Islam*, 51.

Iraq who, when asked "From whom are you?," say "From such and
such a village." For, by God, there would be something between a
man and his brother, if he only knew the tie of affection through
blood kinship (*dikhlah ar-rahim*) between them, which would restrain
one from abusing the other.[126]

This follows from the hadith[127] according to which Muhammad taught
"Learn your lineages so that you can maintain ties of kinship, for maintaining the ties of kinship increases the love amongst families, increases
one's wealth and extends one's age."

According to this, it is preferable that one refer to himself as Johnson,
son of John, rather than as *John the Londoner*. We can interpret this as a
stop against the deracinating potential of *civilization*, of entering into
the *civitas*, the city—of losing our rootedness in the extended family, in
a certain semi-nomadic ruggedness. As civilization progresses there are
those who warn against the danger in becoming too sedentary, paradoxically, so rooted one is uprooted. Here is the mystique that civilized
peoples often feel for those they consider barbarians.

Sacrifice and the Fraternal Foe

If the slayer is the slain, and if the savage and civilized are one, we have
ample support for a doctrine of fraternal enemies. In the play *The Siege of
Numancia* Miguel de Cervantes might present a dual-protagonist: both
the Numantians, Celtiberians in Spain under siege from the Romans, and
the Romans, namely commander Scipio. The Numantines are, however,
ultimately the centerpiece of the play, and their exploits, including their
suicide in evasion of Roman captivity, is described by Cervantes as a figure
for inspiring glory and national unity to the future Spain.[128] Whereas
Scipio rejected both the Numantian offer of peace and friendship and
the possibility of direct confrontation and war-making, preferring to
lay siege, the Numantians opt for virile resistance. Just as in Aeschylus,
a small city (or cities) defeats a large empire, for indeed, the final tragic
lamentation is uttered not by Numantians but by Scipio, who admits
to his having been robbed of victory by the enemy's collective suicide.

The idea of victory in death, of inspiring national renewal by inspiring
the future Spain (even justifying its sacking of Rome under the Spanish
Habsburg Charles V, which Cervantes seems to do[129]) differs from Aeschy-

---

126   Ibn 'Abd al-Barr, *al-Inbah* (Cairo, 1350/1931-1932), 43. Referenced in Franz
Rosenthal's translation of Ibn Khaldun, *The Muqaddimah*, vol. 1 (Princeton: Princ-
eton University Press, 1967), 266n.55, and "The Shuubiya Controversy" by Roy
Mottahedeh, 170-71.

127   Narrated by Abu Hurayrah, reported by al-Tirmidhi and classed as sound
by al-Albani.

128   A. de Armas, F., *Cervantes, Raphael and the Classics.* (Cambridge: Cambridge
University Press, 1998), 83.

129   The Council of Trent had condemned literary and other artistic depictions

lus and may be connected to the use of bread as a symbol in Numancia, so that the death of the city is a sacrificial, even Eucharistic, sacralizing of Spain.[130] Indeed, the play is explicit that Rome was robbed of victory, and Numancia likewise did not receive victory. But it is also explicit that victory in the context of that siege came to a third entity, that of Spain. In this sense, just as a king is both sacrificer and sacrifice, in Cervantes, the sieging and besieged are both flawed protagonists, and the victor is a third entity beyond these (perhaps even a synthesis of them, given that the Spain Cervantes celebrates is a Latin-speaking child of Rome).

Apart from Aeschylus, these themes can also be related to Virgil's *Aeneid* and its attendant tradition: Virgil's celebrated Trojans, at savage enmity with the Greeks, become Roman in part by the guidance of the Sibyl of Cumae, a Greek colony, and later by uniting with the Sabine women, where the Sabines are also said to be of Greek origin. The victor is not Trojan or Greek, but a third people which absorbs both, the Latins.

SACRED KINGSHIP AND SACRED LAW

Ernst Kantorowicz distinguishes between liturgical and legal kingship, or grace-centered and law-centered kingship, the latter legalism becoming prominent in the late Middle Ages and replacing the former liturgical sense. He argues that this shift accompanies the view of king as analogue to God the Father rather than to the *son*, so that the mediatorship of Christ falls to priests, not kings.[131] Ambiguities (already in the Justinian Codex, at least as read by later generations) between *lex digna* and *lex regia*, would eventually lead to the two modern modes: popular sovereignty and absolutist monarchy. Schizophrenia rather than synthesis. We have the revolutionary impulse that stems dialectically from the reactionary disposition to remove creativity or manifestation (the son, and with him, *becoming*) from the principle of power (identified with universal *Being*).

Frederick II of the Hohenstaufen may be the last example of legal kingship which is nonetheless still somehow in line with liturgical mediation. He is described as father and son of justice (not law, but *justice*). This gives us an image of mediation similar to those used in the Gospel. His version of modernity is traditional. For his jurists, the king as "living law" and maker of law, is subject (or in harmony with) the "Mother of all Law"/Reason understood as a sort of Goddess (not yet reason as reason-of-state, for "in legal philosophy she still showed

of suicide not long before Cervantes' writing of this piece (there are also suicides in *Don Quixote*), so that the Castilian author seems to be attacking Roman Catholic institutional pronouncements through the plot itself.

130   A. de Armas, *Cervantes, Raphael and the Classics*, 86.

131   We may disagree with Kantorowicz and argue that this is a shift to viewing the king as analogue to the *Ancient of Days*, where previously he was identified more with the *Son of Man* (the Father of the Trinity is *represented* in that relationship from Daniel's vision, not depicted there).

the features of a goddess"[132]): "For although our imperial majesty is free from all laws, it is nevertheless not altogether exalted above the judgment of Reason, herself the Mother of all Law."[133]

This is more or less John of Salisbury's sense of Christ as above the law, but the law as His will.[134] St. Paul's "all is permitted me but not all is beneficial" (1 Corinthians 10:23). This is analogous to Jove, who is not subject to the world-soul but receives the autozoon from his mother Rhea, which manifests through his kingly/demiurgic agency as the world-soul; or to the prophet Muhammad being exempt from aspects of shariah (having more than four wives, for example) and the Qur'an being considered a miracle of Muhammad, but he is in harmony with the Mother of the Book, the *Umm al-Kitab* (interpreted as prior to the oral recitation of the Qur'an). The banishing of Reason as "Mother of all Law" in late medieval political thought may be equivalent to Josiah's reforms of Jerusalem religion explored by Margaret Barker.[135]

When imminent harmony with that source of law is lost, and law downstream is turned into an idol, or our mental compulsion to decree, we have, again, the dichotomy again, of unstable civilization: pharisee and pharaoh, Sanhedrin and caesar, revolutionary and reactionary, obedience and obsession, iconoclast and idolater, or idolater of the law and idolater of the state; the one who searches for external signs and the one who searches for mental reasons in St. Paul's admonition against both Jew and Greek (1 Corinthians 1:22).

The twin mistakes are William Blake's Puritan and Deist, that is, the one who says "There is no Natural Religion," and therefore relies

---

132   Kantorowicz, *The King's Two Bodies,* 107.
133   Frederick II to the senators and people of Rome, cited by Kantorowicz (*The King's Two Bodies,* 105–6.)
134   Kantorowicz, *The King's Two Bodies,* 105.
135   This is not to say that the reform had nothing to do with a partial degeneration in the guardians of its preceding paradigm. In the late medieval case, perhaps conceiving of the king as father and not son (legalistic and not liturgical) is in fact a reaction to a prior excessive identification with sonship, where the king was receiving birth but not giving forth. He would be subject to the "feminine will" (world as divorced from masculinity), in William Blake's sense, because he was not properly realizing it: he was receiving the autozoon from mother Rhea and not manifesting in the world-soul, leading to static cultural forms and the sacrifice of creative works to that static state, just as Blake identifies human sacrifice with the divorce of the female will from the male. By not participating in the world, one might become subject to the world or one's reification of it (the unbalanced static becomes unbalanced dynamism, excessive lack of movement leads to excessive movement). Frederick II may have represented an unrealized balance between these: a conceiving of king as both ancient of days and son of man, both being and becoming. Giving justice at a lower octave and receiving its higher (abstract) principle. Here Kantorowicz's category of *legal kingship* is one allowing that the king may legislate in ways the previous understanding might have begun to deny, treating the law as static. We are speculating on patterns more than proposing historical trajectories.

on external culture/tradition, avoiding the mistake of seeking pure spontaneity but reifying the transcendent as his inherited tradition, and the one who says "All Religions are One," seeing common underlying principles, avoiding the mistake of sectarianism, but reifying the underlying principle as naturalistic causes. The alternative is to assert both phrases at once, taking both the mediation of culture, tradition, community and also seeing different cultures as encompassed in a single harmony. Here we approach sacred law and its relation to the initiate in terms of this alternative.

Sacred Kingship as Freedom to Legislate, or Of God and gods

The macranthrope, the cosmic body, requires internal diversity, as do all complex systems, and therefore must operate by letting its inner representatives act according to their nature, just as cells differentiate organically in the body. It is logical, then, that laws and customs should vary within the human family according to local character, just as it is good that languages are diverse. With that preamble, we may now address the ability of the king—as a metaphysically empowered representative of the kingdom—to act as king, that is, to rule, or more specifically, legislate.

Plutarch writes that great lawgivers consecrate their people to the gods. Their various laws are outer congealment of the New Law, which is grace and is in the heart, as St. Thomas Aquinas specifies in Christian terms. [136] The king sits as judge on the judgement seat, just as he sacrifices, having been made sacred (sacrifice is the *sacrum facere*, the making sacred). According to the metaphysics we have been discussing—and which we have found contained in the Gospel and elsewhere—particularity is not justified by its exclusive value or as a necessary restraint against agonistic conflict. This is so because no particular form is ultimately identifiable with the Absolute or with Its agency (salvation, in theological terms). In fact, the harmonious interaction of different forms is precisely what displays the Absolute both in Its being beyond form (it produces a plethora of forms because It isn't a form itself) and in Its oneness (those forms cohere and harmonize with each other because a common logic underlies them); ineffability and creativity.

In terms of Biblical scripture, the rejection of such exclusivism is behind St. Paul's rejection of the law. If the law is exclusive (either in its prescriptions or the people to which it is given) and necessary for a particularly exalted degree of salvation (or itself represents an exclusively exalted means to salvation) then its rejection entails a metaphysically grounded rejection of exclusivism. St. Paul opposes the law to the universality of Christ's Atonement. This universality concerns both scope (encompassing all humanity in potentially equal exaltation) and character

---

136   Saint Thomas Aquinas, *Summa Theologica*, vol. 2 (Cambridge: Hackett Publishing Company, 1997), Q.106, art.1; 949–50.

(it is not contained by the particularity of a legal code and pertains instead to something as universal as faith and the command to love).

Ultimately, the point St. Paul makes in various epistles concerning the law and, more generally, the ordinary Christian opinion on this topic, is the same as that of the *Gospel of Thomas* in its 53rd saying:

> His disciples said to him, "is circumcision useful or not?" He said to them, "If it were useful, their father would produce children already circumcised from their mother. Rather, the true circumcision in spirit has become profitable in every respect."

That the *Gospel of Thomas* also speaks of prayer, fasting and charity as unnecessary—however ritualistic the expressions of these practices—indicates it does not mean to reprimand the external acts themselves. Yet it should be noted that in the case of circumcision the text invokes a certain natural law—the state in which one is born—so that, as we have mentioned, a practice that permanently alters the anatomy implies particular restraint of application. Particular cultural expressions of universal principles, though essential, cannot totally subsume the biological and physical facts of human existence.

The Ecumenical Council of Florence, representing something like a common ground between Catholic West and Orthodox East in Europe, includes the following paragraph in its 11th section (dating from 1442), which expresses the European Christian attitude towards the law (I am abridging):

> It firmly believes, professes and teaches that the legal prescriptions of the Old Testament or the Mosaic law...were instituted to signify something in the future...once our lord Jesus Christ who was signified by them had come, came to an end and the sacraments of the New Testament had their beginning. Whoever, after the passion, places his hope in the legal prescriptions and submits himself to them as necessary for salvation and as if faith in Christ without them could not save, sins mortally. It does not deny that from Christ's passion until the promulgation of the gospel they could have been retained, provided they were in no way believed to be necessary for salvation. But it asserts that after the promulgation of the gospel they cannot be observed without loss of eternal salvation. Therefore, it denounces all who after that time observe circumcision, the sabbath and other legal prescriptions as strangers to the faith of Christ...Therefore, it strictly orders all who glory in the name of Christian, not to practice circumcision either before or after baptism, since whether or not they place their hope in it, it cannot possibly be observed without loss of eternal salvation.[137]

---

137   Ecumenical Council of Florence, *Decrees of the Ecumenical Councils*, ed. Norman P. Tanner and original language eds. Giuseppe Alberigo et al. (Georgetown: Georgetown University Press, 1990).

It is not entirely clear from this why a Jewish Christian could not continue to follow the Mosaic prescriptions in the same spirit which is mentioned as possibly belonging to that first generation of disciples, that is: "provided they were in no way believed to be necessary for salvation." It does, however, make clear that the Christian is accepting the Gospel, not the Deuteronomist observance, and, as the Acts of the Apostles (10) emphasizes, the gentile who becomes a Christian remains a gentile.

For Christianity, insofar as the law is justified to set a people apart, or as a (necessary or privileged) means for salvation, it has lost its *raison d'être* in the New Testament. The law is not needed to set people apart by making them holier because being better is not the only or best way to justify difference. Difference is embraced by itself (the mainstream Christian narrative is that national Israel really was holier than other nations, and Jewish opinion varies, including some pluralistic passages in the Torah, but the point, in any case, is that respect and love for diversity does not need anchoring in a hierarchy of value or, in this case, of holiness). Thusly did some church fathers consider the Jewish people to be a people even apart from the question of whether it is legitimate or not for them to continue observing the law.

Keeping apart from theological polemics, we now attempt to draw out the metaphysical view behind St. Paul's epistles. It suffices to point out that, just as Qur'anic criticisms of Christianity in which the latter's doctrines are not correctly represented (speaking of Mary as part of the Trinity, for example) can nonetheless be valid in that they are probably addressing popular distortions of that faith (more important for people than theological arguments) so too St. Paul is addressing a legalistic distortion. As such, his points can also be heeded by traditions with more definite legal prescriptions than Christianity (though ultimately his point is Christ). In any case, many a Sufi or Jewish mystic (of the sort, for example, whose Enoch-centric texts have been cited) would likely not fall afoul of St. Paul's main rebukes.

For St. Paul, Old Testament law (from Abraham to Moses) represents conformity to the Elementals. He observes in it something similar to what the *Bhagavad Gita* teaches regarding the worship of gods. Namely, that it is a failure to understand that the Divine is unconditioned, beyond form. This is particularly salient considering that for St. Paul the Elementals were probably something like the gods. The follower of the law that St. Paul has in mind, like the worshiper of gods as distinct from God in the Gita, is identifying a form with the formless Absolute. Realizing this mistake leads to the justification (in a Biblical sense) of all particularities by relinquishing the exclusive claim of any one of them (including a legal code) to having privileged access to the Absolute. (To this we may add St. Paul's subordinate argument against the idea that actions can by themselves earn salvation.)

St. Paul's talk of Elementals is interpretable as referring to gods or spiritual intelligences tasked with administering the universe but finding themselves in a somewhat twisted state, like humanity after the fall, and anyway being lesser than Christ. The term can also mean literal elemental aspects of life, like the basic features of grammar it is necessary for a child to learn before becoming an adult poet. In any case, Paul views the law as conformity to such entities or base lessons, and such conformity as slavery. Similarly, the *Gospel of Philip* contains the following passages:

> There are two trees growing in Paradise. The one bears animals, the other bears men. Adam ate from the tree which bore animals. He became an animal and he brought forth animals. For this reason the children of Adam worship animals. [138]

And concerning that tree which Adam ate from and that turned him into an animal and his children into animal worshipers, it says that this tree is the law:

> The law was the tree. It has power to give the knowledge of good and evil. It neither removed him from evil, nor did it set him in the good, but it created death for those who ate of it. For when he said, "Eat this, do not eat that," it became the beginning of death. [139]

On the relation of animals to gods, in a fragmented passage the text seems to tell us that certain powers interfere with salvation because "...if man is saved [there will not] be any sacrifices...and animals will not be offered to the powers." [140] It says these animals were offered alive and became dead, whereas men are offered dead to God and become alive. Man, as automaton, sleep-walking through life, passive to the external constraint of that tree which is the law and knowledge of good and evil, feeds the powers, the Elementals, and is spiritually dead. But if he is sacrificed to God, surrendered, he comes alive.

Indian tradition does not disagree. In fact, it uses the same language of becoming or being as an animal and of powers that are served thereby. Consider the *Birhadaranyaka Upanishad* and its warning:

> Now, if a man worships another deity, thinking "He is one and I am another," he does not know. He is like an animal to the gods. As many animals serve a man, so does each man serve the gods. Even if one animal is taken away, it causes anguish to the owner, how much more so when many are taken away! Therefore it is not pleasing to the gods that men should know the truth. [141]

The *Bhagavad Gita* (7:23) adds: "To the gods the god-worshipping go; My worshippers go surely to me." Abhinavagupta expands on the *Gita* (7:23):

---

138   *Nag Hamadi Codex II, 2–7, The Gospel of Philip*, 185.
139   Ibid., 191.
140   Ibid., 54:13–55:3, 149.
141   *Birhadaranyaka Upanishad*, I, iv, 10.

> Those whose minds are taken by various desires worship, according
> to their respective desires, a particular god or goddess Who in real-
> ity are partial manifestations of the higher reality. Therefore, the
> fruit that they attain comes only from the highest Lord. However,
> the fruits that they attain are not permanent. This is because such
> people limit themselves by their desires. Those who as a result of
> their devotion to Indra or other gods perform yajña etc., attain only
> that kind of result that could be granted by Indra and other guards.
> On the other hand, those who perform sacrifice for Me attain Me.

Limited results are attained by people who do not know that God
is beyond form.

Abhinavagupta continues concerning 7:24,

> ...there is no need to insist on giving me any particular name. The
> point here is that one who abandons his desires, and worships
> whichever form of God he chooses, then that given form of God
> eventually culminated in the real form of God, which is pure
> and formless. On the other hand, if the opposite is done and the
> outcome will be limited.[142]

It is when the Elementals are thought of as independent creatures,
not constituents of the cosmos (macro- and micro-; both the world we
encounter and our own form) that they become dangerous, holding power
over us. Crucially, by considering them constituents of the universe and
the human person they are no longer identifiable with the Absolute (of
which they are "partial manifestations"). The blasphemy ceases.

Compare the above, especially what the *Gospel of Philip* teaches concerning the "powers," to the following remarkable passage from St. Clement
of Alexandria (Strom. 4.25:156–57):

> Having become one deed, all the powers of the Spirit produce one
> Son and it is not possible to limit him to the concept of any of
> his individual powers. And the Son neither simply becomes one
> as one, nor many as parts, but he is one as all, and all comes from
> him. For he is the circle of all the powers being bound and united
> into one...That is why to become unitary means to believe in him
> and by him and to become one in him without distraction. On
> the other hand, to disbelieve means to hesitate, to be separated
> and to be divided.[143]

In this way, one who has "become unitary" may command (*Corpus
Hermeticum*, XIII.4:18):

> Powers within me, sign a hymn to the one and the universe. Sign
> together, all you powers within me, for I wish it.... Join me, all

---

142 Abhinavagupta, *Gitartha Samgraha* (Commentary on the *Bhagavad Gita*), 2nd
ed., trans. Boris Marjanovic (Varanasi, India: Indica Books, 2004), 182–83.
143 Discussed here: Ivan Miroshnikov, *The Gospel of Thomas and Plato: A Study of
the Impact of Platonism on the "Fifth Gospel"* (Brill: Leiden, 2018), 113.

you powers, and sign the hymn.... I thank you, father, energy
of my powers. I thank you, God, power of my energies; through
me your word hymns you.... This is what the powers within me
shout...they accomplish what you wish.... Your man shouts this
through fire, through air, through earth, through water, through
spirit, through your creatures...the praise that you have told, I have
also established in my cosmos...in the intellectual cosmos...[144]

We have the imagery of sacred monarchy and initiation wherein the four
corners (fire, air, earth, water) are brought together in a fifth (spirit)
and therefore encompass all (creatures, cosmos, and in fact, *my* cosmos,
the microcosm of man and the realm of his regency). Henry Corbin
describes this in terms of he who becomes an *imam* in the spiritual sense,
leading prayer for the angels, who are also parts of him, contained in
himself, in his microcosm.[145] The striking similitude between ancient
Egyptian sculptural depictions of deities and human bodily organs may
indicate this principle (the rams at Karnak resemble a brain with horns
indicating the hemispheres and the pharaoh beneath as brain stem;
Hathor's cow-face resembles a womb).[146]

    The integration of the gods into one's body appears in the *Pyramid
Texts*. The initiate: "[f]eeds on the lungs of the Wise Ones, and is satisfied
with living on hearts and their heka..." and "it is the pharaoh who eats
their heka, and gulps down their spirits."[147] The Corpus Hermeticum's
powers (deities, Elementals) are no longer autonomous from the person
who is now unitary, and therefore need not be restrained by "the law"
and sacrificed to in the sense of being appeased (for restraint must also
involve appeasement).

    This liberational character occurs in Greek philosophy. Empedocles
tells his student Pausanias that he will learn to change the weather, cure
disease and even raise the dead "if you so wish," a formula taken from
Homer's epics but there applied only to the gods:[148]

> And thou shalt master every drug that e'er
> Was made defense 'gainst sickness and old age—
> ...And thou shalt calm the might of tireless winds,
> ...And if thou wilt, shalt thou arouse the blasts,
> ...And thou shalt
> From Hades beckon the might of perished men.[149]

---

144   *Hermetica: The Greek Corpus Hermeticum and Latin Asclepius*, Brian P. Cophenhaver
(trans.) (Cambridge: Cambridge University Press, 1995), 53.
145   Corbin, *Alone with the Alone: Creative Imagination in the Sufism of Ibn 'Arabi*, 259–60.
146   This similitude is discussed in the *Magical Egypt* documentaries, especially
the upcoming second installment.
147   *Pyramid Texts*, 273–74. Cited by Uzdavinys, *Philosophy as a Rite of Rebirth: From
Ancient Egypt to Neoplatonism*, 214.
148   Kingsley, *Ancient Philosophy, Mystery and Magic*, 224.
149   Fragment III in William Ellery Leonard's translation (Chicago: Open Court
Publishing Company, 1908), 51–52.

In this, Empedocles is critiquing and esoterically clarifying the exoteric religion of Homeric paganism.[150] It is not a doctrine to be subject to the gods but to internalize the gods and their work in the self. This is similar to what the Gospel does to parts of the Old Testament.

Thus, although the *Gospel of Philip* speaks of powers as contrary to man's salvation because they want sacrifices from him, it also compares the man who ploughs his field with domestic animals to the "perfect man" who ploughs with "powers which are submissive." There are rebellious or wild powers as well as submissive ones, therefore, the latter being aligned with the perfect man's purpose. It also seems to teach that a non-legalistic attitude to the law could make appropriate use of the Tree of Knowledge, where knowledge/law is not an idol, not identified with righteousness/sainthood:

> This garden is the place where they will say to me, "[...] eat this or do not eat that, just as you wish." In the place where I will eat all things is the Tree of Knowledge. That one killed Adam, but here the Tree of Knowledge made men alive.[151]

This corresponds to the doctrine according to which Adam was indeed to eventually eat of all the trees in the garden, except that he did so from the Tree of Knowledge of Good and Evil before he was ready. He should have first eaten from the Tree of Eternal Life. In scripture, the knowledge of good and evil is indeed a necessary discernment for kings. But it is by first knowing that all life comes from God (Eternal Life) that we can properly understand the dualities of life. The former is theoria, and the latter theosis. To reach for theosis before knowing theoria (the formal, manifest, before knowing what is beyond it) is to become attached to the phenomenal. This is the mistake of the tyrant, he who does not apply universal paradigms to particular realities. This is also the mistake the *Turba Philosophorum* and other alchemical texts warn against.

Chapter three of the *Gita* states that in the beginning the Lord created men and gods, along with duty/sacrifice, and blessed them saying

> Be thou happy by this sacrifice because its performance will bestow upon you all desirable things. The gods, being pleased by sacrifices, will also please you; thus nourishing one another, there will reign general prosperity for all. In charge of the various necessities of

---

150 "...Empedocles throws in the assurance that Pausanias will be able to change the weather 'if you so wish'.... The phrase...was no doubt chosen deliberately by Empedocles because of its frequent use in Homer and Hesiod when referring to the special divine powers of gods and goddesses." This "explains well why this kind of magic was always bound to bring down on itself the charge of impiety" (Kingsley, *Ancient Philosophy, Mystery and Magic*, 224). Kingsley finds a correspondence with Diodorus Siculus's description of the Telchines, weather-altering shamans from Crete and Rhodes.

151 *Nag Hamadi Codex II, 2–7, The Gospel of Philip*, 191.

life, the gods, being satisfied by the performance of sacrifice, supply all necessities to man. But he who enjoys these gifts, without
offering them to the gods in return, is certainly a thief.

It can be a choice and a matter of coordinating action, but the law is
not any longer a necessary restraint-appeasement of powers/elementals/
deities, which have been recognized as "partial manifestations of the
higher reality" (Abhinava), which is the Son who "it is not possible to
limit...to...any of his individual powers," they are "bound and united
into one" (St. Clement), they are "submissive" and the "perfect man"
ploughs with them (*Gospel of Philip*), they receive that which is due to
them (sacrifices) but these are given in worship of and unto the one
Lord (*Bhagavad Gita*).

Knowledge, law, technology—these must be subject to the *spirit of
the law*, to a properly oriented heart. The begetting of giants by angels
(who Barker identifies with priests) can be considered a titanic creation
where knowledge has been misapplied and not used in conformity with
the harmony of creation, analogous to replacing religion with legalism.
Things renew themselves and lead to prosperity if done in sacrifice, if
offered up to God, not held onto. The duties/sacrifices, and the specific
gods in charge of these or associated with them, are not abolished in
this apophatic all-consuming attitude of offering. They are like the bush
ablaze but not consumed in Divine fire that Moses saw. This is not to
say, however, that such a transformation in holy fire will not look like
abolishment to the pharisaic legalist, who interpreted Jesus's disciples
as violating the Sabbath and blaspheming.

The instrumentalizing of ritual, where the Sabbath is revealed to be
for man and not the other way around, where the rites and laws do
not make us subject to Paul's Elementals or the Upanishads' gods, is
not dissimilar to the idea (explored by anthropologists like Durkheim,
Mauss, etc.) that archaic forms of state structure and public administration were instrumentalized—detachably and detachedly—by paleolithic
societies when the season required it, morphing in and out of opposite
social forms, and not congealed and solidified into brittle procrustean
contraptions (as Blake warns against in *Jerusalem*). Love should be the
substance of law, or the state, and the best way to guarantee that this
is so is to make sure we are using structures appropriately rather than
letting them lead us along by their own inner dynamics (as Heidegger
warns about the inner logic of technology, or as Walter Benjamin saw
in the case of capitalism becoming like a religion, with its own telos,
instead of capital accumulation being exhausted in the pursuit of good).
Seasonal dissolution and reconstitution of these structures, like the
initiate king's ritual death and return ceremony, dipping in and out of
formless potential and formal manifestation (formless love and formal
love), may be the technology ancient peoples utilized to this end. Like

water freezing in winter and melting in spring. Like the Jubilee's periodic forgiveness of debt.

St. Paul rejects the law (as passed on, as understood) because he views it as conformity or sacrifice to Elementals, lesser gods regarded outside a proper understanding of God. After all, Christ is a priest according to the order of Melchizedek (Hebrews 5:5–6), that mysterious king appearing in Genesis who is outside Abraham's covenant and circumcision, while also recognizing and being paid deference to by Abraham. It is a sacred kingship which stands outside and sustains the Abrahamic. Apart from abstractions concerning legalism in religion, then, the specific content of the law, and of central practice St. Paul most often cites, needs attending to in order to determine why the apostle rejects it. Circumcision is widely considered by Biblical scholars to have originally been a substitute for actual human sacrifice of first-born sons on their eighth day (thus the mandate to circumcise on the eighth day after birth).[152]

Indeed, the Greek Theophrastus (in *De Pietate*, cited in Porphyry's *De Abstinentia* II:26) opined that human sacrifice originated with the Israelites, an obvious exaggeration that nonetheless indicates it was known to be practiced by them anciently, noting they did so from compulsion, not desire.[153] There is also evidence that the original—or at least one early—version of Abraham's life included the real slaying of his son Isaac, who is taken into heaven—as illustrated in the *Dura Europos* synagogue in Syria, whose construction would have ended by 244 AD. After this, a substitute was given in the form of an animal to be slain thereafter, as well as circumcision. One Rabbinical tradition points out that since scripture does not tell us the Lord spoke to Abraham after this episode, except by angelic intermediaries, it may be that the patriarch fell short of his mission. After all, he questioned other proposed actions by the Lord, such as the destruction of cities, and negotiated (so to speak) an attenuation of the wrath that was to fall on them. His failure to do so on this occasion might have been met with a distancing of direct Divine communication.

Regardless, it makes sense in light of this possible origin for the practice—human sacrifice, either as a bestowal of prosperity, an apotropaic device to ward off evil or both[154]—that St. Paul should be so specific in condemning it, for such a sacrifice cannot continue if the ultimate sacrifice, that of Christ, has already occurred and really been accepted. It would seem, then, that St. Paul is rejecting, or that the Gospel is distinct from, both the older Hebrew religion, including human sacrifice (apparently being practiced even after the substitute of circumcision was introduced, since Deuteronomy sees fit to condemn it during its reform,

---

152 Barker, *The Mother of the Lord Volume I: The Lady in the Temple*, 36.
153 Cited by Barker, *The Mother of the Lord Volume I: The Lady in the Temple*, 36.
154 Frithjof Schuon somewhere takes a positive view of human sacrifice as having a meaning other than these.

although this may have to do with rare holdouts or a foreign practice being imitated by Israelites) on the one hand, and on the other the Deuteronomist version of religion, which was more iconoclastic, banned various pagan-like practices and rejected the veneration of Lady Wisdom.

Whether Abraham was merely attenuating sacrifice by changing its extreme form (sacrifice of firstborn sons) for lighter ones, is another question. In one sense circumcision is like animal sacrifice or even baptism, representing self-sacrifice (acceptance of death) by an external act. This initiatic character may be perceived in ancient Egyptian or tribal sub-Saharan African examples of the practice and by the word's transposition into the context of spiritual realization by the expression "circumcision of the heart" in Christian scripture.

It is contradicted, however, as is the case for animal sacrifice, by instances in which it is treated as a real and necessary apotropaic act. Further, it affects the body permanently, and in this regard grants cultural symbolism a permanent veto over the human form. For this reason, it can be treated just as animal sacrifice when the latter is understood not to replace spiritual self-sacrifice but as a sacralization of the act of hunting or slaughter which would be carried out anyway in order to acquire meat. Perhaps circumcision can be similarly understood as a symbol for spiritual self-sacrifice when united with necessity, as when, or if, it was practiced because conditions in a particular climate, given a particular state of medicine, caused it to be adopted, or if it were propitious to a particular vocation, such as curbing (or otherwise affecting) sexual activity (which is how Maimonides justifies the practice) for those pursuing a partly renunciatory priestly office, as might have been the ancient Egyptian case.

Margaret Barker notes human sacrifice as a part of the pre-Josian reform of Hebrew religious practice. If we read William Blake's view of history[155] creatively, and together with Barker, his presentation of the negative aspect of the female-will when detached from the male (sentience overtaking consciousness, experience overtaking the experiencer) and its link to human sacrifice (which Blake takes as a historical degeneration) is interesting. Here the coming of Christianity is a recovery of the Lady Wisdom (per Barker) but not of human sacrifice—at least not as actual killing: it is recovered as self-crucifixion and spiritual rebirth. Christianity would, in Blakean terms, be the return of an older female-will, prior to the Druidic cult of blood sacrifice, with female and male in harmony (as in the *Gospel of Philip*) and sacrifice made through bread and wine.

In any case, human sacrifice cannot be accepted as simply another part of pre-Deuteronomist Hebrew observance, since Abraham—whether Isaac really did die or not—was instructed to adopt a non-human form of sacrifice and any continuance of actual human slaying would be a hold-out of something non- or pre-Abrahamic. It is another question

---

155   Frye, *Fearful Symmetry*, 135.

whether the non-human sacrifice (animal, circumcision) is just an atten-uation, maintaining the same fundamentally flawed mentality, or a mere symbol, uniting what was already practiced for quasi-medical or priestly-vocational reasons to a spiritual initiation and ritual death (again, possibly similar to the ancient Egyptian or tribal African version of the practice). The Egyptian practice could have been a vocational, caste-specific priestly initiation, since we have mummified evidence of pharaohs and other Egyptians who were not circumcised, and the two extant ancient illustrations of the practice—the stele of Uha and the tomb of Ankmahor—concern men of the priesthood. Given that Israel is called a priestly nation, it would make sense to have generalized such a practice. In Ugaritic texts it is a practice associated with marriage, which may be to do with limiting the possibility of infection in the context of marital sex, general climate-related hygiene or even an ethos consistent with that of the possible priestly association in Egypt.

Both the attenuation of human sacrifice while retaining its underlying logic and the symbolizing of spiritual initiation by way of a procedure with some context-specific utility are probably true in different senses. In the Christian understanding, the Gospel corrects the first by abolishing its mentality entirely while usually considering the second a legitimate particularity that should not be universalized along with the universally restorative lesson of the crucified and resurrected Christ. The Sabbath is not abolished but becomes a technology to be used, where it is made for man but man is not made for it. (It is a shame, however, that this radical break from sacrificial psychology has not come fully through in history, with assertions of vicarious blood payment and cosmic debts coming out of Christianity itself.)

The *Bhagavad Gita* advises against the total renunciation of ritual, caste and social function, probably in the context of certain Buddhist and Jain attacks on tradition. In a similar vein, the *Chandogya Upanishad* uses the term for human sacrifice in the context of giving up one phase of life to the next—as though recovering the term's original meaning before an aberrant literalization. [156] Human sacrifice is rejected but in the context of asserting a sort of esoteric meaning for the term, as well as ritual and the traditional phases of life. In the *Bhagavatam Purana* (V.9:18), Kali herself (in some ways equivalent to Christianity's Babylon, maybe) stops the sac-rifice of an exalted person by killing her misguided followers. Thus, this ferocious female deity to whom the age of spiritual ignorance corresponds nonetheless is not opposed to order and interrupts sacrifice gone awry.

---

156   It is also possible that some cultures understood human sacrifice not as propi-tiation of the gods but as a willing passage into death in order to carry out some oper-ation. Such a thing would be entirely different from the kinds of sacrifice we observe among the Aztecs, for example. Propitiating the gods with blood in return for favor is precisely the kind of demonic economy the Bible or Zosimos of Panopolis warn of.

"Man is sacrifice" begins the sixteenth Khanda of the *Chandogya Upa-nishad* (III.16:1). It then goes on to describe every part of ritual sacrifice, from initiation, foods, hymn recitations and gifts for priests as a part of the ordinary life of a man, identifying the carrying off of sacrificial vessels that contained *Soma* to be cleansed as his death (III.17:1–5). We read that after one has communicated this view of sacrifice to Krishna, one never thirsts again (III.17:6), which resembles Christ's saying that the living water he gives renders one never again thirsty (John 4:14). The scripture is also appropriately solar, using the knowledge of the sun's luminescence as a symbol for epiphany, the light in the heart and the highest light.[157] As Henk W. Bodewitz notes,[158] the attitude here of incorporating the real meaning of Vedic ritual into quotidian life itself, is similar to that of the Gita (and, we can add, all the more so given its devotion to Krishna).

Jan E. M. Houben writes of an episode that reveals a similar philos-ophy in the *Satapatha Brahmana*, where:

> When the description of the Purusamedha—the sacrifice—reaches the point that the human victims are to be killed, the author switches to a narrative mode ("Now, the victims had had the fire carried round them, but they were not yet slaughtered") and lets the mysterious voice say to the sacrificer and priests: "Purusa, do not consummate (these human victims): if thou wert to con-summate them, man (purusa) would eat man"; next, the *Satapatha Brahmana* continues: "Accordingly, as soon as fire had been carried round them, he set them free, and offered oblations to the same divinities…" (SB 13.6.2.121–3, tr. Eggeling)

Houben adds that whether this and other examples of such interrup-tions of human sacrifice "concerns an earlier actual practice of human sacrifice or just a theoretical possibility is controversial."[159] In any case, it is a similar Divine arresting of blood sacrifice as occurs in Genesis when Abraham readies the death of Isaac and is restrained by an angel.

We have here the inner meaning of sacrifice, its non-literalized, non-caricatured form. Many of the cultures that seem to encode a true metaphysics in their myths, including the Minoans, did, at least during periods of their history, fall into such literalization and practice human sacrifice. The above inner meaning provides the key to what Catherine

157   *The Upanishads*, trans. F. Max Muller. In: *The Sacred Books of the East*, 1879–1884, trans. Various Oriental Scholars (London: Macmillan and Co., Publishers to the University of Oxford, 1879), 50–52.

158   H. W. Bodewitz, "Hindu Ahimsa and its Roots," 17–44. In: *Violence Denied: Violence, Non-Violence and the Rationalization of Violence in South Asian Cultural History*, eds. J. Houben and K. van Kooij (Leiden: Brill, 1999), 39–40.

159   Jan Houben, "To Kill or not to Kill the Sacrificial Animal (yajna-pasu)? Arguments and Perspectives in Brahmanical ethical philosophy," 105–84. In: *Violence Denied: Violence, Non-Violence and the Rationalization of Violence in South Asian Cultural History*, eds. J. Houben and Karel van Kooij (Leiden: Brill, 1999), 120–21.

Pickstock describes as redemption, the allegorizing faculty that can return to the past with ironic removal from its mistakes or degeneracies to see the inner spirit of which even evils were a mere parody or privation (she makes this observation in the context of allegorizing Old Testament violence).[160] Writes Northrop Frye:

> ...the Bible has been seen to have many traces of pre-Biblical thought and ritual...in such episodes of Jephthah's sacrifice of his daughter...or Jacob's setting up of a sacred stone at Bethel...while the parallels are suggestive and even tantalizing.... We might get more sense of direction if we looked at the situation from something closer to the Bible's own point of view...the Bible is providing the antitypes of which Canaanite and other pre-Biblical cults are types. It claims, by implication, to indicate what the symbolism of such cults "really means" by relating them to the worship of the true God.[161]

When William Blake stated that the Antiquities of all nations are as holy and true as that of the Jews, he added (in *Jerusalem* and elsewhere) that a terrible deviation occurred wherein "Druid temples" began spreading human sacrifice. This is also not dissimilar to St. Dionysius the Areopagite who sees the angels of all nations, and the guidance they provided, as having been equivalent, and seems to imply that the widespread adoption of the Bible is a remedy to general apostasy brought about by the nations not properly following that guidance (to all nations prophets were sent, as Islam teaches).

In the case of Biblical religion, which seems to mirror India, we have an old, primordial religion corrupted and grown macabre and a puritanical reaction: figuratively, the libertine and the legalist, the error of going too far and of not going at all. The Gospel is neither of these, but a middle way, one which is not really limited to restoring the Abrahamic as it was before the Deuteronomists. The Abrahamic substitute for human sacrifice is itself substituted by a single sacrifice, that of the cross. Indeed, the Gospel is not even a return to Eden, or not merely that. As the *Gospel of Philip* reads:

> Before Christ came, there was no bread in the world, just as Paradise, the place where Adam was, had many trees to nourish the animals but no wheat to sustain man. Man used to feed like the animals, but when Christ came, the perfect man, he brought bread from heaven in order that man might be nourished with the food of man.[162]

Christ brings something better even than humanity had in Eden.

---

160 Pickstock, *Repetition and Identity*, 227.
161 Northrop Frye, *The Great Code: The Bile and Literature* (Toronto: University of Toronto Press, 2006), 111–12.
162 *Nag Hamadi Codex II, 2–7, The Gospel of Philip*, 55:5–55:36, 151.

Just as mistakes produce good effect in the Bible, such as the felix culpa of expulsion from Eden or the apparently negative conditions which lead to diversity of language and the institution of monarchy in Biblical narrative, so too the terror of human sacrifice is used as an occasion for its meaning to be completely reversed by the cross. If Christ is the God of Israel (and the rest of humanity) Incarnate, he is undoing the confusion wrought by a degenerated Archon (to use the Gospel of John's term) of Israel and humanity.

St. Paul's theology of Christ giving the spiritual powers of the cosmos over to the Father at the end of the Age can be understood as analogous to realizing creation's diversity as an effulging of the One, the singular Creator, and not at all the result of irreducibly distinct entities sharing no single cause of single underlying principles. Those Archons, those powers of the cosmos St. Paul discusses, including that angel through which the law came to Moses, would have fallen into ignorance during the present age or earlier, forgetting or no longer perceiving that there is one principle for all beings, Plato's One, Abraham's Lord. Several points are to be noted here:

1. By inhabiting the structures of the old religion, namely that of the sacrifice of the firstborn, that religion's symbols are entirely conquered, the meaning of its structures being altered while those structures are taken up—it is not opposition but assimilation, which is consistent with the embrace of the cross, for death is indeed to be embraced, but as self-death through which there is life, not as bloody stages and rites (hungry demons received a poisoned meal);

2. The sacrifice of Christ is qualitatively different from how sacrifice is conceived of in certain previous scriptures, as the sacrifice Himself becomes the model to be imitated, that is, not an instrument towards exaltation but itself the protagonist of exaltation and, consequently, the disciple is to imitate the sacrifice by sacrificing himself (like the ancient king wearing an animal hide and thus *being* the sacrificed animal)—the Evangelical commandment to love is a commandment to be willing to die and, in life, to be kenotic, to empty out, to bear one's cross and follow, to not live, but have Christ live in oneself (Galatians 2:20);

3. It is important to realize that the Eucharist is not apotropaic, not a giving something up that the universe might thereby consider us to have already paid our debts and spare us from unexpected pains (the habit of mind of a sufferer of obsessive compulsions), but rather is a joyful participation, a simple receiving of the unearned gift, into which human agency and nature go and are completed (as mentioned earlier, wine and bread are natural elements finished by humanity—grape and wheat worked on by humans—and Divinized in the Eucharist). The Eucharist is not punitive, it is celebratory.

What is legitimate in the apotropaic mentality is purely ascetical: suffering not as an idol, as though pain were virtuous, but as an ascetical discipline in order to mature and pursue vital projects from that state. Ultimately this implies self-sacrifice of the false self and the joyful experience of being. This Christ-like willingness to die achieves what the Upanishads recommend: to locate St. Paul's Elementals in oneself (like the Tantric practitioner writing his school's doctrine and gods on his body) and in the body of Christ. The destructive forces, the Titans, covered in gypsum, give way to the immortal Zagreus whose new body of gypsum can be understood as containing them in a subdued form.

This subordinates them, conceiving of them as parts (or perspectives), rather than worshiping them as external and therefore autonomous (just as anger, outside its proper place in a healthy personality that channels it towards the ends of compassion, becomes an autonomous and destructive emotion). This is precisely what monarchical initiation, the realization of identity with the macranthrope, does. It locates the elements of the universe in the body, for both manifest the same paradigm. To the king, after his epiphany, the Elementals are manifestly not the Absolute or even the whole of manifestation, but parts (this is clear in the *Vedas* and in Tantric initiation). The fact that Tantric initiation—which explicitly maps the cosmic elements and gods onto the body of the devotee—contains a certain antinomianism presents a possible correspondence with St. Paul, whose subordination of the cosmic Elementals and embrace of the body of Christ leads him to reject the law.

Equivalently, "Krishna's later exploits included battles with, and defeats of, the gods Indra, Varun and Shiva...."[163] The manifestation of the one God defeats the gods. This is not a Christian innovation but is the stuff of the perennial spiritual quest. The Elementals of the cosmos are no longer adhered to, but are under judgement (John 16:11) and brought into the body of Christ, for the cosmos is not undone but conquered (John 16:33), made to have faith (John 17:21), because God loved the cosmos (John 3:16), ending the rule by law (which results from adherence to the Elementals) and allowing deliberative, creative, compassionate, communal human agency, if properly subordinate to the Spirit. In a sense this legitimizes the whole of the human political sphere and, beyond history, reveals a perennial epiphany encoded in monarchical investiture and traditions throughout the world.

A perfect summation of this point is found in myths in which Juno, the force of nature, the dynamic world of becoming, is opposed to the hero at the start of the spiritual journey, as in the cases of Hercules and Aeneas, but then finally embraces him. Aeneas reconciles with femininity by marrying Lavinia at the end of his story, Hercules is accepted as a god and, in a more ancient version, Gilgamesh reconciles with the goddess Inanna after

163　*Bhagavad Gita*, trans. W. Sargeant (Albany, NY: SUNY Press, 1984), 14.

quarrelling with her. This is explained in Vaishnavism, Krishna-centric doctrine according to which the goddess *Yogamaya* produces duality so that saints may interact with God as a personal being and engage in play, not as a deception or falling into spiritual ignorance but as a will to creative enjoyment of Divine power. Just as Juno becomes ally to Aeneas and Hercules, the divine feminine ceases to be a force for ignorance and becomes so for creativity. Vala, the shadow of the Divine Feminine *Jerusalem* in Blake's *Prophetic Books*, can have a manifestation which is "animated and vegetated" and a "devouring worm" or can be in "sweet repose" (*Jerusalem*, 12, 2–3), a repose allowing us to perceive the Divine in the world, submitted to the sublime, translucent to the transcendent.

We have to treat the gods as part of us, integrate them and move beyond, like learning the elemental grammar and mastering language (in Galatians St. Paul explicitly uses this pedagogic metaphor). Huston Smith writes in his preface to the *Bhagavad Gita*: "Just as the many gods of the *Vedas* are effective in different situations, so the many yogas are prescribed in the Gita without compromising or subordinating one to another. Mutual paths are allowed to exist in complementarity."[164] Max Mueller's term *henotheism*, coined to describe the Vedic, specifically Rig-Vedic, approach to the gods, is not quite appropriate here, for it is not a question of choosing one god among gods but of choosing God, and considering the gods to be lesser, manifest beings or less universal principles.

The law, or certain ways of adhering to scripture, identifies God with contingent forms, as we have already pointed out. To place God's salvific agency within the stricture of specific legal prescriptions is an intellectual error. If a particular set of practices (such as Mosaic law and the priestly mode of worship represented by it) are identified with the human state's communion with the Divine as such, then idolatry has entered into the religion. The form-transcending nature of God or His agency has not really been accepted. Therefore, one is not accessing the proper spiritual epiphany, just like those Indian worshippers of particular gods do not access liberation (*moksha*). In a sense every religion's exotericism poses this trap, Christianity very much included, although, like other religions, it also contains the medicine to treat the poison, for example in some of St. Paul's rebukes against those the law.

Whether, in the Christian context, this should include Jewish Christians following the Mosaic law under the condition that it not be thought of as a requisite or privileged vehicle for salvation is a question some Church Fathers might well have answered in the affirmative. For his part, the 18th century Orthodox Rabbi Jacob Emden considered condemnations of the law appropriate in Christianity, seeing this religion (and Islam) as legitimate, so long as Jewish adherence to Mosaic law continued. This is also the opinion of Samuel Zinner, whose work we reference elsewhere, and

---

164   Ibid., xxv.

who considers early non-Pauline Jewish Christianity, including continued adherence to Mosaic law, compatible with the Gospel. [165]

On one level the law is always sacred if it seeks to facilitate the harmonious coexistence of people, since harmony is precisely what the kingly epiphany of transcendent unity translates as in the manifest plane: it is the law of the autozoon. In Christianity the Incarnation of the ultimate king is often understood as representing the end of the rule of law, its obsolescence.

Legal systems can be a means for communal harmony but also for articulating an aesthetic (the way certain customs are followed by groups—from nations and professional associations to hobby enthusiasts—who cultivate a cultural character for themselves). They must conform to human flourishing in just the same way as it is a physical or anatomical law that bending one's arm the wrong way will break it. The religious character of sacred law is usually predicated on something like this latter sense of being a physical law, a fact of human flourishing.

However, just as a language like Arabic or Japanese can be sacred and endowed of a function both exclusive and liturgical to Muslim or Shinto observance, respectively, without meaning that the linguistic faculty as such is exhausted or finds its highest possible expression in that language (though both must fully conform to the rules of human nature and coherence) the same applies to sacred laws. So long as a legal code is not considered salvific by itself and is understood as one "language" among a potential multitude, a law-emphasizing approach to religion would be one valid vocation among others.

The above relates to the previous discussion concerning redemption as the act of deeming again or re-naming: Adam's freedom in the garden to give names to its denizens. It is the key to cultural renewal, whereby a deep and abiding essence is given a new name, a lesson is taken out of the historical context of scripture and applied to new contexts, humanity's freedom to a legitimate nominalism is grounded in its submission to metaphysical realism. The essence is real but the name can be changed according to human creativity. Place and cultural particularity can thereby be sacralized. St. Paul is pointing to the Gospel as freedom also for political communities and cultures. This is not the snake as tempter, though temptation rests there as the danger within the saving power, to reverse Holderlin's aphorism.

It is the snake as redeemer, for if the assembled community look upon the snake Moses has impaled in their midst they are saved, the snake that is Christ on the cross, if they can be as wise as serpents (and innocent as doves) (Matthew 10:16). The serpentine way of being must be embraced,

---

165   This, however, would presumably differ from the idea of an Enochic, pre-Josianic Hebrew piety as understood via Andrei Orlov, restored by Jesus according to Margaret Barker.

for, as Pickstock points out, all things must undulate, must contract
and stretch, twist and untwist, embracing the fundamental duality of
advancing even as we retreat into ourselves. This is the embrace of the
cross, dying to things, letting them go so we are free to get something
new, to resurrect. Thus, the cross is revealed as the throne, the suffering
wretch as King. But again, the snake is also temptation, and in politics,
sacralizing place and particularity can be dangerous, as history amply
attests. This leads us to the next section where we make a necessary
distinction between true and untrue sacrifice.

The True and the Perverse Sacrifice: Ex Nihilo Contra Nihilo

The error in the law pointed out by St. Paul and by currents opposed
to legalism (self-flagellation and *apotropaia*) in every tradition, is the
obsessive-compulsive search for stability in ritualized, repetitive action
or thought. Stability of one's own self moment-to-moment, of the forms
around one and particularly of the health of those forms that one values,
desire for whose continuity causes us anxiety. This stability, however,
is a gift freely given, a feature of the cosmos as it is. The apotropaic
impulse, the bartering appeasement of fate by removing something we
value, some enjoyment, and hoping to thusly beat fate to the punch,
so to speak, harming ourselves before life gets a chance to, is a typical
feature of such pathological states of mind. To accept a reality not in
need of sacrifices (in the usual sense of an exchange or barter with the
Divine, not of self-discipline or *making sacred*) is part of the Gospel and
other scriptures. It is part of how St. Paul understands the definitive
sacrifice of Christ and why he rejects continued following of the law
which can be like a continued sacrifice. Bartering is never really required,
so Christ's sacrifice is a making sacred and a displaying of how to live
(by being willing to die but also disbelieving in death), rather than a
strictly vicarious paying of a price. No ritual as such can have saving
status, only relationship to God can.

Again, this is the result of idolatry: of conceiving of Being not as the
Being of beings, within and amidst them, but as a powerful other among
weaker entities. This reification of Being implies it might as well be arbitrary or even evil. We therefore want to appease it through sacrifices, for
being like us except larger, it has need of sustenance. This is paganism,
in Christian terms. Since there is no Being of beings, there is no order
or coherence to reality as such, no ontology of peace. We can only exist
as a function of strife, of mental tension. Anything that presents us with
peaceful beauty, inviting us into a contemplation or aesthetic enjoyment
free of mental tension, is perceived as an annulment, and considered an
enemy. Thusly do the politics of such an existential disposition tend to
be violent and deconstructive. We see this in Dostoyevsky's novels and
their criticism of the revolutionists he had encountered, for example.

By relaxing into the imminent presence of a *hospitable infinity*—an infinity hospitable rather than hostile to the integrity of forms, one supportive of delimitation rather than entropy—we become a locus for hospitability. The source of what we are calling hospitability is Unity as such: not a particular form among forms, but that which manifests forms (unities) and draws forms into harmonious patterns with each other (grander unities). This is apophatic, because Unity is beyond unities, without collapsing into its parody, iconoclasm, because it sees unities as the testifiers of Unity.[166] We have therefore a transforming principle rather than a taxing practice, a baptism rather than a circumcision. The apotropaic barter with Unity pretends Unity is actually a unit among others, and is therefore replaced by Unity's simple presence. The apophatic defeats the apotropaic.

The tendency to disfigure, or partition, forms and to thusly produce stability out of one's incisive agency rather than accepting the ego destabilizing truth of stability being an externally given gift, is present, then, in human sacrifice, in its attenuated substitutes. The essence of the law is this giving up of one thing for another, an instinct which must be controlled, made to serve the cause of social harmony, and not confused for justice proper, which is not retributive or apotropaic but concerns giving each what nature demands (*suum cuique tribuere*[167]). When law is supreme it oppresses justice, where justice is the ideal of a free play in which each part of the whole does its will, unencumbered by the inner compulsion of sin.

True sacrifice is opposed to a mechanistic formalism. The latter stems from a mentality that seeks stability by convincing itself that it can receive safety by giving something up, that it can barter with Heaven, indeed, that it can, more deeply, produce stable ground out of continuous thought and action, out of staying busy. This mentality is at the root of disorders like Obsessive-Compulsive Disorder. Pure felicity, simple happiness, the contemplation of forms as they are, opens one up to a sort of existential vertigo. One has to accept that there is a reality independent of one's cognition and simply rest in what that reality gives one. Thus, any form that resists our mental categories is overlain with them, and, at the extreme, done violence to, so that our agency is physically and directly imposed upon the autonomy of externals.

At some point *might* and *right* must coincide. The purest will towards an end must be a will towards the true end, that is, the telos of the sentient being doing the willing, *because otherwise some part of that sentience, some deep recess, will be unaligned with the will.* In order for an entity to be entirely committed to something it must be something which is desirable to every part of that entity, down (or up) to its profoundest Being, which, theologically speaking, is the personal God's will for it.

---

166   See St. Dionysius and Nicholas of Cusa.
167   Cicero's translation of Plato's Socrates.

Thusly the logic behind Mircea Eliade's claim that accomplished saints or monks can reverse the ontological constructs of reality, putting a hand on fire without burning, and so on, (like the medieval placing a hand on an open flame to prove one's innocence during litigation). We recall Mark 16:15-20: that the disciples will speak in new tongues is interpretable as affecting the significance of signs[168]—in this passage, the causation between drinking poison and damaged health is suspended by the disciple.

At play is the idea that human beings fear collapse into chaos should their ideations fail, as suggests Suzanne Langer. This involves anxious desire for stability leading us to create, sometimes spurious, ideational frameworks and to want to dwell in these thoughts as opposed to giving ourselves over to a vision of reality as it is—a beatific vision, so religion promises. It also often leads us to justify things we like in terms of necessity, and to deny that reality might not be circumscribed in ways that render these things necessary in the strict terms we have chosen to accept. One sometimes hears arguments clearly motivated by an aesthetic love for manual labor justified in terms of the necessity of such labor to human survival and economic prosperity. The point, however, is that the beauty of manual labor, the aesthetic admiration for it and for the states of mind one can cultivate through it, can be asserted in a manner wholly independent of whether or not new technologies can, in fact, render manual labor unnecessary in the limited terms of producing needed provisions or raising GDP. If one is willing, one can let the beauty of something be its justification. Of course, an aesthetic exploration is needed, one that dives all the way down to where beauty meets the good and the true.

During an interview, I put the issue to William Desmond in terms of coming to admire life, ours and that of others, including its struggles, as a work of beauty (though not in the modern sense of aesthetic excitation, but as simple beauty). He pointed out that the "deeper relationship" between the aesthetic and religious begins to be occluded after the beginning of the eighteenth century, whereas beforehand it was taken for granted without being excessively emphasized, one suspects in the same sense in which the hard problem of consciousness was not put in those terms because, really, the modern problematizing of it had not occurred to many thinkers.

In Dostoyevsky's *Demons* the character Kirilov is tormented by the search for an adequate expression of freedom. He describes himself as "bound to believe that [he doesn't] believe" and "bound to show self-will." That which is outside mental machinations is anathema: whatever does not reduce to the narrow cognizing self is experienced as a nullification of that self and must be subjected to egoic violence. The nihilist has perceived a vast annulment, *nihilo*, and guards against it compulsively through frenetic activity, bursts of anxious reasoning and the need to act quickly while

---

168   Thus can the law remain unchanged in jot or tittle, while also revealing that the Sabbath is made for man and not vice versa.

the imminent perception of some conceptual justification for his actions lasts. This is a sacrificial dynamic. Kirilov's opting for suicide is both the paroxysm of this compulsion and an escape from its exhausting exercise.

Shakespeare expresses the same idea in *Macbeth* through the protagonist's tormentors. Those three witches eschew form. They are ambiguous to the point of non-discrete physicality, materializing and dematerializing, an abdication of corporeality equivalent to Kirilov's suicide. Their cauldron is the brew in which mutilated life (animal and human parts) becomes undifferentiated. It is the opposite of a womb. Their freedom finds expression only in effacement and the ruin of men. Again, life subsisting on its own is perceived with hostility as somehow an affront to the self, which must insinuate into everything it perceives. In these cases, the need to do violence is also the need to bring life under control, a *libido deformitate*, so to speak, as corollary to Augustine's *libido dominandi*, for a thing must be secured before it is savaged. Any entity, left unmolested, is too much a reminder that one's psyche is not supreme and is therefore subject to forces beyond itself. That forms should subsist independently of one is clear evidence for the supremacy of that which is beyond one, and of one's being at the mercy of the unpredictability of an outside reality. The act of subduing in order to exact violence is, in fact, precisely the act of subduing through violence.

The tireless superimposition of mental schemes on actually existing life, is the "plurality of gods" who "deserve worship the less they demand it."[169] Against this idolatry we have the "abolition of all sacrifices."[170] Idols persist, and narcissism swells, so long as one's self is identified as the calculative or discursive organ, separate from the rest of reality. As the *Birhadaranyaka Upanishad* warns:

> Now, if a man worships another deity, thinking "He is one and I am another," he does not know. He is like an animal to the gods. As many animals serve a man, so does each man serve the gods. Even if one animal is taken away, it causes anguish to the owner, how much more so when many are taken away! Therefore it is not pleasing to the gods that men should know the truth.[171]

Mere apprehension or contemplation of forms is sacrificed to a tightly ramified pattern of thought. It requires that enjoyment be deferred continuously, for joy implies a level of un-guardedness that makes itself vulnerable to an encounter with "*nihilo*" as pure contingency. Ecstasy is an exit from the self, though it is also the exit by which the real self is discovered (Matthew 16:25).

The sacrifice of Kirilov and the witches (in truth an inversion of sacrifice, for nothing is being *made sacred*) may be described as creation

---

169   St. Augustine, *City of God*, X:16.
170   Ibid.
171   *Birhadaranyaka Upanishad*, I, iv, 10.

contra nihilo, in contrast to the suspension or subdual of mental categories, which allows for creation *ex nihilo.* The latter lets life speak for itself, by way of existing buoyance, beautiful and beastly, responding by calling out, shepherding forth, new expressions according to what is stirred in oneself, one's vocation. This *letting life speak for itself* (as in the Pythagorean preparatory two-year oath of silence) is to practice the virtue of patience.

This is at play in the Heideggerian attitude of caring or stewarding (*Sorge*) in contrast to Theodor Adorno's negative dialectic. The latter risks systematizing the compulsion that violates—negates—every form. Any resolution, any harmony, implies a whole, therefore an imperative in terms of which the free play of parts may be stimmed and in terms of which there is an outside the whole which do not fit, and totalitarianism that way lies, so goes the negative critique. It proceeds from fear that the irreducibility of things will open us up to a totalizing force, that great force by virtue of which things hang together, that infinity which is hospitable to the integrity of forms, gratuity. A terrible, dry asceticism is required, a kill-joy ethic that prioritizes the possibility of totalitarian metastasis in anything aesthetically compelling. The whole is denied and every part as part too, for there are no parts if there is no whole. By systematically negating the whole, we paradoxically create a totalistic system out of our own fear of the whole, a spectral mockery. And a shadow, a photo negative, emerges. Blake saw it all:

> ...they make an Abstract, which is a Negation
> Not only of the substance from which it is derived,
> A murderer of its own Body, but also a murderer
> Of every Divine Member. It is the Reasoning Power,
> And in its Holiness is closed the Abominatio of Desolation!
> (Blake, *Jerusalem*, chapter 1, 10:10–16)

That Blake observed this in the messianic delirium of the industrial Enlightenment reveals how fully some critiques of the Enlightenment in large part conformed to it. The pathology is an ancient one. Against the "transcendental unity of the gift, according to Paul, the generality of the law is expressed in its compulsive (and non-analogical) multiplicity, that is, its attempt to secure a finite, spatial catalogue of virtue, an exhaustive list."[172] That law requires sacrificial logic, logic of exchange, of apotropaic and self-effacing anticipation of harm, placating the void with constantly churning thought (negations of a thought by a new thought), thusly does the Specter would-be murderer of Body and Member, whole and part, say of Los's Children that "the Law of God commands that they be offered upon his Altar" (*Jerusalem*, chapter 1, 10:38–39) (it is the reasoning mind, the Specter of Los, in Blake's poem, that wishes death on his children, the creative works, for creativity proper is not fortification

---

172   Milbank, *The Word Made Strange: Theology, Language, Culture,* 227.

and violence, and is too open to the vertigo of the gift, it is not a logic of exchange, and so the usurping mind rejects it).

Therefore, we can take a care-taking attitude to history and culture, transforming it rather than rejecting it. Enculturating our spiritual epiphanies and spiritualizing what is around us. There is a danger in taking W. B. Yeats's suspicion regarding allegory too far. He favored the artistic use of symbols, celebrating attempts to convey the truth of an item (the *meaning*, poetically construed, of a tulip's indolent grace or of the sinewy ambulances of cats, for example) over its merely culturally derived, conventional connotations. This is an important safeguard against art becoming all-psychological (entertaining the psyche rather than clarifying it to let the *nous*, the eye of the heart, in Patristic language, shine through). However, this should not lead to bypassing cultural allusion altogether, for, as St. Gregory of Nazianzen teaches, "what is not assumed is not saved."

Dante made ample reference to specific events and factional disputes in his poetry. Yet allegory in the hands of a Dante *is* symbolic. It presents the reader with the occasion to colonize politics on behalf of poetics, rather than contaminating poetics with politics. A rigid dichotomy between natural symbol and cultural allegory fails to properly account for either:

> Nature like culture may also be, in one sense, just the way things happen to be ordered for a time, within time. Yet inversely culture, like nature, may also be, in one sense, an intimation of abiding truths of goodness, beauty and ontological truth.[173]

To refuse history, polemic and cultural commitment, to refuse a Dantean aesthetization or sublimation, is to succumb to a sort of Manichean rejection of life in its teeming diversity. To do without history or to wish for its easy resolution, which Voegelin warns against, is to give up on actually-existent life for the sake of phantoms.

We should act out of nothing, not against it. We should embrace the emptiness of forms, in Buddhist terms, rather than trying to distract ourselves from it and placate it with constant thinking. We should surrender utterly to the immediate perception of the true totality, which is gratuity (in meditation, Christian grace and Buddhist emptiness coincide). Culturally this means creating without the need for antagonism, consistent with Milbank's ontology of peace, where adventure does not need to be justified by reacting against an ultimate privation: the animated movies of Hayao Miyazaki come to mind as a virtuous example, and the consummately boring and ambitionless character of American comic-book superheroes who need some evil to act before they do, despite their vast powers, as a negative one.

Creatio contra nihilo is the desire to control. *Creatio ex nihilo* is surrender into what the Orthodox Christian theologian Nikitas Stithatos calls

---

173   Milbank and Pabst, *The Politics of Virtue*, 292.

"abysmal intellections," an abyss containing intellections just as white light contains every color's wavelength. As the *Gospel of Thomas* (77:1) teaches: "Jesus said, 'It is I who am the light which is above them all. It is I who am the all. From me did the all come forth, and unto me did the all extend.'" It is not then a creation out of nothing as usually taken by mainstream theology. This is instead a nothing that is a plenum of everything and therefore is no-thing in particular.[174] In neo-Platonic terms: if nihilo is the primordial waters, it would be like Plato's Crater (goddess Juno), the spatio-temporal matrix of the cosmos, and both it and the Demiurge (god Jove) would be within the preceding monad of the First Paternal Intellect (Saturn/Rhea) and not in any sense outside God. When Mormonism's founder Joseph Smith pointed out the lack of subject in the Hebrew first sentence of Genesis during his King Follett discourse, he missed the apophatic subtlety of creation from the Ineffable.

The scriptural formula itself seems to want to lead us to understand the *nihilo* not as some vacuum somehow other than God (which must subsist beneath *pura natura* Catholicism, where subsistence apart from the Being of beings is somehow possible) but as a genuine absence of forms as we know them, where there is no Being apart from God's and where beings can then occur. As Wolfgang Smith puts it in *Christian Gnosis*,[175] the true doctrine of *creatio ex nihilo* is to be understood as *creatio ex Deo et in Deo* (an understanding Smith reads in the Christian Kabbalists and in Meister Eckhart). Thus, René Guénon's support of a mathematics in which nothingness is not reified, making unity the centerpiece instead:

$$0 \ldots 1/4,\ 1/3,\ 1/2,\ 1,\ 2,\ 3,\ 4 \ldots \infty$$

Here, absolute zero and actual infinity are approached by numbers but never reached (an infinite potentiality exists but actual form must always be finite: the distinction between the *infinitus secundum quid* and *infinitum absolutum*) and where every number is a function of one, for everything is a manifestation of the One. The above contrast with the typical:

$$\ldots -4,\ -3,\ -2,\ -1,\ 0,\ 1,\ 2,\ 3,\ 4 \ldots$$

This has consequences for how we understand the ontological status of evil, of that which is not God. We have denied that nihilo is an actual empty space outside God from which God creates. We should no more reify the *nihilo* of *ex nihilo* than the *privatio* of *privatio boni*. It is the appearance of a privation of good, not a real privation, as that is impossible. And the reason for this illusion must be in the good: the experience for illusion

---

174   "The forms that are part of the world of Intelligence can be neither discerned nor isolated, although they subsist independently of one another.... But (at the same time) all are simultaneous, and each is in every other" (Corbin, *Avicenna and the Visionary Recital*, 54).

175   Wolfgang Smith, *Christian Gnosis: From Saint Paul to Meister Eckhart* (San Rafael, CA: Angelico Press/Sophia Perennis, 2009), 63.

to allow discovery; the experience of struggle for the sake of victory. It is play, *Lila*. As Alan Watts put it, if we could choose the content of our oneiric flights each night, we might think up vast pleasure domes and beautiful dreamscapes, and eventually even terrible adventures, excitement, danger, until we one night choose to forget we are dreaming for the sake of experiencing profounder excitement, profounder danger, and the thrill of discovery, the sheer relief of waking, of emerging from illusion. This is an analogy for the Divine play that creates the world. (And we could treat life itself as Schiller's aesthetic education, entertainment/play as education or, better, vice-versa.)

Rather than seeking a Rousseauian return to the primitive noble savage or the expression of his universality in political systems, or else to an Edenic golden age simplistically construed from religion and myth as spiritually unpolluted by history and culture, we may consider the purpose of the game of history, of the dream, in terms of that inner imaginative potential which the dreamer desires to realize and to reflect upon in his waking. These are the mundane trophies taken into Heaven. The kings of the nations in the Heavenly city. Ours is to win the world for the spirit, the outer sign for an inner significance. This is the resurrection of the particular *as* particular, yet transformed (in Paul the resurrection body is a body, but not flesh).

> A thing of beauty is a joy forever,
> Its loveliness increases; it will never
> Pass into nothingness...
> (opening of John Keats's *Endymion*)

But this means viewing cultural forms and the history that serves as their proximate cause in non-agonistic terms, as we have already argued. Vico calls that which brings about particularity from universal conditions *providence*. Just as virtue can make itself a secret celebrant of vice as the occasion for its own exercise, a proper understanding embraces all substantial forms as manifesting the good and dispels from its fathoming of them the specter of illusion in which they appeared ontologically separate from the good, so that the true evil is in the virtuous's own misperceptions, and this indeed is celebrated, but as the chance for joyful discovery of truth (good). The greater jihad is the inner jihad[176] and all is Lila.

The True Sacrifice and the True Body

René Guénon comments on the Sanskrit word *dharma* as mode or quality of a being or category of beings.[177] It is not a legal prescription for these, though it can crystallize into such at a given time and place

---

176   This is a weak hadith that actually finds support in stronger ones.
177   René Guénon, "The Law of Manu." In: *The Essential René Guénon: Metaphysics, Tradition and the Crisis of Modernity*, ed. John Herlihy (Bloomington, IN: World Wisdom Inc. and Sophia Perennis, 2009), 145.

for the purposes of aiding their coming to know their own vocation or coordinating their action with others (one's vocation may be that of a fisherman, but one still has need of marine biologists to inform one of the migration pattern and population level of this or that species and thus guide one's actions adequately by informing prescribed legal limits). The law, understood as a specific legal code, cannot be considered salvific. Law is not soteriology. The law can only be an aid in discovering and conforming to one's God-given vocation in the manner of Arjuna in the *Bhagavad Gita*. It is the opposite view of the law-centric understanding of salvation St. Paul seems to be reacting against in Galatians.

Yet legal systems ought to be constructed in accordance with the proper spiritual attitude (and therefore as an exoteric aid to the esoteric). St. Paul may be reacting to a degenerate form of pagan and Hebrew religion—akin to the Buddha in the case of the Brahmanism he encountered—but exotericism is not abolished by this reaction. We still have need of the law for a myriad of reasons and we still want to bring every facet of life into conformity with its central religious demand.

Given that the (originally sinful or at least ambivalent) institution of Biblical monarchy serves to set up the lineage in which the Incarnation occurs (Jesus's line descends from David and Solomon, not Moses, though He of course communes with Moses during His transfiguration in Matthew 17:2) and given Christ's symbolic association with kingship, the Bible resolves its narrative not on the side of the supremacy of law but of the rightly guided creative community and its leader's freedom, presumably also a freedom to legislate. Indeed, it is to communal deliberation and solidarity, in full recognition of there being leaders—which is to say, representatives, that is, kings—among believers, that St. Paul entreats the churches he writes to, so rather than Old Testament law they have communal decision making and leadership under the Gospel. (As an aside, it is possible that the Bible presents the coming about of monarchy as negative because those passages were authored by partisans of the supremacy of the law, that is, iconoclasts wanting to mediating realities between their conception of the Absolute Divine agency and Israel.)

Inner freedom wrought by initiation is not legalistic, for it is beyond seeking security in apotropaic sacrifice. This is explicit in Shaktic, Tantric texts, with its antinomian potentials, but is just as clear in the *Bhagavad Gita* (18:66): "Abandon all varieties of religion and just surrender unto Me. I shall deliver you from all sinful reactions. Do not fear." Thus, as the Gospel stresses, if a community or a person are surrendered to Christ, they are spiritually justified. Any legislation thereafter is a matter of coordinating complex social dynamics, coming up with standardized practices to facilitate interaction, and facilitating wellbeing, not a means to that justification.

The medieval understanding of the law as something to be discovered and objectively ascertained does not contradict this, for indeed what is left to us to discover or discern is not already entirely given by revelation (put differently, the principles are revealed, but their application needs determining). As Margaret Barker writes of Josiah's reformers, citing Deuteronomy 4:6, "the Law was to be their Wisdom," and "... poems about Wisdom were later adapted to become poems about the Law."[178] They were also denying that a vision of the Lord was had by prophets like Moses, contradicting earlier texts (Exodus 24:9–10), which goes hand in hand with Deuteronomy's iconoclasm. Consistent with all we have discussed, the vision of the Anthropos, God's revelation of His agency as a human form, which is central to the monarchical investiture as it is the archetype of the *representative body of the king*, and the presence of the divine feminine, Wisdom, contradict the supremacy of legal codes.

But precisely the point of monarchical investiture is that the only human being sacrificed is the initiate, who dies to return, so actual human sacrifice becomes a redundant demonic parody of the real thing, which is where the Old Testament's pre-Josian substitution of human sacrifice comes in, as well as the New Testament's rendering of symbolic death by circumcision obsolete. Eusebius writes that circumcision was an apotropaic act (a warding off of evil by anticipating it and performing a lesser, controlled evil oneself)—it is, in this sense, incompatible with the mindset of initiation as St. Paul saw it. (The Jewish view of circumcision dispenses with any originating act of human sacrifice, and in the Muslim case it is translated over as a part of the *fitrah*—that tradition's view of the proper human norm—being practiced not as religious institution but as medical or hygienic practice, without the initiatic context or need for a religious authority.)

This conception finds a powerful image in the ripping of the temple veil during an earthquake at the death of Jesus (Matthew 27:51). Apart from signaling that that which is behind the veil is revealed in Jesus and His work, this may possibly mean that the death of Jesus corresponds to the tearing of the veil. If religion is what St. Paul sees as subordination to the Elementals and consequently to the law, and Jesus's body corresponds to religion (the temple veil), then Jesus owns as His own body the previously enslaving agency of Elementals, just as the king and tantric initiate maps the cosmic gods onto his body and is thereby sometimes considered beyond ritual prescriptions. Jesus *as* veil then resurrects, so a new veil comes to religion, one diaphanous or more conducive to our understanding, just as the resurrected Jesus reveals Himself more fully than during His ministry.

This stands for life after spiritual epiphany, when the limits and facts of life (the veils) are no longer experienced as a burden (blindness) but as play. His telling Mary Magdalene it is good for her and the other disciples that he should leave may relate to the veil's ripping, in that the

---

178   Barker, *The Mother of the Lord, Volume I: The Lady in the Temple*, 35.

specifics of those contingencies He ministered through (a time, a place, a religion, maybe) are on some level torn at His death, making space for a direct awareness of the Person. This is precisely what allows us to celebrate the veil of life—the many particularities that mediate and hide the plenum from us—for no single contingency is identified with the Absolute, and therefore all contingencies can be considered Its mediators.

In another sense, the temple building is being discarded and Christ— His very body—is revealed as the temple. Here, then, politics, institutions and every form of life, must occur in an organic way, not bricks upon bricks but a living body: forms as congealed love, not as a necessary but separate add-on to love. A certain straightforwardness in medieval associations could be a manifestation of this principle. Our defense of the mysticism of political leadership and representation is not, therefore, a defense of alienating forms of political or religious power or procrustean beds for fitting human relations.

On Currency and the Cross

The Gospel of Luke, for all the detail it provides, does not tell us that Jesus was ever redeemed from the temple as a newborn, per the custom (2:22–24). [179] A mother's firstborn was customarily taken to temple thirty days after its birth, and the parents would pay some monetary compensation. The same was done for the firstborn of animals, but in this case, they were sacrificed by being put to death. We are dealing, then, with the thoroughly mitigated stand-in for human sacrifice or else a human, monetary equivalent of blood sacrifice.

It is the temple's veil that rips upon Jesus's temporary death. The entire lifetime of this subject has passed unredeemed by the priestly authority's standards. This could be a sign that the barter is refused by Jesus and that holding on to debt destroys the temple (the opposite cancellation of debt is a recurring metaphor for salvation, after all—the *Our Father* prayer presents holding on the debt as condemnation and forgiving debt as salvation), or that the temple belonged to Him all along and has no right to demand payment for and from Him. Institutions such as the temple, both religious and political, can no longer legitimate themselves on debt, which is to say, on the apotropaic, sacrificial mentality. Dying unredeemed by the standards of that mentality, He resurrects, redeemed.

A note on the language of the market employed by scripture and its consequences for how we understand the economic sphere is in order. In his study on *Debt*, David Graeber points out that a punitive emphasis on sin *as* debt is used as a starting point but then subverted in religious (specifically Biblical and Vedic) literature, neutering the logic of exchange as spiritually valid. This seems to uphold the forms of a society while dispensing with agonistic justifications (with Milbank's ontology of

---

179   Ibid., 37.

violence), turning them into gift: the scapegoat, the object of cohesion-bestowing group-derision for Girard, remains at the center but now as Lord; money remains in circulation but now (or once more, for anthropology suggests it was so in the remote past) as symbolic exchange, not token of debt (or sin). In a sense, then, Christianity requires the felix culpa, the occlusion in order to reveal, a scapegoat in order to annul scapegoating and teach self-sacrifice.

If Christ's death on the cross, like repentance in the sense of buying back what one sold (the Biblical Hebrew word is used for both salvation and re-buying at market), are symbolic before they are reified (*syn-bole*, a throwing together, a uniting), then the suffering incurred by way of sacrifice is not valuable but for the sake of that which it unites us to. This means that strands of historic Christianity have made an idol of suffering just as certain economic systems make an idol of money, for indeed, both debt-money and commodity-money, like the gold standard, would seem to be technically idolatrous in light of the above.

Christ on the cross is explicitly marred in perception. An obfuscation occurs whereby His relationship to God the Father is no longer perceived and God is referred to as God and not Father for the only time (*Eli*, rather than *Abba*, in the phrase "*Eli Eli lama sabachtani*," "My God, My God, why have You abandoned Me"). Therefore, the perception from the cross, from the place is suffering, from the means, the law, the discipline, is incorrect (to believe in suffering is to disbelieve in the Self, we could say, for Christ is one with God). The focus should be on the resurrection, the ends, grace, *metanoia*. Embracing the cross, but for the sake of the resurrection.

The subtle idolatry that values sacrifice or asceticism for its own sake results in a religion no longer guided by philosophy, love of wisdom, its own original telos. Instead, the instrumental ascetical discipline and the suffering it brings (and, therefore, a focus on empathy for suffering, on a compassion that becomes debilitating and bereft of virile spiritual optimism) becomes its end. Nietzsche considers this to have occurred in Europe,[180] ascribing to such a phenomenon the proliferation of a base human element similar to that which Ortega y Gasset makes the subject of his *Revolt of the Masses*. Social Darwinism aside, we should consider the extent to which he is right in diagnosing the dominance of such a sickly and, as we would put it, idolatrous, ethos in European religiosity and post-religious modernity. The religious instinct can, in such cases, find theism lacking, small,[181] for theism becomes a death-cult. Ultimately, the desire to sacrifice sacrifices everything that has a positive content, even belief in God, to nihilism.[182] It wishes to remain on the

---

180 Nietzsche, *Beyond Good and Evil*, 62.
181 Ibid., 53.
182 Ibid., 55.

cross, to eschew the familiar relationship to the Divine (Abba) for the formal relationship (Eli) and feels itself abandoned, ever trying to please God by way of suffering rather than letting go, dying, and resurrecting.

Poverty and Property, or Heaven Does Not Abolish the Household

Apart from a confusion of means and ends, the error of asserting (poverty-derived) suffering as a value in itself can result from focusing on certain elements in the Gospel (also present in most religious traditions). The celebration of poverty, on the one hand, contrasts with Lord Krishna's bejeweled attire and *gopis*, or Christ's monarchical resplendence in the Apocalypse, on the other. That one should abstain from seeking opulence and power yet receive it in the Divine is similar to the superior ecstatic quality of the conjugal act enjoyed at night by one who abstained from sexual thoughts and incontinence during his day. The natural place of a thing is revealed when it is removed from what is definitely not its place. It is not pleasure's place to be the object sought, and so, when it is not sought, it is truly experienced (the pleasure-seeker experiences less pleasure than one to whom pleasure comes in course of seeking virtue).

Opulence and power are a figure for the eternal nature of divine play, but they cause attachment and pride precisely because they impact the subject by virtue of that which they symbolize, and so human beings require purgation, but if we view that purgation as the figure of the Divine we have become confused: a sick man learns life is fleeting, but if he concludes the resurrected body is sickly he errs by committing that inversion of morals Nietzsche thinks characterizes Christianity.

Apart from poverty's role as ascesis, wealth—or the pleasurable use of material things within relations of friendship—is celebrated. When a woman is reproached by the disciples for using expensive oil to anoint the head of Jesus, He responds

> Why are you bothering this woman? She has done a beautiful thing to me. The poor you will always have with you, but you will not always have me. When she poured this perfume on my body, she did it to prepare me for burial. Truly I tell you, wherever this gospel is preached throughout the world, what she has done will also be told, in memory of her. (Matthew 26:6–13)

Similarly, the traditional commentator on the *Bhagavatam Purana* recommends channeling wealth into worship. The very poor may offer up only thought or water, the rich a more lavish bounty. As the *Purana* says: "My worship in the Deity should be performed with the choicest articles, but it can be performed by my sincere *bhakta* with whatever is available, or even just in the mind" (XI:27.15, 53).

The *Bhagavatam Purana* tells us that Lord Krishna removes material prosperity from one, among other reasons to make that devotee befriend true devotees, in whose company wealth is not valued, "When his endeavors come to nothing, and he becomes despondent in his attempts to gain wealth, then I bestow my favor on him, once he has formed friendships with those devoted to Me" (X:88, 5–10, 168), but also that the four aims of life (the *Purushartha*)—sensual pleasure, material prosperity, righteous duty, and spiritual liberation (*Kama, Artha, Dharma* and *Moksha*)—come from devotion to the Lord (IV:8, 41, 299). It is as though service to God is the fifth element and quintessence between the four aims of life, transcending even spiritual liberation, the spoke of the wheel, just as a king is the fifth function in between the four castes. In any case, it is not a question of rejecting prosperity and victory in life but of being detached from it and in love with God.

Insofar as material prosperity unto righteous duty, in turn unto spiritual liberation, all within service to God, is a legitimate aim in life and comes from God, it is a question of prospering in order to do one's work, which generally includes perpetuating the household. The Gospel's view may be taken as compatible with this, following Christopher Hays in his study on the Gospel of Luke:

> ...the numerous behaviors described by Luke can...be considered contingent expressions of a single, coherent principle, *viz.* that nobody can be Jesus' disciple unless he or she renounces all possessions (14:33). This single coherent principle might be manifested in a variety of ways, contingent upon the disciples' distinctive vocations and relative affluence, though this variety does not devolve into self-contradiction...can refer to a variety of forms of renunciation, from categorical divestiture to an internal rejection.... Luke describes a spectrum of behaviors.... The poor itinerant renounces all by leaving behind his home and occupation.... The rich itinerant, by contrast, renounces all either through giving her possessions to the poor prior to disembarking, or by continually expending her riches to support her fellow itinerants. Non-itinerants are by no means exempt...rather their renunciation takes a form more appropriate to their stationary mode of living. Those who are well-off open their homes to the itinerants, observe justice in all of their dealings, and practice self-sacrificial generosity.[183]

Suggesting correspondingly that "Acts 2–6 depicts early Christians as sharing the use of possessions, but not ownership..."[184] This repudiates the view of Christianity that it endorses economic deprivation as such, what Antonio Escotado calls *pobrismo* or, in English, *povertism*, in his *The Enemies of Commerce*: a celebration of poverty and even misery, which he attributes to Christianity.

---

183   Christopher M. Hays, *Luke's Wealth Ethics* (Tubingen, Germany: Mohr Siebeck, 2010), 267.
184   Ibid., 268.

Detachment from possessions is embraced, and at the same time families or households are delineated by, among other things, a material infrastructure. We may interpret the sharing of resources in the Gospel as compatible with Islam's rejection of earlier tribal social arrangements that lead to unknown parentage, instead turning the clear genealogical delimiting of family units into a religious duty. Sharing resources does not entail the elimination of diverse, discontinuous, households that are proximate to certain specific resources and make a primary use of these for specialized purposes (depending on profession or number of family members and their needs depending, for example, on age). We should avoid certain politically and socially radical appeals to the Gospel's depiction of communal use of wealth that reveal something of what Spengler describes as the return of archaic forms during a civilization's terminal phase, namely the dissolution of family, where, as per radical feminist accounts, patriarchy is defeated by eliminating men's ability to track parentage.

The idea is the same as what we have discussed concerning diverse forms (including nations and cultures and, in this case, propertied households) being revealed as archetypal and harmonious expressions of a single underlying principle rather than as agonistic, ontologically alien entities sharing no common source or depth:

> ...worship gives everything back up to God, hangs onto nothing and so *disallows* any finite accumulation which will always engender conflict. Confident worship also knows that in offering it receives back, so here the temporal world is not denied, but its temporality is restored as gift and thereby rendered eternal.... So no, the Christian man is not a moral man...In absolute trust he gives up trying to be good, to sustain a right order of government within himself.[185]

By disallowing finite accumulation through a worshipful state of being (that "artist of being," in Martin Luther), by giving everything up by never holding on, by being detached, we receive forms, distinction, delineated bodily existence. That seems to be the general attitude to adopt respecting property and wealth according to scripture.

Indeed, Jesus sometimes uses the image of a monarch or patriarch with land, resources, children and servants in parables. Thus, righteous duty involves a material support, including in the form of landed monarchy and lordship. However, this is different from a warrant to social arrangements that cultivate greed or appetitive movement or in which a liquid income usable to control others, where these others are rendered controllable by desperation. Thus, the pooling of resources by early Christians to ensure all have their needs covered, consistent with the kingly provision and periodic Jubilee debt cancellation that

---

185   Milbank, *The Word Made Strange: Theology, Language, Culture*, 230–31.

Old Testament prophets appealed to and that the ministry of Jesus is in continuity with. This is also a recovery of gift cycles, where exact exchange and the calculative mentality is rejected.

The focus is not on the dehumanizing deprivation caused by poverty but precisely on freedom from desperation and from the *libido dominandi*, the lust for domination so easily exercised under conditions of significant wealth inequality. Instead, the focus is on playfulness and friendship. Indeed, many traditions present service to God as coinciding with friendship and play with God.

The identification of spiritual exaltation with suffering, weakness, poverty as deprivation, and everything Nietzsche would have criticized in Christianity (although seeing it as possibly leading to the Overman, for we should not forget that his dichotomy of master-slave moralities is *not* meant to favor the ethos of the master over the slave's) is precisely not in line with the Gospel. St. Gregory of Nyssa saw this, and the history of modern Western philosophy grappled with it:

> Gregory discovers the body and society as a site of pure activity, or of manifestation of the absolute, and even—in Christological terms—its full and unconcealed presence.... When we defend pathos we tend to make pity and suffering ontologically ultimate. Endless continued pity is an insult to the pitied, offers them no good gift and pretends to rob them of their own suffering...tends to make us construe virtue reactively, and to imagine a restricting response to a preceding evil as the highest virtue. This dethrones Charity, which presupposes nothing, much less evil, before its gratuitous giving (or at most the recipients of gifts with and as a primordial giving, as in the case of the Trinity). In contrast with aspects of later Christianity, there is little that could be construed as a cult of weakness in Gregory, and he roundly declares that it is no more praiseworthy to be fearful than to be foolhardy, or to suffer than to enjoy merely temporal pleasure. This robustly objective sense of sin is perhaps now more noticeable and appreciable for an intellectual climate informed by Spinoza and Nietzsche than it was for a certain sickly version of Christian Hegelianism, exalting pathos and dialectical negativity, which has persisted from the nineteenth century into the late twentieth.[186]

Returning to the issue of idolatry and valuing suffering or indeed, pleasure as usually understood, as ends rather than means, in light of Luke 2 it seems that refusing to pay off debt incurred by the very act of living, of being born as a mother's firstborn (like the *head tax* of some nineteenth century economics), that is, resisting the reification of money, which corresponds to the reification of the law—the exclusive attribution of universal principles to one set of particular practices—is the

---

186   Milbank, *The Word Made Strange: Theology, Language, Culture,* 208.

mechanism through which resurrection of the initiate and destruction of the illegitimate structure (the breaking of the temple) is achieved. Psychologically, this means refusing the mental habits of barter and security (*if I give this up I will be justified in indulging this*), the games of compulsive thinking. To refuse the need for specific acts as if these were inexorably and exclusively expressive of universal goods—to refuse legalism—is to fail to pay debts and to be redeemed in the true sense. That legalism is a counterfeit Logos. It does not really believe there is a Logos, an order, and thus attempts to make order up by way of mind games, pretending its constructs are real and transcendent.

THE CORPUS COSMICUM AND THE NARRATIVE BODY

Before moving into analysis of some of the peculiarities of sacred kingship and the articulation of a body politic in a given historical theatre, namely Europe, we may look into how the corpus cosmicum, or rather, the specific corpus micro-cosmicum, manifests in time, in a history, as a story, a narrative, where the king is patriarch and the kingdom a genealogy. We move from cosmic body to body politic (or *micro*-cosmic body) to narrative body (or genealogical/historical body).

The King as Ancestor

When one night, or at the cool of morning after un-relinquishing night, the king holds his queen and looks upon rough engravings from a distant past, since gilded, of illustrious ancestors from a time when dream and archetype had not yet congealed into so heavy a stuff as history. His royal ancestor depicted there, father of his people. He dreams for a moment of that man, that myth. He sees the ever-renewed play of microcosms becoming macrocosms, men and women as nodes whence generations spring, men and women becoming worlds, and feels himself in their company, the company of ancestral worlds and worlds to come. He rouses to look upon his queen again. That which they contain they will give forth.

An important instrument by way of which ancient traditions structured their view of the ecumenic whole had to do with myths of common descent from exalted, often divinized, personages. The initiate-king as ancestor and patriarch is important in revealing that his community was seeded after an experience of transcendent order as an attempt to create an earthly analogue for that order. This analogue is constituted and develops within the constraints of the human ability to relate communally and organize politically, so that it is universal in principle but circumspect in practice (following those considerations that lead Aristotle and the tradition of St. Thomas Aquinas and John of Paris to support limiting the size of political entities). The universality of this community may be conceived of and pursued in explicitly political terms as an imperial expansionist project which will nonetheless at some point fail at global hegemony and produce a distinct cultural sphere (the Roman Empire is now principally a European cultural space, the Umayyad Caliphate is now principally an Afro-Asian continuum stopping at Iran), or it can remain contained in a state cult (as with Bronze Age Egypt and its Near Eastern counterparts).

The previously explored sexual character of kingship and importance of royal coitus renders it easy to understand why the king often becomes an ancestor, that is, a patriarch, why his fecundity should be a matter not only of sustaining the people but of spawning them, along with his queen. He is a horizontal or chronological, as well as vertical or existential, representative. The body of the king becomes a genealogy. The Biblical emphasis on patriarchs as ancestors of Israel is an example of what constitutes an extremely widespread theme, a theme that functions according to that principle which justifies the political representative as microcosm of the represented community, for if one contains the community in one's self, one can give it forth from one's self.

This allows for the ecumene to be understood both as one and as divers. This occurs in the tables of nations produced by Jewish, Christian and Muslim scholars throughout the Middle Ages and, in the Hebrew case, long before. Different peoples known to the scribe were identified as the progeny of this or that Biblical person, accounting for their character (not always flatteringly) in terms of scriptural allegories and therefore explaining diversity while also tracing it back to a common source. This is not an innovation with respect to pagan sources, as these commonly identified different nations with different gods as the latter's offspring. The Egyptian *Book of Pylons* (or *Gates*) provides an account for how the four peoples known to its authors (eastern Semites, southern Africans, norther and western populations and Egyptians themselves) all originated from different activities of the god Horus, Plato provides accounts according to which Europeans and Asians are in the spiritual jurisprudence of different sons of Prometheus, and so on.

Clear examples occur in Genesis, with an expanded version of the categorization of nations according to the sons and grandsons of Noah provided by the *Book of Jubilees*. This latter, or the histories of Flavius Josephus, probably served as a source to St. Jerome's account in his commentary on Genesis 10 and St. Isidore of Seville's *Etymologies*. It may also have inspired some of those equivalent accounts the Muslim historian al-Tabari provides in the second volume of his Histories, according to which "Arabs, the Persians, the Nabateans, the Indians, and the Sindis are among the offspring of Shem b. [son of] Noah."[187] This contradicts other genealogies (as in the Persian case, for example, who are often classed

---

187   al-Tabari, *History of al-Tabari, Vol II: Prophets and Patriarchs*, trans. W. Brinner (New York City: State University of New York Press), 218, 17.

as Japhetic), though it is more or less consistent with *Jubilees*.[188] Some accounts in al-Tabari also class the Egyptians and Syrians as descending from Shem.[189] Not all peoples under Islam at the time of al-Tabari are listed as the progeny of Shem in the accounts he cites, and some are explicitly mentioned as being Japhetites or Hamites. The nations singled out as being of the same community of kinship as Arabs are perhaps those considered most central to the *ummah*, as translator W. Brinner notes.[190]

Indeed, early Arabian conquest in the context of Islam is sometimes related in terms of coming into contact with kin. Al-Tabari provides an account[191] according to which Muhammad said "'When you conquer Egypt, treat its people well, for they are kin [to you] and deserve protection.'" The narrator goes on: "...I asked al-Zuhri 'What is their kinship that the Messenger of God mentioned?' Al-Zuhri answered, 'Hagar, the mother of Ishmael, was one of them.'"[192]

An alternative approach would have been to view that central *ummah* of the early Islamic empire as the meeting of Shem and Ham, Asia and Africa. Ham's descendants are variously identified with portions of the Near East, given that Western commentators sometimes identified the land of Cush son of Ham with Arabia, and Biblical Canaanites are Near Eastern. Indeed, the Arabs descend from Ishmael, son of Abraham and Hagar, Abraham's Egyptian slave, Egyptians being Hamites in this schema (accounts vary, but *Jubilees* and Flavius Josephus, for starters, consider the Egyptians descendants of Ham via his son Mesraim), we could propose that the conception of Arabs as Shemitic-Hamitic fusion might have been operant.

The idea that Ham and Shem together are equivalent to Japheth and might, therefore, constitute a unit, appears in one of al-Tabari's account of the confusion of tongues according to which the lineage of Shem and Ham produced eighteen languages each, and Japheth thirty-six, so that the diversity of the two former equals that of the latter[193] (being seventy-two in total, the nations of Genesis). Although it is patrilineal descent that confers national and tribal affiliation in Islamic tradition, there is precedent for Ishmael's Egyptian matriline[194] being significant

---

188   Anonymous. *The Book of Jubilees*, trans. R. Charles (London: Adam and Charles Black, 1902), 9:2–6, 75–76.
189   al-Tabari, *History*, vol. 2, 217, 16.
190   Ibid., note 61 by trans. W. Brinner, 17.
191   via Ibn Humayd—Salamah—Ibn Ishaq—al-Zuhri—Abd al-Rahman Ibn Abdallah ibn-Ka'b Ibn-Malik Ibn-Ansari.
192   al-Tabari, *History*, vol. 2, 270, 65.
193   Ibid., 220, 18.
194   In Greek mythology Europa is also Egyptian, being the daughter of the king of Memphis, which may reflect the importance of Egypt as teacher to the younger Greek culture, being central to what Proclus considers the root of Hellenism, the Cretan commemoration of Jove's enthronement, where the Cretan Jove is precisely the courter of Europe, and it is significant that Greek cartography awards Europa nominal matronage over the continent of Europe.

in the second volume of al-Tabari's *History*, which often specifies the matriarch of nations as well as patriarch.

The Chinese narrative of the Huangdi or Yellow Emperor, the various nations that descend from him according to the historian Sima Qian and his continued relevance even in the modern era (Deng Xiaoping cited him when expressing his view that China and Taiwan ought to unify) presents a striking example as well.

In the European context, it is the Christian medieval period that saw pre-Christian origins become a sprawling, continent-wide scriptoria, with nations from the Italians to the Icelanders via Snorri Sturluson, asserting themselves as sons and daughters of the famed founder of Rome, the Trojan Aeneas.

We may approach Aeneas as Biblical patriarch. He is the paradigmatic initiate[195] at the start of the archaic occident. Like Jacob, ancestor of king David and Solomon, he was injured on the hip and fathered a royal line (whence the *gens Julia*, including Julius and Augustus Caesar, among other renowned personages) and, like Moses, he shepherded his people through a North African sojourn before delivering them unto their divinely appointed country. In Book 9 of Homer's *Iliad*, Achilles speaks of eleven cities around Troy, the twelfth, which corresponds to the twelve tribes of Israel (the number twelve is ubiquitous in traditional accounts of human and divine order). Troy, like Jerusalem, is destroyed, its people scattered, and a new Troy comes about, becoming the center of the religious life of Europe, Rome. Trojan history displays the same paradigm as Biblical Israel. Indeed, Norse medieval versions of the *Aeneid* present it in a Biblical form. The *Aeneid* is a pan-European, historically extended epic which articulates a cultural space. It is a case study for sacred enculturation and legitimate scripturalization, according to the principle of maintaining the original and deeper spirit of the scriptures.

Myths of common descent when they consider the figures they deal with universal or related to universal deities, as they usually do, implicitly make the whole of international relations into a family affair, expressing the political as the domestic (extended family) and understanding the proliferation of *human diversity in terms of human relatedness*. We will not expound further on this for now, as it is relevant to the following section, titled Ecumene and to the specific examples of ecumenic consciousness to be discussed there.

Catherine Pickstock's commentary on Plato in another context bears relevance to the theme of mythic, hyper-historical parentage and the approach needed to discern its role in history:

> A link between *topos* and *genus*, place and lineage, in the opening question of Plato's Phaedrus . . . posed at the mid-point of a journey,

---

195 Bernardus Silvestris, *Cosmographia* (New York City: Columbia University Press, 1990).

reversing the chronological order of origin and destination, to suggest that the place of origin which constitutes a person's identity is a supplementary place characterised by its open-endedness and recursive structure.[196]

Therefore,

...the journey subsequent to the origin is as much constitutive of that origin as it is dependent upon it. And here the second is not merely that which arrives too late to be first, but is that which permits the first it's priority, in such a way that its constitutive force of delay prevents the origin's primitive autonomy.[197]

Aeneas and the Empire of Heirs

We may investigate the case study mentioned above and trace how a king-as-ancestor myth may sprawl and come to define a civilizational and cultural trajectory, not really as state or institution but as identity and aesthetic. Aeneas, whose testaments Homer and Virgil authored and whose saintly sublimation unto the ages is *Jupiter Indiges*, is aptly rendered by Nietzsche's description of those "rarer and rarely satisfied people who are too expansive to find their satisfaction in any kind of fatherland-ism...those born Mediterraneans, the good Europeans."[198] Aeneas, shipwrecked into destiny by the waves of the Mediterranean, is perhaps the first good European, becoming so by wayfaring across the waters (overcoming changeability to reach solid land). It is true he did not choose to leave his home, the burning Troy, but no child chooses birth (or not as far as it remembers). The adolescent, however, must at some point, in some way, choose maturity, and Aeneas chose the danger of an as yet inexistent Rome over the pleasures of an already prosperous Carthage, like a Trojan Moses, leading his people from exile and North African captivity to comfort rather than chains, into a land promised to him by Jove.

The story of Aeneas, then, is the self-giving epic by way of which many traditions are grounded as one. It is that Dionysian godly progenitor whose dismemberment is, in truth, but the ordeal whereby identity of its limbs with the multiform creation—Cosmos, never chaos—is realized. It is the gored ox from which multiplicity emerges in Book IV of Virgil's *Georgics* (fitting, given Europe's namesake involves the myth of a bull). T. S. Eliot writes of the sacrificial fecundity of Virgil's epic, what we may call a poetic-cultural *imitatio Christi*. He begins:

Nor, on one count or another, can we expect to find the proximate approach to the classic in any modern language. It is necessary to go to the dead languages: It is important that they are dead, because through their death we have come into our inheritance—the fact

---

196   Pickstock, *After Writing: On the Liturgical Consummation of Philosophy*, 180.
197   Ibid., 180–81.
198   Nietzsche, *Beyond Good and Evil*, 147; 254.

that they are dead would in itself give them no value, apart from
the fact that all the peoples of Europe are their beneficiaries. And
of all the great poets of Greece and Rome, I think that it is to
Virgil that we owe the most for our standard of the classic...[199]

This he sees as owing to

...the unique position in our history of the Roman Empire and
the Latin language: A position which may be said to conform to
its destiny. This sense of destiny comes to consciousness in the
Aeneid. Aeneas is himself, from first to last...a man fulfilling his
destiny...by surrendering his will to a higher power behind the
gods who would thwart or direct him.[200]

The civilizational correlate of which is that "...he is the symbol of Rome;
and, as Aeneas is to Rome, so is ancient Rome to Europe."[201] The eternal
city, Rome, is the new Troy, but also, as a civilization, Europe is the new
Troy. The lineaments of Europe begin to look like the story of Aenean
progeny.

Later medieval enculturation of the origin of Roman emperorship into
a Biblical paradigm is made easy by certain similarities in the relevant
narratives. The eldest son of Aeneas's descendent, Proca of Rome, was
called Numitor, but Numitor was deposed by his brother Amulius, who
went to work attempting to snuff out that legitimate lineage, forcing
his niece, Rhea Silvia, daughter of Numitor, to become a vestal priestess
and thus remain virginal, never to experience motherhood.[202] Amulius
thereby abused the religious institution for selfish reasons, compounding
his initial crime of seizing a throne that was not his.

Rhea Silvia, also called Ilia, was therefore a temple priestess, like the
Virgin Mary according to the Infancy Gospel of John. But the virgin would
not be denied children. She became pregnant, but not as virgin, wherein
she differs from Mary. It is related in terms of heavenly interference:

...most writers relate a fabulous story to the effect that it was a
spectre of the divinity to whom the place [a grove] was conse-
crated; and they add that the adventure was attended by many
supernatural signs, including a sudden disappearance of the sun
and a darkness that spread over the sky, and that the appearance
of the spectre was far more marvelous than that of a man both in
stature and in beauty. And they say that the ravisher, to comfort
the maiden (by which it became clear that he was a god), commanded her not to grieve at all at what had happened, since she
had been united in marriage to the divinity of the place and as a
result of her violation should bear two sons who would far excel

199   T. S. Eliot, *What is a Classic?* (London: Faber and Faber, 1944), 28.
200   Ibid., 28.
201   Ibid., 28–29.
202   Livy, *From the Founding of the City*, trans. Rev. Canon Roberts (1905), I:3.

> all men in valor and warlike achievements. And having said this,
> he was wrapped in a cloud and, being lifted from the earth, was
> borne upwards through the air.[203]

She herself apparently declared the father of her children to be the god
Mars.[204] Like Jesus, the fruit of this priestess's pregnancy had to be sent
away to refuge from a jealous Herod. Romulus and Remus, sons of Rhea,
were to be drowned in the river Tiber on order of their uncle Amulius,
but like Moses, they were carried safely by those waters and eventually
found and raised by a she-wolf, a mother-goddess, Rumina. Rhea, for
her part, was married to and became the bride of the deity of that river
Tiber. The heir to the lineage of Sol and Jupiter *Indiges*, the Roman king
Romulus, followed his ancestor Aeneas and eventual successor Numa
Pompilius in not leaving a body behind. He was taken up into Heaven,
specifically during a religious ceremony, according to Plutarch's *Parallel
Lives*. Indeed, it is not only Numa the Pythagorean who links Rome with
Pythagoreanism: The Greek philosophical Pythagorean-Platonic tradi-
tion, is linked to the Trojans in that Pythagoras apparently considered
himself a reincarnation of the Trojan hero Euphorbus.[205]

From such Biblical beginnings come a constellation of national and
dynastic myths. Virgil's "role as a maker of the myth of Europe"[206] is
attested by the fact that the story of Aeneas sprawls into a "Virgilian
historiographical tradition,"[207] or in Frances Yates's words, the "imperial
theme" of "Trojan descent," according to which various European peoples
and lineages were considered Aenean-spawn.[208] Apparently, Aeneas's
descendants followed their ancestor's vector from Carthage to Rome and
pressed northward, as if magnetized by their patriarch's divine patron
in the *Aeneid*, Apollo the Hyperborean. Snorri Sturluson identifies the
company of Aeneas with the Aesir Norse gods,[209] with whom their name
seems to share its root, attributing such significance to the Trojan as to
apparently refer to the European continent as *Enea* on occasion, both in
the *Edda*[210] and in the *Ynglinga saga* of the *Heimskringla*[211] (Sturluson's

---

203   Dionysus of Halicarnassus, *Roman Antiquities*, I:77, 2, 257.

204   Livy, *From the Founding of the City*, I:4.

205   According to Heraclides of Pontus, via Diogenes Laertius' *Lives of Opinions of
Eminent Philosophers* (VIII, 4), Philostratus's *Life of Apollonius of Tyana* (VIII, 7.iv) and
Ovid's *Metamorphoses* (XV, 160–64).

206   Walter R. Johnson, *Darkness Visible: A Study of Vergil's "Aeneid"* (Chicago: The
University of Chicago Press, 1976), 11.

207   Hélène Tétrel, "Trojan Origins and the Use of the Æneid and Related
Sources in the Old Icelandic Brut." *The Journal of English and Germanic Philology*, 109(4)
(2010): 490.

208   Frances A. Yates, *Astraea* (London: Routledge, 1999), 130.

209   Snorri Sturluson, *Edda: Prologue and Gylfaginning*, 2nd ed., ed. A. Faulkes (London: Viking Society for Northern Research, University College London, 2011), xi.

210   Ibid., 3:19; 4.

211   Ibid., *Heimskringla*, 9 (Chapter 1); 6.

histories and etymologies can be wholly contrived, it is the vision of artists that is being attended to). Geoffrey of Monmouth's early twelfth century *Historia regum Britanniae* considers Brutus, storied settler of the British isle, to be a descendent of Aeneas via this latter's son Ascanius, attributing the view that Britons and Romans bear common Aenean descent to Julius Caesar.[212] This lineage would also include King Arthur.

In the 8th century, the *Liber Historiae Francorum* makes the same claim to Trojan origins for the Franks,[213] as does the Chronicle of Fredegar.[214] Charlemagne would thereby be of heroic Trojan extraction. The Holy Roman Emperor, *Pater Europae*, is also referred to as a "second Aeneas" in the medieval *Karolus Magnus et Leo Papa*,[215] so that his realm, sometimes called *Europa* (*vel regnum Caroli*), may, following Sturluson, justifiably be rendered as *Enea*. Some sources teach that the people of Asturias, whence Spain's *Reconquista* was launched, are also of Trojan extraction, named after a certain captain *Astur*.[216, 217, 218]

This occurred in Bulgaria and the Byzantine Empire as well. As Thomas McGinn writes, "[t]he Byzantine emperors considered themselves the rightful successors of Augustus—indeed, of Aeneas."[219] He cites the preamble to the *Nouvellae Constitutiones*, in Latin (Latin *Authenticum*), section forty-seven, which reads "Aeneas Rex Trojanus reipublicae initium dedit, & nos ab illo Aeneadae vocamur; five quis etiam fecunda initia contempletur, quibus."[220]

212   Geoffrey of Monmouth, *History of the Kings of Britain*, trans. A. Thompson (Cambridge, Ontario: In Parentheses Publications, Medieval Latin Series, 1999), IV:1; 54.

213   Anonymous, *Liber Historiae Francorum*, trans. B. Bachrach (Lawrence, KS: Coronado Press, 1973).

214   J. M. Wallace-Hadrill, *Fredegar and the History of France* (Manchester: University of Manchester, 1955), 537.

215   Willem P. Gerritsen and Anthony G. van Melle, *A Dictionary of Medieval Heroes*, trans. T. Guest (Woodbridge, UK: Boydell Press, 1998), 10.

216   Julian del Castillo, *Historia de los Reyes Godos que vinieron de la Scythia de Europa contra el Imperio Romano y a España con Sucesion de ellos hasta los Catolicos Reyes Don Fernando y Doña Isabel* (Madrid: Luis Sanchez, Royal Imprint, 1624), II:i, 64.

217   Floria de Ocampo, *Los Cuatro Libros Primeros de la Crónica General de España* (Zamora: Juan Picardo, at the expense of Juan Pedro Mussetti, 1543), I:xxxviii, 119.

218   A faint parallel appears in St. Isidore's Etymologies (IX.ii.111; 198), where the archbishop considers Galicia to have been settled by Teucer, son of King Telamon (whose exploits are related in Homer's Iliad) entailing Trojan heritage via his maternal grandfather King Laomedon (as well as Greek descent, which, in fact, is what St. Isidore highlights). The term Galicia is used by St. Isidore to denote a Spanish province of which he considers Asturias a part (*Etymologies*, XIV.v.21; 293), although it should be added that he distinguishes Galicians from Asturians, addressing their origins separately (*Etymologies*, IX.ii.112; 198).

219   Thomas A. J. McGinn, *Obligations in Roman Law: Past, Present and Future* (Ann Arbor: University of Michigan Press, 2015), 320.

220   *Novellae Constitutiones, DN Justiniani, Sacratissimi Principis. Ex graeco in latinum controversae et notis illustratae* (Marburgi Cattorum: Impensis Philippi Casimiri Mulleri, 1717), 436.

Constantine Manasses, a twelfth century Byzantine chronicler included the story of the fall of Troy into his chronicles, which were altered later on to emphasize not Bulgaria's prominence but that of Russia.[221] The Russian symbolist Vyacheslav Ivanovich Ivanov linked Aeneas to Moscow as Third Rome, and therefore to the second Rome of Constantinople and Byzantium, in his *Roman Sonnets*. In her national poets, Europe appears as a confederacy of Trojan nations.

The Habsburgs would sometimes be presented as heirs to Aeneas.[222] Supposed Augustan (and therefore Aenean) descent was invoked by the Spanish Habsburgs to confirm Spain's Imperial legitimacy. Janus Secundus sought to adumbrate subtler, older connections, rendering the entry of Habsburg Charles V, called *totius europae dominus*,[223] into Zaragoza a homecoming by presenting his readers with a version of this city's un-contracted name, *Caesarea Augusta*, after its founder, Augustus Caesar.[224, 225]

The *Breta sögur* (Icelandic writings drawing largely from the previously mentioned history of Britain) begin by summarizing Virgil's *Aeneid* and follow Geoffrey of Monmouth's relating British history. The *Hauksbók* version of the *Breta sögur* uses the name of Norse goddess Freya to refer to Venus, and Sif to refer to Juno, while another, longer version of this text uses the name Thor, as well as the Christian derived title of "King of Heaven," to refer to Jove (these documents also occasionally use the Roman appellations for the same deities),[226] thus presenting a pan-European pagan theology and (un-canonized) Christian scripture.

As for the historicity of such accounts, Dr. Eberhard Zangger pointed out during an interview with me that the fact that various Europeans identify as descendants of the loser of the Greek-Trojan conflict is

---

221   Elena Boeck, *The Byzantine Past: Perception of History in the Illustrated Manuscripts of Skylitzes and Manasses* (Cambridge: Cambridge University Press, 2015), 257.

222   Marie Tanner, *The Last Descendent of Aeneas: The Habsburgs and the Mythic Image of the Emperor* (New Haven, CT: Yale University Press, 1993).

223   Anthony Pagden, "Europe: Conceptualizing a Continent." In: *The Idea of Europe: From Antiquity to the European Union*, ed. A. Pagden (Cambridge: Cambridge University Press, 2002), 45.

224   Janus Secundus, *Elegies*, 3:12, cited in David Price, "Negotiating Poetry at Court: Charles V and Janus Secundus." In: S. Hayes-Healy, *Medieval paradigms: Volume I: Essays in Honor of Jeremy duQuesnay Adams* (New York City: Palgrave Macmillan, 2005), 68.

225   Janus Secundus adds (also in his *Elegies*, 3:12) that, since its founder and namesake descended from Venus, it is appropriate that Zaragoza has been blessed by the goddess with beautiful women: "Look, Venus blesses you with beautiful, charming girls and she / devotes herself to you for her Augustan descendant." Cited in David Price, *Janus Secundus* (Tempe, AZ: Arizona State University, 1996), 102. The city's patroness, however, is the Virgin of the Pillar, considered the first Marian apparition, in which Mary is said to have been transported to Hispania in order to help Saint James the elder, who was preaching there.

226   Ryder Patzuk-Russell, *Places, Kings, and Poetry: The Shaping of Breta sögur for the Norse Corpus*. (MA thesis: University of Iceland, 2012), 28.

itself telling. The Roman and medieval identification with Troy is not a boast, at least not by itself and in isolation from identification with later developments, since the Trojans (or possibly Luwians, the ethno-cultural matrix to which the historical Troy belonged) were bested militarily by the Greeks (Bronze Age Myceneans). Of course, medieval claims harken back to Rome, but the original Roman claim is an instance of identifying with the losing side of a conflict. It may indeed be an echo of true events, then, for it is not motivated by the will to appear invincible, as the Trojans came low and were scattered, like the Biblical Israel or disciples after Christ's crucifixion.

The Greeks, one-time rivals of Troy, also joined in this trend by coming to identify with Rome and thereby with Troy. The Byzantine Empire was ancient Rome's successor, and during the Ottoman Empire Greeks would be referred to as *Rum* (Arabic for Roman). To this day, there are Levantines (Syrians, Jordanians, Lebanese and Palestinians, mainly), often Greek Orthodox or Melkite Catholic, who identify as Rum, *Roman*.[227]

Aeneas's Narrative Body and Biblical Narrative

We may look further into the apparent duality of law and liturgy, empire and church. The Christian Roman emperor inherits from the pagan past. He is a virtual heir to Aeneas's initiation, which will lead us into a discussion of his priestly aspect. For now, it is interesting to continue the story above into the Christian era and consider just how Roman, how Aenean, European Christianity was in its origins. It is not only the *translatio* of Israel but of Troy that constitutes European medieval identity.

An important question in Christian civilization is whether a king or emperor as high priest, be he imperial pope or holy emperor, is compatible with Christianity in the first place. Ancient ceremonies of kingship, which are not themselves political in a modern sense, are the basis for Gospel imagery related to Christ's exaltation, including anointing and crowning as self-sacrifice. Christ is a king. The question is perhaps not whether the king should legitimately hold sacred authority as distinct

---

227   Sometimes, but not necessarily, claiming descent from Greek colonists arriving during the Byzantine Roman Empire. There is an older Hellenic or quasi-Hellenic element in the Levant predating Byzantium and the Crusader state, going back to Alexander the Great, and the possible (Biblical) Cretan origin of ancient Philistines (there is apparently some genetic evidence that Bronze Age Philistines had Aegean—that is, Mycenean and possibly Luwian—admixture/origin). On a related note, some historians suggest the Israelite tribe of Dan was of Greek origin. Other accounts of the ethnogenesis of Levantine Christians include descent from ancient Assyrians, Phoenicians and Ghassanid Arabs who moved north from deeper in the Arabic peninsula during pre-Islamic times. These accounts generally reject any difference in origin of local Christians compared to the Muslim majority, although even a Hellenic origin does not necessarily draw an ethnic demarcation between Muslim and Christian compatriots.

from the high priest (or pope) but whether he should be de-politicized as far as possible. Here the Anglican formula and modern constitutional monarchies where the monarch is endowed of theological representation is not unsatisfactory and is not at odds with Biblical and other traditional paradigms. The pope, in this context, more or less acts as an emperor in Roman and ancient terms, that is, as conveyor of the Ecumenic idea, a supra-national source of guidance and representation of sacredness.

Christ's kingdom is not of this world, but Peter is not Christ, and it is on Peter that the Church is built. Further, although His kingdom is not of this world (John 18:36), "all power is given unto [Christ] in heaven and in earth" (Matthew 28:18) and the disciples are instructed to pray that the Father's will be done "on earth as it is in heaven." This suggests His work unfolds organically like a seed in the ground, so that it is not necessarily the case that His kingdom is only received in eschatological discontinuity, and indeed Orthodox commentators often interpret eschatology in terms of historical prophecy (see David Bentley Hart's notes on John's Apocalypse in his translation). The image of a seed and vegetable growth implies development in time and all the filigree and complication of growing branches. This can be interpreted as allowing for historical emergence of political orders whereupon His representatives would act politically, without discounting sudden eschatological arrivals as well.

Such an organic arrival of the kingdom can be compatible with its not being here or there (we are told that we cannot say of it "Lo! Here. Lo! There") but within us or in our midst (Luke 17:21). The kingdom does not arrive by observation (Luke 17:20), it emerges from within and among people organically, so that it seems not to have a singular contingent cause but a cause outside contingency, and is resistant to reification (idolatry) to a contingent form or project. This delivers us back to the idea of a potential plurality of forms, which would indeed mean it is not "here" or "there," but in the midst of these, within these, and not identified with any one particular kingdom or people. This is, again, our ecumenical, pluralistic thesis.

That Christ's kingdom is not of this world (which is perhaps represented by the fact of the Gospel reporting no descendants of Jesus over which legitimacy-battles might be waged) may express that the Logos is not to be situated in this or that thing, for the Logos is not a thing, which does not mean that things (particular forms, practical orders of life, cultural diversity, etc.) are to be eliminated but rather that they are precisely not to be effaced by one another: the Logos is not a color, so it is absurd to claim that blue should replace yellow for it is a more holy color than yellow. Perhaps for this reason it is fortunate for us that Jesus left, as He says, so a new kind of guidance could occur by way of the advocate. John 14:25-26 reads:

These things I have spoken to you while remaining with you. But the advocate, the Spirit, the Holy One which the Father will send in my name, he will teach you everything and will remind you of everything I have told you.

This seems like a statement against deriving theology only from the Bible or Gospel, but also against taking post-Christ revelation in too narrow a sense, as some Muslim apologetics to Christians do, identifying the advocate exclusively with Muhammad. The hyperbole, as G. K. Chesterton once described it, of the Gospel, and its overridingly esoteric character, as perennialists like René Guénon emphasize, is supplemented. It is perhaps this supplementation where political and practical structures arise historically in a Christian context.

Something like this appears in the words of Manfred, one of the sons of Emperor and King of Sicily Frederick II, when he issued a manifesto directed at the Roman people, reiterating his father's conception of emperorship as deriving from Rome, and partly from popular consent, not Papal decision. It reads as follows:

> Rise up, oh Rome, and with frequent meditation consider within the recesses of your heart how hitherto Caesar was publicly elected to the throne of the Empire by the decree of your generals, by the authority of the Senate, and by the affirmation of your people ...the monarchy of our power...proclaims to your attentive obedience that which was written: "For to you it has been given to know the mystery of the Kingdom of God"—both of the restoration of the Empire and of the heling of your Republic—"but to the others only in parables".... Accompanied by our greatest power, and having invoked the name of Christ, we hasten to come to you...[228]

Constantine's earlier installation of holy relics at the newly constructed city of Constantinople, in the Forum of Constantine around a statue of him holding various politically significant items including the statue of Tyche (goddess protector of cities and daughter of Venus and Mercury or Jove) is extremely telling: Baskets and remains of the loaves with which Jesus fed the multitudes (an act of very tangible, perhaps for that reason political, in a certain sense, and very eucharistic caretaking); Noah's axe; The bottle of anointing oil used by Mary Magdalene (in what can be interpreted as an act of kingly anointing, as oil was typical in this context, and such investiture is often associated with feminine agents) and; The statue of Minerva that Aeneas brought from Troy to Rome called the Palladium (significant for representing the new capital's status as Rome, and generally linking the goddess and Rome's first founder, ancestor of emperors, to the new faith, given its peers).

---

228 Armour, "Dante and Popular Sovereignty." In: John Woodhouse, *Dante and Governance*, 27–28.

During his first speech to the assembly as emperor, Constantine apparently cited Virgil's *Eclogues* along with Book VIII of the *Sibylline Oracles*. The *Eclogues* (IV, 1–10) speak of the new Golden Age as that of the Virgin and Saturn (who is the First Paternal Intellect in neo-Platonism), a boy's birth with which the iron age begins to end, and the reign of Apollo, a deity associated with Christ in early Christian art. The relation of Virgil's Eclogues and Christianity—The Father, a virgin, the birth of a child savior—then, are striking. In terms of the Sibylline Oracles, it was also quoted as containing a coded prophecy or reference to Jesus Christ. The first Christian emperor thereby maintained that the pagan, Apollonian Cumaean Sibyl, who guided that hero whose Palladium he placed at the forum, ancestor of Roman rulers, champion of Apollo, Aeneas, was a genuine prophetess. Historically, many would agree, and today she can be seen depicted in the Sistine Chapel among the Old Testament prophets. We have in Constantine an Apollonian, Roman Christianity. This, along with the use of Greek letters to represent Christ after Constantine's famous vision or dream accompanied by the words *In Hoc Signo Vinces*, represented a rooting of the new religion.

Roman law was situated in Christian terms. Under Justinian and by his instruction, the brilliant, though corrupt and pagan, legal scholar Tribonian produced a condensed legal codex, whose legacy remains to this day and was something of a bedrock for European medieval Christendom.

> …mediaeval jurists, as natural, were struck by the grave *solemnity of the ancient Roman Law which, of course*, was inseparable from religion and things sacred in general…[the] Middle Ages had attributed to the legislating Roman Emperors an instrumentality *comparable to that of inspired Prophets and Sibyls*: "Through the mouths of pious Roman Emperors, inspired by God, there were promulgated the venerable Roman Laws" wrote Pope John VIII and his works later penetrated into the collections of Canon Law.[229]

This enculturation of Biblical scripture into Roman emperorship also occurs around the figure of Charlemagne. The entry to the Cathedral he built at Aachen, his new Rome, informs one that it belongs to Mary, and features a Roman, pagan-era statue of a she-wolf, probably Rumina, the form of the goddess who nurtured Romulus and Remus. Tradition holds that if one touches her foot, one will receive good luck and, in the case of women, children. Following this, one finds a depiction of the four rivers of Eden above one's head. Although a modern restoration, the river mosaic may re-propose a medieval motif. If this were the case (and as we have already mentioned earlier) this may suggest a parallel to the four principal rivers of the realm Charlemagne ruled, associated in the main with Mary. Another Biblical reference occurs in Charlemagne's

---

229   Kantorowicz, *The King's Two Bodies*, 126–27.

throne at Aachen, which includes six steps, plus the seat itself as seventh, like that of Solomon according to the Bible.

The original tomb of Charlemagne is also fascinating. It was not the golden casket graven with Germanic kings (rather than the apostles) in which Frederick Barbarossa later placed him, but a Roman-era marble sarcophagus illustrated with engravings of the story of Persephone. The first western Holy Emperor apparently chose this himself. It reminds us of the underworldly journey and feminine guidance in the spiritual quest so clearly evident in the story of the Frankish king's supposed ancestor and first founder of Rome, Aeneas.

The merging of Christian emperorship with the old SPQR legitimacy—the Roman Senate and People—also occurs in the manifesto of Frederick II's son Manfred. Yet this is not the purview of the Hohenstaufen alone, as their towering figures might sometimes suggest, but really belongs to Holy Roman Emperorship as such. The enemies of Frederick II and his sons, the southern French Anjou, were not anti-imperial asserters of Papal supremacy. In their ambitions, the telos of a united Italy and Holy Roman Empire comes through as well, along with the celebration of pagan themes within the fold of Christendom, as it did in that of their rivals. Charles of Anjou defeated Manfred and Frederick II's grandson Conrad, executing the latter. Like Frederick, he moved public administration in a modern direction, at least so far as tax collection was concerned. Charles's own son, Charles II, continued trying to build up a Mediterranean Empire. Under the Anjou, coinage from the late 1200s included a goddess, Roma, with olive wreath like Minerva and world orb in the other hand, along with references to the Roman Senate and its people—SPQR—with the coin's reverse declaring Charles king and Roman senator, *Carolus Rex Senator Urbis*. Thus, the Anjou invoked precisely the source of legitimacy that their Hohenstaufen enemies had been reviving and that the popes might have hoped to quell.

That Nietzsche describes the *Ubermensch* as *Caesar with the soul of Christ* means he on some level considered the *lack* of Caesar—the lack of a clear embrace of power, including political power and historical projection—as the cause of Christianity's deficiency, rather than the *presence* of Christ. This explains his positive assessment of Islam, which includes Jesus in its doctrine and then proceeds to the Caliphate. For our part, in taking Nietzsche seriously, we should look to Aeneas and his sons, actual Christian caesars among them, and wonder whether the lack of explicit enculturation in scripture of Latinity's sacred political paradigms and therefore of politics itself—that is, of creative, directed, willed action, determinations in which power is exerted and allowed to affect others, aesthetic and cultural enterprise—has not allowed the faith to veer towards anarchic naturalism, and whether this is not in fact at the root of the West's playing host to a great explosion of atheistic ideologies and dreams of pure spontaneous order without cultural mediation, history or telos.

From Caesar Augustus's vision in Rome of a virgin birthing a divine son, Emperor Constantine including the Palladium brought by Aeneas to Rome along with Biblical holy relics in his forum, Dante's belief that Aeneas entered Italy just at king David's birth, to the use of the *Aeneid* in medieval histories across Europe from Snorri Sturluson in the *Prose Edda* to Janus Secundus in praise of Charles V, there exists a multi-millennial theme of scripturalization of Aeneas which, were it explicit, might have attenuated the otherworldly, anti-culture digressions of Christian theology in Europe. It can also have avoided the church's presence in Rome seeming arbitrary and at odds with that city's history, even to the church itself. Much of Protestantism is simply a straightforward conclusion from the fact that nothing *Roman* was ever introduced into the scriptures.

In the context of the Roman Christian Empire, theological translation is not between theo-political systems recognizing each other but of the scriptural narrative to the Roman context. It is rather an indigenization. This sort of translation is significant to modern international relations, as will be explored later, where paradigms of peaceful relations and economic prosperity must be imitated and appropriated, that is, translated into a local context, in order to avoid loss of cultural diversity and social destabilization. Destabilization can occur if populations are denied the development they see occurring elsewhere, which leads to a sense of relative deprivation and grievance, but also if such development is imported along with cultural assimilation leading to nationalistic reactions or an erosion of local identity to the point of demoralization and dissolution and disbelief that such development can be sustained by native efforts of industry.

It is in the emperor that the sacred, and not merely secular, dimension of the story of Aeneas and of Roman culture are articulated, given that the institutional Church does not include these in its canon, although it does use symbols of Roman provenance in sacred settings. The emperor draws on the Biblical and Evangelical paradigm as well as on pagan symbols, like the Carolingian link to both Davidic monarchy and to the Trojans, or Charles V's equestrian armor with the Biblical Samson on one side and the pagan Hercules on the other, twin strong men informing the imperial office. Leoni's famous sculpture of the emperor depicts Charles V as Hercules, and Hercules, along with Trajan, appear in the royal palace at Madrid undergoing their apotheosis. None of this means the Empire is outside the Church, on the contrary. We may consider this taking up of paganism part of the real universality of the Church in its not merely institutional sense.

If, as Milbank has argued, kingship, not clergy, is the sight of true and utter reconciliation, this can explain that tradition going back at least to the year 991, of even Archbishops warning that the Antichrist would be a pope,[230] as well as the corresponding prophetic theme of a restorer Holy Roman Emperor. Dante articulates the sacredness of the Roman emperor in his *Convivio*:

> ...there never was, nor shall ever be, a nature more sweet in the exercise of lordship, more firm in its maintenance, nor more subtle in acquiring it, than the nature of the Latin folk (as may be seen by experience) and especially that of the hallowed people in whom the high Trojan blood was infused, God chose that people for such office...herein doth Virgil agree, in the first of the Aeneid, where, speaking in the person of God, he says, "to them (to wit, to the Romans) I assign no limit of things nor of time. To them have I given Empire without end."[231]

Dante thus views Latins and Trojans as chosen for imperial authority, and views the *Aeneid* as true and inspired. Indeed, in the very next chapter of the *Convivio*, Dante, casting himself as a Solomon, addresses the tree of Jesse, the Biblical line of David and its relationship with the Trojans, asserting that Aeneas entered Italy at the same time as King David was born.[232] He goes on to praise Roman history as being so replete with men of noble character and fortunate fates as to be guided by Heaven.

Given the mediaeval Christian Empire's function according to the above, and given it consistently rested its own legitimacy on having been founded by Aeneas, so that exemplar western emperors from Charlemagne to Otto the Great, Frederick II to Charles V, and Byzantine eastern emperors as a rule, all claimed descent from Rome's founder, Aeneas may be confidently treated as Europe's Jacob-Israel. Punctual parallels exist between these two. In this sense, so long as the Holy Roman Empire and Byzantium lasted, it was not a case of Biblical narrative absorbing the Roman Imperial cult, but of both existing in superposition or tandem, just as, in Islam, the Biblical line of Isaac finds its fulfilment in the Incarnation, and that of Ishmael(Isma'il) in Muhammad's Qur'anic recitation and biographical example.

As John Milbank writes in a passage we have already cited, if Christ is to return, then so are Arthur, Charlemagne and Frederick II, and so on. Emperor Barbarossa is also identified with king Arthur,[233] and we should add Constantine XI, last Byzantine Emperor, and many more. This approaches Islamic conceptions of Muhammad as post-Jesus prophet who adds necessary infrastructure to an otherwise quite ascetic or, more correctly, antinomian Gospel text. If certain Islamic approaches are useful here, however, they must be those most moderate in their exaltation of

---

230   Henry Preserved Smith, *Essays in Biblical Interpretation* (London: George Allen and Unwin, 1921), 184.
231   Dante Alighieri, *The Convivio* (London: J. M. Dent and Co., 1903), IV, 244.
232   Ibid., *The Convivio*, V, 247.
233   Kantorowicz, *Frederick the Second*, 409.

Muhammad. Where the latter gave forth sacred law in the Abrahamic key, reforming while canonizing Arab custom, the Holy Roman Emperor restores and legislated from the font of Roman law.

A closer parallel between medieval Holy Roman Emperor and Islam might be found in the Islamic doctrine of the renewer or restorer of religion, the *mujaddid*. The mujaddid periodically iterates the proper application of the spirit of true religion under new and changing conditions. Closer parallels may also occur between European medieval traditions of occluded kings and emperors whose lineage goes back to the initiatic story of Aeneas, and Shia imams.

It should be noted that although we have been focusing on Europe, the translation of Biblical themes into new contexts has occurred elsewhere as well. Ethiopia is a particularly interesting example. The fourteenth century *Kebra Nagast* (Glory of the Kings in Wallis Budge's English rendering) is an Ethiopian text detailing the Solomonic descent of that land's monarchy. Axum is the second Zion by way of the ark of the covenant, said to be in Ethiopia to this day.[234] The text presents all kingly dynasties in the world as descending from Shem, having a certain political program to defend, and of course presents Ethiopia as ruled over by the line of King Solomon and Queen Sheba. David A. Hubbard writes that "[t]o the Ethiopians Zion is not primarily a geographical location but is rather the name of God's dwelling place localized by them in terms of the Ark."[235] Donald N. Levine writes that "these beliefs about Semitic origins are used as means of *ancestral ennoblement* to confirm the superiority of the respective Ethiopian tribes...."[236] Polemics aside, it is striking the extent to which the Bible is indigenized in Ethiopia.

Particularly clear examples of this include Bolivian natives identifying the sacred tree and mountain Sumaj Urqu with the Virgin Mary and the divine child Huayna Potosi with Christ,[237] or the Marian apparition at Guadalupe in Mexico. In the Bolivian case, Tristan Platt emphasizes the Biblical connection by highlighting the similarity between indigenous uses of the tree symbol and the tree of Jesse, also mentioning Constantine's affinity for *Sol Invictus* paralleling the merging of Christian liturgy with native Bolivian solar images.[238]

In the case of Guadalupe, the Virgin appeared to the native St. Juan Diego *Cuauhtlahtoatzin* ("speaks like an eagle"), communicating in his Nahuatl language at the hill of Tepeyac, where a native goddess, Tonantzin,

---

234 David Allan Hubbard, *The Literary Sources of the Kebra Nagast* (University of St. Andrews PhD Thesis, 1956), 349–50.

235 Ibid., 338.

236 Donald N. Levine, *Greater Ethiopia: The Evolution of a Multiethnic Society*. 2nd ed. (London: University of Chicago Press, 2000), 67.

237 Platt, *Simon Bolivar, the Sun of Justice and the Amerindian Virgin. Andean conceptions of the Patria in 19th century Potosi*, 173.

238 Ibid., 174.

had been worshipped. Descriptions imply that she donned Aztec or Mestizo physiognomy. She would appear several times, having Juan Diego collect flowers which she arranged upon his peasant's cloak, or tilma, and which he then took to the bishop of Mexico. When he revealed the flowers, which fell to the ground, an image of the Virgin appeared on the cloak, and is preserved to this day at the Basilica that bears her name. The events leading to this manifestation are recounted in the Nahua language within the 1649 *Nican Mopohua*, "Thus it is Told." Native culture did not cease with the coming of the Spaniards, and this testament is a cornerstone of Nahuatl identity.

She is called the Lady of Guadalupe, although this is possibly a Spanish rendering of *Tequatlasupe*, "She who crushes the Serpent." The image of our Lady Serpent-Crusher manifested wearing the black ribbon worn during pregnancy by Aztec women which, combined with her hairstyle, signaled she was both pregnant and a maiden. Her clothes are decorated with the *Nahui Ollin*, a four-petalled flower representing the Fifth Sun, indicating that the coming of the Age prophesied in Aztec eschatology was fulfilled in Christ.[239] This symbol seems to also represent Ometeotl, the first god, father of four subsequent divinities, indicating that this being is made manifest in the Christ. It is obviously a symbol of the quintessence, like the cross, that is, the fifth element between the cardinal directions.

Further, with her feet upon a crescent moon, a Biblical image, we find further local resonance, given that the name *Mexico* means "center of the moon." She is held up by a cherub whose face and hair are those of a mature man, wearing a typical shirt of native converts, whose wings are those of an eagle—an image, it would seem, of St. Cuauhtlahtoatzin (Juan Diego). He is holding a mantle—possibly representing the sky, for there are stars upon her mantle—with one arm, and the tunic—or earth, whereupon are the flowers—with the other, uniting the two in sainthood.

The above cases represent remarkable instances of theological translation where Christianity becomes indigenized. But the story does not end here. The second ever bishop of Mexico had a reproduction of the cloak made, which he touched to the original and sent across the Atlantic as a gift to the king of Spain, Philip II, who gave it to his brother, Don John of Austria, who bestowed it upon Andrea Doria, with whom he was organizing the Holy League's forces to defend Europe against the Ottoman Empire. Doria had the tilma placed in his vessel's chapel. During battle, overwhelmed by over 400 Turkish ships, he prayed for the Virgin's intercession, whereupon a storm dispersed the enemy fleet. Thereafter, the pope declared that day as belonging to Our Lady of

---

239   If the coming of the fifth age was identified with Quetzocoatl as "white god," and with the person of Hernan Cortes, this apparition and its native Nahuatl features separated the new age from the sense of the culturally foreign and of ethnic privilege.

Victory, and the image of the tilma, with its Aztec symbolism, became an heirloom to the Doria family.

We might say that here the so-called New World came to the aid of the Old. So defeated was the Aztec empire, that its symbols, resurrected as *Christian* symbols, were now victorious in the lands of the foreign conqueror. So conquered was Mexico, that Mexican images now conquered in battles across the world. We have a perfect historical image for the ideal of Evangelization, where to be conquered by Christianity is to become a conqueror. To be humbled by the Gospel is to be exalted.

THE KENOTIC KING'S SOLUBLE STATE, OR THE ANARCHY OF MONARCHY AND WHERE POWER OVERPOWERS ITSELF

The Empire would be within the Church, not tragically outside as a mere dispenser of necessary punishment in a sinful world. In practice, in both the east and west, the emperor had an ecclesial role. In this respect, political Augustinianism contributed to an early rift between east and west. Yet there is a path to unity between these. Charlemagne's Augustinianism (the *City of God* as read by Charlemagne) is not so different from eastern Byzantine conceptions of state and church:

> Augustine himself implies that the Christian emperor will make the empire recede into the Church, and later Western rulers, in particular Charlemagne, read the *City of God* in just this light, and saw themselves as exercising a particular pastoral office (the relation of the Eastern emperors to the Church was a totally different one—they made the Church a "department of state"). Augustine also, as is his attitude to the coercion of the Donatists, opens up almost unlimited possibilities for interpreting most coercion as "pastoral coercion." So that later, a ruler like Charlemagne comes to see himself, without incongruity, as a kind of bishop with a sword, and his court theologians no longer talk, like Pope Gelasius, of two powers, imperial *potestas* and ecclesial *auctoritas* within one *mundus*, but of *potestas* and *auctoritas* within the single *ecclesia*.[240]

Milbank considers this a negative influence towards sacralizing political power, and contrasts it with the Byzantine Empire. Yet, arguably, it was a return to considering necessary political authority (the articulation of life in common) a natural and potentially edifying part of the human condition. The tragic and merely corrective function of politics gives way to that which would exist even if—in Christian terms—there had been no expulsion from Paradise. That the state dissolves into the Church, where the emperor is a Bishop, as in the case of Charlemagne, is not so different from the Byzantine setup of a state including a department that constitutes the institutional, outward church. The end result might be the same, and if Charlemagne was willing to marry Byzantine Empress

240   Milbank, *Theology and Social Theory*, 425.

Irene of Athens, he presumably did not see insurmountable differences. This is a recurrence of traditional structures where the emperor or king is also an officiating high priest. The historical enemy to which John's Apocalypse refers, the Roman Empire as it was, coercive authority and state worship, may be a parody of something which is itself legitimate.

We return to Agamben's study of the *homo sacer*. By exercising its will the sovereign declares a state of exception to the law and creates the homo sacer, who is outside the law and may be killed with impunity. This is like Pontius Pilate washing his hands and letting the mob decide the fate of Jesus, where Jesus's phrase that Pilate received his authority from above may be a reference to the Ancient of Days, to make the narrative fit Daniel's prophecy, so that the Son is sacrificing Himself—Ancient One sacrificing Son of Man (Dante would want to emphasize that this is through the Roman state). The Son is choosing a trial to reveal death's illusion: Odin's "sacrifice of myself to myself"; The cross of light in the *Acts of John* (97–102), wherein Christ is even as he is crucified on a cross of wood, "Thou hearest that I suffered, yet I did not suffer; that I suffered not, yet did I suffer...and in a word, what they say of me, that befell me not. But what they say not, that did I suffer."

In the *homo sacer* we have an analogy for the will that violates the law of habitual thought and thereby murders its mind into a new freedom. The inner unmoving self (Ancient of Days) thereby generates a renewed and free ego able to exert power (Son of Man). This power precisely does without the compulsion to dominate, for it does not conceive of power as the victory over weakness or freedom as victory over oppression in a way that would be complicit with that weakness and oppression. This freedom is not the freedom of master with right over slave/conquered foreigner. It is a freedom whose exercise is not *against*. Thusly does power overpower itself: from the sovereign exception comes a non-domineering sovereignty. The discourse of self-ownership likewise ends up here. We explode Roman law (or modern liberal social constructivism) and assert the medieval recasting of Rome. But this does not necessarily happen dialectically, and the whole affair could be replaced by a pacific realization that never erected a homo sacer as scapegoat for an angry sovereign to cast out. We may *choose* to see that our ethos of freedom as oppression over that which is oppressive, restraint upon that which restrains, is finally self-contradictory.

The radicality of the leader-servant in John's Gospel accompanies the symbology of sacred kingship. The flux of contingent features that avoids identifying kingship as such to the specific traits of this position's occupants might remind us of certain anthropological speculations concerning the Ice Age quoted previously: Those "... 'princes' and 'princesses' of the last Ice Age" their "magnificent isolation, like characters in some kind of fairy-tale or costume drama" who, "[i]f they reigned at all, then

perhaps it was, like the kings and queens of Stonehenge, just for a season."[241] What was torn asunder is here eminently united, modernity's
anarchist and authoritarian excesses were but a single pageantry. *Auctoritas* is anarchic. The state, like the Sabbath in the Gospel, is made for
man, not man for it. The temporary living image of theophany—sacred
monarchy's actor—is not a tyrant and is not allowed to become such,
lest his blasphemy overtake the land.

When suggesting (especially in some of the addenda) that the careers of
historical monarchs (especially Holy Roman Emperors) have manifested
a vocation whose ultimate significance is the epiphany of unity between
time and eternity, body and spirit, the worldly and the heavenly, we cannot
thereby hide that the worldly has become congealed, solidified, turgid
and opaque, and that the state became the very image of this mistake,
like a window ceasing to be a window in its ceasing to be transparent
on account of grime: The anti-philosopher's stone, silhouetted by the
mute testimony of Caesar's slaughtered Gauls, caked with the blood of
Charlemagne's slain Saxons, and all the succeeding atrocities of his successor kings. The state once alternated between sedentary and nomadic
modes, it froze and thawed with summer and winter, and it likewise
dissolved its legal bonds of debt in periodic Jubilee.

But the state stopped being a prop of seasonal use long ago, to become
an idolatrous usurper of all human community, whose members received
the uneasy yoke of the Sabbath's cattle. This corresponds to the king
ceasing to be symbolic of the theophanic body in which we find ourselves, to become an idol, and so kings turn sinners (Apocalypse 18). If
we were to venture further into a political judgement, we could safely
say that a central, far-off, or imperial authority brings its own violence,
but partially restrains local violence—that of a chieftain or of embedded cultural practices, for example. The criterion here, very broadly, is
whether the violence it restrains is more or less just or intense than that
which it inflicts, but also whether it denatures local life in its positive
aspect, that is, in its identity and aesthetic richness.

We should remember that many traditions emphasize the emperor,
or the sacred king, as unmoving, as one who remains outside day-to-day
affairs. The traditional symbols associated with him, like the axis mundi,
the mountain-throne at the center of the world, convey this clearly.
The emperor's role above local regents allows for his distance from
day-to-day politics. The *Tao te Ching* makes its preference for minimal
governance explicit, and the sixteenth century Polish chancellor Jan
Zamoyski expressed the traditional notion that *the king rules but does not
govern*. The union of such remoteness with representation of people (as

---

241   David Graeber and David Wengrow, *How to Change the Course of Human
History (at least, the part that's already happened)*, https://www.eurozine.com/
change-course-human-history/.

well as of the Divine to the demos) should not serve to justify tyranny but agapeic participation, the sort of lordship Christ displayed when washing the feet that followed him.

Imperial dignity as above politics appears in the Chinese distinction between *wen*—pattern, harmony, belonging to the *t'ien-hsia*, the ecumene— and *wu*—the political violence proper to its subordinate kingdoms, the *kuo*:

> The peaceable, primordial correlation between *t'ien-hsia* and *kuo* forms the nucleus for layers of meaning, partly articulated in language symbols, that stress the ritual and cultural aspects of ecumenic rule in opposition to force as represented by the *kuo*. The *t'ien-hsia*, the ecumene in the cultural sense, is associated with *wen*. The symbol *wen* has originally the meaning of markings, or a pattern; it acquires the further meanings of character, ideogram, decoration, and generally of the ornamental aspects of human life; and finally, of the arts of peace, such as dancing, music, and literature, as opposed to those of war, *wu*.[242]

The ecumenic vision should suffuse even as it makes diaphanous, *wen* should take up *wu* and, as Meister Eckhart puts it, the lower should be transformed into the nature of the higher as it is integrated into the higher.

If the Center is Absent, the One is Transcendent, then Monarchy has its Anarchy. Diversity is conceived as beauty rather than defense of one good particularity against bad ones, or as the precarious balance (as in some international relations schools[243]) between ultimately irreducibly antagonistic particularities preferred to the hegemony of one or outbreak of war of all against all. This is one meaning of the phrase in Isaiah (11:6) according to which the wolf lays down with the lamb. Just as diversity is not ultimately supported by agonistic difference where a certain cultural particularity is defended bigotedly as exclusive repository of good or cynically as a way to keep others at bay and extort peace, so too power sheds its agonistic justification as the violent bearing down upon an otherwise disordered world. To assert political authority, but to do so as the assertion of a violence without which there is no order, as the arbitrary pacification of what is itself chaotic, rather than as a coagulation of order in the realm of human community, is to deny the Logos.

The tyrant denies representation as much as the advocate for pure spontaneous direct democracy, as there is no real point in representing what is nothing but clamoring disorder, except in the very superficial and strictly pragmatic sense of appeasing the egos that clamor (which, anyway, is the cynical view that ends up coming across in much modern political practice). The leader must make himself absent for order to be observable as inherent within, and not imposed upon, social relations.

---

242 Voegelin, *Order and History, vol. 4, The Ecumenic Age*, 361.
243 The Realist school, sharing the same underlying assumptions as the Liberal, but not the English School or what Barry Buzan has calls normative Realism.

We are reminded of Christ telling His disciples that it is good for them that He should leave, for in this way they can receive the Spirit. This points to the dissolution of power's coercion by its own inner logic, by that which ultimately justifies it, and the *absent presence* of legitimate authority. Chapter sixty of the *Tao te Ching* makes political recommendations that take this for granted, and it is why Tolkien could describe himself as both a monarchist and anarchist. The mistake of certain liberals and anarchists is in trying to dissolve the pains of power by fleeing from it rather than understanding what legitimate thing it is a parodic hypertrophy of. But the way out is the way through.

Papal or Patriarchal authority as one ideally aloof from politics does not necessitate a terrible duality between time and eternity. It quite naturally responds to the multiplicity of human existence, with its deeper, unmoving, layers and more surface, dynamic ones. Further, it is quite practical. As Pope Gregory I complained, it is difficult to retain the presence of mind and tranquility appropriate to preaching eternal truths when one is involved in politics. A certain specialization may be required, where different people focus on different things. This does not mean the emperor ceases to exert a religious function, only that he receives counsel on religious matters from his Patriarch, who is specifically devoted to them.

Further, as the use of the term *Pontifex Maximus* clearly shows, the pope often identified as Roman Emperor himself, and in a sense was such, as many cases attest. Pope Gregory I, although of a fundamentally monastic disposition, ably administered and influenced affairs all over Europe, Leo I negotiated Rome's safety by dissuading Attila the Hun from laying waste to it and, in a more explicitly military vein, Pope Leo IV organized and lead a navy to defeat an Arab army after Rome was sacked (few net positive military campaigns led by popes come to mind, however).

Even Clement V—despite being thoroughly beholden to King Philip of France and, consequently and apparently spuriously, condemning the Templar Order in an abortion of justice—used his office to achieve such edifying goals as ending a fifteen-year dynastic dispute in Hungary and opening Asian language departments in universities throughout Europe (also affecting Scottish and English politics by excommunicating the Scottish king Robert for killing an enemy in Church and liberating England's Edward I of certain vows).

In discussing the historical relationship between Papacy and states or Holy Roman Empires in western Europe one is often left with the intuition that what should be a superposition (of church and state or church and empire) collapsed into separate competing entities that are mutually exclusive in the territorial sense. The defense of the papal states and territorial prerogative of the papal office has come from popes genuinely interested in exerting a shepherding role as well as from frankly depraved, apart from power-hungry, occupants of the post.

The reduction of the papal states to Vatican City is not, therefore, itself anti-traditional.

The doctrine of the two swords, where the pope may wield both temporal and sacred authority, is relevant here. Theologians such as Bellarmine and Suarez even believed the pope could depose kings and pass local laws. Henri de Lubac considered this view assimilable to the satanic temptation of Jesus in the desert, when Christ was offered all the kingdoms of the earth. Indeed, the case for such authority is dubious even as concerns emperorship. If by the wielding of his office the emperor is to demonstrate a principle of higher authority, it is by no means clear that this ought to allow for the dispossession of rulers in more circumspect realms or the legislating of their affairs. The number three is higher than the number two, but that does not mean it can do what the number two can do, such as divide in halves or double by multiplication.

In any case, far from manifesting the imperial dignity, it could be persuasively argued that insofar as they have been political agents, throughout history popes have usually behaved as local Italian monarchs (in the context of the Papal states). We may take this critique of the historical Papacy further and make another suggestion. It may be the case, though this is arguable, that the imperial office has produced less frankly perverted characters, given that the ranks of (anti-)popes have included not only whoremongers but rapists and perverts. In the history of Christian Europe, and for all the many faults of its occupants, the office of Holy Emperor may have more properly expressed the ideals of Christian civilization and sacred authority than the papacy has. Then again, there have been more popes than emperors, allowing for more disasters, and some excellent servants of the Church among them.

Anyway, since Jesus taught that "the spirit blows where it will" and "such is everyone born of the Spirit" (John 3:8), it is perfectly possible that the more Christlike office has alternated between pope and Holy Roman Emperor, Patriarch and Byzantine Emperor. Some popes may have manifested the principles of Christian civilization better than their contemporary emperors and vice-versa.

To end on the theory of papal and imperial authority, the influential fourteenth century scholar Bartolus of Sassoferrato, employed by Charles V, expressed a well-established view that dominion over the earth had been concentrated in St. Peter and was passed from pope to Roman Emperor,[244] so that anyone claiming that the latter did not enjoy such global authority was a heretic. It seems dubious that St. Peter's transference of authority requires generational enacting rather than simple recognition that a now baptized institution of Holy Roman Emperorship had come about. Peter himself is a married man, father, carries a sword

---

244   Cecil N. Sidney Wolf, *Bartolus of Sassoferrato: His Position in the History of Medieval Political Thought* (Cambridge: Cambridge University Press, 2012), 231, 249.

and administers communities, so insofar as he is pope, the papacy is imperial, monarchical. Either dominion is exerted by Pope-as-Caesar, or the pope is the spiritual minister to an emperor who realizes the Christic and Peternine character of inhabiting human communal life (in John Milbank's sense of Christ as *ultimately* more king than priest). Indeed, *Emperor* is related to the old (Mesopotamian) title *king of kings*, and is a term applied to Christ's second coming, sword in hand, in John's Apocalypse.

None of this is to devalue the monastic or somewhat politically-aloof high pontiff—advisor and herald, a John the Baptist—as far as being a necessary part of the recurring architecture of human politics. Nor is it being argued that the pope has not ever been (or according to some Catholic sources, is not most coherently taken to be) the repository of the imperial function in western Europe, delegating to administrative proxies (but then the term *emperor* is not really appropriate for such a proxy). Nietzsche's desire for a Caesar-Pope is technically coherent in light of these reflections, if, as usual for that thinker, twisted and a bit sinister.

That medieval Christians yearned for this unity is perhaps attested by the popularity of the legend of Prester John. Prester John, descendent of the magi whose Christian kingdom along with the terrestrial paradise is usually situated around India passed the lands of the Muslims (though one Portuguese explorer thought to find it in Abyssinia), represents in the medieval European imagination the unity of sacerdotal and royal powers. He is an eastern wholesomeness, like the dawn, fresh though ancient and free of divisions. In this sense he is as mysterious as Melchizedek, who St. Paul references to highlight Christ's kingship as comprehending His priestly glory. A Melchizedek for their own era, far-off and foreign, like Melchizedek had been foreign to Abraham or the magi to Israel, and untouched by messy history.

V. Ecumene

I N THIS SECTION WE EXPLORE THE ECUMENIC
worldview deriving from the above. We begin with an exploration
of how what we have called a doctrine of correspondence occurs
between polities and traditions (*Translation Requires Transcendence*) and
how the vision of a corporeal body politic is expressed there (*The Corpus Cosmicum and the Ecumene*). We then focus on how these paradigms
play out in two related contexts: Biblical theology (*Biblical Election and
the Ecumene*) and European Middle Ages, specifically its conception of
Empire (*Medieval Empire and the Ecumene*). We should add that this section gives rise to several addenda (VI-X), exploring the Ecumene as it
manifests in Chinese, Islamic, modern European, indigenous American
and technology-driven globalized contexts.

TRANSLATION REQUIRES TRANSCENDENCE

The king prepares for his first official state reception. A well-
choreographed greeting makes its entrance. Through the wide and
heavy doors to the royal hall there enters a cohort of exotically dressed
men and women. Their skin color, physiognomy and garments he has
only ever seen in vivid depictions of ancient wars and treaties, and in
the dignified reserve of that permanently stationed ambassador their
faraway land's regent sent years ago. That regent, the king's own brother
in the burden of leadership—the first he has met—enters in after his
entourage. Their eyes meet and recognize the sight of the beyond in each
other's recognizing, like light shining on light, like mirrors reflecting each
other's reflections. The king rises and moves forward. Protocol is only
strained by the familiarity. It is finally broken when the visitor returns
the gesture with an embrace. A veiled eminence directs herself at the
queen, whereupon a hug and whisper are followed by laughter. Their
husbands affect concern over the beginnings of womanly conspiracy and
friendship is born. Gifts are exchanged. Greeting parties and attendants
dispatched. There are games, spectacles, and dinner before each retires,
rests, and prepares for the morning's formalities. It is during this meeting
that matters of state are negotiated. Once a decision is come to, each
side makes oaths and assurances.

The principles according to which the two kings may trust each
other are invoked. The other speaks in his language, the names whose
sounds he has known from childhood, the tenderness of which most
readily evoke gravity and elicit loyalty. Yet the king understands. Where
one might say *ma'at*, the other hears the autozoon. Where one might

speak of Hathor as a mother, the other hears Juno, and Europa her form. Where one recalls death as Osiris, the other knows it in Dionysus. And where one knows the flaming rebirth of Ra, the other speaks the name of Jove as Cretan solar king, or Apollo. Peace is had, for what are names are names, and what are meanings are meanings, and they trust each other in the latter. Alliances firmly forged, the guests go home. A parting handshake, a goodbye whimper from queen to queen, and final exchange of parting generosities.

Dying to the particular to access the universal and be reborn to the particular allows for re-demption in the sense of re-deeming, deeming again, because a new set of particulars (a name) can be attached to the same universal or abstract principle (a meaning). This means that 1) the particular is understand as expressive of the universal; 2) new circumstances can be adapted to while remaining in conformity with the same principle (using analogy to apply scripture outside its original historic context or legislating on issues that had not previously arisen but according to already existing legal principles), but it also allows for something else, namely; 3) translation, that is, drawing equivalences between cultural forms on the basis of the common principles they express and, therefore, establishing ecumenic, peaceful relations between these.

Theologically, this understanding of the inexhaustibility of general categories to particular designations is present in the ancient tendency to translate the names of gods from one pantheon to another, so that the divine principle or person behind them appears independent form either their Greek or Egyptian name, for example. The Egyptologist Jan Assman understands this phenomenon in terms of translatability, arguing that it can only function if a god represents some cosmic body like the moon, social function like medicine or abstract idea like justice, but must stop short of the God of later monotheism, who is not any of these things but is a person, entirely sovereign.

Professor Assman further understands the politics of translatability as allowing ancient civilizations to draw up accords in which each signatory would swear by his own culture's name for a god, where the latter had to be equivalent to that which his fellow regent was swearing by so that they both felt assured that the other's oath was binding. On this second point, it is not clear that political expediency precedes a genuine theological understanding that divine beings transcend their local names, neither does Assman necessarily imply that it does.

Translatability, as well as a practical requisite for engaging in diplomacy, relies on transcendence. If a thing can be translated it is because it transcends the level at which translation occurs, that is, the level of this or that language and name. If many names can refer to an object it is because that object is not itself a name and is not altered by having different names used for it. That the practical ceremony of conviviality leads us to assert a certain metaphysics, an ontology of peace, as Milbank describes it, is a curious thing.

From third millennium BC Mesopotamian equivalences between Sumerian and Akkadian names for the same deities, to Herodotus's claiming that Greek gods are largely taken from Egyptian religion and simply present different names for these, translation and the metaphysical principles underlying it, seem to constitute the ancient norm across the centuries.

All these ancient cults contained a form of monotheism or monism, for they believed there was a singular source beyond their gods. This is what Assman calls *cosmotheism*, the latent monotheism in all polytheism observed by Eric Voegelin and intuited by Cudworth, as Assman notes. This being the case, those Bronze and Iron Age cults would have had different names for the truly transcendent, singular God, and would probably have considered the equivalent names neighboring peoples used for this God to be legitimate (especially if, as Assman suggests, theological correctness is taken for granted as a condition for establishing political relations, but also given the absence of declarations of religious superiority or greater metaphysical knowledge one finds coming from the kings or high priests of different Bronze Age Near Eastern states, for example).

Contrary to Assman's assertion, the singular God is no more a person than those limited gods who are patrons of principles, functions or objects and can be translated. The kind of principle the supreme Deity is, just like the kind of personhood this Deity represents, would be broader and therefore less capable of being contained in some particular name or set of religious images. It would be all the more translatable as a consequence of its being more universal and less containable in contingent forms than the subordinate gods. It is not monotheism, then, but iconoclasm, that must be understood as the root cause for rejecting translatability.

When Eric Voegelin writes about the cosmological empires that prescinded from political expansion or imperialism, he refers to their worldview as that of the cosmological or *Homeric* ecumene because it is the vision one finds in what remains of the Greek epic cycle. It is likely that Homer's *Iliad* and *Odyssey* are remembering the conflicts that occurred between Mycenean Greeks and, among others, Luwian west Anatolians, including the historical Troy. These are Bronze Age civilizations, and Voegelin's cosmological ecumene is therefore the worldview that dominated the eastern Mediterranean before the 12th century BC end of the Bronze Age. This is not to imply that those societies and relations between them were ideal. They were surely rife with pathologies of various sorts. But they at least benefited from a correct outlook in one area of their political organization (though it did not last).

This theo-political translatability is precisely allowed for by the monarchical rites we have detailed in which the initiate dies to the particular, accesses the universal and is reborn to the particular (like the cosmic man, a dismembered subject delivered into grander identity with the whole cosmos and its underlying principle). Equivalent attempts at expressing cosmic order, for example in the court of Egypt as distinct from that of Babylon, become legitimate, for cosmic order itself has been perceived and, therefore, is known to be neither Egypt nor Babylon, but to nonetheless be present in both insofar as both are ordered.

It may therefore be hypothesized that the prevalence of ceremonies involving ritual death of the monarch and the myth of a cosmic man in the Bronze Age Aegean and Near East might account for what Van den Mieroop calls the Club of Great Powers in which kings referred to each other as equals and brothers in letters and used the metaphor of a village to foster a sense of the proximity and relatedness of their households.

It can be further speculated that, with the end of the Bronze Age in the Eastern Mediterranean as a result of political conflict which, following Dr. Eberhard Zangger's account, might have rendered once prosperous polities bereft of their palaces and temples, the centers of power in which knowledge was stored, this ritual of death and rebirth, along with the theological and political order it was a part of, was interrupted. This would partly explain the rise of predatory expansionism in the case of the Assyrian Empire during the Iron Age, and the anti-monarchism of the Greek city-states that eventually emerged, with their various experiments at composing political life, where kingship only really survives in the relative backwater of Macedonia, farthest away from the Near East and the events that a few centuries before had led to the end of an era.

Eberhard Zangger argues that the collapse of Bronze Age civilization is linked to the excessive concentration of knowledge in temples and palaces. This is compatible with Ken Dark's model of imperialism as rational under circumstances of strong impediments to knowledge transfer. Granted, the attack of the Sea Peoples (potentially a Luwian confederation) on neighboring polities and resulting war with the Myceneans during the 12th Century BC is not an example of imperialist expansion, but it is an upset of political stability, a military transgression that might in some respects have had imperial aspirations and which, in any case, occurs in the context of extreme barriers to knowledge transfer.

As Dr Zangger pointed out during my interview with him,[1] the Luwians had writing many centuries before the Greeks and kept it from their neighbor to the west. The diffusion of other areas of knowledge may have been affected by this hermetic containment. It may explain the initiative Myceneans took in fighting the Luwians: although others had also been attacked by the Sea Peoples, those others had used writing from an earlier date than the Bronze Age Greeks. It seems that after the advent of the Iron Age and following a period of relative stagnation,

---

1   Eberhard Zangger, Interviewed by Carlos Perona on 4 May 2018.

techniques (such as mathematical principles and their architectural applications) known in Babylonia since far earlier times were popularized by
Greek philosophers such as Pythagoras. Thus, a new impetus to spread
rather than concentrate certain types of knowledge and to actively resist
tyrants (such as the Pythagorean conflict with Dionysus of Sicily that
Iamblichus would later relate) perhaps serving as inspiration for the
later Roman Republican distaste for rulers, may have emerged from the
disaster of the opposite tendency. (The caveat in this last sentence is
important, as it is only *certain types of knowledge* that are being popularized,
and precisely Pythagoras and his school emphasized that certain inner
esoteric truths are to be taught only in the context of initiation.) This
reminds us of what Frithjof Schuon has to say about Bronze and Iron
Age state cults, some of which confront us with the sense of a terrible
petrification which desires to bare down upon the uncertainties of
change with the sheer weight of monumental statecraft, where a desire
to ward off uncertainty may partly be what leads to emphasizing the
development of magic and divinatory arts.[2]

A slight aside: Apart from its inner meaning, the historical context
of the very widespread myth of the universal flood likely relates to the
end of the Younger Dryas's glacial conditions.[3] This does not mean,
however, that Plato's account of the end of Atlantis does not also analogize elements of the end of the Bronze Age, as Zangger explores in his
book *The Flood from Heaven*. Robert Graves suggested this compatibility
between an ancient flood and also a metaphorical account of the political
conditions that ended the Bronze Age. The "legend of Atlantis...is not
to be dismissed as pure fancy.... But Plato's version...has apparently
been grafted on a later tradition." If indeed, this coincided with natural disasters, it would remind of the older flood, as the Egyptians tell
Solon in Plato's relating, there have been successive floods.[4] In this case,
Plato would be attributing the immoderate expansionism and hubris of

2   Schuon, *The Essential Frithjof Schuon*, Part I: Theology and Philosophy, note 8, 180–81.
3   As controversial researcher Graham Hancock and geologist Randall Carlson argue.
4   Graves, *The Greek Myths*, 39.2, 146. The later tradition and its political conflagra-
tion would consist of "...the Minoan Cretans who had extended their influence to
Egypt and Italy, were defeated by a Hellenic confederacy with Athens at its head;
and how, perhaps as the result of a submarine earthquake, the enormous harbor
works built by the Keftiu ('sea-people', meaning the Cretans and their allies) on the
island of Pharos, subsided under several fathoms of water... Such an identification
of Atlantis with Pharos would account for Atlas's being sometimes described as a son
of Iapetus—the Japhet of Genesis, whom the Hebrews called Noah's son and made
the ancestor of the Sea-people's confederacy—and sometimes as a son of Poseidon,
patron of Greek seafarers. Noah is Deucalion, and though in Greek myth Iapetus
appears as Deucalion's grandfather, this need mean no more than that he was the
eponymous ancestor of the Canaanite tribe which brought the Mesopotamian Flood
legend rather than the Atlantian, to Greece. Several details in Plato's account such
as the pillar sacrifice of bulls and the hot-and-cold water systems in Atlas's palace,
make it certain that the Cretans are being described, and no other nation."

Atlantis to the Bronze Age polities, and presenting their collapse as a
function thereof. Specifically, the hubris would belong to the polities
behind the Sea Peoples, a Cretan-led and Luwian-allied confederation,
with a presence in Africa, targeting the Myceneans and Egyptians among
others.[5] The Biblical and Apocryphal (in *Jubilees*) idea of oppressive
Edomites allied with Rome (Hebrew *Kittim*, appearing in *Jubilees* as one
faction of mercenaries) against Israel (and Egypt, according to the *Book
of Jashar*) would refer to these events. Rome partly repeated the pattern
of imperialism, but its underlying civilizing mission (represented by
king Numa Pompilius's temple of Janus, whose door of war remained
sealed his entire reign according to Plutarch; the elements in Virgil's
Aeneid that disrupt an imperialist reading, etc.) would result from the
lesson of the failure of the Luwian confederation and the scattering and
recollection of the Trojans in Italy. The link between Biblical narrative
and Pythagorean-Platonic tradition would occur here in their common
condemnation of the imperialism of that Bronze Age alliance, along with
Homer's narration of the end of the age of heroes in John Alvis's reading.

As for the structural reasons for Bronze Age collapse mentioned before,
we should not take it too far, given that the idea that Bronze Age palatial

---

5   Robert Graves speculates that these were part of the same confederation at the
turn of the Bronze Age. Thus, the Trojans (Luwians/future Romans/king Angeas
in the Book of Jashar) would have allied with Edomites against Egypt, Israel and
Mycenean Greece. In Jashar the alliance does not last and Angeas (its version of
Aeneas) does not ultimately attack Egypt, falling out with the Edomites and fighting
these, who ally with the land of Kittim, where his wife is from (perhaps a reference
to the conflict between newcomer Trojans and some of the Italic tribes, as in the
Aeneid). The *Book of Jubilees* (37:10) also mentions Kittim (probably Italians, maybe
Macedonians) as among the various people from whom warriors came to fight with
the Edomites against Jacob, apparently as mercenaries hired by Esau's sons. Let us
speculate freely: the Sea Peoples may be a mercenary force hired to fight Egypt and
Israel (these two being allied with the Myceneans) by near eastern rivals (Edomites)
who are also allied with the Luwians (these latter being close with the Kittim/ancient
Italics, eventually taking refuge in Italy, as well as having a strong presence in Africa,
thus the idea that the Trojans found safe harbor in Carthage and that "Angeas" was
king of Africa). Writes Robert Graves: "*when Joshua conquered Canaan* in the thirteenth
century BC, the men of Gibeon…came as supplicants to Joshua in Greek fashion,
pleading that they were not native Canaanites, but Hivites, i.e., Acheans from overseas. Joshua recognized their rights as foresters of the sacred groves and drawers
of sacred water (Joshua 9). It seems from verse 9 that they reminded Joshua of the
ancient maritime league of Keftiu presided over by Minos of Cnussos, to which
the Acheans and people of Abraham both once belonged. Abraham…married his
sister Sarah to 'Pharoah,' meaning the Cnossean ruler of Pharos" (*The Greek Myths*,
169.6, 715). There is much speculation here, but it fits aspects of other sources. In
Maccabees, the Spartans are considered Abrahamic, brothers to the Jews, and in the
work of Cleodemus Malchus, the Spartans, and Dorians in general, descend from a
daughter of Hercules married to Aphras, the son of Abraham by Keturah. This latter
account is certainly an exception, but we may interpret Maccabees as somehow a
political adoption to do with ancient alliances in an Abrahamic coalition (oriented
towards *gigantomachia*, ridding the land of giants).

economies were highly centralized is dubious, specifically in the case of Mycenean Greece: "It is becoming increasingly clear that Mycenean administrative texts recorded only a fraction of the economic activity,"[6] the non-recorded portion of which would have included entrepreneurial ventures as well. Still, a concentration of knowledge, at least, if not of economic activity generally, may have occurred. Further, the Pythagorean memory of tyrants and militancy against them may not derive only from a general critique of the Bronze Age but also, and more specifically, from the memory of the illegitimate interregnum administrators of Greece who rebelled against their home-coming kings. This is supported by the Pythagorean regard for Homer and, therefore, for Odysseus as Homer presents him, that is, genuinely noble, though flawed.

Homer's age of heroes and tyrants, modern historiography's Bronze Age (given that it involves the fall of Troy), is replaced by one of political heroism or the possibility of such, where spiritual initiation is linked to social participation. This is not an ending that Homer bemoans, just as the author of the *Book of Enoch* considers the passing of those super-human personages in a bygone era fortunate for humanity. In the Iliad, Jove will restrain the production of heroes by limiting or ending divine intermixing with mortals, and those sons of God who bred with mortal women will be retired along with their offspring in the Enochic materials (though apparently in some older antediluvian age). The lower specters of the monarchical archetype will cease to manifest on the earth in a deviated, hyperbolic form. In both the Biblical and Homeric case, this is the Lord's will. Indeed, in Homer, we are implicitly taught that its passing was the purpose of its coming about. These heroic demigods had to display great power and be brought low in order to teach humility to our species.

The Trojan king Priam's hypertrophic polygamy is part of Troy's self-condemnation, and Agamemnon, on the other side of the conflict, claiming for himself the concubine of one of his champions, which is justly protested by Achilles, expresses the same fault, as does the self-regard and fame-obsession of those champions. Goddess Juno at first opposes and ultimate justifies initiates like Hercules and Aeneas, or Apollo and Dionysus. Apart from divine femininity and nature, in these myths she stands for natural morality. She is the principle through which the reign of Jove is able to bring a new age of human moral community (becoming loyal to their marriage bed and closing the age of heroic hubris, as John Alvis writes). She opposes Priam's lavishness but is ultimately (in Virgil, following Homer's) won over to the cause of his subjects, the defeated Trojans, exiled and reborn as Romans under Aeneas.

The logic of imperialism was countered by Greek culture, a point Eric Voegelin observes in *The Ecumenic Age*. From Herodotus's *Histories* to Aeschylus's poetry and Plato's dialogues, the notion that different peoples

---

6   Dimitri Nakassis, *Individuals and Society in Mycenean Pylos* (Boston: Brill, 2013), 2.

ought to respect each other's territorial claims is ubiquitous, including the notion that geography indicates providential borders not to be transgressed. Plato stresses precisely this when, in the *Timaeus*, he cites ceasing to bare prosperity with moderation as the cause for Atlantis's expansionist conquests and consequent chastisement. In this sense, then, Greek philosophy returns to Bronze Age ecumenism by fulfilling the promise of its diplomatic rhetoric of familiarity where different polities are conceived of as households within the same village,[7] but also as a corrective to Bronze Age mistakes and excessive concentration of knowledge. (Indeed, the use of symbols associated with the sacred kings of the Bronze Age for and by mystical sages reminds us of the Chinese doctrine that maintaining proper order requires periods within which the role falls to kings and latterly to sages—from kings to Pythagoras and Plato, from the Duke of Chou to Confucius and Sima Qian, from Davidic monarchy to wilderness prophets: "The burden of reordering the ecumene that formerly was incumbent on the king is now incumbent on the sage."[8])

Apart from claims to universal regency, specific monarchies or pontificates may legitimately represent local unities that, by reason of their historical prolongation and other factors, exercise a degree of legitimate political and ecclesial autonomy. Claims to universal authority, when they are pursued as *de facto* realities, are a confusion of the archetype and the type. An ecumenic vision which refuses to conflate universal archetypes with particular types can impose itself by way of simple pragmatism. In the case of the imperial office, while it is technically speaking always universal, it can become administratively and culturally delineated, whereupon it allows for equivalent counterparts elsewhere, and conceives of the universalism proper to itself as encompassing these multiple counterparts.

Indeed, European Holy Roman Emperors were always considered as representing a universal principle of sovereignty but not as having a de facto right to every kingdom and principality. This is borne out by protestations against certain Papal and Imperial donations of land to the effect that they did not have any real legal right to make them. During the Bronze Age in the Eastern Mediterranean and Near East, the high political and theological station conferred upon regents did not impede the explicit commitment of these, during a certain period at least, to mutual recognition and equivalence, considering each other neighbors and relatives in a metaphorical village (again, as Van den Mieroop documents).

A fascinating later example occurs during the third century split of the Roman Empire into Western and Eastern halves, although there are earlier precedents of joint-emperorship. This took the form of Emperor Diocletian's Tetrarchy system, instituted in 286 AD. The name Tetrarchy

---

7   Marc van den Mieroop, *A History of the Ancient Near East, Ca. 3000–323 BC* (Wiley Blackwell: Oxford, 2016), 137.

8   Voegelin, *Order and History, vol. 4, The Ecumenic Age*, 350.

refers to four emperors though in practice there were two senior ones, Diocletian and his adoptive son and friend, Maximian and even there, Diocletian was senior, taking Jove for his patron god where Maximian's was the junior Hercules, though they were colleagues and both held the title of *Augustus*, their sons in law being Caesares, thus making four. The role of *Augustus* or emperor proper was shared between two persons: one ruler of the west and one of the east. Arguably, this system, which initially lasted only a very short period, later stabilized and endured intermittently for centuries throughout the Middle Ages.

We can interpret the fact that after Pope Leo III's crowing of Charlemagne as emperor (which was intended to make the Frankish king universal emperor, for the Byzantine throne was considered empty) Byzantine emperors continued to rule from Constantinople while, with Otto the Great of Saxony and his successors, Charlemagne's crown endured in the west, as *de facto* a return to Diocletian's Tetrarchy rather than as a terrible theo-political confusion (which on the surface and given a lack of explicit mutual recognition, it also was). Indeed, this strengthens the thesis that actual historical unfolding, often by way of practical necessity, better reflects ecumenical realities than the explicit claims to universal authority this or that polity or office might make for itself.

Later, Suleiman the Magnificent's refusal to refer to Charles V as emperor, for there can be only one emperor (he clearly understood the Holy Roman office as equivalent to the Islamic caliph and, indeed, after taking Constantinople Ottoman regents considered themselves heirs to the Roman Empire, since that city had been the new Rome), is perfectly correct, but misses the point. It is both more practical as well as more poetic to encompass existing representatives of the imperial idea within some wider sense of empire or ecumene rather than trying to physically occupy one's counterparts. We can thereby interpret claims to emperorship of even lesser medieval monarchs as recognitions that their microcosmic fief manifests the same principle as wider structures. The strategy of conquering the counterpart proved disastrous for Suleiman, who was continuously thwarted by terrible Balkan weather during an advance to the gates of Vienna which ultimately represented both the high point and beginning of decline for Ottoman power in Europe.

Translating the gods: Re-Deeming Difference and Rejecting Mimesis

Translating the gods, in Assman's sense, that is, translating the theological and political categories that legitimate a project (be it state, empire, broad political program, ecclesial authority, religious or ideological doctrine) admits that it consists of universals which can inhabit different particulars, the same way translating a word from one language into another admits its meaning is beyond words. This is the basis of the Ecumene, if illegitimate imposition of one particular upon others—illegitimate in its being based on the incorrect notion that this particular is identified with the universal in an exhaustive way—is to be avoided. This means one is re-naming, re-deeming a universal meaning by new words (for example those which other traditions use), in line with Pickstock's discussion of that serpentine movement that coils and stretches, goes inward to find the universal and outward to discover its expression, a discovery which is always a recovery. To desire and seek that universal, understandings its manifestation is ideally pluriform, we avoid desiring after particulars and falling into Girard's mimetic rivalry.

We may reflect on what Frances Yates refers to as the *phantom revival of Empire* in her *Astraea*. Even at its inception with Charlemagne, the idea of Empire in the west is more a metaphor, even a religious concept, than a *de facto* political project. This may be its force. In *The King's Two Bodies*[9] Ernst Kantorowicz notes that political mysticism can lose its mystique outside its native surroundings.

This may be true, but we should add that it also gains from a sense of longing, the nostalgia of what once was, which is a powerful thing. Less sentimentally, its adherents may realize that the specifics of that political mysticism which is now outside its native moment, overrun by history's momentum, were animated by something profounder than those historical specifics, a certain spirit, independent of that particular period in history, evidenced by the fact that its allure survives.

That human beings are prone to idealize the past and imagine recurrences of political, aesthetic and spiritual ideals in new forms can be a positive instinct and should not be ignored. It is not that mysticism should reject the polis, therefore, but it should enable itself to constitute new political projects, or to understand its deepest intuition as universal and capable of different forms, while also preserving that which is essential to its particularity, which requires not wedding this particularity to specific outward political institutions. The political becomes a cultural myth, and is stronger and more versatile in this form; Empire returns as an idea, and even as a consciously local expression of the universal paradigm. In this way, the proliferation of a paradigm in diverse setting can constitute a reminder that humanity is one in its diverse formats; can constitute a renewed vision of ecumene.

Political mysticism can thereby avoid the mistake of some those ancient state-cults Frithjof Schuon describes as "petrified" and "a cosmolatry often accompanied by sanguinary rites, not forgetting a development to excess of magic and the arts of divination." This describes modern totalitarian polities as well as the Bronze and Iron Age excesses he is addressing. The emphasis on divination may partly result from anxiety over passing time and a desire to resist it. Schuon goes on to describe the "marmorean and inhuman side of these paganisms" which "looks

9   Kantorowicz, *The King's Two Bodies.*

like a titanic reaction of space against time," building a fortress against history, perhaps recalling a period when "time was still but a rhythm in a spatial and static beatitude." Such a civilization, as Milbank writes, is one whose wall "seeks to shore life up against death" because ultimately it "always views death as an enemy of life rather than as the passage of life to further life."[10] It has no faith. To steal away from history can stifle religiosity and human creativity and is no longer true to the rhythm which inspired it, but risks becoming a terrible parody of that beatitude, the way puritanism parodies virtue, empowering instead the *thieves of virtue*, as Confucius calls them, the pharisaic legalists.

Rather than building fortresses against time, political mysticism should pack its essential belongings, so to speak, and become agile, as is arguably the case of modern Abrahamic religions, for example, and of Hinduism, which Schuon describes as "a synthesis between the gods of Egypt and the God of Israel."[11] We may leave Buddhism aside because it does not show the same features of political mysticism. As a historical tradition it did not begin by being housed in a specific, foundational polity, the way Judaism and Islam were, as well as Hinduism, depending on what we mean by that panoply of Indian tradition (Christianity is more like Buddhism in that regard).

In Buddhism, the emergence of accounts ascribed to the Buddha written long after the historical Buddha's departure from the world were sometimes legitimated in terms of their relating revelations from the Buddha or his preternatural allies imparted to practitioners during mediation, and also in terms of a doctrine found in the *Uttaravipatti Sutra* (part of the Pali canon) following which if a man converses with a deity whatever is rightly spoken, whatever is correct, constitutes *Dharma* and therefore the word of the Buddha. Thus, post-historical-Buddha scripture is justified. This would inform Mahayana and Vajrayana (Tantric) Buddhism. It also presumably allows a great deal of enculturation.

The previously discussed doctrine of fortunate absence (which is the same as what we termed the *absent center*) contained in the Gospel of John does not so much require that we abandon the polity and political life, but that we allow political mysticism to venture outside its foundational polity to justify the existence of other polities, that we construct our political mysticism and notions of Empire within a sense of ecumenism. On a practical level, this means ideology and allegiance enjoys primacy over institutions. The point here is not only to translate our projects into new contexts and thereby give them a longer and more creative life or lives through which its essentials may be revealed by inhabiting diverse compatible forms, but also to allow sacred scripture to teach us

10   Milbank, *The Word Made Strange: Theology, Language, Culture*, 224.
11   Schuon, *The Essential Frithjof Schuon*, Part I: Theology and Philosophy, note 8, 180–81.

what is going on in our context, not just what went on in ancient times, that is, to sacralize the here and now.

This might yield the impression that the particular, historically coherent cultural mode, in its great artists and long-held aesthetic forms, but even in its struggles and convulsions, is prophetic, for human patterns and imagination reveal archetypal truth. The mysteries will reproduce at every level, like spirals in a Mandelbrot set, so we need not exit particularity to access these. We have already seen that sacralizing the particular means seeing it as a node for the universal. Thus, a sense of uncovering a culture and civilization's sacred lineaments, passed the profane and the overgrowth, amounts to distinguishing between universal and particular without declaring war on the latter on behalf of the former (without sawing off the branch on a tall tree one is sitting on, and expecting to fly into the sky rather than plummet down). But this point has already been belabored.

Exiles and Exaltations, or Communal Initiation as Theological Translation

The translating of sacred symbols to new contexts is a feature of every tradition. Often, we see this when scriptural patterns are observed playing out in the historical and national contexts of newly converted peoples. The exilic return to a promised land is a prominent example. *The detachment of a sacred symbol/scriptural pattern from its original context and its application to a new one mimics the death and rebirth process of individual initiation.* We may therefore speak of communal initiation at the level of traditions and peoples.

Isaiah (19:25) features titles usually reserved for Israel and applies these to enemy nations, specifically—strikingly—the homes of Pharaonic oppression and Assyrian oppression, Egypt and Syria. In a moment of stunning pluralism, a high-hearted love of enemy, like a Hebrew Aeschylus wishing to preserve the Persian foe, the prophet relays: "The Lord of Hosts will bless them, saying, 'Blessed be Egypt My people, Assyria My handiwork, and Israel My inheritance.'"

The consonance of Isaiah with John's Apocalypse or Biblical eschatology generally is manifest in the language of purgation as division. To be dismembered is to be remembered, which is a recovery of something past. To be redeemed is to deem-again something already known. To be an exile and go journeying is to discover homecoming. By losing coordinates one realizes the universal beyond coordinates and can apply that universal more consciously and flexibly to the particular. Isaiah writes that the households of Egypt, prior to their becoming the Lord's people, become divided against themselves (19:2) and Jeremiah has Moab carried off and scattered before being restored, just as Jesus tells us family members will be pitted against one another on his account (Matthew 10:45) (the language is not identical, but similar). This is reminiscent of the iron rod with which Christ will rule and shatter (divide) nations (Apocalypse 2:26–27), which is perhaps the purgatory angels are subject to in 1 Enoch.

But if this receiver of the morning star, bestowed by Christ, who can shatter nations, is endowed of such power by keeping the works of Christ, as is said in the Apocalypse, which are works of humility, then we have here a different relation with the morning star to that which appears in Isaiah 14:12, in which the morning star is a "destroyer of nations" but is brought low by pride rather than being elevated by humility. The shattering of nations in the Apocalypse is not, therefore, a destruction of nations, which latter is the work of a prideful fallen one, not a humble risen one. This adds to our contention that the shattering is like the scattering of Israel which brings forth a nation's holiness through that trial.

The notion of dismemberment is also connected to that of the interruption of normal proceedings of life, a negative breach of health which is nonetheless the occasion for a new, wider encompassing normality. A *better normal*, so to speak. In his *Ecclesiastical History*, Bishop of Caesarea Eusebius Pamphilus, expresses a similar idea, considering Herod as an illegitimate king of Judea according to his reading of the Bible: "Herod was the first foreigner that obtained the government of the Jews, since, as Josephus has written, he was an Idumean by the father's side, and an Arabian by the mother's." This is significant for Eusebius in that it sets the stage for the fulfilment of prophecy: "The government of the Jews, therefore, having devolved on such a man, the expectation of the nations was now at hand according to prophecy: because with him terminated the regular succession of governors and princes...."[12]

Exilic nations, or the theme of leaving one place to establish a new nation, are quite common. From Pythagoras spending some time in captivity—even in Babylon according to some accounts—and establishing colonies upon his return, to the story of the Shona people being led by Mwari (their term for God) to a promised land in Zimbabwe, on route to which they are sustained by supernatural bounties like manna.

In the European context, this theme of collective dispersal and election, mirroring the dismemberment and enthronement of the initiate (history mimicking theurgy) occurs in the many accounts concerning the Trojans. Troy's destruction as one of twelve cities, its population's dispersal and restoration as the new Troy of Rome after North African exile and arrival, by the aid of Jove, to that appointed country in Italy parallels Israel's Biblical travails. Further, the wounding of Aeneas on the hip, his being guided and mythical spawning of royal descendants parallels Jacob, as has been noted. Artists have been aware of this parallel:

> ...for Dante Aeneas is a figure of "salvation history"...Trojan exiles led by Aeneas are understood by Dante as the extension of the journey of the Israelites under Moses. [Ezra] Pound is thus

---

12 Eusebius Pamphilus, *Ecclesiastical History*, trans C. F. Cruse (New York: Thomas N. Stanford, 1856), VI, 29–30.

following a Dantesque tradition in using certain Hebrew voices as
preparation for the inclusion of Aeneas [in Canto LXXIV: 434–35].[13]

Troy embraces its exile, its scattering, its invisibility, as final end.
Rather than being prophetically reconstituted like Israel, it returns in an
entirely new form, as Rome, as Latin. Indeed, it also returns in the form
of a continental civilization, as the many nations and dynasties claiming
Trojan descent, where Europe becomes a Trojan confederacy, and so
precisely by means of being scattered and *remaining* scattered, takes on
a new form. The telos of exile is not the end or reversal of exile but the
new configurations made possible by exile. The king is not only himself
after ritual death, but is the whole cosmos and the whole kingdom. Again,
the phantom quality of Empire that Frances Yates highlights in *Astraea* is
less a political debilitation than the proper realization of a theopolitical
mythos, which can go on to be reinforced and made a widespread creed
in terms of culture, "its reflection in symbolism and poetic imagery."[14, 15]

Even Israel does not really limit itself to reversing the effects of exilic
tribulation, rather, its scattering or crucifixion allows its scriptural
paradigms to be universalized in Christian and Islamic dispensations.
In a sense, forms of statecraft and cultural modalities derived from the
Greco-Roman paradigm have likewise become global, so that Rome, the
Trojan scion, is indeed universal, as well as particular.

Egypt for Isaiah, Moab for Jeremiah, Troy in Virgil's telling and the
disciples in the Gospel and early Church, all non-identically repeat the
paradigm of Israel's Biblical division and scattering (though in historical terms, murky as they are, pre-dating, in the Trojan case, but we are
speaking of archetype), which reinforces the scriptural link between
ordeals of division and being made worthy of election. The lesson is
that of the dismemberment of a primordial man who then becomes the
cosmos, as in the Indian *Rig Veda*, Ymir in Norse mythology, the rending
of Dionysus and Osiris in Greek and Egyptian mythologies, and so on.
The underlying logic is that once external conditions are so altered as to

---

13   Stephen Sicari, *Pound's Epic Ambition: Dante and the Modern World* (New York:
State University of New York Press, 1991), 123–24.
14   Yates, *Astraea*, 2.
15   We imagine a parallel to how in Egypt the "oracular function passed to seers
and pious philosophers…" initiating Roman youths, because "[o]wing to changing
historical and social circumstances, a great number of Egyptian priests and myst-
agogues gained independence from particular temples…. They were the bearers
of ritual *heka* power (*mageia*) and, in some cases, even joined the neo-Platonic circles of those who continued the Iamblichean an Procline chains of transmission"
(Uzdavinys, *Philosophy as a Rite of Rebirth: From Ancient Egypt to Neoplatonism*, 200–1).
Uzdavinys also refers to how sacred animals became the repositories of Divine
symbolism when foreign rulers yoked Egypt and made it impossible for Egyptian
religiosity to treat the monarchical institution as such a repository. This suggests
the state cult becomes mobile, even partly de-institutionalized.

be undone (scattered, dismembered), that which remains—the essence of a thing—can be fathomed directly.

But scattering is not necessarily or exclusively the creation of something new. It is the creation of something old. It is a return. In personal, initiatic terms, the end of ritual death and the experience of dismemberment is to realize oneself, one's true identity is attained. It is not only one's true identity as the *Atman*, in Indian terms, or the Self beyond selves. It is also one's true identity as duty, the vocation in life, the mission to be fulfilled, one's *dharma*. The king dies to himself to realize that transcendent Self but then, by way of this, returns to life in order to do his duty and embody the realm. He is not the petty ego he thought himself to be, but experiences identity with the Beyond, yet also, and consequently, experiences identification with the contingent set of strictures required of him as a king by his kingdom.

This is consistent with the *Aeneid*. The Trojans are, in fact, returning to their origin, as the *Penates* gods express, reporting Apollo's message (III:167–70, trans. John Dryden):

> ...Italia, from the leader's name.
> Iasius there and Dardanus were born;
> From thence we came, and thither must return.
> Rise, and thy sire with these glad tidings greet.
> Search Italy...

We read this again in Book VII (238–43):

> Fate and the gods, by their supreme command,
> Have doom'd our ships to seek the Latian land.
> To these abodes our fleet Apollo sends;
> Here Dardanus was born, and hither tends;
> Where Tuscan Tiber rolls with rapid force,
> And where Numicus opes his holy source.

The Trojans do not only return to their homeland, but are integrated and assimilated into its ethno-cultural context, the Latins. As Juno asks of and is granted by Jove, referring to the marriage of Aeneas and Lavinia:

> when the nuptial bed shall bind the peace,
> (Which I, since you ordain, consent to bless,)
> The laws of either nation be the same;
> But let the Latins still retain their name,
> Speak the same language which they spoke before,
> Wear the same habits which their grandsires wore.
> Call them not Trojans: perish the renown
> And name of Troy, with that detested town.

> Latium be Latium still; let Alba reign
> And Rome's immortal majesty remain.

Jove responds (XII:834–40):

> From ancient blood th'Ausonian people sprung,
> Shall keep their name, their habit, and their tongue.
> The Trojans to their customs shall be tied:
> I will, myself, their common rites provide;
> The natives shall command, the foreigners subside.
> All shall be Latium; Troy without a name;
> And her lost sons forget from whence they came.
> From blood so mix'd, a pious race shall flow,

(This language is similar to that of Plutarch when he refers to the fusion of Romans with Sabines under king Numa Pompilius.)

> Equal to gods, excelling all below.
> No nation more respect to you shall pay,
> Or greater off'rings on your altars lay.

In defending the choice of title for his autobiographical *Spiritual Aeneid* over the more common analogy of *Odyssey* (as in the word *theodyssey* rather than theo-Aeneid), Ronald Knox points out that Odysseus returned home whereas Aeneas discovered a new home (Rome, precisely where Knox finds his religious anchor after setting sail from Anglicanism). But we should add in light of the above that for the Trojan nation the *Aeneid* is in fact an odyssey, a return home, like Odysseus to Ithaca. Just so, the coming of Israelites to Israel in Exodus is a return, for that land was already inhabited by their father Abraham in Genesis.

The exile's return is an encounter analogous to the vision of the Biblical Ancient of Days and the Son of Man. Or in Indian terms, the *Chit* (Reflexive Awareness) perceives its own *Sat* (Being) as that which it wills to worship—the *Bhava* (a form of the Lord specific to a devotee). A return to Being in which Being accommodates us, like Jesus washing the disciples' feet, results in *Ananda* (Joy). The Trojan return to the land of their father in Italy analogizes this, where that which is in place and stable is like Being—the Latin kingdom—and that which is wandering and unstable is like Reflexive Awareness—the Trojans.

The Trojan-Latin dynamic—The idea of a double agency where the returning exile civilizes the local and the local re-naturalizes the exile—occurs throughout political history. For example, in early Zionism, which often viewed the local Arabic-speakers of Palestine as ancient Jewish populations, now Christian and Muslim, with early Jewish settlers imitating the local more authentically "Semitic" dress, etc.[16] Or in

---

16   Biblical themes of exile and return, or of reconciliation between the one who left and the one who remained, can be seen as recurring in the historical conversion of the Judean population to Christianity and Islam (religions that acted as foreign Ecumenic visions with local Israelite roots). This conversion is suggested by various historians, as well as by the first Prime Minister of Israel, Ben Gurion, and second

African-American thought inspired by E. W. Blyden, Martin Delany or Marcus Garvey, who viewed the return of African Americans to Liberia and Africa in general, and their relation with the local African, as a historical mission of modernizing the African while at the same time rediscovering their own African identity.

The theme of a scattered nation becoming holy appears in Nietzsche's discussion of a chosen people, where masters proceed from resentful and displaced slaves, or in Hegel's detailing of how a slave becomes master by acquiring mastery over processes his superior no longer involves himself with, or in Joseph de Maistre's account of hidden and humble lineages emerging to historical prominence from obscurity and spawning geniuses or ruling dynasties. In the *Gay Science*, section 344, Nietzsche tells us that convictions—by which he means hypotheses ardently believed in but unproven—have no right to citizenship. He is asserting the will to truth. It is the exile, the man separated from his familiar and comforting ideas, who will face naked truth nakedly, perhaps beginning with the truth of his own weakness, and therefore the need to remedy it.

These have been *made sacred*, literally sacrificed (again, *sacrum facere* means to make sacred). The entry of nations (whose kings bring their glory and crowns, as if relinquishing in the act of preserving the political) through the twelve gates of the Heavenly city in the Apocalypse is like the initiate entering the holy mountain in other traditions, or the recurrence of this number in the twelve cities of which Troy was one according to the *Iliad* (XI, 128), communities into which Cecrops divided Attica, regions of China, Indian names of the sun god Surya or tribes of Israel. Division of national units or kingdoms into twelve is apparently very widespread in history.[17] The new Jerusalem has twelve gates whereas those mountains are identified with four streams or kings, the quarters of the earth, which twelve is divisible by. Sometimes the number eight appears in this context (as in Frederick Barbarossa's chandelier, placed in the resting place of Charlemagne in Aachen, representing the Heavenly city but featuring eight candles, or perhaps the eight-pointed star symbolizing the agency of the female deity Inanna, identified with Venus the morning star), which is a multiple of four as well.

Indeed, the totalizing quality of that holy city is reinforced by the fact that Genesis mentions a total of seventy-two nations, which is itself divisible by twelve, so that in a sense all peoples "fit" into salvation. The number of "the sealed," one-hundred forty-four thousand (Apocalypse 7:4), is also divisible by twelve and seventy-two, as is three-hundred sixty, the

Israeli President, Ben-Zvi, in their *Eretz Israel in the Past and in the President* (Jerusalem: Ben-Zvi, 1979), 196. Indeed, that this population would come to be referred to as the hated *other* (the *Philistine* enemies of king David) is also readable in terms of Biblical paradigms, for example of Jacob's donning animal skin to appear as Esau.
17　John Mitchell and Christine Rohne, *Twelve-tribe Nations: And the Science of Enchanting the Landscape* (Rochester, VT: Inner Traditions, 1991).

degrees of a circle, usually presented as the shape of the heavenly whole. Twelve, seventy-two and three-hundred sixty are all divisible by six (and three). We have seen all this before.

In Isaiah (19) unity is reached on the basis of higher principles: not on the basis of rejecting some particulars and adopting others but by recognizing that which is beyond. Again, God is worshiped neither on the Samaritan mountain nor in Jerusalem, but in the Spirit (John 4:21–24). Allegory allows these higher principles to be applied across particulars. It keeps a psychic or noetic content without the bodily form in which it previously appeared. As Catherine Pickstock writes and as we have cited before, redemption "consists in a continuous and renewed non-identical repetition of history" there occurs an "endless allegorical return to the past and ironic removal from the meanings of the past (from Old Testament literal violence, for example)."[18] A sacred tradition may rehearse new projects. One can learn from and inhabit the meanings of Genesis and Exodus without savaging Canaan. We have here a kind of *translatio convenantii*, akin to the medieval *translatio imperii* whereby imperial legitimacy is translocated, so to speak, but one that does not abolish the old.

The Eschaton at Elysium, or the Elysian Ecumene

We will see in medieval usage of the term *Empire* that it is not necessarily a literal, singular, hegemonic project but can denote units within units. First, however, let us pursue the meaning of *Empire contra imperialism* at its origin in the West: Rome's political mythology. Indeed, Europe's foundation myth—the *Aeneid*—is in line with mystical ecumenism. Virgil may be read as ecumenic rather than imperialistic, redeeming European universalism by expressing how Roman universality can be ecumenic, a claim to an archetype rather than an actual bid for global hegemony. Like the Chinese Huangdi, Aeneas structures a civilization by means of his monarchy as myth of common descent, and implicitly subverts the drive to turn the ideal of Empire into imperialism.

The *Aeneid* is not utopian, or perhaps it is properly so (*a-topian*, a-*topos*, no-place), advising that the Elysium and what has been encountered there cannot be definitively, stably manifested in history (this might imply that Heaven does not rely on only one earthly vessel).[19] The Elysian vision of Rome is near the metapolis, the autozoon that undergirds all harmonious bodies, including that Roman community Aeneas is entreated to by destiny. Aeneas even fails to heed his father's injunction to show mercy to

18   Pickstock, *Repetition and Identity*, 227.
19   Homer's Odysseus may represent the same principle when he introduces himself as "nobody" to Polyphemus, the Cyclops in Homer, *The Odyssey of Homer*, trans. William C. Bryant (New York City: Harper and Row, 1967), IX:426, 191. By relinquishing his name/ego, Odysseus is able to avoid the wrath of the one-eyed monster (one-eyed egoism, lacking depth-perception owing to its focus on the narrow self, perhaps).

the defeated in the case of his final, fatal dealing with Turnus[20] (which is nonetheless suggested as being some order of righteous). Virgil's view is not the triumphalist historicism of the propagandist. It may be claimed as having avoided the trap of the immanentized eschaton.[21]

However, Virgil's is not a debilitating criticality prone to cerebral or sentimental obfuscation. Aeneas does not relinquish his mission. On the contrary, his father and heavenly descent encourage him unto its fulfillment. "A people without history is not redeemed from time, for history is a pattern of timeless moments" as T. S. Eliot writes in his *Four Quartets*, so that although Aeneas has seen this pattern (timeless,[22] for, again, its monads and moments present themselves without regard for chronology) he, like prince Arjuna in the *Bhagavad Gita*, does not abdicate what filigree his own life might represent within that pattern.

In the *Aeneid*, as in the *Bhagavad Gita*, spiritual epiphany does not foster antinomian abandon. Virtue is essential to Virgil, not as replacing spiritual initiation[23] (in light of the discussion below such a conclusion would appear incorrect) but as preparation for it and as its natural expression. For this reason, Virgil can represent "central European values"[24] for T. S. Eliot—indeed, or any coherent values at all.

To gain a broader understanding of Virgil's approach, another of his works, the *Georgics*, may be addressed. This work's title (meaning agriculture) indicates the irreducible necessity of a certain minimum labor: to live human beings must eat, to eat they must attain food. This is particularly clear in those passages[25] presenting the "law of fate" according to which all earthly things decay,[26] until "stern death's ruthlessness sweeps us away."[27] This is not overridingly somber, however, as it represents a call to activity and adventure: "[t]oil triumphed over every obstacle."[28]

Apart from the general conditions of earthly life, the Georgics do not present politics and, specifically, the Roman project as redemptive in the sense of transforming human nature or the human lot. On the contrary, images of slaughter and putrefaction—the ugliness of the natural world—are associated with it at various points. In describing Rome, Virgil writes that "[t]he putrid blood of slain bullocks has engendered

---

20 Virgil, *The Aeneid*, XII:796; 383.
21 Mittal, *Time and History in Virgil's Aeneid*, 15–16.
22 Aeneas's Elysian visions may be bright with the morning that ends the nightmare of history, but they are not *in* history, they are perpendicular to it, like the vertical beam of a cross. Ending the dream of history is never a historical accomplishment. Immanent eschatons only churn fresh night terrors.
23 Mittal, *Time and History in Virgil's Aeneid*, 18.
24 Eliot, *What is a Classic?*, 7.
25 Zanker, *Some Thoughts on the Term "Pessimism" and Scholarship on the "Georgics,"* 83–84.
26 Virgil, *Virgil: Eclogues. Georgics. Aeneid: Books 1–6*, ed. G. Goold and trans. R. Fairclough (London: Loeb Classical Library, 1999), *Georgics*, I:199–203; 113.
27 Virgil, *Georgics*, III:66–68, 181.
28 Ibid., I:145; 109.

bees."[29] Llewelyn Morgan observes that "[i]f such material makes the Georgics subversive of the Augustan dispensation..." (which it would if the latter were interpreted as an immanent eschaton, an era set to change even physical laws) "...then it is uncompromisingly so...."[30] The golden age to which Virgil alludes, therefore, is self-consciously incommensurable with the originating and eschatological horizon in which the divine draws mankind into harmony with itself. Rather, it is a toiling attempt at piety.

Further, in the outline of Aeneas's journey we see something of Europe's history. One who, when injured, is carried by the gods, as Aeneas was, knows to in turn carry tradition, the broken-footed inheritance, upon his back, even as his home burns. As noted, this image from the distant past is also projected forward, appearing in Catholic eschatology as a limping Holy Emperor.

A civilization like the European which has lost its traditional grounding, exiting what had been mainstream of medieval thought and entering philosophically nominalist territory, can be said to have lost its Creusa, the wholesomeness of its home. Like the burning of Troy, this entailed fire, the revolutions and wars marking the Westphalian state's birth pangs (though the treaty of Westphalia did not actually end Empire) and, later, the new idols that had come to occupy the vacuum left by the death of god. Carrying the broken-footed past, Anchises, out of the doomed city, which itself carries the household gods, preserving tradition despite its biases, its lopsidedness and mis-steps, and attending to its prophecies from Elysian beyonds, it can leave behind modern indulgences foreign to the soul, the comfortable distraction and luxury of a queen Dido, and attend to the promise of Lavinia to be held.

The poet's presentation of Rome as a heritage aloof from history's politics and polemics and the torpors of gross military expansion sheds concern for temporal linearity. This is clear from the non-chronological order in which figures of Roman grandeur are presented to Aeneas during his descent into the underworld and his visit to the Elysian Fields. Further, that the bard is equally unconcerned by historical contingency is attested by his excluding of seditious or rivalrous episodes from Anchises' (Aeneas's father) description of the future career of these figures. They are not their historical selves, although those latter are them (partially, imperfectly).

On the question of *Aeneidian* politics, then, much can be drawn from Book VI of Virgil's epic, in which the hero descends to the underworld, eventually reaching beatific realms where he is shown a vision of Rome. This is not a rendering of history but of that which history renders. Aeneas does not witness a future Rome but Rome's ideal, the mythic

---

29   Ibid., IV:285; 239.

30   Llewelyn Morgan, *Patterns of Redemption in Virgil's Georgics* (Cambridge: Cambridge University Press, 1999), 13.

archetype beneath, just as C. S. Lewis describes the palpitation of a realm called Logres under the surface of mere Britain:

> ...something we may call Britain is always haunted by something we may call Logres. Haven't you noticed that we are two countries? After every Arthur, a Mordred; behind every Milton, a Cromwell: a nation of poets, a nation of shopkeepers...[31]

This veiled dimension to the homeland may be applied to ancient Rome, for according to Lewis, "[e]very people has its own haunter"[32] and, consistently with Virgil, it is not discontinuous with the temporal, for Logres has manifested an often-occluded lineage to prompt Britain's history ("an unbroken succession of Pendragons").[33]

By happy correspondence, Logres (*Loegria*) as appellative for England (rather than for all of Britain, although it ought perhaps to apply to the latter, given that it is likely a Celtic designation for England, so that although it refers to Saxon land, it is owed to pre-Saxon Celts) is said by Geoffrey of Monmouth to derive from king Locrin,[34] oldest son of Brutus, descendant of Aeneas, so that the discoverer and bearer of Rome's Elysian ideal also spawned Albion's spiritual fiber.

The aesthetic admiration for time and history from the perspective of archetypes outside time and history is perhaps responsible for what some commentators have interpreted as pessimism in the *Aeneid*.[35] This approach can militate against reading Virgil as merely political (although it has often been invoked to the opposite end). Virgil's early muse and Callimachus-like aloofness from worldly vainglory (which he makes explicit at the beginning of the sixth *Eclogue*[36]) pulses through even the *Aeneid*'s epic verse.[37] The upset of propaganda can be highlighted, following Steven Shankman, in terms of three ambiguities:[38] Dido's suffering a death undeserved (according to Virgil's narration itself);[39] Aeneas returning from the underworld by way of the gate of false dreams, and the unmerciful treatment meted out to Turnus. Trojans are not without villainy. Virgil shows us their faults and excesses in war. Aeneas does not show mercy to Turnus, just as the Trojans uproot a holy tree

3 1   Clive Staples Lewis, *That Hideous Strength* (Quebec: Samizdat, 2015), 343-44.
3 2   Ibid., 345.
3 3   Ibid., 344.
3 4   Geoffrey of Monmouth, *History of the Kings of Britain*, II:1; 23.
3 5   Andreas T. Zanker, Some Thoughts on the Term "Pessimism" and Scholarship on the "Georgics." *Vergilius* (1959), vol. 57 (The Vergilian Society, 2011), 93.
3 6   Virgil, *The Eclogues of Virgil*, trans. George Mackie (Quebec: Gilbert Stanley, 1847), 27.
3 7   Steven Shankman, *In Search of the Classic: Reconsidering the Greco-Roman Tradition, Homer to Valéry and Beyond* (University Park, PA: The Pennsylvania State University Press, 1994), 222.
3 8   Ibid., 226.
3 9   Virgil, *The Aeneid*, IV: 608; 142.

of the Latins (XII:766–71). Although the cosmic significance of empire (its correspondence with the Cosmos) in the *Aeneid* cannot be denied,[40] a distinction between *Imperium* and imperialism may be made such that these passages subtly undermine the latter.

This is consistent with what Voegelin would identify as a Homeric ecumenism or cosmological empire ("[i]n the epics... the *oikoumene* is not yet a territory to be conquered together with its population," for "[t]he experience of the 'horizon' as the boundary between the physical expanse... and the divine mystery of its being is still fully alive..."[41]) as opposed to an Alexandrian one (a "deadly concupiscence of reaching the horizon,"[42] though one made potentially less deadly, or at least less politically unsavory, if interpreted as sometimes motivated primarily by the curiosity of an explorer[43] rather than by *libido dominandi*). Or, assuming a practical political order across peoples, it is the acceptance of "a plurality of empires within the pragmatic ecumene"[44] as opposed to that previously discussed impulse of "imperial entrepreneurs... to make the jurisdiction of their respective empires coincide with the pragmatic ecumene"[45] by abolishing the plurality of civilizational projects. In short, it is a disposition that does not see universal order and truth as justifying unending political expansion.

That predatory expansion is a parody of true initiation, a kind of misunderstanding of the macro-anthropos and attempt to make it a literal political realm, is also implied by the previously cited passage from a 4th-century Taoist text, Ge Hong's *Baopu Zi Neipian*:

> Methods leading to immortality call for us to extend our love the very frontiers of the universe and to view others as we do ourselves; but the prince absorbs the weak, attacks the ignorant, capitalizes on disorder, and spreads devastation. He opens new lands and extends frontiers. He destroys man's shrines.[46]

The Homeric symbol of an encircling ocean around the earth (*oikos* delineating the oikoumene,[47] the outer waters surrounding the world), beyond which are the dead[48] (which harkens back to Egyptian and Meso-

---

40   Philip R. Hardie, *Virgil's Aeneid: Cosmos and Imperium* (Oxford: Clarendon Press, 1999).

41   Voegelin, *Order and History Volume IV, The Ecumenic Age*, 264.

42   Ibid., 267.

43   Ibid., 267.

44   Ibid., 268.

45   Ibid., 273.

46   James Ware's translation. Fabrizio Pregadio, "Seeking Immortality in Ge Hong's Baopuzi neipian." In David Chai, ed., *Dao Companion to Xuanxue* (Cham: Springer Nature Switzerland, 2020), 27.

47   Voegelin, *Order and History*, vol. 4, *The Ecumenic Age*, 264.

48   Homer, *The Odyssey of Homer*, trans. W. Bryant (New York City: Harper and Row, 1967), XI:25; 225.

potamian myth[49]) is consistent with Virgil's prophecy of Rome reaching

> ...beyond the Libyans and the Indians, to a land that lies beyond the stars, beyond the roads of the year and the sun, where sky-bearing Atlas turns the world, inset with burning stars, on his shoulders.[50]

Although in its most explicit sense this passage describes imperial expansion, it is perhaps less an injunction or prediction of transcontinental political control (although if interpreted in literal terms it has certainly been fulfilled in terms of cultural influence, and even politically insofar as European overseas empires identified themselves with Rome) than of a political order that reaches and reflects that which is altogether beyond the earthly realm and its peoples. The reference later in this passage to a (partial) restoration of the Golden Age may add to this interpretation. There is precedent in the ancient world for nominal, titular claims to universal lordship referring to the universality of the monarchical function and archetype represented by a particular regent or polity, and not to any sort of sincere bid for global political dominance.

While not always acknowledged by Virgil's exegetes (indeed, the *Aeneid* is ambivalent on this score; it might be explicitly expansionistic and implicitly subversive of expansionism), the above is subtly internalized in the literary and pseudo-historiographical tradition the *Aeneid* engendered, and emerges through the figure of Aeneas, beyond Virgil, in those latter accounts, such that dynastic, genealogical links to the Trojan hero may be understood as documents which "record the *translatio* of Trojan Empire, not the expansion."[51]

Writes Wilson-Okamura: "the imperium they celebrate is not that of ultramarine conquest, but of national sovereignty." This is an important insight (albeit it risks misunderstanding medieval pluralism as the later nation-state). According to Otto Gierke, it is precisely in the context of *imperial translation* that Marsilius of Padua expresses the view that the unity of the world (or human form) does not necessitate unity of government, for indeed a plurality can, already and with nothing added, constitute a unity.[52]

Aeneas is an avatar of imperial universality, but within a certain civilization's particularity. It is not only a case of "[t]he societies that emerge from an imperial breakup bear[ing] the imprint of ecumenic-imperial

---

49   Voegelin, *Order and History Volume IV, The Ecumenic Age*, 265.

50   Virgil, *The Aeneid*, VI:704-7; 203.

51   David S. Wilson-Okamura, *Virgil in the Renaissance* (Cambridge: Cambridge University Press, 2010), 223.

52   Marsilius of Padua, *De Translatione Imperii*, XII, quoted by Gierke, *Political Theories of the Middle Ages*, 128. Marsilius's position is, however, open to interpretation. Hwa-Young Lee, *Political Representation in the Later Middle Ages: Marsilius in Context* (Oxford: Peter Lang, 2008), 139.

consciousness...,"[53] but also of a certain potential within the imperial
Roman idea (as construed by certain of its artists and as hymned by
Virgil) becoming ripe. In this sense the medieval corrects the Classical.
Medieval Europe does not inherit an empire; its empire *is* heritage.

This occurs in accord with the poetic image of a triadic structure of
civilization (youthful-barbarous, mature-stately and elder-religious—a
bodily, psychic and spiritual). Aeneas is confronted with Romulus, then
Augustus Caesar and subsequently Numa Pompilius.[54] Although historically they followed a different sequence, the order in which they are
seen corresponds to the above progression. Romulus may reasonably be
identified as savage youth, given that his story largely relates his early
childhood, and given that he was an orphan leader of a war party. Caesar
Augustus, as emperor and reformer attempting to introduce sobriety
into the habits of the Roman establishment represents the disciplining
exertion of adulthood. Finally, Numa Pompilius, temperate and pious,
who ruled according to Pythagorean doctrine,[55] is the wise elder. They
are the founders of Rome's "city...imperium, and...religion,"[56] respectively though not sequentially (or sequentially in some trans-historic
sense, but not chronologically). They are the personalities of Rome's
youth, maturity and sage seniority; the savage and vital, the civilized
and refined, the pious and saintly; *soma, psuche* and *nous.*

Aeneas returns from the underworld by way of an ivory gate, not one
of horn, the portal of false, not true, dreams.[57] This image is taken from
Book XIX of Homer's *Odyssey*, in which Penelope explains that dreams
reach mortals via one of these two portals, so that some are deceptive
and others true.[58] Given that the gates refer to dreams as well as *umbrae*—
that is, shades, the departed—an easy explanation, if not necessarily the
most obvious, is that Aeneas, along with the sibylline guide who has
accompanied him on this descent, are false shades (not being shades at
all, but living mortals), and so must return to the earth by an ivory gate.[59]
More subtly, it may be suggested that the truth of Rome, and of life as
such, is in that Elysian realm Aeneas has glimpsed. The arena of his epic
founding of a temporal Rome, for all its world-historical significance, is
but a surface vapor above the depths he has just plumbed, a stadium for
poetic projects, for exertions inspired by transcendent vistas.

The eternal city seen at Elysium, a collective in which personhood is primary, with denizens whose kingly surpassing sees their "brows...shaded

53   Voegelin, *Order and History Volume IV, The Ecumenic Age,* 372.
54   Virgil, *The Aeneid,* VI: 692–721; 203–4.
55   Plutarch, *Lives,* Numa:6–9; 333–35.
56   Mittal, *Time and History in Virgil's Aeneid,* 245.
57   Virgil, *The Aeneid,* VI: 799; 208.
58   Homer, *The Odyssey of Homer,* XIX:682–83; 157.
59   Nicholas Reed, "The Gates of Sleep in Aeneid 6," *The Classical Quarterly* 23:2
(1973): 311–15; 315.

by civic crown of oak leaves"[60] and other splendors, is shadowed by the imperfection of history and of even Aeneas's actions. The vision itself is, at one level, a monumental history whose effect is to inspire Aeneas and the reader, yet one which must be as critical as it is monumental (to mention two of Nietzsche's categories of historical accounts). Virgil's ignoring of elements considered spurious to greatness (that which Anchises omits from his prophesies of Rome's future) announces a contrast between vocation and historical shortcoming that cannot but result in a kind of critical reading of Roman history (Nietzsche's typology must in this context become confounded).

Misremembering Heaven for the Harpy

We can read the *Aeneid* as anti-imperialism in terms of how Aeneas remembers and misremembers his vision of Elysium. In Book VII of the *Aeneid*, the Trojans share a meal, fruit upon the only table they can improvise—flat bread, like the Israelites, the holy meal of exiles. As juices from the fruit seep down, the old bread softens so they eat this too. Somebody jokes that this is precisely what an angry harpy whose cattle they had inadvertently stolen had hoped for them: that they should end up so hungry as to eat their table. And so, they laugh. But Aeneas now claims to recall that it was his father, Anchises, who told him this would happen, as a sign that they should begin building their new fortresses. Yet no such claim is found in Book VI, when Aeneas speaks to the soul of his departed father in the Elysian realms.

We read this as Aeneas misremembering his father's injunction. He further attributes the words of the harpy—not a prediction so much as an attempted curse—to Anchises, and turns that curse into a sign to go forth and conquer. That his memory of Anchises' prophecy is incorrect can be discerned from the fact that he attributes to it a false augury: that, once the tables have been eaten, no more challenges will come to the Trojans. In fact, much fighting lies ahead. Further indication that this is a mistake on Aeneas's part may be found in the fact that in course of that conquering, he precisely violates what his father *actually* said—that he should show mercy to the defeated foe—for he slays his rival Turnus after this one begs to be spared.

All this is telling of the perils of the spiritual quest. After returning from the beyond, Elysium, without a grounding in the manifest world, we misremember the beyond as a call to escape from the manifest, or to simplify it into the same peace as we perceived. Becoming frustrated, we may impose a merciless uniformity of conquest to parody the Unity of transcendence. Soon the joy we experienced becomes mere ritual.

The gap of silence, and guffaw of laughter, when the Trojans realize they have in fact eaten their tables, but that these were made of bread, is the very

---

60   Virgil, *Georgics*, VI:684; 202.

gap through which the west—latter-day Rome—can be re-thought. But Aeneas reintroduces the harpy's words, now as a curse turned injunction, to pursue the founding of Rome along lines which, we assume, have deviated from those Anchises gave him, deviated from the Elysian paradigm of the heavenly city. Empire is now a burden. The harpy's curse, reinterpreted and appropriated, is now somehow the driver of Empire. Of course, it is tempting to turn a bad omen into good. Our tendency towards superstitious can thereby be utilized, rather than acting as a hindrance to us. But this would compel us unto our path the same way the bad omen threatened that path. We would not be free. The erotic-aesthetic dimension would be occluded. To advance by turning the curse, the omen, into its opposite—a help, a driver, a reason to go forth—is to participate in the ego's dialectic. Our projects should instead be enterprises of free will and love.

To eat our tables is to leave no trace of ourselves: the harpy would have us be entirely apolitical and acultural, leaving no permanence and eating the symbol of shared space, of community. This is the imagined natural state, and it is a vengeance for our past thievery, for stealing from nature, as though we were not its stewards (the Trojans stealing cattle). To eat our table is also to elevate the instrument, the container, the matrix, the technology, to the level of meal. If our anatomy is not designed for it, then we should now adapt, rather than the other way around. So goes the specter of dystopian technocracy. Thus, the harpy's words are both the sinking into a natural state and fleeing into a futuristic event horizon. Indeed, once we give up our shared cultural spaces—the table—we are ripe for technocratic fantasy. This desire to end history, exiting from one side or the other, enters Rome from the harpy, not from Anchises.

The true fulfilment of Rome, which Aeneas remembers correctly, is in his purification and ascension at the river Tiber, and in his eventual succession by Numa Pomipilius, who holds neither the shield of Achilles, depicting two warring cities, nor of Aeneas, depicting a global conquering city, but rather the *Ancile*, the sacred shield, of which twelve images are paraded during the Ides of March: a harmonious manifold. This connects to the medieval mythos of Trojan descent, not as centralized polity but as kinship between many nations.

Translating the Ecumene: From Ethnocentrism to Polycentrism, or the Absent Center and the Plural Center

In terms of the earlier cited reference in Voegelin to the term *ethnos*, Frank Walbank's conclusions concerning the primary (and likely earliest but, in any case, most established[61]) ancient Greek meaning of this word

---

61   "…even if the 'group' meaning came first (which I find highly improbable), it is clear that the ethnic meaning was firmly established by the time of Aristotle and before the hey-day of the federal states." Frank Walbank, *Selected Papers: Studies in Greek and Roman History and Historiography* (Cambridge: Cambridge University Press, 2010), 23.

bears noting, to the effect that it designated "a tribal or kinship basis,"[62] so that "it seems clear that the political organization of the *ethnos* took place within a context of kinship and tribal cohesion...."[63] Plato himself indicates concern for common kinship in the passage from the *Laws* Voegelin is citing (not simply in terms of personal kinship but of groups defined thereby):

> ... had not the bondage that threatened her been warded off by the concerted policy of the Athenians and Lacedaemonians, practically all the Greek races would have been confused together by now, and barbarians confused with Greeks and Greeks with barbarians,—just as the races under the Persian empire today are either scattered abroad or jumbled together and live in a miserable plight.[64]

This concern usually accompanies fear over the end of a religious tradition and precisely counters imperialistic violence (though this can reverse). Biblical examples include Genesis (28), which warns against marrying Canaanites, passage from Exodus in which Joshua is told not to join foreigners after defeating the Canaanites, referring to their habits as sinful, Numbers (33), which claims foreigners will become a prick in the side if they are allowed to live among Israelites, the Book of Tobit, where taking a foreign wife is explicitly prohibited by father to son, Psalm 106, Deuteronomy (32), and so on. Indeed, the *Book of Jubilees* (which is cited as containing truth by St. Justin Martyr, St. Isidore of Seville, St. Epiphanius of Salamis, Origen of Alexandria, Diodorus of Tarsus and St. Isidore of Alexandria and Eutychius of Alexandria) goes so far as to declare that those Israelites who want to give their children in marriage to foreign spouses should die.

We see how the emergence of Voegelin's "distinguishable units in history," then, is often religious. Montgomery Watt notes this in the case of Islam which, in part and in terms of historical processes, united the Arabs. And we may think of Yellow Emperor Taoism and this figure's role in the religious imagination of China and conceptions of a greater (non-exclusive Han) Chinese polity. There is also the striking case of Native American nationhood in the ministry of the late 18th-, early 19th-century Shawnee brothers Tecumseh and Tenskwatawa. Tecumseh was the military leader, Tenskwatawa the ministering mystic. Tecumseh denied that any tribe could sell land to the European settlers unilaterally, as the land belonged to all indigenous tribes as one.

He conceived of Native Americans as having one legal personality, being a singular owner of land, one people. Tenskwatawa's disciple, Odawa chief Le Maigous or "The Trout," taught that since "The Creator's red and

---

62 Ibid., 22–23.
63 Ibid., 22–23.
64 Plato, *Laws*, trans. Robert G. Bury (Cambridge, MA: Cambridge University Press, 1961), III:693; 221–22.

white children are of different colors, they must each be a separate people" where Native Americans become "one great people."[65] Part of the religious character of historical emergence is that it distinguishes people from each other through codified practices as well as reforming the practices of the identity whose emergence into a unified form it is articulating. In the case of Tenskwatawa, this involved prohibiting native Americans from drinking alcohol and dressing in European style clothes, as well as abolishing certain tribal practices considered witchcraft. Again, we cannot resist drawing a parallel to the southern Tupac Katari, who also prohibited the use of Spanish dress and the drinking of alcohol for his followers, as well as the eating of Spanish bread (wheat flour), to be replaced by traditional corn bread.

Keeping a people and religion compact ensures that its cultural character is clear and the psychological affinity between its members is retained, such that a path to spiritual realization is reliably marked out. Coming to understand one's own psychological proclivities and deactivate one's complexes is often a big part of getting to grips with a spiritual practice. These proclivities and complexes are often learnt and inherited from one's context, so that if this context is known and has been traversed many times over, one has a good chance of finding roadmaps from one's own tradition that work relatively well for one. This, combined with an underlying sense that diversity is a good in and of itself, because it teaches us that no single tradition can ever exhaust the great mystery, and because diversity gives different moods or archetypes space to manifest, provides a justification for the texts cited above and their concerns.

Latent (and sometimes fully explicit) in these texts, however, is the danger of dehumanizing the other. Indeed, distinctiveness is frequently defended in agonistic terms, identifying the group that is distinct as holding a monopoly on truth or nobility. But this also often veers into defending diversity simply for the sake of its beauty. And to perceive this beauty is to read in *book of nature* that it "does not just give rise to an indefinite number of, say, cats and dogs, indifferently; rather, this indefinite number is differentiated into a definite plurality of different kinds...," once more quoting Desmond on the "disclosure of the metaxological affinity of being, the presence of unselfconscious community in natural things."[66]

In the *Divine Comedy*, Dante reports the following words as coming from his crusading ancestor, Cacciaguida, in Heaven: "Strains intermingled the beginning were, and cause of evil in the city's life, as excess food in bodies will incur" (*Paradiso* XVI). As Barbara Reynolds writes, "[f]rom these words it is evident that Dante believed in protecting the purity of the blood-line, a view which seven centuries later would be termed politically incorrect, if not racist."[67] However, Dante is not maintaining

---

65   Irwin, *Coming Down From Above*, 192.
66   Desmond, *Desire, Dialectic, and Otherness: An Essay on Origins*, 164.
67   Reynolds, *Dante*, 356.

other peoples are not virtuous or are not included within what he considers the true faith.

St. Thomas Aquinas quotes Sirach (Ecclesiasticus) 13:19 to this effect,[68] "[e]very beast loveth its like: so also every man him that is nearest to himself" (in its original context the passage actually acquires moral connotations, referring to likeness in terms of that which exists among the righteous[69]). The angelic doctor also notes Biblical instances in which fellowship is allowed or disallowed in part (not exclusively) as a function of common kinship, specifically as regards Israelites, descendants of Jacob, and "Idumeans, the children of Esau, Jacob's brother" as opposed to Israelites and Amalekites, as the former "had no fellowship of kindred with them [Amalekites]."[70] The underlying logic for this can be found in the *Summa Theologica*, in terms of how "... likeness, properly speaking, is a cause of love..." and unity in likeness constitutes a certain common self that multiple individuals may participate in.[71]

St. Jerome makes a very similar point in *Against Helvidius*, which refers to kinship as defining national units as one of the bases for social cohesion which scripture gives warrant to. Here, then, diversity is not the accidental result of the bearers of virtue protecting themselves against the profane, but rather is a distributed good. In line with this, in his *Ad Nationes* Tertullian argues against considering Christians a new race for indeed every nation may be Christian, and faith or spiritual exaltation is not a matter of race. The possible danger in this is not so much one of dehumanizing others than of isolationism. However, the ethic emerging from the previous discussion need not opt for defending either different existing identities and cultural forms or new combinations and versions of these, but can instead fully assert both at once.

---

68   Saint Thomas Aquinas, *Summa Theologica*, Third Number (QQ. XC–CXIV), trans. Fathers of the English Dominican Province (London: R. and T. Washbourne, 1915), Q.99:Art.2, 102.

69   The *Gospel of Philip* also uses the idea that like things attract each other and create more like things as an analogy for how spiritual righteousness is attracted to itself (this analogy precisely emphasizes the diversity of manifested righteousness): "The human being has intercourse with the human being. The horse has intercourse with the horse, the ass with the ass. Members of a race usually have associated with those of like race. So spirit mingles with spirit, and thought consorts with thought, and light shares with light." *Nag Hamadi Codex II, 2–7, The Gospel of Philip*, 62:34–63:34, 167.

70   Saint Thomas Aquinas, *Summa Theologica*, Third Number, Q.105:Art.3.

71   "One kind of likeness arises from each thing having the same quality actually: for example, two things possessing the quality of whiteness are said to be alike.... Accordingly the first kind of likeness causes love of friendship or well-being. For the very fact that two men are alike, having, as it were, one form, makes them to be, in a manner, one in that form: thus two men are one thing in the species of humanity, and two white men are one thing in whiteness. Hence the affections of one tend to the other, as being one with him..." (Saint Thomas Aquinas, *Summa Theologica*, vol. 2, Part 2, First Section, Q.27:Art.4).

Islamic tradition has tended to value kinship (diverse lineages in the architecture of humanity) as a matter of utility, although spiritual contemplation is also mentioned in this context. In the Qur'an, kinship seems to function as follows: 1) Serving as a mechanism for identifying others (Qur'an, 49:13); 2) Ordering one's responsibilities by establishing a rank of affection and service, presumably, and in quite practical terms, given the limitations of the human subject to do good, so that he may focus his works on those near him in kinship (Qur'an, 33:6); and 3) Providing occasion for contemplation, whereby the diversity of creation highlights, by way of contrast, the unity of the Creator, and specifically the necessary transcendence of that unity, for all contingent things are diverse, and therefore genuine unity belongs to that which is not contingent.

In terms of the utility of kinship for purposes of identification, this is established as follows:

> O mankind, indeed We have created you from male and female and made you peoples and tribes that you may know one another. Indeed, the most noble of you in the sight of Allah is the most righteous of you. Indeed, Allah is Knowing and Acquainted. (Qur'an, 49:13)

Referring to kinship as indicating an order of affection and responsibility, we read the following:

> The Prophet is more worthy of the believers than themselves, and his wives are [in the position of] their mothers. And those of [blood] relationship are more entitled [to inheritance] in the decree of Allah than the [other] believers and the emigrants, except that you may do to your close associates a kindness [through bequest]. That was in the Book inscribed. (Qur'an, 33:6)

Kinship, now generalized into larger groups and their differentiating features, also constitutes a context for spiritual epiphany (already quoted in another context): And of His signs is the creation of the heavens and the earth and the diversity of your languages and your colors. Indeed, in that are signs for those of knowledge (Qur'an, 30:22). The idea to which this may lead is that permutations on a single theme, that is, variability in terms of communicative faculty or differences in color within the same human form, indicate oneness of principles behind plurality, and ultimately oneness as such.

This third, contemplative, function of kinship is represented throughout creation, also outside the human kingdom:

> Do you not see that Allah sends down rain from the sky, and We produce thereby fruits of varying colors? And in the mountains are tracts, white and red of varying shades and [some] extremely black. (Qur'an, 35:27)

It may be argued that this does not entail valuing human lineage in term of tribal or national belonging, for family is a necessary feature of reproduction and would endure the dissolution of any national or tribal group. It could be argued that combining these precisely restores the Adamic state, in which all three were present, although arguments in the opposite direction might be put forward as well, for if that initial unity was split three-ways, and given that Islam lacks a doctrine of original sin to which such a division might be attributed, it may be a necessary part of creation, just as humanity did not continue to consist of two people (Adam and Eve) but became numerous. Paradise does not consist of only these two original humans, so, similarly, differentiation, as much as proliferation, could be a part of the design for the species. In any case Islamic tradition is ambivalent on this point.

Given that human difference is mentioned along with gender difference as presenting a means for knowing one another (Qur'an, 49:13), one may consider the verse as alluding to sexual union and an intended melting away of difference through intermarriage, or a contrary persistence of difference in the way that gender necessarily remain distinguishable in every generation, following which line of speculation, different "peoples and tribes" would also express archetypal elements in the same way as gender reflects fundamental categories (the Mercy and Majesty of God, in Islamic terms). Yet the fact that a certain condition (difference in humanity's "tongues" and "colors") procures knowledge of a spiritual principle may not entail that this principle is not supposed to pass away, just as ignorance or rebelliousness are mentioned as coming about as a result of God's will, and His punishment of them may constitute a sign of His Majesty, yet are not to be purposefully promoted by human beings, but quite the opposite. The two cases would seem to be different, however, as creation's diversity is not mentioned as being treated punitively. Still, since traditionally Islam considers Arabic the universal language of prayer and religious study, homogenization of some sort seems implied.

The issue is clarified by the apparent preference in early Islam for kinship over locality. Belonging to a city, village, or more generally, country, provides a means of identification, for a person can: 1) Be associated to a geographic provenance or residence as easily as to a family lineage; 2) Have his or her service to others ordered by way of a ranking of priority in terms of doing good works to neighbors who happen to live near one as easily as to one's blood relatives (and sometimes more so), and; 3) The diversity of humanity is contemplatable in terms of its leading to different political communities, and not just kinship-derived ones. On this latter point, the Qur'anic emphasis on kinship may be understandable in terms of its mentioning "color," that is, heritable difference in appearance, so that the contemplation in question is potentiated by physical differences, as well as cultural ones or "tongues." The issue, then, is partly one of heritability: the fact that human beings come about from other human beings and are not equidistant to each other in their causal entry into the world.

If the, at times frankly crass, ethnocentrism of scripture (in many traditions) has meaning beyond a) the elevation of one set of cultural contingencies over all others, which from a metaphysical perspective can only be relative, and b) a counter-intuitive rejection of scriptural narrative by its own offshoots (a sort of Marcionism in the Christian context, for example, where New Testament universalism is used to deny Old Testament specificity), then a middle way is true. This middle way consists in interpreting the narrowness of scripture and its transcending vision as a universalization of particularities.

The singularity of a tradition allows it to properly reflect the singularity of its subject, just as a language can express reason if it is grammatically coherent but not if it takes on pieces of another grammar haphazardly, but 1) loan words can be useful, and 2) the multiplicity and mutual recognizing of different languages is needed in order to understand that the human capacity for reason and for communication is itself beyond the specifics of any language. One perceives the numinous in one's mother's cooking and childhood home, but even if one uses expressions like "you're the best mom ever," these are not intended as a statement of *objective* superiority, if such a thing is even possible, because objectivity is not the point. Our mother is our own, and in the order of things we cannot ever alter who we were born from. Therefore, the universal paradigm of motherhood is necessarily best mediated to us by that one person.

A mirror reflects the sun a single time, indicating correctly that there is but one sun in the sky, and if that mirror is placed into a patchwork with others it might seem there are many suns, yet counter-wise, we have need of many mirrors in order to understand that these are only reflecting, and that their unity is *analogous but not identical* to the actual sun, an understanding made possible if it is known that each mirror is distinct and that its reflection is thus not of another sun but of the same sun as the one reflected by its peers (if the mirrors were not known to be separate, one would conclude a large mirror was reflecting numerous suns). This should also lead us to assert the rights of some new mirror combining features of older ones. If two mirrors reflect the sun from different angles and do so best at different times of the day, we should celebrate the emergence of a new mirror occupying some intermediate angle and therefore literally adding a new perspective. In the field of cultural and political articulation, the human being should be free to pursue its experiments and intuitions.

When combinations of cultural forms emerge, these should constitute themselves as delineable entities. Combinations that become their own category avoid confounding their originators. This principle was already touched on in the introduction, but bears repeating. It is a mistake for a cultural melting pot to be celebrated as superseding or somehow revealing the deficiency of the elements it draws from. Rather, the melting pot should congeal into a new identity with its own integrity and not simply the space in between. If the mirror in between two other mirrors, revealing an intermediate angle, fuses these two precedents together, it creates a seamless continuum which will reflect the sun but once (or, if their angles are preserved, distortedly, elongating at the seams) and fail to express the truth that reflections can be multiple while the reflected object is singular, that contingent forms are ever plural and yet ever manifesting the Absolute. Three mirrors joined at their edges produce a triangular reflection of the sun, four joined in this way produce a square luminosity, and so on, so that the image of the sun is lost. Creation must have borders; the branches can weave in continuum but the trunks are discontinuous.

Just as the basic differentiation of unity into duality manifests the archetypes of masculine and feminine, so we may view the emergence of other differentiations as revelatory of other archetypes. In this way, various traditions have tended to associate themselves and others with numbered elemental or archetypal categories. We should remember the doctrine of macrocosmicality or simultaneous presence of archetypes in a type, so that the identification of a profession or civilization with a single element or cardinal direction is not absolute and makes sense relationally, in terms of its interaction with others.

Indeed, all these traditional classificatory schemes have the virtue of necessarily emphasizing relationship. A thing knows itself as expressive of an archetype in relation to others: a man on his own is less man than in relation to woman. On their own, things are closer to formless potential than in community. In this context, the identification of a cultural and civilizational project with the axis mundi, the spiritual center, the king-archetype, is not itself a mistake. It is a technology by way of which that civilization is made legitimate in just the same way as considering a work of art beautiful—which is to say, recognizing such a thing as beauty and wanting that work to unite with some pre-existent standard of beauty—is the correct way to go about creating art. The mistake is in viewing physical reality as having one exclusive and discrete center, not in considering one's place central. Civilizations should make themselves religious, mythic realities. The opposite approach of radically secularizing and relativizing one's projects leaves them limp, lifeless and, paradoxically, fanatically willing to render the rest of the world likewise limp and lifeless, as recent historical examples of anti-religious movements have shown.

The correct approach is a middle way between radical relativization and secularization that recognizes no spiritual center at all, on the one hand, and an exclusivism that reifies spiritual centrality into an actual, contingent center, on the other. Neither nihilism nor solipsism are the way. We should not consider examples from the past as always being of the latter exclusivist type. There is evidence for their consciously uniting to the archetypal center while understanding it as an archetype which is also available to other polities, as during the Bronze Age's club of great powers.

A particular cultural context can come to be viewed as being as much peripheral to the center of the manifold as others, or else, the attenuation of metaphysical hubris can come by way of considering one's locality the fifth point, center of the four, but embracing the perspectival nature of this judgement, such that every locus is the center from its own vantage. We can consider humanity *as such*, but also *in specific*.

Numbers signify archetypal categories manifesting at the human level in a divinely ordained architecture. The Bible tends to divide the species into three (by way of Noah's three sons and maybe by the earlier three sons of Adam and Eve) rather than four. Here, Israel is the ecumenical whole, though initially situated within the threefold (Jacob—Israel—descends from Shem, one of the three). Christianity and Islam inherit this typology. The former is clear from the histories of saints like Jerome and Isidore of Seville, and the former appears in hadith literature. In Church history, the three Petrine churches of which Pope St. Gregory the Diaologist says "in three places is the See of one"—namely, Alexandria in Africa, Antioch in Asia and Rome in Europe—reflect this scheme, and could be interpreted as corresponding to Ham, Shem and Japhet respectively.

The three colors mentioned in the Qur'an (35:27) as proceeding after the rain from the earth appear also in a hadith,[72] but applied to humans:

> The Prophet—peace and blessings be upon him—said: "Indeed, Allah, the Exalted and Sublime, created Adam from a portion that He took from each part of the earth. For this reason, the Children of Adam appear just as the earth: among them are the red, the white, the black, and hues in between, as well as the soft, the sad, the vile, and the good."

This presents humanity as a threefold, and as linked to elements of the natural world in a manner similar to Frithjof Schuon's considerations regarding the three gunas of Indian thought manifesting as, among other things, branches of humanity. The four temperaments listed at the end can be understood as referring to the phlegmatic, choleric, sanguine and melancholic, in European medieval terms, a common understanding in medieval and antique thought, and in Indian terms would be related to the castes.

If the number four is assumed to refer to archetypal categories such as the elements or cardinal directions, then the ancient Egyptians seem to have relativized themselves into one of these four, rather than centralizing themselves between them. They divided the world roughly between themselves, Near-Easterners, Sub-Saharans and Europeans and Westerners[73] (Northwest Africans and Europeans apparently counted

---

72   Provided by Ibn Kathir, narrated by al-Tirmidhi.
73   Jan Assman, *From Akhenaten to Moses: Ancient Egypt and Religious Change* (Cairo: The American University in Cairo Press, 2014).

as a single category).[74] This humility is attenuated, however, by the fact that they did consider themselves to have received the generic name "Men" in the *Book of Gates*, which details the creation and origin of the four branches of humanity.[75] Interestingly, the modern West seems to have partly inherited Egyptian categories.

In any case the quaternary seems quite important in Egyptian thought. It appears unlikely that the four categories of humanity were considered unrelated to the four corners of the earth and *Duat*, or the four sons of Horus, represented in the four canopic jars containing basic elements of bodily subsistence during mummification, stores of vital organic functions in anticipation of the resurrected subject. The recurrence of the number four in religiously significant contexts is difficult to ignore. Thus, Egyptian mythology may be subtly indicating that Egyptians are only one of the four parts of the human whole as they knew it, yet, from their own perspective, each is the whole and may call itself humanity.

This is, of course, speculative, but the speculation might be bolstered by the fact that human diversity is treated with positive regard in some Egyptian sources, such as the Atum hymn (*Papyrus Cairo* 58038) where diversity originates from Divine will and, in being equally subject to God, consists of equal jurisdictions:

> Atum, creator of humankind,
>> Who distinguishes their characteristics and creates their means
> of subsistence,
>> Who distinguishes their skin color one form another.

(This should not be confused with later similar statements in Amarna hymns. Jan Assman suggests that the Atum hymn has its roots in 1600 BC, and that Akhenaten's 1350 BC suppression of the gods—despite some similar declarations in his own hymns—must be viewed as a *revolutionary* rather than *evolutionary* development with respect to this more ancient ethos.[76])

The fourfold is also important to Incan tradition, where the name of the Incan state, the *Tawantinsuyu*, literally means four regions[77]. The Tawantinsuyu had its capital in Cuzco, divided between the northern Hanansaya and southern Hurinsaya, with the former consisting of the northwestern Chicasuyu and northeastern Antisuyu, and the latter of the southwestern Cuntisuyu and southeastern Collasuyu. Here the gendered two-fold is further divided to make a fourfold.

Sometimes the fourfold appears in relation to the recurring theme of four great ages, as in Hesiod. Greek sources, however, also attribute

---

74   Alfred Cort Haddon, *History of Anthropology* (London: Franklin Classics, 2018), 6.
75   E. A. Wallis Budge, *The Gods of the Egyptians: Or, Studies in Egyptian Mythology*, vol. 1 (New York City: Dover Publications, 1969), 304.
76   Papyrus 58038, cited by Aleida Assman and Sebastian Conrad, *Memory in a Global Age: Discourse, Practices and Trajectories* (New York: Palgrave MacMillan, 2010), 124.
77   Gordon F. McEwan, *The Incas: New Perspectives* (Santa Barbara, CA: ABC Clio), 44.

national characteristics to climate and local deities, which can therefore occur during the same age. Here, the fourfold is not so much a wheel of contemporaries as it is in ancient Egypt, but a series of ages succeeding themselves, giving rise to progressively more perverse iterations of humanity, as in Hindu historiography. The fourfold is describing different realities.

Chinese tradition conceived of a fivefold: four elemental categories corresponding to barbarians at the four corners of the earth, and one central station, the ether or quintessence, corresponding to the middle kingdom of China. The Romantic poet Coleridge, basing himself on the German anthropologist J. F. Blumenbach, also subscribed to a pentagonal schema, placing Caucasians, rather than the Chinese, at its center or pinnacle, although Coleridge ultimately preferred a Biblical threefold, which he considered to reflect a profounder division.[78] This should illustrate the fundamentally relative, perspectival nature of centrality in such models, whereby the conceptual cartographer mapping the human species tends to consider whatever he identifies as to be the center. This sort of chauvinism misapplies a metaphysical principle. If the European error, borne of identifying one's place with the center, is expansionism, the same identification led China to an opposite direction.

The number five appears in Indian tradition. The first Manu is said to have had two sons (Priyavrata and Uttānapāda) and three daughters (Ākūti, Devahūti and Prasuti), that is, five children, where the binary and the threefold are also present.[79, 80] The number five also refers to the five peoples, *pancha jahna*. A hymn mentioning these five appears in both the *Rig-Veda* and *Atharva-Veda*. The language employed arguably suggests the five peoples comprehend all mankind: after a reference to living creatures, "both quadruped and biped," the *Atharva-Veda* reads "…these five human races, for whom, though mortals, Surya as he rises spreads with his rays the light that is immortal."[81] If the five were to be universalized they may be interpreted in terms of Chinese tradition, the four elements and the center, and in Indian terms of the four castes and outsider forest-dwellers (the latter amenable to the preceding four, and not necessarily equivalent to an untouchable class).[82]

The number seven, like the number five, occurs in various traditions. Indian tradition speaks of seven continents or kingdoms, linked, perhaps to the seven sages who rode the arc with the seventh Manu, from whom

78   Peter Kitson, *Romantic Literature, Race, and Colonial Encounter* (New York City: Palgrave Macmillan, 2007), 43.

79   ed. Gaṅgā Rām Garg, *Encyclopaedia of the Hindu World*, vol. 1 (New Delhi, India: Concept of Publishing Company, 1992), 14.

80   Geeta Kasturi, *Srimad Bhagavatam* (Orpington, UK: Pepper Global. 2013), 48.

81   Maurice Winternitz, *A History of Indian Literature*, vol. 1 (Delhi, India: Motilal Banarsidass Publishing, Atharveda, 1927), 147.

82   Jayantanuja Bandyopadhyaya, *Class and Religion in Ancient India* (London: Anthem Press, 2007), 39.

the present humanity descends, in India's equivalent to the universal flood myth. This is alike the 70 Biblical nations divided according to the number of "Sons of El" (according to one reading of Deuteronomy 32:8), or the slightly more than 70 nations listed in Genesis (10) as descending from Noah's three sons, similar to the 70 sons of Athirat and El in Ugaritic religion. There are also the seven orders of angels spoken of in Enoch. Here, just as each entity may consider itself the fifth, quintessence, between the fourfold, each may consider itself white light prior to the six colors of the rainbow, so long as the courtesy of being a center and microcosm is extended to others.

Iranian tradition uses the number seven to organize space, counting the central axis. These it calls the seven *keshvars*:

> There is the central keshvar, called Xvaniratha…the extent of which in itself alone is equal to that of all the six other keshvars, which are arranged around it and separated one from another by the cosmic ocean that surrounds them. There is one eastern keshvar, one western keshvar, two to the north, two to the south.

Thus, this is congruent with the four cardinal directions,

> The keshvar on the eastern side is called Savahi; the one on the western side, Arezahi; the two keshvars to the south are Fradad-hafshu and Vidadhafshu; the two to the north are Vourubareshti and Vourjareshti. The mythical ocean surrounding and dividing them is called Vourukasha. As to their situation, this is deduced astronomically in relation to the keshvar which is the center, whose presence, therefore, has the quality of situating space, before itself being situated in that space. In other words, it is not a matter of a pre-existing, homogeneous, and quantitative space in which regions are distributed but the typical structure of a qualitative space. The eastern keshvar, Savahi, extends from the point where the sun rises on the longest day to the point where it rises on the shortest day. The two southern keshvars extend from this last point to the point where the sun sets on the shortest day. From there to the point where the sun sets on the longest day extends the western climate, Arezahi. Finally, the two northern keshvars extend from this last point to where the sun rises on. Mazdean Imago Terrae the longest day. The names of the six keshvars that surround the central climate of Xvaniratha actually correspond to mythical regions.[83]

These mythical regions were made to correspond with specific peoples known to the Iranians, with Iran in the middle, surrounded by the six: Arabia and Abyssinia, Syria and Egypt, Slavs and Byzantium/Rome, Turkestan, China and Tibet, and Hindustan/India. In the phrases we have emphasized above, Corbin makes the point that this is a transferable way

---

83   Corbin, *Spiritual Body and Celestial Earth: From Mazdean Iran to Shi'ite Iran*, 18–20.

of structuring space, and so the center can shift. If the earth is always sevenfold, it is so inclusive of the central observer.

We find something similar in Eusebius's 4th century *Church History*, but using the twelvefold, dividing the world by the twelve apostles. This also occurs in Paul of Alexandria's late 4th-century *Eisogogue*. Mitchell and Rohne compare the latter to the Biblical Acts (also to Zodiacal signs). The Eisogogue gives us the twelve as Persia, Babylon, Cappadocia, Armenia, Asia, Hellas and Ionia, Libya and Cyrene, Italy, Cilicia and Crete, Syria, Egypt, Red Sea and India. Acts provides Parthians/Medes/Elamites, Mesopotamia, Cappadocia, Pontus, Asia, Phrygia and Pamphylia, Libya and Cyrene, Rome, Crete, Judea, Egypt, Arabia.[84]

That which constitutes a sacred order or division is also that which must be defeated, like the gods to be integrated into the initiate: thus the four winds afflict Aeneas but are also four Edenic rivers; thus Hercules faces twelve trials and "Odysseus has had to face twelve major obstacles which are spiritual tests and phases of his inner transformation"[85] yet they are also the twelve disciples of Christ, the twelve knights of the Round Table, and the twelve parts of humanity in Eusebius and Paul of Alexandria.

We can address case studies in redemption, that is, in *re-deeming what it means to be the center* in terms of that absent center. If we focus our attention on the ubiquitous fourfold model, we may engage in a thought experiment where there are four ways in which civilizations came to terms with the ecumene not corresponding to themselves. A historical experience of entering the ecumenic worldview could be imagined as one of the four corners of the earth, the four modes of the Tantric Sanskrit formula which we previously explored: ahamidam-idamaham: *I am that* and *that is I.*

These four would be the *passive object, passive subject, active object* and *active subject.* By subject we mean *consciousness* and by object *sentience* (respectively the inner experiencer and its experience or capacity to experience, which *must necessarily also occur within subjectivity*). The subject/ consciousness emphasizes its own containment of identity with the universal (China as almost trans-historic center of the earth; modern Europe spurred on by its own ideal past of Roman *Imperium*) and the object/sentience emphasizes experience of the external (Israel as brought along a historical path and the early Islamic polity as responding to the imperial and religious missions around it). *Passivity* refers to a reception of identity with the universal Ecumene with no need for experiential or literal realization of that universality (Israel and China) and *activity* to the realization of identity with the universal Ecumene in an imperial project (Caliphal and European expansions). Each of the four can be treated as an experience unto *unio mystica.*

---

84   Mitchell and Rohne *Twelve-Tribe Nations.*
85   Uzdavinys, *Philosophy as a Rite of Rebirth: From Ancient Egypt to Neoplatonism,* 279.

It is not yet clear what path post-colonial indigenous identities will take, however, we may observe the following: their culture has not been universalized forcing a distinction between what is universalizable and what is their own, as with Israelite scripture (although this may be occurring in some areas); they do not take on the mantle of European colonial empires as their own, as European projects did with Rome; they are not poised to export their own universal project and compete with universalizing projects as the Islamic Caliphate with regards to the empires of Byzantium or Persia; they are a formerly compact *cosmological* ecumene of their own, which were colonized and are now reconnecting with their cultural particularity but wishing to take on elements of west-ern modernity and benefit from them by participating in the world and molding it to fit them (at least this is the Indianist-Katarist program of American, particularly Aymara-Quechua and related, native peoples). Their current trajectory is therefore closest to the Chinese path. Indeed, this latter may be most relevant for most peoples.

Each of the four moments can also be understood as an interaction between Being and self-awareness, *Sat* and *Chit*: Being can be the object which is simply given and which the subject, self-awareness, must relate to, but can also be understood as pure consciousness, of which *Chit* is self-awareness understood as an object, that is, a mind or structured thought patterns and mental contents which the underlying consciousness interacts with. Each mode of interaction between *Sat* and *Chit* must here be recali-brated in order to include *Ananda*, joy understood as harmony, that is, the true order, which is ecumenic in the most positive sense. Thus, each chap-ter exploring a historical trajectory in relation to the Ecumene will attempt to resolve the conceptions of each civilization into that higher ecumenism.

The following chapters concern the Ecumene in relation to the Bib-lical concept of election, first, and of the medieval European concept of Empire, second. These will illustrate principles that are important for our conclusion and, therefore, are in the body of the text below. The rest we include as addenda: the Ecumene in the Chinese, Islamic, modern European, post-Columbine indigenous American, and modern technology-driven globalized trajectories.

THE CORPUS COSMICUM AND THE ECUMENE, OR ECUMENIC INTERNATIONAL RELATIONS

A corporate cosmos implies the political doctrine of *organicism*, staying the hand of the polis. A king who undergoes the above rite of self-sacrifice and identifies with the universe may, within a certain order, narrow his cosmic identity to a more circumspect perimeter, realizing himself as the personification of his kingdom (assuming Heaven condescends its mandate). Gavin Flood provides the following description of what we may describe as *incarnationist monarchism*:

Through consecration the king becomes the analogue of the tantric Brahman. As the divinization of the body is described in the texts, so the king's body is divinized in consecration, and as the body of the practitioner becomes an index of a tradition-specific subjectivity, so the king's becomes an index of the wider social body. In a way not dissimilar to medieval Europe, the king's body points to the health of the society as a whole.[86]

Body and community are spiritualized by way of the same operation. Imagined anatomies are like imagined communities, but the imagination must be baptized and this implies community, tradition. The imagined chakras Gavin Flood discusses, which are real yet become sensate to us through visualization, and whose visualized formula depend on a living tradition, so the kingdom, or the *nation*, in Greek and Biblical terms, those likewise imaged communities, to use Benedict Anderson's popular term, may be real, but they require human imagination in tandem, that is, in tradition, in continuity. In pursuing the above reference to medieval Europe, it is appropriate to cite John Milbank:

> ...collective personalities...were created fictions—yet they were deemed to be real personalities and could be "represented" by symbolic personages—beginning with the Pope himself. This does not, however, mean representation in the modern sense of "necessary substitution," but rather a representation like that of the cognitive *species*, which is based upon a participatory identity: the king's mystical body *is* the sovereign realm; the abbot *is* the monastery, the Pope *is* the Church in person, and so forth.[87]

Once again, Chinese Taoism provides a parallel study. This tradition sometimes presents the functions of political reign over a kingdom as punctually equivalent to those of maintaining a healthy body. Heshang Gong's first century commentary of the *Tao te Ching* has it that:

> If in governing the body one cherishes one's breath, the body will be complete. If in governing the country one cherishes the people, the country will be peaceful. Governing the body means to inhale and exhale Essence and Breath (*jing* and *qi*) without letting one's ears hear them. Governing the country means to distribute virtue (*de*) and bestow grace (*hui*) without letting the lower ones know it.[88]

The monarchical dismemberment or crucifixion accesses of the paradigm beyond the king's empirical body or ego that encodes and contains *in potentia* that and every other corporeal whole, the realization of cosmic identity and the functional adjustment of this spiritual epiphany to operate within the ambit of a particular political realm to be thereby

---

86   Flood, *The Tantric Body: The Secret Tradition of Hindu Religion*, 81.
87   Milbank, *Beyond Secular Order*, 214.
88   Pregadio, *The Encyclopedia of Taoism*, 75.

experienced as the king's extended body (indeed, or of the abbey as body of abbot, guild as body of guild master, and so forth in conformity to the rich variety of medieval society). This provides the underlying metaphysic and theurgy of what Douglas Hedley remarks in the context of my interview:

> It is intriguing how Charles I in *Eikon Basilike* or Louis XVI or even the Romanovs were presented in this quasi-sacrificial, messianic form, that somehow the renewal of people was linked to the death and of course the resurrection of, or renewal of, some messianic figure. The king is dead long live the king...sacrifice as literally the making sacred...why is it important for us that the state should have a sacred foundation, why should we associate the state in any way whatsoever with a sense of the sacred? Well, quite apart from discussions about secularization I think this has to do with our basic need for security and, more deeply, our needs for belonging, and I would say our needs for a home. So the state is part of that, or the nation. But it is so only as part of the greater whole. So think of Eliot in *Little Gidding*, with his emphasis on this spot. Which is England but is more than England. I think that sense of encountering the sacred with the particular, through a place that is contingently precious but is thereby the means to recognition of our belonging to a sacred cosmos that transcends the particularity of the tribe or the nation. And there is a lovely saying of Meister Eckhart that if we have one prayer it should be that of gratitude. And that sense of gratitude for the sacred order of things, I think, lying behind all of this.[89]

This constitutes a defense of human communal identity or polity as sacred project—a church within the Church, an ecclesial jurisdiction. Frithjof Schuon describes this in the context of Japan:

> ...before the founding of the Empire, the population of the Japanese islands was undergoing a process of "chaotic elaboration"; Jimmu Tenno united the tribes and, by "divine mandate," made of the human materia—providentially assembled within the same country—a mirror of humanity and of the Universe: he was in a direct sense son of the solar goddess because, being born of the Spirit, he was without origin and without end.[90]

This passage is consistent with the status of the king as son of a solar goddess across traditions, and with the traditional Christian associations of the eternal Feminine with the Spirit, with the Apocalyptic Woman Clothed in the Sun, as well as with the second (spiritual) birth of the Christian disciple. It also reinforces the point that spiritual initiation can accompany a political role.

---

89   Douglas Hedley, "Interview with Carlos Perona," 7th March 2018.
90   Frithjof Schuon, *Treasures of Buddhism* (New Delhi: Smriti Books, 2003), 187.

That the monarch *is* the kingdom does not mean he ought to be the only person—the only body—in the realm, exiling or executing everybody else. Nor does it imply that he ought to be the only monarch in the world. That the concept *monarchy* is singular does not require that there be only one physically existent monarch, forever and everywhere. A given coordinate of contingency—a particular biographical configuration—need not replace all others in order to do justice to the unity of its capital source—God, the Absolute. This would be absurd. Eric Voegelin describes the corresponding healthy civilizational disposition:

> A society in cosmological form is experienced by its members as an analogically ordered part of the divinely ordered cosmos. The symbolization of its order as an analogue of cosmic order has nothing to do with the size of its population or territory; nor does it carry an obligation to subjugate foreign populations or to expand the territory; and the coexistence of a plurality of such analogues is not experienced as an unbearable contradiction to the oneness of the cosmos. In this sense, therefore, societies in cosmological form are completely self-contained.[91]

According to Voegelin it is this sensibility that leads Plato to "acknowledge the plurality of parallel civilizations in the field of history,"[92] Aeschylus to mourn for his foe, not seeing the extinction of Persia as a glory to Hellas, and Homer to see Greek conflict with Troy as a disturbance.[93]

A human body is not rendered super-galactically obese by identifying with the cosmos. This would be a farcical denial of analogy implying the effacement of lower planes in the wake of realizing higher ones. Yet such farce is at play when unity of principle is taken to demand uniformity of practice, leading to attempts at social pasteurization in which may be intuited an antique heretical dualism. Bodies need not undo their constituents in order to act as a unit. In fact, transgressing the structures of differentiated organs would result in a dysfunctional body. Just so, successful theurgy results in souls possessing a "...noetic perfection, never departing from their pure condition" while simultaneously, "like individual souls, they each possess a single and moving body."[94]

Whereas a principle is irreducible to its multitude declinations, it nonetheless simultaneously exists as an objectified structure which functions as the organic emergent of those subordinates and cannot, therefore, violate them without exiting the realm of actuality. For this reason, violent seekers who rip the dress of *Lady Philosophia*[95] (as Boethius calls her) are tearing at the possibility of their own realization. Unity,

91   Voegelin, *Order and History, vol. 4, The Ecumenic Age,* 202–3.
92   Ibid., 287.
93   Ibid., 157.
94   Shaw, *Theurgy and the Soul,* 67.
95   Boethius, *Consolatio Philosophiae,* I.1; 8.

then, translates into created harmony, not uniformity. The plurality of somatic, psychic and noetic characters appears not as accidental conflict-incitement but as the filigreed buoyancy of providential creativity. This is the lesson of the *theorganics* outlined above.

The consequent social ethic, according to which human community is viewed as a body (an account of which is provided in Plato's *Republic*[96]) must be one of excellence rather than excess, wherein each partial association and vocational pursuit abstains from costing another, as tissues abstain from cancerously transgressing upon each other. Neither should a larger structure do violence to smaller ones except in case of pathology. Attending to the inspired crux of this ethic, it is foremost a call to positive action in that ardor which guards against the siren of imitative and unfocused desire bidding neglect of one's own calling for the sake of quarrelling with neighbors, against which Plato warns.[97] As René Girard observes: "in intense conflict, far from becoming sharper, differences melt away."[98]

Applied to issues of governance, then, (and remaining wedded to the corporeal metaphor) these become more a question of good posture (a straight spine keeping the body in proper alignment) than of cerebral (and necessarily futile) attempts at administering (micro-managing) the affairs of every organ. Communal health is understood as depending on symbolic rather than coercive authority (the latter implying a lack of sensitivity to the former and the former a lack of necessity for the latter). In practical terms, the above corresponds to a thorough application of the principal of subsidiarity (or Johannes Althusius's spheres) as the prioritized vehicle for articulating collective identities.

As explored in the introduction, this can be expressed in terms of language, which is inherent to the human condition, without any one language being inherent itself. According to this (Pentecostal) approach, transcendent things are on a different axis from that along which human culture (*as* culture) differentiates. This is not to argue that one culture cannot be more conducive to genuine human flourishing than another, but that it is also possible for two cultures to be different and equal, for example in the sense in which two words for *chair* can be just as good as one another. Allowing for this difference prevents us from reifying the particulars of one mode of expression or of *being cultural* and equating it with truth or with the human condition as such. Were we unaware of the existence of significantly different grammatical structures (were we to forget that language is a category whose concrete

---

96   Plato, *The Republic*, V.462c–d; 141.
97   Ibid., II.373d; 50.
98   Haven, L. Cynthia, "*Christianity Will Be Victorious, But Only in Defeat*": *An Interview with René Girard*. http://www.firstthings.com/onthesquare/2009/07/christianity-will-be-victorious-but-only-in-defeat. Accessed on: 24/5/15.

instantiations can vary widely, that such variation is even possible), we would lose some knowledge of the diversity and therefore the essence (that which is consistent throughout such diversity) of the linguistic or communicative function *in and of itself.* Such is the core of a defense of difference.

Contact with the eternal feminine, explored in the preceding section, is precisely presented by the traditions as allowing one to perceive diversity holistically and, therefore, to dispel opposition between the parts and the whole, the differentiated and the united. The theme of femininity as articulator and personification of difference, and specifically human difference (with its political implications) can be located in Biblical scripture. From the book of Wisdom:

> And being but one, she can do all things: and remaining in herself the same, she reneweth all things, and through nations conveyeth herself into holy souls, she maketh the friends of God and prophets. (Wisdom 7:27)

This passage emphasizes both the oneness of God's wisdom and its self-conveying through a plurality of forms, including diverse nations. It associates her unitary agency with the plurality of human communities. Indeed, the seventy sons of El (the high God, as distinct from YHWH, the Lord), by whose number and under whose agency the nations are divided according to the Bible (in Deuteronomy 32:8, if this is read following Margaret Barker and others to the effect that the expression "sons of Israel" originally read as "sons of El") are also described as sons of the Lady dressed in the sun in John's Apocalypse.

Thus, the theological current observant of God's Wisdom, Sophia, "…is driven by a desire to celebrate the diversity of reality precisely in its union with God and to do this it uses paradox."[99] This is the corporeal imperative discussed above: a body is one in principle and plural in its internal structures. Corresponding to the Wisdom love of diversity is the Logos and Its keeping things distinct. Writes Margaret Barker: "One of the roles of the Logos was to keep the elements of creation apart and distinct"[100] and, quoting Philo of Alexandria (*On Cultivation*, 10): "The Divine Logos stations himself to keep these elements apart." Since the king is made king by the Divine Feminine, and is united to the Logos (as in Psalm 110) he manifests the Sophianic celebration of diversity through the fundamental political and patriarchal imperative of borders, realms, appropriate limits (not as painful imposition but as simple love of measure, the sort that leads a painter to retire his brush or abstain from making a form more lavish, larger, and harming its sober beauty—what the Japanese call *Shibui*, a subtle, simple beauty).

---

99   Brandon Gallaher, "The Christological Focus of Vladimir Solov'ev's Sophiology." *Modern Theology*, 25(4) (2009): 630. Cited by Martin, *The Submerged Reality*, 155.
100   Barker, *Who Was Melchizedek and Who was His God?*, 8.

Interestingly, Nano Marinatos sees the radiant feminine principle in the form of the Bronze Age symbol of the sun goddess as also linked to life's diversity: "A solar goddess would explain why Minoan wall paintings abound in motifs of lush vegetation, birds, monkeys and ungulates. They celebrate nature as the sun's gift to men."[101] The relationship of sun to diversity, which also has to do with light revealing forms, joins unity to multiplicity, for the sun is simple but feeds the diverse world, and light is formless but allows us to see many forms. The fact that the traditions we encounter are solar (from the Apollonian Pythagoras and Plato and the solar associations of Enoch to Egyptian mythology) and also view the eternal feminine as agent of spiritual epiphany makes sense in terms of this link.

The same insight whereby the integrity of different structures is seen to merit respect leads also to viewing these as united in a common body. Blake odes this vision in his *Jerusalem*: "Let the Human Organs be kept in their perfect Integrity... Everyone knows, we are One Family! One Man blessed forever."[102, 103]

Writes the Central Asian 13th-century Sufi Aziz Ibn Muhammad al-Nasafi (the emphasis on there being only one Perfect Man we understand in terms of everything being ever encompassed by a single pattern or harmony and manifesting a single underlying principle, and that this harmony is, in some sense, human and personal):

> This Perfect Man is always in this world and there is only one perfect man. This is because all creatures are like one person and the perfect man is the heart of that person and creatures cannot exist without a heart.[104]

---

101   Marinatos, *Minoan Kingship and the Solar Goddess: A Near Eastern Koine*, 65.
102   Blake, *Blake: The Complete Poems, Jerusalem, Emanation of Giant Albion*, 36, 781.
103   Neville Goddard describes a visionary experience under the tutelage of William Blake: "...from afar—it is one man.... As you approach it, it becomes unnumbered races and nations of people...a glorious, radiant man. His heart was all like living rubies...and there were unnumbered, innumerable beings making up the heart, and the whole body was made up of races and nations.... When I came close enough I recognized myself. I was he, containing within myself the whole of humanity." This vision contains the idea of ontological layers of reality wherein are different beings (disclosed as a function of the viewer's distance, the resolution of the vision). We may think of the medieval idea that a horse is less real than a human, in that it actually exists at a different level of reality, it is a less conscious creature. And yet *it is actually an extension of our being, a limb of humanity seen from a certain vantage, for it is not merely a less conscious creature but ultimately a part or potential of a larger fully conscious one*. Indeed, Blake discusses this idea of animals actually being parts of the human person in *To the Jews*. Goddard's vision also contains the idea of one's finding oneself to contain that total vision, a fractal set wherein the macrocosm recurs in the particular microcosm of the visionary, and *the visionary finds oneself in and as the whole*. Finally, the above description, in referring to nations, reminds us both of the Bible's use of the term in Revelation and Black Elk's vision of hoops.
104   Uzdavinys, *Philosophy as a Rite of Rebirth: From Ancient Egypt to Neoplatonism*, 213.

We are again reminded of Swedenborg' remarks on all things being one body. All humanity is one human person, whence the myth of the macranthropos, is all human diversity, the Human Organs, and whence also the logic of the representative body of the king to which is indexed the kingdom according to the rites of sacred monarchy. St. Thomas writes "we can consider all men one man," *unus homo*.[105] And the divine feminine Jerusalem encompasses human diversity in its bodily, human unity:

> And thirty-two the nations, to dwell in Jerusalem's Gates.
> O Come ye Nations, Come ye People, Come up to Jerusalem.
> Return, Jerusalem, and dwell together as of old: Return,
> Return... let Jerusalem overspread all Nations
> As in times of old...
>
> *(Jerusalem, Chapter 3, 72, 32–36)*

It is the insight according to which the part is also a whole unto itself (thus to be respected in its integrity) and the whole a part (thus to be preserved in connection with fellow parts beyond itself). As Plotinus puts it in another context, "...each part is a whole and the whole remains an undiminished whole—but matter divides it—and all the parts are one."[106]

This would imply that imperialistic expansionism follows from the same misperception as sedition and nationalist excess, or collectivism from the same root as social and political atomization. Both proceed from forgetting the identity of part with whole (such that a part can be a whole and a whole can contain parts). If some ancient conceptions presented Greece as distinct from Persia, or Europe as distinct from Asia, they followed a logic (an aesthetic) that requires these two be in turn viewed as provinces within a common ecumene. Historically, when this view ceases from prominence, political centralization and fragmentation ensue (the whole asserts its being so by usurping the ambit of its parts; the part articulates its being also a whole by attempting to retire from larger units). Voegelin expresses this in a formula that can apply equally to the movement to expand as to fragmentize: "imperial entrepreneurs..." attempting "to make the jurisdiction of their respective empires coincide with the pragmatic ecumene...."[107] In either case, something very much akin to Girard's mimetic crisis seems to be occurring.

Common, broad identities may or may not receive political articulation, and are, in any case, primarily within the ambit of art, cult, and a sort of political mythology. It is also the case that states may be constituted so as to include peoples of widely divergent groups (this is how the imperial prerogative has often been interpreted during what,

---

105   Insofar as they derive their nature from Adam (*Summa Theologica*, I-II, question 81, a.1.)

106   Plotinus, *Ennead*, trans. Arthur H. Armstrong (Boston, MA: Harvard University Press, Loeb Classical Library, 1984), IV.9:5, 439.

107   Voegelin, *Order and History Volume IV, The Ecumenic Age*, 273.

in its negative aspect, Voegelin describes as history's concupiscential moments). The peril of nationalism is to ignore the transcendent unity represented in the imperial idea, and even local, regional unities. The error of imperialism, correspondingly, is to literalize that ideal, for even when homogenizing policies are not pursued, it brings uniformity about in the wake of global political ambition all the same and (a more profound error) to exclusively identify the archetypal character or center of humanity with a particular people or dynasty.

Thus, no discrete political corollary or single representative *demos* for the total, global ecumene need be constructed (although *ad hoc* treatise and governance institutions can appear naturally in different contexts, operating in transnational and transcontinental ambits as needed). As Michael Martin comments with regard to the vision of Novalis:

> What Novalis upholds here is a notion often interpreted as "cosmopolitanism," but perhaps a better description is "communitarian," as his vision begins at an interpersonal level of common and human flourishing and his idea is explicitly set into a Christian framework. If he is interested in cosmopolitanism, it is in a very restricted sense.[108]

Since this passage identifies the principle in question as Christian, it is worth noting that, for Martin as for Novalis: "Catholicism is universal, but it is not a homogenized singularity, uniform in all aspects: 'In my Father's house there are many mansions.'"[109]

Particular cultural unities can be understood as sinews or coherences in the muscles of the ecumene. As Novalis puts it, "[t]he world must be romanticized. Then one will again find the original sense."[110] With T. S. Eliot in his *Four Quartets*, the historical, cultural, civilizational (indeed, the political) axis can simply be taken up and, precisely thereby, relaxed and de-emphasized: a "sick society must think much about politics, as a sick man must think much of his digestion," as C. S. Lewis[111] puts it. Correspondingly, and in the case of the matter under consideration, once diverse forms are acknowledged in such a way as to preclude their mere existence from appearing as a bellicose instigation (once unity is understood as harmony and not as uniformity) the specifics of one or another of those forms need not be turned into a compulsively announced battle cry by dissenters (assuming their sincerity) against homogenizing pressures, for there is no longer any battle in which to cry.

---

108 Martin, *The Submerged Reality*, 117.
109 Ibid., 116.
110 Novalis, Fragments from the Notebooks. In: ed. Beiser, C. Frederick, *The Early Political Writings of the German Romantics* (Cambridge: Cambridge University Press, 1996), 85. Cited by Martin, *The Submerged Reality*, 119.
111 Clive Staples Lewis, *The Weight of Glory and Other Addresses* (New York City: Harper Collins, 2001), 163.

The rise of more nominalist (as opposed to realist) approaches to metaphysics and systems uninterested in attaining direct apprehension of the metaphysical, the divine condescension (the autozoon which reveals the identity of whole with part and vice-versa) would tend to correspond either with the abandonment of the concept of a coherent *whole* or with its parody in homogenizing centralism.

Historic examples of the above could include the use of God's promise to Japheth in Genesis (9:27) to justify European colonial dominance[112] and the emphasis on the primacy of Arab patrilineal descent (Arabic: *fadl*, *sabiqa*) in the Umayyad caliphate[113] (though the two are not equal in their normativity within these systems[114]). These seem to mirror each other in several ways: 1) opting for unity through a kind of centralism (the preponderance of one group over others) presumably with the ultimate corollary of global homogeneity (on the basis of that group's cultural hegemony); 2) accompanying literalistic or rationalistic theologies[115] and, finally; 3) arising simultaneously with (in the European case) or giving rise to (in the Islamic, Near Eastern, case), bids for political or cultural disconnection as their dialectical negative.

The third of these terms bears some brief specification. In the case of European colonialism, it tended to occur in tandem with the emergence of modern, unitary sovereignty, pursuing itself detachedly from Europe. In terms of Islamic expansion, the question of Arab primacy, including the tying of conversion by non-Arabs with clientage to an Arab patron[116] and the marital suitability or parity (*kafaa'ah*, كفاءة) of a non-Arab woman as spouse for an Arab man despite the unsuitability of the inverse, privileging Arab patrilineal lineage (*nasb*)—which, generally speaking, is the traditionally established consensus in the majority of Sunni jurisprudential schools or *madhhabs*, excepting the *Maliki* school—contributed to the *Shu'ubiyyah* movement.[117] This is discussed in Addendum V.

---

112   Robert Breckenridge, "Hints on Colonization and Abolition." The American Colonization Society, *The African Repository and Colonial Journal*, IX.11 (1834): 321. And for a Catholic example, see Bishop Newton's dissertation, cited in Pius O. Adiele, *The Popes, the Catholic Church and the Transatlantic Enslavement of Black Africans 1418–1839* (Hildesheim: Olms, 2017), 176.

113   Nimrod Hurvitz, *The Formation of Hanbalism: Piety into Power* (New York City: Routledge, 2002), 33.

114   The latter is a more mainstream and long-established opinion in Islam than the former was in Christianity.

115   In the European case, the first thousand years of Christendom did not feature colonialist escapades, indeed, even the Crusades were often reactive. In the case of the Islamic Near East, the clearest emphasis on Arab primacy is perhaps to be found in the Hanbali school, which is also most known for literalism or anthropomorphism (this in spite of its founder Ahmad Ibn Hanbal's high regard for the Sufi Ma'ruf al-Karkhi).

116   Montgomery Watt, *Islam and the Integration of Society* (London: Routledge/The International Library of Sociology and Social Reconstruction, 1961), 151.

117   Ibid., 152.

Membership as Mediation, not Imitation

According to the above, political membership is just that: being a member, a limb of a body (understanding human community as corporeal). This necessarily implies sheaths of mediation: organisms consist of parts assembled into subordinate structures, just as cells form tissues in turn configuring organs, and so forth. Therefore, mediation is always *re*ligious (*re*-linking; connective), for it orients the member of a part towards the whole (an apt description of the movement of *transcendence*). We have the mediating role of orders of organic life (nesting various cells into common tissues, tissues into common organs) as opposed to the imitative drive that effaces diversity of function.

This is expressed by Otto Gierke when condensing the Medieval conception in which "[u]nity was neither absolute nor exclusive." Instead:

> The Total Body is a manifold and graduated system of Partial Bodies.... Between the highest Universality... and the absolute Unity of the individual... we find a series of intermediating units, in each of which lesser and lower units are comprised and combined.[118]

Analogously, the relationship of one's soul to the One (in Platonic terms) is not independent from the mediating agency of gods (or saints and angelic intelligences) as it is in more iconoclastic religiosities. The soul depends on this mediation as a part of the cosmic architecture (although, ultimately, the One is omnipresent, directly sustaining the being of all particular beings: if various grades mediate the divine creativity to our *becoming*, the divine is nonetheless ever immediate to our *being*).

Neither is the relationship between an individual and the state exempt, as in much liberal thought, from the mediation of family, guild, club, and every manner of partial association. Just so, it follows from this vision of organic concentricity that a nation is a branch on some tree, and not one of indefinite rhizomes, not an organ without a body. Just as individuals come in types (rooted, for example, in particular families and professions), so too collective identities are legitimately grouped and comprehended together in wider ones on an ascendant scale. Membership implies mediation.

If the nation, however construed (in practice often in terms of linguistic idiosyncrasy) is afforded exclusive legitimacy to articulate itself through government (and if this is a matter of principle, not just practicality), the resulting dialectic will correspond to that which exists between atomizing individualism and the total state of collectivism[119] (*atomized* meaning an isolated atom, one that does not form a molecule, in turn a cell, in turn an organ, and onwards). To be an atom in this sense, what Jung describes as "a particle in the mass," is to be subject

---

118   Gierke, *Political Theories of the Middle Ages*, 20–21.
119   Nikolai Berdyaev, *The Meaning of History* (London: Transaction Publishers, 2009), 170.

to physical determinism, slavish adherence to whatever concentrates the most mass. On the contrary, it is organization into organic bodies, with their differentiated and hierarchically arrayed sub-structures, that allows for the emergence of complex life capable of volition, of agency:

> The less we understand of what our [forebears] sought, the less we understand ourselves, and thus we help with all our might to rob the individual of his roots and his guiding instincts, so that he becomes a participle in the mass, ruled only by what Nietzsche called the spirit of gravity.[120]

If nation-statism does not argue only from feasibility and convenience in governance (for example, maintaining that a nation-state ought to concentrate functions because it is most practical to deliver certain services to its denizens), but, going further, denies that a nation belongs in wider mediating identities (seeking an ultimate justification for political disunion) then the fulfillment of its project would leave nothing in between itself and an (inorganic) international community. The fact that bids for (thorough and not merely decentralizing) political separation are paired with denials of common identity and are (it may be intuited) motivated by the desire to appropriate the perceived privilege of the nation-state, is consonant with René Girard's analysis.

As Edmund Burke sustains, "[m]en are not tied to one another by papers and seals. They are led to associate by resemblances, by conformities, by sympathies. It is with nations as with individuals"[121] (although elsewhere, Burke expresses a contrasting account, at least in terms of emphasis, more in line with liberal social-contract theory[122]). The analogy between nations and individuals renders mere social-contractualism inappropriate for both, for such a doctrine tends to treat them as functions of self-interested artifice, psychological constructs—and even then, only of a very particular psychic mode—and not as (respectively higher and deeper) spiritual or corporeal constructs (or *growths*), endowed, for example, of the same organic caprice and ornament as a garden. The rejection of the "ideas and usages, religious, legal, moral or social, of this civilized world" by what he terms the "Jacobin Republick"[123] manifests both in the undoing of "…the spirit of European Monarchy…" (which consists for Burke not so much in the endurance of monarchical institutions as of "…classes, orders and distinctions…")[124] and in the "violent breach of

---

120   Carl Jung, *Memories, Dreams, Reflections* (New York City: Random House, 1989), 236.

121   Edmund Burke, *Thoughts on the Prospect of Regicide Peace in a Series of Letters* (London: Printed for J. Owen, no. 168, Piccadilly, 1796), 47.

122   Peter Stanlis, *Edmund Burke: The Enlightenment and Revolution* (London: Transaction Publishers, 1993), 237.

123   Burke, *Thoughts on the Prospect of Regicide Peace in a Series of Letters*, 50.

124   Ibid., 49.

the community of Europe."[125] Rejection of differentiation undoes both the diversity internal to a society and the bonds of the community of nations that this society belongs to. These bonds between nations occur according to the previously mentioned mediating structures.

It is also the case, however, that specific persons may be closer or farther from one another depending on the feature under consideration or, in a more general sense, on their vocation. While some will find it their disposition to contribute to the articulation of some *national* character, others will primarily and instinctively identify with a profession or craft, feeling themselves kin to faraway people by virtue of a common calling which to them represents the overriding project of their lives, the function to which they are most suited (feeling themselves linked with fellow reciters of the Hippocratic Oath, for example, but not much with the co-national). Indeed, even those whose mission it is to be involved in folkloric life and to animate local distinctiveness will find a special connection with each other *across* nationalities, one that they do not share with members of their own community who are not similarly captivated by *amor patriae*.

Apart from differences in vocation between those who are oriented towards the articulation of national identities and those that are not, individuals may prioritize participation in the political structures of different overlapping identities within a territory, from the municipal up to the trans-national, and also in ones that are not nested and may even seem to contradict. The *Euroregions* and other examples of arrangements overlapping national borders illustrate this.

To deny this differential (whether it is articulated in governing institutions or not, which, again, can depend on pragmatic considerations) is to militate against organic order and in favor of a sort of atomization of nations (again, seeing the atom and the group thereof, but not the molecule). In facing the more negative, homogenizing potentials of globalization, the nation-state has need of its context, otherwise it risks becoming less a safeguard against, than a dutiful denizen of, that homogenization. This appeal to context can be described as *associationism*, in line with the *English School* of international relations:

> Associationist approaches would assume that the international system is not so much a society of sovereign states but, rather (as in the early work of the English School, especially the writings of Martin Wright, Herbert Butterfield and Donald Mackinnon), a society of nations and peoples who are bound together by social ties and cultural bonds that are more primary than State guaranteed rights and market contracts.[126]

By mediated membership, then, what is meant is that a *body politic* is structured according to nested (and in some cases overlapping) identities

---

125   Ibid., 51.
126   Milbank and Pabst, *The Politics of Virtue*, 334.

and, indeed, tiers of administrative competency. Each echelon contains multiple subordinates and is contained along with a multitude of peers within a superior grade. *Mimesis*, in contrast, is of necessity destabilizing to this arrangement. Wherever one tier is desirous of another's station, or the constituents of a common grade are desirous of the function of their fellows, imitative aspiration will result in the failure to specialize, per René Girard, and in defining a member of the same body as enemy:

> Negative reciprocity, although it brings people into opposition with each other, tends to make their conduct uniform and is responsible for the predominance of the *same*. Thus, paradoxically, it is both conflictual and solipsistic.[127]

A note of caution against too rigid an understanding of the above is warranted. Should a member of a city within a country find that this city has been razed to the ground while he was away on business, this would not sever him from the country, would not invalidate his passport. It is not as physically irrevocable as a fruit's separation from the trunk of a tree when the twig or branch it stems from is snapped off. In this sense, then, specific local identities, while worthy of respect, need not be the condition *sine qua non* of the wider identities in which they nest. The point, however, is that the seed proceeds from a root, trunk, branch, twig, fruit and contains a design for equivalent roots, trunks, branches, twigs, fruits, not for a simple, undifferentiated, amoebic mass.

Reaching for another metaphor, it is not a gardener's responsibility to preserve every water body that forms along his garden's topography after it rains. Instead, he may let these seep into the soil or evaporate into the air per their natural course. However, it is his responsibility (the lot of high politics) to aid in the fruition of that garden's flora (civilizational output, art, inquiry) by ensuring a safe water supply (the culture and values of a society, whose defined character should not, however, prevent its ever-flowing, like the water cycle).

Maturing in Multiplicity, not Amalgamation

Maturation does not consist in converging at a certain end-point of advancement, just as a man does not cease from his family after arriving at a certain age or receiving a certain degree of education. He may share camaraderie with those who are likewise aged and educated, but his children, wife and siblings remain his own. Similarly, a person's head may have more in common with other people's heads than with that same person's liver, but it would be absurd to conclude from this that the concept of *body* is a malicious social construct.

According to Otto Gierke, in the *Tractatus de Regia Potestate et Papali* John of Paris suggests that God-given natural instinct justifies people living

---

127   René Girard, *The Scapegoat*, trans. Y. Freccero (Baltimore, MD: The Johns Hopkins University Press, 1989), 13–14.

in different states.[128] He seems to make a distinction between unity of principle and multiplicity of practice similar to the above. St. Augustine also favored a humanity arranged in an array of different states.[129] These are examples of "the principle of the Universal State" being "assailed while as yet the principle of the Universal Church was not in jeopardy..." so that some theologians held to

> the doctrine that the Oneness of all Mankind need not find expression in a one and only State, but that on the contrary a Plurality of States best corresponds to the nature of man and of temporal power.[130]

Voegelin renders Plato's view (from the *Laws*) as follows:

> ...the course of history must be understood as an advance of civilization in time through inventions and arts, improvement of transportation and discoveries, population increase and density of settlement to the point when culturally homogeneous peoples in contiguous settlement appear as distinguishable units in history.[131]

The historical emergence of these distinguishable units can be linked to their invention of the role of emperor. The Imperial title comes about when a sense of historical achievement is reached, as in the case of Augustus, articulating the Roman project through his reforms and following from Julius's momentous expansion of its borders, as though it were now in some wise matured, or Qin Shi Huang, first regent of a unified China, who dispensed with the title of king and created that of emperor, *Huangdi*, hearkening to the mythic Yellow Emperor, as though the expansive telos of this latter figure (to whom Sima Qian attributes patronage over different East Asian peoples) had been to some significant degree attained. In fact, the Chinese character *Huang* can be translated as *August*. The Yellow Emperor is also linked to the monarchical symbol of storm or thunder, Jove or Odin in his capacity as storm deity, being said to have been conceived in his mother by a lightning bolt from the Big Dipper.

To reiterate and develop the argument of the present study: Unity manifests in harmonious relations because 1) harmony is unifying (and therefore expressive of unity); 2) a relation, by definition, involves multiple entities, so that no one entity appears as exhausting unity as an isolate; 3) a relation that is harmonious, by definition, involves entities that are different from each other, so that the commonality of entities does not appear as exhausting unity in their uniformity. Therefore, unity manifests

---

128   John of Paris, *Tractatus de Regia Potestate et Papali*, III, referenced in Gierke, *Political Theories of the Middle Ages*, 128.
129   St. Augustine, *De Civitate Dei*, IV:15, referenced in Gierke, *Political Theories of the Middle Ages*, 128.
130   Gierke, *Political Theories of the Middle Ages*, 20.
131   Voegelin, *Order and History Volume IV, The Ecumenic Age*, 285.

as functionally integrated differentiation. The most primal example of this is femininity and masculinity (distinct entities that are harmonious with each other and whose harmony is expressive of unity). This dyad is archetypal, it comprehends a way of relating between differentiated unities that can take many forms but fundamentally manifests unity.

William Desmond writes about "the presence of unselfconscious community in natural things," an instance of "metaxological affinity" for, according to what we have already seen regarding the autozoon, it is coherence, harmony, and therefore involves permutations on the same themes, connectedness, so that things fit together in terms of affinity as well as complementarity:

> Time does not just give rise to an indefinite number of, say, cats and dogs, indifferently; rather, this indefinite number is differentiated into a definite plurality of different kinds...those bound together through their issue from a common origin. Such an interconnectedness of natural kinds might be seen as one disclosure of the metaxological affinity of being, the presence of unselfconscious community in natural things.... Becoming perpetuates the same kinds of particulars in an as yet undetermined sequence of generations.[132]

A thought-experiment: repeating the conditions that produced dogs from wolves may be said to produce genuine Great Danes, with all their attendant propensity for hunting, albeit these would descend from an entirely different group of wolves as existing Great Dane populations (a difference which their genetics would bear out). We may also speculate as to what constitutes a canine to begin with, and whether the *archetype* of canine does not overlap with the marsupial category and *Dasyuromorphia* order to produce the *Thylacinus cynocephalus* (marsupial wolf, also sometimes called marsupial tiger), as it does with the *Carnivora* order to produce the Grey Wolf. I am writing in a consciously unscientific key, although this can be discussed in terms of convergent evolution and adaptation to similar environmental pressures. Consider the idea that the eye (a roughly spherical photon-detector) seems to have several times evolved independently on the earth. Differentiation entails the manifestation of patterns and forms through multiple origins. The point is that the archetypes of things repeat and are therefore ever "safe" within the source of manifestation, the *actual infinite*, as Desmond calls it.

As civilizations take shape and relate to each other, they must express unity by seeking harmonious relations as a fundamental element of the telos of human communal and political projects (see point 1 above). None are legitimately identified as exclusive representatives of unity as such, that

---

132   Desmond, *Desire, Dialectic, and Otherness: An Essay on Origins*, 164.

is, of the total, singular human family as such (see point 2 above). They must conceive of these harmonious relations as occurring through, and being assertive of, the differences between them (see point 3 above). In terms of Voegelin's description of the historical emergence of civilizations, we may understand their doing so according to archetypes—of the archetype behind European or Chinese culture, for example.

Often the different character of civilizations will come through in their relations and be confirmed by the other. When 18th-century Chinese texts described Europeans as displaying a defective nature, for, "[i]n Chinese eyes... [European] complexion was not merely white, it was 'ash-white' *(huibai)*, the exteriorization of the demonological forces that drove the foreign devils to undertake expansion overseas,"[133] reacting against imperialism, whereas European accounts attacked Chinese isolation and technological or social stagnation, these two critiques are not incompatible. They in a sense set up the same dichotomy, one sensitive to the dangers of imperialism, the other to those of stagnation.

Something similar occurs when we compare certain critiques against Europeans provided in Volume Two of al-Tabari's *Histories,* which present these as antinomian by nature, not following a set sharia, with other Muslim polemics emphasizing the consequent lack of known prophets among Europeans (though Islamic doctrine maintains prophets came to all nations). This agrees, in a sense, with the medieval European idea that, as indicated by the etymologies of both *Japheth* and *Europa,* Europeans are expansive, where a corresponding antinomianism (that which is expansive is less obviously fixed by specific strictures) is linked to the non-legalistic aspect of the Gospel (St. Paul's reference to gentiles having an advantage in faith may feed into this). Again, the Muslim critique and the European self-image do not really disagree here.

Of course, during a phase of decline, a culture may become identified with its present torpidity and enter into mimetic subservience to that culture which is on the ascendant. Therefore, the above search for defining characters—essences only discernable in relation—should be engaged carefully and with a long historical view that avoids self-servingly (or masochistically, as the case might be) identifying a culture with the worst or best phase of its history, with those features that are actually universal to periods of decline or prosperity.

Voegelin warns that "cultural differences" among "variants of civilizational evolution" interfere with excessively generalized narratives.[134] One cannot attend to the universals or the commonly emerging features of civilization ("inventions and arts, improvement of transportation and discoveries") and ignore the differences (the *distinguishableness* of those

---

133   Frank Dikotter, *The Discourse of Race in Modern China* (Hong Kong: Hong Kong University Press, 1992), 14.

134   Voegelin, *Order and History Volume IV, The Ecumenic Age,* 286.

"distinguishable units in history"). Technological advance/refinement represents one axis, whereas the culture of a civilization represents another. Voegelin goes on to discuss how, for Plato, proper order can only exist if a certain unit is, in fact, truly a unit:

> a noetically satisfactory order is possible only if the unit in question is indeed culturally an ethnos and not a jumble of former peoples held together by a conquering power as in the Persian case; the population of a multi-civilizational, ecumenic empire is not an ethnos that could organize itself as a federation of paradigmatic poleis (693a).[135]

Such coherence is consequence of organic emergence (given Voegelin's emphasis on advancement in the course of history) but, like anything human, this cannot be conceived as detached from agency. It is neither wilderness nor brick house, but garden. The emergence of distinguishable units is both a function of internal unification and of distinction from other people. Yet distinguishing a people from others also makes that people alike to others, in a sort of benign version of what Girard criticizes as the homogenizing effect of rivalry: In order to make a certain unit commensurate to, and able to protect itself from, other unites, it must adopt features of the other (we see elements of Persian or Byzantine organization in how historical Islam changed how Arab tribes organized; Tenskwatawa adopted elements of European discourse for Native Americans, etc.). To be fruitful is to give forth from within; to continue to be fruitful requires pruning from without, not left wild and wonton with knotted twigs (this is analogous to the lamb and the king in the *Gospel of Philip*, the creature and creator). A YouTube video on the School of Life channel does a great job at summarizing this principle in terms of city planning and architecture:

> The ideal we're seeking is variety and order. This is the idea of a square in Telc in the Czech Republic where every house is the same width and height, but within that pattern, every house has been allowed freedom at the level of form and color, or in Java-Eiland in Amsterdam... that's what more and more cities should have: order and variety. So, as a general rule: too much mess and it's off-putting, but too much simple order and it's boring. What we crave is organized complexity.[136]

The same occurs in the micro, where functions are uniform in some regards across administrations on the same level (so that municipalities or regional governments do not have too widely divergent rights and responsibilities). The differences should come through in their

---

135 Ibid., 285.
136 School of Life, "How to Make an Attractive City," www.youtube.com, retrieved 26th January 2015.

specialization, not in their access to resources. Relative uniformity in the latter allows for the solutions which work in one city, for example, to be easily adopted by others. There is that in which similarity causes mimetic rivalry, and there is that in which similarity allows fair-play and easy collaboration. Thus, while associative and federalist arrangements should be respectful of the local, the excessive proliferation of ad hoc idiosyncratic privileges and special statutes will, following the above principles, result not in "variety and order," but variety and disorder.

Ex Unum et In Unum, Pluribus

Maturing into multiplicity, internal differentiation, means that under his auspices, the king oversees much political and cultural flourishing. It is alike in the Holy Roman Empire, whose "Empire's principal kingdoms were not clearly delineated before the eleventh century" because "[p]olitics involved networks and chains of obligations and responsibilities, not uniform control of clearly bounded territories." But this eventually gave way to

> clearer spatial divisions...[h]owever, this process was neither one of progressive fragmentation into ever-smaller territories, nor the steady evolution of existing subdivisions towards sovereign statehood. Rather, the components changed their size and character throughout the Empire's existence. Some territories indeed fragmented, or became more distinct...[others] were subsumed later within neighbouring territories. Moreover, this process was not an expression of declining central power. Rather, spatial demarcation co-evolved with how the Empire was government.... In short, integration proceeded through demarcating more jurisdictions, rather than trying to bind those already established under tighter central supervision."[137]

With regard to differences emerging within overarching unity, we may think of Denis de Rougemont's remark that "Europe is much older than the nations."[138] Around 1490, the Holy Roman Empire's organization changed such that "[t]he superior jurisdictions associated with the status of imperial Estate now emerged as distinct territories.... This process...has been labelled 'territorialization'...." But, crucially,

> [i]t simultaneously embedded the territories more deeply within the Empire, because each owed its rights and status through recognition from the other territories. In short, status was mutually agreed rather than self-determined, and thus tied to continued membership of the Empire rather than offering the basis for sovereign independence.[139]

---

137 Peter Wilson, *Heart of Europe: A History of the Holy Roman Empire*, 183.
138 Denis de Rougemont, *The Idea of Europe* (New York City: The Macmillan Company, 1966), xi.
139 Peter Wilson, *Heart of Europe: A History of the Holy Roman Empire*, 216.

The relation of part to whole is maintained. But a part may become tumoric. A delegation of semi-nomadic tribal chiefs now arrives at the king's court. They have come a few days' journey from their usual dwellings on the steppes of his realm's western fringe, spurred on by a courtly edict. It seems certain observances proper to the kingdom are going unmarked, and children on that periphery are not learning the language they have in common with its other provinces. Further, time is spent in early youth on pursuits that altogether eclipse the official curriculum with its seven liberal arts, leaving its people at a disadvantage, and more likely to be the life-long wards of local rulers, given their lack of capacity to communicate with their countryman, much less participate in their civilization project. The offending edict seeks to make clear what the tribal chief's obligations are, and to end their dereliction of duties. *However*, they protest, *we are not aware of ourselves as your subjects. Perhaps in bygone times our fathers thought themselves such. But we live differently from how you live and our customs have altered greatly. We have fellowship with those wealthy peoples farthest away on your west more than we have occasion to meet you.* In the word *wealthy* is heard something of the motive animating the assembled group, but there is more to it.

A more radical claim is made, not by the chief orator of the delegation but by an upstart of prestigious birth, who voices what is perhaps the background or the moral reasoning produced to serve as support for his party's present protestation. *And why should any tribe be part of any kingdom, or indeed any man be counted as brother by one man more than another. Only by accident of birth? Are we not all two-armed, two-legged, two-eyed, one-hearted creatures? Do we not all speak and fear death? And I have met a man in the neighboring west alike your lieutenant, and your advisor of fiscal affairs grimaces like a friend of mine from that country. Why should they speak different tongues and live under different allegiances?*

The king responds, *It is true that your commerce is with foreigners, and that you have shared their festivals, and that all notes and all colors are on a spectrum, and resemblances of every sort run through the matrix of the earth, but the branches in a forest seen from above may weave together in seamless texture, whereas from below they are revealed to grow from discontinuous trunks. The question we must answer is whether you, however woven in with our neighbors, are a branch of mine, or of a foreign king. As for our differences and likenesses, the function of a drooping petal is not the same in orchid as in tulip. In one it frames the central portentous bloom, like a falling ember from a firework display, like a playful memento mori, but in the other it appears in protagonist simplicity, lazy, lusty, fresh and wanton as a late morning. A face, taken in its blunt and external features, can be made use of by different characters, iterated to different effects, animated by different habits, becoming wrinkled in old age according to entirely contrasting patterns. A body and its face remain the visible portion of the soul, but for this very reason can only be understood by approaching that soul, by meeting and knowing the person. The very optics of a face change once its bearer is understood. And not only a man's face, but the personality and wishes behind, which he may share with many others, can differ in the uses made of them. The peoples of different kingdoms vary in aspect and affect, appearance and attitude, physique and festivals. Some overlap like the branches on a tree weaving with those of its neighboring, but they nonetheless proceed from different trunks and have different roots.*

The young man of the separatist delegation cuts in by another route, *As individuals we are defined by our choices, and in this regard, we share more with one of a similar will to our own than we might with our own brother. Is a doctor not kin to every doctor in a way that he is not with a neighbor of his who is a carpenter?*

Our king continues, *Do you deny my hand's belonging in my body, because it resembles your own? Surely one hand is more alike another hand than it is similar to the heart or liver of that body it shares blood with, but none demand that all hands be severed for that reason.*

His interlocutor attempts yet another angle of attach, *I see foreigners here in your court. I see ambassadors, experts of various sorts whose skill you have needed. Are they any different from those native to the land your court lays claim upon? And if an ambassador of yours lives for many years in another court, is he not more foreign to you than a man who came from abroad but has been here those same years?*

The king picks this up by means of his previous metaphor, *The fact of organic connection does not deny inorganic participation. My hand is mine because it is connected to my wrist, but when I grow old, my claim to this hand does not invalidate my use of a walking stick, not connected to my hand by nerve or bone, or of a pair of spectacles, artifices which the natural body appropriates. Such is the case for mercenaries, travelling merchants and visiting scholars in cities they are not native to. But now, we turn to you, and to the question of what manner of thing you are, whether a hand to shake in friendship, or to pump my own blood through.*

The king calls his advisors and sibyl and puts the matter to deliberation, though he feels, even now, that these protestors are, in fact, comprehended within the extent of his kingly body, that human region that focuses his life's work, his microcosm of cosmic identity, activated through ritual death and rebirth.

What follows, then, is very similar to what Herodotus recounts in the *Histories* (II:18), when the oracle of Ammon was consulted to settle a similar dispute:[140]

> The men of the cities of Marea and Apis, in the part of Egypt bordering on Libya, believing themselves to be Libyans and not Egyptians, and disliking the injunction of the religious law that forbade them to eat cow's meat, sent to Ammon saying that they had no part of, or lot with, Egypt: for they lived (they said) outside the Delta and did not consent to the ways of its people, and they wished to be allowed to eat all foods. But the god forbade them: all the land, he said, watered by the Nile in its course was Egypt, and all who lived lower down than the city Elephantine

---

140   Donald Lateiner, *The Historical Method of Herodotus* (Toronto: University of Toronto Press, 1989), 129–30.

and drank the river's water were Egyptians. Such was the oracle given to them.[141]

But, begins the king, *tell me of these customs that have grown up among you, by reason of which you claimed a separation from my body.* And so, they relate the form of these, sometimes imitated from foreign peoples near to them, others a recitation and dance or dish originating in some recent artist or in the artistry of accumulated generations. *I see in these growths no weeds, but flowers. There is in your new custom no violence against the human spirit, no necessary strain on your environment.* The king orders they be featured in the yearly processions at the capital, therefore, and gives them his patronage, making loyalists of one-time seditionists.

But he remains pensive. The cause of separatism at the fringes of his domain requires attention. It is because the neighboring kingdoms and their customs are viewed as more prestigious that their own that these delegates wished to recast themselves in a foreign identity. Not all subjects will seek political independence, for not all can plausibly propose it, residing in more central provinces of the kingdom. Yet they may easily adopt the practices of those higher-status foreign kingdoms, enriching them and impoverishing themselves by buying far-off clothes and spices, eventually losing the unique offering they were to give to the world, practicing foreign rites and forgetting the local cult. The king recalls a sage and Confucian advice:

> If the people of far-off lands do not submit, then the ruler must attract them by enhancing the prestige [*tê*] of his culture [*wen*]; and when they have been duly attracted, he contents them. (Confucius, *Analects*, 16:1[142])

Whatever force (*li*) he might exert in the pursual of conflict (*wu*), the king knows it would be but a short-term and probably counter-productive staving off of *cultural* annexation and *moral* defeat. Culture must be won over on culture's terms. Belligerence might help in displaying military prowess and therefore inspiring admiration, but protracted militarily exertion is neither morally nor materially sustainable. Indeed, even a non-protracted escapade would fall short of moral standards, given that no provocation has been issued. To be sure, these delegates from the periphery have likely come to the court only after being seduced by foreigners, having received some assurances in a semi-official capacity, however vain. An attempt to destabilize his kingdom has been made, though tepidly. But it is better to respond with finesse. What is attractive in these neighboring kingdoms are their advancements in various fields, and the romances

---

141   Herodotus, *Histories,* trans. Alfred Denis Godley (Cambridge. Harvard University Press, 1920).

142   Arthur Waley, *The Analects of Confucius* (London: Allen and Unwin, 1956), 203. Quoted by Voegelin, *Order and History, vol. 4, The Ecumenic Age,* 362.

composed about their mythical figures. The latest ink-dying and wool-weaving looms must be adapted to the kingdom's colors and designs, they must be made so they can be bought and fitted at home and packed off to the plazas where crafts-persons and traders are accustomed to working and showing off, leaving social and economic manners formally unchanged, and the king's court must patronize literary excellence and recitation. These poets the people will recompense, for they are lovers of narrative and will remember their love of their old stories, renewed. Foreign technology will be translated into the kingdom, re-minted in its own style.

Theo-Geopolitics: Misery Loves Uniformity, Joy Loves Unity

In Organizational Behavior and Management generally, the term *referent other* is used to designate a subject at the workplace that employees use to index the value ascribed to them and the progress of their career-path. An employee will often seek out someone who is more or less comparable to themselves according to variables he or she considers salient, and determine whether the treatment they receive from the company and the degree to which their career advances is fair by the standards of that company as a function of how well they perform compared to how the company acts with respect to that comparable referent other.

I would suggest that often the referent other becomes a mimetic rival in René Girard's sense. The referent other becomes a rivalrous other. Further, companies sometimes promote a silo culture in order to channel rivalrous impulses away from the company itself and the management. This functions as follows:

- When a company pretends to link benefits, economic or otherwise, to concrete performance indices, it must explain away mismatches, even when these occur for reasons of simple resource scarcity.
- If the management of a given department within a company cannot allocate benefits as a function of performance it will promote the idea to subordinates that other departments receive excessive resources, producing scarcity elsewhere and are therefore responsible for this mismatch of performance to benefit.
- The promotion of this idea results in 1) employees or departments collectively considering other departments their referent other, 2) referent others being perceived as rivals, 3) grievances being channeled away from managers of a department by employees in that department, 4) hostility, lack of porosity and general rivalry between departments (which we may describe as a silo culture), 5) all the benefits and liabilities usually associated with internally competitive corporate atmospheres.

The company does not cease to be a unit, but it polarizes its organs against each other, insulating management. This is precisely what the Italian theoreticians of elites such as Mosca, Michels and Pareto, or Hannah Arendt in her study on totalitarianism, discuss as the precondition for radical concentrations of power: social atomization. Misery loves uniformity. If an elite of twenty persons cannot control twenty thousand, it can control a single individual twenty thousand times. So long as individuals do not draw on the cultural and psychological resources afforded by a larger unit, their heuristics can be affected by means that would usually be described as propaganda.

Similarly, nationalism, in the pejorative sense, does not break with international unity so much as it allows for a kind of unity based on atomized, rivalrous silos, that is, a centralized unity where sub-units are more easily controlled as opposed to a de-centralized unity where sub-units genuinely determine the form of unity (federal arrangements where ad hoc agreements can be reached in the manner championed by Pabst and Milbank in *The Politics of Virtue*).

Before Plato, Herodotus recorded a similar ethic to this latter among several peoples. Just as Achilles ends up displaying prowess during funerary games in honor of the dead and the gods rather than in pursuit of self-glorification, there is a sense in the ancients of trying to establish contest over conquest. Apart from the trespasses of king Xerxes, Herodotus writes that Persians considered themselves rightfully endowed of mastery over one sphere, Asia, and not, therefore, over Greece and Europe.[143] Consonantly, the Greek Themistocles (despite partially ulterior motives), argues against pursuing Persians into their land after defeating them and warding off invasion, for to do so would be a violation, a repetition of the very wrong which had just been made right.[144]

Unfortunately, Themistocles' plea was not always observed. Though his contemporary Persian counterpart, Khosrow II, may have had nefarious designs on Byzantium, even apart from being mad (indeed, a popular revolt deposed Khosrow, not the Byzantines), Emperor Heraclius might nonetheless have done well to spare the place of Zoroaster's birth in Azerbaijan and its nearby fire-temple. Even in Christian terms, was this not the tradition from which the three Magi learnt of Christ's coming? Was this not the religion by whose sciences they observed and knew to follow a star unto Bethlehem? Perhaps.[145] It is a shame that a campaign to retake the true cross destroyed the holy sites of those who witnessed to the birth of the one exalted on that cross. But that came much later in the annals of history.

For their part, Herodotus's *Histories* can be read as drawing "systematic attention to proper realms," to which end he quotes an Egyptian oracle,[146] revealing such attention to legitimate difference and divisions entails a religious dimension, and contrasting this with the impiety of

---

143   Herodotus, *Histories*, IX.116.
144   Ibid., VIII.109, 490–91.
145   The magi were either Persians or Arabs, perhaps from Yemen.
146   Donald Lateiner, *The Historical Method of Herodotus* (Toronto, Ontario: University of Toronto Press, 1989), 129–30.

"Xerxes' disdain" for any limit placed upon his empire.[147] In his *Persians*, Aeschylus seems to express the same distaste for homogenization and coercion through the dream of Atossa, Xerxes' mother. In this dream, Xerxes harnesses two quarreling women, one dressed in Persian raiment and the other in Greek. He affixes them to a single chariot, but one of them rebels and as the contraption loses balance the king falls.[148]

Aeschylus and Herodotus's Themistocles both reject turning their foe's defeat into effacement by conquest. In the poem cited above, Aeschylus at times elicits sympathy for the enemy. This is in line with Isaiah's extension of epithets the Bible ascribes to Israel to other peoples as well, and specifically to enemy polities: "In that day the Egyptians will become weaklings. They will shudder with fear at the uplifted hand that the Lord Almighty raises against them" (Isaiah 19:16) and yet "The Lord Almighty will bless them, saying 'Blessed be Egypt my people, Assyria my handiwork, and Israel my inheritance'" (Isaiah 19:25). One reading of these sources is that conflict is necessary for avoiding amalgamation into foreign projects, but illegitimate in attempting to repeat the same breach, and should instead be followed by reconciliatory embrace of difference and common elevation within that difference.

Following history's contest between Achaean and Assyrian, Greek and Persian, Roman and Carthaginian, and medieval Christian and Muslim, traditional (Platonic, but also pre-Socratic) continental nomenclature as detailed by Herodotus and Genesis congeals into civilizational reality in a case of words preceding the world or, more realistically, a case of both adhering to geography.

Voegelin seems to view civilizations as non-Newtonian fluids or anti-fragile[149] systems. They are stronger when struck. Nietzsche's injunction to love one's enemy, in terms of his own philosophy, is not out of place here. The divided initiate who finds a grander vantage for himself does not literally take over other forms, but he sees them in himself, his very empirical body is a microcosm that includes them, like the beads on a web that reflect all others and bare their image, in turn reflected by each of them. Europe can be said to discover Islam in itself by taking Qur'anic criticisms of popular, vulgar trinitarianism seriously, and the Islamic world can find European Christendom in itself by taking seriously the critique of popular Islam as *Mohammedan*, where an idolatry of the man and of Arab custom may have become part of its theological mainstream. We already mentioned how trinitarianism leads to tawhid (and there is an Islamic equivalent to the Indian *Sat-Chit-Ananda* in Ibn 'Arabi's *wujud*, *wijdan* and *wajd*). Europe may have acted as a sword against Islam's idolatry

---

147   Ibid., 128.
148   Aeschylus, *The Persians*, trans. Walter George Headlam (London: George Bell and Sons, 1909), 180–202, 5.
149   Nassim Nicholas Taleb's term.

as much as the reverse. Therefore, different communities should compete with each other in doing good works, as instructed in the Qur'an (2:148).

In a sense this is a benign version of Girardian mimetic rivalry, where rivals imitate each other, taking on board what is valid in the other's approach, while also polarizing and thereby avoiding being conquered by the other; a sort of romantic rivalry which, however, must nonetheless ultimately discover the validity of difference and embrace a paradigm beyond rivalry, maintaining pluralism without the need for enemies, in a de-polarized state.

Plato suggests a people articulate itself politically and seek common governance structures for its federated parts in order to secure "peace within" and "defense against organized units of a comparable size" without,[150] as Voegelin puts it (still commenting on Book III of the *Laws*). This is the function of personality or personhood: to gather itself and to engage others appropriately—integrity and interaction. It is Carl Schmitt's necessary political discrimination.

Integrity and interaction constitute the two modes of healthy discrimination: appropriate cohesion and appropriate collaboration. Such is an *ordo amoris* according to which the particulars of a person's station in life render the exercise of compassion in a given case more efficacious and more propitious to human flourishing (being with the bounds of duty, *dharma*) than in a certain other case. This needn't always relate to kinship or group-identity, it can also have to do with personal compatibility or positive affect owing to a shared professional vocation.

Apart from similarity, however, there is the issue of compatibility, just as a man bestows a special kind of attention on a woman precisely because of their difference, or a certain personality finds itself more at ease with one that attenuates its extravagancies or compensates for its shortcomings. Both, unity in similarity and union in compatibility, however, bespeak organic linkages whereby one does not participate in the social body in an indiscriminate way, but rather must (cannot help but) be rigorously discriminating. Again, here are the twin pillars of cohesion and collaboration on which civilization must perch. A town must be internally cohesive and also collaborate with other towns; blood cells must flow together and also carry oxygen to other kinds of cells.

It may be remarked, in a momentary aside, that the realization that unity of principle is not properly expressed in uniformity of practice (that the coherence of the category *"human being"* does not prevent human beings from legitimately participating in different projects) contains not a jot of gloomy concession to the fallen and frail condition of human nature. It is rather an optimistic prospect, as picturesque and essential to joyful creativity as the unity and neutrality of sunlight when it, nevertheless, divides into the plural colors of a rainbow (a quite comprehensive cliché).

150   Voegelin, *Order and History, vol. 4, The Ecumenic Age*, 285.

The process of federating, Plato suggests, requires active agency to come about. Voegelin asks the pertinent question as to whether the Hellenes are a people presently, as Plato makes these recommendations, or will become one by way of such recommendations.[151] The answer is that both are true. Just as the Achaeans preexist the Dorian Federation yet are in a sense birthed by it, so too the Greeks are being asked to *make* themselves on the basis of their already existing self. A man exists as an infant, and also becomes himself as an adult.

The effacement of particularity at some eschatological horizon made imminent is therefore out of the question. Instead, wholesome civilizational advance allows for the accentuation of difference. A plurality of examples of successful maturation can be fathomed, and civilizational advance is not conceived in terms of mutual pasteurization into a shared cultural monotony. If, as was previously proposed, membership implies mediation, then maturity implies multiplicity.

Even in the context of universalistic religion, where assertions of the desirability of independent polities within a shared ecumene interact with tradition-specific conceptions of the ecumene, pluralism is often strong. During Catholic expansion in the Americas, for example, when a sense of civilizing mission required or justified intervention abroad on the part of Castile and Portugal, with Papal Bulls encouraging expansion and allocating territory, this gave way by the 1520s to a Spanish intellectual current, in line with Aristotle, St. Thomas Aquinas and the Dominican tradition to which John of Paris and his radical vision of political plurality belonged, emphasizing the need for independent states rather than world empire. But this came about after, or in the course of, establishing a requisite consensus (ending human sacrifice and so forth, which was partly the initiative of local central Americans who were being predated on by the Aztec empire as well as of the Spaniards with whom they allied).[152]

The sixteenth century theologian Francisco de Vitoria was an early codifier of international law. His twin belief in legitimate intervention in the Americas and legitimate native American territorial polities rests on considering Christianity not the Ecumene, but a fruition or maturation thereof. However pagan, the native American is considered to have a *verum dominium* by Vitoria, against other thinkers who thought it necessary to be Christian. Like Dante's *humana universitas*, the ecumene already exists and encompasses many peoples, Christians and heathens. It is subject to the law of nations or *ius gentium* who, crucially, are not outside or opposed to the Ecumenic Order or necessarily even to the Christian Church, as they often are to Israel in the Old Testament.

---

151   Ibid.
152   Oliver O'Donovan, "Christianity and Territorial Right." In: *States, Nations and Borders: The Ethics of Making Boundaries*, eds. Allen Buchanan and Margaret Moore (Cambridge: Cambridge University Press, 2003), 152.

According to this line, preaching to the Native Americans and converting them to Christianity is bringing the child into maturity or the
tree into spring, but it is not what justifies the child or tree's right
not to be impeded in its health. This very right, however, requires that
certain practices, like human sacrifice, be stopped by external agents
and by force, if need be. We can conclude that, while a polity's moral
corruption should be detained, it should then be returned to itself. The
detainer should not thereafter establish permanent dominion over or
enmeshment of governing structures with the now corrected polity. This
implicitly values human cultural and political diversity. Indeed, in his
de Indis, Vitoria argues against a global state under Emperor Charles V
(Charles V, for his part, was not particularly interested in the Americas).

Some of those participating in the Junta de Valladolid debates of 1550–
1551 made the point that there were cruel practices (we may add that these
included human sacrifice) in epochs of European history too. A propensity
for such should not be essentialized as native American, justifying domination by Europeans. Vitoria does, however, justify the interaction between
peoples on the basis of a principle of freedom and reciprocity which, given
the obvious differences in technological advancement between Americans
and Spaniards, could not but favor the penetration of the latter's culture
and institutions into the former, as Eric Voegelin criticizes.[153]

Ancient Thought and Non-Mimetic Politics, or Respect over Rivalry

The organic vision of the world that emerges from the above concords
with a model of concentric identities where lower orders pool together
like cells into organs and organs into bodies. This may be why Isaiah
emphasizes regional integration. Marc van de Mieroop describes the
ruling families of the Bronze Age Near East as operating like a family,
constituting not only an economic but a political club,[154] which echoes
in Isaiah's (Chapter 19) vision of Egypt, Israel and Assyria all connected
by a highway, their peoples dwelling with each other, all having been
made holy nations. It also might provide the political context for a
cultural connection between some of these ancient kingdoms, a connection modern linguistics designate by the term *Afro-Asiatic* language
family, formerly *Hamito-Semitic* (although the family van de Mieroop is
describing includes Indo-European language speakers as well, such as
the Hittites, and others).

This *to each his own* theology is also found in the polytheistic portions
of the Bible, as the Book of Judges (11:23–24) puts it:

> Now, since the Lord, the God of Israel, has driven the Amorites
> out before his people Israel, what right have you to take it over?

153   Eric Voegelin, *History of Political Ideas: Religion and the Rise of Modernity* (London:
University of Missouri Press, 1998), 124–25.
154   Marinatos, *Minoan Kingship and the Solar Goddess: A Near Eastern Koine*, 190.

> Will you not take what your god, Chemosh, gives you? Likewise, whatever the Lord our God has given us, we will possess.

In fact, the idea that different peoples have angelic or divine administrators apportioning land and fortune is found throughout Christian scripture and theology, as in St. Dionysius the Areopagite, as well as in pagan writings, such as those of the Emperor Julian the Apostate (more on which below).

The *Book of Jubilees* seems to accord with the Platonic view to which Herodotus and Aeschylus serve as antecedents. It apparently does not consider difference an incitement to conflict, but rather respect for difference as the condition for peace. After relating the apportionment of certain regions to the sons and grandsons of Noah, it prohibits the transgression of these:

> And thus the sons of Noah divided unto their sons in the presence of Noah their father, and he bound them all by an oath, imprecating a curse on everyone that sought to seize the portion which had not fallen (to him) by lot.[155]

Jubilees then presents homogenization as such, and not only in the context of violent conquest, as negative through the story of the Tower of Babel: "Behold the children of men have become evil through the wicked purpose of building for themselves a city and a tower..."[156] wanting to ascend into Heaven, confusing physical verticality (a tower), which is to say, technical or psychical advance, for spiritual verticality (asceticism, noetic advancement). This is the same confusion by which universality is expressed as uniformity rather than harmony between different forms: The voice of the Lord in the *Book of Jubilees* adds in condemnation, "Behold, they are one people...."[157]

The *Book of Jubilees*, however, considers Heaven's language to be a pronounceable language, like those of man, specifically Hebrew. One culture, then, is holier than others and, presumably, allows privileged communication with higher realms. *Jubilees'* vision of plurality is therefore circumspect, tending to appear as mere precaution against hubris. The question of the language of Heaven and the language of man illustrates different approaches to the universal and particular.

Genesis 10:5 tells us of a linguistic differentiation (among the sons of Javan, son of Japhet) that occurred prior to the confusion of tongues during the fall of the tower of Babel, so that this diversity is not the result of a specific transgression and could be regarded as legitimate from the Biblical perspective. The passage in question might be interpreted as an overview of future events, however, and therefore as referring to the confusion of tongues at Babel, or else it might indeed have to do

---

155   *Jubilees*, 9:14, 77–78.
156   Ibid., 10:18, 82.
157   Ibid., 10:22, 83.

with a pre-Babelic diversity that, in the course of the construction of the tower or prior, was effaced to the point at which only one language was spoken on the earth (Genesis 11:1).

Also contrasting with what *Jubilees* seems to be saying is the view found within Biblical tradition that *angeloglossia*, the speech of angels, is not a language spoken by men, but is a kind of esoteric communication, and maybe a super-verbal (musical?) language. John Poirier highlights examples of this latter view:

> 1 Cor 13.1, the *Book of the Resurrection*, *Ephrem's Hymn* 11, the *Testament of* Job, and the *Apocalypse of Zephaniah*, as well as, less obviously, in 2 Cor 12.1–7, the *Ascension of Isaiah*, the *Apocalypse of Abraham*, and *Genesis Rabbah*.[158]

As Filastrius, Bishop of Brescia, argued in his *Diversarum Hereseon Liber*, it is more important to know that human beings are endowed of reason, than to know by which names they call or called certain objects (during some primordial age).[159] In *De Genesi ad Litteram* St. Augustine argues that the language employed by God in the Garden and before Babel is not a human language with words as we understand them, but a spiritual communication.[160]

Against his own earlier opinion, Dante came to consider the language Adam spoke to have died in ancient times, so that even this first language, either Hebrew or some earlier version of Hebrew, is mortal and a product of human agency, as is every language (*Paradiso*, 26, 124–29). In *Paradiso* 26: 136–38 Dante implies that the Hebrew name for God is a mortal invention that will be replaced by others, so that Hebrew is not the original language of Adam which he says went extinct (that is, for Dante the original language was presumably not recovered after going extinct and taught to Abraham and his descendants, as *Jubilees* has it).

Just as many Church fathers consider Israel a figure (a metaphorical representation) for all humanity in alignment with God's will, and the Church to be Israel, so too the 13th-century Jewish Kabbalist Abraham Abulafia argued that in scripture the term *Hebrew* refers to the proper use of language, not any specific language, encompassing all languages within itself when these are used properly, that is, in accordance with reason and spiritual truth. This position is similar to that of Dante as articulated through Adam in *Paradiso*. It is also similar to the opinion of medieval mysticism according to which "all knowledge, in whatever language it takes verbal form, may depend for its potency on the Adamic" so that, for example "Latin can pose as a reconstituted version of Adamic

---

158   John Poirier, *The Tongues of Angels* (Tübingen, Germany: Mohr Siebeck, 2010), 108.
159   Tim Denecker, "Ideas on Language in Early Latin Christianity." In: *Vigiliae Christianae Supplements*, vol. 142, David Runia and Gerard Rouwhorst, eds. (Leiden: Brill, 2017), 64.
160   Ibid., 89.

language because of its lucidity, its distance from ordinary speakers, and the way it had to be acquired through formal study aided by grace," as Nicholas Watson puts it.[161]

Turning to Catholic mysticism for a moment, although most early Christian theologians assumed Hebrew to have been the original language of humanity, according to Anne Emmerich's visions (such as they have been recorded), the language of Adam and his descendants prior to the confusion of tongues was something closest to Bactrian and the holy language of India, as she puts it, with words in common with her native German—which means she is referring to proto-Indo-European. Hebrew was created in part to set Abraham's descendants apart, according to her. The liturgical status of Latin is defended by Emmerich as having religious importance which, one might intuit, has to do with its being a descendent of that proto-Indo-European. Thus, in Emmerich's visions, there seems to be a possible plurality of holy languages with spiritually important functions, where both Hebrew and Latin (and Sanskrit) have an exalted status. There is some precedence for this idea. In its introduction, the 13th-century *Book of Sydrac* claims to originate with Noah's sons, having surfaced in Toledo, Spain (supposed origin of the Holy Grail myth as well) and been translated from Greek into Latin (so that, presumably, Noah and his sons wrote it down in something like Greek).

The notion that Noah spoke a language whose purest remnant is the holy language of India allows us to collapse Noah into the Sanskrit seventh Manu who survives the global flood in Indian tradition, providing an interesting Catholic rapprochement to Indian religion (although paganism is generally corrupted in the post-flood humanity according to Emmerich).

In any case, we conclude this discussion by highlighting again the scriptural support for angeloglossia as non-human, and the opinions concerning language of the Bishop of Brescia, Filastrius, St. Augustine and Dante as well as some Kabbalistic philosophy, to argue for a western medieval, Biblically and Hellenic inspired pluralism in line with the Book of Judges, Herodotus and Aeschylus (and to a lesser degree *Genesis Apocryphon*). From these sources modern European culture can draw out a non-secularizing, non-disenchanting, pluralistic ethos.

BIBLICAL ELECTION AND THE ECUMENE

In the Christian context, the above considerations are theologically at stake in the question of whether national Israel was or is under the care of an angel like other nations, or not. The latter position belongs to Origen and the former to St. Dionysius. For Origen the difference between Israel and gentile nations is resolved by considering Israel, including the

---

161   Nicholas Watson, "Introduction: King Solomon's Tablets." In: Fiona Somerset and Watson Nicholas, eds., *The Vulgar Tongue: Medieval and Postmedieval Vernacularity* (University Park, PA: Penn State University Press, 2013).

Hebrew language,[162] the original and eschatological identity of humanity, so that, after the first century AD, the particular historical and national character of Israel ceases and, correspondingly, so do all others.

Paradoxically, in Christian theology radical denials of supersessionism tend to be complicit with, and dialectically related to, radical supersession. The features of Israel as Biblical nation will be appropriated by those attaining salvation insofar as these features are identified with humanity's perfected state *as such*. If a distinction (such as Biblical election) is so profound as to constitute the human *telos* itself, it must be undone in due teleological course. On the contrary, and counter-intuitively, the preservation of distinction requires that it be relativized. Identity is a delicate gift, grasp it too tightly, and it suffocates you.

The confusion of the categories *cultural particular* and *metaphysical universal* occurs if the Bible is read as justifying the existence of Israel as national community in terms of the preservation of truth against falsehood (gentile religion). Therefore, it is not only historical Christianity that has at times denied the particularity of national Israel by emphasizing that this nation is defined by a universal which is now the patrimony of all believers. Judaism did as well. There were periods of Jewish proselytism, from the Hasmonean conversion of Idumeans and Itureans to various Roman conversions to Judaism related (often in condemnation) by authors such as Valerius Maximus, Horace, Cicero, Tacitus or Cassius Dio. This is consistent with sources by Jewish authors. There are passages in Philo of Alexandria's *Life of Moses* to the effect that the Septuagint Greek translation of the Torah may cause all peoples to adopt Jewish law, or Flavius Josephus's celebration in *Against Apion* of the fact that Jewish law, such as the keeping of Sabbath and even dietary restrictions, is being adopted far and wide by different peoples. These are significant because they highlight the fact that Hellenized/Romanized Jewish scholars saw gentile adherence not only to Noachide law (prescriptions meant for all descendants of Noah according to the Torah) but to specific aspects of Mosaic law, as a positive development. The categories of Israel in its cultural specificity and humanity/Ecumene tended to coincide not only in Christian thought but in Jewish thought as well.

A defense of election as radical difference champions the identity of an elect community with the saved human condition as such, meaning that as this condition is approached by others the particularity of Israel must cease to be its own and come to belong to all. Contrastingly, in order to assert difference, to legitimize the harmonious emergence of forms, a certain sense of equality is needed (again, Nicholas of Cusa's Equality as the unfolding of form in oneness[163]).

---

162   *Homilies on Jeremiah* 12, 8 cited in Jean Danielou, *Origen*, trans. Walter Mitchell (Eugene, OR: Wipf and Stock, 1955), 233.

163   Nicholas of Cusa, *De Pace Fidei and Cribratio Alkorani*, trans. Jasper Hopkins (Minneapolis, MN: The Arthur J. Banning Press, 1994), VIII:22, 644–45.

In contrast to Origen, St. Dionysius the Areopagite relativizes the role of national Israel in the economy of salvation until it resembles one brother among many who remembers their father's instructions and reminds the rest. He does not, therefore, require an eschatological abolition of national Israel or of the gentiles. In his (authorially disputed) *scholia* on St. Dionysius, St. Maximus summarizes this position: "It is not as if a God has chosen Israel alone.... Is God not also the God of the pagans?... Human beings are free; when they choose, they can have God in their midst." [164]

This is Blake's understanding that "[t]he antiquities of every Nation under Heaven, is no less sacred than that of the Jews. They are the same thing...." He writes in *The Marriage of Heaven and Hell*:

> Then Ezekiel said, "The philosophy of the east taught the first principles of human perception: some nations held one principle for the origin & some another; we of Israel taught that the Poetic Genius (as you now call it) was the first principle and all other others merely derivative, which was the cause of our despising the priests & Philosophers of other countries, and prophecying that all Gods would at last be proved to originate in ours & to be the tributaries of the Poetic Genius; it was this that our great poet King David desired so fervently & invokes so pathetiqly, saying by this he conquers enemies & governs kingdoms; and we so loved our God, that we cursed in his name all deities of surrounding nations, and asserted that they had rebelled; from these opinions the vulgar came to think that all nations would at last be subject to the jews."
>
> This said he, like all firm perswasions, is come to pass, for all nations believe the jews code and worship the jews' god...

Further, St. Dionysius "follows the Hellenic Neoplatonists in...recognizing...as sacred...specific places for specific peoples, under the providential care of specific gods." [165] This approach to Christianity, by granting particularity, refuses that universality is contained in one particularity, it "rules out the possibility that God, like Apollo, might be allotted only a certain nation...." [166] The solution here is simply the old Platonic one, but incorporating the cultural force and revelation of Christianity. In *On Isis and Osiris* Plutarch describes his monotheism in terms of there being one sun and sky above all nations and Celsus recognized Divine Oneness while recommending each nation hold fast to its rites. [167] Here is the *theos ek theon* or god consisting of gods of Porphyry (*Peri Agalmaton*, III:38).

---

164   *In Coel. Hier*, 9, in Balthasar H.v., *Cosmic Liturgy: The Universe According to Maximus the Confessor*, trans. Brian E. Daley (San Francisco: Ignatius Press, 2003), 307.
165   Michael L. Harrington, *Sacred Place in Early Medieval Neoplatonism* (New York: Palgrave Macmillan, 2004), 103.
166   Ibid., 104.
167   Charles Elsee, *Neoplatonism in Relation to Christianity: An Essay* (Cambridge: Cambridge University Press, 1908), 14.

Porphyry acknowledges oracles and prophets from perhaps every tradition he knows of, including the *pietissimus* Christ (*Phil. Orac.*, 141.2–145.10, 180.16–18), having, however, harsher words for Christians elsewhere.[168]

Contrastingly, for Origen the cosmic architecture that allows for nations and, specifically, linguistic difference, is abolished by Christ, whereas for St. Dionysius it is repaired but deemed legitimate. Here asserting radical difference leads dialectically towards homogeneity and relativizing that difference towards pluralism. This is because when a distinction is so profound as to constitute the difference between attaining and not attaining the very purpose of the human condition (for Origen, the unmediated human-Divine relationship) it will be viewed as ending when that telos is reached by those who have not yet done so. If a distinction is made to be quite so profound, it demands its own cessation—this is the whole of the present argument.

At the farther reaches of speculation, it can be suggested that binaries (when they are not gendered and explicitly complementary) are psychologically conducive to images of rivalry, whereas schemas with more numerous categories inspire corporeal differentiation (organs, team members) and therefore images of collaboration. This is roughly consistent with René Girard's understanding of mimetic desire. It is then preferable to structure one's account of cultural diversity in terms of the manifold and not the binary.

For Origen, Christ abolishes the office of national angels so that Christians become the wards of the Lord in an unmediated way,[169] as national Israel was in the Old Testament.[170] He interprets the name Israel as denoting a "race of the soul…as is indicated by the interpretation of the name itself: for 'Israel' is interpreted to mean a 'mind' or 'man seeing God'…"[171] The (righteous) olive tree to which branches from the wild counterpart become grafted according to St. Paul is Christ[172] and Origen urges that this be understood in terms of the idea that membership in Israel is a function of individuals' free will.[173] One suspects Origen would have considered equating the tree into which believers are grafted with national Israel rather than with Christ (entering a nation rather than pre-Babel or pre-lapsed humanity) idolatrous. Applying election-language

---

168   Niketas Siniossoglou, "From Philosophic Monotheism to Imperial Henotheism: Esoteric and Popular Religion in Late Antique Platonism." In: Stephen Mitchell and Peter van Nuffelen, eds., *Monotheism Between Pagans and Christians in late Antiquity* (Leuven: Peeters, 2010), 127-48, 146.

169   *Homilies on Jeremiah* 12, 8, cited in Danielou, *Origen*, 233.

170   *Commentary on Matthew*, 16, 8, cited in Danielou, *Origen*, 236.

171   Origen, *On First Principles*, 4.1.22, ANF 4:371, cited by Michael Vlach, *Has the Church Replaced Israel?: A Theological Evaluation* (Nashville, TN: B&H Publishing Group, 2010), 39.

172   Origen, *Commentary on the Epistle to the Romans*, Books 6–10, trans. T. Scheck (Washington, DC: The Catholic University Press, 2002), 8, 8, 178.

173   Ibid., 8, 11, 180.

to nations other than Israel would be mistaken, but so would applying it to national Israel after the Incarnation.

Origen does not hierarchize the Jew-gentile dichotomy, because for him both are Israel. It is significant that despite this, the fact of recognizing past hierarchy still leaves him no way to assert salvific equality between Israel and the nations other than by eliminating distinction altogether. This is because he grounds past differences structurally (in that national Israel uniquely had no angelic steward, while the gentile nations did). His view identifies the unity of the human condition with one of the particulars of contingent multiplicity (the Hebrew language, etc.). Jean Danielou summarizes this: "... the true Israel is mankind as it was in the beginning... and the carnal Israel is only an image of the true one..."[174] To identify particular cultural elements with the human state in and of itself entails the rejection of difference:

> the political order dependent on the existence of a variety of nations...was henceforth over and done with...he regarded polyarchy as a system going with polytheism.... Monarchy was to appear at the end of the world....[175]

This may signal a contradiction in Origen between believing the cosmos is a harmonious organic body in which each entity has a place determined by free will but so providentially ordered as to fit in with every other, on the one hand, yet also that this was the result of a fall. Even if the fall is interpreted as fortunate, a felix culpa under which human individualities may play out in such a way as to not be undone by the beatific vision of plenitude but, rather, fulfilled, taken up and preserved within it, this is somewhat at odds with the view that human linguistic and political uniformity is the proper expression of divine unity. More succinctly: if plurality is fathomed for persons, why not also for the cultural forms persons are wont to produce? This is, perhaps, a proto-liberal feature in Origen, where the individual is emphasized over and—critically—*against* culture. This proto-liberalism occurs precisely in the context of a proto-Protestant suspicion of (angelic) mediation, strengthening the case made by John Milbank and others that liberalism is always at least quasi-Protestant (iconoclastic, rejecting of mediation).

For Origen, all humanity, including national Israel, will constitute a spiritual Israel, the Church. In Book 6 of his *Commentary on the Epistle to the Romans*, Origen writes that

> as long as Israel remains in its unbelief it will not be possible to say that the fullness of the Lord's portion has been attained. The people of Israel are still missing from the complete picture. But when the fullness of the Gentiles has come in and Israel comes

---

174 Danielou, *Origen*, 233.
175 Ibid., 230–31.

to salvation at the end of time, then it will be the people which, although it existed long ago, will come at the last and complete the fullness of the Lord's portion and inheritance.

This passage treats Israel as a community of descent and not as a general name for the saved. This conveys a more relative point of view than his analysis of Biblical allegorical uses of the name Israel. Ultimately, as he writes elsewhere in Book 6, all Israel, whether Jew or Gentile in the context of pre-eschatological history, is saved, and *is* Israel.

For Origen, in national Israel's entering salvation after the gentiles, its original primacy is reversed, but whether Origen's statement elsewhere that the Jewish community will not regain its original position applies to this eschatological conversion or only to its status in the course of history is unclear. The issue would seem mute, however, since Origen accepted St. Paul's opinion in the Epistle to the Romans that the Jewish people have an advantage in terms of the law and oracles while, however, adding that gentiles have the advantage in terms of faith. Origen is asserting complementary spiritual vocations, both conducive to salvation and both possible within adherence to the true faith.[176] There is no need, then, to restore the primacy of one or uphold that of the other. There is only the need to assert, as Origen does, that the fullness of God's portion and inheritance requires that both be saved, and both, in Christian terms, be considered Israel.

In this vein, Origen interprets scriptural descent as sometimes biological and sometimes not. He points out that the promise made to Abraham about his descendants is made while the patriarch is yet uncircumscribed, concluding that this promise does not apply to the heirs of the rite of circumcision alone. Language of ancestry operates here as it does when Jesus refers to some pharisees as not being children of Abraham but of Satan, or, when the prophet Daniel refers to adulterers as sons of Canaan and not Judah.[177]

If the difference between Israel and the gentiles is structural (having a different relation to God in principle, unmediated by angels) this is a difference not of kind or competence, which can be hierarchical within a particular sphere (the Eskimo language can be better at describing different kinds of snow than the Australian Aboriginal without being better in some general sense), rather it is an overall difference of spiritual caliber. It can only allow for the generalization of its superior quality to all saved mankind, effectively ending its difference, or an everlasting caste system in which the fullness of beatitude is inaccessible outside that nation, coming through its mediation to the gentiles, which elevates the contingent particulars of that nation (scriptural language, heritage,

---

176   Origen, *Commentary on the Epistle to the Romans Books 1–5* (Washington, DC: The Catholic University of America Press, 2001), 2:14, 9, 168.

177   Ibid., 4:2, 8, 250.

specific history, etc.) to the universal quality of the salvific function (contemplation of Divine truths). This confuses the universal with the contingent and must constitute idolatry.

Yet Origen's view that national Israel had no angel, and was cared for only by the Lord, is contradicted by scriptural passages, also militating against the logic of Christian icons. St. Dionysius writes:

> Hence the Word of God, as shewing that Israel elected himself for the worship of the true God, says this, "He became Lord's portion"; and as indicating that he was assigned equally with the other nations, to one of the holy Angels, for the recognition, through him, of the Head of all, said "That Michael became leader of the (Jewish) people…"[178]

And, "[h]ence, the Word of God has assigned our Hierarchy to Angels, by naming Michael as Ruler of the Jewish people, and others over other nations."[179]

The "angel of the Lord" who appears to Joshua, for example, may be the pre-incarnate Christ, but St. Michael is the patron of Israel. As holders of a universal message, they are guided by the angel of the Lord, the Son. But as a particular nation, they have their own angel.

For Dionysius, then, attending to the transmission coming through national angels renders a nation righteous (superficially at least, this disagrees with St. Paul's view that the angels became corrupt):

> …the turning away of the nations to false gods ought not to be attributed to the direct guidance of Angels, but to their own refusal of the true path which leads to God, and the falling away through selflove and perversity, and similarly, the worship of things which they regarded as divine. Even the Hebrews are said to have acted thus, for he says, "Thou hast cast away the knowledge of God and hast gone after thine own heart."

Consistently with Dionysius, the Bible sometimes presents Israel as among the nations.[180] The Hebrew word *Goy*, plural *Goyim*, usually translated as gentiles or *nations* appears when the Lord says to Abraham that He will make of him a great nation and to Sarah that in her womb are two nations. In the New Testament, Christ speaks of being hated by the nations (Matthew 24:9) after referring to His persecution at synagogues (23:34), and in Luke (24:47) we read an injunction to proclaim the gospel to all the nations beginning at Jerusalem, so that Israel seems to be one of these.

---

178   St. Dionysius, *Works* (London: James Parker and Co, 1897). Reproduced in: http://www.documentacatholicaomnia.eu/03d/0450-0525,_Dionysius_Areopagita ,_Works,_EN.pdf The *Celestial Hierarchy*, Chapter 9, Section 4, 128.
179   Ibid., Chapter 9, Section 2, 127.
180   Terence L. Donaldson, *Jews and Anti-Judaism in the New Testament: Decision Points and Divergent Interpretations* (London: Society for Promoting Christian Knowledge, 2010).

The point is that for Dionysius cosmic architecture is restored and brought into alignment by Christ rather than being partially abolished as for Origen. The particular is received as a gift if one seeks first the Absolute (seeking first the kingdom of Heaven, as Jesus advises). Multiplicity is rediscovered through and within the ecstasy of unity (*nation* can be interpreted as this multiplicity, referring to all kinds of categories inside which human beings situate themselves: vocation, personality, metabolism, favorite color, etc.).

In line with Dionysius, Bishop Synesius of Cyrene writes the following fascinating passage in his third hymn:

> Thee, Father of the worlds, Father of the æones, artificer of the *gods*, it is holy to praise. Thee, O king, the intellectual gods sing, thee, O blessed God, the *cosmagi*, those fulgid eyes, and starry intellects, celebrate, round which the illustrious body [of the world] dances. All the race of the blessed sing thy praise, those that are about, and those that are in the world...who govern the parts of the world, wise itinerants, stationed about the illustrious pilots [of the universe,] and which the angelic series pours forth.

The bishop mentions the ministrants of Thrace and Chaldea specifically, so that the angelic intelligences whose bodies are stars are identified as caretakers of human nations and, being that they praise God, are considered pious.

This tradition seems to have survived in some form into the Middle Ages. In line with this, Suhrawardi writes in his *Creed of the Sages*: "The sages hold that just as our bodies have rational souls, so too the spheres have living rational souls that know and passionately love their Creator eternally with a continual ecstasy and ever-renewed pleasure."[181] Perhaps when king Alphonse X of Castile and Leon, Suhrawardi's near contemporary, writes that Spain's first name, *Esperia*, derived from the star Hesperos[182] (from the ancient Greek designation for the evening star, which is Venus at dusk, whence the Latin for *vespers*) in his *General Chronicle of Spain* in the second half of the 13th century he was harkening back to this doctrine of linking nations to stars.

St. Paul can be read as being compatible with Dionysius even though he believes the national angels have become corrupted whereas Dionysius apparently does not. Paul can be read as referring to the *likeness* and Dionysius to the *image* (these are distinct, since according to scripture humans are made in the image and likeness of God), that is, the former to the agency and surface of an entity which can become twisted by sin, and the latter to its legitimate archetype. This may be at the root of Origen's view that there are two angels per nation, one good and one

---

181   Suhrawardi, *Creed of the Sages*, XI, 81.
182   Alphonse X of Castile and Leon, *Primera crónica general*, Section 3, lines 2–4, 6.

bad[183] and of course Dionysius accepts the possibility of nations being led astray by demons who take the place of their angels.

These considerations bring to mind a strange episode from Exodus, when Jehovah tries to kill Moses and has to be persuaded not to. If interpreted as a reference to Israel's angel, instances in which this entity is referred to as Jehovah may refer to its being subordinate and acting in accord with the Logos, whereas instances like this one, when it acts in apparently destructive ways, may be taken as referring to a confounding of the angel, for which reason the *Book of Jubilees* amends the episode from Exodus and refers to the entity who tried killing Moses *Mastema*, that is, the devil (in one of the first Hebrew references to something like the later Christian and Muslim concept of Satan) rather than as Jehovah.

In accord with this, St. Paul considers the sons of the high God, El, or local deities, corrupt and in need of being ordered under Christ. Crucially, following Galatians (3:19), this might include the angels who brought the law to Moses (following Hart, even though Orthodox theologians take the author of the law to be a preincarnate Christ). Israel's angel may be subject to the same confusion befalling other heavenly administrators. The Gospel according to Matthew (19:3-9) also presents the law of Moses as less than morally perfect, and in I Timothy 1:8 we read that the law is for the lawless, not the just, which, by its very wording implies the lawful are not under the law (because it is inside them, not above them). Paul implication that the law has possibly been corrupted in the course of history or even arrived corrupted echoes Matthew 15:1-9, Isaiah 29:13 and Jeremiah 8:8. It is also consistent with Margaret Barker's account of various prophets and the Gospel itself as a return to the religiosity that pre-dated Mosaic law as passed down (the Ezra canon, Mosaic law as understood by Hilkiah and king Josiah).

The Elementals of the cosmos (possibly national angels) are never demonic for St. Paul, but imperfect and, only potentially or in part, malicious, custodial guides. It seems we are dealing with a doctrine not dissimilar to that of the Kali Yuga: a period of history during which awareness of the Divine dims and, therefore, the already present architecture of the cosmos—including angelic intelligences, perhaps—manages its affairs somewhat blindly, as though imitating the impossible *pura natura* idea. With the Incarnation, the Kali Yuga is over *in potentia*, and the coming Golden Age (following Hindu and Hesiodic terminology) is available for whoever enter into that Anointing. The saint in Indian tradition is likewise not bound to the decay of the Kali Yuga, and can transcend it by devotion to God.

We are no longer under custodial guides, (Galatians 3:25). For St. Paul, even—or especially—national Israel, whose guide was good (albeit imperfect), isn't under that guide any longer (the term may refer to a national

183   *Against Celsus*, 1, 24, cited in Danielou, *Origen*, 229.

angel as well as to the priestly office or just legal prescriptions). Yet this may mean that we are not under guides as we were. Just as a student moves on from a teacher, but continues, in traditional custom, to cite his lineage and to pass it on, and just as a child grows up and leaves the parental home but continues to bare the father's name and to pass it on, so the metaphor of a custodial guide in St. Paul allows for its continuity even in its being relinquished. Human diversity is no longer a conflict-inducing agonistic reality but a thing to be celebrated for its aesthetic beauty.

In the same passages, Dionysius celebrates the transcendence of God with language highlighting the aesthetic beauty of diverse forms at the same tier of the created order and in equivalent relation to the "one Providence of the whole."[184] The unity and transcendence of that Providence is thus emphasized and, therefore, the equivalents of forms. This emphasis on the equality or peerage—"Israel ... equally with the other nations"—of created forms within a particular stratum of reality anticipates the previously cited point from Nicholas of Cusa's *De Pace Fidei* according to which equality is the unfolding in oneness.

Scriptural passages in which Israel is described as the portion of the Lord are compatible with St. Dionysius's approach if they refer to a state of affairs that came about through proper, devoted, contemplation by that community's national angel and its wards, but which did not efface angelic mediation, which Israel continued to have in common with other nations. The principal at play is the same as the formula which describes a child as its father's son when it acts in ways particularly reminiscent of the father's behavior (as when Jesus describes some pharisees as not being sons of Abraham on account of faithlessness).

This also relates to a scriptural theme in which lower entities are identified by titles ascribed to, and said to share in the likeness of, higher ones. This occurs when angels communicate the Lord's edicts in the first person, or during throne theophanies that end with the visionary occupying the throne himself, becoming its regent. The phenomenon is not exclusive to Biblical tradition. It seems to describe what Indian Vaishnavism calls *sarupya*, a mode of *moksha* (spiritual liberation) in which the liberated person takes on the likeness of the Divine body.

This fluidity of form is such as permitting one to oscillate between one's own form and assimilation into the likeness of the Lord, and where the beloved male-female couple (Radha-Krishna in this tradition) enter in and out of each other's likeness and seem to form a single being together. When, as recounted in the *Deva Bhagavatam* (IX:13, 52–107),[185]

---

184   St. Dionysius, *Works: The Celestial Hierarchy* (London: James Parker and Co, 1897), Chapter 9, Section 4, 128.
http://www.documentacatholicaomnia.eu/03d/0450-0525,_Dionysius_Areopagita ,_Works,_EN.pdf.
185   The S'Rimad Devi Bhagavatam, *One of the Upapuranas, devoted to the Devi (Goddess)*.

the "four faced Brahma" creator god (along with Vishnu and Vamadeva, a form of Shiva) approaches Lord Krishna:

> Wherever He cast His glance...He saw Sri Krishna, full of the Highest Bliss, of the nature of the Highest Bliss, sitting. All have turned out Krishnas...No difference at all between them whether in form, or in qualities, or in ornaments, or in radiance, in age, in lustre, in no respect no one was inferior to another. No one was imperfect; no one was deficient in lordliness. It was indeed very difficult to make out who was the master and who was the servant...sometimes He comes Formless; sometimes with form; and again sometimes both with and without form.

Even the personalities of the Divine, male and female, enter in and out of each other's likeness:

> Sometimes there is no Radha; there is only Krishna; And sometimes again in every seat there is the Yugal Murti Radha and Krishna combined. Sometimes Râdhâ assumes the form of Krisna. So the Creator Brahmâ could not make out whether Sri Krisna was a female or a male. At last He meditated on Sri Krishna in his heart-lotus and began to chant hymns to Him with devotion and prayed for forgiveness for his misdoings. When Sri Krishna got pleased, the Creator, opening His eyes, saw Sri Krishna on the breast of Sri Radha. There were His attendants on all the sides and the Gopis all around. Seeing this, Brahmâ, Visnu, and Maheshvara bowed down to Him and sang His praises.

Biblical examples include taking on the likeness of the Lord as well as of a holy teacher or saintly patriarch, who is perhaps taken up in the Lord. They include 2 *Enoch* 33:2, where the Lord commands Enoch to write things he has learnt in Heaven, later declaring that He Himself has written them; the *Targum Pseudo-Jonathan on Genesis* in which Jacob sees his own likeness engraved on the throne of the Lord; the Exagoge by Ezekiel the Tragedian in which Moses sees the Heavenly throne and is given a crown and made to sit upon that seat by its occupant; the Testament of Abraham in which its eponymous patriarch ascends to a form upon the Heavenly throne, describing the figure as having the likeness of the Lord but then having it revealed that this is Adam (*Testament of Abraham*, 1:11), and then later seeing another person that to him appears identical to the first but that turns out to be Abel (*Testament of Abraham*, 1:13) and the *Testament of Isaac* (2:1–9) in which the archangel Michael appears as Abraham's double.[186]

We find the same thing at the mosaic in the Martorana at Palermo depicting the investiture of Roger II, in the "striking facial resemblance

---

186   Andrei Orlov notes these in *The Greatest Mirror: Heavenly Counterparts in the Jewish Pseudepigrapha* (Albany, NY: State University of New York Press, 2017). As does David J. Larsen commenting on a paper by Margaret Barker (youtube.com, retrieved 23rd February 2018).

between Roger and Christ," with similar cases occurring in art from Otto's emperorship and also in some imperial coins.[187] The same theme may be conjured when, at the end of their time together in the *Divine Comedy*, Virgil says "Te sopra te," you above yourself, when crowning Dante. Here the Son of Man is encountering the Ancient of Days. At the end of the Divine Comedy, Dante describes the Second Person of the Trinity's circle of light "painted, with its own color, with our own effigy," on which Kantorowicz comments: a "coincidence of God and Son of Man and of Man in general and of the beholder in the state of perfection, each turned back upon himself and to each other."[188]

There is a Sufi account of Muhammad's heavenly ascent wherein he finally sees his own self, for, as Corbin would remind us, the Divine cannot be equated to anything, and so must be expressed by that which perceives It. Thus the hadith in which Muhammad provides an equivalent to the Gospel formula: "You who look at me, look at God."[189] "During the mi'raj, the curtains of heaven were progressively opened; when all the veils were finally lifted, the Prophet saw himself..."[190] In Shia Islam we find this doctrine concerning the Twelfth Imam: "Whoso wishes to behold Adam and Seth, I am Adam and Seth; whoso wishes to behold Noah and his son Shem, I am Noah and his son Shem" repeating the same for Abraham and Ishmael, Moses and Joshua and Jesus and Simon.[191]

In Acts 17 St. Paul cites the *Phaenomena*, a pagan poem by Aratus of Soli, agreeing with the poet to the effect that human beings are the Lord's *genos*, His kin, where the reference in question concerns Zeus. Paul would seem to be indicating that the Greeks know the Lord by the name Zeus (and the Romans by Jove). A higher principle, then, can assimilate mythic forms other than those contained in what Paul knew as scripture.

The Lord and Logos, an interactive *deus revelatus* (pouring forth from the more ineffable aspect of the High God *El Elyon*, in Old Testament terms) is sometimes identified with His subordinate gods or angels, so that the angel of Israel would not be the Lord as such, or is so in the same sense in which stories concerning the Greek countryside sometimes featured the name of Zeus, by which the philosophers, nonetheless, understood a higher principle (not the First Paternal Intellect, presumably a neo-Platonic equivalent to the Hebrew El Elyon, but the Second Paternal Intellect, who Proclus explicitly identifies as Zeus and Logos, and who would be the Old Testament Jehovah, who according to Margaret Barker

---

187   Kantorowicz, *The King's Two Bodies*, 65.
188   Ibid., 494.
189   Edward Henry Palmer, *Oriental Mysticism: A Treaty on the Sufistic and Unitarian Theosophy of the Persians* (London: Luzac and Co., 1938), 52.
190   William Elliott, *The Career of Ibn Qasi as Religious Teacher and Political Revolutionary in 12th Century Islamic Spain*, PhD Thesis (Edinburgh: University of Edinburgh, 1979), 77.
191   A hadith from Ja'far al-Sadiq, provided in: Dennis MacEoin, *The Messiah of Shiraz: Studies in Early and Middle Babism* (Leiden: Brill, 2009), 336.

was treated as equivalent to the New Testament Logos by early Christians, at an ontological octave beneath that High God).

This allows for a wholesome understanding of the Biblical vision of reality. Higher grades of unity encompass lower granularity and integrate diverse forms rather than undoing these. Although a nation can, like a person, attain and thus present a higher theophany (awareness of a grander degree of reality) than its peers, the Logos itself (Origen's *idea of ideas*), underlies the whole of the human condition, so that if It corresponded to one nation directly, skipping over intermediate strata of creation, this nation would lack a layer, specifically the mediation of an angel. Indeed, to view a lack of mediation as bestowing a greater glory is to commit the error of radical iconoclasts. Such a nation would be impoverished rather than raised up, for the whole scale of reality is to be asserted and dispensing with a layer is like skipping organs when making a body from cells. Such a body would be simpler, a lesser testament to the fullness of creation, which includes several orders, and its holiness would not serve to baptize, so to speak, those various layers.

Being the Lord's portion, then, should not efface the agency of intermediate layers of reality, as these layers cannot compromise the immediacy of His agency. Theologically, secondary causation is a direct condescension on the part of God. It is ever subordinate to Him but is the means by which God allows human beings agency, for such agency would be impossible in a cosmos without apparent casuistry and partial occlusion, otherwise everything would occur at once (sequential action would be impossible). Again, considering the direct agency of the Lord as requiring the abolition of other agencies is dangerously iconoclastic.

We find these principles illustrated in the theology of Ismaili Islam. According to this view as described by Henry Corbin, it is the failure of one level of reality (one Angel, in Ismaili terms, or Archetype) to recognize its antecedents, that is, to accept a prior level's mediating of Unity, that produces spiritual ignorance, or a *fall*.[192] An angel's "refusal to recognize their precedence, to hear the appeal, to testify to the Oneness (tawhid)" causes that angel to "stop at himself: he remains in a stupor which gives rise to a gap, a distance between himself and the world of eternal Existentiation..." This is akin to the man who refuses to see that Oneness expresses itself in the unity of forms and harmony between forms, which is a wider unity, ripping the veil of nature, or Lady Philosophy (as Boethius puts it in his *Consolation*) in an iconoclastic tantrum. He refuses medicine, for healing should come from God directly, he refuses relationships, for God's company is enough, he refuses oxygen, for God is sole provider of life, impiously blinding himself to the fact that all these are from God. Proper recognition of Unity, of the Divine Oneness—proper *tawhid*, in Muslim terms—is actually not radical iconoclasm, but is precisely opposed to it.

---

192 Corbin, *Cyclical Time and Ismaili Gnosis*, 40.

This illustrates the profound mistake of Puritanical and Salafist extremism, indeed, its Satanic dimension, for the Angel who asks "Is he not first and alone, originating in himself?," as Corbin puts it, thereby rejecting those who came before him, is very much alike the Satan in John Milton's *Paradise Lost*, who rejects his origin in God and prefers to imagine a lowlier origin springing up from the earth spontaneously, where hubris paradoxically leads to thinking up an inferior and absurd existence for oneself. One account of Ismaili demonology has it that a certain angel, refusing to recognize mediation of the Divine by the Eternal Imam, the Anthropos, the archetypal human form, is assaulted by that Anthropos. The mistake is of misanthropy and iconoclasm, a false monotheism whose piety is impiety, as just described: "without these theophanic figures that the Imam opposes to Azaziel's"—demonic—"claim, monotheism would perish in its own triumph, through the most subtle treason—that by which one imposes on oneself a denial of oneself." [193]

All this suggests the complexity of reality with its various sheaths, including angels, is to be redeemed, not simplified. It suggests that the judgement of angel-shepherds described in *1 Enoch* (90:20-27) is a purgation, not a destruction. This could apply to the destruction of strong kings given over to the Elect in *1 Enoch* 48:1-10 (the earthly subordinated to the spiritual, perhaps). The kings in John's Apocalypse (21) may refer to these purged angels, just as the prophet Daniel (10) seems to refer to angels as the princes of Greece and Persia. In one of his notes on the translation of John's Apocalypse (21:24) David Bentley Hart writes:

> The Byzantine text reads "the nations of the saved," but this is clearly an emendation of the text, and a fairly maladroit one, meant to make the eschatological imagery seem more consistently eschatological. The language used here echoes the prophetic picture (drawn from Isaiah, Micah and Jeremiah) of a restored Jerusalem and a new earthly age in which the peoples of other nations will come to worship Israel's God, rather than a final dispensation beyond all history. [194]

This suggests the justification of national angels is within the ambit of present history and not only beyond it. It is in the ecclesial context that the notion of a nationally delimited Europe seems to emerge:

> The organization of the Council of Constance (1414-1418) into "national" groups of bishops is widely acknowledged as marking the general acceptance of Europe as composed of distinct sovereign jurisdictions. [195]

---

193   Ibid., 173.
194   *The New Testament*, trans. David B. Hart (London: Yale University Press, 2017), 594.
195   Peter Wilson, *Heart of Europe: A History of the Holy Roman Empire*, 170.

Later Catholic tradition concurs, since Church approved Heavenly communications can feature angel-shepherds (the Marian apparition at Fatima included the presence of a benevolent Angel of Portugal, where this entity is benevolent—perhaps the Archangel Michael in or with reference to his role as patron of Portugal). This implies that judgement, purgation or restoration has, in fact, occurred, at least partly.

The universal is accessed by way of the particular, and the universal preserves rather than obliterates the particular. Picking up on Hart's mention of Micah, that prophet is consistent with Dionysius when he writes (Micah 4:5): "All the nations may walk in the name of their gods, but we will walk in the name of the Lord our God for ever and ever."

In this light, Paul's language of grafting gentile branches to the tree of Israel (if Israel is understood not as the righteous race of souls Origen interpreted it to mean, but as a specific nation) becomes more a matter of religious and ritual adoption due to other traditions being more degraded, or a temporary "angelic adoption" due to other national angels having become more corrupted, until the judgement (understood as purgation rather than final destruction) of other national angels described in 1 Enoch.

In any case, the notion that the Israel into which Christians are grafted is the righteous race of souls of Origen finds support in the Gospel. As Jesus says in John 15:5, "I am the vine, you are the branches; the one remaining in me and I in him, this one bears plentiful fruit, because apart from me you can do nothing." Christ is Israel, in the sense of its being a spiritual reality. Just as Israel was scattered, He was crucified, and just as Israel wandered the desert for forty years, He fasted in the wilderness for forty days. As already cited from St. Irenaeus, Christ summed up in Himself all nations and all languages and generations.[196] That into which believers are grafted is Christ Himself, a pre-existing human archetype.

Jesus is a middle term in a ratio, establishing the connection, the *analogy*, between others. Jesus fasted for forty days in the desert, recapitulating the exile of Israel in the desert for forty years and revealing the spiritually preparatory nature of that historical narrative so that it can be reapplied. It makes sense that those nations wanting to put themselves under the kingship of Christ have often produced histories drawing from scripture, describing tragic phases of their history as a sacred history and *imitatio Christi* (more truly than an *imitatio Israeli*).

One may argue that individual mediators are not ultimately interposed between other individuals and Christ, for Jew and gentile are equidistant from Him (Galatians 3:28), so that such intercalation is not what Israel's election means. Even if Galatians were interpreted differently in light of Paul mentioning man and woman in the same context yet also considering

---

196   Saint Irenaeus of Lyon, *Against the Heresies*, III, 22.3; cited in Pickstock, *Repetition and Identity*, 231.

husbands an image of Christ and women of the Church, where the former guides the latter, Jesus also imparts authority to His disciples (Matthew 16:19), so that spiritual mediation would be sought through apostolic succession (in Catholic terms) or discipleship (in Protestant ones), but not through a particular nation's members. Of course, one nation may display human potential and proper relation to the Divine to other nations, just as one person may be an example to other persons, but the biographical accidents of that person must be understood as contingent.

This would not strictly exclude the salvation of nations *as collectives* being mediated by a single nation, however. Yet for Paul Christ seems to put the Archon administrators of national collectives beneath Himself directly, and the polity or communal entity imparting His salvific agency seems to be an invisible center, for His kingdom is not of this world (John 18:36) and is neither here nor there but in the midst of His disciples (Luke 17:21), just as God is worshiped neither in Jprusalem nor on a Samaritan mountain but in the Spirit and in truth (John 21:24). Indeed, in the Gospel of John Jesus precisely says His kingdom is not of this world when asked if He is king of the Judeans, although the issue is complex (He also implies His kingdom will be of this world in the future but, in any case, contrasts it with the Judeans and any particular nation).

The vision of St. Peter in Acts 10 seems to present all peoples—kosher and non-kosher animals—as similarly the manifestation of that fifth element beyond the four corners of the earth which that first pope sees as though lifted by angels, and this leads Peter to make pronouncements such as that persons among all peoples who harken to God are His, and to tell a gentile, the Centurion Cornelius, not to bow to him. St. Peter's vision is deeply ecumenical and leads him to baptize uncircumcised gentiles who remain so: the ritual of conversion does not now affect national membership (the foreskin or generally the body and, symbolically, ethnicity) but the heart (water leaves the body unchanged but is sensed, is felt).

Indeed, it is logical that the contemplation of God comes by way of an invisible center only imperfectly and fleetingly suggested by manifest ones. If election is spiritual centrality (of one people within humanity) and insofar as centrality represents harmony (as was already defined, *movement around, or according to, a fixed or repeating point or pattern*) and therefore represents also the unity of God, it must admit variation in its accidental features lest these become idolatrously identified with centrality as such.

While the priestly vocation *might* by definition refer to spiritual centrality (if united with the regal), there is no reason to consider the emphasis on Mosaic law-observance (as opposed to the "magian"-ritual mode of Parsee piety, or the arcane-astrological mode of the Druze, to name two other priestly nations), or other contingent features such as the Hebrew language, as intrinsic to it. They can only act as such in a given context. Thusly did some Church Fathers admit the continuance of certain Old Testament features for Jewish Christians without considering it the most excellent modality of relationship between humans and God. Origen, for example, asserts the complementary advantages of Jewish law and gentile faith.[197]

As has been noted, history might have a contingent center, so a nation may represent that historical center, but as creation is contingent, it must be a provisional representative of centrality only, and other histories will have different centers. In addition, as the *Bhagavad Gita* and Christ's absence opening space for the Spirit in the Gospel of John both indicate, that which should be given religious attention is the object of religion, that is, the absent center, not the contingency it manifests through. Contemplation of God precisely requires divesting our contemplation of Him of particulars, and then rediscovering particulars in such a way as to witness Him in all of them. One can become a saint without becoming a first century, male carpenter, because becoming a saint is partaking of holiness and holiness is not any of those things. In fact, one must come to understand the Logos as not defined by that biographical configuration. The Son can, necessarily, unite hypostatically with contingencies other than those of the first century Jesus of Nazareth, as St. Thomas Aquinas knew (passages from the *Summa Theologica* have been quoted to this effect).

It should be noted that spiritual centrality is not how election is necessarily understood in Judaism. The United Synagogue of Conservative Judaism declared the following in its 1988 *Emet ve-Emunah* statement:

> God may well have seen fit to enter covenants with many nations ... theological humility requires us to recognize that although we have but one God, God has more than one nation.... It is part of our mission to ... discern those truths in [other] cultures from which we can learn, and to share with them the truths that we have come to know.[198]

There are historic antecedents for this. Flavius Josephus, a first century Jewish scholar, was something of a pluralist, or can be read as such, arguing against the geographic centrality of Jerusalem and Israel:

> Josephus does not use Genesis 10 to argue the eternal centrality and inviobility of Israel among the nations of the world, for, on the one hand, Josephus recognizes that Israel did not always possess the land but, rather, took it by force from its original occupants.... On the other hand, Josephus probably considered it impossible to argue for the eternal inviobility and centrality of Israel in view of both AD 70 and the oppressive reign of Domitian ...[199]

---

197   Origen, *Commentary on the Epistle to the Romans Books 1–5*, 2:14, 9, 168.
198   *Emet ve-Emunah* (New York: Jewish Theological Seminary of America, 1988).
199   James M. Scott, *Paul and the Nations* (Tübingen, Germany: Mohr Siebeck, 1995), 44.

In this vein, Spinoza much later writes that,

> ... election, whether temporal or eternal, insofar as it is merely peculiar to the Jews, regards only their polity and their material interests (since this is all that can distinguish one nation from another)...[200]

The parenthesized words express the point we were making earlier, that contingencies of a certain order should be understood within that order without being exclusivistically attached to whatever transcends them. Somewhat similarly, the 13th-century Abraham Abulafia, who can be read as universalizing the term *Hebrew* to refer to a spiritual category or a properly spiritual use of language, also saw a return to the conditions of the particular Biblical election narrative, namely a Jewish kingdom, as concordant with reason and human nature within the flux of history.[201]

Spinoza's argument, taken from Maimonides' *Guide for the Perplexed*, is that the Bible does not deny proximate causes (like the workings of reason and human nature which Abulafia so unproblematically brings up in this context) for Israel's election but can seem so because it tends to piously ascribe all things to the final cause, God.[202] These proximate causes are the striving for a thing which nonetheless, *seen from above*, one is being *chosen* for. (From above and, really, from *within*, *globally*, with *cleansed doors of perception*, yet this means that one is not being chosen from without but from within, for when the doors of perception are cleansed the perceiver itself is revealed as a manifestation of God—a creature is God's will to be that creature.)

This turns the political form of Biblical election into a participative possibility which is in some sense chosen and not just given, one chooses as well as being chosen. We could go so far as to say that even the great renewal of cycles and return of the Golden Age that Hindu and Hesiodic theogony foretells does not occur unless the subjectivities that compose the world chose it. Although, even if they are not yet aware of it, they will choose it or have already chosen it, for the prophecies that attest to this draw on a perspective outside time. But, counter-wise, in the case of specific religious prophecy we need to beware of speculative and dogmatic accretion, given its politically tempting character and especially as it can lead us to miss the imminence of theophanic *choosing*: The Spirit gives life, the letter kills (2 Corinthians 3:6). Prayer can come true in unexpected ways and prophetic realizations may turn out to be more accommodating

---

200   Baruch Spinoza, *Theological-Political Treatise* (Cambridge: Cambridge University Press, 2017), "On the Vocation of the Hebrews, and Whether the Prophetic Gift Was Peculiar to Them," 13, 56.

201   In any case Abulafia, unlike Spinoza, does at some point refer to the superiority of Israel over other nations.

202   Spinoza might go too far in de-emphasizing final causes by presenting them as rhetorical/perspective-dependent in the Bible.

of history, more flexible, than the more purist dogmas of a tradition would have allowed for.[203] That this should result in a pluralistic theology of election makes sense if we realize that we have here something like the Bhavas of Vaishnavism and the widespread doctrine of God revealing Himself in terms of how we approach Him, and in a form appropriate for us as part of our paradoxical *participation*, which is His mercy.

In the case of Biblical theology, the binary according to which humanity is divided between Mosaic law and Noachide law, or Jew and Gentile, and in which the former in principle manifests a superior piety, gives way to a vision according to which a plurality of projects are conceived as playing out within humanity, and the followers of Mosaic law manifest a specific *kind* of piety rather than necessarily a higher *degree* of piety.

Thus, Jewish and Christian traditions that understand Biblical election as a nation's spiritual superiority over others correspond to what can be described as metaphysical chauvinism. This is perhaps partly identifiable with the seventh century BC reforms of King Josiah as already discussed, contrasting with the earlier version of the faith whose adherents joined Babylonians and took refuge in Arabian and southern Egyptian temples after those reforms. It has also manifested to destructive effect in violently iconoclastic sects of Christianity.

The above contradicts a tendency among modern Christian theologians to criticize supersessionism by emphasizing the exclusivity and historicity of election, rather than its archetypal and allegorical meaning (which can easily accommodate and preserve the historical specifics of scripture as well, albeit altering these in the spirit of the Gospel teaching that the Sabbath is made for man and not man for the Sabbath). Such criticisms are frequently directed at the use of election-language by modern nation-states and the historical tendency of Protestant monarchs to couch disengagement from the Papacy in Old Testament covenantal terms, but their logic is often such as to exclude election-language from any context other than national Israel. We encounter an example of this tendency in a book review by David Bentley Hart:

> a proper biblical appreciation of the everlasting uniqueness of Israel's covenant serves to expose as damnably false the misappropriation of the language of election by many a modern nation-state.[204]

Both the view that election-language should be applied only to one particular and the view that it should only be applied to the Church in its universal aspect miss the possibility that *particularity itself* is being blessed

---

203 An example is the theological translation we have discussed. One case of this might be an Ethiopian prince who sees himself as part of Abraham and Jacob's lineage through king Solomon, but sees his Jerusalem as Axum. In his understanding, there is no need to return to Zion for he is already there.

204 David Bentley Hart, "Church and Israel after Christendom: The Politics of Election." www.firstthings.com, retrieved February 18th 2018.

by scripture—not the particularity of a particular group and not the universal without reference to the particular, but *particularity in each particular*—the epiphany that each part is indeed a microcosm, is indeed a whole.

A strict restriction of election-language to a single community risks desensitizing Christian theology to the promise prophet Isaiah (19:25) countenances when he describes enemy polities with titles usually reserved for Israel (Egypt becomes the Lord's people, Assyria His handiwork, Israel His inheritance). Election-language is being appropriated for these nations by a Biblical prophet. The Israel to which all three epithets belonged is not the Israel mentioned but some broader universal Church that includes Egypt, Assyria and the nation of Israel. The same also occurs in Jeremiah (48:46–47), according to which the children of Moab will be carried away into captivity, like those of Israel, but thereafter Moab's fortunes will be restored. This is consistent with the already referenced passage from John's Apocalypse (21:24), and the image of nations being within the twelve gates identified with the twelve tribes of Israel, that is, within election and beyond curse (22:2–3). It reminds us of the teaching that there are many places in the Father's house (John 14:2).

The Bible seems to teach that the sons of God assigned to guide the nations began receiving idolatrous worship from these. Such would correspond to a form of state-worship and sacrifices that the Biblical narrative is keen to dissociate from Davidic monarchy. In the former, the theophanic function of the king is replaced by a false theophany, a possessing entity, so that he no longer represents the divine, mediating to his people. Then the angel of a nation, a son of God, in Biblical terms, is said to have fallen, which we may understand as producing a false double (as St. Dionysius does not blame the ministering angels for the straying of nations into pagan idolatry). A once lofty station becomes a parodying interloper of what was, and remains, though occluded, the legitimate archetype. The conversion of a deity or ancestral spirit, such as Hachiman becoming a Buddhist in Japan, or identifying Amaterasu with the cosmic Buddha Vairocana, can be interpreted as linking up the particular to the universal, restoring the brokenness of the particular.

Whatever the nations of humanity manifest, it endures in their kings entering Jerusalem in the Apocalypse, in their being a multiple of the gates of Jerusalem, in the very structure of the holy city. The relinquishing of their crowns suggests the end of the state as it has come to be historically. The mediating role enjoyed by these is now purified of idolatry, and in this sense is abolished. We might link this to the promise to Abraham that his seed will be as the stars. In the ancient world, stars were often presented as reigning divinities. In Christianity, patron saints take on functions of angelic intelligences and pagan gods. We may interpret the coming about of saintly patronage over nations, professions and so on as already an eschatological transformation.

It should be noted that such a position is consistent with the Biblical story that introduces the name of Israel. Jacob is not his family's firstborn and therefore not the primary heir to his father's and grandfather's estate, yet he inherits the main of it, that is, of the Lord's promises to Abraham. The theme of inheritance falling to one who was not expected to inherit is ubiquitous in the Bible. Further, Jacob receives the name Israel after wrestling with the angel of the Lord. It is thus a title given to him as a result of his actions. That the history of the Gospel should have consisted of the outsider inheriting the Biblical mission and attaining to the title of Israel as a result of faith would therefore seem consistent with the Biblical ethos, and the principle of the first becoming the last (Matthew 20:16). Just as St. Irenaeus's language (quoted before) in *Against the Heresies* (III) implies, dispersal (from Adam) is a creative coming forth, even if the subject experiences it as a sort of death, and is a universal experience.

To reject the application of Biblical epithets assigned to Israel outside a single, literal national entity is approximately to reject the tradition of the early church and to do so not in an Orthodox (allegorizing) and non-literalistic manner, but just the opposite. Even if what is rejected is only the application of these epithets to particulars, abrogating them for the universal Church exclusive, this position also should be mitigated.

It further risks dialectic inversion, where the emphasis on distinction leads to its necessary effacement, specifically conflating the universal with the particular (treating Israel's Biblical election as so profound a distinction that it constitutes the proper as opposed to improper relationship with God, as Origen does, requires that it be universalized and therefore undone).

Awareness of this dialectic and its dangers is important in navigating prevalent issues of cultural diversity and identity. The temptation to equate the particular with the universal is a difficult thing to resist in the context of legitimately critiquing destructive sorts of relativism. The dilemma and analytic horizon to which the preceding discussion is oriented may be expressed as follows, using the example of language: to articulate what language should do (allow the human intellect to interface with objective reality and communicate this) without forgetting the ultimately necessary-yet-arbitrary nature of any *particular* language and therefore without stigmatizing some in favor of others.

MEDIEVAL EMPIRE AND THE ECUMENE

The Holy Roman Empire and the Biblical Concept of Israel: From "Against the Nations" to Encompassing the Nations

The name Israel can refer both to a certain nation and to *wrestling with the Lord* and *election through exile*. The latter sense is realized in the ecumenic vision and can find expression in an imperial articulation. Here the conceptual Israel in Biblical terms can pass from a particularism set aside from that of the nations to a sanctity capable of encompassing multiple particularisms. We may address this as it occurs in the history of European Christendom, although we will deal with European civilization in its ecumenic dimension later on as well. While outside the purview Jan Assman understands as its natural polytheistic context, this presents a foundational case of *theological translation*, one that incorporates Biblical paradigms into the Roman context rather than an extension of such a translation to non-Christians, so that Assman's central claim remains approximately, historically valid.

With exceptions, in the Bible the nations or peoples (*Ethne* in Greek, *Goyim* in Hebrew) is a concept indexed to Israel (just as "you" is indexed to the subject denoting it, for, to itself that 'you' is an 'I'). When St. Thomas Aquinas writes *Contra Gentiles*, for example, the term gentile refers to those outside Christianity or the Catholic Church, so that the latter occupies the perspective of Biblical Israel. The Spanish philosopher Gustavo Bueno would describe the nation as an *oblique* rather than *straight* concept, one with clear reference to something other. We can describe the thrust of Biblical scripture and its historical uses as one which takes *Israel* from a category against the nations to one encompassing of them. This movement is towards a conception with parallels in other traditions, such as in China: "The *t'ien-hsia* is organized as a manifold of *kuo*, while the *kuo* recognize themselves as parts of the ecumene."[205]

The nation-states of political modernity initially defined themselves by rejecting the Catholic Church and Holy Roman Empire. The nation-state can however, make allowances for the former, tolerating catholic subjects or citizens (indeed, some popes have considered loyalty to local rulers to be almost as important as religious faithfulness, to the point that in 1832 Pope Gregory XVI's *Cum Primum* encyclical, for example, condemned Polish insurrection against Tsarist imposition of Russian Orthodoxy). But it cannot do the same in the case of the Empire, whose very existence as a political structure theoretically contradicts that of the nation-state (though not of the nation).

It may be argued that the Holy Roman Empire was simply its own political entity, alike others, but this is not in keeping with the nature of Empire. In principle, Empire is hierarchically above regents, but still integrating them politically.

Eventually, the Church would grow hostile to symbols of Adamic unity between the sacerdotal and regal authority. On the one hand, we have Papal opposition to emperors like Charles V, and on the other, the view that politics itself is to be treated as a transitory element of fallen humanity, a doctrinal possibility always latent in the Church but which at some point clearly led clergymen to doubt the point of having an emperor at all (and what modern Catholic theologian or priest calls for the return of

---

205   Voegelin, *Order and History, vol. 4, The Ecumenic Age*, 361.

that figure or seriously discusses its theological import?). The Papacy often stood on the same side as nation-states (be they absolutist monarchists or Protestant princes and later republics) against the common foe of Empire.

But in western Europe, the Holy Roman Empire was functionally Israel. We may consider the imperial crown. Writes Habsburg expert Eva Demmerle:

> Our ancestors could still "read" the Imperial Crown and recognise its deep symbolism. It is a "glorious sign" of the firm connection between the sacred and the secular, between rex et sacerdos, king and priest, as with the coronation, the ruler was also ordained a deacon. The octagonal form of the crown refers to the Augustinian vision of the world Sabbath, when humanity will celebrate the eternal eighth day in union with the Divine Glory. The arrangement of each stone and each bead relates to the biblical texts, and the number of beads (240) and stones (120) are each a multiple of twelve. The stones on the front plate are a faithful copy of the stones on the breast plates of the Old Testament priests as described in the second book of Moses.[206]

The connection is also made explicit through the use of Biblical symbolism related to Davidic monarchy, such as the Tree of Jesse on the window of Chartres Cathedral and explicit pronouncements in the *Codex Carolinus* to the same effect. As has been documented in other traditions, royalty is linked to the tree. Chartres Cathedral was built during the Capetian dynasty, harkening back to their Merovingian and Carolingian precursors, as well as to Biblical precedent, also referencing, as the tinted window does, the events of the Crusade of the 1140s.[207] It evidences what Ernst Kantorowicz calls the medieval ruler cult, which in western Europe would begin with the anointing of Pépin, father of Charlemagne.

Of course, Emperor Constantine was technically emperor of the west as well as the east, so that, in a Christian context, he would have been the first to represent the ruler cult, albeit not yet mediaeval, but already Christian. Constantine had himself buried among twelve sarcophagi representing those apostles, as though he were a viceregent of Christ.

But, notwithstanding Constantinian precursors, at Chartres Pépin's anointing is presented as alike that of Old Testament kings, and the consequent ruler cult centers on the Franks, who were strikingly referred to by the Holy See as the "new sacred people of promise" in the *Codex Carolinus* (11, III, 505).[208] The *Codex Carolinus* uses metaphors in which

---

206 Eva Demmerle, "The Imperial Crown: Witness of the Occident." In: *The European Conservative*, 21.
207 James R. Johnson, "The Tree of Jesse Window of Chartres: Laudes Regiae." In: *Speculum*, 36 (1961): 1–22, 20.
208 Quoted in Erns Kantorowicz, *Laudes Regiae: A study in liturgical acclamation and medieval ruler worship* (Berkley: University of California Press, 1958), 56.

the Emperor is described as image of Christ (being anointed, where Christ is *the* Anointed). Consistent with this, Charlemagne was described as *Rex et Sacerdos* by Rome's bishops[209] and as King David, where his biographer Bezaleel is named the "man of talent," a title taken from Exodus (31).[210] Another outstanding example of the sacred status perceived in the Franks occurs in the Song of Roland, which mentions the king blessing people in the name of Jesus and in his own name.[211] In a sense this points to the baptizing of the secular sphere.

We may also refer to Pope Gregory's pronouncements, in the context of Frederick II's rule, concerning the lofty role of the Emperor, for apparently "[b]efore the great breach, Pope Gregory had written that God had installed the Emperor as a Cherub...as a token of resemblance to the only-begotten Son."[212] We have here a kind of Christology after Christ and sacred enculturation. The Holy Empire is included in Christology, so that the Emperor was a cherubic image of likeness of the Son, where the Christ might be thought of as the mast and highest point of the ship and the Empire as its wave breaking prow, the most forward portion, or, where He is the word, the Emperor is the echo.

The Empire precluded nation-states but included nations. There are medieval European sources in which nations are described as being part of the Empire, which finds its logic in the Christian doctrine of the Church or spiritual Israel including different nations and in the pagan conception of, for example, Julian the Apostate for whom the Roman Empire did likewise, as quoted by Jean Danielou:

> Our writers say that the Demiurge is the father of all men and their common king. He has divided the peoples among various gods, whose business it is to watch over the different nations and cities.... Every nation reproduces the natural characteristics of the deity ruling it.[213]

It may also find thematic support in that the Biblically elected Israel is internally diverse, being composed of twelve tribes.

This is the essential and most descriptive meaning of the word *nation*, devoid of autonomous political structure as correlate, where it does not require a state delineated by itself necessarily excluding the possibility of an overarching structure such as the Empire. The Bible often uses the term goyim/ethne to denote theological error (the *gentile* as infidel, which is the sense in which St. Thomas Aquinas uses it as well). In European terms, this is the meaning which falls upon the nation-state and not nationality as such. Just as a pattern or paradigm described

---

209   Johnson, "The Tree of Jesse Window of Chartres," 5.
210   Ibid., 13.
211   Ibid., 5.
212   Kantorowicz, *Frederick the Second*, 199.
213   Danielou, *Origen*, 226–27.

in scripture (such as the nation of Israel) may be applied to different contexts without forcing the original literal context upon these, so too later applications ought not rip former ones (ought not problematizing that original context's continuance). Further, as has been established, Europe constitutes a historically consistent concept, from the ancient Greeks and *Genesis Apocryphon* to modernity.

The European concept of Roman Empire, be it Classical or medieval, is different from the ecumenism of the Bronze Age Aegean and Near East as previously discussed. Whereas thinkers from Julian the Apostate to Dante refer to a diversity of nations within a universal empire, Bronze Age polities lacked that overarching structure, although even here Mesopotamian monarchy (with its Sumerian, Akkadian mystique) included the title *king of kings* (overarching authority) and was considered normative and imitated by courtrooms like the Minoan, so perhaps there was a sense of international Empire. It should also be noted that the Holy Roman Emperor was not a national regent but was elected. He therefore did not represent one nation's dominance over another: not the unity of nations at the level of nationhood but unity at the level of another more encompassing non-national principle of authority.

True, the emperor was almost always considered a descendant of Aeneas the Trojan, but Troy was not an existent European nation. Rather it was a widespread and scattered regal line whose claimants and possible heirs were abundant in various parts of Europe. Thus, Trojan descent as bolstering one's claim to Holy emperorship represented a form of European transnationalism (Trojan descent is a specifically European theme in the pseudo-histories) comparable to Hashemite status in the Muslim world (descent from Prophet Muhammad's grandfather Hashim). This may also be the meaning of that supposed (though disputed) robust polygamy practiced by Hasan, Muhammad's grandson via Ali (the latter being the prophet's son in law, husband to his daughter Fatima, fourth rightly-guided Caliph to the Sunni and first legitimate Caliph to the Shia).

By exceeding the normative maximum of four wives, Hasan produced a widespread possibility of Hashemite status, especially (but by no means exclusively) in the Arab world. In any case, whether via Hasan or not, there exists ample distribution of a feature which, although not a requisite, could add legitimacy to bids for Caliphal authority. In both the Trojan and Hashimite case, power is linked to lineage but not to nationality and, therefore, becomes supra-national and can avoid the sense of national domination and grievance. These formulas retain human community's basis in kinship while building up an international cupula.

The contention that entering the Biblical narrative required gentiles to become circumcised and learn Hebrew would have represented an *equivalent and opposite error* to the (literalistic and often Protestant) support for the nation-state against the Empire. The former mistake is equivalent to a person thinking that in order to peacefully interact with someone else this latter must be assimilated and the latter is like organs within a body conceiving of their integrity as requiring exit from the body.

As an aside: some of what has been said here concerning the accommodation of the nation within a universalistic vision could be said about modern political projects, such as Soviet Marxism. In Leninist and Stalinist conceptions of nationality, Marxist internationalism embraces the nation. However, rather than seeing it as a structurally mediating entity between smaller units such as the family and the total ecumene, in Marxism, the nation's mediation is collapsed into historical, chronological terms. The nation is tolerated, but as a temporary stepping stone to the future borderless collectivity. This is fitting, as Marxism is historicist and immanentizes the eschaton, that is, it treats universality as the annulment of the particular, treating the stratospheric universal as terrestrial reality: universality as uniformity, not as harmony. In any case, the development of modern ideological conceptions of the ecumene, both Marxist and liberal, would be a topic in itself.

The Fractal Empire, or It's Empires All the Way Down (and Up)

We continue exploring the imperial idea in medieval European Christendom. The ecumenical worldview requires that we not transgress with our particularity that which is particular in others, usurping for ourselves the agglutinating role of genuine universals. We may look to European history for examples of retaining, defending and articulating particularity in the context of grander wholes, so that neither part nor whole is denied. Specifically, we may attempt to find in the term Empire a meaning subversive of imperialism by treating part as microcosm of whole, or kingdom of empire in medieval European terms:

> The early thirteenth-century Italian lawyer Azo of Bologna claimed each king was "an emperor in his own kingdom" (*rex imperator in regno suo est*).... England's King John claimed in 1202 that the "kingdom of the English can be compared to an empire"... the crime lese-majeste, previously reserved to protect the emperor, was increasingly employed to defend kings...[214]

It is important that "[i]nitially these arguments were directed primarily at strengthening royal authority within each kingdom, rather than challenging the Holy Roman emperor's pre-eminence."

Spain provides an interesting example. Although some medieval Spanish monarchs had described themselves as *Emperors of all Spain*, this title dispensed with the original universality of the term *Empire*, serving instead to assert a particular unity, that of Spain proper, microcosmically manifesting the same principle as wider *empires*.

---

214   Peter Wilson, *Heart of Europe: A History of the Holy Roman Empire*, 170.

In the twelfth century *Poem of Almeria* recounting the taking of the southern city of Almeria from Islamic authorities by King Alfonso VII, the nation of the Asturians is mentioned, but in the context of its being part of the emperor's dominion and army. Alfonso VII ruled the Spanish territories of Castile, Leon and Galicia, which included Asturias, and used the title *Emperor of all Spain*.

The justification for this desire to rule *all Spain*, and for the Spanish *Reconquista* against Muslim *al-Andalus*, was to recompose the 586 Visigothic *kingdom* of Spain, which in turn inherited the old Roman Hispania.[215] This is what historians call the *neo-gothic ideal*.[216] The term denotes the tendency to pursue or take for granted a united *Hispania*, articulated in St. Isidore's seventh-century histories of the Visigothic Kingdom of Toledo, "*Hispaniae Regnum*," before the kingdoms of Castile and Aragon had even come about.[217] We find this theme in the *Codex Albeldensis* (compiling material from antiquity to the 10th century) and the early 10th century of the *Chronicle of Alfonso III*, which refer to the lost kingdom of Spain, to which we may add a series of fragmentary melancholic medieval songs around the theme of the lost Spain (politically, the Visigothic kingdom).[218]

---

215 Consisting of two, and later three Roman provinces, all referred to as being Hispanian, an adjective used to designate its people generally (as in the work of the AD 4th c. Latinus Pacatus Drepanius, who praised Hispania, in the singular, as motherland of Emperor Theodosius I and loveliest of Roman regions). Just as medieval Spanish kingdoms attempted to recover the united Spain of the Visigoths, each under its aegis, so too prior attempts to recover the peninsular order of Roman Hispania included not only the Visigoths but also the Suebian kingdom of the northwest (Galicia).

216 Marco S. Quesado, *Diccionario de civilización y cultura españolas* (Madrid: ISTMO, 1997), 236.

217 Already in the late sixth, early seventh century, St. Isidore of Seville has a robust sense of Spanish nationhood, as well as a strong allegiance to the Visigoths (Saint Isidore of Seville, *Isidori Hispalensis Historia Gothorum, Vandalorum, Suevorum* [Tubingae: Litteris Schrammianis, 1803], 34). On this, Claudio Sanchez Albornoz's *Spain: A Historical Enigma*, and related works by that historian are perhaps the best source. We may even speculate an Islamic version of this in the trajectory of the Hispano-Gothic clan of the Banu Qasi, whose alliances with their Christian cousins, rivalry with the Arab Umayyads and later Berber Almoravids, and pretension to political leadership, would in some ways be equivalent to the Christian Reconquista treating the *Hispaniae Regnum* as precedent for their project. I am thinking, for example, of Musa Ibn Musa Ibn Qasi, self-proclaimed third king of Spain (*tertius regem d'Isbaniya*) who fought the other two: the Umayyad Muslim lord of Córdoba and the king don Ordoño of Asturias. His victory would have reunified Spain under a Visigoth (although his branch of the Banu Qasi can also lay claim to descent from the third caliph, Uthman, and Musa was one-eighth Arab).

218 The popular conception expressed through medieval songs reminds us that the Reconquista was the military expression of a demographic *Repoblamiento*. The two phenomena are not easily parsed, given that the military push was undergone largely by popular militias. Andalusians, for example, largely descend from northern settlers; eastern Andalusians from Aragonese, western from Leonese, roughly. This process is amply documented, among others, by Claudio Sanchez Albornoz. Modern

It appears in the epic poems of Fernan Gonzalez, el Cid and Jaime I. It is brought together in the 13th-century *Histories of Spain* produced by Alfonso X.

Thus, the *Reconquista* emerges as historical project *cum* hero cycle around the mythic theme of the recovery of a lost kingdom. According to this theme, the Visigothic capital of Toledo was founded by Hercules in ancient times, and was lost because a Gothic king, *Ricaredo*, did not honor the mystery of the caves and secrets installed there by Hercules, where the table of Solomon (with its link to the Holy Grail) was also said to be kept, so that the reconquest of Hispania is a purgative struggle to become worthy of the holy cave/grail, manifesting historico-politically in the restoration of the original kingdom of Toledo, as invoked by Queen Isabel explicitly when she and her husband took Granada, the last Muslim stronghold in Spain, in 1492.

And just as the Reconquista discloses this higher, spiritual principle, it has a wider, political context as well. *Hispania* was part of the Roman Empire. Gothic Spain, *Hispania Gothorum*, was initially a province of the new Rome with its capital at Constantinople. Spain was not the Empire, but a unit within the Empire, and insofar as it was described as itself an Empire, this constituted a pluralization of the term to designate both the macrocosm and microcosms.

The 13th-century Alfonso X, king of Castile and Leon, whom the historian Robert S. Lopez compares to Frederick II, suggesting he was a deeper thinker (and who was the great grandson of Frederick Barbarossa, thereby related to Frederick II), put in a bid for Holy Roman Emperorship. In his elaborate *Partidas*, he lays out a legal structure for the Empire which retains the integrity of its sub-units or kingdoms. We cannot but interpret this in the light of his History (*Estoria*) of Spain, where king Alfonso (and his court scholars) follows *Jubilees*, St. Jerome and St. Isidore in discussing how Europeans descend from Japheth and Spaniards specifically from Tubal, son of Japheth. Here, Spain is too much a particular community to be conceived of as replacing the Holy Roman Empire. Alfonso seems to be moving in the direction of Spain's political integration with the Empire (a vision Charles V's project would fulfill centuries later).

If a *translatio* of emperorship to Spain's monarchy is being suggested in the Partidas, it cannot be simplistically thought of as effacing the particularity of Spain as national community, in terms of which Spain cannot become the *Empire* as such, in universal terms. In line with this, 15th-century political theorists in Spain, such as Alfonso of Cartagena, distinguished between kingdom and Empire, where Empire is a

genetic studies confirm this east-west clinal spread in the peninsula. Columns of northern Christians thusly replaced Moorish colonists (although some *Moriscos*, Moorish converts to Christianity, remained to be later expelled by Philip III, who accused them of acting as a fifth column for the Ottoman Empire by harboring a support network for Ottoman piracy).

coordination of kingdoms or states, not itself a kingdom or state. Likewise, the term *Empire* was later reserved for Charles V's Holy Roman Empire, to be distinguished from Spain, of which he was king Charles I.

In the modern era, however, patriotism often becomes nostalgia for Empire, betraying itself thereby. His rejection of the scientism of 19th- and 20th-century European culture at one point led the Basque Spanish author Miguel de Unamuno, for example, to identify his country not with Europe but with its former Empire. Identifying Spain with its global Empire, then, is to identify her with the coordinating action among certain states. It ignores the "thick" account of identity found in St. Isidore, Alfonso X, Isabel's declaration of restoration of the kingdom of Toledo with the taking of Granada, and the fractal meaning of empire.

This renders Spain no longer kingdom, state or nation. Rather than a form, it becomes the harmony between forms. In the same way that radical supersessionism in Christian theology can lead to the idea that the particular, national Israel is abolished in favor of a universal Israel, so too thinking of a nation as a general, abstract principle of Empire effaces its particularity. I do not mean to attack the idea that the *Hispanidad* (the Spanish-speaking world) should be made a politically actual reality, as well as a transnational identity, only that its proper expression cannot be the confusion of nation with empire. Modern *Hispanistas* who argue that Spain is not Spain, but only a part thereof, for the nation known by this name must include the Americas,[219] are engaging in the very modern, liberal conflation of empire, or commonwealth, with nation.

Apart from a category error, this contradicts the empire's actual legacy and its preservation of indigenous identity (from the semi-autonomous *Indian Republics*, to making native languages co-official with Spanish in the viceregencies where these were spoken). The quasi-medieval character of what became the Spanish empire explains why its overseas territories were not made into colonies with inferior rights to Spain,[220] such that Lima and Mexico City were soon richer than any Iberian city:

---

219   As is the case of Marcelo Gullo Omodeo, *Madre Patria*, 3rd ed. (Barcelona: Espasa, 2021).

220   Culturally, there were policy measures to preserve local cultural forms, in line with Vitoria's recommendations. Catholic clergy grammaticized the indigenous Quechua and Nahuatl languages. In 1575, the viceroy of Peru, Francisco de Toledo, decreed that Aimara, Quechua and Puquina were to be "lenguas mayores" or co-official, in modern terms (Puquino was probably being replaced by the former two, as it was never grammaticized the way the others were, in spite of this decree). Neither is the *demographic* colonialism carried out by Spain comparable to that which went on in North America. Peninsular Spanish population seems to have remained relatively stable over the centuries following the discovery of America. Which is not to say that a large *mestizo* and smaller politically-privileged European-descended population did not come about in the Americas. But it was the result of a small amount (relative to British expansion in North America) of Spaniards moving to the Americas. According to the relevant Spanish archive (*Archivo de Indias* according

> ... an analysis of fiscal data at regional levels ... shows the existence
> of massive revenue redistribution within the colonies, disputing
> the notion of a predatory extractive empire based on endowments
> as the source of original inequality.[221]

It also explains why the very notion of imperial expansion was put on trial early on. The 1550–1551 debates at the Junta of Valladolid included speakers who argued against conquest. King Charles stopped expansion while theologians debated and generally was not inclined towards the American project. This resulted in the laws of Burgos (or *Indias*) and their articulation of the rights of the natives over their land and states, drawing on the same tradition that had led Isabel and Fernando to temporarily imprison Christopher Columbus for his alleged ill-treatment of the natives of Hispaniola.

Philip II would later issue a 1573 *Decree on Discoveries and Pacifications* according to which the word conquest was to be banished, and all further pacifications of America were to take place "peacefully and with utmost charity." The term pacification was compatible with his role as coordinator of states, whereas "conquest" was not. The latter meant Spain was expanding itself, rather than correcting the behavior of others. He also ordered that Spaniards committing crimes against natives be punished more severely than if their crime was committed against a fellow Spaniard.

King Philip, under whose rule Nahuatl became co-official with Spanish in the viceregency of New Spain, just as Quechua and Aymara were in that of Peru, was concerned not to abrogate existing state structures. Whereas he did attempt to bar natives from membership in certain knightly orders, a measure the Pope prevented, and by the 1640s his successors had disallowed them from various careers[222] (some of these restrictions had been put in place prior to Philip II[223]), he simultaneously held to a

---

to Elvira Roca Barea), 45,327 Christians (Spaniards and also others departing from Spain) went to the Americas in the 16th century, of which 10,128 were women. A robust indigenous and partly-indigenous population was maintained. Following Angel Rosenblat's studies, the current population of indigenous people in central and south America is larger than in 1492, to which we may add peoples who are *partly* native-descended. In general, it was difficult to find people willing to go to the Americas, and Spanish policy itself restricted the flow because one had to be going for some specific productive purpose, not merely as a settler, and marine training was difficult. We may speculate that those willing to make the jump were frequently likely not to have a stable position or promising prospects at home, and were therefore unlikely to have the resources to prove their purpose in going to the New World was in fact productive.

221   Regina Grafe and Maria Alejandra Irigoin, "The Spanish Empire and its legacy: fiscal redistribution and political conflict in colonial and post-colonial Spanish America," *Journal of Global History* 1(2) (July 2006): 241–67.

222   Bartolomé Bennassar, *La América española y la América portuguesa siglos XVI-XVIII* (Madrid: Biblioteca de Ensayo, 2001), 208.

223   There had also been a ban on intermarriage between Spaniards in certain positions and local women, set off by an earlier viceregent of Peru, the Count of Nievas.

structure in which indigenous people from autonomous republics could have aristocratic status and in which the rights of mestizos, including the illegitimate sons of Hernan Cortes, were fully recognized.

He was particularly adamant that the Incan state be preserved, imposing a demerit upon viceroy Francisco de Toledo for executing Tupac Amaru I, and writing to the royal Sayri Tupac in 1552 forgiving Incan rebellions, admitting local Spaniards were to blame, and promising never to appoint a Spaniard to rule over Vilcabamba, which would remain under native authority. Similarly, when it was suggested to him that Castilian be made the official language in the kingdom of the Two Sicilies in order to facilitate communication, Philip refused, answering that it was his duty to retain the culture and structure of those states under his rule.

Moving on from the 16th century, despite their problematic aspects, certain modern nation states present us with a recurrence of older structures compatible with a wider identity. In this sense, the Fractal Empire or Ecumenism can conquer even political modernity. Italy, for example, provides a case study for how the emergence of an identity into political prominence can occur within a sense of the greater whole. In the context of Napoleon III's rule, the Italian struggle for political and national self-definition assumes the ecumenic/imperial idea, however degraded. After supporting a Sicilian peasant revolt, Giuseppe Garibaldi, father of modern Italian unity, rode upon and greeted his opponents on the battlefield and called out to hail the king of Italy, as he designated Charles Albert of Sardinia, who was leading the other side. Garibaldi thereby sacrificed republicanism to nationalism, all while being supported by Napoleon III. Here, a local national aspiration finds itself restrained by—but in a sense finally manifested in—the figure of a king, while resting in the framework of a transnational imperial structure.

The cliché that a united Italy comes about only in the context of political modernity in 1861 ignores the extent to which Italian unity was operant in the minds of people before Garibaldi, from constituting a unit within the Roman Empire to king Theodoric and the early modern Cola di Rienzo. The Roman administrative unit of Italy and the Ostrogoth's fifth and sixth century *Regnum Italiae* are the obvious and oldest precedents. The Ostrogoth king Theodoric the Great ruled over Italy and other territories and was a *patricius* of the Roman Empire. Theodoric had replaced Odoacer, previous king of Italy, at the behest of (Byzantine) Emperor Zeno. He also ruled the Visigothic kingdom of Spain after 511 (the *praefectura praetorio Hispaniarum*). He was devoted to classical Roman culture and his Kingdom of Italy was not a national project at odds with a broader, imperial project.

John Norwich refers to a similar project in the later Frederick II, Holy Roman Emperor between 1215 and 1250:

Like virtually all the Hohenstaufen, he had a dream of making
Italy and Sicily a united kingdom within the Empire, with its
capital at Rome; the overriding purpose of the papacy, aided by
the cities and towns of Lombardy, was to ensure that that dream
should never be realized.[224]

In the first half of the 1300s the eccentric Cola di Rienzo, tribune
and senator of Rome, had attempted to unite Italy by extending Roman
citizenship to all Italian cities and was even recognized as an authority
in the Kingdom of Naples. Di Rienzo would inspire artists for centuries.
There is a recurrence of ancient motifs associated with sacred monarchy
in Byron's poetic tribute of di Rienzo, *Childe Harold's Pilgrimage* (Canto
IV: CXIV), from the femininity of the body politic, analogue of the
Church as Bride ("turn we to her Tribune's name") to the arboreal symbol
("Freedom's wither'd trunk puts forth a leaf") and even a remembrance
of the religious provenance of Rome by way of that Pythagorean initiate
who received runes upon a shield from Jove, king Numa Pompilius ("Her
new-born Numa thou!"). Later, Richard Wagner dedicated an opera to
depicting di Rienzo as a Romantic hero.

Di Rienzo's allegiance was to medieval tradition, writing a favorable
commentary on Dante's *de Monarchia* and identifying with Holy Roman
Emperorship (even claiming Emperor Henry VII was his father) but in
a mode that embraced and transformed modern republican and civic
ideas. This is consistent with the fact that even Roman republicanism
was never really broken with by Caesar Augustus, and that Holy Roman
Emperors like the Hohenstaufen (as well as their Anjou rivals) harkened
back to it (consider Frederick II's teaching Roman law in the University
of Naples and his son Manfred's *Manifesto*).

Di Rienzo's initiative might have been spurred on partly by the Papacy's
protracted absence from Italy. When it returned to Rome from France,
national feeling once again articulated itself in the cries of "Romano lo
volemo, o almanco italiano!," by which the city's populace made it known
that they wanted the next pope to be Roman, or at least Italian. They
settled in the end for Pope Urban VI, high pontiff until 1389. That the
Romans felt themselves reflected in this Neapolitan archbishop of Bari
is supported by the fact that their rioting ceased, reveals their Italian
national feeling. It is also highlighted by protestations on the part of
the French cardinals present at the selection process who, feeling themselves displaced, maintained that Urban VI was illegitimate because he
had been selected under the effective threat of Roman revolt, a violent
possibility which his being Italian had quashed (these cardinals went so
far as to schismatically select their own—technically antipope—Clement
VII, who was actually accepted in Naples and several parts of Europe).

---

224   John J. Norwich, *The Popes: A History* (London: Chatto and Windus, 2011), 186.

Centuries later, during the 1500s, the *risorgimento* was anticipated by Pope Clement VII, as John Julius Norwich writes in his *Four Princes*. Pope Clement VII's forming the League of Cognac with French king Francis I seems to have been intended to unite the Italic peninsula (contradicting the French king's Treaty of Madrid with Emperor Charles V and therefore representing a Catholic rather than Protestant subversion of the Holy Roman Empire in favor of the nation-state). Unlike Cola di Rienzo and Garibaldi's enterprises, this would have been a move towards Italian unity at odds, rather than organically within, grander imperial unity (if it was such a move at all).[225]

The Roman Empire itself had treated Italy as a single administrative unit, one that had the privilege of being the center of the state rather than a province like other territories. Spanning from the Alps to the southern coasts, it was organized into eleven subunits under Caesar Augustus, coming to include the islands of Corsica, Sardinia, Malta and Sicily at the end of the third century AD under Diocletian, and remaining united until the sixth century. According to Strabon's *Geographica*, the name of Italy may have originally been used by Greeks to refer specifically to the southern territory of Calabria and later by Romans to refer to everything south of the Rubicon river, so that Italy begins in the south, delineated by sea, and extends north. Indeed, one medieval view, expressed by St. Isidore of Seville in his *Etymologies*, had it that the name Italy originated with a certain king of the Sicilians called *Italus*.[226] From its precedent during the Roman Empire to the later search for a return to Italian unity, and from Theodoric the Great's becoming king of Italy because Emperor Zeno requested it, to di Rienzo's support of the Holy Roman Empire and Garibaldi's support of Napoleon III, Italian nationhood and statehood was historically neither naval-gazing nor opposed to a sense of a broader ecumenic wholesomeness. The nineteenth century emergence of Italian nationalism or unionism was, therefore, more a revolving back to a prior state than an anti-historical revolution.

Thus, in the above we have examples of unitary conceptions of identity (seeking *political* unity) that recognize a larger unit beyond themselves. These should serve to illustrate the principle of ecumenic empire. They should also be taken as examples of a current in history worth highlighting. We are claiming a usage for the word *Empire* that is not related to colonial expansion, but refers instead to the medieval idea of regents as emperors inheriting the Roman order and translating it into a microcosm. As Wilson-Okamura notes, the "translation of Trojan"—*Roman*—"Empire, not the expansion," that is, an "imperium"

---

225   Not to deny that, in practice, final Italian unification proceeded as an annexation and impoverishment of the south (the two Sicilies).

226   St. Isidore of Seville, *Etymologies*, XIV.iv.18, 291.

that is "not that of ultramarine conquest."[227] It is a *little Ecumene*, but one which is corporeal, organic, internally differentiated and externally integrated into wider structures, so that politics and political institutions do not have a pre-defined hard and fast stoppage point, but can cross-cut these structures in a Baroque, medieval sort of way.

Importantly, just as the kingdom/nation can emerge within an empire, and empires can consist of parts that are each a microcosmic empire, constituting an *Empire of empires*, an *Israel of israels*, so too larger empires can exist within a wider harmony. The notion that empires succeeded each other but cannot be multiple, cannot constitute Voegelin's plural ecumenes, derived in Christian Europe from a reading of Daniel according to which "a succession of four 'world monarchies': Babylon, Persia, Macedonia and Rome" meant that "empire was singular and exclusive...[empires] could not coexist, but followed each other in a strict sequence that was epochal."[228] However historically valid this succession turned out to be, and however much leadership in world affairs tends to pass from polity to polity, the theological argument can be undermined by pointing to parallels between Daniel and Ezekiel. Both saw the Ancient of Days, but the beasts who stand for the four world monarchies in Daniel are, in Ezekiel, four cherubim. A higher order of things, then, outside the prophetic pattern that leads to the coming messiah (which is what Daniel is predicting) would allow for simultaneity, just as the four angelic creatures are together, below the Ancient of Days, implying coexistence is possible if there is subordination to God.

Nationalism as Index of a Failed Empire; Imperialism as Index of a Failed Nation

Nationalism here means the modern idea that a local cultural idiosyncrasy is a sufficient and legitimate basis on which to constitute a separate state and, more than this, a legitimate basis on which to construct a narrative according to which the local is not a part or expression of a wider whole, but is at odds with that whole, having a different essence. The Empire whose failure nationalism indicates is an ecumenic body, a fractal empire, and if nationalism is its failure, imperialism is its specter, the way rationalism is the specter of rationality, or the tyrannical ego is the specter of the true self.

The basis for a political unit precedes its parts and must be understood as previous to any specific political institution that expresses it. Milbank describes this as the supplement at the origin, after referring to a mystical consensus in unity, a shared horizon:

---

227   David Wilson-Okamura, *Virgil in the Renaissance* (Cambridge: Cambridge University Press, 2010), 223.
228   Peter Wilson, *Heart of Europe: A History of the Holy Roman Empire*, 38.

...it's not possible for the representative to be merely mandated
by the people, nor do you have the idea the representative is then
going to usurp the voice of the people and simply say what he
thinks. I think the problem—a lot of the crisis that we're seeing
today over populism—is because modern representation, if it's
not seen as mere mandation [merely mandating], tends to be very
usurping, and the people become extremely angry. But I think that
(I've been writing about this since *The Politics of Virtue*), I think that
right from the outset of modern thinking about politics in the
17th century onwards, there's been a tension between notions of
representation in the modern sense (that I've just been talking
about) on the one hand and notions of populist direct democracy on
the other hand. Particularly the idea that states should be founded
on a popular vote or else that representatives should be mandated.
You find this in early Whig politics in early modern England and
of course it's very, very important in the French Revolution. So,
I think that there's always been a tension between populism and
representative democracy. And I think this is suddenly coming to
the surface, and becoming much more intensified. I think populism
and direct democracy—I mean I believe in real local participatory democracy that's integrated with people's ordinary life, but I
distrust the idea of direct democracy, if you like for postmodern
reasons. Because the idea that the people is there before they've
represented themselves to themselves is an illusion. Think of
Derrida here and what he says about a supplement at the origin.
Representation is the supplement at the origin.[229]

It is neither the one nor the many—neither the univocity of the political leader and representative (king) nor the equivocity of the people—but
both or the ratio between, for the king's health indexes that of the kingdom and the kingdom is the king's body, to put it in archaic terms. We
return to the ratio, the metaxy, as center and, indeed, as origin: for it is
in this metaxy that the supplement Milbank refers to is found. It is not
the people as aggregate or the king who already articulates the people
as polity. If the people is the reflexive consciousness and the political
leader/representative is the image of being or unity reflected upon, then
they share the joy of self-discovery and self-externalization resultant of
reflecting upon one's own self, just as consciousness is always at a remove
from its own being and yet is made whole in the awareness of itself.
That which the people discover in their own political representation is
essentially an aesthetic vision: nationhood, with all its cultural particulars,
is an artistic rendering, and art is for the sake of joy. Where the body
is diverse and the mind is singular, there is also a mediating heart. The
metaxy is the balance between part and whole, or whole as composite
and whole as unitary principle. Broad imperial or ecumenical identity

---

229   John Milbank, "Interview with Carlos Perona," 16th March 2018.

should be pursued as a matter of principle that retains the particular.

This occurs in what is perhaps the earliest epic poem in Catalan, the "*Llibre dels Feits*" (Book of Deeds). Its first manuscript dates from the first half of the 14th century, and its authorship is attributed to the 13th-century king of Aragon (including Catalonia), Jaime I. The epic is narrated by the king in the first person. The monarch describes his father, former king of Aragon, as the "most generous king there ever was in Spain,"[230] relates accounts of an angelic apparition foretelling that he himself, Jaime I, would rally against the Muslims "so that evil does not befall Spain,"[231] boasts of his territories (specifically Catalonia) as lovelies in Spain,[232] and congratulates his men with the words "Worthy men, we can go now, for today all Spain is honored."[233] To the text's author and readers, neither Jaime's being regent of one particular part of Spain (Aragon), nor his proclamations in one of that portion's local languages (medieval Catalan), constituted any contradiction with respect to being part of Spain. In the Book of Deeds and these other works from the period,[234] Spain is not only geographic but is a political, religious and national category. Parts of the Iberian geography under Muslim rule are not considered Spain, or are so potentially and still must be taken by *Spain*.

Both centralism and the reaction against it (or, counter-wise, hostile localism and the reaction against this) endanger the above conception. Remaining in the land of the Book of Deeds, we may reflect on what came to be known as the Corpus de Sang, or *body of blood*, which met the Corpus Christi celebrations of 1640 Barcelona with bloody revolt. It was a reaction against the Count-Duke of Olivares' reforms under

---

230   Jaime I of Aragon, *Llibre dels Fets*, trans. D. Smith and H. Buffery (Ashgate: Farnham, 2010), Section 6, 21.

231   Ibid., Section 389, 291.

232   Ibid., Introduction by Damian Smith, 10.

233   Ibid., Section 535, 365.

234   Examples abould. In the 14th century, Bernat Descot records in his *Llibre del rei en Pere d'Arago e dels seus antecessors passats* that, during a French invasion, the Catalan barons told their king, Pedro III, that they desired to go meet this force in the battlefied rather than remain safely in their cities like merchants for, lest they bring shame and a bad name to "Spain's cavalry." On the pivotal battle of the Navas de Tolosa against an Islamic army, Desclot writes "On how the powerful Sarracen entered Spain, and how the three kings of Spain went to meet him and defeated the sarracens." Concerning such joint actions, the 13th/14th-century catalan Ramon Muntaner writes in his *Chronica o descripcio dels fets e hazanyes del inclyt Rey Don Jaume primer* that no power on earth could resist Spain's united monarchs, and that the kings of Spain "*son una carn e una sang*," are one flesh and one blood. Pere Tomich, a Catalan knight who wrote a general history of Catalonia in the 1400s presents the same conception of this region as part of Spain, and as having fought to recover Spain from the loss suffered centuries prior at the arrival of the Umayyad Caliphate's forces. And when the count of Barcelona went to meet the Holy Roman Emperor, he presented himself as *hun cavaller de Spanya*, a knight of Spain, and to the empress as *hun compte de Spanya a qui dien lo compte de Barcelona*, "a count of Spain whom they call count of Barcelona."

king Philip IV. Something of a famine was sweeping Iberia, and The Thirty Years' War was raging beyond France, but Castile, the region which contributed funds to central European war efforts, was exhausted. The Duke proposed something called "the union of arms," according to which other parts of Philip IV's domain would begin contributing funds and men to the war effort. Aragon, Valencia and Catalonia were now subject to new taxation, which Catalonia refused to pay. Partly as a consequence of this, and partly to respond to the French taking of a Spanish fort in what is now the French Catalonia, the Duke sent an army to the region. This army, however, fed itself on what livestock and crops it found, which, given bad harvests, was particularly onerous. Local nobles, unwilling to pay the Duke's new tax, stoked the flames, which led to violence in Barcelona and the murder of the viceroy.

The president of the regional government, Pau Claris, proclaimed a Catalan republic and recognized Louis XIII of France as sovereign. France occupied, and soon, Catalonia was made to finance the troops that Louis XIII, precisely what her nobles had tried to avoid in the case of the Duke of Olivares' reform. King Louis reserved public positions for Frenchmen, and appointed a French viceroy, not a local (indeed, the portion of Catalonia that would remain French would find itself subjected to a cultural homogenization never imposed on its Spanish counterpart). Pedro de Marca, who acted as governor of Catalonia on behalf of the French (the viceroy being de facto occupied with military issues), wrote "I am confirmed in the opinion that, in Catalonia, all bear ill-will towards France and are disposed towards Spain.... I receive fresh confirmation daily...there is no pro-French party." War ensued and, a decade later, the Catalan Generalitat recognized the Spanish monarchy, returning to Spain (albeit without its northern parts).

The episode's consequences were thus reversed except for a portion of Catalonia which remained French, breaking with its history as far back as the Visigothic kingdom of Toledo in the sixth century, and what was called the *Hispanic March* in the days of Charlemagne, although here, crucially, being part of Charlemagne's domain was compatible with being *Hispanic*.

Centralism or homogenization hurts the organic character of an identity just as homogenizing the organs of a body would be absurd, where a contrary reaction on the part of those organs, however, does not have a positive effect if it goes so far as to eject them from the body. Not even one century after the events just mentioned, this principle was understood by another generation of Catalan insurrectionists. On the 11th of September 1714, local government authorities (among other Iberians) revolted against Bourbon Absolutism, setting off the uprising with a letter stating their intention to struggle on behalf of "the freedom of this principality and of all Spain" ("*tot lo Principat i de tota Espanya*") and to avoid "becoming slaves with the rest of misled Spaniards" ("*quedant esclaus ab los demés enganyats espanyols"*).[235] A local, regionalist assertion, then, occurred within the consciousness of a wider identity.[236]

In contrast, modern separatism tends towards centralization, generally conceiving of its hypothetical independent state as a liberal, unitary entity. This approach to sovereignty (de)constructs regional identity as a discrete, disconnected unit, accounting for its identity ahistorically as separate from its immediate context, an inorganic simplicity. It thereby operates according to a conception of sovereignty that traces its lineage through French Republicanism precisely to the monarchical absolutist usurpation of regional (and aristocratic) prerogatives that Barcelona was rebelling against three centuries prior. As Girard notes, when struggle conceals imitative desire, it causes one to become that which is being pushed against. John Milbank and Adrian Pabst make a similar point (without the Girardian angle) in the British context:[237]

> An isolated English nation-state would be a wholly artificial reality, denying the reality of its own Celtic fringes (Cornwall, Cumbria, the Welsh Marches and the Scottish Borders). Similarly, an independent Scottish nation—through adherence to a contrived, post-Calvinist and sometimes pseudo-Gaelic 'Scottishness'—would tend to deny its variously Anglo-Saxon, Norse, Brithonic and religiously Catholic and Episcopalian components, while not doing justice to the real Gaelic legacy of the Highlands and Islands either...[238]

But if unity on the basis of a higher principle is abolished, then the part must assert itself against the whole. We should not default to the view that a sense of grander unity fails first, and then, consequently, the particular compensates by revolting. It may be that the particular fails those principles on the basis of which grander unity manifests by not living up to them. Whatever the case, we may paraphrase Walter Benjamin's "every

---

235   Jaume Sobrequés i Callicó, *L'Onze de Setembre i Catalunya: Guerra, resistència i repressió* (Barcelona: Editorial Base, 2011), 138–40. And again: the principle recurs in 1808, when the *Catalan Song (Cantich català contra los francesos)* railed against Napoleon in the spirit of a regionalism that explicitly considered itself part of a wider identity:

> "Nosaltres som espanyols;
> Y encara que siguem sols
> Contra toda la França;
> Ja mai nos aturdirem.
> Perque amb Deu confiem
> Que es la nostra esperanza."

(We are Spaniards; And even if we are alone Against all of France, We never founder. For with God we trust In that which we hope.)

236   The 11th of September is, contradictorily, used by Catalan separatism for its annual celebration, but is also generally a day of celebration in Catalonia.

237   Although later relating medieval, organic conceptions of political membership to British colonial projects and modern civic patriotism in ways that probably do not fit with my approach.

238   Milbank and Pabst, *The Politics of Virtue*, 355–56.

fascism is the index of a failed revolution" to the effect that nationalism is the index of a failed Empire/Ecumene or, as Miguel de Unamuno said of Basque nationalism, it is a "Carlismo cabreado," that is, an angry *Carlism*—Carlism being a current of conservative Spanish monarchism.[239]

Rejecting the more progressive, politically modernizing wing of the Bourbon royal family (represented by queen Isabel, who ascended to the throne) that took hold in Spain, the ire of supporters of the more conservative Carlism (named after Carlos, Isabel's rival claimant) would be taken up as supposed antecedent by hyper-modern republican nationalists. The idea that they ceased to view themselves as part of the whole (Spain), for the whole seemed to have betrayed itself is not entirely accurate, however. There is a discontinuity between Carlism and liberal separatism, bridged by the latter's rewriting of the former's history. All the same, empire betrays itself when it attempts to become a unitary, homogenizing force, and the nationalism that reacts against this in turn betrays itself when it embraces the very unitary statism it claims to rebel against. Girardian mimetic rivalry is at play.

However, crucially, it is worth noting that it was not so much centralization (for regions like Catalonia were split between supporters and opponents of greater centralization) as the loss of overseas territories and prestige that led the regional bourgeois to adopt liberal nationalism and pivot towards a project that might gain them more advantages and possibly foreign patronage. The Catalan bourgeois had benefitted from Spanish policy more than that of most other regions, to the point that the loss of imperial resources produced a greater sense of relative deprivation.

The Spanish state invested significantly in Catalonia, given that the region borders a receptive market, France (although there were also protected industries elsewhere in the country). The 1755 Royal Company of Barcelona was given a monopoly on goods from certain overseas territories, including Puerto Rico, protectionism under Charles III made Spain a captive market for Catalan cotton,[240] the first steam powered

---

239   This is initially a medievalist rejection of modernity, like a grandmother unhappy with her granddaughters' conduct, as Claudio Sanchez Albornoz analogizes, although it then inverted and phased into hyper-modernist nationalism. Sanchez Albornoz described the Basques as Spain's square root, $\sqrt{Spain}$ (and the Baroque cultural forms of certain others—Portugal, Andalusia, Valencia—as *Spain2*). This view is not far from that which was widely held before the advent of 19th century separatism. Basques largely constituted the ethnogenesis of Castile ("the Basque Country is the mother of Castile and the grandmother of Spain," writes Sanchez Albornoz). More remotely, Basque itself is the last remnant of the non-Celtic pre-Roman Iberian languages, as linguists Jürgen Untermann and Luis Silgo Gauche's work seems to establish.
240   Gabriel Tortella et al. calculated that the excess cost this protectionism represented for the Spanish citizenry (including Catalans) during the 19th century alone amounted, on the lower end of their estimate, to 510,720 million euros in modern terms. See: Jesús Laínz Fernández, *Negocio y traición: La burguesía catalana de Felipe V a Felipe VI* (Madrid: Ediciones Encuentro, 2020).

factory in Spain was installed in Catalonia by the Spanish government, the Bonaplata factory, etc. Even now, the Catalan government controls the region's public-school curriculum, public television, etc.; and, through a special statute, enjoys more autonomy than every other region with the exception of the Basque country. This long-standing position of privilege has been eroded by more recent technological changes (airplanes, high-speed trains, etc.), which no longer make geographic proximity to a developed neighbor as important as it was.

As Mateo Sagasta, who served as Spanish Prime Minister eight times in the late 1800s, remarked, those Catalans complaining about the structure of the Spanish state are part of the same regional class that lobbied for and benefitted from that structure, and many of the dysfunctions of that state resulted from its excessive catering to the Catalan bourgeois.

This issue of "relative deprivation" is important, because it results from a prior privilege which already bespeaks hypertrophy in one region and class of a body politic, rendering part disharmonious with whole. By way of contrast, constituting an example of healthy development of the part and the whole both, we may again consider that late 15th-century "territorialization" of the Holy Roman Empire, which, as we have already seen, "embedded the territories more deeply within the Empire, because each owed its rights and status through recognition from the other territories..." Because "status was mutually agreed rather than self-determined, and thus tied to continued membership of the Empire," it did not constitute a "basis for sovereign independence."[241] For this to work, whole and part must be loyal to each other, and prudent enough not to create situations that may tempt unscrupulous agents, be these at the local or overarching levels of governance.

In Catalonia, bourgeois interests came to use Carlist history and its antecedents (the upheavals of 1640 and 1714) to present a narrative in which they could be sold as a form of nascent separatism. This despite the fact that these movements were explicitly patriotic (on behalf of Spain) and medievalist in outlook (contradicting liberal-nationalist postulates).[242] It is in this sense of reacting to a loss of prestige and repurposing history for a local class project that we may understand Spanish intellectual Pedro Insua's description, following Unamuno, of regional separatism as a *pseudo-morph* of monarchical, Spanish patriotic Carlism.

A more genuine mutation of Carlism, which emerged before separatism, is found in currents akin to Proudhon's anarcho-federalism, represented in the 19th century by Francesc Pi i Margall, who nonetheless considered Spain a nation proper, with regional identities not rising to the level of nations. The idea here was of an indivisible nation whose anatomy

---

241   Peter Wilson, *Heart of Europe: A History of the Holy Roman Empire*, 216.
242   Jesús Laínz Fernández, *España contra Cataluña: Historia de un fraude* (Madrid: Ediciones Encuentro, 2014).

consisted of federated municipalities, which is more or less Plato's idea of a federated poleis, avoiding the problem of highly centralized regional governments that then homogenize themselves to cultivate separatist aspirations. This current would interfere with the bloom of explicit separatism, as well as be taken up by it. Even in the 20th century, when Lluis Companys i Jover (who was the regional Catalan government's president in the era of the Spanish Civil War, overseeing extensive anti-Catholic murders from which he later repented, and who was executed by Franco's government after the war) declared a Catalan state in 1934, this was not an independent state but a state within a proposed Iberian federation more or less in line with Pi i Margall's conception.

It is not always the case that wider units originate this dynamic by conceiving of themselves as a linguistically or otherwise homogenous unit. Sometimes the idea of fractal empire, wherein a unit contains units and is contained within units, falls away because one of those parts abrogates supreme authority for itself. We might term this nationalism. In such a case, the nation usually conceives of itself as supreme locus of sovereignty in strictly political terms. Psychologically or spiritually, however, it will seek adoption into some new idea of the ecumene considered more prestigious. When nationalism caught on in Spanish regions or in overseas colonies, it did not do so only in terms of a new conception of the state, but in terms of a new conception of the ecumene, that is, an Enlightened, liberal Republican international by which it wanted to be recognized. This corresponded to the loss of prestige associated with the quasi-medieval structure of the Spanish Empire, including military losses and a failure of propaganda. In the Americas, the charge for independence was largely led by the European-descended (creole) class and opposed by indigenous peoples, because the former was in greater contact with new, liberal conceptions, and more concerned with being viewed positively by the champions of these emerging European ideas.

Bourbon monarchy did at times fall short of articulating a vision for the ecumene. The Habsburgs had already failed to dedicate adequate attention to this issue, being overwhelmed by Protestant printing campaigns and missing their chance to nip the *Black Legend* in the bud (the so-called Black Legend being a firstly Italian,[243] but mainly Dutch and British, account of Spanish character and historical trajectory as exceptionally inhumane or incompetent, beginning in the sixteenth century).

Some Bourbons may have more or less adopted the Black Legend themselves, at least in part, in order to present their predecessor Habsburgs and Spain's accomplishments under these in a negative light. Proscribing pro-Habsburg historical analysis meant that Spain's 1500s-1600s was

---

243   According to Sverker Arnoldsson, although others argue that early anti-Spanish writings in Italy do not constitute an instance of what will come to be the Black Legend in Dutch and British works.

treated negatively within Spanish academia itself. Rather than political centralization, which never went as far as in other European countries, in Spanish history it is *ideological* failure—failure of propaganda and of ruling class promotion of a patriotic and ecumenic mythos—that will eventually weaken the concept of fractal empire, or local ecumene. Regional nationalism serves as index for this weakening.

The failure was one of *soft power* promotion, of *wen*, in Chinese terms, partly because Spain relied on Catholicism as its geopolitical rationale and ideological justification, but the church did not necessarily reciprocate at the level of promoting a positive view of Spain and, depending on the pope, actually participated in the denigration of Spain. It is as though a firm were to carry on its work on some environmental project while relying on an NGO to promote its activities among stakeholders, but found that the NGO had little interest in such promotion (although supporting and benefiting from aspects of the project). What we have here is a case of falling behind the times in terms of the emergence of propaganda as a modern technology, and of naiveté and even treachery on the part of Spain's kings.

Historically, foreign propaganda against a country or its people has been used by domestic agents to justify radical reform or revolution and eschew traditional arrangements. External critique has often been taken as a programmatic injunction by internal dissenters. In Spain, revolutionaries appealed to the Black Legend.[244] It is important not to see modern deconstructions of dominant cultural modes as disconnected from such older paradigms. 19th century progressives were often nationalistic, but certain prominent iterations of their thought spawned internationalist and post-modern social-constructivist heirs. Modern protests against the 12th of October celebrations of the discovery of America in Spain are part of a global reappraisal of traditional patriotic conceptions, especially of oversees imperial projects, but it would be a mistake to view them as also being disconnected from older foreign propaganda emphasizing the worst of the Spanish presence in the Americas and elsewhere (indeed, modern critics explicitly draw on these centuries-old polemics). The ideological revolt against tradition, the conscious desire to break with the past, as a liberal and progressive prototype to later Marxian and postmodern projects, should not be divorced from a long history of using foreign negative perceptions to justify domestic radicalism.

---

244   The Marxist intellectual Santiago Armesilla Conde, author of *Marxism and the Spanish National Question*, argues that a properly Communist worker's movement failed to develop in Spain partly because the political left—heir to modernizing Bourbon and later progressive bourgeois elites—subscribed to the foreign Black Legend against Spain, and therefore failed to marry revolutionary working class politics to patriotic feeling, which in part accounts for the success of Communist movements elsewhere.

Northern Italian or Catalan nationalism are clear examples of this. In the latter case radical deconstructivism's rejection of history and established modes of identity allies with modern bourgeois nationalism's desire to break with political structures that limit a regional oligarchy's scope for action. In a sense, the radical element of Catalonian separatism represented by factions such as the CDR or CUP rejects Western culture as uniquely oppressive. Its separatism is understood as a blow against that civilization. Similarly, the first member of the Basque terrorist E. T. A. to die, Javier Echevarrieta, wrote in one of his diaries that Basque nationalism was reactionary, but served as a temporary instrument to attain internationalist ends. The moderate element of Catalan separatism, on the other hand, namely the JxC and ex- regional president Jordi Pujol's project, is animated by the perception that, in order to be fully Western, they must break with Spain, which the Black Legend has tended to depict as the exotic *other* with respect to Protestant and, later, secular modernity. Both radical and bourgeois separatism wishes to be embraced by the modern or postmodern world, and is engaged in a Girardian game of mimetic desire. Here is a political project sociologically drawing on a continuity between a version of liberal 18th- and 19th-century nationalism on the one hand, and Marxist and post-Marxist 19th- and 20th-century internationalism on the other.

The desire to become, or be accepted by, the idealized *other* is a powerful thing, as is resentment against perceived obstacles in the way of this becoming. The desire for the ideal of a foreign culture, or for an Enlightened international community, has historically unleashed rivalry between political factions and regions within a country when one of these viewed the others as obstacles to its enjoyment of that desired good. This manifests in the perception, for example, that conservative voters are blocking progressives in their country from being embraced by the forward-thinking peoples of the world, or that poorer, rural parts of a country are preventing denizens of its richer industrial provinces from being treated with all the prestige of a doctor or engineer when they go abroad. That degradation of a national identity causes political disintegration is recognized by Confucius in the Analects when he recommends to a *Kuo* or kingdom that it exert *wen*—in the sense of cultural prestige alike Joseph Nye's *soft power*[245]—and so attract others into its fold.

I once put these ideas to the American hispanist historian Stanley Payne, who did not find them amenable to his understanding of history. We should be wary of excessive academicism. Modern fashions of deconstructing dominant cultural identities and political projects did not come about in a vacuum. They built on the ideologies of the early modern period, whose program relied on foreign animus to support

---

245   Joseph Nye, *Soft Power: The Means to Success in World Politics* (New York: Public Affairs, 2005).

domestic rupture with the past. There is a history of the Black Legend yet to be written, a genealogical history of this dynamic as prototype for the twentieth and twenty-first century political militancy of social-constructivism or post-structuralism and hyper-criticality of established identities as hiding a rivalrous motive. The Ecumene (or Fractal Empire) in which nationhood (as distinct from nationalism in the negative sense) may thrive, requires a defusing of mimetic desire and its deconstructivist consequence, and the articulation of a clear vision of the Good.

Considering René Girard's triangle of desirous Subject, desired Object, and Model who possesses the subject's desired object, we find the model and desired object have merged, because really it is the model's status—the model *as* model—that is desired. The model's higher status is a function of perceiving and projecting a necessary, dialectic, lower status onto others. Being perceived as lower, the subject imitates the model by beginning to perceive and project lower status (and specifically *its own* lower status) onto a separated entity, the Scapegoat. This scapegoat has to simultaneously be identifiable with the model's projection of lower status on the subject and be somehow distant from the subject. This imitation is meant to fuse the subject with the model. It is the northern Italian separatist desire to be considered an extension of central and even northern Europe by taking stereotypes about Italy and projecting them towards another Italy (claiming to be the true Italy or else claiming not to be Italian), or of Spanish regional separatist projecting the Black Legend and foreign prejudices on the rest of Spain in order to gain exemption for himself in foreign eyes. The exoticizing confirmation bias of a foreign caricature is internalized. The subject here tries to confirm foreign denigration, so that the border of high and low status is reestablished, no longer at the Alps or Pyrenees, for example, but slightly south of these.

Justifying this re-drawing of maps requires a corresponding historical narrative, and given that its impetus is a status-seeking adaptation to prejudices whose origin is historically recent, this narrative will be forced. Rather than renegotiating one's place or rethinking one's comparative advantages, separatism represents a political (or merely rhetorical) reaction against structural changes which are not themselves strictly political. The history of Madrid's policies towards Catalonia needs to be ignored in order to present a false narrative of opposition in which Catalonia is a historic victim rather than a member and beneficiary of Spain, for example.

Critically, the oppression narrative or victim mentality does not require genuine grievance, it rather stems from a desire which is really a desire for antagonism and a failure of the creative imagination. Creating zero-sum accounts of identity, of resource needs, or of whatever else, which entail irreducible contradiction and therefore conflict and winners and losers: this is the ontology of violence, the preference of rivalry to creativity. The powerful party that needs a powerless counter to be itself, and vice-versa, the pristine victim who needs an oppressor to have himself an identity (Adorno sees this stereotyped dichotomy as emerging when a society is becoming repressive: "slave morality is indeed bad, it is still the master morality"[246]). It is like wanting one's homeland to be precisely where others live, wanting one's sacred site to be precisely where others have theirs, etc., even in the face of contradictory evidence. It is the rejection of simultaneity, or superposition, of *both/and*, preferring *either/or*. And the desire for irreducible conflict is tied up with wanting to be a victim (for being a victimizer and victims are ever mirrored states), to the desire for *ressentiment*.

To use an image we have already invoked: The mistake is in asserting the perspective from which a certain point of light appears as discontinuous with respect to its neighboring points of light while rejecting the more distant and comprehensive perspective from which the luminosity of various nearby points merge into a single circumference. Nothing stops us from choosing to participate in the life of our locality as the discontinuous self-contained identity, which, from a certain perspective, it is, but we should not therefore reject the existence of wider identities which include it along with others.

It is possible to be made victims not by our being victimized but by our wishing we had been. In this case, we are victims of our own selves the more we act in a spirit of antagonism, wanting to elicit antagonism and justify our self-image. As Girard knew, it is not the object we desire, but rivalry (not against the model that possesses the desired object in this case, unless that object is statehood, but against the entity that blocks access to that object, if the object is recognition by the modern, the cosmopolitan, the *foreign*). The psychology is that of a child resenting his upbringing when he moves away to college, wanting to recreate his personality according to whatever is popular: the numinous is all tied up for us in the new and exotic, for we think it flows from a set of particulars, rather than transcending these and being available in what we knew before. Like Coelho's Alchemist, we go journeying, but our journey is home-bound. Modernity's homogenizing impact is this desire for the shiny exotica of the more "modern" neighbor and the degradation of history, tradition, etc.

---

246 Adorno, *Minima Moralia*, 119, 199.

VI. Conclusion

OUR KING RECLINES ON HIS THRONE, YOUTH and mission spent in the erection of his present estate, a pillar of faith, an elder bastion. He watches with closing eyes as a vaporous curtain dances in the spring wind, punctuating the silhouette of his heirs and grand-heirs playing in the palatial garden. On his shoulder a familiar pressure, the shroud and scent of his queen's hair, cushion of her cheek, fingers down his arm like a scepter. He sees a vision of her form perched on his own soul through the open doors of death. Like an ascending cross of light, he spreads his arms to touch the recurrences of his self across the myriad worlds, all by the same hand wrought. In the expansion of death, he feels this world expand into the split second of eternal "now," whence the Creator picks it ripe like fruit into the night of resurrection. The Creator for whom are the king's last thoughts, forever.

We may summarize the essential scheme of the above, the general narrative of the preceding sections, in the following bullet points:

- Initiation is realization of both ontological unity (Being, *Sat*, First Paternal Intellect, the monad of Saturn/Rhea, analogous to the Father) and harmony between forms (Joy, *Ananda*, analogous to the Spirit, engendering the primordial intellection which is the auto-zoon). It occurs when the personality (the mind, ego, the thought-complex, the *jiva* of Indian thought) is slain/pacified/ecstatically exited. Now the initiate may take on the role of Demiurge, pray *in the name of* Christ. The initiate's Awareness (Reflexive Consciousness, *Chit*, Second Paternal Intellect, Jove) reflects upon its own unitary Being. The primordial experience is Joy: where Awareness finds Joy it knows unitary Being, and where it knows unitary Being it finds Joy. Awareness produces or receives a representation of that unitary Being: the theophany of the archetype, Anthropos, the Ancient of Days. Awareness consists both of its reflecting (the Son of Man) and its representing (the Ancient of Days) of that which is reflected on (Being). The Awareness can identify as both these, wherein is the duality of kingship. Any creativity, any phenomena, has as its motivating root a joyful will to express Unity in multiplicity, and so in the midst of contemplation is the possibility of action, and the demiurgic imperative to make the universe. It is not the case that Awareness brings knowledge of Being into experience, rather it does this *and* paradoxically simultaneously discovers that experience itself is knowledge of Being, presupposes Being: Jove *brings* the autozoon to Juno *and discovers* Juno contains it; they both contain order (the autozoon, containing the principle of the four elements) because they both subsist within Being and yet, in their interacting they manifest that order each as one half of it (two elements as masculine and two as feminine, per Empedocles): just so, microcosms each contain the macro, and yet each may interact as *parts* of it.

- ○ The metaxy between Unity and multiplicity where the auto-zoon perceived, appears at first like a terrible void. This must be crossed as St. Paul recommends in I Corinthians 1, with recourse neither to signs and omens nor to reasoning and thinking. Quoting from a prior section: "Mercy to them who show mercy, the tree of life to them who plant it, the true temple to them that build it: here is the whole meaning of demiurgy/theurgy, that is, receiving heavenly ascent by participating in the heavenly patterns (the Egyptian-rooted Proclean Platonism we have been emphasizing)."

- This occurs through a threefold experience of death, transcendence and rebirth: the personality or empirical self loses itself (ritual death, Katharsis), perceives the universal (*through* the theophanic vision, Theoria), which implies identity with the All, the whole, the cosmic body as manifestation of unitary Being, and returns to inhabit a given station within a sacralized order, which in the case of the king is his kingdom (Theosis).

- Realization of universal selfhood is modulated into conscious occupancy of a social being. Social existence can be endowed of—can be inhabited by—a real being beyond mere psychological construct. A set of concentric and transversal corporate identities constitute a unique view on the whole.

- Perception of the universal and return to the particular is experienced across traditions as a gestation in and rebirth from the Divine womb, the Divine feminine as mother.

- Return to the world is experienced across traditions as entry into, inhabiting of, the extended social body as just that, a body, and as a bride, the Divine feminine as lover. This is the insertion of the universal paradigm of harmony (the autozoon given to the Demiurge by Rhea) which is the intellection produced in the Awareness (*Chit*, Jove) of the fact of ontological Unity (*Sat*, Saturn/Rhea). The initiate therefore dwells outside his body and is present in the extended social body (insemination of the female consort), creating the world like the Demiurge with the Crater (an heir, a child from the female consort).

  - ○ We described the triad of *Sat-Chit-Ananda*/Being-Consciousness-Bliss (or Pure Consciousness/Awareness/Joy) as Unity-Masculinity-Femininity (these are analogous to the lower threefold of stillness-centripetal-centrifugal motions/Porphyry's *hyparxis*, *nous* and *zoe*, the three Indian *gunas*, and so on).

  - ○ Being manifests inside Consciousness as Daniel's Ancient of Days and Throne (representing the male and female modes of Being, Saturn and Rhea) and the Son of Man as Lamb/sacrificial animal represent Awareness proper, with its mind/ego. The autozoon is the principle of theophany: Awareness reflects on Being, experiences the primordial Joy, and wants to express this through creativity in a myriad of dancing forms. It is Joy that causes the autozoon to be thought in Awareness. Indeed, the autozoon's essence is in Joy, which is why it is the Feminine, Rhea, who transmits it.[1] The representations of Being as perfect body (the Ancient of Days and Throne) and harmonious multiplicity (the kingdoms inherited by the Son of Man) are the autozoon. The autozoon is the most general thought of a multiplicity expressing unity.

○ This Awareness appears as effaced-yet-enthroned, for the Son of Man is presented as sacrifice yet heir, Christ: it is an ego-death and epiphany. Thus, far from a reactionary celebration of *Being against subjectivity*, of elderhood over youth, glorification finally occurs in the Son of Man (subjectivity, youth). This is similar to how initiation is not a bringing of order by Awareness to Experience, but also a discovery of order in Experience. The point of sacred monarchy is not only the subject's perception of the monarch as living icon, but also the subject's realization of itself as living icon. Crucially, the reactionary imposition of elder on youth is not being met by a revolutionary replacement of elder by youth: *the Son of Man does not get sacrificed to the Ancient of Days in Daniel's vision, but neither does he slay the Ancient of Days*, like Jove slaying Saturn or the castration of Ouranos (interpreted as overthrow of what came before). And when Christ is visioned in John's Apocalypse, he is described with features of the Ancient of Days (hair as white as wool in Daniel 7:9 and the Apocalypse 1:14)

▪ This is where we locate a defense of participation and artistic contribution (including political assembly, the commons, cooperative institutions and artistic production).

▪ It is also why the periodic dissolution of the state, as in seasonal oscillations between sedentary and nomadic modes (as highlighted by anthropologists) or of state-guarantees (as in the cancellation of debts through a Jubilee) may serve to prevent excessive identification of representation (in an institution) with the represented principle, avoiding idolatry (a one-way relationship of reified Being to Awareness). This reified Being by which Awareness is tyrannized we identify with *political* tyranny (William Blake's Mystery and Tyranny, for Awareness concedes to tyranny because it never turns to Being, so Being remains a mystery in the negative sense).

---

1   In this sense, Proclus's *Being, Eternity* and *Autozoon* as the three triads of Nous can correspond to *Sat, Chit* and *Ananda*, but we have emphasized the autozoon as first intellection. A triad within Nous, that is, within the Awareness, corresponds more closely to the Ancient of Days as symbol of unitary Being, the Son of Man as perceiving Awareness, and the idea of harmonious kingdoms or world-as-organism as Autozoon.

- Through initiatic realization the initiate is not just a part but the whole: The king is central to the kingdom, but not central *in* the kingdom, rather, he is central *as* the kingdom, like a symbolic representation standing outside the kingdom and mirroring the kingdom to itself as well as mirroring that which exceeds the sum of parts of the kingdom, that which its parts cannot know without that microcosmic mirroring in the person of the king, namely, unity, that which must transcend the parts, being prior to them, being their telos, revealing the reason for their differentiations, being transcendent (revealing the oneness that is the essence of reality).
- The distinction between particular and universal, where a proliferation of particulars allows one to understand the universal as a common principle irreducible to any one particular, and the inhabiting of particulars (a social being, including the polity), constitutes the basis for a pluralistic world-order and society, a differentiated Ecumene.
- This ecumenic ethos is a non-imitative ethos, but this is not to assert individualistic self-construction. The less one determines oneself egoically the more one receives oneself, one's true self, from one's own ontic truth, from the Being beyond oneself. The locus of self-determining is beyond, not among fellow forms, and therefore is an escape from mimetic desire and rivalry in favor of that part of the beauty of the whole, that particular aesthetic beauty, appropriate to oneself (as individual person, as extended social being, as polity, etc.).

On one level the above reconciles us to two realities traditionally alienated from religion in the west: politics and sex. Concerning the structure of initiation as laid out above, the personality could be described as thought/mind and is like an echo of the Word, a sprout from the true vine. In Trinitarian terms, Being would correspond to the Father and Joy to the Spirit. Both Being and Joy are realized by the personality upon reflecting on its own consciousness. This reflection is analogous to the theophanic vision of the initiate.

The above orients us away from seeing the sphere of politics and culture as rivalrous and agonistic to aesthetically beautiful in its diversity. This is nothing new. It is the baptizing and crucifying of the world. In terms of politics, it recommends that those wishing to represent others go searching for the reality which allows one thing to be represented by another, and on the basis of which different units can relate harmoniously, by undergoing an ego-death. The prospect of politicians incubating in darkness for several days is likely appealing to many.

We are also justifying the idea of community as coherent entity, and the idea of communal leadership. This leadership would be the locus of a communal, albeit virtual and provisionary, epiphany of the universal. Indeed, all harmony, even the slightest of pacific interactions, is a tacit recognition of the singular cause of all and a realist metaphysical. Where regard for place is replaced by an emphasis on religious institutions as true locus of human conviviality, a simple confusion between what is universal and what is particular has occurred. Whether municipality or dioceses, whether supposedly secular or ecclesial, the point is to honor the particular within the universal.

This does not constitute a defense of the legally designated institution of monarchy or any particular form of the state. Whether representation conforms to this paradigm of sacred kingship is not necessarily conditioned by titles like president, monarch, prime minister, community organizer, television personality, soccer mom, etc. Indeed, the mediating, representational role can be filled by a sacred symbol or structure, prominently that of a temple/palace structure understood as a body and microcosm.

We should aim to reconcile dichotomies such as those between modern political representationalism and archaic sacred kingship, traditional canon and artistic dynamism, otherworldly mysticism and this-worldly participation, and universalist ecumenism and local particularism. The point isn't so much a synthesis as it is a vision of that wholesomeness prior to an only apparent division. On the other hand, there is a synthesis, because we experience that wholesomeness by bringing it into a world where such concepts have been treated as separate. We thereby experience the thrill of bringing together. The joy of union for the sake of which the illusion of separation was brought about in the first place. Yet always remembering that the dichotomy was artificial and, therefore, the synthesis is natural: it does not require an act of forceful harnessing together on our part. If we forget this, we end up treating reality violently by assuming it is violent.

Each entity presents some archetypal potential, some metaphor and Divine thought, and is also a microcosm, presenting the "All" in one particular mode, serving others as an epiphany for the all and therefore that which produces the all (the One). The Anaxagorean "all things are in everything, though in a way that is appropriate to each thing," but also the One which produces all things is omnipresent. Monarchical pomp and ceremonial sacrifice are a making explicit of this microcosmic selfhood as a show of epiphany to other members of the community. In producing differentiated entities, the One encompasses them in the harmony that is expressive of Its oneness. Each delineated unit (of harmoniously interacting units) presents its own kind of microcosmic vision of the Divine (of the All as harmonious and therefore as bearing witness to the fact of oneness and—always apophatically—of the One).

The handing over of the cosmic powers by Christ to the Father at the end of the Age according to St. Paul, ending the apparent autonomy of those ruling powers, recapitulates the creation of diversity as an expression of transcendent unity (rather than as product of ontologically irreducible elements). The discordant parts have been put in harmony again by being subdued and given over to their singular cause, the principle underlying everything, God. We may intuit that the longer-lived or more recurring a given characteristic or pattern is, the more fundamental is the archetype that it manifests. Gender is a fundamental archetypal differentiation expressing harmony (and therefore oneness). Professions, or more properly, personality and vocational types, and the aesthetic flavor of historically prominent cultural and civilizational human projects can be profoundly archetypal, albeit the way they play out in history is often wicked.

Each concrete thing is also an intersection of archetypes, just as shapes can have different colors. Different people will feel more centered around the exploration of permutations of one archetype over another, or around specific intersections thereof (one Chinese man may feel called to explore the Chinese aesthetic as cultural and national project, while his fellow countrywoman may feel called to explore medicine and the meaning of what it is to be a healer, with no felt connection to China, where yet another is fascinated by the aesthetic and philosophy of Chinese medicine).

A particular community (even just a couple in their unity) presents us with a delineated unit as microcosmic vision of the Divine. The constituents of that community can mediate that vision to each other, for otherwise the totality in which they are embedded evades them, the same way in which one cannot see the coherence of one's body as a whole because one is looking out from that body, and so needs a mirror. The sacred king (the initiate-representative) of a community is that mirror. Crucially, it is a mirror that returns one to the understanding of the microcosm-as-community (its parts in harmonious interaction with each other), because the king represents the kingdom in his own body and because monarchical ceremonial, as we have seen across traditions, is sacrificial, is self-absenting, is a *kenotic kingship*. And so even as the community sees itself in its sacred king, its guiding initiate, its beloved teacher, it also thereby is returned to itself, for that teacher makes himself/herself absent in pointing to the transcendent and suggesting that each part of the community enter into relationship with the Divine. By reflecting us, a mirror lets us see ourselves in the act of making us more aware of our actual body than of its reflection.

Corporate representation is a mirror of community, a celebrator, not an abrogator, of community. The Christian conception of the Church, which for St. Gregory of Nyssa is a mirror, bears this out. For Gregory each member of that body has particular virtues because he/she receives these from God for that purpose they are to serve as a part of the body. The individual body which is self-sacrificially absent and present in that absence, and which rules by love from a death-made-life, a cross-revealed-as-throne, is Christ, whose very body is the community—the Church in its cosmic sense—even as He represents to the community what it is. There is never a final physical image of the Church, a final end to creation and creative possibility (even though all possible entities must be encompassed within harmonious relations, that is, within oneness, because no entity proceeds from a cause other than the One). The ultimate King (the ultimate Representative) is God's Anointing, the Anointed One as most encompassing archetype, the *idea of ideas*, the Logos, the Firstborn and First Fruit, not as a particular type (if the particular type is understood as excluding the universal, it is blasphemy: "The Bible or Peculiar Word of God, Exclusive of Conscience or the Word of God Universal is that Abomination, which... is for ever removed..."). The Gospel says that just as Christ left (ascending into the sky) he will be seen to return by the disciples.

This indicates the perennial and eschatological significance of the individual Bridegroom as counterpart of the Church/Bride, the singular (male) partner to (female) diversity, the unique body to the communal one: the representative of unity absents itself and yet returns and reminds diversity of its image, its unity. There is a pulse here, a serpentine oscillation, between the reification of oneness and its giving life to diverse forms by reminding them of themselves, like the reflection reminding the body of itself. Paradoxically, that harmonious or unified diversity is itself actually the reflection of a prior oneness which it expresses. The *Chit*/reflexive awareness contemplating its own *Sat*/Being and experiencing *Ananda*/Joy, where Christ mediates an encounter with Being by absenting himself, by ecstatic self-denial. Again, Blake:

> "Jesus is the Bright Preacher of Life,
> Creating Nature from this fiery Law
> By self-denial and forgiveness of sin.
> Go, therefore, cast out devils in Christ's name,"
> (*Jerusalem*, "To The Christians," 77, 64–66)

What this interaction means in terms of Christ mirroring the Bride (Church, Community, Heavenly City) to Herself as well as the Church mirroring Christ is that the conjunction of Bridegroom and Bride, the ecstasy of their bridal chamber, is a cessation of perceived separation. The community is all king, the contemplation of that king's body ignites a fiery light in which the community perceives itself to be the body. Perhaps this is why there is no temple in the New Jerusalem, "I did not see a temple in the city, because the Lord God Almighty and the Lamb are its temple" (Apocalypse 21:22).

It is not that the Heavenly City disappears, leaving only Christ, it is that it is fully and utterly perceived to be the body of Christ (through what is beyond bodies, the Logos). But there is ever a need for a vantage outside the whole to perceive the whole as a whole: the need for a representation of the whole by a part, the Church as a person in the likeness of the persons who compose it. Paradoxically, in separation (which allows the contemplation of one by the other) is total union (realization of one in the other). A portion of being continues to occur in the midst of the created play of forms (entering contemplation) and a profounder part of being is extinguished in union (contemplatively realized).

Being multiple, the whole is dynamic in that it can display its forms through sequence, although all is simultaneous, as in Gregory of Nyssa's *epektasis*. Beings, though extinguished, are extended. The people of paradise play their games, but every Friday the veil is lifted and all ceases in absorbed awe of God's ineffability, as Islam teaches. Nothing abolished, everything transformed. In one sense the many (community) and the one (individual representative) are equal (as in Milbank's interpretation of Plato's *Parmenides*). The many return to the one and the one proceeds into the many in a simultaneous ecstasy/intasy. But in a grander sense all is contained by One, all is occurring in the midst of One. We can assert the Trinity so long as we are clear about being monotheists.

The question of the many interacting with the one is related to the triadic structure of reality. Being is univocal, the Being of beings, but awareness of being, consciousness or *Chit*, allows multiplicity, for each being is a commentary on (an act of reflection upon) Being. The Son contains all people (St Irenaeus), the Logos is the idea of ideas (Origen), and all who have seen the Son have seen the Father (John 14:9). The Son presents the univocity of the Father to His own externalized plurality (the Church, His bride). The Second Platonic Intellect or Demiurge receives the autozoon from the First. *Chit* has *Ananda* when it reflects on *Sat*, or can reflect on *Sat* when it has *Ananda*. *Joy* then is the essence of the *blueprint of all bodies, it is the instruction to harmonize.* For this reason, the autozoon comes to Jove from Rhea and only manifests when he joins Juno, per our identification of femininity with Joy where masculinity is Awareness (*Ananda* and *Chit* in Sanskrit). This last point is crucial.

Abstaining from imposing generality on particular conditions (abstaining from anticipating that which is generalizable about the particular before actually *listening* to the particular), lets us perceive the archetypal in those conditions. The autozoon is in the metaxy, it is in between Being and Consciousness, it is Joy, for in the encounter with pure Being, which is our own being, our consciousness receives joy. We are dumbfounded by the sheer gratuitous naked being of a tree or a person or whatever else; we feel at home because it is our own pure being we are in the presence of; and we are joyful, we rejoice in its beauty, its harmony, and we will beauty, harmony. This occurs through forms, through senses, through inner contemplation that encompasses outer reality and realizes it as inner reality rather than retreating. Such is the mysticism of Proclus and Meister Eckhart, which "is the natural situation which prevails especially for children."[2]

---

2   Milbank and Zizek, *The Monstrosity of Christ*, 175.

It is what William Desmond calls the "passio essendi." We perceive the kind of encounter with Being to be had in the midst of certain particulars, as the particular creature we are. This leads us to receive that which we abstained from imposing: a vision of reality as ordered, as composed of categories/archetypes, that does not result from the categorizing compulsion of the mind but gives the mind what it seeks. If one fails to interface with the archetypal in this way, one may make of harsh legalism one's categorizing metric or, counter-wise, sentimentality, but either way mere thought and feeling are one's compass. Goethe described the drive of the collector as the civilizing impulse, and we add that such may be a sacred enterprise if one remains porous to the ways that *being* communicates.

Yet this simple contemplation of Being must be a choosing of Joy. Its self-negation is a self-assertion. We cannot attain it without relinquishing the blasphemous piety that denies all assertion of joy and creativity, for in fact to receive joy (the *Ananda* of contemplating *Sat*) we must first believe in it, otherwise we are not really surrendering in faith, and we are not becoming co-participative in Joy. Consider the above quote on "self-denial and forgiveness": "Such are the Laws of Eternity, that each shall mutually Annihilate himself for others' good, as I for thee" (Blake, *Milton*, 39, 35–36).

Reality is kenotic, we learn to lay down our lives for our friends. But where the Gospel of John teaches this, it teaches also creativity, praying in faith and staying in a state of love. It is not a moralistic or morbid self-sacrifice. And so, Blake goes on, rebuking the devil and his institutions:

> Thy purpose & the purpose of thy Priests & of thy Churches
> Is to impress on men the fear of death; to teach
> Trembling & fear, terror, constriction: abject selfishness.
> Mine is to teach Men to despise death & to go on
> In fearless majesty annihilating Self, laughing to scorn
> Thy Laws & terrors, shaking down thy Synagogues, as webs.
> I come to discover before Heav'n & Hell the Self righteousness
> In all its Hypocritic turpitude, opening to every eye
> These wonders of Satan's holiness, shewing to the Earth
> The Idol Virtues of the Natural Heart, & Satan's Seat
> Explore in all its Selfish Natural Virtue & put off
> In Self annihilation all that is not of God alone:
> To put off Self & all I have, ever & ever. Amen.
> (Blake, *Milton*, 39, 37–49)

Should we abstain from rising to the archetypes and true joy, we should not expect to dwell in the vision of ordered reality. If we pray, "Lord give me harmony and beauty if you wish," in truth doubting Divine generosity in our pious pretense, we fall afoul of the hadith and do not surrender in childlike expectation of good. We do not forthrightly unite with that which we wish to discover, we have no part in it, it is not in us, and we are not faithful unto it. This is the great principle of correspondence. Mercy is open to us when we are merciful (the Gospel and traditions from Islam to the Indian and beyond provide ample iterations of this). And what we wish to have manifested we should seek to have in us, to pray as if it were done (Mark 11:24), which is faith, and as the very nature of reality is at base pacific, loving, we cannot participate in co-creation as extensions of the Divine self unless we forgive and love all (recall the Gospel of John, chapters 15 and 16, instructions on how to pray). And if the psyche and body resist our faith, we should have faith in our being made integrally faithful, from the mustard seed of faith which is the point of will inside us, until the whole mind and body are transformed by its robust growth.

Too often the sense of piety subtly becomes a lack of faith, a lack of confidence in the Divine, and we do not pursue what we intuit, we do not discover by creating and stepping confidently into the unknown *yet knowing*. Like Blake's city of Golgonooza built up by the human imagination (purified, relinquishing all resentments) unto the pre-existent Eden, the coming Jerusalem. We do not receive a vision of harmony by denying our sense of harmony, for we receive if we are faithful, and believe in it already, otherwise we are faithless. How many would-be-ascetics stayed in denial, in "neti, neti," as though it were an instruction for every sphere of life, and never stepped into the creative moment, the confidence recommended in the hadiths, the claim to be co-heirs with Christ? How many Arjunas have thought it holy to relinquish action, and fallen into that "lifeless dejection," forgetting that "Strong men know not despair, Arjuna, for this wins neither heaven not earth" and have not heeded the warning, "Fall not into degrading weakness.... Throw off this ignoble discouragement, and arise like a fire that burns all before it" (*Bhagavad Gita*, II:2-3, trans. J. Mascaro).

Self-awareness is joyful (*Ananda*) when it reflects upon the true object (its own being), but hellish when it reflects nothing and simply gyrates in itself, incestuously, onanistically. The consciousness that does not reflect on Being does not encounter joy, but instead plays constant mind games and arms itself against an encounter with being, against immediacy, produces disease, morbid introspection, obsessive-compulsion. The encounter with being may feel like a loss of the conscious self but is actually the path to realizing its own being in joy: it is the ritual death and rebirth we have been discussing. The legalistic, or economistic, technicism of compulsive categorization and false sense of security it elicits is sacrificed to a counter-symbolism of worshipful kenosis whose communal character precisely seeks the metaxy here and now and does not reify the middle in which dwells the autozoon, the metapolis, to place it out there in space somewhere, for "The kingdom of God will not come with observable signs. Nor will people say, 'Look, here it is,' or 'There it is.' For you see, the kingdom of God is in your midst" (Luke 17:20–21). And so, we should see it, not as an externally given arrival but by arriving ourselves at a thing which is here and now in ourselves: "Let every Christian, as much as in him lies, engage himself openly and publicly before all the World in some mental pursuit for the building up of Jerusalem" (*Jerusalem*, "To the Christians," 77).

The *Gospel of Thomas* speaks of a mystical perception, and in truth so does Blake, for that "mental pursuit," whatever external works it might correspond to, is just that, mental, that is, inward, but also open and public and a "building up" as the Gospel so often tells us, we must have faith like children. Without faith we will not heal or move mountains. If we dwell in a state that is not joyful, not grateful in the knowledge of receiving, we are in some wise, in some part of ourselves, not faithful. But for most people the psychological and somatic layers of the self require training, accustoming to joy and gratitude, especially if they have wallowed in the sickness of doubt and pessimism for years. Thus, the vehement tone with which scripture often calls on the believer to shake off the cadaverous version of his old self. It is an active rising up. At that point the sign is inward, it is will, it is not a reliance on constant external confirmation but a fully internalized joy. It is the attitude of a fire which rejects despair in the *Bhagavad Gita*. The danger is in identifying this attitude with the ego, rather than a kenotic faith in God, "Why stand we here trembling around Calling on God for help; and not ourselves in whom God dwells" (Blake, *Jerusalem*, 43, 13–14).

Modern society and particularly the European cultural trajectory, does not need to deny reflexive consciousness, but to again make *Being* its subject of reflection. To a degree this is experienced as a discontinuity, rupture. Such is the alternative Proclean modernity we have mentioned. Milbank explained this when he spoke with me as the way in which ritual openness to the Divine interrupts the mechanistic economic/technological-determinist, processes we produce and become slaves to. The community needs its communal rites to point to something beyond itself just as consciousness must refresh itself with its own being, which is the Being of beings and is actually encountered as if outside itself and then points back to the self.

The courageous way to resolve an existential problem is to abstain from thinking up a solution to the deep spiritual discomfort it yokes us to, and to instead try to encounter being until the whole problematic seems irrelevant. Rather than think, the sufferer should breathe deeply and go into ice water, into a thoughtless intensity. Now, the guardian of the abyss, the vapors of the void, the gargoyles, may assail him when he does, for the mind projects out what it fears in apotropaic anticipation. As we already asked in an early section: who knows what monsters populate emptiness? Here is the "Existential Self at the last gasp" that "will do anything...to avoid taking this disintegrating step into 'non-being',"[3] which we already commented on when discussing the king's initiation. Here is the metaxy, what Crowley described as

> ...the gap in thought between the Real, which is ideal, and the Unreal, which is actual. In the Abyss all things exist...but are without any possible meaning.... They are thus Insane Delusions. Now the Abyss being thus the great storehouse of Phenomena, it is the source of all impressions. And the Triune Principle has invented a machine for investigating the Universe; and this machine is the fourth Principle of Man.[4]

To know the metaxy as the autozoon's dwelling, as the place where *Chit* meets *Sat* unto *Ananda*, we must face its parody: Labyrinthine minotaur, "thicket of delusion," St. John of the Cross's Dark Night guards, Kafkaesque persecutors, Blake's Specter. But we cannot rely on those Upanishadic hungry gods, St. Paul's Elementals, with their ritual and compulsion. We must be outside the law here, we must walk by faith. That way we can know the *nihilo* that allows *creatio ex nihilo*, Nikitas Stithatos "abysmal intellections." The *metaxy* is not the stormy Mediterranean Aeneas struggled to cross, but is overcome and encompassed by imperial Rome after his successful crossing. He knows water no longer as sea but as river, water/matter is in the body, as in Ezekiel and the Apocalypse.

This perilous realm, western occultism's Abyss, must be crossed, for it separates the state of "lifeless dejection" and "doubt" from that of fiery purpose, of friendship and faith in God: "When your intellect crosses beyond The thicket of delusion, then you shall become disgusted With that which is yet to be heard And with that which has been heard (in the Veda)." We have already seen how, for the *Bhagavad Gita* (II:52[5]) this crossing requires stepping out of theistic prescription, "When your intellect stands fixed in deep meditation, unmoving, disregarding Vedic doctrine, then you shall attain Self-realization" (II:53). Like the *Tibetan Book of the Dead*, the instruction is not to rely on externals, for the mind is busy producing ghouls, but on the certainty that these are projections and phantoms, and on inner faith. (Again, we are returning to passages already quoted, but it is important to end with them.)

We are at the point not of reliance on externals but of internalization, of walking in faith. Thusly does scripture imply a maturing into autonomy, co-inheritance, co-creativity, of *choosing* salvation, of will and decision to cease being led by the mind, doubt and even religious law, yet within the epiphany that only God exists. No longer relying on externals, on

---

3   Grant Morrison, "Pop Magic!" In: Richard Metzger, *Book of Lies: The Disinformation Guide to Magick and the Occult* (Red Wheel Weiser, 2003).
4   Crowley, A., *Little Essays Towards Truth, Man: Neschamah.*
5   Winthrop Sargeant's translation.

memory of what we are told is real and possible by our past experiences, we are in the present moment and create from the present moment:

> Do not call to mind former things; pay no attention to the things of old. Behold, I am about to do something new; even now it is coming. Do you not see it? Indeed, I will make a way in the wilderness and streams in the desert. The beasts of the field will honor Me, the jackals and the owls, because I provide water in the wilderness, and rivers in the desert, to give drink to My chosen people. The people I formed for Myself will declare My praise. (Isaiah 43:18–21)

And,

> So from now on we regard no one according to the flesh. Although we once regarded Christ in this way, we do so no longer. Therefore if anyone is in Christ, he is a new creation. The old has passed away. Behold, the new has come! All this is from God, who reconciled us to Himself through Christ and gave us ministry and reconciliation that God; that God was reconciling the world to Himself in Christ, not counting men's trespasses against them... (2 Corinthians 5:16–19)

In order to reduce a limited egoic sense of self and chose another we must make ourselves larger than the small scab of a mind we were previously inhabiting: we must expand until our misperception is small and stands in relation to a larger context, wherein we may perceive it differently and alter it. Such adventure has no reference point in our past (which is why Blake prefers referring to the Imagination, rather than calling the principle muse Memory, as is traditional). For this reason, we often wait until we are in a state of suffering to expand our awareness, for at that point we are desperate to escape, but it can of course be done without suffering. We must expand to fill the abyss, the metaxy, until we are larger than the fears our frightened ego is mushrooming out into that void. Suddenly we perceive ourselves in that substrate and Juno adopts us. When we encounter oneness, we find there every possible bounty, and we are made a one unto giving forth bounty. The dynamic of manifestation is gift, generosity and gratitude forever. Lord Krishna says in the *Gita* that He acts although He has everything, and recommends joyful, faithful (free-of-doubt) action to prince Arjuna.

Communal festivities often present us with monsters, those boogey men of every folklore, and also the initiate in kingly regalia. My sense of the monstrous warebulls of Spanish and other winter carnivals is that some of them represent the initiate having defeated and integrated the animal self: after successfully crossing the Abyss, entering the unconditioned state, the mind of instinct and animal impulse is no longer in chronic cortisone-releasing survival mode, but is our ally, not autonomous from our will, for we are living from the present grace-filled field, where even the beasts render honor, as the prophet Isaiah (43) relates. The farcical chimera actually symbolizes an eschatological awakening to nature: We may consider Blake's idea of animals as parts, limbs, of the human person, to whom we reconcile and who we reintegrate, like the Zoroastrian teaching of animal resurrection on the last day, which the Eriugena apparently also defended. We are the ark, having survived the flood, with the whole animal kingdom in us, in harmony. We who receive dominion over the nations, as in Psalms, contain the nations in us, the diversity of humanity as well as animality, as our own body and soul, and are rulers thereof. Taoist inner alchemy often makes this point, relating animals to our organs.

The outer coarse nature has been taken on by the subtle, and the king and heir secures his inheritance thereby: Jacob dresses in animal hides to receive Esau's birthright from the blind father Isaac. The inner contemplation is Isaac, that Christ-like sacrifice who lived. Blind, with awareness turned inward, it perceives all the coarseness, ruggedness, concreteness of reality in the subtle thing, Jacob. Even if it be faced with Esau later, that is, with the reality of things as they appear to be—as the senses and the habituated mind perceives them—it will nonetheless not repent of his having given their birthright to the subtle thing.[6] He will remain faithful. He will not suffer to have them be his reality, his heir. He has already chosen the subtle thing. The first-born—Esau, the reality as it initially and prominently appears to us—is not what we settle for. The initiate, the noetic athlete, gives his continuance to the subtle one, Jacob. That one is his heir. And thus, man is not subject to the predation of nature but dons the garments of beasts to his own health. This costume play, this animal dress, can serve us as a figure for the initiate, like Jacob pretending to be Esau.

The carnivalesque shakes consciousness from ritual prescription and habit, for ritualization impedes the free fall of faith. The Vedic rites are not with the initiate when he overcomes the Abyss (*Gita*, II:52–53), the human person is not made for the Sabbath. Carnival sucks us into aesthetic contemplation and social communion. Interrelation is crucial because it is where we manifest harmony with other forms. Festivals point to the univocity beyond. But they must be joyful, a ceremony, celebration or contemplation, and all three in one. The way a community of individuals (consciousness as multiple reflections on Being) encounter this reflection on Being is through its symbolic representation as prior to the community itself (the supplement at the origin).

A symbolized/ritualized unity is prior to the community as community, just as Being is prior to consciousness. Otherwise that particular

---

6   This is Neville Goddard's understanding in *Consciousness is the Only Reality*, found in *Five Lessons*.

community would not be a particular community, but simply an aggregate of individuals perhaps belonging to alternative, different communities. Symbolizing themselves culturally, as occurs during folkloric processions, communal rituals, or in political institutions, shows that they are now a community and that their having come together is *unto* something, and perhaps was preceded by that something as invisible cause. The community is not an arbitrary delineation of merely natural elements, it is a cultural specificity.[7]

Now, the subject of politics (or of *life in common*) is neither the one nor the many, the individual representative nor the represented community. It is neither the *individualizing* nor the *individuating* (as Indo-European languages helpfully distinguish) neither reproducing the same nor causing dissimilarity, neither the shape rendered in different colors nor a color used to draw different shapes. Recall that the paradigm of harmony is not outside forms but between forms, the transcendent metaxy is an intersubjective space. There is an invisible king, ratio rex, who is also an invisible kingdom. The subject of politics is the will to non-identically repeat an aesthetic pattern. The creative project of exploring variations on a theme, a *suggestive project of life in common*, as Ortega y Gasset defined it.

The pattern to be non-identically repeated need not be shape or color. If one encounters a multitude of colored shapes and is told to group them by kind, one may do so either by color or shape. And one may realize that one identifies as much with one's favorite shape (one's form, for example, vocation as a doctor) as with one's favorite color (one's substance, for example one's family, or the specific way in which form is rendered in that substance, what it means to be a musician *as* a member of a specific family). Certain authors who have sought to value *being* and traditional static societies over *becoming* and modern technologically-dynamic societies fail to account for substance in their emphasis of form. The point of living in the present epoch may therefore be to take up substance and redeem it from hypertrophy (like retrieving spilt ink from color blots with no particular shape and giving the ink new life by using it to draw or write). Indeed, religion often paradoxically expresses universals through particulars as if to sacralize the particular, as occurs in Biblical narrative, the Bible being more or less the story of a family. Theophanic transformation, salvific theurgy, does not reveal in us the universal and burn off the dross of the particular, it takes up and transforms the particular too.

Once a cake has been prepared and put in the oven, one cannot remove the flour content in the mix, replace it with other similar material, or

---

7   Anthropologists like David Graeber have pointed to the significance that to Native American tribes—who have been romantically/condescendingly depicted almost as *a prioris* of the world—ancient facts of nature, operating in the modern western imagination as their own aesthetic categories, were, of course, consciously chosen, their rites deliberately crafted and participated in.

interchange it with the same material baked into another pastry (however much both might have flour, and however much that flour might even have come from the same wheat stem; the egg in an éclair is not exchangeable with that in a Japanese omelet, and no fresh egg can be integrated into either after the cookery process is complete without compromising the product). It may be said that a son's formal properties include the property of causal inheritance from his father. At a certain point, and in a certain sense, the *telos* of a project takes up its (apparently accidental) chain of causation. Mere secondary or horizontal causation becomes the ornament and clothing of primary, vertical causes: types dance like *corybantes* around their common archetype. This again relates to the idea that peripheral or lower beings (animal minds) are a part of a harmonious integrated whole.

Embracing secondary causation, however, is embracing its ornamenting the archetypes, our purpose, our vision, and not allowing it to determine that purpose. It does not necessarily lead to a sort of conservative disposition, in which we are bogged down by the world as it is. Of course, our starting point is the world, and not some imagined *tabula rasa,* and yet, in a sense, the opposite is true. The ways in which an archetype instantiates through material causes may be so numerous in their variety that we see these corybantic dancers in a vision like armies of jesters, which does not allow us to place too much weight and severity on historical comings and goings. Ours is to pursue creative vision, not be slaves to the past. we chose from our inheritance, discerning between what we will and what we do not will. That which we do, we amplify, that which we do not, we may curse like Jesus cursed the fig tree that would not give fruit.

If some of these causes and secondary features seem at odds with the main of an entity, we can see them as decorative filigree, a momentary change in tempo to contrast and highlight the general pace of the piece. Perhaps even an appearance and not a real substance of our work. The experience of the *Gita*'s "thicket of delusion," the vapors of the void, we can hold to be revealed as unreal, like laughing at shadow puppets *from the knowledge* that they cannot affect our flesh, to be transformed at will by lighting another light, and at memories of a dream when waking relief sweeps over us, containing and superseding the consciousness which feared them and even the possibility of inhabiting that consciousness, but from Eternity overtaking it in the truth.

An abstract principle like "triangle" may manifest across colors and an abstract principle like 'blue' may manifest across shapes. Both form and feature, essence and substance, shape and color, are concepts, unitary ideas which can only manifest in relation to some other set of ideas (a shape must have a color, even if a neutral grey; a color must be in some shape, even if just a blotting stain) and therefore must point to potential varieties. The possibility of manifestation as such is not substance as opposed to form as usually thought of, and has no primary formlessness (if we perceive it, it is always already in some particular form). To quote from the introduction, the mystery and mercy of matter is that "there is no archetypal concept drawing itself in chaotic substance, but only archetypes crisscrossing the great matrix of reality."

Concerning those potential varieties which any form points to (the blue triangle implies a triangle which remains the same shape while being red, and also another shape that is equally blue): We may have narrower and wider identities, forms across wider and narrower ranges of substance, substances across wider and narrower ranges of forms, but we may end up finding out that the subject of politics and of life is a particular range of forms within a particular range of substances, or consciousness and sentience, or being and joyful experiences of being, wherein a certain transcendent third has its home, its body. Perhaps we decide our preferred center is as blue triangle, both blue and triangle. We may have our existential home in that particular bandwidth, without feeling identified with those possibilities beyond it. They perish who go to deep into things, per Islamic teaching. We have spoken of the resurrection of the particular with the revelation of the eternal, of heaven winning trophies from history, of our tragedies and fall into history serving as ornament and filigree within a vision of our true selves in the eternal, of the doctrine of the Apokatastasis or universal salvation. All things offered up to God.[8] Reads the *Gospel of Philip*: "The world has become the Aeon (eternal realm), for the Aeon is fullness for him." [9]

The waters themselves, the fleshy self, the mutable nature, is therefore taken up into the essential:

> The priest is completely holy, down to his very body. For if he has taken the bread, he will consecrate it. Or the cup or anything else that he gets, he will consecrate. Then how will he not consecrate the body also? By perfecting the water of baptism, Jesus emptied it of death. Thus, we do go down into the water, but we do not go down into death ... [10]

It is not only the essence, but the substance, that are taken up, not only the shape but also the color, not only the mirror, but the light as well:

> None can see himself either in water or in a mirror without light. Nor again can you see in light without mirror or water. For this

---

8 The Vaishnavist Jiva Goswami recommends that even sinful actions be offered in devotion to the Lord (Bryant, 2017, 52). Here Bryant provides this translation of Lord Krishna's words in the *Bhagavad Gita* (IX, 30–31): "If even the performer of the most evil deeds worships Me with undivided devotion, he will quickly become righteous and is to be considered saintly, for his determination is perfect."

9 *Nag Hamadi Codex II, 2–7, The Gospel of Philip*, 55:5–55:36, 151.

10 Ibid., 76:27–77:28, 197.

reason, it is fitting to baptize in the two, in the light and the
water. Now the light is the chrism.

And from the *Bundahishn* (the "*Gochihr*" here is apparently a once-fallen
celestial being and Ohrmazd is the Creator):

> Gochihr burns the serpent in the melted metal, and the stench
> and pollution which were in hell are burned in that metal, and
> it (hell) becomes quite pure. He (Ohrmazd) sets the vault into
> which the evil spirit fled, in that metal; he brings the land of hell
> back for the enlargement of the world; the renovation arises in
> the universe by his will, and the world is immortal for ever and
> everlasting. (*Bundahishn*, 30:31–32)

We reproduce a warning from C. S. Lewis not to anticipate the mysteries at the level of lower realities and states of consciousness, however (like that artist who mixes colors on his paint pallet thinking to
recompose the rainbow into its originating sunlight, confusing the oils
of his canvas for the light he observes in the sky). From the preface to
The Great Divorce (my italics):

> ...if we accept Heaven we shall not be able to retain even the
> smallest and most intimate souvenirs of Hell. I believe, to be sure,
> that *any man who reaches Heaven will find that what he abandoned* (even
> in plucking out his right eye) *has not been lost:* that the kernel of
> what he was really seeking even in his most depraved wishes will
> be there, beyond expectation, waiting for him in 'the High Coun-
> tries'. In that sense it will be true for those who have completed
> the journey (and for no others) to say that good is everything and
> Heaven is everywhere. But we, at this end of the road, must not
> try to embrace the false and disastrous converse and fancy that
> everything is good and everywhere is Heaven.
>
> But what, you ask, of earth? Earth, I think, will not be found
> by anyone to be in the end a very distinct place. I think *earth, if
> chosen instead of Heaven, will turn out to have been, all along, only a region
> in Hell: and earth, if put second to Heaven, to have been from the beginning
> a part of Heaven itself.*

Yet, we may add, Heaven being real in a way that hell is not—Good
having *being* where evil is the appearance of impossible non-being—the
Heavenly realization is just that, a genuine realizing of the way things
are, whereas the hellish apprehension is illusory and finds its true being
as a game for Heaven.

Heaven is real, Hell is not. The encounter with Being is real, and the
autozoon, the *Ananda*, which we receive in the metaxy between us (*Chit*)
and our Being (*Sat*) is real but depends on us (the *bhava* of the Vaishnavist
believer depends on his state when he dies during his final lifetime, the
Divine gives us what we ask for in faith); the horrors of the Abyss, the
Specter or thicket of delusion, is not, it is just that, a specter, a delusion.

The meeting with Being produces subsequent thoughts about it, and may even appear to be hastened by thought, by discursive philosophy, just as being is, paradoxically, analogized in communal terms by cultural ritual, which seems like an artifice to the anthropologist if he thinks of humans only as animals who are good at calculating (anthropologists are seldom guilty of this however, it is economists who commit this error). But this is good, for being as such is not encounterable as a thing, so we encounter its presence as if it were being brought about by constituents, yet also as though it were the final cause of those constituents in their coming together.

Cultural rituals in which the community participate as a unit analogize reflexive consciousness's encounter with being as *prior cause yet end of journey*, and therefore they are often about *death and rebirth*. He who dies and is reborn as representing the community is a symbol of Being's univocity to the community (conscious awareness). He who gives his life for his friends (the community) receives life (analogized as the joy of a consciousness aware of its Being; pacified in the safety of that which is not subject to the changing stream of its thoughts). This abrogates Girard's suspicion of folkloric rites as expressing a foundational murder and violence as the basis of community which then is covered up by narrative. We are actually encountering the joyful truth behind the parodic inversion that is legalistic ritualizing of a community which prefers fear to Being, the pharisaic parody of a consciousness that prefers mental masturbation to the kenotic, self-effacing yet self-fulfilling, encounter with its own being.

Consciousness encounters Being in the context of particulars, and is returned from Being to being-in-particulars. If it tries to hold on to one encounter with being it will lose its presence in other possible encounters. If we feel the thrill of being totally present in the moment while bathing in a cold river, and we identify the intensity of that moment with its particular conditions, we may never bother to find the same intensity elsewhere, returning as pilgrims to that river as though the mystery were only there, and allowing other parts of our lives to become mediocre. We received it, but we never became its ministers. We got it and never gave it out, never sought it farther. We were not co-creators of the theatres of revelation, we were too pious and meek for that.

The slavish adherence to outer forms of encounter with Being is like Milbank's reference to human action congealing into mechanistic processes that it originated itself. There is a risk in becoming slaves to another's system, as Blake writes, and also of becoming slaves to our own systems as, I think, Joseph Chilton Pearce warns, although Blake was indeed getting at this: the *Spectre* in his poetry, the egoic mind, can enslave us and must be tamed. Nowadays, this is clearest in terms of technologically-facilitated novelty-addiction. To leave a community's *paideia* to random stories by random people on social media and fail to cultivate disciplined minds in favor of compulsive phone-gazing will likely make for social processes that are prone to slavishly following automatic, mechanized processes right off a cliff.

Joseph Nye and Robert Keohane's *complex interdependence* can disempower people as much as empower, constituting the context for global, stateless, technologically-driven hypnosis of all by all (or all by organized few, but not necessarily), a network of creative community as well as a straight-jacket spiderweb whereon the Elementals may devour us. We should not view technology itself as empowering direct-democratic utopia. Even apart from the dreamy image of pure spontaneous sociability unmediated by culture which this evokes, and which we have been critiquing, the point is that the use of technology depends on the user and the user needs cultivating *as user*, that is, as a point of conscious intention. We should be creators, we should, again, discover by inventing.

One may encounter Being, the purely objective or, in another sense, purely subjective, in that which is not conducive to one's bodily and mental existence or spiritual orientation, or one may encounter Being in that which is conducive to these intimate ends. The metaphor we have used is that of the tiger and the familiar. The tiger's jaws awaken us to the present moment and gifts us with an intensity of gratitude for life which we can take with us thereafter, but we wisely reframe from returning to those jaws. Making love to our spouse likewise awakens us to an intensity of presence and grateful immediacy but, in this case, we may fruitfully return to the experience.

These are like the dual aspects of the king-initiate, who is sacrifice and 'sacrificer'. Embracing himself as sacrifice, and this as source of exaltation, he does not literally suffer himself to die and leave his people, but dies ritually and resurrects in the spiritual epiphany, for the "return of Israel is a return to mental sacrifice," not to literal human sacrifice (Blake's Jerusalem, *To the Jews*). The people who, after the ordeal of persecution and captivity, return to themselves and their prior sacred tradition, do not return with a desire for vengeance or self-effacement (sado-masochistically wanting to become like the oppressing foreigner in order to exact revenge on him). The inner peace and gratitude of the man who survives the jaws of the tiger allow him to proceed awakened, spiritually royal, and do not compel him to return to the place of near-death, wishing death on every tiger, as happens in the pathological case that wishes to relive trauma, Captain Ahab and his vendetta. He remains the sacrifice, brings that awareness into the ritual space of seasonal ceremony, and combines it with legitimate agency as 'sacrificer', the one who makes things sacred—legitimate because he is in a state of inner surrender, of open-handed freedom, kenosis.

In fact, the two are the same, he is sacrificing the self, that is, constantly letting go of egoic delusion, and so is the sacrifice and precisely the one who sacrifices. It is by coming to terms with history in this way that the political/cultural identity which recovers from a period of oppression and suppression can avoid Nietzsche's *ressentiment*, the victim-mentality which inevitably leads to imitating the resented oppressor, further losing one's own identity in a Girardian game of desire and imitation, preventing a centered, deliberate, creative participation in shaping one's self and participating in the ecumene.

Modern, originally western, technological civilization is like earlier European imperialism, intruding on splendidly isolated *israels* who must cease to view themselves as *the people* (as native peoples often self-designate) and realize they are *a people* among others, but also, thereby, becoming able to gift others with their insights (like Israelite scripture), giving away the gift of spiritual centrality with which they previously regarded themselves exclusively, and yet precisely never giving away that which was given specifically to them, but rather gaining a clearer awareness of it by distinguishing it from that which belongs to all ideal humanity (gaining life by giving it away, as the Gospel says).

This can mean articulating their particularity more explicitly, like China after realizing it is not literally the Middle Kingdom, and selectively imitating external, hegemonic, cultural modes, the way early Islamic civilization configured tribal societies into being an equivalent to the Persian, Byzantine and Abyssinian polities. These hegemonic cultural particularities can be taken on (like the European medieval and early modern state vis-a-vis Rome) or kept at arm's length (as in assertions of indigenous identity in post-colonial countries). Western norms can be deemed tiger or spouse, wild or domestic, according to local preference.

Foreign hegemonic technology and organization, along with its cultural baggage, are analogous to the law/rites, which we may use without becoming subjected to the Elementals/gods of St. Paul/the Upanishads. They are as the Sabbath which is made for man. They are like the parts of the cosmos we interface with harmoniously so long as we do not forget that they are not separate from us. So long as we experience ourselves as microcosms, like the initiate-king, a "child Jove" receiving the autozoon from the monadic Rhea. So long as we see them as part of ourselves and not external, so long as we engage in "theological translation," enculturating them into our selves, like the Tantric initiate mapping the cosmos on his body.

If we do not incorporate these advantageous features, we will end up serving the foreign hegemon, for we identify its advantages with itself and do not acquire them for ourselves. We do not see ourselves as participants in an ecumene, but as peripheral. Thus, a slavish mimesis of the Girardian "model," adherence to the dominance of the hegemon, non-deliberate participation in the ecumene, is analogous to slavery to Paul's Elementals or the gods who wish to feed on us in the Upanishads.

When Sir. Woodroffe says that "[f]oreign achievements and culture should be a food for each people eaten and *assimilated*,"[11] referring to post-colonial India, he reminds us of this principle. And it is not only the hegemon but also—perhaps principally—the automatic dynamics of a certain institutionalized procedure that is analogous to the Elementals. The (unspoken, assumed) rules of the game become reified and followed uncritically even when they do not serve their supposed ends (prosperity, etc.). But to map the cosmos onto our body we must *have a body*.

To participate in procedures without being swept up like automata we must have a will of our own. We must be a reflection of transcendent Unity *by being a unit in ourselves* (we become a particular unit by knowing the transcendent Unity, as the Corpus Hermeticum recommends in XIII.4:18: the neo-Platonic reception of the autozoon from the monad, St. Clement of Alexandria's becoming coherent by observing the harmonious body of Christ in *Strom.* 4.25:156–57). Here is the direct involvement in relational action, theurgy, liturgy, and taking the Divine in (through rite or ritual, not *ritualism*, not legalism, not habit and compulsion), serving ourselves as a storehouse for the depths of our Being.

Politically, to be unitary is to have a sense of what culture we are enculturating these foreign and global *techne* into. Like a consciousness reflecting on Being as its own Being, and therefore giving forth Joy from itself. Like a poet giving forth his own emanation. A culture may thereby exert its own cultural attractor, its own *kuo*. This brings together and concludes our discussion of religious legalism and sacred monarchy, on the one hand, and on the other our explorations of political mimesis and identity (in terms of modern nation-states and post-colonial identities and of contrasting historical paths to Voegelin's ecumenic consciousness), and the concluding theme of having a center, of embracing creative agency.

---

11   John Woodroffe, *Bharata Shakti: Collection of Addresses on Indian Culture* (Madras: Ganesh and Co., 1921), 56.

ADDENDA

A Digression on Heliocentrism and Cosmology as Metaphor

I N DISCUSSING THE MEANING OF SOLAR CEN-
trality, we could hardly do better than to quote Wolfgang Smith
on the topic (obviously this does not constitute an endorsement
of his latter conclusions or all his cosmological theories). He begins
by noting that geocentrism and heliocentrism "correspond to different
levels of vision," where:

> heliocentrism is based upon an intellective vision which replaces
> or supersedes the sensory. The crucial point, however, is that
> authentic heliocentrism does not deny that sensory truth, but
> accommodates it, rather, within an enlarged and perforce hier-
> archic vision of reality. Vivekananda has put it well when he said
> that 'Man does not move from error to truth, but from truth to
> truth: from truth that is lower to truth that is higher.'[1]

In any case:

> The heliocentric position corresponds evidently to a more intellec-
> tual or internal kind of vision, inasmuch as it contradicts what might
> be termed the testimony of sense perception. Its iconic truth, more-
> over, derives from the fact that the Sun, as the representative of
> Deity, does by right occupy the center of the universe. As 'the author
> not only of visibility in all visible things, but of generation and
> nourishment and growth',[2] it could not be conceived Ptolemaically
> as a mere planet, one among several that revolve about the Earth.
> Considering the overtly theophanic, one might almost say, 'liturgi-
> cal' outlook of the traditional heliocentric orientation, it is hardly
> surprising that heliocentrism has been especially associated with
> the Pythagorean and Platonist traditions, as opposed to the Aristo-
> telian. Based on the report of Philolaus, the Pythagoreans espoused
> a non-geocentric cosmology in which the Earth revolves around
> a central fire, the so-called Altar of the Universe, which however
> was apparently not identified with the Sun.[3]

As we have seen, that central fire was analogized by the visible sun,
but seems to have been thought of as cuboidal. If it is the quadrangular

---

1 Wolfgang Smith, *The Wisdom of Ancient Cosmology: Contemporary Science in Light of Tradition* (Oakton, VA: The Foundation for Traditional Studies, 2004), 174.
2 Smith is quoting Book VI of Plato's *Republic* here.
3 Ibid., 173.

Egyptian Duat where souls are judged and purged, it is also the cube-throne of deity and most ancient goddess Vesta, so that encounter with that central fire may yield unity with the sun-disk and abode of Ra, the often-cited Apollonian character of sages like Pythagoras and Plato, but it is not reduced to that. It remains an inner, secret sun, a spiritual light.

The identification of inner fire with visible sun, Smith continues, "came about later at the hands of the Neoplatonists, whose cosmology thus became overtly heliocentric." We should add that this is probably not a complete identification but an emphasizing of the correspondence between inner fire and outer sun. He continues:

> Later still, in the Renaissance movement championed by Marsiglio Ficino, the doctrine came alive again, but in a somewhat altered form; one might say that what Ficino instituted was indeed a religion, a kind of neo-paganism. Copernicus himself was profoundly influenced by this movement, as can be clearly seen from numerous passages in the *De Revolutionibus*. To cite but one example (from the tenth chapter of the First Book) which enables us to savor the spirit of those Renaissance times:
>
> *In the middle of all sits the Sun enthroned. In this most beautiful temple, could we place this luminary in any better position from which he can illuminate the whole at once? He is rightly called the Lamp, the Mind, the Ruler of the Universe; Hermes Trismegistus names him the Visible God, Sophocles Electra calls him the All-seeing. So the Sun sits as upon a royal throne ruling his children the planets which circle round him.*
>
> Yet despite these panegyrics, it appears that the light of iconic truth was fast fading. A kind of earth-bound literalism, hostile to the spirit of Platonic philosophy, was beginning to manifest itself, foreboding the advent of the modern age. Neither in Marsiglio Ficino nor in Copernicus do we encounter an authentic revival of Platonist doctrine, nor can it be said that the resultant heliocentrism conforms altogether to its traditional prototype: 'rather was it comparable,' writes Titus Burckhardt, 'to the dangerous popularization of an esoteric truth.'[4] (Smith is quoting *Mirror of the Intellect* by Burckhardt[5])

It may have been positive for Christianity to restrain neo-Platonic cosmological heliocentrism for a time, according to this view. But we should look to the necessary re-enchantment of the world, and re-sacralizing of cosmology, inclusive of cosmological heliocentrism, and by way of the insoluble terminus of materialistic accounts, beginning with the hard problem of consciousness.

Wolfgang Smith wonders whether a traditional anthropocentrism can survive cosmological heliocentrism. Certainly, it has been historically displaced, but in a sense the centrality of human perspective is asserted

---

4   Ibid., 174.
5   Titus Burckhardt, *Mirror of the Intellect* (Albany, NY: SUNY Press, 1987), 22.

in a scheme where coordinates (the very idea of east, west, north and south, as well as up and down) depend on the fact of human intellection. The fact that the universe has become host to that ordering, coordinating perception is enough to justify its value. The fact of multiplicity and of there being movement even in what seems stationary (the earth) and what we determine as relatively central (the sun) is, again, a deference to the transcendence of God, so that even the most exalted physical bodies are not at rest and totally central, for true rest and centrality is not to be sought in particular forms but in the Absolute. Indeed, the Bible, like the Pythagoreans, places fire at the center of the cosmos. It is not a people or place, not a specific cultural mode of humanity that ancient geocentrist accounts supported.

On the question of traditional anthropocentrism, C. S. Lewis notes the following in *The Discarded Image*:

> ... the material cosmos mirrors, hence reverses, the reality, so that what is truly the rim seems to us the hub.... We watch "the spectacle of the celestial dance" from its outskirts. Our highest privilege is to imitate it in such measure as we can. The medieval Model is, if we may use the word, anthropoperipheral. We are creatures of the Margin.

And in *Miracles: A Preliminary Study* Lewis adds:

> The insignificance of Earth was as much a commonplace to Boethius, King Alfred, Dante, and Chaucer as it is to Mr H. G. Wells or Professor Haldane. Statements to the contrary in modern books are due to ignorance.

In any case, the issue is not so much a sticking point of Christian tradition as some have supposed. Melchior Inchofer, an opponent of Galileo during the latter's trial, apparently admitted "I have not found a single one of the Holy Fathers who has dealt with the motion of the earth clearly and positively, as the saying goes."[6]

Given that the idea of centrality and the immobile pole as expressive of exalted status was also well established, it seems that the earth's immobility in a Ptolemaic schema was reversed and identified with grossness, lack of loftiness, and fallenness, and, in its positive connotations, somehow deferred to a realm beyond the spheres, more expressive of exaltation and truly immobile. Thusly does Dante perceive himself no longer to be ascending but penetrating into a center when he passes the seven spheres of Heaven and enters the Empyrean.

In this way, even Ptolemaic geocentrism somehow comes to view the moving heavens as loftier than the immobile earth, and in fact closer to

---

6 Father Melchior Inchofer cited by Richard Blackwell, *Behind the Scenes at Galileo's Trial: Including the First English Translation of Melchior Inchofer's Tractatus syllepticus* (South Bend, IN: University of Notre Dame Press, 2006), 112.

the truly immobile Empyrean, and in this regard exalt the clearest symbol of grandeur in those observable heavens, the sun, as somehow central or expressive of that centrality. For this reason, ancient peoples refer to the sun as royal and to royalty as manifesting the immobile pole. The association is clear, even if their cosmology does not always consider the sun to actually be an immobile center relative to the earth. But ancient cosmology does view the sun as a regulator, a governor. Franz Cumont observes that the Chaldeans had solved the problem of "the irregular courses of the planets" by noting that they were "connected with the revolutions of the sun" and concluding from this that "the sun governed their movements; the sun was, as it were, the chorus-leader who directed the rhythmic evolutions of the wandering stars,"[7] that is, a ruler.

---

7   Franz Cumont, *Astrology and Religion Among the Greeks and Romans* (New York: Putnam, 1912), 128.

ADDENDUM II

The Center at the Periphery
CRETE AS THE HEART OF EUROPE

THE IMPORTANCE OF IDAEAN INITIATION JUS-
tifies reflecting for a moment on the importance of Crete and
Minoan culture. Jove, named *europos* by Homer,[1] is in turn responsible for naming *Europe*. During his earthly exploits, the thunder god and
demiurge established that Cretan ceremonial which Proclus considers
central to Hellenism and, by means of the woman he away'd to the same
island, also this continent its name. The nomenclature bespeaks the
importance of Crete. The initiatic rite at the root of Greece and, therefore,
of the West, is the seating upon Jove's throne at Mount Ida in Crete. It
proceeds from the Bronze Age Minoans to the Mycenaeans.[2] Whether
these peoples had different origins or not, Mycenaean iconography and
ideology is taken from the Minoans.[3] Historian Charles Hawkes argues
for a Bronze Age coherence across Europe on the basis of Mycenaean
culture "in the orbit of Minoan Crete":

> The concept of the Mycenaean achievement as a European pri-
> macy is no mere fancy. Right across Europe in the middle of this
> millennium run the signs of the same pattern of society... [4]

In this vein, Sir Arthur Evans spoke of a *pax minoica* (preceding the
Mycenaean), maybe invoking some continuity with the much later *pax
romana*. Indeed, according to Thucydides (I.4) King Minos was the first
to organize a navy, and in medieval times (sixth and seventh centuries)
it was believed by some scholars that Cretans were the first to use
arrows,[5] indicating some possible memory of their having held a military
advantage. That all of Europe is named after a myth centered on Crete
is therefore fitting. Tying this to the Roman and medieval theme of
Trojan descent, it can be speculated that Troy and Crete were somehow
linked, since according to Virgil Aeneas, who has witnessed his divine
mother in the Anatolian Mount Ida, where he was conceived, initially
seeks refuge in Crete, at a similarly named Mount Ida.

---

1   Denis de Rougemont, *Vingt-huit siècles d'Europe: La conscience européenne à travers les textes, d'Hésiode à nos jours* (Paris: C. de Bartillat, 1990), 8.
2   Louise Schofield, *The Mycenaeans* (London: The British Museum Press, 2007), 144.
3   Marinatos, *Minoan Kingship and the Solar Goddess: A Near Eastern Koine*, 9.
4   C. F. C. Hawkes, *The Prehistoric Foundations of Europe* (New York City: Routledge, 2014), 379.
5   St. Isidore of Seville, *Etymologies*, XVIII.viii.1, 363.

GREEK PHILOSOPHY AND BRONZE AGE THEOLOGY

Zangger sees Pythagoreanism as expanding concepts known to Babylonians, possibly by way of the late Bronze Age or early Iron Age Western Anatolian mediation of the Luwians or their cultural remnants. It is also possible that such knowledge was simply known to the Luwians, not necessarily originating in Babylonia, or having done so a long time prior to the end of Luwian culture. Indeed, many of the defining features of Bronze Age Babylonia, from technical knowledge to religion, were common to Aegean cultures from the period, as Nanno Marinatos notes, calling these features a *Near Eastern Koine*. Be that as it may, this might explain why many of the great Greek philosophers originated in Western Asia Minor, the Luwian homeland. It would mean a Luwian substratum survived in Ionia and Hellenic Anatolia.

Further, Peter Kingsley sees the later neo-Platonism of the early centuries AD as presenting themes identifiable in pre-Socratic fragments of Empedocles and Western Orphism/Italic Pythagoreanism.[6] Plato would have drawn on these. Indeed, the Athenian explicitly ascribed the mythic structure of his *Gorgias* (493a) to a "Sicilian or Italian." Kingsley specifically refers to Zopyrus, a probably Italian Pythagorean invited to Syracuse by Dionysus I to work on artillery weapons and to whom the Orphic poems of the *Krater* and *Net* are attributed (the crater and net being prominent symbols in Plato's *Timaeus*) as a source for the Platonic dialogues. There is also the Pythagorean general and political leader Archytas of Tarentum (Puglia). Empedocles would have taught in this milieu. In taking on certain Orphic and Pythagorean ideas prevalent in that region,[7] Middle and especially Neo-Platonists were simply drinking from the source.

As for the term *Near Eastern Koine*, it seems excessive in its geographic restriction, given the presence of many of the features that define it in Marinatos's account, including the theme of a solar goddess as mother of the king, in cultures as far afield as Japan. Indeed, Professor of Classical Archeology Dimitri Nakassis has written of the temple and palatial economy at (Mycenean) Pylos and possibly also (Minoan) Knossos as having been a response to local social realities rather than as a Near Eastern import, rejecting Moses Finley's characterization of Mycenean culture as fundamentally Near Eastern (which Finley takes to mean economically centralized, highly bureaucratic and statically hierarchical, a set of features that does not, according to modern historiography, apply to Near Eastern palatial economies either). Nakassis argues for undercutting the

---

6   Similar to Jan Assman's highlighting of Renaissance Hermetism as genuinely reiterating ancient Egyptian theology. Indeed, Kingsley considers the Corpus Hermeticum is consistent with the tradition he is delineating as well.

7   Kingsley points out the artificiality of parsing out the Orphic from the Pythagorean. The two would be intimately related.

idea that "the palace is something fundamentally alien and is imported into Greece from the Middle East," adding that "instead of being a monolithic entity that is cut-and-pasted onto [ancient Greek] society, [the temple] is . . . better understood as the product of . . . broader social and historical sources."[8]

Further, the notion that Minoans and Myceneans were genetically (as well as linguistically) distinct peoples and that the former brought the institution of the palace from the Near East, where they originated, is dubious. A 2017 genetic study of the remains of these Bronze Age peoples published in *Nature* titled "Genetic Origins of the Minoans and Mycenaeans" found that, "Minoans and Mycenaeans were genetically similar, having at least three-quarters of their ancestry from the first Neolithic farmers of Western Anatolia and the Aegean, and most of the remainder from ancient populations related to those of the Caucasus and Iran," to which the Mycenean gene pool apparently added a component originating in hunter-gatherers from eastern Europe and Siberia[9] (perhaps accounting for their Indo-European language). None of this necessarily discounts an overridingly Near Eastern origin for temple or palatial monarchic rites in the European Mediterranean, but this account should be complemented by noting the viability of a perennialist approach according to which certain features are widespread because they articulate common human intuitions and insights.

Peter Kingsley maintains Pythagoreanism is substantively Babylonian in the images and concepts it employs. However, given that these features are known to have been quite well established throughout the Bronze Age Eastern Mediterranean (Marinatos's *Near Eastern Koine* or van de Mieroop's *club of the great powers*), that the Greek sources themselves attribute Pythagorean concepts to Egyptian learning, and that Egypt is essentially a Bronze Age civilization that survived into the Iron Age (as noted by Eric Cline in his book on Bronze Age collapse[10]), we may also identify Pythagoreanism and its heir, Platonism, generally as a renaissance of Bronze Age theology and philosophy. This may have been preserved by way of Egypt, Babylon, a West Anatolian residue of the Hittite-related Luwians, remains of Mycenaean Greek culture rooted in Minoan Crete, or all of these. For example, if we take one of the fundamental figures of pre-Socratic Greek philosophy: there is evidence, including in Herodotus, that Elea, the home city of Parmenides,

---

8   Dimitris Nakassis, "The Mycenaeans in Greek History: Orientalism and Master Narratives," youtube.com, retrieved 10th December 2018.
9   Iosif Lazaridis et al., "Genetic origins of the Minoans and Mycenaeans," *Nature* 548 (2017): 214–18.
10   Eric Cline, *1177 BC: The Year Civilization Collapsed* (Princeton, NJ: Princeton University Press, 2015).

practiced religious rites of a Western Anatolian (Luwian) origin, being founded by Ionian Greeks, the Phocaeans, while his poetry is related to Babylonian literature by several scholars. Specifically, the relation of the Underworld to a Goddess, wherein the initiate descends guided by the daughters of the Sun, would be Babylonian (the daughters of Marduk, associated with the sun, leading to the House of Night). There would be a link between Babylonian origins, which we have already discussed as supported by Kingsley and Uzdavinys, and the diffusion of this culture's knowledge into Anatolia, affecting Greek culture, per Zangger's view.[11]

But, again, the Greek sources themselves, from Plato to the second century AD, point to Egypt, where both Pythagoras and Plato are said to have studied, and to Crete, where the surviving ancient Minoan rites of Mount Ida are said by Proclus to constitute the very heart of Hellenism and specifically of the Platonic tradition he belongs to (of course he doesn't call them *Minoan*, as this is a modern name, and Proclus seems to see little discontinuity between the Bronze Age Minoan, Mycenean and the Iron Age and classical Greek antiquity).

Similarly, if Margaret Barker's thesis is correct, Christianity is a harkening back to theological concepts prominent during the Bronze Age that survived into the seventh century BC before being toppled by reformers in Jerusalem, whereupon Iron Age expansionism in the form of the Assyrian empire and Nebuchadnezzar's Babylonian army, laid waste.

In terms of the Luwian element and its possible influence on Greek philosophy, this should not be viewed as disconnected from that Minoan source of Greek wisdom highlighted by Proclus. The much later Virgil's *Aeneid* connects the Anatolian Mount Ida near Troy (which would have been a Luwian city) to the Cretan Mount Ida, so that Aeneas and his surviving Trojan company originally aim to arrive and take refuge in Crete. The Mycenaean war with the Luwians at the close of the Bronze Age—which Dr. Zangger hypothesizes and which Homer's Iliad and Odyssey would recall—would have been a conflict between cultures that actually shared fundamental traits and drew on the same sources.

Pythagoras is said by Iamblichus to emphasize the initiate's identity with Jove, god of lightning and divine king, which concords with what we know of the Luwians, who considered their king a representative of his patron deity, usually the lighting god.[12] Perhaps the Romans, for whom Caesar would be Jupiter incarnate, learnt this by way of some Pythagorean or else Luwian instruction, given accounts of Roma's founding by Aeneas, who would have been a Luwian, and of its being ruled early on by the Pythagorean sage Numa Pompilius. Numa Pompilius was

---

11   Kingsley, *Ancient Philosophy, Mystery and Magic*, 392.
12   Annick Payne, *Iron Age Hieroglyphic Luwian Inscriptions* (Atlanta: Society of Biblical Literature, 2012), 14–15.

a Pythagorean and a Sabine, a people that according to Plutarch were originally Greek settlers from Lacedaemon.[13]

The similarity between Pythagorean-Platonic tradition understood as the philosophy of Voegelin's Homeric ecumene (many Platonists wrote esoteric commentaries on Homer's epics), and Babylonian or general Bronze Age (most clearly Egyptian, but also Luwian) theology highlights its convergence with Christianity. It was mentioned earlier that both Algis Uzdavinys and Peter Kingsley see the figure of Enoch and Hebrew mysticism as having a Babylonian origin. Uzdavinys writes that the "...Enoch literature of Jewish mysticism derives directly from the Assyrian and Babylonian hieratic customs,"[14] in which vein Kingsley suggests that elements of New Testament theology originate in Babylonian religion and were inherited via the *Book of Enoch*.[15] Even if the origin is not strictly, genetically, Babylonian, the same concepts that lead these scholars to ascribe such an origin to Enochic Hebrew and Christian tradition also lead Zangger to ascribe it to Pythagoreanism.

Further, the (Mycenean) Bronze Age Greece that Homer is recalling in his surviving epics radiates chivalry and its norms are approximately those of the Pythagorean-Platonic and Christian tradition (there is no pederasty in Homer, which is consistent with Pythagoras's reported banning of these practices at the colony he founded in Crotona, Plato's *Laws* and Biblical injunctions). Nietzsche's opinion that the Old Testament is Homeric in its ethos would concord with this, apart from also reminding us that we should read much of it creatively and with the same whimsy we use to approach other myths, as it does not really contain the theology of Orthodox Christianity, for example, save elliptically and always allowing for divergent readings, and just as the Bible has need of a tradition of exegetes, so Homer's epics have their philosopher-commentators.

Apart from the Greek and Egyptian legacy, for Christianity, there is also a Persian connection, given the likely Zoroastrian—and specifically monistic or monotheistic *Zurvanist* Zoroastrian—provenance of key Christian theological tenets. These largely originate in the book of Daniel, which presents the view of the afterlife, the resurrection, and the prophecy of the Son of Man which the Gospels will take for granted. Daniel contains images punctually corresponding to the Zoroastrian *Zand-i Vahman Yasht*, such as the mixing of iron and clay as a metaphor for future disaster when the sacred and profane mingle. In addition, of course, the three wise men—the Magi—that read Christ's impending birth in the firmament and follow a wandering star to Bethlehem in

---

13   Plutarch, *Lives*, Numa: 4; 309.

14   Algis Uzdavinys, "Chaldean Divination and the Ascent to Heaven." In: eds. Patrick Curry and Angela Voss, *Seeing with Different Eyes: Essays in Astrology and Divination* (Newcastle: Cambridge Scholars Publishing, 2007), 30.

15   Kingsley, *Ancient Philosophy, Mystery and Magic*, 211.

Matthew may have been Zoroastrians (they may also have been Arabs). The Enoch tradition is also connected to Persia, with 2 (Slavonic) Enoch sharing the Zoroastrian view of animals as having eternal souls destined to bear witness against those humans who were cruel to them in life, and to dwell in paradisiacal pastures after the final judgement.

Obviously, we have been treating ancient Bronze Age and latter pagan insights as spiritually valuable. This requires a word on certain inaccurate characterizations of these. Contrary to a familiar Christian polemic, it is not really the case that ancient mythology precluded the possibility of an afterlife for most people, teaching instead of a slow decomposition in the Greek Hades or Egyptian Duat, in conformity to a dreary, fatalistic and tragic ethos. This is certainly not the case in ancient India, or Hellenic philosophical schools, who entreated people to prepare for death, and it is also not necessarily the case for mainstream religiosity in the West either. As Martin Nilsson suggests, referring to the opinion of archeologist Roberto Paribeni, "...the Minoans besought their gods to give the departed spirit bliss,"[16] an attitude, he adds, that parallels the Egyptian. As for later, post-Mycenean, Greek religion, it was more story than religion, which is a fair summation of Plato's view on it. Furthermore, if a degraded heroism that only embraces tragedy and ultimate futility (rather than the far different attitude of the *Bhagavad Gita*, for example) is found in Homer, it is only partly present, more or less on the surface, and in that portion of the epic cycle corresponding to an already degraded phase of history (we should remember there was once, apparently, a more comprehensive Homeric oeuvre which included the Golden Age[17]). It is likely that Egyptian religion decayed after the Bronze Age as well.

---

16   Martin P. Nilsson, *The Minoan-Mycenaean Religion and Its Survival in Greek Religion* (New York City: Biblo and Tannen, 1950), 429.
17   "Homer's two songs are only the central part of an epic cycle which initially ran from the imagined beginning of the world, the Golden Age, down to the Heroic Age" (Uzdavinys, *Philosophy as a Rite of Rebirth: From Ancient Egypt to Neoplatonism*, 279).

On Giants and Incarnation, or Sacrificial Flesh and Hungry Spirits

I MEAN TO WRITE OF FLESH AND SPIRIT IN TERMS of their union, stressing that this union is not an indiscriminate mingling, but a proper harmony. In Paul, flesh is not body, but fallen body, contrasting with that of the resurrection. When we couple flesh with spirit, therefore, we do not readily imply the fallen and unfallen, or merely low and high. Rather, the words conjure a correspondence of fallen body with fallen psyche.

In such a case, a negative conjunction of flesh and spirit is possible, as occurs in Genesis 6:2-7 when the sons of God come to the daughters of men. These birth giants who must then be slain—*gigantomachia* (war against giants) representing an often overlooked theme in scripture. In Biblical demonology, the departed giants are partly allowed to remain on the earth and inspire the living to offer up flesh. Thus, we have a second, subsequent, negative conjunction of flesh with spirit, that of blood sacrifice.

The Mexican account of this—because there is one, as recorded by Fray Juan de Zumárraga, first Bishop of Mexico—has it that the giants, or *quinametzin*, lived in the era of the sun of water, *Atonatiuh*. We may understand this to mean that the sky was wet, clouded, its air and light made weighty, damp, and the earth robbed of a clear view of what is above it, bereft of direct light, with only diffuse, ambiguous, promiscuous, glow. The connection to water also appears in the tale of how Britain came to be populated by giants, later slain by Brutus the Trojan, as recounted by Geoffrey of Monmouth. It is said that sister princesses first arrived to Britain after being bound and set out upon a ship—led by the waters to a land where they mate with spirits and birth giants. Later, Trojans will sail upon the waters—intentionally, unlike the sisters—arriving to the land and ridding it of its colossal denizens.

If we understand *sky* as referring to a higher faculty, will or cognition, we have here a lethargic or un-lucid mind, whereas the earth, our substance or soul, is deprived of its proper vista and reflects fragmented ghostly images rather than the crisp form of the sun. Such a spirit tends downward, uniting—in the sense of becoming attached to—the flesh. Giants result. Big Thoughts. Obsession. Ideology. Addiction.

These will drown after we clear that which obfuscated our sky, bringing flood, but their recurrences will need slaying, as by Joshua in the

Promised Land. And even after putting the *idee fixe* to the sword, we may find that it leaves us with compulsive apotropaic habits, gestures to ward off the specter of those negative thoughts and feelings, phobias. These are the ghosts of slain giants hankering for sacrifice.

The daughters of men had already, in a way, been sacrificed to spirits. Enoch tells us that, after yielding, they were terribly mistreated by the fallen ones. The subsequent sacrifice is to the spirits of giants, but it is rendered on account of a prior fear. Where there is faith in the salvific economy, there is no need for an economy of blood. Instead of understanding the world as disclosing of Logos, we see it as primal chaos. We forget that matter as matter, is always already formed, always a coincidence of forms. The essence of a blue circle isn't circularity, where blue is only base substrate. Blue is an archetype as much as circularity. St. Gregory of Nyssa is, as ever, the paragon of Orthodoxy here.

We err if instead of conceiving of the Divine Feminine as the power (Shakti) to substantiate, we perceive unformed substance. The tendency of the latter would be towards confusion of forms, which murderous propitiation at once abates and fulfills, suggesting the bloody cup of the whore of Babylon. The true object of appeasement, then, is a feminine specter, as Robert Graves celebrated and William Blake warned against ("the female will"). Thus the appearance of human sacrifice in that version of ancient Judaism which included a goddess ("Asherah," following Raphael Patai and Margaret Barker among others) and which was later reformed by King Josiah (I am consciously constructing a "likely story" here).

What flesh, in relation to what spirit, saves us from all this? Staying with the Biblical narrative, two particularly relevant sources are the Ethiopic *Book of Enoch* (*1 Enoch*), the earliest portions of which are dated to the 2nd century BC, and the 3rd-century Zosimos of Panopolis's *Teleutaia Apochē* (or *Final Abstinence*), focusing on its citations of the treaty *Isis the Prophetess to her son Horus* (in the *Codex Marcianus*).

Zosimos, who was neither a Christian nor Jew, identifies the reliance on blood rites (including human sacrifice) with the sort of magic that 1 Enoch condemns, and maintains that an opposite kind of operation was practiced by King Solomon (*Final Abstinence 2:24-27*). Barker reads 1 Enoch as defending first temple Hebrew religiosity prior to Josiah's reform.

Among the features of the first temple she delineates, we find human sacrifice (Exodus 22:29). However, reading Hosea (6:6-7), "I desire steadfast love, not sacrifice, And knowledge of God, rather than burnt offerings. But man" or "Adam" in the Vulgate, "has transgressed the covenant," she concludes that the Adamic covenant was not believed to have been based on blood offerings. The figure of Solomon comes up here, as his role—and in general that of righteous kingship—is described in terms related to Adam's original vocation of pacification and dominion (1 Kings 4:21, 24).

Providing an overview of universal history, Zosimos likewise defends king Solomon as having been safe from certain malevolent influences (the term "overseers" below refers to Enoch's Nephilim):

> In former days, powerful men kept the overseers at bay. In order to receive prayers, the overseers "hid" (ekrupsan) the art of natural tinctures [natural or edifying alchemy] and replaced them with a 'non-natural' one (aphusikon), asking for sacrifices in exchange for success in these tinctures. After a "revolution of the astrological zones (klimatōn)" and a war, the human race disappeared from "this zone" (ek tou klimatos ekeinou). The temples were deserted and the sacrifices offered to the overseers were consequently neglected. Contacting those left as if in dreams and sending them omens, the overseers continued to exchange success in tincture for the offering of sacrifices.[1]

The notion that Zosimos of Panopolis had a genuine basis for his opinions is supported by the following factors:

1. He is conversant with 1 Enoch, and therefore with Jewish tradition distinct from the reforms of King Josiah.
2. Biblical sources, including Jeremiah, indicate that opponents of Josiah migrated to Egypt (where Zosimos lived centuries later) and preserved a version of Judaism.
3. Zosimos's description is consistent with Biblical descriptions (Jeremiah) of Hebrew refugees in Egypt, who are said not to practice blood sacrifices,[2] and with the descriptions of the Elephantine Papyri (written in Aramaic and discovered in southern Egypt and dated to the 5th century BC). It is also consistent with the 1 Enoch itself (19:1), albeit a portion that shows signs of Hellenization, "...the angels who have connected themselves with women, and their spirits assuming many different forms are defiling mankind and shall lead them astray into sacrificing to demons as gods." Likewise, in the *Book of Jubilees* (2:20; 2:28), Adam and Enoch only offer incense as sacrifice, not blood.[3]
4. As the work of Raphael Patai and Margaret Barker emphasize, pre-Deuteronomic temple worship included a divine mother, Asherah. We may therefore speculate that Zosimos's emphasis on Isis is a further hint or parallel with that ancient Jerusalem observance.

---

1   Olivier Dufault, *Early Greek Alchemy, Patronage and Innovation in Late Antiquity* (Berkeley, CA: University of California Press, 2019), 129.

2   Although it may be believed they practiced the son sacrificed ascribed to Ahaz, condemned by Deuteronomy, Zosimos would not approve of this, and does not ascribe the practice to Jewish traditions he is aware of.

3   It is ambiguous whether all forms of animal sacrifice are being rejected, however. In the (Slavonic) 2 *Enoch*, that patriarch gives instructions on the binding of animals, and the son of Enoch, Methuselah performs animal slaughter at an altar (69:11-16). It may be only the bargain with demonic forces wherein human officiators provide blood is being condemned, and specifically human sacrifice.

In rejecting bloody rites, Zosimos would be distinguishing Isis/ Asherah devotion from its degeneration as practiced by king Ahaz (2 Kings 16:3; 2 Chronicles 28:3), as well as from the Deuteronomic reform, which entirely rejected Asherah, and which would have defined the Jerusalem temple of his day (though not the religion of all Jewish communities in Egypt).

5. The idea that a faction of Hebrew religionists rejected *both* the reform and what they considered perverse ritualism (often translated as *witchcraft*) is reinforced by those texts that Barker identifies as critiquing the Deuteronomists, for these also often condemn the same magical practices that Deuteronomy condemns. This is the case of Isaiah, when he rejects soothsayers (2:6–8), the "tokens of *witches*" (44:24), the "children of *witches*" (57:3). We may also cite prophet Micah, who believes in the heavenly host, a feature of the First Temple, yet speaks against sacrifice:

All the nations may walk in the name of their gods, but we will walk in the name of the Lord our God for ever and ever. (Micah 4:5)

Would the Lord be pleased with thousands of rams, with ten thousand rivers of oil? Shall I present my firstborn for my transgression, the fruit of my body for the sin of my soul? He has shown you, O Mankind, what is good. And what does the Lord require of you, but to act justly, to love mercy, and to walk humbly with your God? (Micah 6:7–8)

We may add that the Abrahamic dispensation contains a critique of this practice. Barker cites accounts in which Isaac was truly killed by Abraham and later resurrected as possibly being the original version of that story (suggested, for example, in the depictions of the Dura Europos synagogue). But even here we find that the narrative would undermine continued practice of sacrifice, just as the resurrection of Jesus is not used to justify crucifixion, and so would not bolster the notion that it was an unproblematic part of Hebrew religion prior to Josiah. Indeed, Isaac's post-resurrection career is essential to Biblical narrative, for he goes on to father a flesh and blood Jacob and, through him, a flesh and blood community. This story would not serve to legitimize sacrifices in which a dead son was not seen to resurrect in a tangible, bodily form. It seems rather to serve as paradigm for a *ritual* of death and rebirth. The widespread identification of such rituals with mountains as symbolic entries into the underworld, as wombs from which the initiate returns, occurs here: Abraham's near-sacrifice takes place at the Mountain of the Lord (Genesis 22:14) in the land of Moriah, and a certain Mount Moriah is elsewhere identified as the place where Solomon would build his temple (2 Chronicles 3:1).

Such a rite is quite different from offering one's life or someone else's to a hungry god. Chaste flesh chastens spirit, giving way to what is deeper than flesh and higher than spirit (understood as psyche). The psycho-somatic organism must not entertain the imagery of a disordered, compulsive psyche. In the treaty Zosimos choses to relate to 1 Enoch, *Isis the Prophetess to her son Horus,* the Egyptian goddess does not yield to the amorous advances of angels, and so is the opposite of the daughters of men in Enoch. She specifically resists two angels, the lunar and the solar:

> Due to her persistent rebuffing of the angel...Isis was able to gain mastery over Amnael, and he revealed to her the alchemical knowledge. It appears that she did not have to mate with him in return, because the moral lesson of this story, which she imparts to Horus, centers on the notion that like begets like...
>
> In the Enochian myth, which is based on Genesis 6:1–4, the angels mate with human women and beget a race of giants called the Nephilim. Isis's claims that such breeding is "against the order of nature" and "engenders monsters" are in full agreement with the sentiments of the Jewish scriptures...Isis to Horus also promotes concepts that Zosimus associates with natural methods. It teaches that alchemists can acquire knowledge from cosmic spirits, such as angels or daemons, but should also resist their influence.[4]

In fact, Zosimos condemns those whose sacrifices to spirits leads to a slavish relationship, and who are deceived by these entities with substitutes for the true gold of alchemy, or else simply do not aspire for that prize, going so far as to recommend the following:

> Then, without being called to do it, offer sacrifices to the daimons, not the useful variety, not those which nourish and comfort them, but those which deter and destroy them, those which Mambres gave to Solomon, king of Jerusalem, and of which he himself has written according to his wisdom. (*Final Abstinence* ll. 24–27)

If we consider the passage from Zosimus's *Final Abstinence* in which a history of alchemy and the daimons or overseers was provided,[5] we may draw an analogy between the degeneration of religion away from "the art of natural tinctures" towards "non-natural" ones, because "powerful men" no longer "kept the overseers at bay," leading to "sacrifices in exchange for success," with the human sacrifices practiced prior to the Deutero-nomic reform in Jerusalem, in contrast to an earlier form of the religion (as Abraham's story must have indicated an end to even earlier, perhaps Chaldean, practices). The "revolution" that left "temples...deserted and the sacrifices offered to the overseers...neglected" would correspond, or be analogous to, the Deuteronomic reform and its iconoclasm: a temple deserted of the old forms and the end of sacrifices.

---

4   Shannon L. Grimes, *Zosimos of Panopolis: Alchemy, Nature and Religion in Late Antiquity* (Los Angeles: Syracuse University Dissertation. 2003), 105–6.
5   Olivier Dufault, *Early Greek Alchemy, Patronage and Innovation in Late Antiquity* (Berkeley: University of California, 2019), 129.

For Zosimos, there is a legitimate alchemy. The choice is not between a demonic, Titanic magic, on the one hand, and a superficial devotional religion in which God remains a big Other, on the other. We may call this third way *liturgy*. The two others can be identified with Paul's Hebrew and Hellenic mentalities (1 Corinthians 1:22): one superstitious, seeking omens, the other rationalistic, thinking obsessively. We may also think of these as the water that floods the earth, on the one hand, and the sun of water, on the other, in previous Mexican tale. They appear as the lunar and solar angels in the story of Isis.

Whereas the Overseers share, among other things, knowledge of metallurgy for the forging of weapons in Enoch, Isis obtains noble metals, silver and gold, from angels of the moon and sun. Where one expands horizontally, quantitatively, through war (again suggesting the idea of gigantism) the other does so vertically. Resisting the angels, she requests their occult knowledge, and receives it. Rather than resulting from illicit fornication—from mental fascination, fixation, wherein we are instrumentalized by what would otherwise be an instrument, including the psyche itself—a kind of alchemy comes from just the opposite, from resisting and thereby receiving knowledge.

If our original analogy holds, the protagonist here is not spirit acting on flesh, but flesh purifying spirit. Treating this story and Zosimos's commentary as a paganism that ends in Christianity,[6] we may connect its symbols to The Lady of John's Apocalypse. Pregnant, dressed in the sun with her feet on the moon, she might be understood as having mastered these cosmic powers. Returning to Mexico, the Lady of Guadalupe is often interpreted as replacing or vanquishing the sun and lunar gods. Mary's virgin birth of Christ is the fulfilment of these pagan themes.

PROPHETS AGAINST GIANTS

Yet the negative conjunction of flesh and spirit can *look* like its true image. In *1 Enoch*, the newborn Noah is suspected by his father to be a child of a Nephilim angel because of his radiance and ability to speak:

> I have begotten a strange son; he is not like a man but is like the children of the Angels of Heaven, of a different type and not like us. And his eyes are like the rays of the Sun and his face glorious. And it seems to me that he is not sprung from me but from the Angels and I am afraid that something extraordinary may be done on the earth in his days. (106: 5–6)

His wife denies this, but he takes the matter to his father, who takes it to Enoch (106: 10–12), who responds: "...now make known to your

---

6   I would reject Eric Voegelin's characterization of Zosimos as a kind of anti-Platonist proto-Marxist revolutionist, although Christianity does contain another kind of revolutionary imperative.

son Lamech that the one who has been born is truly his son" (106: 18). And again, "And now, my son, go, make known to your son Lamech, that this child that has been born, is truly his son, and this is no lie" (107:2).

This means that some of the phenomena brought by adulterous congress with angels are also achievable through a raised spiritual station. One may manifest supernatural light and other wonders as a consequence of being singled out for a special destiny while being entirely human. Indeed, the hypertrophy of the sons of the Nephilim, described as giants, is not present here, for Noah does not grow to be superhuman in stature. His birth is more comparable with descriptions of Lao Tse, who is said to have had white hair from the womb, for example.

The same occurs in 2 *(Slavonic) Enoch* around the birth of Melchizedek, whose priesthood is linked to messiahship and to Jesus. The contrast between Noah or Melchizedek and the giants parallels the contrast in Greek tradition between figures like Pythagoras, said to be incarnations of Apollo, and earlier hubristic demi-gods like Achilles. Following John Alvis's reading of Homer's *Iliad*,[7] Zeus intended to end the heroic age, culminating with Achilles turning away from hubris and vengeance, using his marshal prowess in the context of funerary games in honor of the dead and the gods. But this intention of Zeus is manifested in Hera's will that he be loyal to the marital bed and producing demigods. We began with the flesh responding to the agency of spirit. Here, femininity is celestial, and bids the masculine to cease from its straying.

Returning to Noah, the same line of questioning Lamech engages in with respect to his son is repeated by St. Joseph in the Gospel, only in this case he is told that the fruit of his wife's womb is, in fact, not his, but likewise not the product of adultery, of undue mixture. It is something entirely different, birthed from a substance that received no visible form.

With regards to pagan accounts of demigods born of the union of deities and humans, which is certainly condemned by the Bible and Zosimos, we should nonetheless note that certain of these may relate not to the ritual union of human with non-human entities, but to

1. a sacred vision of the "heavenly double" of one's spouse, as in Joseph and Aseneth, where Joseph's double acts like Metatron, and speaks of Aseneth's celestial counterpart as Metanoia, and
2. a spurious account of a divinely arranged birth.

In the case of Hercules, this latter is the opinion of the Stoic Lucius Annaeus Cornutus and Epictetus, who consider stories of his being a son of Zeus to simply derive from his having been devout. The same opinion occurs in Iamblichus's hagiography of Pythagoras (II) as concerns the philosopher:

---

7   Alvis, *Divine Purpose and Heroic Response in Homer and Virgil.*

...we must not regard the assertions of Epimenides, Eudoxus and Xenocrates who suspect that Apollo at that time, becoming connected with Parthenis [mother of Pythagoras], and causing her to be pregnant from not being so, had in consequence of this predicted concerning Pythagoras from the Delphic prophet: for this is by no means to be admitted.

While it is also the case that "no one can doubt that the soul of Pythagoras was sent to mankind from the empire of Apollo...for this may be inferred both from birth, and all-various wisdom of his soul." Adds Thomas Taylor, in a footnote:

> It must not be admitted that Apollo was actually connected with Pythais [designating Pythagoras's mother]; for this would be absurd to the extreme; but the narrations of Epimenides, Eudoxus and Xenocrates must be considered as one of those mythological narrations in which heroes are said to have Gods for their fathers, or Goddesses for their mothers, and the true meaning of it is as follows: According to the ancient theology, between those perpetual attendants of the divine nature called essential heroes, who are impassive and pure, and the bulk of human souls who descend to earth with passivity and impurity, it is necessary there would be an order of human souls who descend with impassivity and purity. For as there is no vacuum either in incorporeal or corporeal natures, it is necessary that the last link of a superior order should coalesce with the summit of one proximately inferior. These souls were called by the ancients, terrestrial heroes, on account of their high degree of proximity and alliance to such as are essentially heroes. Hercules, Theseus, Pythagoras, Plato, and co., were souls of this kind, who descended into mortality both to benefit other souls, and in compliance with that necessity by which all natures inferior to the perpetual attendants of the Gods are at times obliged to descend.

Heroes are prophetic, boddhisattva-like entities, then. There are pagan, and even neo-Platonic accounts of physical union between the gods and humans, but the above opinion discards it, representing a current of pagan thought compatible with Zosimos and that of the Bible.

Sacred Authority in European Christendom:
EMPERORS AND POPES

W E ADDRESS THE ARTICULATION OF SACRED kingship as a body politic, the body of the kingdom, through the Roman-Imperial idea and its interaction with Biblical theology and the Apostolic idea, so that the emperor (heir to Aeneas) and pope (heir to St. Peter) constitute our principal subjects (recalling the *Saint Paul as Sacred King* discussion).

THE AMBIVALENCES OF CHRISTIAN EUROPE

We may compare what has been looked at so far with Christian Europe's imperial and papal offices. The investiture rites of these typically refer to Christ, the sacrificed and resurrected king and high priest, and in this sense implicitly contain the preceding pattern of religious epiphany.

Further, that pattern is more or less present in the foundational events of both Papacy and emperorship in Europe: St. Peter's vision in Acts and the story of Aeneas, from whom emperors generally claim descent. It is not, however, that Peter is antecedent of popes and Aeneas of emperors. Imperial authority was often explained as coming from that universal dominion Christ gave Peter and the popes bestow on emperors.

Strange as it may be, it seems that the Church-Empire or Pope-Emperor relationship in Christian Europe is somewhat similar to that of the queen-king relationship is societies from Bronze Age Crete to Tantric Indian city-states. The feminine language associated with the Church is explicitly contrasted to the masculine principle of Empire by Dante, who asserts a necessary symmetry between them. The distinction, however, is more a matter of function than gender, where the high priestly, hide-wearing work of Bronze Age kings fell to the pope or Patriarch and cardinals, and the robe of purple pomp to the emperor and kings.

The split is, in a sense, inherited from imperial Rome, where the queen or empress was not really ritually significant. Still, many queen mothers, including the wife of Otto of Saxony, Adelaide, were crowned along with their husbands upon the latter's ascent. Another axis along which European sacred and political authority gendered itself involves the attempt of several western emperors to marry eastern empresses or princesses, as though the west-east divide were a conjugal alienation.

Margaret Barker sees three agents involved in the Gospel's restoration of ancient religion.[1] The first is the solar goddess whose equivalents we have pointed out in multiple traditions, described in John's Apocalypse as a Lady clothed in the sun and referred to in Malachi 4:2: "But for you who revere my name the sun of righteousness will rise with healing in its rays." The second is Elijah, of whom the Lord says in Malachi 4:5 "See, I will send the prophet Elijah to you before that great and dreadful day of the Lord comes." Jesus seems to identify Elijah with John the Baptist, a priestly revealer that baptizes Jesus and reveals his status, though being subordinate to Christ.

Elijah is a herald. Just as Odysseus sets Mycenae in order after his travels, having lost the disruptive parts of the self (the crew), and ending their clamor at his household (the discourteous pretenders), urged on by the fiery Shakti (the presence of the divine feminine in the Odyssey) the newly calmed psyche can accept its Lord. Bizarrely, Ezra Pound noted a discovery of W. H. D. Rouse according to which people in the Aegean still tell stories about Odysseus, but call him by the name of the Hebrew prophet Elijah.[2]

Barker's third agent of restoration is the Lord, Christ Himself. In Christian terms, we might understand these as partly manifested or represented by the earthly avatars of the mother Church, the pope who, like the priestly John the Baptist baptizing Jesus, crowns the emperor, and the emperor himself, an anointed king after the image of Christ. Of course, these are not the only manifestations of those three, just outwardly visible, institutionalized ones.

Offshoots of Islam, such as the Alawites, have a potentially similar conception of threefold divine agency, which the Alawites designate the *meaning*, *name* and *gate*, so that each prophet actually came with two others (Muhammad, the most recent example in their theology, would have been the *name*, Ali, his relative and son in law, the *meaning*, and Salman al-Farsi, a Persian member of Muhammad's company, the *gate*). We might sense something like this in modern Native American history with the Shawnee chief Tecumseh and his younger brother Tenskwatawa, where the former is the warrior and strategist, and the latter the prophet, whose name, adopted after a transformative vision, means *open door*. The Asante empire's founders, conjurer Okomfo Anokye and emperor Osei Tutu, are also analogous to Tenskwatawa and Tecumseh. The prophet of the ghost dance, Wovoka, and the medicine man Black Elk, who received visions during ghost dances, are likewise a similar, less formally political, dyad. The Alawite Name-Gate-Meaning doctrine is similar to the Prophet-King-Priest doctrine of the Bobo Ashanti Rastafarians (one

---

1   Margaret Barker, *King of the Jews: Temple Theology in John's Gospel* (London: Society for Promoting Christian Knowledge, 2017), 150, 156–57.

2   Sicari, *Pound's Epic Ambition*, 122.

of the three major "mansions" or sects of Rastafarianism), according to which pan-Africanist leader Marcus Garvey, Ethiopian Emperor Haile Selassie I and the sect's founder Prince Emmanuel Charles Edwards, form a triad.

Chinese tradition also contains the idea that the 'prophetic' career requires multiple personages linked together. Sima Qian refers to five-hundred-year-long cycles where agency passes from king to sage (Duke of Chou to Confucius to Sima Qian himself), and Mencius apparently refers to the same periods of time to highlight that more than five-hundred years have passed since the Duke of Chou: "But heaven does not yet want the ecumene pacified and ordered. If it wanted the ecumene pacified and ordered in the present generation, who is there but myself?"[3] The Alawite categories are also not too dissimilar, perhaps, to the three initial creations of the prior Divine masculine and feminine in some schools of Hinduism, where Krishna and Radha, the primordial black and white lights, engender Universal Intellect, Basic-Nature and the Embryo-of-Splendor.[4]

Given that an empress was often crowned by the pope with her emperor, and given that the Empire itself also represents a corporate body, we can posit a fourth term, similar to the idealized humanity that Russian theologians such as Solovyov, Bulgakov and Berdyaev identify with Sophia. We may also approach these in perspectival terms and view the Church as mother, corresponding to or representing the Virgin Mary as far as we, as disciples and congregants, are concerned, but to Christ representing His bride, being at a different ontological level. Very simply, to me the archetype of the mother manifests in my mother, but to my father, my mother is a wife, not a mother. To the Empire, the institutional Church can be a feminine counterpart and therefore consort, but to the society at large, Empire and Church appear as paternal and maternal institutions. This is the sort of imagery that Dante uses and would correspond to the Egyptian set of four primary deities, Shu and Tefnut (father and mother) and their children Geb and Nut (son and daughter).[5]

Perspectival shifts are present, it seems, in the Gospel of John. In John 21:5, though Jesus Christ's words to his disciples is often translated as beginning with "Friends," following David Bentley Hart, it is more accurately translated as "children" (Παιδία): "So Jesus says to them, 'Little children, do you have any fish?'." That Jesus should endear himself to his disciples and friends as an adult to children is consistent with

3   Voegelin, *Order and History, vol. 4, The Ecumenic Age*, 350.
4   Karapatri, *Sri Bhagavati tattva*, Siddhanta, V, 1944–45, cited by Alain Danielou, *The Myths and Gods of India: The Classic Work on Hindu Polytheism* (Rochester, VT: Inner Traditions, 1991), 177.
5   Patai, *Hebrew Goddess*, 118.

John 20:21, where He says "As the Father has sent me, I also send you."
If He is to the Father as the disciples are to Him, even though they all
share a common Father (John 20:17), than divine Fatherhood manifests
in different beings along the great chain of Being (similarly to the way
in which angels in the Bible sometimes speak in the first person when
relaying messages from the Lord).

Overall, however, there are ambivalences here, and it must be admitted
that the case of Christian Europe seems to be one in which the same
principle, with differing emphasizes, is used to justify multiple institutions. It is what Frithjof Schuon describes as an "ambiguity in the
imperial function—of which the emperors were conscious to a greater
or less extent" which "partly explains what may be called the traditional
disequilibrium of Christianity."[6] This point, however, can be overstated,
especially when we compare European Christendom to other pre-modern
civilizations and underestimate the internal tensions in these.

In one sense, these ambivalences are not even principally a matter of
doctrine. If Justinian had conquered Italy definitively and joined east to
west, or if a literal marriage between east and west, such as Irene and
Charlemagne or, more viably, Theophanu and Otto II, could have produced lasting effects, some of the above ambiguities would have been mute.

THE ROMAN EMPEROR AS HIGH PRIEST

The fundamental feature that differentiates the Christian European
emperor—by which is meant both eastern Byzantine and western Holy
Roman emperors—from ancient models is his subordination to the pope
of Rome or the Patriarch of Constantinople. Arguably, however, this
distinction is only apparent.

Emperors claim to descend from Aeneas via Augustus Caesar, which
represents not only a secular source of legitimacy but one of pagan-era
theology. The story of Aeneas contains many initiatic themes, and the
reforms and visions of Caesar Augustus mark him out as a figure of
religious significance even to Christianity, given his vision of a Virgin
birthing the Divine.

When medieval European emperorship comes near to fulfilling its
telos—which is to unite the old Roman world, now Christianized, under
itself—it almost always does so by becoming supreme over the *ecclesia*
or, more correctly, by becoming head of the ecclesia. This reveals its
historic character, but is obviously contentious.

In this mode, Christian European emperorship conforms to the ancient
paradigm, in which "the high-priesthood cannot be distinguished...from
kingship" in the following passage Marinatos is discussing Minoan iconography, but here we draw attention to a general principle:

---

6   Schuon, *The Essential Frithjof Schuon*, Part I: Theology and Philosophy, note 8, 180.

This is not to deny that colleges of priests existed in Crete, as they did also in the Near East and Egypt. In Mycenean Greece the Linear B tablets attest to the office of i-je-re-u, namely priest. Nor is it to deny that priests had power (they could even manipulate the king himself during certain periods of history).[7]

While the fundamental insight of the preceding discussion is that religious epiphany leads to the political act par excellence, namely representation (though not necessarily or strictly *political* representation, as one can represent unities other than the *polis*), and therefore that high priesthood's archaic unity with kingship is indeed coherent, this does not mean that a king or emperor has no need of instruction, of reminding, and that a priestly office apart from his cannot fulfil that role, remaining focused on the abstract epiphany of the autozoon (and therefore often monastic) even while the king applies it to—discovers it within—the life of the concrete kingdom. It is true that clerical priority of order is quite universally asserted in European culture. Apart from Byzantine and Holy Roman Emperors, the Bulgar, Serb and Russian Tsar, as well as the Austrian Kaiser, were considered subordinate to the head of the Church (Orthodox and Catholic respectively).

But the structural relationship of pope or high priest to emperor, where the former crowns the latter, is not so clear sign of hierarchy. In the first place, for a time popes had to swear fealty to the emperor during their Papal investiture, creating a curious symmetry of mutual dependence between the offices. If this does not entail that the Holy Roman emperor, even in the west, had an ecclesial position, the issue is clearer in that emperors and kings would sometimes invest their local bishops with sacred authority (using ring and staff, symbols of the sacred). This ended when Pope Calixtus II (albeit reluctantly and hoping it would be provisional) agreed to the monarchical right to invest bishops as part of the Concordat of Worms with Emperor Henry V, but only if the investiture was to do with secular authority, that is, by lance, but no ring or staff (Calixtus II wanted to go further in reducing kingly and imperial power).

Apart from historical backs and forths, the crowning of emperor by pope might not signify superiority, as the Christian tradition includes the precedent of John the Baptist baptizing one greater than himself, Jesus Christ, where a ritual recognition and revelation—even a bringing forth—of the latter's status does not by any means imply that the officiator of that ritual is responsible for bestowing, much less creating, said status. This scriptural paradigm cannot be wholly absent from the minds of devout Christians, and something like it seems to approximate what certain emperors understood, given their, at times explicit, rejections of

---

7   Marinatos, *Minoan Kingship and the Solar Goddess: A Near Eastern Koine*, 32.

the notion that the pope had made them emperors by crowning them as such, as is the case of Frederick Barbarossa. Of course, power-hunger and ambition were often at play, but a conceptual disagreement also existed.

The Minoan parallel is not as incidental as it may seem. Although Marinatos emphasizes its similarity to other Near Eastern (including Anatolian Hittite) theo-monarchical ideologies, it is conspicuous among these for how long it has taken to identify the figure of the king in its iconography. Whereas in other surviving Bronze Age political paraphernalia the king stands out, Minoans apparently did not emphasize him. The Minoan king's plumed crown was often associated with the high priest rather than with the king *as* high priest by modern archeologists and researchers. The de-emphasizing of royal pomp, a certain humility, or the swallowing up of the royal by the priestly at key moments in its ceremonial—however merely stylistic or aesthetic a difference it may pose as regards other contemporary cultures—is quite in keeping with the Roman Republican approach to leadership and the European medieval conception, which strongly harnesses kingship and emperorship to a sense of priestly measure, at least rhetorically and often in practice too. At this point the intuition that Minoan Crete is the basis of Platonic *paideia* and Platonic paideia in turn the basis for much of European medieval practice may be reiterated. We could venture to speak of a Minoan-Medieval ethos, via Platonism.

Indeed, Dimitri Nakassis's characterization of Mycenean society sounds somewhat medieval, rather than fitting the orientalist notion of Bronze Age despotic, centralized polities in the region (which is in any case inaccurate of other polities too). Referring to recent studies, he writes that "[t]his work suggests that the Mycenean social and political order was quite complex, with respect to both the internal operation of the palace and its relationship to other institutions."[8]

From the historical point of view, we may even venture the following thesis: Christian Roman Emperors generally tended towards the classical and ancient unity of sacerdotal and kingly authority. This supports the idea that Empire as such is not really separable from high priesthood (just as spiritual epiphany underpins political representation).

The above is very seldom explicit in European history, however. We often find a theology of division between kingly dignity and the sacred, where law and collective organization is a condescension to sin—Charlemagne's favoring of St. Augustine's *City of God* might be an instance of this. Such a view implies order should be spontaneous and acultural, thereby containing the seed of utopian, anarchic and naturalist ideologies. It is freedom from law, not the freedom to make law, freedom

---

8   Dimitri Nakassis. *Individuals and Society in Mycenean Pylos*. Mnemosyne, Supplements, History and Archaeology of Classical Antiquity, Volume 358 (Leiden: Brill, 2013), 3.

from culture, not freedom to produce culture. The Byzantine east is at least in principle more properly connected to sacred kingship and less prone than the west to the fantasy of acultural human sociability. The idea of society without community (liberal and Marxist) emerges from the European west.

The tendency of Christian emperors to involve themselves in theology is evidence for 1) the ultimate impossibility of divorcing authority from theology and 2) the historical endurance of the sense that emperorship is not inferior to the Papacy, an instinct sometimes made explicit by actions. If this is a hearkening back to and anticipation of the more ancient and initiatic unity of kingship with high priesthood, it is nonetheless not the case that such unity should necessarily have been achieved de facto (analogous to Frederick II's *potential ubiquity* in terms of his office as emperor). Historical processes have their rhythms and anticipating something which a tradition places at the horizon of eschatological changes would obviously have been impious. At the same time, the historical Papacy does not seem for its part to have renounced the political, nor did it assert sacred kingship, instead often allowing itself to be animated by petty localized concerns.

In any case, if sacred kingship is divided in European Christendom, it is divided between emperor *and* pope. Whether one is more excellently the repository of the virtual image of sacred kingship is another matter. Perhaps the last shall be first in this, and the lower dignity of the emperor with respect to pope is esoterically actually reversed.

The current state of affairs, wherein Catholicism has its pope, but Europe has no emperor, is interesting to consider. The final absence of emperorship in Europe signals its inappropriateness for the climate of political modernity, maybe even its being inessential for those dire political and religious circumstances modernity has brought about. Yet maybe lofty things become absent more readily than gross ones. As John Milbank writes, those hidden regents from legend who are prophesied to return (Sebastian of Portugal, King Arthur, Frederick II, and so on) are figures of that yet-to-return Christ. Conspicuously, the pope is not likewise hidden.

The real ambiguity here is that of conversion and how conversion functions. If Roman emperorship takes its spiritual significance from its founder, Aeneas, whose story is initiatic and displays the perennial features of sacred kingship, how does it relate to these same features in the story of St. Peter? That is, how does it relate to the institution of the Petrine Church or Apostolic authority in general? How are two sources of legitimacy, one older and perhaps weakened, the other newer but claiming not to abolish the preceding, relate? Concerning the newer, Peter (or the Apostles in general) receives authority from Christ, and Christ is a fuller revelation of religious significance than otherwise available, so that, from the Christian perspective, that which He establishes must have priority.

Perhaps this priority is not to do with replacing older institutions and mythologies. Not abolishing the law, but fulfilling it; not circumcising, but baptizing with water. Maybe the fortunate absence of Christ (leaving His disciples; the absence of an empirical body; the absence of a dynastic lineage) is best expressed by the baptizing and merging of His revelation with pre-existing dynasties and institutions, rather than the creation of a new locus of authority. Christianity baptizes with water, it does not circumcise, it does not alter the body.

The fact that St. Peter reveals his epiphany of sacred kingship to an Italian centurion whose service and position is pledged to the descendent of Aeneas adds one source of initiation to the other, renewing and deepening. The centurion warrior receives the sacred teaching, like Arjuna in the *Bhagavad Gita*. The priest is higher than the warrior yet the king comes from the warrior caste, and is in a sense highest, the fifth element in between the four castes, and is mentioned in the *Bhagavad Gita* when Lord Krishna declares He is "the king among humans" (10:27) while listing His manifestation in different orders of creation (mount Meru among mountains, etc.).

Multiple interpretations are possible, but the Gospel injunction is to give Caesar what is Caesar's and God what is God's, not to give God what is God's while (or by) refusing Caesar. Some Catholics have interpreted this passage as a statement of subsidiarity, that is, respecting concentric circles of authority. Christ is teaching a spiritual or esoteric truth, not establishing a new Caesar, a new national or political project or abolishing the work of Hebrew prophets in shaping the nation of Israel. The treatment of Caesar is no different to that of Hebrew religion as established. Its hypocritical and calcified elements are treated with antinomian abandon, but in and of itself it is not rejected. In this sense, Aeneas can be taken alongside those Hebrew prophets.

If Jesus was born to the line of King David and the Hebrew context of St. Peter's career relates him to Davidic monarchy, Dante's contention that David was born when the Trojans entered Italy connects the two sources of spiritual authority (Aeneas via his descendants the Emperors and David fulfilled in Jesus and then carried on by Peter) archetypically and in the context of a Christian Roman Empire. Indeed, in theory both are universal, and in practice both delineate a European reality (circumscribed by the culturally less Greco-Roman and non-Christian borders of Islam), while also being present globally.

But how do they relate structurally, as *types* rather than in terms of their archetype, if superimposed in one entity, that is, Christian Roman Emperorship (Holy Roman or Byzantine)? One answer is that the situation is similar to that of two men collecting water from the rain, surviving a drought, thereafter being able to marry and have children. Subsequently, during second drought, one of the men, having water available, offers some to the other. Both survive and are able to educate their children, who are now older. The water itself is from the sky, but families are receptive and can receive help from others in times of need.

A foreign culture can develop a quality that is essential to another, but which that other has allowed to atrophy. Assimilating that foreign culture is therefore a way of achieving a truer expression of the local. This is more or less the Muslim position, insofar as the *fitrah*, or human primordiality, is more or less articulated by those Arab customs Muhammad emphasized. The instinct to identify reception as pollution is misguided in such matters. Indeed, the *Sol Indiges* cult of Rome was renewed by *Sol Invictus*.[9] The meaning of receiving from the outside what fulfils the indigenous is that *essences are occult and transcendent* and *formal entities are porous to each other*.

The key point to remember is that Christianity does not contain an *imperative towards ethnogenesis* the way the story of Aeneas and origin of Rome does. Even any imperative towards a *civilizational project* is extremely subtle compared to Islam, for example, as highlighted by statements from Christ about worshiping God in spirit, neither in Jerusalem nor in the Samaritan mountain.

Here, Montgomery Watt's notion of Islam as issuing from a certain Old Testament mode of prophethood seems appropriate (which in this context we can describe as institutionalizing rather than transforming—setting up a state, legal tradition or national vocation rather than baptizing an existing structure). It can be argued that translation is partially what the Ottoman Empire thought it was doing, considering itself a continuation of Rome in Constantinople, but Caliphal authority was a new, political seat erected by Islam, unlike the Papacy, which sought sacerdotal status and the correcting of worldly rulers, and unlike Christian Roman Emperorship, which was a prior form baptized, not replaced, by the faith.

We may compare Christianity to Buddhism, which at times in its history was translated into existing institutions, transforming but not replacing them. A radical example of this is the Manchu Emperor of China assigning clerical and kingly authority to the Mongolian son of Tushetu Khan in the 17th century, overriding Buddhist Tibetan clergy as separate source of legitimacy. The Buddhist clergy as effective actor was at that time seemingly represented by a pre-Buddhist imperial institution, rather than acting as its own separate institution.

---

9   Europe has always been receptive to the Orient, receiving the Lebanese princess Europa, the Trojans, Christianity, fantasizing about Prester John and, in terms of modern historical accounts, Indo-Aryans (possibly) from the Pontic Caspian area or Anatolian farmers during the Neolithic. *Ex Oriente Lux.*

EMPEROR AS THEOLOGICAL BRIDGE-BUILDER (*PONTIFEX*)

The emperor's relationship to the pope or patriarch often seems to be one in which the latter is a spiritual corrector, counselor, and teacher, rather than superior. Christian Roman emperorship is initiated by Constantine, who is honored as a Saint. Subsequent emperors are somewhat possessed of the confidence implied by such a term, pronouncing on theology and, in the case of Otto of Saxony and his successors, appointing popes, reversing the familiar, if somewhat novel and originally quite *ad hoc*, formula of pope appointing emperor.

Emperors were often bridge builders between east and west and between different Christian sects. The clergy has always been a bit allergic to imperial attempts at relaxing theological differences. Initially the only emperor was in the east, Byzantium. As early as the sixth century the Patriarch of Constantinople had been described as ecumenical, or universal, pontiff, as was the case of a certain Patriarch John in 588 AD, whom Popes Pelagius and later Gregory I rejected, the latter asking the emperor (at the time there was only one, and he was Byzantine) for help in condemning the title, which came to nothing, meeting only with clear support of emperor for patriarch.

The early handling of the Arian controversy by Emperor Constantine is a case in point, displaying Imperial will to ecumenism. At first, he entreated both sides to see that the issue in dispute was not worthy of the polemic it was inciting. When this did not work, he held a Synod and decided in favor of the non-Arianist formulation *homoousia*, of *one essence*, to describe Christ's relation to the Father, telling the followers of Arius, however, that this could be interpreted mystically (which is why the usual translation of one *substance* seems less appropriate to me than one *essence*, for the substances can be different within a *mystical* unity). He later almost reinstated Arius as Bishop, though hostility at the move led him to call for a clarification of Arian views in course of which the problematic theologian died (for his part, Constantine would be baptized by an Arian Bishop). Eventually, however, Constantine's Edict against the Arians imposed the death penalty on whoever did not hand in Arius's writings to be disposed of.

From Constantine's esoteric accommodation of Arians to Justinian's attempted reconciliation of mainstream with Monophysite Christians (along an arguably Orthodox route), Charlemagne's involvement in theological questions related to icon veneration, ensuring these were not considered *worshipable*, Otto of Saxony's paternalistic attempts at correcting Pope John XII and appointment of proper popes, Otto III apparently thinking his office enjoyed primacy over the Papacy, Barbarossa apparently not considering his emperorship to emanate from Papal decision, Byzantine John VIII pushing for the Council of Florence, and Charles V's imputations against Clement VII, it has not been historically clear that emperorship is secondary to the papacy, even in terms of treating theology responsibly.

The fact of being a temporal ruler leads to a vista over sacred truths that is possibly more complete than that of the priest who is not involved in such temporal issues, because temporality is also a part of the creation and is to be restored, revealed in the light of eternity. Milbank's formula about the king *diagonalizing* out from his merely temporal role and being superior to the priest contains this idea. Recall that in Vedic tradition the priestly caste is above that of warriors, the king is a warrior, but the king is in a sense above priests in that Lord Krishna says in the *Bhagavad Gita* that among humans he is the king.

As Schuon puts it, "the temporal power, which appertains to the emperor, represents in this case universality or 'realism' and therefore 'tolerance', and therefore also in the nature of things a certain element of wisdom."[10] Indeed, our whole thesis here is that the spiritual epiphany, a vision of the universal, is the true basis of political representation and leadership (this is expounded on in Addendum IV concerning Christian Roman Emperorship, which traces some of these themes through a historical survey).

The ideal of the Adamology of Empire, the Adam-Emperor in which the sacerdotal and regal are undivided or, what is the same, the Christic king, manifests in European history from radical Ghibellines praising Frederick II in the 1200s to Rosicrucianism's manifestos. The European prophetic tradition of a Holy Caesar repeats many of the same themes to do with sacred kingship found in Mesopotamian, Egyptian, Minoan, Hebrew, Indian, and other mythologies that we looked at previously. From the golden age inaugurated through Caesar Augustus according to Virgil, to the future holy Roman emperor anticipated in early Christian works such as pseudo-Methodius and the Tiburtine Sibyl, medieval prophecies attributed to Merlin of Arthur's return, to the prophecies around figures such as Emperor Barbarossa and his grandson Frederick II, both linked to sacred mountains and said to be dormant, set to return one day, to Dante who reformulates these themes in *Il Convivio*, also referring to Emperor Henry VII as a new Aeneas and, in a letter urging the capture of rebellious Florence, as a new David set to slay Goliath.

Many of the images discussed above recur in Catholic eschatology (which often focuses on Europe in foretelling the restoration of spiritual health, perhaps as a local proxy or analogue for more general considerations) and specifically in the writings of Anne Catherine Emmerich *via* Clemens Brentano. The consistent validity or general theological and metaphysical correctness of these is not taken for granted here, although on several points they display traditional symbolism, as René Guénon

---

10   Schuon, *The Essential Frithjof Schuon*, Part I: Theology and Philosophy, note 8, 180.

pointed out[11]—but pious prudence is called for.[12] Frithjof Schuon, for example, characterizes Emmerich's visions as "purely symbolical images interspaced with historically adequate facts."[13] As St. Paul writes, "Do not despise prophetic utterances. Test everything; retain what is good" (1 Thess. 5:19-21). The Catholic prophetess recounts her visions concerning a future emperor:

> I saw a mountain as of precious stones appear before the Throne of God; it grew and spread. It was in terraces, like a throne; then it changed into the shape of a tower—a tower which enshrined every treasure of the spirit and every gift of grace and was surrounded by the nine choirs of angels.[14]

The "mountain of the prophet," whose name indicates the possibility of its issuing spiritual renewal, shares descriptors with holy mountains in Greco-Latin, Egyptian and Hebraic traditions. Emmerich presents the same superposition of holy mountain, divine throne and tower that Aristotle highlights as an artifact of Pythagorean doctrine according to Simplicius. The most elusive of the Pythagorean associated terms, however, that of *prison*, does not appear in Emmerich's vision, perhaps because in an eschatological restoration this facet no longer operates.

Emmerich's description also features nine angelic choirs, corresponding to the nine Corybantes dancing at Crete's Idaean ceremonial, and to the general recurrence of this number in the context of sacred mountains. Further, this image is linked to the Virgin Mother: "I saw in the sky a

11   René Guénon, *The King of the World*, trans. H. Fohr, ed. S. Fohr (Hillsdale, NY: Sophia Perennis, 2004), 52; 55; 65.

12   From a Catholic perspective, Colin Donovan, Vice President for Theology at EWTN (a Catholic television channel) puts it quite reasonably, writing that private revelations can "lead to a fruitful personal meditation...without being historical in all its details. An example of the principle of God using what is already known by the mystic to form a vision or private revelation is the placement of the nails, and its corollary, the location of the stigmata in those saints who have had them. Scripture doesn't tell us with precision how Jesus was nailed. The Hebrew word in Psalm 22:16 is usually translated hand, but could apply to the wrist or adjacent forearm, as well. Nonetheless, the artistic tradition usually portrays the palm of the hand, while mystics propose a variety of placements from palm to wrist to forearm. On the other hand, the Shroud of Turin and historical studies of crucifixion argue strongly that the Crucified was nailed through the wrist, as the only part which could support a body's weight. Do the differences among mystics, and with the likely actual case (the wrist), make a palm or forearm placement of the wounds inauthentic? Not according to Catholic mystical theology, which recognizes the subjective (personal) element in mysticism, and which therefore allows for differences in such details."

13   Frithjof Schuon, *Sufism: Veil and Quintessence* (Bloomington, IN: World Wisdom, 2006), footnote, 62.

14   Anne Catherine Emmerich, *The Life of the Blessed Virgin Mary: From the Visions of Ven. Anne Catherine Emmerich*, trans. Sir Michael Palairet (Charlotte, NC: TAN Books & Publishers, 2004), 42–43.

figure like a virgin which passed into the tower...."[15] This is paralleled by the association of Mount Ida to Rhea, mother of Jove and, on another level, to Juno, mother of souls, and generally by a host of traditions that imbue holy mountains with maternal connotations.

In occupying Jove's seat, the demiurgically endowed king counts Rhea as his mother, whereas Juno is his spouse, into which he implants the cosmic design so that it might be actualized or ripened. Being corporeal and feminine, both body and bride, there is a parallel here to Christian doctrine as regards the Church in relation to Christ.

---

15 Ibid., 43.

Christian-Roman Emperor

EMPEROR AS GUARDIAN OF THE CHURCH, PART I: IMPERIAL ECUMENISM

The first Western Emperor Charlemagne's possible fit of pique, as John Julius Norwich suggests it be characterized, upon hearing of the Papacy's rapprochement with the eastern Patriarch, is an interesting case of theological involvement. It seems that Rome and Constantinople came together in mutual condemnation of the sort of iconoclasm the Byzantine Emperor Leo III had been promoting a few decades prior, and that Leo IV, Irene's late husband, had at first partly reversed but latterly resumed. Perhaps angry at not having been included, and in a contrarian mood, The Frankish Caesar had his court produce a defense of iconoclasm. The entire issue was settled, however, on account of a mistaken translation. Apparently, Charlemagne was happy to accept *veneration* of holy things, but not *adoration*, which is owed to God alone. The subtle difference is actually not at all subtle and is revealing of the Emperor's creedal orthodoxy. Given how it was resolved, the episode is instructive of correct doctrine (indeed, of an important metaphysical principle) and the Emperor's role in maintaining it. Therefore, we should not automatically impute Charlemagne's interrogation of the clerical ruling with the desire to assert political dominance (on this point, Norwich defaults to assuming a base feeling, as is frequent in his treatment of the personages he discusses, conforming to a certain skeptical style in mainstream historians of his generation, probably stemming from a liberal and Marxist anthropology according to which even history's exceptional moments result from the pursuit of profit and power).

A less edifying episode, one in which Charlemagne could justifiably be thought obstinate, involves his anger at Pope Leo III's defense of the original Nicene creed in order to smooth over differences with the eastern Patriarchate. This involved emphasizing the original creed as it was, which both east and west had agreed on, and which did not include the famous *filioque* clause according to which the Holy Spirit proceeds from the Father *and* from the Son, rather than simply from the Father. Pope Leo III was not rejecting the clause, simply de-emphasizing it, given that it was indeed absent from the original creed as agreed centuries prior. Charlemagne's defense of the addition of the *filioque* wording and interference with the pope's ecumenical project is similar to certain popes using theological issues to emphasize their power, valuing the latter over the cause of peace and terminology-transcending doctrinal substance. The east and west would reconcile on this point centuries later during the 1431 Council of Florence when it was decided that the latterly devised eastern formula of *from the Father and through the Son* was the true meaning of the western *filioque* and perfectly compatible with the original creed.

We may take the Augustinian explanation of the Trinity, compatible with the Hindu *Sat-Chit-Ananda* triad (Being, Consciousness, Bliss). The *filioque* could not be extirpated entirely, it needed a defender, because the locus of understanding is consciousness, although it does originate from Being, because what is understood in the first place, that which reveals itself to its own awareness, is that Being. Even here, therefore, we should view Charlemagne generously (although, again, Leo III wasn't denying the filioque).

In seeing off her husband's iconoclasm, Irene of Athens can be seen as an example of the theological role of the imperial office. It may even be the case that deposing her son Constantine VI (who she blinded, presumably as a way to avoid execution or permanent imprisonment) was in part motivated by his having iconoclastic sympathies like the preceding Emperors Leo IV and Leo III, apart from his military failures, divorce, marriage to a mistress and mutilation of his seditious uncles (this latter he might actually have done under his mother's influence). Such excesses are unremarkable by the standards of the day and would not really warrant Irene's punishment of him, which could explain the popular dislike that finally led to her downfall.

Anyway, the feminine character of the cosmos as multiplicity is somehow expressed by Byzantine history through figures like the Empresses Irene, Euphrosyne and Theodora, who all successfully fought against iconoclasm,[1] which rejects the formal diversity of creation as expressive of the Divine in liturgy.

Charlemagne also endeavored towards east-west, Orthodox-Catholic unity, wanting to marry Byzantine Empress Irene of Athens. The same will to unity appears centuries later when Otto of Saxony regained the long-dormant office, lost in the west since the death of Charlemagne's son Louis. Otto of Saxony was recovering an institution, but doing so under the morally despicable John XII (a notorious trafficker in *pornocracy*, rule by debauchery, as Church histories put it). John XII bestowed this honor, one which Otto had aspired to for years, for similar reasons to those that moved the practically minded and somewhat obscure figure of Leo III to inaugurate western Emperorship in the first place: the need to fight off raiders in Norther Italy by enlisting a militarily strong Germanic state. However, John XII subsequently decided to negotiate with the son of the raiders he had asked Otto to fight off, a betrayal which fully explains Otto's turning against that anti-pope.

---

1   Judith Herrin, *Women in Purple: Rulers of Medieval Byzantium* (Princeton, NJ: Princeton University Press, 2004).

It is also possible that John's disastrous behavior in other matters originated the conflict, for Otto had from the beginning apparently insisted on treating the pontiff of Rome as though he were a reprobate child, lecturing him accordingly, leading the latter to undermine their political alliance. Otto defeated the northern menace as originally agreed, occupied Rome and had the bishops appoint a new pope, Leo VIII, who the Romans myopically rejected, preferring the devil they knew to a foreign appointment. Thus, John XII returned, wrought horrible vengeance, continued squandering Roman treasure and confirming the charges which Otto and the bishops had previously brought against him to justify their selection of a new pope. Otto had to return, once again do away with John and facilitate yet another reasonable pope. A certain primacy of emperorship was manifest in Otto the Saxon's appointing of popes and defeating pornocracy.

Like Charlemagne and his son Louis, Otto shared emperorship with his son, Otto II, to educate him as to the requirements of the office. This is similar to those good caesars, ending with Marcus Aurelius, who appointed their adoptive sons co-emperors so that on their death these would be ready to rule. After Otto II, Otto III's Papal appointments (the relationship of emperor to pope is now explicitly appointer to appointee) consisted of the first German and Frenchman to hold the seat. The second, Gerbert of Aurillac, Archbishop of Ravenna who took the name Sylvester II, led the Papacy into its second millennium. He went about building Europe, from popularizing Arabic numerals and terrestrial and celestial globes, to donating Hungary her crown.

History saw disastrous lapses after this, but the Imperial office would occasionally return to good form and appoint a competent pope, which is not to say that all competent popes were imperial appointments, but it was frequently the case that Rome would see rise a terrible nepotist whom the emperor had to replace with a better man. An example is that of Emperor Henry III's appointment of the able Leo IX after the debauched papacy of Benedict IX, which was even worse than that of his father, also a pope. After a confused three-way competition for the position, Leo IX emerged as tireless crusader against bribery and politicking in the church.

Unfortunately, Leo IX later took it upon himself to fight the mercenary Normans, who were establishing themselves throughout Italy, but who were not heretics, nor even allied with Constantinople, and who, in fact, seem to have treated the pope relatively well when they captured him after his army's defeat in 1053. In this he exceeded his reformist purview and took up arms against people who were part of his civilization, of the Catholic faith, and whose disruptive influence could probably have been absorbed.

The east displays a long history of Imperial ecumenism following Constantine. Emperor Zeno the Isaurian wrote a letter trying to reconcile mainstream and Monophysite Christians without taking a clear position, leading to such ire that the Roman Pope excommunicated the Patriarch of Constantinople (presumably thinking the latter's opinion was that of Zeno) and vice-versa. Granted, the popular rejection of Zeno as a foreigner contributed to this reaction, but something similar occurred again during the rule of Justinian.

St. Justinian, whom the Eastern Orthodox have canonized, tried to reconcile Monophysites and Chalcedonian Christians (like Constantine had done with Arian ones) by getting them to focus on their common condemnation of Nestorians (whose presence in the Empire was between scant and null). This he did by issuing a triple condemnation of Nestorius's teacher and two other obscure theologians, Theodore of Mopsuestia, Theodoret of Cyrus, and Ibas of Edessa. Though partly motivated by his wife Theodora's Monophysite leanings, this must have been an overridingly political move intended to bring peace and, perhaps, theological subtlety to a conflict that modern Orthodox theologians regard as proceeding more from differences in language than real disagreement. David Bentley Hart writes:

> The great tragedy of the Christological controversies was that, for the most part, the churches were divided more by language than by belief. The so-called Monophysites, for instance, never meant to deny the full and inviolable humanity of Christ.[2]

Justinian's desire for unity included military ambitions. He sought to return to the Roman empire, retaking the first Rome and more generally Italy. Dante praises him for his loyalty to the ideal of Roman unity, envisioning him in Paradise in the *Divine Comedy*. Under Justinian, by way of his brilliant general Belisarius, the Ostrogoths lost Ravenna and Rome (though by then Belisarius had been made to take a secondary role) along with other cities, the Vandals of North Africa lost about an eighth of Spain and formerly un-Romanized parts of the Black Sea coast entered the Byzantine fold.

Emperor Justinian was harsh with Pope Vigilius, who went back and forth between conformity to the Emperor and his wife's wishes and earnest disagreement with Justinian's condemnation of obscure Nestorian (or approximately Nestorian) thinkers, preferring a direct attack on the Monophysites. He was finally made to settle on the former position after much vacillation and ultimately imprisonment, dying after his release while attempting to make the journey back home to Rome from the east, by which time his health waned severely. The pope's initial hardline against Monophysites had been shared in Italy, and his later agreement with the Emperor caused the ecclesial authorities of some cities, including

---

2   David Bentley Hart, *The Story of Christianity: A History of 2000 Years of the Christian Faith* (London: Quercus Editions, 2013).

Milan, to temporarily break with Rome. Latter-day Protestant rejection of the Imperial idea and willingness to break with the pope is therefore already present in the sixth century. Like Otto of Saxony and the much later Charles V, Justinian is a champion of Roman unity, viewing himself as having authority to interfere in church matters, taking theological positions and, crucially, being thwarted by local Italian or regional nationalism.

Emperor Heraclius, after Justinian, resolved a theological dispute by arguing Christ has two natures but one energy (Monoenergism), later, one will (Monothelitism). It was Sophronius, Patriarch of Jerusalem who declared it heresy. Eventually the pope excommunicated Constantinople's Patriarch and vice-versa. Again, we have a historically quite consistent clerical tendency to reject reconciliation, even in mystical or esoteric terms, in preference of doctrinal clarity, anathematizing what seems to fall outside it, while the emperor tries his hand (perhaps sometimes clumsily or spuriously) at ecumenical understanding.

Constantine's desire for a mystical interpretation of formulae within which Arianists might find their way to Orthodoxy, Justinian's anticipation of later theologians' realization that the Monophysites were in a way not really outside Orthodoxy, along with attempts like those of Zeno and Heraclius, add to the idea of the Roman Emperor as a kind of high priest.

Back west Frederick Barbarossa presents an interesting case study for the imperial prerogative. When Pope Hadrian was forced to make peace with King William of Sicily, contradicting his agreement with Barbarossa that neither pope nor emperor would unilaterally negotiate with Sicilian Normans (or Byzantines and other third parties), the emperor needed explanations and assurances. The consequent reception of a letter from Hadrian in Barbarossa's court marks an interesting episode, providing as it does evidence for the entrenched conception of the emperorship as an office recognized or ratified but not bestowed by the papacy. The language of the letter employed technicisms proper to describing the relationship of feudal lord and vassal but occurred in the context of the pope's relationship with the emperor. The latter was being reminded that, in the opinion of the letter's author, the pope had made him what he was. When the Papal envoy present at its reception responded to the assemblage's consternation by asking who the emperor received his crown from if not the pope, a member of Barbarossa's company had to be restrained after lunging forward at the fellow with apparently murderous intent.

Otherwise, however, both before and after this episode, Emperor Frederick Barbarossa was not particularly up to the task of articulating a sense of sacred monarchy. The mystic Hildegard of Bingen, so-called Sybil of the Rhine, wrote to Barbarossa that she had seen him in visions "like a little boy, or some madman living before Living Eyes."[3]

---

3   Hildegard of Bingen, Letter 45, in Joseph L. Baird, ed., *The Personal Correspondence of Hildegard of Bingen* (Oxford: Oxford University Press, 2006), 78.

He unnecessarily alienated the recently formed Roman commune by not paying even rhetorical tribute to the glories of Rome and giving no concrete assurances that he would fend for the city's safety, causing Pope Adrian IV to have to crown him emperor outside Rome, a city Frederick was unable to enter on that occasion because it barricaded itself against him. He later absurdly organized a *coup d'ecclesia*, so to speak, infiltrating a pretender to the papacy into the investiture ceremony of Pope Alexander III, Adrian's successor. His chosen antipope, Victor IV, had to hastily steal and, when thwarted, produce a double of the papal garments, sit at the throne, declare himself pope and force some clergymen to recognize him at supreme pontiff as though the whole rite were a matter of words and actions and not context and intent. This caused a schism in the Papacy which eventually resolved itself against Frederick's designs and in favor of Alexander, but not before Frederick entered Rome and delivered one of the worst sacks the city had experienced in a campaign of vicious abandon and impiety. It was all for naught, as a plague, which killed many of his men, forced him back north, where he had to disguise himself for fear of the populace, which understandably hated him. Eventually he resolved most of his disputations with the Papacy by accepting its imperatives, so both he and the imperial office gained little or nothing from the conflict. Frederick would die on crusade crossing the Taurus mountains in southern Anatolia.

One of Barbarossa's sons, Philip of Swabia, married Irene Angelina, daughter of the deposed Byzantine emperor, Isaac II. The marriage was meant to improve relations between east and west, but when Philip asked the west for help against the Byzantine pretender who had ousted his father-in-law, he received it in the form of a terrible Frankish sack of Constantinople that, although it was interpreted by Pope Innocent III as a reprisal against schismatics finally putting an end to the division of Christendom (Franks would stay on the eastern throne for about fifty years thereafter), quite predictably ensured a far harder line against the west on the part of Constantinople. Another son was crowned Emperor Henry VI along with his wife Empress Constance, daughter of Roger II king of Sicily. It is their heir, Frederick Barbarossa's grandson, Frederick II, inheritor of Sicily by way of his mother, who provides a more interesting case than Barbarossa himself as pursuer of sacred monarchy. We have here the first good European according to Nietzsche.[4]

Frederick II showed a diplomatic cunning which his grandfather had largely lacked. The Pope's angry incitement against him for having put off the crusade he had sworn himself to—refusing to see the Hohenstaufen Emperor's envoys in Rome or to accept his account of being genuinely ill and awaiting recovery before setting off to retake the holy land—was met with a reasonable request for understanding in the form of an open letter from Frederick.

---

4   Nietzsche, *Beyond Good and Evil*, 200, 87.

In fact, Frederick II did mount a crusade—though by then he had been excommunicated—but it was a peaceful one, convincing the Muslim Sultan at Cairo to simply give him Jerusalem (the Spaniard Cardinal Pelagius of Albano had previously refused to be given land west of Jerusalem in return for leaving Egypt, but Frederick II maneuvered a similar settlement for himself and Christendom). That Christians at the time found cause for reproach in Frederick's admiration of Arabic culture and consultation with Islamic philosophers should, even by whatever standards they were holding him to, have been a moot point after such an achievement. The fact of entering Jerusalem peacefully and being rejected by religious authorities for precisely that reason presents a Christic parallel (just as some among the Pharisees rejected Jesus peacefully entering Jerusalem, wanting a martial messianic taking of the city).

The Pope and Frederick II reconciled over time, falling out again, and just as emperors had at times favored their antipopes the pope had his anti-kings. Both Frederick II, who died of dysentery during a hunting trip, and his sons, would see their political project thwarted by a jealous papacy (consisting especially of the competent and militantly anti-imperial Gregory) refusing to be purely sacerdotal but also refusing to be imperial, preferring instead regency over the Papal states and the undermining of any possible ecumenical unity—it is sometimes as if the fate of Europe (as well as African and Asian Christians and, in fact, Muslims too) had fallen to a petty state regent:

> European anti-imperialism originated in papal propaganda during the Investiture Dispute and especially with the onset of renewed conflict against the Staufer emperors from the mid-twelfth century…[h]owever, the papacy's own actions simultaneously invalidated its claims to supplant the emperor as universal judge.[5]

Another case of emperor as unifier occurs in the reign of Byzantine John VIII Palaiologos, who pressured the clergy to settle the Council of Florence, ending the centuries long east-west schism in 1439. This was more or less only cosmetic but provides at least a symbolic touchstone for asserting that doctrinal differences between Orthodoxy and Catholicism are more linguistic than truly doctrinal, which was the Council's conclusion.

As for Emperor Charles V, he appointed popes, such as Adrian VI, and had his plans to unite Europe and retake Constantinople thwarted by Pope Clement VII, whose League of Cognac with Francis I of France undermined the earlier treaty of Madrid between the Emperor and French king. In particular, Charles V's letter to Pope Clement VII provides an example of Imperial agency vis-à-vis theology and the Church. In 1526, after the Pope's organizing of the League of Cognac, Charles V wrote two

---

5   Peter Wilson, *Heart of Europe: A History of the Holy Roman Empire*, 169.

letters to Clement VII, which "could hardly have been more outspoken if they had been written by Martin Luther himself"[6] accusing the Pope of failing to live up to his responsibilities.

EMPEROR AS HEAD OF THE CHURCH, PART I: FREDERICK II AND THE GHIBELLINES

Frederick II's perceived crimes against the papacy have to do with something else, a certain pretension. There was a whole mystique about him which is quite concordant with themes of sacred monarchy and which seem to elevate him to the level of high pontiff, pitting him against the Pope.

If we take the split between Emperor and Pope as a sign of historical brokenness, whereas in the Apocalyptic New Earth with Christ's return the two functions are united, then Frederick II could symbolize a *short millennium*, a momentary and partial shining through of the archetype of sacred kingship in its fullness (that is, including the priestly role) within the context of the civilization of Roman Empire:

> A way of expressing the religious side of the imperial mission, as understood in Frederick's circle, was through a form of Adam mysticism. According to these notions, the first Just World Ruler was Adam before the Fall; it is therefore the function of the Just Emperor to establish such a rule upon earth as will lead men back to the state of Adam before the Fall, that is to say, to the Earthly Paradise. This implies a Christ-like redemptive role for the Emperor, though limited to the temporal sphere, and it is related to that interpretation of the golden age as being identical with the Earthly Paradise which Lactantius among others, had worked out in the time of Constantine. It would seem that what is developing here is a species of secular mysticism, or mystical secularism, with the Emperor as a kind of temporal Christ, redeeming man back to the Earthly Paradise with his justice, bringing in a full golden age with his imperial order. Such notions are a very extreme development out of that process of sanctifying the *civitas terrena*, the worldly society, which was implicit in the medieval emperor-idea.[7]

The Adamology of Empire, and the specifically Holy Roman Adamology of the sons of Aeneas, refers both to the unity of humanity in Adam and of the royal and priestly functions, which became divided after expulsion from Eden. However, just as Adam was not created to rest in himself but to unite with Eve, and these two not to be content together but to produce progeny, so too we may consider the return to Adam through Empire not a return to the simplicity of the origin but to the ever-present origin in the midst of diversity. Further, the

---

6 Norwich, *Popes*, 289.
7 Yates, *Astraea*, 8.

eschatological restoration is thus not only an object ahead in time but also beneath or above the timeline, whose tumult sometimes produces waves so high as to lap at its surface. Caesar Augustus in Virgil's work, Emperor Constantine, Frederick II—they symbols associated with these are waves that lick that sacred crown, albeit frothy and alloyed, but the aspiration is unto an archetype.

Concerning the myths of Frederick II, certain purported prophecies seem to have drawn attention to the *puer Apuliae*, the son of Apulia, as early as his birth.[8, 9] Godfrey of Viterbo takes the theme of Merlin and a returning king Arthur from Geoffrey of Monmouth and places it in the Italian context, celebrating the figure of Frederick II.[10] Yet these prophecies identified with Merlin are not, it seems, celebrating a final end, but pointing to partial eschatological realizations, avatars of archetypes, which also bring a certain ambiguity in their results. Thus, we find Ghibelline, pro-imperial, specifically pro-Hohenstaufen, statements alongside a bemoaning of the division of Italy that results from Imperial-Papal rivalry.[11]

Much of the European mythos comes together in this figure. Self-identified heir or continuer of Aeneas and Augustus,[12] he invented renaissance modernity before the fact, teaching *Lex Romana* at the University of Naples rather than canon law as in Paris or Bologna, attempting to standardize weights and measures, offering free education and lodging in return for a period of state service, and so forth. Indeed, his constitution of Malfi has been diligently studied by modern legal scholars.

His legacy is ambiguous in that it anticipates aspects of the modern state which may legitimately be regarded with suspicion. He founded the renaissance before the renaissance, but maintained a more medieval conception than would later prevail, as Kantorowicz (whose biography of the Hohenstaufen is seductive but probably hyperbolic) puts it, "the need of the state is the divine and natural law. For Frederick II this was true—though no longer true for the Renaissance princes."[13] It is a question of "[n]ature recognized as spiritual and law-abiding. Metaphysics was supplanting Transcendentalism."[14]

His identification with the sacrificial figure of that prophecy attributed to Merlin provides a good description of the sort of monarchical initiation described previously: a dismembered lamb that would nonetheless

---

8   Kantorowicz, *Frederick the Second*, 4.
9   Ibid., 447.
10   Hoffman, D., 1994. "Was Merlin a Ghibelline? Arthurian Propaganda at the Court of Frederick II." In: *Culture and the King: The Social Implications of the Arthurian Legend*, eds. Martin Shichtman and James Carley (Albany: SUNY Press), 115.
11   Ibid., 119.
12   Kantorowicz, *Frederick the Second*, 572.
13   Ibid., 245.
14   Ibid., 248.

not be consumed,[15] so that the empirical self is undone but the essence can thereby access the cosmic paradigm which unfolds as all things. The resultant cosmic identity is referred to quite explicit when Frederick II is described as one who "...grasped the cosmos as one gigantic whole...,"[16] for apparently "the Emperor was frequently heard to say 'the bodies of others were dependent on his life—the traitor imperiled the fabric of the world.'"[17]

If these words imply monarchy is sacred, and if Frederick II presented his religious duty and conscience as being outside the church,[18] this explains his difficult relationship with the clergy,[19] which can be understood in terms of the monarch's ultimate surplus over priesthood in Milbank's terms.

The religious epiphany of the cosmic body which the above words from Frederick II imply is linked by this study to organicism and ecumenism. This can explain Frederick II's lack of desire for expansion. His "laws were not issued on the scale of the Roman codes; they did not seek to encompass the whole of human[ity]...."[20] This drew on Roger II, in whose rule "what was revolutionary was the transformation of the idea of monarchy from the universalism of the late-Roman codes into the regional autonomy of the Sicilian kingdom,"[21] though, as seen above, Frederick II had ambitions beyond Sicily, just not necessarily beyond Europe and Christian holy sites. This is not, therefore, really a precursor to the modernity of the nation-state, but it may be a reminder of Plato's defense of the particular in the Gorgias and Laws, and of a positive potential of the modern, or an attenuation of late antiquity's excessively political universalism or imperialism.

Accounts—apparently based on visions—of Frederick II dwelling in the Sicilian Mount Etna,[22] like Empedocles, waiting to return and restore the Holy Roman Empire, further link him to the previous discussion of kingly initiation, which often occurs in a mountain, as Jove in Crete's Mount Ida, and specifically a mountain linked to a goddess, as is the case of Etna. In this context we may remember Goethe's travel diary, where he writes that Sicily is the key to everything (the same is true of Crete). Apart from Frederick's Palermo, Sicily briefly hosted the

15 Ibid., 4.
16 Ibid., 250.
17 Ibid., 243.
18 Ibid., 617.
19 Ibid., 617.
20 David Abulafia, *Frederick II: A Medieval Emperor* (Oxford: Oxford University Press, 1988), 202–3.
21 Ibid., 33.
22 B. Topfer, *Das kommende Reich des Friedens. Zur Entwicklung chiliastischer Zukunftshoffnungen im Hochmittelalter* (Berlin: Akademie-Verlag, 1964), 164–65. Cited by Robert E. Lerner, *The Powers of Prophecy: The Cedar of Lebanon Vision from the Mongol Onslaught to the Dawn of the Enlightenment* (London: Cornell University Press, 2008), 52.

Byzantine Empire's capital, when Islamic expansion made it strategically necessary. Volcanic mountains like Etna and Ida represent the Platonic receptacle and feminine counterpart (Juno) of the active, creator aspect of the Divine (Jove the Demiurge). Indeed, the preface to his *Liber Augustalis* seems to identify the role of emperor to that of the Demiurge, the divine agency at the level of space-time (assuming it is not collapsing its theology of God into the demiurgic function).[23]

Frederick II's dwelling in the mountain is therefore a sign of spiritual exaltation, of becoming a demiurge, as Iamblichus would put it, very much in the same vein as the accounts of Christian *theosis* or divinization one finds in theologians like St. Gregory of Nyssa (compatible with, though perhaps preferable to, those of later Western Catholic thought, like that of St. Thomas Aquinas, whose descriptions tend at times to evoke a more static state, eventually compensated, perhaps, by Western art).

Plato's and the pre-Socratic (as in Empedocles' case) volcanic crater of initiation is also one meaning of the Holy Grail, to which Frederick II is connected,[24] for one version of this story was presumably written by an attendant to the Emperor's court, in addition to which, again, Merlin was supposed to have written a prophecy concerning the Hohenstaufen. Frederick II is also linked to Apollo by Ernst Kantorowicz's imaginative biography, given that the early Apollonian Christianity of Sicily lent many of its titles for *Christ-as-Apollo* to Frederick II or to his pieties. Kantorowicz sees certain kingly titles used in Sicily as deriving from the Sol Invictus cult and being attributed to Frederick II.[25]

This is a Christianity like that of Constantine, who had begun his journey to monotheism minting coins to Sol Invictus and featured a relic of Apollo's champion and Roman founder Aeneas along with Christian ones in his new city's forum. Its presence in Sicily we may connect with the tradition that Parmenides, Empedocles and Plato were priests of Apollo and, in some cases, Apollonian avatars, justifying Christianity's historically Platonist character.

Elsewhere Kantorowicz thinks to intuit Odin in this figure. This again relates to the Holy Grail, which is the Crater constellation (the stars in which Flagetanis read the Holy Grail story from Toledo in Spain according to Wolfram von Eschenbach's version). Indeed, the Crater constellation is traditionally identified as Apollo's cup, and it is between bird and snake constellations (Corvus and Hydra), just as Odin stole the mead of wisdom by becoming eagle and serpent in Norse mythology.

He died in December, with its Christ-like connotations, mirroring Frederick II's birth, near Christmas eve, also in December, in Iesi, Italy,

---

23 Kantorowicz, *Frederick the Second*, 250.
24 Mark A. Pinkham, *Guardians of the Holy Grail: The Knights Templar, John the Baptist and the Water of Life* (Kempton, IL: Adventures Unlimited Press, 2004), 136–38.
25 Kantorowicz, *Frederick the Second*, 202.

which he described as his Bethlehem,[26] a comparison with Jesus he drew in his Jerusalem Manifesto as well. After his death, his followers wrote of his leaving a "sun-son in the west,"[27] and accounts circulated of his having burnt or been cut to pieces,[28] reminding of Christic gods such as Osiris and Dionysus, and the cosmic man's dismemberment.

In the lore surrounding Frederick II the issue of theological translation or analogy, applying Biblical themes of Davidic monarchy and election to an extra-scriptural context, namely Roman Emperorship, meets ancient Greco-Italic pagan roots, those of mountain initiation and its solar connection, specifically in the Sicilian theatre, analogous to the Cretan, and in so doing displays not disordered mixture but reveals underlying unity, for the symbols of those ancient roots are actually the same as those of the Bible, pointing to the Christ or cosmic man. This should be regarded as the ultimate potential and criteria for success of theological translation: to reveal underlying unity and actually embrace and redeem the past (in Christian terms baptizing even the pagan past).

Interestingly, in the *Divine Comedy*, Dante hitches his theology to Frederick II's son, the Hohenstaufen prince Manfred, rather than to papal decree and doctrine. While Frederick II's supposed excesses lead Dante to report his station is in Hell, he witnesses the likewise excommunicated son in Paradise. Here, Dante's *Divine Comedy* explicitly contradicts Church doctrine, arguing that although Manfred must spend a period in purgatory thirty times that which he spent living in excommunication, he will, following this, enter Paradise.

As for Frederick's moral and theological errors, while granting his faults and unscrupulousness in certain areas, most of these probably fall under three types: 1) Dubious or outright false and stemming from unfounded papal propaganda; 2) True but really only falling afoul of bigotry that the church would have been better off without (after all, why not speak Arabic, and why not discuss the physics of an apparently still earth beneath the rotating celestial dome, or of the human soul and its multiple components, with Muslim philosophers?); 3) True, but of a sort no worse than that of other emperors, who likewise seemed to question the papal office, making far less concessions and in truth issuing far more challenges than did Frederick II, achieving less than he did in terms of the papacy's stated aims, such as retaking Jerusalem (though, again, we suspect it is the peaceful nature of that enterprise which made some in the Curia and elsewhere suspicious) and on top of this being just as debauched or more than Frederick II, an indictment we may easily extend to some who have sat on St. Peter's throne. True, Frederick II kept a harem, but many emperors and monarchs who were never excommunicated have had their

---

26 Ibid., 512.
27 Ibid., 686.
28 Ibid., 688.

courtesans, as have some popes, and the Hohenstaufen did not carry on a pornocracy, complete with commonplace rape, like Pope John XII and his relatives had for many years, hated but tolerated by the clergy.

Anyway, Frederick's dynasty and the *Regno* of southern Italy would eventually be lost. The next popes, Urban and Clement, gave their compatriot Charles of Anjou regency over Sicily, but again he began to attempt to unite Italy, and the Empire beyond that, wanting to integrate Constantinople into his vision of Empire. Again, the station's telos imposed itself. Sicilian rebellions against the French and the advent of Spanish Aragonese rule in southern Italy interfered with the house of Anjou, however.

THE EMPEROR AS GUARDIAN OF THE CHURCH, PART II: EUROPA REGINA

In an Emperor-philic vein, Cánovas del Castillo cites as a possible inspiration for Charles V's rebuking of Pope Clement VII the opinion of archbishop D. Pedro Guerrero, published in 1560, to the effect that "all the Church's pains and censures have come from the clergy, and all remedy and quietude from government and the temporal arm." This goes quite far, and we should by no means forget the many outstanding popes that have contributed to stability and the betterment of people's lives.

In any case, Guerroro warned that "princes will have to render accounts before God for the Church they are called to support and repair."[29] This presents an ecclesial function for the Emperor, where his merely earthly authority is like a diagonal line (to use John Milbank's image) not merely horizontal but also vertical, that stretches beyond itself into sacred authority. Such a reading of history is old, and corresponds to an eschatology that views the Antichrist as an (anti-)pope, as proposed by Archbishop Ranieri of Florence among others:

> ...the identification of the Pope with Antichrist, which we have probably supposed to be a Protestant notion, is much older than the Reformation. It is found at least as early as the year 991, and was then openly made by an Archbishop in a Synod at Rheims.[30]

The emperor, then, would be a contrasting holy figure. Charles V specifically can be considered a reformer in his critique of the popes, herald of an alternative Reformation that corrected tradition by way of a refreshed vision of transcendence rather than by way of the literalistic materialism latent in the thought of many of Luther's followers. His attempt at European harmonization, personified in the image of a Europa Regina, the European map depicted as a queen, which was common in imperial propaganda, however, was thwarted by both Protestant princes and the pope.

---

29   Cánovas del Castillo, *Bosquejo historico de la Casa de Austria* (Madrid: Librería General de Victoriano Suárez, 1911), 48–49.
30   Preserved Smith, *Essays in Biblical Interpretation*, 184.

Just as there was a Catholic subversion of Empire with Pope Clement VII and others, there was a potential imperial reform of Catholicism with Charles V. Centuries later, coinciding with the French Revolution, a monarchical and partially imperial, non-Lutheran, impetus to break with the papacy nearly established several national Catholic churches in response to the widespread perception that the Jesuit order was instigating revolts and upheavals and that the Vatican was protecting it. The Bourbon house, whose scions ruled several countries at the time (including Spain, France and the kingdom of Naples) was particularly belligerent against the late 18th and early 19th century Jesuitical establishment.

Cánovas del Castillo writes in his *Bosquejo historico de la Casa de Austria* that it was precisely when Charles V had finished condemning Protestantism in a series of edicts that Pope Clement VII incited against him with the League of Cognac, and that it was just as the Emperor was warring against the Ottomans, with the hope of retaking Constantinople, that Popes Clement VII and Paul IV ran interference with their own armada.[31] Granting his opposition to the Ottoman project, Cánovas del Castillo is nonetheless quite ecumenical. He considers Charles V aligned not only with Catholicism but with civilization in general, and maintains that a close analysis of the Emperor's career does not permit one to think he was aspiring to some sort of global monarchy or really overstretching himself by unwarranted influence beyond his realm, all of which del Castillo would decry. Rather, in del Castillo's estimation, upon proper inspection Charles V emerges as a man of measure, attempting to secure and administer his own realm.

A similar implicit perennialism comes through in the works of 16th century Catholic historians like Pedro de Ribadeneyra, whose *Treatise on the Religion and Virtues That the Christian Prince Must Have to Govern and Conserve His Estates* praises religion as a category unto itself, outside specific theological narrative, including great lawgivers like Lycurgus in Sparta and Numa in Rome (specifically in the discussion concerning Plutarch). More specifically, del Castillo allows us to intuit another sense in which emperorship fulfils an important historical role: that of mediator. Del Castillo's narrative is one of taking the middle way. Emperor Charles V navigates between Protestantism and Papacy, between the disintegration of communal life into a patchwork of local princes and theological experiments, on the one hand, and a clerical institution given over to its physical presence, to naval-gazing worldly politics, not even generous enough to lay Italian ambitions aside until the Ottoman threat to its religious sphere had abated.

The popes themselves behaved as Protestant princes, but may also have been guided by a sense of priestly supremacy similar to Gregory VII's disastrous campaign to assert his office. In general terms, we may idealize

---

31   Cánovas del Castillo, *Bosquejo historico de la Casa de Austria*, 48.

the emperor as mediator or bridge (or bridge-maker, *pontifex*) between the *too worldly* and the *too other-worldly*, the vital and the contemplative, or, again, as a synthesis between nomad hunter and sedentary farmer. emperorship, then, is mediation and moderation.

The sense of unity between temporal and eternal, between secular and sacred, is not something that is conceived as coming in the future. The urgency of the Gospel was taken for granted, and Christianity rather started with and later lost that idea of already-arrived unity:

> At the beginning of the Eastern Empire's long last agony, when Constantinople was already surrounded by Turks (ca. 1394), a Patriarch could rebuke a Prince of Moscow for refusing to have the Emperor prayed for at the Eucharist: "My son, you are wrong to say, *We have a church, but not an emperor*. It is not possible for Christians to have a church and not an emperor. Church and empire are entirely one and interwoven, and cannot be separated."[32]

Apart from highlighting that the nationalist temptation is ever present, this illustrates that the idea of empire, the notion that Jesus's parables of vegetable, organic growth, allows some, even in the theological mainstream, to feel that history was manifesting the eschatological Kingdom, to live already at the center and also at the horizon.

Concerning respect for different spheres of governance, we should emphasize the long pedigree of a reconciliation between tribalism and the Ecumenic/Imperial project through the idea mentioned by Spanish historian Gonzalo Rodriguez Garcia in his study on Celtic Spain concerning an ideological affinity between the cult of the chieftain among those Celtiberians and the Roman understanding of emperor.[33] This is the theoretical compatibility that returns us to those seasonal flows of nomad and citizen which we have discussed. In practice, however, this does not mean that monarchs and emperors have not suppressed the potential of communities to develop structures of conviviality and mutual aid. The Castilian rebellion against Charles V's policies (the *comuneros*) for all their limitations, are reminiscent of a long medieval trajectory whereby many Castilian (and quite a few Aragonese) municipalities systematically reduced monarchical and ecclesial authority, reflecting an ethos of radical decentralization and a canton-like ideal for Castile, which was not later realized.[34] Charles V at least issued a general pardon to those who had participated in the rebellion of Castilian municipalities, the *comuneros* (commoners).

---

32   Oliver O'Donovan, "Christianity and Territorial Right." In: *States, Nations and Borders: The Ethics of Making Boundaries*, eds. Allen Buchanan and Margaret Moore (Cambridge: Cambridge University Press, 2003), 133.

33   Gonzalo Rodriguez Garcia, *Los Celtas, Heroes y Magia* (Madrid: Editorial Almuzara, 2009).

34   This is suggested by Felix R. Mora, *Tiempo, Historia y Sublimidad en el Románico Rural* [*Time, History and Sublimity in Rural Romanesque*] (Madrid: Potlatcht, 2012).

EMPEROR AS HEAD OF THE CHURCH, PART II: HABSBURGS AND HERMETICISTS

Conrad Celtis, a 15th century German thinker and humanist, put forward a more or less explicit case for Imperial autonomy and primacy respecting the Pope. His work railed against the impiety and degeneracy of Papal Rome and presented Germanic emperorship as morally purer.[35] Emperor Maximilian would benefit from Celtis in justifying his Italian wars. Similarly, Erasmus of Rotterdam, in his *Julius Exclusus*, criticized the eponymous Pope in contrast to northern moral, and specifically sexually moral, superiority.[36] Yet German territories did not proceed from the 1400s into becoming the seat of Imperial peace and subordination of a morally corrupt Papal office. Arguably, when the Reformation arrived with Luther, it reversed the political direction represented by a Celtis or an Erasmus, ultimately taking an anti-Imperial line.

In her analysis of the topic, historian Maria Elvira Roca Barea argues that Lutheranism, and Luther himself, acted politically to provide a theological pretext for German princes to rebel against Empire in the person of Charles V. The latter's attempt at European unity, the *Universitas Christiana*, as he termed it, where the Imperial office was explicitly endowed of authority over other regents, was thwarted in favor of religious wars and, crucially, civil wars, including intra-Protestant conflict and persecution, demographically draining the continent's Germanic heartland. The rise of national polities "encouraged new interest in the emperor as arbiter of this potentially violent new order" and the "accumulation of territories in direct Habsburg possession at last gave the emperor the means to intervene effectively in European affairs." However, "French opposition and Charles V's inability to defuse the religious controversy swiftly close this opportunity... this predominantly French and Protestant critique was implicitly hostile to the Empire."[37]

In the 1700s, Europe's Protestant territories were not richer than their Catholic counterparts. This contradicts Max Weber's famous statement of casuistry, a gloss which ignores that "the Protestant work ethic" was, for its first few centuries, largely expended in the production of diverse eccentric iterations of Biblical theology, the pitting of these against Catholicism as well as against one another, and the volumetric spilling of blood.

Yet, if politically Protestantism was largely a revolt against Empire, a certain esoteric Protestantism attempted to institute Empire without Papacy (a Protestant emperor would, by definition, not be subject to the

---

35 Kurt Stadtwald, *Roman Popes and German Patriots: Antipapalism in the Politics of the German Humanist Movement from Gregor Heimburg to Martin Luther* (Librairie Droz: Geneva, 1996), 74–76.

36 Ibid., 80–82.

37 Peter Wilson, *Heart of Europe: A History of the Holy Roman Empire*, 171.

pope). The possibility of esoteric Protestantism as basis for emperorship has gone unfulfilled, however, except perhaps, in some minor way, in the German Kaiser. In the late sixteenth century, there arose an esoterism drawing on John Dee's occult system, the Imperial court of the Habsburg Rudolph II's religious toleration and interest in occultism and on the possibility of a Protestant anti-Habsburg confederacy around the Palatine Elector Frederick V after his marriage to Elizabeth, daughter of King James of England.

Frithjof Schuon considers the basis for this current, or for some of its elements, on the surface so at odds with Luther's reform, to have nonetheless been galvanized by it. Luther's

> exclusive recourse to faith, his tendency to interiorize everything for the sake of the "spirit" and against the "flesh," hence also his reduction of the sacraments with regard to their form and number, all refer logically and mystically to the principle of inwardness or immanence.

Schuon continues,

> If this perspective...were intrinsically false and ineffectual, one could not explain how an esoterist such as Jakob Bohme could flower in such a climate, not to mention other Rosicrucian and Hermetic Lutheran theosophists.

To the name of Boehme, we must add Swedenborg and, emphatically, the prophet-poet Blake (who, however, transcends Protestantism). The principle behind what Schuon is getting at is that "...every form can be abrogated by a more essential form, and with all the more reason by their common essence; a form is never a pure absolute..."[38]

Frances Yates in her *Rosicrucian Enlightenment*, considers the Rosicrucian manifestos to belong to a current of mystical Protestantism. References in these manifestos to an influx of blessings akin to those which once surrounded Adam and which were to occur before the Day of Judgement remind us of that *Adamology of Empire*, the notion that in Adam priestly and kingly functions were one, and that the emperor restores primordial unity, amongst extreme Ghibellines, as well as to the Virgilian theme of a return to the golden age (indeed, the eruption of the age of Saturn in the midst of these latter days is one of the images invoked by medieval references to the returning Adamic force).

Rosicrucian Adamic Emperorship is Apollonian (like that of the Sol Invictus and medieval Hohenstaufen cultism, if we follow Kantorowicz), as emphasized by some editions of the Rosicrucian manifestoes reproducing Trajano Bocallini's work (the *Satira Ragguagli di Parnasso*). Their opposition to the Papacy's conduct is similar to what Cervantes seems

---

38   Schuon, *Christianity/Islam: Perspectives on Esoteric Ecumenism.*

to have in mind in Numantia, which is supportive of Charles V and generally opposes the popes (on account of their interfering with the building up a *Universitas Christiana* by the Spanish Habsburgs). We should remember Bocallini's text is complaining against Protestant heresy and ascribing it to imperial, or specifically Spanish (since Philip II was not technically an emperor like his father) oppression. Religious sectarianism and political fragmentation on the Protestant side, and imperialism and doctrinal rigidity on the Catholic, are criticized.

The Rosicrucian *Fama Fraternitatis* accepts Roman Imperial authority, although anticipating and supporting certain alterations to its character. Reads the *Fama*: "In Politia we acknowledge the Roman Empire and Quartam Monarchiam for our Christian head, albeit we know what alterations be at hand…"[39] The *Confessio Fraternitatis* reads "…we hereby do condemn the East and the West [meaning the Pope and Mahomet] for their blasphemies against our Lord Jesus Christ, and offer to the chief head of the Roman Empire our prayers, secrets, and great treasure of gold."[40]

Elsewhere these texts consider the Pope to be Antichrist, "we do now securely call the Pope Antichrist,"[41] which has a long pedigree even in Catholic sources but especially those exalting the Holy Roman Emperor. The overflow of pagan themes in Frederick V's wedding and court bespeaks an occultist context, along with the support for emperorship in Rosicrucian manifestos, which is connected to him according to Yates.

Rosicrucian circles were also connected to Italian liberalism, modernism or nationalism. Again, Boccalini's *Raggugagli di Parnaso* was included in some editions of Fama. In Boccalini, the god Apollo blames Habsburg tyranny for causing Protestant heresy. Tommaso Campanella also influenced these circles, leading a southern Italian revolt against the Spanish Habsburg presence and writing utopian fiction-manifesto from jail thereafter. Cervantes occupies this literary space as well in his *Journey to Parnassus*, but is supportive of the Habsburgs. Concerning this period's Apollonian utopianism (of which Cervantes is not an exemplar), spiritual intuitions can lead to immanentizing the eschaton, trying to apply grand truths in too literal a way, producing the opposite of utopia. Thus, the link between esotericism and political modernity's attendant revolutionary violence and totalitarian paroxysms.

Indeed, even theology can make itself a nuisance to true religion or, put differently, it is possible to be too religious, too one-sidedly so. Occultism can likewise fascinate, become convoluted, forgetting simpler truths, and even open one up to sinister influences, a spiritual lust, as C. S. Lewis put it. Unfortunately, sometimes, aiming for a high peak can

39 Anonymous, *Fama Fraternitatis and Confession of the Rosicrucian Fraternity*, trans. A. E. Waite from. T. Vaughan (Plano Texas: Stone Guild Publishing, 2009), 25.
40 *Confessio*, I, 30.
41 Ibid., II.

see us fly right off the cliff. Still, some Renaissance Hermeticism can function as part of a legitimate Christian tradition. The West's somehow occultic pursuit of knowledge and technological sophistication could contain auspicious currents and produce useful fruits.

Just so, legitimate authority can be applied overbearingly and forget that it is presiding over life, over real organic dynamics, and that these must be allowed their expression. Perhaps Habsburg rule, or its agents, forgot this in certain theatres. Perhaps Rudolph II's trajectory should have been maintained (without, however, ignoring the very real dangers of the then nascent nation-state). Indeed, Campanella would later write *Monarchy of Spain*, suggesting that he might become pro-Habsburg so long as this dynasty properly ally itself with the Pope, which is a rather interesting example of Hermetic utopianism (which influenced northern Protestant esoterists, as Campanella did) resolving itself into Papal supremacism, always in terms of desire for a universal, global, hegemonic polity. The sort of pro-Imperial Catholic historiography in which Charles V and his antecedents are seen as the correctors of Papal excess would actually seem closer to the sentiment of the Rosicrucian manifestos.

As Yates notes, the Fama ends with *sub umbra alarum tuarum, Jehovah*, the Psalmist *under the shadow of thy wings, Jehovah*. She sees a response, though I would read it as a (maybe involuntarily neutral) commentary, in satirical prints referring to Frederick V's defeat in Bohemia, where his anti-Habsburg ambitions were militarily quashed. The print in question includes the phrase *Under the shadow of my wings the kingdom of Bohemia will flourish*.[42] The eagle whose wings are featured are those of the Habsburg imperial emblem and above it, shining light upon that eagle, is the name of Jehovah. Thus, the wings of the Habsburg eagle belong to Jehovah, and it is *these* that offer refuge to the faithful, including Bohemia. Is this, then, a failure of that program contained in the *Fama Fraternitatis*?

It is interpretable as precisely the fulfillment of that program, albeit in a surprising and unexpected way, especially surprising those who had identified certain projects (Frederick's) with Rosicrucianism. We should remember the staunch support for Roman Emperorship in the *Fama* and *Confessio*, and consider the following concerning the Spanish Habsburgs, specifically Phillip II, son of Charles V, referring to the palace he built in Madrid, the *Escorial*:

> Though the contrast between Madrid and Prague brings out the rift between the Spanish and the German Habsburgs, yet it appears from an article...by Rene Taylor in *Essays in the History of Architecture presented to Rudlf Wittkower* (1967) that the Escorial may have been a 'magical' building, its design influenced by a recent reconstruction

---

42   Frances Yates, *The Rosicrucian Enlightenment* (Routledge: London, 1972), 75.

of the Temple of Solomon, and that its occupant was secretly involved in the Hermetic trends of the age. Both Philip and his intimate friend and adviser, the architect Herrera, were ardent Lullists.[43] Herrera owned two copies of Dee's *Monas Hieroglyphica*, a copy of one of Bruno's works on magic, mnemonics, and a whole range of other examples of Renaissance Hermetic literature. Herrera's mathematical, mechanical, and probably magical interests have suggested to Taylor a comparison between Herrera and Dee. One wonders whether the esoteric interests evidently rife in the Escorial... may have had anything to do with the King's [Philip II] passion for the strange pictures of Hieronymus Bosch.[44]

Indeed, the idea that the Escorial is fruit of the esotericism of Philip II's court is a widespread notion in Spain.

Whatever restoration of Christianity with the Roman Emperor as chief was expected does not seem to have arrived in the ensuing centuries. Perhaps, like Frederick II (Hohenstaufen)'s acolyte-produced literature, it was an eruption of splendor, short-lived but anticipating something farther ahead in time. Attempting to restore what has been lost before the season is right is like eating a fruit before it is ripe, liable to set our teeth on edge. It is normal, then, that some of these texts, from Frederick II to the Rosicrucian manifestos, come across as blasphemous. Their program, if taken as eminently political, can be very damaging.

Virgil's presentation of Caesar Augustus's vocation is related to this. In his *Egyptian Mysteries*, Iamblichus does not consider Virgil to be a genuinely religious poet, properly submitted to the muses (although he does acknowledge the piety of Aeneas), yet the restoration of the age of Saturn that Virgil prophesied did, perhaps, come about, by means of the coming of Christianity. Those first few centuries, however, were tumultuous. Prophecies, we might conclude, come about with imperfect and imprecise cadence so far as historical agents can articulate and determine, neither can we always discern what is fulfilled from what is yet in store.

Renaissance Hermeticism occurs on both sides of the political divide of sixteenth century Europe, that is, the Spanish Habsburgs on the one hand and northern Protestants influenced by Italian intellectual currents on the other. We may fathom a synthesis of Protestant explorations of occultism with Catholic emperorship, following G. K. Chesterton's

---

43   The term Lullist refers to Ramon Lull. Lull was a 13th/14th-century Franciscan mystic from the island of Mallorca, whose father was a knight who moved to the island from Catalonia when Jaime I took it from the Muslims. He wrote in Castilian, Latin, Arabic and (possibly for the first time), Catalan. Whether the alchemical works identified with him have much to do with the historical Lull or not, he in any case produced mystical tracts which very much remind us of the path of the lover, the *fedeli d'amore*.

44   Frances Yates, *Ideas and Ideals in the North European Renaissance* (New York: Routledge, 1984), 212.

thoughts on Protestantism as a centrifugal phase that will yield a return of many spiritual gifts to the bosom of Rome.

In a sense, Philip II's Catholic Hermeticism and defense of quasi-protestants in Spain already presents this synthesis. He protected theologically unconventional figures such as Arias Montano, Fray Jose de Siguenza and the Caritatis group. Indeed, he gave Montano warrant to seek out reconciling elements between the Reformation and Counter-Reformation.

The same is true of king James Charles Stuart VI of Scotland and I of England and Ireland.[45] Referred to as a British Solomon, James was committed to doing in his own kingdom what Philip II had done with the Escorial in Spain, namely present Solomonic wisdom (considered consistent with Pythagorean teachings) in a restored temple, with all its kingly-anointing and liturgical significance. He was also linked to Egyptian knowledge via supposed ancestral Scottish roots in Egypt and so was connected to the in-vogue Egyptian themes of the *Corpus Hermeticum*. His Anglicanism was open to some of the Hermetic currents of Protestantism but rejected the Reformation's defining iconoclasm and was friendly to Catholic and Imperial institutions. His building plans, including his appointment of masons to Holyrood, was opposed by radical Presbyterians for being in their minds a papist project. James even seems to have had a sense of perennial patterns extending into pre-Christian antiquity, commissioning a study of the structure of Stonehenge.

He gave patronage to Fludd and pro-Rosicrucian figures while also opposing his son-in-law Frederick V's (who many considered the fulfiller of the Rosicrucian manifestoes) militant anti-Spanish, anti-Catholic actions. He attempted to restrain Frederick V, who was married to his daughter, and reconcile him to Spain. James Maxwell, who praised king James as Britain's Asclepius, tried to quell hostilities between Protestant and Catholic and focus, in the vein of Charles V, on fighting Ottoman expansion.

Scholars and architects in James's employ such as Inigo Jones and John Drummond seem to have learnt from the Escorial in Madrid, including Lullist mathematics and the *art of memory*, and king James was supported by private Catholics such as Dunfermline and Arundel. Henry Adamson's writings display the nexus that James's court constituted, praising the Escorial as well as Rosicrucian *second sight*. The same comes across in Archbishop of Canterbury William Laud's *The Works of the Most Reverend Father in God* and his refutation of the Puritan *Calling of the Jews*, this latter being both anti-Papal and anti-Monarchical. Archbishop Laud saw radical Protestants as playing into Papist hands, a reinforcing dialectic between apparent opponents, and instead defended peace with Catholic countries, the pro-Spanish politics of king James,

---

45   Marsha Keith Schuchard, *Restoring the Temple of Vision: Cabalistic Freemasonry and Stuart Culture* (London: Brill, 2002), chapter six.

the king's building program and its Solomonic/Pythagorean aspirations, and the desire for religious unity. The Anglicanism of James and Laud feels like an Orthodox national church seeking to be bound and in communion with her sisters, yet also as a desire for the temple. Their intuitions are alike those of Britain's Orthodox Metropolitan Kallistos Ware and other modern Orthodox figures who have praised Barker's temple theology.

The "tree of hate"[46] between Britain and Spain, as the 1621 English play *Dick of Devonshire* calls it, and the Black Legend against Spain in general is, apart from its geopolitical function, more subtly understandable as a block against this historical current represented by Philip and James. They ensure that the anglosphere (and with it, modernity) conceives of itself as a break-away from European civilization (and generally Christendom). They hide the way of return from Protestantism back to unity with Rome, from Hermeticism back to Christianity (for aspects of Frederick V's esoterism and that which followed after James seem too far-gone to be aligned with Christian tradition). They stigmatize the imperial (neo-Ghibelline) Catholicism of Charles V and his son and the latter's selective assimilation of Renaissance Hermetica into a traditional civilizational project.

Where the shade of the temple might have reconciled opposing parties, history veered instead towards a false temple, one of revolutionary anti-clericalism and anti-monarchism. It is not only that Catholic and Protestant mainstreams rejected the temple as kings James and Philip conceived of it, but also that an alternative *esoterism* may have been at play, parodying the temple into a kind of secular, spuriously pagan, technology-obsessed, anarchic-yet-tyrannical[47] direction.

Milbank's *Proclean modernity* might find its most recent and clearest antecedent in the period referred to here, for the temple is the sight of theurgy. It was perhaps a recurrence on the eve of modernity of what Barker identifies as the original temple. Nor is the Pythagorean theme and that of Roman prestige that these monarchs connected themselves with (at least in Philip II's case) extraneous to the hope for a Solomonic restoration: We should remember that the Pythagorean Rome of Numa Pompilius was temple-centric, following Plutarch's account of king Numa's temple to Janus and, more anciently, Aeneas's initiatic journey to the underworld proceeds by the guidance of the Sibyl at the temple to Apollo at Cumae. Rome had by now been re-founded and its

---

46   Philip Wayne Powell, *Tree of Hate: Propaganda and Prejudices affecting United States Relations with the Hispanic World* (Albuquerque: University of New Mexico Press, 1971).
47   To be anarchic and tyrannical, declaring oneself acultural and spontaneous yet ending up subject to a rigid all-colonizing culture (the painful oscillation we already touched on as characterizing some Franciscan thought according to Milbank) is perhaps exactly what William Laud was warning about.

valid ancient institutions taken up. But these early moderns were not rebuilding the temple in Jerusalem, they were rather modelling their own monarchies on its principles, just as the Christian does not seek to die at Cavalry, but makes every hill a new Golgotha. The temple was a symbol for knowledge, synthesized and summarized in one place.

As for the *art of memory* which so interested regents and their scholars, the spatially envisioned features of initiation, the recollection of gnoseological principles, angelic allies and divine names through an envisioned spatial sequence, is an art unto death which appears in various traditions, including the Egyptian, as a means for retaining conscious continuity of the psyche in the wake of death and so avoid being swept up by subconscious tides into the ghostly disintegration of Hades or (in the Tibetan Book of the Dead) an unplanned reincarnation. This is why we pray at death's door, and listen to the priest's last rites as we depart.

Critically, memory allows us to grasp pattern, order, harmony (the presence of the autozoon) by drawing things we have seen into our perception of the things we see and thereby understand that they are in some relation to each other, that they are patterned. The temple is the sight of initiation, theurgy, and a successful death, and therefore also of a non-materialistic civilization.

Beyond even this, we have the recovery of memory as Plato teaches: the knowledge of the whole cosmos that is within the initiate, which the initiate already surveyed upon his empyrean chariot in some pre-natal state, rediscovering that his Being is the same Being as that of the whole cosmos. The temple as microcosm reminds the initiate that he also is a microcosm (thus de Lubicz's term "temple of man"). His own correspondence with the temple reminds him that forms are different instances of that which is itself beyond forms. The ancient cult aims at grasping the pattern that recurs across different structures and at different levels (universe, temple, human body). The temple, to summarize, brings secular authority into the Church, but is, ultimately, the human person.

THE EMPEROR AND EUROPE

Leaving aside the sacral element of emperorship, we briefly discuss Roman emperorship as articulator of the European civilizational realm. This is relevant because emperorship's relationship to ecclesial institutions and the context in which it shows through its own sacredness has a political character, a political direction, and that direction is the articulation of a particular civilization.

It should first be noted that the western emperors do not reject the eastern seat of Constantinople's legitimacy, nor did their office first appear as a rejection of Byzantium. To the contrary, they tend to want to unite with it as a matter of some urgency and Pope Leo III, who crowned the first western emperor, Charlemagne, did so not as a rejection of Constantinople or even within the understanding that a sort of pluralistic arrangement with multiple emperors might be practical. He did so because, by Salic tradition, women could not rule as Empresses, and Constantine VI, the son of the widow Byzantine Empress Irene of Athens, had been removed from power and blinded by his mother. Indeed, the east agreed with this tradition, at least as far as the letter of the law was concerned, for Irene was technically *Emperor*, not *Empress*. The title that she officially took on was legally coded as a male noun. As far as Pope Leo III could see, the emperorship was vacant, and a new emperor could ascend without in any sense implying the seat at Constantinople was illegitimate. This is somewhat dubious considering Irene did have a living male son, but technically not a division of the Empire, although we can read these events as an implicit resurfacing of Diocletian's Tetrarchy (with its dual emperorship).

Furthermore, the first Holy Roman Emperor Charlemagne had wanted to unite with the east by marrying the Empress Irene of Athens, making overtures to which she was apparently positively inclined. The result of such a union, had it occurred, might not have been particularly beneficial, however, as John Julius Norwich speculates in his history of the popes. She was in her forties or fifties and would (probably, though stranger things have happened) not have given him a son to claim rulership over Europe from Pyrenees to the Bosporus (with gaps in between), and Byzantine political intrigue might have mired the king of the Franks. In any case Empress Irene was deposed by her subjects, who were not fond of her, and would probably have likewise rejected her possible foreign husband. Notwithstanding any of this, it is significant that the new western emperor saw union with the east as important. In terms of Charlemagne, as first Emperor of the west, personifying the *Regnum Europae* as Catwulf writes, his military campaigns east and west, even trying to retake Hispania, certainly warrant the characterization.

Later on, Emperor Otto the Saxon married his son, Otto II—who had been made co-emperor just as Charlemagne's son Louis—to the Byzantine princess Theophanu, who was a close relation to the Byzantine emperor at the time, and whose father became emperor in the east soon after her meeting Otto II. Here things were more complicated than they had been under Charlemagne, as there were two distinct emperors (both male, so neither could be denied on grounds of gender), but still the thrust was to unite and end the ambiguity.

Otto II died in his twenties of malaria after stealthily swimming to safety following a loss against a Byzantine-Saracen alliance meant to deny him dominion of Puglia, the heel of the Italian peninsular boot, a Byzantine territory which he viewed as his marriage dowry (and a region whose connection with the western emperorship is a historically recurrent theme given Frederick II's love of it).

The Byzantine Empress Theophanu could not fend for her dead husband's interests in Italy, but went north to secure her son's safety. Otto III is in a sense the first culmination of Europe's *telos*, committed to old Roman unity, with an archaic conception of sacred kingship as exceeding the pope, and being the son of Greek and Saxon, east and west:

> ...Otto III, was an extraordinary child. Succeeding to the imperial throne at the age of three, he grew up combining the traditional ambitions of his line with a romantic mysticism clearly inherited from his mother, forever dreaming of a great Byzantinesque theocracy that would embrace Germans and Greeks, Italians and Slavs alike, with God at its head and himself and the Pope—in that order—His twin Viceroys. Who could be more suited than he—born as he was of a Greek mother—to make this dream a reality?[48]

Apparently, centuries later, Frederick II would consider European royal families one.[49] What Justinian I attempted from the east, Otto III did so from the north, and Frederick II from the south and Charles V from the west. Political failure notwithstanding, this is the *telos* of the emperor.

---

48   Norwich, *Popes*, 86.
49   Kantorowicz, *Frederick the Second*, 572.

On Europe

D ENIS DE ROUGEMONT, HIGHLIGHTING THE
Homeric name for Jove, *Europos*, follows Nietzsche in suggesting
that Europe, and the will to its articulation, belongs to the sensibilities of her "abundant, impetuous"[1] artists or, as he puts it, "the best
spirits of Europe, namely those who see very far."[2] Indeed, as has been
mentioned, Europe appears in many of the sources already referenced,
often in the context of their defense of plurality against miasma and
mimesis. It is presented as one (actual or potential) civilization among
others, as well as, precisely, *one*, that is, a coherent entity. This insight,
then, will in large part constitute the approach taken in what follows:
the building of narrative through attention to artists, philosophers and
pseudo-historians.

CONTINENT AS CIVILIZATION

The Herodotean articulation of Europe in a doctrine that posits
continent-cum-civilization presents a case study for how theological narrative
presented an ethic of geographically delineated spheres. From ancient
Greek, especially Herodotean and Platonic, articulations of large units
within a larger ecumenic whole, to the medieval Christian attribution
of Biblical patriarchs to different national entities, Europe represents a
historically consistent and, in some ways, consistently ecumenical idea. As
is the case of the Yellow Emperor in China and in Chinese perceptions
of related peoples, especially through Sima Qian's histories, the idea of
Europe often appeared in terms of a myth of common descent, namely
from the Biblical Japheth and Roman Aeneas.

Few starting points could be as auspicious in this regard as that of
commending of ourselves to that *corpus* for which western thought serves
as a series of footnotes,[3] that work whose author's name is synonymous
with the archetypes that push and pull, birth and draw, life. Yet even
Plato is too late. We may turn farther back, to that deity of which, by
the testimony of Olympiodorus,[4] the famed Athenian philosopher was
an avatar, Apollo. Perhaps the first reference to Europe as a continent

---

1   Nietzsche, *Beyond Good and Evil*, Section 256; 149.
2   de Rougemont, *Vingt-huit siècles d'Europe*, 8.
3   "The safest general characterization of the European philosophical tradition is
that it consists of a series of footnotes to Plato." A. N. Whitehead, *Process and Reality:
Corrected Edition* (New York, NY: The Free Press, 1985), 39.
4   Olympiodorus, *The Life of Plato and On Plato First Alcibiades*, 1–9, trans. M. Griffin.
(London: Bloomsbury, 2015), 25–30, 72.

appears in the Homeric hymn to this solar Olympian. In it, the god calls on the people of the Peloponnese, Greek islands and Europe, "both they who dwell in rich Peloponnesus and the men of Europe and from all the wave-washed isles," to come to his temple, established for their edification, and seek oracular instruction therefrom.[5]

The pre-Socratic scripture, likely composed in the seventh or sixth century BC, is presenting Europe, as well as those portions of Greece geographically discontinuous with it, as a single jurisprudence, a unit unto the god. While this has been cited by some as evidence for the concept of Europe not yet including the Peloponnesian region and proximate islands, it is precisely a comprehending of these, along with the landmass to their north, in an entity defined by a common center and patron.

Of course, the immediate meaning is to do with the Greek mainland, but nonetheless, it is interesting that the expansive Europe is employed, a term which Herodotus tells us refers to the entire geographically contiguous continent occupying the north of the earth (which relates to Apollo, being the Hyperborean or far-northern god) and whose usage is so ancient that he cannot trace it. It is the case that such usage is confirmed by history, which saw Europe become overridingly Greek in its culture.

Again, in Herodotus, the word *Europe* seems to refer to the Greek mainland and an indefinite northern sprawl: "[a]s for Europe, no one knows whether there is a sea to the east or to the north of it...."[6] Herodotus clarifies its contours in the *Histories*, presenting a recognizably modern cartographic delineation of this continent's edges: Egypt is portioned between Libya (Africa) and Asia, straddling the Nile,[7] although the historian prefers to consider the whole of Egypt as separate from both Libya and Asia, so that the Libyan coast extends from Egypt to the southern side of the straits of Gibraltar.[8] Assyria is Asian, along with Persia and Arabia[9] and Europe begins at the pillars of Hercules north of which are Celtic settlements and the Cynesian "westernmost inhabitants of Europe,"[10] on one end, and at Greece on the other.

The remote origin of this conception Herodotus admits he is not able to trace: "[n]or have I been able to learn who determined their boundaries...."[11] Already in the work of the ancient historian this receives suggestive, extra-geographic, significance when Greece is discussed as being in community with Europe as apart from the Persian,

---

5   In: *Hesiod, the Homeric Hymns and Homerica*, trans. H. G. Evelyn-White (Boston: Loeb Classical Library, 1914), *Homeric Hymn to Apollo*, II.287–93; 62.

6   Herodotus, *Histories*, trans. Pamela Mensch (Indianapolis, IN: Hackett Publishing Company, 2014), IV.45; 218.

7   Ibid., II.16; 87–88.

8   Ibid., II.32; 93.

9   Ibid., IV.39; 215.

10   Ibid., II.33; 94.

11   Ibid., IV.45; 218.

Asian, sphere[12] (a conception attributed to Persian thought, albeit one that flourished prior to Xerxes and perhaps Darius[13]).

The same trans-territorial intimations appear in Plato when common cause is invoked not with all peoples tittering on the edge of Persia's imperial sway, but between Greece and the other inhabitants of Europe,[14] and in the *Gorgias*,[15] which relates Jove's decree that souls proceeding from Europe stand before a common judge, Aeacus, and Asian souls before another, Rhadamanthus (the notion of local tutelary angelic intelligences is not absent from Christian theology[16, 17, 18]). The use of these regions' names is significant, notwithstanding the possibility of other, non-geographically pertinent, meanings also operating in this passage (such as proposed by Olympiodorus,[19] where Asia and Europe become metaphors, but just as Biblical scripture can be read in terms of a spiritual human-wide Israel without stripping it of its local meanings, so too Plato can be read in both senses).

In the first century, Strabo described Europe as bearing its own political culture,[20] and Pliny the Elder referred to Europe as nurse of victorious people,[21] likewise implying more than a geographic category. If these extra-geographic implications with their early attestation in Apollo's Homeric hymn, Herodotus and Plato, were instantiated, it was insofar as a Greco-Celtic culture existed,[22] the midpoint of which would have been Rome, allowing for a certain poetic license (without excluding either older sources of coherence or, of course, cultural continuities across continents).

According to Strabo and Julius Caesar, Greek constituted a language of law and possibly (given references to the Druids, although holy utterance

---

12   Ibid., I.4; 5.
13   Ibid., I.4; 7; IX,116.
14   Plato, *Laws*, III.698b; 239.
15   Plato, *Gorgias*, trans. Edward Meredith Cope (Cambridge: Bell and Daldy, 1864), 524a; 126–27.
16   Karl Barth, *Church Dogmatics*, vol. 3, trans. G. Bromiley and R. Ehrlich (London: T and T Clark, 2006), 208.
17   Peter W. Martens, "On the Confusion of Tongues and Origen's Allegory of the Dispersion of Nations." *The Studia Philonica Annual* (24) (Providence, RI: Brown University, 2012), 111.
18   Daniel, *The Book of Daniel*, ed. R. Charles (New York City: Oxford University Press, 1958), X.13, 115; X.20, 117.
19   Olympiodorus, *Commentary on Plato's Gorgias*, trans. R. Jackson, K. Lycos and H. Tarrant (Brill: Leiden, 1998), 49.2, 312–13.
20   Strabo, "The Nature of This Continent." In: A. Drace-Francis, *European Identity: A Historical Reader* (New York City: Palgrave McMillan, 2013), 6–8.
21   Pliny the Elder, "The Most Beautiful Portion of the Earth." In: A. Drace-Francis, *European Identity: A Historical Reader* (New York City: Palgrave McMillan, 2013), 8–9.
22   Nicholas Laos draws attention to this, also referring to Strabo and Julius Caesar in *The Metaphysics of World Order: A Synthesis of Philosophy, Theology and Politics* (Eugene, OR: Pickwick Publications, 2015), 191.

was apparently recited, not written) sacred rite for some Celts, which would imply no contrast, given how often law and religion are articulated unitarily (in Islam, Arabic is the language of the *Salat* and of the *Sharia*, prayer and law). Strabo writes about Marseilles:

> ...this city for some little time back has become a school for the barbarians, and has communicated to the Galatae such a taste for Greek literature that they even draw contracts on the Grecian model. While at the present day it entices the noblest of the Romans...[23]

Julius Caesar attests to the continuity of such in his *Gallic War*: "In the camp of the Helvetii were found, and brought to Caesar, records written out in Greek letters..."[24] And,

> Druids...learn by heart a great number of verses...they do not think it proper to commit these utterances to writing, although in almost all other matters, and in their public and private accounts, they make use of Greek letters.[25]

Similarly, we observe painted Attic plates and vases in pre-Roman southern Iberian burial chambers, along with a fully developed Greco-Iberian script that was being used in the fourth century BC to write Iberian in what is now the region of Murcia (which was non-syllabic, in contrast to other Iberian alphabets).

Returning to Herodotus's delineation of continents, history has seen this border periodically iterated. Plato himself notes the parallel between Achaean resistance against Assyrian intrusion and the wider Hellenic curbing of Persia.[26] Eric Voegelin reads Plato's *Laws* as suggesting a

> Hellenic federation is supposed to hold its own against Persia; in the power field of the time it is to be a match to the ecumenic empire, as the earlier Doric federation was to be the European counterweight to the "Assyria" in the background of Troy[27]

Later, in something like a prescriptive vein but in clear reference to Roman enmity with Carthage, Virgil describes the conflict-prone fissure through queen Dido's curse on Rome's founder, Aeneas, as he sailed north ("shore against shore").[28]

At the end of the seventh century or beginning of the eighth, a European *demos*-as-audience was proclaimed by the author of the *Life*

---

23   Strabo, *The Geography of Strabo*, vol. 1, trans. H. Hamilton and W. Falconer (London: Bohn's Classic Library, 1854), IV:1.6, 270–71.
24   Julius Caesar, *The Gallic War*, trans. H. Edwards (Cambridge, MA: Harvard University Press, 1917), I:29, 43–45.
25   Julius Caesar, *The Gallic War*, VI:14, 339.
26   Plato, *Laws*, III.685c; 195–97.
27   Voegelin, *Order and History, Volume IV, The Ecumenic Age*, 284–85.
28   Virgil, *The Aeneid*, trans. B. Powell (Oxford: Oxford University Press, 2016), IV.549–51; 139.

of St. Gertrude: "who living in Europa does not know the loftiness, the names and the localities of [Gertrude's] lineage?"[29] Slightly later, *Europe* was being used to describe a political reality, as is the case of a letter by the "probably Anglo-Saxon, possibly Irish" Cathwulf, in which the scribe thanks God for raising Charlemagne "to the honor of the glory of the *regnum Europae*."[30]

During the same period, the term *Europenses* (*Europeans*) was invoked in an Iberian chronicle from AD 754 to denote armies engaged at the battle of Tours against a foe originating south of the Mediterranean. The same record also apparently criticizes those armies for not pushing down to retake Iberia.[31] This reproach is somehow echoed and answered by the Song of Roland, whose eponymous knight dies "in the direction of Spain"[32] (*devers Espaigne*). According to one reading:

> ...we can understand "France" in this poem as not only the physical kingdom of France, but as symbol for the whole of Christendom (Charles's empire).... Roland's gaze towards Spain reflects, there-fore, his determination to make France whole by returning it to Charles and thus to God.[33]

The legendary Spanish knight of the Reconquista, Bernardo del Carpio's connection to the court of Charlemagne strengthens this link, which may explain why Charles V chose to visit Bernardo's tomb and take the medieval hero's sword to Madrid with him.

Indeed, the *telos* of Holy Roman Emperors was generally pan-European, though we should not exaggerate that point. Still, we have the examples of Justinian taking Italy, and western emperors, from Charlemagne trying to marry Irene of Athens, Otto III's career and Charles V trying to unite Europe against the Ottoman Empire, producing print images of the whole continent as one body.

Europe is asserted in the medieval tradition of Biblically-derived speculative pseudo-historiography. This presents Europe, inclusive of portions of Anatolia, as a coherent unity. It corresponds in large part to the general outline presented by Flavius Josephus in the first century and, therefore, to a certain tradition evidenced by Dead Sea Scroll texts (describable as *Enochic*), the *Book of Jubilees* (which was thought to be Pharisaic prior to the discovery of the Dead Sea Scrolls) and the *Genesis*

---

29   Jinty Nelson, "Charlemagne and Europe." *Journal of the British Academy* 2 (2013): 130. This is the earlier Gertrude of Nivelles, O. S. B., not to be confused with the 13th-century Saint Gertrude the Great.
30   Ibid.
31   John V. Tolan, *Saracens: Islam in the Medieval European Imagination* (New York, NY: Columbia University Press, 2002), 82.
32   Anonymous, *The Song of Roland*, trans. J. Crosland (Cambridge, Ontario: In Parentheses Publications, 1999), 168, 46.
33   Molly Robinson Kelly, *The Hero's Place: Medieval Literary Traditions of Space and Belonging* (Washington, DC: Catholic University of America Press, 2009), 173.

Apocryphon.[34] Being dependent on Hellenic cartography,[35, 36] these are consistent with the Herodotean account and present a recognizably modern relief of Europe, which they take to be Japheth's community, descendants of one of Noah's three sons.

In his *Poetices libri septem*,[37] the cantankerous scholar Julius Caesar Scaliger writes of the divine Creator's will to diversity. In line with ancient thought from Plato to St. Dionysius he refers to regional tutelary spirits, and in line with Herodotus and Genesis he divides humanity principally between the three continents of Asia, Europe and Africa (despite writing after the discovery of America), each of which may boast a different character for its inhabitants (the European being "keen-spirited"). He provides a cavalcade of derogation in apparently earnest celebration of national diversity when listing the features of various peoples (there is in his discourse some real comedy, I think, and humility on behalf of others—the author makes a tirade of the many ways humanity may be inept). Other renaissance thinkers considering Europe a unit and praising her character include Abraham Ortelius, Giovanni Botero, Cesare Ripa and Samuel Purchas.

EUROPE IS THE FAITH

Frithjof Schuon and Samuel Zinner suggest that Christianity, in its Greco-Roman form, is in some sense providentially circumscribed roughly to Europe.[38] Schuon specifically mentions the Roman world, reading Christ as legitimizing the Caesar's authority in Mark 12:17 and, therefore, identifying His church (more correctly, one historically prominent manifestation of His Church) with the Roman domain.[39]

---

3 4   The *Book of Jubilees* is generally dated to between 160 and 150 BC, see: James C. Van der Kam, "The Origin and Purpose of the Book of Jubilees." In: M. Albani, J. Frey and A. Lange (eds.), *Studies in the Book of Jubilees* (Tübingen, Germany: Mohr Siebeck, 1997), 20. While the *Genesis Apocryphon* seems partly or largely derivative of Jubilees, this relationship has been reversed by some researchers, but, in any case, both, along with *1 Enoch*, likely date from the same period. See: Joseph Fitzmyer, *The Genesis Apocryphon of Qumran Cave 1 (1Q20): A Commentary*, 3rd ed. (Rome: Pontifical Biblical Institute, 2004), 21.

3 5   Daniel A. Machiela, *The Genesis Apocryphon (1Q20): A Reevaluation of Its Text, Interpretive Character, and Relationship to the Book of Jubilees* (PhD Thesis: University of Notre Dame, 2007), 180, 223–24.

3 6   Katell Berthelot, "Casting Lots and Distributing Territories: The Hellenistic Background of The Book of Jubilees and the Genesis Apocryphon." In: *Sibyls, Scriptures, and Scrolls: John Collins at Seventy*, Joel Baden, Hindy Najman and Eibert Tigchelaar (Leiden: Brill Academic Publishers, 2016), 154.

3 7   Julius Caesar Scaliger, "How God Made Human Diversity." In: Alex Drace-Francis, *European Identity: A Historical Reader* (New York, NY: Palgrave McMillan, 2013), 27–28.

3 8   Of course, Christianity always includes Hellenic features.

3 9   Frithjof Schuon, *The Transcendent Unity of Religions* (Wheaton, IL: Quest Books, 2014), 159.

This interpretation bears equivocation and is best approached as subordinate to the cited Gospel passage's more obvious meaning, where Caesar stands for political authority as such, with the presence of his image on money being invoked as an analogy for the image borne by human beings, that of God. It may also contain a reference to the principle of subsidiarity and political decentralization, if Caesar's authority occurs *within* the kingship of Christ.

In any case, later European culture may be singled out as the clearest heir of Roman civilization. Zinner recognizes as much when he observes, in support of Schuon's position, that "[t]he spread of Islam stopped at Europe's doors."[40] Indeed, after the age of mass conversions and invasions (if such can be so parenthesized, at least as far as a certain historical cycle in a certain part of the world is concerned) Islam's northern borders by and large coincided with the borders of Herodotus's outline of Europe. Those portions of Asia singled out in some texts as allotted to Japheth would correspond partly to Georgia, remembering that the *Book of Jubilees*, Flavius Josephus and medieval pseudo-histories including the work of St. Isidore of Seville, identify all or, more commonly, most of Anatolia with Shem, not Japheth (via *Lud* son of Shem).

This corresponds with the debatable suggestion by some researchers that the author of the Biblical *Acts of the Apostles* was referencing the division of nations between Noah's sons.[41] According to this reading, St. Paul's missionary career can be split between a Shemetic and Japhetic period, such that during the latter he conspicuously avoided regions traditionally regarded as Shemetic, even when they were on his way (Schuon also mentions these limits on Paul's preaching[42]). St. Paul is forbidden to preach at the Roman province of *Asia*, in Anatolia (Acts 16:6).

Instead, he directs himself to (Greek) Macedonia (Acts 16:10) and apparently plans to go farther into Europe, unto Spain. It is apparently not the Roman political domain as such that is being presented as a unit, that is, as the appropriate object of St. Paul's proselytizing efforts during this season of his mission, but Europe.

Zinner further notes that in the New Testament the term *"nations"* appears to refer primarily to the Roman Empire and associated peoples. Such may be interpreted as conforming to the likewise generic treatment of Japheth's descendants found in Genesis, where they are referred to as spreading from the coasts, constituting "nations" (Genesis 10:5). This contrasts with the specificity of national appellatives ascribed to the offspring of Ham and Shem in Genesis (10:6-30). Apart

---

40   Zinner, *Christianity and Islam: Essays on Ontology and Archetype*, 237.
41   James M. Scott, "Luke's Geographical Horizon." In: David W. J. Gill and Conrad Gempf (eds.), *The Book of Acts in its Graeco-Roman Setting (The Book of Acts in Its First Century Setting)*, vol. 2 (Grand Rapids, MI: Eerdmans, 1994), 539-41.
42   Schuon, *The Transcendent Unity of Religions*, 159.

from Mediterranean islands and part of Europe, it is Ham and Shem's territories (North African and western Asia) that exhaust the lands with which it is likely a near eastern scribe would have been concerned, or of which he is likely to have been aware. It therefore appears reasonable to assume that those nations seeded by Japheth in Genesis do, in fact, refer to Europe, consistently with *Jubilees*.

The above provides some semblance of justification for that long-standing tendency to emphasize European civilization when discussing the Christian faith, Hilaire Belloc's "Europe is the faith, the faith is Europe." But this conclusion, proceeding from certain historical usages of the term "nations," and applying as it does to a particular cultural-civilizational vocation, does not exclude other readings of the same scriptural passages, nor does it in any wise deny the theological appropriateness of broader understandings of the Biblical "nations."

If misunderstood, Schuon and Zinner's approach could lead to identifying the European instantiation of universality and of the Christian faith with Christianity in and of itself. But their approach is not untraditional. It is, for example, clearly evidenced in the writings of Pope Pius II. Born Aeneas Sylvius Piccolomini, he shared his name both with Aeneas, founder of Rome, and with this Trojan hero's esoteric exegete, Sylvestris. And he was not indifferent to his heroic namesake, connecting it to the office of pontiff when choosing the Papal name of Pius, which is Virgil's most frequent title for Aeneas: pious Aeneas. In the 15th century, writing to Nicholas of Cusa, this Pope described the fall of Constantinople to the Ottomans as "a second death of Homer and Plato."[43] Such familiarity with the pagans reminds of Dante's finding the souls of the pagans Rhipeus the Trojan and Emperor Trajan in the sixth Heaven in his Paradiso, or John Mauropous's prayer for Plato and Plutarch. Pope Pius II writes:

> In times gone passed we have been wounded in Asia and in Africa, that is to say, in foreign lands; now truly we have been stricken and felled in Europe, that is to say in our own fatherland, in our own house, in our own seat.[44]

The final words, describing Europe as *fatherland*, *house* and *seat*, articulate a unitary identity. He also mentions many of Europe's cities, from Spain to Britain, and the Hellenic character thereof. This constitutes an explicit identification of the Greek (epic and philosophic) legacy with European Christendom. It is fitting that Pope Pius II should be decrying the dishonoring of pagan fathers in the loss of the east, given that

43   Kenneth Setton, *The Papacy and the Levant, 1204–1571: The Fifteenth Century*, vol. 2 (Philadelphia, PA: American Philosophical Society, 1997), 150.
44   Aenea Sylvius Piccolomini (Pope Pius II), "Europe, our own home." In: Drace-Francis, *European Identity: A Historical Reader*, 15.

Byzantium (Constantinople) was in some ways the seat of a profoundly Greek, profoundly pagan, Christianity, as Judith Herrin notes, including the identification by some thinkers of Minerva as a prefigurement of the Holy Virgin, or Plethon's liturgies to pagan deities[45] (though this latter apparently rejected Christianity rather than locating paganism within it). Incidentally, it may be the case that refugees from fallen Constantinople stimulated the rest of Europe's thought, bringing texts little known in the West, along with Byzantine learning, so that tragedy produced fecundity, following the Trojan pattern after the burning of their city, whereby Troy's scions established Rome.

While Mehmet II was at the gates, the final eastern Roman Emperor reminded the Byzantines that they were descendants of Greek and Roman heroes, and told those Italians present that they were one with his Hellenic people. A truly ecumenical mass, annulling the east-west split, was then held at the Hagia Sophia. It is fitting that the assertion of antiquity occurred together with that of Christian unity. A deepening, together with a widening.

That final emperor, Constantine XI, ended his life with the words "the city is lost, but I live," before throwing himself into the fray of battle and, it is said, turning to marble, entering the earth beneath the golden gate, set to return one day, along with the priests of the Hagia Sophia, who melted into the walls and will resume the liturgy from where they left off when the city returns to the fold of Christendom.

Mehmet II, who in any case was known to be superstitious, gave the story enough credence to order the gate in question boarded up. Constantine XI becoming marble is a similar myth to those according to which great kings sleep in mountains and caves, and also emphasizes his continuation with the classical past. A living marble, a Greek statuary, waiting. As Lars Brownworth puts it in the conclusion to this *Twelve Byzantine Rulers*, whereas the west tended to answer Tertullian's question—*what has Athens to do with Jerusalem?*—by choosing one, the east asserted both.

JAPHETIC HISTORIES

The seven sons of Japheth are listed as spawning the peoples of various parts of Europe. This allowed European medieval scholars to account for Europe and its peoples, that is, their own civilizational and cultural context, in Biblical terms, as a tribally structured community of patriarchal provenance, and to do so while also articulating a specific or differentiated cultural or spiritual character. This character is that of *expansiveness* or *width*, as per Genesis 9:27, understood as the taking up by gentiles of Biblical agency and the perhaps antinomian character of the Gospel for peoples who fall outside the Mosaic covenant.

---

45 Judith Herrin, *Byzantium: The Surprising Life of a Medieval Empire* (Princeton, NJ: Princeton University Press, 2007), 330.

Before delving into European identification with Japheth, however, we will briefly touch on the idea that Europe is Abrahamic. Jewish tradition has at times figuratively identified Rome and, by extension, all of Europe or Christendom, with Esau (father of the Edomites/Idumeans), brother of Jacob, drawing an equivalence between the mistreatment of Jacob by Edom and the mistreatment of Judea by the Roman Empire. Where this figurative association has been literalized, it has sometimes been presented in terms of an overlay of Edomite on Japhetite, so that the Japhetic people became Edomites. This is similar to the Islamic context in which Hamites (North Africans, Egyptians and northern Near Eastern Canaanites) became Ishmaelites (becoming Arabized). All the nations of Noah in Genesis would then also be Abrahamic.

This occurs in some Muslim accounts as well, which tend to treat Esau sympathetically as being close to Ishmael and as having done no ill before being feared by his brother (indeed we have cited hadiths which are positive about Roman rule itself[46]): "Esau b. Isaac married the daughter of his paternal uncle, Basmah b. Ishmael b. Abraham, and she bore him al-Rum b. Esau."[47] This is a strange narrative as it personifies Rome. It then adds (in William Brinner's translation) that the "yellow people" descend from him, but as Lawrence I. Conrad notes, "for *Banu I-asfar* read 'the Byzantines,' not the 'yellow people.'"[48] Later we read: "Jacob set out with these two children of his and with his two wives to go to his father's dwelling-place in Palestine, because he was afraid of his brother Esau, though the latter had never done anything but good to him. It has been mentioned that Esau attached himself to his paternal uncle Ishmael and married Ishmael's daughter Basmah, whom he took to Syria and who bore him a number of children. They multiplied until they overcame the Canaanites in Syria. Then they journeyed to the sea and the area of Alexandria, and from there to Byzantium. It is said that Esau was called Edom because of his ruddiness, and that his descendants were thus called the children of the yellow one..."[49]

According to this, the previous "yellow people" or Byzantines may refer in general to people tending to a ruddy or rosy complexion. This idea that Rome (al-Rum) is the origin of all Europe occurs in European sources too, through the theme of Trojan descent, where whole nations are claimed to descend from Trojan Romans, along with their founding personages like king Arthur, Odin and Thor (via Geoffrey of Monmouth, Snorri Sturluson, etc.). Ruddiness and yellow color (perhaps referencing a higher frequency of blonde hair) is also associated with the descendants

---

46   Spoken by 'Amr Ibn al-'As, in *Sahih Muslim*, 2898.
47   al-Tabari, *History*, vol. 2, 354, 134.
48   Book Review of William M. Brinner's English edition of al-Tabari's *History*, *Middle East Journal*, Vol. 43, No. 2, Spring 1989: 313.
49   al-Tabari, *History*, vol. 2, 357, 136.

of Japheth in another account provided by al-Tabari: "The descendants of Japheth settled in al-Safun [Hebrew Safon means "the north"]...[t]here are ruddy-complexioned and blonde people among them."[50] We may therefore see a conflation of Japheth with Esau and Esau's son al-Rum.

We can imagine something like the recurrence of principles across Biblical personalities noted by Jacob Boehme (so that, for example, the sons of Noah—Japheth, Shem and Ham—repeat the personalities of the sons of Adam—Abel, Seth and Cain). In any case, we should note that the standard European and older Hebrew line of descent also appears in al-Tabari (here, as in the Biblical and *Jubilees* versions, the Byzantines or Romans descend from Japhet via Javan): "The Byzantines are descendants of Lanta bin Javan bin Japhet bin Noah."[51] Several hadiths are consistent with this, and specifically establish the Arabian context by stating that Arabs descend from Shem, Byzantines from Japheth and Abyssinians from Ham.[52] (It is also the case that some narratives seem to want to account for new peoples being encountered in later times, so that, roughly, Turks and East Asian populations are given to Japheth, to Shem broadly Caucasoid peoples, and sub-Saharan populations to Ham,[53] but this is different from the original Biblical texts, which do not detail anything south of the Horn of Africa or east of India.[54])

In terms of the hostility between Esau and Jacob, and the teaching that the older brother will serve the younger, the Bible can be read as considering either Esau the elder, for he exited the womb first, or Jacob, for he was conceived first (according to Rashi on Genesis 25:26, citing a Midrash): "Jacob was conceived from the first drop and Esau from the second. Go and learn from a tube with a narrow opening—put in it two stones, one after the other. The one that goes in first will come out last, and the one that goes in last will come out first. It comes out that Esau, who was conceived last, came out first, and Jacob, who was conceived first, came out last." The similarity between this and the Gospel teaching of the last being the first, also reminds us of the exaltation of gentiles by faith. The double primogenity allows for a sort of mutual servitude (like Origen's double advantage: the advantage in oracles for the Jews and the advantage in faith for the gentiles). Further, service is not deprecating but exalting in Biblical and, especially Christian, theology.

---

50   Ibid., II, 220-21, 19.
51   Ibid., 219, 18.
52   al-Tabari provides three narratives stating this in his *History*, vol. 2, 222, 20-21.
53   This is clear in the hadith narrated by Damrah b. Rabi'ah ibn-Ata, however, the one provided from Sa'id Ibn al-Musayyib in al-Tabari places Byzantines with Shemites, Slavs with Turks as Japhethites, and Copts and Berbers with Sudanese as Hamites. The immediate context of the Arabs is thus expanded and includes more far-off peoples into existing categories.
54   There are hadiths that give this account too, but less than the preceding account, to judge from al-Tabari (vol. 2, 223, 21).

The idea that after making Jacob his servant Esau will serve Jacob is also contradicted by Islamic sources in al-Tabari: "Isaac said, 'O my son, a prayer is left for you. Come here and I will invoke it for you.' Then he [Isaac] prayed for Esau, saying, 'May your offspring be as numerous as the dust and may no one rule them but themselves.'"[55] This also links Esau to the promise made to Abraham according to which his descendants would be very numerous. In general, it adds to the prestige associated with Esau and Rome in such Arab Muslim sources. Likewise, the Jewish scholar Samuel David Luzzatto (known also as *Shadal*) maintained that the prophecy of the elder brother serving the younger was already fulfilled in the times of David and John Hyrcanus, and concerned the Edomites whom Israel defeated (not Rome). This is similar to the Orthodox Christian current of interpretation (which David Bentley Hart sees as most consistent with Biblical language) that sees prophecies as often being fulfilled in history (like the prophecy of the nations coming to Jerusalem being a reference to historic mass conversions to Christianity), rather than as referring to final eschatological events discretely detachable from history.

In any case, literal descent from Esau is often attributed to Near Eastern populations. Shadal argues against Ibn Ezra to the effect that the first Christians were in fact Jewish, as well as Greek and Roman, not Edomites, and therefore the Biblical Edom is not to be identified with historical Christendom at large. The title of *Edom*, argues Shadal, was attached to Rome after the destruction of the second Temple (also partly because the Roman-patronized king Herod had been an Edomite) and refers to the oppressive rule of Rome, not to its Christianity or to the Roman Catholic Church generally. Shadal is thus compatible with the European Christian tradition in this regard.[56]

There are also specific references to the Germans. All sorts of speculation and divergent accounts exist,[57] but in the Talmud[58] (though not necessarily in authoritative passages; Shadal, for his part, seems to disagree or to interpret these figuratively) we find reference to "Germanya of Edom" (related to its geographic proximity to Rome as well as to the negative political connotations of Edom). Indeed, Rabbinical sources which identify Edom with Europe mainly do so with regard to Rome and Germany (which is straightforward considering the Holy Roman Empire was a mainly Germanic polity and *translatio* of Roman Imperium: Talmudic references to Edom being restrained so long as

---

55   Ibid., II, 359, 138.
56   Ibn-Caspi agrees with Shadal. Commenting on Deuteronomy, he argues it is acceptable to lend money at interest to Christians, Europeans or Romans, because the prohibition against doing so to Esau does not apply, as these are not Edomites.
57   Including that the Canaanites fled to Germany and are the latter's ancestors.
58   *Megilla* 6b.

these two are in rivalry can be read in terms of rivalry between the Holy Roman Emperors and popes). The issue was debated in scholarly circles, and even included arguments over whether Jewish people could marry German converts in the modern era, in case a prohibition against marrying the descendants of Esau (at least for a few generations after the latter's entering Israel's faith) includes Germans.[59]

They key to the connection between Rome and Edom may be found straightforwardly in Herod's reign (being paralleled by, or projected into, other eras). We may consider texts which draw on the *Book of Jubilees*.[60] Italy would be part of Japhet's portion according to *Jubilees*,[61] as would Germany. However, the Edomites, sons of Esau, would rise to prominence and be supported in their conflict with Jacob's nation, Israel, by the Romans. Some early Christian-era Jewish adaptations of the Jubilees narrative refer to Arodin, the *Herodion* built by king Herod. The *Book of Jashar* (around which there is much controversy[62]) references Rome's founder Aeneas and the Romans (*Kittim*[63]) as being in alliance with the Edomites. Aeneas is referred to through the figure of king Angeas of Dinhabah (Africa, perhaps relating to Aeneas's presence in Carthage), who allies with the Edomites after the death of Jacob.[64] Aeneas, then, is not an Edomite but is favorable to the Edomites initially, though later he refuses to help them against Israel and Egypt, and fights against them.[65]

---

59   Rabbi Josh Waxman's *Parsha* blog provides good discussion of these issues. Apart from identifying modern Edomites, there is also the position of some scholars that, since no explicitly Edomite nation exists today, such rules are universally inapplicable.

60   In *Jalkut*, The *Chronicles of Jerahmeel*, etc., as discussed in a footnote to chapter 37 in Charles Robert Henry's English edition of the *Book of Jubilees* (1902), 214-15.

61   *Jubilees*, IX, 4:11, 77.

62   My readings are of Mr Samuel's translation (New York: M. N. Noah and A. S. Gould, 1840).

63   Chittim, or Kittim, is also translated as "Romans" in the Septuagint's Greek Book of Daniel, and Kittim is one of the sons of Javan son of Japheth in Genesis 10, so this is consistent with broader tradition.

64   Angeas competes with a certain Turnus to wed the beautiful Jania daughter of Uzu from Chittim, land of the *Romim* (Romans) near the river *Tibreu* (Tiber) latterly ruled by one called Latinus: the parallels with the *Aeneid* are obvious, if garbled. The Edomite Zapho's coaxing of a reluctant king Angeas to go to war against the Israelites in Egypt and Egypt itself makes us think of the Sea Peoples incurring on Egypt at the end of the Bronze Age. In the Biblical book of *Joshua* we see reference to Greeks in the Near East reminding the Israelites of their rights (not being Canaanites) as former allies with the Israelites, and Robert Graves considered the Pharaoh in Genesis to refer to a leader of the Cretan-led and Trojan antagonists of the Myceneans, Egyptians and Israelites.

65   The Edomites come under the hand of Chittim and become one kingdom with them, and the grandson of Esau, Zepho, had risen to rulership over Chittim. The two are distinct, however, as the Book of Jashar lists Chittim as one of the descendants of Javan son of Japheth son of Noah (the same as Genesis 10), whereas the Edomites obviously descend from Shem son of Noah, via Abraham. Eventually,

This is similar to *Jubilees* in that a coalition of warriors, including from Kittim, are employed by the Edomites against Israel.

In European Christian tradition, consistently with Shadal's Jewish theological position, there is little or no identification of Christianity, Europe, Rome or Germany with Esau. Writes St. Isidore: "The son of Esau was Edom, from whom descended the Edomites. These are the nations that descend from the stock of Shem, holding the southern lands from the east to the Phoenicians."[66] Europeans are instead principally or exclusively the seed of Japheth, and so scholars and theologians linked Europe's civilizational and cultural character to narratives concerning Japheth in the Bible.

The tradition in question finds its major articulators after *Jubilees* and Flavius Josephus, in the fourth-century commentaries of St. Jerome and seventh-century Etymologies of St. Isidore, along with various accounts such as Snorri Sturluson's or the Georgian Chronicles.[67] Apart from geographic Europe proper, Japheth's progeny is said to include the Caucasus, ancient Phrygia, a Bactrian radiation into the Hindu Kush, the Medes, and a tribe of north African Moors who, according to St. Isidore, descend from the same son of Japheth as the northern Goths. To this St. Isidore adds that the scattered army of Hercules, composed of Armenians, Medes and Persians, settled in North Africa after Hercules' death in Spain (the Numidians descending from Persians and Moors partly from Medes).[68]

There are Greek and Roman accounts to this effect, wherein Sophax, Hercules' son by the widow of Antaeus, ruled over a Greek colony left in North Africa by his father, and wherein certain other Libyans are of Persian origin: "Sophax's son Diodorus subdued many African nations with a Greek army recruited from the Mycenean colonists whom Heracles had settled there," writes Robert Graves citing Pliny, Strabo, Pomponius Mela and Plutarch, adding "[t]he Mauretanians are of eastern origin...descended from certain Persians who accompanied Heracles to Africa"[69] (Graves also writes of *Thraco-Libyans*). We may add Herodotus's account of the north African Maxyans, who he writes claimed to originate in Troy,[70] possibly referencing the group which led some

---

the Latins or Italics (Chittim) ally with the Edomites, but precisely as dissenters against Angeas (Aeneas), so that the final establishment of the Trojan presence and foundation of Rome (following the *Aeneid* and Roman tradition) would here actually be a triumph *against* the Edomites (Zepho) and their allies (dissenting tribes of Italics), countering the identification of Roman imperium with Edom.

66   *Etymologies*, IX, ii, 9.
67   Stephen H. Rapp, *Studies in Medieval Georgian Historiography: Early Texts and Eurasian Context*. (Leuven, Aedibus Peeters, 2003), 175.
68   St. Isidore, *The Etymologies*, IX.ii.115-23, 198-99.
69   Graves, *The Greek Myths*, 21.2, 509.
70   *Histories*, iv, 191, ii, 5-11.

ancient Egyptian sources to apparently classify Europeans and northwest Africans (perhaps Berbers) together.[71]

The *Book of Jubilees* considers the land beginning with the islands off Asia Minor and extending unto Cadiz in southern Spain, including northern regions[72] and northwestern Europe with its islands[73] as well as four landmasses in the sea approaching North Africa,[74] as occupied by the descendants of Japheth. The *Genesis Apocryphon* concurs, describing land across the Mediterranean, from (or including a part of) Asia Minor, until the southern coast of Spain (Cadiz), with the river Don on this community's opposite, eastern, side, as all being "for Japheth and for his sons to inherit as an everlasting inheritance."[75] Flavius Josephus follows suit:

> Japhet, the son of Noah, had seven sons; they inhabited so, that beginning at the mountains Taurus and Amanus, they proceeded along Asia, as far as the river Tanais, and along Europe to Cadiz, and settling themselves on the lands they chose, which none had inhabited before, they called the nations by their own names...[76]

This relevant medieval scholarship includes St. Jerome's commentary on Genesis 10, written in the late fourth century and relating the "seven nations...coming from the stock of Japheth" which "live in the region of the north,"[77] and St. Isidore's influential *Etymologies*, which proceed in similar terms. The various peoples of Europe, along with certain Anatolians, are listed in terms of their Japhetic ancestry. Other European pseudo-histories also add to this narrative, such as the *Lebor gabála Érenn* (the earliest version of which dates from the 11th century) according to which the Irish descend from Magog, son of Japheth,[78] and Alfonso X of Castile's *General Chronicle of Spain*, whose texts date from the end of the 13th and beginning of the 14th centuries. In this latter, apart from identifying Europe with Japheth's progeny,[79] the king specifies that Spain (referring to the Iberian Peninsula) was peopled by

---

71 Jan Assman, *From Akhenaten to Moses: Ancient Egypt and Religious Change* (Cairo: American University in Cairo Press, 2014).

72 *Jubilees*, 9:10, 76–77; 9:12, 77; 9:8, 76.

73 *Jubilees*, 9:9, 76.

74 Ibid., 9:13, 77.

75 Fitzmyer, *The Genesis Apocryphon of Qumran Cave 1 (1Q20): A Commentary*, Column 16, 10–12 and Column 17, 16–18, 97.

76 Flavius Josephus, *Antiquities of the Jews*, I.6, 20.

77 Saint Jerome, *Saint Jerome's Hebrew Questions on Genesis* (Oxford: Clarendon Press, 1995), Gen. 10:2; 39.

78 Anonymous, *Lebor gabála Érenn* (Dublin: Published for the Irish Texts Society by the Educational Company of Ireland, 1938), xxxi; I:10, 23.

79 Alphonse X, King of Castile and Leon, *Primera crónica general: Estoria de España que mandó componer* Alfonso El Sabio y se continuaba bajo Sancho IV en 1289, ed. Ramon Menendez Pidal (Madrid: Bailly-Bailliére é hijos, 1906), Section 812, lines 48–59, 492.

Japheth's son Tubal.[80] Indeed, this conception was still circulating in the 16th century when the German reformer Martin Luther described himself as a natural descendent of Japheth.[81]

European pseudo-historical attributions of nations to Noah's sons is concurred with by later non-Christian accounts, including the narration of al-Harith Ibn Sa'd Hisham and several Islamic hadiths provided in al-Tabari's *History* (specifically in its second volume, addressing prophets and patriarchs). In the hadiths mentioned, Byzantines are distinguished from Arabs and Abyssinians in being descended from Japheth, as opposed to Shem and Ham, respectively, as is the case of the other two. There are, of course, contradictory accounts as well, but accounts presenting this scheme seem to preponderate. Those hadiths that generalize Noah's sons' descendants into broader populations[82] can be considered as providing a different level of resolution, so to speak, such that, again, these sons represent categorical archetypes which can be used to contrast Arabian to Byzantine civilization, but also East Asian to "Western," etc. (again, something like this can draw inspiration from Boehme). In any case, three hadiths with different lineages are provided as sustaining the narrative that "The Messenger of God said, 'Shem was the father of the Arabs, and Japheth was the father of the Byzantines, while Ham was the father of the Abyssinians.'" [83]

According to al-Tabari's rendering of al-Harith, the descendants of Japheth settled in al-Safun ["north"]... as opposed to the southern lands ("al-Darum"), where the children of Ham took root, or the ("al-Majdal") area between the north of Iraq or east of Anatolia (or possibly, though improbably, the mountains of India) and the sea between Yemen and Syria, where the seed of Shem spread (to each of these three is attached a cursory physical description which remains appropriate for the modern inhabitants of these regions).[84] The figure of Shem seems also to serve "to link the major peoples of the early Islamic Empire in their genealogy."

St. Jerome's commentary on Genesis 10, written in the late fourth century, relates the "seven nations...coming from the stock of Japheth"

---

80   Ibid., section 3, line 53, 6; section 3, lines 10–13, 6; section 812, lines 4–8, 493.
81   Martin Luther, *On the Jews and their Lies*, ed. B. Delmont (Raleigh, NC: Lulu, 2010), 10.
82   al-Tabari, *History*, vol. 2, 223, 21. However, these can be interpreted as containing a racism which would likely render them suspect to many Muslims: 'Imran b. Bakkar al-Kala'i-Abu al-Yaman-Ismail ibn-Ayyash-Yahya ibn-Sa'id narrating an account spoken by Sa'id Ibn al-Musayyib; Damrah Ibn Rabi'ah-Ibn 'Ata, his father.
83   Ibid., II, 222, 20–21. These lineages are Ahmad b. Bashir b. Abi 'Abdallah al-Warraq-Yazid b. Zuray-Said-Qatadah-al-Hasan-Samurah; al-Qasim b. Bishr b. Ma'ruf-Rawh-Said b. AN 'Arubah-Qatadah-al-Hasan-Samurah Ibn Jundub; Abu Kurayb-'Uthman b. Said-'Abbad ibn-al-'Awwam-Said-Qatadah-al-Hasan-Samurah. The middle one is translated as Ham begetting the "Blacks" rather than the "Abyssinians."
84   Ibid., II, 220–21, 19.

which "live in the region of the north."[85] These include peoples settled in Asia Minor (Cappadocians and Medes), the territory north of the Black Sea (Scythians) and the rest of Europe (Spaniards, Gauls, Italians, Greeks and Thracians, with the Goths possibly constituting a Scythian offshoot, a view St. Jerome rejects, apparently preferring to consider them of Thracian extraction).[86] Scythia maps onto the (modern) Russian sprawl, beginning with the Kievan Rus territory. It "begins in the Maeotian swamps (i.e., the Sea of Azov), stretching between the Danube and the northern Ocean up to Germania,"[87] it extends "up to the Caspian Sea, which is on its west... spreads in the south to the summits of the Caucasus" and, on its east, to the "Chinese Ocean."[88]

In addition, elements of nomadic Scythians were thought to have contributed to other peoples,[89] namely Bactrians and Parthians, constituting a Japhethic element in the Central Asian region near the Hindu Kush. It should be noted in the case of the Galatians, supposed descendants of Japheth's son Gomer, that while St. Jerome is referring to "Phrygia, the home of the Galatians"[90] and therefore to an Anatolian nation, in the seventh century St. Isidore of Seville, presenting a very similar account of the seven sons of Japheth, identifies the same appellative and patrimony (Galatians, sons of Gomer) with the Gauls,[91] adding that a portion of these settled Galatia (in Asia Minor), becoming *Gallograeci*.[92]

Italians are mentioned by St. Jerome in the context of the Iberian patriarch, "Thubal to the... Spaniards from whom derive the Celtiberians, although certain people suppose them to be the Italians."[93] St. Isidore's influential *Etymologies* proceed in similar terms.[94] Genesis 10 lists one of the sons of Javan son of Japheth as *Kittim*, who is traditionally identified with the Romans. The Greek Septuagint translates the Hebrew word Kittim in the Book of Daniel to "Romans" and Maccabees tells us that Alexander the Great came from Kittim, the idea being that a single patriarchal son of Japheth receives a large portion for his inheritance. Meanwhile the Sabines and Tuscans are identified with Tubal, who in Jerome and Isidore is the patriarch of Spaniards and maybe Italians (in *Jubilees* it is Meshech son of Japheth

---

85   Saint Jerome, *Hebrew Questions on Genesis*, Gen. 10:2; 39.

86   Ibid.

87   St. Isidore, *Etymologies*, XIV.iv.3, 289.

88   Ibid., XIV.iii.31, 288.

89   Ibid., IX.ii.43–44, 194.

90   Saint Jerome, *Hebrew Questions on Genesis,* Commentary by C. Hayward, Chapter 9 verse 2, 139.

91   St. Isidore, *Etymologies*, IX.ii.26; 193.

92   Ibid., XIV.iii.40, 288.

93   Saint Jerome, *Hebrew Questions on Genesis*, Gen. 10:2; 39.

94   St. Isidore, *Etymologies*, IX.ii.37; 193.

to which Spain corresponds). Italy is therefore partly of Javan the Greek patriarch and partly of Tubal the Spanish one.[95]

Cappadocia is east-of-center Asia Minor: "Asia Minor is girt by Cappadocia in the east."[96] An ancient Hittite territory, Herodotus describes it as belonging to the *Leuco-Syri* (White Syrians).[97] "It is located where Syria begins and touches Armenia in the east, Asia Minor in the west, and the Cimmerian Sea and the Themiscyrian plains, which belong to the Amazons, in the north; in the south it reaches the Taurus mountains, under which Cilicia and Isauria stretch out to the Gulf of Cilicia, which faces the isle of Cyprus."[98] Potentially related to Persia, it was latterly Hellenized. As for the Medes, their land, "Media obliquely borders the Parthian kingdoms in the west; in the north it is enclosed by Armenia; in the east it overlooks the Caspians; in the south, Persia. Its soil produces the tree 'Medica,' which is rarely found in any other region."[99]

Some of these descriptions include the peoples of the Caucasus, just as some references to Iberia may be to the eastern land bearing this name. In fact, the Georgian Chronicles, consisting of texts from between the 9th to 14th centuries, begin their history of the region by ascribing descent from Japheth to the inhabitants of the Caucasus.[100] These chronicles tell of Caucas or Kavkasos, great-grandson of Japheth and ancestor of the Caucasian people. According to the 11th-century Leonti Mroveli, this includes the Chechens and Ingush, who would be sired by a descendant of Kavkasos called Vainakhs.

If medieval accounts extend Europe or Japhetic descent to the Caucasus, it is not surprising that they typically comprehend the Trojans (historical Luwians), or the country of Phrygia, in the same community as Europe. According to St. Isidore "Troy is a region of Phrygia,"[101] the latter being a nation sprung from Gotorna, grandson of Japheth via Gomer;[102] following another trail in the Etymologies, the Trojans were apparently formerly called Dardanians,[103] and Dardania in turn was also referred to as Phrygia,[104] Gotorna's issue. The linking of Troy

---

95   This actually corresponds to modern genetic analyses where Italians appear as a spread between Spain and Greece. We should not, therefore, be hostile to the idea that there is some accurate historiography going on in these ancient books.

96   St. Isidore, *Etymologies*, XIV.iii.31, 288.

97   Herodotus, *The Histories*. trans. Rev. W. Beloe (London: Jones and Co., 1830), footnote 10, I.6, 3; Herodotus, *The Histories*, I.71–72, 32.

98   St. Isidore, *Etymologies*, XIV.iii.37, 288.

99   Ibid., XIV.iii.11, 286.

100   Rapp, *Studies in Medieval Georgian Historiography: Early Texts and Eurasian Context*, 175.

101   St. Isidore, *Etymologies*, XIV.v.21, 293.

102   Ibid., IX.ii.33; 193.

103   Ibid., IX.ii.67; 195.

104   Ibid., XIV.iii.41; 288.

to Japheth is clearer in Nennius's ninth century *Historia Brittonum*, which counts the Trojan founder of Rome, Aeneas, Troius (presumably Troy's namesake), and Dardanus (whence Dardania) as Japheth's descendants.[105] Alphonse X of Castile likewise included the Trojans in his list of nations descended from Japheth (by way of "Yauan," Javan, elsewhere the father of Ionia and a part of the Greeks).[106]

This does not lend itself to appearing as a merely geographic link, which St. Isidore's exposition might. Snorri Sturluson does something similar to Nennius in the forward to the *Prose Edda* when he refers to Japheth (spelt *Japhteth*) receiving the "northern lands,"[107] and later to the descent of various European peoples from the Trojan sons of Jove (including mythical figures of Norse tradition).[108] In Sturluson this encompasses the Germanic sagas: "[t]he family tree extends back to the Trojan-Thracian Trór = þórr," that is, Thor, the thunder god, "who was a descendant of Jupiter's son Dardanus. Snorri traced the line back to Japheth, the son of Noah."[109] Later, in the nineteenth century, Noah Webster identified Tiras, a son of Japheth, with Thor,[110] who, being a thunder deity, is generally considered equivalent to Jove (Thursday—Thor's day, in Germanic languages—is named after Jupiter in Romance ones). It is strange, however, that Webster considers Tiras the deity whom Homer describes as "Mars of the Thracians,"[111] but then links this personage to Thor, when the obvious association is to the Norse Tyr, given the similar spelling of the two and being that Tyr was traditionally considered equivalent to Mars, again, by way of weekdays: Tuesday derives from Tyr's day, and in Romance languages is named after Mars.

The narratives of the Trojan men of Aeneas, founder of Rome, grandson to Jove, are merged by these scholars with that of Japheth (indeed, Jove, Thor and Odin's progenitorship assimilates elements of Japheth's). The similarity of sound between the names Japheth and Jupiter may be at play in some of these, though the *Sibylline Oracles* are usually read as identifying Japheth with the Greek Titan Iapetus.[112] Iapetus as son of

---

105 Nennius, *The Historia Brittonum*, trans. Rev. W. Gunn (Cornhill, London: Printed for John and Arthur Arch, 1819), 10–11.

106 Alphonse X of Castile and Leon, *Primera crónica general*, Section 3, lines 44–49, 5.

107 Snorri Sturluson, *The Prose, or, Younger Edda*, trans. G. Dasent (Stockholm: Norstedt and Sons, 1842), Foreword, 2, 99.

108 Ibid., Foreword, 8, 106.

109 Maria E. Dorninger, "Modern Readers of Godfrey." In: ed. T. Foerster, *Godfrey of Viterbo and His Readers: Imperial Tradition and Universal History in Late Medieval Europe* (London: Routledge, 2015), 33.

110 Noah Webster, *Letters to a Young Gentleman Commencing His Education* (New Haven, CT: S. Converse, 1879), Letter VIII, 99–100.

111 Ibid., 100.

112 Anonymous, *The Sibylline Oracles*, trans. M. Terry (New York City: Eaton and Mains, 2001), footnote 357, 14; III.133, 24.

Uranus and Gaia, that is, of Heaven and earth, can be interpreted as the archetypal human being as bridge, pontifex, between the mundane and celestial. The connection between Iapetus and Japheth, however, is dubious even in terms only of mythical correspondences (to say nothing of some purported common origin).[113] British colonial era hoaxes attempting to falsify ancient Indian myth to fit a Biblical schema serves as one example of the danger of excessively enthusiastic seeking of correspondence (specifically attempting to link the three sons of Noah to figures in ancient Sanskrit history).[114]

According to the account Sturluson gives in the Prologue to his *Prose Edda*, Odin is a distant descendent of Thor,[115] although the Icelander's relating of the *Edda* itself declares of Thor that "one should call him Son of Odin."[116] Of these, the more senior person to which the Odinic presence attaches, if such is taken for history and matched to Sturluson's schema, is the father of Thor (or in the Trojan nomenclature according to Sturluson, Trór), a Trojan chieftain named Múnón who married King Priam's daughter (we are historicizing both accounts and pretending they are compatible). However, Odin is here best understood as trans-historic, in which sense the epithet of All-Father properly applies, equivalent to Jove-Pater, whereas the latter's function as storm-god corresponds with Thor, and the latter's as sorcerer with Mercury (Hermes). Thor becomes the Trojan ancestor of a host of Germanic deities by his wife in the north, the Sibyl or Germanic Sif, and is himself, apart from a descendent of Japheth, a descendent in some archetypal sense of Odin, who assimilates the Japhetic function as European progenitor, as does Jove.

JAPHETH AS SYMBOL

Japheth himself is often identified as kingly. He is featured in lists of kings, for example with his son Tubal appearing in Alphonse X's 13th century History of Spain as one of that country's kings, or in Shakespeare's *Henry IV*, when Prince Hal mocks the snobbishness of those who claim to descend from kings: "they will be kin to us, or they will fetch it from Japhet" (II.ii, 117–18).

Apart from somewhat similarly sounding names, Jupiter and Japheth overlap in meaning and function. Jove is *wide-seeing* (europos) and the name Japheth was thought by medieval scholars to derive from *width*.[117] Further, the name Jupiter contains *pater*, father, and describes

113   Joseph Blenkinsopp, *Creation, Un-Creation and Re-Creation: A Discursive Commentary on Genesis 1–11* (New York City: T&T Clark, 2011), 158.
114   William Hales, *A New Analysis of Chronology and Geography, History and Prophecy* (London: Printed for C. J. G. and F. Rivington, 1830), 198.
115   Sturluson, *The Prose Edda*, Prologue: III, 6–7.
116   Ibid., *The Poesy of the Skalds*, IV, 107.
117   St. Isidore of Seville, *The Etymologies*, VII.vi.18, 163.

the patriarch god, head of the divine household who spawned children of Europa (though the expression is taken from an initiatic context[118]) while Japheth was considered to have fathered Europeans. In addition, Jove as king-god would correspond to the kingly character of Japheth and his descendants, as reported in the accounts of several authors according to al-Tabari:

> Others besides Ibn Ishaq have said that Noah prayed that prophets and apostles would be descended from Shem and that he prayed that kings would be among the descendants of Japheth. He began with the prayer for Japheth and, in so doing, gave him precedence over Shem...[119]

This coincides with a certain tenth century astrological text that C. S. Lewis apparently found useful, in which it is said that the west, or Europeans, are under the influence of Jupiter, the planet associated with kingship. Strangely, the passage from al-Tabari apparently contradicts the Islamic doctrine that prophets have come to all peoples, as well as being at odds with the primacy given to Shem in other sources, although the latter can be ascribed to diverging emphases or perspectives.

Yet any association between the Japheth and Jove is seldom made explicit, though it does appear in modern works, such as the 19th-century writing of John Tomas Painter.[120] The connection should be understood as an imaginative exercise, maybe uncovering archetypical connections.

In the *Animal Apocalypse* of 1 Enoch, Noah's sons are described as a black, white and red bull. The case for these being Ham, Shem and Japheth, respectively, is strong.[121] Japheth's status as red bull may bespeak the regal character given to his sons in some traditions, as opposed to the priestly function of Shem, with red signifying the kingly robe and white the clerical or angelic garment (that the European or Japhetic is red or royal and the Near Eastern or Shemetic is white or priestly echoes in the 19th century stereotype that distinguished between a more active Europe and more contemplative orient).

It may also be read in terms of the threefold work of spiritual awakening, the Katharsis, Theoria and Theosis (blackening, whitening and reddening of alchemy. The asceticism of the black work is followed by an ecstatic flight from the world during the whitening and a subsequent return (the mountains were mountains, the mountains ceased to be mountains, and the mountains were again mountains, to approximate the Zen *koan*).

---

118   Porphyry, *On Abstinence from Animal Food.*
119   al-Tabari, *History,* vol. 2, 215, 14.
120   John Thomas Painter, *Ethnology: Or the History and Genealogy of the Human Race* (London: Printed by J. Davis. Steam Works, Old Kent Road, 1879), 79–80.
121   Daniel Olson, *A New Reading of the Animal Apocalypse of 1 Enoch: All Nations Shall Be Blessed* (Leiden: Brill, 2013), 163.

Jove's taking the form of a white bull and copulating with Europa may signify a repossessing of the bodily, a return from *Theoria* (*Albedo*) and completion of *Theosis* (*Rubedo*). Jupiter, as Japheth, would thus pass from being the white bull to being the red, which the slightly ambiguous attributions made in the Animal Apocalypse almost allow for.

The joining of Europa and Jove is, therefore, a spiritual edification, as was already discussed in the context of the Cretan association of the sun with a bull and its consort with the moon, their union being the fulfillment of the alchemical work. That the sun should be a white bull is explained by the sun's white radiance, and the shift from white to red represents entry into the earth from the sun (conjoining with the feminine moon, entering her sub-lunar space, that is, the earth), into the realm of color and, specifically, blood, life's vitality, rather than remaining in pure, luminous contemplation.

As for Shem, he is like Noah, who is also described as a white bull. The theme of greater continuity between Noah and Shem than between Noah and his other sons appears in several Biblical Apocrypha. Perhaps it is only from their middle term of contemplation, the luminosity of father Noah, that the other two functions can emerge: one higher (the regality of Japheth) and the other deeper, as in Simone Weil's interpretation of Ham's darkness (unfortunately, Weil goes on to devalue the spirituality of the peoples she identifies with Noah's sons Shem and Japheth):

> Ham saw Noah's nakedness when the latter was drunk. Doesn't this mean the mystical, Dionysiac drunkenness, and the nakedness that is the opposite of the shame on account of sin which forced Adam and Eve to cover themselves…? Wasn't the curse which fell upon him the curse of affliction, which is inseparable from all contact between man and God, all human purity?[122]

Ham as black bull can be interpreted as originator, the symbol of the primordial womb (or in the sense in which Krishna is said to be dark of color) and, from another perspective, Japheth as red bull represents color, the middle term of balance between light and darkness, white and black, the external and the internal, which are not themselves properly colors, not manifestations. All might claim preeminence, and do so legitimately, while occupying their own perspective.

---

122   Simon Weil, *The Notebooks of Simone Weil*, trans. A Wills (London: Routledge, 1956), 572.

China and the Ecumene, or, the Circumference is not the Center

HINA PROVIDES A FRUITFUL CASE STUDY FOR
how an instance of archetypal categorization applied to international relations can structure a sense of the Ecumene, calcify
into a kind of metaphysical chauvinism and then alter as a result of
contact with foreigners. Where Europe came to identify with the universal Evangelizing mission as a cultural and political project, in tandem
with its inheriting the universal aspirations of Roman Empire, China
contrastingly simply considered itself the unique center. Where the
former saw itself as the circumference, having to transform the globe,
the latter saw itself as the exclusive center.

The Chinese ecumene is the body of the emperor, prototypically the
antediluvian Huangdi. The popular understanding of that ecumenic
body has transitioned from ethnocentrism to pluralism. It has already
been noted in passing that various Taoist texts present the cosmos as
corporeal so that the body of an initiate can become the cosmic body,[1]
also presenting good governance as equivalent to the body's health.[2]

This sometimes occurs in tandem with a specific sense of Chinese
civilizational unity, it accompanies a political, historical project which
is articulated in terms of descent from China's mythic Yellow Emperor.
The Taoist historian Sima Qian's second century BC work, the *Records
of the Grand Historian* (*Shiji*), links various non-Sinitic peoples to China
by postulating descent from this figure.[3] In such accounts the Yellow
Emperor is father to the Han Chinese as well as certain foreign peoples,
from Korea to northern Xiongnu Turkic or Mongolic peoples.[4]

Later, the *Book of Wei*, a canonical history compiled by Wei Shou in
the sixth century, considered the Touba clan of the Xianbei (probably a
mainly proto-Mongolian folk—speakers of a Mongolic language with
Turkic elements[5]—whose scions constituted the northern Wei dynasty

---

1 Pregadio, *The Encyclopedia of Taoism*, 76.
2 Ibid., 75.
3 Byung Ho Lee, *Forging the Imperial Nation: Imperialism, Nationalism and Ethnic Boundaries in China's Longue Duree* (PhD Thesis: The University of Michigan, 2011), 139.
4 Norman J. Girardot, *Myth and Meaning in Early Taoism: The Theme of Chaos (hun-
tun)* (London: University of California Press, 1988), 201-22.
5 Charles Holcombe, "The Xianbei in Chinese History." *Early Medieval China* 19
(2013): 4.

between the fourth and sixth centuries) to also be sons of the Yellow Emperor.[6, 7] Given that Chinese tradition links government functions to parts of the body and to the teachings of the Yellow Emperor (in the *Inner Scripture of the Yellow Emperor, Huangdi neijing*),[8] the tradition of descent from this figure may be interpreted as an expression of his embodying the realm.

Furthermore, China may provide a case study for myths of common descent structuring political circumspection, suggesting a link between the abandonment of these myths and expansionism. According to one reading of Chinese history, certain "conquest dynasties" which rejected the connection between the Yellow Emperor and political unity tended towards the sort of empire Plato and Voegelin criticize:

> ...Jurchen Jin, Mongol Yuan, and Manchu Qing, did not share the ancestral myth of the native Chinese but cherished their own tribal mythologies. They instead pursued the ideal of political uni-fication—a desire to achieve inclusiveness within a unified empire to which all peoples belong. To accommodate all ethnicities, they employed Confucianism as the official state ideology, one that preaches a supra-ethnic cultural universalism as well as a doctrine of "one-world one-ruler"...[9]

If the above presents a valid take on Chinese history, and if René Guénon's account[10] of that culture's tradition as exoterically Confucian and esoterically Taoist is legitimate, then the attitude of some conquering dynasties risked removing Confucianism from its appropriate ambit. The Yellow Emperor is a figure of cultic significance in some types of Taoism, and in this capacity, he represents a politically programmatic facet thereof (an external application of esotericism). This is twofold: as mythic ances-tor he emphasizes the unity of his descendants and thereby de-emphasize the pursuit of (practical) global unification, and; as paradigmatic practi-tioner of *wu wei* or *wei wu wei* (*inaction* or *action without action*)[11] he serves as referent for rulers limiting their exercise of power, encouraging them to represent universality symbolically rather than clumsily grasping at it through undignified shows of conquest and coercion. This is specifically so for the Huang-Lao lineage of Taoism, the texts of which "do not reject rulership. On the contrary, they embrace the role of the ruler and teach that the true ruler should govern by *wu-wei*, following the model of the

---

6   Lee, *Forging the Imperial Nation*, 146.
7   Holcombe, *The Xianbei in Chinese History*, 2.
8   Pregadio, *The Encyclopedia of Taoism*, 75.
9   Lee, *Forging the Imperial Nation*, 148.
10   René Guénon, *Insights into Islamic Esotericism and Taoism*, trans. H. Fohr, ed. S. Fohr (Hillsdale, NY: Sophia Perennis: 2014), 52–66.
11   Theodore de Bary, *The Great Civilized Conversation* (New York City: Columbia University Press, 2013), 294.

Yellow Emperor..."[12] From this perspective the absence of the Yellow Emperor as a legitimizing force behind a Confucian state can be regarded as a deficiency. In fact, Confucianism did in some ways integrate with Huang-Lao Taoism.[13]

Different interpretations or applications of Confucianism[14] aside, it was a less mythic, more rationalistic political theology that was being put forward, presumably in order to justify (or maybe resulting in, or from) a *de facto* expansive imperialism. This partly suggests that former notions of common ancestry from a mythological, foundational figure were not conducive to such an undertaking, however much the polity that was founded on them, as many of its ancient peers, nominally or figuratively claimed to be universal.

We may also suggest that what occurred here was a case of the dialectical, mutually enforcing relationship between the hegemony (and homogenizing agency) of one group, on the one hand, and political fragmentation, on the other:

> Ethnic separatism and hierarchy particularly persisted under the four major alien regimes: the Khitan Liao (907-1125), Jurchen Jin (1115-1234), Mongol Yuan (1206-1368), and Manchu Qing (1644-1911).[15]

These precisely include all of the dynastic groups previously mentioned as rejecting the myth of common descent from the Yellow Emperor. Therefore, it is consistent with the present discussion that:

> ...the unintended consequence of those minority rules was the expansion of the boundaries of the Chinese people by incorporating various alien groups.... In addition, as a result of the massive territorial expansion under the Qing dynasty, the spatial boundaries of the Middle Kingdom as a political definition of China extended beyond the traditional China proper.[16]

To add nuance, it is reasonable to assume that these dynasties could have been more effective at preserving different identities within their empire than those claiming common ancestry for certain peoples. The choice would then be between attempts to attain actual global unification on the one hand and circumspection to one group of peoples on the other, or more likely, between an expansive and conquering state

---

12   Ronnie Littlejohn, *Daoism: An Introduction* (London: I. B. Tauris, 2009), 34, 36.
13   Ronnie Littlejohn, *Confucianism: An Introduction* (London: I. B. Tauris, 2011), 81-100.
14   Although plainly universalist, there may have been an "ethnic awareness in Confucianism itself" (Zarrow, *China in War and Revolution: 1895-1949*, 55). In addition, there might have been Confucians who interpreted the doctrine of global sovereign in a non-politically literal sense.
15   Lee, *Forging the Imperial Nation*, 24.
16   Ibid.

and an isolationist fortress. The latter tendency would entail some measure of homogenization of those peoples within it, considering them to rightfully constitute a unit and therefore treating some degree of homogeneity among them as the legitimate emergence of their shared character. However, the previously listed regimes:

> ...institutionalized the system of ethnic boundary making not only to preserve their ethno-cultural identity but also to maintain their dominant status over the native subjects who were indiscriminately classified as the Han people.[17]

Insofar as they were exclusively or overridingly interested in preserving their own identity and insofar as they, consequently, classed all others under their rule as *Han*, they would have constructed governance structures prone to conform those other peoples to each other, while reducing their own identity to a mere function of privilege, defined in terms of its dominance over others (although it should be noted that the Manchu Qing, at least, did not clearly pursue homogenizing policies for their subjects, and in some cases accomplished the opposite[18]). Something similar appears in the work of those Islamic jurists who divided the Muslim world into Arab and ʿAjam, that is, simply Arab and non-Arab (although ʿAjam could sometimes mean Persian).

In sum, common descent is the historical-narrative manifestation of the previously discussed *incarnationist* dimension of monarchy. Monarchy is often symbolically described in terms of paternity, after all, where the king appears as benevolent father figure. The monarchical aspect in myths of common descent is explicit in the case of China's Yellow Emperor, as it is in the figure of Aeneas. This is consistent with a political ethic respectful of the other's integrity. While familial ties can be constructed to exploitative ends, familiarity can also attenuate internal power relations and, externally, to claim common parentage places implicit limits on the degree to which a polity or cultural space may legitimately expand, for, presumably, if such parentage is invoked to justify one linkage, it also legitimates the cultural autonomy of regions outside it.

In the Chinese case, as in many others, however, the benign aspect of isolation manifested not so much as respect for foreigners than as the identification of the cosmic center with one's own home, where barbarians outside the gates are considered literally peripherally human. But this chauvinism, at least in terms of its cosmological basis, seems to have been upset as a consequence of China's increased interaction with other peoples. Apparently "[f]amiliarity with outgroups led to an increased relativization of the ingroup's cosmological position." This occurred not in terms of diluting the ingroup's sense of identity but by

---

17   Ibid.
18   Zarrow, *China in War and Revolution: 1895–1949*, 55.

questioning its sense of metaphysical centrality and thus "making the ingroup identity increasingly specific," so that "[h]eightened awareness of differences between groups led to a tendency to underestimate the differences within the group." In a sense China began defining itself in terms of foreign perception, which is not necessarily problematic. We often learn about ourselves by interacting with others rather than indulging in splendid isolation.

The term "yellow race" was thus appropriated, having positive connotations in Chinese culture,[19] linked as it is to royalty. Some currents of thought in China also incorporated the Western notion that this category extended beyond China to include Japan, for example, which has a clear, autochthonous precedent in Sima Qian's inclusion of Vietnam and Korea in the community of the Yellow Emperor. Li Hongzhang, writing in 1895, believed in a "perpetual peace and harmony between China and Japan … so that our Asiatic yellow race will not be encroached upon by the white race of Europe."[20] After the Xinhai revolution of 1911, the Chinese government's *Five Races under One Union* policy or ideology presented Mongols, Manchus, Han Chinese, Tibetans and Hui as all spawn of the Yellow Emperor.

This had non-Chinese precedents as well. Written in the 1730s (1732–35), the *History of the Borjigid Clan* by a certain Aci Lomi, himself a Borjigid, that is, a descendent of Genghis Khan, celebrated rather than decrying the Borjigid union with the Manchu dynasty of China against the Ligdan Khan's attempts to reunite the Mongols. Lomi praises the Taitsu Holy Emperor as a restorer of the Mongols who saved them from disintegration and treated their nobility with high honors, both integrating and maintaining the integrity of the Mongolian people (a more exploitative policy towards Mongolia later came about, however).

The theme of the Yellow Emperor appears in the work of Chiang Kaishek, leader of the Kuomintang during China's Civil War, partly justifying his faction's collaboration with Japan against the communists. Although communists initially suppressed the figure of the Yellow Emperor, this was reversed after the passing of Mao, and Deng Xiaoping himself referenced the Emperor when speaking of the desirability of Chinese unification with Taiwan. These ideas have endured into present-day China.[21] Indeed, the current Chinese government rehabilitation of Sun Yet Sen continues this trajectory, as does the attendance of ceremonies at the Yellow Emperor's mausoleum by government officials.

---

19   Dikotter, *The Discourse of Race in Modern China*, 56.
20   Ssu-yu Teng and John King Fairbank, *China's response to the West: A Documentary Survey, 1839–1923* (Cambridge, MA: Harvard University Press, 1954), 126; cited in Dikotter, *The Discourse of Race in Modern China*, 57.
21   Thomas Mullaney, *Coming to Terms with the Nation: Ethnic Classification in Modern China* (London: University of California Press, 2011).

Thus, the displacement of a sense of cosmological centrality can operate to strengthen localized identities. This is so because the belief in a culture's metaphysical superiority as regards others can ultimately function to draw into question its identity *as particular*, for any universalist epiphany will require others adopt the culture conceived in these terms (salvation for gentiles by becoming Israel, for barbarians by becoming Chinese). This cannot truly constitute a defense of any set of cultural forms, for a cultural form is particular and cannot in the long run be rationally equated with the universal. A note of caution: this shift in self-understanding should not necessarily be thought of as leading to a more benign or peaceful orientation, for "[d]uring prolonged contact with an outgroup, the Chinese provincial consciousness was increasingly supplemented with a racial consciousness" which precisely often articulated itself in terms of needing to unite with fellow East Asians like the Japanese in order to react to the threat of European imperialism.

Yet such hostility (justified or not) can be viewed as dialectically containing the possibility of a more authentic ecumenism than was possible while China considered itself the literal and metaphysical center of humanity. It can lead to the conclusion that to unite with the center is not to claim to be the center. But we have already touched on the ambiguity of sacralizing place, the imperative to, (and simultaneous danger from) finding eternal patterns in one's particular cultural forms, forgetting that those patterns may manifest elsewhere.

The Caliphate and the Ecumene, or, the Center is not the Circumference

THE DEVELOPMENT OF ISLAMIC POLITICAL structures does not allow its historical bid for hegemony and an immanentized ecumene to be delineated within or otherwise distinguished from theology, the way the European or Chinese civilizational trajectories do, as we will see later on. We may speak of Arab Imperialism as distinct from Islam, but the former resolves itself into new political arrangements only through Islam and in the course of a history it shares with non-Arab peoples who take on its mantle. We are not dealing with something analogous to China ceasing to consider itself the literal center of the earth, or Europe ceasing to pursue the Europeanization of the world. We are dealing rather with the historical phenomena of accommodating new political expressions for existing theological doctrines: theological translation, not in its most ecumenic sense of recognizing other traditions as valid, but in the sense of applying a tradition's doctrine in new contexts, just as Roman Emperorship took on the ideal of Biblical Davidic monarchy.

On one level, Islam remarkably avoids the complications of Christian theology. There is a sense in which it is more naturalistic, having as little need for the technology of Paul's grafting of gentile branches into the tree of Israel as it does for that of sacramental marriage. The right way is available without these convolutions, the religion of Abraham is as accessible as it is primordial, Divinely-sent messengers have come to all the nations, and the salvation received by observing their laws is equal in kind and degree.

Yet Islam contends with a parallel dynamic according to which the tradition appears to urge allegiance to political projects that can be plausibly considered inheritors to Mohammed. This is only superficially owed to the latter's far more politically involved career in comparison to that of Jesus. If it were only a question of this, then Mohammed's political activities would simply present a useful paradigm for government. The issue is that allegiance to Islam during its foundational and prophetic infancy was intimately connected with allegiance to the state structures it brought, so that Islamic scripture easily creates the impression that conversion should—if the example of its founder and the holistic range of its potentials are to be operant—imply fealty to at least a specific political program, if not an actual structure. Thusly can an eminently important Qur'anic commentator like al-Tabari disagree with what constitutes the preponderance of Islamic tradition in considering the death penalty appropriate not really for religious apostasy but rather for treason against legitimate government (as it has been used in most civilizations). He and the wider tradition draw on the same sources in arriving at what appears exegetically to be subtly divergent positions but which nonetheless make a significant practical difference.

THE *UMMAH*: ONE AND MANY

It is further the case that the political project implied by Islam is linked by much of the tradition to a specific community, namely that of Arab patrilineal descent. The binary of Jew and Gentile in Hebrew and Christian tradition is paralleled by a binary between Arab and non-Arab. Islamic expansion in its early centuries was accompanied by religiously sanctioned, legally established primacy of Arab patrilineal descent (*fadl*, *sabiqa*).[1] The latter is not necessarily incompatible with individual equality between believers, wherein *individuals* are to be judged only in terms of piety but the character of a group is considered more noble than that of another. This included the tying of conversion by non-Arabs to clientage to an Arab patron[2] and the marital suitability or parity (*kafa'a*) of a non-Arab woman as spouse for an Arab man despite the doctrinal unsuitability of the inverse, privileging Arab patrilineal lineage (nasb).

For one classic example, with supporting hadith, of the issue of suitability in marriage, see Ahmad ibn-Naqib al-Misri's *Reliance of a Traveler* (which is in the tradition of the Shafi'i madhhab). Crucially, this does not constitute a prohibition, only a statement of suitability which a woman is free to ignore when there is no objection on the part of her guardian. Nonetheless, it is related to a hadith and illustrates how early Islamic power relations overlap with the shariah:

> The following are not suitable matches for one another: a non-Arab man for an Arab woman, because of the hadith that the Prophet (Allah bless him and given him peace) said, "*Allah has chosen the Arabs above others.*"[3]

This is a traditional position in the majority of Sunni jurisprudential schools or *madhhabs*, excepting the *Maliki* school.

In parts of the Islamic world, and especially Persia, the prevalence of Arab patronage contributed to the *Shu'ubiyyah* movement.[4] The

---

1   Nimrod Hurvitz, *The Formation of Hanbalism: Piety into Power* (New York City: Routledge, 2002), 33.

2   Montgomery Watt, *Islam and the Integration of Society* (London: Routledge/The International Library of Sociology and Social Reconstruction, 1961), 151.

3   Ahmad ibn-Naqib al-Misri, *Reliance of a Traveller*, trans. Nuh Ha Mim Keller (Beltsville, MD: Amana Publications, 1997), 523.

4   Watt, *Islam and the Integration of Society*, 152.

Shu'ūbiyyah polemicized against Arab culture, though in more literary-cultural than concretely political terms.[5] It should be noted, however, that Montgomery Watt considers the early practice of Arab patronage in Islam "a very reasonable thing to do," given the disconnection from one's community that conversion could entail,[6] without denying an unhealthy metastasis in the practice.

Cultural diversity is perfectly well accepted in Islam, but contrasts with Arabizing trajectories, as found even in the Shu'ūbiyya views of Ibn García, who apparently sought equality between Arab and non-Arab but within the adoption of Arab culture and language. The historical defeat of this trajectory, in a sense, allows us to see what is more essential to Islam (what is separable form Arab culture and early historical polities).

Such an understanding may legitimate maintaining the diversity of human identities against a homogenizing force. One is allowed to preserve *nasb* (lineage) in marriage (according to most Sunni jurisprudential schools) and since producing progeny requires two people of different gender this means that the child is of a same *nasb* on both sides. It is Arab women who are denied to non-Arab men by Shafi *fiqh*, after all, even though they cannot pass on the Arab *nasb*, which is considered patrilineal. That Arab women are reserved for Arab men means that a substantively Arab population is being aimed at. In fact, through these schools, the shariah is preserving what it has created. As Montgomery Watt writes:

> If Muhammad, then, had not made himself ruler of all Arabia, yet he had to a great extend unified the Arabs. Through his "Arabic Qur'an," and through the religious and political system he had created, he had developed Arabs' hitherto only implicit awareness of themselves as an ethnological and cultural unit. It was to this unit that the "Arabic Qur'an" was addressed, and it marked them off from Abyssinians, Byzantines, Persians and Jews.[7]

Thus, the nation is preserved. Yet the nation is not the locus of ultimate political articulation or religious piety. Politics, or at least foreign policy, belongs to an initially supra-national religious polity. One is to fight for principles, not clans. And these two should not be thought of as being at odds: the movement towards drawing tribes into discovery of common *Arabity* is the movement towards drawing nations into discovery of common humanity. The body has its organs.

Still, on the plane of history we end up seeing a split between the Ecumene and the historical experience of a conception, a theory and practice, or manifestation, of Ecumene, such as between Islam and the historical experience of the Caliphate(s). The Catholic Church and

---

5   Roy Mottahedeh, "The Shu'ubiyah Controversy and the Social History of Early Islamic Iran." *International Journal of Middle Eastern Studies* 7:2 (1976): 162.
6   Watt, *Islam and the Integration of Society*, 151.
7   Ibid., 224.

Muslim *ummah* are both described as bodies, which may be a statement on humanity and the cosmos being corporeal and internally diverse. Yet, as historic growths they do not in practice correspond with the actual body of humanity, and the fact that part of the human body is outside the body of the faith is not denied.

Arab patronage may share the same logic as St. Paul's language of grafting gentiles to Israel. It is possible, however, that at some points in history it veered into violating Islamic precepts, namely the stipulation according to which an adopted person is not to use the name of a biologically unrelated adoptive parent but that of its own biological parent (assuming it is known). In such cases, claims to Arab descent in certain regions would in part be a matter of imagined prestige or legal fiction, where the legal category of Arab patronage/adoption might have been literalized.[8]

Muhammad at times expresses pride in his lineage. When his family was insulted, he responded that Arabs are best within humanity, the Quraysh tribe are best within Arabs and his family is best within them. This can be taken to mean that we are not good in isolation but individual goodness is cultivated by a family, a tribe and a nation,[9] although piety is generally strictly individual in Islam. At another time, Muhammad called people to Islam declaring himself messenger of God and grandson of 'Abd al-Muttalib, invoking a family prestige known to Qurayshi Arabs. Indeed, there are hadiths according to which Caliphs are meant to be chosen from the Qurayshi tribe of Muhammad.

Some approaches to Islam accept the fixity of Arab (and Qurayshi tribal) leadership as a matter of maintaining the purity of Arabic, the language of the Qur'an, and presiding over the holy sites of Mecca and Medina, while also accepting the role of different groups, even as political leaders of the *ummah*. In his biography of Muhammad, the *Sirat rasul-Allah*, ibn-Ishaq quotes a speech wherein, indeed, the privilege of the Quraysh consists of custody of Mecca and receiving pilgrims.[10]

In line with this de-emphasizing of the political role of Arabs, hadiths such as that according to which if Arabs are humbled Islam is humbled, which closely associates a national group with what is considered a universal religion, can be treated as compatible with hadiths

---

8   Indeed, conversion to Islam seems to have been a slow process in most theaters, initially linked to adoption and clientage rather than population replacement, where the sensationalistic view of its expansion being due to Arab raiders engaging in voluptuous concubinage has little merit. The desire to take pride in an Arab lineage may lead some to downplay this positive aspect of Islamic expansion. An example, perhaps, of a viable avenue for Islamic apologetics being traded in for something approaching Jahiliya.

9   Louise Marlow, *Hierarchy and Egalitarianism in Islamic Thought* (Cambridge: Cambridge University Press, 2002), 23.

10   Goran Larsson, *Ibn-García's Shu'ūbiyya Letter: Ethnic and Theological Tensions in Medieval al-Andalus* (Boston: Brill, 2003), 53.

praising other nations. For starters it is similar to a hadith[11] wherein

> The Messenger of Allah, peace and blessings be upon him, said, "If the people of Syria (al-Shām) are corrupted, then there will be no good in you. A group among my nation will continue to be supported, unharmed by those who fail them until the establishment of the Hour."

Indeed, Syria, al-Sham (which includes Palestine, Lebanon, Jordan) looms large in Islamic theology. There is apparently a hadith that describes al-Sham as the quintessence of the lands of Allah, where the quintessence of His servants go for protection. The Excellence of al-Sham and its People by Gibreel F. Haddad, a Sufi student of Sheikh Nazim Haqqani, compiles several such hadiths in praise of Syrians.

Other hadiths in praise of peoples include sayings according to which Persians have the greatest share in Islam, "the prayer call is for the Ethiopians,"[12] "faith and wisdom are Yemeni"[13] or

> Al-Mustawrid reported: He said in front of 'Amr ibn al-'As that he heard the Messenger of Allah, peace and blessings be upon him, say, "The Hour will be established while the Romans are the majority of people." Amr said, "Be careful what you say." He said, "I have said what I heard from the Messenger of Allah." Amr said, "If the Prophet said that, indeed, there are four good qualities in them: they are the most forbearing of people in tribulation, they are the quickest to recover after a calamity, they are the most eager to return after a retreat, and they are good to the poor, the orphan, and the vulnerable. Their fifth quality is good and beautiful: they are the best at stopping the oppression of their kings."[14]

(Zaid Shakir of Zaytuna College paraphrases this as: "the Europeans are the most forbearing of people in the face of tribulation, the quickest to recover from a calamity, the fastest to rally after incurring a defeat and the most merciful to the weak, the orphans, and the poor.")

Such hadiths are understood within the scriptural doctrine of equality between individual believers and references to kinship groups in something like aesthetic terms as providing an illustration of God's creative power, ultimately not serving as the basis for conflict. Abu Dawud provides a valid hadith according to which pride in nationality is to be relinquished:

> Undoubtedly Allah has removed from you the pride and arrogance of the Age of Jahilliyah and the glorifications of ancestors. Now

---

11 Narrated by Qurrah Ibn Ilyas, considered sahih (authentic) according to al-Tirmidhi, Sunan al-Tirmidhi, 2192.
12 Aḥmad, 2:364.
13 Bukhāri, 4388; Muslim, 52.
14 Sahih Muslim, 2898.

people are only of two kinds: Either believers who are aware or transgressors who do wrong. You are all the children of Adam and Adam was from clay. People should give up their pride in nations because that is a coal from the coals of hellfire. If they do not give this up Allah will consider them lower than the lowly worm which pushes itself through dung.

In his *Mir'aat al-Mafaateeh*, al-Mubaarakfoori writes that *pride* in lineage refers to arrogance, as in the traditional English sense of this word, and that this must imply boasting over others (*pride* as sin is always antagonistic, pride is always against someone or something). In line with this, the modern scholar Zaid Shakir of Zaytuna College writes the following:

> While recognizing the validity of national, racial, tribal, ethnic, and cultural differences, Islam views them as signs of God's creative power, not as the foundation for the creation of mutually destructive political agendas. [15]

Nations are considered facts: peoples as collectives endowed of specific character even unto the faith (as cited above: the prayer call of Ethiopians, the correctness of Syrians and aspects of Muhammad's Sunnah displayed in exemplary fashion by Europeans, for example). Whether this means patriotism is endorsed in conventional terms is an open question. A Shi'ite collection of hadiths states that "love of one's country is part of the faith"[16] but this is not widely acknowledged as valid (it is popular among the Ahmadiyya sect, whose doctrinal divergence to mainstream Islam is in some respects comparable to that of Mormons in Christianity, though without the idiosyncrasy of Mormon materialism). In any case, what is being endorsed is the embrace of national diversity as an occasion for contemplating God's unitary creativity, and emphatically not for hubris and conflict, or even statehood (nation-statism is simply not part of the era in which Islam arose).

CALIPHAL COLLAPSE AND CALIPHATE AS COORDINATION

When attempting to understand the encounter of Islamic and modern (originally western) political theory, we are dealing with the historical experiment of accommodating new practices to existing theological doctrines: theological translation in the sense of finding endogenous doctrinal support for exogenous political concepts. [17]

---

15   Zaid Shakir, *"Islam and the Nationalist Question," Seasons: The Semiannual Journal of Zaytuna Institute* 2(1) (2004–2005).

16   *Mizan al-Hikmah*, hadith #21,928.

17   Just as Roman Emperorship took on the ideal of Biblical Davidic monarchy, as in the Carolingian depiction of the Tree of Jesse at the Cathedral of Chartres, or the ways modern humanism and pluralism drew on medieval theological trajectories such as those of Nicholas of Cusa.

The central Islamic problematic is that the tradition appears to urge allegiance to political projects that can plausibly be considered inheritors of its founding prophet. If it were only a question of prophet Mohammed's political activities, these would simply present a useful paradigm for government. The issue is that allegiance to Islam during its foundational moment was intimately connected with allegiance to the state structures it brought (from the charter of Medina to the first four caliphs and succeeding state). Islamic sources easily give the impression that conversion should—if the example of its founder and the holistic range of its potentials are to be operant—imply fealty to at least a specific political program, if not an actual government. [18]

The degree to which Islamic legal opinion or *fiqh* is conceived of as a repertoire to draw from, reacting to changing historical circumstances, determines the degree to which its religious principles are conceived as detachable from the cultural and political context in which it initially unfolded. This is paramount to promoting the view that Islam does not require a unitary Caliphate, [19] for example, that it is compatible with a plurality of states or that some elements of the *Shariah* are not operant and should not be invoked.

A twin question to that of how much of the shariah is applicable and when, is the question of how Muslims are to pursue change in government. This latter ranges from the position that even tyrannical governments should be obeyed so long as they allow shariah-compliant practice, [20] where obedience also precludes active attempts at changing them, to the idea that it is legitimate for Muslims to pursue not only political reform but even rupture. [21]

We find a scholarly account of Islamically-justified multi-religious citizenship in the work of the Mauritanian Sheikh Abdallah ibn-Bayyah

---

18   Thusly can a Qur'anic commentator of the stature of al-Tabari disagree with what constitutes the preponderance of Islamic tradition when he considers the death penalty appropriate not so much for religious apostasy as for treason against legitimate government. He and the wider tradition draw on the same sources in arriving at markedly different positions, because they disagree on how to parse the teachings that referred to government under Muhammad from those that refer to Muhammad's religion under later governments.

19   As supported by the hadith in *Sahih al-Bukhari*, #7084: "The people used to ask Allah's Messenger about the good but I used to ask him about the evil lest I should be overtaken by them…. He said, 'Stick to the group of Muslims and their Imam (ruler).' I said, 'If there is neither a group of Muslims nor an Imam (ruler)?' He said, 'Then turn away from all those sects even if you were to bite (eat) the roots of a tree till death overtakes you while you are in that state.'" Some interpret this to mean that rather than reconstituting legitimate leadership one should turn away from pretenders. In this sense, it has been cited against the terrorist group Daesh.

20   Invoking Qur'an 4:49 and hadiths such as *Sahih al-Bukhari* #7142, *Sahih -Muslim* #1847, 1852, and 1855.

21   See the writings of Usama al-Azami and the range of traditional opinions discussed by Khalid Abou al-Fadl in his *Rebellion and Violence in Islamic Law*.

and the *Marrakesh Declaration*, which is patronized by the Moroccan monarchy. This considers it correct for Muslims to be committed to different local political entities, which, we may add, will necessarily have diverse cultural characters. Sheikh Ibn Bayyah reads the *Constitution of Medina*[22] under Muhammad as already articulating a concept of citizenship that charged both Muslims and non-Muslims with the responsibility to defend its borders. In this context, he considers the term *ummah* to have included non-Muslims. Legal equality between Muslims and non-Muslims is therefore a sharia-compatible option for the establishment of legal frameworks. Crucially, Ibn Bayyah points to historical precedent where Muslim governors, including early caliphs and possibly companions of Muhammad, did not charge the *jizya* (the shariah's tax on non-Muslims). Ibn Bayyah reads verses stating there is to be no compulsion in matters of religion as abrogating contrary imperatives rather than being abrogated, and considers the constitution of Medina as having collapsed as a result of historical conditions, but not as having ever been theologically superseded.

The question of including Muslims and non-Muslims in a common polity without charging non-Muslims the *jizyah* touches on the theological principle of government and its prerogatives. *Governmental determination of shariah is itself a factor in shariah*. Issues of *Hudud* (that part of Islamic law that deals with specific punishments for specific blameworthy actions) are the prerogative of government in Islam: they do not constitute a general injunction to act for individual believers. Governments have a responsibility to determine the appropriateness of implementing them. Given that some of these punishments, whose intent is to retain religious integrity would, under modern conditions, likely serve to alienate people from the religion in whose name they would be implemented, their contemporary implementation could be contrary to their purpose. According to Hamza Yusuf, an American student of Ibn Bayyah, this can constitute a sufficient ground for governments to abstain from implementing them.

It should be noted that while this is within the fold of scholarly interpretation, such lenient positions do not necessarily represent the preponderance of interpretation. Also, while this opens the door to equal citizenship under Islamic principles of governance for non-Muslims and Muslims, it does not necessarily address the legitimacy of there being a plurality of governments. Historically Islamic scholars disagreed over whether there could be more than one leader over Muslims at any one time.

For most Sunni Muslims, until relatively recently that one leader was the Ottoman Caliph.[23] The emergence of a plurality of states after

---

22 د ستور المدينة, *Dustūr al-Madīna*, also صحيفة المدينة, *Ṣaḥīfat al-Madīnah*, or: ميثاق المدينة, *Mīthāq al-Madina*.

23 This was not the case for most Muslim Moroccans, whose allegiance was to the king of Morocco as successor (and descendent) of prophet Muhammad.

the end of Ottoman rule resulted in the first push towards a modern, somehow Islamic, idea of citizenship. In the Arab world this generally meant adopting what is described as *Haqq al-dam mu'azzaz bi-haqq al-iqlim*, or *jus sanguinis* strengthened by *jus soli*. This stems from the traditional emphasis on patrilineal lineage (Arabic *nasb*). In most newly independent Arabic states, the arrangement was as follows: "When nationality cannot be attributed by paternal descent, maternal descent is taken into account, even if its weakness needs to be supported by birth on the territory of the state."[24] Citizenship is not so much linked to the universal Islamic community or *ummah*, but to the lineage or *nasb* and attachment to a particular place, which is itself a concept within Islamic *shariah*.[25] We therefore have a distinction between the *ummah* and the state, where the state is nonetheless understood as compatible with Islam.[26]

Muhammad's call away from tribalism (Arabic *Jahiliyyah*) and the pacification of human diversity so that it expresses a harmonious underlying unity (Allah's creative agency[27]) and not a basis for conflict, need not be linked to the historic emergence of a singular Caliphal state. It may be conceived of as a kind of theological diplomacy, so to speak—a common adherence to principles that disallow pursuing the nation as antagonistic rival to other nations. There is a tradition according to which Muhammad sent letters to various imperial regents (those of Abyssinia, Persia, Byzantium), offering them Islam without asking that they relinquish their rulership. The result, had they accepted, would presumably have been the integration, rather than replacement, of their multiple political communities. This implies the possibility of a supra-political alliance in which various politically articulated communities is not contrary to Islam (which does not require a global caliphate understood as a state

---

24   Gianluca Parolin, *Citizenship in the Arab World: Kin, Religion and Nation-State* (Amsterdam: IMISCOE Research Amsterdam University Press, 2009), 99.

25   Qur'anic pronouncements bolster the idea of kinship: "The Prophet is more worthy of the believers than themselves, and his wives are [in the position of] their mothers. And those of [blood] relationship are more entitled [to inheritance] in the decree of Allah than the [other] believers and the emigrants, except that you may do to your close associates a kindness [through bequest]. That was in the Book inscribed" (Qur'an 33:6). Also, according to the sharia, nasb is to be retained even in the case of adopted children, who should not take on the name of their non-biological parents.

26   In some countries the legal framework prioritizes nationalization of fellow Arabs and does not really fathom nationalizing foreign workers: "In several of the Arab Gulf states the majority of residents are permanently excluded from citizenship. Citizenship becomes then a minority privilege attached to descent, ethnicity and religion, as it was in the Athenian polis or the late medieval Italian city Republics." G. Parolin, *Citizenship in the Arab World: Kin, Religion and Nation-State* (Amsterdam: IMISCOE Research Amsterdam University Press, 2009), 11.

27   "Do you not see that Allah sends down rain from the sky, and We produce thereby fruits of varying colors? And in the mountains are tracts, white and red of varying shades and [some] extremely black" (Qur'an 35:27).

centered on a single caliph, unless this tradition is interpreted as an offer for these regents to accept Muhammad as caliph).

The collapse of caliphal hegemony and rise of multiple states in a sense repeats the previous end of ethnic Arab leadership following the Umayyad and Abbasid caliphates. Despite some doctrinal support in Sunni fiqh for the primacy (*fadl, sabiqa*)[28] of Arabic lineage, and specifically of Muhammad's tribe (the *Quraysh*), Ottoman Era theology reconceptualized this. Apologists for the Ottoman Caliphate and opponents of burgeoning Arab nationalism argued that hadiths prioritizing Qurayshi rule actually referred to the *ability* to rule that the Quraysh had displayed.[29] Given that the Qurayshi tribe had been powerful and internally coherent, enjoining *'asabiyya* or in-group solidarity, they were able to lead others at the start of historical Islam. Subsequently, this ability was lost to them and gained by others, eventually falling to the Ottomans.

There is a curious dialectic here of denying ethnic *'asabiyya* by asserting it: any particular ethnicity's priority to rule is denied, but those with in-group ethnic cohesion are, by token of this, able to rule. 'Asabiyya is both denied and asserted. Perhaps Arab nationalists could have simply argued that the Ottomans were losing their ability to rule, as evidenced by the very fact of its beginning to be rejected by Arabs, its inability to quell and marshal these, whereas Arabs were gaining it, as evidenced by their newly found sense of in-group cohesion and desire to lead, even in the form of nationalism. This might have been circular, but the Ottoman defense was perhaps not insulated from it. When one argues from conformity to the dictates of history one implicitly accepts historical agents as legitimate contenders who may appropriate one's argument by becoming historically prominent.

Yet there is something in the Ottoman theology, or Islamic theology throughout the Ottoman period, that is consonant with our general thesis: no particular polity is ultimately identifiable with (theo-political) centrality, and the latter must therefore, throughout history, dress in many different particulars (the Ottomans were also unconcerned with linguistic homogenization outside matters of state, distinguishing their rule from early Arab conquest).

There is also a recurring religious motif having to do with Divine action and revelation following human inquiry: Christ is challenged by and responds to people, verses from the Qur'an are revealed in response to specific situations, and Lord Krishna is said to be a Servant to His servants in the *Bhagavatam Purana*. Why, then, should changing historical

---

28   N. Hurvitz, *The Formation of Hanbalism: Piety into Power* (New York: Routledge, 2002), 33.

29   They also argued that Qurayshi Caliphs were those that counted towards the Apocalypse, so that after a certain number of leaders from that tribe the end of days would arrive, but there could theoretically be any number of non-Qurayshi caliphs.

conditions not de-Arabize the practice of Islam (in its political sense)? But this cannot go too far. Islamic scholars might entertain a change concerning to whom the hadith's *Qurayshi* refers, but they cannot likewise strain their sources into accepting a non-Arabian Mecca or prayers in any other language.

What was explicit political power for the Arabs, became a normative role of custodianship over the Arabic language, Medina and Mecca. In the same way, the end of the Ottoman Caliphate does not mean Islam cannot be thought of as supporting certain normative arrangements or institutional frameworks[30] incorporating existing states. This is more or less how Muslims refer to the *ummah* today: not as a rejection of existing states but as an overarching solidarity that ought to structure their relations.

Crucially, these relations would be peaceful but not necessarily non-competitive. Islam contains the principle of competing for good works. In this it may be seen to prefigure elements of *Realist* International Relations theory. The teaching is that religions (umam, adyan, milal, rather than *shu'ub* or nations[31]) ought to compete, but given that Islam teaches that prophets were sent to individual nations, this could be treated as a statement concerning international as well as inter-religious relations. Perhaps the nation as locus of political articulation and even competition is in fact accommodated, but within the pacification of relations commanded in the Qur'an. Indeed, we find statements in the Qur'an in which universal humanity does not correspond specifically to the religion of Islam:

> To each of you We prescribed a law and a method. Had Allah willed, He would have made you one nation [united in religion], but [He intended] to test you in what He has given you; so race to [all that is] good. To Allah is your return all together, and He will [then] inform you concerning that over which you used to differ. (Qur'an 5:48)

The idea that humanity is meant to be diverse and to interact within that diversity is a Qur'anic tenant:

> "And of His signs is the creation of the heavens and the earth and the diversity of your languages and your colors. Indeed in that are signs for those of knowledge." (Qur'an 30:22)

The Muslim tendency to proselytize on behalf of long-defunct political projects rather than to apply the faith to existing cultural categories even when their history is at odds with those past structures is therefore a

---

30 The definition of *Empire* not as a state but as a coordination of states which one finds in the 15th-century scholar Alfonso of Cartagena, for example.
31 The term that appears in the Qur'an 5:48 is that of umam, but the context is that of religious communities.

mistake: the Greek will not become a Turk, nor the Spaniard a Moor, if they become Muslim; the convert does not become a denizen of a now non-existent Ottoman polity or of al-Andalus. For proselytes, the idea should be that just as Christianity did not end Greco-Roman tradition, and despite the more 'political' and culturally thick content of Islamic tradition, should it spread, Islam would expand its expression to accommodate new realities. There is a freedom in the fact that old structures have passed away, but frequently proselytists fail to embrace that freedom. This prevents the possible convert from engaging with Islamic religion as something other than a foreign project. This is all the truer when what is emphasized in these extinct empires is their debt to the foreign initiator and not the indigenous convert.

Iberian Muslims, for example, often fought the Arab aristocracy's political dominance, but histories written from the Muslim perspective frequently deemphasize these and thereby present Islam as a political—and specifically politically *foreign*—presence, which it did, in fact, operate as, but this fails to learn the lesson of the Reconquista. The latter's success represents a native victory against a foreign elite.[32] For European civilization, an ecumenical rapprochement to Islam after its historic conflicts with Muslim civilizational projects should emulate the attitude of Lord Byron, so much the lover of Greece and fighter on behalf of her independence from Ottoman rule, dying during a campaign for Hellenic statehood, and also so sympathetic to Islamic cultures (his wife apparently thought he had become Muslim).

The "dismemberment" of the original form of a tradition and its taking new, local, forms can involve theological innovation or addition, at least to the degree that the old form is linked to political structures or cultural practices that do not accommodate the new local reality. It can also end up being incompatible, so that a figure such as 'Umar Ibn Hafsun's struggle for local rights in 10th-century Spain accompanies his discovery of Christianity. Miguel Asin Palacios, whose study of Ibn 'Arabi is well known (and contested), points to three indigenous Iberian Muslim insurgencies against the caliphs of Cordova and links them to

---

3 2   We may extend the point and critique a tendency to see cultural gains in Muslim polities as specifically Arabic works. The Alhambra building in Granada is a stellar example of Andalusian architecture, which is partly defined by the horse-shoe arch, a Roman feature that was used by the Spanish Visigoths. After encountering this element, Muslim architects used the horse-shoe arch until Egypt, but generally no farther east. The Temple Mount in Jerusalem, which showcases many styles from various periods, only features two such arches in a late Ottoman structure. Monumental Arabian architecture (mainly found in Yemen) is altogether different. If anything, this should be the historico-political angle on proselytism: that local Islamic cultural expressions were just that, local. "If it was not indigenous by origin, at least it was nationalized": Miguel Asin Palacios, *The Mystical Philosophy of Ibn Masarra and His Followers* (Leiden: Brill, 1978), 144.

Sufism (not directly, but in their context).[33] These he supposes to have resulted from or contributed to the caliphal mistrust of certain Sufis, as it was a partly Sufi or semi-mystical context that accompanied the rebellions. Indeed, just as Islamic apologetics emphasize the support gained by Muslim conquerors from Jewish, Monophysite, Ebionite, Arian or lower-class Zoroastrian sidelined communities, contributing to Muslim successes, a lesson to this effect could be extracted also from the failures of later Islamic polities.

The fact of diversity imposes itself in fortunate absence, alike that of Jesus (who tells us it is good that he should leave so that his disciples may receive the Comforter). It is crucifixion of particularity allowing what is universal to take a new form, to re-name, re-deem. The loss of the initial project of political Islam and the emergence of various governments (loyalty to which finds warrant in the *Shariah*) can be interpreted as such. In his *Expansion of the Prophetic Experience* the Iranian scholar Abdulkarim Soroush locates Islam's vocation in this historical unfolding rather than only in its initial centuries. He accepts the historical character of Qur'anic verses and, like Nicholas of Cusa, embraces pluralism (though Soroush's conception of the Divine is often limited). The initial centuries of political Islam would then be something other than its spiritual core, which would survive in various post-Caliphal and non-Arabized contexts.

That theo-political manifestations of the Ecumene have not historically coincided with the total Ecumene, instead becoming chapters and cultural blocks within the human family, allows us to consider the failure of an initial impetus towards *de facto* global hegemony as a *felix culpa*. True, modern liberal institutionalism has come close to creating structures that correspond with the totality of existing polities, but this system of thought's anthropology can be de-sacralizing and its practice is often culturally homogenizing. That *de facto* ecumenism arrives as a parody of itself should give us pause. Instead, the *felix culpa* exposes our limitations, like Jove's purpose in bringing the heroic age to an end in Homer. It leads us to seeing our own form of ecumenism as but one expression, allowing by means of the loss of its initial political form, a truer, more universal vision wherein our jurisdiction, as Voegelin would put it, is allowed to be itself, to be particular. As Frances Yates notes in terms of Roman imperialism: "revivals, not excluding that of Charlemagne, were never politically real or politically lasting; it was their phantoms which endured and exercised an almost undying influence."[34] A European

---

33   Ibn Qasi in Aragon, Ibn Marwan in Extremadura and Ibn Hafsun in the Sierra of Ronda. The Ibn Qasi he refers to is Ibn Qasi of Aragon, not Ibn Qasi of Algarve: that is, not Ibn al-Husayn Ibn Qasi, but another possible member of the Banu Qasi, a clan that largely concentrated in Aragon.

34   Frances Yates, *Astraea* (London: Routledge, 1999), 2.

mythos, like Muslim memories of the Caliphate, are the perdurance in a new form of a particular type of ecumenical wholeness—as myth and memory it is perhaps more genuinely free and universal, while also being free to be particular. The stone temple is destroyed, but the true temple is a body, a personhood.

THE ARABIC QUR'AN AND THE ARCHETYPAL QUR'AN

Historian Mondher Sfar argues[35] that the Heavenly matrix whence revelation issues according to the Qur'an, the *Umm al-Kitab* (*Mother of the Book*) was not initially to be identified with the particular Arabic Qur'an received by Muhammad. This pre-Arabic heavenly "tablet" is sometimes also referred to as the *Kitab Allah*, meaning *decree* rather than *book*, as Khalil Andani points out. Some Muslims might find this position perfectly orthodox (corresponding, for example, with the *Kalam Allah* or divine speech, understood by some Sunni schools as being prior to the Arabic recitation); others might see in it the Mu'tazilite heresy that cropped up under the 'Abbasids, according to which the Book is created rather than uncreated.[36] It is actually consistent with Isma'ili Shi'a theology: the fourteenth Ismaili Imam (and fourth Fatimid Caliph), al-Mu'izz, taught that Muhammad received revelation as a spiritual light which he then, using his own intellect or imagination, conveyed as an Arabic recitation to the community of first Muslims:

> Verily, God sent down the Light (*nūr*) which He mentioned in the Qur'an upon the heart of Muhammad. The Prophet did not send down that Divine Lordly Light upon the hearts of the believers because they lacked the capacity to bear it, since there was a disparity between the Prophet and the believers among the common people. He only conveyed the meanings of the inspiration (*waḥy*) and the Light—its obligations, rulings and allusions—by means of utterances composed with arranged, constructed, intelligible, and audible letters (*bi-alfāz mu'allafa bi-ḥurūf muḥarrafa murakkaba mafhūma masmū'a*). When Prophet constructed (*rakkaba*) these utterances and letters and enclosed in them the meanings that the inspiration contained, the Recitation (*al-qur'ān*) constructed according to the Light that is the revealed inspiration (*al-waḥy al-munazzal*) became the word of the Messenger (*qawl al-rasūl*). Thus, the construction (*al-tarkīb*), the expressions (*al-alfāz*), and

---

35   Mondher Sfar, *In Search of the Original Koran: The True History of the Revealed Text* (Amherst, NY: Prometheus Books, 2008).

36   It also reminds us of the strange career of an AD 8th-century Berghouta Berber king called Salih Ibn Tarif. He claimed to be a prophet and to bring a Qur'an in the Berber language (Amazigh). If the true Book is not the Arabic recitation, the idea of a recitation in Berber or Coptic or Persian might be conceivable (although this contradicts Islamic doctrine, and Ibn Tarif's claims, for his part, were apparently more abrogative than pluralistic).

the composition (*al-ta'līf*) belongs to the Prophet (*li l-nabī*). So it [the Qur'ān] is the Speech of God (*kalām Allāh*) and the word of the Messenger of God (*qawl rasūl Allāh*).[37]

Adds the scholar Khalil Andani: "Based on my research, all major Fatimid Ismaili authors affirm that the revelation or inspiration of the Qur'an to Prophet Muhammad was non-verbal."[38]

It is also compatible with Algis Uzdavinys's exploration of a "particular interpretation of Islamic sacred history" according to which:

> ...the heavenly Qur'an is tantamount to the essential living Being (*autozoon*) of Plato's Timaeus, since this *autozoon* contains...the ideas of all the living creatures that are manifested in the sensible realm.[39]

And,

> The archetypal Qur'an is like the Plotinian *kosmos noetos*: "a completely coherent and comprehensive matrix, timeless, un-generated, immaterial and perfect, of the physical cosmos."[40] The descent of the Book (in its role of the demiurgic Logos and soteriological revelation) and the ascent of Muhammad (in his role of the paradigmatic mystagogue and divine vicegerent, tantamount to the Assyrian sacred king).[41]

Here, Uzdavinys even confirms our relation of sacred king/initiate to the autozoon by seeing Muhammad as conforming to the paradigm of Assyrian sacred kingship and receiving the autozoon (the descent of the Book as mirror to the ascent of the prophet).

The principle is summarized by Samuel Zinner, but as compatible with "the symbolism of the preexistent Book." He points out that the Qur'an describes itself as a sign, and takes the meaning of this term— sign—from semiotics, to understand the oral Qur'an as index of the preexistent *Umm al-Kitab*:

---

37 Al-Muizz, *Kitāb ta'wīl al-sharī'a,* ed. Nadia E. Jamal, trans. Khalil Andani, Chapter 5, Section 49. From: https://www.academia.edu/26605457/Shi_i_Ismaili_Ta_wil_Spiritual_Interpretation_of_the_Qur_an_The_Cycles_of_Prophecy_and_Imamat.

38 Khalil Andani, *Shī'i Ismaili Ta'wil (Spiritual Interpretation) of the Qur'an: The Cycles of Prophecy and Imamat* (Course Material Prepared for Harvard Divinity School, 2019), endnote 3. https://www.academia.edu/26605457/Shi_i_Ismaili_Ta_wil_Spiritual_Interpretation_of_the_Qur_an_The_Cycles_of_Prophecy_and_Imamat.

39 Uždavinys, *Ascent to Heaven in Islamic and Jewish Mysticism.* (London: The Matheson Trust, 2011), 2.

40 M. John Dillon, *Pleroma and Noetic Cosmos: A Comparative Study,* in: *Neoplatonism and Gnosticism,* R.T. Wallis and J. Bregman (eds.) (Albany: SUNY Press, 1992). Cited by Algis Uždavinys, *Ascent to Heaven in Islamic and Jewish Mysticism* (London: The Matheson Trust, 2011), 2.

41 The view of Ismailis and Uzdavinys provides a useful context to understand the idea of "visionary recitals" (as in Corbin's work on ibn-Sina), as though a spiritual initiate could access and give forth qur'anic poetry.

Since the Qur'an describes itself repeatedly as a "sign," or *aya*, and since each verse is called an *aya*-sign, we might be able to find a helpful descriptive label for the Qur'an in the field of semiotics. More fundamental than the Qur'an as an example of inliteration is the oral Qur'an as semiosis.

And crucially:

Of the semiotic sign classes...index is the class which in a theological manner most fittingly parallels the entry of the formless archetypal Word into manifestation as formal words. We could then refer to the oral manifestation of the Qur'an as the "indexation" of the Umm al-Kitab. The semiotic model of indexicality is the class that most appropriately approximates the supra-ontological and ontological continuity between the Words and words, or Idea and articulation...conceptual and the sonic.

Triadically:

Oral Qur'an (Sign)

—

Interpreter's Understanding that Oral Qur'an
Reflects *Umm al-Kitab* (Interpretant)

—

Umm al-Kitab (Object).[42]

Mondher Sfar's thesis does not therefore contradict all historically established Muslim exegesis. Neither does Sfar's approach deny the *theoretical* universal applicability of that Arabic form of revelation, nor, indeed, of Arabizing and imperialistic tendencies in Islamic history. It would, however, imply a greater potential pluralism, a notion of the Arabic Qur'an as having come about in a protean manner and even (here unlike Ismailism) an attitude of admitting imperfection in Muhammad comparable to the way Old Testament prophets are often recognized as flawed by Biblical narrative (Islamic is not comfortable with this). This is more or less also Montgomery Watt's position at the end of *Muhammad: Prophet and Statesman*.

Following Sfar and the evidence from early Islamic sources that the Qur'an included sections that have been lost and that the exact wording was not at first considered all-important, allowing variations (specifically seven possible recitations of the same Qur'an), we can suggest that Islamic tradition has been *over-codified*, confusing cultural and personal elements with the *fitrah*, ignoring imperfection in, and exaggerating the applicability of, Muhammad's example.

The insight that prophets have come to all nations, however, and that salvation and primordial religion is everywhere essentially one,

---

42   Zinner, *Christianity and Islam: Essays on Ontology and Archetype*, 12.

are important to contemplate, especially in the context of a tradition like historical Christianity, whose theologians have tended to lean the weight of eternity on temporal events. Where a medieval Christian might have considered pre-Christian people excluded from Heaven (even if temporarily) due to the historical epoch they lived in, his Muslim contemporary would have thought it offensive that a true follower of any pre-Muhammadan prophet's guidance would for that reason alone, and as a matter of doctrine, be excluded from Paradise.

Now, having discussed the path, the ongoing journey, into ecumenic consciousness, into the building of an ecumenic post-modernity, of the Chinese and Islamic spheres[43]—a compact cosmological and expansive proselytizing project—we may turn to the west, and its fundamental problematic: Biblical election and Roman empire. In these, we find both modes just mentioned: The Biblical chosen nation is a cosmological ecumene in itself, and at least initially is not to expand that ecumene but to cultivate it inwardly; the Roman empire is an ecumene whose mission it is to extend over the whole earth. The possibility of an expansion of Biblical election through the structures of Empire ends up, in medieval conceptions and perhaps a future medievalist modernity, pointing to the *Israel of israels*, that *Empire of empires* we have discussed elsewhere, a universality between forms that each internalize the universal, each translate Biblical scripture and imperial politics for themselves. By each being a microcosm of the same cosmos, we may realize our *cosmosity*—that is, the opposite of chaos: harmony.

---

43   The Iberian Sufism of Ibn Masarra and Ibn al-Husayn Ibn Qasi present the elements we have been discussing in this section: an understanding of spiritual illumination that might assume something like the *Umm al-Kitab* as Uzdavynis describes the "archetypal" or "heavenly" Qur'an and, in Ibn Qasi's politics, a willingness to establish polities in which Muslims and Christians are legally equal. They may thus be examples of the ecumenic consciousness, and politically post-imperial context in which it can emerge, that we have been suggested. In terms of theological translation via that which is transcendent (the autozoon), some of ibn-Masarra's followers apparently went so far as to adopt a *qibla* away from Mecca, in terms of the doctrine of an *inner* qibla (the Sufi understanding of the image of God's throne as having four legs—the fourfold, the four elements—which parallels the Platonic *autozoon*). W. Elliott, *The Career of Ibn Qasi as Religious Teacher and Political Revolutionary in 12th Century Islamic Spain,* PhD Thesis (Edinburgh: University of Edinburgh, 1979), 80.

ADDENDUM IX

The Sufis of al-Rum:
PROPHETOLOGY AND
PARTICULARITY

I T IS INTERESTING THAT A SACRALIZATION OF
figures essential to European civilization sometimes comes by way
of Islam's fringes. Nietzsche described Plato as a Greek Muhammad
attempting to unite the Hellenes as Muhammad did the Arabs in part
through metaphysical teachings.

> [For him] Plato's attempt to found a "Mediterranean state" in
> Sicily acquires overtone of a Greek Muhammad, attempting to
> unite and control his fellow Hellenes in the same way the Prophet,
> nine centuries later, would bring together and forge an identity
> for the Arabs. The fact that Islam gained a brief foothold in Sicily
> underlines the proximity of the analogy, even if Nietzsche fails to
> comment on this directly.[1]

This reminds us of Frederick II, Holy Roman Emperor and in some
ways philo-Islamic, who Nietzsche so admired, the *"first* European after
[his] taste, the Hohenstaufen Frederick II."[2]

There is precedent for this view of Plato, and precisely in Islam,
including but not limited to the peculiar form of Islam that was briefly
established in Sicily for a short time, Ismailism. Other examples include
Ibn 'Arabi's apparently receiving the title Ibn Aflatun, son of Plato, the
16th-century Nev'i, poet and tutor to Ottoman princes, apparently
reporting a hadith according to which Plato was a prophet, seemingly
lacking any traditional lineage[3] and the 17th-century Ottoman Sufi
Niyazi al-Misri, associated with the Khalwati Sufi order, who seems to
have cited that hadith as well.

The tradition around the 12th-century Persian mystic Suhrawardi,
a Platonist whose work Henry Corbin valued highly, also allows for

---

1 Ian Almond, *The New Orientalists: Postmodern Representations of Islam from Foucault
to Baudrillard* (London: I. B. Taurus, 2007), 22.
2 Nietzsche, *Beyond Good and Evil*, Section 200. He takes this quite far in *The
Antichrist* (Section 60, trans. H. L. Mencken): "'War to the knife with Rome! Peace
and friendship with Islam!': this was the feeling, this was the *act*, of that great free
spirit, that genius among German emperors, Frederick II..." However, Nietzsche's
appreciation of Islamic civilization and distaste of Christianity is also the result of
shoddy historical knowledge.
3 Baki Tezcan, "Some Thoughts on the Politics of Early Modern Ottoman Science." In: *Osmanli Arastirmalari: The Journal of Ottoman Studies*, eds. Donald Quataert
and Baki Tezcan (2010): 150.

something similar. In *The Philosophy of Illumination*, Suhrawardi uses the term *al-hukama al-muta'allihin*, meaning *the divine sages*, to describe "theistic ancient philosophers and in particular Plato."[4] He reports a dream in which Aristotle appears to him and informs him of Plato's high station. The Druze also seem to consider persons like Pythagoras and Plato to be prophets in an Islamic sense.

The 9th/10th-century *Mushaf al-Jama'a—Turba Philosophorum*—probably authored in Egypt, gives us a round table of philosophers presided by Pythagoras, and provides so-called pseudo-Empedoclean writings, as does the 9th century *Theology of Aristotle* produced by the al-Kindi circle in Baghdad, a partial translation of Plotinus's *Enneads*. The latter describes Empedocles as a *ghiyath*, a term Peter Kingsley tells us relates to his being considered a saint or even a prophet (although the word ghiyath means "rainmaker"), and more specifically spiritual Pole (Qutb) or sheikh of sheikhs (Shaykh al-shuyukh)—the spiritual authority of his generation. In the later circles of Suhrawardi in Persia, Empedocles was apparently also presented as being of a high status. The 11th/12th-century Persian al-Shahrastani and the 13th-century al-Shahrazuri who wrote in both Arabic and Persian, both produced expositions on the philosophy of pseudo-Empedocles. The latter wrote of Empedocles that he knew and learnt from kings David and Solomon.

Peter Kingsley considers Pseudo-Empedocles to be largely in line with the historic Empedocles, as Henry Corbin seems to:

> The hagiographic legend of the neo-Empedocles that was known in Islam does contain some parts of the authentic biography, even if exaggerated and transformed. According to these authors, Empedocles was chronologically the first of the five great philosophers of Greece: Empedocles, Pythagoras, Socrates, Plato and Aristotle. He was regarded as a hierophant, a prophet, dedicated to spiritual teaching and practice. He lived apart from the world, travelled around the East, and refused all honors. In short, he was seen as one of the prophets prior to Islam who could be contained within the wide context of Islamic prophetology. His moral physiognomy was that of a Sufi, and some of his books were known and quoted ... [5]

And Asin Palacios:

> The legend elaborated in oriental Islam around the person, books, and ideas of Empedocles is indeed interesting and suggestive.... For the Muslims, Empedocles was the first in ancient times, of the five greatest philosophers of Greece: Empedocles, Pythagoras, Socrates, Plato and Aristotle.... He is presented to us, then, as an

---

4   John Walbridge, "Suhrawardi's Creed of the Sages." In: *Illuminationist Texts and Textual Studies: Essays in Memory of Hossein Ziai*, Ali Gheissari, Ahmed Alwishah and John Walbridge (eds.) (Boston: Brill, 2017), 66.
5   Corbin, *History of Islamic Philosophy*, 223.

> interpreter of sacred mysteries and as almost a prophet... [having studied from king David and Solomon]. His moral appearance was that of a Muslim mystic or Sufi. The most salient features of his images were so similar to those of ibn-Masarra that one could easily believe that the latter intended to copy in his soul the moral characteristics of the master whose doctrine he professed...al-Shahrazuri wrote: "The great and divine philosopher Empedocles, son of ibn-Nadir, born in Agrigento, was one of the greatest and principle sages...."[6]

And,

> The importance of this school lies in the fact that it represents, at the Western extremity of the Islamic world, the esoteric Islam that we have come to know in the East, and that it exercised considerable influence. Its existence was, indeed, responsible for the part played at both geographical extremities of Islamic esotericism by the teaching of Empedocles—an Empedocles transformed into a herald of prophetic theosophy.[7]

Both Corbin and Palacios make much of the 9th/10th-century Muhammad Ibn Masarra's Empedocleanism, however, it is now believed that the Spaniard's system was neo-Platonic but not derived from the pseudo-Empedoclean texts.

A politically militant context does seem to have developed from the native Sufism of Ibn Masarra, however, just as it was a tense religious climate,[8] Palacios suggests, that caused the (probably native Iberian[9])

---

6   Miguel A. Palacios, *The Mystical Philosophy of Ibn-Masarra and His Followers* (Leiden: Brill, 1978), 44-45.

7   "Asin Palacios, on the other hand, preferred to see Ibn Masarrah's followers as perpetuating the gnosis of Priscillian (fourth century CE)" (Corbin, *History of Islamic Philosophy*), 221. I would tend to read the Gnosticism—in the sense of early Christian heresies—of these schools the way I have indicated I interpret its presence in William Blake. Corbin summarizes the doctrine attributed to Ibn-Masarra as "principally concerned with the following themes: the pre-eminence and esotericism of philosophy and psychology, leading to the encounter with the *ruhaniyah*, the spiritual person or reality of the hidden being; the absolute simplicity, ineffability and mobile immobility of the first Being; the theory of Emanation; the categories of soul; individual souls as emanations of the Soul of the world; their pre-existence and redemption. The whole doctrine is enormously rich in both Gnostic and neo-Platonic terms" (Corbin, *History of Islamic Philosophy*), 223.

8   Which later on affected Ibn Qasi and Ibn Barrajan, contributing also to the ultimate emigration of Ibn 'Arabi from Spain, according to Henry Corbin (*Alone with the Alone: Creative Imagination in the Sufism of Ibn 'Arabi*), 50.

9   "According to his biographers, Ibn Masarrah, who was born in 269 H/883 AD, was not an Arab by race. We note that his father 'Abd Allah's physical appearance was such that even though he was a native of Cordoba, he was able to pass as a Norman from Sicily on his journeys." Henry Corbin, *History of Islamic Philosophy*, trans. L. Sherrard (London: Kegan Paul International, 2014), 221. Palacios tells us Ibn Masarra's father was client to a Berber patron, meaning his Islam was recent.

mystic to leave his country and journey east in the first place. Upon his
return, he tried to be cautious in sharing his teachings[10] (though his
books were eventually burnt by Muslim clerics[11]). Yet this figure's teachings inspired later Sufis, who were generally disliked by the authorities.
We may interpret this as signifying that political suppression results
in heterodoxy or apostasy becoming an attractive vehicle of political
resistance.

Asin Palacios sees influence of Ibn Masarra on Ibn al-Husayn Ibn
Qasi coming through Ibn al-Arif:

> Abu-l'Abbas Ibn'-Arif set himself up as a master and definer of
> a new religious order (tariqa) which was infused with the most
> sublime ecstatic doctrine and the same extravagant superstitions
> of theosophic occultism of the Masarrian school. Soon a large
> number of adepts grouped around him.... Three of these disciples
> were agents of the spread of the new Sufi order...

Elsewhere he writes:

> ...the Masarrians would also refuse to recognize the false caliph of
> Cordoba...one must not forget the spirit of nationalist restoration
> and of protest against the political yoke of the Arabs, which spirit
> the Batini schools always represented.... Nor must one forget
> the indigenous lineage of ibn-Masarra.[12]

And "[a]ccording to his biographers, Ibn Masarrah, who was born in
269/883, was not an Arab by race"[13] and nor was his politically, militarily
engaged follower, Ibn al-Husayn Ibn Qasi,[14] a *rumi-al-asl* according to
Ibn 'Abbar.

Indeed, politically prominent hispano-roman muslims were often
at odds with the various lords of Cordoba. Consider the prominent
Spanish Visigothic clan of the *Banu Qasi* (from Count Casius) whose
famous scion, Musa ibn-Musa, rebelled against Cordoba and controlled

---

10   M. Palacios, *The Mystical Philosophy of Ibn Masarra and His Followers* (Leiden:
Brill, 1973), 33.
11   Religious orthodoxy did not stop certain leaders of al-Andalus from engaging
in patricide and pederasty, and went together with the brutal treatment (including deportations and massacres, even the death penalty for refusing to eat meat
on Fridays) of Christians, claiming women for tax levies, as well as the copious
production of eunuchs at Lucena (in the province of Córdoba). We may therefore
suggest that opposition to Sufism stemmed from fear of modes of thought that
could interfere with defining religion as needed for use by the powerful. The danger
could be attributed even to the work of Ibn 'Arabi, whose politics were such as to
advise the repression of Christians, and so is much more obvious coming from a
native like Ibn Masarra or Ibn Marwan.
12   Palacios, *The Mystical Philosophy of Ibn Masarra and His Followers*, 109.
13   Corbin, *History of Islamic Philosophy*, 221.
14   The other two are Abu Bakr of Mayurqi in Granada and Ibn-Barrajan in Seville.
Palacios, *The Mystical Philosophy of Ibn Masarra and His Followers*, 121-22.

the northeast and Toledo (sometimes *Banu Lope* on account of the governor of Toledo, Lope ibn-Musa). Or the late 9th, early 10th-century Spartacus-like Umar Ibn Hafsun,[15] who may eventually have converted to Christianity, being renamed Samuel, and had strong ties to the Ismaili Fatimids. Another important *muladi* (native Iberian convert to Islam) was Sa'dun al-Ṣurunbaqi, and his likewise muladi ally, the Sufi Abdul-Rahman Ibn Marwan, known as *the Galician*. At times allied with the Christian Alfonso III of Leon, Ibn Marwan led both muladis and *mozarabs* (local Christians living in Muslim al-Andalus) in rebellion against the Emir of Cordoba in the 9th century, and later became ruler of Badajoz, establishing a dynasty there.[16]

A fellow Hispano-Roman Sufi who lived during the 12th century Sufi in western al-Andalus (Algarve, southern Portugal) was Abu'l-Qasim Ahmad ibn-al-Ḥusayn Ibn Qasi,[17] who rebelled against the Almoravid dynasty and allied with the Christian king of Portugal (also writing a Sufi treaty, *Removing the Sandals*,[18] to which Ibn ʿArabi penned a commentary). Ibn Qasi even at one time used the title of Mahdi (*al-Mahdl bi-Amr Allah*).[19] He led his Sufi order, the *Muridun*, against the Almoravids and eventually gave the city of Silves to the Christian north, whereupon he was assassinated by Muslim defectors. During roughly the same period, we may also consider the "Wolf King" Muhammad Ibn Mardanish (probably a rendering of Martinez or the Merdanix river). He was king of Murcia in southeastern Spain, which city prospered greatly under him, enjoying commercial ties with Genoa. He extended his domains with the help of Christian allies, whose sources call him the "Rex Lupus" or "Rey Lobo," and is said to have administered Almeria in the name of Alfonso VII of Leon, and Alfonso VIII considered him his vassal. Ibn Mardanish

---

15   Dozy provides the standard account of Umar's ancestry according to which he was an Iberian of Visigothic lineage. Reinhart Dozy, *Spanish Islam: A History of the Muslims of Spain* (London: Chatto and Windus, 1913), 316.

16   Indeed, when Ibn Marwan captured Hashim Ibn ʿAbdul-ʿAziz, Prime Minister of Emir Muhammad of Cordoba, the Galician Sufi gave his high-ranking captive to king Alfonso III, whose Asturian subjects had fought with the *muladi* revolt.

17   Possibly a scion of the Banu Qasi and, in any case, a native Iberian, described as *rumi al-asl*—of Roman stock, where Roman was used to refer to local Europeans—by Ibn-al-ʿAbbar.

18   Ibn ʿArabi concludes with a negative assessment of ibn-Qasi, considering him a transmitter and not genuinely accomplished in spiritual matters, which may be related to his view of ibn-Qasi not conforming to Islamic doctrine/practice properly. He attributes the value of *Removing the Sandals* to Ibn Qasi's teacher, Khalaf Allah al-Andalusi.

19   Although apparently in some mystical sense as a spiritual station to be attained, derived from Ibn Masarra's teachings and those of his successor, the Andalusian Isma'il al-Ruayni, rather than a literal eschatological sense. Al-Ruayni, who had claimed imamate, was accused of teaching that one could acquire prophecy (*iktisab al-nubuwwa*) but, again, probably in some specific sense derived from ibn-Masarra's teachings. The north African Ibn Barrajan is also extremely influential in this context.

signaled his loyalty to the Abbasids, but was committed to fighting the Almohads. Muslim sources paint him as an apostate, emphasizing his adoption of Christian custom. For his protection of Christians, he was referred to fondly by Pope Alexander IV.

We are tempted to speculate that, in the case of the more eccentric Sufis, acknowledging figures of a high spiritual rank among the Arab ethnographic category of the *Rum*, or Europeans, namely certain Greek philosophers, implied the possibility of breaking with foreign domination by Arabs insofar as the latter justified itself theologically.

Europe and the Ecumene

I N LINE WITH A CERTAIN HYPER-CRITICALITY towards European civilization and history prevalent in academia, in his *Contemplation on the Eleventh Contentions*, the otherwise brilliant Abdal Hakim Murad (Professor Tim Winter) discusses what he calls Europe's "historic chauvinism."[1] He bombastically distills the question as follows: "Whether God can forgive Europe is perhaps the greatest problem of theodicy." We begin the discussion of Europe and an ecumenic conception thereof with this reference because it is important to understand that such an attitude is relatively widespread, and why.

According to Murad, Islam is less marred by chauvinism because "Arabdom is not congenital" (although true in some circles, this is an inexact and ahistoric claim, as we have seen from the opinion of most Sunni schools concerning Arab lineage). Consequently, for him, history's "traditional contest" has been "between the exclusivist Christian world and the multi-ethnic world of Islam."[2]

Murad suggests elements of the European Enlightenment reckoned positive may proceed from Islam, including respect for the individual, separation of religious from state power and unwillingness to persecute conscience.[3] Meanwhile, the Enlightenment's pathological urging "in Messianic fashion, its patterns of life upon the world," as well as its Holocaustic potentials, may be considered indigenously European, although presumably not insofar as they pervert a positive universalism, for "it was Muslims who invented globalization," since Islam "does not limit itself to the upliftment of any given section of humanity." As for Muslim exclusivism, it may result from zealots who " ... subscribe to ideologized forms of Islam which adopt dimensions of Western modernity in order to secure an anti-Western profile...."[4] Islamic terror is an alien taint, a shadow cast by northern and western monsters. It seems whatever is distinctively European is negative or whatever is definitely negative is European.

As inclusivism cannot be made compatible with (European) exclusivism, the attempt to demonstrate how Islam's broadness can include Europe

---

1 Abdal Hakim Murad, "Muslims and the European Right," *Cambridge Mosque Project*. masud.co.uk., retrieved 1st December 2018.
2 Abdal Hakim Murad, Interviewed by Dr. Enes Karic (Minister of Education Republic of Bosnia-Herzegovina) in *Ljiljan* (Bosnian-language newspaper, 21st September 2003).
3 Abdal Hakim Murad, *Faith in the future: Islam after the Enlightenment* (delivered as *First Annual Altaf Gauhar Memorial Lecture Islamabad*, 23rd December 2002).
4 Ibid.

denies itself. As a form of proselytism, this seems a strategic oddity to anyone who does not share its premise (a kind of *intolerance towards the intolerant* which only begs the question of who is most principally intolerant). By presenting exclusivism as exclusively European, Europe is exclusively excluded.

We have here a brilliant example of the kind of circularity we observed in some kinds of Christian supersessionism. If a certain identity or set of ideas is universal, anyone claiming it as their specific heritage must be wrong, and may have to be denied their specific heritage, so that it can be made the equal property of everyone else. European culture has been universalized, sometimes violently, and if it is to be experienced as legitimately particular, as a particular expression of universals that is accepting of other particular expressions, it will need to conceive of itself in those terms. Yet, currently, much of the Western discourse around this question presents European culture either as a neutral stage of modern, Enlightenment-derived ideas in whose play all other cultural practices are invited to (and, one suspects, ultimately *required* to) be actors, or as a reactionary holdout against the more just, level-ground of that theatre stage.

For Europe, seeing the particular as node for the universal means mounting a reaction against the conflation of universal humanity with European culture, allowing the latter to inhabit itself without corrosion or conquest, without moral obligation to cease from its particularity or to impose it on all and sundry. This is a work for Europe's *Hanifs* in the cultural desert, searching out the universal in their native speech. Historically, the Hanif was a generically Abrahamic monotheist Arab unwilling to convert to Judaism, Christianity or Zoroastrianism, which he viewed as corrupt or as entailing allegiance to foreign powers. Instead, he prayed for and anticipated a revelation in Arabic, toiling in the pagan dunes. Something new in line with the origin, father Abraham. This is an archeological anticipation, a revelation in the roots, alike Odin's uncovering runes in the shallows of the world-tree.

Pythagorean-Platonic tradition comes to mind. Pythagoras's encounter with Abaris and his legislating work at Crotona, Plato's *Laws*, Rome's Pythagorean lawgiver Numa Pompilius and his reception of the sacred rune-graven shield from Jove,[5] the sprawling tradition around Aeneas. The work of these bestowers of European culture's hidden shape inspires deference (especially given their status as Apollonian avatars, in the cases of Pythagoras and Plato or, in that of Numa, given the religious intensity suggested by his having left behind an empty tomb[6]). We may also think of mythical persons like Cecrops, son of Gaia, who ended bloody sacrifices in favor of cake offerings, divided Attica into twelve districts, and was devoted to Minerva. Hercules is likewise linked to the ending of human sacrifices.

---

5   Plutarch, *Lives*, XIII.6, 353.
6   Plutarch, *Lives*, XXII.5, 381.

Peter Kingsley has shown how Plato's *Phaedo* and *Gorgias* present the mythologized account of Sicilian and Campanian geography as a holy land, deriving from local Orphism and native religious traditions and providing a context for initiation (associated with Empedocles and Mount Etna, or Cumae in Campania) similar to how Homeric epics (esoterically interpreted) and Greek geography served the Eleusinian mysteries.[7] No formal writing of these into the script of scripture, no canonizing of Europe's character and custom, took place (as was arguably one of early Islam's functions in the case of Arab culture so far as that tradition's initial exoteric form is concerned) but, all the same, there is a lineage of inspired tradition in European antiquity, there for the discerning.

In Christian terms, there is much that might be baptized in Greco-Roman and specifically Pythagorean-Platonic tradition. We can emphasize the rejection of human sacrifice, the movement to condemn even animal sacrifice in some Platonism, the rejection of spurious stories concerning the gods, specifically the celebration of a primordial age of peace under Kronos against tales of violent overthrow of older gods by younger ones (Plato's *Laws*, 713d-714a), and the belief in a single transcendent God.

At the level of theology, this is arguably already accomplished in the writings of St. Dionysius, and medieval epics and tales did the same for the old myths. Tolkien seemed to locate the Old Testament, with its *praeparatio evangelica*, in the folklore of each people, as for example Beowulf. The latter, along with medieval versions of pagan narrative, from Snorri Sturluson to the emergence of giants in Britain and their cleansing by the Trojans, and indeed the Holy Grail stories, are all explicitly Christian, pointing ultimately to the Incarnation (Sturluson is clear on this).

Dante, for his part, places the two pagans—Emperor Trajan and Ripheus the Trojan—in Heaven near King David, and links Aeneas and David in his chronology. Where the Trojans follow a biblical pattern of exile and entry into the land assigned to them, Rome will eventually be founded by Romulus after killing his brother for transgressing limits (the wall he was building) and re-founded, that is, returned to the auspicious Biblical pattern, by its conversion, drawing out the Jacob rather than the Cain in Romulus's dispute with his brother.

Europe, as mythopoetic idea, has a long history. We may connect it to Homer's title for Jove, *Europos*—wide of sight or having vision—interpreting this latter in terms of seeing the past and future, as well as the present. For the individual, imitating this consists in both recording the past and projecting into the future. Nietzsche advises that a good memory is needed if one is to keep a promise,[8] and surely creation or creative apprehension (beyond the initial inspiring vision and its

---

7   Kingsley, *Ancient Philosophy, Mystery and Magic*, 105, 107.
8   Friedreich Nietzsche, *Human, All Too Human*, trans. R. Hollingdale (Cambridge: Cambridge University Press, 1996), Section 59, 42.

occasional guiding lights) consists in the, sometimes arduous, keeping of a promise. He also cautions that too good a memory stays one's mind from creative work[9] (an excessively captious approach profusely annotates what is or has been, or *appears* to have been, but it hides, lets fall into disregard, what is on offer).

Jove's descriptor is fitting, given that what follows will largely focus on Europe as an example of how to proceed according to these general principles. By seeing widely, then, past and future in one panorama, we may follow the German aphorist in being good Europeans. Later, in the Middle Ages, Europeans from St. Jerome to St. Isidore of Seville and Martin Luther the reformer, drawing on the *Book of Jubilees*, considered themselves descendants of the Biblical son of Noah, Japheth, whose apportioned land after the great flood corresponded with the Greek continental nomenclature just cited.

Interestingly, the significance of Japheth as vehicle for expressing a sense of shared civilizational endeavor serves to highlight a prominent, potentially negative, feature of that civilization. The name Japheth is speculated to derive from the Hebrew enlargement or "may he expand" (תפי)[10] according with the divine promise made to this primeval progenitor in Genesis (9:27) that his territory would be extended (Denis de Rougemont notes this[11]). This is how it is discussed by St. Isidore of Seville in the Etymologies, for example.

This implies a certain antinomianism on the part of Europeans, linked to the character of gentiles according to Origen as having an advantage of faith—whereas, per St. Paul, Jews have the advantage of law and oracles (prophets). This reminds of al-Tabari's description of Europeans as antinomian. The notion that the Occident's character is wide-of-sight, Faustian, that is, in a state of wanderlust for infinite space (Spengler's understanding that "[i]nfinite space is the ideal that the Western soul has always striven to find, and to see immediately actualized ... "[12]), may therefore boast a long pedigree by way of Christian sources (saintly sources, at that), as well as Islamic ones, albeit its "Faustian" sense would be a degeneration.

That Jove's flight to Crete with princess Europa left her name upon the wide land that lay north is fitting because, as has been noted, that name's possible Greek meaning is *wide of countenance*.[13] This would have

---

9   Ibid., Section 122, 241.

10   St. Isidore, *The Etymologies*, VII.vi.18, 163.

11   Denis de Rougemont, *The Idea of Europe*, 20. Cited in Denis Guénoun, *About Europe: Philosophical Hypotheses*, trans. C. Irizarry (Stanford, CA: Stanford University Press, 2013), note 10 to Part I, 238.

12   Oswald Spengler, *The Decline of the West, Vol 1: Form and Actuality*, trans. C. Atkinson (New York City: Alfred A. Knopf, 1926), 175.

13   Harry Peck, Frank Colby Daniel Gilman (eds.), *New International Encyclopedia*, vol. 7 (New York City: Dodd, Mead and Company, 1903), 42.

fed into European medieval self-understanding, corresponding to the etymology of Japheth. The disposition in question is perhaps only properly
described as Faustian or Promethean when it has lapsed into perversity,
when *techne* replaces *poiesis*, in Heideggerian terms, and utility is prioritized over poetry. Life bereft of lyricism constructs itself in the banal
register of sentimentality rather than sanctity, and political correctness
replaces (high) politics and (ethical) correctness both.

The West's vice has been an inclination towards missing the tree for
the forest, a tendency towards abstraction. Politically, this corresponds
to what Voegelin calls the "multi-civilizational, ecumenic empire," representing a naively (merely horizontal) expansive universalism (a Faustian
or Promethean rather than Herculean, technicist rather than poetic,
politics). It is opposed by the homeward-turn to union on the basis
of existing linkages that Plato defends. This latter militates against
the nation-state's historic bid for protagonism, sometimes by way of
overseas adventures.

It is not so simple as the equation between the unity of the human
condition and unitary government. Colonial powers recognized other
colonial powers. What was equated with the unity of humanity is subtler. It is a set cultural and aesthetic expressions. Due to this subtlety,
it endured far beyond the colonial era. Indeed, some could justify the
exportation of European statecraft (with, and even without, a view to
eventual home-rule and the end of foreign domination) in almost the
same way as one can justify the exportation of Greek philosophy, Japanese sword making, Chinese inner alchemy, Persian astrology, and any
science or craft thought to have been perfected by one people more than
others. But the idea that universal humanity is culturally European and
must be made to realize it, is a pervasive and partly unconscious one.

Perhaps because the whole world was thought to be European, there
was no reason to find Europe in Europe. Instead, Europe was to be built
everywhere else, and so, by and large, the project to be pursued was
that of a European matrix and global, colonial holdings. Even the least
modern of European overseas expansions, the Spanish (not technically
colonialism, as conquered land consisted of provinces) proceeded in
the context of popes and Protestants rejecting Charles V's concert of
Europe—the *Regina Europa*, the *Universitas Christiana* (though this was
not its first impetus).

The point is not to uncritically condemn colonialism and subsequent
forms of western hegemony (which may well have spread good practices
as well as doing severe damage), but to note its horizontal compensation
for a loss of verticality. The nation, in the form of a nation-state, which
had previously been part of a whole, could now create its own whole.
The civilizational project built on ancient foundations (Roman Empire
and Medieval Christianity) was lost and a new overseas project replaced

it, just as, progressively, old philosophical and theological conceptions were lost and a new, often utilitarian, worldview received crusading vigor. As Novalis says: "[w]hat had been lost in Europe they sought to regain multifold in other continents, in the furthest Occident and Orient."[14]

The nation-state is the product of Europe's dismemberment, not in terms of politics alone, for Europe was never really politically united under the emperor, but conceptually, through an intellectual rejection of Emperorship. Indeed, the failure of Charles V's European concert could not be reversed by his son, and may be read as leading eventually to European disunity and the definitive shift of political gravity to overseas colonialism. Charles V's focus had been Europe. He apparently does not even mention the Americas in his memoires.[15] But his emperorship was undermined by both popes and Protestant princes. The latter would not articulate a real sense of European unity, despite the possibility of an alternative esoteric Protestant emperorship, possibly suggested in the Rosicrucian manifestos and attempted by Palatine Elector Frederick V. It is difficult to see the later, modernist form of Empire under Napoleon as non-parodic, and, in any case, it did not re-install the institution or redirect modernity.

We may consider the degree to which a culture's artistic canon is often only selectively aligned or, in fact, unaligned with a country's political trajectory. Spanish literature and philosophy were often critical of imperialism. In Cervantes we have an excellent example of myth digesting modernity (*Don Quixote* is perhaps the first modern novel, with self-reflexive narrative voice) and of nationhood as non-expansionistic. The shepherds and the knights of *Don Quixote* do not mention America, although the Peruvian historian Raul Porras Barrenechea described it as a benevolent satire of conquistadores.[16] It is not that he rejects empire (it is possible he penned romances in honor of Hernan Cortes, or planned to do so), but he is also critical of it and does not conflate it with nationhood.

Cervantes, like other authors of the Golden Age of Spanish literature, the *Siglo de Oro*—Luis de Leon, Lope de Vega, Suarez de Figueroa and Gongora—presents a negative image of those who, in his lifetime, were going to the Americas seeking wealth (as in *The Jealous Man from Extremadura*).[17] Correspondingly, Indigenous American nationhood was

14 Novalis, "Christendom or Europe?" In: Michael Martin, *The Heavenly Country: An Anthology of Primary Sources, Poetry, and Critical Essays on Sophiology* (Brooklyn, NY: Angelico Press, 2016), 92.

15 Diane de Armas Wilson, *Cervantes y la "Materia de América."* Transcript of lecture delivered at the Philosophy Department of the National University of Costa Rica, Heredia (Heredia, Costa Rica, 1993), 24.

16 Raúl Porras Barrenechea, *Cervantes, La Camacha Y Montilla, El Inca Garcilaso en Montilla (1561–1614)* (Lima: San Marcos, 1955), 238.

17 Hector Brioso Santos, *Cervantes y América* (Madrid: Fundacion Carolina, Marcial Pons Historia, 2006), 353.

not imaginatively internalized by Spanish artists. However much Spanish culture exists in America, the situation is not symmetrical.

In his final work, *the Labors of Persiles and Sigismunda, a Septentrional History,* Cervantes describes the savage inhabitants of *the barbarian island* as possessed of a desire for future world empire, as well as prone to rage and vengeance. Many of the features of the barbarian, including human sacrifice, are obviously derived from certain of the American natives, yet in his zeal for global rule he is also European. Indeed, Cervantes locates the barbarian island somewhere in northern Europe. Diana de Armas Wilson notes this duality as a subversion, or rather, expansion, of the category of *barbarian.*[18] It is a double critique of cannibalistic savagery and expansionistic civilization. We would add that both the cannibalistic human sacrifice and the desire for global hegemonic government are instances of literalizing spiritual principles, of immanentizing apocalyptic mysteries. We see here how what Vico calls *barbarism of reflection* and *barbarism of sense* are the civilized and primitive reflections of the same vice.

In his *Novelas ejemplares* Cervantes celebrates Charles V and his son Philip II, but he also highlights the cost of interventionism. Cervantes writes the following about himself, by way of autobiographical note, in the prologue to his *Novelas ejemplares* (my translation):

> For many years he was a soldier, and a captive for five and a half, whereupon he learnt patience in the face of adversity. During the battle of Lepanto he lost his left hand to the blast of a long-gun; this wound, which some might think unseemly, he regards as splendid on account of its having been acquired on the most memorable and high occasion to have transpired in these past centuries—nor can future centuries expect better—militating under the triumphant standards of the son of the lightning of war, Charles V, of felicitous memory. (This son of the *lightning of war* is Philip II.)

As Alexander Samson observes, Cervantes' Spanish patriotism coincides with criticism of expansionistic politics.[19] Americo Castro writes that while Cervantes is critical of Philip II's Mediterranean policy in *El trato de Argel, El gallardo español,* he also includes passages of a "a patriotic character shining through with national pride."[20]

This is clear in the play *The Siege of Numancia.* Here, the *Duero* river, who appears as a character along with Spain herself, prophesizes that, even though the pre-Roman Celtiberian city of Numancia will fall, it

18 De Armas Wilson, *Cervantes y la "Materia de América,"* 37–38.
19 Alexander Samson, *Discurso heroico, aspiración imperialista y el mundo mediterráneo en la obra de Cervantes* (VII Congress of the AISO, 2006), 557–62.
20 Américo Castro, *El pensamiento de Cervantes* (Barcelona, Noguer, 1972), 226. Cited by Samson, *Discurso heroico, aspiración imperialista y el mundo mediterráneo en la obra de Cervantes,* 561.

will inspire future greatness. The river's prophecy celebrates the coming Visigothic monarchy, the end of divisions between Spain's sons (even calling for Portugal to return to the Spanish fold) as well as a hostile policy towards the papacy. In Numancia "the idea of patriotism is a defensive one" which challenges imperialism. It is an investigation into "the origin of Spanishness... the meaning of the myth of Numancia in the formulation of a collective national identity" and can be read as containing varying degrees of anti-imperialism, on which the critical literature on Cervantes agrees.[21] In its historical context, Numancia's safeguard against expansionist excess is to root Spain in herself, including Celtiberian antiquity. In this context, Philip II ("second to none") is lionized and his empire is described specifically as one in which Spaniards are to be united.

By conceptualizing Spanish nationhood as rooted in ancient times, focusing on fighting the Ottoman Empire in the Mediterranean, to the shrinkage of other theatres on Spain's geopolitical horizon, the artist is emphasizing the defensive role of military and political strength, not the missionary expansionist vocation. Blake likewise articulated his vision for Britain as contrary to Empire, as Northrop Frye writes:

> It would have been possible, even in Blake's time, for a nation's imaginative energies to become centripetal and national rather than centrifugal and imperial, and in an atmosphere of growing national and racial consciousness his plan might have received more attention.[22]

(Albeit, in practice, the opposite route was taken.) If politics balances the one and the many, the executive and the people (political sovereignty emanating from the popular will and yet constituting a *supplement at the origin* of that emanation), it is the artist who is the joint of this paradox. The artist is the axis of Pickstock's serpentine reology. The exploration of a culture outside or against its own imperialist past can therefore be sought in its great artists.

EXPANSIVENESS OVER EXPANSIONISM

Imperialism, or nostalgia for it, can contradict not only Europe as cultural unity, but also the nation it is built upon. While Milbank is right to identify Britain and Spain as un-modern (or alternatively modern), medieval mini-Empires whose overseas expansion and incorporation of diverse territories was thereby facilitated, we should not lose sight of the organic and historically ancient basis for a state and the lack of such for a large global empire.

---

21   Aaron M. Kahn, *The Ambivalence of Imperial Discourse: Cervantes' la Numancia within the 'Lost Generation' of Spanish Drama (1570–90)* (Oxford: Peter Land, 2008), 79.
22   Northrop Frye, *Fearful Symmetry: A Study of William Blake* (Princeton, NJ: Princeton University Press, 1969), 412.

The nation-state's desire for protagonism is now perhaps in its far-cical rather than tragic iteration (a renewed British Commonwealth, *La Francophonie*, Russo-centric Soviet-nostalgia, and so forth). The legitimate sprawl of an organ occurs within its body: the sphere of the heart is blood, the sphere of the pancreas is its enzymatic secretion, the sphere of the lungs is present throughout oxygenated arterial coursing. These interpenetrate in one organism rather than transgressing its skin.

Intellectual life in the period of the nation-state was proceeding in large part from a metaphysical error. Writes Novalis:

> ...the erudite gain[ed] the more ground the more the history of European humanity approached the age of triumphant erudition, whereas knowledge and faith entered into more decisive opposition.

A scenario in which "Europe were to reawaken" with "hierarchy" as "the principle of unification of states" would require an element "at once secular and superworldly," for "[i]t is impossible for secular forces to put themselves into equilibrium."[23] It would recognize that "...Nature remained so wondrous...in defiance of all the efforts to modernize her."[24]

Novalis's reawakening of Europe through a principle "at once secular and superworldly" would overcome Promethean temptation, which was partly the context in which Western hegemony emerged, the aegis of a technically proficient, rationalistic universalism. This overcoming is also universalistic: it is the universalism of safeguarding diversity by sustaining European tradition as part of that diversity, and of safeguard-ing the specific good in that tradition to the benefit of all humanity, as well as displaying a path out of the negative aspects of modernity and postmodernity (which is appropriate to the degree that they originated in western culture). We will discuss how the Promethean theft, the Faustian magic of modern technology, can be humanized and divorced from global homogenization in a later section.

What is heroic about Prometheus is the willingness to face peril. We are tempted to rehearse the Egyptian opinion about Greeks, according to Plato, and view Europe as a young culture, adolescent, and cast its Promethean ordeal as a rite of passage into adulthood. His is a caution-ary tale against taking on the initiatic crisis in a spirit of pride, outside the orbit of Divine devotion, forgetting that self-mastery is also self-surrender. Therefore, although understanding Europe, and any aesthetic venture, as a still-disclosing category may come across as vitalistic, a kind of constructivism, it is better construed as initiatic. A perilous rite of passage, like any creative act, has need of *kenosis*, self-emptying, which is to say, abandoning the strictures of safety, the coordinates of comfort, and confronting danger. It is a virgin land, verging on ordeal.

---

23   Novalis, "Christendom or Europe?," 98.
24   Ibid., 94.

This kind of emptying is an opening. It does not assume nihilism, although it confronts the appearance of such (Matthew 27:46). Culture in general can be understood in this way. It is an aesthetic, creative gratuity. Why build a Gothic structure and not one according to the standards of the Chinese *Yingzao Fashi*? The question is as profound and meaningless as why a certain tree ought be oak instead of pine. Because *providence*. Culture is just one human endeavor in which such self-emptying and self-receiving (*Christic* creativity) may unfold. No all-encompassing, all-resolving historicism is being proposed here, just as discussing the biography of a particular individual does not imply a grand narrative regarding all others (although all persons and lives must in some way express a paradigm beyond themselves).

Focusing on the medieval world, to link Europe with expansiveness (through the continent's name and that of Japheth) may be justified by the numerous peoples thought to descend from Japheth or by the northerly sprawl of this landmass, although the same could have been plausibly speculated about other groups of peoples and potentially far-extending continents, such as Asia, especially since this continent was known to include India. Regardless, this project would confirm the instincts of its bards. Europeans did go on to expand, both in land and knowledge. Words preceded the shape the world took. This yielded negative effects, the Promethean perversion, as well as positive.

But expansiveness may be edifyingly understood as pluralism, Nietzsche's definition of greatness: "the ability to be both multifarious and whole, both wide and full."[25] (Indeed, recent history furnishes few better examples of a Faustian type than this son of a pastor, who pursued his intuitions into madness but, like Faust's reconciliation to Heaven, might have found a path into the mysteries when finally signing his letters as the *crucified one*.) The Dionysian philologist maintains that Europe, a place so prone to plurality, is also striving after unity.[26] Such a view may seem ill suited to his anti-essentialism, except that the mad prophet attended to imperatives for whose existence he could perhaps not fully account.

Expansiveness as organic plurality is precisely how Ortega y Gasset conceives of Europe:

> In the European overcoming we envision, the continent's present plurality cannot and should not disappear. While the old state annihilated differences and made them inactive, at most conserving them by a kind of mummification, the national idea in its pure dynamism demands that active permanence of that plurality which has always defined the occidental life ... [27]

---

25 Nietzsche, *Beyond Good and Evil*, Section 212; 107.
26 Ibid., Section 256; 148.
27 Jose Ortega y Gasset, *La Rebelion de las Masas* (Madrid: Diario El Pais, 2002),

Given his defense of social and cultural differences, it is significant that Edmund Burke considers Europe a cultural unit:

> It is virtually one great state having the same basis of general law; with some diversity of provincial customs and local establishments.... The nations of Europe have had the very same Christian religion.... The whole of the polity and oeconomy of every country in Europe has been derived from the same sources. It was drawn from the old Germanic or Gothic customary; from the feudal institutions which must be considered as an emanation from that customary; and the whole has been improved and digested into system and discipline by the Roman law.... From this resemblance in the modes of intercourse, and in the whole form and fashion of life, no citizen in Europe could be altogether an exile in any part of it. There was nothing more than a pleasing variety to recreate and instruct the mind; to enrich the imagination; and to meliorate the heart. When a man travelled or resided for health, pleasure, business or necessity, from his own country, he never felt himself quite abroad.[28]

Likewise, Denis de Rougemont maintains not only that Europe is a unity, but also that it precedes diversity (which can imply that it gives rise to that diversity, and therefore that its expansiveness may be one of differentiation). Europe is much older than the nations, he tells us, a contention which may find support (apart from that which its author himself provides, and even apart from the critique of the nation-state as a recent distortion of organic linkage) in the fact that the term *Europenses* predates the appearance of even some of its most rooted regional identities (the founding of the Duchy of Prussia or the proper, literary emergence of the Provençal, Occitan language, for example). In this context, European expansiveness would consist in giving rise to plural manifestations of itself. A good example of how the term *nation* was not thought to imply political structure and could be comprehended in a larger unit may be found in the twelfth century Alphonse VII's *Poem of Almeria*, cited earlier.

Imperial/ecumenic projects do not require homogenization, but breaking up organic units can create counterfeit identities that do not do themselves justice and are against the grain of their history and the forces that molded them (we touched on this in the case of Catalonia within Spain). The European expansiveness (*Japheth*) cited by Denis de Rougemont, therefore, must mean the creation of a (regional, national, continental) unity that is ample enough to allow internal diversification and correspondingly being able to conceive of a unit therein without rejecting the wider context or links.

II:XIV, 9; 230–31.

28   Edmund Burke's *The First Letter on a Regicide Peace*, quoted by Milbank and Pabst, *The Politics of Virtue*, 361.

Furor should not efface folklore, grandeur should not deny the pasture, the sublime does not rend the beautiful. Indeed, the latter may be birthed and nurtured under the auspices of the former. Europe generated great internal diversity of language and custom, with these local features sometimes developing under common political structures, such as the Holy Roman Empire or Papacy, and within common cultural conceptions, such as Latinity and Christendom or identification with Aeneas or Japheth. This may be understood as simultaneous centripetal and centrifugal forces, alternating periods of both or as the internal differentiation of a maturing body. Plato's call for political *making* and *aligning* is hereby repossessed in terms of expansiveness and pluralism.

That nations and states have emerged within a consciousness of wider imperial units, just as Plato praised city-states and also defended Hellenic federalism and understood the ecumene as transcending Greece, bespeaks a historical trajectory that is ignored when European integration is conceived of in terms of dissolving historic unities into a "Europe of the regions." A more organic approach is to seek a Europe of the nations, but not necessarily of the nation-states, or of an educational/ideological emphasis on broader identities combined with political decentralization. That is, a Europe of historic national unities, with their pedigree often hearkening back to provinces of the Roman Empire (Spain, France, Italy, Germany) and therefore to the Roman (Greek-derived) understanding of pre-Roman populations and geographically sensical administrative units, whose unity was pursued and resumed after the fall of Rome. To deny intermediate units like these historic nations is as much a mistake as considering a set of cultural particulars as a legitimate universal imposition through imperialism.

The view that regional units are more rooted, somehow truer, than larger nations and nation-states ignores that those regional identifiers, including local languages, often developed in the context of larger political wholes and within an explicit adherence to broader identities. In the zygote, the genetic code found in every cell of a body pre-exists the differentiation of cells. There was an Hispanian *Regnum* under the Visigoths prior to a Castile or an Aragon and, as Milbank once tweeted about Monmouthshire in east Wales, there are places that feel "deeply and mysteriously pure British" in that what is typically Welsh or English, say, is not separable in them.

Of course, the centralism of French revolutionary, rationalizing fervor should also be rejected, but the reactionary view that those states established in the context of political modernity and liberal republicanism (like Italy and Germany) are mere artifices ignores their pre-modern roots. *Quidquid luce fuit, tenebris agit*—and work that was began in the light of day and finished at night will nonetheless be illumined by the light of the next day. A nocturnal bloom does not rule out congress with the sun.

Criticism of political modernity and the nation-state should, therefore, be nuanced. Even the radical, republican ideas of the French revolution became material for sorting wheat from chaff, with aspects of the new state taken up by a recurrence of traditional political forms. This is particularly clear in the careers of Emperor Napoleon III and his wife Eugenia of Spain. With them, Catholic Counter-Enlightenment ideals seemed to replace Enlightenment radicalism as source of legitimacy more clearly than with their antecedents, as perhaps illustrated by a personal devotion to the Sacred Heart of Jesus, especially in the case of the Empress (while recognizing the many limitations of Napoleon III).

Just as we do not reject a technology because it was invented at a time when certain ideas were in vogue, a love of pre-modern philosophy should not entail a rejection of every modern political or organizational, or even philosophical, insight. Indeed, consider the degree to which pre-modern thought often thought it reasonable that, just as an animal is not as *real* as a human being (in being less *conscious of reality*) some human beings may be less real than others, less actually or even potentially human. To experience the other (for example, by way of modernity's technologically-facilitated travel) provides us now with a tremendous insight into that *other's* full humanity, the *other's* reality as fully equivalent to our own. The expansive, Faustian, Promethean disposition often denotes technological hypertrophy and a desire to go unto the ends of the earth, but this can be a good thing, yielding important lessons.

In a final reconciliation between traditional inheritance and what is valid in political modernity, we should note what elements of the latter are present in the former. Fundamentally, if tradition locates the kingdom and its people in the king's body, we are dealing with representational politics, however anachronistic that might seem. Of course, the representational politics just mentioned does not involve isonomic participation in politics as modern citizenship would articulate it, although the idea of individual equality in matters of law and in relation to the state is not alien to pre-modern thought. It is rather that one interfaces with the whole (the whole as represented by the state, the king) by way of specific estates. This goes along with Milbank's idea that Dante and Eckhart were proto-humanists and that features often thought of as modern were present in their "pious laicization," a project continuous with the merging of "world with monastery" that thinkers like Dostoyevsky also had in mind.[29] The modern cannot be rejected wholesale without thereby rejecting part of tradition and its inherent potentials. This is precisely where we have been headed: European expansiveness must be expansive enough to embrace *and transcend* the political modernity it created and foisted on the world.

---

29   Milbank and Zizek, *The Monstrosity of Christ*, 115–16.

Though expansiveness is linked to the Faustian or Promethean error, it is worth remembering that neither Faust nor Prometheus ultimately ends in perdition. For Goethe the Satanic doctor enters Heaven, just as the haughty Titan is rescued by Hercules in course of the latter's eleventh labor. The demi-god succeeds where Prometheus failed, thereby redeeming the fire-thief's efforts.

We described Nietzsche as Faustian, which is to say, Promethean. It is interesting, then, that he looked forward to the Herculean figure, entreating the good European towards this archetype.[30] Indeed, the textual body in which appears the first mention of Europe-as-continent presents the redemption of the Promethean type. In the Homeric hymn to Hermes, the eponymous character is a fire-maker and thief, but he is redeemed and reconciled to heaven, that is, to Apollo, and pleasing Jove.

Perhaps the same is true of Europe. It may need to play dead, play condemned, like Prometheus, before activating a new life for itself; to play the fool (wisely persisting in his folly); to see Faustian machinations fail before eliciting Heavenly recognition, Herculean rescue, the god who can save us. It could be unwarranted to borrow the latter phrase from Heidegger, given that his conception of a god's arrival might be merely the novelty introduced by chaos, the fluxing lash of negative infinitude, and not the coherent response of the Cosmos, the self-reciting of the Logos. Still, while this characterization rings true of *Being and Time*, there is much in his *Identity and Difference* to give us pause. Writes Voegelin:

> When the contemporary extravaganza of achieving *aphtharsia* in the world of *phthora* has run its course, perhaps the balance of consciousness will be regained in which the participation in the transfiguring movement, without achieving its consummation in this world, will again become bearable as the lot of man.[31]

Voegelin links this extravaganza to western civilization and not only to its modern technologically-driven version, but also somewhat locates the error in St. Paul, who partly seems to have wanted his theophany to instantiate itself as a unifying historical Apocalypse. Some of the post-Christian West's imperialistic and revolutionary tendency might have roots in this. Thus, the Western crisis, "the strand of the grotesque in Western deculturation," owes itself to veering away from religion as well as to some of Christian doctrine's biases. The metaphysical point here, as we have reiterated over and over, is simply that unity of principle is not best expressible as uniformity of practice.

Once the extravaganza has run its course, once the world conqueror achieves "concupiscential defeat," as Voegelin describes it, after a *petit mort*, lustful conquest can return as erotic and marital maturity, no

---

30   Nietzsche, *Beyond Good and Evil*, 243; 134.
31   Voegelin, *Order and History*, vol. 4, *The Ecumenic Age*, 339.

longer impetuous but centered in the manner of the erotic mysticism we have discussed. Jove's closing of the heroic age in Homer has been understood. Achilles has learnt to love. The Faustian character may play dead to jolt new life—burning out and requiring an igniter from Jove's lightning, evidencing the need for grace. This is an ascetical fast or fall, a *felix culpa*, invoked in Heidegger's piously apophatic reflection upon a "godless thinking which...is thus perhaps closer to the divine God."[32] Here, then, is both the cradle and chasm (that birth and draw of life mentioned previously). The abysmally creative leap, the filling of an empty space with one's howling, listening while falling for an answer from the great *out-there* (Matthew 10:39).

It was mentioned that according to the thirteenth century monarch Alphonse X of Castile and Leon, the earlier name for Spain was *Esperia* or *Hesperia*, after the evening star (Venus), to which it was associated as westernmost part of Europe. According to Book III of the *Aeneid*, Hesperia was an ancient name for Italy (presumably from the perspective of the Trojans). The evening star (Hesperus) and morning star (Phosphorus) are both Venus, and the phrase *Hesperus is Phosphorus* dispels semantics to get at the actual object designated. We have here a metaphor for the alchemy of death realized as birth (the West and dusk's identification with the East and dawn), for Europe and Western culture's present need.

Milbank's emphasis on the Western cultural trajectory as allowing (though having lapsed away from) organic relations while avoiding, through a propensity for experimentation and skepticism, organicist rigidity in which individuals are too much identified with particular social functions, concords with Desmond's argument in *Dialectic, Difference and Otherness*[33] regarding the infinite as hospitable to finite beings and limit, beyond both "extreme traditionalist" (calcified, reactionary) impulses for the apparent psychological security of a finite cosmos, as well as excessively revolutionary "extreme modernist" ones, identifying the infinite cosmos and its potentials as warrant to undo and upturn everything known.

This may also mean conceding that a quasi-undetermined canon of images used to communicate the sublime, a certain communal openness to the new forms coming through artists, is preferable to some of the more radical eastern Orthodox criticisms against Renaissance painting and in favor of more firmly set styles of iconography. It is, in this sense, legitimate to consider the Holy Grail mythos Europe's own sacred recitation or qur'an, as Henry Corbin writes, or Rumi's *Mathnavi* the Persian qur'an,[34] as it is often designated. This connects to the Blakean idea

---

32   Martin Heidegger, *Identity and Difference* (London: Harper and Row Publishers, 1969), 72.

33   Desmond, *Desire, Dialectic, and Otherness: An Essay on Origins*, 163.

34   Hamid Dabashi, *The World of Persian Literary Humanism* (Cambridge, MA: Harvard University Press, 2012), 52.

of prophecy, or the minority doctrine that there can be prophets after Muhammad in Islam, so long as they are not law-issuing (the Ahmadiyya, for example, cite a hadith they trace to A'isha in this regard[35]).

We do not dispense with the Western taste for experimentation and innovation. The work of artists has a place within, or in relation to, scriptural canon or established religious forms. It is here that we encounter a redeemed Prometheus, the sacra Japhetica, so to speak, of medieval thinkers like St. Isidore of Seville: a European expansiveness that must repent from the abuses of modernity, technological and economic determinism, industrialization and colonialization, and eliminate within itself the conditions for their emergence.

We are discussing the possibility of a different, pious modernity, not one that collapses the attributes of God into the world, as Blumenberg correctly observes has occurred, but realizes the contrast raised therefrom (infinite and dynamic creation does not "steal" from God what is His, but prevents any form from idolatrously pretending to be God's attribute in an exclusive sense). It is the Proclean modernity of Milbank, and the "stellarization"[36] of the world understood as hieratic, in which astronomy, and artistic and scientific exploration generally, are viewed as occasions for theophany. St. Augustine's warns that this can hide a certain hubris, indeed, information accrual about stars and physical things is not the same as spiritual discipline and knowledge, but such confusion need not occur.

Apart from past territorial, or past and present scientific, expansion, and apart also from the production of internal diversity, then, European *wide-sight* (*Europos*) should be understood in its vertical axis: Prometheus's redemption following a cruciform bind,[37] per certain depictions of Aeschylus's version of the myth (evoking a Christic ordeal, the mastering of the four directions), the Herculean attainment of Olympus. Where the fire-thief is set free by a rightfully divinized bearer of Olympian torch, and where Doctor Faustus is turned from infernal flames to "Love still revealing Flames," that "become clearer! All, cursed with error, Truth be their Healing."[38] All trophies for Heaven.

The pyric images of danger and redemption are fitting. Such is the fluxing fixity of fire's ceremony, the spiritual drama to which it anchors. It is right, then, that the country of that "Japheth [who] is a type of

---

35   There is also the minority idea that Muhammad is the seal of the prophets in the sense of confirming those who came before, the way the seal on a letter confirms its authorship, but does not thereby deny the possibility of later letters, so long as they do not deny sharia.

36   Blumenberg, *The Legitimacy of the Modern Age*, 316.

37   Thomas Gould, *The Ancient Quarrel between Poetry and Philosophy* (Princeton, NJ: Princeton Legacy Library, 1990), 127.

38   Johann W. Goethe, *Faust: A Tragedy*, trans. B. Taylor (New York, NY: Houghton Mifflin Company, 1912), Act V, 303.

the fire-world"[39] in Jacob Boehme's symbology, John Ruskin's "fiery serpent"[40] of Gothicism, a style that defines medieval Europe, Europe as fire, the element of Lucifer as light-maker, Prometheus as fire-thief and Hermes as thieving fire-maker, should experience the boredom of burn-out and modern malaise before reignition.

Something analogous appears in Ibn'Arabi's account of those souls who are of the fire. In order to make the Qur'anic name of Allah *ar-Rahman*, the All-Merciful, compatible with the description of hellfire as everlasting, the Sufi concludes that the punishment will, in the fullness of time, cease to be a punishment, even though its substance, fire, will endure. Pain will become delight and those who remain with the fire will be revealed to be literally in their element. They are constitutionally fiery souls. This is not so different from the Orthodox Christian understanding of the torturing fire of hell being the same as the blissful rays of Heaven, where the latter are experienced as the former so long as the experiencer remains mired in a narrow sense of self, for which the bliss of beatitude appears as painful annulment.

Fire affects other elements, scorching earth, vaporizing water and feeding on oxygen, thus Europe's role in creating and exporting a culture-corroding modernity. Yet in danger is a saving power. The more tragic character of fire, the incineration of the phoenix (again Matthew 27:46) may be only one initial awakening, after which the pattern of the operation is understood as a *poietic* technology: Instead of burning uncontrollably, burning usefully, and not burning once and out, but learning how to reignite vigor with the effortless enthusiasm of the healthy youth and content sage. Eliciting Jove's lightning to reignite. One can learn the pulse of ignition, burn, wane, burnout and re-ignition from fire and utilize it un-tragically, that is, as the necessary rhythm of life, one which every element displays (the *arising and passing away*, in Buddhist terms), like the king of the mountain, who uses the site of initiation as a site of deep mediation in which to rest in wait of future restorations.

The cross is a throne whereon the old self dies and Christ is glorified. The initiate becomes like Dionysus, becomes a bacchant (implying dismemberment) after dying at Mount Ida (by the proxy of an animal sacrifice, as Porphyry recounts of Pythagoras), Jove's throne, and returning, now as Jove's son (from another point of view becoming co-demiurge, another Jove) and that of Europa (following Euripides, who describes initiates as sons of Europa), a consumed flame rekindled by the Divine father's lightning (the thunderstone, again, as Porphyry writes concerning

---

39   Jacob Boehme, *Mysterium Magnum, Part One*, trans. J. Sparrow (Public Domain, 2009), 290. We are reading this in the context of the tradition that identifies Japheth with Europe, although Jacob Boehme's commentary on Genesis is highly symbolic.
40   John Ruskin, *The Genius of John Ruskin: Selections from his Writings* (Charlottesville, VA: University of Virginia Press, 1998), 189.

Pythagoras's initiation), now aware of the perennial life in itself, now flaming as the cosmic central fire (the archetype sun, the Cretan Jove-as-solar-deity, conjoining with his lunar Europa). The enactment of death and rebirth is the fiery self-consumption and grace-received reigniting. The image of fire gives over to that of spiritual center symbolized by the sun. this is the same as another traditional metaphor for spiritual victory, that of water: stilling the waters yields a vision of the stellar firmament reflected on its surface, or the Heavenly baptismal font, rising up and gushing from the Divine throne (Apocalypse 21:5–6; 22:1). A tumultuous sea falling exhausted suddenly reflects the stars, a soil scrambled and tiled suddenly is ready for seed, a windy violence abating suddenly allows the air to carry melody.

If a vision of the universal accompanies dismemberment, if dismemberment occurs to gain such a vision, the universal vision that Europe gained was of a lower type: rationality (not even reason as traditionally understood). In confusing it for the transcendent—in progressively denying the transcendent—this vision's yielded a parody of wisdom. Europe, then, must pursue folly into wisdom, follow through the quest attaining a vision of the universal proper—which is already occurring, since materialistic scientism has encountered its end at the hard problem of consciousness, which, properly understood, is not solved even by pan-psychism (not even by the sophisticated version of pan-psychism proposed by Tononi and Koch's Integrated Information Theory), meaning the future requires a recovery of metaphysics. This recovery should imbue the ancients at the root and stem of European civilization with renewed authority. Thinkers who anticipated this, championing the spiritual import of the Platonic tradition in modern times, from Thomas Taylor to Pierre Grimes, are perhaps still to receive their peak readership.

Of course, we are more aware and knowledgeable of other traditions and their insight than we have been in the past, and the political and cultural assertion of these against western hegemony constitutes something of a leitmotif for many, so that the present predicament is not to do with discovering the value in the archaic west to export or impose. But once discovered, once the revolt against its premises is shown to have been spurious, it seems natural to embrace it. The future European, rather than gleefully declaring *without god all is permitted*, should be a humble paladin, knowing rather that *without God, nothing is possible.*

Indigenous America and the Ecumene, or Imperial Rise and Indigenous Return

W E TURN TO A CASE STUDY OF THE PARTIC- ular in relation to the universal, nation in relation to Empire/ Ecumene: the post-colonial experience of *indigenism* or *indianismo*. This is not a thorough historical survey, only a focusing in on specific examples to draw out specific points. Political modernity has hearkened back to symbols from tradition, and in this sense allowed for the inversion or, rather, rectification, of its own more radical or dubious propositions. The example of certain natives of Bolivia illustrates this point as well as generally highlighting yet another striking correspondence with the symbols we have been exploring.

THE ASSIMILATION OF CHRISTIANITY AND LIBERAL-REPUBLICANISM BY THE MACHA AS PRECEDENT TO THE INDIGENIZATION OF TECHNOLOGICAL MODERNITY

We already noted the translation of Biblical images into local contexts by indigenous Bolivians. Their use of the tree symbol, combined with Incan, Habsburg and Republican images, is similar to the application of the Tree of Jesse to the Carolingians at the Cathedral at Chartres. Here, Republican symbolism by Bolivian natives is appropriated to express a profound tradition largely odds with Enlightenment and Whig thought.

As Tristan Platt observes in his essay "Simon Bolivar, the Sun of Justice and the Amerindian Virgin: Andean Conceptions of the Patria in 19th-century Potosi," Bolivian natives have historically been ambiguous in their attitude towards the independent Republic of Bolivia. There is a historically consistent indigenous desire to retain tributary status, keeping external government at arm's length, maintaining integral tribal land, rather than embracing modern citizenship.[1] An 1830 provincial governor apparently even complained that the natives were less obedient to him than they had been to Spanish authorities before independence.[2]

Native Macha historiography, consisting of succeeding *suns*, each bringing prosperity to the land, did not and does not explicitly account

---

[1] Platt, "Simon Bolivar, the Sun of Justice and the Amerindian Virgin. Andean Conceptions of the Patria in 19th-century Potosí," Journal of Latin American Studies, vol. 25, No. 1 (Feb. 1993): 161.
[2] Ibid., 170.

for Spanish rule or post-Spanish republican government as constituting new eras (new suns).[3] Indeed, indigenous iconography presented an Inka-Habsburg sun,[4] so that the Incan state of Tinguipaya was not considered fundamentally distinct from that which came with the advent of the Spanish emperor. The republican hero Simon Bolivar, after whom the independent state breaking with Spain would be named, appears to have been likewise assimilated.[5] This may be because the suns represent historical epochs of a broader order, like the Indian yugas, in contrast to which recent political transitions are short-lived. In any case, it seems to indicate theological ambivalence to Habsburg Spanish compared to Inca, and Republican compared to Spanish, government.

Platt points out that solar symbolism appears in both Enlightenment Republicanism, the sort that animated Bolivar and the push for independence in the Americas, and among defenders of established monarchies.[6] The Bolivian case is one in which the liberal ideals of the former hearkened to a perennial symbology (overlapping with their rivals) and therefore ended up representing a source of inspiration not for revolutionary novelty but for ancestral heritage (if mistaken conceptions are inverted truths, their correction is not so difficult, indeed, *revolution*, meaning as it does to *re*-turn, to revolve and so find the starting position, implies this). The ambiguity is such that some revolutionaries wanted to establish a new monarchy with an Inka or Bolivar himself as king.[7] Thus,

> ...the New Republican Age could be thought of as intensifying and renewing (rather than abolishing and replacing) the religious and ethical content of an imagery established long before the advent of the liberty tree.[8]

What Platt is referring to is a typical symbol of Republicanism, the tree of liberty (for whose nourishment Thomas Jefferson famously recommended the blood of tyrants and patriots) which was assimilated into the source from which it was probably originally taken: the tree across traditions as Lady (republicans often used a woman as their symbol too, with one breast showing, perhaps hearkening to the milk-giving goddesses of kingly initiation, like Hathor). This tree was related to the Sumaj Urqu mountain, the goddess Pachamama, and the divine child Huayna Potosi was identified with Christ. The native use of these images does not communicate a whiggish view of history or modern republican understanding of citizenry, even when the figure of Simon Bolivar and republican liberal symbols are integrated.

---

3   Ibid., 159–85, 164.
4   Ibid., 166.
5   Ibid., 177
6   Ibid., 175.
7   Ibid., 176.
8   Ibid., 174.

It is important not to fall into promiscuous syncretism and ignore the religious exclusivism of average persons. Likewise, however, we should not ignore the recurrence of archetypes and the presence of preparatio evangelica, from the Christian perspective. The clearest indigenization of Christianity in the Bolivian context, then, is that which occurred when a descendent of the Incan Huayna Capac, Francisco Tito Yupanqui, carved a miraculous image of the Virgin. Crowned by Pope Pius XI, she commands tremendous devotion in Bolivia and Peru (and beyond) as the Virgin of Copacabana. We have here not an adaptation of pre-Christian symbols to Christianity, but the occurrence of Christianity through the local.

Other non-syncretic indigenization events, or *translations*, include the vision of the Lady of Guadalupe given to St. Juan Diego. In the north American case, we may think of Black Elk, the Catholic medicine man who participated in the Ghost Dance movement.[9] In particular, we should recall his account of Christ in a very native context.

> ...I saw twelve men.... I went to the centre of the circle with these men and there again I saw the tree in full bloom. Against the tree I saw a man standing with outstretched arms. As we stood close to him these twelve men said: 'Behold him!' The man with outstretched arms looked at me and I didn't know whether he was a white man or an Indian. He did not resemble Christ. He looked like an Indian, but I was not sure of it. He had long hair which was hanging down loose. On the left side of his head was an eagle feather. His body was painted red. (At that time I had never had anything to do with white men's religion and I had never seen any picture of Christ.) This man said to me "My life is such that all earthly beings that grow belong to me. My Father has said this. You must say this." I stood there gazing at him and tried to recognize him. I could not make him out. He was a nice-looking man. As I looked at him, his body began to transform. His body changed into all colors and it was very beautiful. All around him there was light. Then he disappeared all at once. It seemed as though there were wounds in the palms of his hands. Then those twelve men said to me: "Turn around and behold your nation, your nation's life is such...." The men that I saw were all beautiful and it seemed there were no old men in there. They were all young. There were no children either. "Behold them, your nations life is such. Their way of life you shall take back to the earth." The women were dressed beautifully... [10]

He reflected elsewhere that he thought he had truly seen the son of the Great Spirit.

---

9   Raymond J. DeMallie, *The Sixth Grandfather: Black Elk's Teachings Given to John G. Neihardt* (Lincoln, NE: University of Nebraska Press. 1984), 260.
10   Ibid., 263–64.

THE *RECONQUISTA* OF TEHUANTIN SUYU AND THE CONQUEST OF MODERNITY

Imperial expansion transports positive elements, such as organizational and other kinds of technology, as Ken Dark observes, and hermetic isolation is dangerous, as localized adaptation to specific pathogens can cause widespread population depletions when contact does take place (had America been arrived at by Europeans later than it was, the impact of smallpox may have been even worse). But a political project cannot easily expand without retaining the mark of its ethno-cultural initiator. Indeed, even when this is not a matter of policy (for in the case of Spain, Habsburg policy sought to retain local language and spaces), this tends to result from technological differential. For an empire to truly be a coordination of states and not itself a state, it almost necessarily has to be reinvented as a federation or commonwealth.

It is natural, therefore, that imperial expansion be followed by local reassertion, and that later forms of political collaboration take a federal and diplomatic form. We have arrived again at something we discussed during the introduction: the idea of a pattern into which discontinuous bodies are arranged and that expresses unity as an encompassing harmony rather than a homogenizing hegemony and preserves difference without isolationism.

In the case of the pre-Columbine political subject (or a post-1492 consciousness of the possibility of a political subject continuous with pre-Spanish identities), it has endured in part as a gesture against the Spanish empire, and in part by being embraced by it. It was not natives who fought for independence, the way they had fought the Aztecs, for example. Independence was led mostly by Spanish *criollos*, as the saying goes "la Conquista la hicieron los indios, la independencia los españoles." Natives would also have to endure the post-Spanish Latin American republics, where indigenous peoples were often targeted, representing an impediment to their unitary pretensions.

In Bolivia, it is in the work of Fausto Reinaga that explicit use of the term *Indian* as political subject and identification with that subject are to be sought (Bolivian politicians may have invoked the Indian as political subject before, but without identifying him as political protagonist, so to speak). Reinaga may be thought of as the father of modern Indianism. But soon the term Indian was replaced by "Indigena" in political discourse, which Indianists identify as a disempowering shift, arguing that just as radical groups were appropriating the term Indian as self-designation, the political establishment was denying it by using a euphemism under which they could make symbolic concessions to that category.[11]

---

11   Pedro Portugal and Carlos Macusaya, *El Indianismo Katarista: Un Analisis Critico* (Fundación Friedrich Ebert, 2016), 60–61.

Indianist discourse is frequently one of being modern and politically empowered, without being western. That which makes itself felt is the robustness of an identity which finds it is so distinct from European cultural forms (Spanish or US-American) that it does not identify as *western*, yet knows itself capable of favorably interfacing with foreign intellectual and technological advances. It distinguishes the Ecumene from historical conditions and can imagine a possible Ecumene where the benefits of foreign structures do not convey cultural effacement, such that reciprocity is viable. More precisely, we are discussing what the Bolivian professor Pedro Portugal has dubbed *Katarist Indianism (El indianismo katarista).*[12]

The latter work is very critical of both, and more or less sees modern Katarism as having tended to use class and pseudo-Marxist categories to deemphasize the colonist-colonized axis. Meanwhile, it sees the romanticism of Indianism as complicit with a discourse in which the native American is assimilated to nature, imagined as animalistic, and thereby made subordinate to the European—the positive spin on this, in which a native of the Americas is considered more in touch with natural forces or a noble savage would continue to deny him participation in modernity. His lot is to live at the margins, speaking with the animals as his imagined ancestors did, not to be a player in global games.

Indeed, the *plurinational* state, as modern Bolivia defines itself, is criticized for resting on the atomization of indigenous peoples into a potentially indeterminate plurality of non-state identities receiving blanket recognition rather than tailored concessions or avenues for political articulation. This atomization and indeterminacy would correspond to the idea of the native as a natural fact, as pre-political subject, as pure spontaneous noble savage with no need for deliberative processes and negotiation in the polis. This line of thinking supposes an impediment for virtuous cultural reform or innovation, which is reflexively identified as western neo-colonialism, and where any criticism of a practice among indigenous populations, however harmful, is out of bounds, for such a practice is a brute fact of nature.

We may contrast this with the founding moment of Katarism. Katarism draws its name from Tupac Katari, a late 1700s Aymara native leader who fought the Spaniards and to a degree united Aymara and Quechua. Tupac Katari was quartered and parts of his body sent to different regions of the country, so that he appears as a figure of the dismembered initiate who is also the sacred king who embodies his realm. He reminds us of the last pre-Spanish Incan emperor, Atahualpa (brother of Manco Inca), who died in 1533. Atahualpa inspires the Inkarri myth, according to which an Incan regent was dismembered, his limbs being sent to different provinces, germinating underground until his return. We might imagine Katari's

12   Ibid.

quartering as a recurrence of the Atahualpa/Inkarri, and as related to the four parts of the old Incan state. Further, there are versions of the Inkarri myth as far off as southern Chile, so that it provides the basis for an expanded Incanate. Before dying, Katari famously declared "I return in the millions." Katari's wife, Bartolina Sisa, who was also executed, was an important player in the siege of La Paz and in calling for indigenous rule. She was quoted as saying that the white-face had to be extinguished so that only Indians would rule, reminiscent of the Incan general of Manco Inca, Quizo Yupanqui, whose battle-cry during the 1536 siege of Lima was to push the bearded ones (Spaniards) into the sea.

The enterprise of Tupac Katari would not be one of 1) representing indigenous rights only in generic terms, or 2) the indigenous population as a set of non- or sub-state associations, or 3) as a demographic category within the populations of American republics like Bolivia. We find the defense of a *specific* identity which until relatively recently had its own state, and restorationism on behalf of that Incan state, the Tehuantin Suyu (meaning "Four Regions," referring to its principal divisions). This Empire would have been constituted in the 15th century. Quechua seems to have been used by the Incas as a lingua franca for their empire, although they would originally have spoken other tongues. It fell in 1532, although briefly enjoying a continued existence under (or in uneasy association with) Spain (specifically the conquistador Pizarro), when it was led by Manco Inca, who eventually rebelled against Pizarro and died in 1545. It also endured as the Neo-Incan state of Vilcamba, whose fourth and final monarch, Tupac Amaru, was executed in 1572 (an execution of which the king of Spain, Philip II, did not approve).

The movements led by Tupac Amaru II and Tupac Katari in the 18th century harkened to that state. Indeed, the mid to low tiers of that state endured as part of the Spanish administration (my translation):

> ...the new order did not start from scratch. Although the higher echelons of Incan state organization were disarticulated, other levels were subordinated to the new power. Thus, the *curaca* through which a community related to the Inca and its administrators, gradually became a mediator between the Spanish and the community. He who represented a community before the Inca gradually became an intermediary for the Spanish. Changes like this were operating in other areas such as the *mit'a*. Spanish dominion adopted the mit'a, but not in the way it had functioned during the Incanate, but rather excessively.... [13]

The restoration of the Tehuantin Suyu can thus appeal to more recent precedent than the end of its top tier (the execution of Tupac Amaru). The lower Incan structures of governance and economic relations may be said to exist to this day in Andean villages. Further, its languages

---

13   Pedro Portugal and Carlos Macusaya, *El Indianismo Katarista: Un Analisis Critico*, 44.

are still spoken. The emphasis is therefore more on explicitly political considerations, the use of the state apparatus, rather than more abstract cultural recovery.

The cultural project, however, is significant, and concerns the adoption (digestion) of modern structures. It is not identifiable with liberal-republicanism and Bolivia's independence from Spain, given that the new states at times engaged native populations more viciously than colonial-era authorities. The explicit belief in a caste system or superiority of creole (Spanish decedent) over native seems to have been common among the republican leaders of the independence movement. The degree to which aspects of the new Bolivian state are taken up and fused with the concept of Collasuyu (one of the four Incan regions or *suyu*, partly corresponding territorially with Bolivia) varies from theorist to theorist. But, if it is not a legacy of liberal-republic independence, the enculturation of modernity by the indigenous political subject is by definition likewise not a return to 17th century monarchical Incan resistance.

Pedro Portugal and Carlos Macusaya point out that the namesakes Tupac Katari chose for himself (Tupac Amaru and Tomas Katari) both wanted to improve the lot of natives by having their personal Incan monarchical or chieftain lineages recognized and thus achieving legitimacy under Spanish law for their authority. In contrast, Tupac Katari had no dynastic claims, and did not care to preserve the existing accommodation between the vestiges of Incan rule and Spain. His was therefore a thorough repudiation of Spanish presence.[14] But given his lack of concern for native ruling lineages, his movement was also hostile to entrenched power interests in the post-Incan social configuration (similar to how Tecumseh scorned native chiefs for dealing unilaterally with the United States). Indeed, the fact that the Aymara accepted his leadership despite his being a commoner represents a break from their inherited political culture, as might the active prominence of women like Tupac's sister Gregoria and wife Sisa.

This is where a balance has to be struck: the old Incan state allows an escape from fuzzy categories of indigenous rights for those wanting a more politically definite project, but Tupac Katari provides a qualified precedent for taking up that legacy dynamically, a *translatio*, without needing its old ruling lineages, without romanticizing its ruling class, or taking up its superstitions. In this sense Katarist reimagining of the Tawantin-suyu will tend to conceive of it as distinct from the Incanate's historical dynastic politics, addressing also the reason for its having made enemies of sufficient indigenous tribes as to furnish the Spaniards with ample local allies, such as those who fought with Pizarro against Manco Inca.

Of course, a successful state, like a successful person, will at times stimulate jealousy in its neighbours as a function of their own resentment,

14   Ibid., 79.

rather than any direct antagonism on its part. However, Indianism must account for the two most prominent pre-Columbine states, the Incan and Aztec, having fallen not to the Spaniards, but to a coalition of Spaniards and native peoples (the same is true of the Maya). Let us consider the Nahua people (Mesoamerica). The celebration of the Aztec state is here particularly jarring given the prominence of human sacrifice. Instead, Indianism could coherently harken not to Aztec political theology, but to the people of Tlaxcala and others who defeated the Aztecs after suffering under that yoke, converting to Christianity and expanding into the north. Like the Aztec triple alliance, these also considered themselves continuers of the older Toltec legacy. We may think of the 1570 *Anales of Cuauhtitlan* and its (possibly originally Toltec or Toltec-inspired) account of Quetzalcoatl opposing human sacrifice in favor of self-mastery. Here, the god Quetzalcoatl is identified with a historical ruler of the city of Tollan-Tula, Topiltzin. The story of Quetzocoatl opposing human sacrifice and becoming identified with Venus, the morning star, like the Davidic king in Psalms, can be interpreted as a *praeparatio evangelica*, and his return from the east as the coming of Christianity. If Roman civilization could be Christianized, why not Nahua culture? Finally, the use of *Mexica* symbols in the image of the Virgin of Guadalupe and the Nahuatl account of her apparition cannot be treated as somehow extraneous to indigenous history and identity. Guadalupe Marian devotion is central to Mexican identity (like the Virgin of Copacabana to post-Inca Bolivian and Peruvian identity) and suggests to us a version of Mexican culture in which the indigenous component is extremely prominent.

The danger is that Katari might represent too clear a break from the foreign, just as he seems to have been too impetuous a leader, and that the rejection of western norms, drawing on a total repudiation of the Spanish empire, ends up rejecting norms that are not western, but Christian. Here we see how movements calling for the return of pre-Spanish forms in Mexico, or the Tawantinsuyu in Bolivia and her neighbors, tend to attach themselves to spurious spiritualities or else, seeking to be modern, engage in a base materialism no different from liberal or Marxist and post-Marxist currents. This ends up taking on the worst aspects of post-modernity, and ignores the indigenizing of what once seemed foreign that has already taken place. Again, it was a descendent of the Incan Huayna Capac through whom Bolivia received the image of the Virgin of Copacabana, and it was to an indigenous man that the apparition of the Lady of Guadalupe came.

In any case, for Indianism the point is to address present conditions and accrue economic capital.[15] The focus is on making modernity

---

15   The version of this articulated by Fernando Untoja emphasizes the Katarist lens on native Aymara thought as one in which the rival is a friend and rivalry or competition are a social good.

its own and neutralizing idealizing primitivism. Correspondingly, it is at odds with the *pluri-nationalities* of modern Bolivia and instead specifically asserts the Aymara-Quechua nation, possibly as enfolding other less extended native identities (and obviously assuming a fusion of the Aymara and the Quechua). Indianist Katarism would conceive of indigenous rights in terms distinct from the Marxist and post-Marxist ideologies that have often allied with it. Rather than insulating the native from global competition, it seeks to make him a global player. Mr Portugal's use of *Indianist* as the noun and *Katarist* as the adjective places emphasis on Indianism in order to preserve the romantic core, however in need of modification, but likewise aspires to a synthesis in which the political subject affects modernity (the global market, etc.). Some have spoken of ceasing to be globalized and instead becoming globalizers. The problem of globalization would be that there are too few globalizers, to paraphrase Chesterton on capitalism. Less globalized and more globalizing actors would reduce the homogenizing impact of globalization and so would in fact mean less globalization in the derogatory sense in which that word is often used. Local realities would preserve their integrity to a greater degree and there would be a greater diversity of resultant syntheses.

We are reminded of the Paiute old man Jack Wilson, *Wovoka*, who had visions and began teaching the Ghost Dance, sweeping parts of North America in the late 1800s and inspiring natives, including large numbers of Lakota (Sioux). "Ghost Dancers were thoroughly modern people...[t]heir religion was...a means by which Indians anticipated, internalized, and even debated the economic and political imperatives of the rapidly advancing twentieth century."[16] This was in the spirit of Tenskwatawa: "What Tenskwatawa invoked was not an appeal to the past or a pre-existing cultural perspective; it was a creative reformulation of indigenous identity in the midst of a historical crisis."[17] Wovoka's code was that Indian Americans should go to work, acquire dollars, buy farmland and ranches of their own, send their children to school and attend any Christian denomination's church (for "all these churches are mine"). But in addition to all this, they would practice the Ghost Dance, eventually bringing about an end of European occupation. Christian Indian Americans interpreted Wovoka's messianic prophecy in Christian terms, non-Christian ones did not. But Christian and non-Christian, radical and reformer, past and modernization were, it seems, reconciled in the embrace of the Dance. Ultimately, we may treat Black Elk's visions as a sort of fulfilment of the Ghost Dance.

---

16   Louis S. Warren, *God's Red Son: The Ghost Dance Religion and the Making of Modern America* (Basic Books, 2017), 366.

17   Lee Irwin, *Coming Down from Above: Prophecy, Resistance, and Renewal in Native American Religions* (Norman, OK: University of Oklahoma Press, 2008), 189.

IMPERIAL RISE, INDIGENOUS RETURN

The above is a testament to the phenomenon of historical perspective whereby the past looms larger and longer as time passes and orients minds to the recovery of archaic project. Indeed, the idea that the Aymara require a renaissance comparable to the modern European (re-)discovery of Greek philosophy is invoked by some Bolivian Indianists. The recovery of the archaic is not, then, necessarily the recurrence of primitive forms which Spengler argued occurs when civilizations crumble, or a reactionary romanticism, as Marxist critique might have it. It is, rather, the *possibility of an identity which was integrated and even apparently effaced by foreign structures recovering itself and in turn selectively integrating those foreign structures, reversing colonialism.* This does not mean the foreign structure is reproduced identically—a different kind of state organization might be sought—but it should be possible to integrate features considered positive. "Foreign achievements and culture should be a food for each people eaten and *assimilated*,"[18] writes the expert in Tantrism Sir John Woodroffe, discussing an independent India and its need for a *Religion of Power*, emphasizing Shaktist principles coming from its own tradition but hardly fearful of making foreign advantages its own. This may include the integration of cultural perspectives as well, so that we may conceive of all humanity becoming western so far as its organizational and political technology is concerned, in a sense fulfilling Virgil's prophecy, and all humanity becoming Japanese in its aesthetic philosophy, recognizing the superior insight of *wabi sabi* (侘寂).

The integration of technical refinements into local cultural forms (which includes altering and innovating those technologies but not necessarily excelling in the same areas or at the same pace as others) makes for non-mimetically rivalrous relations, mutual respect and the ability to communicate each other's uniqueness by participating in common structures (like the internet). The imperialist dynamic appears not as the manifestation of the Ecumene but as one half thereof, which is completed by an *indigenist return* (we are now using *indigenist* outside the Latin American sense). (Not to say that imperialism is necessary: the global distribution of a given technology and its drawing into political coherence can be accomplished otherwise.) There is something of Pickstock's serpentine reology here, the snaking quality of objects over time. Such indigenism is universalist: it provides humanity greater diversity and contrast and thereby greater understanding of the amplitude of that human condition which encompasses such diversity and contrast.

This dynamic of imperial expansion and indigenist return is facilitated by what philosopher Gustavo Bueno calls the "generative Empire," as distinct from the predatory kind. A generative Empire seeks symmetry between the metropolis and province, such that the latter becomes a state

---

18   Woodroffe, *Bharata Shakti: Collection of Addresses on Indian Culture*, 56.

on par with that of the former. It is relevant to note in this context what the 19th- and early 20th-century US activist for Indian rights Charles Fletcher Lummis noted about the Spanish presence in the Americas, to the effect that less than twenty years upon arrival in 1492, there was already a faculty of general studies, a hospital and a cathedral (Santo Domingo) available to local peoples in the Americas.

According to 16th-century Spanish theoreticians, Empire is a coordination of states and not a state itself and, in Bueno's model of "generative Empire," it is a mechanism by which provincial polities develop the metropolitan state's model. Provincial independence from the metropolis after a period during which advanced statecraft (or simply statecraft more adapted to international conditions) and other technologies are being learnt proceeds naturally from this, because at a certain point the state-generative mechanism of Empire is completed. In this sense, some indigenist anti-colonial projects can be seen as in part the legitimate legacy of an Empire insofar as it was generative, and empire-nostalgists should embrace these and pursue renewed ties on their basis, not against them.

Furthermore, we cannot know whether an Empire was "generative" only by looking to its technical refinement and the legal rights it allowed others to hold (as Bueno tends to do) for it may have been so different in its outlook from those it conquered that the latter's native cultural characteristics were not intelligible to it and were therefore suppressed as a matter of course. In such a case, should the native identity have its renaissance, it will likely push back strongly against the properly cultural features of the formerly dominant metropolis, even while integrating its detachable features, those that are truly universalizable (indeed, what justifies the empire if not universality?) such as technology or some other universal human capacity which was previously not being tapped.

We have used the encounter between self-aware reflective consciousness, *Chit*, and pure Being, *Sat*, to analogize this. The man who encounters the universal, the intense presence of Being in the jaws of a tiger, may keep that encounter close to his awareness and use it to be grateful every day, but he should not seek to return to the jaws of the tiger, for that might extinguish his life, whereas if he encounters that same intensity of Being in the arms of his wife, he may return there often, and that may enrich both their lives as well as create new life. Both experiences allow access to a universal but one is more compatible with the man's life (the former empire's culture may have bestowed access to a universal human capacity in technology or organization, and yet also be otherwise incompatible with the resurgent native culture's trajectory).

Therefore, an Empire as coordinator of states may endure, or be reimagined at a later time, but *by the same token*, the newly independent state may reimagine pre-Imperial polities (or proceed on the basis of ethno-cultural identities different from that of the former metropolis).[19] Such coordinating action would be diplomatic and confederating, institution-building and state-power balancing, even composed of ad hoc linkages, rather than a return to administrative centralization in the old metropolis. This is more or less what Gustavo Bueno suggests in *Spain before Europe* for Latin America when he discusses Spain as Empire (elsewhere he discusses Spain as nation), and is similar to what Milbank and Pabst touch on in *The Politics of Virtue* for the Commonwealth or Francophonie, although in tandem with a European union. The key is simply to not problematize the overlapping of political associations.

Therefore, we do not deny Empire-derived linkages. However, rehabilitating these has to mean not only that European unity is compatible with political associations on the basis of old overseas Empires, but also that the latter is compatible with (even if separate from) political projects whose identity is in continuity with pre-Empire realities outside Europe such as those based on native American identity in the Americas (equivalent to those features of European culture considered common to various countries and on the basis of which European integration is undergone), as emphasized by currents of thought dubbed de-colonialist, like Bolivian Indianism.

This would precisely be a true taking up of the imperial legacy. The Spanish empire included "Indian Republics" and co-official status of indigenous languages, after all. Indeed, *Hispanistas* who advocate for Spanish-speaking countries to conceive of themselves as a nation, confusing empire with nationality and viewing the indianistas as dealers in absurd anachronism ignore that the Incan state specifically fell *in spite* of the Spanish monarchy. Philip II chastised the viceroy of Peru, Francisco de Toledo, for executing the Incan leader Tupac Amaru, with the words, "I sent you to Peru not to kill kings but to serve them." The king also wrote to Sayri Tupac (nephew of Manco Inca) in 1552 forgiving all previous rebellions by the Incas of Vilcabamba, admitting these were due to local Spaniards, including Pizarro, misbehaving, and promising rulership of Vilcabamba would never be assigned to any Spaniard, and would remain under Indian authority (not so different, perhaps, from Tupac Katari's most radical pronouncements). Philip's vision did not play out, but the population remained of majority indigenous origin and was not enslaved (although types of institutionally maintained economic inequality and the construction of an economy requiring certain kinds of labor are morally equivalent to slavery).

---

19   I mean to suggest some hypocrisy in those who celebrate the Commonwealth, the Hispanidad, or the Francophonie, as politically actionable and as ideologically rehabilitative of former Empires, without granting those who invoke local political structures (like the Incan) which preceded or ran in parallel to such European Empires the same courtesy.

Too often, those who want to emphasize the good of the British or French or Spanish Empires will view anti-colonialist thought and initiatives meant to regenerate local cultural forms (such as language or rites) with suspicion. But the latter are merely doing for their own identity what the Empire-nostalgists do for theirs, as well as rightly emphasizing that which those Empires got wrong, which is also a part of our shared story. Again, the recurrence of empire must take the form of a commonwealth, not a homogenizing bloc that confuses empire with nation, this latter being a large-scale repetition of liberal modernity's errors. Political associationism should emphasize the compatibility of overlapping identities and projects.

Modern Technological Civilization and the Ecumene, or Translating Technology

W HEN BEING IS CONCEIVED OF NOT AS THE Being of beings but, idolatrously, as an excellent being among deficient ones, we judge and punish beings for not conforming to that being's contingent features (for all beings have contingent features). It is like defining circularity as a particular perfect circle, which happens to be red, and insisting that all circles should be painted red. At present we see a hyper-judgmental culture operating in a reified image of Being: the Internet.

Why is the Internet an image of Being? Because it is an apparently permanent record of past utterances. Being is often thought of as permanence, in much the same way as Eternity is thought of as eternal time. The off-color comment can be eternally extracted and judged from the Internet. Public personalities or even wholly private citizens can lose their job over something they wrote a decade past, and indeed, that is taken out of context. This latter point is especially pertinent. Rather than issuing judgement generously, seeking for context and mitigation—the advocacy recommended in the Gospel, as distinct from the accusation, *Satan*—isolated tweets, for example, are removed from a stream of thought and used as fodder for outrage. This isolation of supposed offensive comment from its context is analogous to its social consequence: atomization.

Being understood as inherent to beings and to their relations, that is, the loving community announced by Christ after the resurrection, where God is sought by gathering in love, is obscured by old, idolatrous images of Being as impassible, detached, judge. It is as though the Son of Man in Daniel's vision does not inherent the harmonious multiple kingdoms, but remains a sacrifice to the Ancient of Days.

This is the obscuring of Being that Heidegger describes in *The Question Concerning Technology*. The solution to this obfuscation, this sleepy mechanic of accusation, is to become sensate to human relations, community, compassion:

> [human] dignity lies in keeping watch over the un-concealment…En-framing, which threatens to sweep man away into ordering as the supposed single way of revealing, and so thrusts man into the

danger of the surrender of his free essence—it is precisely in this
extreme danger that the innermost indestructible belongingness
of man...may come to light, provided that we, for our part, begin
to pay heed to the coming to presence of technology.[1]

We can rise to the challenge of proving, of showing-off, that our "innermost indestructible belongingness" is just that, indestructible, by remaining present and sensate even as we instrumentalize technology (therefore
avoid being instrumentalized ourselves).

Such presence may well result in our reimagining digital technology
in particular, by removing the frame, i.e., the screen. I will not explore
this further here. On a collective level, the reimagining of technology in
a way that allows us to retain a sense of ourselves and our community
requires what John Woodroffe describes: "[f]oreign achievements and
culture should be a food for each people eaten and assimilated."[2] This
is the subject of the present section.

The following is an extremely cursory discussion of the translation of
technology into new cultural contexts. If something like Van de Mieroop's
Bronze Age Club of Powers, in which different political entities treat
each other as relatives and pretend to be denizens of the same village[3]
(an ancient global village), is to be established, then it must be done by
way of the instrument Jan Assman finds at work in that era and later
into Iron and Classical periods, namely *translation*. Each must swear by
the name of the deity he recognizes, while also believing his foreign
peer to be swearing by a valid and equivalent name.

This we approach in the overly mercantile but useful language of
developing a national or regional *brand*. That is, commercially-exploitable
cultural prestige (related to Joseph Nye's concept of *soft power*[4]). We
therefore treat prestige as a structuring element of the English School's
model of *international society*. This is approached through five moments:

1. Simplifying technology to reduce functional fixity
2. Reducing functional fixity to increase enculturation
3. Increasing enculturation as development of soft power
4. Developing soft power as a commercial niche
5. Occupying a commercial niche as a reduction of mimetic rivalry

The first and last of these are not strictly relevant to the field of public
administration, with the former providing the sketch of a basis for the
rest in cognitive science and the latter projecting its conclusions into

---

1   Martin Heidegger, *The Question Concerning Technology and Other Essays*, trans. W.
Lovitt (London: Garland Publishing, 1977), 32.
2   Woodroffe, *Bharata Shakti: Collection of Addresses on Indian Culture*, 56.
3   Martin van den Mieroop, *A History of the Ancient Near East, Ca. 3000–323 BC* (Oxford:
Wiley Blackwell, 2016), 137.
4   Joseph Nye, *Soft Power: The Means to Success in World Politics* (New York: Public
Affairs, 2005).

international relations. Before we begin, the following definitions should be brought to the fore:

- Simplifying technology: parsing out relevant components of a technical refinement in order to lay bare its dynamic and make new uses thereof.
- Functional fixity: cognitive bias towards using (and conceiving of the use of) instruments in familiar ways.
- Enculturation (of technology): identifying a technology with a cultural context other than that of its origin or most prominent usage. This identification is dual, consisting both of 1) uses of technology that perpetuate or reinforce culturally-specific institutions or practices and, therefore, social cohesion and the intangible goods associated with the heritage sector 2) the fostering of a psychological association between technical refinement and a given (national/regional) cultural context.
- Soft Power: used in this context to denote national/regional commercially-exploitable prestige; the degree to which point (2) from the preceding leads to increasing the willingness of global consumers to pay a premium for specific national/regional products.
- Commercial Niche: the specific area of commercial success resulting from the preceding.
- Mimetic Rivalry: 1) conflictual dynamics resulting from conceiving of success as a zero-sum game, 2) specifically refers to conflict resulting from desire for the specific niche of a rival, 3) can militate against the pursuit of new markets.

SIMPLIFYING TECHNOLOGY TO REDUCE FUNCTIONAL FIXITY

The professor of Indian religions Sir John Woodroffe (the aforementioned Arthur Avalon) once discussed the assimilation of foreign (organizational or technical) innovations by a body politic or cultural complex as analogous to digestion. If an organism is healthy and does not overeat, there is no reason to suppose the food it consumes will prove fatal. In the case of post-colonial India, he concluded, so long as the country were united and the society culturally sure of itself, western innovation would not become a second, more subtle, form of colonialization: "Foreign achievements and culture should be a food for each people, eaten and assimilated."[5]

In *The Question Concerning Technology* Heidegger discusses modern technology as an anesthetic against *Being*, that is, against the felt, imminent congress of a self-aware, human subject with the reality *out there* and *as such*. His fear can be related to Woodroffe's point above: The less present a digesting entity is, the more it will be conditioned by its food. Put more lucidly: the more automatic a process and the less obvious its dynamics are to our senses, the more it sweeps us into unconsciousness. Automatic

---

5   Woodroffe, *Bharata Shakti: Collection of Addresses on Indian Culture*, 56.

processes can become our default mode of cognition, and we fall into Heidegger's Enframing [*Ge-stell*], for our perception is framed, and we do not act consciously upon this (conceptual) frame. Psychologists may refer to this as a late-modern recurrence of *magical thinking*. Writes Heidegger:

> Enframing means the gathering together... to reveal the real, in the mode of ordering, as standing-reserve. Enframing means that way of revealing which holds sway in the essence of modern technology and which is itself nothing technological.[6]

We have here a general critique of utilitarianism, but for our purposes we may limit the issue to one of decontextualizing a technology: that is, removing a certain technology (or better, its underlying process) from the specific act of "ordering" that it carries out, from the specific way in which it sets resources (even if these be mere data sets) into a "standing-reserve." The result is functional fluidity rather than fixity and the possibility of appropriating technology for purposes that we creatively and deliberately form rather receive. *At the level of a regional or national enculturation of foreign innovation, this means that its culturally specific institutions, rites, patterns, can be reinforced rather than effaced by an active engagement in an increasingly technology-driven globalization.*

A technology whose dynamics are immediately perceptible and cognizable by the user, then, is preferable when there is no particular reason for more complex forms. As Pabst and Milbank argue, "...more advanced technology is not always the most appropriate or the most sophisticated, economic and sustainable in certain circumstances...." In this way, the automatic is understood properly, in its simplicity, and becomes less likely to induce magical thinking: "[s]impler technologies... remain the crucial allies of human reason and creativity...."[7] This partly involves a refutation of the emancipatory potential Walter Benjamin refers to in *The Work of Art in the Age of Mechanical Reproduction*, where the physical object loses its aura. Reducing physical objects to concepts (wherein a book is never interacted with as physical but only as an infinitely reproducible download across devices, for example) may actually render the subject more willing to reduce reality to a concept and to treat the concept as externally received. Again, as Pabst and Milbank suggest, the opposite approach can be as simple as encouraging library use, "lending to significant writings a certain symbolic weight."[8] We may also be reminded of Nietzsche's contention that reverence for books is a sign of refinement.

This describes the individual analogue of collective enculturation of technology discussed by Woodroffe. The simpler, *the more naked a technology* (no more complex than the task for which it is being used), *the more easily its dynamics and parts can be thought about by the user and restructured to fit that*

---

6   Heidegger, *The Question Concerning Technology and Other Essays*, 21.
7   Milbank and Pabst, *The Politics of Virtue*, 304.
8   Ibid., 303.

user's ends and local cultural forms. Karl Ducker's classic 1945 *candle problem* experiment illustrates how loose reward structures and time frames allow for more creative thinking, specifically in terms of using objects at one's disposal in ways one has not seen them previously used. This is what reducing functional fixity refers to. But it is not only functional fixity to which this experiment is relevant. It also serves to bolster the case made by Milbank and Pabst concerning the simplification of technology, that is, its breakup into parts that the interfacing subject is cognizant of, for if a technology's dynamics are not known, they cannot be used in new ways.

REDUCING FUNCTIONAL FIXITY TO INCREASE ENCULTURATION

Let us briefly describe Duncker's candle problem: Subjects were presented with a box of matches, two candles, thumb tacks, and a task, namely, to somehow mount the candles to the wall. The solution was to place the candles on the box and affix the box to the wall with tacks. Those who were presented with a box of matches were less effective than those presented with matches and a box. The objects were the same for all subjects, but the box was cognitively occluded by the former formula ("box of matches") and therefore subjects tended not to view it as a usable category independent of the matches. Its function was fixed in their minds as a holder of matches, and was not appropriated or integrated into the task as a holder of candles. Further, those who did not labor under a time limit and discrete reward scheme were also more effective, generally thinking more creatively and arriving at the solution more often or more quickly.[9]

The conclusion of Duncker's experiment is that creative thinking is potentiated by loose reward systems and time frames, presumably because cognitive resources are not occupied by tracking these and in order that thinking remain diffuse enough to seek lateral solutions, not honing in on a reward or deadline that then becomes the mind's goal, displacing the solution itself.[10]

The dissolution of functional fixity—the divorcing of technical components from their past uses to allow for innovative applications—may be approached through the devolution of technological application to the municipality, where specific needs are likely to be idiosyncratic enough to a given context that they will incentivize such dissolution, or where structural pressures are weak enough to allow for creative reworkings.

9   In Management or Organizational Behavior the conclusion borne out by Karl Duncker's candle problem is instantiated in structures that de-emphasize the supervisor or manager.

10   True, innovation increases under conditions of existential rivalry, largely because greater financial, material and human resources are mobilized to this end by the entity under stress, such as the state in times of war, as well as because those whose sense of duty requires it throw themselves into the pursuit. However, the Karl Ducker's experiment suggests that assimilation of technical processes is well served in non-competitive, or in *competitive as distinct from rivalrous*, contexts.

It is in practice often the case that promoting the spread and local production of innovations occurs by way of a government actor. An environment must be both coherent, so that it works as a unit and does not diffuse its benefits in such a way as to disincentives its players, and also internally cooperative. This defines the successful *technology cluster* whose relation to policymakers is the result of "an 'entrepreneurial vision,' which provides the 'focal points' around which private sector investment decisions can be (both formally and informally) coordinated."[11]

Ho Joon Chang refers to "intermediate institutions" that embed this vision in an economic sector. *The dissolution of functional fixity as presented in Ducker's experiment is analogous to a dissolution of the link between abstracts like prosperity—or specific technologies—and the culture in which they occur.* In his book *Bad Samaritans*, the development economist Ho Joon Chang provides a key to dissolving this knot, namely, the separation of culture from development or, put differently, a broader understanding of development, including economic prosperity and fruitful collaboration within the international system, as being abstract enough to find support in different cultures.

Functional fluidity allows us to think about technology as a separate category from its typical uses, including the cultural character through which it usually manifests, just as the box and the matches are separately usable, objects. The Japanese integration and innovation of technology originally developed by the West is a good example of divorcing the box from the matches.[12] Indeed, Japan ceased pursuing the so-called *Technopolis* (vertically integrated) model in favor of the cluster decades ago, taking advantage of loose incentive structures by allowing private and municipal actors to collaborate on an approximately *ad hoc* basis.[13]

---

11   Ho Joon Chang and Ali Cheema, *Conditions for Successful Technology Policy in Developing Countries—Learning Rents, State Structures and Institutions* (Maastricht: United Nations University, 2001), 28.

12   In this vein, Bhutan may be the most extreme example of carefully digesting foreign technology, as it is judged against the performance of a domestic *happiness index*, with the country's constitution requiring that sixty percent of the country continue being covered by forest and emphasizing that local norms not be eroded (citizens must wear traditional garments in public, etc.).

13   One may object that Japan should not be appealed to as a positive case study, given worrying social dynamics and the unsustainability of its long-term economic policies, both of which are inseparable from, and arguably more fundamental than, any policies of technological innovation and cultural promotion it might be benefiting from. This is a valid point. However, on both counts, the pessimistic narrative is often overplayed. As is typical in international relations, at least insofar as public opinion is concerned (a not incidental factor, given that public perception is often influenced and marshalled to justify foreign policy) antiquated, anecdotal or isolated indices are used to discount or promote the viability of policies. In terms of Japanese society, whatever pathologies are operant, its suicide rate is lower than that of Belgium and the Baltic countries, and the average Japanese citizen works fewer hours than his counterpart in the US or Portugal.

INCREASING ENCULTURATION AS DEVELOPMENT OF SOFT POWER

In applying the above to the development of soft power in international relations (specifically in terms of commercial clout through a strong national "brand"), we begin with a theoretical model: If a country develops a new mining technology and wants to benefit from it but resource rich countries will not adopt that innovation, it may decide to integrate these and force the adoption of its advancement as a matter of policy. This is described by *internalization theory*:

> Internalization theory explains how the boundaries of firms are set at the margin where the advantages of internal coordination are just offset by the costs of supplanting external markets.[14]

Thus,

> ...internalization occurs when a company expects that activities will be more profitable when they are under common control, i.e., this strategy enables the company to minimize transaction costs by further exploring the capabilities underused in the company (such as management and technological skills) which are superior to those of local competitors.[15]

In the international system, "[n]ewly discovered knowledge is a global public good; it is therefore efficient to apply it simultaneously in all territories to which it is relevant." In these terms, historian Ken Dark and others apply internalization theory to states and international relations as a means to understanding the rationale of imperialism: "Although knowledge is a public good, there are obstacles to transferring it between locations." Given such obstacles:

> A knowledge-intensive state frustrated by barriers to knowledge transfer may therefore resort to force and take over (occupy or govern) territories controlled by other states (especially those that refuse to recognize its supremacy).[16]

What happens next decides whether the integrat*ing* (as opposed to integrat*ed*) state settles for Gustavo Bueno's generative or predatory modes of empire. The former is distinguished from the latter in its sharing of technology between center and periphery, creating technologically-enfranchised subjects, so to speak. Such a dynamic is potentially always relevant, so long as innovation occurs:

> These insights suggest that imperialism is a rational response to a specific set of circumstances. They suggest that in a world

---

14   Mark Casson, Ken Dark, Muhammad Azzim Gulamhussen, "Extending internalisation theory: from the multinational enterprise to the knowledge-based empire." *International Business Review*, 18(3) (2009): 236–56, 1.
15   Ibid.
16   Ibid.

where opportunities to discover new knowledge arise continuously, imperialism emerges naturally wherever these circumstances prevail. Obsolescence too is a natural process, and this explains why empires decline. The decline of one empire may generate a gap that some other rising empire may be able to fill.[17]

Internalization can be conceived according to the above criteria if it does not lead to the identification of desirable ends with the particular culture of the internalizing entity, or at least if it only did so in a way that neither led to a mimetic crisis and attendant destabilizing rivalry nor to a loss of desirable cultural particularity in the internalized entity.

We may suggest a mirror-image of Ken Dark's model, according to which imperialism is rational if there are extreme barriers to knowledge transfer. What occurs presently is the reverse, so that modern equivalents to imperialism are themselves the barrier, preventing some societies from fully embracing aspects of modernity due to their being perceived as alien. This prevents those societies from participating in and contributing as much as they otherwise could to the international system. According to this, alternatives to superficial internalization (by foreign cultural modes identified with economic and technical progress) would lead to genuine internalization (into a collaborative and economically integrated international system). The word *internalization* may be used in three distinct senses:

1. Internalization *of a country or economy by another country or economy* (Ken Dark's understanding of imperialism);
2. Internalization *of technological advancements* (and the economic prosperity it potentiates) *by a country*;
3. Internalization *of a country by an international system* in which technological advancement is distributed so as to allow international economic links.

Here, (1) may cause resistance and backlash to (2) thereby preventing (3).

In order to avoid this, soft power can be exerted by an integrating entity in order to attract potential markets towards the adoption of a technology so that it may reap the benefits, but also by an integrated entity in order to engage fruitfully with the integrating entity, becoming a participant in the resulting commercial relationship. The pursuit of self-interest by the integrating entity is not so much opposed as it is reversed. As Confucius advises, the *kuo* (kingdom) must use *wen* (attractiveness) (Confucius, *Analects*, 16:1[18]).

---

17 Ibid.
18 Arthur Waley, *The Analects of Confucius* (London: Allen and Unwin, 1956), 203. Quoted by Voegelin, *The Ecumenic Age*, 362.

SOFT POWER AS DEVELOPMENT OF A COMMERCIAL NICHE

The sort of competition over productivity and exports typical of 19th-century dynamics is mitigated by the technological upgrading and cultural branding of traditional and traditionally low value-added sectors. Rather than seeking to outsource or import from such sectors while developing other more refined ones, the former can be retained and partly serve the function of the latter.[19]

To some degree technology has functioned as the desired objects in something like René Girard's mimetic rivalry:

> Negative reciprocity, although it brings people into opposition with each other, tends to make their conduct uniform and is responsible for the predominance of the *same*. Thus, paradoxically, it is both conflictual and solipsistic.[20]

This corresponds to the traditional emphasis on rupture between pre- and post-industrial social relations (result not from the technologies themselves as much as the modes of production into which they were organized).

As Ho Joon Chang observes, the late 19th and early 20th century was more globalized than the mid-20th, because "Technology only sets the outer boundary of globalization,"[21] the rest is politically decidable. Globalization understood as increasing economic interdependence can function in such a way as to limit mimetic rivalry while allowing for development and the sorts of technical imitation it requires.

Post-war Japan provides an example of this virtuous engagement with globalization. Indeed, among other theatres were technological innovation is brought forward as a matter of sound policy, Ho Joon Chang and Cheema highlight the "development of 'information technology' industries in East Asia."[22] Japan's initial imitative flurry gave way to a highly innovative economy, and its cultural particularities have become

---

19   One can object that a merely well-curated service, tourism or luxury agrobusiness sector will render an economy vulnerable. Certainly, the above should not be used to argue *against* developing high value-added sectors and strong exports, beyond the traditionally low value-added or recession-risky ones that new technologies would raise the profile of. At the same time, the enculturation of technology discussed here is not merely a means to attract more tourism or sell more high-end spices. Again, it should produce internally robust arrangements, overcoming the rift between reaping benefits from technology and accessing global markets, on the one hand, and retaining social stability and leveraging cultural ipseity, on the other.

20   René Girard, *The Scapegoat*, trans. Y. Freccero (Baltimore, MD: Johns Hopkins University Press, 1989), 13-14.

21   Ho Joon Chang, "Myths of Globalization: Noam Chomsky and Ha-Joon Chang in Conversation," truth-out.org, retrieved 29th April 2018.

22   Ho Joon Chang and Ali Cheema, *Conditions for Successful Technology Policy in Developing Countries—Learning Rents, State Structures and Institutions*, 28.

a source of success. The second half of the 20th century was like a second Meiji restoration, taking hold of and indigenized industrialization, shifting from imitation to an appropriate emphasis on:

1. Cultural idiosyncrasies whose attractiveness to foreigners represents a boon for the country's tourism and export sectors. This contrasts to the comprehensive displacement or occlusion of such unique offerings that often accompanies economic modernization, failing to properly exploit the economic potential of cultural difference, while also becoming vulnerable to the emergence of local resentment against the presence of foreign cultural norms.

2. Indigenous innovation, as opposed to an excessively long-term importation of high value-added goods. This contrasts to the failure to transition the economy into a mature capacity for autochthonous innovation, instead remaining dependent on foreign technology. The latter, combined with the perception of relative deprivation, is liable to provide fertile ground for a political mobilization against remaining engaged with the international system. Avoiding this, government regulation was used to control the quality of exports and thus project a positive, competent image of Japan abroad.

It is by now something of a cliché to invoke the dawn (by now midday) of a new industrial revolution. By way of case study, we may engage in a short extrapolative exploration of one particular technologically sophisticated sector on the horizon of the twenty-first century, namely nanotechnology, and its conduciveness to proliferating the above virtuous paradigm, attenuating rivalry between states and societies and having a stabilizing effect on relations. Of course, such promise depends on the ways in which nanotechnology is applied. No deterministic or historicist account is being hazarded, merely an earnest highlighting of its potential. There is much in the possible applications of new technologies that may be dehumanizing, but *in danger is the saving power*, as Heidegger quotes from Holderlin.

Models like that of Atkinson & Stiglitz[23] according to which innovation often occurs as a rearrangement of existing processes and equipment and so localizes in given sectors is not relevant if the object of analysis is a technology of economy-wide applicability, one incubating advances in a range of sectors (such as nanotechnology[24]).

The assumption that some economic activities will increase in competitiveness while others see no creative destruction due to inherent and necessary imbalances in initial investment strategies may therefore

---

23   Anthony Atkinson and Joseph Stiglitz, "A New View of Technological Change." In: *Economic Journal*, Royal Economic Society, vol. 79 (315) (September 1969): 573-78.
24   We may also look to Blockchain Technology in government structures, such as Estonia's X-Road, that avoid the vulnerabilities inherent in the concentration of knowledge.

prove not to be as relevant in economies investing in technologies applicable to all sectors, including traditional ones. Further, reducing un-equal access to new technology between urban and rural areas may increase social cohesion, resulting in the application of high-tech solutions to traditional sectors and elevating traditional sectors in the esteem of development economists and policymakers. This carries the added benefit of avoiding social displacement and a consequent vulnerability to political upheaval during phases of economic modernization, while simultaneously promoting itself as economically dynamic, competent, and capable of innovating (attracting foreign investment and talent).

John Kenneth Galbraith is correct to note that classical Ricardian comparative advantage is *de facto* impossible as a strategy for economic prosperity in *every* country because not every country has its own unique comparative advantage. Yet, crucially, it is also the case that every country does enjoys a stable, if not entirely hermetic, monopoly over its own identity or *brand*. Ho Joon Chang and Ali Cheema note that "knowledge creation and technological change have attributes of pure public goods, i.e., it is both non-rival and non-exclusive in character."[25] The same is true of culture.

It is approximately true that no country enjoys the advantage of another's cultural distinctiveness and the as yet untested ways in which such might be creatively developed and promoted. It is also true that innovation is so broad a category, and presents so numerous a set of possibilities, that proper focus and investment can, hypothetically, yield unique offerings for any sector in any economy (this may strike an excessively optimistic key, but the principle itself does not deserve to be disqualified, if only because it orients policy towards terrain more likely to be fertile than the saturated spheres of competition: a programmatic disengagement from crowded spaces and the constant pursuit of the *niche*).

To a degree, the development of new technologies is itself responsible for allowing a different account of development. Nanotechnology, for example, is applicable to traditionally low value-added economic sectors such as textiles and presumably usable in activities proper to post- and in some cases pre-industrial social arrangements. Relevant applications of nanotechnology likely to facilitate the development of a country's soft power include *the retention and development of traditional sectors,*[26] *the preser-*

---

25   Ho Joon Chang and Ali Cheema, *Conditions for Successful Technology Policy in Developing Countries—Learning Rents, State Structures and Institutions,* 19.
26   Textiles and agriculture present salient examples of production able to benefit from nanotechnology. The former of these may incorporate all manner of technical refinements, from wearable biometrics to aesthetic innovations such as the changing of colors and patterns on a single clothing item. As for agriculture, in parts of the world suffering from water shortages more effective diffusion of water in soil through the use of nanoparticles presents a significant potential windfall.

vation of historically and culturally significant artefacts,[27] and *the empowerment of specialized manufacturing.*[28]

The first of these allows for both the maintenance of social stability during phases of economic modernization, bringing new processes into existing economic activity rather than displacing the latter, and globally decentralized production, with its positive implications as concerns environmental pollution and local job markets. This would presumably have a positive effect on the international system, specifically by rendering a country less susceptible to upheaval and political demagoguery.

The most appropriate means for this integration of technology is the constitution of clusters/hubs and Open Innovation:

> By investing in collaborative research or taking a minority position in high-risk (external) ventures, investing firms learn about this opportunity and in this way decrease the huge uncertainty related to the initial investment.[29]

---

2 7   Turning to the preservation of heritage, the cultivation of a country's cultural attractiveness and the obvious boon to its tourism industry that this entails, requires the preservation and elevation to a state of maximum visual impact of its historically and artistically significant artefacts. There are many relevant examples to note as regards the contribution of nanotechnology in this area. Historically significant wall paintings and limestone renderings can be protected by way of nanoparticles. This has been done for the Masaccio's *Capella Brancacci* and the *Beato Angelico* at the San Marco Abbey. Older artworks, namely the unfortunate city of Pompeii's surviving frescoes, have also been thusly preserved. Neither are paper and wood excluded from the protective potentials of nanomaterials, as the latter can be used to de-acidify and thus preserve such objects, a process from which the Swedish Vasa Warship, which sank in the seventeenth century, has benefited from. Further applications include straightforward but more precise and less potentially damaging cleaning procedures for art pieces.

28   Finally, as regards the third area of nano-technological application relevant to the stimulation of cultural soft power, we may speculate concerning both the preservation of local crafts by the incorporation of technical refinement and the creation of new markets for this marriage of tradition with technology (as well as, secondarily, a renewed market for non-technologically innovative pieces, by way of their distinctiveness). This may be conceived, for example, in terms of crafts-persons improving their pieces by furnishing them with greater durability, for example by applying nano-texturing to surfaces to minimize their accrual of dirt, or by including details that can only be glimpsed by way of ocular aids, adding an aesthetic *curio*. These represent a unique selling point for as long as they remain rare and, in any case, should the market normalize such features, they can represent a vehicle for renewed demand of artisanal work. The stabilizing of this sector's image as technically-refined can render it appealing to new social cleavages. Finally, as mentioned previously, non-new-fangled pieces will likely retain and renew their market, precisely in reaction and by way of contrast to such innovations, so even non-technologically enhanced sectors can be galvanized by new technologies.

29   Henry Chesbrough, Wim Vanhaverbeke and Vareska van de Vrande, "Understanding the Advantages of Open Innovation Practices in Corporate Venturing in Terms of Real Options." *Creativity and Innovation Management* 17.4 (2008): 251–58.

After this learning phase, a firm may invest more substantially or retire from the project. Essentially, investors are unburdened from the need for clear returns on investment and are more able to canvas the array of available investment opportunities without committing excessively. New technologies can thus receive more initial investment and, should they prove promising, can be impelled forward by investing firms. Further, if a technology is not promising as a marketable product, the firm can sell its license to a third party, including a supplier, and benefit from it exogenously, so to speak.

In line with the above, maximizing a system's capacity to innovate may entail the relative independence of entities within that system. This is what policy geared at producing technology clusters assumes in several countries, emphasizing that SMEs should develop away from operating as subcontractors and towards greater autonomy.

A cluster can therefore represent a delimited space within which these virtuous dynamics can occur. The successful innovation cluster combines both the advantages of coherence and focus that an "entrepreneurial vision," as Ho Joon Chang calls it, can provide, directing investment to common goals, and also the laxity (or de-institutionalization) of reward systems and non-mimetic dynamics.

Another reason why the cluster may be conducive to innovation is that it produces a market for technical refinements that do not yet have a market. Entities seeking to increase the degree to which they can turn technological innovation into an advantage can be impeded if the market is unable to receive this innovation. Clayton Christensen describes *disruptive innovation* not necessarily as an advancement in the technology itself, but rather as a demand-oriented change in how a technology is commercialized, often entailing a simpler, paradoxically less disruptive use that the market is more willing to adopt (being more intelligible, more assimilable to existing consumer habits). At least in large part, disruption refers to an upset in the position of market players.

Projects of digital transformation in the public sector often require agile methods not only to learn from end-users (citizens) but also to make the end-user aware of what is on offer so that his demand becomes more specialized. This is sometimes called *continuous business justification*, where demand is assumed to be in flux. As one of the software developers for Estonia's e-Residency program told me, the point is to learn from the end-user and mold the public service on the basis of end-user desires. Here, agile methods become agile ends. The constant alternations based on citizen-feedback are not relegated to designing the service prior to implementation, but are permanent. According to the OECD's typology we are discussing Digital Government, where services are defined by citizens, rather than e-Government, where only service-delivery is. Yet this simultaneously teaches the citizen about the technology and creates a market for a service where previously there was none.

Creating a market does not only mean generating demand but also businesses able to commercialize advances and researchers able to alter a technology in helpful ways.[30] Further, the social and economic benefits of a cluster are mitigated if it fails to substantively bring in different kinds of practitioners, becoming an appendage instead for a foreign entity or entities.[31]

A product is all the more disruptive if the business being displaced is precisely that which developed the technology (often from a position of relative market dominance that allowed it to make the investment it took to bring this innovation about).[32]

It may be beneficial, therefore, for the sake both of increasing innovation and of having a market for it, that an entity endeavors to create its own ideal ecosystem, like a scorpion contributing to desertification or a panther buying Amazonian acreage. Ken Dark's internalization theory of imperialism points to this: if a polity develops a technology it cannot exploit because others will not adopt it, it may be tempted to conquer and force innovation on others. The creation of a new market, however, can occur along more benign lines. A cluster-creator of this sort generates a non-mimetic ecosystem for itself (not one that is free of competition, but one in which competition is a function of prestige wrought from achievement).

Apart from more general cultural considerations, Japan's so-called Galapagos Syndrome (*galapagoska*), denoting its tendency to look inward, is precisely describable in terms of this difficulty on the part of the wider market to pick up on excessively unconventional innovative products and the possibility of creating a market for such rather than being entirely undercut by disrupters who take a new technology into a more conventional direction, adapting it to the market rather than creating a new market.[33]

---

30   Researchers from the University of the Basque Country, Goio Etxebarria and colleagues, describe this principle: "When creating a local nanotechnology cluster, lack of a key agent such as a large firm may lead to failure. Generating a 'local initiative' to strengthen certain fields or clusters is one way of overcoming this problem. This initiative might consist of creating or fostering research groups, forming centers of excellence, local or international coordination and even trying to fill the gap due to the lack of large firms." Goio Etxebarria, Mikel Gomez Uranga and Jon Barrutia Guenaga, *The Dynamics of Regional Clusters of Nanotechnologies: Evidences from German Lander and Two Spanish Autonomous Communities* (University of the Basque Country, 2011), 31–32.
31   Ibid., 32.
32   This approximates the dialectical reversal Hegel describes in *The Phenomenology of Geist*, where the master loses connection to the sort of practical knowledge and skill cultivated in the slave, whose subservience requires of him the sorts of activities that teach him how to attain mastery over practical domains.
33   Parts of the Arab-speaking Islamic world present an almost mirror Galapagos syndrome, often seeing foreign technology as carrying irreligious cultural features and identifying piety with surface features of Muhammad's life, such as the state of technology in Arabia at the time. There is much in the Islamic legal tradition,

Without endorsing all its implications, it is worth referring to the following account of Europe's own potential Galapagos moment from a European think-tank:

> This experience is similar to that experienced by Japanese technology companies. A few years ago, these companies became aware that although Japan made the best 3G phones in the world, they could not find a global market because the rest of the world could not catch up with the technological innovations to use these "perfect" devices. The Japanese have christened this phenomenon the "Galapagos Syndrome." Takeshi Natsuno, who teaches at Tokyo's Keio University, told the New York Times that "Japan's cellphones are like the endemic species that Darwin encountered on the Galápagos Islands—fantastically evolved and divergent from their mainland cousins." Rather than being too big to fail, Japan's phones had become too perfect to succeed. Europe might now be is facing its own "Galápagos moment." It may be that Europe's postmodern order has become so advanced and particular to its environment that it is impossible for others to follow. It evolved in a protective ecosystem, shielded from the more muscular, 'modern' world where most people live.... Europeans will need to spend more time thinking about how to defend Europe's fragile system from external aggression rather than imagining how it will take over the rest of the world. Europe's universalism seems to have morphed into a form of exceptionalism.[34]

Focusing on the particularity, rather than superiority (the exceptionalism, rather than universal applicability) of a political or economic environment, it seems relevant to speak of the development of products and shaping of markets, as well as the development of political cultures and institutions, in ways that are not, as such, globally competitive (though they can be adapted to be), and that opt out of the game of mimetic rivalry and the Hobbesian rule that "if any two desire the same thing, then conflict is inevitable,"[35] instead prioritizing catering to local preferences and needs.

The technology cluster represents a model in which competition can become secondary to local appropriateness. This can be the case insofar as clusters allow for diverse economic entities that, by virtue of their diversity, represent a swath of social interests and thus orient innovation towards those interests, and insofar as it focuses on technologies that upgrade rather than displace artisanship and low-value added sectors, such as (certain applications of) nanotechnology. The cluster can thus

---

however, that can justify and potentiate precisely such assimilation of innovations, allowing for their divorce from a sense of being Westernized and therefore from the twin ills of imitation and rivalry.

34 Mark Leonard, "Europe's Galapagos Moment," ecfr.eu, retrieved 22nd May 2018.
35 Jodok Troy, "Desire for Power or the Power of Desire? Mimetic Theory and the Heart of Twentieth-Century Realism." *Journal of International Political Theory*, 11(1) (2015): 26–41, 31.

move in two potentially countervailing directions: it can allow innovation to produce markets able to receive it and it can cater innovation to local idiosyncrasies. This may also be why if one looks at the percentage of total public expenditure occurring at the sub-national level in EU countries, it correlates positively with a higher rank on the Digital Economy and Society Index (DESI), unless this sub-national expenditure is concentrated at the regional level rather than municipal. In other words: municipal implementation of digital technology (and innovative in general) is key. It adapts to local needs more easily and provides an ecosystem of tight-knit administration and business. This works best in countries where municipal competencies are uniform across the territory, rather than affected by highly differentiated regional competencies.

An organization seeking to promote technical advancements that are relatively unestablished in an economy (possibly as an intermediate institution promoting a government's favored investment focus for the private sector) may do so both by creating an environment for itself (attempting to incentivize researchers, academics, companies, entrepreneurs and regional or municipal public agencies), so that a market able to receive its product comes into being, and at the same time by catering to existing needs and tastes.

DEVELOPING A COMMERCIAL NICHE TO REDUCE MIMETIC RIVALRY

If the international society of states and non-state actors has as its telos the prosperity (both economic and in terms of some conception of human flourishing by way of articulation and protection of rights) of its members, then it must allow the detachment of these from cultural specificity, not in order to promote them as pure abstract principles (but that will nonetheless be married to some unexamined set of cultural norms), but to promote them in diverse cultural contexts. On one level this is a *fait accompli*. There already exists a common reservoir of what C. S. Lewis calls the *Tao* in *The Abolition of Man*: a moral and teleological consensus across humanity, often attributed to and expressed in terms of religious traditions. However, there are genuinely modern phenomena, such as those wrought by technological advances, in need of *detaching*, so to speak. To the degree that a technology and the material prosperity it brings are identified with a foreign cultural imposition, it will provoke what René Girard called mimetic rivalry but, to the degree that its spread is impeded, it will render imperialism sensical in terms of Ken Dark's internalization theory, in turn provoking rivalry.

Technical refinement and culturally idiosyncratic applications thereof represent a non-scarce arena of competition, replacing past competition over volumetric production and exports. The impact of scientific innovations on international relations is not circumscribed to the pursuit of competitive advantage. Technical knowledge or, more correctly, the specific applications found for such knowledge, is not neutral with respect to the form the international system takes. Technology is not always an either effective or ineffective instrument in the game of power-politics or institution-building, but rather can be a means to changing that game.

It may be suggested that the industrial revolution and the two centuries that followed structured international relations into approximate conformity with what René Girard conceptualized as the triangular structure of imitative desire and rivalry: that is, a complex interaction between model, desired good and subject (the three vertices of the triangle). Very simply, the models were countries with early industrial capacity (a *leader country*, in Moses Abramovitz's terms), the desired good was industry and capacity to export, and the subjects were countries without much industry but engaged in its pursuit.

Allowing the model to mediate desire for success (which entails a deviated desire for the model's success rather than for success as such) can result in the importation of the model's cultural and productive output, which is reinforced if the model promotes a strategy towards economic development that requires such importation, usually so far as high-value-added goods are concerned (the pursuit of a low value-added comparative advantage without adequate reinvestment in local high value-added sectors).

This inverts somewhat if rivalry emerges fully, in which case the subject mirrors the model rather than punctually emulating it, that is, the subject attempts to differentiate from the model, but always reactively, according to the model's actions (doing the opposite is still, in a sense, a form of imitation, genuine autonomy would mean imitating selectively, critically).

Much of what characterized industrial-era international relations belongs in a catalogue of perennial features of international relations. This can be conceded without granting that these features are or need always be as prominent as they have been. Industrialization certainly did not inaugurate such a dynamic, but it did likely instantiate a particularly clear form thereof. When one is more captivated by the possessor of admirable features than by those features themselves, and when engagement with that possessor (one's *model*) is conflated with the cultivation of those features, there emerges the risk that one will prioritize competition over the ends competed for. This contrasts with healthy competition and instead constitutes what we will refer to as rivalry. In the international system such subtle shifts in focus (on the part of societies, policymakers, defense departments, etc.) carry with them a not insignificant measure of danger.

Apart from the systemic effects of technology on international relations, the issue can be addressed on a country basis in terms of *scientific diplomacy*, with examples ranging from the Spanish government's stated intention to promote scientific advisory roles at the level of embassies and chambers of commerce, to the Small Advanced Economies Initiative, from within which countries like New Zealand attempt to foster ties and promote advances in areas likely to empower sectors on which their economies are reliant.

Scientific diplomacy should be conceptualized as largely or entirely an instrument of what Nye's *soft power* or Confucian *wen*. As such, it can project a country's culture, competence or charity. These serve to exert attraction (the utility of which can range from expanding the tourist industry to securing foreign investment). Some technologies and applications thereof are significantly conducive to the disengagement of a country's pursuit of status or prestige from rivalry. Technological innovations readily applicable to the cultivation of a country's cultural sector can be formidable instruments in the development of the *national brand*, largely assimilable to soft power. Otherwise, it is the model, or rather, the model-sponsored strategy for development, or, indeed, the importation of technology from the model or adoption of culture from the model, that mediates the subject's desire for success. Merely out-producing other countries does not best define success in the international system. The occlusion of the subject's cultural character or the defining of this character by foreign stereotyping and a corresponding reliance on foreign production of high-tech goods entails a failure to promote its culturally unique selling point and to promote itself as capable of technologically sophisticated production. The subject's unbridled pursuit of the model's success by importing its technology/adopting its culture, results in a lack of cultural attractiveness/soft power, and thus in a lack of success, of recognition and positive foreign perception.

If desire for a given object is mediated by desire for alternative objects that appear commensurate or conducive to the primary one but in reality deviate from it, then the subject's understanding of its own ends may be said to be faulty. Insofar as commercial success in the international system is less to do with outproducing industrial bulk than with competence (technological innovation) and culture (capacity to attract), relations that impede the capacity to develop these should not be allowed to mediate objectives.

Key to Girard's schema is the insight that subjects are less often desirous of a good for its own sake than of that which possessing the good represents. Attaining a particular good can be a way of imitating the model. According to the French anthropologist, the good that is truly being sought is often the status of the model, or, with one less sheath of self-deception, competition as such, the rivalrous dynamic in itself, without which the pursuit of goals ceases to entice.

It may be hazarded that something very similar to this dynamic has served as an instrument to structure hierarchies in the *international society of states* (we should use this latter expression, taken from the English

School of international relations, over the equivalent *international system*, as we are now definitively positing relations between states as analogous to those between individuals in a society). Since this mechanism relies on perception and desire, it is of interest insofar as it plays out in the more benign realities of international relations (those to do with *wen*, apparently deemphasizing, or at least remaining distinct from, military threat).

A model state may utilize imitative desire (desire felt by others towards itself) in order to promote the adoption of a set of norms, so long as these are viewed as conforming their adopter (the subject) to the model's own practice and, therefore, as oriented towards attaining the model's prosperity and even status as a model.[36] Products such as cars, televisions, computers, computer games, phones, and so forth, to some degree become more than the infrastructure in which culture is housed. It is not necessarily that they are themselves carriers of a particular culture (most of the changes they bring about were not a part of any society before even a century ago, and are not what is usually referred to by the word *culture*). Rather, these goods (or technical advances in general) carry and spread the imprint of national *prestige*, of a sense of excellence and competence: a country's brand, its soft power. This brand is difficult to separate from a diffuse admiration and the sense that a country's norms are worthy of emulation (it is here, then, that *culture*, properly speaking, becomes relevant). Rather, success has to do with a country's capacity to define its image, that is, to project culture and competence. This includes wielding soft-power commercially. The subject's desire for success (including recognition/positive foreign perception) is mediated by its brand/soft-power (including technological innovation and proficiency at the service of cultural goods and attractiveness).

One need not go so far as those scenarios of intense conflict in which Girard sees differences melting away (during what is merely the emergence into actuality of that inward conspiracy between the drive to rivalry and the drive to imitate) to note that societies, like individuals, sometimes adopt even the superficial features of those who possess a quality they admire. This is the case because what is being admired is often the capacity to garner admiration itself (success, status, recognition, in the abstract). The subject is not aware of what specific feature allows the model to be successful. Thus, while a country's status might have everything to do with ICT and patents, its fashion and music become objects of imitation

36 If the model links its present prosperity to practices other than those it employed or employs to bring this prosperity about, promoting norms it does not earnestly apply to itself, it can thereby limit the degree to which subjects will attain its levels of success. However valid Girard's ultimate point that imitative desire rests upon, and finally erupts into, rivalry, it would also seem to be the case that if the model is able to carefully leverage such mimetic dynamics and convince its subjects to adopt behaviors that render them relatively torpid, the impulse to rivalry will, even if it does emerge fully, be more or less ineffectual.

abroad (or unrelated sectors—a certain shampoo advertising under the tagline of *German Engineering for your Hair*, to the sound effect of engine noises, provides a humorous real example). This seems perfectly natural and, to a point, quite rational, as the key to success is not always clear and, in any case, potentiating cultural exchange has its obvious benefits.

However, Ho Joon Chang notes that a historically literate approach to economic development is liable to leave its student ambivalent as to what *specific* cultural traits are conducive to technological development. The ambivalence does not concern surface feature, as obviously different languages and similar traits are compatible with scientific research. The issue is that, even beyond this, different cultural sensibilities (from a sort of late liberalism to modern forms of Confucianism) seem to make propitious hosts for technological innovation.[37]

It is therefore recommendable that policy makers engage in earnest efforts to link the abstract drive for status and, indeed, for competition, to its specific, potential sources (technological innovation being an obvious candidate, along with the attractiveness of a cultural brand). Having done so, the model can be treated as empirical repository of strategic precedent, not as foreign policy's reason for being. Here, the fact that the desire for success includes a prominent element of desire for recognition (that is, for being perceived as competent by foreign entities) becomes explicit, and is thus not as prone to opening the subject to manipulation.

Further, a society can turn its own achievements and the cultural attractiveness that results from them into its own model and perhaps that of others as well. Given the above, a divorce of *mere culture* (straightforward cultural features like language and folklore) and the more brute expressions of the mimetic drive, on the one hand, from the desire for status, and specifically for technological innovation, on the other, would seem to hold some potential for pacifying the international society.

This allows for what Kant considered the precondition for federalization and transnational association in his 1795 essay *Perpetual Peace*, namely, relative parity among negotiating partners (although perhaps only possible in a quite limited sense).[38] Such a divorce is made appealing given the possibility of turning cultural particularity itself into a source of attraction (of investment, tourism, and so forth) and, perhaps more profoundly, of Kantian *recognition*.

---

37   This point stands on its own, and should not be taken too much further, for cultures that thwart the intellect can obviously exist, to which we may add that, in any case, technological innovation does not on its own indicate that the culture of the society within which it is taking place is conducive to human flourishing.

38   In terms of Latin American Dependency Theory, this could be conceived of as a strategy for subverting hierarchical arrangements, interfering with the promotion of economically unsound strategies by the model.

INDEX

A

Abaris the Hyperborean, 189, 223, 659

'Abd al-Muttalib, 639

Abd al-Rahman Ibn Abdallah ibn-Ka'b Ibn-Malik Ibn-Ansari, 390 n191

Abdai Khan, 239

Abdal Hakim Murad (Tim Winter), 43, 262, 658

Abdallah al-Warraq-Yazid, 622 n83

Abdulkarim Soroush, 647

Abel, 305, 491, 617

Abhinavagupta, 284, 317, 358–59

Abou al-Fadl, Khalid, 641 n21

Abraham, 45, 129 n28, 133 n37, 181, 189, 191, 213, 260, 269, 338, 357, 363–64, 366, 390, 412, 418 n5, 428, 480–81, 486–87, 490–92, 500–1, 564–65, 616, 635

Abramelin the Mage, 93

Abramovitz, Moses, 705

Abu Bakr of Mayurqi, 655 n14

Abu Dharr, 343 n105

Abu Hurayrah, 342, 352 n127

Abu'l-Barakat, 65 n108

Abu'l-Qasim Ahmad, 656

Abulafia, 480, 498

Abulafia, David, 591 n20

Achilles, 300, 326–28, 391, 419, 438, 474, 567

Adam, 43, 91, 99, 113, 128, 139, 159, 229, 253, 269, 282, 287, 320, 358, 361, 367, 443, 446, 480–81, 491–92, 501, 562–63, 589, 598, 628, 640

Adams Bellows, Henry, 199 n203

Adamson, Henry, 602

Adorno, Theodor Ludwig Wiesengrund, 107, 244, 332 n82, 376, 525

Adrian IV (Pope), 587

Aeneas Sylvius Piccolomini, 614

Aeolus, 197, 224–25, 232

Aeschylus, 352–53, 419, 424, 454, 475, 479, 481, 673

Agamben, Giorgio, 100, 154, 407

Agamemnon, 327, 419

A'isha, wife of prophet Muhammad, 129, 267, 673

Akhenaten, 190–91, 447

Al-Albani, 352 n127

al-Azami, Usama, 641 n21

Al-Barr, 351–52

al-Bukhari, Muhammad ibn Ismā'īl, 15, 342, 641 n19

Alexander III (Pope), 587

Alexander IV (Pope), 657

Alexander the Great, 242, 397 n227, 643

Al-Farabi, 75

al-Farsi, Salman, 570

Al-Harith, Ibn Sa'd Hisham, 622

Ali-Atac, 302

Alighieri, Dante, 36, 48, 71, 91, 99–100, 227, 229–30, 252, 256, 258, 301, 305, 307, 339, 377, 403, 407, 425–26, 440, 480–81, 492, 505, 553, 569, 571, 579, 585, 593, 660, 670

Al-Kala'i-Abu al-Yaman-Ismail ibn-Ayyash-Yahya ibn-Sa'id, 622 n82

al-Karkhi, Ma'ruf, 460 n115

Al-Kindi, 653

Alkmene, 182

Al-Malik, 129 n31

al-Misri, Niyazi, 636, 652

Alphonse X of Castile, 488, 621 n79, 625–26, 672

Al-Qadr, 44

Al-Shahrastani, 653

Al-Shahrazuri, 653–54

Al-Suyuti's al-La'ali, 129 n31

Al-Tabari, 389–91, 467, 616–18, 622, 627, 636, 641 n18, 661

Altan Khan, 239

Althusius, Johannes, 455

Al-Tirmidhi, 352 n127, 639

Alvis, John, 71, 197, 300, 340, 418–19, 567

Al-Zahra, 206 n240

Al-Zuhri, 390

Amaterasu, 203, 249, 293, 500

Amphitryon, 182

Anaxagoras, 184

Anchises, 98, 101, 245, 432, 437-38

Andani, Khalil, 648-49

Anderson, Benedict, 452

Anfortas, 164, 172, 182, 217, 247-48, 252, 255, 272

Angeas in the Book of Jashar, 418 n5, 619-20

Anokye, Okomfo, 292 n176, 570

Apaza, Julian, 72

Aphrodite, 151-52, 215, 221, 233, 281, 283

Apis, 142, 146, 152, 471

Apollonius of Tyana, 394 n205

Aquinas, Thomas (St.), 34, 108, 261, 346, 355, 388, 441, 477, 497, 502, 405, 592

Archytas of Tarentum, 556

Arendt, Hannah, 328, 473

Ariadne, 156

Aristotle, 65, 187, 226, 388, 438 n61, 477, 580, 653

Arjuna, 193, 242, 327, 380, 431, 536, 539, 576

Armesilla Conde, Santiago, 522 n244

Artemis, 106, 158

Arthur (King), 59, 148, 182, 200-1, 395, 403, 433, 575, 579, 590, 616

Arubah-Qatadah-al-Hasan-Samurah Ibn Jundub, 622

Ascanius, 309, 395

Aseneth, 127, 216, 567

Asherah, 106, 134, 181, 190, 203, 205, 209-11, 562-64

Asin Palacios, Miguel, 646, 653-55

Assman, Jan, 112, 191-92, 414, 447, 502, 556 n6, 690

Astarte, 157

Atahualpa (Emperor of the Incas), 200, 680-81

Athena, 106, 116, 222, 283

Athirat of the Ugarit, 203, 449

Athtar, 216

Atkinson, Anthony, 698

Atlas, 161, 417 n4, 435

Atum, 234, 274-75, 282-85, 290, 447

Augustine (St.), 39, 49, 94, 97, 171, 253, 310, 320, 332, 340, 375, 406, 465, 480-81, 574, 673

Augustus Caesar, 192, 203, 311, 339, 391, 396, 402, 436, 465, 512-13, 572, 579, 590

Ault, Donald, 105 n182

B

Ba'al, 293

Bacchus, 107, 280

Bailey, Adrian, 142 n66

Baldr, 322 n54

Baltzly, Dirk, 200 n214

Bangdel, Dina, 136 n48

Barbarossa, Frederik I Hohenstaufen (Emperor), 179, 200, 351 n124, 401-3, 429, 508, 574, 578-79, 586-87

Barlaam of Calabria, 298 n207

Barrutia Guenaga, Jon, 702 n30

Bastida, Micaela, 293 n178

Beatrice, 229, 252, 256, 258

Bekker, Immanuel, 157 n103

Benedict IX (Pope), 584

Benedict X (Pope), 239

Benedict XIV (Pope), 265

Benjamin, Walter, 362, 518, 692

Bennassar, Bartolomé, 510 n222

Bentley Hart, David, 113 n192, 115, 298 n207, 398, 494, 499, 571, 585, 618

Berdyaev, Nicholas, 461 n119, 571

Bergmans, Luc, 55 n82

Bergson, Henri, 28 n35, 30-31, 37, 328

Bernardus Silvestris, 296, 391 n195

Berrens, Stefan, 272 n87

Bethge, Gebhard, 208 n245

Blumenberg, Hans, 12, 673

Bocallini, Traiano, 598-99

Boccaccini, Gabriele, 190 n181

Boehme, Jacob, 252, 598, 617, 622, 674

Boethius, 256, 291, 454, 493, 553

Bolivar, Simon, 204, 210, 676-77

Bosch, Hieronymus, 601

Brahma, 195, 236, 279, 287–88, 344, 491

Brenner, Jan, 227–29

Brinner, William, 389–90, 616

Brioso Santos, Hector, 663 n17

Brown, Christ, 75 n128

Brown, Samuel M., 65 n105

Brownworth, Lars, 615

Bruno, Giordano, 12, 33

Brutus the Trojan, 395, 433, 561

Bryant, Edwin, 5, 40, 174, 543 n8

Buchanan, Allen, 477 n152, 596 n32

Budge, Wallis, 168 n122, 319, 404, 447 n75

Bueno, Gustavo, 72, 502, 685–87, 695

Bulgakov, Sergei, 19 n19, 103 n176, 115–17, 253, 297–98, 571

Burckhardt, Titus, 552

Burke, Edmund, 349, 462, 668

Burnier, Raymond, 296

Buzan, Barry, 409 n243

Byron, George Gordon Noel (Lord Byron), 512, 646

Byung Ho Lee, 629 n3

C

Caesarea Eusebius Pamphilus, 425

Cain, 617

Calixtus II (Pope), 573

Calliope, 230

Campanella, Tommaso, 599–600

Campbell, Leroy A., 146 n71, 151–52

Carley, James, 201 n215, 590 n10

Carlos Macusaya, 293 n178, 679 n11, 681–82

Carlyle, Thomas, 349

Cassius Dio, 482

Cervantes Saavedra, Miguel (de), 41 n59, 352–53, 598–99, 663–65

Chai, David, 323 n59

Chang, Ho-Joon, 694, 697, 699, 701, 708

Charlemagne, 76, 136, 148, 200, 347, 395, 400–3, 406, 421–22, 429, 503–4, 517, 572, 582–84, 604–5, 611, 647

Charles V (Emperor), 352, 396, 402–3, 411, 421, 478, 502, 513, 586, 588, 594–600, 602–3, 606, 611, 664

Charles Albert of Sardinia, 511

Charles of Anjou, 594, 401

Charles Phillips, 136 n50

Chatterji, Prasanna, 78 n131

Chaucer, Geoffrey, 553

Cheema, Ali, 694 n11, 697, 699

Chesbrough, Henry, 700 n29

Chesterton, Gilbert Keith, 399, 684

Chiang Kai-shek, 633

Chomsky, Noam, 697 n21

Chou (Duke of), 126

Chrysostom, Dio, 182

Clement III (Antipope), 240

Clement VII (Pope), 512–13, 579, 588–89, 594–95

Cline, Eric, 557

Cohn, Norman, 211 n270, 293 n180, 337

Colby, Frank, 167 n121, 661 n13

Coleridge, Samuel Taylor, 448

Columbus, Christopher, 510

Commodus, 510

Companys i Jover, Lluís, 521

Confucius, 420, 423, 472, 523, 571, 696

Conrad of Hohenstaufen, 351 n124

Conrad, Sebastian, 447 n76

Constance (Empress), 587

Constantin I (Emperor), 272 n87

Constantine (Emperor), 129 n28, 181, 237, 271–72, 399–400, 402–4, 503, 578, 584–90, 592

Constantine VI (Emperor), 583, 605

Constantine XI (Emperor), 200–1, 306 n221, 615

Coomaraswamy, Ananda Kentish, 23–24, 152 n99

Cope, Edward Meredith, 136 n51, 609 n15

Corbin, Henry, 5, 9, 25, 31, 44, 49, 63–66, 70, 93, 99, 124, 191, 214, 254–55, 268–70, 284, 316, 325, 329–31, 338, 360, 449, 492–94, 652–55, 672

Cornelius (Centurion), 237, 496

Cortes, Hernan, 244 n6, 405 n239, 511, 663

Cratylus of Plato, 125 n18, 178, 296, 301

Creusa, 164, 255, 309, 432

Crowley, Aleister, 140, 538

Cumont, Franz, 282, 554

Cupid, 277

Curry, Patrick, 189 n179, 559 n14

Cuzco, 200, 447

Cybele, 203, 271

Cyllene Mountain, 163

Cyril of Alexandria, 158

D

Daguan, Zhou, 292

Dalai Lama, 239

Dalal, Roshen, 150 n85

Damick, Andrew Stephen, 173

Dan, 123, 154, 397 n227

Daniel, 77, 81, 98–99, 106 n183, 127–29, 145, 177, 181 n143, 486, 514, 559, 623

Danielou, Alain, 482 n162

Danielou, Jean, 485, 504

Danquah, Joseph, 292

Dara Shikoh, Prince, 45

Dardanus, 211, 310, 427, 625

Dark, Ken, 679, 695

David Luzzatto, Samuel, 618

De Armas Wilson, Diana, 352 n128, 663–64

De Lubicz, René Adolphe Schwaller, 213 n271

De Maistre, Joseph, 80

De Young, Stephen, 173 n130

Dechend, Hertha (von), 188

Dee, John, 601

Dehejia, Vidya, 205 n229, 264 n68, 295 n186

Demeter, 186, 203–4, 207

Demiurgus, 130, 180

Desmond, William, 22, 33–34, 38, 53, 81, 92, 107, 176, 268, 286, 304, 347, 374, 440, 466, 535, 672

d'Hoine, Pieter, 51 n75, 56 n90, 200 n214

Dido, 255, 309, 432–33, 610

Diego, Juan, 404–5, 678

Diocletian (Emperor), 192, 420–21, 513, 605

Diodorus Siculus, 162 n116, 186 n165, 361 n150, 620

Diogenes Laertius, 247, 394 n205

Diomede, 247

Dionysus, 106–7, 137, 146, 155–56, 161, 187–88, 202, 221, 283, 308, 414, 419, 426, 593, 674

Dionysius the Areopagite, 6, 73, 108, 173, 273, 290, 297–96, 322, 334, 367, 479, 481, 483–84, 487–90, 495, 500, 612, 660

Dionysius of Halicarnassus, 168, 227–28, 271, 394 n203

Di Rienzo, Cola, 339, 511–13

Doniger, Wendy, 270 n83

Donoso Cortes, Juan, 349

Doria, Andrea, 405–6

Dostoyevsky, Fyodor, 372, 374, 670

Ducker, Karl, 693–94

Dufault, Olivier, 138 n56, 563 n1, 565 n5

Dumezil, Georges, 171 n126, 312

Dumuzid (Mesopotamian God), 148, 246

Durkheim, Émile, 362

Dyczkowski, Mark, 276 n106, 279 n118, 316–17

E

Ebert, Friedrich, 293 n178, 679 n11

Echevarrieta, Javier, 523

Eckhart (Meister), 53, 75, 101, 108, 110, 160, 302, 330, 332, 334, 337, 378, 409, 453, 534, 670

Edward I, 410

Edward the Confessor, 101

Edward Lewis, 323

Egeria (nymph/ goddess), 310

Eliade, Mircea, 241, 301, 374

Elijah, 127, 570

Eliot, Thomas Stearns, 68, 73, 188, 228, 242, 285, 392–93, 431, 453, 459

Elizabeth (Queen), 598

Elliott, William, 142 n63, 492 n190, 651 n43

Elsee, Charles, 483 n167

Emilie Kutash, 200 n214

Emmerich, Anne Catherine, 247, 273, 481, 579–80

Empedocles, 21 n20, 96, 100, 102, 124, 161–62, 180, 184, 186, 223 n289, 247, 276, 281, 283, 361–61, 528, 556, 591–92, 653–54, 660

Enki, 150, 251

Enkidu, 243, 302, 348

Ephesus, 200

Epictetus, 182, 567

Epimenides, 568

Epimetheus, 171

Epiphanius of Salamis, 181, 439

Erasmus, 597

Eriugena, 6, 64, 540

Esau, 98, 418 n5, 429 n16, 441, 540, 616–20

Escotado, Antonio, 385

Esperanza, 518

Etxebarria, 702 n30

Eugenia of Spain, 670

Euphorbus, 394

Euripides, 119 n1, 161, 226, 674

Eusebius, 99, 159, 381, 425, 450

Euthydemus, 122

Eutychius of Alexandria, 439

Evagrios the Solitary, 105

Evans, Arthur, 206, 555

Eve, 282, 443, 446, 589, 628, 113

Ezekiel, 127–28, 150, 154, 196–97, 211–12, 236, 266, 280, 301, 483, 514, 538

Ezekiel the Tragedian, 491

Ezra, 124 n10, 132–33, 190, 212 n270, 425, 489

F

Fakhry, Majid, 142 n64

Fatima (daughter of Muhammed), 206 n240, 254–55, 495, 505

Faust, 661–62, 666–67, 670–73

Felipe VI, 519 n239

Felix R, 169 n125, 596 n34

Ficino, Mars, 296, 552

Figueroa, Suarez de, 663

Finley, Moses, 556

Fisher King, 101, 172–73, 247, 252

Flavius Josephus, 389–90, 482, 497, 611, 613, 620–21

Fletcher Lummis, Charles, 686

Flood, Gavin, 5, 79 n133, 121 n2, 264–65, 292, 294, 297–98, 318, 324–25, 451–52

Florensky, Pavel, 275

Florescano, Enrique, 235 n343

Fludd, Robert, 252, 602

Frankfort, Henri, 319 n42

Frazer, James G., 157

Frederick II, 84, 148, 200–1, 339, 353–54, 399, 401, 403, 508, 511, 575, 579, 587–93, 601, 606, 652

Frederick Barbarossa, 179, 200, 351 n124, 401, 403, 429, 508, 574, 578–79, 586–87

Freya, 199, 233, 322, 396

Frye, Northrop, 5, 196 n198, 285, 341, 367, 665

G

Gabriel, 98, 128 n28, 519 n240

Gaia, 162, 626, 659

Galilei, Galileo, 553

Gallaher, Brandon, 456 n99

Gamkrelidze, Thomas, 146 n70, 291 n171, 318 n33

Ganesh, 155

Garcia Trevijano, Antonio, 337 n91

Garibaldi, Giuseppe, 511, 513

Garvey, Marcus, 429, 571

Ge Hong, 323

Geb, 282–84, 286, 571

Gelasius (Pope), 406

Gemistos Plethon, 298 n207

Genghis Khan, 633

Geoffrey of Monmouth, 395–96, 433, 561, 590, 616

Gerard of Cremona, 187

Gerard Rouwhorst, 480 n159

Germany with Esau, 620

Gerson, Lloyd, 56 n90, 277 n107

Gertrude the Great (St.), 611

Gertrude of Nivelles, 611 n29
Geryon (Titan), 161
Ghassanid Arabs, 227
Gheissari, Ali, 41 n60, 653 n4
Giaquinto, Corrado, 187–88
Gierke, Otto, 435, 461, 464–65
Gilgamesh, 97–99, 124, 146, 150, 152,
    163, 215–16, 284, 302, 306–7, 369
Girard, Rene, 25, 84, 90, 102, 383, 422,
    455, 458, 462, 464, 468, 473, 476, 484,
    518–19, 523–25, 545, 547, 697, 704–7
Goddard, Neville, 32 n40, 457 n103, 540
    n6
Godfrey of Viterbo, 590
Godley, Denis, 472 n141
Goethe the Satanic, 671
Goethe, Johann W., 112, 253, 303, 348,
    535, 591, 671
Goetinck, Glenys W., 273 n89
Gogh, Vincent (van), 158
Golgonooza-Allamanda-Bowlahoola,
    285, 536
Golgotha, 604
Goliath, 579
Gomer, 623–24
Gomez Uranga, Mikel, 702 n30
Gong, Heshang, 452
Gotorna, 624
Gould, Thomas, 673 n37
Graeber, David, 63 n102, 304, 382, 408
    n241, 541 n7
Graves, Robert, 156, 162, 204, 312,
    417–18, 562, 619–20
Gregory (Pope), 410, 578
Gregory VII, 240, 595
Gregory XVI (Pope), 502, 504
Gregory of Nyssa (St.), 6, 55, 60, 90–91,
    94, 122, 124, 138, 220, 329, 387, 532,
    534, 562, 592
Gregory Palamas, 297–98
Griffin, Jasper, 166 n118
Grimes, Pierre, 223, 675
Guangchengzi, 323
Guénon, Rene, 4–5, 12, 44, 46, 54–55, 70,
    288, 345, 378–79, 399, 580, 630
Guénoun, Denis, 661 n11

Guerrero, Pedro D., 594
Gulamhussen, Mohamed Azzim, 695
    n14
Gullo Omodeo, Marcelo, 509
Gurion, Ben, 428

H
Ha Mim Keller, 636 n3
Hachiman, 500
Haddad, Gibreel F., 639
Hadrian IV (Pope), 586
Hagar (Abraham's concubine), 213, 390
Haile Selassie I (Emperor of Ethiopia),
    182, 193, 571
Hales, William, 626 n114
Ham (son of Noah), 390, 446, 613–14,
    617, 622, 627–28
Hamid Dabashi, 672 n34
Hanan, Eshel, 190 n181
Hani, Jean, 10 n3, 191, 300
Hannibal, 307
Haqqani, Nazim, 639
Harrington, Michael, 57 n93, 75
Hathor, 142, 146, 152, 168, 203–4, 207,
    209, 220, 226, 233, 414, 677
Hays, Christopher, 385
Hayy ibn-Yaqzan, 105, 110 n188, 161
Headlam, George, 475 n148
Hecate, 166, 180–81, 186, 203–4
Hector, 327–28
Hedley, Douglas, 5, 68, 453
Hegel, Georg Wilhelm Friedrich, 10,
    331, 702 n32
Heidegger, Martin, 34, 336 n86, 362,
    671–72, 689–92, 698
Heimburg, Gregor, 597 n35
Heimdallr, 199
Heinemann, William, 168 n123
Helen, 309
Helios, 122, 162–65, 207, 293, 302, 308
Henry III (Holy Roman Emperor), 584
Henry IV (Holy Roman Emperor),
    240, 626
Henry VII (King of England), 307, 512,
    579
Hephaestus, 281, 283

Hera, 25 n29, 31, 100, 164, 207, 213, 241, 283

Heracles/Hercules, 96, 102–3, 106, 142, 156, 161–62, 164, 172, 181–82, 197, 213, 217, 223 n289, 241, 303, 369–70, 402, 418–21, 450, 508, 567–68, 608, 620, 659, 671

Heraclius, 474, 586

Herlihy, John, 379 n177

Hermes Trismegistus, 290 n162, 552

Herod (King of Judah), 394, 425, 618–19

Herodotus, 189, 290, 415, 419, 471–72, 474–75, 479, 481, 557, 608–13, 620, 624

Herrin, Judith, 583 n1, 615

Hesiod, 187, 361 n150, 447, 489, 498

Hestia, 117–18, 125, 134, 301, 312

Hildebrand, 239–40

Hildegard of Bingen, 586

Hilkiah, 190, 210, 489

Hippolytus, 129 n28, 141

Hoffman, Donald, 201 n215, 590 n10

Hohenstaufen Frederick II, 44, 351 n124, 353, 401, 512, 587, 590, 592–94, 598, 601, 652

Holcombe, Charles, 629–30

Hölderlin, Friedrich, 371, 698

Hollander, Lee Milton, 199 n210, 209 n255

Homer, 33 n43, 71, 74, 125, 136, 151, 158, 162–63, 184–86, 197, 209–10, 213, 215, 223, 250–51, 290 n162, 301–3, 326–27, 340, 360–61, 391–92, 395 n218, 418–19, 430 n19, 433–36, 454, 555, 558–60, 567, 607–9, 614, 625, 647, 660, 671–72

Horus, 137, 162, 170, 185, 204 220, 232–33, 248–49, 271, 280, 285, 289, 389, 447, 562, 565

Hosea, 139, 193, 562

Huang Lao (Huang-Lao), 201, 630–31

Huangdi (The Yellow Emperor), 201, 323, 391, 430, 465, 629–30

Huayna Capac, 683

Huayna Potosi, 204, 404, 677–78

Hudson, Dennis, 294, 316 n19

Hume, David, 341

Hyrcanus, John, 618

Iamblichus, 107, 121–22, 148, 180, 206, 215, 223, 225, 262, 274–75, 277, 296–99, 315, 317, 319, 417, 558, 592, 601

Iapetus, 417 n4, 625–26

Ibas of Edessa, 585

Ibn'-Arif, 141, 655

Ibn-Arabi, Muhammad ibn 'Alī ibn Muhammad, 130, 190, 208, 263–64, 268, 282, 646, 654–56

Ibn-Ata, 617 n53

Ibn-Barrajan, 654–56

Ibn-Bayyah, 641–42

Ibn-Ezra, 618

Ibn-Garcia, 637–38

Ibn-Hafsun, 647 n33

Ibn-Hafsun, Umar, 646, 656

Ibn-Hanbal, Ahmad, 460 n115

Ibn-Hashim, 505, 656 n16

Ibn-Humayd, 390 n191

Ibn-Ishaq, 390 n19, 627, 638

Ibn-Khaldun, 352 n126

Ibn-Mardanish, 656

Ibn-Marwan, Abdul- Rahman, 647 n33, 655–56

Ibn-Masarra, 651 n43, 654–56

Ibn-Musa, 507 n217, 655–56

Ibn-Nadir, 654

Ibn-Naqib al-Misri, Ahmad, 636

Ibn-Qasi, Ahmad ibn-Al-Husayn, 141–42, 507 n217, 622 n83, 647 n33, 651 n43, 654–56,

Ibn-Qasi of Algarve, 647, 656

Ibn-Qasi of Aragon, 647 n33

Ibn-Rabi'ah-Ibn, 617 n53

Ibn-Sina (Ibn-Sina), 41, 65 n108, 105, 110, 161, 284, 316, 649 n41

Ibn-Tarif, Salih, 648 n36

Innocent III (Pope), 306, 587

Insua, Pedro, 520

Irene Angelina, 587

Irene of Athens, 407, 583, 605, 611

Irwin, Lee, 232 n342, 244 n6, 440 n65, 684 n17

Isaac, 45, 98, 150, 363–66, 403, 540, 564, 618

Isaac Newton, 179
Isabel, 508–10, 519
Isaiah, 16, 41 n59, 123, 128 n28, 133 n37, 424–26, 475, 478, 494, 540, 564
Isauria, 624
Ishmael, 45, 132 n37, 213, 390, 403, 492, 616
Isidore of Seville, 222, 348–49, 389, 395 n218, 439, 446, 507–9, 513, 613, 620–26, 661, 673
Isis, 170, 204, 207, 222, 247, 256, 283–85, 290–91, 314, 318, 562–66
Ivanovich Ivanov, Vyacheslav, 396

J

Jacob (Israel), 35, 98, 150, 217, 247–48, 251, 255, 391, 403, 418 n5, 425, 441, 446, 491, 501, 540, 564, 616–19, 660
Jacob Boehme, 252, 617, 674
Jacob by Edom, 616
Ja'far al-Sadiq, 492 n191
Janus Secundus, 396, 402
Japheth of Genesis, 348, 390, 460, 508, 607, 613–28, 662, 667–69, 673–74
Jasagtu Khan, 239
Jayadeva, 256
Jefferson, Thomas, 677
Jehovah, 219, 292, 489, 492, 600
Jehu, 154
Jephthah, 367
Jeremiah, 16, 424, 426, 494, 563
Jerome (St.), 348–49, 389, 441, 446, 508, 620–23, 661
Jerryson, Michael, 239 n348
Jin, Jurchen, 630–31
Jiutian Xuannu, 292
Jivananda, 79
Job, 71, 139, 480
John VIII, 578, 588
John VIII (Pope), 400
John XII, 578, 583–84, 594
John of Austria, 405
John the Baptist, 412, 570, 573
John of the Cross's Dark Night, 144, 538
John of Paris, 388, 464–65, 477

Johnson, James R., 503 n207
Jonah, 306
Joshua, 133 n39, 219, 418 n5, 439, 487, 492, 561, 619 n64
Josiah, 132–35, 190, 210, 212, 219, 354, 381, 489, 499, 562–64
Joyce, James, 162
Judah, 211 n270, 486
Juergensmeyer, Mark, 239 n348
Julian the Apostate (Emperor), 191, 479, 504–5
Julius Caesar, 391, 395, 465, 609–10, 612
Jung, Carl, 185, 306, 461–62
Jupiter, 107, 121, 130, 171, 181, 221–22, 272, 275, 277, 279, 282, 394, 558, 625–28
Jupiter Indiges, Aeneas, 228

K

Kahn, Aaron M., 665 n21
Kantorowicz, Ernst, 100, 103, 112, 300, 320, 351 n124, 353–54, 422, 492, 503–4, 590, 592, 598
Karic, Enes, 658 n2
Katari, Tomas, 682
Kavkasos, 624
Keats, John, 379
Kepler, Johannes, 179
King Alfonso I the Battler, 182
King Arthur, 59, 182, 200–1, 395, 403, 575, 590, 616
King David, 71, 126, 158, 214–19, 233, 255, 380, 391, 402–3, 429 n16, 483, 504, 576, 579, 653–54, 660
King Fairbank, John, 633 n20
King James of England, 5, 214, 598, 602
King Josiah, 132, 135, 190, 210, 219, 489, 499, 562–63
King Laomedon, 395 n218
King Philip of France, 410, 510
King Priam, 419, 626
King Sebastian of Portugal, 148
King Solomon, 122, 147, 152, 206, 293, 404, 481, 499 n203, 562–63
Kingsley, Peter, 5, 21 n20, 102 n172, 134, 183–89, 223 n289, 361 n150, 556–59, 653, 660

Kramrisch, Stella, 296 n195
Krishna, 15, 45, 60, 78–79, 103, 106, 144, 193, 195–97, 227, 242, 259, 262, 267, 274, 288–89, 316, 325, 344, 366, 369–70, 384, 490–91, 539, 543 n8, 571, 576, 579, 628, 644
Kubeleya, Matar, 203
Kublai Khan, 239
Kurayb-'Uthman, 622 n83

L

Ladon, 161
Lakshmi (Goddess), 18, 103, 106, 109–10, 197–98, 206, 259, 274, 278, 284
Lama Pagspa, 239
Langer, Suzanne, 374
Lao Tse, 201, 275 n98, 567
Larsson, Goran, 638 n10
Laud, William, 5, 602–3
Lavinia, 103, 106, 166, 228–29, 246, 248, 255, 272, 293, 308–9, 369, 427, 432
Lawrence, David, 315
Layton, Bentley, 208 n245
Leibniz, Gottfried Wilhelm von, 48–49
Lenardon, Robert, 228 n316
Leo III, 76, 421, 582–83, 604–5
Leo IV, 582–83, 410
Leo IX, 584
Leo X (Pope), 244 n6
Leroux, Pierre, 49
Leto, 203–5, 213, 222, 302
Lewis, Clive Staples, 433 n31, 459 n111
Liang Kai, 198
Liao, Khitan, 631
Lieber, Andrea, 58 n97
Ligdan Khan, 239, 633
Lipton, Gregory, 282
Liu Yiming, 51
Livy, Titus, 171, 228, 393–94
Loki, 199
Louis XIII, 517
Lovejoy, Arthur, 56
Lubac, Henri de, 43, 411
Lubicz, Schwaller de, 213, 264, 604
Lucian of Samosata, 157
Lucifer, 217–19, 303, 674

Lucius Annaeus Cornutus, 182, 567
Lull, Ramon, 601
Luther, Martin, 386, 589, 594–95, 597–98, 622, 661
Lycurgus in Sparta, 595

M

MacDiarmid, Hugh, 41
MacEoin, Dennis, 492
Mackinnon, Donald, 463
Mahoney, Dhira, 273
Maia, 125, 163
Maimonides, 364, 498
Malachi, 570
Malchus, Cleodemus, 181, 418
Manchu (Emperor of China), 239, 577
Manchurian Qing, 349, 630–33
Manco Inca, 680–82, 687
Manco Kapac, 293
Manfred (son of Frederick II Hohenstauffen), 339, 399, 401, 512, 593
Marcus Aurelius, 80, 584
Marcus Terentius Varro, 168
Marinatos, Nanno, 81, 148, 186, 191–92, 203–7, 221, 249 n23, 302, 347–48, 457, 556–57, 572–74
Mark, Saint, 39, 237 n346
Marsiglio Ficino, 552
Marsilius of Padua, 435
Martin, Michael, 254, 265, 297 n200, 459, 663 n14
Marx, Karl, 86
Mary Magdalene, 42, 158, 381, 399
Mauropous, John, 614
Mauss, Marcel, 81, 304, 362
Maximilian (Emperor), 597
Maxwell, James, 602
McEvilley, Thomas, 168 n124, 315 n6
McGinn, Thomas, 395
Mehmet-Ali Atac, 150 n84, 246 n13, 302
Meister Eckhart, 53, 101, 108, 110, 160, 302, 334, 337, 378, 409, 453, 534
Melchior Inchofer, 553
Melchizedek, 181–82, 189, 218, 338, 347, 363, 412, 567

Mencius, 126, 571

Merlin, 201, 335, 579, 590, 592

Metatron, 127, 189–90, 209, 229, 242, 252–53, 320, 567

Metropolitan Kallistos Ware, 274 n94, 603

Micah, 16, 177, 494–95, 564

Michalowski, Kazimierz, 135 n47

Milbank, John, 5, 22, 49, 80, 110 n187, 148, 192, 261, 297 n201, 332–37, 341, 347, 377, 382, 402–3, 406, 412, 415, 423, 452, 474, 485, 514–15, 518, 534, 537, 545, 575, 579, 591, 603, 665, 669–73, 687, 692–93

Minos, 155–56, 284, 555

Miroshnikov, Ivan, 359 n143

Mises, Ludwig von, 86

Mishima, Yukio, 111

Mitchell, John, 529 n17, 450

Mithra, 97, 99 n159, 151–52, 155–56, 168, 284

Mittal, Rajesh, 65 n106, 167 n119, 431

Miyazaki, Hayao, 377

Mongolian Xiongnu, 348

Montano, Arias, 602

Moore, Margaret, 477 n152, 596 n32

Morgan, Llewelyn, 166 n117, 432

Moses, 61, 96, 104, 122, 124, 126–27, 133–34, 138, 161, 190–91, 211, 290 n163, 302, 347, 357, 362, 368, 371, 380–81, 391, 394, 489, 491–92, 503, 556

Mrnjavčević, Marco, 200

Mroveli, Leonti, 624

Mueller, Max, 370

Muhammad, 42–46, 123–24, 129, 181 n143, 213, 254, 267, 282, 285, 325, 340, 352–54, 390, 399, 403–4, 457, 492, 505, 570, 577, 637–38, 640–44, 648–52, 654, 656, 673, 702 n33

Muhammad of Cordoba (Emir), 656

Murad, Hakim, 43, 262, 658

Musa Ibn Musa Ibn Qasi, 507 n217, 655

Mussetti, Juan Pedro, 395 n217

N

Nakassis, Dimitri, 556–57, 574

Napoleon, 518 n235, 663

Napoleon III, 511, 513, 670

Nasir al-Din al-Tusi, 93

Nelson, Jinty, 611 n29

Nennius, 625

Nephthys, 283, 285

Neptune, 165

Nicholas of Cusa, 5–6, 12, 26, 33, 38, 40, 55–59, 64, 75, 183–85, 221, 274, 277, 373 n166, 482, 490, 614, 640 n17, 647

Nicholson, W. E. Byron, 127 n25

Nickelsburg, George, 123

Nietzsche, Friedrich, 14, 22, 33 n43, 74, 88, 105, 160, 175, 194, 200, 303–8, 331, 383–84, 387, 392, 401, 412, 429, 437, 462, 475, 547, 559, 587, 607, 652, 660, 667, 671, 692

Nilsson, Martin, 148, 560

Norwich, John Julius, 240, 511–13, 582, 589, 605–6

Numa Pompilius (Emperor), 76, 172, 271–72, 300, 310, 394, 418, 428, 436, 438, 512, 558–59, 595, 603, 659

Nye, Joseph, 523, 546, 690, 706

O

Odin/Wotan, 97, 125, 152, 162, 164, 169, 194, 199–200, 203, 209, 215, 217, 224, 247, 251, 273, 284, 301, 308, 321–23, 335, 349–50, 407, 465, 592, 616, 625–26, 659

O'Donovan, Oliver, 337, 477 n152, 596 n32

Odysseus, 103, 162–65, 310, 419, 428, 430 n19, 450, 470

Oghuz Khan, 147

Olivares (Duke of), 516–17

Olivi, Peter John, 244

Olodumare, 42

Olympiodorus, 223 n289, 607–9

Origen of Alexandria, 22, 43, 92, 133 n40, 212 n2, 269, 439, 481–89, 493, 495, 497, 501, 534, 609 n17, 617, 661

Orlov, Andrei, 189–90, 320, 371 n165, 491 n186

Orpheus, 21, 130, 136–37, 161, 164, 187, 223 n289, 255, 273, 287

Ortega y Gasset, Jose, 383, 541, 667

Orunmila, 42

Osei Tutu, 292 n176, 570

Osiris, 121, 126, 137, 139, 149, 152, 180 n139, 185, 187, 189, 209, 225, 242, 247–48, 256, 272, 283–91, 314, 318–19, 323, 414, 426, 593

Ostrom, Elinor, 87

Otto II (Emperor), 320, 572, 584, 605

Otto of Saxony (Emperor), 569, 578, 583–86, 605

P

Pabst, Adam, 22, 297 n201, 332, 474, 518, 687, 692–93

Pageau, Jonathan, 336 n85

Pagspa Lama, 239

Painter, John Thomas, 627

Palairet, Michael, 580 n14

Palamas, Gregory, 297–98

Palatine Elector Frederick V, 311

Pareto, Vilfredo, 473

Paribeni, Roberto, 560

Paris of Troy, 309

Parmenides, 31, 49, 102–3, 122–23, 193–94, 294, 557, 592

Parsifal/Parzival, 182

Patai, Raphael, 115, 129, 283, 286, 562–63

Patanjali, 98, 201, 322

Patriarch of Constantinople, 72, 572, 578, 585

Patriarch John, 578

Patroclus, 327–28

Paul IV (Pope), 595

Paul VI (Pope), 306

Payne, Stanley, 523

Pearce, Joseph Chilton, 25, 545

Pelagius, 578, 588

Penelope, 103, 158, 163, 168, 436

Pericles, 314

Perona Calvete, Carlos, 68 n112, 337 n89, 416 n1

Persephone, 100, 126, 186, 203–4, 207, 281–83, 401

Philip II, 5, 214, 405, 510, 599, 600–3, 664–65, 681, 687

Philip IV, 517

Philo of Alexandria, 103, 114, 181, 250, 269, 456, 482

Philolaus, 185, 187, 551

Phoebus Apollo, 166

Pi I Margall, Francesc, 520

Picardo, Juan, 395 n217

Pickstock, Catherine, 31 n38, 38, 43 n63, 60–61, 64, 73–74, 91–93, 346, 367, 372, 430, 495 n196

Pidal, Menendez, 621 n79

Pinch, Geraldine, 126 n21, 137 n55, 220, 234 n340, 318 n35

Pinchard, Bruno, 55 n82

Pindar, 161, 227

Pius II, 614

Pius XI (Pope), 678

Pizarro, 681–82, 687

Platt, Tristan, 204 n227, 210, 404, 676, 677

Plethon, Gemistos, 298 n207

Pliny, 620

Pliny the Elder, 609

Plotinus, 12, 55, 108, 114, 130, 280, 334, 458

Polyphemus, 430 n19

Pomponius, 620

Pontic Caspian, 577 n9

Pontifex Maximus, 311–12

Pontius Pilate, 154, 407

Porphyry, 51, 116, 134, 146–47, 151, 154, 161, 166, 184, 209–10, 212 n2, 223, 270, 285, 325, 363, 483–84, 528, 674

Porras Barrenechea, Raul, 663

Portugal, Pedro, 293 n178, 679–84

Powell, Barry, 230 n322

Pratt, Orson, 65 n105

Pregadio, Fabrizio, 198 n201, 323, 434 n46

Price, David, 396 n224

Prometheus, 171–72, 217, 231, 303, 309, 389, 666, 671–74

Pseudo-Dionysius (See Dionysius the Areopagite), 6 n7

Pseudo-James, 210 n263
Pujol, Jordi, 523
Purchas, Samuel, 612
Pythagoras, 134, 146–47, 162, 177, 179,
    184, 186, 189, 215, 223, 226, 242, 247,
    270, 394, 417, 420, 425, 457, 552, 558–
    59, 567–68, 653, 659, 674–75

Q
Quetzalcoatl, 97, 234–35, 683
Quirinus, 228

R
Ra-Atum, 234
Rabbi Jacob Emden, 370
Rabelais, 183
Radha (Goddess), 78–79, 103, 106, 195–97,
    256, 262, 267, 274, 277–79, 284, 288–89,
    490–91, 571
Raine, Kathleen, 5 n4, 71
Rama, 103, 205, 274
Ramanuja, 114
Ramses II, 293
Reed, Nicholas, 436
Reinaga, Fausto, 679
Reusch, Helga, 207
Reynolds, Barbara, 307 n223, 440
Rhipeus the Trojan, 614
Robert Henry, Charles, 619 n60
Roca Barea, Maria Elvira, 510 n220, 597
Rodrigo Mora, Felix, 169 n125
Rodriguez Garcia, Gonzalo, 596
Roger II, 491, 587, 591
Rohne, Christine, 429, 450
Romulus, 310, 394, 400, 436, 660
Rosenblat, Angel, 510 n220
Rosenthal, Franz, 352 n126
Rougemont, Denis de, 609, 661, 668–69
Rudolph II, 598–600
Ruskin, John , 674
Ryder Patzuk-Russell, 396 n226

S
Sagasta, Mateo, 520
Sa'id Ibn al-Musayyib, 617 n53, 622 n82
Samson, Alexander, 664

Sanchez Albornoz, Claudio, 507, 519
    n239
Sancho IV, 621 n79
Sargon II, 302
Saturn, 17–18, 95–96, 106–10, 113, 125–
    27, 158, 167, 169–73, 180 n139, 181
    n143, 202, 212, 233, 249–53, 277–80,
    286–87, 378, 400, 527–29, 598, 601
Sayri Tupac, 511, 687
Sayyidna Pir Hasan Kabir al-Din, 45
Schiller, Friedrich, 379
Schmitt, Carl, 100 n166, 476
Schneider, Christoph, 297 n201
Schuchard, Keith, 602 n45
Schuon, Frithjof, 4 n2, 15, 21 n21, 26,
    67 n111, 116, 125 n19, 185, 347, 363
    n154, 417, 422–23, 446, 453, 572, 579–
    80, 598, 612–14
Scipio, 352
Scotus, John Duns, 244
Scruton, Roger, 85
Selassie, Haile, 182, 193, 571
Sfar, Mondher, 648, 650
Shakespeare, William, 80, 375, 626
Shakir, Zaid, 639–40
Shakti, 18, 103–6, 109–10, 113–14, 165,
    206, 246, 256, 274, 276–77, 279, 281,
    284, 286, 288, 291, 295, 297, 299,
    308–9, 317, 380, 562, 570, 685
Shankman, Steven, 433
Shaw, Gregory, 148, 225 n299, 297 n201,
    317 n21, 319 n44
Sheba (Queen), 293, 404
Shem, 389–90, 404, 446, 492, 613–14,
    617, 619 n65, 620–22, 627–28
Shepherd of Hermas, 127, 129, 179, 253
Shi'ur Qomah, 127
Shiva, 18, 60–61, 103, 106, 109–10,
    113, 143 n68, 155, 195, 206, 262, 274,
    276–77, 281, 284, 286, 288, 291, 295,
    299, 318, 369, 491
Shou, Wei, 629
Sibyl of Cumae, 166, 201, 353, 400
Siegfried, 101, 169, 301
Sif, 396, 626
Silgo Gauche, Luis, 519 n239

Silvia, Rhea, 310, 393
Silvius, 309
Sima Qian, 126, 348, 391, 420, 465, 471, 607, 629, 633
Simek, 199
Simplicius, 134, 183, 226 n305, 580
Sinbad the Sailor, 267
Sisa, Bartolina, 293 n178, 681
Sita, 103, 205
Smith, Adam, 84, 86
Smith, Alden, 232 n337
Smith, Joseph, 65 n105, 378
Smith, Wolfgang, 33, 378, 551–52
Sol Indiges, 228–29, 272, 293, 308, 394, 577
Sol Invictus, 271–72, 293, 404, 577, 592, 598
Solomon, 122, 147, 154, 206, 380, 391, 401, 403–4, 499 n203, 508, 562–65, 653–54
Solovyov, Vladimir, 253, 297, 315, 571
Sophax, 620
Spengler, Oswald, 661 n12, 685–86
Spenser, Edmund, 130, 254
Spinoza, Baruch, 387, 498
Sri Krishna, 195, 491
Stevens, Wallace, 323
Stiglitz, Joseph, 698
Stithatos, Nikitas, 274, 290, 377, 538
Strabo, 513, 609–10, 620
Sturluson, Snorri, 199 n207, 224, 332 n55, 349, 391, 394–95, 402, 616, 620, 625–26, 660
Suhrawardi, 41, 52–53, 91, 95 n154, 103–4, 316, 488, 652–53
Suleiman, 421
Sumaj Urqu, 204, 404, 677
Sun Yet Sen, 633
Swedenborg, Emmanuelle, 5 n4, 66, 214, 321, 458, 598
Sybil of the Rhine, 586
Syllepticus, 553 n6
Sylvester II, 584
Sylvius Piccolomini, 614
Symmachus, 133 n40

T
Tacitus, 76, 482
Taleb, Nicholas, 475 n149
Taylor, Rene, 600–1
Taylor, Thomas, 5, 125, 155 n101, 177, 281 n130, 568, 675
Tecumseh, 72, 439, 570, 682
Tefnut, 234, 282–86, 571
Tenskwatawa, 72, 341, 439–40, 468, 570, 684
Tezcan, Baki, 652 n3
Theodora (Byzantine Empress), 583, 585
Theodoric the Great, 511–13
Theodosius I (Emperor), 507 n215
Thompson, David, 229 n319, 395 n212
Thucydides, 555
Tigchelaar, Eibert, 612 n36
Tobias, Jonathan, 265–66
Tolkien, John Ronald Reuel, 410, 660
Tomberg, Valentin, 273, 322
Tomich, Pere, 516 n234
Tononi, Giulio, 675
Tortella, Gabriel, 519 n240
Trajan (Emperor), 402, 614, 660
Tubal, 508, 622–24, 626
Tupac Amaru,72, 293 n178, 511, 681–82, 687
Tupac Katari, 72, 293 n178, 440, 680–82, 687
Tupac Yupanki, 293
Turnus, 166, 232, 431, 433, 437, 619 n64
Tushetu Khan, 239, 577
Tyr, 625

U
Untermann, Jürgen, 519 n239
Untoja, Fernando, 683 n15
Urban VI (Pope), 512
Uzdavinys, Algis, 4–5, 93, 123–24, 131, 152, 189, 202, 223 n289, 276 n104, 280, 282–83, 285, 290, 426 n15, 558–60, 649

V
Valdegamas, Marques de, 349 n121
Valerius Maximus, 277, 482

Valpy, Francis E. J., 349 n117
Van der Kam, C., 612 n34
Van de Mieroop, Marc, 416, 420, 478, 557, 690
Varuna, 151 n89, 294
Vattimo, Gianni, 33 n44
Vico, Giambattista, 36, 67, 379, 664
Villavicencio, Maritza, 293
Virgil, 99, 153, 158, 165–67, 183, 197, 211, 217, 223 n289, 225–30, 245–46, 255, 258, 308, 353, 392–96, 400, 403, 418–19, 426, 430–37, 492, 555, 558, 579, 590, 601, 610, 614, 685
Vishnu, 18, 45, 60–61, 103, 106, 109–10, 195, 206, 259–60, 262, 267, 274, 278, 284–85, 288, 491
Vlach, Michael, 484 n171
Voegelin, Eric, 5, 14, 32–33, 50 n73, 52, 68, 70, 75, 188, 242, 244, 284, 287, 331–32, 377, 415, 419–20, 434–36, 438–39, 454, 458–59, 465, 467–68, 475–78, 514, 548, 559, 566 n6, 610, 630, 547, 662, 672, 696 n18
Voss, Angela, 559 n14
Vulcan (God), 107, 126, 180, 270–71, 280–83, 285
Vyasa, 145, 174, 329

W
Waddell, John, 273, 292–93
Wagner, Richard, 182, 218, 512
Waite, Edward, 171 n128, 218 n279, 599 n39
Walbank, Frank, 438
Watson, Nicholas, 481
Watt, Montgomery, 439, 460 n116, 577, 636–37, 650
Watts, Alan, 379
Weber, Max, 597
Webster, Noah, 625
Weil, Simone, 82–83, 628
Wengrow, David, 63 n102, 304, 408 n241
Whitehead, Alfred North, 341, 607
Whitman, Walt, 41, 96, 316, 321, 324
Whittaker, Thomas, 56
Wilkinson, Toby, 124 n15

Wilson, Horace Hayman, 278 n114
Wilson, Jack, 684
Wilson, Peter, 74 n119, 469, 494 n195, 506 n214, 514 n228, 520 n241, 588 n5, 597 n37
Wilson-Okamura, David S., 513–14
Winter, Tim, 43, 262, 658
Wolfram von Eschenbach, 273, 592
Woodroffe, John George (Arthur Avalon), 296, 548, 685, 690–92
Wovoka, 570, 684
Wright, Martin, 463

X
Xenocrates, 568
Xerxes, 474–75, 609
Xiaoping, Deng, 391, 633

Y
Yahweh, 128 n28, 209, 211 n270, 338
Yates, Frances, 394, 422, 426, 598–601, 647
Yeats, W. B., 32 n40, 111, 377
Ymir, 97, 111, 136, 152, 207, 235, 284, 321–22, 426
Yusuf, Hamza, 642

Z
Zagreus, 146, 157–58, 161, 187, 202, 209, 221–22, 369
Zamoyski, Jan, 408
Zangger, Eberhard, 5, 396, 416–17, 556–59
Zechariah, 219
Zeno (Emperor), 511, 513, 584–86
Zeus, 31, 100, 118, 128, 170, 182, 200, 241, 272, 283, 326–27, 340, 492, 567
Zinner, Samuel, 6 n7, 10, 34 n48, 203, 370, 612–14, 649–50
Zizek, Slavoj, 13, 334
Zopyrus, 556
Zoroaster, 474
Zosimos of Panopolis (or Zosimus of Panopolis), 137–38, 365 n156, 562–68
Zumárraga, Juan de (Fray), 561

CARLOS PERONA CALVETE is a writer for *The European Conservative*, where his contributions range from political philosophy to geopolitics and current affairs. He has a background in International Relations and an M.Sc. in Organizational Behaviour from the LSE. His professional experience includes project management for a number of international institutions. He has also published several fiction pieces.

www.ingramcontent.com/pod-product-compliance
Lightning Source LLC
Chambersburg PA
CBHW020810300326
41914CB00077B/1846/J